Rick Steves'

FRANCE

Rick Steves & Steve Smith

2011

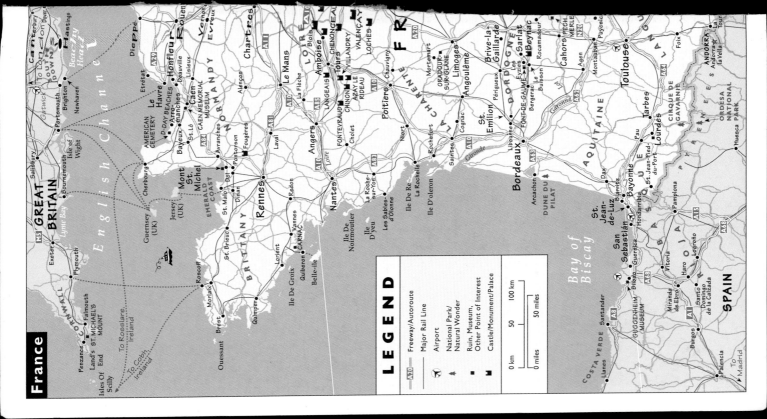

France

LEGEND

- **A10** — Freeway/Autoroute
- Major Rail Line
- ✈ Airport
- ▲ National Park/Natural Wonder
- ■ Ruin, Museum, Other Point of Interest
- ▮ Castle/Monument/Palace

0 km   50   100 km

0 miles   50 miles

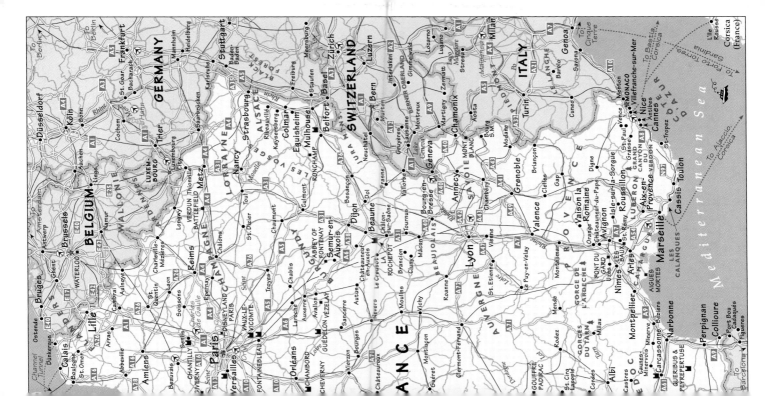

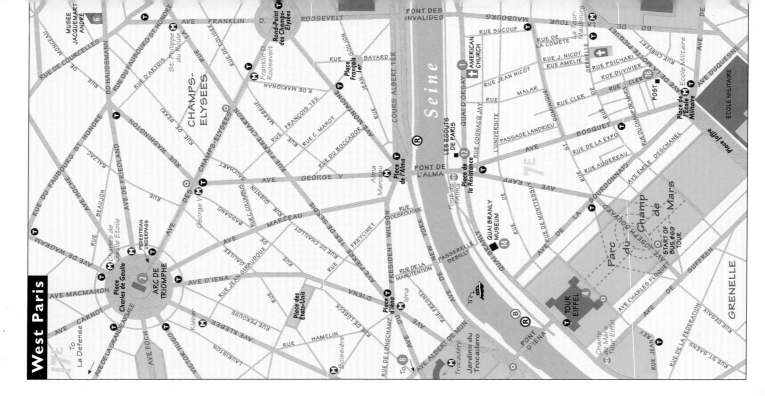

West Paris

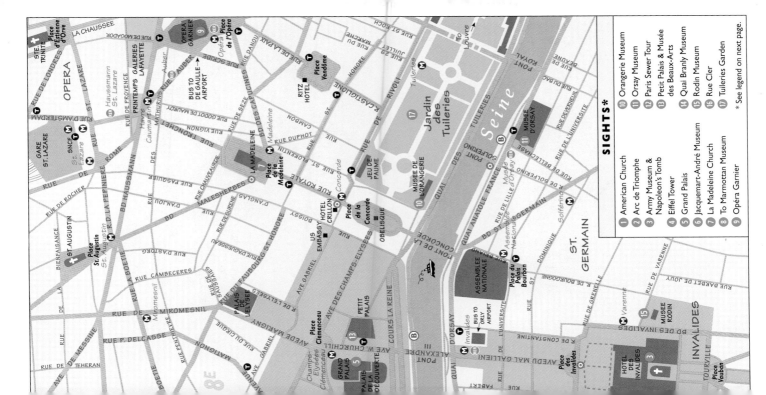

SIGHTS*

1. American Church
2. Arc de Triomphe
3. Army Museum & Napoleon's Tomb
4. Eiffel Tower
5. Grand Palais
6. Jacquemart-André Museum
7. La Madeleine Church
8. To Marmottan Museum
9. Opéra Garnier
10. Orangerie Museum
11. Orsay Museum
12. Paris Sewer Tour
13. Petit Palais & Musée des Beaux-Arts
14. Quai Branly Museum
15. Rodin Museum
16. Rue Cler
17. Tuileries Garden

* See legend on next page.

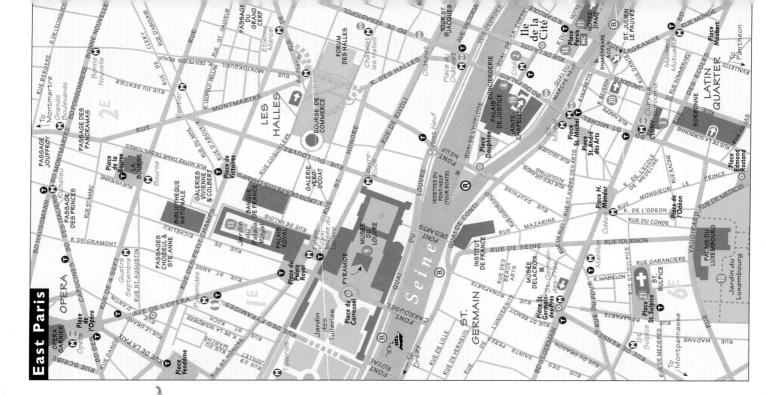

East Paris

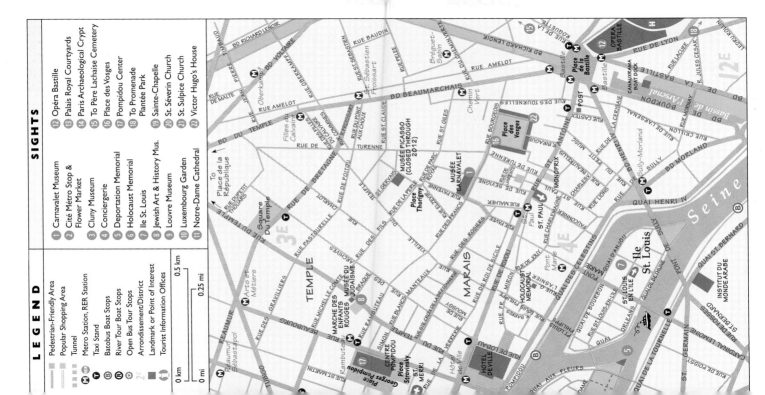

LEGEND

- Pedestrian-Friendly Area
- Popular Shopping Area
- Tunnel
- Ⓜ Metro Station, RER Station
- Ⓣ Taxi Stand
- Ⓑ Batobus Boat Stops
- Ⓡ River Tour Boat Stops
- Ⓞ Open Bus Tour Stops
- Ⓘ Arrondissement/District
- ■ Landmark or Point of Interest
- ⓘ Tourist Information Offices

0 km   0.25 mi
0 mi   0.5 km

SIGHTS

1. Carnavalet Museum
2. Cité Métro Stop & Flower Market
3. Cluny Museum
4. Conciergerie
5. Deportation Memorial
6. Holocaust Memorial
7. Ile St. Louis
8. Jewish Art & History Mus.
9. Louvre Museum
10. Luxembourg Garden
11. Notre-Dame Cathedral
12. Opéra Bastille
13. Palais Royal Courtyards
14. Paris Archaeological Crypt
15. To Père Lachaise Cemetery
16. Place des Vosges
17. Pompidou Center
18. To Promenade Plantée Park
19. Sainte-Chapelle
20. St. Séverin Church
21. St. Sulpice Church
22. Victor Hugo's House

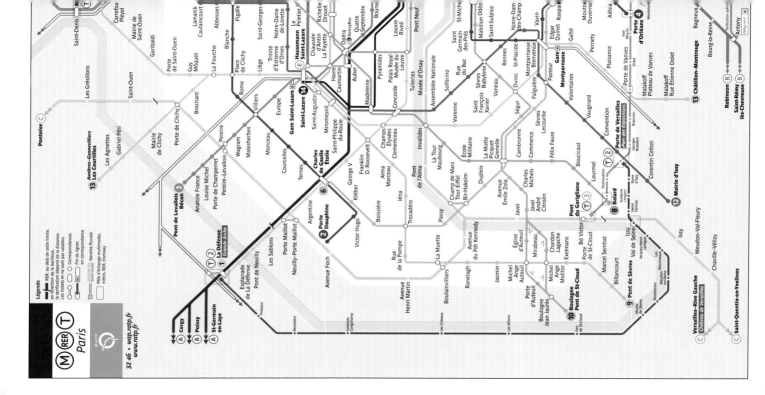

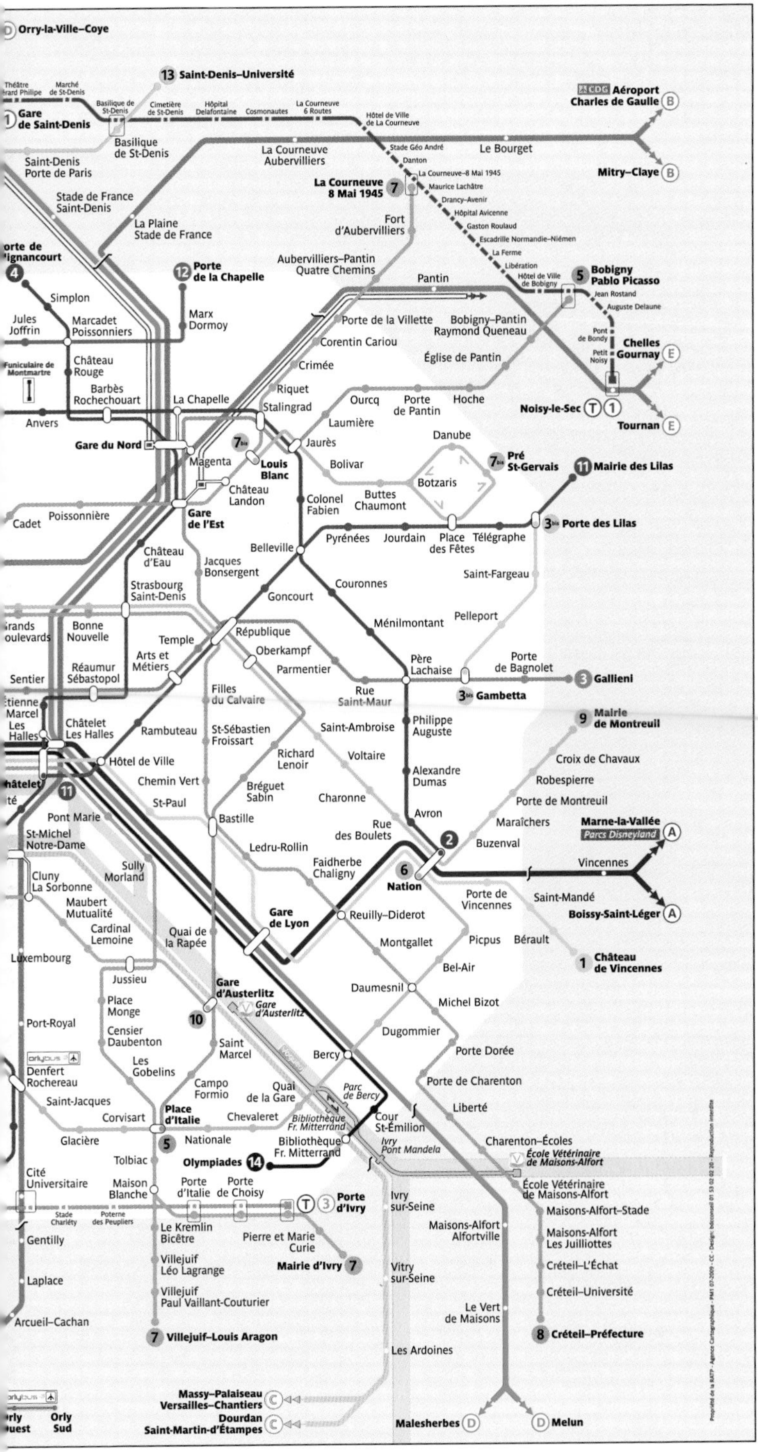

Orry-la-Ville–Coye
13 Saint-Denis–Université
Théâtre
érard Philipe
Marché
de St-Denis
Gare
de Saint-Denis
Basilique de
St-Denis
Cimetière
de St-Denis
Hôpital
Delafontaine
Cosmonautes
La Courneuve
6 Routes
Hôtel de Ville
de La Courneuve
CDG Aéroport
Charles de Gaulle B
Basilique
de St-Denis
Saint-Denis
Porte de Paris
La Courneuve
Aubervilliers
Stade Géo André
Danton
Le Bourget
Mitry–Claye B
La Courneuve
8 Mai 1945
La Courneuve–8 Mai 1945
Maurice Lachâtre
Drancy–Avenir
Hôpital Avicenne
Gaston Roulaud
Escadrille Normandie–Niémen
La Ferme
Libération
Hôtel de Ville
de Bobigny
Stade de France
Saint-Denis
La Plaine
Stade de France
Fort
d'Aubervilliers
orte de
ignancourt
4
12 Porte
de la Chapelle
Aubervilliers–Pantin
Quatre Chemins
5 Bobigny
Pablo Picasso
Jean Rostand
Auguste Delaune
Pantin
Simplon
Jules
Joffrin
Marcadet
Poissonniers
Marx
Dormoy
Porte de la Villette
Bobigny–Pantin
Raymond Queneau
Corentin Cariou
Pont
de Bondy
Petit
Noisy
Chelles
Gournay E
Funiculaire de
Montmartre
Château
Rouge
Crimée
Église de Pantin
Barbès
Rochechouart
La Chapelle
Riquet
Stalingrad
Ourcq
Porte
de Pantin
Hoche
Noisy-le-Sec T 1
Anvers
Laumière
Tournan E
Gare du Nord
7bis
Jaurès
Danube
Magenta
Louis
Blanc
Bolivar
7bis Pré
St-Gervais
11 Mairie des Lilas
Château
Landon
Botzaris
Colonel
Fabien
Buttes
Chaumont
Cadet
Poissonnière
Gare
de l'Est
3bis Porte des Lilas
Pyrénées
Jourdain
Place
des Fêtes
Télégraphe
Château
d'Eau
Belleville
Jacques
Bonsergent
Saint-Fargeau
Strasbourg
Saint-Denis
Couronnes
Goncourt
irands
oulevards
Bonne
Nouvelle
Temple
Ménilmontant
Pelleport
République
Arts et
Métiers
Oberkampf
Réaumur
Sébastopol
Parmentier
Père
Lachaise
Porte
de Bagnolet
Sentier
3 Gallieni
Filles
du Calvaire
Rue
Saint-Maur
3bis Gambetta
tienne
Marcel
Les
Halles
Châtelet
Les Halles
Rambuteau
St-Sébastien
Froissart
Saint-Ambroise
Philippe
Auguste
9 Mairie
de Montreuil
Richard
Lenoir
Voltaire
Croix de Chavaux
hâtelet
Hôtel de Ville
11
ité
Chemin Vert
Bréguet
Sabin
Alexandre
Dumas
Robespierre
St-Paul
Charonne
Porte de Montreuil
Pont Marie
Bastille
Avron
Maraîchers
St-Michel
Notre-Dame
Rue
des Boulets
Marne-la-Vallée
Parcs Disneyland A
Ledru-Rollin
2
Buzenval
Sully
Morland
Faidherbe
Chaligny
6
Nation
Vincennes
Cluny
La Sorbonne
Maubert
Mutualité
Porte de
Vincennes
Saint-Mandé
Boissy-Saint-Léger A
Cardinal
Lemoine
Gare
de Lyon
Reuilly–Diderot
Quai de
la Rapée
Montgallet
Picpus
Bérault
Luxembourg
1 Château
de Vincennes
Jussieu
Bel-Air
Gare
d'Austerlitz
Daumesnil
Place
Monge
V Gare
d'Austerlitz
Port-Royal
10
Michel Bizot
Censier
Daubenton
Saint
Marcel
Dugommier
orlybus
Denfert
Rochereau
Les
Gobelins
Bercy
Porte Dorée
Campo
Formio
Quai
de la Gare
Parc
de Bercy
Porte de Charenton
Saint-Jacques
Corvisart
Place
d'Italie
Chevaleret
Bibliothèque
Fr. Mitterrand
Cour
St-Émilion
Liberté
Glacière
5
Nationale
Bibliothèque
Fr. Mitterrand
Ivry
Pont Mandela
Charenton–Écoles
Tolbiac
Olympiades 14
V École Vétérinaire
de Maisons-Alfort
Cité
Universitaire
Maison
Blanche
Porte
d'Italie
Porte
de Choisy
T 3 Porte
d'Ivry
Ivry
sur-Seine
École Vétérinaire
de Maisons-Alfort
Maisons-Alfort–Stade
Stade
Charléty
Poterne
des Peupliers
Le Kremlin
Bicêtre
Pierre et Marie
Curie
Maisons-Alfort
Alfortville
Maisons-Alfort
Les Juilliottes
Gentilly
Villejuif
Léo Lagrange
Mairie d'Ivry 7
Vitry
sur-Seine
Créteil–L'Échat
Laplace
Villejuif
Paul Vaillant-Couturier
Créteil–Université
Arcueil–Cachan
Le Vert
de Maisons
7 Villejuif–Louis Aragon
8 Créteil–Préfecture
Les Ardoines
Massy–Palaiseau
Versailles–Chantiers C
Dourdan
Saint-Martin-d'Étampes C
orlybus
rly
uest
Orly
Sud
Malesherbes D
D Melun

CONTENTS

France

Bienvenue! You've chosen well. France is Europe's most diverse, tasty, and, in many ways, most exciting country to explore. It's a multifaceted cultural bouillabaisse.

France is a place of gentle beauty, where the play of light transforms the routine into the exceptional. Here, travelers are treated to a blend of man-made and natural beauty like nowhere else in Europe. With luxuriant forests, forever coastlines, truly grand canyons, and Europe's highest mountain ranges, France has a cover-girl beauty from top to bottom. You'll also discover a dizzying array of artistic and architectural wonders—soaring cathedrals, chandeliered châteaux, and museums filled with the cultural icons of the Western world.

In many ways, France is a yardstick of human achievement. Travelers can trace the whole of European history, from the earliest prehistoric cave paintings to Roman ruins that rival Italy's. In medieval times, France cultivated Romanesque and Gothic architecture, erecting the great cathedrals and basilicas of Notre-Dame, Chartres, Vézelay, and a dozen others. With their innovative designs, French architects set the trends for cities throughout Europe—and with their revolutionary thinking, French philosophers refined modern thought and politics. The châteaux of the Loire Valley and the grand palace of Versailles announced France's emergence as the first European superpower and first modern government. It was France that gave birth to Impressionism and the foundations

of modern art. Today's travelers can gaze dreamy-eyed at water lilies in Claude Monet's Giverny, rejoice amid the sunflowers of Provence that so moved a troubled Vincent van Gogh, and roam the sunny coastlines that inspired Picasso and Matisse. And after all these centuries, France still remains at the forefront of technology, fashion, and—of course—cuisine.

There are two Frances: Paris...and the rest of the country. France's top-down government and cultural energy have always been centered in Paris, resulting in an overwhelming concentration of world-class museums, cutting-edge architecture, and historic monuments. Travelers can spend weeks in France and never leave Paris. Many do.

The other France venerates land, tradition, and a slower pace of life. After Paris, most travelers will be drawn to romantic hill towns and castles, meandering rivers and canals, and seas of vineyards that carpet this country's landscape. Village life has survived in France better than in most other European countries because France was slow to urbanize. It was an agricultural country right up until World War II (when a smaller proportion of French citizens lived in cities than Italians did 500 years earlier). And today, even as young people are chasing jobs in the cities, France remains farm country.

Everyone values the soil (*le terroir*) that brings the flavor to their foods and wines and nourishes a rural life that French people dream about. So although the country's brain resides in Paris, its soul lives in its villages—and that's where you'll feel the real pulse of France.

France offers more diversity than any other nation in Europe; moving from region to region, you feel as if you're crossing into a different country. Paris and the region around it (called Ile de France) is the "island" in the middle that anchors France. To the west are the dramatic D-Day beaches and English-style, thatched-roofed homes of Normandy; to the south lie the river valleys of the Loire and Dordogne, featuring luxurious châteaux, medieval castles, and hillside villages. Explore under-the-radar France

to the far south and west, in the Spanish-tinged Languedoc and Basque regions. Closer to Italy, sun-baked and windswept Provence offers Roman ruins and rustic charm, while the Riviera has sunny beaches and yacht-filled harbors. And in the north and east, travelers encounter snow-capped Alps, the venerable vineyards of Burgundy, and the Germanic villages and cuisine of Alsace.

The forte of French cuisine is its regional diversity. You'll enjoy Swiss-like fondue in the Alps, Italian-style pasta and pesto on the Riviera, Spanish paella in Languedoc, and German sauerkraut mixed with fine wine sauces in the Alsace. *C'est magnifique*—you can taste a good slice of Europe without stepping outside of France.

Each region also produces a wine that complements its cuisine—such as rich Burgundy wines that go perfectly with

coq au vin, meaty wines from Languedoc to counter heavy cuisine (such as cassoulet), fruity Côtes du Rhône wines that work well with herb-infused Provençal dishes, and dry whites in Alsace that meld perfectly with the Germanic cuisine. And in Normandy and Brittany, you'll enjoy apple ciders with crêpes and fresh seafood.

As if that weren't enough, France is also famous for its many pâtés, foie gras, hundreds of different cheeses, sizzling

escargots, fresh oysters, *herbes de Provence*, raw meats, fine wine sauces, French fries, duck and lamb dishes, pastries, bonbons, crème brûlée, and sorbets.

L'art de vivre—the art of living—is not just a pleasing French expression; it's a building block for a sound life. With five weeks of paid vacation, plus every Catholic holiday ever invented, the French are forced to enjoy life. It's no accident that France is home to café lounging, fine cuisine, Club Med vacations, barge cruising, and ballooning. You'll run headlong into that mindful approach to life at mealtime. The French insist on the best-quality croissants, mustard, and sparkling water; they linger over lunches; and an evening's entertainment is often no more than a lovingly prepared meal with friends. France demands that the traveler slow down and savor the finer things; a hurried visitor will miss the *what-matters-in-life* barge and blame the French for being lazy. One of your co-authors learned this lesson the hard way while restoring a farm house in Burgundy—and

found that it's counterproductive to hurry a project past its "normal pace."

In spite of lavish attention to relaxation, the French are a productive people. French inventors gave us the metric system, pasteurization, high-speed trains, and Concorde airplanes. More importantly, this country rose from the ashes of two debilitating world wars to generate the world's seventh-largest

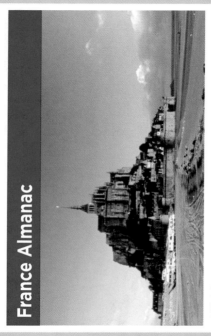

France Almanac

Official Name: It's officially the République Française, but locals, and everyone else, just call it France.

Population: France has 62 million people (nearly twice the population of California). They're a mix of Celtic, Latin, and Teutonic DNA, plus many recent immigrants from around the globe—especially North Africa. Four of five French are (at least nominally) Roman Catholic. Every French citizen is expected to speak French.

Area: At 215,000 square miles, it's Western Europe's largest nation. (But Texas is still 20 percent bigger.)

Latitude and Longitude: 46°N and 2°E (similar latitude to the states of Washington, North Dakota, and Maine).

Geography: The terrain consists of rolling plains in the north and mountains in the southwest (Pyrenees), southeast (Alps), and south-central (Massif Central). Capping the country on both ends are 1,400 miles of coastline (Mediterranean and Atlantic). The Seine River flows east-west through Paris, the Rhône rumbles north-south 500 miles from the Alps to the Mediterranean, and the Loire travels east-west, roughly dividing the country into north and south. Mont Blanc (15,771 feet) is Western Europe's highest point.

Major Cities: Nearly one in five lives in greater Paris (12 million in the metropolitan area, 2.2 million in the city). Marseille, on the Mediterranean coast, has 827,000, and Lyon has 472,000.

Economy: France's gross domestic product is $2.66 trillion (bigger than California's $1.85 trillion); the GDP per capita is $32,800

(America's is $46,400). Though the French produce nearly a quarter of the world's wine, they drink much of it themselves. France's free-market economy is tempered by the government: high taxes (one of Europe's highest rates at 44 percent of GDP—compared to 33 percent in the US), government investment in industry, and social spending (to narrow the income gap between rich and poor). Despite the three-hour lunch stereotypes, the French work as much as their EU neighbors—that is, 20 percent less than Americans (but with greater per-hour productivity).

Government: President Nicolas Sarkozy, elected by popular vote in 2007, heads a conservative government (but by conservative Americans', it's leftist) along with president-appointed Prime Minister, François Fillon. The upper-house Senate (343 seats) is chosen by an electoral college; the National Assembly (577 seats) by popular vote. Though France is a cornerstone of the European Union, many French are Euro-skeptics.

Flag: The Revolution produced the well-known tricolore, whose three colors are vertical bands of blue, white, and red.

The Average Jean: The average French person is 39 years old and will live almost 81 years. This person eats lunch in 38 minutes (twice as fast as 25 years ago) and consumes a glass and a half of wine and a pound of fat a day. The average French citizen pops a bottle of champagne about every four months. The typical French woman is 5' 4", weighs 140 pounds, and wears a size 8-10 dress. The average worker enjoys five weeks of holiday and vacation a year. A dog is a part of one in three French households; cats are animals non grata.

economy. This is thanks in part to determined government intervention that continues today (government spending is 53 percent of GDP). Wine, tourism, telecommunications, pharmaceuticals, cars, and Airbus planes are big moneymakers. France is also the European Union's leading agricultural producer and a chief competitor of the US. You'll pass endless wheat farms in the north, dairy farms in the west, vegetable farms and fruit orchards in the south...and vineyards everywhere.

With no domestic oil production, France has focused on nuclear power generation, which now accounts for more than 75 percent of the country's electricity production. Electricity is expensive, so the French are careful to turn out lights and conserve—something to remember when you leave your hotel room for the day or evening.

Although France's economy may be one of the world's largest, the French remain skeptical about the virtues of capitalism and the work ethic. Business conversation is generally avoided, as it implies a fascination with money that the French find vulgar. (It's considered gauche even to ask what someone does for a living.) In France, CEOs are not glorified as celebrities—chefs are.

The French believe that the economy should support social

good, not vice versa. This has produced a cradle-to-grave social security system of which the French are proud. France's poverty rate is half of that in the US, proof to the French that they are on the right track. On the other hand, if you're considering starting a business in France, think again—taxes are formidable (figure a total small-business tax rate of around 66 percent). France is routinely plagued with strikes, demonstrations, and slow-downs as workers try to preserve their hard-earned rights in the face of a competitive global economy.

As you travel, you'll find that the most "French" thing about France is the French themselves. Be prepared to embrace (or at least understand) the cultural differences between yourself and your French hosts. You'll find the French to be reserved in the north and comparatively carefree in the sunny south. Throughout the country, they're more formal than you are. When you enter a store, you'll be greeted not simply with a "*Bonjour,*" but with "*Bonjour, Monsieur* or *Madame.*" The proper response to the shopkeeper is "*Bonjour, Monsieur* or *Madame.*" If there are others present, you'd say, "*Bonjour, Messieurs* or *Mesdames*"—just to make sure you don't leave anyone out. (For more on the French attitude toward language, see page 1002.)

The French are overwhelmingly Catholic but not very devout, and are quick to separate church from state. They are less active churchgoers than Americans, whom they find *très* evangelical. And in France you don't go to church to socialize or to help in charitable deeds (that's what taxes are for). France is also Europe's largest Muslim nation, with well over five million followers (there are twice as many Muslims in France as Protestants). The influx of Muslim immigrants has led to considerable problems of assimilation and remains one of France's thorniest issues to resolve.

The French don't seem particularly athletic—unless you consider tossing little silver balls in the dirt (*pétanque*, a.k.a. *boules*) a sport. A few jog and exercise regularly, and fewer play on recreational teams—though you will find country lanes busy with bike riders hunched over handlebars

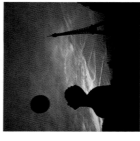

on weekends. The French are avid sports-watchers. Soccer is king (even though the national team disgraced itself at the 2010 World Cup), bike racing is big, and rugby is surprisingly popular for such a refined place. *Le basket* (basketball) is making a move, with a French league and several French NBA stars, including Tony ("Mr. Eva Longoria") Parker.

Another passion the French share with Americans is their love of movies. They admire Hollywood blockbusters, but they've also carved out their own niche of small-budget romantic comedies and thought-provoking thrillers.

Today's France will challenge many of your preconceptions. The French have a Michelin Guide certainty in their judgments and are often frank in how they convey their

opinions. (Just ask about the best wine to serve with any given course.)

Simply put, the French see the world differently than we do. The right to bear arms, the death penalty, miniscule paid vacations, and health care as a privilege rather than a basic human right—these American concepts confound the average Jean. And they don't understand the American need for everyone to be in agreement all of the time. Whether it's Iraq, Vietnam, or globalization, the French think it's important to question authority and not blindly submit to it. Blame this aversion to authority on their Revolution hangover.

The French can be a complicated people to understand for hurried

Rick Steves' France

travelers. But remember where they've come from: In just a few generations, they've seen two world wars destroy entire cities, villages, landscapes, and their self-respect. They've watched as America replaced them as the world's political and cultural superpower. On the bright side, they've seen their country re-emerge as a global force, with nuclear weapons, a space program, an international spy network, and their own ideas about geopolitics. Like Americans, they're trying to find their place in an increasingly global, multicultural world. Today, they just don't want to be taken for granted. And while the French may—or may not—love your country's politics, that has no bearing on how they will treat you as an individual.

As you travel through this splendid country, come with an appetite to understand and a willingness to experience. Welcome new ideas and give the locals the benefit of your doubt. Accept France on its own terms and don't judge. Above all, slo-o-o-ow down. Spend hours in cafés lingering over *un café*, make a habit of making unplanned stops, hop on the *l'art de vivre* barge, and surrender to the play of light as the Impressionists did.

INTRODUCTION

France is nearly as big as Texas, with 62 million people and some 400 different cheeses. *Diversité* is a French forte. This country features three impressive mountain ranges (the Alps, the Pyrenees, and the Massif Central), two coastlines as different as night and day (Atlantic and Mediterranean), cosmopolitan cities (such as Paris, Lyon, Strasbourg, and Nice), and countless sleepy villages. From the Swiss-like Alps to the *molto* Italian Riviera, and from the Spanish Pyrenees to *das* German Alsace, you can stay in France and feel like you've sampled much of Europe—and never be more than a short stroll from a *bon vin rouge*.

We've covered the predictable must-sees while mixing in a healthy dose of Back Door intimacy. Along with seeing the Eiffel Tower, Mont St. Michel, and the French Riviera, you'll take a minivan tour of the D-Day beaches, pedal your way from village to vineyard in the Alsace, marvel at 15,000-year-old cave paintings, and paddle a canoe down the lazy Dordogne River. You'll find a *magnifique* hill-town perch to catch a Provençal sunset, ride Europe's highest mountain lift over the Alps, and touch the quiet Romanesque soul of Burgundian abbeys and villages. You'll learn about each region's key monuments and cities with our thoughtfully presented walking tours and background information. Just as important, you'll meet the intriguing people who run your hotel, bed-and-breakfast, or restaurant. We've also listed our favorite local guides, all well worth the time and money, to help you gain a better understanding of this marvelous country's past and present.

The destinations covered in this book are balanced to include the most interesting cities and intimate villages, from jet-setting beach resorts to the traditional heartland. This book is selective, including only the most exciting sights and romantic villages—for

Top Destinations in France

example, there are hundreds of beautiful châteaux in the Loire region, but we cover only the best. And though there are dozens of Loire towns you could use for a home base, we recommend only the top two: Amboise and Chinon.

The best is, of course, only our opinion. But after spending half of our adult lives writing and lecturing about travel, guiding tours, and gaining an appreciation for all things French, we've developed a sixth sense for what touches the traveler's imagination.

About This Book

Rick Steves' France 2011 is a personal tour guide in your pocket. Better yet, it's actually two tour guides in your pocket: The co-author of this book is Steve Smith. Steve lived in France as a child and has been traveling to France—as a guide, a researcher, a homeowner, and a devout Francophile—every year since 1985. He restored a 300-year-old farmhouse in Burgundy and today keeps one foot on each side of the Atlantic. Together, Steve and I keep this book up-to-date and accurate (though, for simplicity, from

Key to This Book

Updates

This book is updated every year, but things change. For the latest, visit www.ricksteves.com/update, and for a valuable list of reports and experiences—good and bad—from fellow travelers, check www.ricksteves.com/feedback.

Abbreviations and Times

I use the following symbols and abbreviations in this book:

Sights are rated:

▲▲▲ Don't miss
▲▲ Try hard to see
▲ Worthwhile if you can make it
No rating Worth knowing about

Tourist information offices are abbreviated as **TI**, and bathrooms are **WCs**. To categorize accommodations, I use a **Sleep Code** (described on page 23).

Like Europe, this book uses the **24-hour clock.** It's the same through 12:00 noon, then keep going: 13:00, 14:00, and so on. For anything over 12, subtract 12 and add p.m. (14:00 is 2:00 p.m.).

When giving **opening times,** I include both peak season and off-season hours if they differ. So if a museum is listed as "May-Oct daily 9:00-16:00," it should be open from 9 a.m. until 4 p.m. from the first day of May until the last day of October (but expect exceptions).

For **transit** or **tour departures,** I first list the frequency, then the duration. So a train connection listed as "2/hour, 1.5 hours" departs twice each hour, and the journey lasts an hour and a half.

this point "we" will shed our respective egos and become "I").

This book is organized by destination. Each of these destinations is a mini-vacation on its own, filled with exciting sights, strollable towns, homey affordable places to stay, and memorable places to eat. In the following chapters, you'll find these sections:

Planning Your Time suggests a schedule, with thoughts on how best to use your limited time.

Orientation includes specifics on public transportation, helpful hints, local tour options, easy-to-read maps, and tourist information.

Sights describes the top attractions and includes their cost and hours.

Self-Guided Walks take you through interesting neighborhoods, with a Personal tour guide in hand.

Sleeping describes my favorite hotels, from good-value deals to cushy splurges.

Eating serves up a range of options, from inexpensive eateries to romantic bistros.

Connections outlines your options for traveling to destinations by train and bus, plus route tips for drivers.

France: Past and Present gives you a quick overview of French history and its notable citizens.

The **appendix** is a traveler's tool kit, with telephone tips, useful phone numbers, transportation basics (on trains, buses, car rentals, driving, and flights), recommended books and films, festival list, climate chart, handy packing checklist, hotel reservation form, pronunciation guide for place names, and French survival phrases.

Browse through this book and select your favorite sights. Then have a *fantastique* trip! Traveling like a temporary local, you'll get the absolute most out of every mile, minute, and euro. I'm happy that you'll be visiting the places I know and love and meeting my favorite French people.

Planning

This section—with advice on trip costs, when to go, and what you should know before you take off—will help you get started on planning your trip.

Travel Smart

Your trip to France is like a complex play—easier to follow and really appreciate on a second viewing. While no one does the same trip twice to gain that advantage, reading this book in its entirety before your trip accomplishes much the same thing.

Design an itinerary that enables you to visit museums and festivals on the right days. Note holidays, specifics on sights, and days when sights are closed. If you're using public transportation, read up on the tips for trains and buses (see pages 1019 and 1021 in the appendix). If you're renting a car, peruse my driving tips and study the examples of road signs (see page 1026).

Mix intense and relaxed periods in your itinerary. To maximize rootedness, minimize one-night stands (and opt for three-night stays). Every trip—and every traveler—needs at least a few slack days (for picnics, laundry, people-watching, and so on). Pace yourself. Assume you will return.

Reread this book while you travel, and visit local tourist information offices. Upon arrival in a new town, lay the groundwork for a smooth departure; write down the schedule for the train or bus you'll take when you depart, or study the best driving route to your next destination. Use taxis in the big cities.

Get online at Internet cafés or at your hotel, and buy a phone

card or carry a mobile phone: You can get tourist information, learn the latest on sights (special events, English tour schedules, etc.), book tickets and tours, make reservations, reconfirm hotels, research transportation connections, check weather, and keep in touch with your loved ones.

Connect with the culture. Cheer for your favorite bowler at a *pétanque* match, leave no chair unturned in your quest for the best café, find that perfect hill-town view, and make friends with a waiter. Slow down to appreciate the sincerity of your French hosts, and be open to unexpected experiences. Ask questions—most locals are eager to point you in their idea of the right direction. Keep a notepad in your pocket for organizing your thoughts. Wear your money belt, and figure out how to estimate prices in dollars. Those who expect to travel smart, do.

Trip Costs

Five components make up your total trip cost: airfare, surface transportation, room and board, sightseeing and entertainment, and shopping and miscellany.

Airfare: Paris and Nice have the most convenient flights from the US. A basic round-trip flight from the US to Paris or Nice costs $800–1,600—including taxes and fuel charges—depending on where you fly from and when (cheaper in winter).

Within Europe, flights can be cheaper than train travel. Smaller budget airlines provide bargain service from several European capitals to many French cities (see "Cheap Flights" on page 1029 for details). Within France, these inexpensive flights can get you between Paris and other major cities (such as Nice, Marseille, Strasbourg, Toulouse, Lyon, and Bordeaux).

If your trip in Europe covers a wide area, consider saving time and money by flying "open jaw"—into one city and out of another—for example, into Nice and out of Paris. Many find the easygoing Mediterranean city of Nice far easier than Paris as a starting point for their trip.

Surface Transportation: For a three-week whirlwind trip of my recommended destinations, allow $700 per person for public transportation (trains and buses) or $900 per person (based on two people sharing) for a three-week car rental, parking, tolls, gas, and insurance (figure about $250 total per week for just gas and tolls). Leasing is worth considering for trips of three weeks or more. Car rentals and leases are cheapest if arranged from the US. Train passes, normally available only outside of Europe, are usually a good deal, but you may find you'll save money by buying tickets as you go. For details on public transportation, car rental, and leasing, see "Transportation" in the appendix.

Room and Board: You can thrive in France on $135 a day per

France at a Glance

These attractions are listed (as in this book) looping counter-clockwise around France, starting in Paris and ending in Champagne.

Paris World capital of art, fashion, food, literature, and ideas, offering historic monuments, grand boulevards, corner cafés, chic boutiques, cutting-edge architecture, and world-class art galleries, including the Louvre and Orsay.

Near Paris Europe's best palace at Versailles, the awesome cathedral of Chartres, Monet's flowery gardens at Giverny, and a mouse-run amusement park.

Normandy Pastoral mix of sweeping coastlines, half-timbered towns, and exciting cities, including bustling Rouen (Gothic architecture, Joan of Arc sites), the little romantic port town of Honfleur, historic Bayeux (remarkable tapestry on the Battle of Hastings), stirring D-Day sites and museums, and the almost surreal island abbey of Mont St. Michel.

Brittany Windswept and rugged, with a forgotten interior, well-discovered coast, Celtic ties, and two notable towns: Dinan (Brittany's best medieval center) and the beach resort of St. Malo.

The Loire Picturesque towns (such as Amboise and Chinon) and more than a thousand castles and palaces, including Chenonceaux (arcing across its river), the huge Château de Chambord, Villandry (wonderful gardens), lavishly furnished Cheverny, and many more.

Dordogne Prehistoric caves, rock-sculpted villages, lazy canoe rides past medieval castles, market towns such as pedestrian-friendly Sarlat, and nearby, for wine lovers, St. Emilion.

Languedoc Sunny region with a Spanish flair, featuring Albi (fortress-like cathedral and a beautiful Toulouse-Lautrec Museum), medieval Carcassonne (walled town with towers, turrets, and cobblestones), remote Cathar castles, and the lovely coastal village of Collioure.

person for room and board (allow $155 a day for Paris). A $135-a-day budget allows an average of $12 for breakfast, $18 for lunch, $40 for dinner with drinks, and $65 for lodging (based on two people splitting the cost of a $130 double room). That's definitely doable, and it's easy for many travelers to come in under budget. Students and tightwads do it on $50 a day ($25 per bed, $25 for meals and snacks).

Provence Attracts writers and artists, boasts Arles (Van Gogh sights, evocative Roman Arena), Avignon (famous bridge and brooding Palace of the Popes), the ancient Roman aqueduct of Pont du Gard, Orange (Roman Theater), the beautiful Côtes du Rhone wine road, and rock-top villages such as Les Baux, Roussillon, and Vaison la Romaine.

The Riviera A string of coastal resorts, including Nice (big city with seafront promenade and art museums), easygoing Villefranche-sur-Mer, glitzy Monaco (casino), romantic Antibes (silky-sandy beaches), and little hilltop Eze-le-Village, with magnificent Mediterranean views.

The French Alps Spectacular scenery featuring the drop-dead gorgeous town of Annecy, sky-high Mont Blanc, and the world-famous ski resort of Chamonix, with hikes galore and lifts to stunning alpine views.

Lyon Metropolitan city, located between Burgundy and Provence, with two Roman Theaters, a terrific Gallo-Roman Museum, the stirring French Resistance Center, and France's best cuisine at affordable prices.

Burgundy Aged blend of vineyards and spirituality, with the compact town of Beaune (world-famous vineyards), Fontenay (France's best-preserved medieval abbey), Vézelay (magnificent Romanesque church), the one-of-a-kind medieval castle under construction at Guédelon, Cluny's grand medieval abbey, and the modern-day religious community of Taizé.

Alsace Franco-Germanic region dotted with wine-road villages, starring half-timbered Colmar and its world-class art, and high-powered Strasbourg and its sensational cathedral.

Reims and Verdun Champagne-soaked Reims with caves serving the sparkling brew, and nearby Verdun, site of brutal WWI battles, with a compelling, unforgettable memorial.

Sightseeing and Entertainment: In cities, figure about $8–18 per major sight (Louvre–$12, Abbey of Mont St. Michel–$11), $6 for minor ones (climbing church towers), $25 for guided walks, and $40–50 for bus tours and splurge experiences (concerts in Paris' Sainte-Chapelle or a ride on the Chamonix gondola).

An overall average of $25 a day for sightseeing and entertainment works for most people. Don't skimp here. After all, this category is the driving force behind your trip—you came to sightsee, enjoy, and experience France.

Shopping and Miscellany: Figure $5 per ice-cream cone, coffee, or soft drink. Shopping can vary in cost from nearly nothing to a small fortune. Good budget travelers find that this category has little to do with assembling a trip full of lifelong and wonderful memories.

Sightseeing Priorities

Depending on the length of your trip, here are my recommended priorities:

  3 days: Paris and maybe Versailles
  5 days, add: Normandy
  7 days, add: Loire
 10 days, add: Dordogne, Carcassonne
 15 days, add: Provence, the Riviera
 18 days, add: Burgundy, Chamonix
 21 days, add: Alsace, northern France
 23 days, add: Basque Country

For a day-by-day itinerary of a three-week trip, see the sidebars (one for drivers and one for people using trains and buses) in this chapter.

If all you have is a week and it's your first trip to France, do Paris, Normandy, and the Loire.

For a more focused 10- to 14-day trip that highlights Paris, Provence, and the Riviera, fly into Paris and out of Nice. After touring Paris, take the TGV train from Paris to Avignon, rent a car there, and drop it in Nice (or use trains, buses, and minivan tours to get around). This trip also works in reverse.

Travelers with a little more time could add Burgundy and/or the Alps, which are about halfway between Paris and Provence and easy to explore by car or train.

When to Go

Late spring and fall are best, with generally good weather and lighter crowds, though summer brings festivals, reliable weather, and long opening hours at sights.

Europeans vacation in July and August, jamming the Riviera, the Dordogne, and the Alps (worst from mid-July to mid-Aug), but leaving the rest of the country just lively enough for tourists. And though many French businesses close in August, the traveler hardly notices. Winter travel is fine for Paris, Nice, and Lyon, but you'll find smaller cities and villages buttoned up tight (see "Winter Activities" on page 58). Winter weather is gray, noticeably milder in the south (unless the wind is blowing), and colder and wetter in the north. Sights and tourist information offices keep shorter hours, and some tourist activities (such as English-language castle tours) vanish altogether. On the other hand, winter travel allows you to see cities though the lens of a local, as hotels, restaurants, and sights are wonderfully tourist-free. To get the latest weather forecast in English, dial 08 99 70 11 11, then press 1. Also see the climate chart in the appendix.

Thanks to France's relatively mild climate, fields of flowers greet the traveler much of the year:

Mid-April–May: Crops of brilliant yellow colza bloom, mostly in the north (best in Burgundy). Wild red poppies (*coquelicots*) begin sprouting in the south.

June: Red poppies pop up throughout the country. Late in June, lavender blooms begin covering the hills of Provence.

July: Lavender is in full swing in Provence, and sunflowers are awakening. Cities, towns, and villages everywhere overflow with carefully tended flowers.

August–September: Sunflowers flourish north and south.

October: In the latter half of the month, the countryside glistens with fall colors, as most trees are deciduous. Vineyards go for the gold.

Know Before You Go

Your trip is more likely to go smoothly if you plan ahead. Check this list of things to arrange while you're still at home.

You need a **passport**—but no visa or shots—to travel in France. You may be denied entry into certain European countries if your passport is due to expire within three to six months of your ticketed date of return. Get it renewed if you'll be cutting it close. It can take up to six weeks to get or renew a passport (for more on passports, see www.travel.state.gov). Pack a photocopy of your passport in your luggage in case the original is lost or stolen.

Book your rooms well in advance, especially if you'll be traveling during peak season or any major **holidays**. (See the "Major Holidays and Weekends" sidebar on page 14.)

Call your **debit- and credit-card companies** to let them know the countries you'll be visiting, to ask about fees, and more (see page 16).

Do your homework if you want to buy **travel insurance.** Compare the cost of the insurance to the likelihood of your using it and your potential loss if something goes wrong. For more information, see www.ricksteves.com/insurance.

If you're bringing an MP3 player, you can download free information from **Rick Steves Audio Europe,** featuring hours of travel interviews and more (at www.ricksteves.com and on iTunes; for details, see page 1030).

Whirlwind (Kamikaze) Three-Week Trip Through France for Drivers

Day Plan

1 Fly into Paris, pick up your car, visit Giverny, and overnight in Honfleur (1 night). Save Paris sightseeing for the end of your trip.

2 Spend today at D-Day sights: Arromanches, American Cemetery, and Pointe du Hoc (and Caen Memorial Museum, if you're moving fast). Dinner and overnight in Bayeux (1 night).

3 Bayeux Tapestry and church, Mont St. Michel, sleep on Mont St. Michel (1 night).

4 Spend your morning on Mont St. Michel, then head for châteaux country in the Loire Valley. Tour Chambord, then stay in Amboise (2 nights).

5 Do a day trip, touring Chenonceaux and Cheverny or Chaumont. Save time at the end of the day for Amboise and its sights.

6 Head south to the Dordogne region, stopping en route at Oradour-sur-Glane. End in a Dordogne village—your choice of the handful of lodgings I recommend (2 nights).

7 Browse the town and market of Sarlat, take a canoe trip, and tour Font-de-Gaume cave.

8 Head to the Languedoc region, lunch in Puycelci or Albi, and spend the evening in Carcassonne (1 night).

9 Morning in Carcassonne, then on to Provence with a stop at the Pont du Gard aqueduct. Stay in or near Arles (2 nights).

10 All day for Arles and Les Baux.

11 Visit a Provençal hilltown such as Roussillon, then depart for the Riviera, staying in Nice or Villefranche-sur-Mer (2 nights).

12 Sightsee in Nice and Monaco.

13 Make the long drive north to the Alps, and sleep in Chamonix (2 nights).

14 If the weather is clear, take the mountain lifts up to Aiguille du Midi and beyond.

15 A half-day for the Alps (in Chamonix or Annecy). Then head for Burgundy, ending in Beaune for a wine-tasting. Sleep in

If you'll be **traveling with children,** read the list of pre-trip suggestions on page 30.

If you're planning on **renting a car** in France, you'll need your driver's license. An International Driving Permit is recommended (see page 1022).

All **high-speed TGV trains** in France require a seat reservation—book as early as possible, as these trains fill fast. If you're

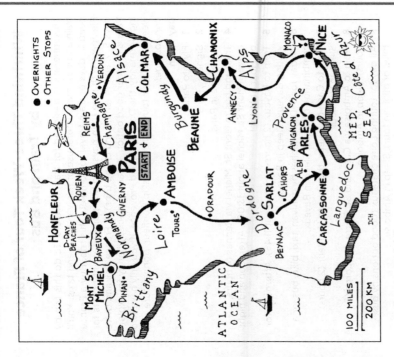

Beaune (1 night).

16 Spend the morning in Beaune, then move on to Colmar (2 nights).

17 Enjoy Colmar and the Route du Vin villages.

18 Return to Paris, visiting Verdun or Reims en route. Collapse in Paris hotel (4 nights).

19 Sightsee Paris.

20 More time in Paris.

21 Finish your sightseeing in Paris, and consider side-tripping to Versailles.

using a railpass, it's especially important to reserve early—there's a tight limit on seat reservations for passholders. If you're taking an overnight train (especially to international destinations), and you need a *couchette* (overnight bunk) or sleeper, and you *must* leave on a certain day, consider booking it in advance through a US agent (such as www.raileurope.com), even though it may cost more. (For more on train travel, see the appendix.)

Whirlwind Three-Week Tour of France by Train and Bus

This itinerary is designed for train travelers. To do this trip by train and bus, make liberal use of minivan tours and taxis. You'll need 12 days of train travel to complete this trip. Buy a France Flexipass with nine train days and buy point-to-point tickets for days 5, 7, and 14 (short and cheap trips). A France Rail and Drive Pass is another good option. A car is especially handy for exploring Normandy, the Dordogne, and Provence. If you only have two weeks, end your tour in Nice and skip Honfleur. *Bonne route and bon courage!*

Day Plan

1 Fly into Paris.

2 Sightsee Paris.

3 More time in Paris.

4 Train and bus to Mont St. Michel via Rennes (4 hours, arrive in Mont St. Michel about 13:00). Afternoon and night on Mont St Michel.

5 Train to Bayeux (2 hours, arrive about 11:45). Afternoon for visiting Bayeux. Sleep in Bayeux.

6 All day for D-Day beaches by minivan, taxi, bike, bus, or a combination of these. Sleep in Bayeux.

7 Train to Caen or Lisieux, then bus to Honfleur (2 hours). Sleep in Honfleur.

8 Train to Amboise via Caen and St. Pierre des Corps (5 hours). Sleep in Amboise.

9 All day for touring Loire châteaux (good options by bus, bike, or minivan tour). Sleep in Amboise.

Because **airline carry-on restrictions** are always changing, visit the Transportation Security Administration's website (www .tsa.gov/travelers) for an up-to-date list of what you can bring on the plane with you...and what you have to check.

Practicalities

Emergency and Medical Help: In France, dial 17 for police help or 15 for a medical emergency. If you get sick, do as the French do and go to a pharmacist for advice. Or ask at your hotel for help— they'll know the nearest medical and emergency services.

Lost or Stolen Passport: To replace a passport, you'll need to go in person to a US embassy or consulate. You'll find the US embassy in Paris and consulates in Lyon, Marseille, Nice, and Strasbourg (see page 1009; full list at www.travel.state.gov). Though not required, having a back-up form of ID (ideally a pho-

10 Early train to Sarlat (6 hours, arrive about 13:30). Afternoon and evening in Sarlat. Sleep in Sarlat.

11 All day for caves and canoes by train and bike or minivan/taxi tour. Sleep in Sarlat.

12 Train or bus to Carcassonne (5.5 hours, leaving about noon is best, though earlier trips are possible). Dinner and evening wall walk. Sleep in Carcassonne.

13 Morning wall walk, then train to Arles (2.5 hours). Afternoon in Arles.

14 Train to Nîmes, then bus to Pont du Gard. Tour the Pont du Gard, then bus to Avignon and spend your afternoon/evening there (consider dinner). Train back to Arles. Sleep in Arles.

15 Morning in Arles or Les Baux (4 hours), afternoon train to Nice (4 hours), set up in Nice. Sleep in Nice.

16 All day for Nice and Monaco. Sleep in Nice.

17 Morning train to Lyon (4 hours). Afternoon and night in Lyon.

18 Train to Chamonix (4 hours, consider a halfway stopover in Annecy—no bag check). Sleep in Chamonix.

19 If the weather is clear, take the mountain lifts up to Aiguille du Midi and beyond. Sleep in Chamonix.

20 Early train to Paris (leave at 6:30, arrive about 13:30). Last afternoon and night in Paris. (Or make it a 23-day tour with a scenic 6.5-hour train through Switzerland to Colmar, spend two nights there, then take the TGV back to Paris.)

21 Fly home.

tocopy of your passport and your driver's license) speeds up the process. For more info, see www.ricksteves.com/help.

Time Zones: France, like most of continental Europe, is generally six/nine hours ahead of the East/West Coasts of the US. The exceptions are the beginning and end of Daylight Saving Time: Europe "springs forward" the last Sunday in March (two weeks after most of North America) and "falls back" the last Sunday in October (one week before North America). For a handy online time converter, try www.timeanddate.com/worldclock.

Business Hours: You'll find much of rural France closed weekdays from noon to 14:00 (lunch is sacred). On Sunday, most businesses are closed (family is sacred), though some small stores such as *boulangeries* (bakeries) are open until noon, special events and weekly markets pop up, and museums are open all day (but public transportation options are fewer). On Monday, some businesses are closed until 14:00 and sometimes all day. Smaller towns

Major Holidays and Weekends

Popular places are even busier on weekends...and inundated on three-day weekends. Holiday weekends can make towns, trains, roads, and hotels more crowded than summer. The French are masters at the long weekend, and you're no match for them when it comes to finding hotels and driving during these peak periods. Book your accommodations and train trips well in advance if you'll be traveling during busy times.

In 2011, expect crowds during these holiday periods: Easter weekend (April 22-25 and the week on either side; Easter Monday is a holiday, too); Ascension weekend (June 2-5); Pentecost weekend (June 10-13, Pentecost Monday is a holiday, too); Bastille Day (July 14) and the week during which it falls; and the winter holidays (Dec 17-Jan 2). Note that Christmas week is quieter than the week of New Year's. Two major holidays—Labor Day (May 1) and WWII Victory Day (May 8)—fall on Sundays in 2011, which should make them unusually quiet. For more information, check the list of festivals and holidays near the end of the appendix.

are often quiet and downright boring on Sundays and Mondays, unless it's market day. Saturdays are virtually weekdays (without the rush hour).

Watt's Up? Europe's electrical system is different from North America's in two ways: the shape of the plug (two round prongs) and the voltage of the current (220 volts instead of 110 volts). For your North-American plug to work in Europe, you'll need an adapter, sold inexpensively at travel stores in the US. As for the voltage, newer electronics or travel appliances (such as hair dryers, laptops, and battery chargers) automatically convert the voltage—if you see a range of voltages printed on the item or its plug (such as "110–220"), it'll work in Europe. Otherwise, you can buy a converter separately in the US (about $20), though these tend to be heavy and unreliable, and get really hot when in use. For small appliances that don't automatically convert voltage, I suggest going without or buying a cheap replacement in France. You can buy low-cost hair dryers and other small appliances at Darty and Monoprix stores, which you'll find in major cities (ask at your hotel for the closest branch).

Discounts: Discounts are not listed in this book. However, seniors (age 60 and over), youths under 18 or even 26, and students and teachers with proper identification cards (www.isic.org) can get discounts. Always ask. Some discounts are available only for EU citizens. To inquire about a senior discount, ask, *"Réduction troisième âge?"* (ray-dook-see-ohn twah-zee-ehm ahzh).

News: Americans keep in touch by reading the *International Herald Tribune* (published almost daily throughout Europe and online at www.iht.com). Other newsy sites are http://news.bbc.co.uk and www.europeantimes.com. Every Tuesday the European editions of *Time* and *Newsweek* hit the stands with articles of particular interest to travelers in Europe. Sports addicts can get their daily fix online or from *USA Today*. Many hotels have CNN and BBC News television channels.

Money

This section offers advice on how to pay for purchases on your trip (including getting cash from ATMs and paying with plastic), dealing with lost or stolen cards, VAT (sales tax) refunds, and tipping.

What to Bring

Bring both a credit card and a debit card. You'll use the debit card at cash machines (ATMs) to withdraw euros for most purchases, and the credit card to pay for larger items. Some travelers carry a third card as a backup, in case one gets demagnetized or eaten by a temperamental machine.

As an emergency backup, bring cash. One of your co-authors brings a few hundred dollars; the other brings a few hundred euros (in either case, denominations of 20 are best). Dollars are pricey to exchange in France at currency booths (banks won't take them), but euros are pricey to buy in the States. The best solution could be to bring along a hundred dollars as a backup, and stock up on euros soon after you arrive in France. Regardless, skip traveler's checks—they're a waste of time (long waits at slow banks) and a waste of money in fees.

Cash

Cash is just as desirable in Europe as it is at home. Small European businesses (hotels, restaurants, and shops) prefer that you pay your bills with cash. Some vendors will charge you extra for using a credit card, and some won't take credit cards at all.

Throughout Europe, ATMs are the standard way for travelers to get cash. To withdraw money from an ATM—known as a *distributeur*, *retrait*, or *point d'argent*—you'll need a debit card (ideally with a Visa or MasterCard logo for maximum usability), plus a PIN code. Know your PIN code in numbers, because there are only numbers—no letters—on European keypads. You could use a credit card for ATM transactions, but it's generally more expensive (because it's considered a "cash advance" rather than a "withdrawal"). For security, it's best to shield the keypad when entering your PIN at the ATM.

Exchange Rate

1 euro (€) = about $1.25

To convert prices in euros to dollars, add about 25 percent: €20 = about $25, €50 = about $65. (To get the latest rate and print a cheat sheet, see www.oanda.com.) Just like the dollar, the euro is broken down into 100 cents. You'll find coins ranging from 1 cent to 2 euros, and bills from 5 euros to 500 euros.

When using an ATM, taking out large sums of money can reduce the number of per-transaction bank fees you'll pay. If the machine refuses your request, try again and select a smaller amount (some cash machines limit the amount you can withdraw—don't take it personally). If that doesn't work, try a different machine. If the ATM dispenses big bills, try to break them at a bank or larger store, because it's easier to pay for purchases at small businesses using smaller bills. Most ATMs in France are located outside of a bank. Try to use the ATM when the branch is open: If your card is eaten by a machine, you can immediately go inside for help.

To keep your cash safe, use a money belt—a pouch with a strap that you buckle around your waist like a belt and wear under your clothes. Pickpockets target tourists. A money belt provides peace of mind, allowing you to carry lots of cash safely. Don't waste time every few days tracking down a cash machine—withdraw a week's worth of money, stuff it in your money belt, and travel!

Credit and Debit Cards

Visa and MasterCard are more commonly accepted than American Express. Although you can use either a credit card or a debit card for most transactions, credit cards offer a greater degree of fraud protection (because debit cards draw funds directly from your account).

Just like at home, credit or debit cards are accepted by larger hotels, restaurants, and shops. I typically use my debit card to withdraw cash from ATMs, and my credit card only in a few specific situations: to book hotel reservations by phone, to make major purchases (such as car rentals, plane tickets, and long hotel stays), and to pay for things near the end of my trip (to avoid another visit to the ATM).

Ask Your Credit- or Debit-Card Company: Before your trip, contact the company that issued your debit or credit cards.

• Confirm your card will work overseas, and alert them that you'll be using it in Europe; otherwise, they may deny transactions if they perceive unusual spending patterns.

• Ask for the specifics on transaction **fees.** When you use your credit or debit card—either for purchases or ATM withdrawals—you'll often be charged additional "international transaction" fees of up to 3 percent (1 percent is normal) plus $5 per transaction.

Some banks have agreements with European partners that reduce or eliminate the $5 transaction fee. For example, Bank of America debit-card holders can use French Parisbas-BNP ATMs without being charged the transaction fee (but they still pay a 1 percent international fee). If your fees are too high, consider getting a card just for your trip: Capital One (www.capitalone.com) and most credit unions have low-to-no international fees.

• If you plan to withdraw cash from ATMs, confirm your daily **withdrawal limit** (€300 is usually the maximum). Some travelers prefer a high limit that allows them to take out more cash at each ATM stop, whereas others prefer to set a lower limit in case their card is stolen.

• Ask for your credit card's **PIN** in case you encounter Europe's "chip-and-PIN" system.

Chip and PIN: If your card is declined for a purchase in Europe, it may be because of chip and PIN, which requires cardholders to punch in a PIN instead of signing a receipt. Much of Europe, including France, Great Britain, Ireland, the Netherlands, and Scandinavia, is adopting this system. Chip and PIN is used by some merchants, and also at automated payment machines—such as those at train and subway stations, toll roads, parking garages, luggage lockers, bike-rental kiosks, and self-serve pumps at gas stations. If you're prompted to enter your PIN (but don't know it), ask if the cashier can print a receipt for you to sign instead, or just pay cash. If you're dealing with an automated machine that won't take your card, look for a cashier nearby who can make your card work. The easiest solution is to carry sufficient cash.

Dynamic Currency Conversion: If merchants offer to convert your purchase price into dollars (called dynamic currency conversion, or DCC), refuse this "service." You'll pay even more in fees for the expensive convenience of seeing your charge in dollars.

Damage Control for Lost Cards

If you lose your credit, debit, or ATM card, you can stop people from using it by reporting the loss immediately to the respective global customer-assistance centers. Call these 24-hour US numbers collect: Visa (410/581-9994), MasterCard (636/722-7111), and American Express (623/492-8427). For another option (with the same results), you can call these toll-free numbers in France: Visa (08 00 90 11 79) and MasterCard (08 00 90 13 87). American Express has a Paris office, but the call isn't free (01 47 77 70 00, greeting is in French only, dial 1 for English). Diners Club has offices in the US (303/799-1504, call collect) and Paris (08 10 31 41 59).

At a minimum, you'll need to know the name of the financial institution that issued you the card, along with the type of card (classic, platinum, or whatever). Providing the following information will allow for a quicker cancellation of your missing card: full card number, whether you are the primary or secondary cardholder, the cardholder's name exactly as printed on the card, billing address, home phone number, circumstances of the loss or theft, and identification verification (your birth date, your mother's maiden name, or your Social Security number—memorize this, don't carry a copy). If you are the secondary cardholder, you'll also need to provide the primary cardholder's identification-verification details. In Europe you can generally receive a temporary card within two or three business days.

If you promptly report your card lost or stolen, you typically won't be responsible for any unauthorized transactions on your account, although many banks charge a liability fee of $50.

Tipping

Tipping (*donner un pourboire*) in France isn't as automatic and generous as it is in the US, but for special service, tips are appreciated, if not expected. As in the US, the proper amount depends on your resources, tipping philosophy, and the circumstances, but some general guidelines apply.

Restaurants: At cafés and restaurants, a 12–15 percent service charge is always included in the bill (*service compris*) and most French never tip (credit-card receipts don't even have space to add a tip). However, if you feel the service was exceptional, it's fine to tip up to 5 percent. When you hand your payment plus a tip to your waiter, you can say, "*C'est bon*" (say bohn), meaning, "It's good" (and you don't want any change back). Never feel guilty if you don't leave a tip.

Taxis: To tip the cabbie, round up. For a typical ride, round up to the next euro on the fare (to pay a €13 fare, give €14); for a long ride, round to the nearest €10 (for a €56 fare, give €60). If the cabbie hauls your bags and zips you to the airport to help you catch your flight, you might want to toss in a little more. But if you feel like you're being driven in circles or otherwise ripped off, skip the tip.

Special Services: It's thoughtful to tip a couple of euros to someone who shows you a special sight and who is paid in no other way. Tour guides at public sights sometimes hold out their hands for tips (€1–2) after they give their spiel. If I've already paid for the tour, I don't tip extra, unless they've really impressed me. At hotels, if you let the porter carry your luggage, it's polite to give him or her a euro for each bag (another reason to pack light). I don't tip the maid, but if you do, you can leave a euro per overnight at the end of your stay.

In general, if someone in the service industry does a super job for you, a small tip (the equivalent of a euro or two) is appropriate …but not required.

When in doubt, ask. If you're not sure whether (or how much) to tip for a service, ask your hotelier or the tourist information office—they'll fill you in on how it's done on their turf.

Getting a VAT Refund

Wrapped into the purchase price of your French souvenirs is a Value-Added Tax (VAT) of about 19.6 percent. You're entitled to get most of that tax back if you purchase more than €175 (about $220) worth of goods at a store that participates in the VAT-refund scheme. Getting your refund is usually straightforward and, if you buy a substantial amount of souvenirs, well worth the hassle. If you're lucky, the merchant will subtract the tax when you make your purchase. (This is more likely to occur if the store ships the goods to your home.) Otherwise, you'll need to do the following:

Get the paperwork. Have the merchant completely fill out the necessary refund document, *Bordereau de Vente à l'Exportation*, also called a "cheque." You'll have to present your passport at the store.

Get your stamp at the border or airport. Process your cheque(s) at your last stop in the EU (most likely the airport) with the customs agent who deals with VAT refunds. It's best to keep your purchases in your carry-on for viewing, but if they're too large or dangerous (such as knives) to carry on, track down the proper customs agent to inspect them before you check your bag. You're not supposed to use your purchased goods before you leave. If you show up at customs wearing your chic new French ensemble, officials might look the other way—or deny you a refund.

Collect your refund. You'll need to return your stamped document to the retailer or its representative. Many merchants work with a service, such as Global Refund (www.globalrefund.com) or Premier Tax Free (www.premiertaxfree.com), which have offices at major airports, ports, or border crossings. These services, which extract a 4 percent fee, can refund your money immediately in your currency of choice (within two billing cycles). You're not supposed to use your purchased goods before you leave. If the retailer handles VAT refunds directly, it's up to you to contact the merchant for your refund. Or you can mail the documents from your point of departure (using a stamped, addressed envelope you've prepared or one that's been provided by the merchant). You'll then have to wait—it can take months.

Customs for American Shoppers

You are allowed to take home $800 worth of items per person duty-free, once every 30 days. The next $1,000 is taxed at a flat 3 percent. After that, you pay the individual item's duty rate. You can also bring in duty-free a liter of alcohol (slightly more than a standard-size bottle of wine; you must be at least 21), 200 cigarettes, and up to 100 non-Cuban cigars.

As for food, you can take home vacuum-packed cheeses; dried herbs, spices, or mushrooms; and canned fruits or vegetables, including jams and vegetable spreads. Baked goods, candy, chocolate, oil, vinegar, mustard, and honey are OK. Fresh fruits or vegetables (even that banana from your airplane breakfast) are not permitted. Meats are generally not allowed, though canned pâtés are permitted if made from geese, duck, or pork. Just because a duty-free shop in an airport sells a food product, that doesn't mean it will automatically pass US customs. Be prepared to lose your investment.

Note that you'll need to carefully pack any bottles of wine, jam, honey, oil, and other liquid-containing items in your checked luggage, due to the three-ounce limit on liquids in carry-on baggage. To check customs rules and duty rates before you go, visit www.cbp.gov, and click on "Travel," then "Know Before You Go."

Sightseeing

Sightseeing can be hard work. Use these tips to make your visits to France's finest sights meaningful, fun, efficient, and painless.

Plan Ahead

Set up an itinerary that allows you to fit in all your must-see sights. For a one-stop look at opening hours in the bigger cities covered in this book, see the "At a Glance" sidebars. Most sights keep stable hours, but you can easily confirm the latest by checking their website or asking the local TI.

Don't put off visiting a must-see sight—you never know when a place will close unexpectedly for a holiday, strike, or restoration. On holidays (see list on page 1035), expect shorter hours or closures.

When possible, visit major sights in the morning (when your energy is best) and save other activities for the afternoon. Hit a sight's highlights first, then see the rest if you have the stamina and time.

Going at the right time helps avoid crowds. This book offers you tips on specific sights. For example, Paris' Louvre, Orsay, and Orangerie museums are open selected evenings, and the Pompidou Center is always open late. Evening visits are usually peaceful with fewer crowds. At Mont St. Michel or Carcassonne, it's by far best to arrive at about 17:00, spend the night, and explore in the morning before the crowds descend. Visit these sights first thing or late: Château de Chenonceau, Les Baux, and Pont du Gard.

Study up. To get the most out of the self-guided tours and sight descriptions in this book, read them before you visit. Several cities offer sightseeing passes that are worthwhile values for busy sightseers; do the math to see if they'll save you money.

At Sights

Here's what you can typically expect: Some important sights may have metal detectors or conduct bag searches that will slow your entry; others require you to check daypacks and coats. They'll be kept safely. If you have something you can't bear to part with, stash it in a pocket or purse. To avoid checking a small backpack, carry it under your arm like a purse as you enter. From a guard's point of view, a backpack is generally a problem whereas a purse is not. If you check a bag, the attendant may ask you (in French) if it contains anything of value—such as a camera, phone, money, or passport—because these cannot be checked.

Flash photography is banned at most major sights, but taking photos without flash is usually OK. Look for signs or ask. Flashes damage oil paintings and distract others in the room. Even without a flash, a handheld camera will take a decent picture (or buy postcards or posters at the museum bookstore). If photos are permitted, video cameras are generally OK, too.

Some museums may have special exhibits in addition to their permanent collection. Some exhibits are included in the entry price; others come at an extra cost (which you may have to pay even if you don't want to see the exhibit).

Many sights offer audioguides, which generally offer useful recorded descriptions in English (about €6, sometimes included with admission). If you bring along your own pair of headphones and a Y-jack, you can sometimes share one audioguide with your travel partner and save money. I've produced free audio tours of the major sights in Paris that you can download before you go (see www.ricksteves.com). Sights are most likely to offer guided tours in English during peak season; these range widely in quality and cost around €8. Some sights run short films featuring their highlights and history. These are generally well worth your time. I make it standard operating procedure to ask when I arrive at a sight if there is a film in English.

Expect changes—artwork can be on tour, on loan, out sick, or shifted at the whim of the curator. To adapt, pick up any available free floor plans as you enter. Ask the museum staff if you can't find a particular painting. Say the title or artist's name, or point to the photograph in this book, and ask for its location by saying, "Où est?" (oo ay).

Important sights often have an on-site café or cafeteria (usually a good place to rest and have a snack or light meal). The WCs at many sights are usually free and nearly always clean (it's smart to carry tissues in case a WC runs out).

Many places sell postcards and guidebooks that highlight their attractions. Before you leave, scan the postcards and thumb through the biggest guidebook (or skim its index) to be sure you haven't overlooked something that you'd like to see.

Most sights stop admitting people 30–60 minutes before closing time, and some rooms close early (generally about 45 minutes before the actual closing time). Guards usher people out, so don't save the best for last.

Every sight or museum offers more than what is covered in this book. Use the information in this book as an introduction—not the final word.

Sleeping

Good-value accommodations in France generally are easy to find. Choose from one- to four-star hotels (two stars is my mainstay), bed-and-breakfasts (*chambres d'hôtes*, usually cheaper than hotels), hostels, campgrounds, and even homes (*gîtes*, rented by the week). I like hotels and B&Bs that are clean, central, friendly, a good value, run with a respect for French traditions, and small enough to have a hands-on owner and stable staff. Four of these six virtues means it's a keeper. For tips on making reservations, see page 30.

Types of Accommodations

Hotels

In this book, the price for a double room ranges from €4 (very simple, toilet and shower down the hall) to €350-plus (grand lobbies, maximum plumbing, and the works), with most clustering at about €80–110 (with private bathrooms).

The French have a simple hotel-rating system based on amenities, indicated in this book by asterisks). One star (asterisk) is modest, two has most of the comforts, and three is generally a two-star with a fancier lobby and more elaborately designed rooms. Four stars offer more luxury than you usually have time

Sleep Code

(€1 = about $1.25, country code: 33)

To help you sort easily through my listings, I've divided the rooms into three categories based on the price for a standard double room with bath:

$$$ **Higher Priced**
$$ **Moderately Priced**
$ **Lower Priced**

I always rate hostels as $, whether or not they have double rooms, because they have the cheapest beds in town.

Prices can change without notice; verify the hotel's current rates online or by email. For other updates, see www .ricksteves.com/update.

To give maximum information in a minimum of space, I use the following code to describe the accommodations. Prices listed are per room, not per person. When a price range is given for a type of room (such as double rooms listing for €100–130), it means the price fluctuates with the season, size of room, or length of stay.

S = Single room (or price for one person in a double).
D = Double or Twin.
T = Triple (generally a double bed with a single).
Q = Quad (usually two double beds).
b = Private bathroom with toilet and shower or tub.
s = Private shower or tub only (the toilet is down the hall).
* = French hotel rating system, ranging from zero to four stars.

According to this code, a couple staying at a "Db-€100" hotel would pay a total of €100 (about $125) for a double room with a private bathroom. You can assume a hotel takes credit cards unless you see "cash only" in the listing. Unless otherwise noted, hotel staff speak basic English and breakfast is not included (but is usually optional).

If I mention "Internet access" in a listing, there's a public terminal in the lobby for guests to use. If I mention "Wi-Fi," you can generally access it in your room (usually for free), but only if you have your own laptop.

to appreciate. Two- and three-star hotels are required to have an English-speaking staff, though nearly all hotels I recommend have someone who speaks English (unless I note otherwise in the listing).

Generally, the number of stars does not reflect room size or guarantee quality. Some two-star hotels are better than many three-star hotels. One- and two-star hotels are inexpensive, but

Types of Rooms

Study the price list on the hotel's website or posted at the desk, so you know your options. Receptionists often don't mention the cheaper rooms (they assume you want a private bathroom or a bigger room). Here are the types of rooms and beds:

une chambre sans douche et WC	room without a private shower or toilet (uncommon these days)
une chambre avec cabinet de toilette	room with a toilet but no shower (some hotels charge for down-the-hall showers)
une chambre avec bain et WC	room with private bathtub and toilet
une chambre avec douche et WC	room with private shower and toilet
chambres communiquantes	connecting rooms (ideal for families)
un grand lit	double bed (55 inches wide)
deux petits lits	twin beds (30–36 inches wide)
un lit single	true single room bed
un lit de cent-soixante	queen-size bed (literally, 160 centimeters, or 63 inches, wide)
le king size	king-size bed (usually two twins pushed together)
un lit pliant	folding bed
un berceau	baby crib
un lit d'enfant	child's bed

some three-star (and even a few four-star) hotels offer good value, justifying the extra cost. Unclassified hotels (no stars) can be bargains or depressing dumps.

Most hotels have lots of doubles and a few singles, triples, and quads. Traveling alone can be expensive, as singles are usually doubles used by one person—so they cost about the same as a double. Room prices vary within each hotel depending on size and whether the room has a bath or shower, twin beds or a double bed (tubs and twins cost more than showers and double beds). A triple is often just a double room with a double (or queen-size) bed plus a sliver-size single. Quad rooms usually have two double beds. Hotels cannot legally allow more in the room than what's shown on their price list. Modern hotels generally have a few family-friendly rooms that open to each other (*chambres communiquantes*).

Keep Cool

If you're visiting France in the summer, the extra expense of an air-conditioned room can be money well spent, particularly in the south. Most hotel rooms with air-conditioners come with a control stick (like a TV remote) that generally has the same symbols and features: fan icon (click to toggle through wind power, from light to gale); louver icon (choose steady airflow or waves); snowflake and sunshine icons (cold air or heat, depending on season); clock ("O" setting: run X hours before turning off; "I" setting: wait X hours to start); and the temperature control (20 or 21 degrees Celsius is comfortable; also see the thermometer diagram on page 1039).

Given the economic downturn, some hoteliers may be willing to make a deal. I'd suggest emailing several hotels to ask for their best price. Comparison-shop and make your choice. As you look over the listings, you'll notice that some hotels promise special prices to my readers who book direct (without using a room-finding service or hotel-booking website, which take a commission). To get these rates, mention this book when you reserve, then show the book upon arrival.

In general, prices can soften up if you do any of the following: offer to pay cash, stay at least three nights, or mention this book. You can also try asking for a cheaper room or a discount. To save money off-season, consider arriving without a reservation and dropping in at the last minute.

Hotels in France must charge a daily tax (*taxe du séjour*) of about €1–2 per person per day. Although some hotels include it in the price list, most add it to your bill.

You can save as much as €25 by finding the rare room without a private shower or toilet. A room with a bathtub usually costs more than a room with a shower and is generally larger. Hotels often have more rooms with tubs than showers and are inclined to give you a room with a tub (which the French prefer).

A double bed is usually cheaper than twins, though rooms with twin beds tend to be larger. Many hotels have queen-size beds (a bed that's 63 inches wide—most doubles are 55 inches). To find out whether a hotel has queen-size beds, ask, "*Avez-vous des lits de cent-soixante?*" (ah-vay-voo day lee duh sahn-swah-sahnt). Some hotels push two twins together under king-size-sheets and blankets to make *le king size*.

If you prefer a double bed (instead of twins) and a shower (instead of a tub), you need to ask for it—and you can save up to €20. If you'll take either twins or a double, ask for a generic *une chambre pour deux* (room for two) to avoid being needlessly turned away.

Hotels lobbies, halls, and breakfast rooms are off-limits to smokers, though they can light up in their rooms. Still, I rarely smell any smoke in the hundreds of rooms I check each year. Some hotels have non-smoking rooms or floors—ask about them if this is important to you. If your room smells of stale smoke, ask for a different one.

Most hotels offer some kind of breakfast, but it's rarely included in the room rates. The price of breakfast correlates with the price of the room: The more expensive the room, the more expensive the breakfast. This per-person charge can add up, particularly for families—so beware. Hotels hope you'll buy their breakfast, but it's optional unless otherwise noted (for more on breakfast, see "Eating," later in this chapter).

Some hotels, especially in coastal resort towns, strongly encourage their peak-season guests to take *demi-pension* (half-pension)—that is, breakfast and either lunch or dinner. By law, they can't require you to take half-pension unless you are staying three or more nights, but, in practice, many do during summer. And though the food is usually good, it limits your ability to shop around. I've indicated where I think *demi-pension* is a good value.

Most hotels rooms have a TV and phone, and Internet access (usually Wi-Fi) is increasingly common. To turn on your TV, press the channel-up or channel-down button on the remote. If it still doesn't work, see if there's a power button on the TV itself, then press the up or down button again.

Towels aren't routinely replaced every day. Hang up your towel to dry. Extra pillows and blankets are sometimes in the closet or available on request. To get a pillow, ask for *"Un oreiller, s'il vous plaît"* (un oh-ray-yay, see voo play).

Hoteliers can be a great help and source of advice. Most know their city well, and can assist you with everything from public transit and airport connections to finding a good restaurant, the nearest Internet café (*café internet*, kah-fay an-ter-net), or a self-service launderette (*laverie automatique*, lah-vay-ree oh-to-mah-teek).

Even at the best hotels, mechanical breakdowns occur: air-conditioning malfunctions, sinks leak, hot water turns cold, and toilets gurgle and smell. Report your concerns clearly and calmly at the front desk. For more complicated problems, don't expect instant results.

If you suspect night noise will be an issue, ask for a quiet room in the back or on an upper floor. To guard against theft in your room, keep valuables out of sight. Some rooms come with a safe, and other hotels have safes at the front desk. Use them if you're concerned.

Checkout can pose problems if surprise charges pop up on your bill. If you settle up your bill the night before you leave, you'll have time to discuss and address any points of contention (before 19:00, when the night shift usually arrives).

Some hoteliers will ask you to sign their *Livre d'Or* ("Golden Book," for client comments). They take this seriously and enjoy reading your remarks.

Modern Hotel Chains: France is littered with sterile, ultra-modern hotels, usually located on cheap land just outside of town, providing drivers with low-stress accommodations. The antiseptically clean and cheap Formule 1 and ETAP chains (about €40–50/room for up to three people), the more attractive Ibis hotels (€80–100 for a double), and the cushier Mercure and Novotels hotels (€110–170 for a double) are all run by the same company, Accor (www.accorhotels.com). Though far from quaint, these can be a good value (particularly if you find deals on their website) and some are centrally located. A smaller chain, Kyriad, offers good prices and quality (Kyriad Prestige offers a bit more comfort, visit www.kyriad.com; this website also works for affiliated chains, including Première Classe and Campanile). For a long listing of various hotels throughout France, see www.france.com.

Bed & Breakfasts

B&Bs (*Chambres d'hôtes*, abbreviated CH) are generally found in smaller towns and rural areas. They're a great deal, offering double the cultural intimacy yet costing much less than most hotel rooms. And though you may lose some hotel conveniences—such as lounges, in-room phones, frequent bed-sheet changes, and the ability to pay with a credit card—I happily make the trade-off for the personal touches and lower rates. Your hosts may not speak English, but they will almost always be enthusiastic and pleasant.

You'll find B&Bs in this book and through local TIs, often listed by the owner's family name. To find small-town TIs online, do a web search for "office du tourisme" with the name of town you want (if that doesn't work start with the nearest large city TI and go from there). Though some CHs post small *Chambres* or *Chambres d'hôte* signs in their front windows, many are found only through the local TI. It's always OK to ask to see the room before you commit.

I recommend reliable CHs that offer a good value and/or unique experience (such as CHs in renovated mills, châteaux, and wine *domaines*). Although *chambres d'hôtes* have their own star-rating system, it doesn't correspond to the hotels' rating system. So, to avoid confusion, I haven't listed these stars for CHs. But most of my recommended CHs have private in-room bathrooms, and some have common rooms with refrigerators. Doubles with breakfast generally cost €55–75 (breakfast may or may not be included—ask).

Tables d'hôte are CHs that offer an optional, reasonably priced home-cooked dinner; the meals are almost always worth springing for, and they must be requested in advance.

Hostels

You'll pay about €20 per bed to stay at a hostel (*auberge de jeunesse*). People of any age are welcome if they don't mind dorm-style accommodations (usually in rooms of four to eight beds) or meeting other travelers. Cheap meals are sometimes offered, and kitchen facilities may be available. Expect youth groups in spring, crowds in the summer, snoring, and variability in quality from one hostel to the next. Family and private rooms are sometimes available on request.

There are two basic types of hostels: official and independent. **Official hostels** belong to the same parent organization, Hostelling International. They adhere to various rules (such as a 17:00 check-in, lockout during the day, and a curfew at night). If you plan to spend at least six nights at official HI hostels, you'll save money if you buy a membership card before you go ($28/year, www.hihostels.com); non-members pay an extra $5 per night.

Independent hostels tend to be more easygoing and colorful than official hostels, but not as reliably organized, clean, or quiet late at night. Independent hostels don't require membership cards or charge extra for non-members, and generally have fewer rules. Various organizations promote independent hostels, including www.hostelworld.com, www.hostelz.com, www.hostelseurope.com, and www.hostels.com.

Camping

In Europe, camping is more of a social than an environmental experience. It's a great way for American travelers to make European friends. Camping costs about €18 per campsite per night, and almost every destination recommended in this book has a campground within a reasonable walk or bus ride from the town center and train station. A tent and sleeping bag are all you need. Many campgrounds have small grocery stores and washing machines, and some even come with cafés and miniature golf. French TIs have camping information. You'll find more detailed information in the annually updated *Michelin Camping France*, available in the US and at most French bookstores.

Gîtes and Apartments

Throughout France, you can find reasonably priced rental homes that are ideal for families and small groups wanting to explore a region more closely.

Gîtes (pronounced "zheet") are country homes—usually urbanites' second homes—that the government rents out to visitors who want a week in the countryside (homes are rented for at least a week at a time, from Saturday to Saturday). The objective of the *gîte* program was to save characteristic rural homes from abandonment and to make it easy and affordable for families to enjoy the French countryside. The government offers subsidies to renovate such homes, then coordinates rentals to make it financially feasible for the owner. Today, France has more than 9,000 *gîtes*. One of your co-authors restored a farmhouse a few hours north of Provence, and even though he and his wife are American, they received the same assistance that French owners get.

Gîtes are best for drivers (they're usually rural, with little public-transport access) and ideal for families and small groups (because they can sleep many for the same price). Homes range in comfort from simple cottages and farmhouses to restored châteaux. Most have at least two bedrooms, a kitchen, a living room, and a bathroom or two—but no sheets or linens (though you can usually rent them for extra). Like hotels, all *gîtes* are rated for comfort from one to four (using ears of corn—*épis*—rather than stars). Two or three *épis* are generally sufficient quality, but I'd lean toward three for more comfort. Prices generally range from €400 to €1,300 per week, depending on house size and amenities such as pools. For more information on *gîtes*, visit www.gites-de-france.com/gites or www.gite.com.

Apartments, less common than *gîtes*, are available in cities and in towns. You'll find long lists of homes and apartments for rent through TIs and on the Internet, though these are usually more expensive than staying in a *gîte*. Here are two good independent sources to consider: **France Homestyle** is run by Claudette, a service-oriented French woman from Seattle who handpicks every home and apartment she lists (US tel. 206/325-0132, www.francehomestyle.com, info@francehomestyle.com). Or try **Ville et Village,** which has a bigger selection of high-end places (US tel. 510/559-8080, www.villeetvillage.com, rentals@villeetvillage.com).

Phoning

To call France from the US or Canada, dial 011-33 and then the local number (drop the local number's initial 0). The 011 is our international access code, and 33 is France's country code.

If calling France from another European country, dial 00-33-local number (drop the local number's initial 0). The 00 is Europe's international access code.

Traveling with Kids

France is kid-friendly for young children, partly because so much of it is rural. (Teenagers, on the other hand, tend to prefer cities.) Both of this book's authors have kids (from 9 to 23 years old), and we've used our substantial experience traveling with children to improve this book. Our kids have greatly enriched our travels, and we hope the same will be true for you.

My kids' favorite places have been Mont St. Michel, the Alps, the Loire châteaux, Carcassonne, and Paris (especially the Eiffel Tower and Seine River boat ride)—and any hotel with a pool. To make your trip fun for everyone in the family, mix heavy-duty sights with kids' activities (playing miniature golf, renting bikes, and riding the little tourist trains popular in many towns). And though Disneyland Paris is the predictable draw, my kids had more fun for half the expense simply by enjoying the rides in the Tuileries Garden in downtown Paris.

Minimize hotel changes by planning three-day stops. Aim for hotels with restaurants, so the older kids can go back to the room while you finish a quiet dinner.

I've listed public pools in many places (especially the south), but be warned: Public pools in France commonly require a small, Speedo-like bathing suit for boys and men (American-style swim trunks won't do)—though they usually have these little suits to loan. At hotel pools, either kind of suit will do.

For breakfast, croissants are a hit, though a good *pain au chocolat* (croissant with chocolate bits) will be appreciated even more. Hot chocolate, fruit, and yogurt are usually available. For lunch and dinner, it's easy to find fast-food places and restaurants with kids' menus, or *créperies*, which have a wide variety of kid-friendly stuffings for both savory crêpes and sweet dessert crêpes. For food emergencies, I travel with a plastic container of peanut butter brought from home and smuggle small jars of jam from breakfast.

Kids homesick for friends can keep in touch with cheap international phone cards and by email. Cybercafés and hotels with Internet access are a godsend for parents with teenagers. Readily available Wi-Fi makes bringing a laptop worthwhile. Some parents find buying a French mobile phone—or roaming

To make calls within France, simply dial the local number. For more tips on calling, see page 1003.

Making Reservations

Given the quality of the places I've found for this book, I'd recommend that you reserve your rooms in advance, particularly during peak season and for Paris any time of year. Book several weeks ahead, or as soon as you've pinned down your travel dates. Note that some national holidays and major events jam things up and merit with an American mobile phone—a helpful investment; adults can stay connected to teenagers while allowing them maximum independence (see page 1007).

Swap babysitting duties with your partner if one of you wants to take in an extra sight, or ask at hotels for babysitting services. And for memories that will last long after the trip, keep a family journal. Pack a small diary and a glue stick. While relaxing at a café over an *citron-pressé* (lemonade), take turns writing down the day's events, and include mementos such as ticket stubs from museums, postcards, or stalks of lavender.

What to Bring: Children's books in English are scarce and pricey in France. My children read more when traveling in Europe than while at home in the US, so don't skimp here. If your kids love peanut butter, bring it from home (hard to find in France)... or help them acquire a taste for Nutella, the tasty hazelnut-chocolate spread available everywhere.

Choose items that are small and convenient for use on planes, trains, and in your hotel room: a lightweight netbook computer (these have a long battery life and take little packing space), compact travel games, a deck of cards, and a handheld video game. Bring your own drawing paper, pens, and crayons (expensive in France). For younger kids, Legos are easily packed and practical (it's also fun to purchase kits overseas, as Legos are sometimes different in Europe from those in the US). Budding fashionistas might enjoy traveling with—and buying new outfits for—a Corelle doll or another 16-inch doll. The French have wonderful doll clothes, with a better selection than you'll typically find in the US.

Car-rental agencies usually rent car seats, though you must reserve one in advance (verify the price ahead of time—you may want to bring your own). And though most hotels have some sort of crib, I brought a portable crib and did not regret it. Cameras are a great investment to get your kids involved. For longer drives, audio books can be fun for the whole family. I recommend Peter Mayle's *A Year in Provence*, available on CD (or put it on your MP3 player/iPod).

your making reservations far in advance (see the "Major Holidays and Weekends" sidebar, earlier). Just like at home, holidays that fall on a Monday, Thursday, or Friday can turn the weekend into a long holiday, so book the entire weekend well in advance.

Requesting a Reservation: To reserve, contact hotels directly by email, phone, or fax. Email is the clearest, most economical way to make a reservation. Or you can go straight to the hotel website; many have secure online reservation forms and can instantly inform you of availability and any special deals. But be sure you use the hotel's official site and not a booking agency's site—otherwise you may pay higher rates than you should. If you're phoning from the US, be mindful of time zones (see page 13). Most hotels listed are accustomed to guests who speak only English.

The hotelier wants to know these key pieces of information (also included in the sample request form in the appendix):

- number and type of rooms
- number of nights
- date of arrival
- date of departure
- any special needs (e.g., bathroom in the room or down the hall, twin beds vs. double bed, air-conditioning, quiet, view, ground floor, etc.).

When you request a room, use the European style for writing dates: day/month/year. For example, for a two-night stay in July, I would request: "1 double room for 2 nights, arrive 16/07/11, depart 18/07/11." Consider carefully how long you'll stay; don't just assume you can tack on extra days once you arrive. Mention any discounts offered—for Rick Steves readers or otherwise—when you make the reservation. If you don't get a reply to your email or fax, it usually means the hotel is already fully booked (but you can try sending the message again, or call to follow up).

Confirming a Reservation: If the hotel's response includes its room availability and rates, it's not a confirmation. You must tell them that you want that room at the given rate. Most hoteliers will request your credit-card number for a one-night deposit to hold the room. And though you can email your credit-card information (I do), it's safer to share that confidential info by phone call, fax, two successive emails, or secure online reservation form (if the hotel has one on its website).

Canceling a Reservation: If you must cancel your reservation, it's courteous to do so with as much advance notice as possible—at least three days. Simply make a quick phone call or send an email. Family-run hotels and *chambres d'hôtes* lose money if they turn away customers while holding a room for someone who doesn't show up. Understandably, many hotels bill no-shows for one night.

Cancellation policies can be strict: Some hotels require seven days' notice of a cancellation, whereas most want three days; otherwise, you might lose a deposit. Or you might be billed for the entire visit if you leave early. Internet deals may require prepayment, with no refunds for cancellations. If concerned, ask about cancellation policies before you book.

If canceling by email, request confirmation that your cancellation was received to avoid being accidentally billed.

Reconfirm Your Reservation: Always call to reconfirm your room reservation a day or two in advance. Smaller hotels and *chambres d'hôtes* appreciate knowing your time of arrival. If you'll be arriving after 17:00, let your hotelier know. On the small chance that a hotel loses track of your reservation, bring along a hard copy of their emailed or faxed confirmation.

Reserving Rooms as You Travel: You can make reservations as you travel, calling hotels or *chambres d'hôtes* a few days to a week before your visit. If everything's full, don't despair. Call a day or two in advance and fill in a cancellation. If you'd rather travel without any reservations at all, you'll have greater success snaring rooms if you arrive at your destination early in the day. When you anticipate crowds (weekends are worst), call hotels around 9:00 or 10:00 on the day you plan to arrive, when the hotel clerk knows who'll be checking out and just which rooms will be available. If you encounter a language barrier, ask the fluent receptionist at your current hotel to call for you.

Eating

The French eat long and well. Relaxed lunches, three-hour dinners, and endless hours sitting in outdoor cafés are the norm. Here, chefs are as famous as great athletes, and mamas hope their babies grow up to be great cooks. Cafés, cuisine, and wines should become a highlight of any French adventure. It's sightseeing for your palate. Even if the rest of you is sleeping in cheap hotels, let your taste buds travel first class in France. (They can go coach in England.)

You can eat well without going broke—but choose carefully: You're just as likely to blow a small fortune on a mediocre meal as you are to dine wonderfully for €20. Carefully read the information that follows, consider my restaurant suggestions in this book, and you'll do fine.

The non-smoking revolution hit France in 2008, when a law mandated that all café and restaurant interiors be smoke-free. Today the only smokers you'll find are at outside tables, which—unfortunately—may be exactly where you want to sit.

Waiters probably won't overwhelm you with friendliness (their tip is included in the bill, so there's less schmoozing than we're used to at home). Notice how hard they work. They almost never stop. Cozying up to clients (French or foreign) is probably the last thing on their minds. They have to deal with client overload, too, because the French rarely hire part-time employees, even to help with peak times. To get a waiter's attention, say, "*S'il vous plaît*" (see voo play)—"please."

To get the most out of dining—slow down. Allow enough time, engage the waiter, show you're serious about food, and enjoy the experience as much as the meal.

Market Day (Jour du Marché)

Market days are a big deal throughout France. They have been a central feature of life in rural areas since the Middle Ages. No single event better symbolizes the French preoccupation with fresh products, and their strong ties to the small farmer, than the weekly market. Many locals mark their calendars with the arrival of fresh produce.

Notice the signs as you enter towns indicating the *jours du marché*—essential information to any civilized soul, and a reminder not to park on the streets the night before (*stationnement interdit* means "no parking"). Try to buy some of your picnics at an open-air market.

Most *marchés* take place once a week in the town's main square and, if large enough, spill onto nearby streets. Markets combine fresh produce; samples of wine and other locally produced beverages (such as brandies and ciders); and a smattering of nonperishable items, such as knives, berets, kitchen goods, and cheap clothing. The bigger the market, the greater the overall selection—particularly for nonperishable goods. Bigger towns (such as Beaune and Arles) may have two weekly markets. The biggest market days are usually on weekends, so that everyone can go.

Market day is as important socially as it is commercially—it's a weekly chance to resume friendships and get the current gossip. Neighbors catch up on Henri's barn renovation, see photos of Jacqueline's new grandchild, and relax over *un café*. Dogs are tethered to café tables while friends exchange kisses. Tether yourself to a café table and observe: three cheek-kisses for good friends (left-right-left, a fourth for friends you haven't seen in a while. (The appropriate number of kisses varies by region—Paris, Lyon, and Provence each have separate standards.) It's bad form to be in a hurry on market day. Allow the crowd to set your pace.

Most perishable items are sold directly from the producers—no middlemen, no Visa cards, just really fresh produce (*du pays* means "grown locally"). Space rental is cheap (about €5-10, depending on the size). Most vendors follow a weekly circuit of markets they feel work best for them, showing up in the same spot every week, year in and year out. Notice how much fun they have chatting up their customers and one another. Many vendors speak enough English to assist you in your selection. Markets end by 13:00—in time for lunch, allowing the town to reclaim its streets and squares.

Breakfast

You'll almost always have the option of breakfast at your hotel, which is usually pleasant and convenient. *Petit déjeuner* (puh-tee day-zhuh-nay) starts with café au lait, hot chocolate, or tea, and a roll with butter and marmalade. Some hotels offer only this classic continental breakfast for about €8, while others put out a buffet breakfast for about €10-15 that I usually spring for (cereal, yogurt, fruit, cheese, croissants, juice, and the occasional hard-boiled egg).

If all you want is coffee or tea and a croissant, the corner café offers more atmosphere and is less expensive (though you get more coffee at your hotel). Go local and ask for *une tartine* (oon tart-een; baguette slathered with butter or jam) with your café au lait. To keep it really cheap, pick up some fruit at a grocery store and pastries at your favorite *boulangerie* (bakery), and have a picnic breakfast, then savor your coffee at the bar (*comptoir*) while standing, like the French do. You could also buy (or bring from home) plastic bowls and spoons, buy a box of cereal and a small box of milk, and eat in your room before heading out for coffee.

Some bakeries offer worthwhile breakfast deals with juice, croissant, and coffee or tea for about €5. If you crave eggs for breakfast, drop into a café and order *une omelette* or *œufs sur le plat* (fried eggs). As a less atmospheric alternative, some fast-food places offer very cheap breakfasts.

Picnics and Snacks

Great for lunch or dinner, French picnics can be first-class affairs and adventures in high cuisine. Be daring. Try the smelly cheeses, ugly pâtés, sissy quiches, and minuscule yogurts. Shopkeepers are accustomed to selling small quantities of produce. Get a tasty salad-to-go and ask for a plastic fork (*une fourchette en plastique*). A small container is *une tranche*. If you need a knife (*couteau*) or corkscrew (*tire-bouchon*), ask to borrow one from your hotelier. And though wine is taboo in public places in the US, it's *pas de problème* in France.

Here are some ideas of what to look for, but don't hesitate if something unknown whets your appetite. Say *"s'il vous plaît"* to get a clerk's attention, then point to what you want.

Gather supplies early for a picnic lunch; you'll want to visit several small stores to assemble a complete meal, and many close at noon for their lunch break. Or visit open-air markets (*marchés*), which are fun and photogenic but shut down around 13:00 (many are listed in this book; French TIs have complete lists).

At the *boulangerie* (bakery), choose some bread. A baguette does the trick, or choose from the many square loaves of bread on display such as *pain aux céréales* (whole grain with seeds), *pain de*

Picnic Vocabulary

English	French	Pronounced
please	*s'il vous plaît*	see voo play
a plastic fork	*une fourchette en plastique*	oon foor-sheht ahn plah-steek
a small box	*une barquette*	oon bar-keht
a knife	*un couteau*	uhn koo-toh
corkscrew	*tire-bouchon*	teer-boo-shohn
sliced	*tranché*	trahn-shay
a slice	*une tranche*	oon trahnsh
a small slice	*une petite tranche*	oon puh-teet trahnsh
more	*plus*	ploo
less	*moins*	mwan (rhymes with man)
It's just right.	*C'est bon.*	say bohn
Thank you.	*Merci.*	mehr-see

campagne (country bread, made with unbleached bread flour), *pain complet* (wheat bread), or *pain de seigle* (rye bread). To ask to have it sliced, say, *"Tranché, s'il vous plaît."*

At the *pâtisserie* (pastry shop, usually the same place you bought the bread), choose a dessert that's easy to eat with your hands. My favorites are *éclairs* (*chocolat* or *café* flavored), individual fruit tartes (*framboise* is raspberry, *fraise* is strawberry, *citron* is lemon), and *macarons* (made of flavored cream sandwiched between two meringues, not coconut cookies like in the US).

At the *crèmerie* or *fromagerie* (cheese shop), choose a sampling of cheeses. I usually get one hard cheese (such as *Comté*, *Cantal*, or *Beaufort*), one soft cow's milk (such as *Brie* or *Camembert*), one goat's milk cheese (anything that says *chèvre*), and one bleu cheese (*Roquefort* or *Bleu d'Auvergne*). Goat cheese usually comes in individual portions. For all other large cheeses, point to the cheese you want and ask for *une petite tranche* (*a small slice*). The shopkeeper will place a knife on the cheese indicating the size of the slice they are about to cut, then look at you for approval. If you'd like more, say *"plus."* If you'd like less, say *"moins."* If it's just right, say *"C'est bon!"*

At the *charcuterie* or *traiteur* (for deli items, prepared salads, meats, and pâtés), I like a slice of *pâté de campagne* (country pâté made of pork) and *saucisson sec* (dried sausages, some with pepper crust or garlic—you can ask to have it sliced thin like salami). I get a fresh salad, too. Typical choices are *carottes râpées* (shredded carrots in a tangy vinaigrette), *salade de betteraves* (beets in vinaigrette), and *céleri rémoulade* (celery root with a mayonnaise sauce).

At a **supermarché**, **épicerie**, or **magasin d'alimentation** (small grocery store or minimart) you'll find plastic cutlery, paper plates, napkins, drinks, chips, and sometimes a meek display of produce. **Supermarchés** are less colorful than smaller stores, but cheaper, more efficient, and offer adequate quality. Department stores often have supermarkets in the basement. On the outskirts of cities, you'll find the monster **hypermarché**. Drop in for a glimpse of hyper-France in action.

In stores, unrefrigerated soft drinks, bottled water, and beer are one-third the price of cold drinks. Bottled water and boxed fruit juice are the cheapest drinks. Avoid buying drinks to-go at streetside stands; you'll find them for far less in a shop. Try to keep a water bottle with you. Water quenches your thirst better and cheaper than anything you'll find in a store or café. I drink tap water throughout France, filling my bottle in hotel rooms as I go.

Sandwiches and Other Quick Bites

Throughout France you'll find bakeries and small stands selling baguette sandwiches, quiche, and pizza-like items to go for about €4. Usually filling and tasty, they also streamline the picnic process. Here are some sandwiches you'll see:

Fromage (froh-mahzh): Cheese (white on beige).

Jambon beurre (zhahn-bohn bur): Ham and butter (boring for most).

Jambon crudités (zhahn-bohn krew-dee-tay): Ham with tomatoes, lettuce, cucumbers, and mayonnaise.

Poulet crudités (poo-lay krew-dee-tay): Chicken with tomatoes, lettuce, maybe cucumbers, and always mayonnaise.

Saucisson beurre (saw-see-sohn bur): Thinly sliced sausage and butter.

Thon crudités (tohn krew-dee-tay): Tuna with tomatoes, lettuce, and maybe cucumbers, but definitely mayonnaise.

Anything served **à la provençale** (ah lah proh-vehn-sahl) has marinated peppers, tomatoes, and eggplant. A sandwich **à la italienne** is a grilled **panini**.

Typical **quiches** you'll see at shops and bakeries are **lorraine** (ham and cheese), **fromage** (cheese only), **aux oignons** (with onions), **aux poirreaux** (with leeks—my favorite), **aux champignons** (with mushrooms), **au saumon** (salmon), or **au thon** (tuna).

Café Culture

French cafés and brasseries provide user-friendly meals and a refuge from sightseeing overload. They're not necessarily cheaper than restaurants. Their key advantage is flexibility: they offer long serving hours, and you're welcome to order just a salad, a sandwich, or a bowl of soup, even for dinner. It's also OK to split starters and

Coffee and Tea Lingo

By law, the waiter must give you a glass of tap water with your coffee or tea if you request it; ask for *"Un verre d'eau, s'il vous plaît"* (uhn vayr doh, see voo play).

Coffee

French	Pronounced	English
un café allongé (also called *café longue*)	uhn kah-fay ah-lohn-zhay (kah-fay lohn)	closest to an American cup of coffee
un express	uh nex-press	shot of espresso
une noisette	oon nwah-zeht	espresso with a shot of milk
café au lait	kah-fay oh lay	coffee with lots of steamed milk (closest to an American latte)
un grand crème	uhn grahn krehm	big café au lait
un petit crème	uhn puh-tee krehm	small café au lait
un décaffiné	uhn day-kah-fee-nay	decaf—available for any of the above drinks

Tea

French	Pronounced	English
un thé nature	uhn tay nah-tour	plain tea
un thé au lait	uhn tay oh lay	tea with milk
un thé citron	uhn tay see-trohn	tea with lemon
une infusion	oon an-few-see-yohn	herbal tea

desserts, though not main courses.

Cafés and brasseries usually open by 7:00, but closing hours vary. Unlike restaurants, which open only for dinner and sometimes for lunch, some cafés and all brasseries serve food throughout the day (though with a more limited menu than at restaurants), making them the best option for a late lunch or an early dinner. (Note that many cafés in smaller towns close their kitchens from about 14:00 until 18:00.)

If you're a novice, it's easier to sit and feel comfortable when you know the system. Check the price list first, which by law must be posted prominently (if you don't see one, go elsewhere). There are two sets of prices: You'll pay more for the same drink if you're seated at a table (*salle*) than if you're seated at the bar or counter (*comptoir*). For tips on coffee and tea, see "Coffee and Tea Lingo" above.

Standard Menu Items: *Croque monsieur* (grilled ham-and-cheese sandwich) and *croque madame* (*monsieur* with a fried egg on top) are generally served day and night. Sandwiches are least expensive but very plain (*boulangeries* serve better ones). To get more than a piece of ham (*jambon*) on a baguette, order a sandwich *jambon crudité*, which means garnished with veggies. Omelets come lonely on a plate with a basket of bread. The daily special—*plat du jour* (plah dew zhoor), or just *plat*—is your fast, hearty, and garnished hot plate for €10–18. At most cafés, feel free to order only entrées (which in French means the starter course); many find these lighter and more interesting than a main course. A vegetarian can enjoy a tasty, filling meal by ordering two entrées. Regardless of what you order, bread is free; to get more, just hold up your bread basket and ask, *"Encore, s'il vous plaît."*

Salads: They're typically large—one is perfect for lunch or a light dinner. To get salad dressing on the side, order *"la sauce à part"* (lah sohs ah par). These salads are among the classics:

Salade niçoise (nee-swahz), a specialty from Nice, usually includes green salad topped with green beans, boiled potatoes, tomatoes, anchovies, olives, hard-boiled eggs, and lots of tuna.

Salade au chèvre chaud is a mixed green salad topped with warm goat cheese on small pieces of toast.

Salade composée is "composed" of any number of ingredients, such as *lardons* (bacon), Comté (a Swiss-style cheese), Roquefort (bleu cheese), *œuf* (egg), *noix* (walnuts), and *jambon* (ham, generally thinly sliced).

Salade paysanne usually comes with potatoes (*pommes de terre*), walnuts (*noix*), tomatoes, ham, and egg.

Salade aux gesiers is a salad with chicken gizzards (and often slices of duck).

Restaurants

Choose restaurants filled with locals. Consider my suggestions and your hotelier's opinion, but trust your instinct. If a restaurant doesn't post its prices outside, move along. Refer to my restaurant recommendations to get a sense of what a reasonable meal should cost.

French restaurants usually open for dinner at 19:00 and are typically most crowded about 20:30 (the early bird gets the table). Last seating is about 21:00 or 22:00 in cities (even later in Paris and on the Riviera, and earlier in small villages during the off-season.

If a restaurant serves lunch, it generally begins at 11:30 and goes until 14:00, with last orders taken at about 13:30. In contrast, most cafés and brasseries offer a minimal menu (or more) all day (described earlier under "Café Culture").

French Wine-Tasting 101

France is peppered with wineries and wine-tasting opportunities. The American wine-tasting experience (I'm thinking Napa Valley) is generally informal, chatty, and entrepreneurial (logo-adorned baseball caps and golf shirts). In France, your hosts are not there to make small talk; you're likely to find them "all business." For some people, it can be overwhelming to try to make sense of the vast range of French wines, particularly when faced with a no-nonsense winemaker or sommelier. Take a deep breath, do your best to follow the instructions in this sidebar, and don't linger anywhere you don't feel welcome. (I've tried to identify which vineyards are most accepting of wine novices.) Visit several private wineries, or stop by a *cave coopérative*—an excellent opportunity to taste wines from a number of vintners in a single, less intimidating setting. You'll have a better experience if you call ahead to let them know you're coming—even if the winery is open all day, it's good form to announce your visit (ask your hotelier for help). Avoid visiting places between noon and 14:00, when many are closed—and those that are open are staffed by people who would rather be at lunch.

Winemakers are happy to work with you...*if* they can figure out what you want (which they expect you to already know). When you enter a winery, it helps to know what you like (drier or sweeter, lighter or full-bodied, fruity or more tannic, and so on). The people serving you may know those words in English, but you're wise to know and use the key words in French (see "French Wine Lingo" on the next page).

French wines usually have a lower alcohol level than American or Australian wines. Whereas many Americans like a big, full-bodied wine, most French tend to prefer more subtle flavors. They judge a wine by virtue of how well it pairs with a meal—and a big, oaky wine would overwhelm most French cuisine. The French also enjoy sampling younger wines to determine how they will taste in a few years, allowing them to buy at cheaper prices and stash the bottles in their cellars. Americans want it now—for today's picnic.

Remember that the vintner is hoping that you'll buy at least a bottle or two. If you don't buy, you may be asked to pay a minimal fee for the tasting. They know that Americans can't take much wine with them, and they don't expect to make a big sale,

If you ask for the *menu* (muh-noo) at a restaurant, you won't get a list of dishes; you'll get a fixed-price meal. *Menus*, which usually include two or three courses, are a good value if you're hungry. A three-course *menu* lists several options per course for you to choose from. You'll select a starter (*entrée*), your choice of several main courses with vegetables (*plats principal*), plus a cheese course or a choice of desserts. Two-course *menus* always include the *plat* but they do hope you'll look for their wines in the US. Some of the places I list will ship your purchase home—ask.

French Wine Lingo

Here are the steps you should follow when entering any wine-tasting:

1. Greetings, Sir/Madam: *Bonjour, Monsieur/Madame.*
2. We would like to taste a few wines.
   Nous voudrions déguster quelques vins
   (noo voo-dree-ohn day-goo-stay kehl-kuh van).
3. We want a wine that is _____ and _____
   Nous voudrions un vin _____ et _____
   (noo voo-dree-ohn uhn van _____ ay _____).

Fill in the blanks with your favorites from this list:

English	French	Pronounced
wine	*vin*	van
red	*rouge*	roozh
white	*blanc*	blahn
rosé	*rosé*	roh-zay
light	*léger*	lay-zhay
full-bodied, heavy	*robuste*	roh-boost
fruity	*fruité*	frwee-tay
sweet	*doux*	doo
tannic	*tannique*	tah-neek
jammy	*confituré*	koh-fee-tuh-ray
fine	*fin, avec finesse*	fahn, ah-vehk fee-nehs
ready to drink (mature)	*prêt à boire*	preh ah bwar
not ready to drink	*fermé*	fair-may
oaky	*goût de la chêne*	goo duh lah sheh-nuh
from old vines	*de vieille vignes*	duh vee-yay-ee veen-yah
sparkling	*pétillant*	pay-tee-yahn

principal and usually offer you a choice between *entrée* and *dessert* (*entrée et plat* or *plat et dessert*). Restaurants that offer a *menu* for lunch often charge about €5–10 more for the same *menu* at dinner. Many restaurants offer a reasonable *menu-enfant* (kids' menu). If all you want is a salad or soup, go to a café instead.

Ask for *la carte* (lah kart) if you want to see a menu and order à la carte, rather than get a fixed-price meal. Request the waiter's help in deciphering the French. Consider his or her recommendations and anything *de la maison* (of the house), as long as it's not an organ meat (tripes, *rognons*, and andouillette). For more ideas on what to order, see "French Cuisine," later. Galloping gourmets should bring a menu translator; the *Rick Steves' French Phrase Book & Dictionary*, with a menu decoder, works well for most travelers. Wines are often listed on a separate *carte des vins*.

Customers ordering à la carte typically get *une entrée and un plat*, or *un plat and un dessert*, or just *un plat*. Two people can split an *entrée* or a big salad (as small-size dinner salads are usually not offered *á la carte*) and then each get a *plat principal*. At better restaurants, it's considered inappropriate for two diners to share one main course.

At the end of your meal, your server is likely to ask if you're finished: *"Vous-avez terminé?"* (voo-zah-vay tehr-meen-nay), and then ask if you'd like anything else: *"Desirez-vous autre chose?"* (day-zee-ray-voo oh-truh shohz).

Restaurants are almost always a better value in the countryside than in Paris. If you're driving, look for red-and-blue *Relais Routier* decals on main roads outside cities, indicating that the place is recommended by the truckers' union. These truck-stop cafés offer inexpensive and hearty fare.

Beverages

Water: The French are willing to pay for bottled water with their meal (*eau minérale*; oh mee-nay-rahl) because they prefer the taste over tap water. Badoit is my favorite carbonated water (*l'eau gazeuse*; loh gah-zuhz). If you prefer a free pitcher of tap water, ask for *une carafe d'eau* (oon kah-rahf doh). Otherwise, you may unwittingly buy bottled water.

Coffee and Tea: See the "Coffee and Tea Lingo" sidebar, earlier.

Wine and Beer: House wine at the bar is generally cheap and good (about €3/glass at modestly priced places). At a restaurant, a bottle or carafe of house wine costs €8–18. To get inexpensive wine, order regional table wine (*un vin du pays*; uhn van duh pay) in a pitcher (*un pichet*; uhn pee-shay—only available when seated and when ordering food), rather than a bottle. Note, though, that finer restaurants usually offer only bottles of wine.

If all you want is a glass of wine, ask for *un verre de vin rouge* for red wine or *blanc* for white wine (uhn vehr duh van roozh/ blahn). A half-carafe of wine is *un demi-pichet* (uhn duh-mee pee-shay); a quarter-carafe (ideal for one) is *un quart* (uhn kar).

The local beer, which costs about €4 at a restaurant, is cheaper on tap (*une pression*; oon pres-yohn) than in the bottle (*bouteille*; boo-teh-ee). France's best beer is Alsatian; try Kronenbourg or the heavier Pelfort. *Une panaché* (oon pah-nah-shay) is a tasty French shandy (beer and lemon soda).

Regional Specialty Drinks: For a refreshing before-dinner drink, order a *kir* (pronounced keer)—a thumb's level of *crème de cassis* (black currant liqueur) topped with white wine. If you like brandy, try a *marc* (regional brandy; e.g., *marc de Bourgogne*) or an Armagnac, cognac's cheaper twin brother. *Pastis*, the standard southern France aperitif, is a sweet anise (licorice) drink that comes on the rocks with a glass of water. Cut it to taste with lots of water.

Soft Drinks: For a fun, bright, nonalcoholic drink of 7-Up with mint syrup, order *un diabolo menthe* (uhn dee-ah-boh-loh mahnt). For 7-Up with fruit syrup, order *un diabolo grenadine* (think Shirley Temple). Kids love the local orange drink, *Orangina*, a carbonated orange juice with pulp and without caffeine. They also like the flavored syrups mixed with bottled water (*sirops à l'eau*; see-roh ah loh). In France *limonade* (lee-moh-nahd) is Sprite or 7-Up.

Ordering: Be very clear when ordering drinks—you can easily pay €8 for an oversized Coke and €12 for a huge beer. When you order a drink, state the size in centiliters (don't say "small," "medium," or "large," because the waiter might bring a bigger drink than you want). For something small, ask for 25 cl (about 8 ounces); for a medium drink, order 33 cl (about 12 ounces)—a normal can of soda; a large is 50 cl (about 16 ounces); and a super-size is one liter (about a quart—which is more than I would order in France). The ice cubes melted after the last Yankee tour group left.

French Cuisine

The following listing of items found commonly throughout France should help you navigate a typical French menu. For dishes specific to each region, see the "Cuisine Scene" section in every chapter but Paris (which borrows cuisines from all regions).

First Course (*Entrée*)

Crudités: A mix of raw and lightly cooked fresh vegetables, usually including grated carrots, celery root, tomatoes, and beets, often with a hefty dose of vinaigrette dressing. If you want the dressing on the side, say "*La sauce à côté, s'il vous plaît*" (lah sohs ah koh-tay, see voo play).

Escargots: Snails cooked in parsley-garlic butter. You don't even have to like the snail itself. Just dipping your bread in garlic butter is more than satisfying. Prepared a variety of ways, the classic is *à la bourguignonne* (served in their shells).

Foie gras: Rich, buttery in consistency, and pricey, this pâté is made from the swollen livers of force-fed geese (or ducks, in *foie* *gras de canard*). Spread it on bread with your knife, and never add mustard. For a real French experience, try this dish with some sweet white wine (often offered by the glass for an additional cost). For more on foie gras, see the sidebar on page 438.

Huîtres: Oysters, served raw any month, are particularly popular at Christmas and on New Year's Eve, when every café seems to have overflowing baskets in their window.

Pâtés and terrines: Slowly cooked ground meat (usually pork, though game, poultry liver, and rabbit are also common) is highly seasoned and served in slices with mustard and *cornichons* (little pickles). Pâtés are smoother than the similarly prepared but chunkier *terrines*.

Salades: With the exception of a *salade mixte* (simple green salad, often difficult to find), the French get creative with their *salades*. (See page 39 for good salad suggestions.)

Soupe à l'oignon: Hot, salty, and filling, French onion soup is a beef broth served with a baked cheese-and-bread crust over the top.

Main Course (*Plat Principal*)

Duck, lamb, and rabbit are popular in France, and each is prepared in a variety of ways. You'll also encounter various stew-like dishes that vary by region. The most common regional specialties are available almost everywhere and are described here.

Bœuf bourguignon: A Burgundian specialty, this classy beef stew is cooked slowly in red wine, then served with onions, potatoes, and mushrooms.

Confit de canard: A Southwest favorite from the Dordogne region is duck that has been preserved in its own fat, then cooked in its fat, and often served with potatoes (cooked in the same fat). Not for dieters. (Note that *magret de canard* is sliced duck breast and very different in taste.)

Coq au vin: This Burgundian dish is rooster marinated ever so slowly in red wine, then cooked until it melts in your mouth. It's served (often family-style) with vegetables.

Daube: Generally made with beef, but sometimes lamb, this is a long and slowly simmered dish, typically paired with noodles or other pasta.

Escalope normande: A favorite from Normandy, this is turkey or veal in a cream sauce.

Gigot d'agneau: A specialty of Provence, this is a leg of lamb often grilled and served with white beans. The best lamb is *pré salé*, which means the lamb has been raised in salt-marsh lands (like at Mont St. Michel).

Poulet rôti: Found everywhere, it's roasted chicken on the bone—French comfort food.

Saumon and *truite*: You'll see salmon dishes served in various styles. The salmon usually comes from the North Sea and is always served with sauce, most commonly a sorrel (*oseille*) sauce. Trout (*truite*) is also fairly routine on menus.

Steak: Referred to as *pavé* (thick hunk of prime steak), *bavette* (skirt steak), *faux fillet* (sirloin), and *entrecôte* (rib steak). French steak is usually thinner than American steak and is always served with sauces (*au poivre* is a pepper sauce; *une sauce roquefort* is a bleu-cheese sauce). You will also see *steak haché*, which is a lean, gourmet hamburger patty served *sans* bun. When it's served as *steak haché à cheval*, it comes with a fried egg on top.

By American standards, the French undercook meats: Their version of rare, *saignant* (seh-nyahn), means "bloody" and is close to raw. What they consider medium, *à point* (ah pwan), is what an American would call rare. Their term for well-done, *bien cuit* (bee-yehn kwee), would translate as medium for Americans.

Steak tartare: This wonderfully French dish is for adventurous types only. It's very lean, raw hamburger served with spices (usually Tabasco, capers, raw onions, salt, and pepper on the side) and topped with a raw egg yolk. This is not hamburger as we know it, but freshly ground beef.

Cheese Course (Le Fromage)

In France, the cheese course is served just before (or instead of) dessert. It not only helps with digestion, it gives you a great opportunity to sample the tasty regional cheeses. There are more than 400 different French cheeses to try. Some restaurants will offer a cheese platter from which you select a few different kinds. A good cheese platter has four cheeses: a hard cheese (such as Emmentaler—a.k.a., "Swiss cheese"), a flowery cheese (Brie or Camembert), a bleu or Roquefort cheese, and a goat cheese.

Those most commonly served are *brie de Meaux* (mild and creamy, from just outside Paris), Camembert (semi-creamy and pungent, from Normandy), *chèvre* (goat cheese with a sharp taste, usually from the Loire), and Roquefort (strong and blue-veined, from south-central France).

If you'd like a little of several types of cheese from the cheese plate, say: *"Un assortiment, s'il vous plaît"* (uhn ah-sor-tee-mahn, see voo play). If you serve yourself from the cheese plate, observe French etiquette and keep the shape of the cheese. It's best to politely shave off a slice from the side or cut small wedges.

Dessert (Le Dessert)

If you order espresso, it will always come after dessert. To have coffee with dessert, ask for *"café avec le dessert"* (kah-fay ah-vehk luh day-sayr). See the list of coffee terms earlier in this chapter.

How Was Your Trip?

Were your travels fun, smooth, and meaningful? If you'd like to share your tips, concerns, and discoveries, please fill out the survey at www.ricksteves.com/feedback. I value your feedback. Thanks in advance—it helps a lot.

Here are the types of treats you'll see:

Baba au rhum: Pound cake drenched in rum, served with whipped cream.

Café gourmand: An assortment of small desserts selected by the restaurant—a great way to sample several desserts and learn your favorite.

Crème brûlée: A rich, creamy, dense, caramelized custard.

Crème caramel: Flan in a caramel sauce.

Fondant au chocolat or Moelleux au chocolat: A molten chocolate cake with a runny (not totally cooked) center.

Fromage blanc: A light dessert similar to plain yogurt (yet different), served with sugar or herbs.

Glaces: Ice cream—typically vanilla, chocolate, or strawberry (fraise).

Ile flottante: A light dessert consisting of islands of meringue floating on a pond of custard sauce.

Mousse au chocolat: Chocolate mousse.

Profiteroles: Cream puffs filled with vanilla ice cream, smothered in warm chocolate sauce.

Riz au lait: Rice pudding.

Sorbets: Known to us as sherbets, these light, flavorful, and fruity ices are sometimes laced with brandy; citron (lemon) and citron-vert (lime) are particularly popular and refreshing.

Tartes: Narrow strips of fresh fruit, baked in a crust and served in thin slices (without ice cream).

Tarte tatin: Apple pie like grandma never made, with caramelized apples cooked upside-down, but flipped after baking and served upright.

Traveling as a Temporary Local

We travel all the way to Europe to enjoy differences—to become temporary locals. You'll experience frustrations. Certain truths that we find "God-given" or "self-evident," such as cold beer, ice in drinks, bottomless cups of coffee, hot showers, and bigger being better, are suddenly not so true. One of the benefits of travel is the eye-opening realization that there are logical, civil, and even better alternatives.

With a history rich in human achievement, France is an understandably proud country. To enjoy its people, you need to celebrate the differences. A willingness to go local ensures that you'll enjoy a full dose of French hospitality.

The French generally like Americans. But if there is a negative aspect to their image of us, it's that we are big, loud, aggressive, impolite, rich, and a bit naive.

The French place a high value on speaking quietly in restaurants and on trains. Listen while on the bus or in a restaurant—the place can be packed, but the decibel level is low. Try to adjust your volume accordingly to show respect for their culture.

Although the French look bemusedly at some of our Yankee excesses—and worriedly at others—they nearly always afford us individual travelers all the warmth we deserve. Judging from all the happy feedback I receive from travelers who have used this book, it's safe to assume you'll enjoy a great, affordable vacation—with the finesse of an independent, experienced traveler.

Thanks, and *bon voyage!*

Back Door Travel Philosophy
From *Rick Steves' Europe Through the Back Door*

Travel is intensified living—maximum thrills per minute and one of the last great sources of legal adventure. Travel is freedom. It's recess, and we need it.

Experiencing the real Europe requires catching it by surprise, going casual..."Through the Back Door."

Affording travel is a matter of priorities. (Make do with the old car.) You can eat and sleep—simply, safely, and enjoyably—anywhere in Europe for $120 a day plus transportation costs. In many ways, spending more money only builds a thicker wall between you and what you traveled so far to see. Europe is a cultural carnival, and time after time, you'll find that its best acts are free and the best seats are the cheap ones.

A tight budget forces you to travel close to the ground, meeting and communicating with the people. Never sacrifice sleep, nutrition, safety, or cleanliness to save money. Simply enjoy the local-style alternatives to expensive hotels and restaurants.

Connecting with people carbonates your experience. Extroverts have more fun. If your trip is low on magic moments, kick yourself and make things happen. If you don't enjoy a place, maybe you don't know enough about it. Seek the truth. Recognize tourist traps. Give a culture the benefit of your open mind. See things as different, but not better or worse. Any culture has plenty to share.

Of course, travel, like the world, is a series of hills and valleys. Be fanatically positive and militantly optimistic. If something's not to your liking, change your liking.

Travel can make you a happier American, as well as a citizen of the world. Our Earth is home to six and a half billion equally precious people. It's humbling to travel and find that other people don't have the "American Dream"—they have their own dreams. Europeans like us, but with all due respect, they wouldn't trade passports.

Thoughtful travel engages us with the world. In tough economic times, it reminds us what is truly important. By broadening perspectives, travel teaches new ways to measure quality of life.

Globetrotting destroys ethnocentricity, helping us understand and appreciate other cultures. Rather than fear the diversity on this planet, celebrate it. Among your most prized souvenirs will be the strands of different cultures you choose to knit into your own character. The world is a cultural yarn shop, and Back Door travelers are weaving the ultimate tapestry. Join in!

PARIS

Paris—the City of Light—has been a beacon of culture for centuries. As a world capital of art, fashion, food, literature, and ideas, it stands as a symbol of all the fine things human civilization can offer. Come prepared to celebrate, rather than judge the cultural differences, and you'll capture the romance and *joie de vivre* that Paris exudes.

Paris offers sweeping boulevards, chatty crêpe stands, chic boutiques, and world-class art galleries. Sip decaf with deconstructionists at a sidewalk café, then step into an Impressionist painting in a tree-lined park. Climb Notre-Dame and rub shoulders with the gargoyles. Cruise the Seine, zip up the Eiffel Tower, and saunter down avenue des Champs-Elysées. Master the Louvre and Orsay museums. Save some after-dark energy for one of the world's most romantic cities.

Planning Your Time

For up to five very busy but doable days in Paris, I've listed sights in descending order of importance in the planning sections that follow. Therefore, if you have only one day, just do Day 1; for two days, add Day 2; and so on. When planning where to plug in Versailles (see next chapter), keep in mind that that the Château is closed on Mondays and especially crowded on Sundays and Tuesdays—try to avoid these days. For other itinerary considerations on a day-by-day basis, check the "Daily Reminder" on page 58.

Day 1

Morning: Follow this chapter's Historic Paris Walk, featuring Ile de la Cité, Notre-Dame, the Latin Quarter, and Sainte-Chapelle.

Afternoon: Tour the Louvre.

Evening: Enjoy the Trocadéro scene and a twilight ride up the Eiffel Tower.

Day 2

Morning: Wander the Champs-Elysées from the Arc de Triomphe down the grand avenue des Champs-Elysées to the Tuileries Garden.

Afternoon: Cross the pedestrian bridge from the Tuileries Garden, then tour the Orsay Museum.

Evening: Take one of the nighttime tours by taxi, bus, or retro-chic Deux Chevaux car. (If you're staying more than two days, save this for your last-night finale.)

Day 3

Morning: Catch the RER suburban train by 8:00 to arrive early at Versailles (before it opens at 9:00). Tour the palace's interior.

Midday: Have lunch in the gardens at Versailles.

Afternoon: Spend the afternoon touring the gardens, the Trianon Palaces, and Domaine de Marie-Antoinette.

Evening: Have dinner in Versailles town or return to Paris. For dessert, cruise the Seine River.

Day 4

Morning: Visit Montmartre and the Sacré-Cœur Basilica. Have lunch on Montmartre.

Afternoon: Continue your Impressionist theme by touring the Orangerie and the Rodin Museum, or change themes entirely and tour the Army Museum and Napoleon's Tomb.

Evening: Enjoy dinner on Ile St. Louis, then a floodlit walk by Notre-Dame.

Day 5

Morning: Ride scenic bus #69 to the Marais and tour this neighborhood, including the Pompidou Center.

Afternoon: Tour the Opéra Garnier (English tours available), and end your day enjoying the glorious rooftop views at the Galeries Lafayette and Printemps department stores.

Evening: Stroll the Champs-Elysées at night.

Orientation to Paris

Paris (population of city center: 2,170,000) is split in half by the Seine River, divided into 20 arrondissements (proud and independent governmental jurisdictions), circled by a ring-road freeway (the *périphérique*), and speckled with Métro stations. You'll find

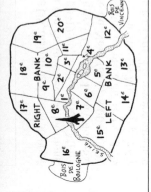

Paris easier to navigate if you know which side of the river you're on, which arrondissement you're in, and which Métro stop you're closest to. If you're north of the river (the top half of any city map), you're on the Right Bank (Rive Droite). If you're south of it, you're on the Left Bank (Rive Gauche). The bull's-eye of your Paris map is Notre-Dame, which sits on an island in the middle of the Seine.

Most of your sightseeing will take place within five blocks of the river.

Arrondissements are numbered, starting at the Louvre and moving in a clockwise spiral out to the ring road. The last two digits in a Parisian zip code indicate the arrondissement number. The abbreviation for "Métro stop" is "Mo." In Parisian jargon, the Eiffel Tower is on *la*

Paris Arrondissements

Rive Gauche (the Left Bank) in the *7ème* (7th arrondissement), zip code 75007; Mo: Trocadéro.

Paris Métro stops are used as a standard aid in giving directions, even for those not taking the Métro. As you're tracking down addresses, these words and pronunciations will help: Métro (may-troh), *place* (plahs—square), *rue* (roo—road), *avenue* (ah-vuh-noo), *boulevard* (boo-luh-var), and *pont* (pohn—bridge).

Tourist Information

Paris' TIs have long lines, offer little information, and may charge for maps. All you really need are this book and one of the freebie maps available at any hotel (or in the front of this book). On the plus side, TIs sell individual tickets to sights (see "Avoiding Lines with Advance Tickets" in "Helpful Hints," later) as well as Paris Museum Passes, but if you plan to get a Museum Pass, it's quicker to buy these at participating sights. Paris' TIs share a single phone

Paris Neighborhoods

number: 08 92 68 30 00 (from the US, dial 011 33 8 92 68 30 00).

If you must visit a TI, you can do so at several locations, including **Pyramides** (daily 9:00–19:00, at Pyramides Métro stop between the Louvre and Opéra), **Gare de Lyon** (Mon–Sat 8:00–18:00, closed Sun), **Gare du Nord** (daily 8:00–18:00), and **Montmartre** (two branches: one on place du Tertre, daily 10:00–19:00, and the other above the Anvers Métro stop, daily 10:00–18:00). The official website for Paris' TIs is www.parisinfo.com. Both **airports** have handy information offices (called ADP) with long hours and short lines (see "Airports" on page 203).

Pariscope: The weekly €0.40 *Pariscope* magazine (or one of its clones, available at any newsstand) lists museum hours, art exhibits, concerts, festivals, plays, movies, and nightclubs. Smart sightseers rely on this for the latest listings.

Other Publications: Look for the *Paris Times*, which provides helpful English information and fresh insights into living in Paris (available at English-language bookstores, French-American establishments, and the American Church). *L'Officiel des Spectacles* (€0.35), which is similar to *Pariscope*, also lists goings-on around town (in French). The *Paris Voice*, with snappy reviews of concerts, plays, and current events, is available only online at www.parisvoice.com. For a schedule of museum hours and English museum tours, get the free *Musées, Monuments Historiques, et Expositions* booklet at any museum.

American Church and Franco-American Center: This

interdenominational church—in the rue Cler neighborhood, facing the river between the Eiffel Tower and Orsay Museum—is a nerve center for the American expat community. Worship services are held every Sunday (traditional services at 9:00 and 11:00, contemporary service at 13:30; the coffee hour after church and the free Sunday concerts (generally Sept–June at 17:00—but not every week) are a good way to get a taste of émigré life in Paris (reception open Mon–Sat 9:00–12:00 & 13:00–22:00, Sun 14:30–19:00, 65 quai d'Orsay, Mo: Invalides, tel. 01 40 62 05 00, www.acparis.org). It's also a handy place to pick up free copies of *Paris Times* (described earlier) and *France–USA Contacts* (an advertisement paper with info on housing and employment for the 50,000 Americans living in Paris, www.fusac.fr).

Arrival in Paris

For a comprehensive rundown of the city's train stations and airports, see "Paris Connections," near the end of this chapter. For information on parking for drivers, see page 57.

Helpful Hints

Theft Alert: Troublesome thieves thrive near famous monuments and on Métro and RER lines that serve high-profile tourist sights. Beware of pickpockets working busy lines (e.g., at train station ticket windows). Pay attention when it's your turn and your back is to the crowd—keep your bag firmly gripped in front of you.

In general, it's smart to wear a money belt, put your wallet in your front pocket, loop your day bag over your shoulders, and keep a tight grip on your purse or shopping bag. Muggings are rare, but they do occur. If you're out late, avoid the dark riverfront embankments and any place where the lighting is dim and pedestrian activity is minimal.

Paris is taking action to combat crime by stationing an abundance of police at monuments, on streets, and on the Métro, as well as security cameras at key sights. You'll go through quick and reassuring airport-like security checks at many major attractions.

Tourist Scams: Be aware of the latest scams, including these current favorites. The "found ring" scam involves an innocent-looking person who picks up a ring off the ground, and asks if you dropped it. When you say no, the person examines the ring more closely, then shows you a mark "proving" that it's pure gold. He offers to sell it to you for a good price—several times more than he paid for it before dropping it on the sidewalk.

In the "friendship bracelet" scam, a vendor approaches you and asks if you'll help him with a demonstration. He

Paris Museum Pass

In Paris there are two classes of sightseers—those with a Paris Museum Pass, and those who stand in line. The pass admits you to many of Paris' most popular sights, allowing you to skip ticket-buying lines. Serious sightseers save time and money by getting this pass.

Buying the Pass

The pass pays for itself with four key admissions in two days (for example, the Louvre, Orsay, Sainte-Chapelle, and Versailles), and lets you skip the ticket line at most sights (2 days/€32, 4 days/€48, 6 days/€64, no youth or senior discount). It's sold at participating museums, monuments, FNAC department stores, and TIs (even at airports; see "Paris Connections," near the end of this chapter). Try to avoid buying the pass at a major museum (such as the Louvre), where the supply can be spotty and lines long. For more info, visit www.parismuseumpass.com or call 01 44 61 96 60.

Tally up what you want to see from the list on the next page—and remember, an advantage of the pass is that you skip to the front of most lines, which can save you hours of waiting, especially in summer. Note that at a few sights (including the Louvre, Sainte-Chapelle, Notre-Dame's tower, and the Château de Versailles), everyone has to shuffle through the slow-moving baggage-check lines for security—but you still save time by avoiding the ticket line.

Families: The pass isn't worth buying for children and teens, as most museums are free or discounted for those under 18 (teenagers may need to show ID as proof of age). Kids can usually skip ticket lines if you have a Museum Pass, although a few places (such as the Arc de Triomphe and Army Museum) require you to stand in line to collect your child's free ticket. Of the few museums that charge for children, some allow kids in for free if their parents have a Museum Pass, whereas others charge admission, depending on age (the cutoff age varies from 5 to 18). The free directory that comes with your pass lists the current hours of sights, phone numbers, and the price that kids pay.

What the Paris Museum Pass Covers

Most of the sights listed in this chapter are covered by the pass. Notable exceptions are the Eiffel Tower, Montparnasse Tower,

Marmottan Museum, Opéra Garnier, Notre-Dame Treasury, Jacquemart-André Museum, Grand Palais, La Grande Arche at La Défense, Catacombs, Montmartre Museum, Sacré-Cœur's dome, Dalí Museum, Museum of Erotic Art, and the ladies of Pigalle.

Here's a list of included sights and their admission prices without the pass:

Louvre (€9.50)	Notre-Dame Tower (€8)
Orsay Museum (€8)	Paris Archaeological Crypt (€4)
Orangerie Museum (€7.50)	Paris Sewer Tour (€4.30)
Sainte-Chapelle (€8)	Cluny Museum (€8.50)
Arc de Triomphe (€9)	Pompidou Center (€10-12)
Rodin Museum (€6)	Jewish Art and History Museum (€7)
Army Museum (€9)	National Maritime Museum (€7)
Conciergerie (€7)	Delacroix Museum (€5)
Panthéon (€8)	Quai Branly Museum (€8.50)

Versailles (€25 total—€15 for Château, €10 for Trianon Palaces and Domaine de Marie-Antoinette)

Activating and Using the Pass

Think ahead to make the most of your pass. Validate it only when you're ready to tackle the covered sights on consecutive days. Make sure the sights you want to visit will be open (many museums are closed Mondays or Tuesdays). The Paris Museum Pass even covers most of Versailles (your other option for Versailles is the Le Passeport pass; see next chapter). Keep in mind that sights such as the Arc de Triomphe and Pompidou Center are open later in the evening, and that the Louvre and Orsay have late hours on selected evenings, allowing you to stretch the day for your Paris Museum Pass. On days that you don't have pass coverage, visit free sights as well as those not covered by the pass (see page 79 for a list of free sights).

The pass isn't activated until the first time you use it (write the starting date on the pass).

To use your pass at sights, boldly walk to the front of the ticket line (after passing security, if necessary), hold up your pass, and ask the ticket-taker: "*Entrez, pass?*" (ahn-tray pahs). You'll either be allowed to enter at that point or you'll be directed to a special entrance. For major sights, such as the Louvre and Orsay museums, I've identified passholder entrances on the maps in this book.

With the pass you can pop into sights as you're walking by (even for a few minutes) that otherwise might not be worth the expense (e.g., the Conciergerie or Paris Archaeological Crypt).

proceeds to make a friendship bracelet right on your arm. When finished, he asks you to pay for the bracelet he created just for you. And because you can't easily take it off on the spot, he counts on your feeling obliged to pay up.

Distractions by a stranger—often a "salesman," or someone asking you to sign a petition, or posing as a deaf person to show you a small note to read—can all be tricks that function as a smokescreen for theft. As you try to wriggle away from the pushy stranger, an accomplice picks your pocket.

In popular tourist spots (such as in front of Notre-Dame) young ladies politely ask if you speak English, then pretend to beg for money while actually angling to get your wallet.

To all these scammers, simply say "no" firmly. Don't apologize, don't smile, and step away purposefully.

Street Safety: Parisian drivers are notorious for ignoring pedestrians. Look both ways (many streets are one-way) and be careful of seemingly quiet bus/taxi lanes. Don't assume you have the right of way, even in a crosswalk. When crossing a street, keep your pace constant and don't stop suddenly. By law, drivers are allowed to miss pedestrians by up to just one meter—a little more than three feet (1.5 meters in the countryside). Drivers carefully calculate your speed so they won't hit you, provided you don't alter your route or pace.

Watch out for bicyclists when you're crossing streets. This popular—and silent—transportation may come at you from unexpected places and directions—cyclists have a right to use lanes reserved for buses and taxis. Also, bikes commonly go against traffic, as many bike paths are on one-way streets. Again, always look both ways.

Museum Strategies: The worthwhile Paris Museum Pass, covering most sights in Paris, is sold at TIs, museums, FNAC stores, and monuments. For detailed information, see the "Paris Museum Pass" sidebar. For other museum strategies, see "Sightseeing," on page 20.

Avoiding Lines with Advance Tickets: Throughout Paris, TIs and FNAC department stores sell individual *coupe-file* tickets, which allow you to use the Museum Pass entrance at sights and thereby skip ticket lines. TIs sell these tickets for no extra fee, but FNAC stores add a surcharge of 10–20 percent (possibly worth it, given the convenience of FNAC's many locations). For sights that can otherwise have long waits (such as the Arc de Triomphe, Opéra Garnier, Versailles, and Monet's gardens in Giverny), these tickets are a good idea. (Note that Versailles and the Arc de Triomphe are covered by the Paris Museum Pass—also sold, without surcharge, at TIs and FNAC stores.)

You can go online to buy Paris Museum Passes and tickets for several major sights at no surcharge (no more than three weeks in advance, http://en.parisinfo.com/express-booking). You'll print out vouchers, which you'll need to redeem at a Paris TI for the actual passes or tickets (or you can opt to have the passes or tickets mailed to you in the US, allow 5–7 days, postage fee added).

Bookstores: Paris has many English-language bookstores, where you can pick up guidebooks (at nearly double their American prices). Most stores carry this book.

My favorite is the friendly **Red Wheelbarrow Bookstore** in the Marais neighborhood, run by mellow Penelope (Mon 10:00–18:00, Tue–Sat 10:00–19:00, Sun 14:00–18:00, 22 rue St. Paul, Mo: St. Paul, tel. 01 48 04 75 08).

Other options include the following:

Shakespeare and Company (some used travel books, Mon–Fri 10:00–23:00, Sat–Sun 11:00–23:00, 37 rue de la Bûcherie, across the river from Notre-Dame, Mo: St. Michel, tel. 01 43 25 40 93).

W. H. Smith (Mon–Sat 9:00–19:00, Sun 12:30–19:00, 248 rue de Rivoli, Mo: Concorde, tel. 01 44 77 88 99).

Village Voice (Mon 14:00–19:30, Tue–Sat 10:00–19:30, Sun 12:00–18:00, near St. Sulpice Church at 6 rue Princesse, tel. 01 46 33 36 47).

San Francisco Book Company (Mon–Sat 11:00–21:00, Sun 14:00–19:30, 17 rue Monsieur le Prince, tel. 01 43 29 15 70).

Public WCs: Public toilets are free (though it's polite to leave a small tip if there's an attendant). Modern, sanitary street-booth toilets provide both relief and a memory (don't leave small children inside unattended). The restrooms in museums are free and the best you'll find. Or walk into any sidewalk café like you own the place, and find the toilet in the back. Keep toilet paper or tissues with you, as some WCs are poorly supplied.

Parking: Street parking is generally free at night (19:00 to 9:00), all day Sunday, and anytime in August, when many Parisians are on vacation. To pay for streetside parking, you must go to a *tabac* and buy a parking card (*une carte parking*), sold in €10, €20, and €30 denominations. Insert the card into the meter and punch the desired amount of time (generally €1–2/hour), then take the receipt and put it inside your windshield. Meters limit street parking to a maximum of two hours. For a longer stay, park for less at an airport (about €10/day) and take public transport or a taxi into the city. Underground lots are numerous in Paris—you'll find them under Ecole Militaire, St. Sulpice Church, Les Invalides, the Bastille, and the Panthéon; all charge about €27–36/day (€58/3 days, €10/day

Daily Reminder

Sunday: Many sights are free on the first Sunday of the month, including the Louvre, Orsay, Rodin, Cluny, and Delacroix museums, the Arc de Triomphe (Oct-March only), and Pompidou Center. These free days at popular sights attract hordes of visitors.

Versailles is more crowded than usual on Sunday—but on the upside, the garden's fountains are running (April-Oct).

Look for organ concerts at St. Sulpice and possibly other churches. The American Church often hosts a free concert (often classical piano and vocals, generally Sept-June at 17:00—but not every week). Summer brings puppet shows to Luxembourg Garden and the Champ de Mars park.

Most of Paris' stores are closed on Sunday, but shoppers will find relief along the Champs-Elysées and in the Marais neighborhood's lively Jewish Quarter, where many stores are open. Many recommended restaurants in the rue Cler neighborhood are closed for dinner.

Monday: These sights are closed today: Orsay, Rodin, Marmottan, Carnavalet, Catacombs, Petit Palais, Victor Hugo's House, Montmartre Museum, Quai Branly, and Paris Archaeological Crypt. Outside of Paris, the Château and the Trianon Palaces and Domaine de Marie-Antoinette area at Versailles are closed. The Louvre and Eiffel Tower are more crowded because of these closings. From fall through spring, the Army Museum (and Napoleon's Tomb) is closed the first Monday of every month. Some small stores don't open until

more after that, for locations see www.vincipark.com). Some hotels offer parking for less—ask your hotelier.

Tobacco Stands (*Tabacs*): These little kiosks—usually just a counter inside a café—sell cards for parking meters, some public-transit tickets, postage stamps (though not all sell international postage—to mail something home, use two domestic stamps, or go to a post office), prepaid phone cards, and...oh yeah, cigarettes. To find one anywhere in Paris, just look for a *Tabac* sign and the red cylinder-shaped symbol above certain cafés. For details on prepaid phone cards, see page 1006.

Winter Activities: The City of Light sparkles year-round. For background on what to do and see here in winter months, see www.ricksteves.com/pariswinter.

Getting Around Paris

Paris is easy to navigate. Your basic choices are Métro (in-city subway), RER (suburban rail tied into the Métro system), public bus,

14:00. Market streets such as rue Cler and rue Mouffetard are dead today. Some banks are closed. It's discount night at many cinemas.

Tuesday: Many sights are closed today, including the Louvre, Orangerie, Cluny, Pompidou, National Maritime, and Delacroix museums, as well as the Grand Palais. The Eiffel Tower, Orsay, and Versailles are particularly busy today.

Wednesday: All sights are open (Louvre until 21:45). The weekly *Pariscope* magazine comes out today. Most schools are closed, so many kids' sights are busy, and in summer the puppet shows play in Luxembourg Garden and the Champ de Mars park. Some cinemas offer discounts.

Thursday: All sights are open except the Sewer Tour. The Orsay is open until 21:45 (last entry 21:00). Some department stores are open late.

Friday: All sights are open (Louvre until 21:45; last entry 21:00) except the Sewer Tour. Afternoon trains and roads leaving Paris are crowded; TGV train reservation fees are higher. Restaurants are busy—it's smart to book ahead at popular places.

Saturday: All sights are open except the Jewish Art and History Museum and the Holocaust Memorial. The fountains run at Versailles (April–Oct). Department stores are jammed. The Jewish Quarter is quiet. In summer, puppet shows are held at Luxembourg Garden and the Champ de Mars park. Restaurants get packed; reserve in advance if you have a particular place in mind.

and taxi. (Also consider the hop-on, hop-off bus and boat tours, described under "Tours in Paris," later.) You can buy tickets and passes at Métro stations and at many *tabac* shops. Keep change on hand, as some smaller Métro stations don't have staffed ticket windows, only ticket-vending machines, for which you'll need coins (some take bills; none takes American credit cards).

Public-Transit Tickets: The Métro, RER, and buses all work on the same tickets. You can make as many transfers as you need on a single ticket, except when transferring between the Métro/RER system and the bus system, which requires using an additional ticket. A **single ticket** costs €1.70. To save money, buy a *carnet* (kar-nay) of 10 tickets for €12 (cheaper for ages 4–10). *Carnets* can be shared among travelers.

Passes: The transit system has introduced a chip-embedded card, called the **Passe Navigo** (though for most tourists, *carnets* are still the better deal). You pay a one-time €5 fee for the Navigo card itself (which also requires a postage stamp-size photo of

Métro Basics

- The same tickets are good on the Métro, RER (within the city), and city buses (but not to transfer between Métro/RER and bus).
- Save money by buying a *carnet* of tickets or a Passe Navigo.
- Find your train by its end-of-the-line stops.
- Insert your ticket into the turnstile, retrieve it, and keep it until the end of your journey.
- Beware of pickpockets, and don't buy tickets from men roaming the stations.
- Transfers (*correspondances*) within the Métro and RER system are free.
- At the end of your trip, choose the right exit (*sortie*) to avoid extra walking.
- Dispose of used tickets after you complete your ride and leave the station (not before), to avoid confusing them with fresh ones.
- On some trains you must activate the door by pushing a button (but most open automatically).

Key Words for the Métro and RER

French	Pronounced	English
direction	dee-rek-see-ohn	direction
ligne	leen-yuh	line
correspondance	kor-res-pohn-dahns	connection/transfer
sortie	sor-tee	exit
carnet	kar-nay	discounted set of 10 tickets

yourself—bring your own, or use the €4 photo booths in major Métro stations). For a weekly (*behdomadaire*) version, you'll pay €22.50, which gives you free run of the bus, Métro, and non-suburban RER system from Monday to Sunday (expiring on Sunday, even if you buy it on Friday). A monthly version for €60 is good for one calendar month.

To use the Passe Navigo, whether at a Métro turnstile or on the bus, touch the card to the purple pad, wait for the green validation light and the "ding," and you're on your way. The basic pass covers only central Paris, not regional destinations such as Versailles.

Navigo or Carnet? It's hard to beat the *carnet*. Two 10-packs of *carnets*—enough for most travelers staying a week—cost €23.40, are shareable, and don't expire until they're used. The Passe Navigo only becomes worthwhile for visitors who stay a full week or more and use the system a lot.

French	Pronounced	English
Pardon, madame/ monsieur.	par-dohn, mah-dahm/ mes-yur	Excuse me, ma'am/ sir.
Je descends.	juh day-sahn	I'm getting off.
Donnez-moi mon porte-monnaie!	duh-nay-mwah mohn port-moh-nay	Give me back my wallet!

Etiquette

- When your train arrives, board only after everyone leaving the car has made it out the door.
- Avoid using the hinged seats near the doors of some trains when the car is crowded; they take up valuable standing space.
- If you find yourself blocking the door at a stop, step out of the car to let others off, then get back on.
- Talk softly in the cars. Listen to how quietly Parisians communicate and follow their lead.
- On escalators, stand on the right and pass on the left.
- When leaving a station, hold the door for the person behind you.

Other Passes: A handy one-day bus/Métro pass (called **Mobilis**) is available for €5.90. The overpriced **Paris Visite** passes are poorly designed for tourists, and offer minor reductions at minor sights (1 day/€9, 2 days/€15, 3 days/€20, 5 days/€29).

By Métro

In Paris, you're never more than a 10-minute walk from a Métro station. Europe's best subway allows you to hop from sight to sight quickly and cheaply (runs daily 5:30–24:30 in the morning). Learn to use it. Begin by studying the color Métro map at the beginning of this book, free at Métro stations, and included on freebie Paris maps at your hotel.

How the Métro Works: To get to your destination, determine the closest "Mo" stop and which line or lines will get you there. The lines are color-coded and numbered, and are known by their end-of-the-line stops. For example, the La Défense/Château de

Vincennes line, also known as line 1 (yellow), runs between La Défense, on its west end, and Vincennes on its east end. Once in the Métro station, you'll see the color-coded line numbers and/or blue-and-white signs directing you to the train going in your direction (e.g., *direction: La Défense*). Insert your ticket in the automatic turnstile, reclaim your ticket, pass through, and keep it until you exit the system (some stations require you to pass your ticket through a turnstile to exit).

Be warned that fare inspectors regularly check for cheaters and accept absolutely no excuses—keep that ticket or pay a minimum fine of €25.

Transfers are free and can be made wherever lines cross, provided you do so within 1.5 hours. When you transfer, follow the appropriately colored line number for your next train, or find orange *correspondance* (connection) signs leading you to the part of the station where you'll find your next line.

Be prepared to walk significant distances within Métro stations to reach your platform (especially when you transfer). Escalators are common, but they're often out of order. To limit excessive walking, avoid transferring at these sprawling stations: Montparnasse–Bienvenüe, Châtelet–Les Halles, Charles de Gaulle–Etoile, Gare du Nord, and Bastille. (Taking buses require less walking than the Métro—for more, see "By City Bus," later.)

When you reach your destination, look for the blue-and-white *sortie* signs pointing you to the exit. Before leaving the station, check the helpful *plan du quartier* (map of the neighborhood) to get your bearings. At stops with several *sorties*, you can save lots of walking by choosing the best exit.

After you exit the system, toss or tear your used ticket so you don't confuse it with unused tickets—they look almost identical.

Beware of Pickpockets: Thieves dig the Métro and RER. Be on guard. For example, if your pocket is picked as you pass through a turnstile, you end up stuck on the wrong side (after the turnstile bar has closed behind you) while the thief gets away. Stand away from Métro doors to avoid being a target for a theft-and-run just before the doors close. Any jostling or commotion—especially when boarding or leaving trains—is likely the sign of a thief or a team of thieves in action. Make any fare inspector show proof of identity (ask locals for help if you're not certain). Never show anyone your wallet.

By RER

The RER (Réseau Express Régionale; air-ay-air) is the suburban arm of the Métro, serving outlying destinations such as Versailles, Disneyland Paris, and the airports. These routes are indicated by thick lines on your subway map and identified by the letters A, B, C, and so on.

Within the city center, the RER works like the Métro and can be speedier if it serves your destination directly, because it makes fewer stops. Métro tickets and the Passe Navigo card are good on the RER when traveling in the city center. You can transfer between the Métro and RER systems with the same ticket. But to travel outside the city (to Versailles or the airport, for example), you'll need to buy a separate, more expensive ticket. Unlike the Métro, not every train stops at every station along the way; check the sign over the platform to see if your destination is listed as a stop ("*toutes les gares*" means it makes all stops along the way), or confirm with a local before you board. For RER trains, you may need to insert your ticket in a turnstile to exit the system.

By City Bus

Paris' excellent bus system is worth figuring out. Buses don't seem as romantic as the famous Métro and are subject to traffic jams, but savvy travelers know that buses can have you swinging through the city like Tarzan in an urban jungle. Buses require less walking and fewer stairways than the Métro, and you can see Paris unfold as you travel.

Bus stops are everywhere, and every stop comes complete with all the information you need: a good city bus map, route maps showing exactly where each bus that uses this stop goes, a frequency chart and schedule, a *plan du quartier* map of the immediate neighborhood, and a *soirées* map explaining night service, if available.

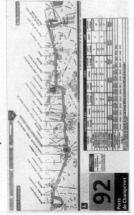

Just like with the Métro, every bus stop has a name, and every bus is headed to one end-of-the-line stop or the other. The photo on page 64 shows the route for bus #69. First, find your stop on the chart. It says "*vous êtes ICI*" ("you are HERE") at esplanade des Invalides. Next, find your destination stop—let's say Bosquet-Grenelle, located a few stops to the west. Now, find out exactly where to catch the bus going in that direction. On the map showing the bus route, notice the triangle-shaped arrows pointing in the direction the bus is headed. You'll see

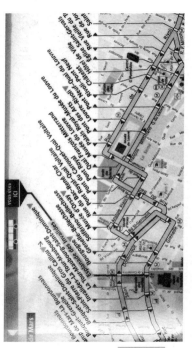

that esplanade des Invalides has two different bus stops—one for buses headed east and one for the bus going west. You want to go west to Bosquet-Grenelle, so you head for that street corner to catch the bus. (With so many one-way streets in Paris, it's easy to get on the bus in the wrong direction.) When the bus pulls up, double-check that the sign on the front of the bus has the end-of-the-line stop going in your direction—to "Champ de Mars," in this case.

Buses use the same tickets and passes as the Métro and RER. One Zone 1 ticket buys you a bus ride anywhere in central Paris within the freeway ring road (*le périphérique*). Use your Métro ticket or buy one on board for €0.10 more. (The ticket system has a few quirks—see "More Bus Tips," below.)

Board your bus through the front door (or on long buses, you can push the green button by the other doors to open them). If you already have a ticket, validate it in the yellow machine. If you have a Passe Navigo, scan it on the purple touch pad. Otherwise, buy a ticket from the driver. Keep track of what stop is coming up next by following the on-board diagram or listening to recorded announcements. When you're ready to get off, push the red button to signal you want a stop, then exit through the rear door. Even if you're not certain you've figured out the system, do some joyriding.

More Bus Tips: Avoid rush hour (Mon–Fri 8:00–9:30 & 17:30–19:30), when buses are jammed and traffic doesn't move. Not all city buses are air-conditioned, so they can become rolling greenhouses on summer days. You can transfer from one bus to another on the same ticket (within 1.5 hours, re-validate your ticket

PARIS

Scenic Bus Route #69

Why pay €25 for a tour company to give you an overview of Paris, when city bus #69 can do it for the cost of a Métro ticket? Get on the bus and settle in for a ride through some of the city's most interesting neighborhoods. Or hop on and off using this tour as a fun way to lace together many of Paris' most important sightseeing districts (your ticket gives you 90 minutes in one direction). This scenic route crosses the city east-west, running between the Eiffel Tower and Père Lachaise Cemetery, and passing these great monuments and neighborhoods: Eiffel Tower, Ecole Militaire, rue Cler, Les Invalides (Army Museum and Napoleon's Tomb), Louvre Museum, Ile de la Cité, Ile St. Louis, Hôtel de Ville, Pompidou Center, Marais, Bastille, and Père Lachaise. You don't have to do the whole enchilada; get on and off wherever you like.

You'll learn how great the city's bus system is—and you'll wonder why you've been tunneling by Métro under this gorgeous city. And if you're staying in the Marais or rue Cler neighborhoods, line #69 is a useful route for just getting around town.

You can hop on daily until 22:30 (last departure from Eiffel Tour stop). It's best to avoid weekday rush hours (8:00–9:30 & 17:30–19:30) and hot days (no air-conditioning). Sundays are quietest, and it's easy to get a window seat. Evening bus rides are magical from fall through spring (roughly Sept–April), when it gets dark early enough to see the floodlit monuments before the bus stops running. In the rue Cler area, catch bus #69 eastbound at the Eiffel Tower on avenue Joseph Bouvard (the first stop is at the southwestern end of the avenue, across from the Eiffel Tower; the second stop is at the eastern end).

in the next bus's yellow machine), but you can't do a round-trip or hop on and off on the same line. Neither can you transfer between the bus and the Métro/RER systems on a single ticket. Also, you can't transfer between buses with a ticket bought on board—go figure.

Handy bus-system maps (*plans des autobus*) are available in any Métro station (and in the €6 *Paris Pratique* map book sold at newsstands). For longer stays, consider buying the €6 *Le Bus* book of bus routes. While the Métro shuts down at about 24:30 in the morning, some buses continue much later (called Noctilien lines, www.noctilien.fr).

For a list of Paris' most scenic and convenient routes, see "Key Buses for Tourists" on the next page. I've also listed the handiest bus routes for each recommended hotel neighborhood in the "Sleeping in Paris" section, later.

Key Buses for Tourists

Of Paris' many bus routes, these are some of the most scenic. They provide a great, cheap, and convenient introduction to the city.

Bus #69 runs east-west between the Eiffel Tower and Père Lachaise Cemetery by way of rue Cler (recommended hotels), quai d'Orsay, the Louvre, and the Marais (recommended hotels). For more on the route, see "Scenic Bus Route #69" on page 65.

Bus #87 also links the Marais and rue Cler areas, but stays mostly on the Left Bank, connecting the Eiffel Tower, St. Sulpice, Luxembourg Garden (more recommended hotels and restaurants), St. Germain-des-Prés, the Latin Quarter, the Bastille, and Gare de Lyon.

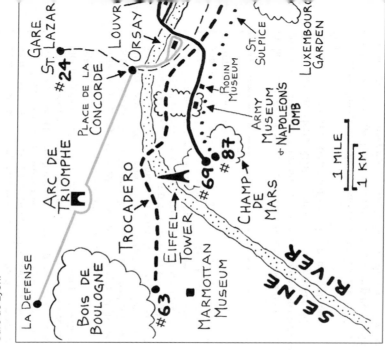

Bus #24 runs east-west along the Seine riverbank from Gare St. Lazare to Madeleine, place de la Concorde, Orsay Museum, the Louvre, St. Michel, Notre-Dame, and Jardin des Plantes, all the way to trendy Bercy Village (cafés and shops).

Bus #63 is another good east-west route, connecting the Marmottan Museum, Trocadéro (Eiffel Tower), pont de l'Alma, Orsay Museum, St. Sulpice, Luxembourg Garden, Latin Quarter/Panthéon, and Gare de Lyon.

Bus #73 is one of Paris' most scenic lines, starting at the Orsay Museum and running westbound around place de la Concorde, then up the Champs-Elysées, around the Arc de Triomphe, and down avenue Charles de Gaulle to La Défense.

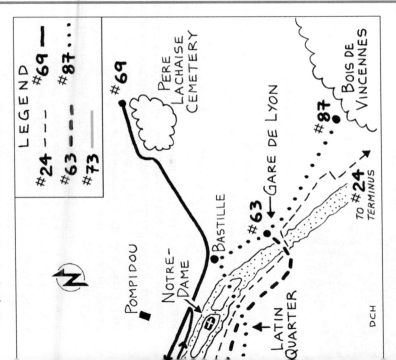

By Taxi

Parisian taxis are reasonable, especially for couples and families. The meters are tamper-proof. Fares and supplements (described in English on the rear windows) are straightforward and tightly regulated.

A taxi can fit three people comfortably, and a fourth for €3 extra. (Cabbies are legally required to accept four passengers, though they don't always like it.) Groups of up to five can use a larger vehicle, which must be booked in advance—ask your hotelier to call. For a sample taxi tour of the city at night, see page 140.

Rates: All Parisian taxis start with €2.20 on the meter, and have a minimum charge of €6.10. A 20-minute ride (e.g., Bastille to Eiffel Tower) costs about €20 (versus €1.20/person to get anywhere in town using a *carnet* ticket on the Métro or bus). Drivers charge higher rates at rush hour and at night, all day Sunday, and to any of the airports. Each piece of luggage you put in the trunk is €1 extra (though it won't appear on the meter, it is a legitimate charge). To tip, round up to the next euro (at least €0.50).

How to Catch un Taxi: You can try waving down a taxi, but it's often easier to ask someone for the nearest taxi stand (*"Où est une station de taxi?"*, oo ay ewn stah-see-ohn duh "taxi"). Taxi stands are indicated by a circled "T" on good city maps, and on many maps in this book. To order a taxi, call 3607, or ask your hotelier for help. When you summon a taxi by phone, the meter starts running as soon as the call is received, often adding €6 or more to the bill.

Taxis are tough to find during rush hour, when it's raining, and on Friday and Saturday nights, especially after the Métro closes (around 24:30 in the morning). If you need to catch a train or flight early in the morning, book a taxi at least the day before (especially for weekday departures). Some taxi companies require a €5 reservation fee by credit card for weekday morning rush-hour departures (7:00–10:00) and only have a limited number of reservation spots.

By Bike

Paris is surprisingly easy by bicycle. The city is flat, and riders have access to more than 370 miles of bike lanes and the many priority lanes for buses and taxis. I biked along the river from Notre-Dame to the Eiffel Tower in 15 wonderfully scenic minutes.

Urban cyclists will find Paris a breeze. First-timers will get the hang of it quickly enough by following some simple rules. Always stay to the right in your lane, bike single-file, stay off sidewalks, watch out for opening doors on parked cars, signal with your arm before making turns, and use bike paths when available. Obey the traffic laws as if you were driving a car.

Parisians use the same road rules as Americans, with two exceptions: When passing vehicles or other bikes, always pass on the left (it's illegal to pass on the right); and where there is no stoplight, always yield to incoming traffic on your right. You'll find a bell on your bike; use it like a horn to warn pedestrians who don't see you.

The TIs have a helpful "Paris à Vélo" map, which shows all the dedicated bike paths. Many other versions are available for sale at newsstand kiosks, some bookstores, and department stores.

Both bike companies listed below rent bikes at good rates, sell maps, and also offer organized tours by bike (listed under "Tours in Paris," next).

Bike About Tours is your best bet for bike rental. Their bikes are also foldable, which allows you to collapse your bike and jump on the Métro if the weather turns bad or you tire too early (€15/day during office hours, €20/24 hours; includes locks, helmets, and comfy gel seats; daily 9:00–12:30 & 14:00–16:30, closed mid-Dec–mid-Feb, shop located near Hôtel de Ville at 4 rue de Lobau in Vinci parking garage—see map on page 122, Mo: Hôtel de Ville, www.bikeabouttours.com, info@bikeabouttours.com). They sell detailed maps for €6 (free for Rick Steves readers with bike rental) and are full of advice for routes and things to see.

Fat Tire Bike Tours has some bikes for rent—call ahead to check availability (€4/hour, €25/24 hours, includes helmets and locks, credit-card imprint required for deposit, €3 discount with this book for daily rental, office open daily 9:00–18:30, May–Aug bike rental only after 11:30 as priority is given to those taking a tour, ask for their map of suggested routes, 24 rue Edgar Faure—see map on page 103, Mo: Dupleix, tel. 01 56 58 10 54, www.fattirebiketoursparis.com).

Bike Freedom for Parisians: You're sure to see Vélib' rental bikes and racks around town—the bikes are geared mainly for residents to rent (the machines take chip-embedded European credit cards, and American Express cards—but otherwise no other American cards). For tourists, the plus side of the popular, highly touted Vélib' program is that it has prompted the city to add more bike paths, and has helped Parisian drivers learn to share the road with bicycles.

By Scooter

Left Bank Scooters will deliver and pick-up rental scooters to daring travelers over 20 years old with a valid driver's license (€70–90/

day, price depends on size of the scooter and how long you keep it, tel. 06 82 70 13 82, www.leftbankscooters.com).

Tours in Paris

By Bus

Bus Tours—**Paris Vision** offers bus tours of Paris, day and night (advertised in hotel lobbies). I'd consider a Paris Vision tour only for their nighttime tour (see page 139). During the day, the hop-on, hop-off bus tours and the Batobus (both described in this section) are a better value, providing both transportation between sights as well as commentary.

Hop-on, Hop-off Bus Tours—Double-decker buses connect Paris' main sights, allowing you to hop on and off along the way. You get a disposable set of ear plugs to listen to a basic running commentary (dial English for the so-so narration). You can get off at any stop, tour a sight, then catch a later bus. These are best in good weather, when you can sit up top. There are two companies: L'Open Tours and Les Cars Rouges (pick up their brochures showing routes and stops from any TI or on their buses). You can start either tour at just about any of the major sights, such as the Eiffel Tower (both companies stop on avenue Joseph Bouvard).

L'Open Tours uses bright-yellow buses and provides more extensive coverage (and slightly better commentary) on four different routes, rolling by most of the important sights in Paris. Their Paris Grand Tour (the green route) offers the best introduction. The same ticket gets you on any of their routes within the validity period. Buy your tickets from the driver (1 day–€29, 2 days–€32, kids 4–11 pay €15 for 1 or 2 days, allow 2 hours per tour). Two to four buses depart hourly from about 10:00 to 18:00; expect to wait 10–15 minutes at each stop (stops can be tricky to find—look for yellow signs; tel. 01 42 66 56 56, www.paris-opentour.com). A combo-ticket covers both the Batobus boats (described next) and L'Open Tours buses (€44, kids under 12 pay €20, valid 3 days).

Les Cars Rouges' bright red buses offer largely the same service, with only one route and just nine stops, for less (recorded narration, adult–€24, kids 4–12 pay €12, good for 2 days, 10 percent cheaper when booked online, tel. 01 53 95 39 53, www.carsrouges.com).

By Boat

Seine Cruises—Several companies run one-hour boat cruises on the Seine. For the best experience, cruise at twilight or after dark. (To dine while you cruise, see "Dinner Cruises" on page 195.) Two of the companies—Bateaux-Mouches and Bateaux Parisiens—are

convenient to the rue Cler hotels, and both run daily year-round (April–Oct 10:00–22:30, 2–3/hour; Nov-March shorter hours, runs hourly). Some offer discounts for early online bookings.

Bateaux-Mouches, the oldest boat company in Paris, departs from pont de l'Alma's right bank, and has the biggest open-top, double-decker boats (higher up means better views). But this company often has too many tour groups, causing these boats to get packed (€10, kids 4–12 pay €5, tel. 01 40 76 99 99, www.bateaux-mouches.com).

Bateaux Parisiens has smaller covered boats with handheld audioguides, fewer crowds, and only one deck. It leaves from right in front of the Eiffel Tower (€11, kids 3–12 pay €5, half-price if you have a valid France or France–Switzerland railpass—does not use up a day of a flexipass, tel. 01 76 64 14 45 or toll 08 25 01 01 01, www.bateauxparisiens.com).

Vedettes du Pont Neuf offers essentially the same one-hour tour as Bateaux Parisiens, but starts and ends at pont Neuf, closer to recommended hotels in the Marais and Luxembourg Garden neighborhoods. The boats feature a live guide whose delivery (in English and French) is as stiff as a recorded narration—and as hard to understand, given the quality of their sound system (€12, kids 4–12 pay €6, tip requested, check for online advance-purchase discounts, nearly 2/hour, daily 10:30–22:30, tel. 01 46 33 98 38, www.vedettesdupontneuf.com).

Hop-on, Hop-Off Boat Tour—Batobus allows you to get on and off as you like at any of eight popular stops along the Seine: Eiffel Tower, pont Alexandre III (closest to Champs-Elysées), Orsay/place de la Concorde, the Louvre, Notre-Dame, the Institut de France (closest to St. Germain-des-Prés), Hôtel de Ville, and Jardin des Plantes. Safe glass enclosures turn the boats into virtual ovens on hot days (1 day–€12, 2 days–€16, 5 days–€20, boats run June–Aug 10:00–21:30, mid-March–May and Sept–Oct 10:00–19:00, Nov–early Jan and Feb–mid-March 10:30–16:30, no service last three weeks in Jan, every 15–20 minutes, 45 minutes one-way, 1.5-hour round-trip, worthless narration, www.batobus.com). If you use this for getting around—sort of a scenic, floating alternative to the Métro—it can be worthwhile, especially with a 5-day pass. But if you just want a guided boat tour, Batobus is not as good a value as the regular tour boats described above.

Connecting with the Culture

Paris offers *beaucoup* ways for you to connect with locals—and thereby make your trip more personal...and more memorable.

I'm amazed at the number of groups that help travelers meet locals. These get good reviews:

Meeting the French puts you in touch with "regular" Parisians by organizing dinners in private homes, workplace tours to match your interests/career, and more (tel. 06 73 65 62 19, www.meetingthefrench.com).

Paris Greeter is an all-volunteer organization that connects travelers with English-speaking Parisians who want to share their knowledge of Paris. These volunteer "guides" are not licensed to give historical tours; rather, they act as informal companions who can show you "their Paris"—it's like seeing Paris through the eyes of a friend. The tours are free (though donations are welcome), and you must sign up five weeks before your visit (www.parisgreeter.org).

Enjoy Your Paris offers social events for small groups of Parisians interested in connecting with travelers and for travelers wanting the same from Parisians. Events include everything from conversation over a drink to expositions, tastings, sporting events (such as *boules*—see page 1033), walks, tours, concerts, and shows. Some events are free; others involve a charge. Indicate your interests by filling out the questionnaire on their website, and you're in business (http://fr.enjoyourparis.com).

Wine-Tasting: Young and enthusiastic Olivier Magny and his team of sommeliers teach fun and informative wine-tasting classes at **Ô Château** wine school near the Louvre, in the 17th-century residence of Madame de Pompadour, the favorite mistress of King Louis XV. Olivier's goal is to "take the snob out of wine." At all of the informal classes, you'll learn the basics of French wine regions, the techniques of tasting, and how to read a French wine label. Classes include Introductory Tasting (€30, 1 hour), Tour de France of Wine (€50, 2 hours), and Wine and Cheese lunches (€75, 2 hours). Register online using code "RS2011" for a €10 discount (68 rue Jean-Jacques Rousseau, Mo: Louvre-Rivoli, tel. 01 44 73 97 80 or toll 08 00 80 11 48, www.o-chateau.com).

Conversation Swap: Parler Paris is a free-form conversation group organized for native French and English speakers who want to practice in a relaxed environment. In a small group, you'll discuss interesting topics—for the first 45 minutes in French, then for 45 minutes in English. Your first visit is free; after that it's €10 a session (several meetings per week possible, tel. 01 48 42 26 10 or 01 40 27 97 59, www.parlerparlor.com, info@parlerparlor.com).

Low-Key Cruise on a Tranquil Canal—**Canauxrama** runs a lazy 2.5-hour cruise on a peaceful canal out of sight of the Seine. Tours start from place de la Bastille and end at Bassin de la Villette (near Mo: Stalingrad). During the first segment of your trip, you'll pass through a long tunnel (built at the order of Napoleon in the early 19th century, when canal boats were vital for industrial transport). Once outside, you glide—not much faster than you can walk—through sleepy Parisian neighborhoods and slowly climb through four double locks as a guide narrates the trip in French and English (€16, check online for discounts for advance booking, departs at 9:45 and 14:30 across from Opéra Bastille, just below boulevard de la Bastille, opposite #50—where the canal meets place de la Bastille, tel. 01 42 39 15 00, www.canauxrama.com). The same tour also goes in the opposite direction, from Bassin de la Villette to place de la Bastille (departs at 9:45 and 14:45). It's OK to bring a picnic on board.

On Foot

Paris Walks—This company offers a variety of two-hour walks, led by British and American guides. Tours are thoughtfully prepared and entertaining. Don't hesitate to stand close to the guide to hear (€12-15, generally 2/day—morning and afternoon, private tours available, family guides and Louvre tours a specialty, call 01 48 09 21 40 for schedule in English, or check printable online schedule at www.paris-walks.com). Tours focus on the Marais (4/week), Montmartre (3/week), medieval Latin Quarter (Mon), Ile de la Cité/Notre-Dame (Mon), the "Two Islands" (Ile de la Cité and Ile St. Louis, Wed), the Revolution (Wed), and Hemingway's Paris (Fri). Call a day or two ahead to hear the current schedule and starting point. Most tours don't require reservations, but specialty tours (such as the Louvre or Chocolate tour) require advance reservations and prepayment with credit card (not refundable if you cancel less than two days in advance).

Context Paris—These "intellectual by design" walking tours are geared for serious learners and led by docents (historians, architects, and academics). They cover both museums and specific neighborhoods (see website for details). It's best to book in advance—groups are limited to six participants and can fill up (€55-90/person plus admissions, generally 3 hours long, tel. 01 72 81 36 35, US tel. 800-691-6036, www.contextparis.com). They also offer private tours and excursions outside Paris.

Classic Walks—The antithesis of Context Paris' walks, these low-brow, low-information, but high-fun walking tours are run by Fat Tire Bike Tours. Their 3.5-hour "Classic Walk" covers most major sights (€20, March-Oct, daily at 10:00, meet at their office—see their listing under "By Bike," next page). They also do two-hour walks on various themes and neighborhoods: Montmartre, French Revolution, World War II, and Latin Quarter (€12–20, €2 discount on all walks with this book, leaves several times a week—see website for details, 24 rue Edgar Faure, Mo: Dupleix, tel. 01 56 58 10 54, www.classicwalksparis.com).

Local Guides—For many, Paris merits hiring a Parisian as a personal guide. **Arnaud Servignat** is an excellent licensed guide (€160/half-day, €270/day, also does car tours of the countryside around Paris for a little more, tel. 06 68 80 29 05, www.french-guide.com, arnotour@me.com). **Thierry Gauduchon** is a terrific guide well worth his fee (€180/half-day, €350/day, tel. 01 56 98 10 82, mobile 06 19 07 30 77, tgauduchon@aol.com. **Elizabeth Van Hest** is another likeable and capable guide (€160/half-day, €270/day, tel. 01 43 41 47 31, elisa.guide@gmail.com).

By Bike

Paris is terrific by bike (see "Getting Around Paris—By Bike," earlier) and made easier by bike tour. Both companies below sell bottled water and bike maps of Paris, and can give advice on biking routes of the city. Their tour routes cover different parts of the city, so you could do both tours without much repetition.

Bike About Tours—Run by Christian (American) and Paul (New Zealander), this company offers easygoing tours with a focus on the eastern half of the city.

The four-hour tours run daily year-round at 10:00 (also at 15:00 June–Aug). You'll meet at the statue of Charlemagne in front of Notre-Dame, then walk to the nearby rental office to get bikes (in Vinci parking garage at corner of rue de Lobau and rue de Rivoli). The tour includes a good back-street visit of the Marais, the Rive Gauche outdoor sculpture park, the Ile de la Cité, the heart of the Latin Quarter (with a lunch break), the Louvre, Les Halles, and the Pompidou Center. Group tours have a 12-person maximum—reserve online to guarantee a spot, or show up and take your chances (€30, €5 discount with this book, maximum 2 per book, 15 percent discount for families, includes helmets upon request, private tours available, see listing on page 69 for contact info).

Fat Tire Bike Tours—A hardworking gang of young American expats runs an extensive program of bike, Segway, and walking tours.

Their high-energy guides run four-hour bike tours of Paris, by day and by night. Reservations aren't necessary—just show up. On the day tour, you'll pedal with a pack of 10–20 riders, mostly in parks and along bike lanes, with a lunch stop in the Tuileries Garden (€28, show this book for a €3/person discount, maximum 2 discounts per book, English only, tours leave daily rain or shine at 11:00, April–Oct at 15:00 as well). Night tours are more lively, and include a boat cruise on the Seine (€28, €3 discount with this book, April–Oct daily at 19:00, March daily at 18:00, end of Feb and all of Nov Tue, Thu, and Sat–Sun at 18:00, no night tours Dec–mid-Feb). Both tours meet at the south pillar of the Eiffel Tower, where you'll get a short history lesson, then walk six minutes to the Fat Tire office to pick up bikes (helmets available upon request at no extra charge, for contact info see listing on page 69). They also run bike tours to Versailles and Giverny (reservations required, see website for details). Their office has Internet access with English keyboards.

Fat Tire's pricey four-hour **City Segway Tours**—on stand-up motorized scooters—are novel in that you learn to ride a Segway while exploring Paris (you'll get the hang of it after about half an hour). These tours take no more than eight people at a time, so reservations are required (€75, daily at 9:30, April–Oct also at 14:00 and 18:30, March and Nov also at 14:00, www.citysegway tours.com).

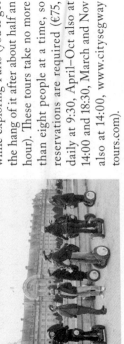

Excursions from Paris

Most of the **local guides** listed earlier (see page 74) will do excursion tours from Paris using your rental car. Or consider these companies, which provide transportation:

Paris Webservices, a reliable outfit, offers many services, including day trips with English-speaking chauffeur-guides in cushy minivans for private groups to all the destinations covered in this book (figure €90–120/person for groups of 4 or more, 10 percent discount for Rick Steves readers—use promo code "RSteves07," see contact info in listing on page 1010).

Many companies offer bus tours to regional sights, including all of the day trips described in this book. **Paris Vision** runs minivan and bus tours to several popular regional destinations, including the Loire Valley, Champagne region, D-Day beaches, and Mont St. Michel. Minivan tours are pricier, but more personal and given in English, and most offer convenient pickup at your hotel (€90–190/person). Their full-size bus tours are multilingual, mass-marketed, and nothing special, but cheaper than the minivan tours—worthwhile for some travelers simply for the ease of transportation to the sights (about €70, destinations include Versailles and Giverny). Paris Vision's full-size buses depart from 214 rue de Rivoli (Mo: Tuileries, tel. 01 42 60 30 01, www.paris vision.com).

Self-Guided Walk

Historic Paris Walk

(This information is distilled from the Historic Paris Walk chapter in *Rick Steves' Paris*, by Rick Steves, Steve Smith, and Gene Openshaw. A free audio tour version of this walk is available to use with an iPod or other MP3 player at www.ricksteves.com, or search for "Rick Steves Audio Tours" in iTunes. There's also a multimedia, interactive version of this tour for sale on iTunes.)

Allow four hours to do justice to this three-mile walk. Start where the city did—on the Ile de la Cité. Face Notre-Dame and follow the gray line on the "Historic Paris Walk" map.

• *Start at Notre-Dame Cathedral on the island in the River Seine, the physical and historic bull's-eye of your Paris map. The closest Métro stops are Cité, Hôtel de Ville, and St. Michel, each a short walk away.*

On the square in front of the cathedral, stand far enough back to take in the whole facade. View it from the bronze plaque on the ground marked "Point Zero" (30 yards from the central doorway). You're standing at the center of France, the point from which all distances in France are measured. Find the circular window in the center of the cathedral's facade.

▲▲▲Notre-Dame Cathedral

This 700-year-old cathedral is packed with history and tourists. Study its sculpture and windows, take in a Mass, eavesdrop on guides, and walk all around the outside.

Cost and Hours: Free, cathedral open daily 8:00–18:45, Sat–Sun until 19:15; Treasury–€3, not covered by Museum Pass, daily 9:30–18:00, Sat–Sun until 18:30; audioguide–€5, ask about free English tours—normally Wed and Thu at 14:00, Sat at 14:30; Mo: Cité, Hôtel de Ville, or St. Michel. Tel. 01 42 34 56 10, www .cathedraledeparis.com. The international Mass is held Sun at 11:30, with an organ concert at 16:30. Call or check the website for a full schedule. On Good Friday and the first Friday of the month at 15:00, the (physically underwhelming) relic known as Jesus' Crown of Thorns goes on display.

⊙ Self-Guided Tour: The **cathedral facade** is worth a close look. The church is dedicated to "Our Lady" *(Notre Dame)*. Mary is center stage—cradling God, right in the heart of the facade, surrounded by the halo of the rose window. Adam is on the left and Eve is on the right.

Below Mary and above the

Historic Paris Walk

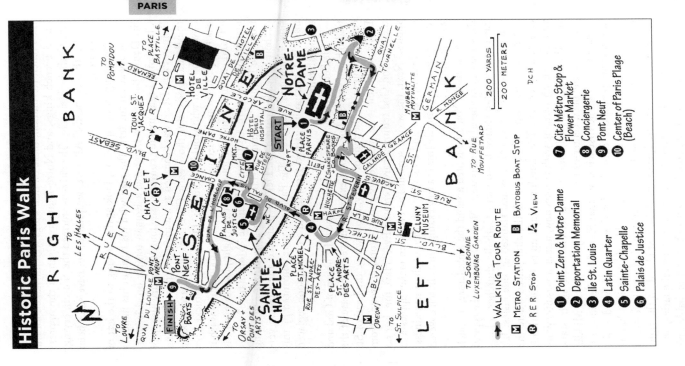

PARIS

Legend:

- → WALKING TOUR ROUTE
- B BATOBUS BOAT STOP
- ⚊ VIEW
- Ⓜ METRO STATION
- Ⓡ RER STOP

1. Point Zero & Notre-Dame
2. Deportation Memorial
3. Ile St. Louis
4. Latin Quarter
5. Sainte-Chapelle
6. Palais de Justice
7. Cité Métro Stop & Flower Market
8. Conciergerie
9. Pont Neuf
10. Center of Paris Plage (Beach)

200 YARDS
200 METERS

RIGHT BANK
LEFT BANK
SEINE
NOTRE DAME
SAINTE-CHAPELLE
HOTEL DE VILLE
HOTEL DIEU HOSPITAL
PALAIS DE JUSTICE
CLUNY MUSEUM
TOUR ST. JACQUES
CHATELET
START
FINISH

TO POMPIDOU
TO PLACE BASTILLE
TO LES HALLES
TO LOUVRE
TO ORSAY + PONT DES ARTS
TO ST. SULPICE
TO ODEON
TO SORBONNE + LUXEMBOURG GARDEN
TO RUE MOUFFETARD

arches is a row of 28 statues known as the Kings of Judah. During the French Revolution, these biblical kings were mistaken for the hated French kings, and Notre-Dame represented the oppressive Catholic hierarchy. The citizens stormed the church, crying, "Off with their heads!" All were decapitated, but have since been recapitated.

Speaking of decapitation, look at the carving to the left of the doorway on the left. The man with his head in his hands is St. Denis. Back when there was a Roman temple on this spot, Christianity began making converts. The fourth-century bishop of Roman Paris, Denis was beheaded as a warning to those forsaking the Roman gods. But those early Christians were hard to keep down. The man who would become St. Denis got up, tucked his head under his arm, headed north, paused at a fountain to wash it off, and continued until he found just the right place to meet his maker: Montmartre. (Although the name "Montmartre" comes from the Roman "Mount of Mars," later generations—thinking of their beheaded patron, St. Denis—preferred a less pagan version, "Mount of Martyrs.") The Parisians were convinced by this miracle, Christianity gained ground, and a church soon replaced the pagan temple.

Medieval art was OK if it embellished the house of God and told biblical stories. For a good example, move to the base of the central column (at the foot of Mary, about where the head of St. Denis could spit if he were really good). Working around from the left, find God telling a barely created Eve, "Have fun, but no apples." Next, the sexiest serpent I've ever seen makes apples à la mode. Finally, Adam and Eve, now ashamed of their nakedness, are expelled by an angel. This is a tiny example in a church covered with meaning.

Step inside. You'll be routed around the ambulatory, in much the same way medieval pilgrims were. Notre-Dame has the typical basilica floor plan shared by so many Catholic churches: a long central nave lined with columns and flanked by side aisles. It's designed in the shape of a cross, with the altar placed where the crossbeam intersects. The church can hold up to 10,000 faithful, and it's probably buzzing with visitors now, just as it was 600 years ago. The quiet, deserted churches we see elsewhere are in stark contrast to the busy, center-of-life places they were in the Middle Ages. Don't miss the **rose windows** that fill each of the transepts. Just past the altar is the "**choir**," enclosed with carved-wood walls, where more intimate services can be held in this spacious building. Circle the choir—the back side of the choir walls features **scenes of the resurrected Jesus** (c. 1350). Just ahead on the right is the **Treasury**. It contains lavish robes, golden reliquaries, and the humble tunic of King (and St.) Louis IX, but it probably isn't

Affording Paris' Sights

Paris is an expensive city for tourists, with lots of pricey sights, but—fortunately—lots of freebies, too. Smart, budget-minded travelers begin by buying and getting the most out of a **Paris Museum Pass** (see page 54), then considering these frugal sightseeing options.

Free Museums: Museums that are always free (with the possible exception of special exhibits) include the Carnavalet, Petit Palais, Victor Hugo's House, and Fragonard Perfume Museum. Many of Paris' most famous museums offer free entry on the first Sunday of the month, including the Louvre, Orsay, Rodin, Cluny, Pompidou Center, and Delacroix museums (expect big crowds on these days). You can also visit the Orsay Museum for free at 17:00 (or Thu at 21:00), an hour before the museum closes. One of the best everyday values is the Rodin Museum's garden, where it costs just €1 to experience many of Rodin's finest works in a lovely outdoor setting.

Other Freebies: Many worthwhile sights don't charge entry, including the Notre-Dame Cathedral, Père Lachaise Cemetery, Deportation Memorial, Holocaust Memorial, Paris Plage (summers only), Sacré-Cœur Basilica, St. Sulpice Church (with organ recital), and La Défense (though there is a charge to enter La Grande Arche).

Paris' glorious, entertaining parks are free, of course. These include Luxembourg Garden, Champ de Mars (under the Eiffel Tower), Tuileries Garden (between the Louvre and place de la Concorde), Palais Royal Courtyards, Jardin des Plantes, the Promenade Plantée walk, and Versailles' gardens (except on Fountain Spectacle weekends).

Reduced Price: Several museums offer a discount if you enter later in the day, including the Louvre (after 18:00 on Wed and Fri), Orsay (Fri-Wed after 16:15 and Thu after 18:00), Army Museum and Napoleon's Tomb (one hour before closing), and Versailles' Château (after 15:00) and Trianon Palaces and Domaine de Marie-Antoinette (after 16:00).

Free Concerts: Venues offering free or cheap (€6-8) concerts include the American Church, Hôtel des Invalides, St. Sulpice Church, La Madeleine Church, and Notre-Dame Cathedral. For a listing of free concerts, check *Pariscope* magazine (under the "Musique" section) and look for events marked *entrée libre*.

Good-Value Tours: At €12-15, Paris Walks' tours are a good value. The €10-12 Seine River cruises, best after dark, are also worthwhile. The Scenic Bus Route #69, which costs only the price of a transit ticket, could be the best deal of all.

Pricey…but worth it? Certain big-ticket items—primarily the Eiffel Tower, Louvre, and Versailles—are expensive and crowded, but offer once-in-a-lifetime experiences. Think of it as you would a spree in Vegas—budget in a little "gambling" money you expect to lose, then just relax…and enjoy.

worth the €3 entry fee.

Back outside, walk around the church through the park on the riverside for a close look at the **flying buttresses.** The Neo-Gothic 300-foot **spire** is a product of the 1860 reconstruction of the dilapidated old church. Around its base (visible as you approach the back end of the church) are apostles and evangelists (the green men) as well as Eugène-Emmanuel Viollet-le-Duc, the architect in charge of the work. The apostles look outward, blessing the city, while the architect (at top) looks up the spire, marveling at his fine work.

Nearby: The **archaeological crypt** is a worthwhile 15-minute stop if you have a Paris Museum Pass (€4 without Museum Pass, Tue–Sun 10:00–18:00, last entry 30 minutes before closing, closed Mon, enter 100 yards in front of cathedral). You'll see remains of the many structures that have stood on this spot in the center of Paris: Roman buildings that surrounded a temple of Jupiter; a wall that didn't keep the Franks out; the main medieval road that once led grandly up the square to Notre-Dame; and even (wow) a 19th-century sewer.

Tower: You can climb to the top of the facade between the towers, and then to the top of the south tower, 400 steps total, for a grand view (€8, covered by Museum Pass but no bypass line for passholders, daily April–Sept 10:00–18:30, June–Aug Sat–Sun until 23:00, Oct–March 10:00–17:30, last entry 45 minutes before closing, arrive before 10:00 or after 17:00 to avoid long lines).

• *Behind Notre-Dame, cross the street and enter through the iron gate into the park at the tip of the island. Look for the stairs and head down to reach the…*

▲Deportation Memorial
(Mémorial de la Déportation)

This memorial to the 200,000 French victims of the Nazi concentration camps (1940–1945) draws you into their experience. France was quickly overrun by Nazi Germany, and Paris spent the war years under Nazi occupation. Jews and dissidents were rounded up and deported—many never returned.

As you descend the steps, the city around you disappears. Surrounded by walls, you have become a prisoner. Your only freedom is your view of the sky and the tiny glimpse of the river below.

Enter the dark, single-file chamber up ahead. Inside, the circular plaque in the floor reads, "They went to the end of the earth and did not return." The hallway stretching in front of you is lined with 200,000 lighted crystals, one for each French citizen who died. Flickering at the far end is the eternal flame of hope. The tomb of the unknown deportee lies at your feet. Above, the inscription reads, "Dedicated to the living memory of the 200,000

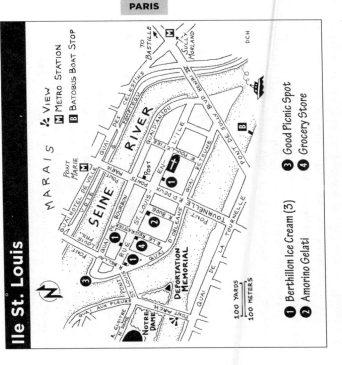

Ile St. Louis

- **1** Berthillon Ice Cream (3)
- **2** Amorino Gelati
- **3** Good Picnic Spot
- **4** Grocery Store

☆ View
Ⓜ Metro Station
Ⓑ Batobus Boat Stop

French deportees sleeping in the night and the fog, exterminated in the Nazi concentration camps." The side rooms are filled with triangles—reminiscent of the identification patches inmates were forced to wear—each bearing the name of a concentration camp. Above the exit as you leave is the message you'll find at many other Holocaust sites: "Forgive, but never forget."

Cost and Hours: Free, daily April–Sept 10:00–12:00 & 14:00–19:00, Oct–March 10:00–12:00 & 14:00–17:00, Mo: Cité.

• *Back on street level, look across the river (north) to the island called...*

Ile St. Louis

If the Ile de la Cité is a tug laden with the history of Paris, it's towing this classy little residential dinghy, laden only with high-rent apartments, boutiques, characteristic restaurants (see page 185), and famous ice-cream shops.

This island wasn't developed until much later than the Ile de la Cité (17th century). What was a swampy mess is now harmonious Parisian architecture and one of Paris' most exclusive neighborhoods.

If you won't have time to return here for an evening stroll (see page 138), consider taking a brief detour across the pedestrian bridge. Pont St. Louis connects the two islands, leading right to rue St. Louis-en-l'Ile. This spine of the island is lined with interesting shops and reasonably priced restaurants. A short stroll takes you to the famous Berthillon ice cream parlor at #31 (there are two more—one across the street, and yet another around the corner on rue Bellay). Gelato-lovers head instead to Amorino Gelati at #47. Loop back to the pedestrian bridge along the parklike quays (walk north to the river and turn left). This walk is about as peaceful and romantic as Paris gets.

• *From the Deportation Memorial, cross the bridge onto the Left Bank and enjoy the riverside view of Notre-Dame; window-shopping among the green book stalls; and browsing through used books, vintage posters, and souvenirs. Page through books at the atmospheric* **Shakespeare and Company,** *a reincarnation of the original 1920s shop (37 rue de la Bûcherie), then venture inland a few blocks, basically arcing through the Latin Quarter. Before returning to the island, walk a block behind Shakespeare and Co. and take a spin through the...*

▲Latin Quarter

This area's touristy fame relates to its intriguing, artsy, bohemian character. This was perhaps Europe's leading university district in the Middle Ages, when Latin was the language of higher education. The neighborhood's main boulevards (St. Michel and St. Germain) are lined with cafés—once the haunts of great poets and philosophers, now the hangouts of tired tourists. Though still youthful and artsy, much of this area has become a tourist ghetto filled with cheap North African eateries. Exploring a few blocks up or downriver from here gives you a better chance of feeling the pulse of what survives of Paris' classic Left Bank. For colorful wandering and café-sitting, afternoons and evenings are best.

Walking along rue St. Séverin, you can still see the shadow of the medieval sewer system. The street slopes into a central channel of bricks. In the days before plumbing and toilets, when people still went to the river or neighborhood wells for their water, flushing meant throwing it out the window. At certain times of day, maids on the fourth floor would holler, *"Garde de l'eau!"* ("Watch out for the water!") and heave it into the streets, where it would eventually wash down into the Seine.

Consider a visit to the Cluny Museum for its medieval art and unicorn tapestries (see page 110). The Sorbonne—the University of Paris' humanities department—is also nearby; visitors can ogle the famous dome, but they are not allowed to enter the building (two blocks south of the river on boulevard St. Michel).

This square, place St. Michel (facing the pont St. Michel), is the traditional core of the Left Bank's artsy, liberal, hippie, bohemian district of poets, philosophers, and winos. In less commercial times, place St. Michel was a gathering point for the city's malcontents and misfits. In 1830, 1848, and again in 1871, the citizens took the streets from the government troops, set up barricades Les Miz–style, and fought against royalist oppression. During World War II, the locals rose up against their Nazi oppressors (read the plaques under the dragons at the foot of the St. Michel fountain).

In the spring of 1968, a time of social upheaval all over the world, young students battled riot batons and tear gas, took over the square, and declared it an independent state. Factory workers followed their call to arms and went on strike, challenging the de Gaulle government and forcing change. Eventually, the students were pacified, the university was reformed, and the Latin Quarter's original cobblestones were replaced with pavement, so future scholars could never again use the streets as weapons. Even today, whenever there's a student demonstration, it starts here.

• From place St. Michel, look across the river and find the prickly steeple of the Sainte-Chapelle church. Head toward it. Cross the river on pont St. Michel and continue north along the boulevard du Palais. On your left, you'll see the doorway to Sainte-Chapelle.

You'll need to pass through a strict security checkpoint to get into the Sainte-Chapelle complex. (This is more than a tourist attraction—France's Supreme Court meets to the right of Sainte-Chapelle.) Past security, you'll enter the courtyard outside Sainte-Chapelle, where you'll find WCs and information about upcoming church concerts (for concert details, see page 136). The ticket-buying line into the church may be long.

If you have a Museum Pass or a Conciergerie combo-ticket, you may be able to skip some of the security line (look for signs), and can certainly bypass the ticket-buying line. You can also bypass it by buying your ticket or Museum Pass from the tabac shop across the street from the security entrance.

Enter the humble ground floor.

▲▲▲Sainte-Chapelle

This triumph of Gothic church architecture is a cathedral of glass like no other. It was speedily built between 1242 and 1248 for King Louis IX—the only French king who is now a saint—to house the supposed Crown of Thorns. Its architectural harmony is due to the fact that it was completed under the direction of one architect and in only five years—unheard of in Gothic times. Recall that Notre-Dame took over 200 years.

Inside, the layout clearly shows an ancien régime approach to worship. The

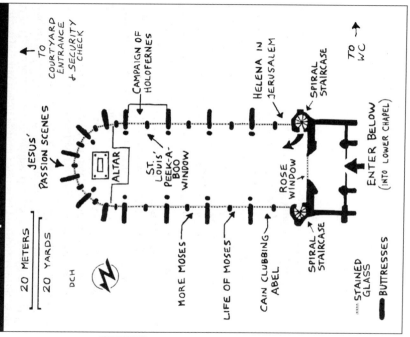

Sainte-Chapelle

TO COURTYARD ENTRANCE + SECURITY CHECK

JESUS' PASSION SCENES

CAMPAIGN OF HOLOFERNES

HELENA IN JERUSALEM

SPIRAL STAIRCASE

TO WC

ALTAR

ST. LOUIS' PEEK-A-BOO WINDOW

ENTER BELOW (INTO LOWER CHAPEL)

ROSE WINDOW

CAIN CLUBBING ABEL

LIFE OF MOSES

MORE MOSES

SPIRAL STAIRCASE

20 METERS
20 YARDS

DCH

····· STAINED GLASS
■■■ BUTTRESSES

low-ceilinged basement was for staff and other common folks—worshipping under a sky filled with painted fleurs-de-lis, a symbol of the king. Royal Christians worshipped upstairs. The paint job, a 19th-century restoration, helps you imagine how grand this small, painted, jeweled chapel was. (Imagine Notre-Dame painted like this....) Each capital is carved with a different plant's leaves.

Climb the spiral staircase to the Chapelle Haute. Fill the place with choral music, crank up the sunshine, face the top of the altar, and really believe that the Crown of Thorns is there, and this becomes one awesome space.

Fiat lux. "Let there be light." From the first page of the Bible, it's clear: Light is divine. Light shines through stained glass like God's grace shining down to earth. Gothic architects used their new technology to turn dark stone buildings into lanterns of light. The glory of Gothic shines brighter here than in any other church.

There are 15 separate panels of stained glass (6,500 square

feet—two thirds of it 13th-century original), with more than 1,100 different scenes, mostly from the Bible. These cover the entire Christian history of the world, from the Creation in Genesis (first window on the left, as you face the altar), to the coming of Christ (over the altar), to the end of the world (the round "rose"-shaped window at the rear of the church). Each individual scene is interesting, and the whole effect is overwhelming.

The altar was raised up high to better display the Crown of Thorns, the relic around which this chapel was built. The supposed crown cost King Louis three times as much as this church. Today, it is kept by the Notre-Dame Treasury (though it's occasionally brought out for display).

Cost and Hours: €8, €11 combo-ticket with Conciergerie, kids under 18 free, covered by Museum Pass, March–Oct daily 9:00–18:00, Wed in summer until 21:30, Nov–Feb daily 9:00–17:00, last entry 30 minutes before closing, English tours most days at 10:45 and 14:45, 4 boulevard du Palais, Mo: Cité. Leave sharp metal objects at home or lose them to security.

• *Exit Sainte-Chapelle. Back outside, as you walk around the church exterior, look down to see the foundation and take note of how much Paris has risen in the 750 years since Sainte-Chapelle was built.*

Next door to Sainte-Chapelle is the...

Palais de Justice

Sainte-Chapelle sits within a huge complex of buildings that has housed the local government since ancient Roman times. It was the site of the original Gothic palace of the early kings of France. The only surviving medieval parts are Sainte-Chapelle and the Conciergerie prison.

Most of the site is now covered by the giant Palais de Justice, built in 1776, home of the French Supreme Court. The motto *Liberté, Egalité, Fraternité* over the doors is a reminder that this was also the headquarters of the Revolutionary government. Here they doled out justice, condemning many to imprisonment in the Conciergerie downstairs or to the guillotine.

• *Now pass through the big iron gate to the noisy boulevard du Palais. Cross the street to the wide, pedestrian-only rue de Lutèce and walk about halfway down.*

Cité "Metropolitain" Métro Stop

Of the 141 original early-20th-century subway entrances, this is one of only a few survivors—now preserved as a national art

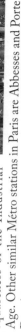

treasure. (New York's Museum of Modern Art even exhibits one.) It marks Paris at its peak in 1900—on the cutting edge of Modernism, but with an eye for beauty. The curvy, plantlike ironwork is a textbook example of Art Nouveau, the style that rebelled against the erector-set squareness of the Industrial Age. Other similar Métro stations in Paris are Abbesses and Porte Dauphine.

The flower and plant market on place Louis Lépine is a pleasant detour. On Sundays this square flutters with a busy bird market. And across the way is the Préfecture de Police, where Inspector Clouseau of *Pink Panther* fame used to work, and where the local resistance fighters took the first building from the Nazis in August of 1944, leading to the Allied liberation of Paris a week later.

• *Pause here to admire the view. Sainte-Chapelle is a pearl in an ugly architectural oyster. Double back to the Palais de Justice, turn right onto boulevard du Palais, and enter the...*

▲Conciergerie

Though pretty barren inside, this former prison echoes with history (and is free with the Museum Pass—remember that passholders can skip any ticket-buying lines). Positioned next to the courthouse, the Conciergerie was the gloomy prison famous as the last stop for 2,780 victims of the guillotine, including France's last *ancien régime* queen, Marie-Antoinette. Before then, kings had used the building to torture and execute failed assassins. (One of its towers along the river was called "The Babbler," named for the pain-induced sounds that leaked from it.) When the Revolution (1789) toppled the king, the building kept its same function, but without the torture. The progressive Revolutionaries proudly unveiled a modern and more humane way to execute people—the guillotine.

Inside, pick up a free map and breeze through. See the spacious, low-ceilinged Hall of Men-at-Arms (Room 1), used as the guards' dining room, with four large fireplaces (look up the chimneys). This big room gives a feel for the grandeur of the Great

Hall (upstairs, not open to visitors), where the Revolutionary tribunals grilled scared prisoners on their political correctness. You'll also see a re-creation of Marie-Antoinette's cell, which houses a collection of her mementos. In another room, a list of those made "a foot shorter at the top" by the "national razor" includes ex-King Louis XVI, Charlotte Corday (who murdered the Revolutionary writer Jean-Paul Marat in his bathtub), and—oh, the irony—Maximilien de Robespierre, the head of the Revolution, the man who sent so many to the guillotine.

Cost and Hours: €7, €11 combo-ticket with Sainte-Chapelle, covered by Museum Pass, daily March–Oct 9:30–18:00, Nov–Feb 9:00–17:00, last entry 30 minutes before closing, 4 boulevard du Palais, Mo: Cité, tel. 01 53 40 60 97, www.monum.fr.

• *Back outside, turn left on boulevard du Palais and head north. On the corner is the city's oldest public clock. The mechanism of the present clock is from 1334, and even though the case is Baroque, it keeps on ticking.*

Turn left onto quai de l'Horloge and walk west along the river, past "The Babbler" tower. The bridge up ahead is the pont Neuf, where we'll end this walk. At the first corner, veer left into a sleepy triangular square called place Dauphine. Marvel at how such coziness could be lodged in the midst of such greatness. At the equestrian statue of Henry IV, turn right onto the old bridge and take refuge in one of the nooks on the Eiffel Tower side; or continue through the park to the end of the island (the departure point for Seine river cruises offered by Vedettes du Pont Neuf; described under "By Boat" on page 71).

Pont Neuf

This "New Bridge" is now Paris' oldest. Built during Henry IV's reign (about 1600), its arches span the widest part of the river. Unlike other bridges, this one never had houses or buildings growing on it. The turrets were originally for vendors and street entertainers. In the days of Henry IV, who promised his peasants "a chicken in every pot every Sunday," this would have been a lively scene. From the bridge, look downstream (west) to see the next bridge, the pedestrian-only pont des Arts. Ahead on the Right Bank is the long Louvre Museum. Beyond that, on the Left Bank, is the Orsay. And what's that tall black tower in the distance?

• *As for now, you can tour the Seine by boat, continue to the Louvre, or (if it's summer) head to the...*

Paris at a Glance

▲▲▲**Notre-Dame Cathedral** Paris' most beloved church, with towers and gargoyles. **Hours:** Cathedral daily 8:00–18:45, Sat–Sun until 19:15; tower daily April–Sept 10:00–18:30, June–Aug Sat–Sun until 23:00, Oct–March 10:00–17:30; Treasury daily 18:00, Sat–Sun until 18:30. See page 76.

▲▲▲**Sainte-Chapelle** Gothic cathedral with peerless stained glass. **Hours:** March–Oct daily 9:00–18:00, Wed in summer until 21:30, Nov–Feb daily 9:00–17:00. See page 83.

▲▲▲**Louvre** Europe's oldest and greatest museum, starring Mona Lisa and Venus de Milo. **Hours:** Wed–Mon 9:00–18:00, most wings stay open Wed and Fri until 21:45 (except on holidays), closed Tue. See page 91.

▲▲▲**Orsay Museum** Nineteenth-century art, including Europe's greatest Impressionist collection. **Hours:** Tue–Sun 9:30–18:00, Thu until 21:45, closed Mon. See page 99.

▲▲▲**Eiffel Tower** Paris' soaring exclamation point. **Hours:** Daily mid-June–Aug 9:00–24:45 in the morning, Sept–mid-June 9:30–23:45. See page 103.

▲▲▲**Arc de Triomphe** Triumphal arch with viewpoint, marking start of Champs-Elysées. **Hours:** Always viewable; inside daily April–Sept 10:00–23:00, Oct–March 10:00–22:30. See page 117.

▲▲▲**Versailles** The ultimate royal palace (Château), with a Hall of Mirrors, vast gardens, a grand canal, plus a queen's playground (Trianon Palaces and Domaine de Marie-Antoinette). **Hours:** Château April–Oct Tue–Sun 9:00–18:30, Nov–March Tue–Sun 9:00–17:30, closed Mon. Trianon/Domaine April–Oct Tue–Sun 12:00–18:30, Nov–March Tue–Sun 12:00–17:30, closed Mon; in winter only the two Trianon Palaces are open. Gardens generally open daily 9:00 until sunset, Nov–March closed Mon. See page 210.

▲▲**Orangerie Museum** Monet's water lilies, plus works by Utrillo, Cézanne, Renoir, Matisse, and Picasso, in a lovely setting. **Hours:** Wed–Mon 9:00–18:00, closed Tue. See page 98.

▲▲**Army Museum and Napoleon's Tomb** The emperor's imposing tomb, flanked by museums of France's wars. **Hours:** Daily April–Sept 10:00–18:00, Sun until 18:30 and Tue until 21:00, July–Aug tomb stays open until 19:00; daily Oct–March 10:00–17:00, Sun until 17:30. See page 108.

▲▲**Rodin Museum** Works by the greatest sculptor since Michelangelo, with many statues in a peaceful garden. **Hours:** Tue–Sun 10:00–17:45, closed Mon. See page 109.

▲▲**Marmottan Museum** Untouristy art museum focusing on Monet. **Hours:** Tue 11:00–21:00, Wed–Sun 11:00–18:00, closed Mon. See page 110.

▲▲**Cluny Museum** Medieval art with unicorn tapestries. **Hours:** Wed–Mon 9:15–17:45, closed Tue. See page 110.

▲▲**Champs-Elysées** Paris' grand boulevard. **Hours:** Always open. See page 115.

▲▲**Jacquemart-André Museum** Art-strewn mansion. **Hours:** Daily 10:00–18:00. See page 119.

▲▲**La Défense and La Grande Arche** The city's own "little Manhattan" business district and its colossal modern arch. **Hours:** Daily 10:00–19:00. See page 120.

▲▲**Pompidou Center** Modern art in colorful building with city views. **Hours:** Wed–Mon 11:00–21:00, Thu until 23:00 when special exhibits are on, closed Tue. See page 123.

▲▲**Carnavalet Museum** Paris' history wrapped up in a 16th-century mansion. **Hours:** Tue–Sun 10:00–18:00, closed Mon. See page 125.

▲**Sacré-Cœur** White basilica atop Montmartre with spectacular views. **Hours:** Daily 6:00–23:00. See page 127.

▲**Panthéon** Neoclassical monument celebrating the struggles of the French. **Hours:** Daily 10:00–18:30 in summer, until 18:00 in winter. See page 113.

▲**Opéra Garnier** Grand belle époque theater with a modern ceiling by Chagall. **Hours:** Generally daily 10:00–16:30, July-Aug until 17:30. See page 118.

▲**Père Lachaise Cemetery** Final home of Paris' illustrious dead. **Hours:** Mon–Sat 8:30–17:30, Sun 9:00–18:00. See page 126.

▲**Luxembourg Garden** Grand, sprawling park filled with flowers, fountains, and Parisian flair. **Hours:** Open daily dawn until dusk. See page 112.

Paris Sights

TO LA DEFENSE & LA GRANDE ARCHE

GALLERIES LAFAYETTE

OPERA GARNIER

BLVD.

MADELEINE

PLACE VENDOME

RUE

ORANGERIE

TUILERIES GDN.

ORSAY

ST. GERMAIN

BLVD.

RASPAIL

PLACE DE LA CONCORDE

PETIT PALAIS

SEINE R.

BLVD.

DOMINIQUE

ARMY MUSEUM & NAPOLEON'S TOMB

RODIN MUSEUM

TO MONTPARNASSE TOWER & CATACOMBS

8

JACQUEMART-ANDRE MUSEUM

CHAMPS-ELYSEES

GRAND PALAIS

RIVER CRUISES

SEWER TOUR

RUE CLER

QUAI BRANLY MUSEUM

ECOLE MILITAIRE

DCH

ARC DE TRIOMPHE

RIVER CRUISES

CHAMP DE MARS

PARC DU

EIFFEL TOWER

15

AVE KLEBER

16

TO MARMOTTAN MUSEUM

TROCA-DERO

MARITIME MUSEUM

QUAI

RER RAIL TO VERSAILLES

N

VIEW   PARIS PLAGE

GRAY NUMBERS INDICATE
ARRONDISSEMENTS (DISTRICTS)

Paris Plage (Beach)

The Riviera it's not, but this fanciful faux beach—assembled in summer along a two-mile stretch of the Seine on the Right Bank—is a fun place to stroll, play, and people-watch on a sunny day. Each summer since 2002, the Paris city government has closed the embankment's highway and trucked in potted palm trees, hammocks, lounge chairs, and 2,000 tons of sand to create a colorful urban beach. You'll also find "beach cafés," climbing walls, prefab pools, trampolines, *boules*, a library, beach volleyball, badminton, and Frisbee.

Cost and Hours: Free, mid-July–mid-Aug daily 7:00–24:00, no beach off-season; on Right Bank of Seine, just north of Ile de la Cité, between pont des Arts and pont de Sully.

Map labels: GARE DU NORD, GARE DE L'EST, CANAL ST. MARTIN, PLACE DE LA RÉPUBLIQUE, AVE DE LA RÉPUBLIQUE, PÈRE LACHAISE CEMETERY, BLVD. MAGENTA, BLVD. ST. MARTIN, SEBASTOPOL, POMPIDOU, JEWISH MUSEUM, PICASSO MUSEUM (CLOSED), MARAIS, CARNAVALET MUSEUM, PLACE DES VOSGES, PROMENADE PLANTÉE, GARE DE LYON, BLVD. DIDEROT, OPÉRA, PLACE BASTILLE, ST. ANTOINE, HÔTEL DE VILLE, HOLOCAUST MEM., ILE ST. LOUIS, GARE D'AUSTERLITZ, ½ MILE, .5 KM, TO MONTMARTRE & SACRE-COEUR, HAUSSMANN, PALAIS ROYAL, FORUM LES HALLES, BLVD. DE RIVOLI, PLACE CHATELET, ILE DE LA CITÉ, NOTRE DAME, LOUVRE, RIVER CRUISES, SAINTE-CHAPELLE, LATIN QUARTER, CLUNY MUS., SORBONNE, PANTHEON, RUE MOUFFETARD, ST. MICHEL, BLVD. ST. MICHEL, ST. SULPICE, LUXEM-BOURG GARDEN

Sights in Paris

Major Museums Neighborhood

Paris' grandest park, the Tuileries Garden, was once the private property of kings and queens. Today it links the Louvre, Orangerie, Jeu de Paume, and Orsay museums. And across from the Louvre are the tranquil, historic courtyards of the Palais Royal.

▲▲▲Louvre (Musée du Louvre)

This is Europe's oldest, biggest, greatest, and second-most-crowded museum (after the Vatican). Housed in a U-shaped, 16th-century palace (accentuated by a 20th-century glass pyramid), the Louvre is Paris' top museum and one of its key landmarks. It's home to

Mona Lisa, Venus de Milo, and hall after hall of Greek and Roman masterpieces, medieval jewels, Michelangelo statues, and paintings by the greatest artists from the Renaissance to the Romantics (mid-1800s).

Touring the Louvre can be overwhelming, so be selective. Focus on the Denon wing (south, along the river), with Greek sculptures, Italian paintings (by Raphael and da Vinci), and—of course—French paintings (Neoclassical and Romantic). For extra credit, tackle the Richelieu wing (north, away from the river), displaying works from ancient Mesopotamia (today's Iraq), as well as French, Dutch, and Northern art; or the Sully wing (connecting the other two wings), with Egyptian artifacts and more French paintings. You'll find my self-guided tour of the Louvre's highlights on page 94.

Expect Changes: The sprawling Louvre is constantly in flux. Rooms are periodically closed for renovation, and pieces are removed from display if they're being restored or loaned to other museums. In 2011, for example, the pre-Classical Greek section is closed; sections of the Greek Antiquities Wing (including areas covered by our tour) are being rearranged; and construction continues on the exciting new Islamic art wing due in 2012. To find the artwork you're looking for, ask the nearest guard for its new location.

Cost: €9.50, €6 after 18:00 on Wed and Fri, free on first Sun of month, covered by Museum Pass. Tickets good all day; reentry allowed. Optional additional charges apply for temporary exhibits.

Hours: Wed–Mon 9:00–18:00, most wings stay open Wed and Fri until 21:45 (except on holidays), closed Tue. Galleries start shutting down 30 minutes early. The last entry is 45 minutes before closing.

When to Go: Crowds are worst on Sun, Mon, Wed, and mornings. Evening visits are peaceful, and the glass pyramid glows after dark.

Getting There: You have a variety of options:

By Métro: The Métro stop Palais Royal–Musée du Louvre is closer to the entrance than the stop called Louvre-Rivoli. From the Palais Royal–Musée du Louvre stop, you can stay underground to enter the museum, or exit above ground if you want to go in through the pyramid (more details on the next page).

By Bus: Handy bus #69 runs every 10–20 minutes. Buses headed west from the Marais drop off passengers next to the

Major Museums Neighborhood

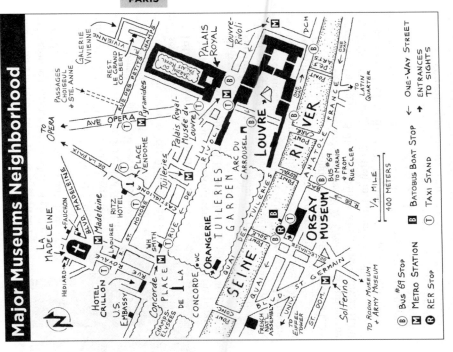

Palais Royal–Musée du Louvre Métro stop on rue de Rivoli. Buses headed east from rue Cler drop off along the Seine River (at quai François Mitterand).

By Taxi: You'll find a taxi stand on rue de Rivoli, next to the Palais Royal–Musée du Louvre Métro station.

Getting In: Enter through the pyramid, or opt for shorter lines elsewhere.

Main Pyramid Entrance: There is no grander entry than through the main entrance at the pyramid in the central courtyard, but metal detectors (not ticket-buyers) can create a long line.

Museum Pass/Group Entrance: Museum Pass-holders can use the group entrance in the pedestrian passageway (labeled *Pavillon Richelieu*) between the pyramid and rue de Rivoli. It's under the arches, a few steps north of the pyramid; find the uniformed guard at the security checkpoint entrance, at the down escalator.

Carrousel du Louvre

Underground Mall Entrance: You can enter the Louvre from its less crowded underground entrance, accessed through the Carrousel du Louvre shopping mall. Enter the mall at 99 rue de Rivoli (the door with the red awning) or directly from the Métro stop Palais Royal–Musée du Louvre (stepping off the train, exit at the end of the platform, following signs to *Musée du Louvre–Le Carrousel du Louvre*). Museum Pass–holders can skip to the head of the underground-mall security line.

Information: Pick up the free *Plan/Information* in English at the information desk under the pyramid as you enter. Tel. 01 40 20 53 17, recorded info tel. 01 40 20 51 51, www.louvre.fr.

Buying Tickets: Located under the pyramid, the self-serve ticket machines are faster to use than the ticket windows (machines accept euro notes, coins, and Visa cards). The *tabac* in the underground mall at the Louvre sells tickets to the Louvre, Orsay, and Versailles, plus Museum Passes, for no extra charge.

Tours: Ninety-minute English-language **guided tours** leave twice daily except Sun from the *Accueil des Groupes* area, under the pyramid between the Sully and Denon wings (normally at 11:00 and 14:00, sometimes more often in summer; €5 plus your entry ticket, tour tel. 01 40 20 52 63). Digital **audioguides** provide eager students with commentary on about 130 masterpieces (€6, available at entries to the three wings, at the top of the escalators). I prefer the self-guided tour described below, which is also available as a **free audio tour** for use with an iPod or other MP3 player (download from www.ricksteves.com or search for "Rick Steves Audio Tours" in iTunes). You'll also find English explanations throughout the museum.

Baggage Check: The free *Bagagerie* is under the pyramid, to the right of the Denon wing entrance. Large bags must be checked, and you can also check small bags to lighten your load. They will not take coats unless they're stuffed into bags. (The coat check, or *Vestiaire,* is near the Richelieu wing.) The baggage-claim clerk might ask you in French, "Does your bag contain anything of value?" You can't check cameras, money, passports, or other valuables.

Services: WCs are located under the pyramid, behind the escalators to the Denon and Richelieu wings. Once you're in the galleries, WCs are scarce.

Photography: Photography without a flash is allowed. (Flash photography damages paintings and distracts viewers.)

 ⊙ Self-Guided Tour: Start in the Denon Wing and visit the

The Louvre

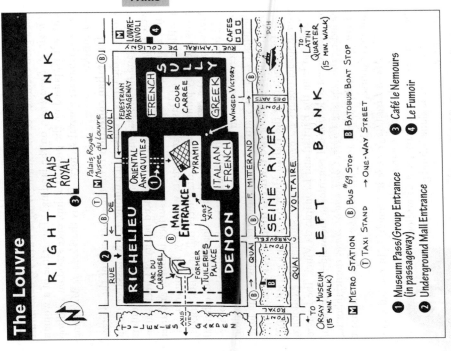

RIGHT BANK

PALAIS ROYAL

③ Palais Royale
Ⓜ Musée du Louvre

RICHELIEU

Arc du Carrousel

FORMER TUILERIES PALACE

Ⓜ MAIN ENTRANCE

Louis XIV

Oriental Antiquities ①▪▪Ⓜ

PYRAMID

ITALIAN & FRENCH

DENON

FRENCH

SULLY

COUR CARREE

GREEK

WINGED VICTORY

PEDESTRIAN PASSAGEWAY

RIVOLI

RUE DE RIVOLI

DE

L'AMIRAL DE COLIGNY

Ⓜ LOUVRE-RIVOLI ④

☐ ☐ ☐
CAFES
☐ ☐ ☐

TO LATIN QUARTER (15 MIN. WALK)

PONT DES ARTS

PONT DU CARROUSEL

QUAI VOLTAIRE

Ⓜ F. MITTERAND

SEINE RIVER

LEFT BANK

TO ORSAY MUSEUM (15 MIN. WALK)

AXIS VIEW

TUILERIES GARDEN

QUAI ROYAL

PONT ROYAL

Ⓜ METRO STATION   Ⓑ BUS #69 STOP   Ⓑ BATOBUS BOAT STOP
Ⓣ TAXI STAND   → ONE-WAY STREET

① Museum Pass/Group Entrance (in passageway)
② Underground Mall Entrance
③ Café le Nemours
④ Le Fumoir

highlights, in the following order (thanks to Gene Openshaw for his help writing this tour).

Find the famous **Venus de Milo** *(Aphrodite)* statue. This goddess of love (c. 100 B.C., from the Greek island of Melos) created a sensation when she was discovered in 1820. Most "Greek" statues are actually later Roman copies, but *Venus* is a rare Greek original. She, like Golden Age Greeks, epitomizes stability, beauty, and balance. After viewing *Venus*, wander through the **ancient Greek and Roman works** to see the Parthenon frieze (stone fragments that once decorated the exterior of the greatest Athenian temple), mosaics from Pompeii, Etruscan sarcophagi, and Roman portrait busts.

Later Greek art was Hellenistic, adding motion and drama. For a good example, see the exciting **Winged Victory of Samothrace** (*Victoire de Samothrace*, on the landing). This statue of a woman with wings, poised on the prow of a ship, once stood on a hilltop to commemorate a naval victory. This is the *Venus de Milo* gone Hellenistic.

The **Italian collection** is on the other side of the *Winged Victory* in the Grand Gallery. In painting, the Renaissance meant realism, and for the Italians, realism was spelled "3-D." Painters were inspired by the realism and balanced beauty of Greek sculpture. Painting a 3-D world on a 2-D surface is tough, and after a millennium of Dark Ages, artists were rusty. Living in a religious age, they painted mostly altarpieces full of saints, angels, Madonnas-and-bambinos, and crucifixes floating in an ethereal gold-leaf heaven. Gradually, though, they brought these otherworldly scenes down to earth. (The Italian collection—including the *Mona Lisa*—is scattered throughout the rooms of the long Grand Gallery—look for **two Botticelli frescoes** as you enter.)

Two masters of the Italian High Renaissance (1500–1600) were Raphael (see his *La Belle Jardinière*, showing the Madonna, Child, and John the Baptist) and Leonardo da Vinci. The Louvre has the greatest collection of Leonardos in the world—five of them, including the exquisite *Virgin, Child, and St. Anne*; the neighboring *Virgin of the Rocks*; and the androgynous *John the Baptist*. His most famous, of course, is the *Mona Lisa*.

The **Mona Lisa** (*La Joconde* in French) is in the Salle des Etats, midway down the Grand Gallery, on the right. After several years and a €5 million renovation, Mona is alone behind glass on her own false wall.

Leonardo was already an old man when François I invited him to France. Determined to pack light, he took only a few paintings with him. One was a portrait of a Lisa del Gioconda, the wife of a wealthy Florentine merchant. When Leonardo arrived, François immediately fell in love with the painting, making it the centerpiece of the small collection of Italian masterpieces that would, in three centuries, become the Louvre museum. He called it *La Gioconda* (*La Joconde* in French)—both her last name and a play on the Italian word for "happy woman." We know it as a contraction of the Italian for "my lady Lisa" —*Mona Lisa*. Warning: François was impressed, but *Mona* may disappoint you. She's smaller than you'd expect, darker, engulfed in a huge room, and hidden behind a glaring pane of glass.

The overall mood is one of balance and serenity, but there's also an element of mystery. *Mona's* smile and long-distance beauty are subtle and elusive, tempting but always just out of reach, like strands of a street singer's melody drifting through the Métro tunnel. *Mona* doesn't knock your socks off, but she winks at the patient viewer.

The huge canvas opposite *Mona* is Paolo Veronese's *The Marriage at Cana*, showing the Renaissance love of beautiful things gone hog-wild. Venetian artists like Veronese painted the good life of rich, happy-go-lucky Venetian merchants.

Now for something **Neoclassical.** Exit behind *Mona Lisa* and turn right into the Salle Daru to find *The Coronation of Napoleon* by Jacques-Louis David. Neoclassicism, once the rage in France (1780–1850), usually features Greek subjects, patriotic sentiment, and a clean, simple style. After Napoleon quickly conquered most of Europe, he insisted on being made emperor (not merely king) of this "New Rome." He staged an elaborate coronation ceremony in Paris, and rather than let the pope crown him, he crowned himself. The setting was Notre-Dame Cathedral, with Greek columns and Roman arches thrown in for effect. Napoleon's mom was also added, because she couldn't make it to the ceremony. A key on the frame describes who's who in the picture.

The **Romantic** collection, in an adjacent room (Salle Mollien), has works by Théodore Géricault (*The Raft of the Medusa*—one

of my favorites) and Eugène Delacroix (*Liberty Leading the People*). Romanticism, with an emphasis on motion and emotion, is the flip side of cool, balanced Neoclassicism, though they both flourished in the early 1800s. Delacroix's *Liberty*, commemorating the stirrings of democracy in France, is also a fitting tribute to the Louvre, the first museum ever opened to the common rabble of humanity. The good things in life don't belong only to a small, wealthy part of society, but to everyone. The motto of France is *Liberté, Égalité, Fraternité*— liberty, equality, and the brotherhood of all.

Exit the room at the far end (past the Café Mollien) and go downstairs, where you'll bump into the bum of a large, twisting male nude looking like he's just waking up after a thousand-year nap. The two *Slaves* (1513–1515) by Michelangelo are a fitting end to this museum—works that bridge the ancient and modern worlds. Michelangelo, like his fellow Renaissance artists, learned from the Greeks. The perfect anatomy, twisting poses, and idealized faces appear as if they could have been created 2,000 years earlier. Michelangelo said that his purpose was to carve away the marble to reveal the figures God put inside. The *Rebellious Slave*, fighting against his bondage, shows the agony of that process and the ecstasy of the result.

Although this makes for a good first tour, there's so much more. After a break (or on a second visit), consider a stroll through a few rooms of the Richelieu wing, which contain some of the Louvre's oldest and biggest pieces. Bible students, amateur archaeologists, and Iraq War vets may find the collection especially interesting.

Palais Royal Courtyards

Across from the Louvre are the lovely courtyards of the stately Palais Royal. Although the palace is closed to the public, the courtyards are open. Enter through a whimsical (locals say tacky) courtyard filled with stubby, striped columns and playful fountains (with fun, reflective metal balls). Next, you'll pass into another, perfectly Parisian garden. This is where in-the-know Parisians come to take a quiet break, walk their poodles and kids, or enjoy a rendezvous—amid flowers and surrounded by a serene arcade and a handful of historic restaurants. Bring a picnic and create your own quiet break, or have a drink at one of the outdoor cafés at the courtyard's northern end. This is Paris.

Exiting the courtyard at the side facing away from the Seine brings you to the Galeries Colbert and Vivienne, good examples of shopping arcades from the early 1900s and worth a look.

Cost and Hours: Courtyards are free and always open. The Palais Royal is directly north of the Louvre on rue de Rivoli (Mo: Palais Royal–Musée du Louvre).

▲▲Orangerie Museum (Musée de l'Orangerie)

Step out of the tree-lined, sun-dappled Impressionist painting that is the Tuileries Garden, and into the Orangerie (oh-rahn-zheh-ree), a little bijou of select works by Claude Monet and his contemporaries. You'll start with the museum's claim to fame: Monet's water lilies. These eight mammoth-scale paintings are displayed exactly as

Monet intended them—surrounding you in oval-shaped rooms—so you feel as though you're immersed in his garden at Giverny. Working from his home there, Monet built a special studio with skylights and wheeled easels to accommodate the canvases—1,950

square feet in all. Each canvas features a different part of the pond, painted from varying angles at distinct times of day—but the true subject of these works is the play of reflected light off the surface of the pond. Downstairs you'll find a tight selection of works by Utrillo, Cézanne, Renoir, Matisse, and Picasso. Together they provide a snapshot of what was hot in the world of art, circa 1920.

Cost and Hours: €7.50, mandatory temporary exhibitions may raise price, €13 combo-ticket with Orsay Museum valid four days (one visit per sight), under 18 free, covered by Museum Pass, audioguide-€5, Wed–Mon 9:00–18:00, closed Tue, located in Tuileries Garden near place de la Concorde, Mo: Concorde. Tel. 01 44 77 80 07, www.musee-orangerie.fr.

▲▲▲Orsay Museum (Musée d'Orsay)

The Musée d'Orsay (mew-zay dor-say) houses French art of the 1800s and early 1900s (specifically, 1848–1914), picking up where the Louvre's art collection leaves off. For us, that means Impressionism, the art of sun-dappled fields, bright colors, and crowded Parisian cafés. The Orsay houses the best general collection anywhere of Manet, Monet, Renoir, Degas, Van Gogh, Cézanne, and Gauguin.

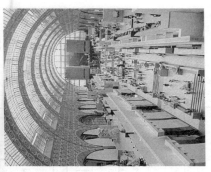

The museum shows art that is also both old and new, conservative and revolutionary. You'll start on the ground floor, with the Conservatives and the early rebels (like Manet and Gustave Courbet) who paved the way for the Impressionists. Here, sappy soft-focus Venuses (popular with the 18th-century bourgeoisie) are displayed alongside the grittier work of the Realists. For most visitors, the most important part of the museum is the Impressionist collection on the top floor, which is closed until fall of 2011 (see "Renovation," later).

If the top floor is open, this is where you can study many pictures you've probably seen in books, such as Renoir's *Dance at the Moulin de la Galette*, Monet's *Cathedral of Rouen*, Degas' *The Dance Class*, James Abbott McNeill Whistler's *Portrait of the Artist's Mother*, Van Gogh's *The Church at Auvers-sur-Oise*, Cézanne's *The Card Players*, and Henri de Toulouse-Lautrec's *Jane Avril Dancing*. You'll also see Primitive works by Gauguin and Henri Rousseau. As you approach these beautiful, easy-to-enjoy paintings, remember that there is more to this art than meets the eye.

Orsay Museum—Ground Floor

SEINE RIVER

PONT ← ROYAL

RUE DU BAC

TO LOUVRE (15 MIN. WALK)

BUS #69 FROM RUE CLER TO LOUVRE + MARAIS

ESCALATOR UP TO IMPRESSIONISM

MANET

REALISM

CONSERVATIVE ART

❶

❷

START

ENTRANCE

FOR PASS HOLDERS

FOR NON-PASS HOLDERS

SECURITY

VESTIAIRE (BAGGAGE CHECK)

BOOKS

BOOKSTORE

QUAI ANATOLE FRANCE

RUE DE LA LEGION D'HONNEUR

RUE DE BELLECHASSE

DCH

TO ⓂSOLFERINO (5 MIN. WALK) + RODIN MUSEUM

Ⓣ TAXI STAND

→ ONE-WAY STREET

SOLFERINO PED BRIDGE

→ TO ORANGERIE

Ⓑ BUS #69 FROM MARAIS TO RUE CLER + EIFFEL TOWER

MUSÉE D'ORSAY

Ⓑ BUS #69 STOP

Ⓜ METRO STATION

Ⓡ RER STOP

Ⓑ BATOBUS BOAT STOP

❶ Temporary Impressionist & Post-Impressionist Rooms

❷ Temporary Van Gogh & Gauguin Rooms

Background: Here's a primer on Impressionism: After the camera was invented, it threatened to make artists obsolete. A painter's original function was to record reality faithfully, like a journalist. Now a machine could capture a better likeness faster than you could say "Etch-a-Sketch."

But true art is more than just painting reality. It gives us reality from the artist's point of view, with the artist's personal impressions of the scene. Impressions are often fleeting, so you have to work quickly.

The Impressionist painters rejected camera-like detail for a quick style more suited to capturing the passing moment. Feeling stifled by the rigid rules and stuffy atmosphere of the Academy, the Impressionists took as their motto, "Out of the studio, into the open air." They grabbed their berets and scarves and went on excursions to the country, where they set up their easels (and newly invented tubes of premixed paint) on riverbanks and hillsides, or they sketched in cafés and dance halls. Gods, goddesses, nymphs, and fantasy scenes were out; common people and rural landscapes were in.

The quick style and everyday subjects were ridiculed and called childish by the "experts." Rejected by the Salon (where works were displayed to the buying public), the Impressionists staged their own exhibition in 1874. They brashly took their name from an insult thrown at them by a critic who laughed at one of Monet's "impressions" of a sunrise. During the next decade, they exhibited their own work independently. The public, opposed at first, was slowly won over by the simplicity, the color, and the vibrancy of Impressionist art.

Cost: €8, €5.50 Fri–Wed after 16:15 and Thu after 18:00, free first Sun of month, covered by Museum Pass. Tickets are good all day. Combo-tickets are available with the Orangerie Museum (€13, valid four days) or Rodin Museum (€12, valid same day).

Hours: Tue–Sun 9:30–18:00, Thu until 21:45, closed Mon, last entry one hour before closing (45 minutes before on Thu). When open, the top-floor Impressionist galleries begin closing 45 minutes early, frustrating unwary visitors. Tuesdays are particularly crowded, because the Louvre is closed.

Free Entry near Closing Time: Right when the ticket booth stops selling tickets, you're welcome to scoot in free of charge (Tue–Wed and Fri–Sun at 17:00, Thu at 21:00; they won't let you in much after that, however). Make a beeline for the Impressionist galleries (if they're open), which start shutting down first.

Renovation: The Orsay's top-floor Impressionist and Post-Impressionist rooms are closed for renovation until fall of 2011. Until then, some paintings may be in storage or on loan. Fortunately, most are temporarily displayed on the ground floor.

After the reopening, the Impressionist art will return to the top floor, but some Post-Impressionist art may be moved downstairs to the second level. Regardless of when you visit, you'll see most of the Orsay's masterpieces.

Getting There: The museum sits above the RER-C stop called Musée d'Orsay. The nearest Métro stop is Solférino, three blocks southeast of the Orsay. Bus #69 from the Marais neighborhood stops at the museum on the river side (quai Anatole France); from the rue Cler area, it stops behind the museum on the rue du Bac. From the Louvre, catch bus #69 along rue de Rivoli; otherwise, it's a lovely 15-minute walk through the Tuileries Garden and across the river on the pedestrian bridge. The museum is at 1 rue de la Légion d'Honneur. A taxi stand is in front of the entrance on quai Anatole France. The Batobus boat also makes a stop here (see page 71).

Getting In: The ticket-buying line can be long, but if you have a Museum Pass or advance ticket, you can waltz right in (tickets can be purchased in person at FNAC department stores and TIs, or online for pick-up in Paris; for options and fees, see the Orsay website, www.musee-orsay.fr). As you face the front of the museum from rue de la Légion d'Honneur (with the river on your left), passholders and ticket-holders enter on the right side of the museum (Entrance C). Ticket-purchasers enter closer to the river (Entrance A).

Information: The booth inside the entrance provides free floor plans in English that can help you navigate the museum while it's under renovation. Tel. 01 40 49 48 14, www.musee-orsay.fr.

Tours: Audioguides cost €6. English guided tours usually run daily (except Sun) at 11:30 (€7.50/1.5 hours). Occasionally, some tours are offered at other times (inquire when you arrive). I recommend my **Rick Steves self-guided tour,** which is available as a free audio tour for use with an iPod or other MP3 player (download from www.ricksteves.com or search for "Rick Steves Audio Tours" in iTunes).

Cloakroom (*Vestiaire*): Checking bags or coats is free. Day bags (but nothing big) are allowed in the museum. No valuables can be stored in checked bags. The cloakroom clerk might ask you in French not to check cameras, passports, or anything particularly precious.

Photography: Photography is forbidden.

Cuisine Art: A pricey but *très* elegant restaurant is on the second floor, with affordable tea and coffee served 14:45–17:30 (daily except Thu). A fifth-floor café is sandwiched between the Impressionists.

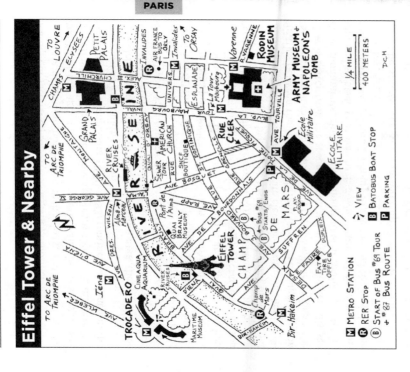

Eiffel Tower & Nearby

TO LOUVRE
TO ARC DE TRIOMPHE
PETIT PALAIS
INVALIDES
AIR FRANCE BUS TO ORLY
Invalides
TO ORSAY
CHAMPS - ELYSEES
CHURCHILL
Varenne
RODIN MUSEUM
R. VARENNE
ALEX III
UNIVERS.
GRAND PALAIS
ESPLANADE
La Tour-Maubourg
AVE MONTAIGNE
RIVER CRUISES
QUAI D'ORSAY
SEWER TOUR
AMERICAN CHURCH
S E I N E
BLVD. LA TOUR-MAUBOURG
ARMY MUSEUM + NAPOLEON'S TOMB
RUE CLER
AVE BOSQUET
SNCF BOUTIQUE
RUE ST. DOMINIQUE
RIVE R
AVE GEORGE V
Alma-Marceau
Pont de l'Alma
RUE DE GRENELLE
AVE RAPP
AVE BOURDONNAIS
AVE DE LA BOURDONNAIS
Bus #69 STARTS/ENDS
AVE TOURVILLE
Ecole Militaire
¼ MILE
400 METERS
DCH
TO ARC DE TRIOMPHE
AVE KLEBER
AVE D'IENA
AVE PIERRE 1ER DE SERBIE
Iéna
AVE DU PRES. WILSON
Quai Branly Museum
CINEAQUA AQUARIUM
TROCADERO
RIVER CRUISES
IENA
PONT D'IENA
Eiffel Tower
C H A M P
D E
M A R S
AVE DE SUFFREN
AVE DE LA MOTTE-PIQUET
Champ de Mars
ECOLE MILITAIRE
MARITIME MUSEUM
Bir-Hakeim
AVE DE SUFFREN
FAT TIRE OFFICE
E. FAURE
PLAY-GROUND
AVE DUPLEIX
AVE DE LA MOTTE-PICQUET

M METRO STATION
R RER STOP
B START OF BUS #69 TOUR + #87 BUS ROUTE
🔭 VIEW
B BATOBUS BOAT STOP
P PARKING

Eiffel Tower and Nearby

▲▲▲**Eiffel Tower (La Tour Eiffel)**—It's crowded, expensive, and there are probably better views in Paris, but this 1,000-foot-tall ornament is worth the trouble. Visitors to Paris may find *Mona Lisa* to be less than expected, but the Eiffel Tower rarely disappoints, even in an era of skyscrapers.

Built a hundred years after the French Revolution (and in the midst of an industrial one), the tower served no function but to impress. In 1889, the first visitor to Paris' Universal Exposition walked beneath the "arch" formed by the newly built Eiffel Tower and entered the fair grounds. The World's Fair celebrated both the centennial of the French Revolution and France's position as a global superpower. Bridge-builder Gustave

Eiffel (1832–1923) won the contest to build the fair's centerpiece by beating out rival proposals as a giant guillotine.

To a generation hooked on technology, the tower was the marvel of the age, a symbol of progress and human ingenuity. Not all were so impressed, however; many found it a monstrosity. Writer Guy de Maupassant (1850–1893) routinely ate lunch in the tower just so he wouldn't have to look at it.

Delicate and graceful when seen from afar, the Eiffel Tower is massive—even a bit scary—close up. You don't appreciate its size until you walk toward it; like a mountain, it seems so close but takes forever to reach. But despite the tower's 7,300 tons of metal and 60 tons of paint, it is so well-engineered that it weighs no more per square inch at its base than a linebacker on tiptoes.

There are three observation platforms, at 200, 400, and 900 feet. (The higher you go, the more you pay.) To get to the top, you need to take two different elevators. The first takes you to the second level. (You must bypass the first level on the way up and see it on the way back down.) A separate elevator—with another line—shuttles between the second and third levels. Although being on the windy top of the Eiffel Tower is a thrill you'll never forget, the view is better from the second level, where you can actually see Paris' monuments. Budget three hours to wait in line, get to the top, and sightsee your way back down. With online reservations and/or no crowds, figure 1.5 hours to the top and back (with time for sightseeing).

The stairs—yes, you can walk up to the first and second levels—are next to the entrance to the pricey Jules Verne restaurant. As you ascend through the metal beams, imagine being a worker, perched high above nothing, riveting this thing together.

The **top level**, called *le sommet*, is tiny. (It can close temporarily without warning when it reaches capacity.) All you'll find here are wind and grand, sweeping views. The city lies before you, with a panorama guide. On a good day, you can see for 40 miles.

The **second level** (400 feet) has the best views because you're closer to the sights, and the monuments are more recognizable. (The best views are up the short stairway, on the platform without the wire-cage barriers.) This level has souvenir shops, public telephones to call home, and a small stand-up café. Although you won't save money, consider taking the elevator up and the stairs down (five minutes from second level to first, five minutes more to ground) for good exercise and views.

The **first level** (200 feet) has more great views, all well-described by the tower's panorama displays. There are a number of photo exhibits on the tower's history, WCs, a conference hall (closed to tourists), an ATM, and souvenirs. A small café sells pizza and sandwiches (outdoor tables in summer). The 58 Tour

Eiffel restaurant (listed on page 176) has more *accessible* prices than the Jules Verne Restaurant, and also is run by Alain Ducasse (for Jules Verne, allow $250/person for dinner or weekend lunch at the restaurant, $115 for weekday lunch, reserve three months in advance). In winter, part of the first level is set up for winter activities (most recently as an ice-skating rink).

Videos shown in the small theater (some permanent, some rotating) document the tower's construction, paint job, place in pop culture, and a century of fireworks, capped by the entire millennium blast.

Seeing It All: If you don't want to miss a single level, here's a plan for getting the most out of your visit. Ride the elevator to the second level, then immediately line up for the other elevator to the top. Enjoy the views on top, then ride back down to the second level. Frolic there for a while and take in some more views. When you're ready, head to the first level by taking the stairs (no line) or lining up for the elevator. Explore the shops and exhibits on the first level and have a snack. Once you're ready to leave, you can line up for the elevator, but it's quickest and most memorable to take the stairs back to earth.

Cost: €13.10 all the way to the top, €8.10 if you're only going up to the two lower levels, not covered by Museum Pass. You can skip the elevator line and climb the stairs to the first and second level for €4.50, or for €3.50 if you're under 25. (Elevators and stairs are both free going down.) Once inside the tower, you can buy your way to the top with no penalty—ticket booths and machines on the first and second levels sell supplements for €5 (€3.50 if you're under 25; walkers need to climb to second level to ride elevator up).

Hours: Daily mid-June–Aug 9:00–24:45 in the morning, last ascent to top at 23:00 and to lower levels at 24:00; Sept–mid-June 9:30–23:45, last ascent to top at 22:30 and to lower levels at 23:00 (elevator) or 18:00 (stairs). During windy weather, the top level may close to tourists.

Reservations: At www.toureiffel.fr, you can book an entry time (e.g., June 12 at 16:30) and skip the line—at no extra cost. You just pay online with a credit card and print your own ticket (or have confirmation sent to your mobile phone). At the tower, go to the entrance for *visitors with reservation*, where attendants scan your ticket and put you on the first available elevator. Note that even if you have a reservation, when you want to get from the second level to the summit, you'll still have to wait in line like everybody else (and show your ticket again).

The website is easy, but here are a few tips: First, when you "Choose a ticket," make sure you select "Lift entrance ticket with access to the summit" in order to go all the way to the top. For "Type of ticket," it doesn't really matter whether you pick "Group" or "Individual"; a "Group" ticket just gives you one piece of paper covering everyone in your party. You must enter a "Mobile phone number" for identification purposes, so if you don't have one, make one up—and jot it down so you won't forget it. To print the ticket, follow their specifications carefully (white paper, blank on both sides, etc.). If you're on the road without a printer, try forwarding your email confirmation notice to your hotel reception. They can click on a link to the website, where you can enter your information and print out your ticket.

When to Go: For the best of both worlds, arrive with enough light to see the views, then stay as it gets dark to see the lights. The views are grand whether you ascend or not. At the top of the hour, a five-minute lighting display features thousands of sparkling lights (best viewed from place du Trocadéro or the grassy park below).

Avoiding Lines: Crowds overwhelm this place much of the year, with one- to two-hour waits to get in. Weekends and holidays are worst, but prepare for ridiculous crowds almost any time. The best solution is to make an online reservation (see above). If you don't have a reservation, go early; get in line 30 minutes before it opens. Going later is the next-best bet (after 19:00 May–Aug, after 17:00 off-season; see "Hours," earlier, for last ascent times). If you're in line to buy tickets, estimate about 20 minutes for every 100 yards, plus 30 minutes more after you reach the security check near the ticket booths. You can bypass some (but not all) elevator lines if you have a reservation at either of the tower's view restaurants. There's less of a line for the stairs.

Getting There: The Bir-Hakeim and Trocadéro Métro stops, and the Champ de Mars-Tour Eiffel RER stop, are each about a 10-minute walk away. The Ecole Militaire Métro stop in the rue Cler area is 20 minutes away. Buses #69 and #87 stop nearby on avenue Joseph Bouvard in the Champ de Mars park.

Nearby: Before or after your tower visit, you can catch the Bateaux Parisiens boat for a Seine cruise (near the base of Eiffel Tower, see page 71).

Information: An Eiffel Tower information office is between the north and east pillars. Each level on the tower has displays pointing out the landmarks and monuments visible below. Tel. 01 44 11 23 23, www.toureiffel.fr.

Pickpockets: Tourists in crowded elevators are like fish in a barrel for predatory thieves. *En garde.*

Security Check: Bags larger than 19" × 8" × 12" are not allowed and there is no baggage check. All bags are subject to a security search. No knives, glass bottles, or cans are allowed.

Services: There are free WCs at the base of the tower, behind the east pillar. Inside the tower itself, WCs are on all levels, but they're small, with long lines.

Photography: All photos and videos are allowed.

Best Views: The best place to view the tower is from place du Trocadéro to the north. It's a 10-minute walk across the river, a happening scene at night, and especially fun for kids. Consider arriving at the Trocadéro Métro stop for the view, then walking toward the tower. Another delightful viewpoint is the Champ de Mars park to the south. However impressive it may be by day, the tower is an awesome thing to see at twilight, when it becomes engorged with light, and virile Paris lies back and lets night be on top. When darkness fully envelops the city, the tower seems to climax with a spectacular light show at the top of each hour...for five minutes.

Quai Branly Museum (Museé du Quai Branly)—This is the best collection I've seen anywhere of so-called Primitive Art from Africa, Polynesia, Asia, and America. It's presented in a wild, organic, and strikingly modern building that caused a stir in Paris when it opened in 2006. Masks, statuettes, musical instruments, clothes, voodoo dolls, and a variety of temporary exhibits and activities are artfully presented and exquisitely lit. It's not, however, accompanied by much printed English information—to really appreciate the exhibit, use the €5 audioguide. It's a 10-minute walk east (upriver) of the Eiffel Tower, along the river. Even if you skip the museum, drop by its garden café for its fair prices and fine Eiffel Tower views (closes 30 minutes before museum).

Cost and Hours: €8.50, more for temporary exhibits, covered by Museum Pass, Tue–Sun 11:00–19:00, Thu–Sat until 21:00, closed Mon, 37 quai Branly, RER: Champ de Mars-Tour Eiffel or Pont de l'Alma. Tel. 01 56 61 70 00, www.quaibranly.fr.

National Maritime Museum (Musée National de la Marine)—This extensive museum houses an amazing collection of ship models, submarines, torpedoes, cannonballs, *beaucoup* bowsprits, and naval you-name-it, including a small boat made for Napoleon. Don't miss the model and story of how the obelisk on place de la Concorde was delivered from Egypt to Paris entirely by waterways; look for the model and story (behind stairs leading down to special exhibits space). Your ticket (or Museum Pass) includes a good audioguide that explains key exhibits and adds important context to your visit. Kids love it, too.

Cost and Hours: Adults–€7, 18 and under free but pay €2 for audioguide, more during special exhibits, covered by Museum Pass, Wed–Mon 10:00–18:00, closed Tue, on left side of place du Trocadéro with your back to Eiffel Tower. Tel. 01 53 65 69 69, www.musee-marine.fr.

▲**Paris Sewer Tour (Les Egouts de Paris)**—Discover what happens after you flush. This quick, interesting, and slightly stinky visit (a perfumed hanky helps) takes you along a few hundred yards of water tunnels in the world's first underground sewer system. Pick up the helpful English self-guided tour, then drop down into Jean Valjean's world of tunnels, rats, and manhole covers. (Victor Hugo was friends with the sewer inspector when he wrote *Les Misérables*.) You'll pass well-organized displays with helpful English information explaining the history of water distribution in Paris, from Roman times to the present. The evolution of this amazing network of sewers is surprisingly interesting. More than 1,500 miles of tunnels carry 317 million gallons of water daily through this underworld. It's the world's longest sewer system—so long, they say, that if it was laid out straight, it would stretch from Paris all the way to Istanbul.

Ask about the slideshow in the gift shop and occasional tours in English. The WCs are just beyond the gift shop.

Cost and Hours: €4.30, covered by Museum Pass; Sat–Wed May–Sept 11:00–17:00, Oct–April 11:00–16:00; closed Thu–Fri; located where pont de l'Alma greets the Left Bank—on the right side of the bridge as you face the river, Mo: Alma-Marceau, RER: Pont de l'Alma. Tel. 01 53 68 27 81.

▲▲Army Museum and Napoleon's Tomb (Musée de l'Armée)

—The Hôtel des Invalides—a former veterans' hospital built by Louis XIV—houses Napoleon's over-the-top-ornate tomb, as well as Europe's greatest military museum. Visiting the Army Museum's different sections, you can watch the art of war unfold from stone axes to Axis powers.

At the center of the complex, the Napoleon lies majestically dead inside several coffins under a grand dome—a goose-bumping pilgrimage for historians. The dome overhead glitters with 26 pounds of thinly pounded gold leaf, and tombs of other French war heroes surround the emperor. Follow signs to the crypt to find Roman Empire–style reliefs that list the accomplishments of Napoleon's administration.

Your visit continues through an impressive range of military museums that surround a central courtyard, complete with good English explanations. See medieval armor, Napoleon's stuffed and mounted horse, Louis XIV–era uniforms and weapons, and much more. The best part is the section dedicated to the two World Wars, especially World War II.

Cost: €9, ticket includes Napoleon's Tomb, all museums within Les Invalides complex, and audioguide for tomb. All covered by the Museum Pass except for €1 audioguide. Price drops to

€7 an hour before closing time; always free for all military personnel in uniform.

Hours: Daily April–Sept 10:00–18:00, Sun until 18:30 and Tue until 21:00, July–Aug tomb stays open until 19:00; daily Oct–March 10:00–17:00, Sun until 17:30; last tickets sold 30 minutes before closing; Oct–June closed first Mon of every month, Charles de Gaulle Museum (within the complex) closed Mon year-round.

Location: The Hôtel des Invalides is at 129 rue de Grenelle; Mo: La Tour Maubourg, Varenne, or Invalides. Tel. 01 44 42 38 77 or toll 08 10 11 33 99, www.invalides.org.

▲▲**Rodin Museum (Musée Rodin)**—This user-friendly museum is filled with passionate works by the greatest sculptor since Michelangelo.

Auguste Rodin (1840–1917) sculpted human figures on an epic scale, revealing through the body their deepest thoughts and feelings. Like many of Michelangelo's unfinished works, Rodin's statues rise from the raw stone around them, driven by the life force. With missing limbs and scarred skin, these are prefab classics, making ugliness noble. Rodin's people are always moving restlessly. Even the famous *Thinker* is moving—though

he's plopped down solidly, his mind is a million miles away.

Rodin worked with many materials—he chiseled marble (though not often), modeled clay, cast bronze, worked plaster, painted, and sketched. He often created different versions of the same subject in different media.

Rodin lived and worked in this mansion, renting rooms alongside Henri Matisse, poet Rainer Maria Rilke (Rodin's secretary), and dancer Isadora Duncan. The well-displayed exhibits trace Rodin's artistic development, explain how his bronze statues were cast, and show some of the studies he created to work up to his masterpiece (the unfinished *Gates of Hell*). Learn about Rodin's tumultuous relationship with his apprentice and lover, Camille Claudel. Mull over what makes his sculptures some of the most evocative since the Renaissance. And stroll the gardens, packed with many of his greatest works (including *The Thinker*, *Balzac*, the *Burghers of Calais*, and the *Gates of Hell*). The beautiful gardens are ideal for artistic reflection.

Cost and Hours: €6, under 18 free, free on first Sun of the month, €12 same-day combo-ticket with Orsay Museum, covered by Museum Pass. It costs €1 to get into the gardens only—which may be Paris' best deal, as many works are on display there (also

covered by Museum Pass). Audioguides are €4, and baggage check is mandatory. Open Tue–Sun 10:00–17:45, closed Mon, gardens close at 18:45, last entry 30 minutes before closing. It's near the Army Museum and Napoleon's Tomb, 79 rue de Varenne, Mo: Varenne. Tel. 01 44 18 61 10, www.musee-rodin.fr.

▲▲**Marmottan Museum (Musée Marmottan Monet)**—The Marmottan has the best collection of works by master Impressionist Claude Monet. In this mansion on the fringe of urban Paris, you can walk through Monet's life, from black-and-white sketches to colorful open-air paintings to the canvas that gave Impressionism its name. The museum's highlights are scenes of his garden at Giverny, including larger-than-life water lilies. In addition, the Marmottan features a world-class collection of works by Berthe Morisot.

The ground floor usually displays Paul Marmottan's eclectic collection of non-Monet objects—period furnishings, a beautifully displayed series of illuminated manuscript drawings, and non-Monet paintings created in the seamless-brushstroke style that Monet rebelled against. The permanent collection (mainly Monet) is generally in the basement and on the first floor. The basement displays Monet's large-scale works from his gardens at Giverny, whereas the first floor hosts special exhibits and paintings by Impressionist colleagues Pierre-Auguste Renoir, Camille Pissarro, Berthe Morisot, and more.

Cost and Hours: €9, not covered by Museum Pass, Tue 11:00–21:00, Wed–Sun 11:00–18:00, closed Mon, last entry 30 minutes before closing, 2 rue Louis-Boilly, Mo: La Muette. Tel. 01 44 96 50 33, www.marmottan.com.

Left Bank

Opposite Notre-Dame, on the left bank of the Seine, is the Latin Quarter. (For more information, see the "Historic Paris Walk," earlier.)

▲▲**Cluny Museum (Musée National du Moyen Age)**—This treasure trove of Middle Ages *(Moyen Age)* art fills old Roman baths, offering close-up looks at stained glass, Notre-Dame carvings, fine goldsmithing and jewelry, and rooms of tapestries. The highlights are several original stained-glass windows from Sainte-Chapelle, and the exquisite *Lady and the Unicorn* series of six tapestries: A delicate, as-medieval-as-can-be noble lady introduces a delighted unicorn to the senses of taste, hearing, sight, smell, and touch. This museum helps put the Middle Ages in perspective,

Left Bank

TO ORSAY MUSEUM
TO RODIN MUSEUM
RIGHT BANK
SEINE
TO LOUVRE VIA PONT DES ARTS
ST. GERMAIN-DES-PRÉS
CAFÉS DEUX MAGOTS + LA FLORE
DELACROIX MUSEUM
SAINTE-CHAPELLE
ILE DE LA CITÉ
NOTRE DAME
BLVD. ST. GERMAIN
PLACE ST. MICHEL
CLUNY MUSEUM
RUE ST. SÉVERIN
LATIN QUARTER
ST. MICHEL
ÉCOLE MUTUALITÉ
RUE MONGE
MAUBERT-MUTUALITÉ
PLACE MONGE
ÉD. LENOIR
RUE MONGE
THÉATRE ODÉON
ODÉON
SORBONNE
ST. ÉTIENNE DU MONT
PANTHÉON
RUE MOUFFETARD
ST. SULPICE
FOUR
R. MABILLON
RUE DU VIEUX COLOMBIER
SHOPPING AREA
SÈVRES-BAB.
BON MARCHÉ
RUE DE VARENNE
BLVD. RASPAIL
RENNES
BLVD.
RUE VAUGIRARD
N.D. DES CHAMPS
LE SELECT CAFÉ
LA COUPOLE CAFÉ
MONTPARNASSE TOWER
VAVIN
TO CATACOMBS
LUXEMBOURG GARDEN
POND
KIDS' PLAY AREA
RUE D'ASSAS
RUE DE FLEURUS
PORT ROYAL
BLVD.
ST. JACQUES
SOUFFLOT
RUE DES ÉCOLES
PLACE ST. SULPICE

LATIN QUARTER
M METRO STATION
Ⓡ RER STOP

SÈVRES-BABYLONE TO ST. SULPICE BOUTIQUE STROLL

¼ MILE
400 METERS
DCH

reflecting a time when Europe was awakening from a thousand-year slumber and Paris was emerging on the world stage. Trade was booming, people actually owned chairs, and the Renaissance was moving in like a warm front from Italy.

Cost and Hours: €8.50, free on first Sun of month, covered by Museum Pass, Wed–Mon 9:15–17:45, closed Tue, last entry at 17:15, near corner of boulevards St. Michel and St. Germain at 6 place Paul Painlevé; Mo: Cluny–La Sorbonne, St. Michel, or Odéon. Tel. 01 53 73 78 16, www.musee-moyenage.fr.

St. Germain-des-Prés—A church was first built on this site in A.D. 452. The church you see today was constructed in 1163 and is all that's left of a once sprawling and influential monastery. The colorful interior reminds us that medieval churches were originally painted in bright colors. The surrounding area hops at night with venerable cafés, fire-eaters, mimes, and scads of artists (free, daily 8:00–20:00, Mo: St. Germain-des-Prés).

▲**St. Sulpice Church and Organ Concert**—This grand church was featured in *The Da Vinci Code*, and has since become a trendy stop for the book's many fans. But the real reason to visit is to see and hear its intimately accessible organ. For pipe-organ enthusiasts, this is one of Europe's great musical treats. The Grand Orgue at St. Sulpice Church has a rich history, with a succession of 12 world-class organists—including Charles-Marie Widor and Marcel Dupré—that goes back 300 years. Widor started the tradition of opening the loft to visitors after the 10:30 service on Sundays. Daniel Roth (or his understudy) continues to welcome guests in three languages while playing five keyboards. (See www.danielrothsaintsulpice.org for his exact dates and concert plans.)

The 10:30–11:30 Sunday Mass (come appropriately dressed) is followed by a high-powered 25-minute recital. Then, at noon, the small, unmarked door is opened (left of entry as you face the rear). Visitors scamper like 16th notes up spiral stairs, past the 19th-century StairMasters that five men once pumped to fill the bellows, into a world of 7,000 pipes. You can see the organ and visit with Daniel (or his substitute, who might not speak English). Space is tight—only 15 people are allowed in at a time, and only a few can gather around the organist at once—you need to be quick to allow others a chance to meet him. You'll likely have about 20 minutes to kill before watching the master play during the next Mass (church views are great and there's a small lounge to wait in); you can leave at any time. If you're late or rushed, show up around 12:30 and wait at the little door (last entry is at 13:00). As someone leaves, you can slip in, climb up, and catch the rest of the performance. Tempting boutiques surround the church, and Luxembourg Garden is nearby.

Cost and Hours: Free, church open daily 7:30–19:30, Mo: St. Sulpice or Mabillon.

Delacroix Museum (Musée National Eugène Delacroix)—

This museum for Eugène Delacroix (1798–1863) was once his home and studio. A friend of bohemian artistic greats—including George Sand and Frédéric Chopin—Delacroix is most famous for the flag-waving painting *Liberty Leading the People*, which is displayed at the Louvre, not here.

Cost and Hours: €5, free on first Sun of the month, covered by Museum Pass, Wed–Mon 9:30–17:00, Sat–Sun until 17:30 in summer, closed Tue, last entry 30 minutes before closing, 6 rue de Furstenberg, Mo: St. Germain-des-Prés. Tel. 01 44 41 86 50, www.musee-delacroix.fr.

▲Luxembourg Garden (Jardin du Luxembourg)—Paris'

most beautiful, interesting, and enjoyable garden/park/recreational area, le Jardin du Luxembourg, is a great place to watch Parisians

at rest and play. These 60-acre gardens, dotted with fountains and statues, are the property of the French Senate, which meets here in the Luxembourg Palace. Luxembourg Garden has special rules governing its use (for example, where cards can be played, where dogs can be walked, where joggers can run, and when and where music can be played). The brilliant flower beds are completely changed three times a year, and the boxed trees are brought out of the orangery in May. Children enjoy rentable toy sailboats, pony rides, and marionette shows (Les Guignols, or Punch and Judy). Challenge the card and chess players to a game (near the tennis courts), or find a free chair near the main pond and take a well-deserved break (park open daily dawn until dusk, Mo: Odéon, RER: Luxembourg).

The grand Neoclassical-domed Panthéon (next listing), now a mausoleum housing the tombs of great French notables, is three blocks away.

If you enjoy Luxembourg Garden and want to see more green spaces, you could visit the more elegant **Parc Monceau** (Mo: Monceau), the colorful **Jardin des Plantes** (Mo: Jussieu or Gare d'Austerlitz, RER: Gare d'Austerlitz), or the hilly and bigger **Parc des Buttes-Chaumont** (Mo: Buttes-Chaumont).

▲**Panthéon**—This state-capitol-style Neoclassical monument celebrates France's illustrious history and people, balances

Foucault's pendulum, and is the final home of many French VIPs. Inside the vast building (360' × 280' × 270') are monuments tracing the celebrated struggles of the French people: a beheaded St. Denis (painting on left wall of nave), St. Geneviève saving the fledgling city from Attila the Hun, and scenes of Joan of Arc (left transept).

Foucault's pendulum swings gracefully at the end of a 220-foot cable suspended from the towering dome. It was here in 1851 that scientist Léon Foucault first demonstrated the rotation of the Earth. Stand a few minutes and watch the pendulum's arc (appear to) shift as you and the earth rotate beneath it.

Stairs in the back lead down to the crypt, where a pantheon of greats is buried. Rousseau is along the right wall as you enter,

Voltaire faces him across the hall. Also buried here are scientist Marie Curie, Victor Hugo (*Les Misérables*, *The Hunchback of Notre-Dame*), Alexandre Dumas (*The Three Musketeers*, *The Count of Monte Cristo*), and Louis Braille, who invented the script for the blind.

From the main floor you can climb 206 steps to the dome gallery for great views of the interior as well as the city (accessible only with an escort). Visits leave every hour until 17:30 from the bookshop near the entry—see schedule as you go in.

Cost and Hours: €8, covered by Museum Pass, daily 10:00–18:30 in summer, until 18:00 in winter, last entry 45 minutes before closing, Mo: Cardinal Lemoine. Ask about occasional English tours or call ahead for schedule. Tel. 01 44 32 18 00, www.monum.fr.

Montparnasse Tower (La Tour Montparnasse)—This sadly out-of-place 59-story superscraper has one virtue: its sensational

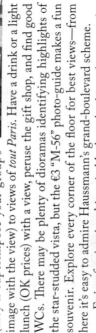

views are cheaper and far easier to access than the Eiffel Tower's. Come early in the day for clearest skies and be treated to views from a comfortable interior and from up on the rooftop. (Some say it's the very best view in Paris, as you can see the Eiffel Tower clearly...and you can't see the Montparnasse Tower at all.) Exit the elevator at the 56th floor, passing the eager photographer (they'll superimpose your group's image with the view) to views of *tout Paris*. Have a drink or a light lunch (OK prices) with a view, peruse the gift shop, and find good WCs. There may be plenty of dioramas identifying highlights of the star-studded vista, but the €3 "M-56" photo-guide makes a fun souvenir. Explore every corner of the floor for best views—from here it's easy to admire Haussmann's grand-boulevard scheme.

Enjoy fascinating historic black-and-white photos, and a plush little theater playing a worthwhile video that celebrates the big views of this grand city (free, 12 minutes, shows continuously). Climb to the open terrace on the 59th floor to enjoy the surreal scene of a lonely man in a box, and a helipad surrounded by the window-cleaner track. Here, 690 feet above Paris, you can scan the city with the wind in your hair, noticing the lush courtyards hiding behind grand street fronts.

Cost and Hours: €11.50, not covered by Museum Pass, daily April–Sept 9:30–23:30; Oct–March 9:30–22:30, Fri–Sat until 23:00; last entry 30 minutes before closing, sunset is great but views are disappointing after dark, entrance on rue de l'Arrivée, Mo: Montparnasse-Bienvenüe—from the Métro stay inside the station and follow the signs for *La Tour*. The tower is an efficient stop when combined with a day trip to Chartres (see next chapter for details). Tel. 01 45 38 52 56, www.tourmontparnasse56.com.

▲**Catacombs**—These underground tunnels contain the anonymous bones of six million permanent Parisians. In 1786, the citizens of Paris decided to relieve congestion and improve sanitary conditions by emptying the city cemeteries (which traditionally surrounded churches) into an official ossuary. They found the perfect locale in the many miles of underground tunnels from limestone quarries, which were, at that time, just outside the city. For decades, priests led ceremonial processions of black-veiled, bone-laden carts into the quarries, where the bones were stacked into piles five feet high and as much as 80 feet deep behind neat walls of skull-studded tibiae. Each transfer was completed by placing a plaque, indicating the church and district where the bones came from and the date that they arrived. Note to wannabe Hamlets: An attendant checks your bag at the exit for stolen souvenirs. A flashlight is handy. Being under 6'2" is helpful.

Cost and Hours: €8, not covered by Museum Pass, Tue–Sun 10:00–17:00, ticket booth closes at 16:00, closed Mon. Be warned that lines are long (figure an hour wait) and hard to avoid. Arrive no later than 14:30 or risk not getting in. Take the Métro to Denfert-Rochereau, then find the lion in the big traffic circle; if he looked left rather than right, he'd stare right at the green entrance to the Catacombs at 1 place Denfert-Rochereau. Tel. 01 43 22 47 63.

Champs-Elysées and Nearby

▲▲**Champs-Elysées**—This famous boulevard is Paris' backbone, with its greatest concentration of traffic. From the Arc de Triomphe down avenue des Champs-Elysées, all of France seems to converge on place de la Concorde, the city's largest square. And though the Champs-Elysées has become as international as it is Parisian, a walk here is still a must.

In 1667, Louis XIV opened the first section of the street as a short extension of the Tuileries Garden. This year is considered the birth of Paris as a grand city. The Champs-Elysées soon became *the* place to cruise in your carriage. (It still is today; traffic can be gridlocked even at midnight.) One hundred years later, the café scene arrived.

From the 1920s until the 1960s, this boulevard was pure

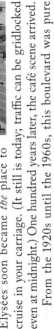

Champs-Elysées & Nearby

½ MILE

1 KM

◼ METRO STATION

To MONTMARTRE + SACRÉ-COEUR

GALLERIES LAFAYETTE

OPÉRA GARNIER

FRAGONARD PERFUME

BLVD. HAUSSMANN

PRINTEMPS

CAFÉ DE LA PAIX

PLACE VENDÔME

JACQUEMART-ANDRÉ MUSEUM

St-PHILIPPE du ROULE

MADELEINE

Madeleine

Con- corde

To LOUVRE

TUILERIES GARDEN

ORANGERIE

FRIEDLAND

CHAMPS-ELYSÉES

F.D.R.

PLACE DE LA CONCORDE

PETIT PALAIS

SEINE

Charles DeGaulle-Etoile

George V

AVE. MONTAIGNE

GRAND PALAIS

RIVER CRUISES

To Army Museum + Napoleon's Tomb

To LA DEFENSE

ARC DE TRIOMPHE

To TROCADERO

DCH

elegance. Parisians actually dressed up to come here. It was mainly residences, rich hotels, and cafés. Then, in 1963, the government pumped up the neighborhood's commercial metabolism by bringing in the RER (commuter train). Suburbanites had easy access, and *pfft*—there went the neighborhood.

The *nouveau* Champs-Elysées, revitalized in 1994, has new benches and lamps, broader sidewalks, all-underground parking, and a fleet of green-suited workers who drive motorized street cleaners. Blink away the modern elements, and it's not hard to imagine the boulevard pre-1963, with only the finest structures lining both sides all the way to the palace gardens.

◑ Self-Guided Walk: To reach the top of the Champs-Elysées, take the Métro to the Arc de Triomphe (Mo: Charles de Gaulle–Etoile), then saunter down the grand boulevard (Métro stops every few blocks, including Charles de Gaulle-Etoile, George V, and Franklin D. Roosevelt). Start here, then head downhill, following this commentary.

Fancy car dealerships include **Peugeot,** at #136 (showing off its futuristic concept cars, often alongside the classic models), and **Mercedes-Benz,** a block down at #118, where you can pick up a Mercedes watch to go with your new car. In the 19th century this was an area for horse stables; today, it's the district of garages, limo companies, and car dealerships. If you're serious about selling cars in France, you must have a showroom on the Champs-Elysées.

Next to Mercedes is the famous **Lido,** Paris' largest cabaret (and a multiplex cinema). You can walk all the way inside, if you ask nicely, until 18:00. Paris still offers the kind of burlesque-type spectacles combining music, comedy, and scantily clad women that have been performed here since the 19th century. Moviegoing on the Champs-Elysées provides another kind of fun, with theaters showing the very latest releases. Check to see if there are films you recognize, then look for the showings (*séances*). A "v.o." (*version originale*) next to the time indicates the film will be shown in its original language.

The flagship store of leather-bag makers **Louis Vuitton** may be the largest single-brand luxury store in the world. Step inside. The store insists on providing enough salespeople to treat each customer royally—if there's a line, it means shoppers have overwhelmed the place.

Fouquet's café-restaurant (#99), under the red awning, is a popular spot among French celebrities, serving the most expensive shot of espresso I've found in downtown Paris (€8). Opened in 1899 as a coachman's bistro, Fouquet's gained fame as the hangout of France's WWI biplane fighter pilots—those who weren't shot down by Germany's infamous "Red Baron." It also served as James Joyce's dining room.

Since the early 1900s, Fouquet's has been a favorite of French actors and actresses. The golden plaques at the entrance honor winners of France's Oscar-like film awards, the Césars (one is cut into the ground at the end of the red carpet). Look for the plaques for Gérard Depardieu, Catherine Deneuve, Roman Polanski, Juliette Binoche, and many famous Americans (but not Jerry Lewis). Recent winners are shown on the floor just inside.

The hushed interior is at once classy and intimidating—and also a grand experience...if you dare (to say "I'm just looking" in French, say "*Je regard*"—zhuh ruh-gard"). The outdoor setting is more relaxed. Fouquet's was recently saved from foreign purchase and eventual destruction when the government declared it a historic monument. For his election-night victory party in 2007, the flamboyant President Sarkozy celebrated at Fouquet's, along with France's glitterati—including the "French Elvis," Johnny Hallyday. France's first lady, Carla Bruni-Sarkozy, is often seen dining here.

Ladurée (two blocks downhill at #75, with green-and-purple awning) is a classic 19th-century tea salon/restaurant/*pâtisserie*. Its interior is right out of the 1860s. Nonpatrons can discreetly wander in through the door farthest downhill and peek into the cozy rooms upstairs (no photos). A coffee here is *très élégant* (only €3.50). The bakery sells traditional *macarons*, cute little cakes, and gift-wrapped finger sandwiches to go (your choice of four mini-*macarons* for €7.50).

▲▲▲**Arc de Triomphe**—Napoleon had the magnificent Arc de Triomphe commissioned to commemorate his victory at the battle

of Austerlitz. There's no triumphal arch bigger (165 feet high, 130 feet wide). And, with 12 converging boulevards, there's no traffic circle more thrilling to experience—either from behind the wheel or on foot (take the underpass).

The foot of the arch is a stage on which the last two centuries of Parisian history have played out—from the funeral of Napoleon to the goose-stepping arrival of the Nazis to the triumphant return of Charles de Gaulle after the Allied liberation. Examine the carvings on the pillars, featuring a mighty Napoleon and excitable Lady Liberty. Pay your respects at the Tomb of the Unknown Soldier. Then climb the 284 steps to the observation deck up top, with sweeping skyline panoramas and a mesmerizing view down onto the traffic that swirls around the arch.

Cost and Hours: Outside—free, always viewable. Interior—€9, under 18 free, free on first Sun of month Oct–March, covered by Museum Pass, daily April–Sept 10:00–23:00, Oct–March 10:00–22:30, last entry 30 minutes before closing, place Charles de Gaulle, use underpass to reach arch, Mo: Charles de Gaulle-Etoile. Tel. 01 55 37 73 77, www.arc-de-triomphe .monuments-nationaux.fr.

▲**Opéra Garnier**—This gleaming grand theater of the belle époque was built for Napoleon III and finished in 1875. The building is huge—though the auditorium itself seats only 2,000. The real show was before and after the performance, when the elite of Paris—out to see and be seen—strutted their elegant stuff in the extravagant lobbies. Think of the grand marble stairway as a theater. As you wander the halls and gawk at the decor, imagine the place filled with the beautiful people of its day. The massive foundations straddle an underground lake (inspiring the mysterious world of the *Phantom of the Opera*). Visitors can peek from two boxes into the actual red-velvet performance hall to view Marc Chagall's colorful ceiling (guided tours take you into the performance hall; you can't enter when they're changing out the stage). Note the box seats next to the stage—the most expensive in the house, with an obstructed view of the stage...but just right if you're here only to be seen.

The elitism of this place prompted President François Mitterrand to have a people's opera house built in the 1980s, symbolically on place de la Bastille, where the French Revolution started in 1789. This left the Opéra Garnier home only to ballet and occasional concerts. The library/museum will interest opera buffs, but anyone will enjoy the second-floor grand foyer and Salon du Glacier, iced with decor typical of 1900.

For a novel souvenir, pick up a jar of honey cultivated from beehives on the Opéra's roof. The hives are tended by staff and can be seen from the seventh floor of Galleries Lafayette (behind the Opéra).

Cost and Hours: €9, not covered by Museum Pass, generally daily 10:00–16:30, July–Aug until 17:30, closed during rehearsals (schedule on website), 8 rue Scribe, Mo: Opéra, RER: Auber, www.operadeparis.fr.

Tours: English tours of the building run during summer and off-season on weekends and Wed, usually at 11:30 and 14:30—call to confirm schedule (€12.50, includes entry, 1.5 hours, tel. 08 25 05 44 05, press 2 for tours).

Nearby: The Fragonard Perfume Museum (next) is on the left side of the Opéra, and the venerable Galeries Lafayette department store (marvelous views from roof terrace) is just behind. Across the street, the illustrious Café de la Paix has been a meeting spot for the local glitterati for generations. If you can afford the coffee, this spot offers a delightful break.

Fragonard Perfume Museum—Near Opéra Garnier, this perfume shop masquerades as a museum. Housed in a beautiful 19th-century mansion, it's the best-smelling museum in Paris—and you'll learn a little about how perfume is made, too (ask for the English handout).

Cost and Hours: Free, daily 9:00–17:30, 9 rue Scribe, tel. 01 47 42 04 56, www.fragonard.com.

▲▲Jacquemart-André Museum (Musée Jacquemart-André)—This thoroughly enjoyable museum (with an elegant café) showcases the lavish home of a wealthy, art-loving, 19th-century Parisian couple. After wandering the grand boulevards, get inside for an intimate look at the lifestyles of the Parisian rich and fabulous. Edouard André and his wife Nélie Jacquemart—who had no children—spent their lives and fortunes designing, building, and then decorating this sumptuous mansion. What makes the visit so rewarding is the excellent audioguide tour (in English, free with admission, plan on spending an hour with the audioguide). The place is strewn with paintings by Rembrandt, Botticelli, Uccello, Mantegna, Bellini, Boucher, and Fragonard—enough to make a painting gallery famous.

Cost and Hours: €10, not covered by Museum Pass, daily 10:00–18:00, 158 boulevard Haussmann, Mo: Miromesnil or Saint-Philippe de Roule, bus #80 makes a convenient connection to Ecole Militaire. Tel. 01 45 62 11 59, www.musee-jacquemart-andre.com.

After Your Visit: Consider a break in the sumptuous museum tearoom, with delicious cakes and tea (daily 11:45–17:30). From here walk north on rue de Courcelles to see Paris' most beautiful park, Parc Monceau.

▲**Petit Palais (and its Musée des Beaux-Arts)**—This free museum displays a broad collection of paintings and sculpture from the 1600s to the 1900s. It's a museum of second-choice art, but the building itself is impressive, and there are a few 19th-century diamonds in the rough, including pieces by Courbet, Monet, the American painter Mary Cassatt, and other Impressionists. The Palais also has a pleasant garden courtyard and café.

Cost and Hours: Free, Tue–Sun 10:00–18:00, Thu until 20:00 for temporary exhibits, closed Mon, across from Grand Palais on avenue Winston Churchill, a 1-o-o-ong block west of place de la Concorde. Tel. 01 53 43 40 00, www.petitpalais.paris.fr.

Grand Palais—This grand exhibition hall, built for the 1900 World's Fair, is used for temporary exhibits. The building's Industrial Age, erector-set, iron-and-glass exterior is grand, but the steep entry price is only worthwhile if you're interested in any of the several different exhibitions (each with different hours and costs, located in various parts of the building). Many areas are undergoing renovations, which may still be underway during your visit. Get details on the current schedule from the TIs, in *Pariscope*, or from the website.

Cost and Hours: Admission prices and hours vary with each exhibition. It's open daily, though some parts of the building are closed Mon, and others are closed Tue. Major exhibitions are usually €11 and not covered by Museum Pass. Generally open 10:00–20:00, Wed 10:00–22:00, closed between exhibitions, avenue Winston Churchill, Mo: Rond Point or Champs-Elysées. Tel. 01 44 13 17 17, www.grandpalais.fr.

▲**La Défense and La Grande Arche**—Though Paris keeps its historic center classic and skyscraper-free, this district, nicknamed "le petit Manhattan," offers an impressive excursion into a side of Paris few tourists see: that of a modern-day economic superpower. La Défense was first conceived more than 60 years ago as a US-style forest of skyscrapers that would accommodate the business needs of the modern world. Today La Défense is a thriving business and shopping center, home to 150,000 employees and 55,000 residents.

For an interesting visit, take the Métro to the La Défense, Grande Arche stop and ride the elevator to the top of La Grande Arche for great city views. Then stroll among the glass buildings to the Esplanade de la Défense Métro station, and return home from there.

La Grande Arche de la Fraternité is the centerpiece of this ambitious complex. Inaugurated in 1989 on the 200th anniversary of the French Revolution, it was, like the Revolution, dedicated to human rights and brotherhood. The place is big—Notre-Dame Cathedral could fit under its arch. The "cloud"—a huge canvas canopy under the arch—is an attempt to cut down on the wind-tunnel effect this gigantic building creates.

Glass capsule elevators whisk you scenically up to a grand open-air view, a thrilling 20-minute movie (with English subtitles) on the mammoth construction project, and models of the arch. You can also visit an exhibit on computer history, and take advantage of its free Internet access. Kids like the small video-game museum, and everyone seems fascinated by the set of digital portraits by French artist Dimitri, illustrating *remanence*—"after imagery." After staring at one of these colorful portraits for 30 seconds, close your eyes and see a clear image of the face...behind your eyelids.

Cost and Hours: La Grande Arche elevator and exhibits–€10, kids–€8.50, family deals, not covered by Museum Pass, check online for discounts, daily 10:00–19:00, RER or Mo: La Défense, Grande Arche, follow signs to *La Grande Arche.* Tel. 01 49 07 27 55, www.grandearche.com.

After Your Visit: If you're hungry, head over to glassy Le Dome, which serves good sandwiches and salads to go. Have lunch with a view on the steps of La Grande Arche (cafés also available nearby).

The Esplanade: La Défense is much more than its eye-catching arch. Wander from the arch back toward the city center (and to the next Métro stop) along the Esplanade (a.k.a. "le Parvis")—a virtual open-air modern art gallery, sporting pieces by Joan Miró (blue), Alexander Calder (red), and Yaacov Agam (the fountain with colorful stripes and rhythmically dancing spouts), among others. *La Défense de Paris,* the statue that gave the area its name, recalls the 1871 Franco-Prussian war—it's a rare bit of old Paris out here in the 'burbs. Notice how the Wallace Fountain and *boules* courts are designed to integrate tradition into this celebration of modern commerce. Walking toward the Nexity Tower, you'll come to the Esplanade de la Défense Métro station, which zips you out of all this modernity and directly back into town.

Marais Neighborhood and Nearby

The Marais neighborhood extends along the Right Bank of the Seine, from the Pompidou Center to the Bastille. With more

Marais Neighborhood & Nearby

pre-Revolutionary lanes and buildings than anywhere else in town, the Marais is more atmospheric than touristy. It's medieval Paris, and the haunt of the old nobility. During the reign of Henry IV, this area—originally a swamp (*marais*)—became the hometown of the French aristocracy. In the 17th century, big shots built their private mansions (*hôtels*) close to Henry's stylish place des Vosges. With the Revolution, the aristocratic splendor of this quarter passed, and the Marais became a working-class quarter, filled with gritty shops, artisans, immigrants, and a Jewish community. Today this thriving, trendy, real community is a joy to explore.

It looks the way much of the city did until the mid-1800s, when Napoleon III had Baron Georges-Eugène Haussmann blast out the narrow streets to construct broad boulevards (wide enough for the guns and ranks of the army, too wide for revolutionary barricades), thus creating modern Paris. When strolling the Marais, stick to the west-east axis formed by rue Ste. Croix de la Bretonnerie, rue des Rosiers (heart of Paris' Jewish community), and rue St. Antoine. On Sunday afternoons, this trendy area pulses with shoppers and café crowds.

Don't waste time looking for the **Bastille**, the prison of Revolution fame. It's Paris' most famous nonsight—the building is long gone and just the square remains.

▲**Place des Vosges**—Henry IV (r. 1589-1610) built this centerpiece of the Marais in 1605 and called it "place Royal." As he'd hoped, it turned the Marais into Paris' most exclusive neighborhood. Walk to the center, where Louis XIII on horseback gestures, "Look at this wonderful square my dad built." He's surrounded by locals enjoying their community park. You'll see children frolicking in the sandbox, lovers warming benches, and pigeons guarding their fountains while trees shade this escape from the glare of the big city (you can refill your water bottle in the center of the square).

Study the architecture: nine pavilions (houses) per side. The two highest—at the front and back—were for the king and queen (but were never used). Warm red brickwork—some real, some fake—is topped with sloped slate roofs, chimneys, and another quaint relic of a bygone era: TV antennas. Victor Hugo lived at #6—at the southeast corner of the square, marked by the French flag—from 1832 to 1848. This was when he wrote much of his most important work, including his biggest hit, *Les Misérables*. Inside you'll wander through eight plush rooms and enjoy a fine view of the square (free, optional special exhibits cost about €7—usually not worth paying for, Tue–Sun 10:00–18:00, closed Mon, last entry at 17:40, 6 place des Vosges, tel. 01 42 72 10 16, www.musee-hugo .paris.fr).

Leave the place des Vosges through the doorway at the southwest corner of the square and pass through the elegant **Hôtel de Sully** (great example of a Marais mansion, grand courtyard open daily 10:00–19:00, fine bookstore inside) to rue St. Antoine.

▲▲**Pompidou Center (Centre Pompidou)**—One of Europe's greatest collections of far-out modern art is housed in the Musée National d'Art Moderne, on the fourth and fifth floors of this colorful exhibition hall. The building itself is "exoskeletal" (like Notre-Dame or a crab), with its functional parts—the pipes, heating ducts, and escalator—on the outside, and the meaty art inside. It's the epitome of Modern architecture, where "form follows function." Created ahead of its time, the 20th-century art in this collection is still waiting for the world to catch up.

Buy your ticket on the ground floor, then ride up the escalator (or run up the down escalator to get in the proper mood). When you see the view, your opinion of the

Pompidou's exterior should improve a good 15 percent. Find the permanent collection—the entrance is either on the fourth or fifth floor (it varies). Enter, show your ticket, and get the current floor plan (*plan du musée*).

The 20th century—accelerated by technology and fragmented by war—was exciting and chaotic, and the art reflects the turbulence of that century of change. In this free-flowing and airy museum (with great views over Paris), you'll come face to face with works by Henri Matisse, Pablo Picasso, Marc Chagall, Salvador Dalí, Andy Warhol, Wassily Kandinsky, Max Ernst, Jackson Pollock, and many more. After so many Madonnas-and-children, a piano smashed to bits and glued to the wall is refreshing.

Cost and Hours: €10-12 depending on current exhibits, free on first Sun of month, Museum Pass covers permanent collection and view escalators (but not special exhibitions), Wed–Mon 11:00–21:00, open Thu until 23:00 when special exhibits are on, closed Tue, ticket counters close at 20:00, Mo: Rambuteau or farther-away Hôtel de Ville. Tel. 01 44 78 12 33, www.centrepompidou.fr.

View from the Pompidou: Even if you don't go inside, you can ride the escalator for a great city view from the top (€3 Panorama ticket covers ride but not exhibit, also covered by museum ticket or Museum Pass).

Nearby: The Pompidou Center and the square that fronts it are lively, with lots of people, street theater, and activity inside and out—a perpetual street fair. Kids of any age enjoy the fun, colorful fountain (called *Homage to Stravinsky*) next to the Pompidou Center. Consider either eating at the good mezzanine-level café, or for a light meal or snack, try the places lining the Stravinsky fountain: Dame Tartine and Créperie Beaubourg, both with reasonable prices (to the right as you face the museum entrance).

▲Jewish Art and History Museum (Musée d'Art et Histoire du Judaïsme)

—This fine museum, located in a beautifully restored Marais mansion, tells the story of Judaism in France and throughout Europe, from the Roman destruction of Jerusalem to the theft of famous artworks during World War II. Displays illustrate the cultural unity maintained by this continually dispersed population. You'll learn about the history of Jewish traditions, from bar mitzvahs to menorahs, and see the exquisite traditional costumes and objects central to daily life. The museum also displays paintings by famous Jewish artists, including Marc Chagall, Amedeo Modigliani, and Chaim Soutine. The English explanations posted in many rooms provide sufficient explanation for most; free audioguides provide greater detail.

Cost and Hours: €7, more during special exhibits, includes audioguide, covered by Museum Pass, Mon–Fri 11:00–18:00, Sun 10:00–18:00, closed Sat, last entry 45 minutes before closing, 71 rue du Temple, Mo: Rambuteau or Hôtel de Ville a few blocks farther away. Tel. 01 53 01 86 60, www.mahj.org.

Rue des Rosiers–Jewish Quarter—Located along rue des Rosiers, the tiny yet colorful Jewish district of the Marais was once considered the largest in Western Europe. Today, rue des Rosiers is lined with Jewish shops and kosher eateries—and the district is being squeezed by the trendy boutiques of modern Paris (visit any day but Saturday, when most businesses are closed—best on Sunday). The intersection of rue des Rosiers and rue des Ecouffes marks the heart of the small neighborhood that Jews call the Pletzl ("little place"). Lively rue des Ecouffes, named for a bird of prey, is a derogatory nod to the moneychangers' shops that once lined this lane.

If you're visiting at lunchtime, you'll be tempted by kosher pizza and plenty of cheap fast-food joints selling falafel "to go" (*emporter*). The falafel at LAs du Falafel, with its bustling New York–deli atmosphere, is terrific (at #34, sit-down or to go). The Sacha Finkelsztajn Yiddish bakery at #27 is also good (Polish and Russian cuisine, pop in for a tempting treat, sit for the same price as take-away). Nearby, recommended Chez Marianne cooks up traditional Jewish meals and serves excellent falafel to go (at corner of rue des Rosiers and rue des Hospitalières–St.-Gervais; long hours daily). The Jewish Quarter is also home to the Holocaust Memorial (described later).

▲▲**Picasso Museum (Musée Picasso)**—This museum, currently closed for a major renovation that will last several years, contains the world's largest collection of Picasso's paintings, sculptures, sketches, and ceramics, along with his small collection of Impressionist art.

▲▲**Carnavalet Museum (Musée Carnavalet)**—The tumultuous history of Paris—starring the Revolutionary years—is well-portrayed in paintings, models, and a few original artifacts. You'll get a good overview of everything from Louis XIV period rooms to Napoleon to the belle époque. The sprawling Carnavalet is housed in two Marais mansions connected by a corridor; it can be hard to navigate but is great for browsing. The first half of the museum (pre-Revolution) dates from a period when people generally accepted the notion that some were born to rule, and most were born to be ruled. Lovers of Louis XIV-, XV-, and XVI-period furniture will enjoy this section. Others can see it quickly, then concentrate on the Revolution and beyond.

The Revolution is the museum's highlight. A dozen rooms of fascinating exhibits cover this bloody period of French history, when atrocious acts were committed in the name of government "by, for, and of the people." The exhibits take you from events that led up to the Revolution to the storming of the 100-foot-high walls of the Bastille to the royal beheadings, and through the reigns of terror that followed. The rest of the museum traces the rise and fall of Napoleon, France's struggle between monarchy and democracy, the Paris Commune, and the elegance of Paris during the belle époque. Though explanations are in French only, many displays are fairly self-explanatory.

Cost and Hours: Free, occasional fees for optional temporary exhibits, Tue–Sun 10:00–18:00, closed Mon; avoid lunchtime (12:00–14:00), when many rooms close; 23 rue de Sévigné, Mo: St. Paul. Tel. 01 44 59 58 58, www.carnavalet.paris.fr.

Holocaust Memorial (Mémorial de la Shoah)—Commemorating the lives of the more than 76,000 Jews deported from France in World War II, this memorial's focal point is underground, where victims' ashes are buried. Displaying original deportation records, the museum takes you through the history of Jews in Europe and France, from medieval pogroms to the Nazi era.

Cost and Hours: Free, Sun–Fri 10:00–18:00, Thu until 22:00, closed Sat and certain Jewish holidays, 17 rue Geoffroy l'Asnier. Tel. 01 42 77 44 72, www.memorialdelashoah.org.

Promenade Plantée Park (Viaduc des Arts)—This two-mile-long, narrow garden walk on an elevated viaduct was once used for train tracks and is now a good place for a refreshing stroll. Botanists appreciate the well-maintained and varying vegetation, and runners adore the separated pathway. At a few spots, gaps in the planted path have you walking along the street for a bit until you pick up the next segment. The shops at street level below the viaduct's arches take creative advantage of once-wasted urban space, and make for entertaining window shopping (mostly modern furnishings).

Cost and Hours: Free, opens Mon–Fri at 8:00, Sat–Sun at 9:00, closes at sunset (17:30 in winter, 20:30 in summer). It runs from place de la Bastille (Mo: Bastille) along avenue Daumesnil to Saint-Mandé (Mo: Michel Bizot), passing within a block of Gare de Lyon. From place de la Bastille (exit the Métro following *Sortie rue de Lyon*), walk a l-o-o-ong block down rue de Lyon hugging the Opéra on your left. Find the steps up the red brick wall a block after the Opéra.

▲Père Lachaise Cemetery (Cimetière du Père Lachaise)—Littered with the tombstones of many of the city's most illustrious dead, this is your best one-stop look at Paris' fascinating, romantic past residents. Enclosed by a massive wall and lined with 5,000 trees, the peaceful, car-free lanes and dirt paths of Père Lachaise cemetery encourage parklike meandering. Named for Father (*Père*) La Chaise, whose job was listening to Louis XIV's sins, the cemetery is relatively new, having opened in 1804 to accommodate Paris' expansion. Today, this city of the dead (pop. 70,000) still accepts new residents, but real estate prices are sky high (a 21-square-foot plot costs more than €11,000).

The 100-acre cemetery is big and confusing, with thousands of graves and tombs crammed every which way, and only a few pedestrian pathways to help you navigate. The maps available from any of the nearby florists will direct you to the graves of Frédéric Chopin, Molière, Edith Piaf, Oscar Wilde, Gertrude Stein, Jim Morrison, Héloïse and Abélard, and many more.

Cost and Hours: Free, Mon–Sat 8:30–17:30, Sun 9:00–18:00. It's two blocks from Mo: Gambetta (not Mo: Père Lachaise) and two blocks from bus #69's last stop. Tel. 01 55 25 82 10, www.pere-lachaise.com.

Montmartre

Stroll along Paris' highest hilltop (420 feet) for a different perspective on the City of Light. Walk in the footsteps of the people who've lived here—monks stomping grapes (1200s), farmers grinding grain in windmills (1600s), dust-coated gypsum miners (1700s), Parisian liberals (1800s), Modernist painters (1900s), and all the struggling artists, poets, dreamers, and drunkards who came here for cheap rent, untaxed booze, rustic landscapes, and cabaret nightlife. With vineyards, wheat fields, windmills, animals, and a village tempo of life, it was the perfect escape from grimy Paris.

Getting There: To reach Montmartre, you have several options: You can take the Métro to the Anvers stop (to avoid the stairs up to Sacré-Cœur Basilica, buy one more Métro ticket and ride the funicular, though it's sometimes closed for maintenance). The Abbesses stop is closer but less scenic. Or you can go to place Pigalle, then take the tiny electric Montmartrobus, which drops you right by place du Tertre, near Sacré-Cœur. A taxi to the top of the hill saves time and avoids sweat (about €13, €20 at night). For restaurant recommendations, see page 193.

▲▲**Sacré-Cœur**—The Sacré-Cœur (Sacred Heart) Basilica's exterior, with its onion domes and bleached-bone pallor, looks ancient, but was finished only a century ago by Parisians humiliated by Germany invaders. Otto von Bismarck's Prussian army laid siege to Paris for more than four months in 1870. Things got so bad for residents that urban hunting for dinner (to cook up dogs, cats, and finally rats) became accepted behavior. Convinced they

Montmartre

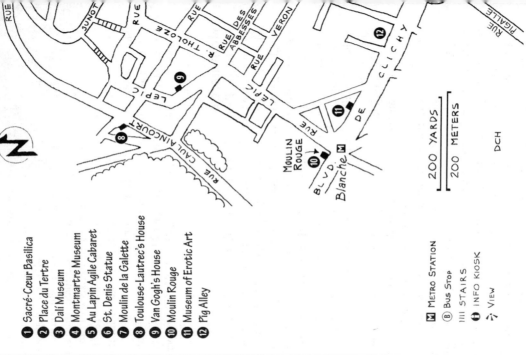

1. Sacré-Cœur Basilica
2. Place du Tertre
3. Dali Museum
4. Montmartre Museum
5. Au Lapin Agile Cabaret
6. St. Denis Statue
7. Moulin de la Galette
8. Toulouse-Lautrec's House
9. Van Gogh's House
10. Moulin Rouge
11. Museum of Erotic Art
12. Pig Alley

M METRO STATION
B BUS STOP
||| STAIRS
ℹ INFO KIOSK
👁 VIEW

200 YARDS
200 METERS

DCH

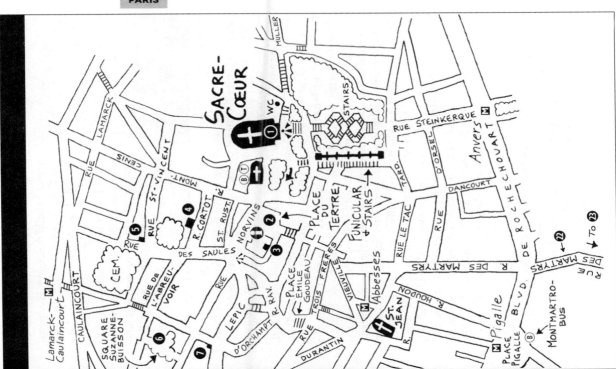

were being punished for the country's liberal sins, France's Catholics raised money to build the church as a "praise the Lord anyway" gesture. The five-domed, Roman-Byzantine–looking basilica took 44 years to build (1875–1919). It stands on a foundation of 83 pillars sunk 130 feet deep, necessary because the ground beneath was honeycombed with gypsum mines. The exterior is laced with gypsum, which whitens with age.

Take a clockwise spin around the crowded interior to see impressive mosaics, and to give St. Peter's bronze foot a rub. For an unobstructed panoramic view of Paris, climb 260 feet (300 steps) up the tight and claustrophobic spiral stairs to the top of the dome (especially worthwhile if you have kids with excess energy).

Cost and Hours: Church interior free, open daily 6:00–23:00, last entry at 22:15; €5 to climb dome, not covered by Museum Pass, daily June–Sept 9:00–19:00, Oct–May 10:00–18:00.

The Heart of Montmartre—One block from the church, the **place du Tertre** was the haunt of Henri de Toulouse-Lautrec and the original bohemians. Today, it's mobbed with tourists and unoriginal bohemians, but it's still fun (to beat the crowds, go early in the morning). From here follow rue des Saules (a block west, passing near the Dalí Museum—described next), and find Paris' lone vineyard and the **Montmartre Museum** (described later). Return uphill, then follow rue Lépic down to the old windmill, **Moulin de la Galette,** which once pressed monks' grapes and farmers' grain, and crushed gypsum rocks into powdery plaster of Paris (there were once 30 windmills on Montmartre). When the gypsum mines closed (c. 1850) and the vineyards sprouted apartments, this windmill turned into the ceremonial centerpiece of a popular outdoor dance hall. Farther down rue Lépic, you'll pass near the former homes of **Toulouse-Lautrec** (at rue Tourlaque—look for the brick-framed art-studio windows under the heavy mansard roof) and **Vincent van Gogh** (54 rue Lépic).

Dalí Museum (L'Espace Dalí)—This beautifully lit black gallery (well-described in English) offers a walk through statues, etchings, and paintings by the master of Surrealism. The Spaniard found fame in Paris in the 1920s and '30s. He lived in Montmartre for a while, hung with the Surrealist crowd in Montparnasse, and shocked the world with his dreamscape paintings and experimental films. Don't miss the printed interview on the exit stairs.

Cost and Hours: €10, not covered by Museum Pass, daily

10:00–18:00, July–Aug until 20:00, 11 rue Poulbot. Tel. 01 42 64 40 10, www.daliparis.com.

Montmartre Museum (Musée de Montmartre)—This 17th-century home re-creates the traditional cancan and cabaret Montmartre scene, with paintings, posters, photos, music, and memorabilia.

Cost and Hours: €8, includes good audioguide, not covered by Museum Pass, Tue–Sun 11:00–18:00, closed Mon, 12 rue Cortot. Tel. 01 49 25 89 39, www.museedemontmartre.fr.

Pigalle—Paris' red light district, the infamous "Pig Alley," is at the foot of Butte Montmartre. *Ooh la la.* It's more racy than dangerous. Walk from place Pigalle to place Blanche, teasing desperate barkers and fast-talking temptresses. In bars, a €150 bottle of (what would otherwise be) cheap champagne comes with a friend. Stick to the bigger streets, hang on to your wallet, and exercise good judgment. Cancan can cost a fortune, as can can artists in topless bars. After dark, countless tour buses line the streets, reminding us that tour guides make big bucks by bringing their groups to touristy nightclubs like the famous Moulin Rouge (Mo: Pigalle or Abbesses).

Museum of Erotic Art (Musée de l'Erotisme)—Paris' sexy museum has five floors of risqué displays—mostly paintings and drawings—ranging from artistic to erotic to disgusting, with a few circa-1920 porn videos and a fascinating history of local brothels tossed in. It's in the center of the Pigalle red light district.

Cost and Hours: €8, €6/person for small groups of four or more, no...it's not covered by Museum Pass, daily 10:00–2:00 in the morning, 72 boulevard de Clichy, Mo: Blanche. Tel. 01 42 58 28 73, www.musee-erotisme.com.

Shopping in Paris

Even staunch anti-shoppers may be tempted to indulge in chic Paris. Wandering among elegant and outrageous boutiques provides a break from the heavy halls of the Louvre, and, if you approach it right, a little cultural enlightenment.

Here are some tips for avoiding *faux pas* and making the most of the experience.

French Etiquette: Before you enter a Parisian store, remember the following points:

- In small stores, always say, *"Bonjour, Madame or Mademoiselle or Monsieur"* when entering. For extra credit, apologize for bothering the clerk: *"Excusez-moi de vous déranger."* And remember to say *"Au revoir, Madame or Mademoiselle or Monsieur"* when leaving.
- The customer is not always right. In fact, figure the clerk is

doing you a favor by waiting on you.

- Except in department stores, it's not normal for the customer to handle clothing. Ask first before you pick up an item: *"Je peux?"* (zhuh puh), meaning, "Can I?"
- For clothing size comparisons between the US and France, see page 1038 in the appendix.
- Forget returns (and don't count on exchanges).
- Saturday afternoons are *très* busy and not for the faint of heart.
- Observe French shoppers. Then imitate.
- Stores are generally closed on Sunday, except at the Carrousel du Louvre (underground shopping mall at the Louvre), and some shops near Sèvres-Babylone, along the Champs-Elysées, and in the Marais.
- Some small stores don't open until 14:00 on Mondays.
- Don't feel obliged to buy. If a shopkeeper offers assistance, just say, *"Je regarde, merci."* The expression for "window-shopping" in French is *faire du lèche-vitrines* (window-licking).

Here are a few of your options for shopping Parisian-style.

Souvenir Shops—Avoid souvenir carts in front of famous monuments. You can find cheaper gifts around the Pompidou Center, on the streets of Montmartre, and in some department stores (see below). The riverfront stalls near Notre-Dame sell a variety of used books, old posters and postcards, magazines, refrigerator magnets, and other tourist paraphernalia in the most romantic setting. You'll find better deals at the souvenir shops that line rue d'Arcole between Notre-Dame and Hôtel de Ville and on rue de Rivoli, alongside the Louvre.

Department Stores (*Les Grands Magasins*)—Like cafés, department stores were invented here (surprisingly, not in America). Parisian department stores begin with their showy perfume sections, almost always central on the ground floor, and worth a visit to see how much space is devoted to pricey, smelly water. Helpful information desks are usually near the perfume section (handy floor plans in English). Some have a good selection of souvenirs; all sell toys at (relatively) fair prices; most have reasonable restaurants; and some have view terraces. Choose from these great Parisian department stores: Galeries Lafayette (Mo: Chaussée d'Antin–La Fayette, Havre–Caumartin, or Opéra), Printemps (next door to Galeries Lafayette), and Bon Marché (Mo: Sèvres-Babylone). Department stores generally are open Monday through Saturday from 10:00 to 19:00. Some are open later on Thursdays, and all are jammed on Saturdays and closed on Sundays (except in December).

Boutiques—Give yourself a vacation from your sightseeing-focused vacation by sifting through window displays, pausing at corner cafés, and feeling the rhythm of neighborhood life (or have you been playing hooky and doing this already?) Though smaller shops are more intimate, sales clerks are more formal—so mind your manners. Here are three very different areas to lick some windows:

A stroll linking **Bon Marché with St. Sulpice square** allows you to sample smart clothing boutiques and clever window displays while enjoying one of Paris' more attractive neighborhoods. Start at the elegant Bon Marché department store and follow rues de Sèvres and du Vieux Colombier. For sustenance along the way, there's La Maison du Chocolat (19 rue de Sèvres), selling handmade chocolates in exquisitely wrapped boxes; the *très* atmospheric Au Sauvignon Café (10 rue de Sèvres); or Poilâne Bakery (8 rue du Cherche-Midi), where you can find Paris' most celebrated bread.

The ritzy streets connecting **place de la Madeleine and place Vendôme** form a miracle mile of gourmet food shops, glittering jewelry stores, four-star hotels, exclusive clothing boutiques, and people who spend more on clothes in one day than I do all year. Fauchon, at #30 place de la Madeleine, is a bastion of over-the-top food products has faded from its glory days. Today it caters to a largely tourist clientele—though it can still make your mouth water and your pocketbook ache. Hédiard, across the square at #21, is an older, more appealing, and more accessible gourmet food shop. Two doors down, at #19, La Maison des Truffles sells black mushrooms for up to €1,000 a pound, and white truffles from Italy for €2,500 a pound. Small jars of black truffles cost €40.

For more eclectic, avant-garde boutiques, peruse the artsy shops between place des Vosges and the Pompidou Center in the **Marais.** Start at place des Vosges and stick to the west-east axis formed by rue des Francs-Bourgeois, rue des Rosiers, and rue Ste. Croix de la Bretonnerie. This area is rich with jewelry, shoes, and trendy clothing boutiques. On Sunday afternoons, when the rest of Paris naps, the neighborhood comes alive with shoppers and café crowds, and enjoys little car traffic. But it's quiet on Saturdays, when the Jewish community rests.

Flea Markets—Paris' sprawling flea markets (*marché aux puces*; mar-shay oh-poos; *puce* is French for "flea") are oversized garage sales. They started in the Middle Ages, when middlemen sold old, flea-infested clothes and discarded possessions of the wealthy at bargain prices to eager peasants. Buyers were allowed to rummage through piles of aristocratic garbage.

Today **Puces St. Ouen** (poos sahn-wahn), at Porte de Clignancourt, carries on that tradition. This is the mother of all flea markets, with more than 2,000 vendors selling everything from flamingos to faucets, but mostly antiques (Sat 9:00–18:00, Sun 10:00–18:00, Mon 11:00–17:00, closed Tue–Fri, pretty dead the first 2 weeks of Aug, tel. 01 58 61 22 90, www.st-ouen-tourisme .com and www.parispuces.com).

This market shows off Paris', gritty, suburban underbelly and can be intimidating (in Paris, the have-nots live in the burbs, while the haves want to be as central as they can get). No event brings together the melting-pot population of Paris better than this carnival-like market. Some find it claustrophobic, overcrowded, and threatening; others find French *diamants*-in-the-rough and return happy. The markets actually get peaceful the farther in you go. You can bargain a bit (best deals are made with cash at the end of the day), though don't expect swinging deals here.

Wear your money belt and avoid using ATMs at flea markets, as many are tampered with by con artists.

Puces de Vanves is comparatively tiny and civilized, and preferred by many flea-market connoisseurs who find better deals at less famous markets (Sat–Sun 7:00–17:00, many stalls close at 13:00, closed Mon–Fri; Mo: Porte de Vanves). The mega-**Puces de Montreuil** is the least organized and most traditional of them all, with chatty sellers and competitive buyers (Sat–Mon 8:00–18:00, closed Tue–Fri, Mo: Porte de Montreuil).

Market Streets—Several traffic-free street markets overflow with flowers, produce, fish vendors, and butchers, illustrating how most Parisians shopped before there were supermarkets and department stores. Good market streets include rue Cler (Mo: Ecole Militaire), rue Montorgueil (Mo: Etienne Marcel), and rue Mouffetard (Mo: Censier Daubenton). Browse their shops to collect a classy picnic (open daily except Sun afternoons, Mon, and lunchtime throughout the week from 13:00 to 15:00).

Entertainment in Paris

Paris is brilliant after dark. Save energy from your day's sightseeing and experience the City of Light lit. Whether it's a concert at Sainte-Chapelle, a boat ride on the Seine, a walk in Montmartre, a hike up the Arc de Triomphe, or a late-night café, you'll see Paris at its best. Night walks in Paris are wonderful.

The *Pariscope* magazine (€0.40 at any newsstand, in French) offers a complete weekly listing of music, cinema, theater, opera, and other special events. The *Paris Voice* website, in English, has a helpful monthly review of Paris entertainment (www.parisvoice .com).

Music

Jazz and Blues Clubs—With a lively mix of American, French, and international musicians, Paris has been an internationally acclaimed jazz capital since World War II. You'll pay €12–25 to enter a jazz club (may include one drink; if not, expect to pay €5–10 per drink; beer is cheapest). See *Pariscope* magazine under "Musique" for listings, or, even better, the American Church's *Paris Voice* website for a good monthly review. You can also check each club's website (all have English versions), or drop by the clubs to check out the calendars posted on their front doors. Music starts after 21:00 in most clubs. Some offer dinner concerts from about 20:30 on. Here are several good bets:

Caveau de la Huchette, a characteristic, old jazz/dance club, fills an ancient Latin Quarter cellar with live jazz and frenzied dancing every night (admission about €12 on weekdays, €14 on weekends, €6–8 drinks, daily 21:30–2:30 in the morning or later, 5 rue de la Huchette, Mo: St. Michel, recorded info tel. 01 43 26 65 05, www.caveaudelahuchette.fr).

For a spot teeming with late-night activity and jazz, go to the two-block-long rue des Lombards, at boulevard Sébastopol, midway between the river and the Pompidou Center (Mo: Châtelet). **Au Duc des Lombards** is one of the most popular and respected jazz clubs in Paris, with concerts nightly in a great, plush, 110-seat theater-like setting (admission €20–30, cheap drinks, shows at 20:00 and 22:00, 42 rue des Lombards, tel. 01 42 33 22 88, www .ducdeslombards.fr). **Le Sunside,** run for 16 years by Stephane Portet, is just a block away. The club offers two little stages (ground floor and downstairs): "le Sunset" stage features more traditional and acoustic jazz—Dixieland and big band (concerts range from free to €20, check their website, generally at 21:00, 60 rue des Lombards, tel. 01 40 26 21 25, www.sunset-sunside.com).

For a less pricey—and less central—concert club, try **Utopia.** From the outside it's a hole in the wall, but inside it's filled with devoted fans of rock and folk blues. Though Utopia is officially a private club (and one that permits smoking), you can pay €3 to join for an evening, then pay a reasonable charge for the concert (usually €10 or under, concerts start about 22:00). It's located in the Montparnasse area (79 rue de l'Ouest, Mo: Pernety, tel. 01 43 22 79 66, www.utopia-cafeconcert.fr).

Old-Time Parisian Cabaret on Montmartre: Au Lapin Agile—This historic cabaret maintains the atmosphere of the heady days when bohemians would gather here to enjoy wine, song, and sexy jokes. For €24 (€17 for students) you gather with about 25 French people in a dark room for a drink and as many as 10 different performers—mostly singers with a piano. Performers range from sweet and innocent Amélie types to naughty Maurice Chevalier types. And though tourists are welcome, it's exclusively French, with no accommodation for English speakers (except on their website), so non-French-speakers will be lost. You sit at carved wooden tables in a dimly lit room, taste the traditional drink (brandy with cherries), and are immersed in a true Parisian ambience. The soirée covers traditional French standards, love ballads, sea chanteys, and more. The crowd sings along, as it has here for a century (€7 drinks, Tue–Sun 21:00–2:00 in the morning, closed Mon, best to reserve ahead, 22 rue des Saules, tel. 01 46 06 85 87, www.au-lapin-agile.com).

A Modern Cabaret near Canal St. Martin: Chez Raymonde—
This club proves that the art of dinner cabaret is still alive in Paris. Your evening begins with a good three-course dinner (including apéritif, wine, a half-bottle of champagne, and coffee) in an intimate dining room, where you get to know your neighbors. Around 22:00 the maître d'hôtel and the chef himself kick off the performance with a waltz together. Then it's feather boas, song, and dance—audience participation is encouraged (€55–100/person based on how elaborate a *menu* you choose, Fri-Sat evenings only, dinner starts at 20:00 when *le chef* greets you in person, performance usually finishes about 23:00, reservations necessary, 119 avenue Parmentier, Mo: Goncourt, Parmentier, or République, tel. 01 43 55 26 27, www.chez-raymonde.com). On Sunday afternoons, you can also attend a performance over lunch (same prices, starts at 12:30).

Classical Concerts—For classical music on any night, consult *Pariscope* magazine (check "Concerts Classiques" under "Musique" for listings) and look for posters at tourist-oriented churches.

From March through November, these churches regularly host concerts: St. Sulpice, St. Germain-des-Prés, La Madeleine, St. Eustache, St. Julien-le-Pauvre, and Sainte-Chapelle.

At **Sainte-Chapelle**, it's well worth the money for the pleasure of hearing Mozart, Bach, or Vivaldi, surrounded by the stained glass of the tiny church (unheated—bring a sweater). The acoustical quality is surprisingly good. There are usually two concerts per evening, at 19:00 and 20:30; specify which one you want when you buy or reserve your ticket. "Prestige" tickets get you a seat in the first seven rows; "normal" tickets are everything else. Seats are unassigned, so arrive at least 30 minutes early to snare a good view and to get through the security line. Two companies put on concerts—pick up schedules and tickets during the day at the small ticket booth to the left of the chapel entrance gate (€30 prestige, €25 normal; 4 boulevard du Palais, Mo: Cité; call 01 42 77 65 65 or 06 67 30 65 65 for schedules and reservations, you can leave your message in English—just speak clearly and spell your name; www.archetspf.asso.fr). Flavien from Euromusic offers discounts with this book (limit 2 tickets per book, prestige tickets discounted to €16, normal discounted to €25, offer applies to Euromusic concerts and must be purchased with cash only at the

Sainte-Chapelle ticket booth). The evening entrance is at 4 boulevard du Palais, between the gilded gate of the Palais de Justice and the Conciergerie. You'll enter through the law courts hall, directly into the royal upper chapel, just as St. Louis once did.

The **Salle Pleyel** hosts world-class artists, from string quartets and visiting orchestras to international opera stars. Tickets are usually expensive and hard to come by, so it's best to order online in advance (252 rue du Faubourg Saint-Honoré, Mo: Ternes, tel. 01 42 56 13 13, www.sallepleyel.fr).

Look also for daytime concerts in parks, such as the Luxembourg Garden. Even the Galeries Lafayette department store offers concerts. Many concerts are free (*entrée libre*), such as the Sunday atelier concert sponsored by the American Church (generally Sept–June at 17:00 but not every week, 65 quai d'Orsay, Mo: Invalides, RER: Pont de l'Alma, tel. 01 40 62 05 00, www.acparis.org).

Opéra—Paris is home to two well-respected opera venues. The **Opéra Bastille** is the massive modern opera house that dominates place de la Bastille. Come here for state-of-the-art special effects and modern interpretations of classic ballets and operas. In the spirit of this everyman's opera, unsold seats are available at a big discount to seniors and students 15 minutes before the show. Standing-room-only tickets for €15 are also sold for some performances (Mo: Bastille). The **Opéra Garnier**, Paris' first opera house, hosts opera and ballet performances. Come here for less expensive tickets and grand belle époque decor (Mo: Opéra). To get tickets for either opera house, it's easiest to reserve online at www.operadeparis.fr, or call 01 71 25 24 23 outside France or toll tel. 08 92 89 90 90 inside France. You can also go direct to the Opéra Bastille's ticket office (open daily 11:00–18:00).

Art in the Evening

Various museums are open late on different evenings, offering the opportunity for more relaxed, less crowded visits (see "Daily Reminder" on page 58).

In summer, sound-and-light displays at the Notre-Dame Cathedral illuminate its history. They generally run twice a week (free, in French with English subtitles, usually Thu and Sat at 21:00 but schedule varies—check www.cathedraledeparis.com). There is also an elaborate sound-and-light show at the Château in Versailles on Saturdays (€21, June–Aug at 21:00, www.chateauversailles.fr).

Night Walks

Go for an evening walk to best appreciate the City of Light. Break for ice cream, pause at a café, and enjoy the sidewalk entertainers as you join the post-dinner Parisian parade. Remember to avoid poorly lit areas and stick to main thoroughfares. Consider the following suggestions:

▲▲▲**Trocadéro and Eiffel Tower**—This is one of Paris' most spectacular views at night. Take the Métro to the Trocadéro stop and join the party on place du Trocadéro for a magnificent view of the glowing Eiffel Tower. It's a festival of hawkers, gawkers, drummers, and entertainers. To enjoy the same view from a comfortable seat with a drink in your hand, find **Café de l'Homme** on the west side of the terrace (daily 12:00 until "the heart of the night," but closed on occasion for private events, 17 place du Trocadéro, enter through Musée de la Marine, tel. 01 44 05 30 15).

Walk down the stairs, passing the fountains and rollerbladers, then cross the river to the base of the tower, worth the effort even if you don't go up (tower open daily mid-June–Aug until 24:45, Sept–mid-June until 23:45). See "Eiffel Tower" on page 103.

From the Eiffel Tower you can stroll through the Champ de Mars park past tourists and romantic couples, and take the Métro home (Ecole Militaire stop, across avenue de la Motte-Picquet from far southeast corner of park). Or there's a handy RER stop (Champ de Mars–Tour Eiffel) two blocks west of the Eiffel Tower.

▲▲**Champs-Elysées and the Arc de Triomphe**—The avenue des Champs-Elysées glows after dark. Start at the Arc de Triomphe (observation deck open daily, April–Sept until 23:00, Oct–March until 22:30), then stroll down Paris' lively grand promenade. A right turn on avenue George V leads to the Bateaux-Mouches river cruises. A movie on the Champs-Elysées is a fun experience (weekly listings in *Pariscope* under "Cinéma"), and a drink or snack at Renault's futuristic car café is a kick (at #53, toll tel. 08 11 88 28 11).

▲**Ile St. Louis and Notre-Dame**—This stroll features floodlit views of Notre-Dame and a taste of the Latin Quarter. Take the Métro (line 7) to the Pont Marie stop, then cross pont Marie to Ile St. Louis. Turn right up rue St. Louis-en-l'Ile, stopping for dinner—or at least a Berthillon ice cream (several locations) or Amorino Gelati at #47. At the end of Ile St. Louis, cross pont St. Louis to Ile de la Cité, with a great view of Notre-Dame. Wander to the Left Bank on quai de l'Archevêché, and drop down to the river to the right for the best floodlit views. From May through September you'll find several permanently moored barges (*péniches*) that operate as bars. Although I wouldn't eat dinner on one of these barges, the atmosphere is great for a drink, often including live music on weekends (daily until 2:00 in the morning, closed Oct–April, live music often Thu–Sun from 21:00). End your walk on place du Parvis Notre-Dame in front of Notre-Dame (on Sat–

Sun June–Aug, tower open until 23:00), or go back across the river to the Latin Quarter.

After-Dark Tours

Several companies offer evening tours of Paris. You can take a traditional, mass-produced bus tour for €28 per person, or for about the same price (€90 for 3 people) take a vintage car tour with a student guide. Do-it-yourselfers can save money by hiring a cab for a private tour (€50 for one hour). All options are described here.

▲▲▲**Deux Chevaux Car Tours**—If rumbling around Paris, sticking your head out of the rolled-back top of a funky old 2CV car à la Inspector Clouseau sounds like your kind of fun, do this. Paris Authentic has assembled a veritable fleet of these "tin-can" cars (not made since 1985) for giving tourists tours of Paris day and night. Night is best.

The student-guides are informal, speak English, and are passionate about showing you their city. The tours are flexible—you tell them where you'd like to go (use the taxi tour route described later). Trust your guide's detour suggestions and ask to get out as often as you like. Appreciate the simplicity of the vehicle you're in (France's version of the VW "bug"). Notice the bare-bones dashboard. Ask your guide to honk the horn, to run the silly little wipers, and to open and close the air vent—*c'est magnifique!* They'll pick you up and drop you at your hotel or wherever you choose (€80/hour for 1–2 person tour, €90/hour for 3 people, their 2-hour tour includes Montmartre and a bottle of champagne, 10 percent tip is appropriate, 23 rue Jean Jacques Rousseau, mobile 06 64 50 44 19, www.parisauthentic.com, paris@parisauthentic.com).

Nighttime Bus Tours—I list two different tours run by Paris Vision. Tickets are sold through your hotel (no booking fee, brochures in lobby) or directly at the Paris Vision office at 214 rue de Rivoli, across the street from the Tuileries Métro stop.

The nightly **Paris Vision** tour connects all the great illuminated sights of Paris with a 100-minute bus tour in 12 languages. The double-decker buses have huge windows, but the most desirable front seats are sometimes reserved for customers who've bought tickets for the overrated Moulin Rouge. Left-side seats are better. Visibility is fine in the rain.

These tours are not for everyone. You'll stampede on with a United Nations of tourists, get a set of headphones, dial up your language, and listen to a recorded spiel (which is interesting, but includes an annoyingly bright TV screen and a pitch for the other, more expensive excursions). Uninspired as it is, the ride provides an entertaining overview of the city at its floodlit and scenic best.

Bring your city map to stay oriented as you go. You're always on the bus, but the driver slows for photos at viewpoints (€28/person, kids under 12 ride free, 1.5 hours, departs from 214 rue de Rivoli at 19:00 Nov–March, at 22:00 April–Oct, reserve one day in advance, arrive 30 minutes early to wait in line for best seats, tel. 01 42 60 30 01, www.parisvision.com). Skip the pricier minivan night tours.

L'Open Tour uses open-top, double-decker buses, and the guides don't hawk other packages (€25–30, departs from 2 rue des Pyramides at 22:00, 1.5 hours, daily July–Sept, closed Oct–May, must book in advance, tel. 01 42 66 56 56, www. parislopentour.com). If it's warm out, this is a great option.

▲▲▲**Do-It-Yourself Floodlit Paris Taxi Tour**—Seeing the City of Light floodlit is one of Europe's great travel experiences and a great finale to any day in Paris. For less than the cost of two seats on a big bus tour, you can hire your own cab (maximum four passengers) and have a glorious hour of illuminated Paris on your terms and schedule. The downside: You don't have the high vantage point and big windows, and taxi drivers can be moody. The upside: It's cheaper, you go when and where you like, and you can jump out anywhere to get the best views and pictures. I recommend a loop trip that takes about an hour and connects these sights: the Louvre Museum, Hôtel de Ville, Notre-Dame, Ile St. Louis, the Orsay Museum, esplanade des Invalides, Champ de Mars park at place Jacques Rueff (five-minute stop), Eiffel Tower from place du Trocadéro (five-minute stop), Arc de Triomphe, Champs-Elysées, and place de la Concorde. The trip should cost you about €45 (taxis have a strict meter of €33/hour plus about €1/km).

Sleeping in Paris

I've focused most of my recommendations in four safe, handy, and colorful neighborhoods: the village-like rue Cler (near the Eiffel Tower), the artsy and trendy Marais (near place de la Bastille), the historic core (on the two islands in the Seine, Ile St. Louis and Ile de la Cité), and the lively and Latin yet classy Luxembourg (on the Left Bank). Before choosing a hotel, read the descriptions of the neighborhoods closely. Each offers different pros and cons, and your neighborhood is as important as your hotel for the success of your trip.

Reserve ahead for Paris—the sooner, the better. In August and at other times when business is slower, some hotels offer lower rates to fill their rooms. Check their websites for the best deals. For advice on booking rooms, see "Making Reservations" on page 30.

If you're arriving on an overnight flight or train, your room probably won't be ready first thing in the morning. You should be

Sleep Code

(€1 = about $1.25, country code: 33)

S = Single, **D** = Double/Twin, **T** = Triple, **Q** = Quad, **b** = bathroom, **s** = shower only, ***** = French hotel rating system (0–4 stars). Unless otherwise noted, hotel staff speak basic English, credit cards are accepted, and breakfast is not included (but is usually optional). All hotels in these listings have elevators, air-conditioning, Internet access (a public terminal in the lobby for guests to use), and Wi-Fi for travelers with laptops, unless otherwise noted. "Wi-Fi only" means there's no public computer available.

To help you easily sort through these listings, I've divided the rooms into three categories based on the price for a standard double room with bath during high season:

$$$ **Higher Priced**—Most rooms €150 or more.
$$ **Moderately Priced**—Most rooms between €100-150.
$ **Lower Priced**—Most rooms €100 or less.

Prices can change without notice; verify the hotel's current rates online or by email. For other updates, see www.ricksteves.com/update.

---

able to safely check your bag at the hotel and dive right into Paris.

Old, characteristic, budget Parisian hotels have always been cramped. Retrofitted with toilets, private showers, and elevators (as most are today), they are even more cramped. French hotels must charge a daily room tax (*taxe du séjour*) of about €1–2 per person per day. Some hotels include it in the price list, but most add it to your bill. Get advice from your hotel for safe parking (for parking basics, see page 57).

In the Rue Cler Neighborhood
(7th arrondissement, Mo: Ecole Militaire, La Tour Maubourg, or Invalides)

Rue Cler, lined with open-air produce stands six days a week, is a safe, tidy, village-like pedestrian street. It's so French that when I step out of my hotel in the morning, I feel like I must have been a poodle in a previous life. How such coziness lodged itself between the high-powered government district and the wealthy Eiffel Tower and Les Invalides areas, I'll never know. This is a neighborhood of wide, tree-lined boulevards, stately apartment buildings, and lots of Americans. The American Church and Franco-American Center (see page 52), American Library, American University, and many of my readers call this area home. Hotels here are a relatively good value, considering the elegance of the neighborhood and the higher prices of the more cramped hotels in other central areas. And for sightseeing, you're within walking distance of the Eiffel Tower, Army Museum, Quai Branly Museum, Seine River, Champs-Elysées, and Orsay and Rodin museums.

Become a local at a rue Cler café for breakfast, or join the afternoon crowd for *une bière pression* (a draft beer). On rue Cler you can eat and browse your way through a street full of cafés, pastry shops, delis, cheese shops, and colorful outdoor produce stalls. Afternoon *boules* (outdoor bowling) on the esplanade des Invalides is a relaxing spectator sport (look for the dirt area to the upper right as you face the front of Les Invalides; see sidebar on page 1033). The manicured gardens behind the golden dome of the Army Museum are free, peaceful, and filled with flowers (at southwest corner of grounds, closes at about 19:00).

Though hardly a happening nightlife spot, rue Cler offers many low-impact after-dark activities. Take an evening stroll above the river through the parkway between pont de l'Alma and pont des Invalides. For an after-dinner cruise on the Seine, it's a 15-minute walk to the river and the Bateaux-Mouches (see page 71). For a post-dinner cruise on foot, saunter into the Champ de Mars park to admire the glowing Eiffel Tower. For more ideas on Paris after hours, see "Entertainment in Paris," earlier.

Services: There's a large **post office** at the end of rue Cler on avenue de la Motte-Picquet, and a handy **SNCF Boutique** at 80 rue St. Dominique (Mon–Sat 8:30–19:30, closed Sun, get there when it opens to avoid a long wait). At both of these offices, take a number and wait your turn. A smaller post office is closer to the Eiffel Tower on avenue Rapp, one block past rue St. Dominique toward the river.

Markets: Cross the Champ de Mars park to mix it up with bargain-hunters at the twice-weekly open-air market, **Marché Boulevard de Grenelle**, under the Métro, a few blocks southwest of the Champ de Mars park (Wed and Sun until 12:30, between Mo: Dupleix and Mo: La Motte-Picquet–Grenelle). Two grocery stores, both on rue de Grenelle, are open until midnight: **Epicerie de la Tour** (at #197) and **Alimentation** (at corner with rue Cler). **Rue St. Dominique** is the area's boutique-browsing street and well worth a visit if shopping for clothes.

Internet Access: Two Internet cafés compete in this neighborhood: **Com Avenue** is best (about €5/hour, shareable and multiuse accounts, Mon–Sat 10:00–20:00, closed Sun, 24 rue du

Champ de Mars, tel. 01 45 55 00 07); **Cyber World Café** may close in 2011 and is more expensive, but stays open later (about €7/hour, Mon–Sat 12:00–22:00, Sun 12:00–20:00, 20 rue de l'Exposition, tel. 01 53 59 96 54).

Laundry: Launderettes are omnipresent; ask your hotel for the nearest. Here are three handy locations: on rue Augereau (between rue St. Dominique and rue de Grenelle), on rue Amélie (between rue St. Dominique and rue de Grenelle), and at the southeast corner of rue Valadon and rue de Grenelle.

Métro Connections: Key Métro stops are Ecole Militaire, La Tour Maubourg, and Invalides. The useful RER-C line runs from the pont de l'Alma and Invalides stations, serving Versailles to the southwest; the Marmottan Museum to the northwest; and the Orsay Museum, Latin Quarter (St. Michel stop), and Austerlitz train station to the east.

Bus Routes: Smart travelers take advantage of these helpful bus routes (see "Rue Cler Hotels" map for stop locations):

Line #69 runs east-west along rue St. Dominique and serves Les Invalides, Orsay, Louvre, Marais, and Père Lachaise Cemetery (see sidebar on page 65).

Line #63 runs along the river (the quai d'Orsay), serving the Latin Quarter along boulevard St. Germain to the east (ending at Gare de Lyon), and Trocadéro and the Marmottan Museum to the west.

Line #92 runs along avenue Bosquet, north to the Champs-Elysées and Arc de Triomphe (far better than the Métro) and south to the Montparnasse Tower and Gare Montparnasse.

Line #87 runs from avenue Joseph Bouvard in the Champ de Mars park up avenue de la Bourdonnais and serves St. Sulpice, Luxembourg Garden, the Sèvres-Babylone shopping area, the Bastille, and Gare de Lyon (also more convenient than Métro for these destinations).

Line #80 runs on avenue Bosquet, crosses the Champs-Elysées, and serves Gare St. Lazare.

Line #28 runs on boulevard de la Tour Maubourg and serves Gare St. Lazare.

Line #42 runs from avenue Joseph Bouvard in the Champs de Mars park (same stop as #87) to Gare du Nord—a long ride but less tiring than the subway if you're carrying suitcases.

In the Heart of Rue Cler

Many of my readers stay in the rue Cler neighborhood. If you want to disappear into Paris, choose a hotel elsewhere. The first six hotels listed in this section are within Camembert-smelling distance of rue Cler; the others are within a five- to ten-minute stroll.

Rue Cler Hotels

1. Hôtel Relais Bosquet
2. Hôtel du Cadran
3. Hôtel de la Motte Picquet
4. Hôtel Valadon
5. Hôtel Beaugency
6. Grand Hôtel Lévêque
7. Hôtel du Champ de Mars
8. Hôtel Duquesne Eiffel
9. Hôtel La Bourdonnais
10. Hôtel de France
11. Hôtel de Turenne
12. Hôtel de Londres Eiffel
13. Hôtel de la Tulipe
14. Hôtel St. Dominique
15. Hôtel de la Tour Eiffel
16. Hôtel Kensington
17. Hôtel Les Jardins d'Eiffel
18. Hôtel Tour Eiffel Invalides
19. Hôtel Muguet
20. Hôtel de l'Empereur
21. Best Western Eiffel Park
22. Hôtel Eber Mars
23. Hôtel Prince
24. Hôtel la Serre
25. Hôtel Royal Phare
26. Paris Home Studios
27. SNCF Boutique
28. Internet Cafés (2)
29. Launderettes (3)

- **M** Metro Station
- **B** Bus Stop w/ Route #
- **P** Parking
- **T** Taxi Stand
- Pedestrian Zone

(map of Rue Cler hotels with streets: RUE, AVENUE D'ALMA, RAPP, AVENUE, MONT., AVENUE, R. VALENTIN, RUE LOGES, BOSQUET, R. DE L'EXPO., RUE, AUGER, LA BOURDON, RUE DE, AVE DE, RUE BOURDON, TO SEINE RIVER, TO EIFFEL TOWER, CHAMP DE MARS, KIDS' PLAY AREA + PUPPETS, KIDS' PLAYGROUND)

Bus routes: #80, #92, #87, #42, #28

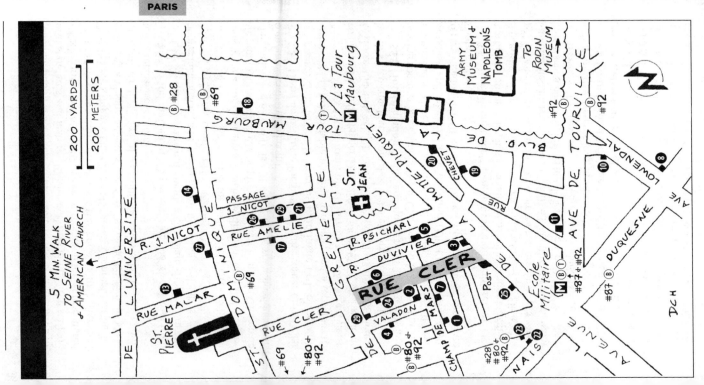

$$$ Hôtel Relais Bosquet*** is an excellent value with generous public spaces and comfortable rooms that are large by local standards and feature effective darkness blinds. The staff are politely formal and offer a 10 percent discount on top of discounted rates to anyone booking direct with this book in 2011 (standard Db-€185–205, bigger Db-€225–245, good €15 breakfast buffet with eggs and sausage, extra bed-€30, 19 rue du Champ de Mars, tel. 01 47 05 25 45, fax 01 45 55 08 24, www.relaisbosquet.com, hotel@relaisbosquet.com).

$$$ Hôtel du Cadran***, perfectly located a *boule* toss from rue Cler, is daringly modern—with a chocolate shop/bar in the lobby, efficient staff, and stylish rooms featuring cool colors, mood lighting, and every comfort (Db-€210–240, 10 percent discount and free (big) breakfast by using the code "RickSteves" when you book by email or through their website, discount not valid on website promo rates, which can be far better deals; 10 rue du Champ de Mars, tel. 01 40 62 67 00, fax 01 40 62 67 13, www.hotelducadran .com, info@cadranhotel.com).

$$$ Hôtel de la Motte Picquet***, at the corner of rue Cler and avenue de la Motte-Picquet, is an intimate little place with narrow halls, comfortable but pricey rooms, and a terrific staff (Moe and Tina). Get a room off the street to avoid street noise (standard Db-€200, bigger Db-€250, Tb/Qb-€300, 30 avenue de la Motte-Picquet, tel. 01 47 05 09 57, fax 01 47 05 74 36, www .hotelmottepicquetparis.com, book@hotelmottepicquetparis.com).

$$$ Hôtel Valadon**, cute and quiet, rents 12 spacious and pleasing rooms a block from the rue Cler action. It's owned by the recommended Hôtel du Cadran (listed above), where you'll have breakfast, and offers the same discounts (Db-€155–165, Tb-€190, 16 rue Valadon, tel. 01 47 53 89 85, www.hotelvaladon.com, info @hotelvaladon.com).

$$ Hôtel Beaugency***, a good value on a quieter street a short block off rue Cler, has 30 small rooms with standard furnishings and a lobby you can stretch out in (Sb-€112–125, Db-€125–165, occasional discounts for Rick Steves readers—ask when you book, 21 rue Duvivier, tel. 01 47 05 01 63, fax 01 45 51 04 96, www .hotel-beaugency.com, infos@hotel-beaugency.com).

Warning: The next two hotels are super values, but very busy with my readers (reserve long in advance).

$$ Grand Hôtel Lévêque**, ideally located on rue Cler, greets travelers with red and gray tones, and a sliver-sized slow-dance elevator. This busy hotel has a sleek breakfast room that doubles as a lounge, but no real lobby. Half the rooms have been nicely renovated and cost more, some need new carpets, and those on rue Cler come with fun views but morning noise as the market sets up (S-€75–95, Db-€95–145, Tb-€140–175, 29 rue Cler, tel.

01 47 05 49 15, fax 01 45 50 49 36, www.hotel-leveque.com, info @hotel-leveque.com, helpful staff).

$ Hôtel du Champ de Mars**, with adorable rooms and serious owners Françoise and Stephane, is a cozy rue Cler option. This plush little hotel has a small-town feel from top to bottom. The rooms are snug but lovingly kept, and single rooms can work as tiny doubles. It's an excellent value despite the lack of air-conditioning. This place gets mixed reviews from readers, who wish the management was more professionally good-natured at all times (Sb–€95, Db–€98, Tb–€129, 30 yards off rue Cler at 7 rue du Champ de Mars, tel. 01 45 51 52 30, fax 01 45 51 64 36, www.hotelduchampdemars.com, reservation@hotelduchampdemars.com).

Near Rue Cler, Close to Ecole Militaire Métro Stop

The following listings are a five-minute walk from rue Cler, near Métro stop Ecole Militaire or RER: Pont de l'Alma.

$$$ Hôtel Duquesne Eiffel***, a few blocks farther from the action, is calm, hospitable, and expertly run. It features handsome rooms (some with terrific Eiffel Tower views for only €20 more), a welcoming lobby, and a big, hot breakfast for €13 (Db–€180–230, price grows with room size, Tb–€250, 10 percent less with this book in 2011, check website for better discounts, 23 avenue Duquesne, tel. 01 44 42 09 09, fax 01 44 42 09 08, www.hde.fr, hotel@hde.fr).

$$$ Hôtel La Bourdonnais*** is *très* Parisian, mixing an Old World feel with creaky, comfortable rooms and generous public spaces. Its mostly spacious rooms are traditionally decorated, and its bathrooms are due for an upgrade (Db–€180–210, Tb–€210, Qb–€235, Sophie promises a 10 percent discount on these prices with this book through 2011, check website for better deals, 111 avenue de la Bourdonnais, tel. 01 47 05 45 42, fax 01 45 55 75 54, www.hotellabourdonnais.fr, hlb@hotellabourdonnais.fr).

$$ Hôtel de France** is a good mid-range option away from most other hotels I list. It's well-run by a brother-sister team (Alain and Marie-Hélène) with a small bar/lounge and 60 fairly priced and well-maintained rooms, some with knockout views of Invalides' golden dome. Rooms on the courtyard are very quiet (Sb–€95, standard Db–€115, bigger Db–€155, Tb–€165, connecting rooms possible for families, no air-con, 102 boulevard de la Tour Maubourg, tel. 01 47 05 40 49, fax 01 45 56 96 78, www.hoteldefrance.com, hoteldefrance@wanadoo.fr).

$ Hôtel de Turenne** is modest, with the cheapest air-conditioned rooms I've found and a lobby with windows on the world. Rooms are simple but comfortable, and the price is right. There are five true singles and several connecting rooms good for families (Sb–€70, Db–€84–104, Tb–€130, Wi-Fi only, 20 avenue de Tourville, tel. 01 47 05 99 92, fax 01 45 56 06 04, www.hotel -turenne-paris.com, hotel.turenne.paris7@wanadoo.fr).

Near Rue Cler, Closer to Rue St. Dominique (and the Seine)

$$$ Hôtel de Londres Eiffel*** is my closest listing to the Eiffel Tower and the Champ de Mars park. Here you get immaculate, warmly decorated rooms (several are connecting for families), cozy public spaces, and a service-oriented staff. Some rooms are tight—request a bigger room. Show them this book in 2011 for a free Seine cruise (inquire upon arrival). It's less convenient to the Métro (10-minute walk), but handy to buses #69, #80, #87, and #92, and to RER-C: Pont de l'Alma (Sb-€165, small Db-€190, bigger Db-€205, DB with Eiffel Tower view-€230, Tb-€260, 1 rue Augereau, tel. 01 45 51 63 02, fax 01 47 05 28 96, www.londres -eiffel.com, info@londres-eiffel.com). The owners also run a good two-star hotel with similar comfort in the cheaper Montparnasse area, **$$ Hôtel Apollon Montparnasse** (Db-€115–145, look for web deals, 91 rue de l'Ouest, Mo: Pernety, tel. & fax 01 43 95 62 00, www.paris-hotel-paris.net, apollonm@wanadoo.fr).

$$$ Hôtel de la Tulipe***, three blocks from rue Cler toward the river, feels pricey but unique. The 20 small but artistically decorated rooms—each one different—come with stylish little bathrooms and surround a seductive, wood-beamed lounge and a peaceful, leafy courtyard (Db-€160, Tb-€180, two-room suite for up to five people-€295, no air-con, no elevator, pay Wi-Fi, 33 rue Malar, tel. 01 45 51 67 21, fax 01 47 53 96 37, www.paris-hotel -tulipe.com, hoteldelatulipe@wanadoo.fr).

$$ Hôtel St. Dominique**, well-located in the thick of rue St. Dominique, has fair rates, formal service, an inviting lobby, a small courtyard, a lovely breakfast room and traditionally decorated rooms—most with minibars (standard Db-€140, big Db-€160, extra bed-€20, no air-con, no elevator, Wi-Fi only, 62 rue St. Dominique, tel. 01 47 05 51 44, fax 01 47 05 81 28, www.hotel stdominique.com, saint-dominique.reservations@wanadoo.fr).

$ Hôtel de la Tour Eiffel** is a good two-star value on a quiet street near several of my favorite restaurants. The rooms are well-designed but have thin walls, and some are desperately in need of new carpets (snug Db-€89–105, bigger Db-€105–129, no air-con, no breakfast offered, Wi-Fi only, 17 rue de l'Exposition, tel. 01 47 05 14 75, fax 01 47 53 99 46, www.hotel-toureiffel.com, hte7 @wanadoo.fr).

$ Hôtel Kensington* is a good budget value close to the Eiffel Tower and run by elegant, though formal, Daniele. It's an unpretentious place with mostly small, simple, but well-kept rooms (Sb-€63, Db-€80, big Db on back side-€96, Eiffel Tower views for those who ask, no air-con, pay Internet access, 79 avenue de la Bourdonnais, tel. 01 47 05 74 00, fax 01 47 05 25 81, www.hotel-kensington.com, hk@hotel-kensington.com).

Near La Tour Maubourg Métro Stop

The next four listings are within three blocks of the intersection of avenue de la Motte-Picquet and boulevard de la Tour Maubourg.

$$$ Hôtel Les Jardins d'Eiffel*, on a quiet street, feels like the modern motel it is, with professional service, its own parking garage (€24/day), and a spacious lobby. Rooms are spacious and peaceful (for Paris) and come in modern or traditional decor (Db–€215–240; 15 percent Rick Steves discount for direct booking through 2011, or check website for special discounts; 8 rue Amélie, tel. 01 47 05 46 21, fax 01 45 55 28 08, www.hoteljardinseiffel.com, paris@hoteljardinseiffel.com).

$$$ Hôtel Tour Eiffel Invalides* advertises its Best Western status proudly and offers a generous-size lobby with a small courtyard and good, traditionally decorated rooms with big beds but no firm prices (the Internet decides). Allow about €210 for a double, but look for better rates on their website (35 boulevard de la Tour Maubourg, tel. 01 45 56 10 78, fax 01 47 05 65 08, www.timhotel.fr, invalides@timhotel.fr).

$$$ Hôtel Muguet*, a peaceful, stylish, immaculate refuge, gives you three-star comfort for a two-star price. This delightful spot offers 43 tasteful rooms, a greenhouse lounge, and a small garden courtyard. The hands-on owner, Catherine, gives her guests a restful and secure home in Paris (Sb–€115, Db–€150–200, Tb–€205, 11 rue Chevert, tel. 01 47 05 05 05 Db with view–€175–205, fax 01 45 50 25 37, www.hotelmuguet.com, muguet@wanadoo.fr, gentle Jacqueline runs reception).

$$$ Hôtel de l'Empereur is well-run and offers good service. It delivers smashing views of Invalides from most of its very comfortable and tastefully designed rooms. Fifth-floor rooms have small balconies, and all rooms have queen-size beds (Sb–€115, Db–€150–175, Tb–€195, two-room Qb–€340, 2 rue Chevert, tel. 01 45 55 88 02, fax 01 45 51 88 54, www.hotelempereurparis.com, contact@hotelempereur.com).

Lesser Values in the Rue Cler Area

Given how nice this area is, these are acceptable last choices.

$$$ Best Western Eiffel Park* is a dead-quiet concrete business hotel with all the comforts, 36 pleasant if sterile rooms, and a rooftop terrace (Db–€270, bigger "premium" Db–€340, check online for promotional rates, 17 bis rue Amélie, tel. 01 45 55 10 01, fax 01 47 05 28 68, www.eiffelpark.com, reservation@eiffelpark.com).

$$ Hôtel Eber Mars** has larger-than-most rooms with weathered furnishings, oak-paneled public spaces, and a beam-me-up-Jacques coffin-sized elevator. Half the rooms are newly renovated, air-conditioned, and pricey; the higher rates listed are for those rooms (Db–€130–190, 20 percent cheaper Nov–March and July–Aug, first breakfast free with this book in 2011, 117 avenue de la Bourdonnais, tel. 01 47 05 42 30, fax 01 47 05 45 91, www.hotelebermars.com, reservation@hotelebermars.com).

$$ Hôtel Prince**, across from the Ecole Militaire Métro stop, has a spartan lobby, drab halls, and plain-but-acceptable rooms for the price (Sb–€90, Db with shower–€115, Db with tub–€130, Tb–€150, Wi-Fi only, 66 avenue Bosquet, tel. 01 47 05 40 90, fax 01 47 53 06 62, www.hotelparisprince.com, paris@hotel-prince.com).

$$ Hôtel la Serre**, a modest place with basic comfort, some rough edges, and acceptable rates, is right on rue Cler (D–€80–120, 24 rue Cler, tel. 01 47 05 52 33, fax 01 40 62 95 66, www.hotella serreparis.com, hotellaserre@wanadoo.fr).

$ Hôtel Royal Phare**, facing the busy Ecole Militaire Métro stop, is a humble place. The 34 basic, pastel rooms are unimaginative but sleepable. Rooms on the courtyard are quietest, with peek-a-boo views of the Eiffel Tower from the fifth floor up (Sb–€84, Db with shower–€98, Db with tub–€108, Tb–€120, fridges in rooms, no air-con but fans, no Wi-Fi, 40 avenue de la Motte-Picquet, tel. 01 47 05 57 30, fax 01 45 51 64 41, www.hotel-royalphare-paris .com, hotel-royalphare@wanadoo.fr, friendly manager Hocin).

In the Marais Neighborhood
(4th arrondissement, Mo: Bastille, St. Paul, and Hôtel de Ville)

Those interested in a more SoHo/Greenwich Village-type locale should make the Marais their Parisian home. Once a forgotten Parisian backwater, the Marais—which runs from the Pompidou Center to the Bastille (a 15-minute walk)—is now one of Paris' most popular residential, tourist, and shopping areas. This is jumbled, medieval Paris at its finest, where classy stone mansions sit alongside trendy bars, antiques shops, and fashion-conscious boutiques. The streets are a fascinating parade of artists, students, tourists, immigrants, and baguette-munching babies in strollers. The Marais is also known as a hub of the Parisian gay and lesbian scene. This area is *sans doute* livelier (and louder) than the rue Cler area.

In the Marais you have these major sights close at hand: the

Carnavalet Museum, Victor Hugo's House, the Jewish Art and History Museum, the Pompidou Center, and the Picasso Museum (closed for a multiyear renovation). You're also a manageable walk from Paris' two islands (Ile St. Louis and Ile de la Cité), home to Notre-Dame and Sainte-Chapelle. The Opéra Bastille, Promenade Plantée park, place des Vosges (Paris' oldest square), Jewish Quarter (rue des Rosiers), the Latin Quarter, and nightlife-packed rue de Lappe are also walkable. Strolling home (day or night) from Notre-Dame along the Ile St. Louis is marvelous. (For Marais sight descriptions, see page 121; for the Opéra, see page 137.)

Most of my recommended hotels are located a few blocks north of the Marais' main east-west drag, rue St. Antoine/rue de Rivoli.

Tourist Information: The nearest TI is in Gare de Lyon (Mon–Sat 8:00–18:00, closed Sun, all-Paris TI toll tel. 08 92 68 30 00).

Services: Most banks and other services are on the main street, rue de Rivoli, which becomes rue St. Antoine. Marais **post offices** are on rue Castex and at the corner of rue Pavée and rue des Francs Bourgeois. There's a busy **SNCF Boutique** where you can take care of all train needs on rue St. Antoine at rue de Turenne (Mon–Sat 8:30–20:30, closed Sun). A quieter SNCF Boutique is nearer Gare de Lyon at 5 rue de Lyon (Mon–Sat 8:30–18:00, closed Sun).

Markets: The Marais has two good open-air markets: the sprawling **Marché de la Bastille,** along boulevard Richard Lenoir, on the north side of place de la Bastille (Thu and Sun until 14:30, arts market Sat 10:00–19:00); and the more intimate, untouristy **Marché de la place d'Aligre** (Tue–Sun 9:00–14:00, closed Mon, closed Mon, cross place de la Bastille and walk about 10 blocks down rue du Faubourg St. Antoine, turn right at rue de Cotte to place d'Aligre; or, take Métro line 8 from Bastille in the direction of Créteil-Préfecture, get off at the Ledru-Rollin stop, and walk a few blocks southeast). A small **grocery** is open until 23:00 on rue St. Antoine (near intersection with rue Castex). To shop at a Parisian Sears, find the **BHV** next to Hôtel de Ville. Paris' oldest covered market, **Marché des Enfants Rouges,** lies a 10-minute walk north of rue de Rivoli.

Bookstore: The Marais is home to the friendliest English-language bookstore in Paris, **Red Wheelbarrow.** Penelope sells most of my guidebooks at good prices, and carries a great collection of other books about Paris and France for both adults and children (Mon 10:00–18:00, Tue–Sat 10:00–19:00, Sun 14:00–18:00, 22 rue St. Paul, Mo: St. Paul, tel. 01 48 04 75 08).

Internet Access: Try **Paris CY** (Mon–Sat 8:00–20:00, Sun 13:00–20:00, 8 rue de Jouy, Mo: St. Paul, tel. 01 42 71 37 37).

Marais Hotels

1. Hôtel Castex
2. Hôtel Bastille Spéria
3. Hôtel de la Place des Vosges
4. Hôtel du 7ème Art
5. Grand Hôtel Jeanne d'Arc
6. Hôtel Lyon-Mulhouse
7. Hôtel Daval
8. Hôtel Sévigné
9. Hôtel du Sully
10. MIJE Hostels (3)
11. Hôtel Caron de Beaumarchais
12. Hôtel de la Bretonnerie
13. Hôtel Beaubourg
14. Hôtel de Nice

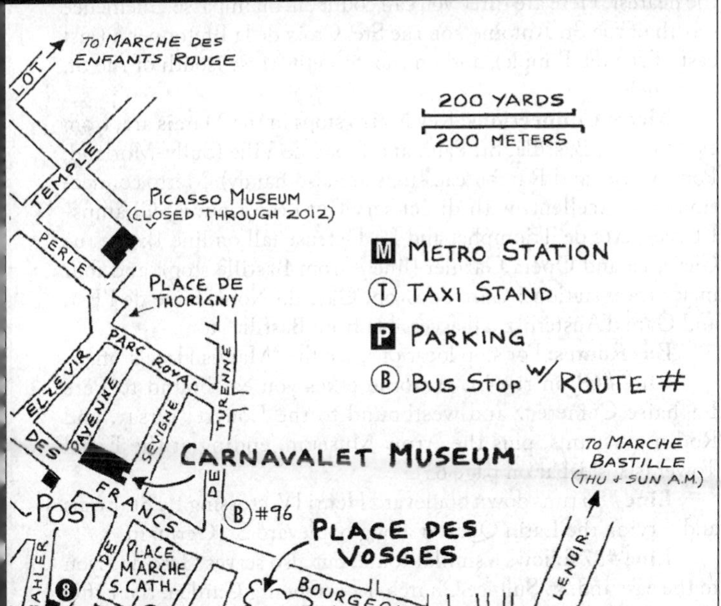

To Marche des Enfants Rouge
200 Yards
200 Meters
Picasso Museum (Closed through 2012)
Metro Station
Taxi Stand
Parking
Bus Stop w/ Route #
Place de Thorigny
Carnavalet Museum
To Marche Bastille (Thu + Sun A.M.)
Place des Vosges
Place Marche S. Cath.
Rue St. Antoine Exit
Place de la Bastille
Opera Bastille
Canauxrama Boat Dock
Sully Morland
Bastille
Lot
Temple
Perle
Parc Royal
Elzevir
Payenne
Sevigne
Turenne
Des Francs Post
Mahler
Rue de
Bourgeois
Beaumarchais
Rich. Lenoir
R. Roquette
Rue de Lappe
Rue St. Antoine
St. Paul
Biraque
Beautrellis
Charles
Castex
Post
Blvd. Henri IV
Rue de Petit Musc
#69
#96
#65
#86 + #87

⓯ Hôtel du Loiret
⓰ Hôtel Saint-Louis Marais
⓱ Hôtel du Vieux Marais
⓲ SNCF Boutique
⓳ BHV Department Store
⓴ Late-Night Grocery
㉑ Red Wheelbarrow Books
㉒ Internet Café
㉓ Launderettes (3)

Laundry: There are many launderettes; ask your hotelier for the nearest. Here are three you can count on: on impasse Guémenée (north of rue St. Antoine), on rue Ste. Croix de la Bretonnerie (just east of rue du Temple), and on rue du Petit Musc (south of rue St. Antoine).

Métro Connections: Key Métro stops in the Marais are, from east to west: Bastille, St. Paul, and Hôtel de Ville (Sully-Morland, Pont Marie, and Rambuteau stops are also handy). Métro connections are excellent, with direct service to the Louvre, Champs-Elysées, Arc de Triomphe, and La Défense (all on line 1); the rue Cler area and Opéra Garnier (line 8 from Bastille stop); and four major train stations: Gare de Lyon, Gare du Nord, Gare de l'Est, and Gare d'Austerlitz (all accessible from Bastille stop).

Bus Routes: For stop locations, see the "Marais Hotels" map.

Line #69 on rue St. Antoine takes you eastbound to Père Lachaise Cemetery and westbound to the Louvre, Orsay, and Rodin museums, plus the Army Museum, ending at the Eiffel Tower (see sidebar on page 65).

Line #86 runs down boulevard Henri IV, crossing Ile St. Louis and serving the Latin Quarter along boulevard St. Germain.

Line #87 follows a similar route, but also serves Gare de Lyon to the east and St. Sulpice Church/Luxembourg Garden, the Eiffel Tower, and the rue Cler neighborhood to the west.

Line #96 runs on rues Turenne and François Miron and serves the Louvre and boulevard St. Germain (near Luxembourg Garden), ending at Gare Montparnasse.

Line #65 runs from Gare de Lyon up rue de Lyon, around place de la Bastille, and then up boulevard Beaumarchais to Gare de l'Est and Gare du Nord.

Taxis: You'll find taxi stands on place de la Bastille (where boulevard Richard Lenoir meets the square), on the south side of rue St. Antoine (in front of St. Paul Church), behind the Hôtel de Ville on rue du Lobau (where it meets rue de Rivoli), and a quieter one on the north side of rue St. Antoine (where it meets rue Castex).

Near Place des Vosges

$$$ Hôtel Castex****, on a quiet street near place de la Bastille, is a well-managed place with tile-floored rooms (that amplify noise). Their clever system of connecting rooms allows families total privacy between two rooms, each with its own bathroom. The 30 rooms are narrow. Your fourth night is free in August and from November through February, except around New Year's (Sb–€130, Db–€160, Tb–€230, 5 percent discount and free but mediocre buffet breakfast with this book through 2011, just off place de la Bastille and rue St. Antoine at 5 rue Castex, Mo: Bastille, tel. 01

42 72 31 52, fax 01 42 72 57 91, www.castexhotel.com, info@castexhotel.com).

$$$ **Hôtel Bastille Spéria***, a short block off place de la Bastille, offers business-type service in a great location. The 42 well-configured rooms are modern and comfortable, with big beds (Sb-€140, Db-€160–180, child's bed-€20, good buffet breakfast-€13, 1 rue de la Bastille, Mo: Bastille, tel. 01 42 72 04 01, fax 01 42 72 56 38, www.hotelsperia.com, info@hotelsperia.com).

$$ **Hôtel de la Place des Vosges***, is a shy, low-brow place brilliantly located between rue St. Antoine and place des Vosges. Rooms are spare, there's no air-con, and the elevator skips floors 5 and 6, but the price is right (Db-€107, 12 rue de Biraque, tel. 01 42 72 60 46, fax 01 42 72 02 64, www.hotelplacedesvosges.com, contact@hpdv.net).

$$ **Hôtel du 7eme Art***, two blocks south of rue St. Antoine toward the river, is a young, carefree, Hollywood-nostalgia place with a full-service café-bar and Charlie Chaplin murals. Its 23 good-value rooms have brown 1970s decor, but are comfortable enough. Sadly, smoking is allowed in all rooms, so you might detect an odor. The large rooms are American-spacious (small Db-€95, standard Db-€110, large Db-€125–150, Tb-€145–170, extra bed-€20, no elevator, 20 rue St. Paul, Mo: St. Paul, tel. 01 44 54 85 00, fax 01 42 77 69 10, www.paris-hotel-7art.com, hotel7art@wanadoo.fr).

$ **Grand Hôtel Jeanne d'Arc***, a lovely little hotel with thoughtfully appointed rooms, is ideally located for (and very popular with) connoisseurs of the Marais. It's a good value and worth booking way ahead (three months in advance, if possible). Sixth-floor rooms have views, and corner rooms are wonderfully bright in the City of Light. Rooms on the street can be noisy until the bars close (Sb-€63–91, Db-€91, larger twin Db-€118, Tb-€148, good Qb-€162, no air-con, Wi-Fi only, 3 rue de Jarente, Mo: St. Paul, tel. 01 48 87 62 11, fax 01 48 87 37 31, www.hoteljeannedarc.com, information@hoteljeannedarc.com).

$ **Hôtel Lyon-Mulhouse***, well-managed by gregarious Nathalia, is located on a busy street barely off place de la Bastille. Though less intimate than some, it is a solid deal, with pleasant, relatively large rooms—five are true singles with partial Eiffel Tower views (Sb-€74, Db-€100, Tb-€130, Qb-€150, 8 boulevard Beaumarchais, Mo: Bastille, tel. 01 47 00 91 50, fax 01 47 00 06 31, www.1-hotel-paris.com, hotelyonmulhouse@wanadoo.fr).

$ **Hôtel Daval***, an unassuming place on the *wild side* of place de la Bastille, is ideal for night owls. The rooms are tiny and the halls are narrow, but the rates are good for an air-conditioned place. Ask for a quieter room on the courtyard side if sleep matters (Sb-€81, Db-€89–98, Tb-115, Qb-€130, Wi-Fi only, 21 rue

Daval, Mo: Bastille, tel. 01 47 00 51 23, fax 01 40 21 80 26, www.hoteldaval.com, hoteldaval@wanadoo.fr, Didier).

$ Hôtel Sévigné**, run by straight-faced owner Monsieur Mercier, is a simple little hotel with lavender halls and 30 tidy, comfortable rooms at good prices (Sb–€72, Db–€86–97, Tb–€100–117; one-night, no-refund policy for any cancellation; Wi-Fi only, air-con turned off overnight, 2 rue Malher, Mo: St. Paul, tel. 01 42 72 76 17, fax 01 42 78 68 26, www.le-sevigne.com, contact@le-sevigne.com).

$ Hôtel du Sully, sitting right on rue St. Antoine, is basic, cheap, central, and run by friendly Monsieur Zeroual. The rooms are frumpy, dimly lit, and can smell of smoke, and the entry is narrow, but the hotel offers a fair deal (Db–€68–70, Tb–€84, Qb–€94, no elevator, no air-con, Wi-Fi only, 48 rue St. Antoine, Mo: St. Paul, tel. 01 42 78 49 32, fax 01 44 61 76 50, www.sullyhotelparis.com, sullyhotel@orange.fr).

$ MIJE Youth Hostels: The Maison Internationale de la Jeunesse et des Etudiants (MIJE) runs three classy old residences, ideal for budget travelers. Each is well-maintained, with simple, clean, single-sex (unless your group takes a whole room), one- to four-bed rooms for travelers of any age. The hostels are **MIJE Fourcy** (biggest and loudest, €11 dinners available with a membership card, 6 rue de Fourcy, just south of rue de Rivoli), **MIJE Fauconnier** (no elevator, 11 rue du Fauconnier), and **MIJE Maubisson** (smallest and quietest, no elevator, no outdoor terrace, 12 rue des Barres). None has double beds or air-conditioning; all have private showers in every room (all prices per person: Sb–€50, Db–€37, Tb–€33, Qb–€31, credit cards accepted, includes breakfast but not towels, required membership card–€2.50 extra/person, 7-day maximum stay, rooms locked 12:00–15:00, curfew at 1:00 in the morning). They all share the same contact information (tel. 01 42 74 23 45, fax 01 40 27 81 64, www.mije.com, info@mije.com) and Métro stop (St. Paul). Reservations are accepted (six weeks ahead online, 10 days ahead by phone), though you must show up by noon, or call the morning of arrival to confirm a later arrival time.

Near the Pompidou Center

These hotels are farther west, closer to the Pompidou Center than to place de la Bastille. The Hôtel de Ville Métro stop works well for all of these hotels, unless a closer stop is noted.

$$$ Hôtel Caron de Beaumarchais***, on a busy corner, feels like a fluffy folk museum, with 20 pricey but cared-for and character-filled rooms. Its small lobby is cluttered with bits from an elegant 18th-century Marais house (small Db in back–€160, larger Db facing the front–€185, Wi-Fi only, 12 rue Vieille du Temple, tel. 01 42 72 34 12, fax 01 42 72 34 63, www.carondebeaumarchais.com, hotel@carondebeaumarchais.com).

$$ Hôtel de la Bretonnerie*, three blocks from the Hôtel de Ville, makes a good Marais home. It has a warm, welcoming lobby and 29 well-appointed, good-value rooms with an antique, open-beam warmth (standard "classic" Db-€135, bigger "charming" Db-€165, Db suite-€195, Tb/Qb-€200, Tb/Qb suite-€220, no air-con, between rue Vieille du Temple and rue des Archives at 22 rue Ste. Croix de la Bretonnerie, tel. 01 48 87 77 63, fax 01 42 77 26 78, www.bretonnerie.com, hotel@bretonnerie.com).

$$ Hôtel Beaubourg* is a solid three-star value on a small street in the shadow of the Pompidou Center. The lounge is inviting, and the 28 rooms are comfy, well-appointed, and quiet (standard Db-€140, bigger twin or king-size Db-€160 and worth the extra cost, rates vary wildly by season, 11 rue Simon Le Franc, Mo: Rambuteau, tel. 01 42 74 34 24, fax 01 42 78 68 11, www.hotel beaubourg.com, reservation@hotelbeaubourg.com)

$$ Hôtel de Nice, on the Marais' busy main drag, features a turquoise-and-fuchsia "Marie-Antoinette-does-tie-dye" decor. Its narrow halls are littered with paintings and layered with carpets, and its 23 Old World rooms have thoughtful touches and tight bathrooms. Twin rooms, which cost the same as doubles, are larger and on the street side—but have effective double-paned windows (Sb-€95, Db-€120, Tb-€145, extra bed-€25, Wi-Fi only, reception on second floor, 42 bis rue de Rivoli, tel. 01 42 78 55 29, fax 01 42 78 36 07, www.hoteldenice.com, contact@hoteldenice.com, laissez-faire management).

$ Hôtel du Loiret* is a centrally located and rare Marais budget hotel. It's basic, but the rooms are surprisingly sharp, considering the price and location (Db-€70–90, Tb-€100, no air-con, pay Internet access, no Wi-Fi, expect some noise, 8 rue des Mauvais Garçons, tel. 01 48 87 77 00, fax 01 48 04 96 56, www.hotel-loiret .fr, hotelduloiret@hotmail.com).

Lesser Values in the Marais

These hotels are located on the map on page 152.

$$ Hôtel Saint-Louis Marais, small and tranquil, is tucked away on a residential street between the river and rue St. Antoine. The lobby and 19 rooms have character, but need attention (small Db-€115, standard Db-€140, Tb-€160, no air-con, no elevator, pay Wi-Fi only, parking-€20, 1 rue Charles V, Mo: Sully Morland, tel. 01 48 87 87 04, fax 01 48 87 33 26, www.saintlouismarais.com, marais@saintlouishotels.com).

$$ Hôtel du Vieux Marais, with a quirky owner and modern rooms but a lobby perpetually under construction, lies on a quiet street two blocks east of the Pompidou Center. Say *bonjour* to friendly bulldog Leelou, who runs the little lobby (Sb-€110–125,

Db-€130–165, Wi-Fi only, just off rue des Archives at 8 rue du Plâtre, Mo: Rambuteau or Hôtel de Ville, tel. 01 42 78 47 22, fax 01 42 78 34 32, www.vieuxmarais.com, hotel@vieuxmarais.com).

In the Historic Core of Paris

(4th arrondissement; Mo: Pont Marie, Sully-Morland, and Cité; RER: St-Michel)

This area is smack-dab in the middle of the city, in the peaceful kernel of this busy metropolis. You won't find any budget values here, but the island's village ambience and proximity to the Marais, Notre-Dame, and the Latin Quarter help compensate for higher rates. For background on these two islands, see the "Historic Paris Walk" on page 76.

On Ile St. Louis

The peaceful, residential character of this river-wrapped island, its brilliant location, and its homemade ice cream have drawn Americans for decades, allowing hotels to charge dearly. All of the following hotels are on the island's main drag, rue St. Louis-en-l'Ile, where I list several restaurants (see page 185). Use Mo: Pont Marie or Sully-Morland.

$$$ **Hôtel du Jeu de Paume***** , occupying a 17th-century tennis center, is the most expensive hotel I list in Paris. When you enter its magnificent lobby, you'll understand why. Greet Scoop, *le chien*, then take a spin in the glass elevator for a half-timbered-tree-house experience. The 30 quite comfortable rooms are carefully designed and *très* tasteful, though small for the price (you're paying for the location and sensational public spaces—check for deals on their website). Most rooms face a small garden; all are pin-drop peaceful (standard Db-€335, larger Db-€420, deluxe Db-€480, check for Web deals, €18 breakfast, 54 rue St. Louis-en-l'Ile, tel. 01 43 26 14 18, fax 01 40 46 02 76, www.jeudepaumehotel.com, info@jeudepaumehotel.com).

$$$ **Hôtel de Lutèce*** charges top euro for its island address but comes with a sit-awhile wood-paneled lobby, a real fireplace, and warmly designed rooms. Twin rooms are larger and the same price as double rooms (Db-€200, Tb-€235, 65 rue St. Louis-en-l'Ile, tel. 01 43 26 23 52, fax 01 43 29 60 25, www.hoteldelutece.com, info@hoteldelutece.com).

$$$ **Hôtel des Deux-Iles*** is bright and colorful, with marginally smaller rooms than other hotels on this street (Db-€200, Wi-Fi only, 59 rue St. Louis-en-l'Ile, tel. 01 43 26 13 35, fax 01 43 29 60 25, www.hoteldesdeuxiles.com, info@hoteldesdeuxiles.com).

$$$ **Hôtel Saint-Louis*** has less personality but good enough rooms with parquet floors and comparatively good rates.

Hotels & Restaurants on Ile St. Louis

☼ VIEW
Ⓜ METRO STATION
Ⓑ BATOBUS BOAT STOP

① Hôtel du Jeu de Paume
② Hôtel de Lutèce & Grocery
③ Hôtel des Deux-Iles
④ Hôtel Saint-Louis
⑤ Le Tastevin Rest.
⑥ Rests. La Taverne du Sergeant Recruteur & Nos Ancêtres les Gaulois
⑦ La Brasserie de l'Ile St. Louis
⑧ L'Orangerie & Auberge de la Reine Blanche
⑨ Café Med
⑩ Berthillon Ice Cream (3)
⑪ Amorino Gelati
⑫ Good Picnic Spot

The hotel will be entirely renovated by 2011, so expect some change in rates (Db-€150-165, superior Db-€240, extra bed-€50, Wi-Fi only, 75 rue St. Louis-en-l'Ile, tel. 01 46 34 04 80, fax 01 46 34 02 13, www.hotelsaintlouis.com, slouis@noos.fr).

On Ile de la Cité

$$ Hôtel Dieu Hospitel Paris is the only Paris hotel with an Ile de la Cité address. It's located in the oldest city hospital of Paris, on the square in front of Notre-Dame (find the hospital on the map on page 77). The present building dates from 1877. Originally intended to receive families of patients, it now offers rooms for tourists as well. With just 14 rooms, you must book well in advance. You'll be surprised by the modern, comfortable decor and may even forget you're in a hospital (Sb-€125, Db-€135, some rooms have peek-a-boo views of Notre-Dame, 1 place du Parvis, tel. 01 44 32 01 00, www .hotel-hospitel.com, hospitelhoteldieu@wanadoo.fr). Enter the hotel's main entrance, turn right, follow signs to wing B2, and take the elevator to the sixth floor.

Luxembourg Garden Area
(St. Sulpice to Panthéon)

(5th and 6th arrondissements, Mo: St. Sulpice, Mabillon, Odéon, and Cluny–La Sorbonne; RER: Luxembourg)

This neighborhood revolves around Paris' loveliest park and offers quick access to the city's best shopping streets and grandest café-hopping. Hotels in this central area are expensive; sleeping in the Luxembourg area offers visitors a true Left Bank experience without a hint of the low-end commotion of the nearby Latin Quarter tourist ghetto. The Luxembourg Garden, boulevard St. Germain, Cluny Museum, and Latin Quarter are all at your doorstep. Here you get the best of both worlds: youthful Left Bank energy and the classic trappings that surround the monumental Panthéon and St. Sulpice Church.

Having the Luxembourg Garden as your backyard allows strolls through meticulously cared-for flowers, a great kids' play area, and a purifying escape from city traffic. Place St. Sulpice presents an elegant, pedestrian-friendly square and quick access to some of Paris' best boutiques. Sleeping in the Luxembourg area also puts several movie theaters at your fingertips (at Métro stop: Odéon), as well as lively cafés on boulevard St. Germain, rue de Buci, rue des Canettes, place de la Sorbonne, and place de la Contrescarpe, all of which buzz with action until late.

Although it takes only 15 minutes to walk from one end of this neighborhood to the other, I've located the hotels by the key monument they are close to (St. Sulpice Church, the Odéon Theater, and the Panthéon). Most hotels are within a five-minute walk of the Luxembourg Garden (and none is more than 15 minutes away).

Services: The nearest **TI** is across the river in Gare de Lyon (Mon–Sat 8:00–18:00, closed Sun, all-Paris TI toll tel. 08 92 68 30 00). There are two useful **SNCF Boutiques** for easy train reservations and ticket purchase: at 79 rue de Rennes and at 54 boulevard St. Michel (Mon–Sat 8:30–18:00, closed Sun).

Markets: The colorful street market at the south end of rue Mouffetard is a worthwhile 10- to 15-minute walk from these hotels (Tue–Sat 8:00–12:00 & 15:30–19:00, Sun 8:00–12:00, closed Mon, five blocks south of place de la Contrescarpe, Mo: Place Monge).

Bookstores: The **Village Voice** bookstore carries a full selection of English-language books (including mine), and is near St. Sulpice. Say hello to Michael but don't ask his opinion of *The Da Vinci Code* (Mon 14:00–19:30, Tue–Sat 10:00–19:30, Sun 12:00–18:00, 6 rue Princesse, tel. 01 46 33 36 47). **San Francisco Book Company** is a welcoming bookstore (Mon–Sat 11:00–21:00, Sun 14:00–19:30, 17 rue Monsieur le Prince, tel. 01 43 29 15 70).

Internet Access: You'll find it at **Le Milk** (always open, between the Luxembourg Garden and Panthéon at 17 rue Soufflot).

Métro Connections: Métro lines 10 and 4 serve this area (10 connects to the Austerlitz train station, and 4 runs to the Montparnasse, Est, and Nord train stations). Neighborhood stops are Cluny–La Sorbonne, Mabillon, Odéon, and St. Sulpice. RER-B (Luxembourg station is handiest) provides direct service to Charles de Gaulle airport and Gare du Nord trains, and access to Orly airport on the Orlybus (transfer at Denfert-Rochereau).

Bus Routes: Buses #63, #86, and #87 run eastbound through this area on or near boulevard St. Germain, and westbound along rue des Ecoles, stopping on place St. Sulpice. Lines #63 and #87 provide direct connections west to the rue Cler area. Line #63 also serves the Orsay, Army, Rodin, and Marmottan museums to the west and Gare de Lyon to the east. Lines #86 and #87 run east to the Marais, and #87 continues to Gare de Lyon. Line #96 stops at place St. Sulpice southbound enroute to Gare Montparnasse and runs north along rue de Rennes and boulevard St. Germain into the Marais.

Hotels near St. Sulpice Church

These hotels are all within a block of St. Sulpice Church and two blocks from famous boulevard St. Germain. This is nirvana for boutique-minded shoppers—and you'll pay extra for the location. Métro stops St. Sulpice and Mabillon are equally close.

$$$ Hôtel de l'Abbaye**** is a lovely refuge just west of Luxembourg Garden, and is a find for well-heeled connoisseurs of this area. The hotel's four-star luxury includes refined lounges inside and out, with 44 sumptuous rooms and every amenity at surprisingly reasonable rates (standard Db–€240–260, bigger Db–€352–380, suites and apartments available for €550, includes breakfast, 10 rue Cassette, tel. 01 45 44 38 11, fax 01 45 48 07 86, www.hotel-abbaye.com, hotel.abbaye@wanadoo.fr).

$$$ Hôtel le Récamier,** romantically tucked in the corner of place St. Sulpice, is high-end defined, with designer public spaces, elaborately appointed rooms, and professional service (classic Db–€260, deluxe Db–€290, traditional Db–€330, deluxe rooms offer best value, fitness room, 3 bis place St. Sulpice, tel. 01 43 26 04 89, fax 01 43 26 35 76, www.hotelrecamier.com, contact@hotelrecamier.com).

$$$ Hôtel Relais St. Sulpice*,** burrowed on the small street just behind St. Sulpice Church, is a little boutique hotel with a cozy lounge and 26 pricey and stylish rooms, most surrounding a leafy glass atrium. Top-floor rooms get more light and are worth requesting (Db–€213–260 depending on size, much less off-season, includes breakfast, sauna free for guests, Wi-Fi only, 3

Hotels near Luxembourg Garden

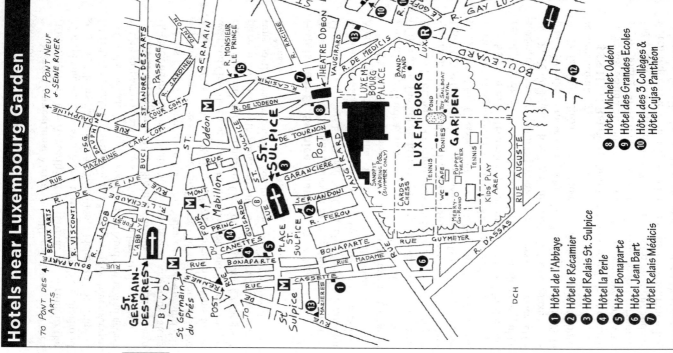

1 Hôtel de l'Abbaye
2 Hôtelle Récamier
3 Hôtel Relais St. Sulpice
4 Hôtel la Perle
5 Hôtel Bonaparte
6 Hôtel Jean Bart
7 Hôtel Relais Médicis
8 Hôtel Michelet Odéon
9 Hôtel des Grandes Ecoles
10 Hôtel des 3 Collèges & Hôtel Cujas Panthéon

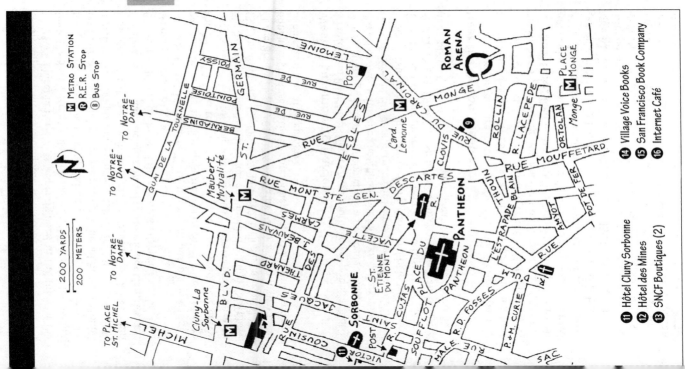

M METRO STATION
R R.E.R. STOP
B BUS STOP

200 YARDS
200 METERS

11 Hôtel Cluny Sorbonne
12 Hôtel des Mines
13 SNCF Boutiques (2)

14 Village Voice Books
15 San Francisco Book Company
16 Internet Café

rue Garancière, tel. 01 46 33 99 00, fax 01 46 33 00 10, www.relais-saint-sulpice.com, relaisstsulpice@wanadoo.fr).

$$$ Hôtel la Perle*** is a spendy pearl in the thick of the lively rue des Canettes, a block off place St. Sulpice. At this snappy, modern, business-class hotel, sliding glass doors open onto the traffic-free street, and you're greeted by a fun lobby built around a central bar and atrium (standard Db-€210, bigger Db-€225, luxury Db-€250, check website or call for last-minute deals within five days of your stay, includes breakfast, 14 rue des Canettes, tel. 01 43 29 10 10, fax 01 46 34 51 04, www.hotellaperle.com, booking @hotellaperle.com).

$$ Hôtel Bonaparte**, an unpretentious place wedged between boutiques, is a few steps from place St. Sulpice. Although the 29 Old World rooms don't live up to the handsome entry, they're plenty comfortable and spacious by Paris standards, with big bathrooms, traditional decor, and molded ceilings (Sb-€107–132, Db-€140-163, big Db-€175, Tb-€182, includes basic breakfast, 61 rue Bonaparte, tel. 01 43 26 97 37, fax 01 46 33 57 67, www.hotel bonaparte.fr, reservation@hotelbonaparte.fr; helpful Fréderic, Sabine, and Eric at reception).

West of Luxembourg Garden

$ Hôtel Jean Bart** feels like it's from another era—prices included. Run by smiling Madame Lechopier, it's a rare budget hotel find in this otherwise swanky neighborhood, one block from Luxembourg Garden. Beyond the dark, retirement home-like lobby, you'll find 33 simple, spotless rooms with creaking floors and tight bathrooms. The cheapest rooms share one shower on the first floor (S-€53, Sb-€71, D-€54, Db-€72, cash only, no air-con, 9 rue Jean-Bart, tel. 01 45 48 29 13, fax 01 45 48 10 79, hotel.jean.bart@gmail.com).

Near the Odéon Theater

These two hotels are between the Odéon Métro stop and Luxembourg Garden (five blocks east of St. Sulpice), and may have rooms when others don't. In addition to the Odéon Métro stop, the RER-B Luxembourg stop is a short walk away.

$$$ Hôtel Relais Médicis*** is perfect in every way—if you've always wanted to live in a Monet painting and can afford it. A glassy entry hides 16 rooms surrounding a fragrant little garden courtyard and fountain, giving you a countryside break fit for a Medici in the heart of Paris. This delightful refuge is taste-fully decorated with floral Old World charm, and is permeated with thoughtfulness (Sb-€172, Db-€208-228, deluxe Db-€258, Tb-€298, Qb-€388, €30 cheaper mid-July-Aug and Nov-March, includes extravagant continental breakfast, faces the Odéon Theater at 23 rue Racine, tel. 01 43 26 00 60, fax 01 40 46 83 39,

Hotels & Restaurants near Rue Mouffetard

1. Hôtel de France
2. Young & Happy Hostel
3. Port-Royal-Hôtel
4. Hôtel de l'Espérance
5. Bar-Restaurant les Papillons
6. Cave de Bourgogne

200 YARDS
200 METERS

Ⓜ METRO STATION

www.relaismedicis.com, reservation@relaismedicis.com).

$$ Hôtel Michelet Odéon** sits in a corner of place de l'Odéon with big windows on the square. Though it lacks personality, it's a fair value in this pricey area, with 24 simple rooms with modern decor and views of the square (Db-€115-135, Tb-€170, Qb-€190, no air-con, pay Wi-Fi, 6 place de l'Odéon, tel. 01 53 10 05 60, fax 01 46 34 55 35, www.hotelmicheletodeon.com, hotel @micheletodeon.com).

Near the Panthéon and Rue Mouffetard

$$ Hôtel des Grandes Ecoles* is idyllic. A private cobbled lane leads to three buildings that protect a flower-filled garden courtyard, preserving a sense of tranquility rare in this city. Its 51 rooms are French-countryside-pretty, spotless, and reasonably spacious, but have no air-conditioning. This romantic spot is deservedly popular, so book ahead, though reservations are not accepted more than four months in advance (Db-€118-143 depending on size, extra bed-€20, Wi-Fi only, 75 rue du Cardinal Lemoine, Mo: Cardinal Lemoine, tel. 01 43 26 79 23, fax 01 43 25 28 15, www.hotel-grandes-ecoles.com, hotel.grandes.ecoles @wanadoo.fr, mellow Marie speaks English, Mama does not).

$$ Hôtel des 3 Collèges** greets clients with a bright lobby, narrow hallways, and unimaginative rooms...but fair rates (Sb-€83–108, Db-€108–150, Tb-€150–170, pay Wi-Fi only, 16 rue Cujas, tel. 01 43 54 67 30, fax 01 46 34 02 99, www.3colleges.com, hotel@3colleges.com).

$ Hôtel Cujas Panthéon** gives traditional two-star comfort *sans* air-conditioning at fair prices (Db-€99–110, Tb-€149, Wi-Fi only, 18 rue Cujas, tel. 01 43 54 58 10, fax 01 43 25 88 02, www .hotelcujaspantheon.com, hotel-cujas-pantheon@wanadoo.fr).

$ Hôtel Cluny Sorbonne** is a modest place warmly run by Monsieur and Madame Berber. It's located in the thick of things across from the famous university and below the Panthéon. Rooms are well-worn with thin walls, but are clean and comfortable (small Db-€95, really big Db/Tb/Qb-€160, check website for deals, no air-con, Wi-Fi only, 8 rue Victor Cousin, tel. 01 43 54 66 66, fax 01 43 29 68 07, www.hotel-cluny.fr, cluny@club-internet.fr).

South of Luxembourg Garden

$$$ Hôtel des Mines** is less central but worth the walk. Its 50 well-maintained rooms are a fair value, and come with updated bathrooms and an inviting lobby (Db-€165, Tb-€195, Qb-€225, less for last-minute bookings and for 3 nights or more, frequent Web deals, between Luxembourg and Port-Royal stations on the RER-B line, a 10-minute walk from Panthéon, one block past Luxembourg Garden at 125 boulevard St. Michel, tel. 01 43 54 32 78, fax 01 46 33 72 52, www.hoteldesminesparis.com, hotel @hoteldesminesparis.com).

Budget Accommodations away from the Center

Acceptable budget accommodations in central neighborhoods are few and far between in Paris. I've listed the best I could find in the neighborhoods above, most at about €100 for a double room. These are great (moderate) budget options, but if you want lower rates or greater selection, you need to look farther away from the river (prices drop proportionately with distance from the Seine). Below you'll find more budget listings in less-central, but still-appealing neighborhoods. You'll spend more time on the Métro or bus getting to sights, but find fewer tourists and save money by sleeping in these areas.

Bottom of Rue Mouffetard

These hotels, away from the Seine and other tourists in an appealing workaday area, offer more room for your euro. Rue Mouffetard is the bohemian soul of this area. Two thousand years ago, it was the principal Roman road south to Italy. Today, this small, meandering street has a split personality. The lower half thrives in the daytime as a pedestrian shopping street. The upper half sleeps during the day, but comes alive after dark. Use Métro stop Censier Daubenton or Les Gobelins. A terrific Saturday market sprawls along boulevard Port Royal, just east of the Port Royal Métro stop.

$$ Hôtel de France**, on a busy street, offers modern rooms with little character. The best and quietest are *sur la cour* (on the courtyard). Stay here only if you score a great promo deal when room prices drop by over 50 percent, which is not unusual (Db-€135–155, Tb-€150–175, 108 rue Monge, Mo: Censier Daubenton, tel. 01 47 07 19 04, fax 01 43 36 62 34, www.hotelfrancequartier latin.com, hotel.de.fce@wanadoo.fr).

$ Young & Happy Hostel is easygoing, well-run, and English-speaking, with Internet access, kitchen facilities, and acceptable hostel conditions. It sits dead-center in the rue Mouffetard action... which can be good or bad (all rates per person: bunk in 4- to 10-bed dorm-€26, in 3- to 5-bed dorm-€28, in double room-€30, includes breakfast, sheets-€2.50, credit cards accepted, no air-con, no lockers but safety box at reception, 11:00–16:00 lockout but reception stays open, no curfew, 80 rue Mouffetard, Mo: Place Monge, tel. 01 47 07 47 07, fax 01 47 07 22 24, www.youngandhappy.fr, smile@youngandhappy.fr).

$ Port-Royal-Hôtel* has only one star, but don't let that fool you. Its 46 rooms are polished top to bottom and have been well-run by the same proud family for 68 years. You could eat off the floors of its spotless, comfy rooms...but you won't find air-conditioning, Internet access, or Wi-Fi. Ask for a room away from the street (S-€42–56, D-€56, Db-€80–90 depending on size, big shower down the hall-€3, cash only, nonrefundable cash deposit required, on busy boulevard de Port-Royal at #8, Mo: Les Gobelins, tel. 01 43 31 70 06, fax 01 43 31 33 67, www.hotelportroyal.fr, portroyal hotel@wanadoo.fr).

$ Hôtel de L'Espérance** is a terrific two-star value. It's quiet and cushy, with soft rooms, canopy beds, and nice public spaces (Sb-€75–80, Db-€80–90, Tb-€107, 15 rue Pascal, Mo: Censier Daubenton, tel. 01 47 07 10 99, fax 01 43 37 56 19, www.hotelde lesperance.fr, hotel.esperance@wanadoo.fr).

Montmartre

Montmartre is surprisingly quiet once you get away from the touristy top of the hill. The neighborhood is young, trendy, and popular with the *bobo* crowd (*bourgeois bohemian*, French for "hipster"). Young and budget-minded travelers will find good deals on hotel rooms and a lively atmosphere.

Most of the action is centered around rue des Abbesses,

Hotels & Restaurants in Montmartre

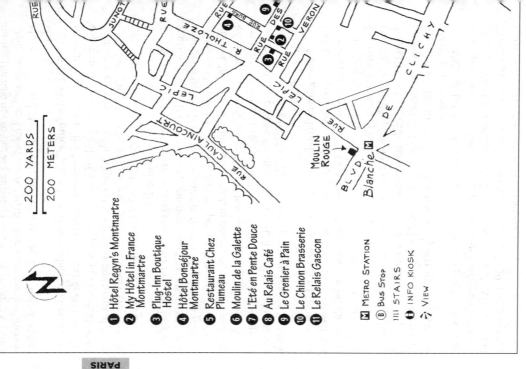

200 YARDS
200 METERS

1 Hôtel Regyn's Montmartre
2 My Hôtel in France Montmartre
3 Plug-Inn Boutique Hostel
4 Hôtel Bonséjour Montmartre
5 Restaurant Chez Plumeau
6 Moulin de la Galette
7 L'Eté en Pente Douce
8 Au Relais Café
9 Le Grenier à Pain
10 Le Chinon Brasserie
11 Le Relais Gascon

M METRO STATION
B BUS STOP
IIII STAIRS
INFO KIOSK
VIEW

starting at place des Abbesses, and stretching several blocks to rue Lépic. Rue Lépic is also lively, but the lower you go the seedier it gets—scammers and shady characters swarm the base of the hill after hours (along boulevard Clichy and boulevard Rouchechouart where you'll find what's left of Paris' red light district). Métro line 12 is the handiest (use the Abbesses stop). Line 2 is also close, using the Blanche, Pigalle, or Anvers stops,

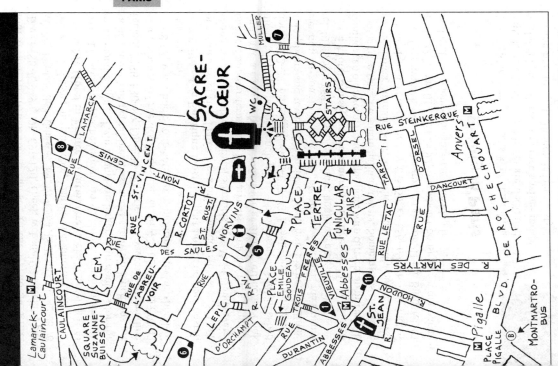

but requires a four-block uphill walk to reach my recommended hotels. There's only one bus line here—the Montmartobus electric bus—which connects Pigalle, Abbesses, and Place du Tertre in 10 minutes (4/hour). For restaurant suggestions, see page 193.

$$ Hôtel Regyn's Montmartre** is located directly on the lively Abbesses square, with 22 small but comfortable rooms, no air-conditioning, and mediocre bathrooms. Rooms in the front come with pleasant views and noise from the square. Guests in fourth- and fifth-floor rooms can see all the way to the Eiffel Tower (Sb-€79–99, Db-€91–120, check website for specials, pay Wi-Fi, 18 place des Abbesses, tel. 01 42 54 45 21, fax. 01 42 23 76 69, www.hotel-regyns-paris.com, hrm18@club-internet.fr).

$ My Hôtel in France Montmartre, a chain hotel, has 41 basic but well-maintained rooms on six floors, with no elevator or air-conditioning. Twin rooms are larger than doubles for the same price. Continental breakfast and a sandwich lunch-box are included (Sb-€80–89, Db-€90–99, prices vary greatly depending on occupancy, 57 rue des Abbesses, tel. 01 42 51 50 00, fax 01 42 51 08 68, www.book-your-hotel.com, montmartre@my-hotel-in -france.com).

$ Plug-Inn Boutique Hostel is part hotel and part hostel, but with a hotel vibe. Half a block off of rue des Abbesses, it has a young clientele, bathrooms in all 30 rooms, free Wi-Fi, and several public computer terminals. Early arrivals can leave their luggage and take a shower. Not all rooms are available online, so book direct (all prices per person: bunk in 4-bed dorm-€23–29, in 6-bed dorm-€22–28, private Db room-€33–43, female-only rooms available, sheets and towels-€2, includes breakfast, kitchen facilities, elevator, 24-hour front desk staff, no curfew, 7 rue Aristide Bruant, tel. 01 42 58 42 58, www.plug-inn.fr, bonjour@plug-inn.fr).

$ Hôtel Bonséjour Montmartre, run by eager Michel and his family, is an old, worn, hostelesque place with dirt-cheap prices. All rooms share one public shower on main floor, and others have oddly placed shower cabins right next to the bed (S-€35–50, D-€56–69, Tb-€78, higher price for private shower, no elevator, no air-con, 11 rue Burq, tel. 01 42 54 22 53, fax 01 42 54 25 92, www.hotel-bonsejour-montmartre .fr, hotel-bonsejour-montmartre@wanadoo.fr).

Eating in Paris

The Parisian eating scene is kept at a rolling boil. Entire books (and lives) are dedicated to the subject. Paris is France's wine-and-cuisine melting pot. Though it lacks a style of its own (only French onion soup is truly Parisian), it draws from the best of France. Paris could hold a gourmet Olympics and import nothing.

Cafés and brasseries are happy to serve a *plat du jour* (garnished plate of the day, about €12–18) or a chef-like salad (about €10–12) day or night, whereas restaurants expect you

Restaurant Price Code

To help you choose among these listings, I've divided the restaurants into three categories, based on the price for a typical main course.

$$\$ \$\$ $$ **Higher Priced**—Most main courses €25 or more
$$\$ \$ $$ **Moderately Priced**—Most main courses between €15–25.
$$\$ $$ **Lower Priced**—Most main courses €15 or less.

to enjoy a full dinner. Restaurants open for dinner at about 19:00, and small local favorites get crowded after 21:00. Most of the following restaurants accept credit cards. Before choosing a seat outside, remember that smokers love outdoor tables.

To save money, review the budget eating tips on page 33. Go to bakeries for quick take-out lunches, or stop at a café for a lunch salad or *plat du jour*, but linger longer over dinner. To save even more, consider picnics (tasty take-out dishes available at charcuteries).

Good Picnic Spots: The Palais Royal (across place du Palais Royal from the Louvre) and place des Vosges in the Marais make exquisite spots for peaceful, royal picnics. The little triangular Henry IV park on the west tip of Ile de la Cité and the bench-equipped pedestrian pont des Arts bridge, across from the Louvre, offer great river views. Parks, such as the Tuileries and Luxembourg Garden, make for ideal picnics—as do the gardens behind Les Invalides, and the Champ de Mars park below the Eiffel Tower (eat at the sides of the park; the central area is off-limits). Parks, including the grassy area on the place des Vosges, close at dusk. For an urban setting and terrific people-watching, try the Pompidou Center (by the *Homage to Stravinsky* fountains) or the courtyard around the pyramid of the Louvre.

Restaurants

My recommendations are centered on the same great neighborhoods listed in "Sleeping in Paris"; you can come home exhausted after a busy day of sightseeing and find a good selection of restaurants right around the corner. And evening is a great time to explore any of these delightful neighborhoods, even if you're sleeping elsewhere. Most restaurants I've listed in these areas have set-price *menus* between €15 and €30. In most cases, the few extra euros you pay are well-spent, and open up a variety of better choices. You decide. Remember that service is always included (so little or no tipping is expected), and consider dinner picnics (great take-out dishes available at charcuteries).

If you plan to travel outside of Paris, save your splurges for the countryside, where you'll enjoy regional cooking for less money. Many Parisian department stores have supermarkets in the basement, along with top-floor cafeterias offering not-really-cheap but low-risk, low-stress, what-you-see-is-what-you-get meals.

In the Rue Cler Neighborhood

The rue Cler neighborhood caters to its residents. Its eateries, while not destination places, have an intimate charm. I've provided a full range of choices from cozy ma-and-pa diners to small and trendy boutique restaurants to classic big, boisterous bistros. For all restaurants listed in this area, use the Ecole Militaire Métro stop (unless another station is listed).

On Rue Cler

$ **Café du Marché** boasts the best seats, coffee, and prices on rue Cler. The owner's philosophy: Brasserie on speed—crank out good food at great prices to chic locals and savvy tourists. It's high-energy, with young waiters who barely have time to smile...*très* Parisian. This place is ideal if you don't mind a limited section and want to eat an inexpensive one-course meal among a commotion of people. The chalkboard lists your choices: good, hearty €10 salads or more filling €10–12 *plats du jour*. If coming for dinner, arrive before 19:30; it's packed at 21:00, and service can be slow (Mon–Sat 11:00–23:00, Sun 11:00–17:00, at the corner of rue Cler and rue du Champ de Mars, 38 rue Cler, tel. 01 47 05 51 27).

$ **Tribeca Italian Restaurant**, next door to Café du Marché, is run by the same people with essentially the same formula and an Italian accent. They offer similar value and more space, a calmer ambience, and more patient service. This family-friendly eatery offers €12 pizzas and €13 Italian *plats* (open daily).

$ **Le Petit Cler** is a popular, tiny café with long leather booths, a traditional interior, a handful of outdoor tables, and fine, inexpensive dishes (€9 omelets, €7 soup of the moment, €12 salads, €14 *plats*, mouthwatering *petit-pots* of chocolate or vanilla pudding, closed Mon, next to Grand Hôtel Lévêque at 29 rue Cler, tel. 01 45 50 17 50).

$ **Crêperie Ulysée en Gaule** offers cheap seats on rue Cler with crêpes to go (€3–10). Readers of this book don't have to pay an extra charge to sit if they buy a drink. The family adores its Greek dishes, but their crêpes are your least expensive hot meal on this street (28 rue Cler, tel. 01 47 05 61 82).

$ **Petite Brasserie PTT**, a simple traditional café delivering fair-value fare, reminds Parisians of the old days on rue Cler. Rick Steves diners are promised a free *kir* with their dinner (closed Sun, 2-minute walk from most area hotels, opposite 53 rue Cler).

Close to Ecole Militaire, Between Rue de la Motte-Picquet and Rue de Grenelle

$$ Le Florimond is good for a special occasion. The setting, though spacious and quiet, is also intimate and welcoming. Locals come for classic French cuisine with elegant indoor or breezy streetside seating. Friendly English-speaking Laurent—whose playful ties change daily—and Bénédicte gracefully serve one small room of tables and love to give suggestions. Try the explosively tasty stuffed cabbage (€36 *menu*, closed Sun, reservations smart, good house wine by the carafe, affordable wine selection, 19 avenue de la Motte-Picquet, tel. 01 45 55 40 38).

$$ Restaurant Pasco, perched elegantly overlooking Les Invalides, is semi-dressy and has a special enthusiasm for fish. The hardworking owner, Pasco Vignes, attracts a loyal following with selections that change daily. The modern Mediterranean cuisine is generously endowed with olive oil. There's some outdoor seating, but I'd come for the cozy red-brick interior (€20 *plats*, €22–36 *menus*, daily, reservations smart, 74 boulevard de la Tour Maubourg, Mo: La Tour Maubourg, tel. 01 44 18 33 26).

$$ Café le Bosquet is a modern, chic Parisian brasserie with dressy waiters and your choice of a mod-elegant interior or sidewalk tables on a busy street. Come here for a bowl of French onion soup; a good-value deal featuring roast chicken with fries and a dessert (€14); or a full meal with inexpensive fish and meat choices. There's always one *plat du jour* for about €11. Say *bonjour* to lanky owner Jean-François (a.k.a. Jeff). The escargots are tasty, and the house red wine is plenty good (€15–20 *plats*, continental breakfast for €5–6, free Wi-Fi, closed Sun, reservations smart Fri-Sat, corner of rue du Champ de Mars and avenue Bosquet, 46 avenue Bosquet, tel. 01 45 51 38 13).

$$ La Terrasse du 7ème is a sprawling, happening café with grand outdoor seating and a living room–like interior with comfy love seats. Located on a corner, it overlooks a busy intersection with a constant parade of people. Chairs are set up facing the street, as a meal here is like dinner theater—and the show is slice-of-life Paris (€16 daily *plats*, no fixed-price *menu*, good €12 *salade niçoise* and €14–18 *plats*, daily until at least 24:00 and sometimes until 2:00 in the morning, at Ecole Militaire Métro stop, tel. 01 45 55 00 02).

Between Rue de Grenelle and the River, East of Avenue Bosquet

$$ Le Petit Niçois is all about fish. Come here for everything from *bouillabaisse* to bass to paella to mussels and enjoy the area's top seafood at fair prices. The *marmite du pêcheur*—my favorite—is a delicious version of *bouillabaisse*; the puréed potatoes are sinful; and the *café gourmand* dessert just about did me in. The atmosphere

Rue Cler Restaurants

1. Café du Marché & Tribeca Italian Rest.
2. Le Petit Cler
3. Créperie Ulysée en Gaule
4. Petite Brasserie PTT
5. Le Florimond
6. Restaurant Pasco
7. Café le Bosquet
8. La Terrasse du 7ème
9. Le Petit Niçois
10. Chez Pierrot
11. Au Petit Tonneau
12. To 58 Tour Eiffel & Jules Verne
13. Le P'tit Troquet
14. Billebaude Bistro
15. La Casa Campana
16. "The Constant Line-Up"
17. To Pâtisserie de la Tour Eiffel
18. La Varangue
19. La Gourmandise Pizzeria
20. Late-Night Groceries (2)
21. Café la Roussillon
22. O'Brien's Pub
23. La Fontaine de Mars
24. L'Ami Jean

M METRO STATION
(B) BUS STOP W/ ROUTE #
P PARKING
(T) TAXI STAND
PEDESTRIAN ZONE

TO SEINE RIVER

AVENUE BOSQUET

RUE D'ALMA

R. VALENTIN

RUE LOGES

AVENUE

TO EIFFEL TOWER

MONT.

R. DE L'EXPO.

RUE AUGER

RUE LA

RUE BOURDON

AVE DE

TO EIFFEL TOWER

CHAMP DE MARS

KIDS' PLAY AREA & PUPPETS

KIDS' PLAYGROUND

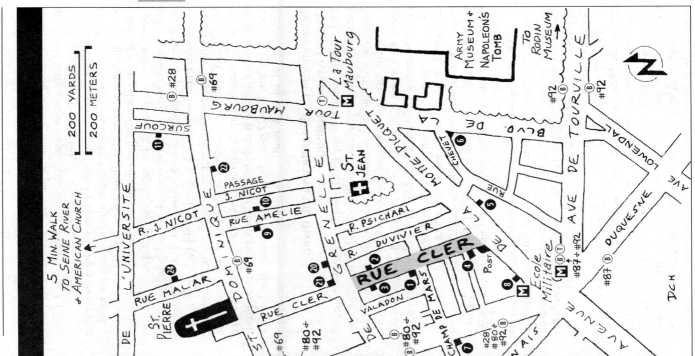

200 YARDS
200 METERS

5 MIN. WALK
TO SEINE RIVER
& AMERICAN CHURCH

ARMY MUSEUM +
NAPOLEON'S TOMB

To RODIN
MUSEUM →

La Tour Maubourg

R. J. NICOT

PASSAGE
J. NICOT

RUE AMELIE

SURCOUF

TOUR MAUBOURG

ST. JEAN

RUE DE L'UNIVERSITE

R. J. NICOT

RUE MALAR

ST. PIERRE

GRENELLE

R. PSICHARI

R. DUVIVIER

MOTTE-PICQUET

RUE CHEVET

RUE DE

BLVD. DE LA MOTTE-PICQUET

AVE DE TOURVILLE

AVE LOWENDAL

DUQUESNE

RUE CLER

VALADON

CHAMP DE MARS

RUE CLER

École Militaire

AVENUE

NAIS

DE DCH

#28

#69

#92

#92

#87 + #92

#87

#69

#80 +
#92

#69

#80 +
#92

#28 +
#80 +
#92

11

22

10

9

24

20

21

2

3

1

4

8

5

6

7

is warm though formal, the welcome is genuine, and the cuisine is excellent—though some find the portions small (€29 two-course *menu*, €32 three-course *menu*, daily, 10 rue Amélie, Mo: La Tour Maubourg, tel. 01 45 51 83 65).

$$ Chez Pierrot, across from Le Petit Niçois, is an inviting 14-table bistro, drawing mostly tourists who appreciate the low-key setting and large portions of traditional fare. Dishes from Lyon are a specialty—try the *salade lyonnaise* and the quenelles (fish dumplings in white cream sauce). The *pot-au-feu*—beef stew—is tasty, as is the *canard à l'orange*—duck in orange sauce (€18 *plats*, good wine list, 9 rue Amélie, Mo: La Tour Maubourg, tel. 01 45 51 50 08).

$$ Au Petit Tonneau is a souvenir of old Paris. Fun-loving owner-chef Madame Boyer prepares everything herself, wearing her tall chef's hat like a crown as she rules from her family-style kitchen. The small, plain dining room doesn't look like it's changed in the 30 years she's been in charge. Her steaks and lamb are excellent (€10 starters, €18–22 *plats*, daily, 20 rue Surcouf, Mo: La Tour Maubourg, tel. 01 47 05 09 01).

Between Rue de Grenelle and the River, West of Avenue Bosquet

$$$ 58 Tour Eiffel is in the Eiffel Tower's first level (about 300 feet up). It's the latest creation of famed French chef Alain Ducasse. Reserve at least a month in advance for a view table on a weekend, or a few days ahead for a viewless spot on weekdays. Lunch is first-come, first-served (€20 lunches, €65 dinners, daily 11:30–23:00, dinner seatings at 18:30 and 21:00; Mo: Bir-Hakeim or Trocadéro, RER: Champ de Mars–Tour Eiffel; within France dial toll tel. 08 25 56 66 62; if calling outside France, use tel. 01 76 64 14 64; www.restaurants-toureiffel.com). Drop by the kiosk between the north/nord and east/est pillars to buy your Eiffel Tower ticket. You can skip the line for the elevator to the first level (lunchtime rate–€4.50, dinnertime rate–€13).

$$$ La Fontaine de Mars is a longtime favorite, charmingly situated on a tiny, jumbled square with tables jammed together for the serious business of eating. Reserve in advance for a table on the ground floor or on the square. Skip the upstairs room (€20–30 *plats du jour*, superb foie gras, superb-er desserts, 129 rue St. Dominique, tel. 01 47 05 46 44).

$$ Le P'tit Troquet, a petite eatery taking you back to the Paris of the 1920s, is gracefully and earnestly run by Dominique. The fragile elegance makes you want to hug a flapper. Dominique is particularly proud of her foie gras and lamb, and of her daughter's breads and pastries. The delicious three-course €31 *menu* comes with traditional choices. Delicate charm and gourmet flair make this restaurant a favorite of connoisseurs (opens at 18:00, closed Sun, reservations smart, 28 rue de l'Exposition, tel. 01 47 05 80 39).

$$ Billebaude, run by patient Pascal, is an authentic Parisian bistro popular with locals. The focus is on what's fresh, including catch-of-the-day fish and meats from the hunt (available in the fall and winter). Chef Sylvain, an avid hunter, is determined to deliver quality at a fair price (€31 *menu,* closed Sun–Mon, 29 rue de l'Exposition, tel. 01 45 55 20 96).

$$ La Casa Campana, is worth a visit if you're sleeping in the rue Cler area and crave Italian food. The gentle owners moved to Paris from southern Italy, bringing their delicious and unspoiled cuisine with them. The handmade ravioli are bellisimo (*menus* from €20, daily, 20 rue de l'Exposition, tel. 01 45 51 37 71).

$$–$$$ The Constant Lineup: Ever since leaving the venerable Hôtel Crillon, famed chef Christian Constant has made a career of taking the "snoot" out of French cuisine—and making it accessible to people like us. Today you'll find four of his restaurants strung along one block of rue St. Dominique between rue Augereau and rue de l'Exposition, each offering a different experience and price range. The restaurants go from the lively **$$ Café Constant** (my favorite, described below), to the refined **$$$ Le Violon d'Ingres** (where Christian won his first Michelin star and reservations are essential), to **$$ Les Cocottes** (a trendy, bar-stool-only place serving simple dishes in small iron pots to yuppie Parisians), to **$$$ Les Fables de la Fontaine** (a tiny, classy place serving fish only, reservations necessary). For more details, check out www.leviolondingres.com.

$$ Café Constant is a cool, two-level place that feels more like a small bistro-wine bar than a café. Delicious and affordably priced dishes are served in a fun setting to a well-established clientele. Arrive early to get a table (downstairs seating is better); the friendly staff speaks English (€11 entrées, €16 *plats,* €7 desserts, closed Sun–Mon, no reservations, corner of rue Augereau and rue St. Dominique, next to recommended Hôtel Londres Eiffel, tel. 01 47 53 73 34).

$$ L'Ami Jean offers top Basque specialties at fair prices with tight but fun seating. The chef has made his reputation on the quality of his cuisine. Arrive by 19:30 or call ahead (€38 menu, closed Sun–Mon, 27 rue Malar, Mo: La Tour Maubourg, tel. 01 47 05 86 89).

$ Pâtisserie de la Tour Eiffel offers inexpensive salads, quiches, and sandwiches. Enjoy the views of the Eiffel Tower (daily, outdoor and indoor seating, one block southeast of the tower at 21 avenue de la Bourdonnais, tel. 01 47 05 59 81).

$ La Varangue is an entertaining one-man show featuring English-speaking Philippe, who lives upstairs, and has found his niche serving a mostly American clientele, who are all on a first-name basis. The food is cheap and basic, the tables are few, and he opens at 17:30. Norman Rockwell would dig his miniscule dining room—with the traditional kitchen sizzling just over the counter. Philippe is so fun and accessible that you are welcome to join him in the kitchen and help cook your meal. Try his snails and chocolate cake..but not together (€12 *plats*, €18 *menu*, always a vegetarian option, closed Sun, 27 rue Augereau, tel. 01 47 05 51 22).

$ La Gourmandise is a kid-friendly cheap pizzeria across from La Varangue (closed Sun, eat in or take out, 28 rue Augereau, tel. 01 45 55 45 16).

Picnicking near Rue Cler

Rue Cler is a moveable feast that gives "fast food" a good name. The entire street is clogged with connoisseurs of good eating. Only the health-food store goes unnoticed. A festival of food, the street is lined with people whose lives seem to be devoted to their specialty: polished produce, rotisserie chicken, crêpes, or cheese.

For a magical picnic dinner at the Eiffel Tower, assemble it in no fewer than five shops on rue Cler. Then lounge on the best grass in Paris, with the dogs, Frisbees, a floodlit tower, and a cool breeze in the Champ de Mars park (picnics are allowed off to the sides of the central area, which is off-limits).

Asian delis (generically called *Traiteur Asie*) provide tasty, low-stress, low-price take-out treats (€8 dinner plates, the one on rue Cler near rue du Champ de Mars has tables). **Crêperie Ulysée en Gaule**, the Greek restaurant on rue Cler across from Grand Hôtel Lévêque, sells take-away crêpes (described earlier). There's a small **late-night grocery** at 197 rue de Grenelle (open daily until midnight), and another where rues Cler and Grenelle cross.

Breakfast on Rue Cler

Hotel breakfasts, though convenient, are generally not a good value. For a great rue Cler start to your day, drop by the **Petite Brasserie PTT**, where Alexi promises Rick Steves readers a *deux pour douze* breakfast special (2 "American" breakfasts—juice, a big coffee, croissant, bread, ham, and eggs—for €12; closed Sun, 53 rue Cler). For a continental breakfast for about €6, try nearby **Café le Bosquet** (closed Sun, 46 avenue Bosquet).

Nightlife in Rue Cler

This sleepy neighborhood was not made for night owls, but there are a few notable exceptions. **La Terrasse du 7éme** and **Café du Marché** (both listed earlier) attract a Franco-American crowd until at least midnight, as does the younger **Café la Roussillon** (good French pub atmosphere, corner of rue de Grenelle and rue Cler). **O'Brien's Pub** is a relaxed Parisian rendition of an Irish pub, full of Anglophones (77 avenue St. Dominique, Mo: La Tour Maubourg).

In the Marais Neighborhood

The trendy Marais is filled with diners enjoying good food in colorful and atmospheric eateries. The scene is competitive and changes all the time. I've listed an assortment of eateries—all handy to recommended hotels—that offer good food at decent prices, plus a memorable experience.

On Romantic Place des Vosges

This square offers Old World Marais elegance, a handful of eateries, and an ideal picnic site until 20:30, when the park closes (use Bastille or St. Paul Métro stops). Strolling around the arcade after dark is more important than dining here—fanciful art galleries alternate with restaurants and cafés. Choose a restaurant that best fits your mood and budget; most have arcade seating and provide big space heaters to make outdoor dining during colder months an option. Also consider a drink or dessert on the square at Café Hugo or Carette after eating elsewhere.

$$$ Ma Bourgogne is a vintage eatery where you'll sit under warm arcades in a whirlpool of Frenchness, as bow-tied and black-aproned waiters serve you traditional French specialties: blood-red steak (try the *brochette de bœuf*), piles of fries, escargot, and good red wine. Monsieur Cougoureux (koo-goo-ruh) has commanded this ship because de Gaulle was sniveling at Americans. He offers anyone with this book a free *amuse-bouche* ("amusement for your mouth") of his homemade *steak tartare*. This is your chance to try this "raw spiced hamburger" delicacy without dedicating an entire meal to it (€37 *menu*, daily, cash only, at northwest corner at #19, tel. 01 42 78 44 64).

$$ Carette is a welcoming, modern café specializing in desserts, fine teas, big salads, and bistro fare served with smiles under the arcades (€16 dinner salads, €20 *plats*, daily from 12:00, 28 place des Vosges, tel. 01 48 87 94 07).

$$ Royal Turenne is smothered in Auvergnant (south-central France) culture and serves up mostly meat-based dishes at good prices. Try the *marquise de bœuf* or the beefy salad topped with foie gras. Clients take their cue from the gregarious owner Philippe—don't come here for a romantic soirée. There's live music on weekends and lively crowds most evenings (daily, where rue de Turenne meets the place des Vosges at 24 rue de Turenne, tel. 01 42 72 04 53).

$$ Les Bonnes Soeurs, barely off the square, blends modern and traditional fare with light-hearted and contemporary ambience. Portions are big and inventive. The delicious and filling *pressé de chèvre* starter (a hunk of goat cheese topped with tapenade and tomatoes) begs to be shared. The French hamburger would feed a soccer team and comes with a salad, and easygoing owner Cécile

Marais Restaurants

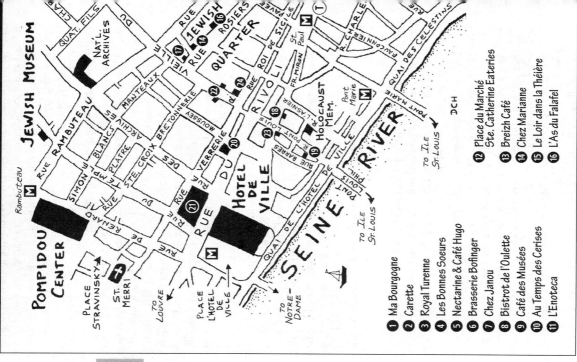

1 Ma Bourgogne
2 Carette
3 Royal Turenne
4 Les Bonnes Soeurs
5 Nectarine & Café Hugo
6 Brasserie Bofinger
7 Chez Janou
8 Bistrot de l'Oulette
9 Café des Musées
10 Au Temps des Cerises
11 L'Enoteca
12 Place du Marché / Ste. Catherine Eateries
13 Breizh Café
14 Chez Marianne
15 Le Loir dans la Théière
16 L'As du Falafel

PARIS

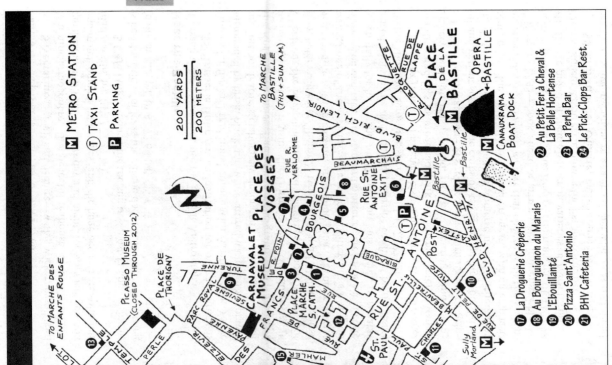

- **M** METRO STATION
- **T** TAXI STAND
- **P** PARKING

200 YARDS
200 METERS

To MARCHE DES ENFANTS ROUGE

PICASSO MUSEUM (CLOSED THROUGH 2012)

PLACE DE THORIGNY

CARNAVALET PLACE DES VOSGES
MUSEUM

RUE R. VERLOMME

BEAUMARCHAIS

BLVD. RICH. LENOIR

To MARCHE BASTILLE (THU + SUN A.M.)

PLACE DE LA BASTILLE

OPERA BASTILLE

Canauxrama BOAT DOCK

Bastille

RUE ST. ANTOINE EXIT

RUE ST. ANTOINE

BLVD. HENRI IV

RUE DE LAPPE

RUE DE LA ROQUETTE

BOURGEOIS

PLACE MARCHE S. CATH.

RUE DE SEVIGNE

FRANCS

PARC ROYAL

ELZEVIR

TURENNE

PAYENNE

PERLE

TEMPLE

LOT

R. FOIN

RUE DE TURENNE

MAHLER

ST. PAUL

RUE ST. PAUL

RUE BEAUTREILLIS

RUE DU PETIT MUSC

CHARLES

Sully Morland

- ⑰ La Droguerie Crêperie
- ⑱ Au Bourguignon du Marais
- ⑲ L'Ebouillanté
- ⑳ Pizza Sant'Antonio
- ㉑ BHV Cafeteria
- ㉒ Au Petit Fer à Cheval & La Belle Hortense
- ㉓ La Perla Bar
- ㉔ Le Pick-Clops Bar Rest.

serves the best fries I've tasted in Paris (*plats* from €16, no *menu*, daily, 8 rue du pas de la Mule, tel. 01 42 74 55 80).

$ Nectarine is small and demure—with a wicker, pastel, and feminine atmosphere. This peaceful teahouse serves €11 salads, quiches, and €13 *plats du jour* day and night. Its *menu* lets you mix and match omelets and crêpes, and the huge desserts are splittable (daily, at #16, tel. 01 42 77 23 78).

$ Café Hugo, named for the square's most famous resident, is best for drinks only, as the cuisine does not live up to its setting (daily, at #22, tel. 01 42 72 64 04).

Near the Bastille

To reach these restaurants, use the Bastille Métro stop.

$$ Brasserie Bofinger, an institution for over a century, is famous for fish and traditional cuisine with Alsatian flair. You're surrounded by brisk, black-and-white-attired waiters. The sprawling interior features elaborately decorated rooms reminiscent of the Roaring Twenties. Eating under the grand 1919 *coupole* is a memorable treat (as is using the "historic" 1919 WC downstairs). Check out the boys shucking and stacking seafood platters out front before you enter. Their €25 two-course and €32 three-course *menus*, while not top cuisine, are a good value. If you've always wanted one of those picturesque seafood platters, this is a good place—you can take the standard platter or create one à la carte (open daily for lunch and for dinner, fun kids' menu, reasonably priced wines, 5 rue de la Bastille, don't be confused by the lesser "Petite" Bofinger across the street, tel. 01 42 72 87 82).

$$ Chez Janou, a Provençal bistro, tumbles out of its corner building and fills its broad sidewalk with happy eaters. At first glance, you know this is a find. Don't let the trendy and youthful crowd intimidate you—it's relaxed and charming, with helpful and patient service. The curbside tables are inviting, but I'd sit inside (with very tight seating) to immerse myself in the happy commotion. The style is French Mediterranean, with an emphasis on vegetables (€16-19 *plats du jour* that change with the season, daily from 19:45—book ahead or arrive when it opens, 2 blocks beyond place des Vosges at 2 rue Roger Verlomme, tel. 01 42 72 28 41). They're proud of their 81 different varieties of *pastis* (licorice-flavored liqueur, €3.50 each, browse the list above the bar).

$$ At **Bistrot de l'Oulette,** Parisians pile into a tiny spot to test the creative inventions of a talented chef who gives traditional dishes a modern twist (€30 *menu*, closed Sun, reservations smart, 38 rue des Tournelles, tel. 01 42 71 43 33).

$ Café des Musées is the real thing—an unspoiled, zinc-countered bistro serving traditional dishes with little fanfare and a €19 daily *menu* special that's hard to beat. The place is just far enough away to be overlooked by tourists (daily, 49 rue de Turenne, tel. 01 42 72 96 17).

$ Au Temps des Cerises is a *très* local wine bar, with a woody 1950s atmosphere, tight seating, and wads of character. Although they serve three-course, €16 lunch *menus*, I'd come here for dinner. "Dinner" is limited to bread, dry sausage, cheese, and wine served by goateed Yves, Michele, or Sara. Their small mixed plate of cheese (€5), meat (€5), and a carafe of good wine (€4–8) surrounded by the intimate Old World setting can make a good light meal (Mon–Sat until about 22:00, closed Sun, at rue du Petit-Musc and rue de la Cerisaie, tel. 01 42 72 08 63).

In the Heart of the Marais

These are closest to the St. Paul Métro stop.

$$ L'Enoteca, high-spirited and half-timbered, serves affordable Italian cuisine (no pizza) with a tempting *antipasti* bar. It's a fun, open setting with busy, blue-aproned waiters serving two floors of local eaters (€17 pastas, €30 three-course *menu*, good-value wines, daily, across from L'Excuse at rue St. Paul and rue Charles V, 25 rue Charles V, tel. 01 42 78 91 44).

$ On place du Marché Ste. Catherine: This small, romantic square, just off rue St. Antoine, is an international food festival cloaked in extremely Parisian, leafy-square ambience. On a balmy evening, this is clearly a neighborhood favorite, with a handful of restaurants offering €20–30 three-course meals. Study the square, and you'll find two popular French bistros (**Le Marché** and **Au Bistrot de la Place**, each open daily with €23 three-course *menus* and tight seating on flimsy chairs indoors and out) and other inviting eateries serving a variety of international food—Russian, Korean, Italian, and so on. You'll eat under the trees, surrounded by a futuristic-in-1800 planned residential quarter.

$ Breizh (Brittany) Café is a find for lovers of things pure and unaffected. This simple Breton place serves organic crêpes and small rolls made for dipping in rich sauces and salted butter. Try a sparkling cider, a Breton cola, or my favorite—*lait ribot*, a buttermilk-like drink (€7–11 dinner crêpes and *plats*, serves nonstop from 12:00 to late, closed Mon–Tue, 109 rue du Vielle du Temple, tel. 01 42 72 13 77).

$ Several hardworking **Asian fast-food eateries**, great for a €8 meal, line rue St. Antoine.

On Rue des Rosiers in the Jewish Quarter

To reach the Jewish Quarter, use the St. Paul Métro stop.

$ Chez Marianne is a neighborhood fixture that blends delicious Jewish cuisine with Parisian *élan*. Choose from several indoor zones with a cluttered wineshop/deli feeling, or sit outside. You'll select from two dozen *Zakouski* elements to assemble your €15 *plat*. Vegetarians will find great options (€8 falafel sandwich—only €6 if you order it to go, long hours daily, corner of rue des Rosiers and rue des Hospitalières-St.-Gervais, tel. 01 42 72 18 86). For take-out, pay inside first and get a ticket before you order outside.

$ Le Loir dans la Théière is a cozy, mellow teahouse offering a welcoming ambience for tired travelers. It's ideal for weekend brunch, baked goods, and hot drinks (Mon–Fri 12:00–19:00, Sat–Sun 10:00–19:00, 3 rue des Rosiers, tel. 01 42 72 90 61).

$ L'As du Falafel rules the falafel scene in the Jewish quarter. Monsieur Isaac, the "Ace of Falafel" here since 1979, brags, "I've got the biggest pita on the street…and I fill it up." (Apparently it's Lenny Kravitz's favorite, too.) Your inexpensive meal comes on plastic plates, in a bustling setting that seems to prove he's earned his success. The €7 "special falafel" is the big hit, but many Americans enjoy his lighter chicken version (*poulet grillé*) or the tasty and filling *assiette de falafel*. Their take-out service draws a constant crowd (day and night until late, closed Sat, air-con, 34 rue des Rosiers, tel. 01 48 87 63 60).

$ La Droguerie, a full-service outdoor crêpe stand a few blocks farther down rue des Rosiers, is an option if falafels don't work for you, but cheap does (€5 dinner crêpes, closed Sun–Mon, rue des Rosiers).

Closer to Hôtel de Ville

These eateries appear on the map on page 180. To reach them, use the Hôtel de Ville Métro stop.

$$ Au Bourguignon du Marais is a handsome wine-bar/bistro for Burgundy-lovers, where excellent wines (Burgundian only, available by the glass) blend with a good selection of well-designed dishes and efficient service. The *œufs en meurette* were the best I've ever had, and the *bœuf bourguignon* could feed two (€10–14 starters, €18–22 *plats*, closed Sun–Mon, pleasing indoor and outdoor seating, 52 rue François Miron, tel. 01 48 87 15 40).

$ L'Ebouillanté is a breezy crêperie-café, romantically situated near the river on a broad, cobbled lane behind a church. With great outdoor seating and an artsy, cozy interior, it's perfect for an inexpensive and relaxing tea, snack, or lunch—or for dinner on a warm evening. Have a *Brick*, a Tunisian-inspired dish that looks like a stuffed omelet (several filling options) and comes with a small salad; it left me stuffed (€13 *plats* and big salads, Tue–Sun 12:00–21:30, closed Mon in winter, 6 rue des Barres, tel. 01 42 71 09 69).

$ Pizza Sant'Antonio is bustling and cheap, serving up €11 pizzas and salads on a fun Marais square (daily, barely off rue de

Rivoli on place du Bourg Tibourg, 1 rue de la Verrerie).

$ BHV Department Store's fifth-floor cafeteria provides nice views, good prices, and no-brainer, point-and-shoot cafeteria cuisine (Mon-Sat 11:30–18:00, closed Sun, at intersection of rue du Temple and rue de la Verrerie, one block from Hôtel de Ville).

Picnicking in the Marais

Picnic at peaceful place des Vosges (closes at dusk) or on the Ile St. Louis *quais* (described later). Stretch your euros at the basement supermarket of the **Monoprix** department store (closed Sun, near place des Vosges on rue St. Antoine). You'll find small **groceries** open until 23:00 at 48 rue St. Antoine and on the Ile St. Louis.

Nightlife in the Marais

Trendy cafés and bars—popular with gay men—cluster on rue des Archives and rue Ste. Croix de la Bretonnerie (closing at about 2:00 in the morning). There's also a line of bars and cafés providing front-row seats for the buff parade on rue Vieille du Temple, a block north of rue de Rivoli (the horseshoe-shaped **Au Petit Fer à Cheval** bar-restaurant and the atmospheric **La Belle Hortense** bookstore/wine bar are the focal points of the action). Nearby, rue des Rosiers bustles with youthful energy, but there are no cafés to observe from. **La Perla** is full of Parisian yuppies in search of the perfect margarita (26 rue François Miron).

$ Le Pick-Clops bar-restaurant is a happy peanuts-and-lots-of-cocktails diner with bright neon, loud colors, and a garish local crowd. It's perfect for immersing yourself in today's Marais world—a little boisterous, a little edgy, a little gay, fun-loving, easygoing...and no tourists. Sit inside on old-fashioned diner stools, or streetside to watch the constant Marais parade. The name means "Steal the Cigarettes,"—but you'll pay €11 for your big salad (daily 7:00–24:00, 16 rue Vieille du Temple, tel. 01 40 29 02 18).

The best scene for hardcore clubbers is the dizzying array of wacky eateries, bars, and dance halls on **rue de Lappe.** Just east of the stately place de la Bastille, it's one of the wildest nightspots in Paris and not for everyone.

The most enjoyable peaceful evening may be simply mentally donning your floppy "three musketeers" hat and slowly strolling place des Vosges, window-shopping the art galleries.

In the Historic Core, on Ile St. Louis

This romantic and peaceful neighborhood is filled with promising and surprisingly inexpensive possibilities—it merits a trip for dinner even if your hotel is elsewhere. Cruise the island's main street for a variety of options, from cozy *crêperies* to Italian eateries to traditional brasseries and romantic bistros. After dinner, sample

Paris' best ice cream and stroll across to the Ile de la Cité to see a floodlit Notre-Dame. These recommended spots line the island's main drag, rue St. Louis-en-l'Ile (see map on page 159; to get here use the Pont Marie Métro stop).

$$$ Le Tastevin is an intimate mother-and-son-run restaurant serving top-notch traditional French cuisine with white-tablecloth, candlelit, gourmet elegance under heavy wooden beams. The romantic setting (and the elegantly romantic local couples enjoying the place) naturally makes you whisper. The three-course *menus* start at about €39–52 and offer a handful of classic choices that change with the season to ensure freshness (daily, reserve for late-evening dining, good wine list, 46 rue St. Louis-en-l'Ile, tel. 01 43 54 1731, owner Madame Puisieux and her gentle son speak just enough English).

$$$ Medieval Theme Restaurants: La Taverne du Sergeant Recruteur, famous for its rowdy, medieval-cellar atmosphere, is ideal for hungry warriors and their wenches who like to swill hearty wine. For as long as anyone can remember, they've served up a rustic all-you-can-eat buffet with straw baskets of raw veggies and bundles of sausage (cut whatever you like with your dagger), massive plates of pâté, a meat course, and all the wine you can stomach for €41. The food is just food; burping is encouraged. If you want to eat a lot, drink a lot of wine, be surrounded with tourists (mostly French), and holler at your friends while receiving smart-aleck buccaneer service, this food fest can be fun. And it comes with a historic twist: The "Sergeant Recruiter" used to get young Parisians drunk and stuffed here, then sign them into the army (daily from 19:00, #37 rue St. Louis-en-l'Ile, tel. 01 43 54 75 42). Next door, **Nos Ancêtres les Gaulois** is a bit goofier and grittier, and serves the same basic formula. As the name implies ("Our Ancestors the Gauls"), this place makes barbarians feel right at home (tel. 01 46 33 66 07). You might swing by both and choose the..."ambience" is not quite the right word...that fits your mood.

$$ La Brasserie de l'Ile St. Louis is situated at the prow of the island's ship as it faces Ile de la Cité, offering purely Alsatian cuisine (try the *choucroute garnie* for €18), served in a vigorous, Teutonic setting with no-nonsense, slap-it-down service and winestained paper tablecloths. This is a good balmy-evening perch for watching the Ile St. Louis promenade. If it's chilly, the interior is plenty characteristic for a memorable night out (closed Wed, no reservations, 55 quai de Bourbon, tel. 01 43 54 02 59).

$$ L'Orangerie is an inviting place with soft lighting and comfortable seating where diners speak in hushed voices so that everyone can appreciate the delicious cuisine and tasteful setting (€35 three-course *menu*, €27 two-course *menu*, closed Mon, open at 19:00, 28 rue St. Louis-en-l'Ile, tel. 01 46 33 93 98).

$ Auberge de la Reine Blanche's friendly owner Michel welcomes diners willing to rub elbows with their neighbors in a cozy setting while enjoying delicious cuisine at unbeatable prices (€20 two-course *menu*, €25 three-course *menu*, daily from 18:00, 30 rue St. Louis-en-l'Ile, tel. 01 46 33 07 87).

$ Café Med, near the pedestrian bridge to Notre-Dame at #77, has inexpensive salads, crêpes, *plats*, and a €14–20 *menu* served in a tight but cheery setting (open daily, limited wine list, tel. 01 43 29 73 17). Two similar *crêperies* are just across the street.

Riverside Picnic for Impoverished Romantics

On sunny lunchtimes and balmy evenings, the *quai* on the Left Bank side of Ile St. Louis is lined with locals who have more class than money, spreading out tablecloths and even lighting candles for elegant picnics. And tourists can enjoy the same budget meal. A handy grocery store at #67 on the main drag (Wed–Mon until 22:00, closed Tue) has tabouli and other simple, cheap take-away dishes for your picnicking pleasure.

Ice-Cream Dessert

Half the people strolling Ile St. Louis are licking an ice-cream cone, because this is the home of *les glaces Berthillon.* The original **Berthillon** shop, at 31 rue St. Louis-en-l'Ile, is marked by the line of salivating customers (closed Mon–Tue). Another Berthillon shop is across the street, and there's one more around the corner on rue Bellay (all are located on map on page 159). The three shops are so popular that the wealthy people who can afford to live on this fancy island complain about the congestion they cause. For a less famous but at least as satisfying treat, the homemade Italian gelato a block away at **Amorino Gelati** is giving Berthillon competition (no line, bigger portions, easier to see what you want, and they offer little tastes—Berthillon doesn't need to, 47 rue St. Louis-en-l'Ile, tel. 01 44 07 48 08). Having some of each is not a bad thing.

In the Luxembourg Garden Area

Sleeping in the Luxembourg neighborhood puts you near many appealing dining and after-hours options. Because my hotels in this area cluster near St. Sulpice Church and the Panthéon (see page 161), I've organized restaurant listings the same way. Restaurants around St. Sulpice tend to be boisterous; those near the Panthéon are calmer; it's a short walk from one area to the other. Anyone sleeping in this area is close to the inexpensive eateries that line the always-bustling rue Mouffetard. You're also within a 15-minute walk of the *grands cafés* of St. Germain and Montparnasse (with Paris' first café and famous artist haunts).

Restaurants near Luxembourg Garden

① La Crêpe Rit du Clown
② Lou Pescadou–Chez Julien
③ Boucherie Rouliere & Santa Lucia
④ Chez Georges
⑤ To La Cigale Récamier &
   Au Sauvignon Café
⑥ Brasserie Bouillon Racine
⑦ La Méditerranée Restaurant
⑧ Restaurant Polidor
⑨ Restaurant Perraudin
⑩ Le Vin Qui Danse

PARIS

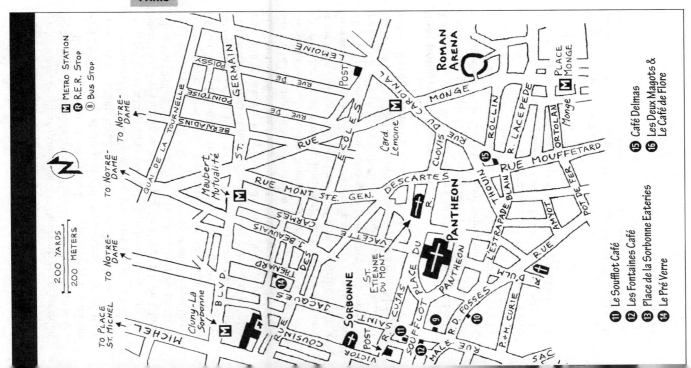

M METRO STATION
R R.E.R. STOP
B BUS STOP

200 YARDS
200 METERS

11 Le Soufflot Café
12 Les Fontaines Café
13 Place de la Sorbonne Eateries
14 Le Pré Verre

15 Café Delmas
16 Les Deux Magots &
Le Café de Flore

Near St. Sulpice Church: Rue des Canettes and Rue Guisarde

For locations, see the map on page 188. These eateries are served by the St. Sulpice, Mabillon, and St. Germain-des-Prés Métro stops.

Roam the streets between the St. Sulpice Church and boulevard St. Germain, abounding with restaurants, *crêperies*, wine bars, and jazz haunts (use Mo: St. Sulpice). Find rue des Canettes and rue Guisarde, and window-shop the many French and Italian eateries—most with similar prices, but each with a slightly different feel. For yummy crêpes, try **$ La Crêpe Rit du Clown** (Mon–Sat 12:00–23:00, closed Sun, 6 rue des Canettes, tel. 01 46 34 01 02). For comfortable atmosphere and above-average bistro fare in a zone where every restaurant looks the same, consider **$$ Lou Pescadou–Chez Julien** (daily, some outdoor seating, 16 rue Mabillon, tel. 01 43 54 56 08). Another option is **$$ Boucherie Roulière**, crammed with locals in search of a good steak or other meat dish (€7 *entrées*, €16 *plats*, €7 desserts, closed Mon, 24 rue des Canettes). **$ Santa Lucia** draws rave reviews with wood-fired pizza, good pasta, and killer tiramisu (€12–14 pizza and pastas, closed Mon–Tue, 22 rue des Canettes, tel. 01 43 26 42 68).

And for a bohemian pub lined with black-and-white photos of the artsy and revolutionary French '60s, have a drink at **Chez Georges.** Sit in a cool little streetside table nook, or venture downstairs to find a hazy, drippy-candle, traditionally French world in the Edith Piaf-style dance cellar (cheap drinks from old-fashioned menu, Tue–Sat 14:00–2:00 in the morning, closed Sun–Mon and in Aug, 11 rue des Canettes, tel. 01 43 26 79 15).

Near Boulevard St. Germain

A five-minute walk from St. Sulpice Church, this venerable boulevard is home to some of Paris' most famous cafés and best pre- or post-dinner strolling. Consider a light dinner with a table facing the action at Hemingway's **Les Deux Magots** or at Sartre's **Le Café de Flore** (figure about €10 for an omelet and €16–25 for a salad or *plat*). A block north (toward the river), **rue de Buci** offers a lineup of bars, cafés, and bistros targeted to a young clientele who are more interested in how they look than how the food tastes. It's terrific theater for passersby.

Near Sèvres-Babylone

$$ La Cigale Récamier is a classy place for a quiet meal with appealing indoor and outdoor seating. It's about 10 minutes west of place St. Sulpice, on a short pedestrian alley a block off rue de Sèvres (€20 *plats*, à la carte only, closed Sun, 4 rue Récamier, Mo: Sèvres-Babylone, tel. 01 46 48 86 58).

Near the Odéon Theater

To reach these, use the Odéon Métro stop. In this same neighborhood, you'll find the historic Café le Procope, Paris' more-than-300-year-old café.

$$ Brasserie Bouillon Racine takes you back to 1906 with an Art Nouveau carnival of carved wood, stained glass, and old-time lights reflected in beveled mirrors. The over-the-top decor, energetic waiters, and affordable prices combine to give it an inviting conviviality. Check upstairs before choosing a table. Their roast suckling pig (€18) is a house favorite, but I'd skip their bouillon soups. There's good beer on tap and a fascinating history on the menu (€18–23 *plats*, €31 *menu*, a few fish options and lots of meat, daily 12:00–14:00 & 19:00–23:00, 3 rue Racine, tel. 01 44 32 15 60, Phillipe).

$$ La Méditerranée is all about having fish in a pastel and dressy setting...with similar clientele. The scene and the cuisine are sophisticated yet accessible, and the view of the Odéon is *formidable*. The sky-blue tablecloths and the lovingly presented dishes add to the romance (€27 two-course *menus*, €32 three-course *menus*, daily, smart to book ahead, facing the Odéon at 2 place de l'Odéon, tel. 01 43 26 02 30).

$ Restaurant Polidor, a bare-bones neighborhood fixture since the 19th century, is much loved for its unpretentious quality cooking, fun old-Paris atmosphere, and fair value. Stepping inside, you know this is a winner—noisy, happy diners squeeze in at shared tables as waiters chop and serve fresh bread. The selection features classic bourgeois *plats* from every corner of France; their *menu fraîcheur* is designed for lighter summer eating (€12–15 *plats*, €20–30 three-course *menus*, daily 12:00–14:30 & 19:00–23:00, cash only, no reservations, 41 rue Monsieur-le-Prince, tel. 01 43 26 95 34).

Near the Panthéon

For locations, see the map on page 188. These eateries are served by the Cluny-La Sorbonne Métro stop and the RER-B Luxembourg station.

$$ Restaurant Perraudin is a family-run, red-checkered-tablecloth eatery understandably popular with tourists. Monsieur Correy serves classic *cuisine bourgeoise* with an emphasis on Burgundian dishes in air-conditioned comfort (€20 lunch *menus*, €30 dinner *menus*, daily, *bœuf bourguignon* is a specialty here, between the Panthéon and Luxembourg Garden at 157 rue St. Jacques, tel. 01 46 33 15 75).

$$ Le Vin Qui Danse is a warm little place serving a good selection of tasty dishes and well-matched wines to appreciative clients (€27 two-course *menu*, add €15 for three wines selected to complement your meal, daily, 4 rue des Fossés Saint-Jacques, tel. 01 43 54 80 81).

$ Le Soufflot Café, between the Panthéon and Luxembourg Garden, is well-positioned for afternoon sun and soft light in the evening. It has a nifty library-like interior, lots of outdoor tables, point-blank views of the Panthéon, and happy waiters (Frédéric and Serge are owners). The cuisine is café-classic, day or night: good €10 salads and omelets, and €12–15 *plats du jour* (daily, a block below the Panthéon on the right side of rue Soufflot as you walk toward Luxembourg Garden, tel. 01 43 26 57 56).

$ Les Fontaines Café offers similar café fare and ambience on the other side of rue Soufflot, but has a more elaborate wine list and features glass-enclosed sidewalk tables with protected views of the Panthéon (daily, 9 rue Soufflot, tel. 01 43 26 42 80).

$ *Place de la Sorbonne*: This cobbled and green square, with a small fountain facing the Sorbonne University just a block from the Cluny Museum, offers several opportunities for a quick outdoor lunch or light dinner. At amiable Carole's tiny **Baker's Dozen**, you'll pay take-away prices for light fare you can sit down to eat (€5 salads and sandwiches, Mon–Fri until 15:30, closed Sun). **Café de l'Ecritoire** is a typical, lively brasserie with happy diners enjoying €11 salads, €13 *plats*, and fine square seating (daily, tel. 01 43 54 60 02). **Patios**, with appealing decor inside and out, serves inexpensive Italian fare, including pizza (daily until late, tel. 01 45 38 71 19).

$ Le Pré Verre, a block from the Cluny Museum, is a chic wine bistro—a refreshing alternative in a part of the Latin Quarter mostly known for low-quality, tourist-trapping eateries. Offering imaginative, modern cuisine at fair prices, the place is always packed. The bargain lunch *menu* includes a starter, main course, glass of wine, and coffee for €14. At €29, the three-course dinner *menu* is worth every penny. They pride themselves equally on their small-producers' wine list, so follow your server's advice (closed Sun–Mon, 8 rue Thénard, reservations necessary, tel. 01 43 54 59 47).

On Rue Mouffetard

Lying several blocks behind the Panthéon, rue Mouffetard is a conveyor belt of comparison-shopping eaters with wall-to-wall budget options (fondue, crêpes, Italian, falafel, and Greek). Come here to sift through the crowds and eat cheap (you get what you pay for). This street stays up late and likes to party (particularly around place de la Contrescarpe). The gauntlet begins on top, at thriving place de la Contrescarpe, and ends below where rue Mouffetard stops at St. Médard Church. Both ends offer fun cafés where you can watch the action. The upper stretch is pedestrian and touristy;

the bottom stretch is purely Parisian. Anywhere between is no-man's land for consistent quality. Still, strolling with so many fun-seekers is enjoyable, whether you eat or not. To get here, use the Censier Daubenton Métro stop.

$$ Café Delmas, at the top of rue Mouffetard on picturesque place de la Contrescarpe, is *the* place to see and be seen. Come here for a before- or after-dinner drink on the broad outdoor terrace, or for typical but pricey café cuisine (€15 salads, €22 *plats*, great chocolate ice cream, daily).

$ Bar-restaurant Les Papillons is a down-and-dirty local diner where a few outdoor tables tangle with pedestrians, and no one seems to care. Join the fun. As smiling owner Eric says, "Everyone sings after zee wine" (€12 *plats*, closed Sun–Mon, 129 rue Mouffetard, tel. 01 43 31 66 50).

$ Cave de Bourgogne, a young and local hangout, has reason-ably priced café fare at the bottom of rue Mouffetard. The outside has picture-perfect tables on a raised terrace; the interior is warm and lively (€13–16 *plats*, specials listed on chalkboards, daily, 144 rue Mouffetard).

In Montmartre

Much of Montmartre is extremely touristy, with mindless mobs following guides to cancan shows. But the ambience is undeniably fun, and an evening overlooking Paris is a quintessential experi-ence in the City of Light.

Near Sacré-Cœur

The steps in front of Sacré-Cœur are perfect for a picnic with a view, though the spot comes with lots of company. Along the touristy main drag (near place du Tertre and just off it), several fun piano bars serve crêpes along with great people-watching. To reach this area, use the Anvers Métro stop. For locations, see the map on page 168.

$$ Restaurant Chez Plumeau, just off jam-packed place du Tertre, is touristy yet moderately priced, with formal service but great seating on a tiny, charming square (elaborate €17 salads, €18–22 *plats*, closed Wed, place du Calvaire, tel. 01 46 06 26 29).

$$ Moulin de la Galette lets you dine with Renoir under the historic windmill in a comfortable setting with good prices. Find the old photos scattered about the place (€17 two-course *menu*, €25 three-course *menu*, daily, 83 rue Lépic, Mo: Abbesses, tel. 01 46 06 84 77).

$ L'Eté en Pente Douce is a good Montmartre choice, hiding under the generous branches of street trees. Just downhill from the crowds on a classic neighborhood corner, it features cheery indoor and outdoor seating, €10 *plats du jour* and salads, vegetarian options, and good wines (daily, many steps below Sacré-Cœur to the left as you leave, down the stairs below the WC, 23 rue Muller, tel. 01 42 64 02 67).

$ Au Relais, on the backside of Montmartre with no hint of tourists, is a neighborhood café, offering a two-course lunch *menu du jour* with a coffee for €11 and good-value dinners (daily, 48 rue Lamarck, at the intersection with rue Mont Cenis, outdoor seating, tel. 01 46 06 68 32). From place du Tertre, walk north on rue Mont Cenis, down two long staircases to rue Lamarck. If you don't want to brave the steps back up after you've finished your meal, head for the closest Métro stop, Lamarck-Caulaincourt (turn right out of the café).

Near Rue des Abbesses

At the bottom of Montmartre, residents pile into a long lineup of brasseries and cafés along rue des Abbesses (Mo. Abbesses). The food is average; the atmosphere is anything but. Come here for a lively, tourist-free scene. The street is perfect for a picnic-gathering stroll with cheese shops, delis, wine stores, and bakeries. In fact, the baker at **Le Grenier à Pain** won the award for the Best Baguette in Paris in 2010 (Thu–Mon 7:30–20:00, closed Tue–Wed, 38 rue des Abbesses, tel. 01 42 23 85 36). For locations, see the map on page 168.

$ Le Chinon Brasserie offers good seating inside and out and is the best bet for café/wine bar ambience and fare (daily, 49 rue des Abbesses, tel. 01 42 62 07 17).

$ Le Relais Gascon serves giant salads (€12) topped with their signature garlic *frites* and a selection of grilled meats (€12–15) in a narrow dining room on two floors (nonstop service daily 10:30–24:00, 6 rue des Abbesses, just after the post office as you leave place des Abbesses, tel. 01 42 58 58 22).

Elsewhere in Paris
Next to the Galerie Vivienne, Behind the Palais Royal

$$$ Le Grand Colbert, appropriately located in the elegant Galerie Colbert, gives its clients the feel of a luxury restaurant at relatively moderate prices. It's a stylish, grand brasserie with hurried waiters, leather booths, and brass lamps, serving all the classic dishes from steak *frites* to escargots (*menus* from €42, daily, 4 rue Vivienne, Mo: Palais Royal/Musée du Louvre or Pyramides, tel. 01 42 86 82 38).

Along Canal St. Martin, North of République

Escape the crowded tourist areas and enjoy a breezy canalside experience. Take the Métro to place de la République and walk down rue Beaurepaire to Canal St. Martin. There you'll find a few worthwhile cafés with similarly reasonable prices. **$ La Marine** is a good choice (daily, 55 bis quai de Valmy, tel. 01 42 39 69 81). In summertime most bars and cafés offer beer and wine to go (*à emporter*), so you can take it to the canal's edge and picnic there with the younger crowd.

Dinner Cruises

The following companies offer dinner cruises (reservations required). Bateaux-Mouches and Bateaux Parisiens have the best reputations and the highest prices. They offer multicourse meals and music in aircraft carrier–size dining rooms with glass tops and good views. For both, proper dress is required—no denim, shorts, or sport shoes; Bateaux-Mouches requires a jacket and tie for men. The main difference between these companies is the music: Bateaux-Mouches offers violin and piano to entertain your romantic evening, whereas Bateaux Parisiens boasts a lively atmosphere with a singer, band, and dance floor.

Bateaux-Mouches, started in 1949, is hands-down the most famous. You can't miss its sparkling port on the north side of the river at Pont de l'Alma. The boats usually board 19:30–20:15, depart at 20:30, and return at 22:45 (€95–130/person, RER: Pont de l'Alma, tel. 01 42 25 96 10, www.bateauxmouches.com).

Bateaux Parisiens leaves from Port de la Bourdonnais, just east of the bridge under the Eiffel Tower. Begin boarding at 19:45, leave at 20:30, and return at 23:00 (€65/person for 18:30 departure with dinner, €100–145/person for 20:30 departure, price depends on view seating and *menu* option, tel. 01 76 64 14 45, www.bateaux parisiens.com). The middle level is best. Pay the few extra euros to get seats next to the windows—it's more romantic and private, with sensational views.

Le Capitaine Fracasse offers the budget option (€50/person, €70 with wine and coffee; tables are first-come, first-serve, so get there early; boarding times vary by season and day of week, closed Mon, walk down stairs in the middle of Bir Hakeim bridge near the Eiffel Tower to Iles aux Cygne, Mo: Bir-Hakeim or RER: Champ de Mars-Tour Eiffel, tel. 01 46 21 48 15, www.croisiere -paris.com).

Paris Connections

When leaving Paris, get to your departure point early to allow time for waiting in lines. Figure on 2–3 hours for an overseas flight; 1–2 hours for flights within Europe (particularly if flying with one of the budget airlines, which tend to have long check-in lines); and 40 minutes for a train trip or long-distance bus ride, if you're doing anything beyond simply boarding (Eurostar trains require you to check in at least 30 minutes early). Whether arriving or departing, always keep your luggage safely near you. Pickpockets prey on jet-lagged tourists on shuttle trains and buses.

Don't take an unauthorized taxi from cabbies greeting you on arrival. Official taxi stands are well-signed.

Trains

Paris is Europe's rail hub, with six major stations and one minor one, each serving different regions:

- Gare du Nord (northern France and Europe)
- Gare Montparnasse (northwestern France and TGV service to France's southwest)
- Gare de Lyon (southeastern France and Italy)
- Gare de l'Est (northeastern France and eastbound international trains)
- Gare St. Lazare (northwestern France)
- Gare d'Austerlitz (southwestern France and Europe)
- Gare de Bercy (smaller station, departure point for most night trains to Italy)

All six main train stations have banks or currency exchanges, ATMs, train information desks, telephones, cafés, newsstands, and clever pickpockets (pay attention in ticket lines—keep your bag firmly gripped in front of you). Because of security concerns, not all have baggage checks.

Any train station has schedule information, can make reservations, and can sell tickets for any destination. Buying tickets is handier from an SNCF neighborhood office. See the sidebar on page 201 for a more extensive list.

Each station offers two types of rail service: long distance to other cities, called Grandes Lignes (major lines); and suburban service to nearby areas, called Banlieue, Transilien, or RER. You also may see ticket windows identified as *Ile de France*. These are for Transilien trains serving destinations outside Paris in the Ile de France region (usually no more than an hour from Paris).

Paris train stations can be intimidating, but if you slow down, take a deep breath, and ask for help, you'll find them manageable and efficient. Bring a pad of paper for clear communication at ticket/info windows. All stations have helpful information booths (*accueil*); the bigger stations have roving helpers, usually wearing red or blue vests. They're capable of answering rail questions more quickly than the staff at the information desks or ticket windows. I make a habit of confirming my track number and departure time with these helpers.

To make your trip go more smoothly, be sure to review the many train tips on page 1019.

Paris' Train Stations

Here's an overview of Paris' major train stations. Métro and RER trains, as well as buses and taxis, are well-marked at every station. When arriving by Métro, follow signs for *Grandes Lignes-SNCF* to find the main tracks.

Gare du Nord

The granddaddy of Paris' train stations serves cities in northern France and international destinations north of Paris, including Copenhagen, Amsterdam (see "To Brussels and Amsterdam by Thalys Train," later), and the Eurostar to London (see "To London by Eurostar Train," later). Arrive early to allow time to navigate this station. Monet-esque views over the trains and peaceful, air-conditioned cafés hide on the upper level near Eurostar ticket windows (find the cool view WCs down the steps in the café).

Key Destinations Served by Gare du Nord Grandes Lignes: **Brussels** (about 2/hour, 1.5 hours), **Bruges** (about 2/hour, 2.5 hours, change in Brussels), **Amsterdam** (8–10/day, 3.5 hours direct), **Berlin** (6/day, 9 hours, 1–2 changes, via Belgium, better connections from Gare de l'Est), **Koblenz** (6/day, 5 hours, change in Köln, more from Gare de l'Est that don't cross Belgium), **Copenhagen** (7/day, 14–18 hours, two night trains), and **London** by Eurostar Chunnel train (12–15/day, 2.5 hours, toll tel. 08 36 35 35 39).

By Banlieue/RER Lines: Charles de Gaulle Airport (4/hour, 30 minutes, runs 5:00–24:00, track 4).

Gare Montparnasse

This big, modern station covers three floors, serves lower Normandy and Brittany, and has TGV service to the Loire Valley and south-western France, as well as suburban service to Chartres.

Air France buses to Orly and Charles de Gaulle Airports stop outside the exit to the far right. City buses are out the front of the station (down the escalator through the glassy façade). Bus #96 is good for connecting to Marais and Luxembourg area hotels, while #92 is best for rue Cler hotels (easier than the Métro).

Key Destinations Served by Gare Montparnasse: Chartres (10/day, 65 minutes), **Amboise** (12/day in 1.5 hours with change in St. Pierre-des-Corps, requires TGV reservation; non-TGV trains leave from Gare d'Austerlitz), **Pontorson/Mont St. Michel** (7/day, 3.5–4 hours, via Rennes or Dreux, some with bus from Rennes), **Dinan** (6/day, 4 hours, change in Rennes and Dol), **Bordeaux** (20/day, 3.5 hours), **Sarlat** (7/day, allow 6 hours; 3/day with change in Bordeaux-St. Jean or Libourne, then TGV; 4/day to Souillac, then bus), **Toulouse** (13/day, 5–7 hours, most require change, usually in Bordeaux or Montpellier), **Albi** (6/day, 6–7.5 hours, change in

Paris Train Stations

Paris Train Stations & Destinations

1 *Gare du Nord:* To London, Brussels, Amsterdam, Copenhagen & N. France (also Chantilly & Auvers-sur-Oise)

2 *Gare Montparnasse:* To Spain, SW France (Languedoc & Dordogne), Loire Valley, Brittany & Mont St. Michel (also Chartres)

3 *Gare de Lyon:* To Italy & SE France (Burgundy, Alps, Provence & Riviera; also Fontainebleau & Melun/Vaux-le-Vicomte)

4 *Gare de Bercy:* Night trains to Italy

5 *Gare de l'Est:* To NE France (Reims, Champagne & Alsace), Germany, Switzerland and Austria

6 *Gare St. Lazare:* To Normandy (incl. Caen, Bayeux & Vernon/Giverny)

7 *Gare d'Austerlitz:* To Spain, SW France & Loire Valley

Toulouse, also night train), **Carcassonne** (14/day, 6.5 hours, most require changes in Toulouse or Montpellier, direct trains take 8 hours, night train also available), **Tours** (18/day, 1 hour), **Madrid** (3/day, 13.5 hours), and **Lisbon** (1/day, 21.5 hours via Irun).

Gare de Lyon

This huge, bewildering station offers TGV and regular service to southeastern France, Italy, and other international destinations (for more trains to Italy, see "Gare de Bercy," next). Don't leave this station without visiting the recommended Le Train Bleu Restaurant lounge, up the stairs opposite track G.

Grande Ligne trains arrive and depart from street level, but are divided into two areas (tracks A–N in the blue area, and 5–23 in the yellow area). Monitors will show either yellow or blue even before the track is posted, so you know which general area your train leaves from. The two areas are connected by the hallway adjacent to track A and opposite track 9.

"Les Cars" Air France buses to Montparnasse (easy transfer to Orly Airport) and direct to Charles de Gaulle Airport stop outside the station's main entrance (opposite tracks A–L, walk across the parking lot—the stop is opposite the Café Européen on the right; €16, 2/hour, normally at :15 and :45 after the hour).

Key Destinations Served by Gare de Lyon: Vaux-le-Vicomte (train to Melun, 2/hour by train, 30 minutes; 3/hour by RER, 45 minutes), **Fontainebleau** (nearly hourly, 45 minutes), **Disneyland** (RER line A-4 to Marne-la-Vallée-Chessy, at least 3/hour, 45 minutes), **Beaune** (nearly hourly, 2.5 hours, most require change in Dijon), **Dijon** (nearly hourly, 1.5 hours), **Chamonix** (6–8/day, 6–8 hours), **Annecy** (13/day, 4–5 hours, many with change in Lyon), **Lyon** (at least hourly, 2 hours), **Avignon** (9/day in 2.5 hours to Avignon TGV station, 5/day in 3.5 hours to Avignon Centre-Ville station, more connections with change—3–4 hours), **Arles** (11/day, 2 direct TGVs in 4 hours, 9 with change in Avignon in 5 hours), **Nice** (10/day, 6 hours, may require change, 11-hour night train possible out of Gare d'Austerlitz), **Venice** (3/day, 4/night, 10–13 hours with change in Milan; 1 direct overnight, 13 hours, important to reserve ahead), **Rome** (3/day, 13–16 hours, plus several overnight options, important to reserve ahead), **Bern** (9/day: 1 direct—4.5 hours, otherwise 5.5 hours; faster trains from Gare de l'Est), **Interlaken** (5/day, 6–6.5 hours, 1–3 changes, 6 more from Gare de l'Est), and **Barcelona** (3/day, 9 hours, 1–2 changes; night train possible from Gare d'Austerlitz).

Gare de Bercy

This smaller station handles some night train service to Italy (Mo: Bercy, one stop east of Gare de Lyon on line 14, exit the Métro station and it's across the street). Facilities are limited—just a WC and a sandwich-fare takeout café.

Gare de l'Est

This two-floor station (with underground Métro) is easy to navigate. All trains depart at street level from tracks 1–30. A train information office is opposite track 17, and ticket sales are at each end of the station through the halls opposite tracks 8 and 25. All other services are down the escalator through the hall opposite tracks 12–20 (baggage lockers, car rental, post office, WC, small grocery store, and Métro access).

Key Destinations Served by Gare de l'Est: Colmar (12/day with TGV, 3.5 hours, change in Strasbourg), **Strasbourg** (hourly with TGV, 2.5 hours), **Reims** (12/day with TGV, 45 minutes), **Verdun** (9/day with TGV, 1.5–3 hours with transfer in Metz or Châlons-sur-Marne), **Bern** (9/day, 4.5–5 hours, 1–2 changes), **Interlaken** (6/day, 5.5–6 hours, 1–2 changes, 5 more from Gare de Lyon), **Zürich** (roughly hourly, 4.5–5 hours, 4 direct, others with change in Strasbourg or Mulhouse and Basel), **Vienna** (7/day, 12–17 hours, 1–3 changes, night train via Munich or Frankfurt), **Prague** (5/day, 12–18 hours, night train via Mannheim or Berlin), **Munich** (4/day, 6–7 hours, most with 1 change, 1 direct night train), and **Berlin** (6/day, 8–9 hours, 1–2 changes; 1 direct night train, 11.25 hours).

Gare St. Lazare

This compact station serves upper Normandy, including Rouen and Giverny. All trains arrive and depart one floor above street level. The station is undergoing renovation, so be prepared for the temporary displacement of shops and services.

Key Destinations Served by Gare St. Lazare: Giverny (train to Vernon, 8/day Mon–Sat, 6/day Sun, 45 minutes), **Rouen** (hourly, 1–1.5 hours), **Honfleur** (13/day, 2–3.5 hours, via Lisieux, then bus), **Bayeux** (9/day, 2.5 hours, some change in Caen), **Caen** (14/day, 2 hours), and **Pontorson/Mont St. Michel** (2/day, 4–5.5 hours, via Caen; more trains from Gare Montparnasse).

Gare d'Austerlitz

This small station provides non-TGV service to the Loire Valley, southwestern France, and Spain. All tracks are at street level. The information booth is opposite track 17, and all ticket sales are in the hall opposite track 10. To get to the Métro and RER, you must walk outside and along either side of the station.

Key Destinations Served by Gare d'Austerlitz: Versailles (RER line C, 4/hour, 30–40 minutes), **Amboise** (6/day direct in 2 hours, 5/day with transfer in Blois or Les Aubrais–Orléans; faster TGV connection from Gare Montparnasse), **Cahors** (5/day, 5 hours, 1 direct night train; other slower trains from Gare Montparnasse), **Barcelona** (1/night, 12 hours; day trains from Gare de Lyon), and **Madrid** (2/night, 13 hours direct, 16 hours via Irun; day trains from Gare Montparnasse).

SNCF Boutiques

You can save time and stress by buying train tickets or making train reservations at an SNCF Boutique. These small branch offices of the French national rail company are conveniently located throughout Paris, with offices near most of my recommended hotels and museums and at Orly and Charles de Gaulle Airports. Arrive when they open to avoid lines (generally open Mon-Sat 8:30-19:00 or 20:00, closed Sun). For a complete list, see www.megacomik.info/boutiquesncf.htm.

Historic Core

- 18 rue du Pont Neuf, Mo: Pont Neuf

Marais

- 2 rue de Turenne, Mo: St. Paul
- 5 rue de Lyon, Mo: Gare de Lyon

Near Major Museums

- Musée d'Orsay RER station, below Orsay Museum
- Forum des Halles shopping mall, basement sublevel -4, returns office (*Salle d'Echanges*), Mo: Châtelet-Les Halles

Champs Elysées

- 229 rue du Faubourg Saint-Honoré, Mo: Saint-Philippe-du-Roule

Farther North on the Right Bank

- 53 rue Chaussée d'Antin, Mo: Chaussée d'Antin (near Opéra Garnier and Galeries Lafayette)
- 32/34 rue Joubert, Mo: Haussman-St. Lazare (near Gare St. Lazare)
- 71/73 boulevard Magenta, Mo: Gare du Nord (Gare du Nord)
- 82 avenue de la Grande Armée, Mo: Porte Maillot (near Hôtel Concorde-Lafayette and Beauvais Airport bus stop)

Montmartre

- 27 rue Lépic, Mo: Blanche

Eiffel Tower/Rue Cler

- 80 rue Saint Dominique, Mo: La Tour Maubourg
- 19 rue de Passy, Mo: Passy (near Marmottan Museum)
- Invalides Métro/RER station

Latin Quarter/Luxembourg Garden

- 54 boulevard St. Michel, Mo: Cluny-Sorbonne
- 79 rue de Rennes, Mo: St. Sulpice

Farther South on the Left Bank

- 17 rue Littré, Mo: Montparnasse-Bienvenüe (near Luxembourg Garden and grand cafés)
- 68 avenue du Maine: Mo. Montparnasse-Bienvenüe (near grand cafés)
- 30 avenue d'Italie, in Centre Commerciale Galaxie, Mo: Place d'Italie

To Brussels and Amsterdam by Thalys Train

The pricey Thalys train has the monopoly on the rail route between Paris and Brussels (for a cheaper option, try the Eurolines bus, described later). Without a railpass you'll pay about €80–100 second class for the Paris–Amsterdam train (compared to €45 by bus) or about €60–80 second class for the Paris–Brussels train (compared to €25 by bus). Even with a railpass, you need to pay for train reservations (second class–€26; first class–€41–54, includes a meal). Book at least a day ahead, as seats are limited (www.thalys.com). Or hop on the bus, Gus.

To London by Eurostar Train

The fastest, most convenient way to get from the Eiffel Tower to Big Ben is by rail. Eurostar, a joint service of the Belgian, British, and French railways, is the speedy passenger train that zips you (and up to 800 others in 18 sleek cars) from downtown Paris to downtown London (at least 15/day, 2.5 hours) faster and more easily than flying. The actual tunnel crossing is a 20-minute, silent, 100-mile-per-hour nonevent. Your ears won't even pop. Eurostar's monopoly expired at the beginning of 2010, and Air France has already announced plans to start a competing high-speed rail service between London and Paris (possibly in 2011).

Eurostar Fares: Channel fares are reasonable but complicated. Prices vary depending on how far ahead you reserve, whether you can live with restrictions, and whether you're eligible for any discounts (children, youths, seniors, roundtrip travelers, and railpass holders all qualify).

Fares can change without notice, but typically a one-way, full-fare ticket (with no restrictions on refundability) runs about $425 first-class and $300 second-class. Cheaper seats come with more restrictions and can sell out quickly (figure $100–160 for second-class, one-way). Those traveling with a railpass that covers France or Britain should look first at the passholder fare ($85–130 for second-class, one-way Eurostar trips). For more details, visit my Guide to Eurail Passes (www.ricksteves.com/eurostar) or Rail Europe (www.raileurope.com), or go directly to Eurostar (www.eurostar.com).

Buying Eurostar Tickets: Because only the most expensive (full-fare) ticket is fully refundable, don't reserve until you're sure of your plans. But if you wait too long, the cheapest tickets will get bought up.

As soon as you're confident about the time and date of your crossing, you can check and book fares by phone or online. Ordering online through Eurostar or major agents offers a print-at-home e-ticket option. You can also order by phone through Rail Europe at US tel. 800-EUROSTAR for home delivery before you

Eurostar Routes

EUROSTAR
--- CHANNEL TUNNEL
...... OTHER RAIL

ENGLAND
LONDON
EBBS FLEET
ASHFORD
CALAIS FRETHUN
LILLE
PARIS
FRANCE
BELG.
BRUSSELS
NETH.
AMSTERDAM
N

50 MI
100 KM

go, or through Eurostar (French toll tel. 08 92 35 35 39, priced in euros) and pick up your ticket at the train station. In Europe you can buy your Eurostar ticket at any major train station in any country, at neighborhood SNCF offices (see "SNCF Boutiques," earlier), or at any travel agency that handles train tickets (expect a booking fee). You can purchase passholder discount tickets at Eurostar departure stations, through US agents, or by phone with Eurostar, but they may be harder to get at other train stations and travel agencies, and are a discount category that can sell out.

Remember France's time zone is one hour later than Britain's. Times printed on tickets are local times (departure from Paris is French time, arrival in London is British time).

Taking the Eurostar: Eurostar trains depart from and arrive at Paris' Gare du Nord. Check in at least 30 minutes in advance for your Eurostar trip. It's very similar to an airport check-in: You pass through airport-like security, fill out a customs form, show your passport to customs officials, and find a TV monitor to locate your departure gate. The currency-exchange booth here has rates about the same as you'll find on the other end.

Buses

The main bus station is Gare Routière du Paris-Gallieni (28 avenue du Général de Gaulle, in suburb of Bagnolet, Mo: Gallieni, tel. 01 49 72 51 51). Buses provide cheaper—if less comfortable and more time-consuming—transportation to major European cities. The bus is also the cheapest way to cross the English Channel; book at least two days in advance for the best fares. Eurolines' buses depart from here (toll tel. 08 36 69 52 52, www.eurolines.com). Look on their website for offices in central Paris.

Airports

Charles de Gaulle Airport

Paris' primary airport has three terminals: T-1, T-2, and T-3 (see map). Most flights from the US use T-1 or T-2. To find out which terminal serves your airline, check your ticket or contact the airport (toll tel. 3950, www.adp.fr).

The RER (Paris suburban train, connecting to Métro) stops

Charles de Gaulle Airport

Legend:
- ® RER STOP
- P PARKING
- ® AIR FRANCE/ROISSY BUS STOP
- ▬ CDGVAL SHUTTLE TRAIN + STATION

N (compass)

TERMINAL 1
- UNDERGROUND WALKWAYS
- CONTROL TOWER
- P PARKING

To ROISSY-EN-FRANCE,
2, A-1 FREEWAY + PARIS

TERMINAL 3
- P PARKING

To LILLE + BRUSSELS

TERMINAL 2
- 2 A, 2 B, 2 C, 2 D, 2 E, 2 F
- CONTROL TOWER
- TRAIN STATION (TGV + ®) + SHERATON HOTEL
- DCH

To DISNEYLAND PARIS,
DIJON, LYON + AVIGNON

1 Hôtel Ibis & Novotel
2 To Hôtel Ibis, Hôtel Campanile,
Hôtel Kyriad Prestige & B&B Hôtel

at T-2 and T-3; the TGV (high-speed train) station is at T-2. The free CDGVAL automated shuttle train links the three terminals and two parking garages (free, every 5 minutes, 24/7). Allow 30 minutes to get between terminals and 60 minutes total travel time between your gates at T-1 and T-2.

Baggage storage is available but pricey, and requires a six-hour minimum (€16, inquire at any info desk or call Baggage du Monde at 01 34 38 58 97). I'd stash my bag at a Paris train station instead.

Terminal 1 (T-1): This circular terminal has one main entry and three key floors—arrival (*arrivées*), departure (*départs*, one floor down), and CDGVAL shuttle trains and shops/boutiques (basement level). For information on getting to Paris, see "Transportation Between Charles de Gaulle Airport and Paris," later.

Arrival Level (*niveau arrivée*): After passing through customs, you'll exit at Gate 36. Nearby are information counters with English-speaking staff, a café, a newsstand, and an ATM. Walk clockwise around the terminal to find gates with Air France and Roissy buses to Paris, Disneyland shuttles, car rentals, and taxis.

Departure Level (niveau départ): Flight check-in, access to basement level and CDGVAL shuttle trains are on this level. Those with boarding passes can access several restaurants, a post office (PTT), a pharmacy, boutiques, and a handy grocery store one floor below the ticketing desks (niveau 2 on the elevator).

Terminal 2 (T-2): This long, horseshoe-shaped terminal is divided into six subterminals (or halls), labeled A through F. The RER and TGV stations are below the Sheraton Hotel (prepare for long walks to reach them). To locate stops for Air France buses and Roissy-Buses—marked on the map on page 204—follow *Paris by Bus* signs and see "Transportation Between Charles de Gaulle Airport and Paris," next. Car-rental offices, post offices, pharmacies, and ATMs (distributeurs) are also well-signed. Confused? Orange ADP information desks are located near Gate 6 in each hall (ask where to buy a Paris Museum Pass).

Transportation Between Charles de Gaulle Airport and Paris: Three public-transportation routes, airport vans, and taxis link the airport's terminals with central Paris. If you're traveling with one or two companions, carrying lots of baggage, or are just plain tired, taxis are worth the extra cost (avoid the airport vans going in the airport-to-Paris direction; see why later in this section).

RER-B trains from the airport to Paris stop at T-2 and near T-3 (connections from T-1 on the CDGVAL shuttle train), then stop in central Paris at Gare du Nord, Châtelet–Les Halles, St. Michel, and Luxembourg (€9.50, 4/hour, runs 5:00–24:00, 30 minutes to Gare du Nord). Follow *Paris by Train* signs, then *RER* signs. The RER station at T-2 mixes with a busy main train station, so pay attention—look for green *Paris/Ile de France* (Paris and Suburbs) ticket windows and expect lines. It's faster to buy tickets from the machines (coins required, break your bills at an airport shop) as lines can be long at ticket windows. The T-3 RER station is less crowded and just five minutes away by CDGVAL shuttle train.

RER-B trains from Paris to the airport run about every 20 minutes. Make sure the sign over the platform shows *Roissy–Charles de Gaulle* as a stop served (the line splits, so not every line B train serves the airport). If you're not clear, ask another rider (air-o-por sharl dub Gaul?). Beware of pickpockets; wear your money belt.

Roissy-Buses run to the Opéra Métro stop (€9.40, 4/hour, runs 6:30–21:00, 50 minutes, buy ticket on bus). You'll arrive at a bus stop on rue Scribe on the left side of the Opéra building. To get to the Métro entrance, turn left out of the bus and walk counterclockwise around the lavish Opéra building. The Métro station entrance faces the Opéra's front. You can also take a taxi (about

Public Transportation to Recommended Hotels

You have many options for traveling between Charles de Gaulle Airport and Paris. These are especially handy for getting to recommended hotels.

Rue Cler area: Take Roissy-Bus to Opéra, then take Métro line 8 (direction: Balard) and get off at the La Tour Maubourg or Ecole Militaire stop. Or take RER-B to the St. Michel stop, transfer to RER-C toward Versailles Rive Gauche, and get off at the Pont de l'Alma stop.

Marais: Take "Les Cars" Air France bus (#4) to Gare de Lyon, enter the train station to find the Métro, then take a quick trip on Métro line 1, direction: La Défense. Get off at the Bastille, St. Paul, or Hôtel de Ville stop. Or take RER-B from the airport to the Châtelet– Les Halles stop and transfer to Métro line 1, direction: Château de Vincennes (long walk in a huge station), and get off at Hôtel de Ville, St. Paul or Bastille.

Luxembourg Garden: RER-B to the Luxembourg stop.

€12) to any of my listed hotels from behind the Opéra (the stand is in front of Galeries Lafayette department store).

"Les Cars" Air France buses serve central Paris on two routes (€16, at least 2/hour, runs 5:45–23:00, toll tel. 08 92 35 08 20, www.cars-airfrance.com). Bus #2 runs between the airport and the Arc de Triomphe and Porte Maillot (45 minutes). Bus #4 runs to Gare de Lyon (45 minutes) and continues to the Montparnasse Tower/train station (1 hour). A third line runs to Orly Airport (see page 209).

Taxis cost about €60 for up to three people with bags (more if traffic is bad). Your hotel can call for a taxi to the airport. Specify that you want a real taxi (un taxi normal), and not a limo service that costs €20 more (and gives your hotel a kickback).

Airport vans work like those at home, packing several passengers from different hotels into a van and taking them to or from the airport. They work best for trips from your hotel to the airport. They don't work as well for trips from the airport because you must book a set pick-up time in advance, even though you don't know exactly when you'll arrive, get your baggage, and so on (the exception is Paris Webservices, which meets you inside the terminal). The hotel-to-airport service takes longer than a taxi because you make several hotel stops on the way, but is a particularly good deal for single travelers or families of four or more (which is too many people for a taxi). If your hotel doesn't work with a van service, reserve directly (book at least a day in advance—most hoteliers will make the call for you). Airport vans cost about €30 for one person, €43 for two, and €55 for three. Here are a couple of companies to consider: **Paris Shuttles Network** (tel. 01 45 26 01 58, www. shuttlesnetwork.com), **Airport Connection** (tel. 01 43 65 55 55, www.airport-connection.com), and **Paris Webservices** (meets you inside the terminal, €155/up to 4 people round-trip, €185/up to 6 people, use promo code "RSteves 07" for 10 percent discount, excursions available—see page 75, sells Museum Passes with no extra fee—order ahead, tel. 01 53 62 02 29, fax 01 53 01 35 84, www.pariswebservices.com, contactpws@pariswebservices.com).

A **Disneyland shuttle van** is at each terminal (€17, runs every 20 minutes daily 8:30–20:00ish, 30 minutes). TGV trains also run to Disneyland from the airport in 10 minutes, but leave less frequently (hourly) and require shuttle buses at each end—take the shuttle van instead.

Sleeping at or near Charles de Gaulle Airport

$$ Hôtel Ibis**, outside the T-3 RER stop, is huge and offers standard airport accommodations (Db–€95-130, tel. 01 49 19 19 19, fax 01 49 19 19 21, www.ibishotel.com, h1404@accor.com).

$$ Novotel*** is nearby and the next step up (Db–€130–180, can rise to €280 for last-minute rooms, tel. 01 49 19 27 27, fax 01 49 19 27 99, www.novotel.com, h1014@accor.com). Both places have restaurants, and are cheapest when booked well in advance.

Orly Airport

This airport feels small, but it has all the services you'd expect at a major airport: ATMs and currency exchange, car-rental desks, cafés, shops, a post office, a TI, and more (flight info tel. 3950—€0.35/minute, www.adp.fr). It's good for rental-car pickup and drop-off, as it's closer to Paris and far easier to navigate than Charles de Gaulle Airport.

Orly has two terminals: Ouest (west) and Sud (south). Air France and a few other carriers arrive at Ouest, and most others use Sud. At both terminals, arrivals are on the ground level and departures are on level one. You can connect the terminals with the free Orlyval shuttle train (departs from Ouest departures level at exit A; from Sud at exit K), or with any of the shuttle buses (*navettes*) that also travel into downtown Paris.

Transportation Between Orly Airport and Paris: Choose between shuttle buses (*navettes*), the RER, taxis, and airport vans. They all connect Paris with either terminal.

"Les Cars" Air France buses run to Gare Montparnasse, Invalides, and Etoile Métro stops, all of which have connections to several Métro lines. Bus #1 goes only to Gare Montparnasse. Bus #1* (with an asterisk) hits Gare Montparnasse, Invalides, and Etoile. For the rue Cler neighborhood, take the #1* bus to

Invalides, then the Métro to La Tour Maubourg or Ecole Militaire. Both buses depart from Ouest exit D or Sud exit L: Look for signs to *navettes* (€11.50, buy ticket from driver, 4/hour, 40 minutes to Invalides).

The **Orlybus** goes directly to the Denfert-Rochereau Métro stop. From there you can catch the Métro or RER-B to central Paris, including the Luxembourg area, Notre-Dame Cathedral, and Gare du Nord. The Orlybus departs from Ouest exit D and Sud exit H (€6.60, 2/hour, 30 minutes).

A different bus called **"Paris par le train"** takes you to the Pont d'Orly RER station, where you can catch the RER-C to Gare d'Austerlitz, St. Michel/Notre-Dame, Musée d'Orsay, Invalides (change here for rue Cler hotels), and Pont de l'Alma. Catch this bus at Ouest exit G or Sud exit F (€6.50 total, 4/hour, 40 minutes).

The **Orlyval shuttle train** takes you to the Antony RER station, where you can catch RER-B to Luxembourg and many recommended hotels, Châtelet-Les Halles, St. Michel, and Gare du Nord. Catch the Orlyval at Ouest exit A or Sud exit K (€10.50 total, 6/hour, 40 minutes).

Taxis are to the far right as you leave the terminal, at Gate M. Allow €38 with bags for a taxi into central Paris.

Airport vans are good for single travelers or families of four or more (too many for a taxi) if going from Paris to the airport (see page 206; from Orly, figure about €23/1 person, €30/2 people, less per person for larger groups and kids).

The Val d'Europe (VEA) **shuttle bus to Disneyland** departs from Ouest exit D or the Sud bus station (€17, daily 8:30–19:45, 45 minutes).

Beauvais Airport

Budget airlines such as Ryanair use this small airport, offering dirt-cheap airfares but leaving you 50 miles north of Paris. Still, this airport has direct buses to Paris (see below), and is handy for travelers heading to Normandy or Belgium (car rental available). The airport is basic, waiting areas are crowded, and services are sparse, but improvements are gradually on the way as Beauvais deals with an increasing number of passengers (airport toll tel. 08 92 68 20 66, www.aeroportbeauvais.com; Ryanair toll tel. 08 92 68 20 73, www.ryanair.com).

Transportation Between Beauvais Airport and Paris: Buses depart from the airport when they're full (about 20 minutes after flights arrive) and take 1.5 hours to reach Paris. Buy your ticket (€14 one-way) at the little kiosk to the right as you exit the airport. Buses arrive at Porte Maillot on the west edge of Paris (on Métro line 1 and RER-C). The closest taxi stand is at Hôtel Concorde-Lafayette.

Buses heading to Beauvais Airport leave from Porte Maillot about 3.25 hours before scheduled flight departures. Catch the bus in the parking lot on boulevard Pershing next to Hôtel Concorde-Lafayette. Arrive with enough time to purchase your bus ticket before boarding (bus toll tel. 08 92 68 20 64).

Trains connect Beauvais' city center and Paris' Gare du Nord (20/day, 80 minutes).

Taxis run from Beauvais Airport to Beauvais' train station or city center (€14) or central Paris (allow €125).

Connecting Paris' Airports

"Les Cars" Air France buses directly and conveniently link Charles de Gaulle and Orly airports (bus #3, stops at Charles de Gaulle terminals 1 and 2 and Orly Ouest Gate 3 or Sud Gate L, roughly 2/hour, 5:45–23:00, 60 minutes, €19).

RER line B connects Charles de Gaulle and Orly but requires a transfer to the Orlyval train. It isn't as easy as the Air France bus mentioned above, though it's faster when there's traffic (5/hour, 1.5 hours, €18). This line splits at both ends: Heading to Orly, take trains that serve the Antony stop (then transfer to Orlyval train); heading to Charles de Gaulle, take trains that end at the airport ("Roissy-CDG"), not Mitry-Claye.

Three **Val d'Europe (VEA) buses** a day run between Beauvais and Charles de Gaulle or Orly airports (€16, www.vea-shuttle .co.uk).

You can connect to a train to Beauvais Airport at Gare du Nord (see "Beauvais Airport," earlier).

Taxis are easiest, but pricey (about €80 between Charles de Gaulle and Orly, €115 between Charles de Gaulle and Beauvais, €135 between Orly and Beauvais).

NEAR PARIS

Versailles • Chartres • Giverny • Disneyland Paris

Efficient trains bring dozens of day trips within the grasp of temporary Parisians. Europe's best palace at Versailles, the awesome cathedral of Chartres, the flowery gardens at Giverny that inspired Monet, and a mouse-run amusement park await the traveler looking for a refreshing change from urban Paris.

Versailles

If you've ever wondered why your American passport has French writing in it, you'll find the answer at Versailles (vehr-"sigh")—every king's dream palace. The powerful court of Louis XIV at Versailles set the standard of culture for all of Europe, right up to modern times. Today, if you're planning to visit just one palace in all of Europe, make it Versailles.

Visiting Versailles can seem daunting because of its size and hordes of visitors. But it's manageable. Arm yourself with a pass to skip ticket-buying lines; arrive early or late to avoid the crowds; and use this self-guided tour to focus on the highlights. I've provided all the details in "Orientation,"

Near Paris

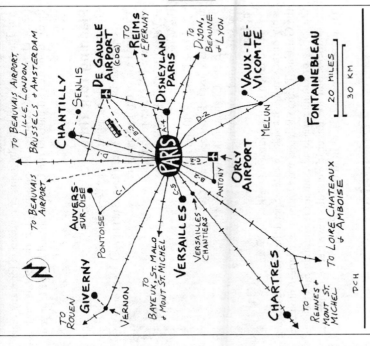

Near Paris map labels:

N

TO ROUEN

GIVERNY

VERNON

TO BEAVAIS AIRPORT, LILLE, LONDON, BRUSSELS + AMSTERDAM

CHANTILLY

SENLIS

DE GAULLE AIRPORT (CDG)

TO REIMS + EPERNAY

DISNEYLAND PARIS

TO DIJON, BEAUNE + LYON

VAUX-LE-VICOMTE

FONTAINEBLEAU

20 MILES

30 KM

TO BEAVAIS AIRPORT

AUVERS-SUR-OISE

PONTOISE

PARIS

MELUN

D-2

A-4

B-3

C-1

D-1

ANTONY

ORLY AIRPORT

VERSAILLES

VERSAILLES CHANTIERS

C-5

B-2

B-4

TO BAYEUX, ST. MALO + MONT ST. MICHEL

CHARTRES

TO RENNES + MONT ST. MICHEL

TO LOIRE CHATEAUX + AMBOISE

PCH

Legend:

—†— SNCF (LONG DIST.) TRAINS

A-4 ═══ RER COMMUTER TRAINS W/ LINE INDICATED

--- BUS

······· OTHER TRANSPORT (BIKE, TAXI, CAR...)

One-Way Travel Times from Paris via Train

CDG Airport: 30 min	Fontainebleau: 50 min
Orly Airport: 30–40 min	Vernon (Giverny): 60 min
Versailles: 30–40 min	Chartres: 65 min
Chantilly: 25–50 min	Amboise/Loire Valley: 90 min
Auvers-sur-Oise: 25–90 min	Beaune: 2.5 hrs
Disneyland Paris: 45 min	Bayeux/Caen (D-Day Beaches): 2–2.5 hrs
Reims: 45 min	Pontorson (Mont St. Michel): 3.5–4 hrs
Vaux-le-Vicomte: 45–60 min	St. Malo (Mont St. Michel): 3 hrs

later. First-timers can simply follow my recommended strategy in "Planning Your Time," next.

The entire complex has been under renovation for many years (some changes and closures are possible), but the serious work is finally done and all parts of the Château should be open for your visit.

Planning Your Time

Here's what I'd do on a first visit to Versailles:

Get a pass in advance (see "Passes," next page). Use your Paris Museum Pass, or buy Le Passeport online, at a FNAC store in Paris, at Versailles' Café Bleu Roi, or at the Versailles TI.

Leave Paris by 8:00 and arrive at the palace just before it opens at 9:00. Tour the Château following my self-guided tour, which hits the highlights.

Have lunch in the Gardens, at one of the sandwich kiosks or cafés. Spend the afternoon touring the Gardens, Trianon Palaces, and Domaine de Marie-Antoinette. On spring or summer weekends, catch the Fountain Spectacles in the Gardens. Stay for dinner in Versailles town (see recommended restaurants on page 225), or head back to Paris.

Orientation

Cost: I recommend buying either a Paris Museum Pass or Versailles' "Le Passeport" Pass, both of which give you access to the most important parts of the complex (see "Passes," next page). As costs, hours, entries, and special events at Versailles can change from season to season, get the latest information at the helpful Versailles website—www.chateauversailles.fr.

If you don't get a pass, you can buy individual tickets for each of the three different sections:

The Château, the main palace, costs €15 (€13 after 15:00, under 18 always free, includes audioguide). Your Château ticket includes the famous Hall of Mirrors, the king and queen's living quarters, many lesser rooms, and any temporary exhibitions. On the first Sunday of off-season months (Nov–March), entry is free.

The Trianon Palaces and Domaine de Marie-Antoinette costs €10 (€6 after 16:00 and Nov–March, under 18 always free). This ticket gives you access to the far corner of the Gardens, the small palaces called the Grand Trianon and

Petit Trianon, the queen's Hamlet, and a smattering of nearby buildings.

The Gardens are free, except on certain days (generally weekends April–Oct) when the fountains blast, and then the price is €8 (see "Fountain Spectacles in the Gardens," on page 217).

Passes: The following passes can save money and allow you to skip the long ticket-buyer lines (though everyone must endure security checks before entering the palaces).

The **Paris Museum Pass** (see page 54) covers the Château and the Trianon/Domaine area (a €25 value) and is the best solution for most, but doesn't include the Gardens on Fountain Spectacle days (you'll have to buy an extra ticket for that).

The **Le Passeport** one-day pass covers your entrance to the Château, the Trianon/Domaine area, and the Gardens, including the weekend Fountain Spectacles. Le Passeport costs €18 except when the fountains play, when it costs €25.

Buying Passes and Tickets: The Château box office (to the left as you face the palace) usually has long lines. It's best to buy tickets or Le Passeport in advance. In the city of Versailles, you can get them at the TI (but only Le Passeport, not tickets) or at Café Bleu Roi (on the right side of the parking lot as you approach the Château, 7 rue Colbert—see map on page 226). They're also available at any Paris FNAC department store, or online at www.chateauversailles.fr (print out your pass/ticket or pick it up near the entrance).

Hours: The **Château** is open April–Oct Tue–Sun 9:00–18:30, Nov–March Tue–Sun 9:00–17:30, closed Mon.

The **Trianon Palaces and Domaine de Marie-Antoinette** are open April–Oct Tue–Sun 12:00–18:30, closed Mon; Nov–March Tue–Sun 12:00–17:30, closed Mon (off-season only the two Trianon Palaces are open, not the Hamlet or other outlying buildings).

The **Gardens** are open April–Oct daily 9:00–20:30, but may close earlier for special events; Nov–March Tue–Sun 8:00–18:00, closed Mon.

Last entry to all of these areas is 30 minutes before closing.

Crowd-Beating Strategies: Versailles is a zoo May–Sept 10:00–13:00, especially Tue and Sun. Lines to buy tickets and go through security are long, and the Château is a slow shuffle of shoulder-to-shoulder tourists.

You can skip the ticket-buying line by using a Paris Museum Pass or Le Passeport, by buying tickets in advance, or by booking a guided tour (discussed later). Everyone—including advanced ticket and passholders—must wait in line

Versailles

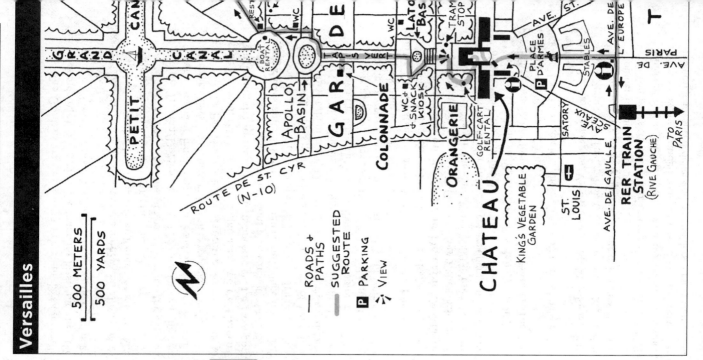

GRAND CANAL

PETIT CANAL

ROUTE DE ST. CYR (N-10)

APOLLO BASIN

BOAT RENTAL

GAR. DE

TAPIS VERT

COLONNADE

WC + SNACK KIOSK

LATO BAS

TRAM STOP

ORANGERIE

GOLF-CART RENTAL

CHATEAU

KING'S VEGETABLE GARDEN

ST. LOUIS

ORANGERIE

AVE. ST.

AVE. DE L'EUROPE

PLACE D'ARMES

STABLES

SATORY

AVE. DE SCEAUX

AVE. DE GAULLE

RER TRAIN STATION (RIVE GAUCHE)

TO PARIS

AVE. DE PARIS

500 METERS
500 YARDS

N

— ROADS + PATHS
— SUGGESTED ROUTE
P PARKING
VIEW

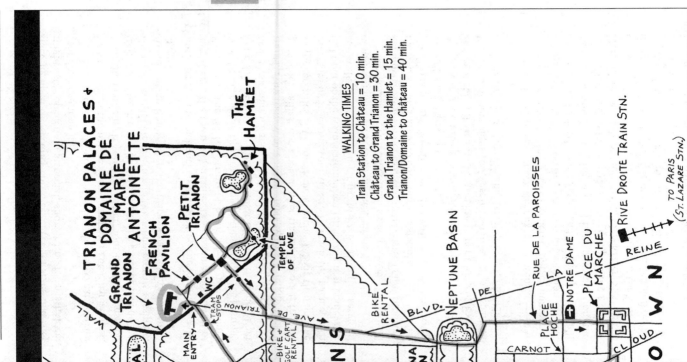

TRIANON PALACES &
DOMAINE DE
MARIE-
ANTOINETTE

THE HAMLET

GRAND TRIANON

FRENCH PAVILION

PETIT TRIANON

TEMPLE OF LOVE

WALKING TIMES
Train Station to Château = 10 min.
Château to Grand Trianon = 30 min.
Grand Trianon to the Hamlet = 15 min.
Trianon/Domaine to Château = 40 min.

WALL

MAIN ENTRY

TRAM STOPS

WC

BIKE & GOLF CART RENTAL

AVE. DE TRIANON

BIKE RENTAL

NEPTUNE BASIN

BLVD. DE

RUE DE LA PAROISSES

LA

PLACE HOCHE

NOTRE DAME

PLACE DU MARCHE

CARNOT

RIVE DROITE TRAIN STN.

TO PARIS (ST. LAZARE STN.)

REINE

CLOUD

OWN

to go through security (longest lines 10:00–12:00). Before queuing up at the security entrance, check for signs that they might have opened up a special, shorter line for passholders (but don't count on it).

For fewer crowds, go early or late. If you go early, arrive by 9:00 (when the palace opens), and tour the Château first, then the Gardens. If you arrive later, tour the Gardens first (remembering that the Trianon/Domaine area opens at noon), then visit the Château after 13:00, when crowds dissipate. Avoid Tue and Sun, when the place is packed from open to close.

Pickpockets: Assume pickpockets are working the tourist crowds.

Getting There: The town of Versailles is 30 minutes southwest of Paris. Take the **RER-C train** (4/hour, 30–40 minutes one-way, €6.20 round-trip) from any of these Paris RER stops: Gare d'Austerlitz, St. Michel, Musée d'Orsay, Invalides, Pont de l'Alma, and Champ de Mars. Scan the list of departing trains. Any train whose name starts with a V (e.g., "Vick") goes to Versailles; don't board other trains. Get off at the last stop (Versailles R.G., or "Rive Gauche"). Exit through the turnstiles by inserting your ticket. To reach the palace, turn right out of the train station, then left at the first boulevard, and walk 10 minutes. To return to Paris, all trains serve all downtown Paris RER stops on the C line.

Versailles has two other train stations—Rive Droite and Chantiers—that are not as useful to travelers. Trains run from Paris' Gare St. Lazare to both of these stations.

Taxis for the 30-minute ride (without traffic) between Versailles and Paris cost about €55.

By **car**, get on the *périphérique* freeway that circles Paris, and take the toll-free A13 autoroute toward Rouen. Exit at Versailles, follow signs to "Versailles Château," and park in the huge pay lot at place d'Armes (€5.50/2 hours, €10/4 hours, €14.80/8 hours).

Information: Before you go, check their excellent website—www .chateauversailles.fr. The palace's general contact number is tel. 01 30 83 78 00. Versailles has two information offices, and both sell Paris Museum Passes and Le Passeport. You'll pass the (uncrowded, helpful) town TI on your walk from the main RER station to the palace—it's just past the Pullman Hôtel (daily April–Sept 9:00–19:00, Oct–March 9:00–18:00, tel. 01 39 24 88 88). The information office at the Château (long waits) is on the left side of the courtyard as you face the Château (toll tel. 08 10 81 16 14). Pick up the free, useful map as you enter the sight.

Guided Tours: The 1.5-hour English guided tour gives you access to a few extra rooms (the line-up varies) and lets you skip ticket-buying lines. Ignore the tours hawked as you leave the train station. Book at the information office in the Château courtyard; bypass the ticket-buying line and find the guided tour desk just to the right of the ticket office. Reserve immediately upon arrival, because tours can sell out by 13:00 (€14.50, or €7.50 if you already have Château admission or pass, runs about every 45 minutes 9:00–15:00).

Audioguide Tours: A free audioguide to the Château is included in admission. A free Rick Steves audio tour is available for users of iPods and other MP3 players at www.ricksteves.com or on iTunes. Other podcasts and digital tours are available in the "multimedia" section at www.chateauversailles.fr.

Length of This Day Trip: With the usual lines, allow 1.5 hours each for the Château, the Gardens, and the Trianon/Domaine. Add another two hours for round-trip transit, plus another hour for lunch...and, at around eight hours, Versailles is a full day trip from Paris.

Baggage Check: To enter the Château and the two Trianons, you must use the free baggage check if you have large bags or baby strollers (your best bet is to use a baby backpack or hire a babysitter for the day).

WCs: Reminiscent of the days when dukes urinated behind the potted palm trees, WCs at the Château are few and far between, and some come with long lines. There are WCs immediately upon entering the Château (Entrance H); near the Grand Café d'Orléans; in the Gardens near the Latona Basin; at the Grand Canal; in the Grand Trianon and Petit Trianon; and at several other places scattered around the grounds. Any café generally has a WC.

Cuisine Art: To the left of the Château's Royal Gate entrance, the Grand Café d'Orléans has a restaurant (€13 salads, €20 *plats*) and a take-out bar (€5 sandwiches, great for picnicking in the Gardens). In the Gardens, you'll find several restaurants, cafés, and snack stands. Most are clustered near the Latona Fountain (less crowded) and the Grand Canal (more crowds and more choices, including two restaurants).

In the **town**, restaurants are on the street to the right of the parking lot (as you face the Château). A handy McDonald's (with WC) is immediately across from the train station (Internet café next door). The best choices are on rue de Satory between the station and the palace, and on the lively place du Marché Notre-Dame in the town center (see page 225).

Photography: Allowed, but no flash indoors.

Fountain Spectacles in the Gardens: On spring and summer weekends, the Gardens charge a mandatory admission fee for these spectacles. Loud classical music fills the king's backyard, and the Garden's fountains are in full squirt. Louis XIV had his engineers literally reroute a river to fuel these gushers. Even by today's standards, they are impressive.

The fountains run April–Oct Sat–Sun 11:00–12:00 & 15:30–17:00, with the finale 17:20–17:30. On these "spray days," the Gardens cost €8. (Pay at the Gardens entrance; covered by Le Passeport but not Paris Museum Pass.) The calendar of spectacles also includes a few music-only days (on the rare Tue, €7) and elaborate sound-and-light displays on Sat June–Aug at 21:00 (€21). Check the Versailles website for what's happening during your particular visit.

Starring: Luxurious palaces, endless gardens, Louis XIV, Marie-Antoinette, and the *ancien régime.*

Overview

The main sights to see at Versailles are the Château, the landscaped Gardens in the "backyard," and the Trianon Palaces and Domaine de Marie-Antoinette, located at the far end of the Gardens. If your time is limited, skip the Trianon/Domaine, which is a full 40-minute walk from the Château.

In the Château, the highlights are the State Apartments of the King and Queen and the Hall of Mirrors.

Self-Guided Tour

Welcome to Versailles

This commentary, which leads you through the various attractions at Versailles, covers just the basics. For background, first read the "Kings and Queens and Guillotines" sidebar on page 222. For a detailed room-by-room rundown, consider *Rick Steves' Paris* (buy in the US or at any of the English-language bookstores in Paris listed in this book) or the guidebook called *The Châteaux, the Gardens, and Trianon* (sold at Versailles).

Stand in the huge courtyard and face the palace, or Château. The original golden Royal Gate in the center of the courtyard, nearly 260 feet long and decorated with 100,000 gold leaves, is a recent replica of the original. The ticket-buying and guided-tour offices are to the left. The entrance to the Château (once you have your ticket or pass) is through the modern concrete-and-glass security checkpoint,

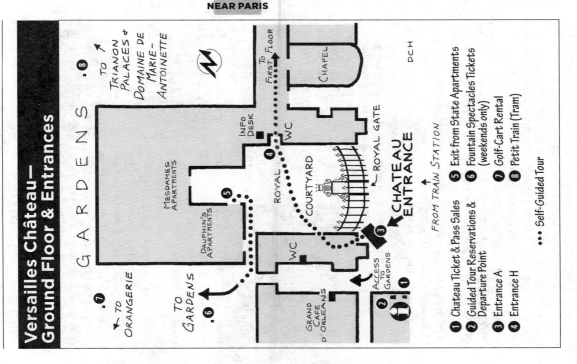

Versailles Château—
Ground Floor & Entrances

GARDENS .8

TO TRIANON PALACES + DOMAINE DE MARIE-ANTOINETTE

N

.7 TO ORANGERIE

TO GARDENS

.6

MESDAMES APARTMENTS

DAUPHIN'S APARTMENTS

INFO DESK

CHAPEL

To FIRST FLOOR

WC

ROYAL GATE

ROYAL COURTYARD

CHATEAU ENTRANCE

FROM TRAIN STATION

WC

GRAND CAFÉ D'ORLEANS

ACCESS TO GARDENS

DCH

① Chateau Ticket & Pass Sales
② Guided Tour Reservations & Departure Point
③ Entrance A
④ Entrance H
⑤ Exit from State Apartments
⑥ Fountain Spectacles Tickets (weekends only)
⑦ Golf-Cart Rental
⑧ Petit Train (Tram)

••• Self-Guided Tour

marked Entrance A.

After passing through security at Entrance A, you spill out into the open-air courtyard inside the golden Royal Gate. Enter the Château from the courtyard at Entrance H—the State Apartments. Once inside, you'll find an info desk (get a free map), WCs, and free audioguides.

The Château: The one-way walk through the palace leads you past the dazzling 700-seat **Royal Opera House;** by the intimate, two-tiered **Royal Chapel**; and through the glamorous **State Apartments**. In the **King's Wing** you'll see a billiard room, a royal make-out room, the Swiss bodyguard room, Louis' official bedroom, and his grand throne room (the **Apollo Room**)—with a 10-foot-tall canopied throne—and war rooms.

Next you'll visit the magnificent **Hall of Mirrors**—250 feet long, with 17 arched mirrors matching 17 windows looking out upon royal garden views. The mirrors—a luxury at the time—reflect an age when beautiful people loved to look at themselves. In another age altogether, this was the room in which the Treaty of Versailles was signed, ending World War I.

You'll finish in the **Queen's Wing,** where you'll see the Queen's bedchamber, the guard room where Louis XVI and Marie-Antoinette surrendered to the Revolution, and Napoleon's coronation room.

Getting Around the Gardens: It's a 40-minute walk from the palace, down to the Grand Canal, past the two Trianon palaces, to the Hamlet at the far end of Domaine de Marie-Antoinette. Allow more time if you stop along the way. After enduring the slow Château shuffle, stretching your legs out here feels pretty good.

A **bike** rental station by the Grand Canal gives you the most freedom to explore the Gardens economically (€6.50/hour or €15/half-day, kid-size bikes available). Although you can't take your bike inside the grounds of the Trianon/Domaine, you can park it near an entrance while you sightsee inside.

The fast-looking, slow-moving *petit train* (tram) leaves from behind the Château (north side). It stops at the Grand Canal and at the Grand and Petit Trianons (two of the entrance points to the Trianon/Domaine). You can hop on and off as you like (€7 day pass, €3.50 single trip, free for kids under 11, 4/hour). Another option is to rent a **golf cart** for a fun drive through the Gardens (€30/hour, rent down by the canal or at Orangerie side of palace).

Palace Gardens: The Gardens offer a world of royal amusements. The warmth from the Sun King was so great that he could even grow orange trees in chilly France. Louis XIV had a thousand of these to amaze his visitors. In winter they were kept in the greenhouses (beneath your feet) that surround the courtyard. On sunny days they were wheeled out in their silver planters and scattered around the grounds.

With the palace behind you, it seems as if the grounds stretch out forever. Versailles was laid out along an eight-mile axis that included the grounds, the palace, and the town of Versailles itself, one of the first instances of urban planning since Roman times and a model for future capitals, such as Washington, DC, and Brasília. A promenade leads from the palace to the Grand Canal, where France's royalty floated up and down in imported Venetian gondolas.

Trianon Palaces and Domaine de Marie-Antoinette:

Versailles began as an escape from the pressures of kingship. But in a short time the Château had become as busy as Paris ever was. Louis XIV needed an escape from his escape and built a smaller palace out in the boonies. Later, his successors retreated still farther from

the Château and French political life, ignoring the real world that was crumbling all around them. They expanded the Trianon area, building a fantasy world of palaces and pleasure gardens—the enclosure called Marie-Antoinette's Domaine.

The beautifully restored **Grand Trianon Palace** is as sumptuous as the main palace, but much smaller. With its pastel-pink colonnade and more human scale, this is a place you'd like to

call home. Nearby are the **French Pavilion,** Marie-Antoinette's **Theater,** and the octagonal **Belvedere** palace.

You can almost see princesses bobbing gaily in the branches as you walk through the enchanting forest, past the white marble **Temple of Love** to the queen's fake-peasant **Hamlet** (*le Hameau*).

Kings and Queens and Guillotines

• *You could read this on the train ride to Versailles. Relax...the palace is the last stop.*

Come the Revolution, when they line us up and make us stick out our hands, will you have enough calluses to keep them from shooting you? A grim thought, but Versailles raises these kinds of questions. It's the symbol of the *ancien régime*, a time when society was divided into rulers and the ruled, when you were born to be rich or to be poor. To some it's the pinnacle of civilization; to others, the sign of a civilization in decay. Either way, it remains one of Europe's most impressive sights.

Versailles was the residence of the king and the seat of France's government for a hundred years. Louis XIV (r. 1643–1715) moved out of the Louvre in Paris, the previous royal residence, and built an elaborate palace in the forests and swamps of Versailles, 10 miles west. The reasons for the move were partly personal—Louis XIV loved the outdoors and disliked the sniping environs of stuffy Paris—and partly political.

Louis XIV was creating the first modern, centralized state. At Versailles he consolidated Paris' scattered ministries so that he could personally control policy. More importantly, he invited France's nobles to Versailles in order to control them. Living a life of almost enforced idleness, the "domesticated" aristocracy couldn't interfere with the way Louis ran things. With 18 million people united under one king (England had only 5.5 million), a booming economy, and a powerful military, France was Europe's number-one power.

Around 1700, Versailles was the cultural heartbeat of Europe, and French culture was at its zenith. Throughout Europe, when you said "the king," you were referring to the French king—Louis XIV. Every king wanted a palace like Versailles. Everyone learned French. French taste in clothes, hairstyles, table manners, theater, music, art, and kissing spread across the Continent. That cultural dominance continued, to some extent, right up to the 20th century.

Louis XIV

At the center of all this was Europe's greatest king. He was a true Renaissance man, a century after the Renaissance: athletic,

Marie-Antoinette's happiest days were spent at the Hamlet, under a bonnet, tending her perfumed sheep and manicured gardens in a thatch-happy wonderland.

The **Petit Trianon** is a masterpiece of Neoclassical architecture. Despite her bad reputation with the public, Marie-Antoinette was a sweet girl from Vienna who never quite fit in with the fast, sophisticated crowd at Versailles. Here at the Petit Trianon, she could get away and re-create the simple home life she remembered good-looking, a musician, dancer, horseman, statesman, art-lover, lover. For all his grandeur, he was one of history's most polite and approachable kings, a good listener who could put even commoners at ease in his presence.

Louis XIV called himself the Sun King because he gave life and warmth to all he touched. He was also thought of as Apollo, the Greek god of the sun. Versailles became the personal temple of this god on earth, decorated with statues and symbols of Apollo, the sun, and Louis XIV himself. The classical themes throughout underlined the divine right of France's kings and queens to rule without limit.

Louis XIV was a hands-on king who personally ran affairs of state. All decisions were made by him. Nobles, who in other countries were the center of power, became virtual slaves dependent on Louis XIV's generosity. For 70 years he was the perfect embodiment of the absolute monarch. He summed it up best himself with his famous rhyme—"*L'état, c'est moi!*" (lay-tah say-mwah): "The state, that's me!"

Another Louis or Two to Remember

Three kings lived in Versailles during its century of glory. Louis XIV built it and established French dominance. Louis XV, his great-grandson (Louis XIV reigned for 72 years), carried on the tradition and policies, but without the Sun King's flair. During Louis XV's reign (1715–1774), France's power abroad was weakening, and there were rumblings of rebellion from within.

France's monarchy was crumbling, and the time was ripe for a strong leader to re-establish the old feudal order. They didn't get one. Instead, they got Louis XVI (r. 1774–1792), a shy, meek bookworm, the kind of guy who lost sleep over Revolutionary graffiti...because it was misspelled. Louis XVI married a sweet girl from the Austrian royal family, Marie-Antoinette, and together they retreated into the idyllic gardens of Versailles while Revolutionary fires smoldered.

from her childhood. Here she played, while in the cafés of faraway Paris, revolutionaries plotted the end of the *ancien régime*.

If you have more time to spend at Versailles, consider one of the following, lesser sights near the palace:

The Equestrian Performance Academy (Académie du Spectacle Equestre): The art of horseback riding has returned to Versailles. On most weekends from May through mid-December, you can watch the basic training sessions (no choreography), or enjoy choreographed performances—including "equestrian fencing"—performed to classical music (€12 training sessions, Sat-Sun and some Thu at 11:15; €25 musical shows, Sun and some Thu at 15:00 plus Sat at 20:00 May–July and at 18:00 Sept–Dec, but schedule is sporadic—check website for closure dates and extra performances; information tel. 01 39 02 07 14, reservations toll tel. 08 92 68 18 91, www.acadequestre.fr). The stables (Grandes Écuries) are across the parking square from the Château, next to the post office.

The King's Vegetable Garden (Le Potager du Roi): When Louis XIV demanded fresh asparagus in the middle of winter, he got it, thanks to his vegetable garden. The 22-acre garden—still productive—is open to visitors. Stroll through symmetrically laid-out plots planted with vegetables both ordinary and exotic, among thousands of fruit trees. The garden is surrounded by walls and sunk below street level to create its own microclimate. Overseeing the central fountain is a statue of the agronomist Jean de la Quintinie, who wowed Louis XIV's court with Versailles-sized produce. Even today the garden sprouts 20 tons of vegetables and 50 tons of fruit a year, which you can buy in season (€4.50 weekdays, €6.50 weekends, April–Oct Tue–Sun 10:00–18:00, closed Mon; limited hours in winter, 10 rue du Maréchal Joffre, tel. 01 39 24 62 62, www.potager-du-roi.fr).

Sleeping in Versailles

For a less expensive and laid-back alternative to Paris, within easy reach of the big city by RER train (4/hour, 30–40 minutes), Versailles can be a good overnight stop, especially for drivers. Park in the palace's main lot while looking for a hotel, or leave your car there overnight (€5.50/2 hours, €14.80/8 hours). Get a map of Versailles at your hotel or at the TI.

$$$ **Hôtel de France***, in an 18th-century townhouse, offers Old World class, with mostly air-conditioned, appropriately royal rooms, a pleasant courtyard, elaborate public spaces, a bar, and a restaurant (Db-€141, Tb-€180, Qb-€240, Wi-Fi, just off parking lot across from Château at 5 rue Colbert, tel. 01 30 83 92 23, fax 01 30 83 92 24, www.hotelfrance-versailles.com, hotel-de-france -versailles@wanadoo.fr).

$$ **Hôtel le Cheval Rouge** **, built in 1676 as Louis XIV's stables, now houses tourists. It's a block behind the place du Marché in a quaint corner of town on a large, quiet courtyard with free parking, free Wi-Fi, and crisp, sufficiently comfortable rooms, many with open beams (Ds-€80, Db-€95, Tb-€118, Qb-€128, 18 rue André Chénier, tel. 01 39 50 03 03, fax 01 39 50 61 27, www .chevalrougeversailles.fr, chevalrouge@sfr.fr).

Sleep Code

(€1 = about $1.25, country code: 33)

S = Single, **D** = Double/Twin, **T** = Triple, **Q** = Quad, **b** = bathroom, **s** = shower only. Everyone speaks English and accepts credit cards.

To help you easily sort through these listings, I've divided the rooms into three categories, based on the price for a standard double room with bath.

$$$ Higher Priced—Most rooms €125 or more.
$$ Moderately Priced—Most rooms between €80-125.
$ Lower Priced—Most rooms €80 or less.

Prices can change without notice: verify the hotel's current rates online or by email. For other updates, see www .ricksteves.com/update.

$ Hôtel Ibis Versailles** offers a good weekend value and modern comfort, with 85 air-conditioned rooms but no character and a disinterested staff (Db-€78 Fri–Sun, €110 Mon–Thu, extra bed-€10, parking-€10, across from RER station, 4 avenue du Général de Gaulle, tel. 01 39 53 03 30, fax 01 39 50 06 31, www .ibishotel.com, h1409@accor.com).

$ Hôtel du Palais, facing the RER station and next to Starbucks, rents 24 very clean and simple rooms—the cheapest I list in this area. Ask for a quiet room off the street (Db-€62, Tb-€77, piles of stairs and no elevator, 6 place Lyautey, tel. 01 39 50 39 29, fax 01 39 50 80 41, www.hotelsversailles.net, info @hotelsversailles.net).

Eating in Versailles

In the pleasant town center, around place du Marché Notre-Dame, you'll find a thriving open market (Sun, Tue, and Fri mornings until 13:00), a variety of reasonably priced restaurants and cafés, and a few cobbled lanes. The square is a 15-minute walk from the Château (veer left when you leave the Château).

On or near place du Marché Notre-Dame: This square is lined with colorful and inexpensive eateries. Troll the intriguing options or try one of these: **La Bœuf à la Mode**, right on the square, is a bistro with traditional cuisine and a passion for red meat (€18 *plats*, €30 three-course dinner *menu*, open daily, 4 rue au Pain, tel. 01 39 50 31 99). A la **Côte Bretonne** is your best bet for crêpes in a friendly, cozy setting. Yann-Alan and his family have served up the cuisine of their native Brittany region since 1951 (€4–10

Versailles Town Hotels & Restaurants

ROADS + PATHS
P PARKING
VIEW

500 METERS
500 YARDS

TO TRIANON PALACES + DOMAINE DE MARIE-ANTOINETTE

GARDENS

COLONNADE

ORANGERIE

KING'S VEGETABLE GARDEN

NEPTUNE BASIN

LATONA BASIN

TRAM STOP

BIKE RENTAL

WC + SNACK KIOSK

GOLF-CART RENTAL

CHATEAU

RUE DE LA PAROISSES

NOTRE DAME

PLACE HOCHE

PLACE DU MARCHE

PLACE D'ARMES

STABLES

CARNOT

AVE. ST.

AVE. DE L'EUROPE

AVE. DE SCEAUX

SATORY

AVE. DE PARIS

AVE. DE GAULLE

RER TRAIN STATION (RIVE GAUCHE)

ST. LOUIS

TOWN

RIVE DROITE TRAIN STN.

REINE

BLVD. DE

AVE. DE CLOUD

TO PARIS (ST. LAZARE STN.)

TO PARIS

Hotels

1 Hôtel de France & Café Bleu Roi (Pass/Ticket Sales)
2 Hôtel le Cheval Rouge
3 Hôtel Ibis Versailles
4 Hôtel du Palais

Restaurants

5 La Bœuf à la Mode Rest.
6 A la Côte Bretonne Rest.
7 Chez Lazare Restaurant
8 Equestrian Performances
9 Town TI (Le Passeport Sales)

crêpes from a fun and creative menu, Tue–Sun 12:00–14:30 & 19:00–22:30, closed Mon, good indoor and outdoor seating, a few steps off the square on traffic-free rue des Deux Portes at #12, tel. 01 39 51 18 24).

On rue de Satory: This pedestrian-friendly street is on the south side of the Château (10-minute walk, angle right out of the Château). The street is lined with a rich variety of restaurants, ranging from cheap ethnic to more pricey and formal French.

Friendly **Chez Lazare** is a good value inside or out, with €14–18 *plats* (closed Sun–Mon, 18 rue de Satory, tel. 01 39 50 41 45).

Chartres

Some of the children who watched Chartres' old church burn to the ground on June 10, 1194, grew up to build Chartres Cathedral and attend its dedication Mass in 1260. That's astonishing, considering that other Gothic cathedrals, such as Paris' Notre-Dame, took hundreds of years to build. Having been built so quickly, Chartres is arguably Europe's best example of pure Gothic, with a unity of architecture, statues, and stained glass that captures the spirit of the Age of Faith.

Chartres is an easy day trip from Paris and gives travelers a pleasant break in a lively, midsize town. Its pedestrian-friendly old center is overshadowed by its great cathedral, but it merits exploration. Discover the picnic-perfect park behind the cathedral and wander the quiet alleys and peaceful lanes down to the river. With affordable hotels and restaurants, Chartres also makes a worthwhile overnight stop. Dozens of Chartres' most historic buildings are brilliantly illuminated at night (May–Sept), adding to the town's after-hours appeal.

Tourist Information

The TI is a natural stop as you walk to the cathedral from the train station. At the TI pick up the English brochure with a good map and basic information on the town and cathedral (TI open Oct–March Mon–Sat 9:00–18:00, Sun 9:30–17:00, 100 yards in front of church, tel. 02 37 18 26 26, www.chartres-tourisme.com). The TI has specifics on cathedral tours with Malcolm Miller (described later), and also rents audioguides for the often-missed old town (€5.50, €8.50/2 people, about 2 hours, available only at the TI, leave passport as a deposit). A branch TI is on place de la Poissonerie.

Arrival in Chartres

Chartres is a 65-minute train trip from Paris' Gare Montparnasse (10/day, about €13 one-way). Allow an hour and a half from Paris to cathedral doorstep (see page 197 for Gare Montparnasse details).

Upon arrival at Chartres' train station, plan ahead and jot

Chartres Town

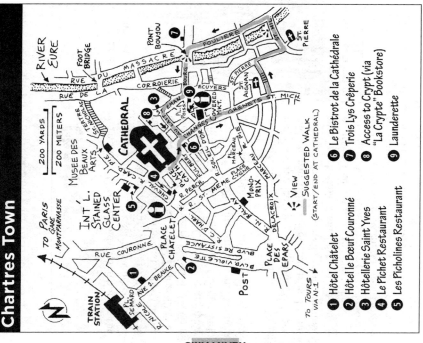

1 Hôtel Châtelet
2 Hôtelle Bœuf Couronné
3 Hôtellerie Saint Yves
4 Le Pichet Restaurant
5 Les Picholines Restaurant

6 Le Bistrot de la Cathédrale
7 Trois Lys Crêperie
8 Access to Crypt (via "La Crypte" Bookstore)
9 Launderette

★ View
Suggested Walk (start/end at cathedral)

down return times to Paris (last train generally departs Chartres around 21:00). Exiting Chartres Station, you'll see the spires of the cathedral dominating the town, a 10-minute walk up avenue Jehan de Beauce (€6.50 for a taxi).

Sights in Chartres

▲▲▲ Chartres Cathedral

The church is (at least) the fourth church on this spot dedicated to Mary, the mother of Jesus, who has been venerated here for some 1,700 years. In 876 the church acquired the torn veil (or birthing gown) supposedly worn by Mary when she gave birth to Jesus. The 2,000-year-old veil (now on display—see page 231) became the focus of worship at the church. By the 11th century, Mary (a.k.a. "Queen of All Saints") was hugely popular. God was obscure and scary, but motherhood was accessible, and Mary provided a

handy go-between for Christians and their Creator. Chartres, a small town of 10,000 with a prized relic, found itself in the big time on the pilgrim circuit.

When the fire of 1194 incinerated the old church, the veil was feared lost. Lo and behold, several days later, they found it miraculously unharmed in the crypt (beneath today's choir). The people were so stoked, they worked like madmen to erect this grand cathedral in which to display it. The small town built a big-city church, one of the most impressive structures in all of Europe. Thinkers and scholars gathered here, making Chartres a leading center of learning in the Middle Ages (until the focus shifted to Paris' university).

Cost: Church entry is free; climbing the 300-step north tower costs €7 (free on first Sun of the month, and for those under 18). Skip the Chartres Pass sold at the TI.

Hours: Church open daily 8:30–19:30. Tower open May–Aug Mon–Sat 9:30–12:30 & 14:00–18:00, Sun 14:00–18:00; Sept–April closes at 16:30 (entrance inside church after bookstore on left). Mass held Mon–Fri at 11:45 (in the crypt) and 18:15, Sat at 11:45 (in the crypt) and 18:00, and Sun at 9:15 (Gregorian) and 11:00.

Restoration: In 2011, the interior is undergoing some restoration work. You may see scaffolding, especially around the choir area and above the main entry.

Bring: Binoculars, if you got 'em. You can rent binoculars for cheap at a souvenir shop near the south porch of the church (at 10 cloître Notre-Dame), but you must leave a deposit.

Information: The church has two **bookstores.** One is inside near the entrance; the other—called La Crypte—is outside near the south porch (church tel. 02 37 21 59 08, www.diocese-chartres .com).

Cathedral Tours by Malcolm Miller: This fascinating English scholar, who moved here 50+ years ago when he was 24, has dedicated his life to studying this cathedral—and sharing its wonder through his guided lecture tours. His 75-minute tours are riveting, even if you've taken my self-guided tour (later). No reservation is needed; just show up—but there's no tour if he doesn't get at least eight takers (€10, €5 for students; includes headphones that allow him to speak softly, offered Mon–Sat at 12:00 and 14:45, no tours last half of Aug and Jan–Feb). Some visitors take two tours on the same day, as every tour is different. Tours begin inside the church at the orange-and-purple *Visites de la Cathédrale* sign by the bookstore. Consult this sign for changes or cancellations. He also offers private tours (private tour info tel. 02 37 28 15 58, fax 02 37 28 33 03, millerchartres@aol.com). For a detailed look at Chartres' windows, sculpture, and history, pick up Malcolm Miller's two guidebooks (sold at cathedral).

Audioguides: You can rent audioguides from the bookstore inside the cathedral near the entrance. Routes include the cathedral (€4.20, 45 minutes), the choir only (€3.20, 25 minutes), or both (€6.20, 70 minutes).

Crypt Tours: The crypt (which means "hidden" in Latin) is the foundation of the previous ninth-century church. Today these foundations can be visited only as part of a very boring guided tour in French (€2.70; April–Oct at 11:00, 14:15, 15:15, and 16:30; June–July also at 17:15, 2/day Nov–March, 30-minute tours start in La Crypte bookstore, English handout, located outside church near south porch, tel. 02 37 21 75 02).

Length of This Tour: Allow one hour. The additional three hours you'll spend in transit means that Chartres is effectively an all-day excursion from Paris.

❻ Self-Guided Tour: Chartres' soaring (if mismatched) **steeples** announce to pilgrims that they've arrived. The right (south) tower, with a Romanesque stone steeple, survived the fire. The left (north) tower lost its wooden steeple in the 1194 fire. In the 1500s, it was topped by a steeple bigger than the tapered lower half was meant to hold.

Enter the church (from a side entrance, if the main one is closed) and wait for your pupils to enlarge. The place is huge—the **nave** is 427 feet long, 20 feet wide, and 120 feet high.

Try to picture the church in the Middle Ages—painted in greens, browns, and golds (like colorful St. Aignan Church in the old town; see "Chartres Town," later). It was full of pilgrims, and was a rough cross between a hostel, a soup kitchen, and a flea market.

Walk up the nave to where the transept crosses. As you face the altar, north is to the left. The three big, round "rose" (flower-shaped) **windows** over the entrances receive sunlight at different times of day. All three are predominantly blue and red, but each has different "petals," and each tells a different part of the Christian story in a kaleidoscope of fragmented images.

Now walk around the altar to the right (south) side and find the **Blue Virgin window** with a big, blue Mary (second one from the right). Mary, dressed in blue on a rich red background, cradles Jesus, while the dove of the Holy Spirit descends on her. This very old window (from 1150) was the central window behind the altar of the church that burned in 1194. It survived and was reinserted into this frame in the new church around 1230. Mary's glowing dress is an example of the famed "Chartres blue," a sumptuous color made by mixing cobalt oxide into the glass (before cheaper materials were introduced).

The **Zodiac Window** (two windows to the left) shows the 12 signs of the zodiac (in the right half of the window; read from the bottom up—Pisces, Aries, Gemini in the central cloverleaf, Taurus, Cockroach, Leo, Virgo, etc.).

The **choir** (enclosed area around the altar where church officials sat) is the heart (*coeur*) of the church. A stone screen rings it with 41 statue groups illustrating Mary's life. The **plain windows** surrounding the choir date from the 1770s, when the dark mystery of medieval stained glass was replaced by the open light of the French Enlightenment.

Find the chapel with Mary on a pillar. A 16th-century **statue of Mary and baby**—draped in cloth, crowned and sceptered—sits on a 13th-century column in a wonderful carved-wood alcove. This is today's pilgrimage center, built to keep visitors from clogging up the altar area.

Double back a bit around the ambulatory, heading toward the back of the church. In the next chapel you encounter (Chapel of the Sacred Heart of Mary), you'll find a gold frame holding a fragment of Mary's venerated **veil**. These days it's kept—for its safety and preservation—out of the light and behind bulletproof glass.

Return to the west end and find the last window on the right (near the tower entrance), the **Noah Window.** Read Chartres' windows in the medieval style: from bottom to top. In the bottom diamond, God tells Noah he'll destroy the earth. Up near the top (diamond #7), a rainbow (symbolizing God's promise never to bring another flood) arches overhead, God drapes himself over it, and Noah and his family give thanks.

To climb the north tower, find the entrance nearby. Then exit the church (through the main entrance or the door in the south transept) to view its **south side.** Six flying buttresses (the arches that stick out from the upper walls) push against six pillars lining the nave inside, helping to hold up the heavy stone ceiling and sloped, lead-over-wood roof.

The **south porch** may be covered by scaffolding when you visit (it's being cleaned, a process that could take several years). The three doorways of the south entrance show the world from Christ to the present, as Christianity triumphs over persecution.

Reach the north side by circling around the back end of the church (great views) or by cutting through the church. In "the Book of Chartres," the **north porch** is chapter one, showing the Creation up to the coming of Christ. Imagine all this painted and covered with gold leaf in preparation for the dedication ceremonies in 1260, when the Chartres generation could finally stand back and watch as their great-grandchildren, carrying candles, entered the cathedral.

Chartres Town

Chartres' old town thrives (except on Monday) and deserves some time. You can rent an audioguide or, better, just wander, following the route marked on the free tourist map (audioguide and map at TI—see "Tourist Information" on page 227). The walk takes you on a 45-minute loop from the cathedral down along the river and back.

In medieval times Chartres was actually two towns—the pilgrims' town around the cathedral, and the industrial town along the river, which powered the mills. Notice the streets with evocative names, including rue des Changes (pilgrims needed to change money), rue au Lait (milk), and rue aux Herbes (folks smoked hemp). You'll pass the former fish market, the sky-blue open-air produce market, the unadorned church of St. Aignan, and the Church of St. Pierre (great photo-op of flying buttresses and a pretty interior). The Eure River is another photogenic spot, with old buildings, humpback bridges, and cathedral steeples in the distance.

Back at the cathedral, consider a stop at the **International Stained Glass Center** to learn the techniques behind the mystery of this fragile but enduring art (Centre International du Vitrail, €4, Mon–Fri 9:30–12:30 & 13:30–18:00, Sat 10:00–12:30 & 14:30–18:00, Sun 14:30–18:00, just 50 yards from cathedral, tel. 02 37 21 65 72, www.centre-vitrail.org).

Sleeping in Chartres

(€1 = about $1.25, country code: 33)

Hotels in Chartres are a good value, and you generally won't have trouble finding a room. The town has several launderettes. The most central is a few blocks from the cathedral by the branch TI at 16a place de la Poissonerie (daily 7:00–21:00). For Internet access, look for Internet cafés near the train station on avenue Jehan de Beauce, or ask at the TI.

$$ Hôtel Châtelet*, a block up from the train station, is friendly and comfortable. Don't let the facade fool you—inside is a cozy place with a huge fireplace in the lobby and 40 spotless, spacious, and well-furnished rooms. Several have connecting rooms for families and many have partial cathedral views (Db–€107-133, Tb–€141, most rooms have bathtub-showers, all have minibars, air-con, handy and safe parking–€8, 6 avenue Jehan de Beauce, tel. 02 37 21 78 00, fax 02 37 36 23 01, www.hotelchatelet.com, reservation@hotelchatelet.com).

$ Hôtel le Bœuf Couronné** is a vintage two-star hotel, warmly run by Madame Vinsot, with 18 freshly renovated, simple, good-value rooms and a handy location halfway between the station and cathedral (Db–€66-75, elevator, Wi-Fi, no air-con, 15 place Châtelet, tel. 02 37 18 06 06, fax 02 37 21 72 13, leboeuf couronne@hotmail.fr).

$ Hôtellerie Saint Yves, which hangs on the hillside just behind the cathedral, delivers well-priced simplicity with 50 spick-and-span, linoleum-floored rooms in a renovated monastery (Sb–€39, Db–€59, Tb–€72, small but workable bathrooms, Wi-Fi and TV in the lounge only, 1 rue Saint Eman, tel. 02 37 88 37 40, fax 02 37 88 37 49, www.hotellerie-st-yves.com, contact@hotellerie-st-yves.com).

Eating in Chartres

Le Pichet, just below the TI, is run by Marie-Sylvie and Xavier, the friendliest couple in Chartres. This local-products shop and cozy bistro makes an ideal lunch stop, with cheap homemade soups and a good selection of *plats*—split the pot-au-feu three ways or try the rabbit with plums (€10-15 *plats*, 19 rue du Cheval Blanc, near TI, tel. 02 37 21 08 35).

Les Picholines is a colorful favorite for Mediterranean-inspired cuisine. Come here to get your fix of tapas and olives, or to feast on €11-14 pastas and salads (€16-19 lunch *menu*, €20-26 dinner *menu*, daily, rue du Cheval Blanc, tel. 02 37 36 85 84).

Le Bistrot de la Cathédrale offers classic French fare in a comfortable interior or on its terrace, which features point-blank views of the cathedral (*menus* from €20, *plats* from €13, daily, south side of cathedral at 1 cloître Notre-Dame, tel. 02 37 36 59 60).

Trois Lys Crêperie, in a historic building, makes good, cheap crêpes (€13 two-course meals, closed Sun-Mon, located five minutes below cathedral across river on pont Boujou, 3 rue de la Porte Guillaume, tel. 02 37 28 42 02).

Giverny

Claude Monet's gardens at Giverny are like his paintings—brightly colored patches that are messy but balanced. Flowers were his brushstrokes, a bit untamed and slapdash, but part of a carefully composed design. Monet spent his last (and most creative) years cultivating his garden and his art at Giverny (zhee-vayr-nee), the Camp David of Impressionism. Visiting the Marmottan and/or the Orangerie museums in Paris before your visit here will heighten your appreciation of these gardens.

In 1883, middle-aged Claude Monet, his wife Alice, and their eight children from two families settled into a farmhouse here, 50 miles west of Paris. Monet, at that point a famous artist and happiest at home, would spend 40 years in Giverny, traveling less with each passing year. He built a pastoral paradise complete with a Japanese garden and a pond full of floating lilies.

Getting to Giverny

By Tour: Big tour companies do a Giverny day trip from Paris for around €70. If you're interested, ask at your hotel—but note that you can easily do the trip yourself by train and bus for about €30.

By Car: From Paris's Périphérique ring road, follow A-13 toward Rouen, exit at *Sortie 14* to Vernon, and follow *Centre Ville* signs, then signs to *Giverny*. You can park right at Monet's house or at one of several nearby lots.

By Train to Vernon: Take the Rouen-bound train from Paris' Gare St. Lazare station to Vernon, about four miles from Giverny (normally leaves from tracks 20–25, 45 minutes one-way, about €24 round-trip, no baggage check). The first train leaves Paris at around 8:15 and is ideal for this trip, with more departures about every two hours after that (8/day Mon–Sat, 6/day Sun). Before boarding, use an information desk in Gare St. Lazare to get return times from Vernon to Paris.

From Vernon's Train Station to Giverny: From the Vernon train station to Monet's garden (4 miles one-way), you have four good options: by bus, taxi, bike, or on foot.

The Vernon–Giverny **bus** meets every train from Paris for the 15-minute run to Giverny and connects to every return train to Paris. To reach the bus stop to Giverny, walk through the station, then follow the tracks—the stop is across from the L'Arrivée de Giverny café (don't dally—the bus leaves soon after your train

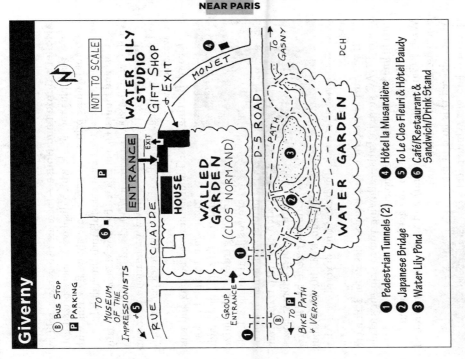

Giverny

Ⓑ Bus Stop
Ⓟ Parking

NOT TO SCALE

N

WATER LILY STUDIO

GIFT SHOP → EXIT

❹

MONET

To GASNY

ENTRANCE

EXIT →

Ⓟ

D-5 ROAD

PATH

CLAUDE

HOUSE

WALLED GARDEN
(CLOS NORMAND)

TO MUSEUM OF THE IMPRESSIONISTS
→ ❺

RUE

❻

❶

❷

WATER GARDEN

❸

DCH

GROUP ENTRANCE

Ⓑ → TO Ⓟ, BIKE PATH & VERNON

❶

❶ Pedestrian Tunnels (2)
❷ Japanese Bridge
❸ Water Lily Pond

❹ Hôtel la Musardière
❺ To Le Clos Fleuri & Hôtel Baudy
❻ Café/Restaurant & Sandwich/Drink Stand

arrives). A bus-and-train timetable is posted at this stop and at the Giverny stop (note return times). The bus leaves Giverny from the same stop where it drops you off (see map).

If you take a **taxi**, allow €12 for up to three people, €13 for four (tel. 06 77 49 32 90, or 02 32 21 31 31). With buses meeting every train, taxis are unnecessary (unless you miss the bus). Taxis wait in front of the station in Vernon.

You can rent a **bike** at L'Arrivée de Giverny, the café opposite the train station (€12, tel. 02 32 21 16 01), and follow a paved bike path (*piste cyclable*) that runs from near Vernon along an abandoned railroad right-of-way (figure about 30 minutes to Giverny). Get the easy-to-follow map to Giverny with your bike, and you're in business.

Hikers can go on **foot** to Giverny, following the bike instructions above, and take a bus or taxi back.

Sights in Giverny

▲**Monet's Garden and House**—There are two gardens, split by a busy road, plus the house, which displays Monet's prized collection of Japanese prints. The gardens are always flowering with something—they're at their most colorful April through July.

Cost and Hours: €6, not covered by Paris Museum Pass, daily April–Oct 9:30–18:00, last entry at 17:30, closed Nov–March.

Information: Tel. 02 32 51 90 31, www.fondation-monet.com and www.giverny.org. An audioguide is being developed and may be available when you visit—ask.

Crowd-Beating Tips: Though lines may be long and tour groups may trample the flowers, true fans still find magic in the gardens. Minimize crowds by arriving a little before 9:30, when it opens (catch the first train from Paris), or late, before it closes. Crowds recede briefly during lunch (12:00–13:30), but the busiest time of year here is May and June.

descend en masse after lunch. The busiest time of year here is May and June.

If you can't arrive early or late, buy your tickets for a bit more at any FNAC store in Paris—allowing you to skip the ticket-buying line here and use the group entrance.

Visiting the Garden: After you get in, go directly into the Walled Garden (Clos Normand) and work your way around clockwise. Smell the pretty scene. Monet cleared this land of pine trees and laid out symmetrical beds, split down the middle by a "grand alley" covered with iron trellises of climbing roses. In his careless manner, Monet throws together hollyhocks, daisies, and poppies. But each flowerbed has an overall color scheme that contributes to the look of the whole garden.

In the far corner of the Walled Garden you'll find a pedestrian tunnel that leads under the road to the Water Garden. Cross under the road and follow the meandering path to the Japanese bridge, under weeping willows, over the pond filled with water lilies, and past countless scenes that leave artists aching for an easel. Find a bench. Monet landscaped like he painted—he built an Impressionist pattern of blocks of color. After he planted the gardens, he painted them, from every angle, at every time of day, in all kinds of weather.

Back in the main garden, continue your visit with a wander through Monet's mildly interesting home (pretty furnishings, Japanese prints, old photos, and a room filled with copies of his paintings). The gift shop at the exit is the actual sky-lighted studio where Monet painted his water-lily masterpieces (displayed at the Orangerie Museum in Paris). Many visitors spend more time in this tempting gift shop than in the gardens themselves.

Nearby Sights—The bright, modern **Museum of the Impressionists** (Musée des Impressionnismes) houses temporary exhibits of Impressionist art—check its website for current shows or just drop in—and has picnic-pleasant gardens in front (€6.50, daily April-Oct 10:00–18:00, closed Nov–March; to reach it, turn left after leaving Monet's place and walk 200 yards; tel. 02 32 51 94 00, www.mdig.fr).

If you have time to kill at Vernon's station, take a five-minute walk into **town** and sample untouristy France.

Sleeping and Eating in Giverny

(€1 = about $1.25, country code: 33)

$$ Hôtel la Musardière** is nestled in the village of Giverny two blocks from Monet's home (exit right when you leave Monet's). Carole welcomes you with 10 sweet rooms that Claude would have felt at home in, a reasonable and homey *crêperie*-restaurant (€8–10 crêpes, €26 non-crêpe *menu*), and a lovely yard with outdoor tables (Db-€83–95, Tb-€105–125, Qb-€140, 123 rue Claude Monet, tel. 02 32 21 03 18, fax 02 32 21 60 00, www.lamusardiere.fr, resa @lamusardiere.fr).

$ Le Clos Fleuri is a family-friendly *chambre d'hôte* in a modern house with three nice rooms, handy cooking facilities, and a lovely garden. It's a 15-minute walk from Monet's place and is run by charming, English-speaking Danielle, who serves up a generous breakfast (Db-€80 for 2 or more nights, €95 for one night, includes breakfast, cash only, Wi-Fi, 5 rue de la Dîme, tel. 02 32 21 36 51, www.giverny-leclosfleuri.fr).

A flowery **café/restaurant** and a **sandwich/drink stand** sit right next to the parking lot across from Monet's home. Enjoy your lunch in the nearby gardens of the Museum of the Impressionists.

Rose-colored **Hôtel Baudy**, once a hangout for American Impressionists, offers an appropriately pretty setting for lunch or dinner (outdoor tables in front, *menus* from €23, popular with tour groups, closed Mon eve, 5-minute walk past Museum of the Impressionists at 81 rue Claude Monet, tel. 02 32 21 10 03). Don't miss a stroll through the artsy gardens behind the restaurant.

Disneyland Paris

Europe's Disneyland is a remake of California's, with most of the same rides and smiles. The main difference is that Mickey Mouse speaks French, and you can buy wine with your lunch. My kids went ducky.

Disneyland is easy to get to, and may be worth a day, if Paris is handier than Florida or California.

Getting to Disneyland Paris

By Train from Paris: The slick 45-minute RER trip is the best way to get to Disneyland from downtown Paris. Take RER line A-4 to Marne-la-Vallée-Chessy (check the signs over the platform to be sure Marne-la-Vallée-Chessy is served, because the line splits near the end). Catch it from Paris' Charles de Gaulle-Etoile, Auber, Châtelet-Les Halles, or Gare de Lyon stations (at least 3/hour, drops you 45 minutes later right in the park, about €8 each way). The last train back to Paris leaves shortly after midnight. When returning, remember to use the same RER ticket for your Métro connection in Paris.

By Bus and Train from the Airport: Both of Paris' major airports have direct shuttle buses to Disneyland Paris (every 20 minutes, 30 minutes, daily 8:30–20:00ish, about €17). Fast TGV trains run from Charles de Gaulle to Disneyland in 10 minutes, but they're less frequent and pricier—the shuttle bus makes more sense.

By Car: Disneyland is about 40 minutes (20 miles) east of Paris on the A-4 autoroute (direction Nancy/Metz, exit #14). Parking is about €10/day at the park.

Dis-orientation

The Disneyland Paris Resort is a sprawling complex housing two theme parks (Disneyland Paris and Walt Disney Studios), a few entertainment venues, and several hotels. Opened in 1992, it was the second Disney resort built outside the US (Tokyo was first). With upward of 15 million visitors a year, it quickly became Europe's leading single tourist destination. Mickey has arrived.

Disneyland Paris: This park has a corner on the fun market, with the rides and Disney characters you came to see. You'll find familiar favorites wrapped in French packaging, like Space Mountain (a.k.a. *De la Terre à la Lune*) and Pirates of the Caribbean (*Pirates des Caraïbes*).

Walt Disney Studios: This zone, which opened in 2002 next to the amusement park, has a Hollywood focus geared for an older crowd, with animation, special effects, and movie magic "rides." The highlight is the Stunt Show Spectacular, filling a huge backlot stadium five times a day for 45 minutes of car chases and thriller filming tips.

Skipping Lines: The free FASTPASS system is a worthwhile timesaver for the nine most popular rides. At the ride, insert your park admission ticket into the FASTPASS machine, which spits out a ticket printed with your return time—often within 45 minutes (you may only have one FASTPASS ticket at a time). You'll also save time by buying your park tickets ahead (at airport TIs, some Paris Métro stations, or along the Champs-Elysées at the Disney Store or Virgin Megastore).

Cost: Disneyland Paris and Walt Disney Studios charge the same. You can pay separately for each or buy a combined "Hopper" ticket for both. A one-day pass to either park is about €53 for adults and €45 for kids aged 3–11 (check their website for special offers). Kids under 3 are free. In the summer, save 25 percent by going after 17:00.

A one-day Hopper ticket for entry to both parks is about €67 for adults (less for kids). Two- and three-day deals are available. Regular prices are discounted about 25 percent Nov–March, and promotions are offered occasionally (check www.disneylandparis .com).

Hours: Disneyland—daily 10:00–19:00, until 23:00 mid-July–Aug, hours fluctuate with the seasons—check website for precise times. Walt Disney Studios—summer daily 9:00–18:00; winter Mon-Fri 10:00–18:00, Sat-Sun 9:00–18:00.

Information: Disney brochures are in every Paris hotel. For more info and to make reservations, call 08 25 30 60 30 (€0.15/minute) or try www.disneylandparis.com or www.mickey-mouse .com.

Avoiding Crowds: Saturday, Sunday, Wednesday, public holidays, and any day in July and August are the most crowded. After dinner, crowds are gone.

Eating with Mickey: Food is fun and not outrageously priced. (Still, many smuggle in a picnic.)

Sleeping at Disneyland

Most are better off sleeping in reality (Paris), though with direct buses and freeways to both airports, Disneyland makes a convenient first- or last-night stop. Seven different Disney-owned hotels offer accommodations at or near the park in all price ranges. Prices are impossible to pin down, as they vary by season and by the "package deal" you choose (deals that include park entry are usually a better value). To reserve any Disneyland hotel, call 01 60 30 60 30 (€0.15/minute), fax 01 60 30 60 65, or check www.disneylandparis.com.

The prices you'll be quoted include entry to the park. The cheapest is **Davy Crockett's Ranch,** but you'll need a car. **Hôtel Santa Fe**** offers a fair midrange value, with frequent shuttle service to the park. The most expensive is the **Disneyland Hotel******, right at the park entry, about twice the price of the Santa Fe. The **Dream Castle Hotel****** is another higher-end choice, with nearly 400 rooms done up to look like a lavish 17th-century palace (40 avenue de la Fosse des Pressoirs, tel. 01 64 17 90 00, www.dreamcastle-hotel.com, info@dreamcastle-hotel.com).

NORMANDY

Rouen • Honfleur • Bayeux • D-Day Beaches • Mont St. Michel

Sweeping coastlines, half-timbered towns, and thatched roofs decorate the rolling green hills of Normandy. Parisians call Normandy "the 21st arrondissement." It's their escape—the nearest beach. The Brits also consider this area close enough for a weekend away (the BBC comes through loud and clear on my car radio).

Despite the peacefulness you feel today, the region's history is filled with war. Normandy was founded by Viking Norsemen who invaded from the north, settled here in the ninth century, and gave the region its name. A couple hundred years later, William the Conqueror invaded England from Normandy. His victory is commemorated in a remarkable tapestry at Bayeux. A few hundred years after that, France's greatest cheerleader, Joan of Arc (Jeanne d'Arc), was convicted of heresy in Rouen, and burned at the stake by the English, against whom she rallied France during the Hundred Years' War. And in 1944, Normandy hosted a World War II battle that changed the course of history.

The rugged, rainy coast of Normandy harbors both wartime bunkers and enchanting fishing villages like Honfleur. And, on the border it shares with Brittany, the almost surreal island abbey of Mont St. Michel rises serene and majestic, oblivious to the tides of tourists.

Planning Your Time

Honfleur, the D-Day beaches, and Mont St. Michel each merit overnight visits. At a minimum, you'll want a full day for the D-Day beaches and a half-day each in Honfleur and on Mont St. Michel.

If you're driving between Paris and Honfleur, Giverny (see

Normandy

previous chapter) or Rouen (covered in this chapter) are worthwhile stops; by train, they're best as day trips from Paris. The WWII memorial museum in Caen works well as a stop between Honfleur and Bayeux (and the D-Day beaches). Mont St. Michel must be seen early or late to avoid the masses of midday tourists. Dinan, just 45

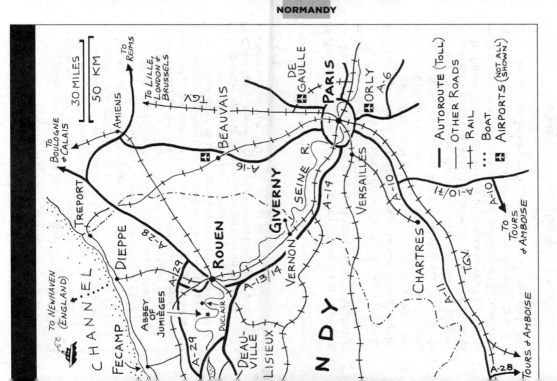

minutes by car from Mont St. Michel, offers a great introduction to Brittany (see next chapter). Drivers can enjoy Mont St. Michel as a day trip from Dinan.

For practical information in English about Normandy, see http://normandy.angloinfo.com.

Getting Around Normandy

This region is ideal with a car. If you're driving into Honfleur from the north, take the impressive but pricey Normandy Bridge (pont

Camembert Cheese

This cheap, soft, white, Brie-like cheese is sold all over France (and America) in distinctive, round, wooden containers. Camembert has been known for its cheese for 500 years, but local legend has it that today's cheese got its start in the French Revolution, when a priest on the run was taken in by Marie Harel, a Camembert farmer. He repaid the favor by giving her the secret formula from his own hometown—Brie.

From cow to customer, Camembert takes about three weeks to make. High-fat milk from Norman cows is curdled with rennet, ladled into round, five-inch molds, sprinkled with *Penicillium camemberti* bacteria, and left to dry. In the first three days, the cheese goes from the cow's body temperature to room temperature to refrigerator cool (50 degrees).

Two weeks later, the ripened and aged cheese is wrapped in wooden bands and labeled for market. Like wines, Camembert cheese is controlled by government regulations and must bear the "A.O.C." (*Appellation d'Origine Contrôlée*) stamp of approval.

de Normandie, €5 toll). If you're driving from Mont St. Michel into Brittany, follow my recommended scenic route to the town of St. Malo (see page 325).

Trains from Paris serve Rouen, Caen, Bayeux, Mont St. Michel (via Pontorson or Rennes), and Dinan, though service between these sights can be frustrating. Plan ahead: For bus information in English, check with the local TI. Buses make Giverny, Honfleur, Arromanches, and Mont St. Michel accessible to train stations in nearby towns, though Sundays have little—if any—bus service. Mont St. Michel is a challenge by train, except from Paris. Enterprising hotel owners in Bayeux operate a minivan service between Bayeux and Mont St. Michel for €58 round-trip per person—a great help to those without cars (see page 286). Bus companies commonly offer multiride discounts—for example, Bus Verts, which serves Le Havre, Honfleur, and Caen, offers a 20 percent discount if you buy just four tickets (even if you share them with another person).

Normandy's Cuisine Scene

Normandy is known as the land of the four Cs: Calvados, Camembert, cider, and *crème*. The region specializes in cream sauces, organ meats (sweetbreads, tripe, and kidneys—the "gizzard salads" are great), and seafood (*fruits de mer*). Dairy products are big here. Local cheeses are Camembert (mild to very strong; see sidebar), Brillat-Savarin (buttery), Livarot (spicy and pungent),

Pavé d'Auge (spicy and tangy), and Pont l'Évêque (earthy flavor).

What, no wine? That's right. You're in the rare region of France where wine is not a local forte. Still, you won't die of thirst. Normandy is famous for its many apple-based beverages. You can't miss the powerful Calvados apple brandy or the Bénédictine brandy (made by local monks). The local dessert, *trou Normand*, is apple sorbet swimming in Calvados. The region also produces three kinds of alcoholic apple ciders: *cidre* can be *doux* (sweet), *brut* (dry), or *bouché* (sparkling—and the strongest). You'll also find bottles of Pommeau, a tasty blend of (unfermented) apple cider and Calvados (sold in many shops), as well as *poiré*, a tasty pear cider. And don't leave Normandy without sampling a *kir Normand*, a mix of crème de cassis and cider.

Remember, restaurants serve only during lunch (11:30–14:00) and dinner (19:00–21:00, later in bigger cities); cafés serve food throughout the day.

Rouen

This 2,000-year-old city mixes Gothic architecture, half-timbered houses, and contemporary bustle like no other place in France. Busy Rouen (roo-ohn) is France's fifth-largest port and Europe's biggest food exporter (mostly wheat and grain). Although its cobbled old town is a delight to wander, the city feels less welcoming at night (you'll notice a surprising number of panhandlers). Rouen works best for me as a day trip from Paris, or as a stop between Paris and Honfleur.

Rouen is nothing new. It was a regional capital during Roman times, and France's second-largest city in medieval times (with 40,000 residents—only Paris had more). In the ninth century, the Normans made the town their capital. William the Conqueror called it home before moving to England. Rouen walked a political tightrope between England and France for centuries. An English base during the Hundred Years' War, Joan of Arc was burned here (in 1431).

Rouen's historic wealth was based on its wool industry and trade—for centuries, it was the last bridge across the Seine River before the Atlantic. In April 1944, as America and Britain weakened German control of Normandy prior to the D-Day landings, Allied bombers destroyed 50 percent of Rouen. And though the industrial suburbs were devastated, most of the historic core survived, keeping Rouen a pedestrian haven. On summer evenings, a sound-and-light show transforms the facade of its Notre-Dame Cathedral into the changing colors of Monet's Impressionist canvas (mid-June–mid-Sept).

Planning Your Time

If you want a dose of a smaller—yet lively—French city, Rouen is an easy day trip from Paris, with convenient train connections to Gare St. Lazare (nearly hourly, 1.5 hours). Considering the convenient Paris connection and Rouen's handy location in Normandy, drivers can save money and headaches by taking the train to Rouen and picking up a rental car there. Leave the car (with your bags in it) in the secure rental lot, and visit Rouen before heading out (for car-rental companies, see "Helpful Hints," later). Even if you don't have a car, you can easily visit Rouen on your way from Paris to other Normandy destinations, thanks to the good bus and train service (free daytime bag check available Wed–Mon at the Museum of Fine Arts, closed Tue).

Orientation to Rouen

Although Paris embraces the Seine, Rouen ignores it. The area we're most interested in is bounded by the river to the south, the Museum of Fine Arts (esplanade Marcel Duchamp) to the north, rue de la République to the east, and place du Vieux Marché to the west. It's a 20-minute walk from the train station to the Notre-Dame Cathedral or TI. Everything else of interest is within a 10-minute walk of the cathedral or TI.

Tourist Information

Pick up the map with information on Rouen's museums at the TI, which faces the cathedral. The TI also has audioguide tours covering the cathedral and Rouen's historic center, for €5 per person, though this book's self-guided walk is enough for most (May–Sept Mon–Sat 9:00–19:00, Sun 9:30–12:30 & 14:00–18:00; Oct–April Mon–Sat 9:30–12:30 & 13:30–18:00, closed Sun; 25 place de la Cathédrale, tel. 02 32 08 32 40, www.rouenvalleedeseine .com). A small office in the TI changes money (closed during lunch year-round).

Arrival in Rouen

By Train: Rue Jeanne d'Arc cuts down from Rouen's train station through the town center to the Seine River. Day-trippers should **walk** from the station down rue Jeanne d'Arc to rue du Gros Horloge—a busy pedestrian mall in the medieval center. This

Rouen

200 YARDS
200 METERS

M METRO STATION
P PARKING

TRAIN STATION

POST

BLVD. I'YSER

JOAN OF ARC TOWER MUSEUM

MUSEUM OF CERAMICS

BLVD. MARNE

SQUARE VERDREL

PLACE DU VIEUX MARCHE (GRAY)

Covered Market

POST

R. THIERS

R. GANTERIE

R. JULES

R. DU GROS

Big Clock

RUE

JOAN OF ARC CHURCH

WC

JOAN OF ARC MUSEUM

CHARETTES

QUAI HAVRE

Bus STN.

THEATRE DES ARTS

QUAI BOURSE

R. GEN. LECLERC

RUE ORS

Post

Horloge

OLD CITY

Palace of Justice

R. ST. ROMAIN

NOTRE-DAME

WC

QUAI P. CORNEILLE

MUSEUM OF FINE ARTS

MUSEUM OF IRONWORKS

R. HOPITAL

PUBLIC

ST. OUEN

RUE FAULX

EAU-DU-ROBEC

R. AMIENS

DAME

R. ALSACE

NIC.

NON-D-DAME

PLAGUE CEMETERY

ST. MACLOU

MARTAIN-VILLE

SEINE R.

TO A-5 FREEWAY & PARIS

DCH

1 Hôtel Mercure
2 Hôtel de la Cathédrale
3 Hôtel le Cardinal
4 Crêperie le St. Romain, Dame Cakes & Fayencerie Augy China Shop
5 Chez Nous Restaurant
6 Flunch Cafeteria
7 Le Maupassant Rest.
8 Monoprix Dept. Store/Grocery
9 Internet Café
10 ABC Books
11 SNCF Boutique (Train Tickets)

cobblestone street connects place du Vieux Marché and Joan of Arc Church (to your right, the starting point of my self-guided walk) with Notre-Dame Cathedral (to your left). Note that the station has no baggage storage. If you have luggage, walk or taxi a few blocks down from the station to the Museum of Fine Arts, where you can check your bags for free (for museum hours, see page 258). You can enjoy this lovely museum at the end of your walking tour.

Rouen's **subway** (Métrobus) whisks travelers from under the train station to the Palais de la Justice in one stop (€1.60, descend and buy tickets from machines one level underground, then validate ticket on subway two levels down). From the station, take a train headed to Technopole or Georges Braque. Returning to the station, take the direction Boulingrin and get off at Gare-Rue Verte.

Taxis (to the right as you exit station) will take you to any of my recommended hotels for about €7.

By Bus: Rouen's bus station is just off rue Jeanne d'Arc, near the river (information office open Mon–Fri 7:00–19:00, Sat 9:30–17:30, closed Sun, tel. 02 35 52 52 52, www.tcar.fr). As you exit the station, turn left and walk up rue Jeanne d'Arc, then turn right on pedestrian-friendly rue du Gros Horloge to reach most hotels and the cathedral. (To find the start of my self-guided walk, turn left on rue du Gros Horloge.)

By Car: Assume you'll get lost—then follow signs for *Centre-Ville* and *Rive Droite* (right bank). Park near place du Vieux Marché or the cathedral (parking garages available at both—see map). You can park for free overnight along the river (metered until 19:00), or pay for more secure parking in one of many well-signed underground lots. La Haute Vieille Tour parking garage, between the cathedral and the river, is handy (about €12/day). If you get turned around (likely, because of the narrow, one-way streets), aim for the highest cathedral spires you spot.

If leaving Rouen for Honfleur, the fastest way is to follow blue autoroute signs to *Le Havre*, then *Caen*.

Helpful Hints

Closed Days: Most of Rouen's museums are closed on Tuesday, and many sights also close midday (12:00–14:00). The cathedral is closed Monday morning and during Mass (Tue–Sat at 10:00, July–Aug also at 18:00; Sun and holidays at 8:30, 10:30, and 12:00). The Joan of Arc Church is closed Fri and Sun mornings, and during Mass.

Market Days: The best open-air market is on place St. Marc, a few blocks east of St. Maclou Church. It's filled with antiques and other good stuff (all day Tue, Fri, and Sat; on Sun until about 12:30). There's also a smaller market on place du

Vieux Marché, near the Joan of Arc Church (Tue–Sun until 13:30, closed Mon). The TI has a complete list of all weekly markets.

Supermarket: It's inside the **Monoprix**, at the back of the store (Mon–Sat 8:30–21:00, closed Sun, on rue du Gros Horloge).

Internet Access: Surf with a view of the Joan of Arc Church at **Cybernet** (Mon–Sat 10:00–21:00, Sun 14:00–19:00, has English keyboards and Wi-Fi, 47 place du Vieux Marché, tel. 02 35 0773 02).

English Bookstore: ABC Books has nothing but English-language books—some American but mostly British (Tue–Sat 10:00–18:00, closed Sun–Mon, south of Eglise St. Ouen at 11 rue des Faulx, tel. 02 35 71 08 67).

Taxi: Call **Les Taxis Blancs** at 02 35 61 20 50 or 02 35 88 50 50.

Car Rental: Agencies with an office in the train station include **Europcar** (Mon–Fri 8:00–12:00 & 14:00–19:00, Sat 8:30–12:00 & 14:00–17:00, closed Sun, tel. 02 32 08 39 09), **Avis** (tel. 02 35 88 60 94), and **Hertz** (tel. 02 35 70 70 71).

SNCF Boutique: For train tickets, visit the SNCF office in town at the corner of rue aux Juifs and rue Eugène Boudin (Mon–Sat 10:00–19:00, closed Sun).

Self-Guided Walk

Welcome to Rouen

On this 1.5-hour walk, you'll see the essential historical Rouen sights. Remember that many sights are closed midday (12:00–14:00). This walk is designed for day-trippers coming by train (it begins a 10-minute downhill walk from the station). Drivers should park at or near place du Vieux Marché (parking garage available).

You'll start at place du Vieux Marché, then walk the length of rue du Gros Horloge to Notre-Dame Cathedral. From there, walk four blocks west to the plague cemetery, loop up to the church of St. Ouen, and return along rues de l'Hôpital and Ganterie, ending at the Museum of Fine Arts (a five-minute walk to the train station). The map on page 250 highlights our route.

• *If arriving by train, walk down rue Jeanne d'Arc and turn right on rue du Guillaume le Conquérant. This takes you to our starting point...*

Place du Vieux Marché

• *Stand near the entrance of the Joan of Arc Church.*

Surrounded by half-timbered buildings, this old market square has a covered produce market, a park commemorating Joan of Arc's burning, and a modern church named after her. A few steps away, a tall aluminum cross planted in a flowery garden marks the spot

Welcome to Rouen Self-Guided Walk

NORMANDY

where Rouen publicly punished and executed people. The pillories stood here, and during the Revolution, the town's guillotine made 800 people "a foot shorter at the top." In 1431, Joan of Arc—only 19 years old—was burned at this site. As the flames engulfed her, an English soldier said, "Oh my God, we've killed a saint." (Nearly 500 years later, Joan was canonized, and the soldier was proved right.)

The modern **Joan of Arc Church** (Eglise Jeanne d'Arc)—worth ▲▲—is a tribute to the young woman who was canonized in 1920 and later became the patron saint of France. The church, completed in 1979, feels Scandinavian inside and out—another reminder of Normandy's Nordic roots. Sumptuous 16th-century windows, salvaged from a church lost during World War II, were worked into the soft architectural lines (the €0.40 English pamphlet gives you some church background and describes the stained-glass scenes). Similar to churches designed by the architect

200 YARDS
200 METERS

P PARKING
M METRO STATION

1 Place du Vieux Marché
2 Joan of Arc Church
3 Joan of Arc Museum
4 Les Larmes de Jeanne d'Arc
5 Big Clock
6 Palace of Justice
7 Notre-Dame Cathedral
8 Rue St. Romain
9 Fayencerie Augy
10 St. Maclou Church
11 Half-Timbered Buildings
12 Plague Cemetery
13 Museum of Fine Arts

Le Corbusier, this is an uplifting place to be, with a ship's-hull vaulting and sweeping wood ceiling that sail over curved pews and a wall of glass below. Take time to savor this unusual place (free; April–Oct Mon–Thu and Sat 10:00–12:00 & 14:00–18:00, Fri and Sun 14:00–17:30; Nov–March daily 14:00–18:00; closed during Mass). There's a public WC 30 yards straight ahead from the church doors.

• Turn left out of the church and step over **ruins** of a 15th-century church that once stood on this spot (destroyed during the French Revolution).

A waxy **Joan of Arc Museum** is straight ahead (enter through a souvenir shop sandwiched between big restaurants). It tells the story of this inspirational teenager of supreme faith who, after hearing voices for several years, won the confidence of her countrymen, was given an army, and rallied the French against their English invaders. Those touched by her story will enjoy this little museum, with excellent English information and nifty models

Joan of Arc
(1412–1431)

The cross-dressing teenager who rallied French soldiers to drive out English invaders was the illiterate daughter of a humble farmer. One summer day, in her dad's garden, 13-year-old Joan heard a heavenly voice accompanied by bright light. It was the first of several saints (including Michael, Margaret, and Catherine) to talk to her during her short life.

In 1429, the young girl was instructed by the voices to save France from the English. Dressed in men's clothing, she traveled to see the king and predicted that the French armies would be defeated near Orléans—as they were. King Charles VII equipped her with an ancient sword and a banner that read "Jesus, Maria," and sent her to rally the troops.

Soon "the Maid" (*la Pucelle*) was bivouacking amid rough soldiers, riding with them into battle, and suffering an arrow wound to the chest—all while liberating the town of Orléans. On July 17, 1429, she held her banner high in the cathedral of Reims as Charles was officially proclaimed king of a resurgent France.

Joan and company next tried to retake Paris (1429), but the English held out. She suffered a crossbow wound through the thigh, and her reputation of invincibility was tarnished. During a battle at Compiègne (1430), she was captured and turned over to the English for £10,000. In Rouen, they chained her by the neck inside an iron cage, while the local French authorities (allied with the English) plotted against her. The Inquisition—insisting that Joan's voices were "false and diabolical"—tried and sentenced her to death for being a witch and heretic.

On May 30, 1431, Joan of Arc was tied to a stake on Rouen's old market square (place du Vieux Marché). She yelled, "Rouen! Rouen! Must I die here?" Then they lit the fire; she fixed her eyes on a crucifix and died chanting, "Jesus, Jesus, Jesus."

After her death, Joan's place in history was slowly rehabilitated. French authorities proclaimed her trial illegal (1455), prominent writers and artists were inspired by her, and the Catholic Church finally beatified (1909) and canonized her (1920) as St. Joan of Arc.

throughout (€4, daily mid-April–Sept 9:30–19:00, Oct–mid-April 10:00–12:00 & 14:00–18:30, tel. 02 35 88 02 70, www.jeanne-darc .com).

• *Leave the square with Joan's church on your left and join the busy pedestrian street, rue du Gros Horloge—the town's main shopping street since Roman times.*

A block up on your right (at #163) is Rouen's most famous

chocolate shop, **Les Larmes de Jeanne d'Arc,** which would love to tempt you with its chocolate-covered almond "tears (*larmes*) of Joan of Arc." Although you must resist touching the chocolate fountain, you are welcome to taste a tear. The first one is free; a small bag costs about €8.50.

• *Your route continues past a medieval McDonald's and across busy rue Jeanne d'Arc to the...*

Big Clock (Gros Horloge)

This impressive, circa-1528 Renaissance clock, le Gros Horloge (groh oar-lohzh), decorates the former city hall. Is something missing? Not really. In the 16th century, an hour hand offered ample precision; minute hands became necessary only in a later, faster-paced age. The lamb at the end of the hour hand is a reminder that wool rules—it was the source of Rouen's wealth. The town medallion features a sacrificial lamb, which has both religious and commercial significance. The black-and-silver orb above the clock makes one revolution in 29 days. The clock's artistic highlight fills the underside of the arch (walk underneath and stretch your back), with the "Good Shepherd" and lots of sheep.

To see the inner workings and an extraordinary panorama over Rouen (including a memorable view of the cathedral), climb the clock tower's 100 steps. You'll tour several rooms with the help of an audioguide narration. The big bells ring on the hour—a deafening experience if you're in the tower (€6, includes audioguide; April–Oct Tue–Sun 10:00–12:00 & 13:00–18:00, closed Mon; Nov–March Tue–Sun 14:00–18:00, closed Mon).

• *Walk under le Gros Horloge and take a one-block detour left on rue Thouret to see the...*

Palace of Justice (Palais de Justice)

This flamboyantly Gothic building, once the home of Normandy's *parlement,* had been covered with grime, but years of cleaning are near an end. The result is striking; think of this as you visit Rouen's other Gothic structures, which are awaiting baths of their own. You'll see pockmarks on the side of the building that faces rue Jeanne d'Arc—leftovers from bombings during the Normandy invasion. Look for the English-language plaques on the iron fence—they provide some history and describe the damage and the tedious repair process.

• *Double back and continue up rue du Gros Horloge. You'll soon see a plaque dedicated to Cavelier de la Salle (high on the left), who explored the mouth of the Mississippi River, claimed the state of Louisiana for France, and was assassinated in Texas in 1687. Soon you'll reach...*

▲▲Notre-Dame Cathedral (Cathédrale Notre-Dame)

This cathedral is a landmark of art history. You're seeing essentially what Claude Monet saw as he painted 30 different studies of this frilly Gothic facade at various times of the day. Using the physical building only as a rack upon which to hang light, mist, dusk, and shadows, Monet was capturing "impressions." One of the results is in Rouen's Museum of Fine Arts; four others are at the Orsay Museum in Paris. Find the plaque showing two of these paintings (in the corner of the square, about 30 paces to your right if you were exiting the TI). Look up at the soaring facade and find the recently cleaned sections, with

bright statues on either side of the central portal—later, we'll meet some of their friends face to face inside the cathedral.

Enter the cathedral (Tue–Sun 8:00–19:00, Mon 14:00–19:00; closed during Mass Tue–Sat at 10:00, July–Aug also at 18:00, Sun at 8:30, 10:30, and 12:00; also closed Nov–March daily 12:00–14:00).

• *Stand at the back and look down the* **nave.**

This is a classic Gothic nave—four stories of pointed-arch arcades, the top filled with windows to help light the interior. Today, the interior is lighter than intended, because the original colored glass (destroyed mostly in World War II) was replaced by clear glass. Why such a big cathedral in a small town? Until the 1700s, Rouen was the second largest city in France—rich from its wool trade and its booming port.

• *Circle counterclockwise three-quarters of the way around the church along the side aisle.*

The side chapels and windows have descriptions in English. These chapels display an assortment of styles through the centuries—for example, windows with bold blues and reds are generally from the 13th century. Look for photos halfway down on the right that show devastating WWII bomb damage to the cathedral.

Passing through an iron gate after the high altar (closed during Mass, but often open on the opposite side even during Mass), you come to several **stone statues.** These figures were lifted from the facade during a recent cleaning and will eventually be installed in a museum. For us, it's a rare chance to stand toe-to-toe with a saint (weird feeling).

There are several **stone tombs** on your left, dating from when Rouen was the Norman capital. The first tomb is for Rollo, the first duke of Normandy in 933 (and great-great-great-grandfather

The Hundred Years' War
(1336–1453)

It would take a hundred years to explain all the causes, battles, and political maneuverings of this century-plus of warfare between France and England, but here it goes:

In 1300, before the era of the modern nation-state, the borders between France and England were fuzzy. French-speaking kings had ruled England, English kings owned the south of France, and English merchants dominated trade in the north. Dukes and lords in both countries were aligned more along family lines than by national identity. When the French king died without a male heir (1328), both France and England claimed the crown, and the battle was on.

England invaded the more populous country (1345) and—thanks to skilled archers using armor-penetrating long-bows—won big battles at Crécy (1346) and Poitiers (1356). Despite a truce, roving bands of English mercenaries stayed behind and supported themselves by looting French villages. The French responded with guerrilla tactics.

In 1415, the English took still more territory, with Henry V's big victory at Agincourt. But rallied by the heavenly visions of young Joan of Arc, the French slowly drove the invaders out. Paris was liberated in 1436, and when Bordeaux fell to French forces (1453), the fighting ended without a treaty.

---

of William the Conqueror, seventh duke of Normandy, c. 1028). As the first duke, Rollo was chief of the first gang of Vikings (the original "Normans") who decided to settle here. Called the "Father of Normandy," Rollo died at the age of 80, but he is portrayed on his tomb as if he were 33 (as was the fashion, because Jesus died at that age). Because of later pillage and plunder, only Rollo's femur is inside the tomb.

And speaking of body parts, the next tomb contains the heart of Richard the Lionhearted. (The rest of his body lies in the Abbey of Fontevraud, described on page 405 in the Loire chapter.) A descendant of William the Conqueror, Richard was both a king of England and the 12th duke of Normandy. A photo mounted on the wall opposite Richard shows damage from a violent 1999 storm that blew the spire off the roof and sent it crashing to the cathedral floor.

• Circle behind the altar. Look back above the entry to see a rare black-and-white rose window (its medieval colored glass is long gone).

Continue a few paces, then look up to the ceiling over the nave.

Looking directly above Rollo's femur, you can see the patch-work in the ceiling where the spire crashed through the roof. Perhaps this might be a good time to exit? Pass through the small iron gate, turn right, and leave through the side door (north transept).

• *Stepping outside, look back at the* **facade.**

The fine carved tympanum (the area over the door) shows a graphic Last Judgment. Jesus stands between the saved (on the left) and the damned (on the right). Notice the devil grasping a miser, who clutches a bag of coins. Look for the hellish hot tub, where even a bishop (pointy hat) is eternally in hot water.

Most of the facade has been cleaned—blasted with jets of water—but the limestone carving is still black. It's too delicate to survive the hosing, and instead awaits a more expensive laser cleaning (as do many other monuments in Rouen).

• *From this courtyard, a gate deposits you on a traffic-free street. Turn right and walk along...*

Rue St. Romain

This street has half-timbered buildings and lanes worth a look. In a short distance, you can look through an arch, back at the cathedral's spire. Made of cast iron in the late 1800s—about the same time Gustave Eiffel was building his tower in Paris—the spire is, at 490 feet, the tallest in France. You can also see the former location of the missing smaller (green) spire—downed in that 1999 storm.

• *Farther down the street, find a shop that shows off a traditional art form in action.*

At **Fayencerie Augy** (at #26), Monsieur Augy welcomes potential shoppers to browse his studio/gallery/shop and see Rouen's clay "china" being made the traditional way. First, the clay is molded and fired. Then it's dipped in white enamel, dried, lovingly hand-painted, and fired a second time. Rouen was the first city in France to make faience, earthenware with colored glazes. In the 1700s, the town had 18 factories churning out the popular product (Tue–Sat 9:00–19:00, closed Sun, 26 rue St. Romain, VAT tax refunds nearly pay for the shipping, www.fayencerie-augy.com). For more faience, visit the local Museum of Ceramics (described later, under "Sights in Rouen").

• *Continue along rue St. Romain, which (after crossing rue de la République) leads to the fancy...*

St. Maclou Church

This church's unique, bowed facade is textbook Flamboyant Gothic (sadly, its doorways are blackened by pollution—visualize the brilliant exterior of the Palais de Justice, and what a world without pollution would be like). Notice the flame-like tracery decorating its gable. Because this was built at the very end of the Gothic age—and construction took many years—the doors are from the next age: the Renaissance (c. 1550). The pretty interior is worth a quick peek (Fri–Mon 10:00–12:00 & 14:00–17:30, closed Tue–Thu).

• *Leaving the church, turn right, and then take another right (giving the little boys on the corner wall a wide berth). Wander past a fine wall of half-timbered buildings fronting rue Martainville, to the end of St. Maclou Church.*

Half-Timbered Buildings

Because the local stone—a chalky limestone from the cliffs of the Seine River—was of poor quality (your thumbnail is stronger), and because local oak was plentiful, half-timbered buildings became a Rouen specialty from the 14th through 19th centuries. Cantilevered floors were standard until the early 1500s. These top-heavy designs made sense: City land was limited, property taxes were based on ground-floor square footage, and the cantilevering minimized unsupported spans on upper floors. The oak beams provided the structural skeleton of the building, which was then filled in with a mix of clay, straw, pebbles...or whatever was available.

• *A block farther down on the left, at 186 rue Martainville, a covered lane leads to the...*

Plague Cemetery (Aître St. Maclou)

During the great plagues of the Middle Ages, as many as two-thirds of the people in this parish died. For the decimated community, dealing with the corpses was an overwhelming task. This half-timbered courtyard (c. 1520) was a mass grave, an ossuary where the bodies were "processed." Bodies would be dumped into the grave (where the well is now) and drenched in liquid lime to help speed decomposition. Later, the bones would be stacked in alcoves above the colonnades that line this courtyard. Notice the ghoulish carvings (c. 1560s) of gravediggers' tools, skulls, crossbones, and characters doing the "dance of death." In this *danse macabre*, Death, the great equalizer, grabs people of all social classes (free, daily mid-March–Oct 8:00–20:00, Nov–mid-March 8:00–19:00). The place is now an art school. Peek in on the young artists. As you leave, spy the dried black cat (died c. 1520, in tiny glass case to the left of the door). To overcome evil, it was buried during the building's construction.

Farther down rue Martainville, at place St. Marc, a colorful market blooms Sunday until about 12:30 and all day Tuesday, Friday, and Saturday. If it's not market day, you can double back to the cathedral and rue du Gros Horloge, or continue with me to explore more of Rouen and find the Museum of Fine Arts (back toward the train station).

• *To reach the museum, turn right upon leaving the boneyard, then right* *again at the little boys (onto rue Damiette), and hike up antique row to the vertical Church of St. Ouen (a seventh-century abbey turned church in the 15th century, fine park behind). Turn left at the church on rue des Faulx (an English bookstore, ABC Books, is a block to the right—open Tue–Sat 10:00–18:00, closed Sun–Mon), and cross the busy street. (The horseman you see to the right is a short yet majestic Napoleon Bonaparte, who welcomes visitors to Rouen's city hall.) Continue down rue de l'Hôpital's traffic-free lane, which becomes rue Ganterie. A right at the modern square on rue l'Ecrueuil leads you to the **Museum of Fine Arts** and the **Museum of Ironworks** (both described next, under "Sights in Rouen"). This is the end of our tour. The tower where Joan of Arc was imprisoned (also explained under "Sights in Rouen") is a few blocks uphill, on the way back to the train station.*

Sights in Rouen

The first three museums are within a block of one another, closed on Tuesdays, never crowded, and can all be visited with the same €5.50 combo-ticket (www.rouen-musees.com).

▲**Museum of Fine Arts (Musée des Beaux-Arts)**—Paintings from many periods are beautifully displayed in this museum, including works by Caravaggio, Peter Paul Rubens, Paolo Veronese, Jan Steen, Théodore Géricault, Jean-Auguste-Dominique Ingres, Eugène Delacroix, and the Impressionists. Don't miss Monet's painting of Rouen's Notre-Dame Cathedral, and the room dedicated to Géricault. Pick up the museum map at the ticket desk. Important rooms have excellent handheld English descriptions. The audioguide is good, but spotty in its coverage (€3, occasional temporary exhibitions cost extra, Wed–Mon 10:00–18:00, 15th–17th-century rooms closed 13:00–14:00, closed Tue, a few blocks below train station at 26 bis rue Jean Lecanuet, tel. 02 35 71 28 40).

Museum of Ironworks (Musée le Secq des Tournelles, a.k.a. Musée de la Ferronnerie)—This deconsecrated church houses iron objects, many of them more than 1,500 years old. Locks, keys, tools, coffee grinders—virtually anything made of iron is on display. You can duck into the entry area for a glimpse of a medieval iron scene without passing through the turnstile (€2.50, no English explanations, Wed–Mon 10:00–13:00 & 14:00–18:00, closed Tue, behind Museum of Fine Arts, 2 rue Jacques Villon, tel. 02 35 88 42 92).

Museum of Ceramics—Rouen's famous faïence (earthenware), which dates from the 16th to the 18th centuries, fills this fine old mansion. Unfortunately, there is not a word of English (same hours and cost as Museum of Ironworks, above; 1 rue Faucon, tel. 02 35 07 31 74).

Joan of Arc Tower (Le Tour Jeanne d'Arc)—This tower (1204), part of Rouen's brooding castle, was Joan's prison before her untimely death (€1.50, Wed–Sat and Mon 10:00–12:30 & 14:00–18:00, Sun 14:00–18:30, closed Tue, one block uphill from the Museum of Fine Arts on rue du Bouvreuil, tel. 02 35 98 16 21).

Near Rouen

The Route of the Ancient Abbeys (La Route des Anciennes Abbayes)—This route—punctuated with abbeys, apples, and Seine River views—provides a pleasing detour for drivers connecting Rouen and destinations farther west (if you're traveling *sans* car, skip it). Follow D-982 west of Rouen to Jumièges (visit its abbey), then cross the Seine on the car ferry at Duclair (about €2).

Drivers can stop to admire the gleaming Romanesque church at the **Abbey of St. Georges de Boscherville** (but skip the abbey grounds). The romantically ruined, twin-towered **Abbey of Jumièges** is the top sight to visit on this route. Founded in A.D. 654, it was destroyed by Vikings and rebuilt by William the Conqueror, only to be torn down again by French Revolutionaries. Today, nature is gradually reclaiming its stone, as there is no roof to protect the abbey (€5, helpful English handout, more detailed booklet for €6, daily mid-June–mid-Sept 9:30–18:30, mid-Sept–mid-June 9:30–13:00 & 14:30–17:30, last entry 30 minutes before closing, tel. 02 35 37 24 02). Several decent lunch options lie across the street from the abbey.

Sleeping in Rouen

Although I prefer Rouen by day, sleeping here presents you with a mostly tourist-free city (most hotels cater to business travelers). These hotels are perfectly central, within two blocks of Notre-Dame Cathedral.

$$$ Hôtel Mercure*, ideally situated a block north of the cathedral, is a concrete business hotel with a professional staff, a big lobby and bar, and 125 rooms loaded with modern comforts. Suites come with views of the cathedral, but are overpriced and not much bigger than a double. Look for promotional rates (Db-€290, suite-€290, air-con, elevator, free Internet access and Wi-Fi, parking garage-€12/day, 7 rue Croix de Fer, tel. 02 35 52 69 52, fax 02 35 89 41 46, www.mercure.com, h1301@accor.com).

$$ Hôtel de la Cathédrale** is run by friendly Nathalie and Alexandra, who welcome you with a flowery courtyard, a cozy, wood-beamed breakfast room, and frumpy but mostly country-French decor. Some rooms have hardwood floors, and most have basic bathrooms and poor sound insulation (Sb-€60–80, Db-€70–100, Tb-€120, Qb-€130, extra bed-€15, elevator, free Internet

Sleep Code

(€1 = $1.25, country code: 33)

S = Single, **D** = Double/Twin, **T** = Triple, **Q** = Quad, **b** = bathroom, **s** = shower only, ***** = French hotel rating system (0–4 stars). Unless otherwise noted, credit cards are accepted and English is spoken.

To help you easily sort through these listings, I've divided the rooms into three categories based on the price for a standard double room with bath:

$$$ Higher Priced—Most rooms €90 or more.
$$ Moderately Priced—Most rooms between €60–90.
$ Lower Priced—Most rooms €60 or less.

Prices can change without notice; verify the hotel's current rates online or by email. For other updates, see www .ricksteves.com/update.

access and Wi-Fi; nearby parking–€5 overnight or €10/24 hours, 12 rue St. Romain, a block from St. Maclou Church, tel. 02 35 71 57 95, fax 02 35 70 15 54, www.hotel-de-la-cathedrale.fr, contact @hotel-de-la-cathedrale.fr).

$$ Hôtel le Cardinal** offers rooms facing the cathedral, without the street appeal of the Hôtel de la Cathédrale. It's run by English-speaking, born-and-raised-Rouennais Pascal and his wife, Agnes. Nearly all of its 18 sufficiently comfortable rooms look right onto the cathedral, and a few are good for families. Rooms on the fourth floor are best, with small balconies and great cathedral views (Sb–€58-68, Db–€68-78, Db with balcony–€80-90, Tb–€98, Qb–€110, extra bed–€15, non-smoking rooms available, breakfast–€8, elevator, free Wi-Fi, 1 place de la Cathédrale, tel. 02 35 70 24 42, fax 02 35 89 75 14, www.cardinal-hotel.fr, cardinal hotel.rouen@wanadoo.fr).

Eating in Rouen

Near the Cathedral

Crêperie le St. Romain, between the cathedral and St. Maclou Church, is an excellent budget option. It's run by gentle Mr. Pegis, who serves filling €8 crêpes with small salads in a warm setting (lunch Tue–Sat, dinner Thu–Sat, closed Sun–Mon, 52 rue St. Romain, tel. 02 35 88 90 36).

Dame Cakes is ideal if it's lunchtime or teatime and you need a Jane Austen fix. The decor is from another, more precious era, and the baked goods are out of this world (€12–15 salads and *plats*, garden terrace in the back, Mon–Sat 11:00–18:00, closed Sun, 70 rue St. Romain, tel. 02 35 07 49 31).

Chez Nous is a sharp place with efficient owners serving well-prepared dishes at fair prices. There's lots of contemporary music and lots of yellow (€17 for 2-course *menu*, €21 for 3-course *menu*, closed Sun–Mon, 234 rue Martainville, tel. 02 35 89 50 02).

At **Flunch** you'll find family-friendly, cheap, point-and-shoot, cafeteria-style meals in a fast-food setting (€6 *menu* includes salad bar, main course, and drink; good kids' menu, open daily until 22:00, a block from cathedral at 66 rue des Carmes, tel. 02 35 71 81 81).

On Place du Vieux Marché

A fun lineup of restaurants—where locals wouldn't be caught dead—faces place du Vieux Marché, across from the Joan of Arc Church. **Le Maupassant** stands out as more welcoming, with an outdoor terrace and three lively floors filled with orange leather booths (regional *menus*—lunch from €16, dinner from €30, daily, 39 place du Vieux Marché, tel. 02 35 07 56 90).

Rouen Connections

Rouen is well-served by trains from Paris, via Amiens to other points north, and Caen to other destinations west and south.

From Rouen by Train to: Paris' Gare St. Lazare (nearly hourly, 1.5 hours), **Bayeux** (6/day, 2 hours, change in Caen; more trips possible via Paris' Gare St. Lazare, 4–5 hours), **Pontorson–Mont St. Michel** (2/day, 4 hours, change in Caen; more with change in Paris, 7 hours).

By Train and Bus to: Honfleur (6/day Mon–Sat, 3/day Sun, 1-hour train to Le Havre, then easy transfer to 30-minute bus over Normandy Bridge to Honfleur—Le Havre's bus and train stations are adjacent).

Honfleur

Gazing at its cozy harbor lined with skinny, soaring houses, it's easy to overlook the historic importance of this port. For more than a thousand years, sailors have enjoyed Honfleur's (ohn-flur) ideal location, where the Seine River greets the English Channel. William the Conqueror received supplies shipped from Honfleur. Samuel de Champlain sailed from here in 1608 to North America, where he discovered the St. Lawrence River and founded Quebec City. The town was also a favorite of 19th-century Impressionists:

Eugène Boudin (boo-dan) lived and painted in Honfleur, attracting Monet and other creative types from Paris. In some ways, modern art was born in the fine light of idyllic little Honfleur.

Honfleur escaped the bombs of World War II, and today offers a romantic port enclosed on three sides by sprawling outdoor cafés.

Long eclipsed by the gargantuan port of Le Havre just across the Seine, Honfleur happily uses its past as a bar stool...and sits on it.

Orientation to Honfleur

All of Honfleur's engaging streets and activities are within a short stroll of its old port (Vieux Bassin). The Seine River flows just east of the center, the hills of the Côte de Grâce form its western limit, and rue de la République slices north–south through the center to the port. Honfleur has two can't-miss sights—the harbor and Ste. Catherine Church—along with a handful of other tempting spots. But really, the town itself is its best sight.

Tourist Information

The TI is in the flashy glass public library (Mediathèque) on quai le Paulmier, two blocks from Vieux Bassin toward Le Havre (July–Aug Mon–Sat 9:30–19:00, Sun 10:00–17:00; Sept–June Mon–Sat 9:30–12:30 & 14:00–18:00, Sun 10:00–13:00; free WCs inside, tel. 02 31 89 23 30, www.ot-honfleur.fr). Pick up the town map, as well as tourist maps of Normandy and the Calvados region. You can also find information on the D-Day beaches here. Skip the useless museum pass. Ask about concerts, special events, and guided visits of Honfleur (tours usually Wed at 15:00, €6, 1.5 hours, smart to reserve by calling TI).

Arrival in Honfleur

By Bus: Get off at the small bus station (*gare routière*), and confirm your departure at the helpful information counter. To reach the TI and old town, turn right out of the station and walk five minutes up quai le Paulmier.

By Car: Follow *Centre-Ville* signs, then find your hotel (easier said than done) and unload your bags (double-parking is OK for a few minutes). Parking is a headache in Honfleur, especially on summer and holiday weekends. Some hotels offer parking...for a price (otherwise, your hotelier knows where you can park for free). The central Parking du Bassin (across from the TI) is pricey (€2/

hour, €12/day). Across the causeway is Parking du Môle, which is cheaper (only €3/day), but a bit less central (see map). Street parking, metered during the day, is free from 20:00 to 8:00.

Helpful Hints

Market Day: The area around Ste. Catherine Church becomes a colorful open-air market every Saturday (9:00–13:00). A smaller organic food-only market takes place here on Wednesday mornings, and a flea market takes center stage here the first Sunday of the month.

Grocery Stores: The **Carrefour Market** is the biggest in town (a 10-minute walk down rue de la République from Vieux Bassin, on place Sorel). There's also a good **Casino Grocery** near the TI (daily July–Aug, closed Mon off-season, 16 quai le Paulmier).

Regional Products with Panache: Visit **Produits Regionaux Gribouille** for any Norman delicacy you can dream up. Say *bonjour* to Monsieur Gribouille (gree-boo-ee) and watch your head—his egg-beater collection hangs from above (open 364 days a year, 9:30–13:00 & 14:00–19:00, 16 rue de l'Homme de Bois, tel. 02 31 89 29 54).

Internet Access: Cyberpub has unpredictable hours but plenty of computers (at Hôtel de la Diligence, 55 rue de la République, tel. 02 31 89 95 83).

Laundry: Lavomatique is a block behind the TI, toward the port (daily 7:00–20:00, 4 rue Notre-Dame).

Taxi: Call 06 16 18 38 38 or 02 31 98 87 59.

Tourist Train: Honfleur's *petit train* toots you up the Côte de Grâce—the hill overlooking the town—and back in about 50 minutes (€7, daily 10:30–11:30 & 14:30–17:30, departs from across gray swivel bridge that leads to Parking du Môle).

Sights in Honfleur

In Honfleur

Vieux Bassin—Stand near the water facing Honfleur's square harbor, with the merry-go-round across the lock to your left, and survey the town. The word "Honfleur" is Scandinavian, meaning the shelter (*fleur*) of Hon (a Norse settler). Eventually, the harbor was fortified by a big wall with twin gatehouses (the one surviving gatehouse, *la*

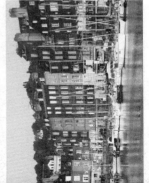

Honfleur

100 YARDS
100 METERS

JETTY WALK →

JARDIN RETROUVEE

MAISONS SATIE

BOUDIN MUSEUM

STE-CATHERINE

PLACE DU PUITS

To COTE DE GRACE & ⑤

1 Hôtel le Cheval Blanc
2 l'Absinthe Hôtel & Rest. & Le Bouilland Normand Rest.
3 Les Maisons de Léa
4 Hôtel du Dauphin
5 Hôtel Monet
6 Etap Hôtel
7 La Cour Ste. Catherine & Travel Coffee Shop
8 Le Fond de la Cour
9 To Madame Bellegarde's Rooms
10 Le Bréard Restaurant
11 P'tit Mareyeur Restaurant
12 Le Vintage Café
13 La Tortue Rest.
14 La Commanderie Rest.
15 La Cidrerie Bar & Crêperie
16 Café de l'Hôtel de Ville
17 Waterfront Crêpe Stand
18 "Nighttime Food to Go"
19 Le Marin, Le Perroquet Vert & L'Albatross Bars
20 Carrefour Market
21 Casino Grocery
22 Produits Regionaux Gribouille
23 Internet Café
24 Launderette
25 Tourist Train Stop
26 Art Gallery Row

P PARKING

BOAT EXCURSIONS

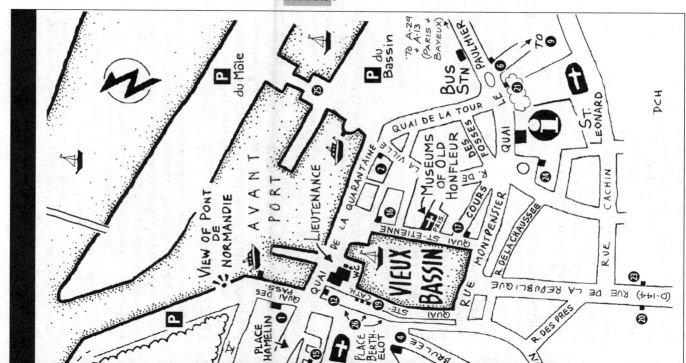

Lieutenante, is on your right) and a narrow boat passage protected by a chain. Those skinny houses on the right side were designed at a time when houses were taxed based on their width, not height. Wouldn't you love a room on the top floor, with no elevator? Imagine moving a piano into one of these units today. The spire halfway up the left side of the port belongs to Honfleur's oldest church and is now home to the Marine Museum.

The port, once crammed with fishing boats, is now home to sleek sailboats. Walk toward the gatehouse (*La Lieutenance*). In front of the barrel-vaulted arch (once the entry to the town), you can see a bronze bust of Samuel de Champlain—the explorer who sailed with an Honfleur crew 400 years ago to make his discoveries in Canada.

Turn around to see various tour and fishing boats and the high-flying Normandy Bridge (described later, under "Near Honfleur") in the distance. Fisherfolk catch flatfish, scallops, and tiny shrimp daily and bring them here. On the left you may see fishermen's wives selling *crevettes* (shrimp). You can buy them *cuites* (cooked) or *vivantes* (alive and wiggly). They are happy to let you sample one (rip off the cute little head and tail, and pop the middle into your mouth—*délicieuse!*) or buy a cupful to go (€2, daily in season).

You're likely to see artists sitting at easels around the harbor, as Boudin and Monet did. Many consider Honfleur the birthplace of Impressionism. This was a time when people began to revere, not fear, the out-of-doors, and started to climb mountains "because they were there." Pretty towns like Honfleur and the nearby coast were ideal subjects to paint—and still are—thanks to what locals called the "unusual luminosity" of the region. Artists would set up easels along the harbor to catch the light playing on the line of buildings, slates, timbers, geraniums, clouds, and reflections in the water. Monet came here to visit the artist Boudin, a hometown boy, and the battle cry of the Impressionists—"Out of the studio and into the light!"—was born.

If you're an early riser, you can watch what's left of Honfleur's fishing fleet prepare for the day, and you just might experience that famous luminosity.

▲▲**Ste. Catherine Church (Eglise Ste. Catherine)**—The unusual wood-shingled exterior suggests that this church has a different story to tell than most. Walk inside. You'd swear that if it were turned over, it would float—the legacy of a community of sailors and fishermen, with plenty of boat-builders and no cathedral architects. When workers put up the first nave in 1466, it soon became apparent that more space was needed—so the second was built in 1497. Because it felt too much like a market hall, they added side aisles. Notice the oak pillars, some full-length and others supported by stone bases. Trees come in different sizes, yet each pillar had to be the same thickness. In the last months of World War II, a bomb fell through the roof—but didn't explode. The pipe organ behind you is popular for concerts, and half of the modern pews are designed to flip so that you can face the music. Take a close look at the many medieval instruments carved into the railing below the organ—a 16th-century combo band in wood (free, daily July-Aug 9:00–18:30, Sept-June 9:00–17:15).

The church's bell tower is equally unusual. It was not built atop the church, but across the square—to lighten the load of the wooden church's roof and to minimize fire hazards. Peek inside, where you'll find a tiny museum with a few church artifacts (not worth the entry fee but free with your ticket to the Eugène Boudin Museum; April–Sept Wed–Mon 10:00–12:00 & 14:00–18:00; Oct-March Wed–Mon 14:00–18:00 only, closed Tue).

▲**Eugène Boudin Museum**—This pleasing little museum has three interesting floors with many paintings of Honfleur and the surrounding countryside. The first floor displays Norman folk costumes, the second floor has the Boudin collection, and the third floor houses the Hambourg/Rachet collection and the Katia Granoff room.

Cost and Hours: €6.50, €2 extra during special exhibits—English audioguide-€2 (no English explanations on display—but none needed); mid-March–Sept Wed–Mon 10:00–12:00 & 14:00–18:00, closed Tue; Oct–mid-March Wed–Fri and Mon 14:30–17:30, Sat–Sun 10:00–12:00 & 14:30–17:30, closed Tue; elevator, no photos, rue de l'Homme de Bois, tel. 02 31 89 54 00.

⊙ **Self-Guided Tour:** Pick up a map at the ticket counter, tip your beret to Eugene Boudin, and climb the stairs (or take the elevator).

First Floor (Costumes): Monsieur and Madame Louveau (see their photo as you enter) gave Honfleur this quality collection of local traditional costumes. The hats, blouses, and shoes are supported by paintings that place them in an understandable historical and cultural context. Of special interest are the lace bonnets, typical of 19th-century Normandy. You could name a woman's village by her style of bonnet. The dolls are not toys for tots, but marketing tools for traveling clothing merchants—designed to show off the latest fashions. The men's department is in the back of the room.

Second Floor (Boudin Collection and More): A right off the stairs leads you into a large room of appealing 20th-century paintings and sculpture, created by artists who produced most of their works while living in Honfleur. A left off the stairs leads you through a temporary exhibition hall into a fine gallery of 19th-century paintings (in the room on the left). Boudin's artwork here

Eugène Boudin (1824–1898)

Born in Honfleur, Boudin was the son of a harbor pilot. As an amateur teenage artist, he found work in an art-supply store that catered to famous artists from Paris (such as Jean-Baptiste-Camille Corot and Jean-François Millet) who came to paint the seaside. Boudin studied art in Paris but kept his hometown roots. Thanks to his Paris connections, Boudin's work was exhibited at the Paris salons.

At age 30 Boudin met the teenage Claude Monet. Monet had grown up in nearby Le Havre, and, like Boudin, sketched the world around him—beaches, boats, and small-town life. Boudin encouraged him to don a scarf, set up his easel outdoors, and paint the scene exactly as he saw it. Today, we say: "Well, duh!" But "open-air" painting was unorthodox for artists trained to thoroughly study their subjects in the perfect lighting of a controlled studio setting. Boudin didn't teach Monet as much as give him the courage to follow his artistic instincts.

In the 1860s and 1870s, Boudin spent summers at his farm (St. Siméon) on the outskirts of Honfleur, hosting Monet, Edouard Manet, and others. They taught Boudin the Impressionist techniques of using bright colors and building a figure with many individual brushstrokes. Boudin adapted those "strokes" to build figures with "patches" of color. In 1874, Boudin joined the renegade Impressionists at their "revolutionary" exhibition in Paris.

is arranged chronologically, from Romanticism through Realism to Impressionism (the heart of this museum). Find the glass display case in the rear titled *Précurseur de l'Impressionisme*, with little pastel drawings, and start here.

Upon showing their work in Paris, local artists—such as Eugène Boudin—created enough of a stir that Normandy came into vogue; many Parisian artists (including Monet and other early Impressionists) traveled to Honfleur to tune in to the action. Boudin himself made a big impression on the father of Impressionism. This collection of his paintings—which he gave to his hometown—provides a good study of the evolution from realistic portrayals of subjects (outlines colored in, like a coloring book) to masses of colors catching light (Impressionism). Boudin's beach scenes, showing aristocrats taking a healthy saltwater dip, helped fuel that trend. His skies were good enough to earn him the nickname "King of Skies."

Third Floor (Hambourg/Rachet Collection): Follow the steps that lead from the Boudin room to the small Hambourg/

Rachet collection (and a smashing painting of Honfleur). In 1988, André Hambourg and his wife, Nicole Rachet, donated their art to this museum. The collection is enjoyably Impressionistic, but with artwork from the mid-20th century.

Third Floor (Salle Katia Granoff): Retrace your steps back to the main stairway to reach the other third-floor room, where you'll find a worthwhile collection of 20th-century pieces by artists who lived and learned in Honfleur. Check out the few paintings by Raoul Dufy (a French Fauvist painter) and compare his imaginative scenes of Honfleur with others you've seen. Don't miss the brilliant view of the Normandy Bridge through the windows.

Art Galleries—Eugène Boudin ignited Honfleur's artistic tradition that still burns today. The town is a popular haunt of artists, many of whom display their works in Honfleur's terrific selection of art galleries (the best ones are along the streets between Ste. Catherine Church and the port). As you walk around the town, take the time to enjoy today's art.

▲**Maisons Satie**—This peaceful museum, housed in composer Erik Satie's birthplace, presents his music in a creative and enjoyable way. As you wander from room to room with your included audioguide, infrared signals transmit bits of Satie's music, along with a first-person story (in English). As if you're living as an artist in 1920s Paris, you'll drift past winged pears, strangers in the window, and small girls with green eyes. (If you like what you hear...don't move; the infrared transmission is sensitive, and the soundtrack switches every few feet.) The finale—performed by you—is the *Laboratory of Emotions* pedal-go-round. For a relaxing sit, enjoy the 12-minute movie (4/hour) featuring modern dance springing from Satie's collaboration with Picasso types (€6, includes audioguide; May–Sept Wed–Mon 10:00–19:00, closed Tue; Oct–Dec and mid-Feb–April Wed–Mon 11:00–18:00, closed Tue; closed Jan–mid-Feb; last entry one hour before closing, 5-minute walk from harbor at 67 boulevard Charles V, tel. 02 31 89 11 11).

Museums of Old Honfleur—Two side-by-side folk museums combine to paint a picture of daily life in Honfleur during the time when its ships were king and the city had global significance. The curator creatively supports the artifacts with paintings, making the cultural context clearer. Both museums have booklets with English explanations.

The **Museum of the Navy** (Musée de la Marine) faces the port and fills Honfleur's oldest church (15th century) with a cool collection of ship models, marine paraphernalia, and paintings. The **Museum of Ethnography and Norman Popular Art** (Musée d'Ethnographie et d'Art Populaire), located in the old prison and courthouse, re-creates typical rooms from various eras and crams them with objects of daily life (€3.30 each or €4.60 for both; both museums open April–Sept Tue–Sun 10:00–12:00 & 14:00–18:30, closed Mon; March and Oct–mid-Nov Tue–Fri 10:00–12:00 & 14:30–17:30, Sat–Sun 10:00–12:00 & 14:00–17:30, closed Mon; closed mid-Nov–Feb).

Walks

▲**Côte de Grâce Walk**—For good exercise and a bird's-eye view of Honfleur and the Normandy Bridge, take the steep 20-minute walk (or quick drive) up to the Côte de Grâce viewpoint—best in the early morning or at sunset. From the church of Ste. Catherine, walk or drive up rue du Puits, then follow the blue-on-white sign to reach the splendid view. *Piétons* (walkers) should veer right up la Rampe du Mont Joli; drivers should keep straight. Two hundred yards past the top, the **Chapel of Notre-Dame de Grâce** merits a visit. Built in the early 1600s by the mariners and people of Honfleur, the church oozes seafaring mementos. Model boats hang from the ceiling, pictures of boats balance high on the walls, and what's left is decorated by stained-glass images of sailors praying to the Virgin Mary while at sea. Even the holy water basins to the left and right of the entrance are in the shape of seashells.

Just below the chapel, a second lookout point offers a sweeping view of the super-industrial Le Havre, with the Manche (English Channel) to your left and the Normandy Bridge to your right.

Jetty/Park Walk—Take a level stroll in Honfleur along the water past the Hôtel le Cheval Blanc to see the mouth of the Seine River and big ships at sea. You'll pass kid-friendly parks, well-endowed with flowers and grass, and continue past the lock connecting Honfleur to the Seine and the sea. Grand and breezy vistas of the sea reward the diligent walker (allow one hour out and back for best views).

Near Honfleur

Boat Excursions—Boat trips in and around Honfleur depart near Hôtel le Cheval Blanc (Easter–Nov usually about 11:00–17:00). The tour boat *Calypso* takes good 45-minute spins around Honfleur's harbor (€6, tel. 02 31 89 07 77). You'll also find several boats with cruises to the Normandy Bridge (see below), which, unfortunately, include two boring trips through the locks (about €8, 50 minutes, details at TI).

▲**Normandy Bridge (Pont de Normandie)**—The 1.25-mile-long pont de Normandie is the longest cable-stayed bridge in the Western world (€5 toll each way). This is a key piece of a super-expressway that links the Atlantic ports from Belgium to Spain. View the bridge from Honfleur (better from an excursion boat or the Côte de Grâce viewpoint, and best at night, when bridge is floodlit). Also consider visiting the bridge's free Exhibition Hall (under tollbooth on Le Havre side, daily 8:00–19:00). The Seine finishes its winding 500-mile journey here, dropping only 1,500 feet from its source. The river flows so slowly that in certain places, a stiff breeze can send it flowing upstream.

▲**Etrétat**—France's answer to the White Cliffs of Dover, these chalky cliffs soar high above a calm, crescent beach (from Honfleur it's about 50 minutes by car or 2 hours by bus via Le Havre). Walking trails lead hikers from the small seaside resort of Etrétat along a vertiginous route with sensational views (and crowds of hikers in summers and on weekends). You'll recognize these cliffs—and the arches and stone spire that decorate them—from countless Impressionist paintings, including several at the Eugène Boudin Museum in Honfleur. The small, Coney Island–like town holds plenty of cafés and a **TI** (place Maurice Guillard, tel. 02 35 27 05 21, www.etretat.net).

Getting There: Etrétat is north of Le Havre. To get here by car, cross the Normandy Bridge and follow A-29, then exit at *sortie Etrétat*. Buses serve Etrétat from Le Havre's *gare routière*, adjacent to the train station (8/day Mon–Sat, 1 hour, www.cars-perier.com).

Sleeping in Honfleur

(€1 = about $1.25, country code: 33)

Though Honfleur is popular in summer, it's busiest on weekends and holidays (blame Paris). English is widely spoken (Honfleur is a popular weekend getaway for Brits). A few moderate accommodations remain, but most hotels are pretty pricey. Budget travelers should consider the *chambres d'hôtes* listed.

Hotels

$$$ Hôtel le Cheval Blanc***, a Best Western, is a waterfront splurge with port views from all of its 32 plush rooms (many with queen-size beds and high-tech showers), plus a rare-in-this-town elevator (small Db with lesser view–€85–130, Db with full port view–€150–200, bigger Db–€135–200, family rooms/suites–€180–425, must cancel by 16:00 the day before or forfeit deposit, free Wi-Fi, 2 quai des Passagers, tel. 02 31 81 65 00, fax 02 31 89 52 80, www.hotel-honfleur.com, info@hotel-honfleur.com).

$$$ L'Absinthe Hôtel*** offers 12 tastefully restored rooms, all with king-size beds. Rooms in the "old" section come with wood-beamed decor and Jacuzzi tubs, and share a cozy public lounge with a fireplace (Db–€115–150). Five rooms have port views and four-star, state-of-the-art comfort, including air-conditioning and saunas (Db–€165–250, Db suite–€250; breakfast–€12, private parking-€12, 1 rue de la Ville, check in at L'Absinthe restaurant across alley, tel. 02 31 89 23 23, fax 02 31 89 53 60, www.absinthe.fr, reservation@absinthe.fr).

$$$ Les Maisons de Léa* ** boasts Honfleur's most handsome shell but charges dearly for its 30 adorable rooms and tasteful decor. This hotel delivers a homey feel, with French-country wood furnishings, pleasing public spaces, a library that may keep you inside even in good weather, and the only spa in town (€30 for 30-minute massage). The highest rates listed are for weekends, whereas the lowest rates apply to nonsummer weekdays (Db-€120–220, suites-€200–325, €235–325 for cottage that sleeps up to 5 and has a full kitchen, pricey €15 breakfast, free Internet access and Wi-Fi, across from the church on place Ste. Catherine, tel. 02 31 14 49 49, fax 02 31 89 28 61, www.lesmaisonsdelea.com, contact @lesmaisonsdelea.com).

$$ Hôtel du Dauphin ** is Honfleur's best midrange value, with a colorful lounge/breakfast room, many stairs, an Escher-esque floor plan, and helpful staff. The 30 rooms—some with open-beam ceilings, most with queen- or king-size beds—are all comfortable and well-maintained. If you need a lower floor or bigger bed, request it when you book (Db-€70–100, Tb-€120–130, lovely Qb-€149–165, free Wi-Fi, a stone's throw from Ste. Catherine Church at 10 place Pierre Berthelot, tel. 02 31 89 15 53, fax 02 31 89 92 06, www.hotel dudauphin.com, hotel.dudauphin@wanadoo.fr).

$$ Hôtel Monet ** , on the road to the Côte de Grâce and a 10-minute walk down to the port (longer back up), is an overlooked find. This tranquil spot is an ivy-covered brick home with 10 mostly tight but good-value rooms facing a courtyard, each with a patio made for picnics. You'll meet welcoming owners Christoph and Sylvie, who plan to add six new rooms in 2011 (Db-€64–120, Tb-€75–110, Qb-€92–120, highest rates are for July–Sept, free and easy parking, free Wi-Fi, Chartière du Puits, tel. 02 31 89 00 90, fax 02 31 89 97 16, www.hotel-monet.fr, contact@hotel-monet -honfleur.com).

$ Etap Hôtel is modern, efficient, tight, and cheap, with antiseptically clean rooms (Sb-€40, Db/Tb-€48, €6 for each extra person, reception is closed 21:00–6:00 but automatic check-in with credit card available 24 hours, elevator, pay Wi-Fi, across from bus station and main parking lot on rue des Vases, tel. 08 92 68 07 81, fax 02 31 89 77 88, www.etaphotel.com).

Chambres d'Hôtes

The TI has a long list of Honfleur's many *chambres d'hôtes* (rooms in private homes), but most are too far from the town center. All four are good values.

$$ La Cour Ste. Catherine is an enchanting bed-and-breakfast run by the open-hearted Madame Giaglis ("call me Liliane") and her big-hearted husband, Monsieur Liliane. Her six big, modern rooms—each with firm beds and a separate sitting area—surround a perfectly Norman courtyard with a small terrace, fine plantings, and cool coffee shop. The rooms are as cheery as the owner (Db-€80, Db suite-€100, extra bed-€25, includes breakfast, small apartments that sleep up to 6 and cottage with kitchens also available, cash only, free Internet access and Wi-Fi, free parking in 2011 with this book, 200 yards up rue du Puits from Ste. Catherine Church at 74 rue du Puits, tel. 02 31 89 42 40, www.giaglis.com, coursaintecatherine@orange.fr). If you can't find a room in Honfleur, talk to Liliane—she wants to help, even when her place is full.

$$ Le Fond de la Cour lies kitty-corner to La Cour Ste. Catherine and is another top value (don't let the bleak exterior fool you). British expat Amanda Ferguson and big dog Pataud offer a spanking-new two-floor cottage that could sleep six (Db-€100, €20 extra/person). The cottage has a private garden and a full kitchen, and the converted stable/main house has two sharp rooms (Db-€70, Tb-€100), including one ideal for three people (breakfast-€6, free Wi-Fi, free street parking, private parking-€9, 29 rue Eugène Boudin, tel. 09 62 31 24 30, mobile 06 72 20 72 98, www.lefonddelacour.com, Amanda.ferguson@orange.fr).

$ Sweet Madame Bellegarde offers two simple rooms in her traditional home (Db-€37–42, family-friendly Tb with great bathroom view-€64, cash only, 54 rue St. Léonard, 10-minute uphill walk from TI, 3 blocks up from St. Léonard Church in untouristy part of Honfleur, look for small *chambres* sign in window, she'll try to hold a parking spot if you ask, tel. 02 31 89 06 52).

Eating in Honfleur

Eat seafood or cream sauces here. It's a tough choice between the irresistible waterfront tables of the many look-alike places lining the harbor, and eateries with more solid reputations elsewhere in town. Trust my dinner suggestions below and consider your hotelier's opinion. It's best to call ahead to reserve at most restaurants in Honfleur (particularly on weekends).

Le Bouilland Normand hides a block off the port on a pleasing square and offers a true Norman experience at reasonable prices (inside and out). Charming Annette serves while her chef-husband (who excels in sauces and seafood) manages *la cuisine*. Annette and daughter Claire are happy to help you select your courses (€18–26 *menus*, closed Sun and Wed, on rue de la Ville, tel. 02 31 89 02 41).

Le Bréard serves exquisite modern French cuisine presented with care, style, and ingenuity. The chef has returned after several years in Paris' finer restaurants, bringing his considerable talent back to Honfleur. Book ahead, then savor a delicious, slow meal in a formal yet appealing setting—all for a fraction of the price you'd pay in Paris (€29–49 *menus*, closed Mon–Tue, 7 rue du Puits, tel. 02 31 89 53 40).

P'tit Mareyeur is whisper-formal, intimate, all about seafood, and a good value. Reservations are particularly smart here (€25 *menu*, try the bouillabaisse *bonfleuraise*, closed Mon–Tue and Jan, 4 rue Haute, tel. 02 31 98 84 23, friendly owner Julie speaks some English).

Le Vintage, just off the port, is a happening bar/café with live piano and jazz some nights. Casual outside seating and a vigorous interior make this a good choice if you value liveliness over fine cuisine. For dinner, sit upstairs and enjoy port views and a nice atmosphere (€13–21 *plats*, €18 *menu*, €12–24 French-style tapas platters, closed Tue, 8 quai des Passagers, tel. 02 31 89 05 28).

La Tortue combines marvelous ambience on both floors with authentic Norman cuisine and decent rates. Main courses are small but delicious (€22, good three courses from €22, good vegetarian options, closed Mon–Tue, 36 rue de l'Homme de Bois, tel. 02 31 81 24 60).

La Commanderie, specializing in pizza and crêpes, is cozy and welcoming (daily July–Aug, closed Mon–Tue off-season, across from le Corsaire restaurant on place Ste. Catherine, tel. 02 31 89 14 92).

L'Absinthe is a handsome place with wicker chairs and big windows facing the outer port. If you want a mini-splurge, this is a solid option (*menus* from €28, 1 rue de la Ville, tel. 02 31 89 04 24).

La Cidrerie is a purely Norman cider bar with crêpes made in the traditional style, Calvados apple brandy, and an inviting atmosphere (closed Tue–Wed, set back on cathedral side of place Hamelin at #26, tel. 02 31 89 59 85).

Travel Coffee Shop is an ideal breakfast or lunch option for travelers wanting conversation (in either English or French) and good food at very fair prices (Thu–Tue 8:00–19:00, closed Wed, 74 rue du Puits).

Along the Waterfront: If the weather cooperates, or you just need to see the water, slide down to the harbor and table-shop the joints that line the high side. Several places have effective propane heaters that keep outdoor diners happy when it's cool. Although the cuisine is mostly mediocre, the setting is uniquely Honfleur—

and, on a warm evening, hard to pass up. Take a stroll along the port to orient yourself and compare restaurant views, chair comfort, and menu selection (all of these places look the same to me). Then dive in and remember that you're paying for the setting, not the cuisine.

For a portside drink, **Café de l'Hôtel de Ville** owns the best afternoon sun exposure (and charges for it), and looks across to Honfleur's soaring homes (open daily July–Aug, closed Tue off-season, place de l'Hôtel de Ville, tel. 02 31 89 07 29).

Breakfast: If it's even close to sunny, skip your hotel breakfast and enjoy ambience for a cheaper price by eating on the port, where several cafés offer *petit déjeuner* for about €7–12, depending on the *menu* you select. Morning sun and views are best from the high side of the harbor. If price or companionship matter, head to the Travel Coffee Shop for the best breakfast deal in town (described earlier).

Dessert: If you need a Ben & Jerry's ice cream fix or a scrumptious dessert crêpe, find the waterfront stand at the southeast corner of Vieux Bassin.

Nighttime Food to Go: There's a salad, *frites*, and kebab place at 6 rue de l'Homme du Bois (until 21:00, closed Wed).

Nightlife: Nightlife in Honfleur centers on the old port. Three bar/cafés sit almost side by side, halfway up the high-building side of the port: **Le Marin** (most local), **L'Albatross** (pub-like), and **Le Perroquet Vert** (existential).

Honfleur Connections

Buses connect Honfleur with Le Havre, Caen, Deauville, and Lisieux (all with direct rail service to Paris), where you'll catch a train to other points. Coming from Paris, the best train-to-bus transfers are usually in Lisieux or Deauville, but if you want to visit Rouen on the way, the bus via Le Havre works fine. Although train and bus service usually are coordinated, ask at Honfleur's helpful bus station for the best connection for your trip (information desk open Mon–Fri 9:00–12:00 & 13:00–18:00, in summer also Sat–Sun, tel. 02 31 89 28 41, www.busverts.fr). Railpass-holders will save money by connecting through Deauville, as bus fares increase with distance.

From Honfleur by Bus and/or Train to: Caen (express buses 2/day at about 7:30 and 16:55, 1 hour, €10.50; more scenic *par la côte* 9/day, 2 hours, €7.50; or 1-hour, €4 bus to Lisieux, then 30-minute train to Caen), **Bayeux** (8/day, 1.5–3 hours by bus and train; 1-hour express bus or 2-hour bus via the coast to Caen, then 20-minute train to Bayeux; or 1-hour, €4 bus to Lisieux, then 1-hour train to Bayeux via Caen), **Rouen** (6/day Mon–Sat, 3/day

Sun, €4 bus-and-train combo involves 30-minute bus ride over Normandy Bridge to Le Havre, then easy transfer to 1-hour train to Rouen), **Paris'** Gare St. Lazare (13/day, 2–3.5 hours by bus to Lisieux, Deauville, or Le Havre, then 2-hour train to Paris; buses from Honfleur meet most Paris trains).

Bayeux

Only six miles from the D-Day beaches, Bayeux was the first city liberated after the landing. Incredibly, the town was spared the bombs of World War II. After a local convent chaplain made sure London knew that this was not a German headquarters and was of no strategic importance, a scheduled bombing raid was canceled—making Bayeux the closest city to the D-Day landing site not destroyed. Even without its famous tapestry and proximity to the D-Day beaches, Bayeux would be worth a visit for its enjoyable town center and awe-inspiring cathedral, beautifully illuminated at night. Bayeux makes an ideal home base for visiting the area's sights, particularly if you lack a car.

Orientation to Bayeux

Tourist Information

The TI is on a small bridge two blocks north of the cathedral—conveniently located on the pedestrian street that connects place St. Patrice (with its recommended hotels and a Saturday market) and the tapestry. Pick up the free *Exploration and Emotion: D-Day Landings* map, bus schedules to the beaches, and regional information, and ask about special events and concerts (July–Aug Mon–Sat 9:00–19:00, Sun 9:00–13:00 & 14:00–18:00; April–June and Sept–Oct daily 9:30–12:30 & 14:00–18:00; Nov–March Mon–Sat 9:30–12:30 & 14:00–17:30, closed Sun; on pont St. Jean leading to rue St. Jean, tel. 02 31 51 28 28, www.bessin-normandie .com).

For a **self-guided walking tour**, pick up the map called *Découvrez Vieux Bayeux* at the TI. Follow the bronze plates embedded in the sidewalk, and look for information plaques with English translations that correspond to your map.

Arrival in Bayeux

By Train and Bus: Trains and buses share the same station (no bag storage). It's a 15-minute walk from the station to the tapestry, and 15 minutes from the tapestry to place St. Patrice (and several recommended hotels). To reach the tapestry, the cathedral, and the

Bayeux

N

200 YARDS
200 METERS

To ARROMANCHES via D-516

To CAEN via N-13

TO A-84

To ST-LÔ + MONT ST. MICHEL

TRAIN STATION

BAYEUX TAPESTRY

CATHEDRAL

BATTLE OF NORMANDY MUSEUM

PUBLIC BUS STOP FOR D-DAY BEACHES

1. Hôtel Churchill & Marché Plus Grocery
2. Hôtel le Lion d'Or
3. Hôtel Tardif
4. Le Castel B&B
5. Logis les Remparts B&B
6. Chambre d'Hôte le Petit Matin
7. Hotel Reine Mathilde & Brasserie
8. Hôtelle Bayeux
9. Hôtel d'Argouges
10. Hôtel Mogador
11. Hôtel le Maupassant & Café
12. La Chaumière Deli
13. La Reine Mathilde Patisserie
14. La Rapière & La Fringale Rests.
15. La Coline d'Enzo Rest.
16. L'Assiette Normande Rest.
17. Le Pommier Restaurant
18. Lace Conservatory
19. Launderettes (3)
20. Bike Rental
21. Scauto Car Rental
22. Lewis Pub (Wi-Fi)

hotels, cross the major street in front of the station and follow rue Cremel toward *l'Hôpital*, then turn left on rue Nesmond (follow the huge spire). Taxis are usually waiting at the station, though you may have to ask someone to call one for you. Allow €7 for a taxi from the train station to any recommended hotel or sight in Bayeux, and €20 to Arromanches (more after 19:00 and on Sundays, taxi tel. 06 70 40 07 96 or 02 31 92 92 40).

By Car: Look for the cathedral spires and follow signs for *Centre-Ville*, and then signs for the *Tapisserie* (tapestry) or your hotel (individual hotels are well-signed from the ring road—wait for yours to appear). Drivers connecting Bayeux with Mont St. Michel should use the speedy, free A-84 autoroute (closest entrance/exit for Bayeux is at Villers-Bocage; from Bayeux to A-84, take the underpass by the train station to Tilly-sur-Seulles, then Villers-Bocage).

Helpful Hints

Market Days: The Saturday open-air market on place St. Patrice is much larger than the Wednesday market on pedestrian rue St. Jean. Both end by 13:00. Don't leave your car on place St. Patrice on a Friday night, as it will be towed early Saturday.

Grocery Store: Marché Plus, at rue St. Jean 14, is next to the recommended Hôtel Churchill (Mon–Sat 7:00–21:00, Sun 8:30–12:00).

Internet Access: Across from the TI, the souvenir shop **Aure du Common** has several computers upstairs (daily 9:30–19:30). For Wi-Fi, try **Lewis Pub** near the tapestry at 38 rue de Nesmond (daily 10:00 until late, tel. 02 31 92 05 35).

Laundry: There's a launderette with big machines a block behind the TI, on rue Maréchal Foch. Two more launderettes are near place St. Patrice: One is at 4 rue St. Patrice and the other is at 69 rue des Bouchers (both open daily 7:00–21:00).

Bike Rental: Vélos Location, run by amiable Mr. Decaen, has what you need and will deliver to outlying hotels (€10/half-day, €15/day, €5 picnic lunch, daily April–Oct 8:00–20:30, closes earlier off-season, across from the TI at Impasse de Islet, tel. 02 31 92 89 16).

Taxi: Call 06 70 40 07 96 or 02 31 92 92 40.

Car Rental: Bayeux offers few choices. **Scauto** is handiest, just below the train station at the BP gas station (16 boulevard Sadi-Carnot, tel. 02 31 51 18 51, fax 02 31 51 18 30, www .scauto.fr).

Day Trip to Caen Memorial Museum: France's best D-Day museum (described on page 307) is a manageable day trip from Bayeux, thanks to frequent and quick (20-minute) rail service between Bayeux and Caen, and easy access to the museum from Caen's train station. It's a 30-minute drive from Bayeux to the museum.

Sights in Bayeux

▲▲▲**Bayeux Tapestry (Tapisserie de Bayeux)**—Made of wool embroidered onto linen cloth, this historically precious document is a 70-yard-long cartoon. The tapestry tells the story of William the Conqueror's rise from duke of Normandy to king of England, and shows his victory over Harold at the Battle of Hastings in 1066. Long and skinny, it was designed to hang in the nave of Bayeux's cathedral.

Your visit consists of three separate parts that tell the basic story of the battle, provide historical context for the event, and explain how the tapestry was made. First, you'll enter the courtyard, which contains a full-size replica of the boats William used to cross the Channel and rout out Harold. Inside, your visit starts with the actual tapestry, accompanied by an included audioguide that gives a top-notch, fast-moving 20-minute scene-by-scene narration complete with period music (if you lose your place, find subtitles in Latin). Next you'll climb upstairs into a room filled with informational displays, mannequins, models of castles (who knew that the Tower of London was a Norman project?), medieval villages, and good explanations of events surrounding the invasion and the subsequent creation of the tapestry. Your visit finishes with a worthwhile 15-minute film that ties it all together one last time (in the cinema—up one flight, about every 40 minutes, in English).

Remember, this is Norman propaganda—the English (the bad guys, referred to as *les goddamns*, after a phrase the French kept hearing them say) are shown with mustaches and long hair; the French (*les* good guys) are clean-cut and clean-shaven—with even the backs of their heads shaved for a better helmet fit.

Cost and Hours: €8; includes worthwhile audioguide for adults and a special kids' version, daily May-Aug 9:00-18:15, March-April and Sept-Oct 9:00-17:45, Nov-Feb 9:30-11:45 & 14:00-17:15—these are first and last entry times, tel. 02 31 51 25 50, www.tapisserie-bayeux.fr. To avoid crowds, arrive by 9:00 or late in the day. When buying your ticket, ask when they'll show the English version of the 15-minute battle film.

▲▲**Bayeux Cathedral**—This massive building, as big as Paris' Notre-Dame, dominates the small town of Bayeux. (Make it a

Bayeux History—The Battle of Hastings

Because of this pivotal battle, the most memorable date of the Middle Ages is 1066. England's king, Edward the Confessor, was about to die without an heir. The big question: Who would succeed him—Harold, an English nobleman and the king's brother-in-law, or William, duke of Normandy and the king's cousin? Edward chose William and sent Harold to Normandy to give William the news. On the journey, Harold was captured. To win his release, he promised he would be loyal to William and not contest the decision. To test his loyalty, William sent Harold to battle for him in Brittany. Harold was successful, and William knighted him. To further test his loyalty, William had Harold swear on the relics of the Bayeux cathedral that when Edward died, he would allow William to ascend the throne. Harold returned to England, Edward died... and Harold grabbed the throne.

William, known as William the Bastard, invaded England to claim the throne. Harold met him in southern England at the town of Hastings, where their forces fought a fierce 14-hour battle. Harold was killed, and his Saxon forces were routed. William—now "the Conqueror"—marched to London, claimed his throne, and became king of England (though he spoke no English) as well as duke of Normandy.

The advent of a Norman king of England muddied the political waters and set in motion 400 years of conflict between England and France—not to be resolved until the end of the Hundred Years' War (1453). The Norman conquest of England brought that country into the European mainstream (but still no euros). The Normans established a strong central English government. Historians speculate that had William not succeeded, England would have remained on the fringe of Europe (like Scandinavia), and French culture (and language) would have prevailed in the New World. Hmmm.

point to see the cathedral after dark, when it's beautifully illuminated.) To start your visit, find the small square opposite the front entry (information board about the cathedral is in the corner). Notice the two dark towers—originally Romanesque, they were capped later with tall Gothic spires. The west façade is structurally Romanesque, but with a decorative Gothic "curtain" added.

Before entering, head to the left of the cathedral and drop down to the walking lane that runs along its side. The little rectangular stone house atop the near tower was the **watchman's home,** from which he'd keep an eye out for incoming English troops during the Hundred Years' War...and for Germans five centuries later (it didn't work—the Germans took the town in 1940). Bayeux was liberated on D-Day plus one: June 7. About the only casualty was the German lookout—shot while doing just that from the window of this stone house.

Now step inside the cathedral (free, daily July–Aug 8:30–19:00, Sept–June 8:30–18:00). The view of the **nave** from the top of the steps shows a mix of Romanesque and Gothic. Historians believe the Bayeux tapestry originally hung here. Imagine it proudly circling the Norman congregation, draped around the nave below the arches. The nave's huge, round lower arches are Romanesque (11th century) and decorated with the same zigzag pattern that characterizes this "Norman" art in England. This section is so brightly lit because of the huge windows above, in the Gothic half of the nave. The glass was originally richly colored (see the rare surviving 13th-century bits in the high central window above the altar). The most stunning example of 13th-century "Norman" Gothic is in the choir (the fancy area behind the central altar). Each column is decorated with Romanesque carvings. But those carvings lie under a Gothic-style stone exterior (with characteristic tall, thin lines adding a graceful verticality to the overall feel of the interior).

For maximum 1066 atmosphere, step into the spooky **crypt** (beneath the central altar), which was used originally as a safe spot for the cathedral's relics. The crypt displays two freestanding columns and bulky capitals with fine Romanesque carving. During a reinforcement of the nave, these two columns were replaced. Workers removed the Gothic veneer and discovered their true inner Romanesque beauty. Orange angel-musicians add color to this somber room.

River Walk—Join the locals and promenade along the meandering walking path that follows the little Aure River for about 2.5 miles through Bayeux. The path runs both ways from the TI (find the water wheel behind the TI and keep walking; path marked on city maps).

Lace Conservatory (Conservatoire de la Dentelle)—Notable for its carved 15th-century facade, the Adam and Eve house (find Adam, Eve, and the snake) offers a chance to watch workers design and weave intricate lace, just as artisans did in the 1600s. You can also see examples of lace from the past (free, Mon–Sat 10:00–12:30 & 14:00–17:00, closed Sun, across from cathedral entrance, tel. 02 31 92 73 80).

Baron Gérard Museum—This museum, which houses a modest painting gallery and a collection of porcelain and lace, is closed until 2012.

▲**Battle of Normandy Memorial Museum (Musée Memorial de la Bataille de Normandie)**—This museum provides an excellent overview of WWII's Battle of Normandy, with elaborate English explanations throughout. The well-conceived exhibits cover the historical context of the invasion's intense battles and highlight several aspects of the battles, including the challenges faced by doctors and war correspondents, General de Gaulle's contributions to the invasion, and the key role played by aviation. An enlightening 25-minute film is shown near the end (4 showings/day, note the times as you enter). It's like a small, cheaper Caen Memorial Museum—and worthwhile if you won't be visiting that more impressive museum (€6.50, included with Normandy Pass—see page 293, daily May–mid-Sept 9:30–18:30, mid-Sept–April 10:00–12:30 & 14:00–18:00, on Bayeux's ring road, 20 minutes on foot from center, tel. 02 31 51 46 90, www.normandie memoire.com).

Just beyond the museum is a **British Military Cemetery,** decorated with 4,144 simple gravestones marking the final resting places of these fallen soldiers. The memorial's Latin inscription reads, "In 1944, the British came to free the homeland of William the Conqueror." A **Monument to Reporters** is along the footpath exiting the museum, to the right. The grassy walkway is lined with white roses and stone monuments listing, by year, the names of reporters who have died in action from 1944 to today.

Sleeping in Bayeux

(€1 = about $1.25, country code: 33)

Hotels are a good value here. Drivers should also see "Sleeping in Arromanches" on page 297.

Near the Tapestry

$$$ Hôtel Churchill*,** on a traffic-free street across from the TI, could not be more central or more service-oriented. They have 32 plush rooms with wood furnishings, big beds, and convivial public spaces. The professional owners, the Heberts, were made for this business, and they take excellent care of their clients (standard Db-€102–112, superior Db-€135, deluxe Db-€162, Tb-€162, Qb-€180, Internet access and Wi-Fi, comfortable bar/lounge, easy and free parking, at 14 rue St. Jean, tel. 02 31 21 31 80, fax 02 31 21 41 66, www.hotel-churchill.fr, info@hotel-churchill.fr). This hotel also runs a shuttle van to Mont St. Michel (see "Bayeux Connections," later).

$$$ Hôtel le Lion d'Or*,** Eisenhower's favorite hotel in Bayeux, draws an older clientele willing to pay top euro for its Old World character, professional service, and elegant restaurant (standard Db-€125, bigger Db-€150, still bigger Db-€180–200, suite Tb-€245, extra bed-€30, breakfast-€13, no elevator, Wi-Fi, easy €9 parking, 71 rue St. Jean, tel. 02 31 92 06 90, fax 02 31 22 15 64, www.liondor-bayeux.fr, lion.d-or.bayeux@wanadoo.fr).

$$ At Hôtel Tardif, you'll sleep like Napoleon in a central six-room manor house that dates from the emperor's era but feels more like a bed-and-breakfast. Run by friendly Anthony, it's at once *très elegant* and intimate, with traditional touches, a grand garden, and a smashing wooden spiral staircase (standard Db–€75, big Db–€120, massive Db–€160, Tb–€130–190, Qb–€210, Wi-Fi, 16 rue Nesmond, tel. 02 31 92 67 72, www.hoteltardif.com, hotel tardif@orange.fr). The same owner has recently opened a B&B, called **Le Castel**, a short walk away (Db–€65–85, superior Db–€95–115, 1 boulevard Sadi Carnot, tel. 02 31 92 67 72, www .castelbayeux.com, castelbayeux@orange.fr).

$$ Logis les Remparts is a delightful, three-room bed-and-breakfast run by charming Christèle and situated above an atmospheric Calvados cider tasting shop. Rooms are big, comfortable, and homey—one is a huge, two-room suite (Db–€60–70, Tb–€70–90, cash only for payments under €100, includes breakfast, Wi-Fi downstairs in shop, a few blocks above the cathedral on the park-like place Charles de Gaulle at 4 rue Bourbesneur, tel. 02 31 92 50 40, www.bayeux-bandb.com, cidrelecornu@wanadoo.fr).

$$ Chambre d'Hôte le Petit Matin is a block above the cathedral (but may change location in 2011). You'll enter into a small courtyard garden, then climb to one of three homey rooms. Helpful Pascal runs the place and offers very reasonable rates (Db–€65–75, Tb–€85, Qb–€85, 23 rue Larcher, tel. 02 31 92 08 13, www .hotel-bayeux-reinemathilde.fr, hotel.reinemathilde@wanadoo.fr).

$$ Hôtelle Bayeux**, the closest hotel I list to the train station (600 yards away), is a last resort, with its long halls, bright colors, and 29 basic rooms. The rates are impossible to pin down and can be twice those listed here (Db–€60–90, Tb–€80–140, Qb–€95–180, many family rooms with bunk beds, easy parking, a block from cathedral's right transept at 9 rue Tardif, tel. 02 31 92 70 08, fax 02 31 21 15 74, www.lebayeux.com, lebayeux@gmail .com).

Near Place St. Patrice

These hotels are just off the big place St. Patrice (easy parking), but a 10-minute walk up rue St. Patrice, a 15-minute walk from the TI (a 15-minute walk to the tapestry).

$$$ Hôtel d'Argouges*** (dar-goo-zhah) makes an impression as you enter. Named for its builder, Lord d'Argouges, this tranquil retreat has a mini-château feel, with classy public spaces, lovely private gardens, and standard-comfort rooms. The hotel is run by its helpful owners, formal Madame Ropartz and easygoing son Frédéric, who have renovated every aspect of the hotel except the bathrooms—which they plan to do soon (Db-€110-124, Tb-€150, fine family suites-€190, deluxe mega-suite for up to 6 and good for two couples-€285, extra bed-€15, secure parking-€5, just off huge place St. Patrice at 21 rue St. Patrice, tel. 02 31 92 88 86, fax 02 31 92 69 16, www.hotel-dargouges.com, dargouges @aol.com).

$ Hôtel Mogador** is a fair value, with engaging Monsieur Mencaroni at the helm. Choose between simple, wood-beamed rooms on the busy square, or quiet, more colorful, modern rooms off the street. There are no public areas beyond the small breakfast room and tiny courtyard (Sb-€47, Db-€57, Tb-€70, Qb-€83, breakfast-€6, Wi-Fi planned for 2011, 20 rue Alain Chartier at place St. Patrice, tel. 02 31 92 24 58, fax 02 31 92 24 85, www .hotelmo.fr, lemogador@gmail.com).

$ Hôtel le Maupassant offers 10 no-star, no-frills rooms with just enough comfort. The rooms are above a central café, and the bartender doubles as the receptionist (S-€30, Ds-€41, Ts-€70, WCs down the hall, 19 rue St. Martin, tel. 02 31 92 28 53, h.lemaupassant@orange.fr).

Countryside Accommodations near Bayeux

Drivers will pass scads of good-value *chambres d'hôtes* on the way from Bayeux to Arromanches, and on the road from Arromanches to the American Cemetery (for locations, see the map on page 288).

$$$ L'Atre Fleuri, 20 minutes west of Bayeux, is well-run by Americans Margaret and James. You get the run of the house, including the living room, dining room (no picnics, please), lots of English books, and five immaculate rooms with quilts and other homey touches (Db-€95-125, Tb-€125, includes breakfast, Wi-Fi, in the village of Balleroy, 12 rue des Etangs, tel. 02 31 51 03 20, www.normandynights.com).

$$ La Ferme du Pressoir is a lovely, traditional B&B on a big working farm, immersed in Norman landscapes about 20 minutes south of Bayeux. The five rooms filled with wood furnishings are vintage French—and so are the kind owners, Jacques and Odile (Db-€85, Tb-€105, Qb-€125, 5 people-€145, includes good breakfast, tel. 02 41 53 04 96, Le Haut St. Louet, just off A-84, exit at Villers-Bocage, www.bandbnormandie.com, lafermedupressoir @bandbnormandie.com).

Eating in Bayeux

Drivers can also consider the short drive to Arromanches for seaside dining options (see page 298).

On or near Traffic-Free Rue St. Jean

This street is lined with cafés, *créperies*, and inexpensive dining options.

La Chaumière is the best charcuterie (deli) in town; you'll find salads, quiches, and prepared dishes to go (Tue–Sun open until 19:30, closed Sun 13:00–15:00 and all day Mon; on rue St. Jean across from Hôtel Churchill). The grocery store across the street has what you need to complete your picnic. And for dessert, **La Reine Mathilde Patisserie** is the pride of the town for its pastries (19 rue St. Martin).

La Rapière is a traditional wood-beamed eatery filled with locals enjoying a refined meal and a rare-these-days cheese platter for your finale (€28–35 *menus*, closed Wed–Thu, 53 rue St. Jean, tel. 03 31 21 05 45).

La Fringale is a good choice for a simple meal on this pedestrian street. Warmly run by Franck, this place makes you feel at home and lets you eat very well without paying too much (€9 salads, €16 *menu*, closed Wed off-season, indoor and outdoor seating, 43 rue St. Jean, tel. 02 31 21 34 40).

La Coline d'Enzo works for diners wanting to taste creative, nontraditional cuisine at fair prices. The dining room is an appealing blend of modern and traditional decor, overseen by gracious owner Delfine. A few tables line the side street outside (€22–34 *menus*, closed Sun–Mon, 2 rue des Bouchers, tel. 02 31 92 03 01).

La Reine Mathilde Brasserie is a service-oriented restaurant offering bistro fare all day. It also has a welcoming outside terrace (daily with non-stop service from 12:00–21:00, a block from rue St. Jean at 23 rue Larcher).

Near the Cathedral

L'Assiette Normande is a lighthearted and popular eatery with lots of groups. It's kid-friendly and serves well-presented local dishes in lively rooms with many choices at fair prices (the veal, rump steak, and *parmentier de cochon*—andouille with potatoes—are all good). Show this book for a free *kir Normand*, and don't miss dessert (*menus* from €15, closed Mon, 3 rue des Chanoines, tel. 02 31 22 04 61).

Le Pommier, with street appeal both inside and out, is a good place to sample regional products with clever twists in a relaxed yet refined atmosphere. Owner Thierry mixes old and new in his cuisine and decor. His *lotte* (whitefish) is satisfying no matter how he prepares it, and his meat dishes and desserts are also tasty—try the three crème brûlées (two-course *menu* from €19, three courses from €24, great-value €12 lunch *menu* is filling, open daily, 38 rue des Cuisiniers, tel. 02 31 21 52 10).

Bayeux Connections

From Bayeux by Train to: Paris' Gare St. Lazare (9/day, 2.5 hours, some require change in Caen), **Amboise** (12/day, 4–6 hours, 4 hours via Caen and Tours' St. Pierre des Corps, or 6 hours via Paris–Montparnasse and Tours' St. Pierre des Corps), **Rouen** (6/day, 2 hours, change in Caen; more trips possible via Paris' Gare St. Lazare, 4–5 hours), **Caen** (18/day, 20 minutes), **Honfleur** (8/day, 1.5–3 hours by train and bus; 20-minute train to Caen, then 1-hour express bus to Honfleur or more scenic 2-hour bus via the coast; or 1-hour train to Lisieux then 1-hour bus to Honfleur; for bus information, call 02 31 89 28 41), **Pontorson–Mont St. Michel** (2–3/day, 2 hours to Pontorson, then bus to Mont St. Michel; also consider Hôtel Churchill's faster shuttle van—described below).

By Bus to the D-Day Beaches: Bus Verts du Calvados offers minimal service to D-Day beaches with stops in Bayeux at place St. Patrice and at the train station (schedules at TI, tel. 08 10 21 42 14, www.busverts.fr). Lines #74/#75 run east to Arromanches and Juno Beach (3–5/day, none on Sun Sept–June; 30 minutes to Arromanches, 50 minutes to Juno Beach), and line #70 runs west to the American Cemetery and Vierville-sur-Mer (4/day in summer, 1–2/day off-season, 35 minutes to American Cemetery, 45 minutes to Vierville-sur-Mer). Because of the schedules, you're usually stuck with either too much or too little time at either sight if you try to take the bus round-trip; consider a taxi one way and a bus the other (for taxi information, see page 278).

By Shuttle Van to Mont St. Michel: The recommended **Hôtel Churchill** runs a shuttle van to Mont St. Michel for €58 per person round-trip (€50 one-way, 1.5 hours each way; available to the general public, though hotel clients get a small discount). The van leaves Bayeux at 8:30 and returns by 14:30 (in time for the train to Paris), allowing travelers three hours at Mont St. Michel. For details, see www.hotel-churchill.fr.

D-Day Beaches

The 75 miles of Atlantic coast north of Bayeux, stretching from Ste. Marie-du-Mont to Ouistreham, is littered with WWII museums, monuments, cemeteries, and battle remains left in tribute to the courage of the British, Canadian, and American armies that successfully carried out the largest military operation in history: D-Day. (It's called *Jour J* in French—the letters "D" and "J" come from the first letter for the word "day" in either English or French.) It was on these serene beaches, at the crack of dawn on June 6, 1944, that the Allies finally gained a foothold in France, and Nazi Europe was doomed to crumble.

> *"The first 24 hours of the invasion will be decisive...The fate of Germany depends on the outcome...For the Allies, as well as Germany, it will be the longest day."*
> —Field Marshal Erwin Rommel to his aide, April 22, 1944 (from the movie *The Longest Day*)

June of 2009 marked the 65th anniversary of the landings. It was hailed as the last of the great D-Day commemorations, as there likely won't be any veterans alive for the 70th. But that doesn't mean these events will end. All along this rambling coast, locals will not soon forget what the troops and their families sacrificed all those years ago. A warm regard for Americans has survived political disputes, from de Gaulle to "Freedom Fries." This remains particularly friendly territory for Americans—a place where their soldiers are still honored and the image of the US as a force for good has remained largely untarnished.

Planning Your Time

You'll want at least one full day to explore the D-Day beaches. If you only have one day, I'd spend it entirely on the beaches and—regretfully—miss the Caen Memorial Museum. (If you want to squeeze in the museum, visit it on your way to or from the beaches—but remember that the American Cemetery closes at 17:00, or at 18:00 in May–Sept—and you need at least an hour there.) I've listed the D-Day sites in the order of importance, with the most visit-worthy first (note that several are closed in January). Most Americans prefer to focus on the American sector (west of Aromanches), rather than the British and Canadian sectors (east of Aromanches), which have been overbuilt with resorts, making it harder to re-create the events of June 1944. For more information on touring the D-Day beaches, www.normandiememoire.com is a useful resource.

D-Day Beaches

NORMANDY

By Car: Begin on the cliffs above Arromanches and see the movie at the Arromanches 360° Theater to set your mood. Walk or drive a quarter-mile downhill to the town and visit Port Winston and the D-Day Landing Museum, then continue west to Longues-sur-Mer. Spend your afternoon visiting the American Cemetery, walking on the beach at Vierville-sur-Mer, and exploring the Pointe du Hoc Ranger Monument. Those with time can continue to the strategic town of Ste. Mère Eglise and learn about the paratroopers' role in the invasion. Make a quick stop at the German Military Cemetery on your way back. Canadians will want to start at the Juno Beach Centre and Canadian Cemetery (in Courseulles-sur-Mer, 10 minutes east of Arromanches), then pick up the itinerary described above.

Sans Car: It's easiest to take a minivan tour or taxi from

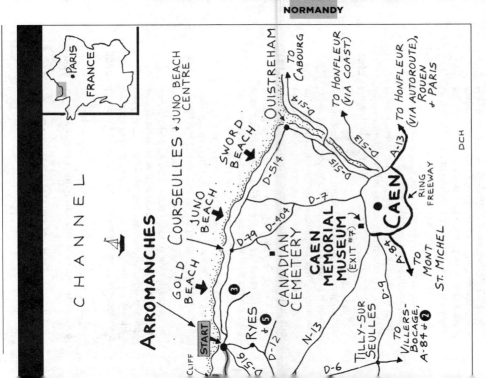

Bayeux, or—for a really full day—combine a visit to the Caen Memorial Museum with their guided minivan tour of the beaches. Public transport is available, though very limited. Many find that a one-day car rental works best.

Getting Around the D-Day Beaches

On Your Own: Though the minivan excursions listed on page 291 teach important history lessons—drawing Americans and Canadians out of their cars—**renting a car** is ideal, particularly for three or more people (see Bayeux's "Helpful Hints" for rental suggestions, on page 278). Park in monitored locations at the sites, since break-ins have been a problem—particularly at the American Cemetery. Hardy souls can **bike** between the sites (though distances are long enough to discourage most). Very limited

Countdown to D-Day

1939 On September 1, Adolf Hitler invades the Free City of Danzig (today's Gdańsk, Poland), sparking World War II.

1940 Germany's "Blitzkrieg" ("lightning war") quickly over-whelms France. Nazis goose-step down the avenue des Champs-Elysées, and the country is divided into Occupied France (the north) and Vichy France (the south, ruled by right-wing French). Just like that, nearly the entire Continent is fascist.

1941 The Allies (Britain, the Soviet Union, and others) peck away at the fringes of "fortress Europe." The Soviets repel Hitler's invasion at Moscow, while the Brits (with American aid) battle German U-boats for control of the seas. On December 7, Japan bombs the US naval base at Pearl Harbor, Hawaii. The US enters the war against Japan and its ally, Germany.

1942 Three crucial battles—at Stalingrad, El-Alamein, and Guadalcanal—weaken the German forces and their ally, Japan. The victorious tank battle at El-Alamein in the deserts of North Africa soon gives the Allies a jumping-off point (Tunis) for the first assault on the Continent.

1943 More than 150,000 Americans and Brits, under the command of George Patton and Bernard ("Monty") Montgomery, land in Sicily and begin working their way north through Italy. Meanwhile, Germany has to fend off tenacious Soviets on their eastern front.

1944 On June 6, 1944, the Allies launch "Operation Overlord," better known as D-Day. The Allies have amassed three million soldiers and six million tons of *matériel* in England to prepare for the biggest fleet-led invasion in history—across the English Channel

bus service links Bayeux, the coastal town of Arromanches, and the most impressive sites of D-Day (see Bus Verts du Calvados information on page 286). Consider a bus one way and taxi the other. For small groups, hiring a **taxi for the day** is far cheaper than taking a minivan tour, but you don't get the history.

By Taxi: Taxi minivans shuttle up to seven people between the key sites at surprisingly fair rates (allow €160/day). Approximate prices per taxi (not per person): €22 one-way from Bayeux to Arromanches, €40 round-trip with one hour of wait time; €33 one-way from Bayeux to the American Cemetery, €62 round-trip with one hour of wait time; €90 round-trip for the American Cemetery to France, then eastward to Berlin. The Germans, hunkered down in northern France, know an invasion is imminent, but the Allies keep the details top secret. On the night of June 5, 150,000 soldiers board ships and planes, not knowing where they are headed until they're under way. Each one carries a note from General Dwight D. Eisenhower: "The tide has turned. The free men of the world are marching together to victory."

At 6:30 on June 6, 1944, Americans spill out of troop transports into the cold waters off a beach in Normandy, code-named Omaha. The weather is bad, seas are rough, and the prep bombing has failed. The soldiers, many seeing their first action, are dazed, confused, and weighed down by heavy packs. Nazi machine guns pin them against the sea. Slowly, they crawl up the beach on their stomachs. More than a thousand die. They hold on until the next wave of transports arrives.

All day long, Allied confusion does battle with German indecision—the Nazis never really counter-attack, thinking D-Day is just a ruse, not the main invasion. By day's end, the Allies have taken several beaches along the Normandy coast and begun build-ing artificial harbors, providing a tiny port-of-entry for the reconquest of Europe. The stage is set for a quick and easy end to the war. Right.

1945 Having liberated Paris (August 26, 1944), the Allied march on Berlin from the west bogs down, hit by poor supply lines, bad weather, and the surprising German counterpunch at the Battle of the Bulge. Finally, in the spring, the Americans and Brits cross the Rhine. Soviet soldiers close in on Berlin, Hitler shoots himself, and—after nearly six long years of war—Europe is free.

and Pointe du Hoc with two hours of total wait time at the sites (50 percent surcharge after 19:00 and on Sun, taxi tel. 02 31 92 92 40).

By Minivan Tour: An army of small companies offers all-day excursions to the D-Day beaches from Bayeux or nearby for about €90 per person or about €475 for groups of up to eight (most don't visit museums, but those that do usually include entry fees—ask).

Most of these tours prefer to pick up in or near Bayeux, and a few levy a small surcharge for Caen pickup. Whereas some companies discourage children, others embrace them. Half-day trips (€45) are offered by **Normandy Sightseeing Tours** and, when things are quiet, **Victory Tours.** Most companies deliver riveting commentary to these moving sites. The ones listed below all offer quality tours that I trust. Because they pick up and drop off at select train stations, they are popular with day-trippers from Paris. Book these tours well in advance, or hope for last-minute cancellations.

British-owned **Battlebus**, with its top-notch guides, offers a full slate of tour options from Bayeux and gets the best reviews from historians (full-day tours only, limited service during the winter, tel. 02 31 22 28 82 or 06 72 02 50 74, www.battlebus.fr, tours@battlebus.fr).

Dale Booth is a superb guide, historian, and passionate storyteller. He can lead tours of the American, Canadian, and British sectors but only guides five days a week so book him well ahead (tel. 02 33 71 53 76, www.daleboothnormandytours.com, dbooth holidays@sfr.fr).

D-Day Battle Tours is for true enthusiasts. British owner and zealot Ellwood von Seibold drives a WWII Dodge Command Car, lives in a home where an American paratrooper landed in the garden, and owns a café in Ste. Mère Eglise (C-47 Café) that has the rudder of a WWII-era C-47 plane as its centerpiece (can you say "fanatic"?). His specialty is the American sector, though he has colleagues who do the British and Canadian sectors (for multiday tours). Tours begin with a military briefing at his café on Ste. Mère Eglise's main square, or he'll meet you at the train station in Carentan (8-person maximum, book well in advance, 4 rue Eisenhower, tel. 02 33 94 44 13, mobile 06 32 67 49 15, www.ddaybattletours.com, ellwood @ddaybattletours.com).

Victory Tours is a one-man show run by friendly Dutchman Roel (pronounced "rule"), who covers sites mostly in the American sector and offers half-day, all-day, and two-day tours. His tours are informal and entertaining, but sufficiently informative for most people (departs from Bayeux only, tel. 02 31 51 98 14, fax 02 72 68 61 66, www.victorytours.com, victorytours@orange.fr).

Nigel Stewart is a low-key yet very capable British guide licensed to lead tours throughout Normandy. Nigel can meet you anywhere in Normandy, and can drive his vehicle or join you in yours (mobile 06 71 55 51 30, www.dday-guide.com, nigel .normandy@gmail.com).

Normandy Battle Tours are led by Stuart Robertson, a likeable and gentle Brit who loves teaching visitors about the landings (tel. 02 33 41 28 34, www.normandybattletours.com, enquiries @normandybattletours.com). He also owns a bed-and-breakfast in Ste. Mère Eglise and offers worthwhile accommodations and tour deals.

Normandy Sightseeing Tours delivers a French perspective through the voices of its small fleet of licensed guides. They offer the most flexibility of all the tours I list, as they will pick you up anywhere you like (for a price) and are happy to do just half-day tours. Because there are so many guides, the quality of their teaching is less consistent—guides David and Karinne get the best reviews (half-day tours from €40, tel. 02 31 51 70 52, fax 02 31 51 74 74, www.normandywebguide.com, fredericguerin@wanadoo.fr).

The **Caen Memorial Museum** runs a busy program of full-day tours covering the American and Canadian sectors in combination with a visit to their museum. This option works well for those who have limited time (see museum listing on page 307). They also have more guides, thus they are more likely to have availability when others don't.

Helpful Hints

Normandy Pass: If you plan to visit several D-Day sites, you can save a few euros by buying the Normandy Pass (€1 added to the full-price admission at your first site). You'll save €1 at most subsequent sites and €4 at the Caen Memorial Museum—but for the best value, don't visit the Memorial first since you have to pay full price at your first site. The pass is valid for one month and is transferrable to anyone.

Good Map: The free and well-done *Exploration and Emotion: D-Day Landings* map gives succinct reviews of 29 D-Day museums and sites with current opening times. It also suggests several driving itineraries that are linked to roadside signposts, helping you understand the significance of the area you are passing through. The map is available at TIs.

Sleeping near the D-Day Beaches

(€1 = about $1.25, country code: 33)

For more options, see "Sleeping in Arromanches" on page 297.

$$ Le Mas Normand, 10 minutes east of Arromanches in Ver-sur-Mer, is the child of *Provençale* Mylène and *Normand* Christian. Here you get a warm welcome and the best of both worlds: four lovingly decorated, Provence-style rooms wrapped in 18th-century Norman stone (a fifth room is in a renovated, four-person gypsy caravan). There's a lovely yard with ample grass, two dogs, some geese, and no smoking (Db-€70–90, Tb-€120, Qb-€140, Nov–March discounts for longer stays, includes breakfast, Wi-Fi; drive to the east end of little Ver-sur-Mer, turn right at Hôtel P'tit Bouchon, take another right where the road ends at a T, and find the sign at 8 impasse de la Rivière; tel. & fax 02 31 21 97 75, www.lemasnormand.com, lemasnormand@wanadoo.fr). Book ahead for Christian's home-cooked gourmet dinner, including wine, cider, and coffee (€45/person, requires 4 people, kids' menus available).

$$ Hôtel du Casino** is a good place to be one with the D-Day invasions and Omaha Beach. This average-looking hotel has surprisingly comfortable rooms and sits alone, overlooking the beach in Vierville-sur-Mer, between the American Cemetery and Pointe du Hoc. The halls have pebble walls, and all rooms have views, but the best face the sea—ask for *côté mer*. Don't expect an effusive greeting. Introverted owner Madame Clémenceau will leave you alone with the sand, waves, seagulls, and your thoughts (Db-€76, view Db-€82–85, extra bed-€16, view restaurant with *menus* from €26, café/bar on the beach below, tel. 02 31 22 41 02, fax 02 31 22 41 12, hotel-du-casino@orange.fr).

$ At André and Madeleine Sebire's B&B, you'll experience a real Norman farm. Its hardworking owners offer four modest, homey, and dirt-cheap rooms in the middle of nowhere (two miles from Arromanches). It's worth the effort to track it down in the tiny village of Ryes at Ferme du Clos Neuf (Sb-€33, Db-€38, Tb-€43, includes breakfast, tel. 02 31 22 32 34, emmanuelle.sebire @wanadoo.fr, little English spoken). Try these directions: Follow signs into Ryes, then locate the faded green *Chambres d'Hôte* sign opposite the village's lone restaurant. Follow that sign (rue de la Forge), cross a tiny bridge, turn right onto rue de la Tringale, and follow that for half a mile until you see a small sign on the right to *Le Clos Neuf*. Park near the tractors. If the Sebires prove too elusive, call from Ryes and they'll come get you.

Arromanches

This small town was ground zero for the D-Day invasion. Almost overnight, it sprouted the immense Port Winston, which gave the Allies a foothold in Normandy, allowing them to begin their victorious push to Berlin and end World War II. The post-war period brought a decline. Only recently has the population of tiny Arromanches finally returned to its June 5, 1944, numbers. You'll find a good museum, an evocative beach and bluff (with an interesting film), and a touristy-but-fun little town that offers a pleasant cocktail of war memories, cotton candy, and beachfront trinket shops. Arromanches makes a great base for sightseeing

(I've listed accommodations under "Sleeping in Arromanches," later). Sit on the seawall after dark and listen to the waves lick the sand while you contemplate the events that took place here more than 65 years ago.

Orientation to Arromanches

Tourist Information

The TI has the *Exploration and Emotion: D-Day Landings* map, bus schedules, a photo booklet of area hotels, a list of *chambres d'hôtes*, and easy parking (daily June–Aug 9:30–18:00, Sept–May 10:00–12:00 & 14:00–17:00, opposite the recommended Hôtel d'Arromanches at 2 avenue Maréchal Joffre, tel. 02 31 22 36 45, www.ot-arromanches.fr).

Arrival in Arromanches

The main parking lot, on the road toward Courseulles-sur-Mer, costs €2. If traffic seems bad, try the free lot at the Iveco market a few blocks above (across from Mountbatten Hôtel) and stroll three blocks down to the museum and town center; or try the free lot near the water past the mini-golf course.

Helpful Hints

Post Office: The main **post office** (PTT)—which has an ATM—is opposite the museum.

Supermarket: There's a little **supermarket** a few blocks above the beach, just below the main post office.

Taxi: To get an Arromanches-based **taxi**, call 06 66 62 00 99.

D-Day Sites in Arromanches

I've linked Arromanches' D-Day sites, below, with some self-guided commentary.

▲▲**Port Winston Artificial Harbor**—Start on the cliffs above the town, overlooking the site of the impressive World War II harbor.

Getting There: Drive two minutes toward Courseulles-sur-Mer and pay €2 to park, or park in Arromanches and walk up. Non-drivers can hike 10 minutes uphill from Arromanches, or take the free white train from the museum to the top of the bluff (runs daily June–Sept, Sat–Sun only Oct–May).

۞ **Self-Guided Tour:** This commentary will lead you around the site.

• *Find the concrete viewpoint overlooking the town and the beaches. Beyond Arromanches to the left is the American sector, with Omaha Beach and then Utah Beach (notice the cliffs); below and to the right lie the British and Canadian sectors (more level terrain).*

Now get this: At a makeshift harbor below, the Allies arrived in the largest amphibious attack ever, launching the liberation of Western Europe. On June 7, 1944—after some pretty serious aerial and seaborne bombing—17 old ships sailed 90 miles across the English Channel under their own steam. The crews sunk them so that each bow faced the next ship's stern, forming the first sea barrier. Then 500 tugboats towed 115 football-field-size cement blocks (called "Mulberries") across the channel. These were also sunk, creating a four-mile-long breakwater located a mile and a half offshore. Finally, engineers set up seven floating steel "pierheads" with extendable legs; they then linked these to shore by four mile-long floating roads made of concrete pontoons. Soldiers placed anti-aircraft guns on the Mulberries and pontoons, protecting a port the size of Dover, England. Within just six days of operation, 54,000 vehicles, 326,000 troops, and 110,000 tons of goods had crossed the English Channel. An Allied toehold on Normandy was secure. Eleven months later, Hitler was dead and the war was over.

The **Arromanches 360° Theater** behind you shows a moving film, *The Price of Freedom*, with D-Day footage that flashes back from quiet farmlands and beaches to June 1944. It's a noisy montage of videos on a 360° screen—stand as near to the center as you can (€4.20, Feb–Dec daily 10:00–18:00, closed Jan, 2 shows/hour at :10 and :40 past the hour, 20 minutes, tel. 02 31 22 30 30).

• *Head down to the town's main parking lot and find the round bulkhead on the seawall, near the D-Day Landing Museum entry. Stand facing the sea.*

The world's first prefab harbor was created out there by the British. Since it was Churchill's brainchild, it was named Port Winston. Designed to be a temporary harbor, it was supposed to get washed out to sea over time—which is exactly what happened with its twin harbor at Omaha Beach (that one only lasted 12 days, thanks to a terrible storm). If the tide is out you'll see several rusted floats mired on the sand close in—these supported the pontoon roads. If you stare hard enough at the concrete blocks in the sea to the right, you'll see that one still has what's left of an anti-aircraft gun on it. Look behind the museum to view a section of a pontoon and an anti-aircraft gun. On the hill above the museum, you'll spot a Sherman Tank, one of 50,000 deployed during the landings. If you can, walk down to the beach and wander among the concrete and rusted litter of the battle—and be thankful that all you hear are birds and surf.

▲**D-Day Landing Museum (Musée du Débarquement)**—The D-Day Landing Museum, facing the harbor, makes a worthwhile

45-minute visit and is the only way to get a full appreciation of how the artificial harbor was built. While gazing through windows at the site of this amazing endeavor, you can study helpful models, videos, and photographs illustrating the construction and use of the prefabricated harbor. Those blimp-like objects tethered to the port prevented German planes from getting too close (though the German air force had been made largely irrelevant by this time). Ponder the remarkable undertaking that resulted in this harbor being built in just 12 days, while battles raged. You're welcome to join an English tour if one is in progress. One video (8 minutes, ground floor) recalls D-Day; the other (15 minutes, upstairs) features the construction of the temporary port—ask for times when it is shown in English (€6.50, daily May-Aug 9:00-19:00, Sept-Dec and Feb-April 9:30-12:30 & 13:30-17:00, closed Jan, pick up English flier at door, tel. 02 31 22 34 31, www.arromanches -museum.com).

Sleeping in Arromanches

(€1 = about $1.25, country code: 33)

Arromanches, with its pinwheels and seagulls, has a salty beach-town ambience that makes it a good overnight stop. Park in the town's main lot at the museum (€1/hour, free from 19:00 to 9:00). For evening fun, try the cheery bar at **Hôtel d'Arromanches-Restaurant "Le Pappagall"** (see "Eating in Arromanches"), or, for more of a nightclub scene, have a drink at **Pub Marie Celeste,** around the corner on rue de la Poste.

$$ Hôtel de la Marine*** has one of the best locations for D-Day enthusiasts, with point-blank views to the artificial harbor site from most of its 28 adequately comfy, modern, non-smoking rooms (non-view Db-€68-80, view Db-€82-110—most about €94, highest prices are for summer, Tb-€145, good family rooms for up to five-€155-185, elevator, Wi-Fi, view restaurant, half-board strongly encouraged—figure €85/person, quai du Canada, tel. 02 31 22 34 19, fax 02 31 22 98 80, www.hotel-de-la-marine.fr, hotel .de.la.marine@wanadoo.fr).

$$ Hôtel d'Arromanches-Restaurant "Le Pappagall"** (French slang for "parakeet") sits behind Hôtel de la Marine and is a good value, with nine smartly appointed rooms (some with water views), some tight stairways, and a cheery restaurant (Db-€68, Tb-€90, breakfast-€9, Wi-Fi, 2 rue Colonel René Michel, tel. 02 31 22 36 26, fax 02 31 22 23 29, www.hoteldarromanches.fr, reservation@hoteldarromanches.fr).

$ Mountbatten Hôtel**, located a long block up from the water, is an eight-room, two-story, motel-esque place with generous-size, clean, and good-value lodgings. Upstairs rooms have a little view over the sea (Db-€54–65, Tb-€64–75, easy parking, short block below the main post office at 20 boulevard Gilbert Longuet, tel. 02 31 22 59 70, fax 02 31 22 50 30, www.hotelmount batten.com, mountbattenhotel@wanadoo.fr).

Eating in Arromanches

You'll find cafés, *crêperies*, and a few shops selling sandwiches to go (ideal for beachfront picnics). The following restaurants offer reliable dining.

Hôtel d'Arromanches-Restaurant "Le Pappagall" has good mussels, filling fish *choucroute*, "*les feesh and cheeps*," salads, and a full menu with fair prices (€18–27 *menus*, may be closed on Thu, see hotel listing earlier).

Lose the crowds at *crêperie* **La Ripaille**, a short block inland from the busy main drag. Sweet Sylvie will serve you a filling deep-dish crêpe for €9 (daily June-Sept, closed Mon Oct–May, 14 rue du Colonel René Michel, tel. 02 31 51 02 31).

Hôtel de la Marine allows you to dine or drink in style on the water. The cuisine gets mixed reviews, but the view doesn't disappoint (*menus* from €24, cool bar with same views, daily, see hotel listing earlier).

Arromanches Connections

From Arromanches by Bus to: Bayeux (bus #74/#75, 3–5/day, Sept–June no bus Sun, 30 minutes), **Juno Beach** (bus #74/#75, 20 minutes). The bus stop is near the main post office, four long blocks above the sea (the stop to go to Bayeux is on the sea side of the street; the stop for visiting Juno Beach is on the post office side).

American D-Day Sites West of Arromanches

The American sector is divided between Omaha and Utah beaches. Omaha Beach starts a few miles west of Arromanches and has the most important sites for visitors, including the American Cemetery and Pointe du Hoc (four miles west of Omaha). Utah Beach sites are farther away (on the road to Cherbourg), and though they may be less visited, they were no less important to the ultimate success of the Normandy invasion. The American Airborne sector covers a broad area behind Utah Beach and centers on Ste. Mère Eglise. You'll see memorials sprouting up all around the countryside.

Omaha Beach D-Day Sites

▲Longues-sur-Mer Gun Battery

This site is always open and free (€5 booklet helpful, skip the €4 tour). Four German casemates (three with guns intact)—built to guard against seaborne attacks—hunker down at the end of a 10-minute drive west of Arromanches (follow *Port en Bessin* signs; once in Longues-sur-Mer, follow *Batterie* signs). The guns, 300 yards inland, were arranged in a semicircle to maximize the firing range east and west, and are the only original coastal artillery guns remaining in place in the D-Day region. (Much was scrapped after the war, long before people thought of tourism.) This battery was a critical link in Hitler's Atlantic Wall defense, which consisted of over 15,000 structures stretching from Norway to the Pyrenees. The guns could hit targets up to 12 miles away with relatively fine accuracy if linked to good target information. The Allies had to take them out.

Enter the third bunker you pass. It took seven soldiers to manage each gun, which could be loaded and fired six times per minute (the shells weighed 40 pounds). Judging from the echoes you hear inside the bunker, you can imagine the terrible noise that was made each time the gun fired. Outside, climb above the bunker and find the hooks that were used to secure camouflage netting, making it impossible for bombers to locate them.

A lone observation bunker (look for the low-lying concrete bunker roof on the cliffs) was designed to direct the firing; field telephones connected the bunker to the gun batteries by underground wires. Walk to the observation bunker to appreciate the strategic view over the channel. From here you can walk along the glorious *Sentier du Littoral* (coastal path) above the cliffs and see Arromanches in the distance. Or enjoy more views by driving five minutes down to the water (continue on the small road past the parking lot).

▲▲▲WWII Normandy American Cemetery and Memorial

"Soldiers' graves are the greatest preachers of peace."
—Albert Schweitzer

Crowning a bluff just above Omaha Beach and the eye of the D-Day storm, 9,387 brilliant white-marble crosses and Stars of David glow in memory of Americans who gave their lives to free Europe on the beaches below. You'll want to spend at least 1.5 hours at this stirring site (in Colleville, near St. Laurent).

Cost and Hours: Free, daily May–Sept 9:00–18:00, Oct–April

9:00–17:00, tel. 02 31 51 62 00, www.abmc.gov. Park carefully, as break-ins have been a problem. You'll find good WCs and water fountains at the parking lot. Guided tours are offered a few times a day in high season—call ahead for times.

○ Self-Guided Tour: Your visit begins at the impressive **Visitors' Center.** Pass security, pick up the handout, sign the register, and allow time to appreciate the superb exhibit. On the arrival floor, computer terminals provide access to a database containing the story of each US serviceman who died in Normandy.

Descend one level, where you'll learn about the invasion preparations and the immense logistical challenges they presented. And, most importantly, you'll get a sense of the personal sacrifices that were made here. This is the heart of the center, highlighting the individuals who gave their lives to liberate people they did not know, by telling their stories and showing the few possessions they died with. This adds a personal touch to the D-Day landings and prepares visitors for the fields of white crosses and Stars of David outside. The pressure on these men to succeed in this battle is palpable here. There are a manageable number of display cases, a few powerful videos (including an interview with Dwight Eisenhower), and a must-see 16-minute film (cushy theater chairs, on the half-hour, you can enter late).

A lineup of informational plaques provides a worthwhile and succinct overview of key events from September 1939 to June 5, 1944. Starting with June 6, 1944, the plaques present the progress of the landings in three-hour increments. Amazingly, Omaha Beach was secured within six hours of the landings.

A path from the visitors' center leads to a bluff overlooking the piece of Normandy **beach** called "that embattled shore—portal of freedom." It's quiet and peaceful today, but the horrific carnage of June 6, 1944, is hard to forget. A good orientation table looks over the sea. Nearby, steps lead down to the beautiful beach below. A walk on the beach is a powerful experience and a must if you are *sans* both car and tour. Visitors with cars can drive to the beach at Vierville-sur-Mer (see next listing).

In the **cemetery,** you'll find a striking memorial with a soaring statue representing the spirit of American youth. Around the statue, giant reliefs of the Battle of Normandy and the Battle of Europe are etched on the walls. Behind is the semicircular Garden of the Missing, with the names of 1,557 soldiers who were never found. A small metal knob next to the name indicates one whose body was eventually found—there aren't many.

Finally, wander among the peaceful and poignant sea of headstones. Notice the names, home states, and dates of death (but no birth dates) inscribed on each. Dog-tag numbers are etched into the lower backs of the crosses. During the campaign, the dead were buried in temporary cemeteries throughout various parts of Normandy. After the war, the families of the soldiers could decide whether their loved ones should remain with their comrades or be brought home (61 percent opted for repatriation).

A disproportionate number of officers are buried here, including General Theodore Roosevelt, Jr., who died from a heart attack one month after D-Day (you can find both Ted's and his brother Quentin's graves along the sea, in the second grouping of graves just after the row 27 marker). Families knew that these officers would want to be buried alongside the men with whom they fought. Also buried here are two of the Niland brothers, now famous from *Saving Private Ryan* (in the middle of the cemetery, before the circular chapel, turn right just after the letter "F").

France has given the US permanent free use of this 172-acre site. It is immaculately maintained by the American Battle Monuments Commission.

▲Vierville-sur-Mer

This worthwhile detour for drivers allows direct access onto Omaha Beach. From the American Cemetery, drive west along D-514 into St. Laurent, then follow *Vierville par la Côte* on D-517 to the beach. A right turn along the water leads to **Le Ruquet** (where the road ends), a good place to appreciate the challenges that American soldiers faced on D-Day. The small German bunker and embedded gun protected this point, which offered the easiest access inland from Omaha Beach. It was here that the Americans would establish their first road inland.

Find your way out to the beach and stroll to the right, below the American Cemetery, to better understand the assignment that American forces were handed on June 6: You're wasted from a lack of sleep and nervous anticipation. Now you get seasick too, as you're about to land in a small, flat-bottomed boat, cheek-to-jowl with 35 other soldiers. Your water-soaked pack feels like stone, and your gun feels heavier. The boat door drops open, and you run for your life for 500 yards through water and sand onto this open beach, dodging bullets from above (the landings had to occur at low tide so that mines would be visible).

The hills above were heavily fortified, and a single German machine gun could fire 1,200 rounds a minute. That's right—1,200. It's amazing that anyone survived. The highest casualty rates in Normandy occurred at Omaha Beach, nicknamed "Bloody Omaha." Though there are no accurate figures for D-Day, it is estimated that on the first day of the Normandy campaign, the Allies suffered 10,500 casualties (killed, wounded, and missing)—6,000 of whom were Americans. Estimates for Omaha Beach casualties range from 2,500 to 4,800 killed and wounded on that day. But thanks to an overwhelming effort and huge support from the US and Royal Navy, 34,000 Americans would land on the beach by day's end.

If the tide's out, you'll notice some remains of rusted metal objects. Omaha Beach was littered with obstacles to disrupt the landings. Thousands of metal poles, miles of barbed wire, and more than four million mines were scattered along these beaches. At least 150,000 tons of metal were taken from these beaches after World War II, and they still didn't get it all. They never will.

Back in your car, retrace your route along the beach (look for worthwhile information boards along the sea) and hug the coast past the flags heading toward the Pointe de la Percé cliff, which, from here, looks very Pointe du Hoc–like (American Army Rangers mistook this cliff for Pointe du Hoc, costing them time and lives).

Park near Hôtel Casino and walk to the beach. It was here that the Americans assembled their own floating bridge and artificial harbor (à la Arromanches). The harbor functioned for 12 days before being destroyed by an unusually vicious June storm. Have a seaside drink or lunch at the casino's café, and contemplate a stroll toward the jutting Pointe de la Percé.

On the road leaving Vierville-sur-Mer, just above the Hôtel Casino you'll pass the pontoon bridge that was installed at this beach. After the storm, it was moved to Arromanches and used as a second off-loading ramp. It was discovered only a few years ago... in a junkyard.

▲▲Pointe du Hoc Ranger Monument

The Germans' most heavily fortified position was located here. The new building at the east end of the parking lot was built for the 60th anniversary of the invasion and has WCs, fliers, and an information desk. Head out to the site, navigating through the lunar landscape. Get as close to the water as you can and spy the wall of cliffs below, then climb to the nearby observation platform. (Work is underway to stabilize a bunker at risk of sliding down the cliff, so expect some disruption to your visit.)

For the American landings to succeed, the Allies determined that they had to run the Germans off this cliff. So they bombed it to smithereens. Heavy bombing occurred during April and May—and most intensely on June 6—making this the most massively bombarded site of the D-Day targets. Then 300 handpicked US Army Rangers attempted a castle-style assault of the cliffs, using grappling hooks and ladders from London fire departments. Rockets fired the grappling hooks with climbing ropes attached while fire-engine ladders extended from below, giving the Rangers a head start up the cliff. Timing was critical, as they had just 30 minutes before the rising tide would overcome the men below. Only about a third of the Rangers survived the assault. After finally succeeding in their task, the Rangers found that the German guns had been moved (commander Erwin Rommel had directed that all coastal guns not under the cover of roofs be pulled back due to air strikes). Still, the taking of this jutting cliff was important to securing the safe landing of American forces.

The large monument at the end of the bluff is the Ranger "Dagger," planted firmly in the ground. The German bunkers and the bombed-out landscape remain as they were found. Picnicking is forbidden here—the bombed bunkers are considered gravesites (free, daily May–Sept 9:00–18:00, Oct–April 9:00–17:00, 20 minutes by car west of American Cemetery, tel. 02 31 51 62 00). A museum dedicated to the Rangers is in nearby Grandcamp-Maisy.

▲German Military Cemetery

To ponder German losses, drop by this somber, thought-provoking resting place of 21,000 German soldiers. While the American Cemetery is the focus of American travelers, visitors here speak in hushed German. The site seems appropriately bleak, with two graves per simple marker and dark crosses in groups of five. It's just south of Pointe du Hoc (daily April–Oct 8:00–19:00, Nov–March until 17:30; right off N-13 in village of La Cambe, 3.5 miles west of Bayeux, follow signs reading *Cimetière Allemand*; tel. 02 31 22 70 76).

Utah Beach D-Day Sites

Ste. Mère Eglise

This celebrated village is 40 minutes east of the Pointe du Hoc and was the first village to be liberated by the Americans, due largely to its strategic location on the Cotentin Peninsula. The area around Ste. Mère Eglise was the center of action for American paratroopers, whose objective was to land behind enemy lines in support of the American landing at Utah Beach.

For *The Longest Day* movie buffs, Ste. Mère Eglise is a necessary pilgrimage. It was around Ste. Mère Eglise that many paratroopers, facing terrible weather and heavy anti-aircraft fire, landed off-target—and many landed in the town. One American paratrooper dangled from the town's church steeple for two hours (a parachute has been snagged—though not in the correct corner). And though many paratroopers were killed in the first hours of the invasion, the Americans eventually overcame their poor start and managed to take the town. They played a critical role in the success of the Utah Beach landings by securing roads and bridges behind enemy lines. Today, the village greets travelers with flag-draped streets and a handful of worthwhile sights.

At the center of town, the 700-year-old **medieval church** on the town square was the focus of the action during the invasion. It now holds two contemporary stained-glass windows that acknowledge the heroism of the Allies. One features St. Michael, patron saint of paratroopers.

Also worth a visit is the **Airborne Museum.** Housed in two parachute-shaped structures, its collection is dedicated to the daring aerial landings that were essential to the success of D-Day. In one building, you'll see a Waco glider (104 were flown into Normandy at first light on D-Day) used to land supplies in fields to support the paratroopers. Each glider could be used only once. Feel the canvas fuselage and check out the bare-bones interior. The second, larger building holds a Douglas C-47 plane that dropped parachutists, along with many other objects essential to the successful landings (€7, daily April–Sept 9:00–18:30, Oct–March 9:30–12:00 & 14:00–18:00, 14 rue Eisenhower, tel. 02 33 41 41 35, www.musee-airborne.com).

Dead Man's Corner Museum

In 1944, the Germans used this French home as a regional headquarters. Today, a tiny museum recounts the terrible battles that took place around the town of Carentan June 6–11. A swampy inlet marked the division between Omaha and Utah beaches. It was critical for the Americans to take this land, allowing the armies on each beach to unite and move forward. But the Germans resisted, and a battle that was supposed to last one afternoon endured five days, leaving more than 2,000 Americans dead. American soldiers named the museum "Purple Heart Lane."

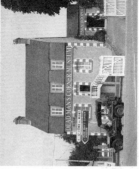

The museum, 15 minutes south of Ste. Mère Eglise, is ideal for enthusiasts and best for collectors of WWII paraphernalia (but overkill for the average traveler). Every display case shows incredible attention to detail. Dutch owner/collector/perfectionist Michel Detrez displays only original material. He acquired much of his collection from American veterans who wanted their "souvenirs" to be preserved for others to see. The museum doubles as a sales outlet, with a remarkable collection of D-Day items for sale—both original items and replicas (€6, daily 9:00–18:00, in St. Côme du Mont, well-signed two exits north of Carentan on N-13, tel. 02 33 42 00 42).

Canadian D-Day Sites East of Arromanches

Juno Beach Centre

Located on the beachfront in the Canadian sector, about 15 minutes east of Arromanches in Courseulles-sur-Mer, this facility is dedicated to teaching travelers about the vital role Canadian forces played in the invasion, and about Canada in general. (Canada declared war on Germany two years before the United States, a fact little recognized by most Americans today.) After attending the 50th anniversary of the D-Day landings, Canadian veterans were saddened by the absence of information on their contribution (after the US and Britain, Canada contributed the largest number of troops—14,000), so they generated funds to build this place (the plaques in front honor key donors). Your visit includes a short film, then many thoughtful exhibits that bring to life Canada's unique ties with Britain, the US, and France, and explain how the war affected daily life in Canada. The Centre also has rotating exhibits about Canada's geography, economy, and more (€6.50, €10 with guided tour, daily April–Sept 9:30–19:00, Oct and March 10:00–18:00, Nov–Feb 10:00–13:00 & 14:00–17:00, tel. 02 31 37 32 17, www.junobeach.org).

The Centre's one-hour English-guided **tours** of Juno Beach are worthwhile (€4.50 for tour alone, or €10 with Centre admission; April–Oct at 11:00 and 15:00; July–Aug nearly hourly from 10:00–16:00; verify times prior to your visit). Your charming guide will be one of four red-shirted young Canadians who spend four months a year in France as a part of the Centre's plan to improve ties between France and Canada.

A beach walk along the other side of the harbor from the Centre leads past several memorials marking the spots where Canadians landed. You'll eventually come to photos of the landings at the House of the Queen's Own Rifles.

Canadian Cemetery

This small, touching cemetery hides a few miles above the Juno Beach Centre and makes a modest statement when compared with other, more grandiose cemeteries in this area. To me, it captures the understated nature of Canadians perfectly. Surrounded by farmland, with distant views to the beaches, the graves are marked with the names of the soldiers, and all have live flowers or plants in their honor. It's located between Courseulles-sur-Mer and Caen, just off D-79.

Caen

Though it was mostly destroyed by WWII bombs, today's Caen (pronounced "kahn," population 115,000) is a thriving, workaday city packed with students and a few tourists. The brilliant WWII museum and the vibrant old city are the targets for travelers, though these sights come wrapped in a big city with rough edges. And though Bayeux or Arromanches—which are smaller—make the best base for most D-Day sites, train travelers with limited time might find urban Caen more practical because of its buses to Honfleur and easy access to the Caen Memorial Museum.

Orientation to Caen

The looming château, built by William the Conqueror in 1060, marks the city's center. West of here, modern rue St. Pierre is a popular shopping area and pedestrian zone. To the east, the more historic Vaugueux quarter has many restaurants and cafés in half-timbered buildings. A marathon race in honor of the Normandy invasion is held every June 8th and ends at the Memorial Museum.

Tourist Information

The TI is opposite the château on place St. Pierre, 10 blocks from the train station (take the tram to the St. Pierre stop). Pick up a map and free visitor's guide filled with practical information (Mon–Sat 9:30–13:00 & 14:00–18:30, Sun 10:00–13:00—April–Sept only, drivers follow *Parking Château* signs, tel. 02 31 27 14 14, www .tourisme.caen.fr).

Arrival in Caen

These directions assume you're headed for the town's main attraction, the Caen Memorial Museum.

By Car: Finding the memorial is quick and easy. It's a half-mile off the ring-road expressway (*périphérique nord*), take *sortie* #7, look for white signs reading *le Memorial*). When leaving the

NORMANDY

museum, follow *Toutes Directions* back to the ring road.

By Train: Caen is two hours from Paris (14/day) and 20 minutes from Bayeux (18/day). Caen's modern train station is next to the *gare routière*, where buses from Honfleur arrive. There is no baggage storage at the station, though free baggage storage is available at the Caen Memorial Museum. The efficient tramway runs right in front of both stations, and taxis usually wait in front. For detailed instructions on getting to the Caen Memorial Museum, see "Getting There" in the next section.

By Bus: Caen is one hour from Honfleur by express bus (2/day), or two hours by the scenic coastal bus (9/day). Buses stop near the train station.

Sights in Caen

▲▲▲Caen Memorial Museum (Le Mémorial de Caen)

Caen, the modern capital of lower Normandy, has the most thorough and by far priciest WWII museum in France. Located at the site of an important German headquarters during World War II, its official name is the "The Caen Memorial: Center for the History for Peace" (*Le Mémorial de Caen: La Cité de l'Histoire pour la Paix*). With two video presentations and numerous exhibits on the lead-up to World War II, the actual Battle of Normandy, the

Cold War, and more, it effectively puts the Battle of Normandy into a broader context.

Cost and Hours: €17.50, or €13.50 with a Normandy Pass purchased elsewhere (see page 293), free for all veterans and kids under 10 (ask about family rates). A one-hour audioguide is available (€4) that streamlines your visit by providing helpful background for each area of the museum. Open March–Oct daily 9:00–19:00 (mid-July–Aug until 20:00); Nov–Feb Tue–Sun 9:30–18:00, closed Mon and most of Jan; last entry 1.25 hours before closing, tel. 02 31 06 06 44—as in June 6, 1944, fax 02 31 06 06 70, www.memorial-caen.fr.

Getting There: Taxis normally wait in front of the train station and are the easiest solution (about €14 one-way, 15 minutes), particularly if you have bags. To reach the museum by public transport (allow 30 minutes for the one-way trip), take the tram from in front of the station. It's the first tram shelter after you leave the train station—do not cross the tram tracks (line A or B, buy

€1.20 ticket from machine before boarding, ticket good for one hour, validate it on tram, departs every few minutes). Get off at the third tram stop (Bernières), then transfer to frequent bus #2 (4–6/hour Mon–Sat, 2/hour Sun). To reach the bus stop (which is signed from the tram stop), exit the tram, cross the street to the left in front of the tram, and walk up rue de Bernières until you see the bus shelter for #2 (your tram ticket is valid on the bus). To experience the heart of Caen, get off the tram at the next stop, St. Pierre, and explore the pedestrian streets near the church and the château (and the TI), then head down rue Saint-Jean to rue de Bernières, turn right, and find bus #2 again.

Returning from the museum by bus and tram is a snap (taxi there and bus/tram back is a good compromise). Bus #2 waits across from the museum on the street's right side (the museum has the schedule), and whisks you to the Quatrans stop in downtown Caen (follow the stop diagram in bus as you go), where you'll transfer to the tram and get off at the Gare SNCF (€1.20 ticket good for bus and tram).

Services: The museum provides free baggage storage and free supervised babysitting for children under 10 (for whom exhibits may be too graphic). There's a large gift shop with plenty of books in English, an excellent and reasonable all-day sandwich shop/café above the entry area, and a restaurant with a garden-side terrace (lunch only, located in the Cold War wing). Picnicking in the gardens is also an option.

Minivan Tours: The museum offers good-value minivan tours covering the key sites along the D-Day beaches. Two identical half-day tours leave the museum: one at 9:00 (€60/person) and one at 13:00 or 14:00—depends on season (€76/person); both include entry to the museum. The all-day "D-Day Tour Package" (€112, includes English information book) is designed for day-trippers and includes pick-up from the Caen train station (with frequent service from Paris), a tour of the Caen Memorial Museum followed by lunch, then a four-hour tour in English of the American sector. Your day ends with a drop-off at the Caen train station in time to catch a train back to Paris or elsewhere. Contact the museum for details, reservations, and advance payment.

Planning Your Museum Time: Allow a minimum of 2.5 hours for your visit, including 50 minutes for the movies. You could easily spend all day here; in fact, tickets purchased after 13:00 are valid for 24 hours, so you can return the next day. The museum is divided into two major wings: the "World Before 1945" (the lead-up to World War II and the battles and related events of the war), and the "World After 1945" (Cold War, nuclear threats, world peacemakers, and so on). And though each wing provides stellar exhibits and great learning, I'd focus on the "World Before 1945."

The museum is brilliant, but it overwhelms some with so many interesting exhibits (all well-described in English). Limit your visit to the WWII sections and be sure to read the blue "Context" information boards that give a helpful overview of each subarea. Then feel free to pick and choose which displays to focus on. The audioguide provides similar context to the exhibits.

My recommended plan of attack: Start your visit with the *Jour-J* movie that sets the stage, then tour the WWII sections and finish with the second movie (*Espérance*).

◆ **Self-Guided Tour:** Begin by watching *Jour J (D-Day)*, a powerful 30-minute film that shows the build-up to D-Day itself and the successful campaign from there to Berlin (every 40 minutes from 10:00 to 19:00, pick up schedule as you enter, works in any language). Although snippets come from the movie *The Longest Day*, most of the film consists of footage from actual battle scenes.

On the opposite side of the entry hall from the theater, find *Début de la Visite* signs and begin your museum tour with a downward spiral stroll (almost psychoanalyzing) the path Europe followed from the end of World War I to the rise of fascism to World War II.

The lower level gives a thorough look at how World War II was fought—from General Charles de Gaulle's London radio broadcasts to Hitler's early missiles to wartime fashion to the D-Day landings. Videos, maps, and countless displays relate the many side stories of World War II, including the Battle of Britain, the French Resistance, German death camps, and the Battle of Stalingrad. Remember to read the blue "Context" panels in each section, and then be selective about how much detail you want after that. Several powerful exhibits summarize the terrible human costs of World War II (Russia alone saw 21 million of its people die during the war; the US lost 300,000).

After touring the WWII sections, try to see the second movie (*Espérance—"Hope"*), a thrilling sweep through the pains and triumphs of the 20th century (hourly, 20 minutes, good in all languages, shown in the main entry hall).

The Cold War wing sets the scene for this era with audio testimonies and photos of European cities destroyed during World War II. It continues with a helpful overview of the bipolar world that followed the war, with fascinating insights into the psychological battle waged by the Soviet Union and the US for the hearts and minds of their people until the fall of communism. The wing culminates with a major display recounting the fall of the Berlin Wall.

The museum also celebrates the irrepressible human spirit in the Gallery of Nobel Peace Prizewinners. It honors the courageous and too-often-inconspicuous work of people such as Andrei

Sakharov, Elie Wiesel, and Desmond Tutu, who understand that peace is more than an absence of war.

A new exhibit (*Taches d'Opinion*) highlights the role of political cartoonists in expressing dissatisfaction with a range of government policies, from military to environmental to human rights issues.

The finale is a walk through the US Armed Forces Memorial Garden (Vallée du Mémorial). On a visit here, I was bothered by the mindless laughing of lighthearted children unable to appreciate their blessings. Then I read on the pavement: "From the heart of our land flows the blood of our youth, given to you in the name of freedom." Then their laughter made me happy.

Mont St. Michel

For more than a thousand years, the distant silhouette of this island abbey sent pilgrims' spirits soaring. Today, it does the same for tourists. Mont St. Michel, among the top four pilgrimage sites in Christendom through the ages, floats like a mirage on the horizon—though it does show up on film. Today, several million visitors—far more tourists than pilgrims—flood the single street of the tiny island each year.

Orientation to Mont St. Michel

Mont St. Michel is connected by a half-mile causeway to the mainland and is surrounded by a vast mudflat. The fortified abbey soars above a petite village, with just one main street on which you'll find all the hotels, restaurants, and trinkets. Between 11:00 and 16:00, tourists trample the dreamscape (much like earnest pilgrims did 800 years ago). A ramble on the ramparts offers

mudflat views and an escape from the tourist zone. Though four tacky history-in-wax museums tempt visitors, the only worthwhile sights are the abbey at the summit of the island, and views from the ramparts and quieter lanes as you descend.

Daytime Mont St. Michel is a touristy gauntlet—worth a stop, but a short one will do. The tourist tide recedes late each afternoon. On nights from autumn through spring, the island stands serene, its floodlit abbey towering above a sleepy village.

Arrive late and depart early. The abbey interior should be open

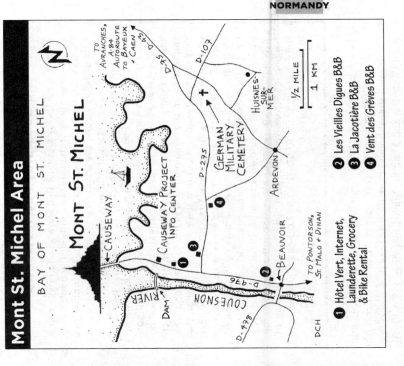

Mont St. Michel Area

BAY OF MONT ST. MICHEL

MONT ST. MICHEL

CAUSEWAY

Causeway Project Info Center

COUESNON RIVER

DAM

TO PONTORSON, St. Malo & Dinan

D-976

BEAUVOIR

ARDEVON

D-275

GERMAN MILITARY CEMETERY

HUISNES-SUR-MER

D-107

D-75

TO AVRANCHES, A-84 AUTOROUTE TO BAYEUX & CAEN

DCH

D-478

½ MILE

1 KM

1 Hôtel Vert, Internet, Launderette, Grocery & Bike Rental
2 Les Vieilles Digues B&B
3 La Jacotière B&B
4 Vent des Grèves B&B

until 23:00 in July and August (Mon–Sat). To avoid the human traffic jam on the main drag, follow the detour path up or down the mount (described on page 317).

Tourist Information

The claustrophobic TI and a WC are to your left as you enter Mont St. Michel's gates. The TI has listings of *chambres d'hôtes* on the mainland, English tour times for the abbey, tour times for walks outside the island, bus schedules, and the tide table *(Horaires des Marées),* which is essential if you plan to explore the mudflats outside Mont St. Michel (daily July–Aug 9:00–19:00, March–June and Sept–Oct 9:00–12:30 & 14:00–18:00, Nov–Feb 10:00–12:00 & 14:00–17:00; tel. 02 33 60 14 30, www.ot-montsaintmichel.com). A post office (PTT) and ATM are 50 yards beyond the TI.

Arrival in Mont St. Michel

By Train: The nearest train station is in Pontorson (called Pontorson–Mont St. Michel). The few trains that stop here are met by a bus waiting in front to take passengers to Mont St. Michel

The Causeway and Its Demise

In 1878, a causeway was built that allowed pilgrims to come and go regardless of the tide (and without hip boots). And though this increased the flow of visitors, it stopped the flow of water around the island. The result: Much of the bay has silted up, and Mont St. Michel is no longer an island. But an ambitious project is underway to return the island to its original form. Plans involve realigning the causeway to the right of its current path, where it will meet a sleek footbridge (allowing water to flow underneath). Visitors will be shuttled from parking lots to the pedestrian bridge, which will lead them the remaining 300 yards to the island. The first phase—the construction of the dam (*barrage*) on the Couesnon River—was completed in 2010, and gives visitors a great view of the abbey from its sleek wood benches. Next up is the construction of huge parking lots, followed by the footbridge. The entire project should be completed by 2014 (but don't hold your breath). There's a good little information center (*Infos Chantier*) about the project in the parking lot across from the Hôtel de la Digue at the foot of the causeway (daily 10:00-12:30 & 14:00-18:00, www.projet montsaintmichel.fr).

(12 buses/day July-Aug, 8/day Sept-June, fewer on Sun, 15 minutes). The bus takes you to the entry gate of Mont St. Michel (the bus driver also will stop at hotels before the causeway if you ask). Taxis between Pontorson and Mont St. Michel cost about €18 (€25 after 19:00 and on weekends/holidays; tel. 02 33 60 33 23 or mobile 02 33 60 26 89). If you plan to arrive on Saturday night, beware that Sunday train service from Pontorson is almost non-existent.

By Bus: Buses from Rennes and St. Malo run directly to Mont St. Michel (for details, see "Mont St. Michel Connections" at the end of this chapter). From Bayeux, it's faster to arrive on Hôtel Churchill's minivan shuttle (see page 286).

By Car: Keep your eyes peeled for views of the abbey's profile long before you reach it. Coming from the north on D-275, detour into the Biscuiterie de la Baie du Mont St. Michel, just before turning onto D-976. Here you'll find the best views of the island from the parking lot (it's close, and there are no parked cars in your frame), along with free samples of the famous cookies inside (made with sea-salted butter). I like the thicker ones. You'll also find free and clean WCs, cold drinks, coffee, and picnic tables. If approaching from Pontorson, you can get the same good cookies from the shop's outlet, but no view.

At the Hôtel de la Digue, the new Couesnon River dam meets the start of the causeway—the first part of an ambitious project to make the island an island again (see "The Causeway and Its Demise" sidebar). Continue onto the causeway (minding absentminded tourists), and park in the pay lot near the base of the island (€5, free after 19:00, ticket valid all day). If sleeping on the island, you can park closer; tell the attendant and you'll be instructed where to go. The highest tides rise to the edge of the causeway, leaving it high and dry but floating forgotten cars left below. (You'll be instructed where to park under high-tide conditions.) There's plenty of parking, except midday in high season. Jot down your parking sector and plan on a 10-minute walk to the island. Don't leave any luggage visible in your car.

Helpful Hints

Tides: The tides here rise above 50 feet—the largest and most dangerous in Europe, and second in the world after the Bay of Fundy between New Brunswick and Nova Scotia, Canada. High tides (*grandes marées*) lap against the TI door (where you'll find tide hours posted).

Internet/Laundry/Groceries/Bike Rental: The industrious **Hôtel Vert,** located at the beginning of the causeway on the right, has Internet access and Wi-Fi for a fee, a 24-hour self-service launderette, a grocery store, and bikes for rent (daily 8:00–20:00). The only Wi-Fi connection on the island itself is available for a fee at the **Hôtel Croix Blanche.** (Both hotels are described under "Sleeping in Mont St. Michel," later.)

Taxi: Call 02 33 60 33 23 or mobile 02 33 60 26 89.

Guided Walks: The **TI** may offer guided walks of the village below the abbey in 2011 (ask ahead). They also have information on inexpensive guided walks across the bay (with some English). **La Traversée Traditionelle** traces the footsteps of pilgrims, starting across the bay at Le Bec d'Andaine and walking over the mudflat to Mont St. Michel (verify that the guide speaks some English, weekends only, May–Oct; about €6, 4 miles—or 1.75 hours—each way, round-trip takes 4.5 hours, including one hour on Mont St. Michel; ask at TI or call 02 33 89 80 88, www.cheminsdelabaie.com). For a tour within the **abbey** itself, see my self-guided tour on page 317.

Crowd-Beating Tips: Arrive after 16:00 and leave by 11:00 to avoid the worst crowds. The island's main drag is wall-to-wall people from 11:00 to 16:00. Bypass this mess by following this book's suggested walking routes (under "Sights in Mont St. Michel").

Best Light: Because Mont St. Michel faces southwest, morning light from the causeway is eye-popping. Take a memorable walk before breakfast. And don't miss the illuminated island after dark (also best from the causeway).

These sights are listed in the order you approach them from the mainland.

Sights in Mont St. Michel

Surrounding the Island

The Bay of Mont St. Michel—The vast Bay of Mont St. Michel has long played a key role. Since the sixth century, hermit monks in search of solitude lived here. The word "hermit" comes from an ancient Greek word meaning "desert." The next best thing to a desert in this part of Europe was the sea. Imagine the desert this bay provided as the first monk climbed the rock to get close to God. Add to that the mythic tide, which sends the surf speeding eight miles in and out with each tide cycle. Long before the causeway was built, when Mont St. Michel was an island, pilgrims would approach across the mudflat, aware that the tide swept in "at the speed of a galloping horse" (well, maybe a trotting horse—12 m.p.h., or about 18 feet per second).

Quicksand was another peril. A short stroll onto the sticky sand helps you imagine how easy it would be to get one or both feet stuck as the tide rolled in. The greater danger for adventurers today is the thoroughly disorienting fog and the fact that the sea can encircle unwary hikers. (Bring a mobile phone.) Braving these devilish risks for centuries, pilgrims kept their eyes on the spire crowned by their protector, St. Michael, and eventually reached their spiritual goal.

▲▲**Stroll Around Mont St. Michel**—To resurrect that Mont St. Michel dreamscape and evade all those tacky tourist stalls, you can walk out on the mudflats around the island (to reach the mudflats, pass through the *gendarmerie*, or guard station, on the left side of the island as you face it). At low tide, it's reasonably dry and a great memory-maker. But this can be hazardous, so don't go alone, don't stray far, and be sure to double-check the tides—or consider a guided walk (described under "Helpful Hints," earlier). Remember the scene from the Bayeux tapestry where Harold rescues Normans from the quicksand? It happened somewhere in this bay. Water taps to rinse muddy feet are inside the *gendarmerie*.

The Village Below the Abbey

Visitors usually enter the island through a stone arch at the lower left (where buses park). However, during very high tides, you'll enter through the gray door in the tower, where the causeway meets Mont St. Michel. The island's main street (rue Principale, or "Grande Rue"), lined with shops and hotels leading to the abbey, is grotesquely touristy. It is some consolation to remember that, even in the Middle Ages, this was a commercial gauntlet, with stalls

Mont St. Michel

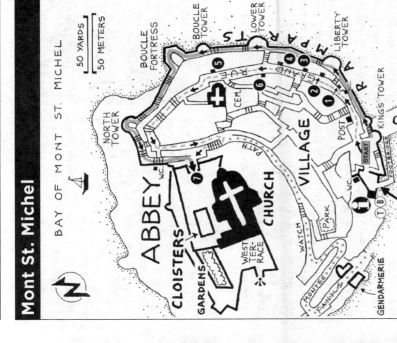

BAY OF MONT ST. MICHEL

50 YARDS
50 METERS

- **View**
- **P** Parking
- **T** Taxi Stand
- **B** Bus Stop
- **→** Ramparts Walk up to Abbey
- **→** Direct Route up to Abbey
- **·····** Less Crowded Route up to Abbey

1. Hôtel St. Pierre
2. Hôtel Croix Blanche
3. Hôtel du Guesclin & Rest.
4. Hôtel le Mouton Blanc & Chez Mado Rest.
5. Hôtel la Vieille Auberge & Restaurant
6. Restaurant le St. Michel
7. Entry to Abbey

selling souvenir medallions, candles, and fast food. With only 30 full-time residents, the village lives solely for tourists. After visiting the TI, check the tide warnings posted on the wall and pass through the imposing doors.

Before the drawbridge, on your left, peek through the door of Restaurant la Mère Poulard. The original Madame Poulard (the maid of an abbey architect who married the village baker) made quick and tasty omelets here (*omelette tradition*). These were popular for pilgrims, who, in pre-causeway days, needed to beat the tide to get out. They're still a hit with tourists—even at the rip-off price they charge today (they're much cheaper elsewhere). Pop in for a minute, just to enjoy the show as old-time-costumed cooks beat eggs.

You could continue the grueling trudge uphill to the abbey, through the masses and past several gimmicky museums (all island hotel receptions are located on this street). But if the abbey's your goal, bypass the worst crowds and tourist kitsch by climbing the first steps on your right after the drawbridge and following the ramparts in either direction up and up to the abbey (quieter if you go right; ramparts described on page 320). If crowds really get in your craw, go back out the island's entry arch and make a hard right, passing under the *gendarmerie*, and follow the cobbled ramp up to the abbey (this is also the easiest route up thanks to the long ramps, which help you avoid most stairs).

Free public WCs are next to the TI at the town entry, partway up the main drag, and at the abbey entrance. You can attend Mass at the tiny St. Pierre Church (daily at 11:00, also Sat at 18:00, opposite Hôtel la Vieille Auberge).

▲▲Abbey of Mont St. Michel

Mont St. Michel has been an important pilgrimage center since A.D. 708, when the bishop of Avranches heard the voice of Archangel Michael saying, "Build here and build high." With brilliant foresight, Michael reassured the bishop, "If you build it..they will come." Today's abbey is built on the remains of a Romanesque church, which stands on the remains of a Carolingian church. St. Michael, whose gilded statue decorates the top of the spire, was the patron saint of many French kings, making this a favored site for French royalty through the ages. St. Michael was particularly popular in Counter-Reformation times, as the Church employed his warlike image in the fight against Protestant heresy.

This abbey has 1,200 years of history, though much of its story was lost when its archives were taken to St. Lô for safety during World War II—only to be destroyed during the D-Day fighting. As you climb the stairs, imagine the centuries of pilgrims and monks who have worn down the edges of these same stone steps.

Cost and Hours: €8.50; May–June daily 9:00–19:00; July–Aug Mon-Sat 9:00–23:00, Sun 9:00–19:00; Sept–April daily 9:30–18:00; closed Dec 25, Jan 1, and May 1; last entry one hour before closing (tel. 02 33 89 80 00). Buy your ticket to the abbey and keep climbing. Mass is held daily, except Monday, at 12:15 in the abbey church.

Visiting the Abbey: Allow 20 minutes to hike at a steady pace from the TI. To avoid crowds, arrive by 10:00 or after 16:00 (the place gets really busy by 11:00). In summer evenings, when the abbey is open until 23:00 and crowds are gone, visits come with music and mood lighting. It's worth paying a second admission to see the abbey so peaceful (nighttime program starts at 19:00; daytime tickets aren't valid for re-entry, but you can visit before 19:00 and stay on).

Tours: You'll find no English explanations in the abbey (except for a small leaflet). Follow my self-guided tour, below. For more detail, rent the excellent audioguide (€4.50, or €6/2 people) or take a 1.25-hour English-language guided tour (free, tip requested, 4 tours/day, first and last tours usually around 10:00 and 16:00, confirm tour times at TI, meet at top terrace in front of church). The guided tours, which can be good, come with big crowds. You can start a tour, then decide if it works for you—but I'd skip them.

⊕ **Self-Guided Tour:** Tour the abbey by following a one-way route. Keep climbing to the ticket booths and turnstile, then climb some more. Pass a public WC, a room with interesting models of the abbey through the ages, a guides' desk (posting the time of the next tour), and—finally—the terrace.

• *Walk to the round lookout at the far end and face the church.*

West Terrace: In 1776, a fire destroyed the west end of the church, leaving this grand view terrace. The original extent of the church is outlined with short walls (as well as the stonecutter numbers, generally not exposed like this—a reminder that they were paid by the piece). The buildings of Mont St. Michel are made of granite stones quarried from the Isles of Chausey (visible on a clear day, 20 miles away). Tidal power was ingeniously harnessed to load, unload, and even transport the stones, as barges hitched a ride with each incoming tide.

As you survey the Bay of Mont St. Michel, notice the polder land—farmland reclaimed by Normans in the 19th century with the help of Dutch engineers. The lines of trees mark strips of land used in the process. Today, this reclaimed land is covered by salt-loving plants and grazed by sheep whose salty meat is considered a local treat. You're standing 240 feet above sea level, at the summit of what was an island called "the big tomb." The small island just farther out is "the little tomb."

The bay stretches from Normandy (on the right as you look to the sea) to Brittany (on the left). The Couesnon River below marks the historic border between the two lands. Brittany and Normandy have long vied for Mont St. Michel. In fact, the river used to pass Mont St. Michel on the other side, making the abbey part of Brittany. Today, it's just barely—but thoroughly—on Norman soil. Construction on the new dam across this river (easy to see from here) was completed in 2010. Central to the dam is a system of locking gates that retain water upriver during high tide and release it at low tide, in effect flushing the bay and returning it to a mudflat at low tide (see "The Causeway and Its Demise" sidebar, earlier). The dam is the first phase of the project to restore Mont St. Michel's island status.

• *Now enter the…*

Abbey Church: Sit on a pew near the altar, under the little statue of the Archangel Michael (with the spear to defeat dragons and evil, and the scales to evaluate your soul). Monks built the church on the tip of this rock to be as close to heaven as possible. The downside: There wasn't enough level ground to support a sizable abbey and church. The solution: Four immense crypts were built under the church to create a platform to support each of its wings. While most of the church is Romanesque (round arches, 11th century), the light-filled apse behind the altar was built later, when Gothic arches were the rage. In 1421, the crypt that supported the apse collapsed, taking that end of the church with it. Few of the original windows survive (victims of fires, storms, lightning, and the Revolution).

• *After the church, enter the…*

Cloisters: A standard feature of an abbey, this was the peaceful zone that connected various rooms, where monks could meditate, read the Bible, and tend their gardens (growing food and herbs for medicine). The great view window is enjoyable today (what's the tide doing?), but it was of no use to the monks. The more secluded a monk could be, the closer he was to God. (A cloister, by definition, is an enclosed place.) Notice how the columns are staggered. This efficient design allowed the cloisters to be supported with less building material (a top priority, given the difficulty of transporting stone this high up). The carvings above the columns feature various plants and heighten the Garden-of-Eden ambience the cloister offered the monks. The statues of various saints, carved among some columns, were de-faced—literally—by French Revolutionary troops.

• *Continue on the tour to the…*

Refectory: This was the dining hall where the monks consumed both food and the word of God in silence—one monk read in a monotone from the Bible during meals (pulpit on the right near the far end). The monks gathered as a family here in one undivided space under one big arch (an impressive engineering feat in its day). The abbot ate at the head table; guests sat at the table in the middle. The clever columns are thin but very deep, allowing maximum light while offering solid support. From 966 until 2001, this was a Benedictine abbey. In 2001, the last three Benedictine monks checked out, and a new order of monks from Paris took over.

• *Stairs lead down one flight to a...*

Round Stone Relief Sculpture of St. Michel: This scene depicts the legend of Mont St. Michel: The archangel Michael wanted to commemorate a hard-fought victory over the devil with the construction of a monumental abbey on a nearby island. He chose to send his message to the bishop of Avranches (St. Aubert), who saw Michael twice in his dreams. But the bishop did not trust his dreams until the third time, when Michael drove his thumb into the bishop's head, leaving a mark that he could not deny.

• *Continue down the stairs another flight to the...*

Guests' Hall: St. Benedict wrote that guests should be welcomed according to their status. That meant that when kings (or other VIPs) visited, they were wined and dined without a hint of monastic austerity. This room once exploded in color, with gold stars on a blue sky across the ceiling. (The painting of this room was said to be the model for Sainte-Chapelle in Paris.) The floor was composed of glazed red-and-green tiles. The entire space was bathed in glorious sunlight, made divine as it passed through a filter of stained glass. The big double fireplace, kept out of sight by hanging tapestries, served as a kitchen.

• *Hike the stairs through a chapel to the...*

Hall of the Grand Pillars: Perched on a pointy rock, the huge abbey church had four sturdy crypts like this to prop it up. You're standing under the Gothic portion of the abbey church— this was the crypt that collapsed in 1421. Notice the immensity of the columns (15 feet around) in the new crypt, rebuilt with a determination not to let it fall again.

• *To see what kind of crypt collapsed, walk on to the...*

Crypt of St. Martin: This simple 11th-century Romanesque vault has minimal openings, since the walls needed to be solid and fat to support the buildings above. As you leave, notice the thickness of the walls.

• *Next, you'll find the...*

Ossuary (identifiable by its big treadwheel): The monks celebrated death as well as life. This part of the abbey housed the hospital, morgue, and ossuary. Because the abbey graveyard was small, it was routinely emptied, and the bones were stacked here.

During the Revolution, monasticism was abolished. Church property was taken by the atheistic government, and from 1793 to 1863, Mont St. Michel was used as an Alcatraz-type prison. Its first inmates were 300 priests who refused to renounce their vows. (Victor Hugo complained that using such a place as a prison was like keeping a toad in a reliquary.) The big treadwheel—the kind that did heavy lifting for big building projects throughout the Middle Ages—is from the decades when the abbey was a prison. Teams of six prisoners marched two abreast in the wheel—hamster-style—powering two-ton loads of stone and supplies up Mont St. Michel. Spin the rollers of the sled next to the wheel. Look down the steep ramp (another sled hangs just below). Notice the parking lot and the crowds down there. When the tide is very high, careless drivers can become carless drivers. A few years ago, a Scottish bus driver (oblivious to the time and tide, and very busy in a hotel room) lost his bus...destroyed by a salty bath. Local police tethered it to the lot so it wouldn't float away. If you're spending the night, enjoy the small number of cars and the complete absence of buses after dinner.

Finish your visit by walking through the Promenade of the Monks, under more Gothic vaults, and into the vast **Scriptorium Hall** (a.k.a. Knights Hall), where monks decorated illuminated manuscripts. You'll then spiral down to the gift shop, turn right, and follow signs to *Jardin*. The room after the shop holds temporary exhibitions about the history and future of Mont St. Michel.

• *Exit the room and walk out into the rear garden. From here, look up at the miracle of medieval engineering.*

The "Merveille": This was an immense building project—a marvel back in 1220. Three levels of buildings were created: the lower floor for the lower class, the middle floor for VIPs, and the top floor reserved for the clergy. It was a medieval skyscraper, built with the social strata in mind. (Remember looking out of those top windows earlier?) The vision was even grander—the place where you're standing was to be built up in similar fashion, to support a further expansion of the church. But the money ran out, and the project was abandoned.

• *Stairs lead from here back into the village. To avoid the crowds on your descent, turn right when you see the sign for Musée Historique and find your own route down or, at the same place, follow chemin des Remparts to the left and bike down via the...*

Ramparts: Mont St. Michel is ringed by a fine example of 15th-century fortifications. They were built to defend against a new weapon: the cannon. They were low, rather than tall—to make a smaller target—and connected by protected passageways, which enabled soldiers to zip quickly to whichever zone was under attack. The five-sided Boucle Tower (1481, see map on page 315) was crafted with no blind angles, so defenders could protect it and the nearby walls in all directions. And though the English conquered all of Normandy in the early 15th century, they never took this well-fortified island. Because of its stubborn success against the English in the Hundred Years' War, Mont St. Michel became a symbol of French national identity.

After dark, the island is magically floodlit. Views from the ramparts are sublime. For the best view, exit the island and walk out on the causeway a few hundred yards.

Near Mont St. Michel

German Military Cemetery (Cimetière Militaire Allemand)—Located three miles from Mont St. Michel, near tiny Huisnes-sur-Mer (well-signed east of Mont St. Michel, off of D-275), this somber but thoughtfully presented cemetery-mortuary houses the remains of 12,000 German WWII soldiers brought to this location from all over France. (The stone blocks on the steps up indicate the regions in France from where they came.) It offers insight into their lives with letters they sent home (English translations). From the lookout, take in the sensational views over Mont St. Michel.

Sleeping in Mont St. Michel

(€1 = about $1.25, country code: 33)

Sleep on or near the island so that you can visit Mont St. Michel early and late. What matters is being here before or after the crush of tourists. Sleeping on the island—inside the walls—is a great experience for medieval romantics (like one of your co-authors) who don't mind the headaches associated with spending a night here, including average rooms and baggage hassles. To reach a room on the island, you'll need to carry your bags about 10-15 minutes uphill (consider taking only what you need for one night in a smaller bag, but don't leave any luggage visible in your car). Hotels and *chambres d'hôtes* (rooms) near the island are quite a bit cheaper and require less walking between your car and the hotel.

On the Island

There are eight small hotels on the island, and because most visitors day-trip here, finding a room is generally no problem (but finding an elevator is). Though some pad their profits by requesting that guests buy dinner from their restaurant, *requiring* it is illegal. Higher-priced rooms generally have bay views. On arrival, remember to tell the parking attendant that you're staying at a hotel on the island, which allows you to park closer. Several hotels are closed from November until Easter.

The following hotels are listed in order of altitude; the first hotels are lowest and closest to the parking.

$$$ Hôtel St. Pierre* and **Hôtel Croix Blanche***, which share the same owners and reception desk, sit side by side (reception at St. Pierre). Each provides comfortable rooms, some with good views (which you'll pay dearly for). Both have several family-run loft rooms (non-view Db-€120-130, view Db-€190, €200 for luxury Db in wood-beamed annex—*Logis du Château*, non-view Tb-€180, Internet access, pay Wi-Fi, tel. 02 33 60 14 03, fax 02 33 48 59 82, www.auberge-saint-pierre.fr, aubergesaintpierre @wanadoo.fr).

$$ Hôtel du Guesclin* has the cheapest rooms I list on the island and is the only family-run hotel here. Rooms have traditional decor and are perfectly comfortable. Check in at the bar on the main street level (Db-€74-90, Tb-€100, tel. 02 33 60 14 10, fax 02 33 60 45 81, www.hotelduguesclin.com, hotel.duguesclin @wanadoo.fr).

$$ Hôtel le Mouton Blanc* presents a good value, with 15 rooms that are split between two buildings. The main building (*bâtiment principal*) is cozier, with wood beams in most rooms, whereas the "annex" is brighter and more modern (Db-€98, loft Tb-€120, loft Qb-€140, tel. 02 33 60 14 08, fax 02 33 60 05 62, www.lemoutonblanc.com, contact@lemoutonblanc.fr).

$$ Hôtel la Vieille Auberge* is run by Hôtel St. Pierre. Its eight basic rooms are available at OK rates. The place feels neglected, but talk is afoot that the rooms will undergo major renovation by 2011—so be prepared for a change in these rates (Db-€90, view Db-€130-155, Tb/Qb-€110-140, extra bed-€25; contact through Hôtel St. Pierre, listed above).

On the Mainland

Modern hotels gather at the mainland end of the causeway. These have soulless but cheaper rooms with easy parking and many tour groups. Hôtel Vert rents bikes, offering easy access to the island.

$ Hôtel/Motel Vert, which offers many services (see "Helpful Hints," page 313), is big and cheap. Hotel rooms provide standard comfort at good rates; the motel is a compound of funky little bungalows that are bare-bones simple, cheap, and fun for families (hotel: Db-€64-78, Tb-€74-93, Qb-€90-110; motel bungalows about €30 less; tel. 02 33 60 09 33, fax 02 33 60 20 02, www .le-mont-saint-michel.com, stmichel@le-mont-saint-michel.com).

Chambres d'Hôtes

Simply great values, these converted farmhouses are near the village of Ardevon, a few minutes' drive from the island toward Avranches.

$ Les Vieilles Digues, where delightful Danielle pampers you, is two miles toward Pontorson on the main road (on the left if you're coming from Mont St. Michel). There's a lovely garden and seven nicely furnished and homey rooms with Asian touches, all with showers and exterior entrances (but no Mont St. Michel views). Ground-floor rooms have patios on the garden (D–€60, Db–€70, Tb–€90, includes good breakfast, easy parking, Internet access and Wi-Fi, 68 route du Mont St. Michel, tel. 02 33 58 55 30, fax 02 33 58 83 09, www.bnb-normandy.com, danielle.tchen @wanadoo.fr).

$ La Jacotière, charming Claudine Brault's stone farmhouse, is closest to Mont St. Michel and walkable to the causeway. She has six immaculate rooms and views of the island from her back-yard (Db–€64, studio with great view from private patio–€66, extra bed–€12, includes a tasty breakfast, Wi-Fi, tel. 02 33 60 22 94, fax 02 33 60 20 48, mobile 06 78 30 25 47, www.lajacotiere.fr, la.jacotiere@wanadoo.fr).

$ Vent des Grèves is about 1.5 kilometers down D-275 from Mont St. Michel (green sign; if arriving from the north, it's just after Auberge de la Baie). Sweet Estelle (who speaks English) offers five bright, modern rooms with good views of Mont St. Michel and a common deck with tables to let you soak in the view (Sb–€35, Db–€45, Tb–€55, Qb–€65, includes breakfast, credit cards OK, Wi-Fi, tel. 02 33 48 28 89, www.ventdesgreves.com, ventdes greves@orange.fr).

Eating in Mont St. Michel

Puffy omelets (*omelette montoise,* or *omelette tradition*) are Mont St. Michel's specialty. The menus at most of the island's restaurants require the most expensive fixed-price *menu* option to get. Also look for mussels (best with crème fraîche) and seafood platters, locally raised lamb (a saltwater-grass diet gives the meat a unique taste), and Muscadet wine (dry, white, and cheap).

The menus at most of the island's restaurants look like carbon copies of one another (with *menus* from €18 to €28, cheap crêpes, and full à la carte choices). Some places have better views or more appealing decor, and a few have outdoor seating with views along the ramparts walk—ideal when it's sunny. If it's too cool to sit outside, window-shop the places that face the bay from the ramparts walk and arrive early to land a bay-view table. Here's a rundown of what you'll find.

Restaurant le St. Michel is lighthearted, reasonable, family-friendly, and run by helpful Patricia (decent omelets, mussels, and pasta, open daily for lunch, summers only for dinner, test its stone toilet, across from Hôtel du Mouton Blanc, tel. 02 33 60 14 37).

Chez Mado is a stylish three-story café-*crêperie*-restaurant one door up from the Hôtel Mouton Blanc. It's worth considering for its upstairs terrace, which offers the best outside table views up to the abbey (open daily). **La Vieille Auberge** has a broad terrace with the next-best views to the abbey and good bay views from inside. **La Croix Blanche** owns a small deck with abbey views and fine window-front tables with bay views.

Hôtel du Guesclin is the best place for a traditional meal, with white tablecloths and beautiful views of the bay from its inside-only tables (book a window table in advance).

Picnics: This is the romantic's choice. The small lanes above the main street hide scenic picnic spots, such as the small park at the base of the ancient treadwheel ramp to the upper abbey. You'll catch late sun by following the ramp that leads you through the *gendarmerie* and down behind the island (on the left as you face the main entry to the island). Sandwiches, pizza by the slice, salads, and drinks are all available to go at shops along the main drag. But you'll find the best selection at the modest **supermarket** located on the mainland at Hôtel Vert (see "Helpful Hints," earlier).

Mont St. Michel Connections

By Train, Bus, or Taxi

Bus and train service to Mont St. Michel is a challenge. Depending on where you're coming from, you may find that you're forced to arrive and depart early or late—leaving you with too much or too little time on the island.

From Mont St. Michel to Paris: There are several ways to get to Paris. Most travelers take the regional bus from Mont St. Michel to Rennes or Dol de Bretagne (about €11, not covered by railpass, www.keolis-emeraude.com/en) and connect directly to the TGV (4/day, 4 hours total from Mont St. Michel to Paris' Gare Montparnasse). You can also take the quick bus ride to Pontorson (see next) and catch one of a very few trains from there (2/day, 5.5 hours, transfer in Caen, St. Malo, or Rennes). In July and August (and on April–June and Sept weekends), you can take the SNCF bus to Villedieu les Poêles, and transfer there to the train to Paris' Gare Montparnasse (1/day, 4 hours total, bus and train covered by railpass).

From Mont St. Michel to Pontorson: The nearest train station to Mont St. Michel is five miles away, in Pontorson (called

Pontorson–Mont St. Michel). It's connected to Mont St. Michel by a 15-minute bus ride (12/day July-Aug, 8/day Sept-June, fewer on Sun) or taxi (€18 by day, €25 at night and on weekends, tel. 02 33 60 33 23, mobile 06 33 60 26 89).

From Pontorson by Train to: Bayeux (2/day, 2 hours; also see Hôtel Churchill's shuttle van service—page 286), **Rouen** (2/day via Caen, 4 hours; 4/day via Paris, 7 hours), **Dinan** (3/day, 2 hours, transfer in Dol), **St. Malo** (3/day, 1-2 hours, transfer in Dol), **Amboise** (2-3/day; 5.5-7.5 hours via transfers in Caen and Tours, or via Rennes, Le Mans, and Tours).

From Mont St. Michel by Bus to: St. Malo (€5.50, 2/day Mon-Sat—usually about 9:20 and 15:45, 1/day Sun, 2 hours with change at the Pontorson train station; the 9:20 bus from Mont St. Michel with Pontorson transfer arrives in St. Malo at 11:00, where you can catch buses to Dinan—TI has schedules), **Rennes** (4/day direct, 1.75 hours). Keolis buses provide service to St. Malo and Rennes (tel. 02 99 19 70 80, www.keolis-emeraude.com/en).

Taxis are more expensive, but are helpful when trains and buses don't cooperate. Figure €75 from Mont St. Michel to St. Malo, and €85 to Dinan, or much more on Sundays and at night.

By Car

From Mont St. Michel to St. Malo, Brittany: The direct (and free) freeway route takes 40 minutes. For a scenic drive into Brittany, take the following route: Head to Pontorson, then follow D-19 signs to St. Malo, then look for *St. Malo par la Côte*, and join D-797, which leads along *la Route de la Baie* to D-155 and on to the oyster capital of Cancale. In Cancale, keep tracking *St. Malo par la Côte* and *Route de la Baie* signs. You'll be routed through the town's port

(good lunch stop) then emerge on D-201 to savor Pointe du Grouin, then continue west on D-201 as it hugs the coast to St. Malo (see page 341 in Brittany chapter). If continuing on to Dinan: From St. Malo, signs direct you to Rennes, then Dinan. This drive adds about 2.5 hours (with stops; takes longer on weekends and in summer) to the fastest path between Mont St. Michel and Dinan, but is well worth it when skies are clear. For more details on this drive, see "Scenic Drive Between St. Malo and Mont St. Michel" on page 346 in the Brittany chapter.

From Mont St. Michel to Bayeux: Take the free and zippy A-84, and be ready to navigate if new signs to Bayeux are not yet in place (keep asking, "oo ay Bayeux?").

BRITTANY

Dinan • St. Malo

The broad peninsula of Brittany is windswept and rugged, with a well-discovered coast, a forgotten interior, strong Celtic ties, and a craving for crêpes and cider. This region of independent-minded locals is linguistically and culturally different from Normandy—and, for that matter, the rest of France. The Couesnon River skirts the western edge of Mont St. Michel, marking the border between Normandy and Brittany. Tradition is everything here, where farmers and fishermen still play a big part in the region's economy.

In 1491, the French King Charles VIII forced Brittany's 14-year-old Duchess Anne to marry him (at Château de Langeais in the Loire Valley). Their union made feisty, independent Brittany a small cog in a big country (the Kingdom of France). Brittany lost its freedom, but with Anne as queen gained certain rights, such as free roads. (Even today, more than 500 years later, Brittany's highways come with no tolls, which is unique in France.)

Locals take great pride in their distinct Breton culture. In Brittany, music stores sell more Celtic albums than anything else. It's hard to imagine that this music was forbidden as recently as the 1980s. During a more repressive time, many of today's Breton pop stars were underground artists. And not long ago, a child would lose French citizenship if christened with a Celtic name.

But the freckled locals are now free to wave their flag, sing their songs, and speak their language (there's a Breton TV station and radio station). Like their Irish counterparts, Bretons—many with red hair—are chatty, their music is alive with struggles against an oppressor, and their identities are intrinsically tied to the sea. The coastal route between Mont St. Michel and St. Malo—through the town of Cancale (famous for oysters and a good lunch stop) and Pointe du Grouin (fabulous ocean views)—gives travelers with limited time a worthwhile glimpse at this photogenic province.

Getting Around Brittany

By Car: This is the ideal way to scour the ragged coast and watery towns. Autoroutes are free, and the traffic is generally negligible (except in summer along the coast).

By Train and Bus: Trains provide barely enough service to Dinan and St. Malo (and on Sundays, service all but disappears). Key transfer points by train include the big city of Rennes and the small town of Dol-de-Bretagne. Some trips are more convenient by bus (Rennes to Dinan and Dinan to St. Malo).

By Minivan Tour: Westcapades runs daylong minivan tours covering Dinan, St. Malo, and Mont St. Michel (designed for day-trippers from Paris, trips officially begin at the train station in St. Malo and end at the train station in Rennes). These tours are flexible. Because the guides are based in Dinan, you can do the entire round-trip from Dinan (about 9:45–19:30). Alternatively, you can start in St. Malo (at 10:30) and finish either in Dinan (about 19:30) or in Rennes (about 19:00), where you can catch the TGV train to Paris. You can also get off at Mont St. Michel (described in the Normandy chapter)—making this tour a convenient way to reach that remote island abbey (€80/day, tel. 02 96 39 79 52, www.westcapades.com, marc@westcapades.com).

Brittany's Cuisine Scene

Though the endless coastline suggests otherwise, there is more than seafood in this rugged Celtic land. Crêpes are to Bretons what pasta is to Italians: a basic, reasonably priced, daily necessity. *Galettes* are savory buckwheat crêpes, commonly filled with ham, cheese, eggs, mushrooms, spinach, seafood, or a combination. Purists insist that a *galette* should not have more than three or four fillings—overfilling it masks the flavor (which is the point at certain places).

Oysters (*huîtres*) are the second food of Brittany, and are available all year. Mussels, clams, and scallops are often served as main courses, and you can also find crêpes with scallops and *moules marinières* (mussels steamed in white wine, parsley, and shallots). Farmers compete with fishermen for the hearts of locals by growing fresh vegetables, such as peas, beans, and cauliflower.

For dessert, look for *far breton*, a traditional custard often served with prunes. Dessert crêpes, made with white flour, come with a variety of toppings. Or try *kouign amann*, a puffy, caramelized Breton cake made with buckwheat dough (in Breton, *kouign* means "cake" and *amann* means "butter"). At bakeries, look for *ker-y-pom*, traditional Breton shortbread biscuits with butter, honey, and apple-pie fillings.

Cider is the locally produced drink. Order *une bolée de cidre* (a traditional bowl of hard apple cider) with your crêpes.

Remember, restaurants serve food only during lunch (11:30–14:00) and dinner (19:00–21:00, later in bigger cities); cafés offer food throughout the day.

Dinan

If you have time for only one stop in Brittany, do Dinan. Hefty ramparts corral its half-timbered and cobbled quaintness into Brittany's best medieval town center. And though it has a touristic icing—plenty of *crêperies*, shops selling Brittany kitsch, and colorful Breton flags—it's a workaday Breton town filled with about 10,000 people who appreciate the beautiful place they call home. This impeccably preserved ancient city, which escaped the bombs of World War II, is peaceful and conveniently located (about a 45-minute drive from Mont St. Michel). For a memorable day, spend your morning exploring Dinan and your afternoon walking, biking, or boating the Rance River.

Orientation to Dinan

Dinan's old city, contained within its medieval ramparts, sits on a hill well above the Rance River. Cobbled lanes climb steeply from Dinan's small river port to the vast place du Guesclin (gek-lahn). There you'll find lots of parking, Château de Dinan, and the TI. Place des Merciers, just north of place du Guesclin, is the center of most shopping activities.

Tourist Information

At the TI, pick up a free map and bus and train schedules, ask about boat trips on the Rance River, and check your email at the Internet terminal (July–Aug Mon–Sat 9:00–19:00, Sun 9:00–12:30 & 14:30–18:00; Sept–June Mon–Sat 9:00–13:00 & 14:00–18:00, closed Sun; just off place du Guesclin near Château de Dinan at 9 rue du Château, tel. 02 96 87 69 76, www.dinan-tourisme.com).

BRITTANY

Arrival in Dinan

By Train: To get to the town center from Dinan's Old World train station (no lockers or baggage storage), find a taxi (see "Helpful Hints," below) or walk 20 minutes (see map on next page). If walking, head left out of the train station, make a right at Hôtel de la Gare up rue Carnot, turn right on rue Thiers following *Centre-Ville* signs, and go left across big place Duclos-Pinot, passing just left of Café de la Mairie. To reach the TI and place du Guesclin, go to the right of the café (on rue du Marchix).

By Bus: Dinan's key intercity bus stop is in front of the post office on place Duclos-Pinot, 10 minutes above the train station and five minutes below place du Guesclin. To reach the historic core, cross the square, passing to the left of Café de la Mairie (for more bus information, see "Dinan Connections," later).

By Car: Dinan is confusing for drivers; follow *Centre-Ville* signs and park on the massive place du Guesclin (free parking 19:00–9:00 except July-Sept and on market days on Thu). If you enter Dinan near the train station, drive the route described above (see "By Train"), and keep to the right of Café de la Mairie to reach place du Guesclin. Check with your hotelier before leaving your car overnight on place du Guesclin; it will be towed before 8:00 on market or festival days.

Helpful Hints

Market Days: On Thursday, a big open-air market is held on place du Guesclin (8:00–13:00). In July and August, Wednesday is flea-market day on place St. Sauveur.

Internet Access: The TI has computers (small fee) but no Wi-Fi. Ask at your hotel or the TI for Wi-Fi availability.

Laundry: Pressing-Laverie's Madame Heurlin can usually do your laundry in a few hours (€8/wash and dry, Tue–Fri 8:30–12:00 & 14:00–19:00, Sat 8:30–18:00, closed Sun–Mon, a few blocks from place Duclos at 19 rue de Brest, tel. 02 96 39 71 35).

Supermarkets: Groceries are upstairs in the **Monoprix** (Mon–Sat 9:00–19:30, closed Sun, 7 rue du Marchix). On Sundays, try **Marché Plus**, on place Duclos-Pinot (Mon–Sat 7:00–19:00, Sun 9:00–13:00).

Bike Rental: The TI has up-to-date information on bike-rental places. Rent a bike at the port to avoid riding down and back up a big hill. **Vélo Corsaire** has what you need, including kids' bikes, child trailers, and baskets. Ask about one-way rentals for the 20-mile ride to St. Malo (closed Sun, near the train station at 13 rue Carnot, tel. 02 96 85 11 11).

Taxi: Call 02 96 39 67 29 or 06 08 54 09 22 (8-seat minivan,

Dinan

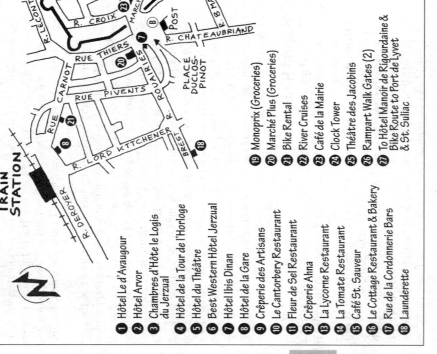

TRAIN STATION

1 Hôtel Le d'Avaugour
2 Hôtel Arvor
3 Chambres d'Hôte le Logis du Jerzual
4 Hôtel de la Tour de l'Horloge
5 Hôtel du Théâtre
6 Best Western Hôtel Jerzual
7 Hôtel Ibis Dinan
8 Hôtel de la Gare
9 Crêperie des Artisans
10 Le Cantorbery Restaurant
11 Fleur de Sel Restaurant
12 Crêperie Ahna
13 La Lycorne Restaurant
14 La Tomate Restaurant
15 Café St. Sauveur
16 Le Cottage Restaurant & Bakery
17 Rue de la Cordonnerie Bars
18 Launderette
19 Monoprix (Groceries)
20 Marché Plus (Groceries)
21 Bike Rental
22 River Cruises
23 Café de la Mairie
24 Clock Tower
25 Théâtre des Jacobins
26 Rampart Walk Gates (2)
27 To Hôtel Manoir de Rigourdaine & Bike Route to Port de Lyvet & St. Suliac

taxilemoine@volia.fr). Figure about €50 to St. Malo and €85 to Mont St. Michel.

Car Rental: Loc n' Drive has the best deals for short-term rentals (same office as Vélo Corsaire at 13 rue Carnot, www.locndrive .fr).

Minivan Excursions: Helpful Marc Le Meur runs **Westcapades,** with guaranteed minivan departures at least three times a week from Dinan to St. Malo and Mont St. Michel (see page 327).

Petit Train: This train runs a circuit connecting the port and upper old town (€6, runs every 40 minutes, leaves in the old town from in front of the Théâtre des Jacobins, a block off place du Guesclin).

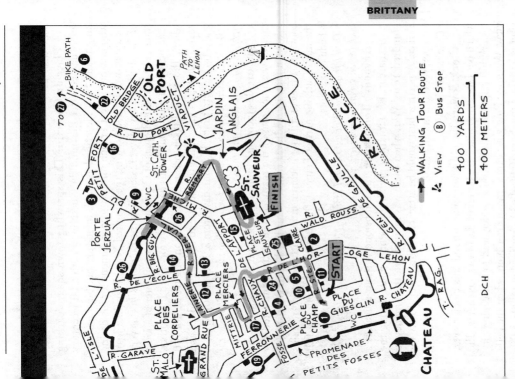

Picnic Park: The small but flowery Jardin Anglais hides behind the Church of St. Sauveur.

Self-Guided Walk

Welcome to Dinan

Frankly, I wouldn't go through a turnstile in Dinan. The attraction here is the town itself. Enjoy the old town center, ramble around the ramparts, and explore the old riverfront harbor. Here are some ideas, laced together as a relaxed one-hour walk (not including exploring the port). Start near the TI, and as you wander, notice the pride locals take in their Breton culture.

• *Start in the center of place du Guesclin, and find the statue of the horseback rider.*

Place du Guesclin: This sprawling town square/parking lot is named after Bertrand du Guesclin, a native 14th-century knight and hero (described as small in stature but big-hearted) who became a great French military leader, famous for his daring victories over England during the Hundred Years' War (like Joan of Arc, he was a key player in defeating the English). On this very square, he beat Sir Thomas of Canterbury in a nail-biter of a joust that locals still talk about to this day. The victory freed his brother, whom Thomas had taken prisoner in violation of a truce. For 700 years, merchants have filled this square to sell their produce and crafts (in modern times, it's Thursdays from 8:00 to 13:00).

• *With the statue of Guesclin behind you, follow rue Ste. Claire to the right, into the old town and to the...*

Théâtre des Jacobins: Fronting a pleasant little square, the theater was once one of the many convents that dominated the town. In fact, in medieval times, a third of Dinan consisted of convents. (They're still not uncommon in Brittany, which remains the most Catholic part of France.) The theater today offers a full schedule of events.

• *Turn left and walk down rue de l'Horloge ("Clock Street") toward the clock tower, where on your left, you'll see...*

Anybody's Tombstone: The tombstone without a head is a town mascot. It's actually a prefab tombstone, made during the Hundred Years' War, when there was more death than money in France. A portrait bust would be attached to this generic body for a proper, yet economical, burial.

• *Continue to the...*

Clock Tower: The old town spins around this clock tower, which has long symbolized the power of the town's merchants. The tower's 160 steps (the last few on a ladder) lead to a sweeping city view. Warning: Plug your ears at the quarter-hour, when the bells ring (€3, daily June–Sept 10:00–18:30, April–May 14:00–18:00, closed Oct–March).

• *Past the tower, take the first left into Dinan's historic commercial center, place des Merciers. Stop under a porch.*

Old Town Center: The arcaded, half-timbered buildings around you are Dinan's oldest. They date from the time when property taxes were based on the square footage of the ground floor. To provide shelter from both the rain and taxes, buildings started with small ground floors, then expanded outward as they got taller. Because trees did not come in standard lengths, it was easier to adjust the size of the pedestals.

Medieval shopkeepers sold goods in front of their homes under the shelter of leaning walls. Most streets are named for the key commerce that took place there. Picturesque rue de la Cordonnerie ("Shoe Street," to the left of the pretty restaurant La Mère Pourcel) is a good example of a medieval lane, with overhanging buildings whose roofs nearly touch. After a disastrous 18th-century fire, a law required that the traditional thatch be replaced by safer slate. A detour up rue de la Cordonnerie and into the small maze of streets is time well-spent. Find "pub row" and the modern market stalls of La Cohue.

• *Continue working your way through place des Merciers. (The building with the arched stone facade at the end of the square—Les Cordeliers—used to be a Franciscan monastery during the Middle Ages; today, it's a middle school...wrap your brain around that change.) Turn right on rue de la Lainerie ("Street of Wool Shops"), which becomes...*

Rue du Jerzual: This spiraling road was the primary medieval link to the port and the focus of commercial activity in old Dinan. The steep cobbled street (slippery when wet) was chock-a-block with potential customers making their way between the port and the upper city. Notice the waist-high stone and wooden shelves that front many of the buildings. Here, medieval merchants could display their products and tempt passersby. You can continue all the way down to the port (described later, under "Sights in Dinan"); it's a 10-minute walk down (remember, what goes down must come back up). If your knees balk, follow the path to the ramparts, described next.

• *For the best look at Dinan's impressive fortified wall, turn right after passing under the massive medieval gate (Porte du Jerzual) and work your way up the curving road. Turn right on rue Michel, then turn right again through the green iron gate to walk along the...*

Ramparts: In the Middle Ages, this elevated walkway was connected with Château de Dinan (it's about a mile in either direction to the château from here).

Although the old port town was repeatedly destroyed, these ramparts were never taken by force. If an attacker got by the *contrescarpe* (second outer wall, now covered in vegetation) and through the (dry) moat, he'd be pummeled by ghastly stuff dropped through the holes lining the ramparts. Today, the ramparts protect the town's residential charm and private gardens. Venture out on the (second) huge Governor's Tower to see how the cannon slots enabled defenders to shoot in all directions. The St. Malo tower is the last one you can see as you look uphill. Our next destination is the farthest visible tower to the right (with your back to the upper old town).

• *Double back to rue Michel and turn right. Take the first left, onto rue du Rempart. Walk to the round tower (in the corner of the park), called...*

St. Catherine's Tower: This part of Dinan's medieval defense system allows strategic views of the river valley and over the old port (for more on the port, see below). Find the medieval bridge below and the path that leads along the river to the right to Léhon (described later, under "Sights in Dinan"). To the left you can follow the Rance River downstream as it meanders toward the sea. The English gardens behind you are picnic-pleasant.

• *Walk through the gardens to the church behind you, and dip into the...*

Church of St. Sauveur: Enter this asymmetrical church (typical in Brittany) to see striking, modern stained-glass windows and a beautifully lit nave. Pick up the English explanation and learn the church's raison d'être. The church is a thousand years old—the wood balcony in the entry confirms that, as it heaves under the weight of the organ. When built, the church sat lonely on this hill, as all other activity was focused around the port.

• *Your tour is over. Good lunch cafés are across the square (see "Eating in Dinan"), and you are a block below the main rue de l'Horloge.*

Sights in Dinan

Dinan's Old Port

Following the self-guided walk, you can reach Dinan's modest little port by continuing down rue du Jerzual (which becomes rue du Petit Fort). Notice the unusual wood-topped building just before the port (across from Le Cottage restaurant). This was a leather tannery. Those wooden shutters could open to dry the freshly tanned hides while the nearby river flushed the toxic waste products (happily, swimming was not in vogue then). The last business before the port is a killer bakery with delicious local specialties, including *far breton* and *kouign amann* (you'll also find good picnic fixings and drinks to go). Try the *pomme* crumble. You deserve a baked break.

The port was the birthplace of Dinan a thousand years ago. For centuries, this is where people lived and worked, and today it's a great place for a riverside drink or snack. This once-thriving port is connected to the sea—15 miles away—by the Rance River. By taxing river traffic, the town grew prosperous. The tiny Vieux Pont (Old Bridge) dates to the 15th century. Because the port area was so exposed, the townsfolk retreated to the bluff behind its current fortifications. Notice the viaduct high above, built in 1850 to alleviate congestion and to send traffic around the town. Until then, the main road crossed the tiny Old Bridge, heading up rue du Jerzual to Dinan.

▲Rance River Valley

The best thing about Dinan's port is the access it provides to lush riverside paths that amble along the gentle Rance River Valley. You can walk, bike, drive, or boat in either interesting direction (perfect for families).

On Foot: For a breath of fresh Brittany air and an easy walk, visit the flower-festooned village of **Léhon.** Cross the Old Bridge in Dinan's port, turn right, and follow the level river trail for 30 minutes. You'll come to pristine little Léhon (a town of character, as the sign reminds you). Visitors are greeted by a beautiful ninth-century abbey that rules the roost (find the cloisters; interior closed to visitors). Explore the village's flowery cobbled lanes, but skip the town-topping castle ruin (free, 9:00–19:00). Enjoy a drink—or, even better, a meal at the adorable **La Marmite de l'Abbaye** café/restaurant, with seating inside or out. Your hostess, sweet Breton Madame Borgnic, serves wood-fire–grilled meats for lunch and dinner (closed Tue off-season, tel. 02 96 87 39 39). The trail continues on well past Léhon, but you'll need a bike to make a dent in it. The villages of Evran and Treverien are both reachable by bike (allow 45 minutes from Dinan to Evran, and an additional 25 minutes to Treverien).

By Bike: The Rance River Valley could not be more bike-friendly, as there's nary a foot of elevation gain (for bike rentals, see "Helpful Hints," earlier). Here's what I'd do with three hours and a bike: Pedal to Léhon (following the "On Foot" route, above), then double back to Dinan and follow the bike path along the river downstream to the Port de Lyvet.

To reach the Port de Lyvet, ride through Dinan's port, staying on the old city side of the river. You'll join a parade of ocean-bound boats as the river opens up, becoming more like an inlet of the sea. It's a breezy, level 30-minute ride past rock faces, cornfields, and slate-roofed farms to the tiny **Port de Lyvet** (cross small dam to reach village, trail ends a short distance beyond). **L'Effet Mer café/restaurant** is well-positioned in the village (open daily for lunch, dinner, or a refreshing drink on its wooden deck, closed Wed off-season, tel. 02 96 83 21 10). Serious cyclists should continue on to St. Suliac via La Vicomte (described later, under "By Car").

By Boat: Boats depart from Dinan's port, at the bottom of rue du Jerzual, 50 feet to the left of the Old Bridge on the Dinan side (schedules depend on tides, get details at TI). The snail-paced, one-hour cruise on the *Jaman IV* runs upriver to Léhon (the trip is better on foot or bike), taking you through a lock and past pretty scenery (€11, runs April–Oct, 2–4/day, tel. 06 07 87 64 90). A longer cruise with **Compagnie Corsaire** goes to St. Malo (€30, runs April–Sept, 1/day, slow and scenic 2.5 hours one-way, schedule changes with the tide, tel. 08 25 16 81 20, www.compagniecorsaire.com, or ask at TI). Enjoy St. Malo (described later in this chapter), then take the bus or train back (or do the reverse—bus/train to St. Malo, then boat back). Get the bus schedule before leaving Dinan (4–6/day, 1 hour, no buses on Sun except in summer). For families, renting a small motorboat from **Danfleurenn Nautic** is an enjoyable option (€35/hour, 5 people max, 21 rue du Quai, tel. 06 07 45 89 97, book ahead for a half-day or full day).

By Car: Meandering the Rance River Valley by car requires a good map (orange Michelin #309 worked for me). Drivers connecting Dinan and St. Malo can include this short Rance joyride detour: From Dinan, go down to the port, then follow D-12 with the river to your right toward Taden, then toward Plouër-sur-Rance (Dinan's port-front road is occasionally blocked, in which case you'll join this route beyond the port). Stay straight through La Hisse, then drop down and turn right, following signs to *Le Vicomte*. Cross the Rance on the small dam and find the cute **Port de Lyvet** (lunch café described earlier), then continue to La Vicomte and find D-29 north. Track your way to **St. Suliac,** a pretty little port town with a handful of restaurants, a small grocery store, and a photogenic *boulangerie*. Stroll the ancient alleys, find a bench on the grassy waterfront, and contemplate lunch. **La Ferme du Boucanier Bistrot** is a good bet (*menus* from €29, closed Tue–Wed, open for lunch weekends only, 2 rue de l'Hôpital, tel. 02 23 15 06 35). From here, continue on to St. Malo or return to Dinan.

Sleeping in Dinan

Dinan is popular. Weekends and summers are tight; book ahead if you can. Dinan likes its nightlife, so be wary of rooms over loud bars, particularly on lively weekends.

In the Old Center

$$$ Hôtel Le d'Avaugour*** is Dinan's reliable three-star hotel, with an efficient staff, stay-awhile lounge areas, and a backyard garden oasis. It faces busy place du Guesclin, near the town's medieval wall. The wood-furnished rooms have comfortable queen- or king-sized beds and modern hotel amenities, though the prices are impossible to pin down and the likeable owner strongly encourages two-night stays (streetside Db–€120–150, garden-side Db–€120–220, third person–€16, suites available, prices vary greatly by season, rooms over garden are best, breakfast–€13.50, elevator, bikes available, 1 place du Champ, tel. 02 96 39 07 49, fax 02 96 85 43 04, www.avaugourhotel.com, contact@avaugourhotel.com).

$$ Hôtel Arvor** is a good-value place with a fine stone facade, ideally located in the old city a block off place du Guesclin.

Sleep Code

(€1 = $1.25, country code: 33)

S = Single, **D** = Double/Twin, **T** = Triple, **Q** = Quad, **b** = bathroom, **s** = shower only, * = French hotel rating system (0–4 stars). Unless otherwise noted, credit cards are accepted and English is spoken.

To help you sort easily through these listings, I've divided the rooms into three categories based on the price for a standard double room with bath:

$$$ Higher Priced—Most rooms €90 or more.
$$ Moderately Priced—Most rooms between €60–90.
$ Lower Priced—Most rooms €60 or less.

Prices can change without notice; verify the hotel's current rates online or by email. For other updates, see www.ricksteves.com/update.

It's run by a delightful couple, with 24 modern and comfortable rooms (standard Db–€58–75, Tb–€75–85, €15/person extra for larger rooms accommodating up to 6 people, elevator, Wi-Fi, free but limited parking, 5 rue Pavie, tel. 02 96 39 21 22, fax 02 96 39 83 09, www.hotelarvordinan.com, hotel-arvor@wanadoo.fr).

$$ Chambres d'Hôte le Logis du Jerzual is just about as cozy as it gets, with five warmly decorated rooms and period furnishings and thoughtful touches throughout. Ideal hostess Sylvie Ronserray welcomes guests. Enjoy the terraced yard in this haven of calm close to the action: It's just up from the port but a long, steep walk below the main town (Db–€75–100, extra bed–€20, includes breakfast, 25 rue du Petit Fort, tel. 02 96 85 46 54, fax 02 96 39 46 94, www.logis-du-jerzual.com, ronsseray@wanadoo.fr). Drive up rue du Petit Fort from the port (it's well-signed) and drop off your bags. Parking is nearby.

$$ Hôtel de la Tour de l'Horloge** is a terrific two-star bet burrowed deep in the town's center, with 12 imaginatively decorated and impeccably maintained rooms fronting the bar-lined rue de la Chaux (some rooms can be noisy on weekends). Madame Diard gives a warm welcome and runs the place with grace (Db–€70–75, Tb–€86, Wi-Fi, 5 rue de la Chaux, tel. 02 96 39 96 92, fax 02 96 85 06 99, www.hotel-dinan.com, hotel.pbdelatour@orange.fr).

$ Hôtel du Théâtre is good for serious budget travelers, with seven simple and slightly smelly (but clean) rooms above a scrappy café/bar, across from Hôtel Arvor (S/D–€24, Db–€29, Tb–€39, €4 more July-Aug, 2 rue Ste. Claire, tel. 02 96 39 06 91, owner Patrick speaks some English).

At the Port

\$\$\$ Best Western Hôtel Jerzual* fronts the port and feels *très americain*, with a spacious lobby, a pool, a Jacuzzi, a pool table, an exercise room, a restaurant, and a riverfront bar/lounge. The comfortable rooms have big beds, and several of them are connecting, which works well for families (standard Db-€112-124, poolside Db-€120-145, Db suite-€175-195, extra person-€30, 26 quai des Talard, tel. 02 96 87 02 02, fax 02 96 87 02 03, www.bestwesterndinan.fr, reservation@bestwesterndinan.fr).

Closer to the Train Station

\$\$ Hôtel Ibis Dinan* , with its shiny, predictable comfort, stands tall between place du Guesclin and the train station. It works especially well for bus and train travelers, as it's central, reasonably priced, and next to the bus stop—convenient for hitting regional destinations such as St. Malo. They may have rooms when others don't (Db-€85, Tb-€118, Qb-€135, cheaper on weekends, 1 place Duclos, tel. 02 96 39 46 15, fax 02 96 85 44 03, www.ibishotel.com, h5977@accor.com).

\$ Hôtel de la Gare* faces the station and offers the full Breton Monty, with *charmant* Laurence and Claude (who both love Americans), a local-as-it-gets café hangout, and surprisingly quiet, clean, and comfy rooms for a bargain. Don't let the hallways scare you. The hotel has no email of its own, but offers free Wi-Fi thanks to the owners' teenage son (D-€28, Ds-€36, Db-€50, Tb/Qb-€50-65, breakfast-€6, place de la Gare, tel. 02 96 39 04 57, fax 02 96 39 02 29).

Near Dinan

\$\$ Hôtel Manoir de Rigourdaine* is *the* place to stay if you have a car and two nights to savor Brittany. Overlooking a splendid scene

of green meadows and turquoise water, this well-renovated farmhouse comes with wood beams, pleasant public spaces, immaculate grounds, and three-star rooms (many with views) for two-star prices. It's so well-run by ever-so-helpful Patrick and Anne-France that you won't want to leave (Db-€82-89, extra person-€15, I prefer the upstairs rooms, Internet access and Wi-Fi, 15-minute drive north of Dinan, tel. 02 96 86 89 96, fax 02 96 86 92 46, www.hotel-rigourdaine.fr, hotel.rigourdaine@wanadoo.fr). From Dinan, drop down to the port and follow D-12 toward Taden, then follow signs to *Plouër-sur-Rance*, then *Langrolay*, and look for signs to the hotel. If coming from the St. Malo area, take N-137 toward Rennes, then N-176 toward Dinan, take the Rance Plouër exit, and follow signs to *Langrolay* until you see hotel signs. From Rennes, take N-137 toward St. Malo, then N-176 toward Saint-Brieuc, take the Plouër-sur-Rance exit, and look for signs to *Langrolay* and then the hotel.

Eating in Dinan

Dinan has good restaurants for every budget. Since *galettes* (savory crêpes) are the specialty, *crêperies* are a nice, inexpensive choice—and available on every corner. Be daring and try the crêpes with scallops and cream, or go for the egg-and-cheese crêpes. Ham-filled crêpes can be salty. For a good dinner, book Le Cantorbery or Le Cottage, and think hard about walking, riding, or driving to nearby Léhon for a charming village experience (see page 335).

Crêperie des Artisans is well worth the walk for its delicious crêpes and warm ambience. Sincere owner Michel is adamant about using only traditional fresh ingredients, and makes the most authentic (and best) crêpes in town (both the mushroom-and-cheese and the caramel-and-salted-butter crêpes are terrific). Try his *lait ribot* (a frothy, slightly sour milk drink) or the delicious handmade cider (€9-14 *menus*, closed Mon, 6 rue du Petit Fort, halfway down to the port, tel. 02 96 39 44 10).

Le Cantorbery is a warm place (literally), where meats are grilled in the cozy dining-room fireplace *à la tradition*. The seafood is *très* tasty (*menus* from €26, open daily, just off place du Guesclin at 6 rue Ste. Claire, indoor dining only, two floors, tel. 02 96 39 02 52, well-run by sincere Madame Touchais).

Fleur de Sel is a soft, white-tablecloth place with a good reputation (particularly for its seafood) and reasonable prices (*menus* from €20, closed Sun–Mon, 7 rue Ste Claire, tel. 02 96 85 15 14).

Crêperie Ahna is perennially busy, satisfying its loyal clientele with tasty crêpes and salads (inside seating only, closed Sun, 7 rue de la Poissonnerie, tel. 02 96 39 09 13).

La Lycorne is Dinan's place to go for a healthy serving of mussels prepared 20 different ways (€13, served with fries of course, many other dishes available as well). The ambience is fine inside or out, as it's situated on a traffic-free street (closed Mon, 6 rue de la Poissonnerie, tel. 02 96 39 06 13).

La Tomate dishes up good pizza and pasta for €10-12 and has fun indoor or outdoor seating (closed Sun–Mon off-season, 4 rue de l'Ecole, tel. 02 96 39 96 12).

Café St. Sauveur is a local watering hole/café with good prices and a hard-to-beat setting...when it's sunny (€6.50 for lunch salads and *plats*, open daily, across from the church at 19 place St. Sauveur, tel. 02 96 85 30 20). The café next door offers a similar menu and prices.

At the Old Port: You'll find several restaurants at the old port. Have a pre-dinner drink—or a meal if the waterfront setting matters more than the cuisine—at one of the places on the river (La Terrasse is decent). Or you can hold out for dinner at **Le Cottage,** which merits the long walk along a cobbled lane, serving beautifully presented dishes to a happy clientele inside or out (*menus* from €18, daily, 78 rue du Petit Fort, tel. 02 96 87 96 70).

Nightlife: So many lively pub-like bars line the narrow, pedestrian-friendly **rue de la Cordonnerie** that the street is nicknamed "rue de la Soif" ("Street of Thirst"). When the weather is good, you can sit outside at the picnic tables and strike up a conversation with a friendly, tattooed Breton.

Dinan Connections

Locals take the bus to St. Malo or to Rennes, then catch trains from there (trains from Dinan require several changes, take longer than buses for regional destinations, and barely run on Sundays). Regional bus service is provided by Tibus (www.tibus.fr) or Illenoo (www.illenoo-services.fr).

From Dinan by Train to: Paris: Gare Montparnasse (6/day, 4 hours, change in Dol and Rennes), **Pontorson–Mont St. Michel** (3/day, 2 hours, change in Dol, then bus or taxi from Pontorson, see "Mont St. Michel Connections" on page 324), **St. Malo** (5/day, 1–2 hours, transfer in Dol, bus is better—see next), **Amboise** (6/day, 5–6 hours, via Rennes, then TGV to Paris with no station change needed in Paris; or better via Rennes, Le Mans, and Tours—2/day, 5–6 hours).

By Bus to: Rennes (with good train connections to many destinations, 7/day, 1 hour), **St. Malo** (5/day, none on Sun except in summer, 1 hour; faster and better than train, as bus stops in both cities are more central), **Mont St. Michel** (2/day, 3–4 hours, includes transfer with 1-hour wait in St. Malo or in Dol de Bretagne), **Dinard** (2/day, Mon–Sat only, 1 hour). Buses leave from the train station and from place Duclos-Pinot, near the main post office.

St. Malo

Come here to experience a true Breton beach resort. The old center (called Intra Muros) is your target, with pretty beaches, powerful ramparts that hug the entire town, and island fortifications that litter the bay. The inner city has an eerie, almost claustrophobic feeling, thanks to the concentration of tall, dark stone buildings hemmed in by the towering ramparts (though a few pedestrian streets buck

that sensation). The town feels better up top on the walls, which is *the* sight here. St. Malo is packed in summer, when the 8,000 people who call the old city home are joined by 12,000 additional daily "residents." But if you're willing to brave the crowds, it's an easy 45-minute drive—or a manageable bus or train ride—from Mont St. Michel or Dinan. (However, there's no baggage storage anywhere.) If you have almost a whole day here, circumnavigate St. Malo, then take the foot ferry to Dinard.

Orientation to St. Malo

Tourist Information

St. Malo's TI is across from the main city gate (Porte St. Vincent) on Esplanade St. Vincent (July–Aug Mon–Sat 9:00–19:30, Sun 10:00–18:00; Sept–June daily 9:00–13:00 & 14:00–18:00; tel. 08 25 13 52 00, www.saint-malo-tourisme.com). Pick up the helpful city map, along with schedules for the bus, train, or ferry (to Dinard).

Arrival in St. Malo

By Train: The modern TGV station serves all trains and is a 20-minute walk to the old center (signs lead to *Centre-Ville*). Walk for 15 minutes straight out of the station, then track the pointed spire in the distance.

By Bus: The main bus stops are near the Porte St. Vincent TI (closer to town) and at the train station (confirm which stop your bus uses—some stop at both).

By Car: Follow *Centre-Ville* signs to the old center (signs lead to *Intra-Muros*), and park as close as possible to the Porte St. Vincent (at the merry-go-round). A big underground parking lot is opposite the Porte St. Vincent, and smaller surface lots are scattered around the walls.

Helpful Hints

Internet Access: The most central place to get online (inside the walls) is at **Mokamalo** (5 rue de l'Orme, tel. 02 99 56 60 17).

Laundry: Inside the walls, you'll find a launderette on rue Petit Degris (daily 8:00–20:00).

Bike Rental: There are several places to rent bikes near the train station and TI. Ask at the TI.

Car Rental: You'll find both **Avis** (tel. 02 99 40 18 54) and **Europcar** (tel. 02 99 56 75 17) inside the train station.

Foot Ferry: A nifty little ferry (*Bus de Mer*) shuttles passengers between St. Malo and Dinard in 10 minutes (€7 round-trip, runs 9:00–18:00, later in summer). Boats depart from the Esplanade de la Bourse, on the west side of the old city.

Minivan Tour: **Westcapades** guarantees minivan departures at least three times a week from St. Malo. Tours include Dinan and Mont St. Michel, and officially end at the Rennes train station so you can connect to Paris (see page 327 for more details).

Sights in St. Malo

▲St. Malo's Ramparts

Climb the stairs inside the Porte St. Vincent and tour the walls counterclockwise. It's a rewarding mile-long romp around the medieval fortifications (the oldest segments date from the 1100s).

Stairs provide access at each door (*porte*). Walk down to the **beaches** if the tides allow (along with Mont St. Michel, St. Malo has Europe's greatest tidal changes). You'll see tree trunks planted like little forests on the sand—these form part of St. Malo's breakwater and must be replaced every 20 years. Storms blast in off the English Channel and bring surges of waves that pound the sea-walls.

The **fortified islands** were built during the Hundred Years' War (late 1600s) by Louis XIV's military architect, Vauban, to defend the country against England. You can tour the closer forts when tides allow (each costs €5 to enter). **Fort National** is the first you'll come across; farther along, you'll see **Fort du Petite Bé**, which sits on Ile du Grand Bé (where the famous poet Chateaubriand is buried). The longer, low-slung island even farther out has no buildings and is off-limits until World War II mines are completely removed. Speaking of WWII, St. Malo was decimated by American bombs during the war as part of the campaign to liberate France. Eighty percent of St. Malo was leveled, so most of the town's buildings date from 1945 or later.

As you walk along the wall, soon after the recommended Le Corps de Garde Créperie, you'll pass a *Chiens du Guet* restaurant

St. Malo

BEACH

To Mont St. Michel via Scenic Route

FORT NATIONAL

BEACH

N

100 YARDS
100 METERS

PORTE DES CHAMPS VAUVERTS

RAMPARTS

BEACH

PORTE ST-THOMAS

CHATEAU

PLACE CHATEAU-BRIAND

BUS STOP Ⓑ

ESPLANADE ST-VINCENT

To TRAIN STN. & DINAN

RUE CERF

RUE STE-BARBE

RUE CORNE DE CERF

PORTE ST-VINCENT

QUAI ST-TROUIN

QUAI ST-VINCENT

CHAUSSÉE SILON

BASSIN VAUBAN

VIEW

RUE VICTOIRE

ST-VINCENT

R. PORCON

RUE JACQUES CARTIER

GRANDE PORTE

PORTE ST-LOUIS

QUAI ST-LOUIS

To CAR FERRY TERMINAL & ALET

RUE BROUSSAIS

R. GRANDE RUE

RUE CORDIERS

RUE BOUCHERIE

RUE FOSSE

PORTE DE DINAN

QUAI ST-VINCENT

CHAUSSÉE TABARLY

DCH

POST

PLACE FRÈRES-LAMM.

R. BOYER

PLACE DU GUET

R. PIEQUI BOITT

RUE ST-SAUVEUR

R. D'ESTRÉES

RUE DE DINAN

RUE DE TOULOUSE

CORSAIRES TICKET OFFICE

Foot FERRY

To DINARD

To GRAND BE ISLAND & FORT DU PETIT BE

BEACH

POTERNE D'ESTRÉE

QUAI DE DINAN

JETTY

Legend:
- ❶ Hôtel France et Chateaubriand & Le Chateaubriand Restaurant
- ❷ Hôtel le Nautilus
- ❸ Le Corps de Garde Crêperie
- ❹ Internet Café
- ❺ Launderette

sign. At one time, bulldogs were kept in the small, enclosed area behind the restaurant, then let loose late at night to patrol the beaches.

Nearby the **Québec flags** fly in honor of St. Malo's sister city, Québec City. (Jacques Cartier, who visited the future site of Québec City and is credited as the discoverer of Canada, lived in and sailed from St. Malo.)

You'll eventually come to a long, concrete **jetty** that offers good views back to the ramparts. Across the bay is the belle époque resort city of Dinard (described later). Farther along, look for long, concrete-bordered *pétanque* (a.k.a., *boules*) courts below the walls (you may encounter games of *boule bretonne*—more like lawn bowling and with bigger balls). The **Corsaires ticket office,** located just before the commercial port, marks the departure point for the foot ferry to Dinard (you'll enjoy great views on your return ride to St. Malo).

From here, find your way inside the walls along rue de Dinan, and return to the Porte St. Vincent on surface streets. The shopping streets rue de la Vieille Boucherie and rue Porcon de la Barbinais are among the most appealing.

Alet

The village of Alet is just a few minutes' drive past St. Malo's port (a 20-minute walk from the ramparts), but it feels a world apart. A splendid walking path leads around this small point with stunning views of crashing waves, the city of Dinard, the open sea, and, finally, St. Malo (allow 30 minutes at a relaxed pace, go in a clockwise direction). World War II bunkers cap the small hill, and there's a memorial you can visit. Several popular cafés face the bay back near the Tour de Solidor.

To get to Alet (easiest by car—see map page 347), follow signs to *Centre-Ville*, then *Intra-Muros*. With the rampart walls on your right and the Bassin Vauban port on your left, follow *Toutes Directions* signs south until you spot *Alet* signs, and park near the Tour de Solidor or a block farther at place St. Pierre. To reach the start of the walking path, walk several blocks (with the sea on your left).

Sleeping in St. Malo

(€1 = $1.25, country code: 33)

Spending a night here gives you more time to enjoy the sunset and sea views from the town walls.

$$$ Hôtel France et Chateaubriand*** is a venerable establishment near the Porte St. Vincent, with 80 rooms at decent rates (Db-€100–170, most rooms around €110, breakfast-€11, Wi-Fi, 12 place Chateaubriand, tel. 02 99 56 66 52, fax 02 99 40 10 04, www.hotel-chateaubriand-st-malo.com).

$$ Hôtel le Nautilus** is a good place run by affable Loïck inside the walls near the Porte St. Vincent (Db-€65-70, Tb-€82, breakfast-€7.50, elevator, Internet access, free Wi-Fi, 9 rue de la Corne de Cerf, easiest to park outside walls and walk in through the Porte St. Vincent, tel. 02 99 40 42 27, www.lenautilus.com, info@lenautilus.com).

Eating in St. Malo

St. Malo is all about seafood and crêpes. There's no shortage of restaurants, many serving the local specialty of mussels (*moules*) and oysters (*huîtres*). Look also for bakeries selling *ker-y-pom*, traditional Breton apple-filled shortbread biscuits that are the best-tasting treat in town, especially when warmed.

Le Corps de Garde Crêperie is my favorite lunch stop. It's up on the walls, with St. Malo's only view tables. They serve original crêpes at fair prices from noon to 22:00, with cool ambience indoors or out (daily, 3 montée Notre Dame, tel. 02 99 40 91 46).

Le Chateaubriand, inside the Porte St. Vincent, delivers grand Old World elegance and offers a full range of choices at decent prices (*menus* from €18, open daily, inside and outdoor dining, place Chateaubriand, tel. 02 99 56 66 52).

St. Malo Connections

From St. Malo by Train to: Dinan (5/day, 1–2 hours, transfer in Dol, bus is better—see below), **Pontorson** (3/day, 1–2 hours, transfer in Dol).

By Bus to: Dinan (5/day, none on Sun except in summer, 1 hour; faster and better than train, as bus stops in both cities are more central), **Mont St. Michel** (2/day Mon–Sat, 1/day Sun, 2 hours via Pontorson), **Rennes** (4/day). Regional bus service is provided by Tibus (www.tibus.fr) or Illenoo (www.illenoo-services.fr).

Near St. Malo

Dinard

This upscale-traditional resort comes with a kid-friendly beach and an old-time, Coney Island–style, beach-promenade feel (2 buses/day from Dinan, Mon–Sat only, 1 hour). The small passenger-only ferry from St. Malo (*Bus de Mer*) provides the most scenic arrival (€7 round-trip, runs 9:00–18:00, later in summer, departs Dinard from below Promenade du Clair de Lune at Embarcadere).

The **TI**, between the casino and place de la République parking lot, is at 2 boulevard Féart (daily 9:30–12:30 & 14:00–18:00, July–Aug until 19:00, tel. 02 99 46 94 12, www.ot-dinard.com). To get to the TI from place de la République, walk toward the water, take your first right, and make another right onto boulevard Féart.

Dinard is a 10- to 20-minute drive from St. Malo. Leaving St. Malo, follow *Barrage de la Rance* signs through the unappealing port; in Dinard, follow *Centre-Ville* signs, and park on place de la République.

▲▲Scenic Drive Between St. Malo and Mont St. Michel

If you have a car, consider this lovely ride—worth ▲▲▲ if it's clear. This quick taste-of-Brittany driving tour samples a bit of the rugged peninsula's coast. Allow two hours for the drive between Mont St. Michel and St. Malo, including stops (a more direct route takes 45 minutes). On a weekend or in summer, the drive will take longer—start early. These directions are from St. Malo to Mont St. Michel, but the drive works just as well in reverse order.

St. Malo to the Emerald Coast: From St. Malo, take the scenic road hugging the coast east on D-201 to Pointe du Grouin, where the appropriately named Emerald Coast (Côte d'Emeraude) begins. Leave St. Malo, following *Cancale* signs and passing countless roundabouts, then look for signs to *Rothéneuf*, where you'll access D-201, which skirts in and out of camera-worthy views. Brown signs lead to short worthwhile detours to the coast; these are my favorites:

Ile Besnard and Dunes de Chevets: A five-minute detour off D-201 leads to this pretty, sandy beach arcing alongside a crescent bay. There are rocks rising from the water to scramble on, a nature trail above the beach, and a view restaurant by the campground (Les Chevets Bar/Restaurant, closed Mon–Tue). From the hamlet of La Guimorais, a 10-minute drive from Rothéneuf, follow signs to *Ile Besnard* and *Dunes de Chevets* to the very end (past the campground), and park at the far end of the lot.

Pointe du Grouin: This striking rock outcrop yields views from easy trails in all directions. Park near Hôtel du Grouin (outdoor café with views), and continue on foot. Pass the *semaphore du grouin* (signal station), where paths lead everywhere. Breathe in the sea air. Can you spot Mont St. Michel in the distance? The big rock below is L'Ile des Landes, an island earmarked for a fort during the French Revolution. The fort was never built, and the island remains home to thousands of birds. What fool would build on an island in this bay?

Cancale: Return to your car and leave Pointe du Grouin, following signs to *Cancale*, Brittany's appealing oyster capital. Its

St. Malo to Mont St. Michel

AUTOROUTE
OTHER ROADS
SCENIC DRIVE

ENGLISH CHANNEL

TO PLYMOUTH, CHANNEL ISLANDS + PORTSMOUTH (BRITAIN)

ILE BESNARD + DUNES DE CHEVETS

POINTE DU GROUIN

CANCALE

EMERALD COAST

ROTHE-NEUF

ST. MALO

DINARD

TO BREST

RANCE

DINAN

TO RENNES

BRITTANY

NORMANDY

MONT ST. MICHEL

AVRANCHES

TO CAEN + PARIS

TO PARIS

TO FOUGERES

PARIS

harbor (le port) is lined with restaurants, all offering oysters and mussels. Upon arrival in Cancale, follow par la côte signs to arrive on the port side. Slurp oysters here.

Cancale to Mont St. Michel: Cancale is a 45-minute drive from Mont St. Michel. Head out of Cancale toward Mont St. Michel on D-155, then D-797, and drive along la Route de la Baie, which skirts the bay and passes big-time oyster farming, windmill towers (most lacking their sails), flocks of sheep, and, at low tide, grounded boats waiting for the sea to return. On a clear day, look for Mont St. Michel in the distance. On a foggy day, look harder.

Fougères

The very Breton city of Fougères, worth ▲, is a handy stop for drivers traveling between the Loire châteaux and Mont St. Michel. Fougères has one of Europe's largest medieval castles, a lovely old city center, and a panoramic park viewpoint. Drivers follow *Centre-Ville* signs, then *Château*, and park at the free lot just past the château.

For a memorable, leg-stretching stroll, start from the parking lot near the château. Walk into Fougères with the water-filled moat on your left, then follow *Jardin Public* signs. Stop for a peek in the handsome church of St. Sulpice (English handout inside); the woodwork is exceptional, from the paneled walls and ceiling to the choir stalls and the carved altar. Then let the *Jardin Public* signs lead you through back streets, passing gingerbread-like Breton homes, up into the lush park. Walk through manicured gardens to the base of St. Léonard Church and find the floral panorama. Double back most of the way you came, then veer right to the château and under the stone gate. There's no reason to enter the château unless you need more exercise or a town map (€5, daily 10:00–12:30 & 14:00–18:00). For a good view of the castle without the previous climb, walk a block above the castle (up rue de la Pinterie) and find the short ramparts across from the *crêperie* recommended next.

Eating in Fougères: You'll find a gaggle of cafés and *crêper-ies* near the castle with good choices and prices. **Le Bonheur Est Dans le Blé** is a notch above the others, serving tasty crêpes on a lovely little terrace overlooking the valley (closed Tue evening, a block up from the château at 3 rue Fourchette, tel. 02 99 94 99 72).

THE LOIRE

Amboise • Chinon • Beaucoup de Châteaux

As it glides gently east to west, officially separating northern from southern France, the Loire River has come to define this popular tourist region. The importance of this river, and the valley's prime location in the center of the country just south of Paris, has made the Loire a strategic hot potato for more than a thousand years. Because of its history, this region is home to more than a thousand castles and palaces in all shapes and sizes. When a "valley address" became a must-have among 16th-century hunting-crazy royalty, rich Renaissance palaces replaced outdated medieval castles.

Hundreds of these castles and palaces are open to visitors, and it's castles that you're here to see (you'll find better villages and cities elsewhere). Today's Loire Valley is carpeted with fertile fields, crisscrossed by rivers, and laced with rolling hills. It's one of France's most important agricultural regions. It's also under some development pressure, thanks to TGV bullet trains that link it to Paris in an hour, and cheap flights to England that make it a prime second-home spot for many Brits, including Sir Mick Jagger.

Choosing a Home Base

This is a big, unwieldy region for travelers, so I've divided it into two halves, each centered around a good, manageable town to use as a base: Amboise or Chinon. Châteaux-holics and gardeners stay longer and sleep in both towns. Amboise is east of the big city of Tours, and Chinon lies to Tours' west. It's over an hour drive from Amboise to Chinon; if you sleep on one side of Tours and intend to visit castles on the other side, you're looking at a long round-trip

The Loire

- 🏰 CHATEAU
- ╬╬ RAIL
- ━━ AUTOROUTE (TOLL)
- ── OTHER ROADS
- ☐ SEE DETAIL MAPS

10 MILES
10 KM

NOTE: NOT ALL ROADS SHOWN

TO LE MANS, NORMANDY & BRITTANY

TOURS

VILLANDRY
LANGEAIS
USSE
AZAY-LE-RIDEAU
CHINON

VIENNE RIVER

ABBAYE ROYALE DE FONTEVRAUD

TO SAUMUR & ANGERS

TO POITIERS & DORDOGNE

DCH

drive—certainly doable, but not my idea of good travel. Instead, sleep in the town nearest the castles you plan to visit, and do what you can to avoid crossing the traffic-laden city of Tours.

Amboise is the best home base for first-timers to this area, as it offers handy access to these important châteaux: Chenonceau, Blois, Chambord, Cheverny, Fougères-sur-Bièvre, Chaumont-sur-Loire, Loches, and Valençay. Amboise also has better train connections from Paris and better public transportation options to nearby sights, making it the preferable choice if you don't want to rent a car or bike.

Chinon and its nearby châteaux don't feel as touristy, and appeal to gardeners and road-less-traveled types. The key sights in this area include the châteaux of Azay-le-Rideau, Langeais, Villandry, Chatonnière, Rivau, Ussé, and the Abbaye Royale de Fontevraud. Chinon is also optimal for cyclists, with quicker access to a bike path and more interesting destinations within pedaling distance.

Loches and **Azay-le-Rideau** are two other home-base options for drivers, who should also consider the tempting rural accommodations listed throughout this chapter.

Planning Your Time

With frequent, convenient trains to Paris and a few direct runs to Charles de Gaulle Airport, the Loire can be a good first or last stop on your French odyssey (more than 20 trains/day between Paris' Gare Montparnasse or Gare d'Austerlitz and Amboise, 1.5–2 hours; some trains from Gare d'Austerlitz require an easy transfer in Blois or Les Aubrais–Orléans, and all trains from Montparnasse require a change in St. Pierre-des-Corps; 6 trains/day between Charles de Gaulle Airport and Tours, 2 hours; easy car rental at St. Pierre-des-Corps Station, 15 minutes from Amboise).

A day and a half is sufficient to sample the best châteaux. Don't go overboard. Two châteaux, possibly three (if you're a big person), make up the recommended daily dosage. Famous châteaux are least crowded early and late in the day. Most open at about 9:00 and close between 18:00 and 19:00. During the off-season, some close at 17:00 and midday 12:00–14:00. The Festival of Gardens at Chaumont runs May to mid-October from 10:00 to 20:30.

Drivers: For the single best day in the Loire, consider this plan: Sleep in or near Amboise and visit Chenonceau early (arrive by 9:00), when crowds are small; spend midday at Chambord (30-minute drive from Chenonceau); and enjoy Chaumont or

Cheverny on the way back to your hotel (the hunting dogs are fed at 17:00 on most days at Cheverny). Remember to allow time to visit Amboise. With a second full day, move to Chinon, visiting Villandry and Langeais en route, then devote your afternoon to Chinon.

The best map of the area is Michelin #518, covering all the sights described in this chapter (the TI's free map of Touraine, the area surrounding Tours, is also quite good).

Try to see one château on your drive in (for example, if arriving from the north, visit Chambord, Cheverny, or Blois; if coming from the west or the south, see Azay-le-Rideau, Chinon, Langeais, or Villandry). If you're coming from Burgundy, don't miss the remarkable Château de Guédelon (see page 883 in the Burgundy chapter). If you're driving to the Dordogne from the Loire, the A-20 autoroute via Limoges (near Oradour-sur-Glane) is fastest and toll-free until Brive-la-Gaillarde.

Without a Car: On a tight budget, bike or catch the public bus, a shuttle van (summers only), or the train from Amboise to the town of Chenonceaux (1–2 buses/day Mon–Sat, none on Sun, 20 minutes; 8 trains/day, 1 hour, requires transfer; tour Chenonceau (the château), then spend the afternoon enjoying Amboise, its château, and Leonardo's last stand at Clos-Lucé. With a second day, the best (but pricier) option is a minivan excursion directly from Amboise to Chambord and Cheverny. If you're watching your wallet, take the train to Blois, tour its castle and old town, then take the excursion bus (runs mid-April–mid-Sept) or taxi from there to Chambord and Cheverny. (For more train and bus specifics, see "Amboise Connections" on page 374 and "Blois Connections" on page 383.) Those connecting Paris with Amboise or Chinon can lay over in Blois en route (baggage check available at château). Budget travelers based in Chinon can bike to Langeais, Ussé, and Villandry, and/or take the train via Tours to Azay-le-Rideau and Langeais (the train trips are long, and not a good option for most).

A limited visit to the Loire is doable as a day trip from Paris. Several minivan and bus tours make getting to the main châteaux a breeze (see "By Bus or Minivan Excursion").

Getting Around the Loire Valley

If you're looking to hunt down remote châteaux, rent a car. Day rentals are easy in Amboise and at the St. Pierre-des-Corps train station in Tours (but not in Chinon). Trains, buses, minivan tours, bikes, or taxis help non-drivers reach the well-known châteaux (all described later). To get to the less-famous châteaux without a car, you can take a taxi, arrange for a custom minivan excursion (affordable for small groups), or hop aboard a bike (great option for those with enough time and stamina).

By Train

With easy access from Amboise and Chinon, the big city of Tours is the transport hub for travelers bent on using the train or buses to explore the Loire (but it has little else to offer visitors—I wouldn't sleep there). Tours has two important train stations and a major bus station (with service to several châteaux). The main train station is called Tours SNCF, and the smaller, suburban TGV station (located between Tours and Amboise) is St. Pierre-des-Corps. Check the schedules carefully, as service is sparse on some lines. The châteaux of Amboise, Blois, Chenonceau, Chaumont (via the town of Onzain plus a long walk), Langeais, Chinon, and Azay-le-Rideau have train and/or bus service from Tours' main station; Amboise, Blois, Chaumont, and Chenonceau are also served from St. Pierre-des-Corps. Look under each sight for specifics, and seriously consider a minivan excursion (described next).

By Bus or Minivan Excursion

A few bus and shuttle van routes and minivan excursions offer painless transportation to the valley's châteaux. These organized itineraries make life far easier for those without a car, and can save you time (in line) and money (on admissions) when you purchase your château ticket at a discounted group rate from the driver. TIs in the region should have details on the options listed here, and on others offering similar services.

Although the minivan companies listed here don't visit all the castles in this chapter, they organize custom excursions to more remote châteaux, and will pick up your small group in Amboise, Chinon, or Azay-le-Rideau (€20–35/person for half-day itineraries from Tours, €45–50 for all day; figure €220 for groups of up to 7 for 4 hours, €390 all day).

From Amboise to Châteaux East of Tours: This area's three big-name castles—Chenonceau, Chambord, and Cheverny—are reachable by bus or shuttle van; minivan tours offer visits to the same three, and quick glances at a few others.

By Bus: If you're on a budget and visiting in high season, the region's buses aren't a bad option. An excursion bus that's a great deal departs from the Blois train station—an easy train ride from Amboise (14/day, 20 minutes)—and runs between Blois, Chambord, and Cheverny three times a day, allowing visits to both châteaux with your pick of three return times. This service runs mid-April–mid-September (departures from Blois train station are at 9:10, 11:10, and 13:40). You can stay at Chambord (the first stop) for two, five, or seven hours, then catch the next bus to Cheverny (where you can spend 2 hours), or head back to Blois (€6 includes bus fare and good discounts on château entries, buy tickets and get schedule from TI or bus driver; as you leave

Loire Valley Châteaux at a Glance

Which châteaux should you visit—and why? Here's a quick summary. Remember, TIs sell bundled tickets for several châteaux that save you money and time in ticket lines (see page 362).

Châteaux East of Tours

▲▲▲**Chenonceau** For sheer elegance arching over the Cher River, and for its lovely gardens. **Hours:** Daily mid-March–mid-Sept 9:00–19:00, closes earlier off-season. See page 375.

▲▲**Blois** For its urban setting, beautiful courtyard, and fun sound-and-light show. **Hours:** Daily April–Sept 9:00–18:30, July–Aug until 19:30; Oct 9:00–17:30, Nov–March 9:00–12:30 & 14:00–17:30. See page 381.

▲▲**Chambord** For its grandeur (440 rooms), fun rooftop views, and evocative setting surrounded by a forest still popular with hunters. **Hours:** Daily April–Sept 9:00–18:15, Oct–March 9:00–17:15. See page 384.

▲▲**Cheverny** For its intimate feel, lavishly furnished rooms, and daily feeding of the hunting dogs. **Hours:** Daily July–Aug 9:15–18:45, April–June and Sept 9:15–18:15, Oct 9:45–17:30, Nov–March 9:45–17:00. See page 387.

▲▲**Chaumont-sur-Loire** For its imposing setting over the Loire River, intriguing rooms, and impressive Festival of the Gardens. **Hours:** Daily May–mid-Sept 10:00–18:00; April and late Sept 10:30–17:30, Oct–March 10:00–17:00. See page 389.

▲**Amboise** For terrific views over Amboise and Leonardo da Vinci memories. **Hours:** Daily April–June 9:00–18:30, July–Aug 9:00–19:00, Sept–Oct and March 9:00–18:00, Nov–Jan 9:00–12:00 & 14:00–16:45, Feb 9:00–12:00 & 13:30–17:30. See page 358.

Fougères-sur-Bièvre For its medieval architecture and presentation of castle-construction techniques. **Hours:** May–mid-Sept daily 9:30–12:30 & 14:00–18:30; mid-Sept–April Wed–Mon 10:00–12:00 & 14:00–17:00, closed Tue. See page 389.

the Blois train station, look to the left for the TLC bus marked *Chambord/Cheverny*). When combined with a visit to the château in Blois, this makes a good, full-day side-trip from Amboise. As an alternative, taxi excursions from Blois' train station to one or both château can be affordable when split between several people. For details, see the Blois section on page 381, or call the Blois TI at tel. 02 54 90 41 41.

Valençay For its Renaissance design, lovely gardens, and kid-friendly summer events. **Hours:** Daily June 9:30–18:30, July–Aug 9:30–19:00, April–May and Sept 10:00–18:00, Oct 10:20–17:30, closed Nov–March. See page 392.

Châteaux West of Tours

▲▲**Azay-le-Rideau** For its magnificent setting in a romantic reflecting pond, and for its beautifully furnished rooms. **Hours:** Daily July–Aug 9:30–19:00, April–June and Sept–Oct 9:30–18:00, Nov–March 10:00–12:30 & 14:00–17:30. See page 400.

▲▲**Villandry** For the best gardens in the Loire Valley. **Hours:** Daily April–Sept 9:00–19:00, March and Oct 9:00–18:00, Nov–Feb 9:00–17:00. See page 403.

▲**Chinon** For its dramatic setting over the Vienne River, Joan of Arc history, and glorious views. **Hours:** Daily April–Sept 9:00–19:00, Oct–March 9:30–17:00. See page 393.

▲**Langeais** For its fortress-like setting above an appealing little village, handsome rooms, and parapet walk. **Hours:** Daily July–Aug 9:00–19:00, April–June and Sept–mid-Nov 9:30–18:30, mid-Nov–March 10:00–17:00. See page 402.

Château de Chatonnière For its overflowing flower display in spring and early summer. **Hours:** Daily mid-March–mid-Nov 10:00–19:00. See page 404.

Château du Rivau For its lovely vegetable and flower gardens based on designs from medieval tapestries. **Hours:** Easter–mid-Nov Wed–Mon 10:00–12:30 & 14:00–19:00, closed Tue except July–Aug, closed mid-Nov–Easter. See page 405.

Ussé For an exterior look at its architecture, which inspired the romantic Sleeping Beauty story. **Hours:** Daily April–Aug 10:00–19:00, mid-Feb–March and Sept–mid-Nov 10:00–18:00, closed mid-Nov–mid-Feb. See page 405.

By Shuttle Van: **Quart de Tours** runs a summer-only van service between Amboise and the Château de Chenonceau (€15 round-trip, €2.50 château discount, 5/day). For details, see page 374.

By Minivan Excursion: **Aco-Dispo** is a small, well-run minibus company based in Amboise with good all-day château tours from Amboise and Tours. Costs vary with the itinerary (from

Amboise—€34/half-day, €52/day; from Tours—€20/half-day, €50/day; daily, free hotel pick-ups, 18 rue des Vallées, Amboise, tel. 06 82 00 64 51, fax 02 47 57 67 13, www.accodispo-tours.com). English is the primary language. While on the road, you'll usually get a fun and enthusiastic running commentary covering each château's background, as well as the region's contemporary scene—but you're on your own at each château. (You're responsible for entry fees but can buy tickets from the driver at group rates—a good savings.) All-day tours depart 8:30–10:30 (varies by itinerary); afternoon tours depart 13:20–13:50. Both return to Amboise at about 18:30. Several itineraries are available; most include Chenonceau, and some throw in a wine tasting. If possible, reserve a week ahead by email, or two or three days ahead by phone. Groups are small, ranging from two to eight château-hoppers. (Day-trippers from Paris find this service convenient; after a one-hour TGV ride to Tours, you're met near the central station and returned there at day's end.) Acco-Dispo also runs multiday tours of the Loire and Brittany.

Loire Valley Tours offers all-day itineraries from Amboise to either châteaux near Amboise or châteaux near Chinon. The tours are fully guided and include admissions, lunch, and wine-tasting (about €120/person, tel. 02 54 33 99 80, www.loire-valley-tours.com, contact@loire-valleytours.com).

Quart de Tours provides transportation from Tours to châteaux near Amboise (from €22/person, tel. 06 85 72 16 22, fax 02 47 49 98 57, www.quartdetours.com).

From Chinon to Châteaux West of Tours: Tours is a one-hour train ride from Chinon (12 trains or SNCF buses/day). Minivan excursions leave from Tours' TI to many châteaux, including Azay-le-Rideau and Villandry. Try **Acco-Dispo** or **Quart de Tours**, with daily three-hour tours to Azay-le-Rideau and Villandry for about €22 (both companies described earlier).

By Bike

Cycling options are endless in the Loire, where the elevation gain is generally manageable. (However, if you have only a day or two, rent a car or stick to the châteaux easily reached by buses and minivans.) Amboise, Blois, and Chinon all make good biking bases and have rental options. A network of nearly 200 miles of bike paths and well-signed country lanes connect many châteaux near Amboise. Pick up the free bike-path map, *Le Pays des Châteaux à Vélo*, at any TI, or buy the more detailed map available at any TI. (I also list several accommodations with easy access to these bike paths.)

Near Chinon, a 30-mile bike path runs along the Loire River, passing by Ussé and Langeais, then meeting the Cher

Hot-Air Balloon Rides

In France's most popular regions, you'll find hot-air balloon companies eager to take you for a ride (Burgundy, the Loire, Dordogne, and Provence are best suited for ballooning). It's not cheap, but it's unforgettable—a once-in-a-lifetime chance to sail serenely over châteaux, canals, vineyards, Romanesque churches, and villages. Balloons don't go above 3,000 feet and usually fly much lower than that, so you get a bird's-eye view of France's sublime landscapes.

Most companies offer similar deals and work this way: Trips range from 45 to 90 minutes of air time, to which you must add two hours for preparation, champagne toast, and transport back to your starting point. Deluxe trips add a gourmet picnic, making it a four-hour event. Allow about €190 for a short tour, and about €270 for longer flights. Departures are, of course, weather dependent, and are usually scheduled first thing in the morning or in early evening. If you've booked ahead and the weather turns bad, you can reschedule your flight, but you can't get your money back. Most balloon companies charge about €25 more for a bad-weather refund guarantee; unless your itinerary is very loose, it's a good idea.

Flight season is April–October. It's smart to bring a jacket for the breeze, though temperatures in the air won't differ too much from those on the ground. Air sickness is usually not a problem, as the ride is typically slow and even. Baskets have no seating, so count on standing the entire trip. Group (and basket) size can vary from 4 to 16 passengers. Area TIs have brochures. **France Montgolfières** gets good reviews and offers flights in the areas that I recommend (tel. 02 54 32 20 48, fax 02 54 32 20 07, www.france-montgolfiere.com). Others are **Aérocom Montgolfière** (www.aerocom.fr) and **Touraine Montgolfière** (www.touraine-montgolfiere.fr).

River at Villandry and continuing along the Cher to Tours and beyond. To follow this route, pick up the *La Loire à Vélo* brochure at any area TI.

Tours-based **Detours du Loire** can help you plan your bike route and will deliver rental bikes to most places in the Loire for reasonable rates (35 rue Charles-Gilles, tel. 02 47 61 22 23, www.locationdevelos.com). Bikes are available to rent in Amboise, Chenonceaux, Blois, and Chinon (see "Helpful Hints" for each city).

By Car

You can rent a car most easily at Tours' St. Pierre-des-Corps train station, or in Amboise (see page 363). I've listed specific driving instructions for each destination covered in this chapter.

The Loire Valley's Cuisine Scene

Here in "the garden of France," locally produced food is delicious. Loire Valley rivers yield fresh trout (*truite*), salmon (*saumon*), and smelt (*éperlan*), which are often served fried (*friture*). *Rillettes*, a stringy pile of cooked and whipped pork, makes for a cheap, mouthwatering sandwich spread (use lots of mustard and add a baby pickle, called a *cornichon*). The area's wonderful goat cheeses include Crottin de Chavignol (*crottin* means horse dung, which is what this cheese, when aged, resembles), Saint-Maure Fermier (soft and creamy), and Selles-sur-Cher (mild). For dessert, try a delicious *tarte tatin* (upside-down caramel-apple tart).

The best and most expensive white wines are the Sancerres, made on the less-touristed western edge of the Loire. Less expensive, but still tasty, are Touraine Sauvignons and the sweeter Vouvray, whose grapes are grown near Amboise. Vouvray is also famous for its light and refreshing sparkling wines (called *vins pétillants*)—locals will tell you the only proper way to begin any meal in this region is with a glass of it, and I can't disagree (try the *rosé pétillant* for a fresh sensation). The better reds come from Chinon and Bourgueil.

Remember, restaurants serve food only during lunch (11:30–14:00) and dinner (19:00–21:00, later in bigger cities); bigger cafés offer eats throughout the day.

East of Tours

Amboise

Straddling the widest stretch of the Loire River, Amboise slumbers in the shadow of its hilltop château. A castle has overlooked the Loire from Amboise since Roman times. Leonardo da Vinci retired here...just one more of his many brilliant ideas. Amboise's sister city in Italy is named Vinci. Perfect.

As the royal residence of François I (r. 1515–1547), Amboise wielded far more importance than you'd imagine from a lazy walk through its pleasant, pedestrian-only commercial zone. In fact, its 14,000 residents are quite conservative, giving the town an attitude—as if no one told them they're no longer the second capital of France. The locals keep their wealth to themselves;

consequently, many grand mansions hide behind nondescript facades. There's even a Royalist element in Amboise (and the duke of Paris, the guy who'd be king if there was one, lives here).

The half-mile-long "Golden Island" is the only island in the Loire substantial enough to be flood-proof and to have permanent buildings (including a soccer stadium and a 13th-century church). It was important historically as the place where northern and southern France, divided by the longest river in the country, came together. Truces were made here. The Loire marked the farthest point north that the Moors conquered as they pushed through Europe from Morocco. (Loire means "impassable" in Arabic.) Today, this region still divides the country—for example, weather forecasters say, "north of the Loire...and south of the Loire..."

With or without a car, Amboise is an ideal small-town home base for exploring the best of château country.

Orientation to Amboise

Amboise (pop. 14,000) covers ground on both sides of the Loire, with the "Golden Island" (l'Île d'Or) in the middle. The train station is on the north side of the Loire, but nearly everything else is on the south (château) side, including the TI and steady traffic. Pedestrian-friendly rue Nationale parallels the river a few blocks inland and leads from the base of Château d'Amboise through the town center and past the clock tower—once part of the town wall—to the striking Romanesque Church of St. Denis. Drivers and pedestrians should use caution: Traffic crossing or entering Amboise's main riverfront drag from side streets has the right-of-way.

Tourist Information

The information-packed TI moves to a new location on quai du Général de Gaulle in 2011 (May-Sept Mon-Sat 9:30-18:30, Sun 9:30-13:00 & 14:00-17:00; Oct-April Mon-Sat 10:00-13:00 & 14:00-18:00, Sun 10:00-13:00; tel. 02 47 57 09 28, www.amboise-valdeloire.com). Pick up the brochure with a self-guided walking tour in and around the city, and consider prepurchasing tickets to key area châteaux (saving time in ticket lines—explained under "Helpful Hints," later). Ask about sound-and-light shows in the region (generally summers only). The TI stores bags (€2.50/piece), books local guides, and can reserve a room for you in a hotel or chambre d'hôte (for a €2.50 fee), but first peruse the photo album of regional chambres d'hôtes. Their free English-speaking service, SOS Chambres d'Hôtes, can tell you which rooms are still available when the TI is closed (tel. 02 47 23 27 42).

Amboise

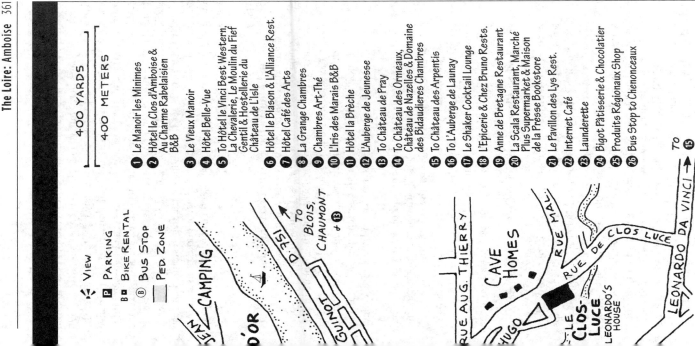

400 YARDS

400 METERS

1 Le Manoir les Minimes
2 Hôtel le Clos d'Amboise & Au Charme Rabelaisien B&B
3 Le Vieux Manoir
4 Hôtel Belle-Vue
5 To Hôtel le Vinci Best Western, La Chevalerie, Le Moulin du Fief Gentil & Hostellerie du Château de l'Isle
6 Hôtel le Blason & L'Alliance Rest.
7 Hôtel Café des Arts
8 La Grange Chambres
9 Chambres Art-Thé
10 L'Iris des Marais B&B
11 Hôtel la Brèche
12 L'Auberge de Jeunesse
13 To Château de Pray
14 To Château des Ormeaux, Château de Nazelles & Domaine des Bidaudieres Chambres
15 To Château des Arpentis
16 To L'Auberge de Launay
17 Le Shaker Cocktail Lounge
18 L'Epicerie & Chez Bruno Rests.
19 Anne de Bretagne Restaurant
20 La Scala Restaurant, Marché Plus Supermarket & Maison de la Presse Bookstore
21 Le Pavillon des Lys Rest.
22 Internet Café
23 Launderette
24 Bigot Pâtisserie & Chocolatier
25 Produits Régionaux Shop
26 Bus Stop to Chenonceaux

⚲ View
P Parking
B■ Bike Rental
Ⓑ Bus Stop
‖ Ped Zone

Arrival in Amboise

By Train: Amboise's train station is birds-chirping peaceful. You can't store bags here, but you can leave them at the TI (see 359). Turn left out of the main station (you may have to cross under the tracks first), make a quick right, and walk down rue Jules Ferry five minutes to the end, then turn right and cross the l-o-o-ong bridge leading over the Loire River to the city center. It's a €6 taxi ride from the station to central Amboise, but taxis seldom wait at the station (taxi tel. 02 47 57 13 53 or 02 47 57 30 39).

By Car: Drivers set their sights on the flag-festooned château that caps the hill. Most recommended accommodations and restaurants cluster just downriver (west) and either have or can help you locate free parking.

Helpful Hints

Save Time and Money: The TI sells tickets to many area sights and châteaux around Amboise and Chinon that are bundled in groups of three (called "le Pass"). This will save you some on entry fees—and, more importantly, time spent in line at each sight (for example, Clos-Lucé and the châteaux of Amboise and Chenonceau for €29, saving €3 over buying tickets individually). You can also get cheaper tickets if you take a minivan tour (see "Getting Around the Loire Valley" on page 352).

Market Days: Open-air markets are held on Friday (smaller but more local, food only) and Sunday (the big one) in the parking lot behind the TI on the river (both 8:30–13:00).

Regional Products: Produits Régionaux, at 29 rue Nationale, sells fine food products from the Loire (daily 9:30–19:00).

Supermarket: Marché Plus is near the TI (Mon–Sat 7:00–21:00, Sun 9:00–13:00), though the shops on pedestrian-only rue Nationale are infinitely more pleasing.

Internet Access: Playconnect Cyber C@fe has good rates and long hours (119 rue Nationale, tel. 02 47 57 18 04).

Bookstore: Maison de la Presse is a good bookstore with a small selection of English novels and a big selection of maps and English guidebooks—such as Michelin's Green Guide *Châteaux of the Loire* (English version costs €16; bookstore open Mon 14:00–19:00, Tue–Sat 8:00–19:00, Sun 9:00–13:00, across from the TI at 5 quai du Général de Gaulle).

Laundry: The handy coin-op **Lav'centre** is near the TI, up allée du Sergent Turpin at #9 (allow €7/load, daily 7:00–20:00, last wash at 19:00, English instructions). The door locks at closing time; leave beforehand, or you'll trigger the alarm.

Bike Rental: You can rent a bike (roughly €11/half-day, €14/day, leave your passport or a photocopy) at either of these reliable places: **Locacycle** (daily 9:00–12:30 & 14:00–19:00, full-day rentals can be returned the next morning, 2 rue Jean-Jacques Rousseau, tel. 02 47 57 00 28) or **Cycles le Duc** (good bikes, Tue–Sat 9:00–12:00 & 14:30–19:00, closed Sun–Mon, 5 rue Joyeuse, tel. 02 47 57 00 17). The signed bike route to Chenonceaux leads past Leonardo's Clos-Lucé.

Taxi: Call 02 47 57 13 53 or 02 47 57 30 39 (allow €25 to Chenonceaux, €35 in the evening or on Sun).

Car Rental: You can rent cars at the St. Pierre-des-Corps train station (TGV service from Paris), a 15-minute drive from Amboise. On the outskirts of Amboise, **Garage Jourdain** rents cars (roughly €48/day for a small car with 100 kilometers/62 miles free, Mon–Fri 7:45–12:00 & 14:00–18:00, Sat 9:00–12:00 & 14:00–17:00, closed Sun, about a mile downriver from the TI at 105 avenue de Tours, tel. 02 47 57 17 92, fax 02 47 57 77 50). Pricier **Europcar** is outside Amboise on route de Chenonceaux (about €65/day for a small car, tel. 02 47 57 07 64, fax 02 47 23 25 14, www.europcar.com). Figure €7 for a taxi from Amboise to either place.

Chocolate Fantasy: An essential and historic stop for chocoholics is **Bigot Pâtisserie & Chocolatier** (daily, one block off the river, where place Michel Debré meets rue Nationale, tel. 02 47 57 04 46).

Tours: At **Loire Uncorked,** British expats Tom and Amanda want to share their love of local wines with other anglophiles. Their tour includes lunch and wine tastings (€145/person, flexible itineraries, tel. 02 47 59 12 61, www.loireuncorked.com).

Sights in Amboise

▲**Château du Clos-Lucé and Leonardo da Vinci Park**—In 1516, Leonardo da Vinci packed his bags (and several of his

favorite paintings, including the *Mona Lisa*) and left an imploding Rome for better wine and working conditions here, in the Loire Valley. He accepted the position of engineer, architect, and painter to the French king. This "House of Light" is the plush palace where he spent his last three years. (He died May 2, 1519.) France's Renaissance king, François I, set Leonardo up here just so he could enjoy his intellectual company. François I was 22 when his 65-year-old mentor moved in.

Cost and Hours: The €12.50 entry price is steep, and worthwhile only for Leonardo fans with two hours to take full advantage of this sight (€3 cheaper Nov–March, €7 for kids and students); daily April–Oct 9:00–19:00, Nov–Dec and Feb–March 9:00–18:00, Jan 9:00–17:00, follow the helpful free English handout, tel. 02 47 57 00 73, www.vinci-closluce.com.

Getting There: It's a 10-minute walk uphill from Château d'Amboise, past troglodyte homes. If you drive, note that the parking lot near Clos-Lucé is unsafe—don't leave anything visible in the car.

Visiting the Château and Gardens: Your visit begins with a tour of Leonardo's elegant yet livable Renaissance home. Find the touching sketch in Leonardo's bedroom of François I comforting his genius pal on his deathbed, and see copies of Leonardo's most famous paintings (including the *Mona Lisa*). The house was built in 1450—just within the protective walls of the town—as a guest house to the Château d'Amboise. Today it thoughtfully re-creates (with a good English brochure and Renaissance music) the everyday atmosphere Leonardo enjoyed while he lived here—pursuing his passions to the very end.

The basement floor is filled with sketches recording the storm patterns of Leonardo's brain and models of his remarkable inventions (inspired by nature and built according to his notes). It's hard to imagine that this Roman candle of creativity died nearly 500 years ago. Notice the steps leading down to the long tunnel that connected this house with the château—created so the king could come and go as he pleased. The adjacent garden café is reasonable and appropriately meditative.

Your visit finishes with a stroll through the whimsical park grounds, with life-size models of Leonardo's inventions (including some that function, such as a "revolving bridge"), "sound stations" (in English), and translucent replicas of some of his paintings. Here it's clear that everything Leonardo observed and created was based on his intense study of nature.

▲**Château d'Amboise**—This historic royal residence was partially designed by Leonardo da Vinci. The king who did most of the building (Charles VIII) is famous for accidentally killing himself by walking into a doorjamb on his way to a tennis match (seriously). Later occupants were shorter—including his successor, Louis XII, who moved the royal court to Blois. François I brought

the Renaissance here in 1516 (through Leonardo da Vinci). Though several rooms are well-decorated, no one room stands out as exceptionally furnished or compelling, and this place pales when compared to other area châteaus. Still, it's close and offers terrific views over Amboise that alone almost merit the entry fee.

Cost and Hours: €10, daily April–June 9:00–18:30, July–Aug 9:00–19:00, Sept–Oct and March 9:00–18:00, Nov–Jan 9:00–12:00 & 14:00–16:45, Feb 9:00–12:00 & 13:30–17:30, tel. 02 47 57 00 98, www.chateau-amboise.com.

Visiting the Château: Pick up the good English handout, which provides a helpful historical perspective for the three floors you'll visit.

After climbing the long ramp, our first stop is the lacy, petite chapel where Leonardo da Vinci supposedly is buried. This flamboyant little Gothic chapel comes with two fireplaces "to comfort the king" and two plaques "evoking the final resting place" of Leonardo (one in French, the other in Italian). Where he's actually buried, no one seems to know. Look up at the ceiling to appreciate the lacy design.

Rooftop views escort you to the castle entry. Inside, you'll tour rooms lined with high-backed chairs and massive stone fireplaces. Look in the Salle des Gardes for plans showing the château's original size, and appreciate delicate columns in the gothic Salle de Conseil.

The rose-colored top-floor rooms are well-furnished from the post-Revolutionary 1800s and demonstrate the continued interest in this château among French nobility. What a difference in comfort a few hundred years make.

Climb to the top of the Minimes Tower for grand views. From here the strategic value of this site is clear: The visibility is great and the river below provided a natural defense. The bulky tower climbs 130 feet in five spirals—designed for a mounted soldier in a hurry.

Your visit ends in the gardens, where you'll find more good views of the château and river.

▲**Château d'Amboise Sound-and-Light Show**—If you're into S&L, this is considered one of the best shows of its kind in the area. Although it's entirely in French, you can buy the English booklet for €5. Volunteer locals from toddlers to pensioners recreate the life of François I with costumes, juggling, impressive light displays, and fireworks. Dress warmly, and be prepared for a long show (€15–22, Wed and Sat late June–July 22:30–24:00, Aug 22:00–23:30, get details at TI or call 02 47 57 14 47, www.renaissance-amboise.com). The ticket window is on the ramp to the château and opens at 20:30. And though you may feel locked in, you're welcome to leave at any time.

Mini-Châteaux—This scruffy five-acre park on the edge of Amboise (on the route to Chenonceaux) shows the major Loire châteaux in 1:25-scale models, forested with 2,000 bonsai trees and laced together by a model TGV train and river boats. For children, it's a fun introduction to the real châteaux they'll be visiting (and a cool toy store). Essential English information is posted throughout the sight (adults-€14, kids-€10, daily June-Aug 10:00-19:00, Sept-Oct 10:00-18:00, April-May 10:30-19:00, closed Nov-March, last entry one hour before closing, tel. 02 47 23 44 44, www.mini-chateaux.com).

You'll find other kid-oriented attractions at Mini-Châteaux; skip the donkey show, but consider playing a round of mini-golf and feeding the fish in the moat (a great way to get rid of that old baguette).

Caveau des Vignerons—This small *cave* offers free tastings of cheeses and regional wines from 12 different vintners (mid-March-mid-Nov daily 10:00-19:00; under Château d'Amboise, across from recommended l'Epicerie restaurant; tel. 02 47 57 23 69).

Biking from Amboise—Allow an hour to Chenonceaux (about 8 miles one-way). The first two miles are uphill, and the entire ride is on a road with light traffic. White-and-green biking signs will guide you past Clos-Lucé to Chenonceaux. Serious cyclists can ride to Chaumont (see page 389) in 1.5 hours, connecting Amboise, Chenonceaux, and Chaumont in an all-day, 37-mile pedal (see "Recommended Bike Route" on the map on page 376).

Canoe Trips from Amboise or Chenonceau—Paddling under the Château de Chenonceau is a memorable experience. **Canoe Company** offers canoe rentals on the Loire and Cher rivers (€12-22/person depending on how far you go, tel. 06 70 13 30 61, www.canoe-company.fr).

Near Amboise

Wine-Tasting in Vouvray—In the nearby town of Vouvray, 10 miles toward Tours from Amboise, you'll find wall-to-wall opportunities for wine-tasting, including a convenient, top-quality winery, **Marc Brédif.** They have a good selection of Vouvray wines, as well as red wines from Chinon and Bourgueil (the most reputed reds in the Loire). Reserve ahead for their wine and cheese tastings, where five wines are paired with different cheeses. You can also take a €5 tour of their impressive 1.2 miles of cellars dug into the hillside (free tasting room, Mon-Fri 9:00-12:00 & 14:00-18:00, Sat 10:30-12:00 & 13:00-18:00, Sun 10:30-13:00, tel. 02 47 52 61 44). Coming from Amboise, you'll pass it on D-952 after Vouvray in the direction of Tours; it's on the right, a few hundred yards after you enter Rochecorbon. (For tips on wine-tasting, see "French Wine-Tasting 101" on page 40.)

ZooParc de Beauval—If you need a zoo fix, this is France's biggest and most impressive one, with thousands of animals from the land and sea. It's about 30 minutes southeast of Amboise toward Vierzon—pick up details at the TI (adults-€20, kids-€14, daily from 9:00 to dusk, tel. 02 54 75 50 00, www.zoobeauval.com).

Sleeping in Amboise

Amboise is busy in the summer, but there are lots of reasonable hotels and *chambres d'hôtes* in and around the city; the TI can help with reservations (for a €2.50 fee).

In the Center

$$$ Le Manoir les Minimes**** is a good place to experience the refined air of château life in a 17th-century mansion, with antique furniture and precious art objects in the public spaces. Its 15 large, modern rooms work for those seeking luxury digs in Amboise (tall folks take note: top-floor attic rooms have low ceilings). Several rooms have views of Amboise's château (standard Db-€125-140, larger Db-€175-190, suite-€270, 3- to 4-person suites-€460, extra bed-€25, air-con, Wi-Fi, 3 blocks upriver from bridge at 34 quai Charles Guinot, tel. 02 47 30 40 40, fax 02 47 30 40 77, www.manoirlesminimes.com, reservation@manoirlesminimes.com, helpful Patrice and Eric).

$$$ Hôtel le Clos d'Amboise*** is a solid value if you want good comfort without the financial hit. This smart, upper-range urban refuge opens onto beautiful gardens and a small pool, and offers well-designed rooms that mix a touch of modern with a classic, traditional look (standard Db-€90–100, bigger Db-€120–140, Db suites-€145–175, Tb-€145, extra person-€20, good buffet breakfast-€12, funky air-con, Wi-Fi, fitness room, sauna, 27 rue Rabelais, tel. 02 47 30 10 20, fax 02 47 57 33 43, www.leclos amboise.com, contact@leclosamboise.com, helpful Patricia is ever-present).

$$$ Le Vieux Manoir* is an entirely different high-end splurge. American expats Gloria and Bob Belknap have restored this secluded but central one-time convent with an attention to detail that Martha Stewart could learn from. The gardens are lovely, as are the atrium-like breakfast room, sitting lounge, and six bedrooms that would make an antique collector drool. Eager-to-help Gloria

is a one-person tourist office (Db-€140–185, cottages-€215–305 and require 3-night minimum stay, includes hearty breakfast, non-smoking, air-con, Internet access and Wi-Fi, free parking, 13 rue Rabelais, tel. & fax 02 47 30 41 27, www.le-vieux-manoir.com, info@le-vieux-manoir.com).

$$ Hôtel Belle-Vue* is a centrally located and traditional place overlooking the river where the bridge hits the town. Rooms are comfortable and well-appointed; many have views up to the château and are quieter (Db-€68–78, Tb-€88, two-room Tb-€98, two-room Qb-€125, elevator, Wi-Fi in lobby, 12 quai Charles Guinot, tel. 02 47 57 02 26, fax 02 47 30 51 23, bellevuehotel .amboise@wanadoo.fr).

$$ Hôtel le Vinci Best Western* is well-run and modern, providing solid midrange comfort a mile from the town center toward Chenonceaux (standard Db-€79–86, superior Db-€96, extra person-€20, 12 avenue Emile Gounin, tel. 02 47 57 10 90, fax 02 47 57 17 52, www.vinciloirevalley.com, reservation@vinciloire valley.com).

$ Hôtel le Blason* has 25 rooms in a 15th-century, half-timbered building five blocks from the river on a busy street. It's run by helpful Damien and Beranger, who speak English. The rooms—some with ship-cabin-like bathrooms—are tight and bright, and have double-paned windows. There's air-conditioning on the top floor (Sb-€50, Db-€60, Tb-€70, Qb-€80, quieter rooms in back and on top floor, free Internet access and Wi-Fi, secure parking-€3, 11 place Richelieu, tel. 02 47 23 22 41, fax 02 47 57 56 18, www .leblason.fr, hotel@leblason.fr).

$ Café des Arts feels more like a hostel, with seven spartan rooms lodged above a local bar/café next to the château. It's best to call, as email isn't their forte (S-€27, D-€40, T-€52, 32 rue Victor Hugo, tel. & fax 02 47 57 25 04, www.cafedesarts.net, cafedesarts @free.fr).

Chambres d'Hôtes

The heart of Amboise offers several solid bed-and-breakfast options.

$$$ Au Charme Rabelaisien is a drop-dead-gorgeous place run by drop-dead-charming Madame Viard. Big doors from the street open onto a grand courtyard with manicured gardens, a heated pool, and three sumptuous rooms surrounding it (small Db-€92, roomy Db-€150-170, €20 for third person—child only, includes breakfast, air-con, Wi-Fi, private parking, 25 rue Rabelais, tel. 02 47 57 53 84, fax 02 47 57 53 84, www.au-charme-rabelaisien .com, aucharmerabelaisien@wanadoo.fr).

$$ La Grange Chambres welcomes with an intimate, flowery courtyard. Each of the four comfortable rooms has been tastefully restored with modern conveniences and big beds. There's also a common room with a fridge, a couch, and tables for do-it-yourself dinners (Db-€82, Tb-€82-90, Qb-€95-100, includes breakfast, cash only, where rues Châptal and Rabelais meet at 18 rue Châptal, tel. 02 47 57 57 22, www.la-grange-amboise.com, info@la-grange -amboise.com). Adorable Yveline Savin also rents a small two-room cottage (€430-550/week, 2- to 3-day stays possible).

$$ At Chambres Art-Thé, three simple but reasonably priced and well-situated rooms hide above a small *salon de thé* next to the château (Db-€65, Tb-€75, bigger rooms-€110-130, includes breakfast, 8 place Michel Debré, tel. 02 47 30 54 00, mobile 06 30 10 50 71, aude.art-the@hotmail.fr).

$ L'Iris des Marais, run by animated Katia Frain, offers two family-oriented *chambres* in a fun, ramshackle building on a busy road. The rooms are modest and a good value, and the artsy garden will make you smile. The upstairs room provides basic comfort; the garden accommodation is cushier and worth booking early (Db-€50-60, cash only, includes a good breakfast, 14 quai des Marais, tel. 02 47 30 46 51, www.irisdesmarais.com, vianney.frain @wanadoo.fr).

Near the Train Station

$$ Hôtel la Brèche*, a sleepy place near the station, has 14 good-value rooms, some with small bathrooms, and a good restaurant. Many rooms overlook the peaceful graveled garden; those on the street are generally larger and louder (Sb-€52, Db-€65, Tb-€76, Qb-€92, room for up to five-€100, breakfast-€7, free Wi-Fi,

15-minute walk from city center and 2-minute walk from station, 26 rue Jules Ferry, tel. 02 47 57 00 79, fax 02 47 57 65 49, www.labreche-amboise.com, info@labreche-amboise.com).

Hostel: $ L'Auberge de Jeunesse (Centre Charles Péguy) is ideally located on the western tip of the "Golden Island," a 10-minute walk from the train station. Open to people of all ages, and popular with student groups, it's friendly and easy on the wallet. There are a handful of double rooms—some with partial views to the château—so book ahead (D–€26, bunk in 3- to 4-bed room–€13, sheets–€3, no surcharge for non-members, breakfast–€4.50, dinner–€10, reception open daily 15:00–20:00, no curfew, Ile d'Or, tel. 02 47 30 60 90, fax 02 47 30 60 91, www.mjcamboise.fr, cis@mjcamboise.fr).

Sleeping near Amboise

The area around Amboise is replete with good-value accommodations of every shape, size, and price range. This region offers drivers the best chance to experience château life at affordable rates—and my recommendations justify the detour. Also consider the recommended accommodations in Chenonceaux and the Hôtel du Grand St. Michel at Chambord.

Within 10 Minutes of Amboise

$$$ Château de Pray**** is a 750-year-old fortified castle with hints of its medieval origins revealed beneath its Renaissance elegance. The 14 rooms in the main château come with appropriately heavy furniture, lots of character, and tubs in most bathrooms. A newer annex offers four contemporary rooms (sleeping up to three each), with lofts, terraces, and cool views of the castle. An overflowing

pool and the restaurant's vegetable garden lie below the château (small Db in main building–€150–200, Db in annex–€145, family room–€250, extra bed–€40, breakfast–€15, no air-con, 3-minute drive upriver from Amboise toward Chaumont on D-751, tel. 02 47 57 23 67, fax 02 47 57 32 50, http://praycastel.online.fr, praycastel@online.fr). The dining room is splendid and the service is tops—it's a relaxing place to splurge and feel good about it (four-course menus from €54, reservations required).

$$$ Châteaux des Ormeaux Chambres d'Hôte is run by attentive owners, and rents four plush rooms in a lovingly restored

19th-century château and two nice rooms in outbuildings. The place has a pool and a grand terrace overlooking the forest (Db-€120–170, includes breakfast, Wi-Fi, across the river from Amboise in Nazelles, Route de Noizay, tel. 02 47 23 26 51, fax 02 47 23 19 31, www.chateaudesormeaux.fr, contact@chateaudesormeaux.fr).

$$$ At **Château de Nazelles Chambres,** gentle owners Veronique and Olivier Fructus offer five rooms in a 16th-century hillside manor house that was once home to Chenonceau's original builder. It comes with a cliff-sculpted pool, manicured gardens, a guest's kitchen (picnics are encouraged), views over Amboise, trails to the forest above, and a classy living room with billiards, computer access, and Wi-Fi. The two bedrooms in the main building are just grand, while the rooms cut into the rock come with private grass terraces and rock-walled bathrooms (Db-€110, bigger Db-€145, includes breakfast, tel. & fax 02 47 30 53 79, www .chateau-nazelles.com, info@chateau-nazelles.com). From Amboise, take D-952 toward Tours, turn right on D-5, and then turn left in Nazelles-Négron on D-1. Quickly veer right above the post office (PTT) to 16 rue Tue-la-Soif. Look for the sign on your left, and enter through the archway on the right.

$$$ **Château des Arpentis***, a medieval château-hotel centrally located just minutes from Amboise, makes a fun splurge. Flanked by woods and acres of grass, and fronted by a stream and a moat, you'll come as close as you can to château life during the Loire's golden age. Rooms are big, with Old World decor—some have incredible wood ceilings—and the pool is even bigger (Db-€115–165, family suites-€180–370, air-con, Wi-Fi, near the village of Saint-Règle, tel. 02 47 23 00 00, fax 02 47 52 62 17, www.chateau desarpentis.com, contact@chateaudesarpentis.com).

$$ **L'Auberge de Launay,** five miles upriver from Amboise, gets rave reviews for its easy driving access to many châteaux, its warm welcome, and its cozy restaurant. Owners François and Hélène are natural hosts at this very comfortable 15-room hotel and restaurant (roadside Db-€63, garden-side Db-€69–75, Wi-Fi, about 4 miles from Amboise, across the river toward Blois, at 9 rue de la Rivière in Limeray; tel. 02 47 30 16 82, www.aubergede launay.com, info@aubergedelaunay.com). The star of this place is the country-elegant restaurant, with *menus* from €25 (closed Sun).

$ **La Chevalerie** owner Martine Martine Aleksic rents four simple bargain *chambres* that are family-friendly in every way. You'll get a warm reception and total seclusion in a farm setting, with a swing set, tiny fishing pond, shared kitchens, and connecting rooms (Sb-€40, Db-€50, Tb-€60, Qb-€76, includes breakfast with fresh eggs, cash only, in La Croix-en-Touraine, tel. 02 47 57 83 64, lyoubisa .aleksic@orange.fr). From Amboise, take D-31 toward Bléré, look for the *Chambres d'Hôte* sign on your left at about three miles, and then turn left onto C-105.

Within 20 Minutes of Amboise

$$$ Domaine des Bidaudieres Chambres, just outside Vouvray, offers eight rooms in a gleaming 18th-century château overlooking a large pool, with a pond and the forest beyond. This kid-friendly place, with room to roam, features big air-conditioned rooms. There's also ping-pong, a fitness room, and an elevator (Db-€135, Tb-€155, two-room troglodyte apartment that sleeps up to five-€170, small cottage ideal for four-€150, includes breakfast in a striking atrium, tel. 02 47 52 66 85, fax 02 47 52 62 17, www.bidaudieres.com, contact@bidaudieres.com). It's located off D-46 on the Amboise end of Vouvray—from D-952 at Vouvray, follow D-142, then D-46 toward Vernou.

$$ Le Moulin du Fief Gentil is a lovely 16th-century mill house set on four acres. Amenities include a backyard pond (fishing possible in summer, dinner picnics anytime), the possibility of home-cooked dinners by formal owner Fleurance (four-course dinner *menu* with wine-€29), and large, smartly decorated rooms (twin Db-€82, bigger Db-€100, 2-room apartment-€135, extra person-€22, includes breakfast, cash only, tel. 02 47 30 32 51, mobile 06 64 82 37 18, www.fiefgentil.com, contact@fiefgentil.com). It's located on the edge of Bléré, a 15-minute drive from Amboise and Chenonceaux—from Bléré, follow signs toward *Luzille*, and it's on the right.

$$ Hostellerie du Château de L'Isle feels like you've stepped into an Impressionist painting. Here, faded Old World comfort comes wrapped in a lush park on the Cher River with a pond and acres of grass. Located in Civray-de Touraine, just 15 minutes south of Amboise and two minutes from Chenonceaux (from the center of Civray-de Touraine, follow D-81 toward Tours), it offers 12 sufficiently comfortable rooms (standard Db-€70, big Db-€85-105, tel. 02 47 23 63 60, www.chateau-de-lisle.com, chateau delisle@wanadoo.fr). The gazebo-like restaurant, as lovely as a Monet painting, features the owner's cooking (€26-36, limited choices).

Eating in Amboise

Amboise is filled with inexpensive and forgettable restaurants, but a handful of places are worth your attention. Many local eateries offer a good, end-of-meal cheese platter—a rarity in France these days. The epicenter of the city's dining action is along rue Victor Hugo and across from the château entrance. After dinner, make sure to cross the bridge for floodlit views of the castle, and consider a view drink at **Le Shaker Cocktail Lounge** (daily from 18:00 until later than you're awake, 3 quai François Tissard).

L'Epicerie, across from the château entry, attracts a few locals and many hungry tourists. It serves tasty traditional cuisine at fair prices outdoors facing the château, or inside beneath wood beams (*menus* from €22, July–Sept daily, Oct–June closed Mon–Tue, reserve ahead, 46 place Michel Debré, tel. 02 47 57 08 94).

Anne de Bretagne is an appealing brasserie, offering well-prepared and classic-but-simple dishes (such as crudités, crêpes, omelets, and French onion soup) at good prices. It's well-run by gregarious Patricia and Patrick. The outdoor tables are perfect for surveying the street scene, and the indoor tables come with cozy decor (nonstop service daily 12:00–22:00, place du Château, tel. 02 47 57 05 46).

Chez Bruno is a basic budget place with a focus on wine, where you can dine inside or out, across from the château. The food is average, but the prices are good. Come for a pre-dinner glass of wine (good prices and selection)—some made by the owners (€6 starters, €8–10 *plats*, closed Sun–Mon, 40 place Michel Debré, tel. 02 47 57 73 49).

La Scala is a low-stress, low-cost, happy-go-lucky Italian bistro with friendly service, a lively interior, and ample sidewalk seating (€10 pizza and pasta dishes, non-stop service daily 12:00–22:00, across from the TI at 6 quai du Général de Gaulle, tel. 02 47 23 09 93).

L'Alliance is a handsome restaurant run by a young couple (Pamela and Ludovica) trying to make their mark in Amboise. You'll dine well on creatively prepared regional specialties in a calming outdoor "greenhouse," or inside with more formal decor. Service can be slow (*menus* from €21–40, closed Wed, next to the Hôtel le Blason at 14 rue Joyeuse, tel. 02 47 30 52 13).

Le Pavillon des Lys is where locals go for a dressy meal and formal service at nearly affordable prices. Enjoy a drink on the terrace or in the candlelit lounge, before sitting down to a formal dinner in an intimate, elegant setting (*menus* from €40, closed Tue and late Nov–Jan, reserve ahead, 9 rue d'Orange, tel. 02 47 30 01 01, www.pavillondeslys.com).

Near Amboise

These places—also recommended for their accommodations—merit the short drive. It's best to call ahead to reserve. For a royal experience, consider making the quick drive to **Château de Pray** (see page 370). For a warm welcome and good cuisine, call to find out if Hélène can take you at **L'Auberge de Launay** (page 371), or if Laurent has a table available at **Hôtel la Roserie** in nearby Chenonceaux (page 379).

Amboise Connections

By Bus and Taxi

From Amboise to Nearby Châteaux: For easiest access to area châteaux, see "Getting Around the Loire Valley" on page 352.

By Bus to: Chenonceaux (1–2/day, Mon–Sat only, none on Sun, 20 minutes, one-way–€1.10; departs Amboise about 9:50, returns from Chenonceaux about 12:25, allowing you about an hour and 20 minutes at the château; in summer, there's also an afternoon departure at about 14:55, with a return from Chenonceaux at about 17:10; the Amboise stop is on quai du Général de Gaulle on the non-river side of the street opposite the post office—look for the green-and-yellow sign at bus stop, confirm times with the TI; the Chenonceaux stop is across the street from the TI, tel. 02 47 05 30 49); **Tours** (8/day Mon–Sat, none on Sun, buses are cheaper than trains—about €2.50).

By Shuttle Van: Quart de Tours runs five round-trips per day (summers only) between Amboise and Chenonceaux (€15 round-trip, €10 one-way, includes €2.50 discount for château, 15-minute trip, book ahead as seats are limited, tel. 06 69 12 24 55). As this service is new, check with the Amboise TI for details and pick-up locations.

By Taxi: Most châteaux are too expensive by cab, but a taxi from Amboise to Chenonceaux costs about €25 (€35 on Sundays and after 19:00, tel. 02 47 57 13 53 or 02 47 57 30 39). The meter doesn't start until you do.

By Train

Destinations Within the Loire

From Amboise by Train to: Chenonceaux (trains are a workable, if slower, option than the bus; 8/day, 1 hour, transfer at St. Pierre-des-Corps), **Blois** (14/day, 20 minutes, bus or taxi excursions from there to Chambord and Cheverny—see "Getting Around the Loire Valley" on page 352), **Tours** (12/day, 25 minutes, allows connections to châteaux west of Tours), **Chinon** (9/day, 1.5 hours, transfer in Tours).

Beyond the Loire

Twelve 15-minute trains link Amboise daily to the regional train hub of St. Pierre-des-Corps (in suburban Tours). There you'll find reasonable connections to distant points (including the TGV to Paris' Gare Montparnasse). Transferring in Paris can be the fastest way to reach many French destinations, even in the south.

From Amboise by Train to: Paris (12/day, 1.5 hours to Paris' Gare Montparnasse with change to TGV at St. Pierre-des-Corps, requires TGV reservation; 6/day, 2 hours direct to Paris' Gare d'Austerlitz, no reservation required; more to Gare d'Austerlitz or Paris RER stations with same travel time and transfers in Blois or Les Aubrais–Orléans), **Sarlat** (4/day, 5–6 hours, several routes possible, best is to change at St. Pierre-des-Corps, then TGV to Libourne or Bordeaux–St. Jean, then train through Bordeaux vineyards to Sarlat; it's a bit slower on the route via Les Aubrais–Orléans to Souillac then scenic SNCF bus to Sarlat), **Limoges** (near Oradour-sur-Glane, 9/day, 4 hours, change at St. Pierre-des-Corps and Vierzon or at Les Aubrais–Orléans and Vierzon, then tricky bus connection from Limoges to Oradour-sur-Glane—see page 456), **Pontorson–Mont St. Michel** (2–3/day, 5.5–7.5 hours by transfers at Caen and Tours or Rennes, Le Mans, and Tours), **Bayeux** (12/day, 4 hours by handy train via St. Pierre-des-Corps and Caen, otherwise 6 hours via St. Pierre-des-Corps and Paris's Gare Montparnasse), **Beaune** (2/day, 5 hours, transfer in Dijon; plus 12/day, 6 hours, with changes in Paris and in Dijon—arrive at Paris' Gare d'Austerlitz or Gare Montparnasse, then Métro to Gare de Lyon).

Chenonceaux

This one-road, sleepy village—with a knockout château—makes a good home base for drivers and a workable base for train travelers who don't mind connections. Note that Chenonceaux is the name of the town, and Chenonceau (no "x") is the name of the château, but they're pronounced the same: shuh-nohn-soh.

Orientation to Chenonceaux

The small TI is on the main road as you enter the village (Mon–Sat 10:00–12:30 & 14:00–18:30, closed Sun, tel. 02 47 23 94 45).

The **bus stops** are at the TI; the Amboise-bound stop is unsigned and across the street from the TI (1–2 buses/day to Amboise, Mon–Sat only, none on Sun, 15 minutes).

La Maison des Pages has some bakery items, cold drinks to go, and just enough groceries for a modest picnic (on the main drag between Hostel du Roy and Hôtel la Roseraie). You can rent **bikes** at the recommended Relais Chenonceaux hotel (May–Sept daily 9:00–19:00; see "Sleeping in Chenonceaux," later).

Sights in Chenonceaux

▲▲▲Château de Chenonceau

Chenonceau is the toast of the Loire. This 16th-century Renaissance palace arches gracefully over the Cher River and is impeccably

Châteaux near Amboise

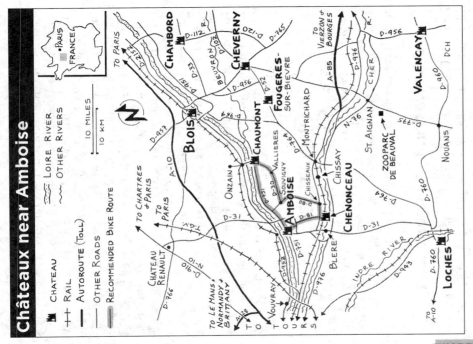

Legend:
- 🏰 CHATEAU
- ╬ RAIL
- ▬ AUTOROUTE (TOLL)
- ━ OTHER ROADS
- ▬ RECOMMENDED BIKE ROUTE
- ～ LOIRE RIVER
- ～ OTHER RIVERS

10 MILES
10 KM

maintained, with fresh flower arrangements in the summer and roaring log fires in the winter. Understandably popular, Chenonceau is the third-most-visited château in France (after Versailles and Fontainebleau)—so carefully follow my crowd-beating tips, next page. Plan on a 15-minute walk from the parking lot to the château. Warning: Because this parking lot is not patrolled, don't leave any luggage visible in your car.

Cost and Hours: Château–€10.50, wax museum–€2, daily mid-March–mid-Sept 9:00–19:00, closes earlier off-season, tel. 02 47 23 90 07, www.chenonceau.com. Consider a moonlit **evening**

walk—*"promenade nocturne"*—on the château grounds (€5, July-Aug daily 21:30–23:30, only Fri-Sun in June, none Sept-May).

Crowd-Beating Tips: Chenonceau's crowds are worth planning around. This place gets slammed in high season, when it's best to come early (by 9:00) or after 17:00. Avoid slow ticket lines by purchasing your ticket in advance (at area TIs) or from the ticket machines (US credit cards work).

Tours: The interior is fascinating—but only if you take full advantage of the free, excellent 20-page **booklet** (included with entry), or rent an audioguide. Two different **iPod video/audio-guide tours** are available (45 and 60 minutes); the 45-minute tour is plenty. There's also a 45-minute audioguide for kids (€4 for any audioguide, leave ID as deposit). Pay for the audioguide when you're buying your ticket (before entering the château grounds), then pick up the iPod just inside the château's door. Or, before you visit, download the tour from www.chenonceau.com to your own iPod or other MP3 player for €3.

Services: WCs are available by the ticket office and behind the wax museum.

Wax Museum, Play Area, and Traditional Farm: The wax museum (La Galerie des Dames–Musée de Cires)—located in the château stables—puts a waxy face on the juicy history of the château (adds €2 to ticket price, tickets only available at the château ticket office). Some information is posted in English. You'll see lots of men in tights and women in fancy gowns from the 16th to 17th centuries, and get your wardrobe bearings from this elegant age. A kids' play area (*Kindergarten*) lies just past the wax museum, and a few steps beyond that you can stroll around a traditional farm and imagine the production needed to sustain the château (free, always open).

Cuisine Art: A reasonable cafeteria is next door to the wax museum. Fancy meals are served in the orangerie behind the stables. There's a cheap *crêperie*/sandwich shop at the entrance gate.

Boat Trips: In summer, the château has rental **rowboats**—an idyllic way to savor graceful château views (€2/30 minutes, July-Aug daily 10:00–19:00, 4 people/boat).

Background: Although earlier châteaux were built for defensive purposes, Chenonceau was the first great pleasure palace. Nicknamed "the château of the ladies," it housed many famous women over the centuries. The original builder's wife oversaw the construction of the main part of the château. In 1547, King Henry II gave the château to his mistress, Diane de Poitiers, who added an arched bridge across the river to access the hunting grounds. She enjoyed her lovely retreat until Henry II died (pierced in a jousting tournament in Paris) and his vengeful wife, Catherine de Médicis, unceremoniously kicked her out (and into the château of

Chaumont, described on page 389). Catherine added the three-story structure on Diane's bridge. She died before completing her vision of a matching château on the far side of the river, but not before turning Chenonceau into *the* place to see and be seen by local aristocracy. (Whenever you see a split coat of arms, it belongs to a woman—half her husband's and half her father's.)

◆ Self-Guided Tour: Strut like an aristocrat down the tree-canopied path to the château. (There's a fun plant maze partway up on the left.) You'll cross three moats and two bridges, and pass an old round tower, which predates the main building. Notice the tower's fine limestone veneer, added so the top would better fit the new château.

The main château's original **oak door** greets you with the coats of arms of the first owners. The knocker is high enough to be used by visitors on horseback. The smaller door within the larger one could be for two purposes: to slip in after curfew, or to enter during winter without letting out all the heat.

Once inside, you'll tour the château in a clockwise direction (turn left upon entering). Take time to appreciate the beautiful brick floor tiles (called *tomettes*) and lavishly decorated ceilings. As you continue, read your pamphlet or listen to your audioguide, and also pay attention to these details:

In the **guard room,** the best-surviving original floor tiles are near the walls—imagine the entire room covered with these tiles. And though the tapestries kept the room cozy, they also functioned to tell news or recent history (to the king's liking, of course). You'll see many more tapestries in this château.

The superbly detailed **chapel** survived the vandalism of the Revolution because the fast-thinking lady of the palace filled it with firewood. Angry masses were supplied with mallets and instructions to smash everything royal or religious. While this room was both, all they saw was stacked wood. The hatch door provided a quick path to the kitchen and an escape boat down-stairs. The windows, blown out during World War II, are replace-ments from the 1950s.

The centerpiece of the **bedroom of Diane de Poitiers** is a severe portrait of her rival, Catherine de Médicis, at 40 years old. After the queen booted out the mistress, she placed her own portrait over the fireplace, but she never used this bedroom. The 16th-century tapestries are among the finest in France. Each one took an average of 60 worker-years to make. Study the complex compositions of the *Triumph of Charity* and the violent *Triumph of Force.*

At 200 feet long, the three-story **Grand Gallery** spans the river. (The upper stories house double-decker ballrooms and art exhibits.) Notice how differently the slate and limestone of the checkered floor wear after 500 years. Imagine grand banquets here. Catherine, a contemporary of Queen Elizabeth I of England, wanted to rule with style. She threw wild parties and employed her ladies to circulate and soak up all the political gossip possible from the well-lubricated Kennedys and Rockefellers of her realm. Parties included grand fireworks displays and mock naval battles on the river.

In summer and during holidays, you can take a quick walk outside for more good palace **views:** Cross the bridge, pick up a re-entry ticket, then stroll the other bank of the Cher (across the river from the château). The river you crossed marked the border between free and Nazi France in World War II. Back then, Chenonceau witnessed many prisoner swaps. During World War I, the Grand Gallery also served as a military hospital, where more than 2,200 soldiers were cared for—picture hundreds of beds lining the gallery.

Double back through the gallery to find the sensational state-of-the-art (in the 16th century) **kitchen** below. It was built near water (to fight the inevitable kitchen fires) and in the basement; because heat rises, the placement helped heat the palace. Cross the small bridge (watch your head) to find the stove and landing bay for goods to be ferried in and out.

The staircase leading **upstairs** wowed royal guests. It was the first nonspiral staircase they'd seen...quite a treat in the 16th century. The balcony provides lovely views of the gardens—originally functional with vegetables and herbs. (Diane built the one to the right, Catherine the one to your left.) The estate is still full of wild boar and deer—the primary dishes of past centuries. You'll see more lavish bedrooms on this floor. Find the small side rooms that show fascinating old architectural sketches of the château. The walls, 20 feet thick, were honeycombed with the flues of 224 fireplaces and passages for servants to do their pleasure-providing work unseen. There was no need for plumbing. Servants fetched, carried, and dumped everything pipes do today. The long room stretching over the river usually contains a temporary modern-art exhibit.

The third floor is worth a peek for its black bedroom, designed by a widow whose husband was murdered by a monk.

Sleeping in Chenonceaux

(€1 = about \$1.25, country code: 33)

Hotels are a good value in Chenonceaux.

\$\$ Hôtel la Roseraie***, lovely as an Impressionist painting, has a flowery terrace and 17 warmly decorated French-country rooms. Laurent and Sophie try their best to spoil you in their

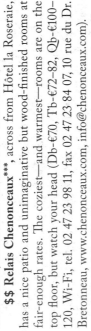

entirely non-smoking hotel (standard Db-€72–85, big Db-€99–129, Tb-€90–129, a few grand family rooms-€140–200, buffet breakfast-€10.50, closed mid-Nov–mid-March, queen- or king-size beds, air-con, Internet access, free Wi-Fi in lobby, free parking, heated pool, across from Hôtel du Bon Laboreur at 7 rue du Dr. Bretonneau, tel. 02 47 23 90 09, fax 02 47 23 91 59, www.hotel-chenonceau.com, info@hotel -chenonceau.com). The traditional dining room and delightful terrace are ideal for a nice dinner, available for guests and non-guests alike. Just be sure to reserve ahead (€29–45 *menus*, open 19:00–21:00, closed Mon and mid-Nov–mid-March).

$$ Relais Chenonceaux***, across from Hôtel la Roseraie, has a nice patio and unimaginative but wood-finished rooms at fair-enough rates. The coziest—and warmest—rooms are on the top floor, but watch your head (Db-€70, Tb-€72–82, Qb-€100–120, Wi-Fi, tel. 02 47 23 98 11, fax 02 47 23 84 07, 10 rue du Dr. Bretonneau, www.chenonceaux.com, info@chenonceaux.com).

$ Hostel du Roy** offers 32 basic budget rooms, some in a quiet garden courtyard, and a mediocre but inexpensive restaurant (Db-€46–60, Tb-€65, one-room Qb-€64, two-room Qb-€98, room for up to five-€110, Wi-Fi, 9 rue du Dr. Bretonneau, tel. 02 47 23 90 17, fax 02 47 23 89 81, www.hostelduroy.com, hosteldu roy@wanadoo.fr).

Eating in Chenonceaux

Reserve ahead to dine at **Hôtel la Roseraie** (closed Mon). **Relais Chenonceaux**, with its pleasant interior and exterior terrace, serves up crêpes, salads, and *plats* at decent prices (daily). Both of these are listed earlier, under "Sleeping in Chenonceaux."

Chenonceaux Connections

From Chenonceaux by Train to: Tours (8/day, 30 minutes), **Amboise** (8/day, 1 hour, transfer at St. Pierre-des-Corps), **Chinon** (8/day, 1.5 hours, transfer in Tours).

By Bus to: Amboise (1–2/day, Mon–Sat only, none on Sun, 20 minutes, one-way-€1.10, departs Chenonceaux at about 12:25, and in summer also at about 17:10, catch bus across the street from the TI, tel. 02 47 05 30 49).

By Shuttle Van: Quart de Tours runs five round-trips per day (summers only) between Chenonceaux and Amboise (see

THE LOIRE

"Amboise Connections" on page 374).

By Taxi to: Amboise (€25, €35 on Sun and after 19:00).

Blois

Bustling Blois (pronounced "blah") feels like a megalopolis after all those rural villages. Blois owns a rich history, dolled-up pedestrian areas, a handsome château, and access to Chambord and Cheverny by excursion bus, taxi, or car (see "Getting Around the Loire Valley" on page 352). Good train service to Paris and Amboise enables easy stopovers in Blois (luggage lockers at château).

Orientation to Blois

Unlike most other Loire châteaux, Blois' Château Royal sits right in the city center, with no forest, pond, or river to call its own. It's an easy walk from the train station, near ample underground parking, and just above the TI.

Arrival in Blois

Train travelers can walk 10 minutes straight out of the station down avenue Jean Laigret to the TI and château (follow small brown *Château* signs), or take a two-minute taxi from in front of the station. Although there's no **bag check** at the station, there are large, free lockers at the château—so you can drop off your luggage, visit the château and the town, and even take the excursion bus or a taxi tour to Chambord and Cheverny (provided you're back in Blois to reclaim your bag before the château closes).

Drivers follow *Centre-Ville* and *Château* signs (metered parking along avenue Jean Laigret or inside at Parking du Château—first 30 minutes free, then €2/2.5 hours).

Tourist Information

The cramped TI is just across from the château entrance (April–Sept Mon–Sat 9:00–19:00, Sun 10:00–19:00; Oct–March Mon–Sat 9:30–12:30 & 14:00–18:00, Sun 10:00–13:00; 23 place du Château, tel. 02 54 90 41 41). Save time as you explore the center of Blois by using the TI's handy walking-tour brochure (€0.20; brown and purple routes are best). The TI also has information on bike rentals.

Sights in Blois

▲▲**Château Royal**—Louis XII and François I each called this château home, and it's here that Catherine de Médicis spent her last night. At the castle's ticket office, pick up the helpful English brochure, then read the well-presented English displays. Free tours are available but usually are in French, though English tours are possible if you call ahead or get lucky—ask.

Begin in the courtyard, where four different wings—ranging from Gothic to Neoclassical—underscore this château's importance over many centuries. (Find the model of the château to get your bearings.) Visit the interior counterclockwise. After entering the courtyard, begin to the right, in the dazzling Hall of the Estates-General; continue to a great display of gargoyles and models in a small lapidary museum; then go upstairs through several richly tiled and decorated royal rooms (can you say busy?). Your visit ends with a walk through the mini fine-arts museum, with a 16th-century who's-who portrait gallery where you can see what the château's inhabitants looked like.

Cost and Hours: €9.50, €15 combo-ticket with House of Magic—described later, kids under 18–€5; daily April–Sept 9:00–18:30, July–Aug until 19:30, Oct 9:00–17:30, Nov–March 9:00–12:30 & 14:00–17:30, free lockers available with entry—same hours, tel. 02 54 55 26 26, www.chateaudeblois.fr.

Sound-and-Light Show: This simple "show" takes place in the center courtyard and features projections on château walls. An English version of the show runs on Wednesday, though the French version is worthwhile any day if you're sleeping in Blois (€7, €13 combo-ticket also covers daytime château entry, €20 gets you both plus the House of Magic; daily April–Sept at about 22:00).

House of Magic—The home of Jean-Eugène Robert-Houdin, the illusionist whose name was adopted by Harry Houdini, offers an interesting but overpriced history of illusion and magic. Kids enjoy the gift shop. Several daily shows have no words, so they work in any language (30 minutes; "séance" schedule posted at entry—usually at 11:15, 15:15, and 17:15, but hours may change in summer; adults–€8, kids under 18–€5, €14 combo-ticket with château, daily 10:00–12:30 & 14:00–18:30, at the opposite end of the square from the château).

Biking from Blois—Blois is well-positioned as a starting point for biking forays into the countryside. Cycling from Blois to Chambord is a level, 70-minute, one-way ride along a well-marked route that gets more scenic the closer you get to Chambord, and allows connections to a good network of other bike paths (the TI's free *Le Pays des Châteaux à Vélo* map shows the bike routes in this area). Adding Cheverny makes a full-day, 30-mile round-trip. The TI has info on bike-rental shops in Blois.

Sleeping in Blois

(€1 = about $1.25, country code: 33)

If you need to bed down in Blois, do so at the friendly and non-smoking **$ Hôtel Anne de Bretagne**** (Sb–€46, Db–€56, Tb–€60–74, Qb–€78–84, Wi-Fi, 150 yards uphill from Parking du Château, 5-minute walk below the train station at 31 avenue Jean Laigret, tel. 02 54 78 05 38, fax 02 54 74 37 79, http://annedebretagne.free.fr, annedebretagne@free.fr).

Eating in Blois

If you're stopping in Blois around lunchtime, plan on eating at **Le Marignan**, located on a breezy, traffic-free square in front of the château (daily, good salads and crêpes, €13–15 *menus*, fast service, 5 place du Château, tel. 02 54 74 73 15). At the top of the hour, you can watch the stately mansion opposite the château become "the dragon house," as monsters crane their long necks out its many windows.

Blois Connections

From Blois by Train to: Amboise (14/day, 20 minutes), **Chinon** (9/day, 2 hours, transfer in Tours), **Paris** (14/day, 1.5 hours).

By Bus: The TLC excursion buses to **Chambord** and **Cheverny** leave from the Blois train station—look for them immediately to the left as you leave the station (€6, 3/day mid-April–mid-Sept; see "Getting Around the Loire Valley" on page 352).

By Taxi: Blois taxis wait 30 steps in front of the station and offer excursion fares to **Chambord, Chaumont,** or **Cheverny** (€29 one-way from Blois to one location, €90 round-trip to Chambord and Cheverny, €45 more to add Chaumont, 8-person minivans available, tel. 02 54 78 07 65). These rates are per cab, making the per-person price downright reasonable for groups of three or four people.

Château de Chambord

With its huge scale and prickly silhouette, Château de Chambord, worth ▲▲, is the granddaddy of all châteaux in the Loire. It's surrounded by Europe's largest enclosed forest park, a game preserve defined by a 20-mile-long wall and teeming with wild deer and boar. Chambord (shahn-bor) began as a simple hunting lodge for bored Blois counts and became a monument to the royal sport and duty of hunting. (Apparently, hunting was considered important to keep the animal population under control and the vital forests healthy.)

The château, six times the size of most, has 440 rooms and a fireplace for every day of the year. It consists of a keep in the shape of a Greek cross, with four towers and two wings surrounded by stables. It has four floors, with 46 stairs in between thanks to the high ceilings. The ground floor has reception rooms, the first floor up houses the royal apartments, the second floor up houses a World War II exhibit and temporary art exhibits, and the rooftop offers a hunt-viewing terrace. Special exhibits describing Chambord at key moments in its history help animate the place. Because hunting visibility is best after autumn leaves fall, Chambord was a winter palace (which helps explain the 365 fireplaces). Only 80 of Chambord's rooms are open to the public—and that's plenty. This place would be great for hide-and-seek.

Cost and Hours: €9.50, daily April–Sept 9:00–18:15, Oct–March 9:00–17:15, last entry 30 minutes before closing (but you'll need more time there anyway), parking–€3, tel. 02 54 50 50 40, www.chambord.org. There are two ticket offices: one in the village in front of the château, and another inside the château. Call ahead to verify hours, guided tour times, horse shows, and evening visits.

Getting There: The Blois excursion bus is best (€6, three daily departures from Blois station mid-April–mid Sept, taxis from Blois are reasonable as well; see "Getting Around the Loire Valley" on page 352 for bus and taxi details).

Information and Tours: This château requires helpful information to make it come alive. Most rooms have adequate English explanations (the free brochure is useless). You can rent an audioguide for a thorough history of the château and its rooms (€4, two can share one audioguide with volume turned to max). Or, before you visit, you can download the tour from www.podibus.com to your own iPod or other MP3 player for free.

Services: There's a fantastic bookshop in the château with a good selection of children's books. Among the collection of shops near the château, you'll find a TI (April–Oct daily 9:30–13:00 & 14:00–18:00, closed Nov–March, tel. 02 54 33 39 16), an ATM, WCs, local souvenirs, a wine-tasting room, and cafés. You can rent bikes, rowboats, and electric boats across the tiny road by the canal—which is small, so room for boating is limited.

Horse-Riding Demonstrations: The horses put on a 45-minute show opposite the château entrance (€9.50, July–Aug daily at 11:45 and 16:30, May–June and Sept–early Oct Tue–Sun at 11:45 only, tel. 02 54 20 31 01, www.ecuries-chambord.com).

Views: For the best views, cross the small river in front of the château and turn right. The recommended Hôtel du Grand St. Michel has a broad view terrace, ideal for post-château refreshment.

Background: Starting in 1518, François I created this "weekend retreat," using 1,800 workmen over 15 years. (You'll see his signature salamander symbol everywhere.) François I was an absolute monarch—with an emphasis on absolute. In 32 years of rule (1515–1547), he never once called the Estates-General to session (a rudimentary Parliament in *ancien régime* France). This grand hunting palace was another way to show off his power. Charles V—the Holy Roman Emperor and most powerful man of the age—was invited here and was, like, totally wowed.

⊕ **Self-Guided Tour:** This tour covers the highlights.

The ground-floor **reception rooms** offer little to see, except for a subtitled video with helpful information on the château's construction, a room showing animals of the hunt, and the magically monumental **double-spiral staircase** (read the wall banner's description to the right of stairway). Climb the staircase, which was likely inspired by Leonardo da Vinci, who died just as construction was starting. Allowing people to go up and down without passing each other (look up the center from the ground floor), it's a masterpiece of the French Renaissance. Peek at other visitors through the openings as you climb, and admire the ingenious design.

The first floor up offers the most interesting rooms. Tour this floor basically clockwise, starting in the room behind the loom display (worthwhile explanations are posted about the loom and the ceramic stove). You'll enter the very royal apartments in the **king's wing** and pass through the grand bedrooms of Louis XIV, his wife Maria Theresa, and, at the far end, François I (follow *Logis de François 1er* signs). Gaze at their portraits and get to know them. I liked Louis' commode shortcut, but overall I'm partial to François' stage-set bedroom—because he was a traveling king, his furniture was designed to be easily disassembled and moved with him (seems pretty thrifty for a king).

Find your way back to the double-spiral stairway (the outside walkway is most fun, but expect to get turned around a few times) and visit the rooms devoted to the **Count of Chambord**, the final owner of the château. This 19th-century count, last of the French Bourbons, was next in line to be the king when France decided it didn't need one. He was raring to rule—you'll see his coronation outfits and even souvenirs from the coronation that never happened. Check out his boyhood collection of little guns, including a working mini-cannon. It was during this period that Chambord was lived in and enjoyed the most.

The second floor up has beautiful coffered ceilings (notice the "F" for you-know-who) and holds a series of ballrooms that once hosted post-hunt parties. To see what happens when you put 365 fireplaces in your house (still used today to heat the palace in winter), climb to the **rooftop**. A pincushion of spires and chimneys decorates a viewing terrace, where the ladies would enjoy the spectacle of their ego-pumping hunters. On hunt day, a line of beaters would fan out and work inward from the distant walls, flushing wild game to the center, where the king and his buddies waited. The showy lantern tower of the tallest spire glowed with a nighttime torch when the king was in. From the rooftop, view the elegant king's wing—marked by *FRF (François Roi de France)* and bristling with fleurs-de-lis.

Finish your visit back on the ground floor, and take a quick spin through the classy **carriage rooms** and the fascinating **lapidary rooms** (in the far right wing of the château, as you face the château from the courtyard entry). Here you'll come face-to-face with original stonework from the roof, including the bulky lantern cupola. Imagine having to move that load. The volcanic tuff stone used to build the spires was soft and easy to work, but not very durable—particularly when so exposed to the elements.

Sleeping near Chambord and Cheverny

(€1 = about $1.25, country code: 33)

$$ Hôtel du Grand St. Michel lets you wake up with Chambord outside your window. It's an Old World, hunting-lodge kind of place with rooms in pretty good shape and a trophy-festooned dining room (*menus* from €20). Sleep here and you'll have a chance to roam the château grounds after the peasants have been run out (small Db-€62–70, bigger Db-€75, Db facing château-€83–115 and worth the extra euros, Tb-€90–120, extra bed-€15, tel. 02 54 20 31 31, fax 02 54 20 36 40, on place Saint Louis, www.saintmichel-chambord.com, hotelsaintmichel@wanadoo.fr).

$$ Chambres la Flânerie, on the bike route from Chambord to Cheverny, offers two family rooms in an adorable home. It's riddled with flowers, crawling with ivy, and surrounded by wheat fields and forests. The gentle Delabarres speak enough English and loan bikes to their fortunate guests (Db–€62, Tb–€80, Qb–€96, includes breakfast, 25 rue de Gallerie, tel. 02 54 79 86 28, mobile 06 75 72 28 41, www.laflanerie.com, laflanerie@laflanerie.com). Coming from Blois on D-765, it's before Cheverny in the hamlet of Les Fées. Turn right where you see wooden bus shelters flanking the road, and follow signs to *Eric Auge Menuiserie*.

Cheverny

This stately hunting palace, a ▲▲ sight, is the most lavishly furnished of all the Loire châteaux. Those who complain that the Loire châteaux have stark, barren interiors missed Cheverny (shuh-vehr-nee). Because the palace was built and decorated from 1604 to 1634, and is immaculately preserved, it offers a unique architectural harmony and unity of style. From the start, this château has been in the Hurault family, and Hurault pride shows in its flawless preservation and intimate feel. The viscount's family still lives on the third floor. (You'll see some family photos.) Cheverny was spared by the French Revolution; the owners were popular then, as today, even among the village farmers.

The château is flanked by a pleasant village, with a small grocery, cafés offering good lunch options, and a few hotels. You can get to Cheverny by bus from Blois or by minivan tour from Amboise (see "Getting Around the Loire Valley" on page 352).

Cost and Hours: €8, family deals, daily July–Aug 9:15–18:45, April–June and Sept 9:15–18:15, Oct 9:45–17:30, Nov–March 9:45–17:00, tel. 02 54 79 96 29, www.chateau-cheverny.fr.

THE LOIRE

❶ **Self-Guided Tour:** Walking across the manicured grounds, you approach the gleaming château, with its row of Roman emperors, including Julius Caesar (above the others in the center). The entire top floor was occupied until 1985 by the viscount's family, who now live in the section to the far right. As you enter the château, pick up the excellent English tour brochure, which describes the interior beautifully.

Your visit starts in the lavish **dining room,** decorated with leather walls and a sumptuous ceiling. As you climb the stairs to the private apartments, look out the window and spot the orangerie across the grass. It was here that the *Mona Lisa* was hidden (along with other treasures from the Louvre) during World War II.

On the first floor up, you'll tour the I-could-live-here family apartments with silky bedrooms, kids' rooms, and an intimate dining room.

You'll pass though the **Arms Room** before landing in the **King's Bedchamber**—literally fit for a king. Study the fun ceiling art, especially the "boys will be boys" cupids. You'll find a Raphael painting, a grandfather clock with a second hand that's been ticking for 250 years, a family tree going back to 1490, and a letter of thanks from George Washington to this family for their help in booting out the English.

Barking dogs remind visitors that the viscount still loves to hunt. The **kennel** (200 yards in front of the château, look for *Chenil* signs) is especially interesting at dinnertime, when the 70 hounds are fed (April–mid-Sept daily at 17:00, mid-Sept–March Mon and Wed–Fri at 15:00). The dogs—half English foxhound and half French Poitou—are bred to have big feet and bigger stamina. They're given food once a day, and the feeding *(la soupe des chiens)* is a fun spectacle that shows off their strict training. Before chow time, the hungry hounds fill the little kennel rooftop and watch the trainer bring in troughs stacked with delectable raw meat. He opens the gate, and the dogs gather enthusiastically around the food, yelping hysterically. Only when the trainer says to eat can they dig in. You can see the dogs at any time, but the feeding show is fun to plan for. The adjacent trophy room is stuffed with more than a thousand antlers and the heads of five wild boar.

Nearby, **Tintin** comic lovers can enter a series of fun rooms designed to take them into a Tintin adventure (called les Secrets de Moulinsart, €12 combo-ticket with castle); hunters can inspect an antler-filled **trophy room;** and gardeners can prowl the château's fine **vegetable and flower gardens** (free, behind the dog kennel).

Near the Château: Opposite the entry to the château sits a slick wine-tasting room, **La Maison des Vins,** featuring all 33 wines made in Cheverny. Let the hostess get you oriented, then sample from the cool automated dispensers (€6.50 for small tastes of 7 wines, €6–9 bottles, daily 11:00–19:00, tel. 02 54 79 25 16).

Fougères-sur-Bièvre

The feudal castle of Fougères-sur-Bièvre (foo-zher sewr bee-ehv) dominates its hamlet and is worth a stop, even if you don't go inside (but I would). Located a few minutes from Cheverny on the way to Chenonceaux and Amboise, Fougères-sur-Bièvre was constructed for defense, not hunting, and was built over a small river (to provide an unlimited water supply during sieges). Leveled in the Hundred Years' War, then rebuilt in the 1500s, it's completely restored. Although there are no furnishings (there weren't many in the Middle Ages in any case), it gives you a good look at how castles were built.

Follow the route with the helpful English handout (brief English explanations are also provided in most rooms). You'll see models of castle-construction techniques, including interesting exhibits on the making of half-timbered walls (oak posts and crossbeams provided the structural skeleton, and the areas between were filled in with a mix of clay, straw, and pebbles). Walk under medieval roof supports, gaze through loopholes, and stand over machicolations (holes for dropping rocks and scalding liquids on attackers) in the main tower. Seeing the main tower from within adds an entirely new appreciation of these structures' complexity, and the two medieval latrines demonstrate how little toilet technology has changed in 800 years. Before leaving, take a few minutes to visit the re-created medieval vegetable garden.

Cost and Hours: €5; May–mid-Sept daily 9:30–12:30 & 14:00–18:30, mid-Sept–April Wed–Mon 10:00–12:00 & 14:00–17:00, closed Tue; last entry 30 minutes before closing, tel. 02 54 20 27 18, http://fougeres-sur-bievre.monuments-nationaux.fr.

Getting There: Fougères-sur-Bièvre has no easy public-transport link from Amboise...or anywhere else. If you're *sans* rental car or bike, arrange for a custom minivan tour—or skip it.

Chaumont-sur-Loire

A castle has been located on this spot since the 11th century; the current version is a ▲▲ sight. The first priority at Chaumont (show-mon) was defense. You'll appreciate the strategic location on the long climb up from the village below. (Drivers can avoid the uphill hike except off-season—explained later.) Gardeners will appreciate the elaborate Festival of Gardens that unfolds next to the château every year, and

modern-art lovers will enjoy how works have been incorporated into the gardens, château, and stables.

Cost and Hours: Château and stables–€9; château open daily May–mid-Sept 10:00–18:00, April and late Sept 10:30–17:30, Oct–March 10:00–17:00, last entry 30 minutes before closing; stables close daily 12:00–14:00; English handout available, tel. 02 54 51 26 26, www.domaine-chaumont.fr.

Festival of Gardens: This annual exhibit, with 25 elaborate gardens arranged around a different theme each year, draws rave reviews from international gardeners (Garden Festival–€9.50; château, stables, and Garden Festival–€15; May–mid-Oct daily 10:00–20:30, tel. 02 54 20 99 22, www.domaine-chaumont.fr). When the festival is on, you'll find several little cafés and reasonable lunch options scattered about the festival hamlet (festival ticket not needed).

Getting There: There is no public transport to Chaumont, although the train between Blois and Amboise can drop you in Onzain, a 25-minute walk across the river to the château (8/day). Bikes, taxis (reasonable from Blois train station), and chartered minivans also work for non-drivers (see "Getting Around the Loire Valley" on page 352).

From May to mid-October, drivers can park up top, at an entrance open only during the Festival of Gardens (you don't need to buy tickets for the garden event). From the river, drive up behind the château (direction: Montrichard), take the first hard right turn (following *Stade du Tennis* signs), and drive to the lot beyond the soccer field.

Background: The Chaumont château you see today was built mostly in the 15th and 16th centuries. Catherine de Médicis forced Diane de Poitiers to swap Chenonceau for Chaumont; you'll pick up tidbits about both women inside. Louis XVI, Marie-Antoinette, Voltaire, and Benjamin Franklin all spent time here. Today's château offers a good look at the best defense design in 1500: on a cliff with a dry moat, big and small drawbridges with classic ramparts, loopholes for archers, and machicolations—hot oil, anyone?

⊙ Self-Guided Tour: Your walk through the palace—restored mostly in the 19th century—is well-described by the English flier you'll pick up when you enter. As the château has more rooms than period furniture, your tour will be peppered with modern-art exhibits that fill otherwise empty spaces. The rooms you'll visit first (in the east wing) show the château as it appeared in the 15th and 16th centuries. Your visit ends in the west wing, which features furnishings from the 19th-century owners.

The castle's medieval **entry** is littered with various coats of arms. As you walk in, take a close look at the two drawbridges (a new mechanism allows the main bridge to be opened with the touch of a button). Once inside, the heavy defensive feel is replaced with palatial luxury. Peek into the courtyard—during the more stable 1700s, the fourth wing, which had enclosed the courtyard, was taken down to give the terrace its river-valley view.

Entering the château rooms, signs direct you along a one-way loop path (*sens de la visite*) through the château's three wings. Catherine de Médicis, who missed her native Florence, brought a touch of Italy to all her châteaux, and her astrologer (Ruggieri) was so important that he had his own (plush) room—next to hers. **Catherine's bedroom** has a case with ceramic portrait busts dating from 1770, when the lord of the house had a tradition of welcoming guests by having their portrait sketched, then giving them a ceramic bust made from this sketch when they departed. Find Ben Franklin's medallion. The bedroom has a private balcony that overlooks the chapel, handy when the lord (or lady) wanted to go to church on a bad hair day. The exquisitely tiled **Salle de Conseil** has a grand fireplace designed to keep this conference room warm. The treasury box in the **guard room** is a fine example of 1600s-era locksmithing. The lord's wealth could be locked up here as safely as possible in those days, with a false keyhole, no handles, and even an extra box inside for diamonds.

A big spiral staircase leads down to rooms decorated in 19th-century style. The **dining room**'s fanciful limestone fireplace is exquisitely carved. Find the food (frog legs, snails, goats for cheese), the maid with the bellows, and even the sculptor with a hammer and chisel at the top (on the left). Your visit ends with a stroll through the 19th-century library, the billiards room, and the living room.

In the **courtyard**, test the 165-foot-deep well for echoes. Study the entertaining spouts and decor on the courtyard walls. What's left of the château's **kitchens** lie below the main entry, but there's little to see.

The **stables** (*écuries*) were entirely rebuilt in the 1880s. The medallion above the gate reads *pour l'avenir* (for the future), which shows off a real commitment to horse technology. Inside, circle clockwise—you can almost hear the horses walking about. Notice the deluxe horse stalls, padded with bins and bowls for hay, oats, and water, complete with a strategically placed drainage gutter. The horses were named for Greek gods and great châteaux. The Horse Kitchen (Cuisine des Chevaux) produced mash twice weekly for the horses. The horse gear was rigorously maintained for the safety of carriage passengers. The covered alcove is where the horse and carriage were prepared for the prince, and the round former kiln was redesigned to be a room for training the horses.

The estate is a **tree garden**, set off by a fine lawn. Trees were imported from throughout the Mediterranean world to be enjoyed—and to fend off any erosion on this strategic bluff. Skip the dog cemetery (*cimetière des chiens*). During the annual Festival of Gardens, you can find cafés and snacks behind the stables.

Loches and Valençay

Loches

The overlooked town of Loches (lohsh), located about 30 minutes south of Amboise, makes a good base for drivers wanting to visit sights east and west of Tours (in effect triangulating between Amboise and Chinon), but has no easy train or bus connections. This pretty town sits on the region's loveliest river, the Indre, and holds an appealing mix of medieval monuments, stroll-worthy streets, and fewer tourists. Its château dominates the skyline and is worth a short visit. The Wednesday street market is small but lively.

Sleeping in Loches: For an overnight stay, try **$$ Hôtel George Sand*****, located on the river, with a well-respected restaurant, an idyllic terrace, and rustic, comfortable rooms (Db-€57–67, luxury Db-€135, Tb-€92, Qb-€145, Wi-Fi, no elevator, 300 yards south of TI at 39 rue Quintefol, tel. 02 47 59 39 74, fax 02 47 91 55 75, www.hotelrestaurant-georgesand.com, contactGS @hotelrestaurant-georgesand.com). **$$$ Le Logis du Bief**, a fine, welcoming *chambre d'hôte* in the center of town with four lovely, air-conditioned rooms, has a riverfront terrace and cozy living spaces (Db-€80–95, Tb-€120, includes breakfast, 21 Rue Quintefol, tel. 02 47 91 66 02, mobile 06 83 10 46 64, www.logisloches .com).

Valençay

The nearby Renaissance château of Valençay (vah-lahn-say) is a massive, luxuriously furnished structure with echoes of its former owner Talleyrand (Napoleon's prime minister) and lovely gardens. It has many kid-friendly activities and elaborate big toys, and lots of summer events such as fencing demonstrations and candlelit visits (€11, ask about family rates, free audioguide covers château and gardens, daily June 9:30–18:30, July–Aug 9:30–19:00, April–May and Sept 10:00–18:00, Oct 10:20–17:30, closed Nov–March, tel. 02 54 00 10 66, www.chateau-valencay.fr).

West of Tours

Chinon

This pleasing town straddles the Vienne River and hides its ancient streets under a historic royal fortress. Today's Chinon (shee-nohn) is better known for its popular red wines. But for me it makes the best home base for seeing the sights west of Tours: Azay-le-Rideau (sound-and-light show), Langeais, Villandry, Chatonnière, Rivau, Ussé, and the Abbaye Royale de Fontevraud. Each of these worthwhile sights is no more than a 20-minute drive away. Trains provide access to many châteaux but are time-consuming, so you're better off with your own car or a minivan excursion (see "Getting Around the Loire Valley," on page 352, and "Chinon Connections," later in this section).

The famous Renaissance writer and satirist François Rabelais was born here in the late 1400s—you'll see many references to him in his proud town. His best-known works, *Gargantua* and *Pantagruel*, describe the amusing adventures of father-and-son giants.

Orientation to Chinon

Chinon stretches out along the Vienne River, and everything of interest to travelers lies between it and the hilltop fortress. Charming place du Général de Gaulle—ideal for café-lingering—is in the center of town.

Tourist Information

The TI is in the town center, near the base of the hill and a 15-minute walk from the train station. You'll find *chambre d'hôte* listings, wine-tasting details (wine-route maps available for the serious taster), bike-rental information, and an English-language self-guided tour of the town (May-Sept daily 10:00-19:00; Oct-April Mon-Sat 10:00-12:00 & 14:00-18:00, closed Sun; in village center on place Hofheim, tel. 02 47 93 17 85, www.chinon-valdeloire.com). Free public WCs are around the back of the TI.

Helpful Hints

Market Days: A market takes place all day Thursday on place Jeanne d'Arc (western end of town). There's a sweet little market on Sunday, around place du Général de Gaulle.

Groceries: Carrefour City is across from the Hôtel de Ville, on place du Général de Gaulle (Mon-Sat 7:00-20:00,

Chinon

1. Best Western Hôtel de France & Le Café des Arts
2. L'Etape en Chinonais B&B & Bike Rental
3. Hôtel Diderot
4. Hôtel Agnès Sorel
5. To Le Clos de Ligré B&B
6. La Treille Hôtel-Rest.
7. Les Années 30 Rest.
8. L'Océanic Restaurant
9. La Cave Voltaire Wine-Tastings
10. Caves Plouzeau Wine-Tastings
11. Panoramic Elevator
12. Launderette
13. Canoe Rental
14. Grocery Store

☙ VIEW

Sun 9:00–13:00).

Laundry: Salon Lavoir is near the bridge at #7 quai Charles VII (daily 7:00–21:00).

Bike Rental: Try **L'Etape en Chinonais** (across from TI, €8/half-day, €15/day).

Taxi: Call 02 47 98 37 98.

Car Rental: It's best to book a car at the St. Pierre-des-Corps train station in Tours (see page 363).

Best Views: You'll find terrific rooftop views from rue du Coteau St. Martin (between St. Mexme Church and the fortress—see map), and rewarding river views to Chinon by crossing the bridge in the center of town and turning right.

Sights in Chinon

▲**Fortresse Royale de Chinon**—Don't underestimate this medieval fortress, especially if you're looking for a contrast to all those softie hunting-lodge palaces you've seen. Three medieval

THE LOIRE

structures occupy the hilltop—Fort St. Georges and Fort Coudray protected the residential château that lies between them. The fortress' history, and the sensational views it affords, justify your visit. Henry II, Eleanor of Aquitaine, and their son, Richard the Lionhearted, all called this home at one time. Most importantly, it was in this castle that Joan of Arc pleaded with Charles VII to muster the courage to take the throne back from the nasty English. Charles had taken refuge in this well-fortified castle during the Hundred Years' War, making Chinon France's capital city during that period.

Thanks to recent renovations to the fortress, visitors get a thorough understanding of the castle's turbulent history and its key characters through films, videos, and posted information, all in English.

Your visit will likely begin with a film presenting the castle's history, then continue on through the various towers and the 16-room interior, which was in ruins prior to the ambitious renovation. You'll learn much about the castle's most famous inhabitant, Joan of Arc.

Cost and Hours: €7, daily April–Sept 9:00–19:00, Oct–March 9:30–17:00. Tel. 02 47 93 13 45, www.forteresse-chinon.fr.

Getting There: It's a bracing walk up from town, or you can take the free "panoramic" elevator from behind the TI (daily 8:00–22:00). Drivers can park near the entry at the top.

Tours: Try to join one of the excellent English-language tours of the château (45 minutes, free with entry ticket, 5/day in summer, 4/day off-season, call château for tour schedule). The tours focus on the big picture—why the castle was built here, how it differed from others in the Loire, the importance of Joan's visit, and how châteaux are rebuilt.

Touring the Old City—Chinon offers a tasty cocktail of quiet cobbled lanes, historic buildings, and few tourists. By following the TI's self-guided tour and reading plaques at key buildings, you'll gain a good understanding of this city's historic importance. Stop for a drink on place du Général de Gaulle, and consider popping into the **Museum of Art and History** (Musée des Arts et d'Histoire, located in the 15th-century Grand Carroi) to better understand Chinon's rich heritage (€3.50, daily May–Oct 14:00–18:00, closed Tue Nov–April, 44 rue Haute Saint-Maurice). Cross the river for the best views of the castle.

Wine-Tasting—Chinon reds are among the most respected in the Loire, and there are a variety of ways to sample them. The most convenient is at **La Cave Voltaire,** where retired English-speaking sommelier Patrice would love to help you learn about his area's wines. He serves inexpensive appetizers and has wines from all regions of France (daily 10:00–22:00, near place du Général de Gaulle at 13 rue Voltaire, tel. 02 47 93 37 68).

At **Caves Plouzeau,** you'll walk through long, atmospheric caves—complete with mood lighting—that extend under the château to a (literally) cool tasting room and reasonably priced wines (€2, April–Sept Tue–Sat 11:00–13:00 & 15:00–19:00, closed Sun–Mon and Oct–March, at the western end of town on 94 rue Haute St-Maurice, tel. 02 47 93 16 34).

▲Biking from Chinon—Many good options are available from Chinon. Most cyclists can do the pleasant bike ride from Chinon to Ussé—though you encounter a monumental hill when you're leaving Chinon. From there you can join a quiet lane (signed as a bike route) that crosses the Indre River, then follows the Loire River to Langeais and Villandry. After Villandry, the path follows the Cher River into Tours. Connecting these three châteaux is a full-day, 40-mile round-trip ride that only those in fit condition will enjoy.

Canoeing from Chinon—The campground across the lone bridge in Chinon rents plastic canoes and kayaks from May through September, and will shuttle you upriver for a relaxing float on the pretty Vienne River (€17/person for 3-hour float from Chinon to Candes, tel. 06 23 82 96 33).

Sleeping in Chinon

(€1 = about $1.25, country code: 33)

Hotels are a good value in Chinon. If you stay overnight here, walk out to the river and cross the bridge for a floodlit view of the château walls.

$$$ Best Western Hôtel de France*** offers sufficient comfort without the personal touches of the other hotels I list. Still, I like the location—at Chinon's best square—as well as the open patios inside the hotel (Db-€85-120, most are about €94, Tb/Qb-€124-145, several rooms have balconies over the square, some have thin walls, Wi-Fi, 49 place du Général de Gaulle, tel. 02 47 93 33 91, fax 02 47 98 37 03, www.bestwestern-hoteldefrance-chinon.com, elmachinon@aol.com).

$$ L'Etape en Chinonais is a *chambre d'hôte* renting five cushy, traditional, just-like-Grandma's rooms in a very central location (Db-€75-100, extra person-€15, includes breakfast, Wi-Fi, 27 rue Jean-Jacques Rousseau, tel. 02 47 95 92 08, mobile 06 37 80 25 73, fax 02 47 95 92 08, www.chambredhotes37.com, etape.en.chinonais@orange.fr).

$$ Hôtel Diderot** is *the* place to stay in Chinon. This handsome 18th-century manor house on the eastern edge of town is the closest hotel I list to the train station (drivers, look for signs from place Jeanne d'Arc). It's a family affair, run by spirited Laurent and his equally spirited sisters, Françoise and Martine, who will adopt you into their clan if you're not careful. The hotel surrounds a carefully planted courtyard, and has a full bar with a good

selection of area wines. Rooms in the main building vary in size and decor, but all are well-maintained, with personal touches. Ground-floor rooms are a bit dark, but they have private patios. The four good family rooms have connecting rooms, each with a private bathroom. Breakfast includes a rainbow of homemade jams (Sb–€65, Db–€64-82, Db–€86-94, extra bed–€12, Wi-Fi, limited parking–€6/day, 4 rue de Buffon, tel. 02 47 93 18 87, fax 02 47 93 37 10, www.hoteldiderot.com, hoteldiderot@hoteldiderot.com).

$ Hôtel Agnès Sorel, at the western end of town, is right along the river and handy for drivers, but a 30-minute walk from the train station. Of its ten sharp rooms, three have river views, two have balconies, and five surround a small, flowery courtyard. A few are air-conditioned (Db–€50-75, most are €60, big Db suite–€100, T/Qb suite–€120, 4 quai Pasteur, tel. 02 47 93 04 37, fax 02 47 93 06 37, www.agnes-sorel.com, pierre.catin@orange.fr).

$ Le Café des Arts is ideal for budget travelers, with six simple, spotless rooms above Chinon's most atmospheric square (D–€38, Db–€42, 4 rue Jean-Jacques Rousseau, tel. & fax 02 47 93 09 84, contact@hotelrestaurant-cafedesarts-37chinon.com).

Outside Chinon, near Ligré

$$$ Le Clos de Ligré lets you sleep in farmhouse silence, surrounded by vineyards and farmland. A 15-minute drive from Chinon, it has plenty of room to roam, a pool overlooking the vines, a billiards room with a baby grand piano, and stay-awhile indoor and outdoor spaces. Let English-speaking Martine Descamps spoil you with her cavernous and creatively decorated rooms that enclose a lovely old courtyard (Db–€100-110, good family rooms, includes breakfast, €35 dinner includes the works, cash only, 37500 Ligré, tel. 02 47 93 95 59, mobile 06 61 12 45 55, www.le-clos-de-ligre.com, mdescamps@club-internet.fr). From Chinon, cross the river and go toward Richelieu on D-760, turn right on D-115, and continue for about five kilometers (3 miles). Turn left, following signs to Ligré, and look for signs to *Le Clos de Ligré* (see map on page 394).

Eating in Chinon

For a low-stress meal with ambience, choose one of the cafés on the photogenic place du Général de Gaulle. The recommended **Le Café des Arts** hotel has great outdoor tables and a modern interior, and serves reasonably priced café fare with €10 salads, omelets, and €12 *plats* (closed Wed). But if food quality trumps outdoor ambience, try one of the next three restaurants.

La Treille Hôtel-Restaurant is a good choice for dining on regional dishes at fair prices. The cuisine is fresh, creative, and delicious (*menus* from €17, closed Wed-Thu, 4 place Jeanne d'Arc, tel. 47 93 0771).

Les Années 30 welcomes you with consistently good, classic

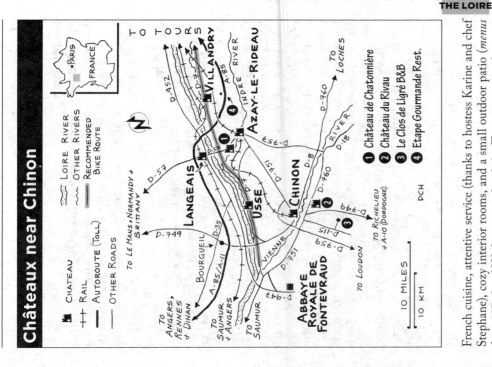

Châteaux near Chinon

Legend:
- 🏛 CHATEAU
- ⊣⊢ RAIL
- ▬ AUTOROUTE (TOLL)
- — OTHER ROADS
- ≋ LOIRE RIVER
- ∿ OTHER RIVERS
- ▬ RECOMMENDED BIKE ROUTE

① Château de Chatonnière
② Château du Rivau
③ Le Clos de Ligré B&B
④ Etape Gourmande Rest.

French cuisine, attentive service (thanks to hostess Karine and chef Stephane), cozy interior rooms, and a small outdoor patio (*menus from €27, closed Wed year-round and also Tue in winter, at the western end of town at 78 rue Haute St. Maurice, tel. 02 47 93 37 18*).

L'Océanic, in the thick of the pedestrian zone, is where locals go for seafood and tasty desserts. It has the best wine list in town, formal indoor or relaxed outdoor seating, and chic Marie-Poule to take your order (*menus from €24, closed Sun–Mon, 13 rue Rabelais, tel. 02 47 93 44 55*).

Near Chinon

For a memorable countryside meal, drive 25 minutes to **Etape Gourmande at Domaine de la Giraudière**, in Villandry (see page 404). This combines well with visits to Villandry and Azay-le-Rideau.

Chinon Connections

By Minivan

From Chinon to Loire Châteaux: Acco-Dispo and **Quart de Tours** offer fixed-itinerary minivan excursions from Tours. Take the train to Tours from Chinon, or get several travelers together to book your own van from Chinon (see "Getting Around the Loire Valley" on page 352).

By Train

Twelve trains and SNCF buses link Chinon daily with the city of Tours (1 hour), connections to other châteaux and minibus excursions from Tours—see "Getting Around the Loire Valley" on page 352) and to the regional rail hub of St. Pierre-des-Corps in suburban Tours (TGV trains to distant destinations, and the fastest way to Paris). Traveling by train to the nearby châteaux (except for Azay-le-Rideau) requires a transfer in Tours and healthy walks from the stations to the châteaux. Fewer trains run on weekends.

From Chinon to Loire Châteaux: Azay-le-Rideau (7/day, 20 minutes direct, plus long walk to château), **Langeais** (5/day, 2 hours, transfer in Tours), **Amboise** (9/day, 1.5 hours, transfer in Tours), **Chenonceaux** (8/day, 1.5 hours, transfer in Tours), **Blois** (9/day, 2 hours, transfer in Tours).

To Destinations Beyond the Loire: Paris' Gare Montparnasse (9/day, 2 hours), **Sarlat** (4/day, 5–6 hours, change at St. Pierre-des-Corps, then TGV to Libourne or Bordeaux–St. Jean, then train through Bordeaux vineyards to Sarlat), **Pontorson–Mont St. Michel** (3/day, 6 hours with change at Tours main station and Caen, then bus from Pontorson; or 8 hours via Paris TGV with changes at St. Pierre-des-Corps and Paris' Gare Montparnasse, then bus from Rennes), **Bayeux** (9/day, 5 hours with change in Caen and Tours, or 7 hours via St. Pierre-des-Corps and Paris' Gare Montparnasse).

By Bus

From Chinon to Langeais and Azay-le-Rideau: Ask at the TI about buses to these towns (2/day to each).

Azay-le-Rideau

About 30 minutes west of Tours, Azay-le-Rideau (ah-zay luh ree-doh) is a pleasant little town with a small but lively pedestrian zone and a château that gets all the attention. Azay-le-Rideau works as a base for visiting sights west of Tours by car, bike, or train (though the train station is a half-mile walk from the town center), and tempts travelers to bed down here with a fun sound-and-light show at its château.

Orientation to Azay-le-Rideau

Tourist Information

Azay-le-Rideau's TI is just below place de la République, a block to the right of the post office (Tue–Sat April–Oct 9:00–13:00 & 14:00–18:00, Nov–March 14:00–18:00, closed Sun–Mon year-round, 4 rue du Château, tel. 02 47 45 44 40). Pick up information on the sound-and-light show and on bike rentals in Azay.

Arrival in Azay-le-Rideau

It's about a 25-minute walk from the station to the town center (taxi tel. 06 60 94 42 00). Walk down from the station, turn left, and follow *Centre-Ville* signs. Drivers can head for the château and park there.

Sights in Azay-le-Rideau

▲▲Château d'Azay-le-Rideau

This handsome 16th-century château floats magnificently in a romantic reflecting pond. Come for the serene setting, and enjoy the well-furnished rooms. You'll see more elaborately furnished châteaux elsewhere, but this one has that water thing going on.

Azay-le-Rideau's builder—a government bureaucrat—wanted to design the most glorious castle of the time (there was no lack of ego in this region 500 years ago). He came close enough to draw the attention of the king (François I). This was what he wanted, but not what he needed—the bureaucrat, who was France's treasurer, soon landed in jail for tax fraud.

Rooms are well-described in English, between the free hand-out and English plaques in most rooms. For the unabridged version, rent a €4 audioguide (€6/2 people). The château's manageable interior offers a collection of warmly furnished rooms where you'd like to hang your beret. Try to recognize familiar faces among the portraits of those who stayed here. You'll see many bed chambers and antechambers, a dining room, a kitchen, and a not-to-be-missed 19th-century billiard room with a nifty scoring board. The gardens are a big grassy area with good views from benches to the château.

Cost and Hours: €8, daily July–Aug 9:30–19:00, April–June and Sept–Oct 9:30–18:00, Nov–March 10:00–12:30 & 14:00–17:30, last entry 45 minutes before closing, tel. 02 47 45 42 04, http://azay-le-rideau.monuments-nationaux.fr/en.

Sound-and-Light Show: The château hosts a sound-and-light show from 21:00 in July and August (€10, call to see if times have been added for non-summer months). These shows allow you to stroll the grounds with interesting lighting and a musical background.

Sleeping in Azay-le-Rideau

(€1 = about $1.25, country code: 33)

The town's appealing center may convince you to set up here (a good idea if you plan to see the sound-and-light show).

$ Hôtel de Biencourt** is ideally located on a traffic-free street between place de la République (easy parking) and the château. This sharp little hotel is a restored convent. Rooms are quite comfortable, with a few big family rooms and a pleasing garden terrace (Db–€62, Tb–€74, Qb–€86, Wi-Fi, open March-mid-Nov, 7 rue de Balzac, tel. 02 47 45 20 75, fax 02 47 45 91 73, www.hotelbiencourt.com, biencourt@infonie.fr).

Eating in Azay-le-Rideau

For dining, consider **Ridelloise**, which is small, central, and budget-friendly (*menus* from €13, open daily, 34–36 rue Nationale, tel. 02 47 45 46 53). The nearby **Crêperie du Roy** is good and cheap (24 rue Nationale, tel. 02 47 45 91 88). If you have a car, by all means drive 10 minutes to **Domaine de la Giraudière** in Villandry (see page 404).

Azay-le-Rideau Connections

From Azay-le-Rideau by Bus to: Chinon and **Langeais** (2/day, ask at TI).

By Train to: Tours (8/day, 30 minutes), **Chinon** (7/day, 20 minutes).

Langeais

One of the most imposing fortresses of the Middle Ages, Langeais—rated ▲—towers above its appealing little village. It

comes with a moat, a drawbridge, lavish defenses, and turrets. It's a well-furnished fort with enough rooms to hold your interest, many beautifully displayed tapestries, and useful English descriptions throughout. The attractive little town houses a handful of good eating options just below the château.

This castle was built on the ruins of a 10th-century fortress—you'll see the lone remnant in the garden as you enter. Langeais served a strategic role in the 1400s as a French outpost, facing the troublesome duchies of Anjou and Brittany. Its 15 minutes of fame came when it witnessed the secret marriage of King Charles VIII and 14-year-old Anne (the Duchess of Brittany), a union that brought independent Brittany into France's fold. You can witness the wedding in a large room outfitted with wax figures; a mini sound-and-light show explains the event in English (ask for times at entry). The scene raises the obvious question: How could such a short person rule such a big country? Ponder that question while you walk along the parapet with great views (through chicken wire) over the town.

Cost and Hours: €8.50, daily July–Aug 9:00–19:00, April–June and Sept–mid-Nov 9:30–18:30, mid-Nov–March 10:00–17:00, last entry one hour before closing, tel. 02 47 96 72 60, www .chateau-de-langeais.com.

Getting There: Nine trains a day link Langeais and **Tours** (20 minutes), with about five connections a day from there to **Chinon** (2 hours total, faster by bike). Drivers should turn right at the foot of the castle and follow the road left (around the castle) to find the parking lot on the right.

THE LOIRE

Villandry

Villandry (vee-lahn-dree) has an unremarkable castle, but its grounds make it a ▲▲ sight (worth ▲▲▲ for gardeners). Built in 1536 as the home of the finance minister, this château has the Loire's best gardens, immaculately maintained and arranged in elaborate geometric patterns. Pick up the excellent English handout that describes the four garden types and suggests a good walking route. The viewpoint behind the château is terrific. The 10-acre Italian Renaissance–style garden (designed c. 1530) is full of symbolism. Even the herb and vegetable sections are artistic—design mattered to the monks who first planted these gardens (only vegetables used in the 16th century are still grown). Paying extra for the château interior isn't worth it, but it does include a 15-minute *Four Seasons of Villandry* slide show (with period music) that offers a look at the gardens throughout the year. You can stay as late as you like in the gardens, though you must enter before the ticket office closes.

Cost and Hours: €9, €6 for gardens only, daily April–Sept 9:00–19:00, March and Oct 9:00–18:00, Nov–Feb 9:00–17:00, tel. 02 47 50 02 09, www.chateauvillandry.com.

Eating and Sleeping in Villandry

The pleasant little village of Villandry offers several cafés and restaurants, a small grocery store, a bakery, and good rates at the nice little **$ Hôtel-Restaurant le Cheval Rouge** (Db–€60–70, Tb–€70–80, Qb–€90–100, dinner *menus* from €20, tel. 02 47 50 02 07, www.lecheval-rouge.com).

Eating near Villandry

Etape Gourmande at Domaine de la Giraudière offers a rustic farmhouse dining experience. Owner Beatrice provides great service and country-good cuisine from her limited menu (ask her how she landed here). The *salade gourmande* makes a good lunch or a hearty first course for dinner (consider splitting it). The *cochon au lait* (melt-in-your-mouth pork, not available in summer) and the nougat dessert are also tasty (€17–33 *menus*, mid-March–mid-Nov daily 12:00–15:00 & 19:30–21:00, closed mid-Nov–mid-March, a half-mile from Villandry's château toward Druye, tel. 02 47 50 08 60, fax 02 47 50 06 60). This place works best for lunch, as it's between Villandry and Azay-le-Rideau. It also works for dinner when combined with a visit to Azay-le-Rideau's sound-and-light show.

More Château Gardens

Gardeners will be tempted by these untouristy "lesser châteaux" because of their pleasing plantings.

Château de Chatonnière features romantic paths through exquisitely tended gardens of various themes. Surrounded by fields of wildflowers (my favorite part), it's a must-visit for gardeners and flower fanatics in May to early July, when the place positively explodes in fragrance and color. At other times, when flowers are few, the entry fee is not worth it for most (€6, mid-March–mid-Nov daily 10:00–19:00, château interior closed to visitors, between Langeais and Azay-le-Rideau just off D-57, tel. 02 47 45 40 29, www.lachatonniere.com).

Château du Rivau is well off the beaten path, a lovely 10-minute drive from Chinon. This gleaming-white medieval château sits smack in the middle of wheat fields, with owners who are busily re-creating the fine gardens as they were 500 years ago (using medieval tapestries as models). Although you're here for the flower and vegetable gardens, you'll also see a medieval castle interior (€8, Easter–mid-Nov Wed–Mon 10:00–12:30 & 14:00–19:00, closed Tue except July–Aug, closed mid-Nov–Easter; in Lémeré on D-759—from Chinon follow *Richelieu* signs, then signs to the château; tel. 02 47 95 77 47, www.chateaudurivau.com).

Ussé

This château, famous as an inspiration for Charles Perrault's classic version of the Sleeping Beauty story, is worth a quick photo stop for its fairy-tale turrets and gardens, but don't bother touring the interior of this pricey pearl. The best view, with reflections and a golden-slipper picnic spot, is from just across the bridge (€13, daily April–Aug 10:00–19:00, mid-Feb–March and Sept–mid-Nov 10:00–18:00, closed mid-Nov–mid-Feb, tel. 02 47 95 54 05, www.chateaudusse.fr).

Abbaye Royale de Fontevraud

The Royal Abbey of Fontevraud (fohn-tuh-vroh) is a 15-minute journey west from Chinon. This vast 12th-century abbey provides a keen insight into medieval monastic life. Here you'll meet Richard the Lionhearted and Eleanor of Aquitaine, and get a better grip on the important role medieval abbeys played in pulling Europe out of the Dark Ages. This is one of Europe's largest abbeys, where you can still feel echoes of the economic engine it was 900 years ago. You can almost hear the gears grinding as you tour this elaborate monastic complex.

Cost and Hours: €8.50, daily 9:30–18:30, €4 English-language tours may be offered a few times a day June–Sept in 2011, call or email for times in any season, tel. 02 41 51 71 41, www.abbaye-fontevraud.com, resa@abbayedefontevraud.com. If there's no tour when you visit, spring for the helpful €4 audioguide (the free English leaflet gives light coverage). The best book on the abbey is *Fontevraud, Royal Abbey—Between Chinon and Saumur* by Francis Collombert (€12).

Visiting the Abbey: Thanks to the audioguide, this abbey is well-presented for English speakers. Your visit begins in the bright **church** (Eglise Abbatiale). Sit on the steps, savor the ethereal light and the cavernous setting, and gaze down at the nave. In the last row of the nave, Eleanor of Aquitaine lies close to her second husband, Henry II Plantagenet. Next to them lies their son Richard the Lionhearted.

You'll leave through the right transept into the Grand Moutier **cloister.** This was the center of the abbey, where the nuns read, exercised, checked their email, and washed their hands. Next you'll find the **chapter house** (salle capitulaire), where the nuns' meetings took place, as well as the **community room**—the only heated room in the abbey, where the nuns would embroider linen. You'll also see a wooden framework under the roof of the dormitories (where most of the nuns of the Grand Moutier slept), an elegant **refectory,** and a portion of underground **tunnels** (accès souterrain). Your visit ends in the honeycombed 12th-century **kitchen,** with five bays covered by 18 chimneys to evacuate smoke.

While visiting the abbey, remember that monastic life was very simple: nothing but prayers, readings, and work. Daily rations were composed of a loaf of bread and half a liter of wine per person, plus soup and smoked fish.

Sleeping and Eating near Abbaye Royale de Fontevraud

(€1 = about $1.25, country code: 33)

$$$ Hôtel la Croix Blanche**, 10 steps from the abbey, welcomes travelers with open terraces and will have you sleeping and dining in comfort. This ambitious restaurant-hotel combines a hunting-lodge feel with polished service, comfortable open spaces, a pool, and rooms with classic French decor (Db–€90–130, Db suites–€100–150, free Wi-Fi, place Plantagenets, tel. 02 41 51 71 11, fax 02 41 38 15 38, www.fontevraud.net, info@fontevraud.net). Their three restaurants meet every need: The elegant country restaurant has menus from €25, the brasserie has café fare, and **Le 7** serves less-pricy cold plates (12:00–18:00).

The **boulangerie** opposite the entrance to the abbey serves mouthwatering quiche and sandwiches at impossibly good prices. You'll also find a few crêperies and cafés near the abbey.

DORDOGNE AND NEARBY

Sarlat • Dordogne River Valley • Cro-Magnon Caves • Oradour-sur-Glane • St. Emilion • Rocamadour • Lot River Valley

The Dordogne River Valley is a rich brew of natural and man-made beauty. Walnut orchards, tobacco plants, and cornfields carpet the valley, while stone fortresses patrol the cliffs above. During much of the on-again, off-again Hundred Years' War, this strategic river—so peaceful today—separated warring Britain and France. Today's Dordogne River carries more travelers than goods, as the region's economy relies heavily on tourism.

The joys of the Dordogne include rock-sculpted villages, fertile farms surrounding I-should-retire-here cottages, memory-card-gobbling vistas, lazy canoe rides, and a local cuisine worth loosening your belt for. But its big draw is its concentration of prehistoric artifacts. Limestone caves decorated with prehistoric artwork litter the Dordogne region.

Planning Your Time

Although tourists inundate the region in the summer, the Dordogne's charm is protected by its relative inaccessibility. Given the time it takes to get here, I'd allow a minimum of two nights (ideally three) and most of two days...or I'd skip it. Your sightseeing obligations, in order of priority, are as follows: prehistoric cave art; the Dordogne River Valley, nearby villages, and castles; the town of Sarlat; and, if you have a bit more time, the less-traveled Lot River Valley (most efficiently viewed when heading to or from the south). Wine-lovers work in a pilgrimage to St. Emilion, two hours west.

If you're connecting the Dordogne with the Loire region by car, the fastest path is on the A-20 autoroute (exit at Souillac for Sarlat and nearby villages). Break up your trip from the north by stopping in Oradour-sur-Glane: Take autoroute A-20 to Limoges and follow *Angoulême* signs, then follow signs to *Oradour-sur-Glane.* If you need to spend the night in this area, consider tiny Mortemart. If you're connecting the Dordogne and Carcassonne, explore the Lot River Valley on your way south. If heading west, taste the Bordeaux wine region's prettiest town, St. Emilion.

Those serious about visiting the Dordogne's best caves (especially with a relatively rare English-speaking tour) need to book well in advance (explained on page 451).

The following three-day itinerary is designed for drivers, but it's doable—if you're determined—by taxi rides, a canoe trip (the best way to see the Dordogne regardless of whether you've got a car), and a minivan tour.

Day 1: Enjoy a morning in Sarlat (ideally on a market day—Sat or Wed), then spend the afternoon on a canoe trip, with time at the day's end to explore Beynac and Castelnaud. If it's not market day in Sarlat, do the canoe trip, Beynac, and Castelnaud first, and enjoy the late afternoon and evening in Sarlat. (Because all of the town's essential sights are outdoors, my Sarlat self-guided walk works great after dinner.) The sensational views from Castelnaud's castle and Domme are best in the morning; visit Beynac's castle or viewpoint late in the day for the best light. With a little lead time, canoe-rental companies can pick up non-drivers in Sarlat. Taxis are also reasonable between Sarlat and the river villages.

Day 2: Drivers can begin at Lascaux II (the best cave art intro in the area, even though it's a replica). Then follow the scenic *Vézère* River toward Les Eyzies-de-Tayac, stopping for lunch in idyllic little St. Léon before going on to the caves at La Roque St. Christophe (no reservations needed; doesn't close for lunch, unlike other caves). In Les Eyzies-de-Tayac, visit the museum of prehistory, then see the real thing at the cave or caves of your choice (I prefer Grotte de Font-de-Gaume and Grotte de Rouffignac). If you lack a car, this day's full list of activities is only possible by taxi or minivan tour. By train, you can link Sarlat and Les Eyzies-de-Tayac (where you can tour the Grotte de Font-de-Gaume and the National Museum of Prehistory).

Day 3: Head east and upriver to explore Rocamadour, Gouffre de Padirac, and storybook villages such as Carennac, Autoire, and Loubressac. And though Rocamadour is accessible by train and a short taxi ride, the rest of these places are feasible only with your own wheels, by taxi, or on a minivan tour.

Choosing a Home Base

Sarlat is the only viable solution for train travelers, but those with a car should sleep riverside in La Roque-Gageac (a beautiful village with good hotels) or Beynac (a spectacular and photogenic village with good *chambres d'hôtes* and hotels). For a grand château hotel experience that won't break the bank, sleep near the Lascaux caves at Château de la Fleunie (30 minutes north of Sarlat, see page 453). For the best view hotel I've found in the area, try Hôtel de l'Esplanade in Domme (see page 432). If you'd rather frolic on a real farm, sleep near Les Eyzies-de-Tayac at Auberge Veyret (see page 450). I recommend several other rural places that are good for drivers (see page 440). For a list of good *chambres d'hôtes* near Sarlat, check www.chambres-perigord.com (in French, but easy to navigate—click *Entrée*, then on the upper-left, click *Chambres/Auberges*).

Getting Around the Dordogne

This region is a joy with a car, and tough without one. Consider renting a car for a day, renting a canoe or bike, or taking a minivan excursion. If you're up for a splurge, consider a hot-air balloon ride (see page 357).

By Train: Though it's possible to get into the region by train, once there, connecting the Dordogne's sights by train is difficult. The only helpful train is the one from Sarlat to Les Eyzies-de-Tayac, where you can see the Grotte de Font-de-Gaume and the National Museum of Prehistory (3/day, transfer in Le Buisson, 15-minute walk from station to museum, 30-minute walk from station to caves).

By Car: Roads are small, slow, and scenic. There is no autoroute near Sarlat, so you'll need more time than usual to get into, out of, and around this remote region. Little Sarlat is routinely snarled in traffic, so passing through it is slow going. You can rent a car in Sarlat (see page 417), though bigger cities, such as Bordeaux and Brive-la-Gaillarde, offer greater drop-off flexibility. In summer (mid-June–mid-Sept), you'll pay to park in most riverfront lots between 10:00 and 19:00. Leave nothing in your car at night—thieves enjoy the Dordogne, too.

By Taxi: For taxi service from Sarlat to Beynac or La Roque-Gageac, allow €27 (€35 at night and on Sun); from Sarlat to Les Eyzies-de-Tayac, allow €38 one-way (€57 at night and on Sun) or €76 round-trip. Philippe (see next) can often pick you up within a few minutes if you call. Corinne, who runs Beynac-based **Taxi Corinne**, is helpful, speaks a little English, and is eager to provide good service to tourists (tel. 05 53 29 42 07, mobile 06 72 76 03 32, www.taxicorinne.com, corinne.brouqui@wanadoo.fr).

By Custom Taxi/Minivan Excursion: You have two good options. **Allô-Philippe Taxi** is run by amiable Philippe, who speaks English and has a comfortable minivan with raised seats for better viewing. Philippe will custom-design your tour, help with cave reservations, and provide some commentary during your

The Dordogne Region

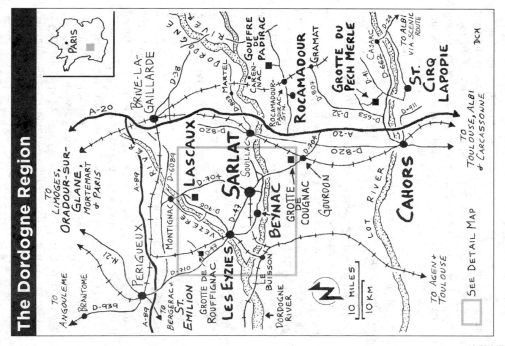

excursion. He can pick you up anywhere—including Bordeaux's airport (€310) and remote train stations. His general rates are €35/hour for up to six people (€52.50/hour on Sun). Some sample fares: from Sarlat area to Lascaux II, €88 round-trip; from Sarlat to Beynac, €27 (€35 at night); from Sarlat to Les Eyzies-de-Tayac, €38 (€57 at night). These prices are estimates only. Book early (tel. 05 53 59 39 65, mobile 06 08 57 30 10, http://allophilippetaxi.monsite.wanadoo.fr, allophilippetaxi@wanadoo.fr).

Découverte et Loisirs is run by Christine, who offers minivan tours for one to eight people. Compared with Philippe, she offers mostly fixed-itinerary tours and few custom ones. Her three weekly afternoon itineraries in English are the Dordogne Valley villages and castles; the prehistoric-focused sights of Lascaux II, La Roque St. Christophe, and the National Museum of Prehistory in Les Eyzies-de-Tayac; and Rocamadour (allow €34–44/person, tel. 05 65 37 19 00, mobile 06 22 70 13 76, www.decouverte-loisirs.com, decouverte.loisirs@wanadoo.fr). Although her fixed tours don't include Grotte de Font-de-Gaume, she can make a custom tour for you that does, and will make the necessary cave reservations if you book with her early enough.

By Boat: Non-drivers should rent a canoe, my favorite mode of transportation for exploring a slice of this region. A canoe offers easy access to the river's sights and villages, and canoe companies will pick you up in Sarlat for no extra charge. Since a canoe costs €11–16/person (for the trip I recommend, from Vitrac Port to Beynac), and you can spend all day on and off the river touring sights I cover, this is a swimmingly good deal. For the same scenery with less work, you can also take a boat cruise from Beynac or La Roque-Gageac. Details on all these options are covered later in this chapter.

By Bike or Moped: Cyclists find the Dordogne beautiful but hilly, with lots of traffic on key roads. Mopeds are an option. You can rent bikes and mopeds in Sarlat (see page 415).

The Dordogne's Cuisine Scene

Gourmets flock to this area for its geese, ducks, and wild mushrooms. The geese produce (involuntarily) the region's famous foie gras. (They're force-fed, denied exercise during the last weeks of their lives, and slaughtered for their livers, meat, and fluffy down—see sidebar on page 438.) Foie gras tastes like butter and costs like gold. The duck specialty is confit de canard (duck meat preserved in its own fat—sounds terrible, but tastes great).

Pommes de terre sarladaises are mouthwatering, thinly sliced potatoes fried in duck fat and commonly served with confit de canard. Wild truffles are dirty black tubers that grow underground, generally on the roots of oak trees. Farmers traditionally locate them with sniffing pigs and then charge a fortune for their catch (roughly $250 per pound). Native cheeses are Cabécou (a silver-dollar-size, pungent, nutty-flavored goat cheese) and Echourgnac (made by local Trappist monks). You'll find walnuts (noix) in salads, cakes, liqueurs, salad dressings, and more.

Wines to sample are Bergerac (red, white, and rosé), Pecharmant (red, must be at least four years old), Cahors (a full-bodied red), and Monbazillac (sweet dessert wine). The *vin de noix* (sweet walnut liqueur) is delightful before dinner.

Remember, restaurants serve only during lunch (11:30–14:00) and dinner (19:00–21:00, later in bigger cities); bigger cafés serve food throughout the day.

Dordogne Markets

Markets are a big deal in rural France, and nowhere more so than in the Dordogne. I've listed good markets for every day of the week, so there's no excuse for drivers not to experience a Dordogne market. Here's what to look for:

Strawberries (*fraises*): For the French, the Dordogne is the region famous for the very tastiest strawberries. Available from April to November, they're gorgeous, and they smell even better than they look. Buy *une barquette* (small basket), and suddenly your two-star hotel room is a three-star. Look also for *fraises des bois*, the tiny, sweet, and less visually appealing strawberries found in nearby forests.

Fresh Veggies: Outdoor markets allow you to meet the farmer, and give you a chance to buy direct. (See what's fresh, and look for it on your menu this evening.) Subtly check out the hands of the person helping customers—if they're not gnarled and rough from working the fields, move on.

Cheeses (*fromages*): The region is famous for its Cabécou goat cheese (described earlier), though often you'll also find Auvergne cheeses (St. Nectaire and Cantal are the most common) from just east of the Dordogne (usually in big rounds).

Truffles (*truffes*): Only the bigger markets will have these ugly, jet-black tubers on display. Truffle season is our off-season (Nov–Feb), when you'll find them at every market. If you see truffles displayed at other times, they are sterilized. On Sarlat market days, there's usually a guy in the center of place de la Liberté with a photo of his grandfather and his truffle-hunting dog.

Anything with Walnuts (*aux noix*): *Pain aux noix* are thick-as-a-brick bread loaves chock-full of walnuts. *Moutarde de noix* is walnut mustard. *Confiture de noix* is a walnut spread for hors d'oeuvres. *Gâteaux de noix* are tasty cakes studded with walnuts. *Liqueur de noix* is a marvelous creamy liqueur, great over ice or blended with a local white wine.

Goose or Duck Livers and Paté (foie gras): This spread is made from geese (better) and ducks (still good), or from a mix of the two. You'll see two basic forms: *entier* and *bloc*. Both are 100 percent foie gras; *entier* is a piece cut right from the product, whereas *bloc* has been blended to make it easier to spread—*mousse* has been whipped for an even creamier consistency. Foie gras is best accompanied by a sweet white wine (such as the locally produced Monbazillac, or Sauterne from Bordeaux). You can bring the unopened tins back into the US, *pas de problème*. For more on foie gras, see the sidebar on page 438.

Confit de Canard: At butcher stands, look for hunks of duck smothered in white fat, just waiting for someone to take them home and cook them up.

Dried Sausages (*saucissons secs*): Long tables piled high with dried sausages covered in herbs or stuffed with local goodies are a common sight in French markets. You'll always be offered a mouthwatering sample. Some of the variations you'll see include *porc, canard* (duck), *fumé* (smoked), *à l'ail* (garlic), *cendré* (rolled in ashes), *aux myrtilles* (with blueberries), *sanglier* (wild boar), and even *âne* (donkey)—and, but of course, *aux noix* (with walnuts).

Olive Oil (*huile d'olive*): You'll find stylish bottles of various olive oils, as well as vegetable oils flavored with truffles, walnuts, chestnuts (*châtaignes*), and hazelnuts (*noisettes*)—good for cooking, ideal on salads, and great as gifts. Pure walnut oil, pressed at local mills from nuts grown in the region, is a local specialty, best on salads. Don't cook with pure walnut oil, as it will burn quickly.

Olives and Nuts (*olives et noix*): These interlopers from Provence find their way to every market in France.

Liqueurs: Although they're not made in this region, Armagnac, Cognac, and other southwestern fruit-flavored liquors are often available from a seller or two. Try the *liqueur de pomme verte*, and sample Armagnac in the tiny plastic cups.

Dordogne Market Days

The best markets are in Sarlat (Sat and Wed, in that order), followed by the markets in Cahors on Saturday, St. Cyprien on Sunday, and Le Bugue on Tuesday. Markets usually shut down by 13:00.

Sunday: St. Cyprien (lively market, 10 minutes west of Beynac, difficult parking), Montignac (near Lascaux), and St. Génies (a tiny, intimate market with few tourists; halfway between Sarlat and Montignac)

Monday: Les Eyzies-de-Tayac (Grotte de Font-de-Gaume caves are here) and a tiny one in Beynac

Tuesday: Cénac (you can canoe from here) and Le Bugue (great market 20 minutes west of Beynac)

Wednesday: Sarlat (big market)

Thursday: Domme

Friday: Souillac (transfer point to Cahors, Carcassonne)

Saturday: Sarlat and Cahors (both are excellent), and the little *bastide* village of Belvès (small market)

Sarlat

Sarlat (sar-lah) is a pedestrian-filled banquet of a town, serenely set amid forested hills. There are no blockbuster sights—the only thing worth going inside for is the cathedral (and that just barely). Still, Sarlat delivers a seductive tangle of traffic-free, golden cobblestone lanes peppered with beautiful buildings, lined with foie gras shops (geese hate Sarlat), and stuffed with tourists. The town is warmly lit at night and ideal for after-dinner strolls. It's just the right size—large enough to have a theater with four screens, but small enough so that everything is an easy meander from the town center. And though undeniably popular with tourists, it's the handiest home base for those without a car.

Orientation to Sarlat

Rue de la République slices like an arrow through the circular old town. Sarlat's smaller half has few shops and many quiet lanes. The action lies east of rue de la République.

Tourist Information

The TI, with English-speaking staff, is 50 yards to the right of the Cathedral of St. Sacerdos as you face the front entrance (April–June and Sept–Oct Mon–Sat 9:00–12:00 & 14:00–18:00, Sun 10:00–13:00 & 14:00–17:00; July–Aug Mon–Sat 9:00–19:00, Sun 10:00–12:00 & 14:00–18:00; Nov–March closes at 18:00 and all day Sun, on rue Tourny, tel. 05 53 31 45 45, www.sarlat-tourisme.com). Ask for an English version of the free city map, and pick up brochures on most regional sights. Their *Guide Pratique* booklet is good for rental information on cars, bikes, and canoes. They also sell the handy, laminated *City of Sarlat* walking-tour map for €6, as well as booklets on sights throughout the region. For €2, the TI can also reserve you a hotel room or a time slot for a prehistoric cave visit (for more on cave reservations, see page 451). The TI also has hiking guides in English, listing suggested trails through the hills and by the Dordogne River.

Arrival in Sarlat

By Train: The sleepy train station keeps a lonely vigil (without a shop, café, or hotel in sight). It's a mostly downhill, 20-minute walk to the town center (consider a taxi, about €7—see "Helpful Hints"). To walk into town, turn left out of the station and follow the *Centre-Ville* sign down avenue de la Gare as it curves downhill, then turn right at the bottom on avenue Thiers. Some trains (such as those from Limoges and Cahors) arrive at nearby Souillac, which is connected to Sarlat's train station by an SNCF bus.

By Car: Sarlat's limited-access downtown funnels cars through narrow streets and creates long backups, although a new bypass road should bring some relief by the time you visit. Parking can be a headache, particularly on market days. Try parking along avenue Gambetta (at the north end of town), or in one of the signed lots on the ring road. The closest parking is metered (free Mon–Sat 12:00–14:00 & 19:00–9:00 and all day Sun).

Helpful Hints

Market Days: Sarlat has been an important market town since the Middle Ages. Outdoor markets thrive on Wednesday morning and all day Saturday. Saturday's market swallows the entire town and is best in the morning (produce and food vendors leave at noon). Come before 8:00 to watch them set up, and, once the market is underway, plant yourself at a well-positioned café to observe the civilized scene. Don't miss the market action in the former Church of Ste. Marie. In summer months, a small organic market enlivens the town's lower (southern) side (Thu 18:00–22:00, place du 14 Juillet). For tips on what to look for at the market, see "Dordogne Markets," earlier.

Supermarket: There's a **Petit Casino** grocery at 32 rue de la République (Tue–Sat 8:30–12:30 & 14:00–19:00, Sun 8:30–12:30, closed Mon).

Internet Access: Ask the TI where you can get connected. The recommended **Brasserie le Glacier** and **Café de la Mairie** have Wi-Fi for customers (described later, under "Eating in Sarlat").

Laundry: Madame Mazzocato runs a good launderette across from the recommended Hôtel la Couleuvrine (self-serve daily 6:00–22:00, drop-off/pickup Mon–Fri 8:00–12:00 & 14:00–18:30, Sat 8:00–12:00, none Sun, 10 place de la Bouquerie). And for my readers, she will drop off laundry at your (Sarlat) hotel.

Biking: Sarlat is surrounded by beautiful country lanes that would be ideal for biking were it not for all those hills. Villages along the Dordogne River make good biking destinations though expect some traffic and hills between Sarlat and the river (the TI and bike rental places can advise quieter routes).

You can rent bikes at **CycleO** (44 rue des Cordeliers, tel.

Sarlat

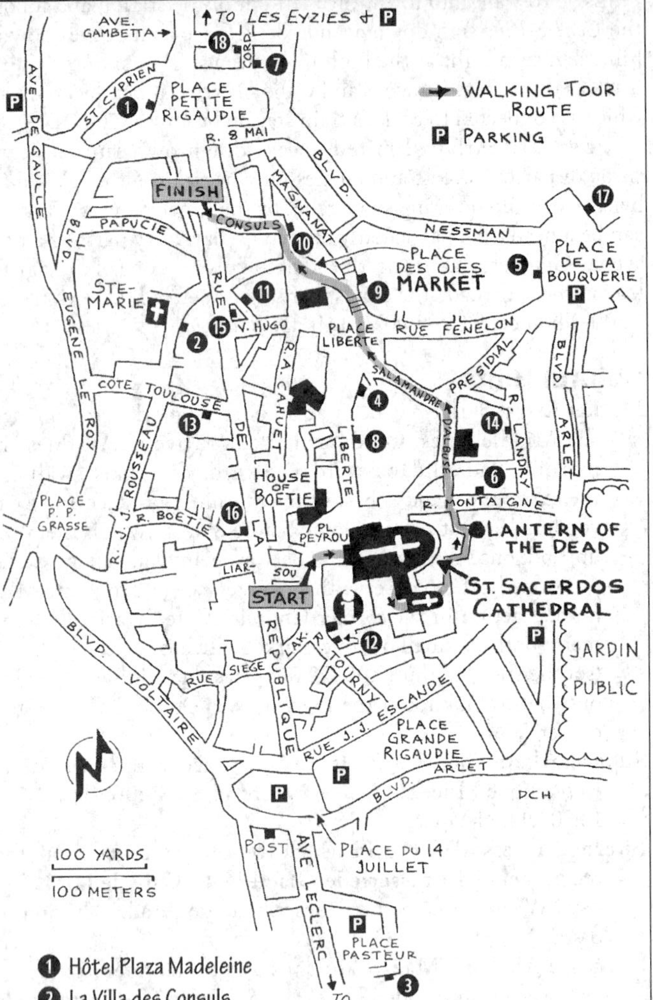

→ WALKING TOUR ROUTE
P PARKING

1 Hôtel Plaza Madeleine
2 La Villa des Consuls
3 Hôtel Montaigne
4 Hôtel de la Mairie
5 Hôtel/Rest. la Couleuvrine
6 La Lanterne Rooms
7 Les Cordeliers Rooms
8 Les Chambres du Glacier & Brasserie
9 La Maison du Notaire Royal
10 La Mirandol Restaurant
11 Le Petit Manoir Restaurant
12 Chez le Gaulois Restaurant
13 Pizzeria Romane
14 Le Présidial Restaurant
15 Lemoine Café
16 Petit Casino Grocery
17 Launderette
18 Bike Rental

05 53 31 90 05, www.cycleo.fr). The TI has information on bike rental outside Sarlat including outfits that deliver bikes to your countryside hotel.

Taxi: Call Philippe of **Allo-Philippe Taxi** (tel. 05 53 59 39 65, mobile 06 08 57 30 10, also available for regional day trips—see page 409) or **Taxi Sarlat** (tel. 05 53 59 02 43, mobile 06 80 08 65 05).

Car Rental: Try **Europcar** (Le Pontet, at south end of avenue Leclerc on roundabout, place du Maréchal de Lattre de Tassigny, tel. 05 53 30 30 40, fax 05 53 31 10 39).

Tours: Passion Périgord is a two-man tour company run by passionate guides Jeff and Pierre. They offer €5 walks of Sarlat in English to small groups (even just two people). Book a few days ahead (countryside walks also possible, tel. 05 53 30 42 55, mobile 06 25 60 59 16, best to email passionperigord @yahoo.fr).

Self-Guided Walk

Welcome to Sarlat

This short walk starts facing the Cathedral of St. Sacerdos (a few steps from the TI). Although it's designed for daytime (when the cathedral is open), it also works beautifully after dinner, when the gas-lit lanes and candlelit restaurants twinkle. See the map on page 416 to help navigate this walk.

Place du Peyrou: An eighth-century Benedictine abbey once stood where the Cathedral of St. Sacerdos is today. It provided the stability for Sarlat to develop into an important trading city during the Middle Ages. The old Bishop's Palace, built right into the cathedral (on the right, with its top-floor Florentine-style loggia), recalls Sarlat's Italian connection. The Italian bishop was the boyfriend of Catherine de Médicis (queen of France)—a connection that got him this fine residence. After a short stint here, he split to Paris with lots of local money. And though his departure scandalized the town, it left Sarlat with a heritage of Italian architecture. (Notice the fine Italianate house of Etienne de la Boëtie on the opposite side of the square, and the similar loggia to its right.)

Another reason for Sarlat's Italo-flavored urban design was its loyalty to the king during wartime. Sarlat's glory century was from about 1450 to 1550, after the Hundred Years' War (see sidebar on page 255). Loyal to the French cause—through thick and thin and a century of war—Sarlat was rewarded by the French king, who gave the town lots of money to rebuild itself in stone. Sarlat's new nobility needed fancy houses, complete with ego-boosting features. Many of Sarlat's most impressive buildings date from this prosperous era, when the Renaissance style was in vogue, and everyone wanted an architect with an Italian résumé.

• *Take a closer look (opposite the cathedral) at...*

The House of Etienne de la Boëtie: This house was a typical 16th-century merchant's home—family upstairs and open ground floor (its stone arch now filled in) with big, fat sills to display retail goods. Pan up, scanning the crude-but-still-Renaissance carved reliefs. It was a time when anything Italian was trendy (when yokels "stuck a feather in their cap and called it macaroni"). La Boëtie (lah bow-ess-ee), a 16th-century bleeding-heart liberal who spoke and wrote against the rule of tyrannical kings, remains a local favorite.

Notice how the house just to the left arches over the small street. This was a common practice to maximize buildable space in the Middle Ages. Sarlat enjoyed a population boom after the Hundred Years' War ended in 1468.

• *If you're doing this walk during the day, head into the cathedral now. If you're doing this walk after hours, skip ahead to the Lantern of the Dead (below): Face the cathedral, walk around it to the left, up the lane, and through the little door in the wall to the rocket-shaped building on a bluff 30 yards behind the church.*

Cathedral of St. Sacerdos: Though the cathedral's facade has a few well-worn 12th-century carvings, most of it dates from the 18th and 19th centuries.

Step inside the only historic Sarlat interior that merits a visit. The faithful believed that Mary delivered them from the great plague of 1348, so you'll find a full complement of Virgin Marys here and throughout the town. The Gothic interiors you'll see in this part of France are simple, with clean lines and nothing extravagant. The first chapel on the left is the baptistery. Locals would come here to give thanks after they made the pilgrimage to Lourdes for healing and returned satisfied. A column on the right shows a long list of hometown boys who gave their lives for France in World War I.

• *Exit the cathedral from the right transept (through a padded brown door) into what was once the abbey's cloisters. Snoop through two quiet courtyards, then turn left, making your way around to the back of the church, where you'll climb steps (above the monks' graveyard) to a bluff behind the church. You'll find a bullet-shaped building ready for some kind of medieval take-off, known as the...*

Lantern of the Dead (Lanterne des Morts): Dating from 1147, this is the oldest monument in town. In four horrible days, a quarter of Sarlat's population died in a plague (1,000 out of 4,000). People prayed to St. Bernard of Clairvaux for help. He blessed their bread—and instituted hygiene standards while he was at it, stopping the disease. This lantern was built in gratitude.

• *From the Lantern of the Dead, exit downhill and to the right, toward an adorable house. Cross one street and keep straight, turn left a block later on impasse de la Vieille Poste, make a quick right on rue d'Albusse, and then take a left onto...*

Rue de la Salamandre: The salamander—unfazed by fire or water—was Sarlat's mascot. Befitting its patriotic animal, Sarlat was also unfazed by fire (from war) and water (from floods). Walk several steps down this "Street of the Salamander" and find the Gothic-framed doorway just below on your right. Step back and notice the tower that housed the staircase. Staircase towers like this (Sarlat has about 20) date from about 1600 (after the wars of religion between the Catholics and Protestants), when the new nobility needed to show off.

• *Continue downhill, passing under the salamander-capped arch, and pause near (or better, sit down at) the café on the...*

Place de la Liberté: This has been Sarlat's main market square since the Middle Ages. Sarlat's patriotic town hall stands behind you (with a café perfectly situated for people-watching). Top shops line the road between here and the cathedral. These tourist-pleasing stores are filled with the finest local products (truffles, liquors, foie gras, and so on).

You can't miss the dark **stone roofs** topping the buildings across the square. They're typical of this region: Called *lauzes* in French, the flat limestone rocks were originally gathered by farmers clearing their fields, then made into cheap, durable roofing material (today few people can afford them). The unusually steep pitch of the *lauzes* roofs—which last up to 300 years—helps distribute the weight of the roof over a greater area. Although most *lauzes* roofs have been replaced by more affordable roofing materials, a great number remain. The small window is critical—it provides air circulation, allowing the lichen that coat the porous stone to grow—sealing gaps between the stones and effectively waterproofing the roof. Without that layer, the stone would crumble after repeated freeze-and-thaw cycles.

The bulky building with the *lauzes* roof (on the right) was the parish Church of Ste. Marie, which was converted into a gunpowder factory in 1789. Today, it's an indoor market (daily 8:30–13:00). Marvel at its tall, strangely modern, seven-ton doors. Climb the small lane past the big doors to meet the "boy of Sarlat"—marking the best view over place de la Liberté. Notice the cathedral's tower, with a salamander swinging happily from its spire.

• *Turn left (behind the boy) and trickle like medieval rainwater down the ramp into an inviting square. Here you'll find a little gaggle of geese.*

Place des Oies: Feathers fly when geese are traded on this "Square of the Geese" on market days (Nov–March). The birds are serious business here, and have been since the Middle Ages. Trophy homes surround this cute little square on all sides. Check out the wealthy merchant's home front and center, with a tower built big enough to match his ego. Just past the square on rue des Consuls (before the recommended restaurant Le Mirandol), a 14th-century vault leads to a fountain. For generations, this was the town's only source of water, protected by the Virgin Mary. Opposite the restaurant and fountain, enter the wooden doorway (open only July–Aug) and pass through one room to find the massive Renaissance stairway. These showy stairways, which replaced more space-efficient spiral ones, required a big house and a bigger income. Impressive.

• *Follow the curve along rue des Consuls, and enter the straight-as-an-arrow...*

Rue de la République: This modern thoroughfare dates from the mid-1800s, when blasting big roads through medieval cities was standard operating procedure. It wasn't until 1963 that Sarlat's other streets would become off-limits to cars, thanks to France's forward-thinking minister of culture, André Malraux. The law that bears his name has served to preserve and restore important monuments and neighborhoods throughout France. Eager to protect the country's architectural heritage, private investors, cities, and regions worked together to create traffic-free zones, rebuild crumbling buildings, and make sure that no cables or ugly wiring marred the ambience of towns like this. Without the Malraux Law, Sarlat might well have more "efficient" roads like rue de la République slicing through its once-charming old town center.

Your tour is over, but make sure you take time for a poetic ramble—ideally after dark—through this town. This is the only town in France illuminated by gas lamps, which cause the warm limestone to glow, turning the romance of Sarlat up even higher.

• *From here you can cross rue de la République and wander through Sarlat's quiet, less commercial side, or find a café and raise a toast to Monsieur Malraux.*

Sleeping in Sarlat

Even with summer crowds, Sarlat is the train-traveler's best home base. Note that in July and August, some hotels require half-pension, and hotels in downtown Sarlat book up first. Parking can be a headache—drivers will find rooms and parking more easily just outside of town (see "Near Sarlat" on page 424) or in the nearby villages and destinations described later, under "The Best of the Dordogne River Valley" (most are a 15-minute drive away).

Sleep Code

(€1= about $1.25, country code: 33)

S = Single, **D** = Double/Twin, **T** = Triple, **Q** = Quad, **b** = bathroom, **s** = shower only, * = French hotel rating system (0–4 stars). Unless otherwise noted, credit cards are accepted and English is spoken.

To help you sort easily through these listings, I've divided the rooms into three categories based on the price for a standard double room with bath:

$$$ Higher Priced—Most rooms €95 or more.

$$ Moderately Priced—Most rooms between €70–95.

$ Lower Priced—Most rooms €70 or less.

Prices can change without notice; verify the hotel's current rates online or by email. For other updates, see www.ricksteves.com/update.

Hotels in the Town Center

$$$ Hôtel Plaza Madeleine* is a central and sharp three-star value with professional service, comfortable lounges, and 39 handsome rooms with every comfort. You'll find a generously sized pool out back, exercise bikes, a sauna, and a Jacuzzi—all free for guests (standard Db–€105-125, most at €105; bigger Db–€135-155, Tb–€180, several connecting rooms for families–€210-250, air-con, elevator, Internet access and Wi-Fi, garage–€10/day, at north end of ring road at 1 place de la Petite Rigaudie, tel. 05 53 59 10 41, fax 05 53 31 03 62, www.hoteldelamadeleine-sarlat.com, hotel.madeleine@wanadoo.fr).

$$ La Villa des Consuls*, in a 17th-century home buried on Sarlat's quiet side, has 12 lovely, spacious rooms with microwave ovens and refrigerators; most have a kitchen and a living room. The rooms surround a small courtyard and come with wood floors, private decks, and high ceilings. Helpful David helms the ship and prices his rooms to encourage longer stays. These rates are for stays of 2–6 nights (Db–€69-89, big Db/Tb/Qb–€97-142, 10 percent more for 1-night stays, less for 7 or more days, air-con, Internet access and Wi-Fi, free washers and dryers, garage–€9/day, train station pickup–€7, 3 rue Jean-Jacques Rousseau, tel. 05 53 31 90 05, fax 05 53 31 90 06, www.villaconsuls.fr, villades consuls@yahoo.fr).

$$ Hôtel Montaigne, Sarlat's best two-star value, is located a block south of the pedestrian zone. It's sharper than its simple lobby lets on, and is well-run by the welcoming Martinats. The rooms are spotless, spacious, and comfortable, and about half are air-conditioned. Of the hotels I recommend, this one is nearest the train station (Db-€58–74, extra person-€15, two-room family suites-€95, elevator, Internet access and Wi-Fi, laundry service, easy parking, place Pasteur, tel. 05 53 31 93 88, fax 05 53 31 99 71, www.hotelmontaigne.fr, contact@hotelmontaigne.fr).

$ Hôtel de la Mairie plays second fiddle to its café, which can keep hotel guests awake late. The hotel is young, frumpy, and basic, but well-located, with rooms right on the main square (Db-€56, Tb-€66–76, Qb-€90, rooms #3 and #6 have the best views, Wi-Fi, reception in café, place de la Liberté, tel. 05 53 59 05 71, fax 05 53 59 59 95, www.hotel-mairie-sarlat.com, hoteldelamairie@orange.fr).

$ Hôtel la Couleuvrine** offers faded comfort at fair rates. It's in a historic building with a great location—across from the launderette and near the park—with easy parking (for Sarlat). Families enjoy *les chambres familles* (#19 and #20 are in the tower), and there are three family suites. Some rooms have tight bathrooms, some could use new carpets, and a few have private terraces (Db-€66, Db suite-€80, Tb-€85, Qb-€95–110, elevator, on ring road at 1 place de la Bouquerie, tel. 05 53 59 27 80, fax 05 53 31 26 83, www.la-couleuvrine.com, lacouleuvrine@wanadoo.fr). Half-pension is encouraged during busy periods and in the summer—figure €62 per person for room, breakfast, and a good dinner in the classy restaurant. The hotel also has a jazzy stone-vaulted wine bar that serves light meals and good wine by the glass.

Hotels North of Town

The following hotels are a 10-minute walk north of the old town on avenue de Selves. All have easy parking.

$$$ Hôtel Clos la Boëtie**** is *the* place to stay if you need four-star comfort a short walk from Sarlat. Located on the same grounds as the Hôtel de Selves (listed next), no expense has been spared in decorating this 11-room luxury hotel, where your every need is attended to (Db-€210–280, Db suite-€300–340, elaborate breakfast-€20, Wi-Fi, pool, sauna, massages possible, parking-€12, 95 avenue de Selves, tel. 05 53 29 44 18, fax 05 53 28 61 40, www.closlaboetie-sarlat.com, hotel@closlaboetie-sarlat.com).

$$$ Hôtel de Selves*** feels American, with a spacious lobby, professional staff, and 40 well-equipped rooms in a modern shell. Reliable comfort is sold at fair prices, including a sauna, a year-round swimming pool, and lovely gardens (Db-€95, bigger Db-€115–125, Db with balcony-€145, Tb-€150, two-room family suites-€210–230, all rooms non-smoking, air-con, elevator, Internet access and pay Wi-Fi, outside parking-€8, garage-€12/day, 93 avenue de Selves, tel. 05 53 31 50 00, fax 05 53 31 23 52, www.selves-sarlat.com, hotel@selves-sarlat.com).

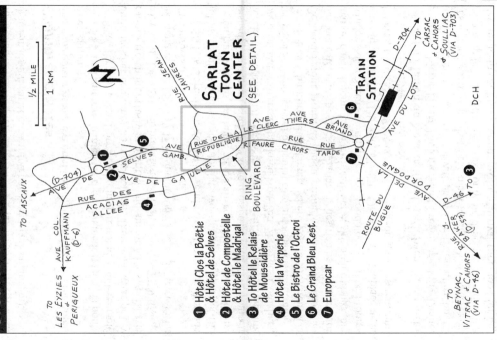

Greater Sarlat

1. Hôtel Clos la Boëtie & Hôtel de Selves
2. Hôtel de Compostelle & Hôtel le Madrigal
3. To Hôtel le Relais de Moussidière
4. Hôtel la Verperie
5. Le Bistro de l'Octroi
6. Le Grand Bleu Rest.
7. Europcar

$$ Hôtel de Compostelle*** features a sleek, open lobby and bright, modern, mostly spacious rooms, including several big rooms for families (Db-€78-92, Tb-€140, Qb-€154 for 4-6 people, air-con, elevator is one floor up, Wi-Fi, backyard terrace, parking-€7, 64 avenue de Selves, tel. 05 53 59 58 53, fax 05 53 30 31 65, www.hotel-compostelle-sarlat.com, info@hotel-compostelle -sarlat.com).

$$ Hôtel le Madrigal**, one block past Hôtel de Compostelle, is a well-maintained 11-room hotel with solid two-star rooms, all with queen-size beds and small bathrooms (Db-€68-74,

Tb/Qb–€76–90, air-con, Wi-Fi, small fitness room, parking-€7, 50 avenue des Selves, tel. 05 53 59 21 98, fax 05 53 30 31 65, www.hotel-madrigal-sarlat.com, info@hotel-madrigal-sarlat.com).

Chambres d'Hôtes

These *chambres d'hôtes* are central and compare well with the hotels listed earlier.

$$$ La Lanterne, named for the monument it faces, is home to Brits Terri and Roy Bowen, who have restored a 500-year-old building that could not be more central. Their somewhat pricey rooms are thoughtfully appointed and surround a sweet little courtyard (Db–€80–115, breakfast-€8, cash only, Wi-Fi, 9 bis rue Montaigne, tel. 05 53 59 17 79, mobile 06 33 42 19 57, www.sarlat.biz, info@sarlat.biz).

$$ Les Cordeliers, owned by gentle Brits Chris and Amanda Johnson, offers four-star comfort at two-star prices. Most of the seven cushy rooms are huge; all are air-conditioned and well-furnished; and a small kitchen is at your disposal with serve-yourself snacks and drinks (Db–€79–89, extra bed-€15, 2-night minimum, big breakfast with eggs-€6, closed Nov-Feb, 51 rue des Cordeliers, tel. 05 53 31 94 66, www.hotelsarlat.com, info@hotelsarlat.com).

$ Les Chambres du Glacier, where gentle Monsieur Da Costa offers four cavernous and surprisingly classy rooms above an outdoor café, is in the thick of Sarlat's pedestrian zone (perfect for market days). Rooms come with café noise, sky-high ceilings, big windows over Sarlat's world, polished wood floors, and bathrooms you can get lost in (Db–€60, Tb–€70, Qb–€82, Wi-Fi, place de la Liberté, tel. 05 53 29 99 99, www.chambres-du-glacier-sarlat.com, carlos.da.costa.24@wanadoo.fr).

$ La Maison du Notaire Royal, with friendly, English-speaking Pierre-Henri Toulemon and French-speaking Diane, has four large rooms with a private entry in a 17th-century home. It's located a few steps above the main square (Db–€45, €8/extra person up to 5, breakfast-€6, cash only, no deposit required, call a day ahead to confirm your approximate arrival time, look for big steps from northeast corner of place de la Liberté, 4 rue Magnanat, tel. 05 53 31 26 60, mobile 06 08 67 76 90, www.toulemon.com, p-h.toulemon@wanadoo.fr). They also rent two cottages with living rooms and kitchens a few blocks from the town center. One has two bedrooms and sleeps four; the other has three bedrooms and can sleep seven (3-day minimum, easy parking).

Near Sarlat

Many golden stone hotels (with easy parking) surround Sarlat; these listings are good for drivers who prefer to be close to Sarlat, yet in a semi-rural location.

$$$ Hôtel le Relais de Moussidière***, a five-minute drive from Sarlat (on the way to Beynac), offers affordable luxury in a lush setting. This nontraditional hotel has a huge pool, private decks, and an almost tropical feel. Faye Dunaway stayed here for a month while filming *The Messenger: The Story of Joan of Arc* (standard Db-€130, bigger Db-€160-180, Tb-€160-190, includes buffet breakfast, most rooms have air-con; in Moussidière Basse: leave Sarlat to the south, direction Bergerac, watch for hotel sign on left just after Citroën garage; tel. 05 53 28 28 74, fax 05 53 28 25 11, www.hotel-moussidiere.com, contact@hotel-moussidiere.com).

$ Hôtel la Verperie** ("Green Fields") is aptly named—it sits barely above Sarlat, surrounded by a park-like setting. Ideal for budget-minded families, the hotel has 25 rooms, a pool, table tennis, swings, restaurant, affordable rates, and adequate comfort in the bungalow-like rooms, each with a simple terrace (Db-€57-67, Tb-€77-87, Qb-€100-110, half-pension requested in high season-€65 per adult per day, a 15-minute walk just west of Sarlat, look for brown signs to *La Verperie* above the town's eastern side, tel. 05 53 59 00 20, fax 05 53 28 58 94, www.laverperie.com, hotel laverperie@wanadoo.fr).

Eating in Sarlat

Sarlat is slammed with restaurants that cater to tourists, but you can still dine well and cheap. The following places have been reliable; the last two are the most formal. If you have a car, consider driving to Beynac (see page 434) or La Roque-Gageac (page 432) for a riverfront dining experience. Wherever you dine, sample a glass of sweet Monbazillac wine with your foie gras.

La Mirandol, a high-energy spot in a town of sleepy restaurants, satisfies local diners with several floors of jam-packed rooms. Those in the know come here for hearty, affordable regional cuisine, thanks to the owner's commitment to providing good food at fair prices. Cap your meal with a wander through their mysteriously lit *cave* (reasonable salads, *plats du jour*, terrific €14-29 *menus*, daily, a block off rue de la République at 7 rue des Consuls, tel. 05 53 29 53 89).

Le Petit Manoir offers a creative fusion of regional classic cuisine served in a quiet, almost elegant setting. Ambience is best in the lovely courtyard, prices are reasonable (€17 and €32 *menus*), and the desserts deserve your attention (closed Mon; just off rue de la République, near the western end of Sarlat, at 3 Passage Payen; tel. 05 53 29 82 14).

Chez le Gaulois is a welcome change from the many traditional Dordogne places. Pyrenees-raised Olivier and Belgian-born

Beatrice serve a hearty mountain cuisine featuring fondue, raclette, *tartiflette* (roasted potatoes mixed with ham and cheese—comes with a good salad for €12), and thinly sliced ham (Olivier spends all evening slicing away). Ask about the daily special and trust Beatrice's advice. They have a few sidewalk tables, but the fun is inside and the service is English-fluent. The ceiling is cluttered with ham hocks, and the soundtrack is jazz (good salads, daily April–Oct, Nov–March closed Sun–Mon, near the TI at 1 rue Tourny, tel. 05 53 59 50 64).

Brasserie le Glacier offers great main-square views from its outdoor tables and good café fare at reasonable prices. Come here for friendly service, a big salad or *plat*, and a view of the lights warming the town buildings (daily, place de la Liberté, tel. 05 53 29 99 99, also rents rooms—see "Sleeping in Sarlat," earlier).

Le Bistro de l'Octroi, a few blocks north of the old town, is convenient to many hotels I list. Because it's a walk from the town center, it has to provide top cuisine and competitive prices to draw locals—and it does. This easygoing place serves fine bistro fare (mostly meat dishes) on a generous garden terrace and within the welcoming interior (several cheap *menus*, €18 three-course *menu*, daily, 111 avenue des Selves, tel. 05 53 30 83 40).

Pizzeria Romane is a cheap, spacious, and family-friendly eatery where you can watch your pizza cook (€9 pizza, closed Sun–Mon, on the quiet side of Sarlat at 3 côte de Toulouse, tel. 05 53 59 23 88).

Hôtel la Couleuvrine reeks of ambience, with heavy wood beams and white tablecloths. Choose between reliable regional cuisine in a fancy dining room or less expensive, simpler fare in the jazzy bistro (€20–26 *menus*, daily; also listed under "Sleeping in Sarlat," earlier).

Le Présidial is a lovely place for a refined meal in a historic mansion. The setting is exceptional—you're greeted with beautiful gardens (where you can dine in good weather), and the interior comes with high ceilings, stone walls, rich wood floors, and formal service (€27–40 *menus*, closed Sun, reservations smart, rue Landry, tel. 05 53 28 92 47).

Le Grand Bleu is the talk of Sarlat, having earned a Michelin star in under a year. Everyone raves about the contemporary cuisine (fish is a specialty) and the fair prices for a starred restaurant—book ahead (€33–70 *menus*, closed Mon, near the train station at 43 Avenue de la Gare, tel. 05 53 31 08 48, www.legrandbleu.eu).

Lemoine is a classy café where you can enjoy rich chocolate cake (you may know it as Chocolate Decadence) with a hot drink, or buy a few slices to go (daily, 13 rue de la République).

Sarlat Connections

Sarlat's TI has train schedules. Souillac and Périgueux are the train hubs for points within the greater region. For all the following destinations, you can go west, on the Libourne/Bordeaux line (transferring in either city, depending on your connection) or east, by SNCF bus to Souillac (covered by railpass, bus leaves from Sarlat train station). I've listed the fastest path in each case. Sarlat train info: tel. 05 53 59 00 21.

From Sarlat by Train to: Paris (7/day, allow 6 hours: 3/day with change in Libourne or Bordeaux–St. Jean, then TGV; and 4/day by bus to Souillac, then train with possible change in Brive-la-Gaillarde), **Amboise** (4/day, 5–6 hours, via Libourne or Bordeaux–St. Jean, then TGV to Tours' St. Pierre-des-Corps, then local train to Amboise), **Limoges/Oradour-sur-Glane** (slow and difficult trip with lots of changes, 5/day, 3–4 hours: 3/day by bus to Souillac and train to Limoges, then 15-minute walk to catch bus to Oradour-sur-Glane; and 2/day with change in Le Buisson and Périgueux), **Cahors** (5/day, 3 hours, bus to Souillac or Siorac, then train to Cahors), **Albi** (6/day, 5–7 hours with 2–3 changes, some require bus from Sarlat to Souillac), **Carcassonne** (4/day, 5.5–7.5 hours, 1–2 changes, some require bus from Sarlat to Souillac), **St. Emilion** (3–4/day, 2 hours, no transfer, or 3/day to nearby Libourne, then bus or taxi to St. Emilion).

To Beynac, La Roque-Gageac, Castelnaud, and Domme: These are accessible only by taxi (allow €19–25) or bike (best rented in Sarlat). See Sarlat's "Helpful Hints" on page 415 for specifics.

The Best of the Dordogne River Valley

The most striking stretch of the Dordogne lies between Carsac and Beynac. Traveling by canoe is the best way to savor the highlights of the Dordogne River Valley, though several scenic sights lie off the river and require a car or bike. Following my "Dordogne River Valley Scenic Loop" directions (next page), you can easily link Sarlat with La Roque-Gageac, Beynac and its château, and Castelnaud before returning to Sarlat.

Planning Your Time

Drivers should allow a minimum of a half-day to sample the river valley (a full day if they toss in a cave visit). Vitrac Port (near Sarlat) is the best place to park for a canoe ride down the river. La Roque-Gageac, Beynac, and Domme have good restaurants. There are a few good places to witness the *gavage* (feeding of the geese and ducks to make foie gras) between Beynac and Sarlat (their dinner time is generally about 18:00).

Self-Guided Tours

▲▲Dordogne River Valley Scenic Loop

Following these directions, beginning and ending in Sarlat, you can see this area by car or bike (27 hilly miles). Cyclists can cut 10 miles off this distance and see most of the highlights by aiming for La Roque-Gageac first (leave Sarlat to the south, then follow signs to *La Roque-Gageac* to pick up the driving tour described below). For a somewhat longer, more scenic bike trip that still avoids a busy road, follow D-704 from Sarlat toward Cahors, then take the Montfort turn-off (well-signed at a roundabout)—see map on page 430. From Montfort, follow the river downstream to La Roque-Gageac.

The Tour Begins: Follow signs as you leave Sarlat on D-704 toward *Cahors* and *Carsac*. Not long after leaving Sarlat, pass the foie gras outlet store, then the limestone quarry that gives the houses in this area their lemony color. The cornfields are busy growing food for ducks and geese—locals are appalled that humans would eat the stuff.

Don't miss the little signposted exit on the right to the *Église de Carsac* (Church of Carsac), just before **Carsac.** Set peacefully among cornfields, with its WWI monument, bonsai-like plane trees, and simple Romanesque exterior, the church is part of a vivid rural French scene. Take a break here and enter the church if it's open.

From here, continue on, following signs to *Montfort.* About a half-mile (1 kilometer) west of Carsac, pull over to enjoy the scenic viewpoint (overlooking a bend in the river known as Cingle de Montfort). Across the Dordogne River, fields of walnut trees stretch to distant castles, and the nearby hills are covered in oak trees. This region of the Périgord is nicknamed "black Périgord" for its thick blanket of oaks, which stay leafy throughout the winter. The fairy-tale castle you see is **Montfort,** which was once the medieval home of Simon de Montfort, who led the Cathar Crusades in the early 13th century. Today it's considered mysterious by locals. (The hometown rumor is that the castle is now the home of a brother of the emir of Kuwait.)

Continue on, passing under Montfort's castle (not worth a stop). If you're combining a canoe trip with this drive, cross the river following signs to *Domme,* and find my recommended canoe rental on the right side (see "Dordogne Canoe Trip," next). The very touristy *bastide* (fortified village) of **Domme** is worth a side-trip from Vitrac Port or La Roque-Gageac for its sensational views. Our driving route continues to the more important riverfront villages of **La Roque-Gageac**, then on to **Castelnaud**, and finally to **Beynac** (all described later in this chapter). From Beynac, it's a quick run back to Sarlat.

▲▲▲Dordogne Canoe Trip

For a refreshing break from the car or train, explore the riverside castles and villages of the Dordogne by canoe.

You can rent plastic boats—which are hard, light, and inde-structible—from many outfits in this area. Whether a one-person kayak or a two-person canoe, they're stable enough for beginners. Many rental places will pick you up at an agreed-upon spot (even in Sarlat, provided that your group is big enough, and they aren't too busy). All companies let you put in anytime between 9:30 and 16:00 (if you start at 16:00, they'll pick you up at about 18:00). They all charge about the same (€11–16/person for two-person canoes, €17–23 for one-person kayaks). You'll get a life vest and, for a few extra euros, a watertight bucket in which to store your belongings. (The bucket is too big for just a camera, watch, wallet, and cell phone, so bring a resealable plastic baggie or something similar for dry storage on the canoe.)

The trip is fun even in light rain (if you don't mind getting wet)—but heavy rains can make the current too fast to handle, so be sure to check on river levels. If you don't see many other canoes in the river, that's a sign that the river is too high—ask before you rent.

Beach your boat wherever it works to take a break—it's light enough that you can simply drag it up high and dry to go explore. (The canoes aren't worth stealing, as they're cheap and clearly color-coded for their parent company.) It's OK if you're a com-plete novice—the only whitewater you'll encounter will be the rare wake of passing tour boats...and your travel partner frothing at the views.

Of the region's many canoe companies, only **Copeyre Canoë** has a pull-out arrangement in Beynac (to get to their Vitrac put-in base, cross the river at Port Vitrac toward Cénac, and turn right). Readers of this book get a 10 percent discount in 2011, and they'll even pick you up in Sarlat for free (this allows non-drivers a chance to explore the riverfront villages for the price of a canoe trip—tip the driver a few euros for this helpful service, tel. 05 53 28 23 82, mobile 06 83 27 30 06, www.canoe-copeyre.com). Allow time to explore Beynac after your river paddle and before the return shuttle trip.

Dordogne Canoe Trips

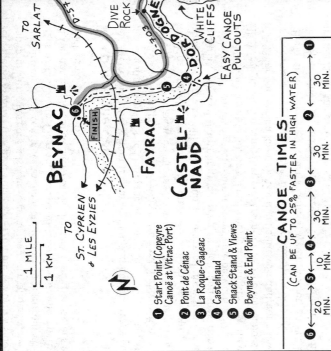

1 MILE
1 KM

TO
SARLAT

TO
ST. CYPRIEN
& LES EYZIES

N

DIVE ROCK

WHITE CLIFFS

DORDOGNE

BEYNAC

FINISH

FAYRAC

CASTEL-NAUD

EASY CANOE PULLOUTS

1 Start Point (Copeyre Canoe at Vitrac Port)
2 Pont de Cénac
3 La Roque-Gageac
4 Castelnaud
5 Snack Stand & Views
6 Beynac & End Point

CANOE TIMES
(CAN BE UP TO 25% FASTER IN HIGH WATER)

1 ← 30 MIN. → 2 ← 30 MIN. → 3 ← 30 MIN. → 4 ← 10 MIN. → 5 ← 20 MIN. → 6

The Nine-Mile, Two-Hour Paddle from Vitrac Port to Beynac:

This is the most interesting, scenic, and handy trip if you're based in or near Sarlat. Vitrac Port, on the river close to Sarlat, is a good starting point. And, with its mighty castle and pleasant hotels and restaurants, Beynac delivers the perfect finale to your journey.

Here's a rundown of the two-hour Vitrac–Beynac adventure: Leave Vitrac Port, paddling through lush, forested land. The fortified hill town of Domme will be dead ahead. Pass through Heron Gulch, and after about 45 minutes you'll come to La Roque-Gageac (one of two easy and worthwhile stops before Beynac).

Paddle past La Roque-Gageac's wooden docks (where the tour boats normally tie up) to the stone ramp at the town. Do a 180-degree turn and beach thyself, dragging the boat high and dry. From there you're in La Roque-Gageac's tiny town center, with a TI and plenty of restaurants nearby. Enjoy the town (described on page 432) before heading back to your canoe and into the water.

When leaving La Roque-Gageac, float backward to enjoy the village view. About 15 minutes farther downstream, you'll approach

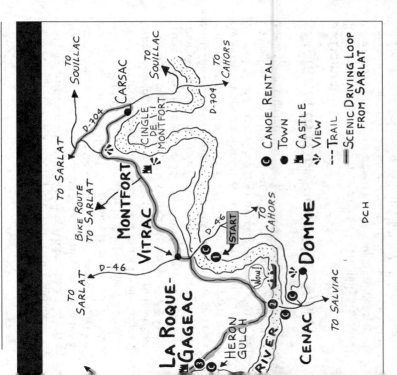

DORDOGNE AND NEARBY

views of the feudal village and castle of Castelnaud. Look for the castle's huge model of a medieval catapult silhouetted menacingly against the sky (it's a steep but worthwhile climb to tour this castle—see page 434). Two grassy pullouts flank the bridge below the castle, and the bridge arches make terrific frames for castle views. Just past the grass there's a small market and charcuterie with all you need for a picnic, and a café/restaurant.

Another 15 minutes downstream brings sweeping views of Château de Fayrac on your left. The lords of Castelnaud built this to better spy on Beynac during the Hundred Years' War. Now on to your last stop: Beynac. The awesome Beynac castle—looming high above the town—gets better and better as you approach. Slow down and enjoy the ride (sometimes there's a snack stand with the same views at the bridge on the right). Keep to the right of the river as you approach the Copeyre Canoë depot at the downstream end of town. You'll see the ramp just before the parking lot and wooden dock (where the tour boats generally tie up). Do another 180-degree turn, and beach yourself hard. The office is right there. Return your boat, and explore Beynac (described on page 434).

Other Canoe Options: All along the river you'll see canoe companies, each with stacks of plastic canoes. Depending on their location and relations with places to pull out, each one works best on a particular stretch of the river. All have essentially the same policies. Below Domme in Cénac, **Dordogne Randonnées** has canoes and kayaks for the scenic two-hour stretch to a pullout near Beynac (to reach their office coming from Sarlat or Beynac, take the first left after crossing the bridge to Cénac, tel. 05 53 28 22 01, randodordogne@wanadoo.fr). In La Roque-Gageac, **Canoe-Dordogne** rents canoes for the appealing two-hour float to Château des Milandes, allowing canoers to stop in Beynac before the pullout (tel. 05 53 29 58 50). **Copeyre Canoë** also arranges a 14-mile trip from Carsac to Beynac, adding the gorgeous Montfort loop, called *Cingle de Montfort* (they also do a longer two-day trip, tel. 05 53 28 23 82, www.canoe-copeyre.com). For a lazier no-paddle alternative, try a boat cruise on the river to Castelnaud and back, either from Beynac (see page 434) or La Roque-Gageac (see below). Both trips are great for landlubbers (€8-9, 50-60 minutes).

Sights in the Dordogne River Valley

▲▲Domme

This overrun little town merits a stop for its stunning view, and is best early or late, when crowds are fewer and the light is best. Follow signs up to *La Bastide de Domme*. Park at a pay lot in the town (parking meters are checked), then follow *Le Panorama* signs. You'll find picnic-perfect benches and a café with views at the panorama, and many forgettable restaurants in the town.

$$$ Hôtel de l'Esplanade turns its back on the touristy village and delivers the valley's most sensational views from many of its comfortable bedrooms and restaurant tables. If you must choose, come for the restaurant (book ahead), where chef Pascal is turning heads with his exquisite regional dishes (Db-€90-125, view Db-€140-150; two-course menu-€25, three-course menu-€32; tel. 05 53 28 31 41, fax 05 53 28 49 92, www.esplanade-perigord.com, esplanade.domme@wanadoo.fr).

▲▲▲La Roque-Gageac

Whether you're joyriding or paddling the Dordogne, La Roque-Gageac (lah rohk-gah-zhahk) is an essential stop—and a strong contender on all the "cutest towns in France" lists. Called by most simply "La Roque" ("The Rock"), it looks sculpted out of the rock between the river and the cliffs. At the upstream end of town, you'll find plenty of parking; the **TI** (Easter-Sept daily 10:00-12:00 & 14:00-18:00, closed off-season, tel. 05 53 29 17 01); a WC; swings and slides for kids; canoe rental; and *pétanque* (*boules*) courts, which are lively on summer evenings (17:00–21:00). A small market brightens La Roque-Gageac on Friday mornings. Though busy with day-trippers, the town is tranquil at night.

La Roque-Gageac is a one-street town stretching along the river. Cars and strollers compete for the same riverfront space.

Walk above the river, past the boat docks and trees, and survey the town: The highest stone work (on the far right) was home to the town's earliest inhabitants, in the 10th century. The 12th-century cave-dwellers' village (to the left, high above the Hôtel Belle Etoile) was built during the era of Norman (Viking) river raids. Long after the Vikings were tamed, French soldiers used this lofty perch as a barracks while fighting against England in the Hundred Years' War.

Now locate the exotic foliage by the church on the right. Tropical gardens (bamboo, bananas, lemons, and so on) are a village forte, because limestone absorbs heat.

Every winter, La Roque-Gageac endures a flood that would leave you (standing where you are now) underwater. When there's a big rain in central France, La Roque-Gageac floods two days later. The first floors of all the riverfront buildings are vacated off-season. (A house about five buildings downriver from Hôtel Belle Etoile shows various high-water marks—*inondation* means "flood.") Looking farther downstream, notice the fanciful castle built in the 19th century by a British aristocrat (whose family still nurtures Joan of Arc dreams in its turrets). The old building just beyond that (downstream end of town) actually is historic—it's the quarantine house, where lepers and out-of-town visitors who dropped by in times of plague would be kept (after their boats were burned).

On the river you'll see small tour boats. Though modern, they're modeled after boats called *gabarres*, originally built here to take prized oak barrels filled with local wine down to Bordeaux. Unable to return against the river current, those boats were routinely taken apart for their lumber. Today, tourists, rather than barrels, fill the boats as they make a scenic round-trip on one-hour cruises to Castelnaud and back (€9, 2/hour, April–Nov daily, tel. 05 53 29 40 44). If you're experiencing a movie-based déjà vu, it's because these actual boats (dolled up, of course) were used by Johnny Depp, who delighted viewers and Juliette Binoche alike, in the movie *Chocolat*.

Climb into the town by strolling up the cobbled lane to the right of the Hôtel Belle Etoile. The path ends where a right turn takes you to the exotic garden and viewpoint (in front of the simple church), and a left turn takes you to the privately owned Fort Troglodytique (likely closed due to damage from a small avalanche). When it's open, the fort—with lots of steps, grand views, and piles of rocks in caves evoking medieval paranoia—is worth the money and energy only if you won't be visiting the similar but much better La Roque St. Christophe (described on page 455).

▲▲Château de Castelnaud

This crumbling castle looks less mighty than Château de Beynac (across the river), but it packs a powerful medieval punch. Now

a museum, every room in the château has a story to tell. Several rooms display weaponry and artifacts from the Hundred Years' War, and others have videos (with English subtitles), interactive computers (in English), and castle models. From the armory to the kitchen, the whole experience is designed to teach you about daily castle life, from the battlefield to the dinner table. The upper courtyard has a 150-foot-deep well (drop a pebble). The rampart views are as unbeatable as the siege machines (located outside the walls) are formidable. Pick up the free, essential English explanations and follow *Suite de la Visite* signs to stay the course (€8, daily July-Aug 9:00–20:00, April-June and Sept 10:00–19:00, Oct and Feb-March 10:00–18:00, Nov-Jan 14:00–17:00, last entry one hour before closing; from the river, it's a steep 20-minute hike through the village, or drive to the €3 parking lot at the castle gate; daily demonstrations of medieval warfare mid-July-Aug, several restaurants near the castle's parking lot, tel. 05 53 31 30 00, www .castelnaud.com).

You can stop at Castelnaud on your canoe trip, or hike an hour from Beynac along a riverside path (though it's tricky to follow in parts—it hugs the river as it passes through campgrounds and farms—determined walkers do fine).

▲▲▲Beynac

Four miles downstream from La Roque-Gageac, Beynac (bay-nak) is the other must-see, picture-perfect Dordogne village. It comes with a big, foreboding bonus: one of the most imposing castles in France.

This feudal village tumbles down a steep hill from its majestic castle to the river far below. You'll have the Dordogne River at your doorstep and a perfectly preserved medieval village wind-

ing, like a sepia-tone film set, from the beach to the castle above. Except for the castle, there's nothing to "tour." The purely stone village—with steep streets that still have their Languedoc (old French) names—is just plain pretty. The floodlit village is always open for evening strollers.

Orientation: The **TI** is across from the recommended Hôtel du Château (daily 10:00–12:30 & 14:00–17:30, tel. 05 53 29 43 08). Pick up the *Plan de Beynac* in English for a simple self-guided walking tour, and get information on hiking and canoes. A few steps down from the TI is the post office (which has an ATM). If you need a lift, call Beynac-based **Taxi Corinne** (see page 409). From June to September, there's a sweet little market on Monday mornings in the river parking lot. In summer (mid-June–mid-Sept), drivers pay to park at lots located on the river, way up at the castle (follow signs to *Château de Beynac*), or halfway between. The same parking ticket works up at the château if you decide against the climb.

Hikes—A too-busy road separates Beynac from its river. The village climbs steeply uphill from river to château—the farther you get from the road, the more medieval the village feels. (You can drive up via a long lane looping around the back of town.) A trail, which begins across from Hôtel Bonnet at the eastern end of town, follows the river toward Castelnaud, with great views back toward Beynac and—for able route-finders—a healthy one-hour hike to Castelnaud. Make time to walk at least a few hundred yards along this trail to enjoy the view to Beynac.

▲▲**Château de Beynac**—Beynac's brooding, cliff-clinging château soars 500 feet above the Dordogne River. During the Hundred Years' War (see sidebar on page 255), the castle of Beynac housed the French, while the British set up camp across the river at Castelnaud. From the condition of the castles, I'd say France won. This sparsely furnished castle is best for its valley views, but it still manages to evoke a powerful medieval feel. (These castles never had much furniture in any case.) Stone oil lamps light the way; swords, spears, and crossbows keep kids entertained.

I like the soldiers' party room best—park your sword at the door and hang your crossbow on the hooks above, *s'il vous plaît*. Notice the list across from the ticket window showing *Beynac et Ses Barons* (the barons of Beynac; *croisade* means "Crusade," and *Coeur de Lion* means "Lionheart."—Richard the Lionhearted spent 10 years here). The current owner lives above the ticket booth. Authentic-looking wooden stockades were installed for the 1998 filming of the movie *The Messenger: The Story of Joan of Arc*. You're free to wander on your own, though you might be required to follow a tour after 17:00. Pick up the English explanations (€0.15) or spring for the excellent €5 pamphlet (€7.50, daily June–Sept 10:00–18:30, April–May and Oct closes at 18:00, Nov–March at 16:00 or 17:00—depending on weather and whim, last entry 45 minutes before closing, tel. 05 53 29 50 40).

Viewpoints—Even if you pass on the castle, hike or drive up to the town lookout for a commanding top-of-the-village view, which overlooks several castles and the river. Walk outside the village at the top (parking available), turn right (passing the little cemetery), and walk uphill until the view opens up. Castelnaud's castle hangs on the hill in the distance straight ahead; Château de Fayrac (owned by a Texan) is by the bridge just in front of Castelnaud, and was originally constructed by the lords of Castelnaud to keep a closer eye on the castle of Beynac. The Château de Marqueyssac is on a hill a bit to the left, and was built by the barons of Beynac to keep a closer eye on the boys at Castelnaud. More than a thousand such castles were erected in the Dordogne alone during the Hundred Years' War (1336–1453).

Two exceptional views of Beynac lie far below. The first is along the riverside path opposite Hôtel Bonnet (walk as far as you can for great views back to Beynac); for the second, drive about a half-mile toward La Roque-Gageac, turn right at the Ferme du Château restaurant, and follow the road to its end. But for the best (and easiest) village view, simply step up on the short wall between the parking lot and the river—just try fitting it all in your camera's viewfinder.

Boat Trips—Boats leave from Beynac's riverside parking lot for relaxing, 50-minute river cruises to Castelnaud and back (€8, nearly hourly, departures Easter–Oct daily 10:00–12:30 & 14:00–18:00, more frequent trips July–Aug, written English explanations, tel. 05 53 28 51 15).

Foie Gras Farms

During the evenings, many farms in this area let you witness the force-feeding of geese for the "ultimate pleasure" of foie gras. Look for *Gavage* signs, but beware: It's hard for the squeamish to watch (read the sidebar on the next page for a description before you visit). Of the three places listed below, the first is by far the best, with the only real tour. The second is a short walk from the Beynac castle (and therefore very handy), and the last is tiny, homey, and has the most flexible hours. For locations, see the map on page 444.

Elevage du Bouyssou, a big, homey goose farm a short drive from Sarlat, is run by a couple who enjoy their work. Denis Mazet (the latest in a long line of goose farmers here) spends five hours a day feeding his gaggle of geese. His wife, Nathalie—clearly in love with country life—speaks wonderful English and enthusiastically shows guests around their idyllic farm. Each evening, she leads a one-hour, kid-friendly tour. You'll meet the geese babies, do a little unforced feeding, and hear how every part of the goose (except heads and feet) is used—even feathers (for pillows). Nathalie explains why locals see the force-feeding as humane (comparable to raising any other animal for human consumption) before you step into the dark barn where about a hundred geese await another dinner. The tour finishes in the little shop. They raise and slaughter a thousand geese annually, producing about 1,500 pounds of foie gras—most of which is sold directly to visitors at good prices. In July and August, Nathalie includes a tasting of her products paired with a sweet wine (tours daily at 18:30 year-round, groups welcome, English tour on request at any time, tel. 05 53 31 12 31, elevage.bouyssou@wanadoo.fr). To get to the farm, leave Sarlat on the Carsac-bound road (D-704), go about seven kilometers (4.5 miles) in the direction of Carsac, turn left at the cement plant, and follow *Bouyssou* signs until you reach the farm.

Madame Gauthier, a small farm where you can also observe the *gavage* and buy the product, is just down the road behind Château de Beynac. You can park there or walk 10 minutes from the château through the parking lot and away from the river—you'll see signs (demonstrations most days 17:30–19:30, call ahead to confirm, best to come at 17:30, no tour, tel. 05 53 29 51 45).

La Ferme de l'Angle is a tiny goose farm in the scenic middle of nowhere, a short distance north of Sarlat. Christiane (who speaks English) and son Cyril (who speaks goose) enjoy playing host to the guests who drop by. While there's no formal tour here and only a handful of geese, this is an easy way to see the *gavage* in action—Cyril will demonstrate at just about any time (daily 10:30–12:00 & 16:30–18:00, tel. 05 53 31 16 63). To get to the farm, located three miles from Sarlat, take D-704 (direction: Brive/Montignac), at Restaurant la Vieille Grange, take a left and follow signs.

Foie Gras and Force-Feeding the Geese and Ducks

Force-feeding geese and ducks has the result of quickly fattening their livers, in order to make the Dordogne specialty, foie gras. The practice is as controversial among animal rights' activists as bullfighting. And though some view these birds as tortured prisoners, here's the (politically incorrect) perspective of those who produce and consume such farm-raised animals:

French enthusiasts of *la gavage* (as the force-feeding process is called) say the animals are calm, in no pain, and are designed to take in food in this manner, because of their massive gullets and expandable livers (used to store lots of fat for their long migrations). Geese and ducks do not have a gag reflex, and the linings of their throats are tough (they swallow rocks to store in their gizzards for grinding the food they eat). They can eat lots of food easily, without choking. They live lives at least as comfy as the chickens, cows, and pigs that many people have no problem eating, and are slaughtered as humanely as any nonhuman can expect in this food-chain existence.

The quality of foie gras depends on a stress-free environment; the birds do best with the same human feeder and a steady flow of good corn. These mostly free-range geese and ducks live six months (most of our factory-farmed chickens in

▲Château de Commarque

This mystical medieval castle ruin is ripe for hikers wanting to get away from it all. From the remote and secluded parking lot, it's a 20-minute walk down through a forest of chestnut trees to a clearing, where the mostly ruined castle appears like a mirage. Pay the entry fee, pick up the English brochure, and you're free to scour the sight at will. The main event is the castle, but you'll also discover the remains of a chapel and several other buildings. Owner Hubert de Commarque bought the castle in 1968 and has been digging it out of the forest ever since. During the summer, you may see archaeology students doing excavating work (€6.50, daily 10:00–19:00, until 20:00 in summer, last entry one hour before closing, WCs back at the parking lot, off D-47 and D-6 between Sarlat and Les Eyzies-de-Tayac—see map on page 444, www .commarque.com). From Sarlat, follow signs to *Les Eyzies*, then follow the D-6 to Marquay. As you pass through Marquay, keep the US live less than two months, and are plumped with hormones). Their "golden weeks" are the last three or four, when they go into the pen to have their livers fattened. With two or three feedings a day, their liver grows from about a quarter-pound to nearly two pounds. A goose with a fattened liver looks like he's waddling around with a full diaper under his feathers. (Signs and placards in the towns of the region show geese with this unique and, for foie gras-lovers, mouthwatering shape.) The same process is applied to ducks to get the marginally less exquisite and less expensive duck-liver foie gras.

The varieties of product you'll be tempted to buy (or order in restaurants) can be confusing. Here's a primer: first, *foie gras* means "fattened liver"; *foie gras d'oie* is from a goose, and *foie gras de canard* is from a duck (you'll also see a blend of the two). *Pâté de foie gras* is a "paste" of foie gras combined with other meats, fats, and seasonings (think of liverwurst). Most American consumers get the chance to eat foie gras only in the form of pâtés.

The *foie gras d'oie entier* (a solid chunk of pure goose liver) is the most expensive and prized version of canned foie gras, costing about €18 for 130 grams (about a tuna-can-size tin). The *bloc de foie gras d'oie* is made of chunks of pure goose liver that have been pressed together; it's more easily spreadable (figure €14 for 130 grams). The *medaillons de foie gras d'oie* must be at least 50 percent foie gras (the rest will be a pâté filler, about €8 for 130 grams). A small tin of blended duck-and-goose foie gras costs about €5.

After a week in the Dordogne, I leave feeling a strong need for foie gras detox.

right, following *Commarque* signs, then go about two kilometers (1.25 miles) and turn right. Notice that this is very close to the Abri du Cap Blanc Cro-Magnon cave (see page 452).

Maison de Reignac

For over 700 years, a powerful lord ruled from this unusual home carved out of a rock face high above the Vézère River. It's a short but steep hike to the entry. From there you'll climb through several floors of well-furnished rooms, some with fireplaces lit. Kids love this tree house of a place. Your tour concludes in a room that houses torture devices and highlights man's creative abilities to inflict pain...and a slow death. You'll see full-size models of interrogation chairs, a spike-covered rack, a guillotine, and a warden's corset. The loaner English handout provides good context (€7, daily 10:00–18:00, May–Sept until 19:00, just north of the village of Tursac, tel. 05 53 50 69 54, www.maison-forte-reignac.com).

Sleeping and Eating in the Dordogne River Valley

(€1= about $1.25, country code: 33)

Those with a car can enjoy plush and tranquil rural accommodations at great prices. Here are a handful of good-value places located within a 15-minute drive of Sarlat. I like them for their cozy village locations, the comfort they provide, the views they offer, or for a combination of these qualities. Read about the villages they're in (listed earlier), then make your choice—you can't go wrong.

Sleeping and Eating in and near La Roque-Gageac

Along with Beynac, this is one of the region's most beautiful villages. Park in the lot at the eastern end of town if you're staying in La Roque-Gageac, and take everything of value out of your car.

$$ Hôtel la Belle Etoile**, located on the river in the center of La Roque-Gageac, is a very well-managed hotel and restaurant. Hostess Danielle and chef Régis (ray-geez)—who greets every diner—make the ideal team, with a loyal staff. Rooms are comfy and well-maintained; most have river views. The hotel is closed from November through March (non-riverview Db-€55, riverview Db-€66 or €76 for better view—I like the €66 rooms, gorgeous suite-€120-150, reserve private parking ahead, tel. 05 53 29 51 44, fax 05 53 29 45 63, www.belleetoile.fr, hotel.belle-etoile @wanadoo.fr). I discovered this place through its **restaurant**—it's where locals go for a fine meal. They serve a memorable dinner of classic French cuisine in a romantic setting. The serving sizes are not great, but the quality is (*menus* from €27, closed for lunch Wed and all day Mon).

$$ Hôtel le Périgord** sits alone a few bends upriver from La Roque-Gageac. This newer hotel lies across the river below the hill town of Domme, and rents traditional rooms at fair rates with nice gardens, a view pool, tennis courts, a game room, and a good restaurant (Db-€61-71, extra person-€16, dinner *menus* from €23, Port de Domme, tel. 05 53 28 36 55, fax 05 53 28 38 73, www .hotelleperigord.eu, bienvenue@hotelleperigord.eu).

$ L'Auberge des Platanes**, across from the TI and parking lot, rents 13 rooms above a sprawling café and a restaurant. Guests take a back seat to café clients, but the staff is friendly and rooms are traditional, comfortable, and a good value (Sb-€36, Db-€46-51, Tb-€56-66, tel. 05 53 29 51 58, fax 05 53 31 19 32, www.aubergedesplatanes.com, contact@aubergedesplatanes .com).

Sleeping in Beynac

My favorite village on the river comes with some traffic noise and the region's greatest castle. Pay to park at the riverside lot (daily mid-June–mid-Sept) or park for free 300 yards up the road toward the castle. All parking is free overnight (19:00–10:00) and off-season. Parked cars are appealing to thieves.

$$ Hôtel du Château**, on the river at Beynac's only—but busy—intersection, is run by an enterprising couple. There's a full café/bar, a good restaurant, and a small swimming pool. It's run by eager-to-please Sarissa and Christoph, a French-Dutch couple with three children. The 16 rooms, most with queen-size beds, are humble and bright. Some have street noise, though it's mitigated by air-conditioning (available in some rooms) and insulated windows. Other rooms have terraces facing the river; four rooms can sleep up to four people, and one has a full kitchen. Their half-pension is a good value (Sb–€45–65, Db–€60–78, price range is from mid- to high season, breakfast-€8, free Internet access and Wi-Fi, tel. 05 53 29 19 20, fax 05 53 28 55 56, www.hotelduchateau-dordogne .com, info@hotelduchateau-dordogne.com).

$ Le Petit Versailles does its name justice, with five immaculate rooms that Louis would have appreciated. The place has a quiet terrace and garden, and—best of all—the welcoming Fleurys, Jean-Claude, and Françoise, who speak just enough English (Db–€60, three rooms have fine views, all have big beds, includes large English breakfast, cash only, no smoking anywhere, reserve ahead for a terrific home-cooked dinner-€20, Internet access and Wi-Fi, laundry facilities, route du Château, tel. 06 71 88 59 72, www.le petitversailles.fr, info@lepetitversailles.fr). With the river on your right, take the small road—wedged between the hill and Hôtel Bonnet—for a half-mile, turn right when you see their sign and continue 100 yards, then take a right down a steep driveway.

Eating in Beynac

Beynac has a handful of worthwhile restaurants and a bakery with handy picnic-ready lunch items (across from the TI). Have a drink up high at the café opposite the castle entry, or down below at the café that hides right on the river (walk down the steps across from Hôtel du Château), and stay for dinner if the spirit moves you.

Hôtel du Château features a handsome dining room, air-conditioned comfort, generous servings, and reasonable prices (€16 salad/pasta bar, dinner *menus*–€23–36, great *omelet aux cèpes*–€19, daily, see hotel listing earlier).

Taverne/Café des Remparts, Beynac's scenic eatery, faces the castle at the top of the town and serves copious salads, good omelets, and *plats*. I can't imagine leaving Beynac without relaxing at their view-perfect café for at least a drink; it's best at night, but call ahead to be sure they're open (July–Aug daily for lunch and maybe dinner, otherwise open daily for lunch, across from castle, tel. 05 53 29 57 76).

La Petite Tonnelle, cut into the rock, has a romantic interior and a fine terrace out front. Locals love it for its tasty cuisine served at fair prices. It's a block up from Hôtel du Château (€16 two-course *menu*, €30 three-course *menu*, €34 gastronomic *menu*, May–Sept daily, Oct–April closed Tue–Wed, on the road to the castle, tel. 05 53 29 95 18).

Sleeping near Castelnaud

This village, ideally situated between La Roque-Gageac and Beynac, has three excellent B&B choices nearby.

$$ La Tour de Cause is where California refugees Albert and Caitlin have found their heaven, amid their renovated farmhouse with five top-quality rooms, a big pool, and, best of all, a *pétanque* court. Albert restores homes in California, and has brought his considerable talent to France (Sb–€75, Db–€92, includes breakfast, cash only, 2-night minimum, en-suite bathrooms—some with immense walk-in showers, closed Nov–April, Internet access, tel. 05 53 30 30 51, US tel. 707/527-5051, www.latourdecause.com, info@latourdecause.com). From the Dordogne River, cross the bridge to Castelnaud, follow signs toward *Daglan*, and turn right in the hamlet of Pont de Cause; park at the green gate.

$$ Château Nineyrol is a relaxed, welcoming place run by British expat Anne Penfold, who is as excited about this region as you are. She has five guest rooms with personality: two big rooms (each sleeps up to four) and three smallish doubles; all the rooms have en-suite bathrooms. Enjoy the large pool and terrace with views of Castelnaud castle (Db–€65-85, Tb–€78-105, Qb–€86-136, dinner by arrangement-€25/person includes drinks, laundry service, tel. 05 53 30 46 01, mobile 06 33 61 34 63, www.nineyrol.com, admin@nineyrol.com). From Beynac, it's on the road to La Roque-Gageac on your left, 100 yards past the turnoff for Castelnaud.

$ Le Lys de Castelnaud is run by French medieval enthusiasts Nathalie and Dominique. Nathalie is a Joan of Arc fanatic and speaks sufficient English to explain her passion. The decor is steeped in the Middle Ages, with knights in armor, tapestries, and old swords. The four rooms are well-priced (three have Castelnaud views) and have all the modern conveniences (Db–€55-65, Tb/Qb–€80-100, cash only, Internet access, tel. 05 53 28 20 27, mobile 06 09 57 21 97, www.chambres-dordogne.com, lysdecastelnaud@aol.com). It's well-signed at the foot of the road that leads across the river to Castelnaud.

Sleeping in Montfort

There's more to this castle-topped village than meets the eye—leave most tourists behind and find a few cafés, a pizzeria, and a handful of *chambres d'hôtes*, including this recommended listing.

$$ Chambres la Barde is where Steve and Bronwen offer five sumptuous rooms in their warm, modern stone home. They have a swimming pool, a cozy lounge, a big grass yard, a communal kitchen, a *pétanque* court, a game room, and views to Montfort castle from each room's terrace (Db-€56–87, extra person-€10, breakfast-€7, one room sleeps five, cash only, Wi-Fi, below Montfort castle—green signs guide you there, tel. 05 53 28 24 34, mobile 06 21 96 51 90, www.perigord-dordogne-sarlat.com, steve .houghton@wanadoo.fr).

Cro-Magnon Caves

The towns and sights of the Dordogne region—including Les Eyzies-de-Tayac, Grotte de Font-de-Gaume, Abri du Cap Blanc, Grotte de Rouffignac, Lascaux II, and Grotte de Cougnac—have a rich history of prehistoric cave art. The paintings you'll see here are famous throughout the world for their remarkably modern-looking technique, beauty, and mystery. To fully appreciate them, take time to read the following information, written by Gene Openshaw, on the purpose of the art and the Cro-Magnon style of painting.

Cave Art 101

From 18,000 to 10,000 B.C., long before Stonehenge, before the pyramids, before metalworking, farming, and domesticated dogs, back when mammoths and saber-toothed cats still roamed the earth, prehistoric people painted deep inside limestone caverns in southern France and northern Spain. These are not crude doodles with a charcoal-tipped stick. They're sophisticated, costly, and time-consuming engineering projects planned and executed by dedicated artists supported by a unified and stable culture—the Magdalenians.

The Magdalenians (c. 18,000–10,000 B.C.): These hunter-gatherers of the Upper Paleolithic period (40,000–10,000 B.C.) were driven south by the Second Ice Age. (Historians named them after the Madeline archaeological site.) The Magdalenians flourished in southern France and northern Spain for eight millennia—long enough to chronicle the evolution and extinction of several animal species. (Think: Egypt lasted a mere 3,000 years; Rome lasted 1,000; America fewer than 250 so far.)

Physically, the people were Cro-Magnons. Unlike hulking,

Cro-Magnon Caves near Sarlat

beetle-browed Neanderthals, Cro-Magnons were fully developed *Homo sapiens* who could blend in to our modern population. We know these people by the possessions found in their settlements: stone axes, flint arrowheads, bone needles for making clothes, musical instruments, grease lamps (without their juniper wicks), and cave paintings and sculpture. Many objects are beautifully decorated.

The Magdalenians did not live in the deep limestone caverns they painted (which are cold and difficult to access). But many did live in the shallow cliffside caves that you'll see throughout your Dordogne travels, which were continuously inhabited from prehistoric times until the Middle Ages.

The Paintings: Though there are dozens of caves painted over a span of more than 8,000 years, they're all surprisingly similar.

These Stone Age hunters painted the animals they hunted—bison or bulls (especially at Lascaux and Grotte de Font-de-Gaume), horses, deer, reindeer, ibex (mountain goats), wolves, bears, and cats, plus animals that are now extinct—mammoths (the engravings at Grotte de Rouffignac), woolly rhinoceros (at Grotte de Font-de-Gaume), and wild oxen.

Besides animals, you'll see geometric and abstract designs, such as circles, squiggles, and hash marks. There's scarcely a *Homo sapiens* in sight (except the famous "fallen hunter" at Lascaux), but there are human handprints traced on the wall by blowing paint through a hollow bone tube around the hand. The hunter-gatherers painted the animals they hunted...but none of the plants they gathered.

Style: The animals stand in profile, with unnaturally big bodies and small limbs and heads. Black, red, and yellow dominate (with some white, brown, and violet). The thick black outlines are often wavy, suggesting the animal in motion. Except for a few friezes showing a conga line of animals running across the cave wall, there is no apparent order or composition. Some paintings are simply superimposed atop others. The artists clearly had mastered the animals' anatomy, but they chose to simplify the outlines and distort the heads and limbs for effect, always painting in the distinct Magdalenian style.

Many of the cave paintings are on a Sistine Chapel–size scale. The "canvas" was huge: Lascaux's main caverns are more than a football field long; Grotte de Font-de-Gaume is 430 feet long; and Grotte de Rouffignac meanders six miles deep. The figures are monumental (bulls at Lascaux are 16 feet high). All are painted high up on walls and ceilings, like the woolly rhinoceros of Grotte de Font-de-Gaume.

Techniques: Besides painting the animals, these early artists also engraved them on the wall by laboriously scratching outlines into the rock with a flint blade, many following the rock's natural contour. A typical animal might be made using several techniques—an engraved outline that follows the natural contour, reinforced with thick outline paint, then colored in.

The paints were mixed from natural pigments dissolved in cave water and oil (animal or vegetable). At Lascaux, archaeologists have found more than 150 different minerals on hand to mix paints. Even basic black might be a mix of manganese dioxide, ground quartz, and a calcium phosphate that had to be made by heating bone to 700 degrees Fahrenheit, then grinding it.

No paintbrushes have been found, so artists probably used a sponge-like material made from animal skin and fat. They may have used moss or hair, or maybe even finger-painted with globs of pure pigment. Once they'd drawn the outlines, they filled everything in with spray paint—either spit out from the mouth or blown through tubes made of hollow bone.

Imagine the engineering problems of painting one of these caves, and you can appreciate how sophisticated these "primitive" people were. First, you'd have to haul all your materials into a cold, pitch-black, hard-to-access place. Assistants erected scaffolding to reach ceilings and high walls, ground up minerals with a mortar and pestle, mixed paints, tended the torches and oil lamps, prepared the "paintbrushes," laid out major outlines with a connect-the-dots series of points...then stepped aside for Magdalenian Michelangelos to ascend the scaffolding and create.

Dating: Determining exactly how old this art is—and whether it's authentic—is tricky. (Because much of the actual paint is mineral-based with no organic material, carbon-dating techniques are often ineffective.) As different caves feature different animals, prehistorians can derive which caves are relatively older and younger, since climate change caused various animal species to come and go within certain regions. In several cases, experts confirmed the authenticity of a painting because the portrayals of the animals showed anatomical details not previously known—until they were discovered by modern technology. (For instance, in Grotte de Rouffignac, the mammoths are shown with a strange skin flap over their anus, which was only discovered during the 20th century on a preserved mammoth found in Siberian permafrost.) They can also estimate dates by checking the amount of calcium glaze formed over the paint, which can sometimes only be seen by infrared photography.

Why? No one knows the purpose of the cave paintings. Interestingly, the sites the artists chose were deliberately awe-inspiring, out of the way, and special. They knew their work here would last for untold generations, as had the paintings that came before theirs. Here are some theories of what this first human art might mean:

It's no mystery that hunters would paint animals, the source of their existence. The first scholar to study the caves, Abbé Henri Breuil, thought the painted animals were magic symbols made by hunters to increase the supply of game. Or perhaps hunters thought that if you could "master" an animal by painting it, you could later master it in battle. Some scholars think the paintings teach the art of hunting, but there's very little apparent hunting technique shown. Did they worship animals? The paintings definitely depict an animal-centered (rather than a human-centered) universe.

The paintings may have a religious purpose, and some of the caverns are large and special enough that rituals and ceremonies could have been held there. But the paintings show no priests, sacrifices, rituals, or ceremonies. Scholars writing on primitive art in other parts of the world speculate that art was made by shamans in a religious or drug-induced trance, but France's paintings are very methodical.

The order of paintings on the walls seems random. Could it be that the caves are a painted collage of the history of the Magdalenians, with each successive generation adding its distinct animal or symbol to the collage, putting it in just the right spot that established their place in history?

The fact that styles and subject matter changed so little over the millennia might imply that the artists purposely chose timeless images to relate their generation with those before and after. Or they simply lived in a stable culture that did not value innovation. Or these people were too primitive to invent new techniques and topics.

Maybe the paintings are simply the result of the universal human drive to create, and these caverns were Europe's first art galleries, bringing the first tourists.

Very likely there is no single meaning that applies to all the paintings in all the caves. Prehistoric art may be as varied in meaning as current art.

Picture how a Magdalenian would have viewed these paintings: You'd be guided by someone into a cold, echoing, and otherworldly chamber. In the darkness, someone would light torches and lamps, and suddenly the animals would flicker to life, appearing to run around the cave, like a prehistoric movie. In front of you, a bull would appear, behind you a mammoth (which you'd never seen in the flesh), and overhead a symbol that might have tied the whole experience together. You'd be amazed that an artist could capture the real world and reproduce it on a wall. Whatever the purpose—religious, aesthetic, or just plain fun—there's no doubt the effect was (and is) thrilling.

Today, you can visit the caves and share a common experience with a caveman. Feel a bond with these long-gone people... or stand in awe at how different they were from us. Ultimately, the paintings are as mysterious as the human species.

Helpful Hints

Drivers Fare Best: All of the prehistoric caves listed here are within a short drive of Sarlat. Considering the scarcity of public transit, if you don't have a car, you're like a caveman without a spear (see page 409 for guided tours that connect some of these sights).

Book Ahead: July, August, and holiday weekends are busiest, so book as far ahead as you can during these times. Saturdays are generally quiet. Four caves take reservations (by phone, fax, or email): Lascaux II (July–Aug only), Grotte de Font-de-Gaume, Abri du Cap Blanc, and Grotte du Pech Merle. The rest are first-come, first-served. Remember that Sarlat's TI and some hotels can reserve cave visits for you (and are likely to be more effective in landing a reservation).

Cave Tips: Read "Cave Art 101" (earlier) to gain a better understanding of what you'll see. Tours can last up to an hour. Tours are all a steady, chilly 55 degrees Fahrenheit, with 98 or 99 percent humidity. While on tour, lag behind the group to have the paintings to yourself for a few moments. Photos, day packs, big purses, and strollers are not allowed. (You can take your camera—without using it—and check the rest at the site.)

Local Guide: Angelika Siméon is a qualified **local guide** eager to teach you about the caves (€125/half-day, €215/day, tel. 05 53 35 19 30, mobile 06 24 45 96 28, angelika.simeon @wanadoo.fr).

Les Eyzies-de-Tayac

This single-street town is the touristy hub of a cluster of Cro-Magnon caves, castles, and rivers, and merits a stop only for its National Museum of Prehistory and the Grotte de Font-de-Gaume cave (a 10-minute walk outside of town; described later, under "Caves near Les Eyzies-de-Tayac"). Les Eyzies-de-Tayac is world-famous because it's where Monsieur Magnon first discovered the original Cro-Magnon man in 1870. That breakthrough set of bones was found just behind the hotel of Monsieur Magnon—Hôtel le Cro-Magnon, which is in business to this day on the main street in Les Eyzies-de-Tayac. The name "Cro-Magnon" translates as "Mr. Magnon's Hole."

Orientation: Les Eyzies-de-Tayac's TI rents bikes (Mon-Sat July-Aug 9:00-19:00, Sept-June 10:00-12:00 & 14:00-18:00, closed Sun except June-Sept 10:00-12:00 & 14:00-17:00, tel. 05 53 06 97 05, fax 05 53 06 90 79, www.leseyzies.com). The train station is a level 500 yards from the town center (turn right out of the station to get into town).

Sights in Les Eyzies-de-Tayac

▲▲National Museum of Prehistory (Musée National de Préhistoire)

This modern museum houses more than 18,000 bones, stones, and crude little doodads that were uncovered locally. It takes you through prehistory—starting 400,000 years ago—and is good preparation for your cave visits. The museum does a great job presenting its exhibits, although you have to work at following the serious teaching style.

Appropriately located on a cliff that's been inhabited by humans for 35,000 years (above Les Eyzies-de-Tayac's TI), the museum's sleek design is intended to help it blend into the surrounding rock. Inside, you'll see worthwhile exhibits, including videos demonstrating scratching designs, painting techniques, and how spearheads were made. You'll also see full-size models of Cro-Magnon people and animals who stare at racks of countless arrowheads.

Cost and Hours: €5; June-Sept daily 9:30–18:00; Oct–May Wed–Mon 9:30–12:00 & 14:00–17:30, closed Tue; tel. 05 53 06 45 65, www.musee-prehistoire-eyzies.fr.

Information: For context, read "Cave Art 101," earlier, before you go.

Tours: To get the most out of your visit, consider a private or semi-private English-language guided tour of the museum; for details, call 05 53 06 45 65 or email reservation.prehistoire @culture.gouv.fr.

Visiting the Museum: Pick up the museum layout with your ticket. Enter by walking in the footsteps of your ancestors, then greet the 10-year-old *Turkana Boy*, whose bone fragments were found in Kenya in 1984 by Richard Leakey and date from 1.5 million years ago.

The first floor sets the stage, describing human evolution and the fundamental importance of tools. Find the numbered English info sheets provided at regular intervals, and match them to exhibit numbers to make sense of what you're seeing.

The second (and better) floor up highlights prehistoric artifacts found in France. Some of the most interesting things you'll see are displayed in this order: a handheld arrow launcher, a 5,000-year-old flat-bottomed boat (pirogue) made from oak, prehistoric fire pits, amazing cavewoman jewelry (including a necklace made of 70 stag teeth—pretty impressive, given that stags only have two teeth each...do the math), engravings on stone (don't miss the unflattering yet impressively realistic female figure), a handheld lamp used to light cave interiors (*lampe à manche*), and beautiful rock sculptures of horses (much like the paintings at the cave of Abri du Cap Blanc).

Your visit ends on the cliff edge, with a Fred Flintstone–style photo op on a stone ledge (through the short tunnel) that some of our ancient ancestors once called home.

Sleeping in and near Les Eyzies-de-Tayac

Train travelers wanting to see the museum and famous cave will find Les Eyzies-de-Tayac a practical place to sleep, as will drivers interested in a fun farm experience.

$$ Auberge Veyret, a 15-minute drive from Les Eyzies-de-Tayac, is as real a farm experience as it gets, with beefy cows and plump pigs. Mama greets you with a huge smile and nary a word of English, her son cooks, and her daughter (Laurence) and husband (Patrick) do everything else. The rooms are spotless and furnished like Grandma's, but with modern conveniences. Several family-friendly wooden chalets have two rooms, private decks, and kitchenettes. You'll be expected to dine here—and you'd be a fool not to, since dinner includes everything from apéritif to *digestif*, with five courses in between and wine throughout (Db-€62/person, lower rates for kids, includes breakfast and dinner; 4-person chalet-€110 per night plus linen fee; cash only, large pool, en route to Abri du Cap Blanc—look for any sign that says *Veyret*, tel. 05 53 29 68 44, fax 05 53 31 58 28, www.auberge-veyret.com, contact @auberge-veyret.com).

$ Madame Bauchet (call her "Nanou") owns the closest rooms to the Les Eyzies-de-Tayac train station, and they're a good, clean value. Madame Bauchet does not speak English, but she's a creative communicator and will pick you up at the station if you ask ahead (Db-€39, Tb/Qb with air-con-€53, breakfast-€5.50, cash only, closed Nov–March, 200 yards from the station at 40 avenue de la Préhistoire—look for the brown *Chambres* sign, tel. 05 53 06 97 71, http://chez.nanou.pagespro-orange.fr, bauchetgerard @orange.fr).

Caves near Les Eyzies-de-Tayac

▲▲▲Grotte de Font-de-Gaume

Even if you're not a connoisseur of Cro-Magnon art, you'll dig this cave—the last one in France with prehistoric multicolored (polychrome) paintings still open to the public. (Lascaux—just down the road—has replica caves for visitors instead.) This cave, made millions of years ago—not by a river, but by the geological activity that created the Pyrenees Mountains—is entirely natural. It contains 15,000-year-old paintings of 230 animals, 82 of which are bison.

On a carefully guided and controlled 100-yard walk, you'll see about 20 red-and-black bison—often in elegant motion—painted with a moving sensitivity. When two animals face each other, one is black, and the other is red. Your guide, with a laser pointer and great reverence, will trace the faded outline of the bison and explain how, 15 millennia ago, cave dwellers used local minerals and the rock's natural contours to give the paintings dimension. Some locals knew about the cave long ago, when there was little interest in prehistory, but the paintings were officially discovered in 1901 by the village schoolteacher.

Cost and Hours: €7, reservation fee—€1.50/group, free first Sun of the month Nov–May, open Sun–Fri mid-May–mid-Sept 9:30–17:30, mid-Sept–mid-May 9:30–12:30 & 14:00–17:30, closed Sat, last departure 1.5 hours before closing, no photography or large bags, tel. 05 53 06 86 00, fax 05 53 35 26 18, fontdegaume @monuments-nationaux.fr. Those planning to also visit the Abri du Cap Blanc cave (described next) can reserve and buy tickets here.

Getting a Ticket: To preserve the precious and fragile art, the number of daily visitors allowed is strictly regulated (180 people per day, in groups of 12). Of the 180 spots available, 140 tickets are allotted to visitors who call or email to make advance reservations, and 40 are kept open for those wanting to enter badly enough to come early and wait for a ticket. In July and August (when spots get booked up months in advance), you'll need to reserve ahead by phone or email, or arrive by 8:00; the rest of the year, you should be OK if you pop in by 9:00. If you reserve by email, you can request an English-language tour (and cross your fingers that space is available); allow a few days for a response (no reservations possible the first Sunday of the month in Nov–May, when the caves are free). They'll send you a form to fill out; provide your name and credit-card number to hold your spot. You can call the site (10:30–12:00 or 14:30–16:00) to see if spots happen to be open (they often are) before doing the early-morning bit. You must check in 15 minutes before your tour, or you'll lose your place to the sightseeing vultures waiting to snatch up the spots of late arrivals. You can join this flock and try to snag a place if you don't have a reservation (many don't show).

Drivers who can't get a ticket here should try the caves at Grotte de Rouffignac (see page 454), or aim for the more remote Grotte du Pech Merle, about 30 minutes east of Cahors (see page 475).

Tours: Because English tours are limited to two per day (usually at 11:00 and 15:00, May–Sept only), you'll likely make the visit with a French guide. Though the English-info flier is useless, the actual tour is little more than pointing out legs, eyes, heads, and bellies of the bison, so don't fret if you're not on an English tour. Pierre Fanlac Editeur's *The Font-de-Gaume Cave* guidebook, sold for €6 in the shop, is an excellent substitute.

Getting There: The caves are a 15-minute walk from Les Eyzies-de-Tayac (toward Sarlat). From the ticket house, walk 400 yards on an uphill path to the cave entrance (where there's a free, safe bag check and a WC). There's easy on-site parking.

▲Abri du Cap Blanc

In this prehistoric cave (a 10-minute drive from Grotte de Font-de-Gaume), early artists used the rock's natural contours to add dimension to their sculpture. Your guide spends the tour in a single stone room explaining the 14,000-year-old carvings. The small museum (with English explanations) helps prepare you for your visit, and the useful English handout describes what the French-speaking guide is talking about. Look for places where the artists smoothed or roughened the surfaces to add depth. Impressive as these carvings are, their subtle majesty is lost on some. You must take one of the 45-minute tours to see the sculptures (€7, 7 tours/day, call to verify tour times, cave open Sun–Fri mid-May–mid-Sept 9:30–18:30, mid-Sept–Oct and April–mid-May 9:30–12:30 & 14:00–17:30, closed Sat and Nov–March, no photos, walk 200 yards down from parking lot, tel. 05 53 59 21 74). Tickets and reservations are also available at the Font-de-Gaume cave (font degaume@monuments-nationaux.fr). Abri du Cap Blanc is well-signed, located two miles after Grotte de Font-de-Gaume on the road to Sarlat. Views of the Château de Commarque (described on page 438) are terrific as you arrive.

More Cro-Magnon Caves

▲▲Lascaux II

The region's—and the world's—most famous cave paintings are at Lascaux, 14 miles north of Sarlat and Les Eyzies-de-Tayac. The Lascaux caves were discovered accidentally in 1940 by four kids and their dog. From 1948 to 1963, more than a million people climbed through this prehistoric wonderland—but these visitors tracked in fungus on their shoes and changed the temperature and humidity with their heavy breathing. In just 15 years, the precious art deteriorated more than during the previous 15,000 years, and the original caves were closed. A copy cave—accurate to within one centimeter, reproducing the best 40-yard-long stretch, and showing 90 percent of the paintings found in Lascaux—was opened next to the original in 1983. Guides assure visitors that the original is every bit as crisp and has just as much contrast as the facsimile you'll see.

At impressive Lascaux II, the reindeer, horses, and bulls of Lascaux I are painstakingly reproduced by top artists using the same dyes, tools, and techniques their predecessors did 15,000 years ago. Of course, seeing the real thing at the other caves is important, but come here first (taking one of the scheduled English-language tours) for a great introduction to the region's cave art. Although it feels a bit rushed—40 people per tour are hustled through the two-room cave reproductions—the guides are committed to teaching, the paintings are astonishing, and the experience is mystifying. (Forget that they're copies, and enjoy being swept away by the prehistoric majesty of it all.)

Cost and Hours: €8.50; July–Aug daily 9:00–19:00; April–June and Sept daily 9:30–18:30; Oct–Dec and Feb–March Tue–Sun 10:00–12:00 & 14:00–17:30, closed Mon; closed Jan.

Touring the Replica Cave: You'll see Lascaux II with a 40-minute English tour (4–6/day May–Sept, usually at about 11:50 and 14:20, about 2/day off-season, call 05 53 51 96 23 for ticket availability and English tour times, reservations possible July–Aug only). Unless you're visiting in winter (Oct–March), you must buy your ticket before coming to Lascaux; the ticket office is next to the TI in Montignac, five minutes away by car. Deep-blue signs direct drivers to *La Billetterie* in Montignac (follow signs for *Centre-Ville*, then look for *La Billetterie*, and don't double-park); Lascaux is well-signed from there. In July and August, tours are usually sold out by 13:00, so book ahead. The cave is a constant 56 degrees year-round, so dress warmly. Pleasant Montignac is worth a wander if you have time to kill.

Sleeping near Lascaux: **$$$ Château de la Fleunie*** offers regal 15th-century château accommodations surrounded by pastures and mountain goats, the biggest private pool I've seen in France, tennis courts, and a restaurant with *beaucoup d'ambiance*. Rooms are either in the château or in the modern annex—book ahead to snag a château room (Db-€110–145, most around €125, extra person-€20, prices rise July–Aug-€80–90/tower room for two-€185, half-pension required July–Aug, *menus* from €30, *menus* from €30, 10-minute drive north of Montignac on road to

Brive-la-Gaillarde, in Condat-sur-Vézere, tel. 05 53 51 32 74, fax 05 53 50 58 98, www.lafleunie.com, lafleunie@free.fr).

▲▲Grotte de Rouffignac

Rouffignac provides a different experience from other prehistoric caves in this area. Here you'll ride a clunky little train down a giant subterranean riverbed, exploring about half a mile of this six-mile-long gallery. The cave itself was known to locals for decades—hence the oblivious graffiti (with dates going back to the 18th century) that litters the ceiling—but the 13,000-year-old paintings were discovered only in 1956.

Cost and Hours: €6.40, daily July-Aug 9:00–11:30 & 14:00–18:00, April-June and Sept-Nov 10:00–11:30 & 14:00–17:00, closed Dec-March, one-hour guided tours run 2/hour, no reservations, tel. 05 53 05 41 71, www.grottederouffignac.fr. Dress warmly. It's really crowded only mid-July–August—especially in the afternoons. Weekends tend to be quietest.

Getting There: Grotte de Rouffignac is well-signed from the route between Les Eyzies-de-Tayac and Périgueux; allow 25 minutes from Les Eyzies-de-Tayac.

Visiting the Cave: Your tour likely will be in French (guides may answer questions in English), but here's the gist of what they're saying on the stops of your train ride:

The cave was created by the underground river. It's entirely natural, but it was much shallower before the train-track bed was excavated. As you travel, imagine the motivation and determination of the painters who crawled so deep into this dark and mysterious cave. They left behind their art...and the wonder of people who crawled in centuries later to see it all.

All along the way, you'll see crater-like burrows made by hibernating bears long before the first humans painted here. There are hundreds of them—not because there were so many bears, but because year after year, a few of them would return, preferring to make their own private place to sleep (rather than using some other bear's den). After a long winter nap, bears would have one thing on their mind: Cut those toenails. The walls are scarred with the scratching of bears in need of clippers (look to the right as you ride).

Stop 1: The images of woolly mammoths etched into the walls can be seen only when lit from the side (as your guide will demonstrate). As the rock is very soft here, these were simply gouged out by the artists' fingers.

Stop 2: Look for images of finely detailed rhinoceroses in black paintings. The rock is harder here, so nothing is engraved.

Stop 3: On the left you'll see woolly mammoths and horses engraved with tools in the harder rock. On the right is the biggest composition of the cave: a herd of peaceful mammoths. A mysterious calcite problem threatens to cover the paintings with ugly white splotches.

Off the Train: When you get off the train, notice how high the original floor was (the bear-crater level), and imagine both the prehistoric makers and viewers of this art crawling back here with pretty lousy flashlight-substitutes. Here, the ceiling is covered with a remarkable gathering of animals. You'll see a fine 16-foot-long horse, a group of mountain goats, and a grandpa mammoth. Art even decorates the walls far down the big, scary hole. When the group chuckles, it's because the guide is explaining how the mammoth with the fine detail (showing a flap of skin over its anus) helped authenticate the paintings: These paintings couldn't be fakes, because no one knew about this anatomical detail until the preserved remains of an actual mammoth were found in Siberian permafrost in modern times. (The discovery explained the painted skin flap that had long puzzled French prehistorians.)

▲La Roque St. Christophe

Five fascinating terraces carved by the Vézère River have provided shelter to people here for 50,000 years. Although the terraces were inhabited in prehistoric times, there's no prehistoric art on display—the exhibit (except for one small cave) is entirely medieval. The official recorded history goes back to A.D. 976, when people settled here to steer clear of the Viking raiders who'd routinely sail up the river. (Back then, in this part of Europe, the standard closing of a prayer wasn't "amen," but "and deliver us from the Norseman, amen.")

A clever relay of river watchtowers kept an eye out for raiders. When they came, cave-dwellers gathered their kids, hauled up their animals (see the big, re-created winch), and pulled up the ladders. Although there's absolutely nothing old here except for the carved-out rock (with holes for beams, carved out of the soft limestone), it's easy to imagine the entire village—complete with butcher, baker, and candlestick-maker—in this family-friendly exhibit. This place is a dream for kids of any age who hold fond tree-house memories.

It's simple to visit: There's a free parking lot across the stream, with picnic tables, a WC, and—adjacent to the babbling brook—a pondside café (providing good salads, omelets, and drinks—the nearby pretty village of St. Léon provides more lunch choices). Borrow the English guidebooklet (or buy it for €2) at the turnstile; stop to take in the picture showing its medieval buildings; and climb through the one-way circuit, which is slippery when damp.

Cost and Hours: €7.50, daily April–Sept 10:00–18:30, July–Aug until 20:00, March and Oct 10:00–18:00, Nov–Feb

11:00–17:00, last entry 45 minutes before closing, lots of steps, 5 miles north of Les Eyzies-de-Tayac, follow signs to *Montignac*, tel. 05 53 50 70 45. When planning your day, note that this sight is very near the Maison de Reignac (described on page 439). It's also one of the rare sights that stays open through lunch.

▲Grottes de Cougnac

Located 19 miles south of Sarlat (and three well-signed miles north of Gourdon on D-704), this cave holds fascinating rock formations and the oldest (14,000–25,000-year-old) paintings open to the public. Less touristy than others, it provides a more intimate look at cave art, because guides have more time to explain the paintings. You'll get some explanations in English (unless it's high season), and see about 10 drawings of ibex and deer (with rust or black outlines) as well as a few representations of humans.

Cost and Hours: €7; these hours correspond to first/last tour times: July–Aug daily 10:00–18:00; April–June and Sept daily 10:00–11:30 & 14:30–17:00; Oct Mon-Sat 14:00–16:00, closed Sun; closed Nov–March; English book available, 1.25-hour tours, some in English—call ahead, tel. 05 65 41 47 54, www.grottesdecougnac .com.

Oradour-sur-Glane

Located two hours north of Sarlat and 15 miles west of Limoges, Oradour-sur-Glane is one of the most powerful sights in France— worth ▲▲▲. French schoolchildren know this town well; most make a pilgrimage here.

Village des Martyrs, as it is known, was machine-gunned and burned on June 10, 1944, by Nazi troops. The Nazis were either seeking revenge for the killing of one of their officers (by French Resistance fighters in a neighboring village) or simply terrorizing the populace in preparation for the upcoming Allied invasion (this was four days after D-Day). With cool attention to detail, the Nazis methodically rounded up the entire population of 642 townspeople. The women and children were herded into the town church, where they were tear-gassed and machine-gunned. Plaques mark the place where the town's men were grouped and executed. The town was then set on fire, its victims left under a blanket of ashes. Today, the ghost town, left untouched for more than 60 years, greets every pilgrim who enters with only one English word: Remember.

Follow *Village des Martyrs* signs and start at the rust-colored **underground museum** (Centre de la Mémoire), which provides a good social and political context for the event (with English explanations and audioguide), including home movies of locals before the attack and disturbing footage of similar events (don't miss the 12-minute film with English audioguide translations). Then, with hushed visitors, walk the length of Oradour's main street, past gutted, charred buildings in the shade of lush trees, to the underground memorial on the market square (rusted toys, broken crucifixes, town mementos under glass). The plaques on the buildings provide the names and occupations of the people who lived there (*laine* means wool; a *sabotier* is a maker of wooden shoes; a *quincaillerie* is a hardware store; *cordonnier* is shoe repair; a *menuisier* is a carpenter; and *tissus* are fabrics). Visit the cemetery where most lives ended on June 10, 1944, and finish at the church, with its bullet-pocked altar.

Cost and Hours: Entering the village is free, whereas the museum costs €8 (audioguide-€2). Both are open daily mid-May–mid-Sept 9:00–19:00, off-season until 17:00 or 18:00, last visit one hour before closing, tel. 05 55 43 04 30, www.oradour.org.

Getting There: Public transport here is a challenge. Bus #12 connects Limoges with Oradour in 30 minutes (4/day, 15-minute walk from Limoges train station to bus stop on place Winston Churchill). Consider a taxi. Limoges is a stop on an alternative train route between Amboise and Sarlat (Limoges TI tel. 05 55 34 46 87).

Sleeping and Eating in Oradour-sur-Glane: $ Hôtel La Glane** is the best hotel in the modern town, with the most respected restaurant. Both are cheap and good enough (Db-€50, *menus* from €16, next to Hôtel de Ville on place de la Mairie, tel. 05 55 03 10 43, fax 05 55 03 15 42).

Near Oradour-sur-Glane

Mortemart

With a car and extra time, visit this bucolic village (15-minute drive northwest of Oradour-sur-Glane on D-675). You'll find a medieval market hall, a smattering of appealing buildings, one café, and a sweet château (good picnic benches behind).

Sleeping in Mortemart: $ Hôtel Relais** offers travelers a sleepy overnight stop. Located on the main road, it has five small but comfortable rooms over a fine restaurant. Formal Madame Pradeau speaks no English, but she'll work with you (Db-€54, Tb-€70, *menus* from €19, closed Mon-Tue, 1 place Royale, tel. & fax 05 55 68 12 09, www.le-relais-mortemart.fr, dominique .pradeau189@wanadoo.fr).

St. Emilion and Bordeaux Wine Country

Two hours due west of Sarlat and just 40 minutes from Bordeaux, St. Emilion is another pretty face just waiting to flirt with you. Unlike other French lookers, this one seduces in English—the historic presence of British interest in the wine industry has given the town an almost bilingual feel. It's an easy place for Anglophones.

Carved like an amphitheater into the bowl of a limestone hill, St. Emilion's tidy streets connect a few inviting squares with heavy cobbles and scads of well-stocked wine shops. There's little to do in this town of well-heeled and well-wined residents other than enjoy the setting, and, of course, sample the local sauce. Wine has been good to St. Emilion, though it accounts for barely 5 percent of Bordeaux's famous red-wine production (about 60 percent of the grapes you see are Merlot). Also try a tasty home-made *macaron*, sold at many shops. Sunday is market day in St. Emilion.

Orientation to St. Emilion

Tourist Information

The TI is a critical stop, at the top of the town on place des Créneaux, across from the town's highest bell tower. It's located in a onetime abbey and connected to pretty cloisters (that go ignored by most tourists—find the door in the rear of the TI). The TI is well-armed with good information in English about anything you need (daily mid-June-mid-Sept 9:30–19:00, mid-Sept-mid-June 9:30–12:30 & 13:30–18:30 except Nov-March closes at 18:00, place Pioceau, tel. 05 57 55 28 28, fax 05 57 55 28 29, www.saint-emilion -tourisme.com, st-emilion.tourisme@wanadoo.fr).

The TI has information on St. Emilion's few sights, and has a helpful booklet on *chambres d'hôtes*. Check the bulletin board for English-language **tours** of the city, the underground church, and the vineyards (vineyard and underground tours described later, under "Sights in St. Emilion"). The TI also rents **bikes,** and has English-language handouts outlining several self-guided cycling and **walking routes** through the vineyards.

Arrival in St. Emilion

By Train: It's a 20-minute walk through the vineyards from St. Emilion's train station into town; taxis don't wait at the station, but you can call one (see "Helpful Hints—Taxi and Local Guide," below; 6 trains/day Mon–Fri from Bordeaux, 4/day Sat–Sun). You can also get off in Libourne (five miles away, with better train service including TGV trains, and easy car rental). From Libourne you can catch a cab (€15) or take an infrequent bus to St. Emilion (3/day) from the bus station (*gare routière*) next to the train station.

By Car: If you're coming from Sarlat, take the autoroute from Périgueux and save 40 minutes over the local roads. If coming from the Loire, take the autoroute to Poitiers, then follow N-10 south toward Angouleme, then Bordeaux. You'll find parking (about €1/hour) in lots at the upper end of the town, or along the wall.

Helpful Hints

Taxi and Local Guide: Jolly **Robert Faustin,** who drives a comfortable station wagon and speaks enough English, can advise you and arrange visits to wineries (he knows them all), and is an enjoyable person to spend time with (tel. & fax 05 57 25 17 59, mobile 06 77 75 36 64, www.taxi-saintemilion.com, robert.faustin@wanadoo.fr).

Tourist Train: A *petit train* toots you from St. Emilion through vineyards and back in 30 minutes (€6, 2/hour, stop is behind TI by vineyards).

Sights in St. Emilion

Wine-Tasting—A fair starting point for oenophiles is the **Maison du Vin,** located next to the TI, where you get an introduction to wine, beginning with an hour-long video (played on the hour, English subtitles). In the next room, read the description of the winemaking process and sniff cool glass cylinders that let you smell elements in the wines before you taste them (free, daily 9:30–12:30 & 14:00–18:30, tel. 05 57 55 50 55, www.vins-saint-emilion.com).

The TI offers **guided walks and bus excursions** through the vineyards (in English and French) that include tastings. Both leave from the TI (usually May–mid Sept only; verify times). The walking tour takes you through vineyards, where you'll get to inspect the vines up close, then visit a winery (€12, 1.5-hour tour usually leaves at 15:30 and includes about 45 minutes of walking). The bus trips provide an introduction to the region with one château-winery visit (€18, 3 hours, usually leaves at 14:00).

St. Emilion's many **wine shops** offer a free and easy way to sample the array of local wines (see "French Wine-Tasting 101" on page 40). Keepers of small shops greet visitors in flawless English, with a central tasting table, maps of the vineyards, and several open bottles (most shops open daily 10:00–19:00, until 20:00 in summer). And though it's hard to distinguish these classy wine stores from each other, you'll be pleasantly surprised at the passionate shopkeepers' welcoming attitude. Americans may represent only about 15 percent of the visitors, but we buy 40 percent of their wine. Although the owners hope that you'll buy a bottle (particularly if you taste many wines), and shipping is easy (except to California and Texas), there's no pressure or fee for the tastings.

Vignobles & Châteaux is a polished wine shop offering wine-tasting classes at their "Ecole de Vin" upstairs (about €30 for 1.5-hour class, offered 3/week, more extensive classes and visits to prestigious wineries available; 4 rue du Clocher, tel. 05 57 24 61 01, www.vignobleschateaux.fr).

I also like the easygoing **Cercle des Oenophiles**, where you can taste wines and tour nearby cellars storing more than 400,000 bottles of wine (free, daily 10:00–19:00, at 12 rue Guadat, tel. 05 57 74 45 55).

Views over St. Emilion—You can climb the **bell tower** in front of the TI for a good view (€1.25, give ID at TI in exchange for the key, open daily same hours as TI), but the view is best from the **Tour du Roy** several blocks below (€1.25, daily 14:00–18:00).

Underground Tours of St. Emilion—The TI offers frequent, somewhat interesting 45-minute tours with three stops: the catacombs (sorry, no bones); the underground monolithic church, which literally rocks; and Trinity Chapel. Learn who St. Emilion was, and be impressed that it took dedicated Benedictine monks 300 years to dig this monolithic church out of one big rock (9th–12th centuries). You'll also learn that there are about 125 miles of underground tunnels in the St. Emilion area. Originally dug as quarries, they're ideal for wine storage today. The tour is mandatory if you want to see these sights (€7, 1–3 English tours/day, always one at 11:00, more in French, thorough English handout given on French tours). If time's limited and you can't get on an English tour, skip this sight.

Quickie Vineyard Loop by Car or Bike—Leave the upper end of St. Emilion on D-243 and head to St. Christophe des Bardes. After passing through the village, follow signs to the right to *St. Laurent des Combes*. Joyride your way down through hillsides of vines, then find signs looping back to St. Emilion's lower end via D-245.

Sleeping in St. Emilion

(€1 = about $1.25, country code: 33)

There are no cheap hotels in St. Emilion. (Those that exist are fine, but they're more costly than elsewhere in France.) *Chambres d'hôtes* offer a better value. Hotel prices skyrocket during the VinExpo festival at the end of June, and during harvest time (the end of Sept).

Hotels

The first two places are a few doors apart, at the upper end of the city.

$$$ Au Logis des Remparts*** offers top comfort in tasteful rooms, plus a pool and a tranquil garden with vineyards to touch (standard Db–€105, nicer Db with bathtubs–€144, Db with garden views–€165, suites–€250–400, air-con, pay Wi-Fi, book ahead for limited on-site parking, tel. 05 57 24 70 43, fax 05 57 74 47 44, www.logisdesremparts.com, contact@logisdesremparts.com).

$$ L'Auberge de la Commanderie** welcomes visitors with a neon entry and Modernist decor in its two buildings—a main hotel and an annex. Run by an amiable owner, the hotel's 16 rooms are well-maintained and have ceiling fans. Rooms in the main building come with loud paintings; annex rooms have more subtle stone walls and more space (small Db–€85, bigger Db–€90–110, Tb–€115, two-room apartment for up to four–€150, closed Jan-Feb, elevator, Internet access and pay Wi-Fi, free parking, tel. 05 57 24 70 19, fax 05 57 74 44 53, www.aubergedelacommanderie.com, contact @aubergedelacommanderie.com).

Chambres d'Hôtes

$$$ La Maison d'Aline is central and welcoming, and comes with splendid views over the village (Db–€110, includes breakfast; 2 blocks past L'Auberge de la Commanderie, across from Cordeliers winery at 7 rue Port Brunet, tel. 05 57 24 65 47, mobile 06 23 77 38 90, www.alinebb.com, mcclemot@alinebb.com).

$$ Le Logis de la Tourelle rents five simple-but-spacious rooms at the lower end of town for fair rates (Db–€65–75, on rue Guadet, tel. 05 57 24 79 65, mobile 06 25 14 51, fax 05 57 74 05 51, restaurant.lacotebraisee@wanadoo.fr). Check in at La Côte Braisée restaurant at 3 rue du Tertre de la Tente, and they'll escort you to the rooms several blocks away.

Near St. Emilion

The vineyards that surround St. Emilion hide many good-value *chambres d'hôtes*. Places below the town are scattered among the villages and are hard to find—get good directions before you go. You can meander the villages just outside St. Emilion's upper entry point, then pick the place you prefer (the village of Montagne has many good *chambres d'hôtes*). Or stop by the TI for a long list with small photos (no room-booking fee).

\$\$ Moulin la Grangère, dreamily wrapped in hills of vineyards, offers the perfect haven from which to appreciate the Bordeaux wine country. Charming Marie-Annick and Alain Noel rent three modern rooms in a well-renovated, blue-shuttered 19th-century mill with manicured gardens, a big pool, a *pétanque* court, and sublime scenery in every direction (Db-€70, Tb/Qb-€90–100, includes breakfast, cash only, Internet access and Wi-Fi, tel. 05 57 24 72 51, www.moulin-la-grangere.com, alain.noel125@orange .fr). It's 10 minutes from St. Emilion: Follow D-122 from below St. Emilion and turn left on D-245. After two kilometers, look for signs on the left to *St. Christophe des Bardes*, then look for the small *Moulin la Grangère* signs (on the left in about 100 yards) and follow them.

\$ Château Meylet is where Madame Favard rents four traditional rooms in her workaday wine *domaine*. The château is a pleasant quarter-mile walk from St. Emilion's doorstep (Db-€53–69, Tb-€74, includes breakfast, cash only, shared kitchen, washer/dryer and bikes available; from the top of St. Emilion, follow D-243 toward Libourne, at 1.5 kilometers turn left at signs to *Château Meylet*; tel. 05 57 24 68 85, http://chateau.meylet.free.fr, chateaumeylet@free.fr).

Eating in St. Emilion

Skip the cafés lining the street by the TI and instead head to the melt-in-your-chair square, place du Marché.

Amelia-Canta Café is *the* happening spot on place du Marché for lunch or dinner on a warm evening. It has café fare, salads, and veggie options (€16–25 *menus*, daily March–Nov, 2 place de l'Eglise Monolithe, tel. 05 57 74 48 03).

L'Envers du Décor wine bar-bistro is about fun, wine, and food—in that order. It's perfect for this wine-happy town: The restaurant's tabletops are wooden wine crates, and the floor is paved with cool blue-and-brown tiles. Meat dishes are their forte (lunch *menus* from €30, dinner *menus* from €19, daily, a few doors from the TI at 11 rue du Clocher, tel. 05 57 74 48 31).

L'Huitrier Pie, a local favorite, serves up the town's best oysters, fish, and other seafood. Cool terraces flank the restaurant (€33 standard *menu*, €50 tasting *menu*, closed Tue–Wed, at the lower/south end of town on 11 rue de la Porte Bouqueyre, tel. 05 57 24 69 71).

Les Girons'dines, a few blocks down from the TI, is a charming place run by a mother-daughter team. The cuisine is traditional and reasonable, served in a pleasant interior or on their sweet terrace (5 rue des Girondins, tel. 05 57 24 77 72).

Rocamadour

An hour east of Sarlat, this historic town with its dramatic rock-face setting is a ▲▲ sight after dark. Once one of Europe's top pilgrimage sites, today it feels more tacky than spiritual. Still, if you can get into the medieval mindset, its peaceful and dramatic setting—combined with the memory of the countless thousands of faithful who trekked from all over Europe to worship here—over-whelms the kitschy tourism, and it becomes a nice (short) stop.

Those who visit only during the day might wonder why they bothered, as there's little to do here except climb the pilgrims' steps (with people who aren't pilgrims) to a few churches, and then stare at the view. Travelers who arrive late and spend the night enjoy fewer crowds—and a floodlit spectacle.

Orientation to Rocamadour

Rocamadour has three basic levels, connected by steps or elevators. The bottom level (La Cité Medievale, or simply La Cité) is a single pedestrian street lined with shops and restaurants. The sanctu-ary level (Cité Religieuse) is up 223 holy steps. Its centerpiece is a church with seven chapels gathered around a small square. A switchback trail, the Way of the Cross (Chemin de la Croix), leads to the top level (called l'Hospitalet) and château (closed to the pub-lic) that crowns the cliff and offers a great view and free parking. For most, the goal is the sanctuary at midlevel.

Tourist Information

There are two TIs in Rocamadour: the glassy TI that drivers come to first, in the village of l'Hospitalet above Rocamadour (daily July–Aug 9:30–19:30, April–June and Sept–Oct 10:00–12:00 & 14:00–18:00, Nov–March until 17:00), and another on the level pedestrian street in **La Cité Medievale** (roughly the same hours, tel. 05 65 33 22 00). On the same pedestrian street, you'll find an ATM next to the post office (PTT).

Arrival in Rocamadour

By Train: Five daily trains (transfer in Brive-la-Gaillarde) leave you 2.5 miles from the village at an unstaffed station. It's a €10 taxi ride to Rocamadour (see "Helpful Hints—Taxi," next page). Start at the Cité Medievale (lower level), and visit from there.

By Car: Drivers have two options: You can park at the bottom of town (follow signs to *La Cité*) and walk to the end of the long pedestrian street (in La Cité Medievale), then either climb or take the elevator to the chapels. Or, for less walking, park above the town (from l'Hospitalet, follow *Château* signs) to a free lot and hike or take the elevator down.

By Elevator: For pilgrims preferring not to climb steps on their knees, this vertical town has two handy, if pricey, elevators. *Ascenseur Cité* (€2.50 one-way, €3 round-trip) connects the lower town with the church but skips the holy stairs. *Ascenseur Incliné* (€2.50 one-way, €4 round-trip) connects the church with the château and parking lot at the top but skips the zigzag Way of the Cross. Each is run like any other elevator: on demand. Managed by two different companies, they're connected within 50 yards at the church level.

Helpful Hints

Views After Dark: If you're staying overnight, don't miss the views of a floodlit Rocamadour from the opposite side of the valley (doable by car, on foot, or by tourist train; see below). It's best as a half-hour (round-trip) stroll. From the town's southeast end, follow the quiet road down, cross the bridge, and head up the far side of the gorge opposite the town. Leave before it gets dark, as the floodlighting is best at twilight. Wear light-colored or reflective clothing, or take a flashlight—it's a dark road with no shoulder. Within the town, climb the steps to just below the sanctuary, and consider a drink with a view at the Hôtel Sainte Marie.

Tourist Train: You can take the cheesy but convenient *petit train* to enjoy the view after dark (runs evenings only), complete with 50 other travelers, a bad sound system blaring worthless commentary in four languages, a flashing yellow light, and a rooftop crimping your view (€5, 30-minute round-trip, 2 trips/evening, departures starting at twilight—the first one is by far the best, check at the TI or call 05 65 33 67 84). Or you can walk the same route in 30 minutes (see above), and take much better photos.

Grocery Store: It's on place de l'Europe, in the upper city (open daily 8:00–20:00).

Taxi: Call 06 73 44 79 98 or 06 81 60 14 60.

Sights in Rocamadour

In the Upper Town (l'Hospitalet)

If you're coming from Sarlat or from the north, your first view of Rocamadour is the same one that medieval pilgrims first saw—at the top of the gorge from the hamlet of **l'Hospitalet**, named for the hospitality it gave pilgrims. Stop here for the sweeping views (and its glassy TI). Imagine the impact of this sight in the 13th century, as awestruck pilgrims first gazed on the sanctuary cut out

Rocamadour's Religious History

Rocamadour was once one of Europe's top pilgrimage sights. Today tourists replace the pilgrims, enjoying a dramatically situated one-street town under a pretty forgettable church—all because of a crude little thousand-year-old black statue of the Virgin Mary.

Of France's roughly 200 "Black Virgins," this was perhaps the most venerated. Black Virgins began at the end of the pagan era—when Europe was forcefully being Christianized. In Europe's pagan religions, black typically symbolized fertility and motherhood. For newly converted (and still reluctant) pagans, it was easier to embrace the Virgin if she was black.

A thousand years ago, many Europeans expected the world to end, and pilgrimages became immensely popular. About that time, the first pilgrims came here—to a little cave in a cliff over a gorge created by the Alzou River—to pray to a crude statue of a Black Virgin. Then, in 1166, a remarkably intact body was found beneath the threshold of the troglodyte chapel. People assumed this could only be a hermit (certainly a saintly hermit) who had lived in this cave. He was given the name Amadour (servant of Mary), and the place was named Rocamadour (the rock of the servant of Mary).

Suddenly, this humble site was on the map. The Benedictines moved in to develop the spot, building a church over the cave. Like Mont St. Michel, a single-street town sprouted at its base to handle the needs of its growing pilgrim hordes. During Europe's great age of pilgrimages (12th and 13th centuries), the greatest of pilgrims (St. Louis, St. Dominique, Richard the Lionhearted, and so on) all trekked to this spot to pray. Rocamadour became a powerful symbol of faith and hope.

During the 14th-century Golden Age of Rocamadour, up to 8,000 people lived here, earning their living off of the pilgrims—who arrived in numbers of up to 20,000 a day. But with the 16th-century wars of religion and the Age of Enlightenment (in the 18th century), pilgrimages declined... and so did Rocamadour.

During the Romantic Age of the 19th century, pilgrimages were again in vogue, and Rocamadour rebounded. Local bishops rebuilt the château above the sanctuary, making it a pilgrims' reception center, and connecting it to the church with the Way of the Cross. (Most of the current buildings in the Sanctuary of Our Lady of Rocamadour date from the 19th century.) But there hasn't been a bona fide miracle here for eight centuries...and that's not good for the pilgrimage business. Since the mid-20th-century, Rocamadour has become more of a tourist attraction, and today, Rocamadour's 650 inhabitants earn a living off its million visitors a year. The vast majority of those who climb the holy steps to the sanctuary are tourists—more interested in burning calories than incense.

of the limestone cliffs. It was through l'Hospitalet's fortified gate that medieval pilgrims gained access to the "Holy Way," which led from l'Hospitalet to Rocamadour.

Château—Dating from the 14th century, the "château" fortified a bluff that was an easy base for bandits to attack the wealthy church below. Today's structure is a 19th-century private house that was transformed into a reception spot for pilgrims. It's privé unless you are a pilgrim (in which case you can sleep here). All it offers tourists is a short rampart walk for a grand view (not worth the €2 fee, turnstile requires exact change).

The zigzag **Way of the Cross** (Chemin de la Croix—a path marked with 14 Stations of the Cross, with a chapel for each station at each corner) gives religious purpose to the 15-minute hike between the château and the sanctuary below.

Grotte Préhistorique des Merveilles—This cave, located next to the upper TI, has the usual geological formations and a handful of small, blurred cave paintings. It's of no interest if you have seen or will see other prehistoric caves—its sole advantages are that it requires little effort to visit (with only about 10 steps down), and the guide can answer questions in English on the 40-minute tour (€6, daily July–Aug 9:30–19:00, April–June and Sept 10:00–12:00 & 14:00–18:00, Oct until 17:00, closed Nov–March, decent handout available, tel. 05 65 33 67 92, www.grotte-des-merveilles.com).

In the Lower Town (La Cité Medievale)

Rocamadour's town is basically one long street traversing the cliff below the sanctuary. For eight centuries it has housed, fed, and sold souvenirs to the site's countless visitors. There's precious little here other than tacky trinket shops, but I enjoyed popping into the **Galerie le Vieux Pressoir** (named for its 13th-century walnut millstone). It fills a medieval vaulted room with the fine art of a talented couple: Richard Begyn and Veronique Guinard.

Of Rocamadour's 11 original **gates**, 7 survive (designed to control the pilgrim crowds). In the 14th century, as many as 20,000 people a day from all over Europe would converge on this spot. From the western end of town, 223 steps lead up to the church at the sanctuary level. Traditionally, pilgrims kneel on each and pray an "Ave Maria" to Our Lady.

Between the Upper and Lower Towns, at the Sanctuary Level (La Cité Religieuse)

These sights form the heart of your rock-face sightseeing. From the western end of the lower town, climb the steps as pilgrims did, passing a plaque listing key medieval pilgrimages starting with St. Bernard. From the upper town, take the Way of the Cross path down. Or take the easy way out, and take an elevator (from above or below). Either way, your destination will be signed *Sanctuaires*.

▲▲**The Sanctuary of Our Lady of Rocamadour**—Stand in the small square with the cliff to your left, and look up to the open door of the Church of St. Saveur. Though the buildings originated much earlier, most of what you see was rebuilt in the 19th century. Crammed onto a ledge on a cliff, the church couldn't follow the standard floor plan, so its seven chapels surround the square (called the *le parvis*) rather than the church. The Bishop's palace is behind you and to your right, and houses a gift shop selling various pilgrimage mementos, including modern versions of the medallions that pilgrims prized centuries ago as proof of their visit. The two most historic chapels are to your left on either side of the steps.

Walk up the flight of steps to the cliff, where a tomb is cut into the rock. This is where the miraculously preserved body of St. Amadour was found in 1166. Places of pilgrimage do better with multiple miracles, so, along with its Black Virgin and the miracle of St. Amadour's body (see sidebar on page 465), Rocamadour has the **Sword of Roland**. The rusty sword of Charlemagne's nephew sticks in the cliffside, 10 yards above Amadour's tomb. According to medieval sources, when Roland was about to die in battle, the great warrior didn't want his sword to fall into enemy hands. He hurled it from the far south of France, and it landed here—stuck miraculously into the Rocamadour cliffs just above the Black Virgin. (The sword is clearly from the 18th century, but never mind.)

St. Michael's Chapel is built around the original cave to your left (open only to pilgrims, with little to see inside). To your right, the **Chapel of the Virgin** (Chapelle Notre Dame) is the focal point for pilgrims. Step inside. High above the altar is the much-venerated Black Virgin, a 12th-century statue (covered with a thin plating of blackened silver—see sidebar on page 465) that depicts Mary presenting Jesus to the world. The oldest thing in the sanctuary—from the ninth century—is a simple rusted bell hanging from the ceiling. The suspended sailboat models are a reminder that sailors relied on Mary for safe passage.

The adjacent **Church of St. Saveur** is the sanctuary's main place of worship. In front of a central pillar, a copy of the Black Virgin is displayed to give visitors a closer look. The double wooden balcony (newly rebuilt) was for the monks. Imagine attending a Mass here in centuries past, when the church was filled with pilgrims, and monks lined the balconies. While Rocamadour's church seems more like a tourist attraction, it remains a sacred place of worship. A sign reminds tourists "To admire, to contemplate, to pray. You're welcome to respectfully visit" (free, open daily generally 8:00–19:00).

From here you can walk under the Church of St. Saveur and find the Way of the Cross (Chemin de la Croix) and elevators up (*Château par ascenseur*) or down (*La Cité par ascenseur*).

Near Rocamadour

▲Gouffre de Padirac—

Twenty minutes from Rocamadour is the huge sinkhole of Padirac, with its underground river and miles of stalagmites and stalactites (but no cave art). Though it's an impressive cave, if you've seen caves already, it's slow in comparison, with an insufficient payoff (lots of climbing and not a word of English). But the mechanics of the visit are easy, and there's not much to communicate anyway. Here's the drill: After paying, hike the stairs (with big views of the sinkhole—a round shaft about 100 yards wide and deep), or ride the elevator to the river level. Line up and wait for your boat. Pack into the boat with about a dozen others for the slow row past a fantasy world of hanging cave formations. Get out and hike a big circle with your group and guide, enjoying lots of caverns, underground lakes, and mighty stalagmites and stalactites. Get back on the boat and retrace your course. Two elevators zip you back to the sunlight. The visit takes 1.5 hours (crowds make it take longer in summer, when I'd skip it). Dress warmly.

Cost and Hours: €9.50, daily July 9:30–18:00, Aug 8:30–18:30, April–June and Sept–early Nov 9:30–17:00, closed early Nov–March, long lines at 14:00, tel. 05 65 33 64 56, www.gouffre-de-padirac.com. For a knickknack Padirac, don't miss the shop.

Sleeping in Rocamadour

(€1= about $1.25, country code: 33)

Hotels are a deal here. Choose from hotels in the upper city, La Cité Religieuse (near l'Hospitalet), which has views down to Rocamadour; or below, within the medieval city, called La Cité Medievale. Parking is easier up top, but the spirit of St. Amadour is more present below (I prefer the lower medieval city). Every hotel—including the ones I recommend—has a restaurant where they'd like you to dine.

In La Cité Religieuse

$ Hôtel Belvédère** has 18 well-maintained, modern, and appealing rooms, 12 of which have views over Rocamadour (rooms #14–18 have best views, Db with no view–€55–64, Db with view–€71–76, tel. 05 65 33 63 25, fax 05 65 33 69 25, www.hotel-le-belvedere.fr, lebelvedere-rocamadour@orange.fr).

In La Cité Medievale

$ Hôtel-Restaurant le Terminus des Pelerins**, at the western end of the pedestrian street in La Cité Medievale, has immaculate, comfortable rooms with wood furnishings; the best have balconies and face the valley. Helpful owner Geneviève was born in this hotel (Db-€53, Db with view and balcony-€71, Tb-€75, tel. 05 65 33 62 14, fax 05 65 33 72 10, www.terminus-des-pelerins.com, contact@terminus-des-pelerins.com).

Near Rocamadour

$$ Moulin de Fresquet is a dreamy *chambre d'hôte* five miles east of Rocamadour. Gracious Gérard and his wife, Claude, have lovingly restored an ancient mill in a lush, park-like setting. The four antique-furnished rooms come with wood beams and oodles of character. You're free to enjoy the outdoor terraces, chaise lounges, and duck pond (with ducks for pets, not for dinner). If you're really on vacation, stay here, and if Claude is cooking, eat here (dinner with wine-€27, daily except Thu). Book as far ahead as possible—this place is popular for a reason (Db-€69-97, fine Db suite-€114, Tb suite-€136, includes breakfast, cash only, closed Nov-March, in Gramat, tel. 05 65 38 70 60, mobile 06 08 85 09 21, fax 05 65 33 60 13, www.moulindefresquet.com, info@moulindefresquet.com). Go to Gramat, then follow signs through town to *Figeac*. The *chambre d'hôte* is well-signed at the east end of Gramat—at the last roundabout, take the exit marked *Moulin de Fresquet*.

Eating in Rocamadour

Hôtel Belvédère, in the upper town, has the best interior view from its modern dining room. Book ahead for a window-side table, ideally for a meal just before sunset (*menus* from €19, daily, tel. 05 65 33 63 25; also listed under "Sleeping in Rocamadour," earlier).

The **Bar l'Esplanade** hunkers cliffside below Hôtel Belvédère and owns unobstructed views from the tables in its garden café. It's open for lunch, dinner, drinks, and snacks (daily, tel. 05 65 33 18 45).

Near Rocamadour: The Overlooked Eastern Dordogne

Many find this remote, less-visited section of the Dordogne (Quercy *département*) even more beautiful than the area around Sarlat. For a good introduction to this area, follow this self-guided driving tour.

Self-Guided Driving Tour

Welcome to the Eastern Dordogne

Follow the Dordogne heading east, driving about an hour upriver from Souillac, to connect these worthwhile stops: Martel, Carennac, Château de Castelnau-Bretenoux, Loubressac, and Autoire, Rocamadour lies just beyond this area, as do the Tom Sawyer–like Gouffre de Padirac caves (both described earlier in this chapter). Allow 45 minutes from Sarlat to Souillac, then 15 minutes to Martel, and 20 minutes to Carennac (Château de Castelnau-Bretenoux and Loubressac are within 10 minutes of Carennac). From Carennac it's 25 minutes south to Rocamadour.

• *From Souillac's center, take D-803 east to...*

Martel: A well-preserved medieval town of 1,500 souls and 7 towers, this peaceful place has a lovely pedestrian area with many shops (good chance to stock up on picnic items). Neither on a river nor crowning a hilltop, Martel is largely overlooked by tourists. The town is named for Charles Martel (Charlemagne's grandfather and role model), who made his name by stopping the Moors as they marched into northern France in 732. A good walking tour of Martel starts at its fine main square (place des Consuls, with a medieval covered market), and connects the seven towers.

• *From Martel, continue east on D-803 toward Castelnaud, Vayrac, and Bétraille, then cross the Dordogne on D-20 to find...*

Carennac: This riverside town demands to be photographed. Park along the river by the fortified Prieuré St.-Pierre. Explore the evocative church and examine its exquisitely carved tympanum. It was built as an outpost of the Cluny Abbey in the 10th century, and then fortified in the 1500s during the wars of religion. For a memorable meal inside or out, head to **Le Prieuré Créperie**, with a warm interior, good salads, and filling crêpes (closed Mon, lunch served all day, across from the church, tel. 05 65 39 76 74). Cross the small bridge behind the *créperie* for more village views.

• *From here, head east on D-30, tracking the Dordogne River. Turn left, following signs to...*

Château de Castelnau-Bretenoux: A splendidly situated and once-powerful military castle, this château has views in all directions and several well-furnished rooms. The reddish-golden stone and massive 12th-century walls make an impression, as does its height—almost 800 feet. Cross the moat to the castle courtyard, and climb the round military tower for sensational views, then join a 30-minute, mercifully brief French-only tour (€7, €2 to park, or park for free at the restaurant/café lot if you plan to have a snack or lunch, daily July–Aug 10:00–19:00, Sept–June 10:00–12:30 &

Near Rocamadour

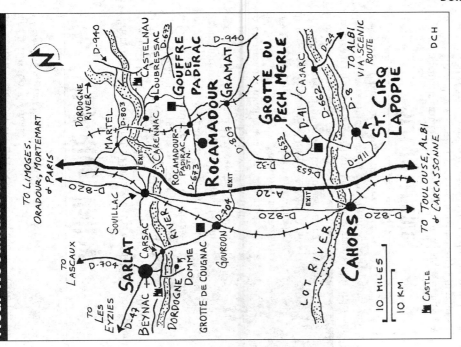

14:00–17:30, Oct–March closed Tue, last entry one hour before closing, tel. 05 65 10 98 00).

• *Return to D-30, cross it, and continue straight up D-14. You'll come to...*

Loubressac: Arguably the most beautiful village in France, Loubressac hangs atop a beefy ridge, with outlandish views and a gaggle of adorable homes at its eastern end. You'll find an Old World café and a modern hotel-restaurant, **$$ Le Relais de Castelnau*****, which rents 40 rooms with a view terrace and a pool (Db-€90, Tb-€106, Qb-€112, half-pension-€76/person, tel. 05 65 10 80 90, fax 05 65 38 22 02, www.relaisdecastelnau.com, rdc46 @orange.fr).

• *From here it's a short hop on D-118 to lovely little...*

Autoire: The *other* most beautiful village in France, this one lies a few minutes beyond Loubressac. Visit and decide which village is fairest of them all.

• From here you can follow signs to Gramat, then on to Rocamadour.

Lot River Valley

Ninety minutes south of the Dordogne, the overlooked Lot River meanders through a strikingly beautiful valley under stubborn cliffs and past tempting villages. The fortified bridge at Cahors, the prehistoric cave paintings at Grotte du Pech Merle, and the breathtaking town of St. Cirq Lapopie are worthwhile sights in this valley—each within a half-hour of the others. These sights can be combined to make a terrific day for travelers willing to invest the time (doable as a long day trip from the Sarlat area). They also work well as a day trip from Rocamadour, and are worthwhile for drivers connecting the Dordogne with Albi or Carcassonne. (If you're going to or coming from the south, you can scenically connect this area with Albi via Villefranche-de-Rouergue and Cordes-sur-Ciel.) With extra time, spend a night in St. Cirq Lapopie, which makes a good base for visiting the area.

St. Cirq Lapopie

This spectacularly situated village, clinging to a ledge sailing above the Lot River, knows only two directions—straight up and way down. In St. Cirq Lapopie, there's little to do but wander the rambling footpaths, inspect the flowers and stones, and thrill over the vistas. You'll find picnic perches, a handful of galleries and restaurants, and views from the bottom and top of the village that justify the pain.

St. Cirq Lapopie is well-signed 30 minutes east of Cahors, an hour south of Rocamadour, and just 20 minutes from the cave paintings of Grotte du Pech Merle.

Orientation to St. Cirq Lapopie

Although you need to be careful of weekend and high-season (July–Aug) crowds, St. Cirq Lapopie has not been blemished by too many boutiques. It remains pin-drop peaceful after-hours in any season. Arrive later in the day and spend the night to best appreciate where you are—your first views of St. Cirq Lapopie are eye-popping enough to convince you to stay.

Tourist Information

The TI is located across from the recommended Auberge du Sombral (May–Sept daily 10:00–13:00 & 14:00–18:00 except July–Aug 10:00–19:00, Oct–April until 17:00 and closed Sun, tel. 05 65 31 29 06). Pick up the visitor's guide in English, with brief descriptions of 22 historic buildings, and ask for information on hikes in the area.

Arrival in St. Cirq Lapopie

By Car: Arriving by car from the west, you'll pass the town across the Lot River, then cross a narrow bridge and climb. There are three well-signed parking options: a small, free, dirt parking lot partway up, leaving you with a hefty uphill walk; a much closer pay lot at village level (€3, exact change required); and a third lot that lies at the top (€3, great views from here). Pull over for photo stops as you climb.

Sights in St. Cirq Lapopie

Chemin de Halage—This is a beautiful riverside trail below St. Cirq Lapopie, originally used for pulling flat-bottomed boats upriver. Long sections of the trail are cut into the limestone cliff. Once riverside, walking downriver toward Cahors, you'll reach the cut-out section in about 20 minutes. It's a steep hike down and a long climb back up (trail leads from across from the TI or by walking through the village to the bottom). Get details at the TI.

Sleeping in St. Cirq Lapopie

(€1= about $1.25, country code: 33)

The village has all of 18 rooms, none of which is open off-season (mid-Nov–March).

$$$ Château de Saint-Cirq-Lapopie is a quirky, artsy, and ancient *chambre d'hôte* housed in the 16th-century château perched on a rock cliff below the old church. Rooms are spacious (all with double beds), and some have dramatic views over the Lot River. There's a grotto-like swimming pool under the castle, and the château is often filled with fine art and sculpture exhibits (Db-€95–140, limited free parking, tel. 05 65 31 27 48, www.lapopie.fr, info@lapopie.fr).

$$ Auberge du Sombral**, run with panache by Madame Hardeveld and daughter Marion (who speaks English), is a good value in the town center below the TI. They'll welcome you with an oh-so-cozy lobby area and eight comfortable rooms above in various sizes, most with double beds (small Sb–€50, Db–€75–80, tel. 05 65 31 26 08, fax 05 65 30 26 37, www.lesombral.com, aubergesombral@gmail.com). The good restaurant serves lunch every day but Thursday, as well as dinners on Friday and Saturday nights (€15 lunch *menus*, €25 dinner *menus*).

Eating in St. Cirq Lapopie

Dinner is tricky here; reliable help seems to be a problem, leaving restaurants understaffed at busy times. But this town was made for picnics; consider picking up dinner fixings in the hamlet of La Tour de Faure. (There's a small grocery store on the other side of the river just west of the bridge to St. Cirq Lapopie, and a bakery a short way east of the bridge.)

As restaurants go, **Lou Boulat Brasserie** works for me. It serves low-risk lighter meals (salads, crêpes, and *plats*) in a low-stress setting, with good views from the side terrace (closed Wed, located at the upper end of town, off the main road by the post office/PTT, tel. 05 65 30 29 04).

L'Oustal is the most traditional restaurant in town, with a handful of cozy tables inside and out on a little terrace (€16 and €32 *menus*, €15 *plats du jour*, closed Mon, beneath the towering church, tel. 05 65 31 20 17).

The **Gourmet Quercynois** is another place with good regional cuisine and terrific ambience inside and out (*menus* from €20, daily, tel. 05 65 31 21 20).

Auberge du Sombral serves reliable cuisine within a lovely dining room or out front on a photogenic terrace (*menus* from €27, daily, described earlier, under "Sleeping in St. Cirq Lapopie").

More Sights in the Lot River Valley

▲**Cahors and the Pont Valentré**—One of Europe's best medieval monuments, this fortified bridge was built in 1308 to keep the English out of Cahors. It worked. Learn the story of the devil on the center tower. The steep trail on the non-city side leads to great views (views are actually better partway up; be careful if the trail is wet) and was once part of the pilgrimage route to Santiago de Compostela in northwest Spain. Imagine that cars were allowed to cross this bridge until recently.

If you need an urban fix, stroll the pedestrian-friendly alleys between Cahors' cathedral and the river, a thriving place filled with good lunch options. To find this area by car, follow *Centre-Ville* and *St. Urcisse Eglise* signs, and park where you can.

▲▲**Grotte du Pech Merle**—This cave, about 30 minutes east of Cahors, has prehistoric paintings of mammoths, bison, and horses—rivaling the better-known cave art at Grotte de Font-de-Gaume. Although this cave is easier to view, as more people per day are allowed in (700), that also makes the cave a bit less special. Still, it has brilliant cave art and interesting stalactite and stalagmite formations. I like the mud-preserved Cro-Magnon footprint. Allow a total of two hours for your visit, starting at the small museum, continuing with a 20-minute film subtitled in English, and finishing with the caves. It's smart to reserve your spot in advance (by phone or online) as private groups can fill the cave's quota. Book a week ahead in summer; if you visit without a reservation, arrive by 9:30 and line up. If you can't join an English tour, ask for the English-translation booklet.

Cost and Hours: €8, daily March–mid-Nov 9:30–12:00 & 13:30–17:00, closes earlier off-season, fewer visitors on weekends, tel. 05 65 31 27 05, fax 05 65 31 20 47, www.pechmerle.com. Before you visit, read "Cave Art 101" on page 443.

BASQUE COUNTRY

Euskal Herria: St. Jean-de-Luz • Bayonne • Biarritz •
San Sebastián • Guernica • Bilbao

Straddling two nations on the Atlantic Coast—stretching about 100 miles from Bayonne, France south to Bilbao, Spain—lies the ancient, free-spirited land of the Basques. The Basque Country is famous for its sunny beaches and scintillating modern architecture...and for its feisty, industrious natives.

It's also simply beautiful: Bright, white chalet-style homes with deep-red and green shutters scatter across lush, rolling hills, the Pyrenees Mountains soar high above the Atlantic, and surfers and sardines share the waves.

Insulated from mainstream Europe for centuries, the plucky Basques have just wanted to be left alone for more than 7,000 years. An easily crossed border separates the French *Pays Basque* from the Spanish *País Vasco*, allowing you to sample both sides from a single base (in France, I hang my beret in cozy St. Jean-de-Luz; in Spain, I prefer fun-loving San Sebastián).

Much unites the French and Spanish Basque regions: They share a cuisine, Union Jack–style flag (green, red, and white), and common language (Euskara), spoken by about a half-million people. (Almost everyone also speaks French or Spanish.) And both have been integrated by their respective nations, sometimes forcibly. The French Revolution quelled French Basque ideas of independence; 130 years later, Spain's Generalísimo Francisco Franco attempted to tame his own separatist-minded Basques.

But over the last generation, things have started looking up. The long-suppressed Euskara language is enjoying a resurgence. And, as the European Union celebrates ethnic regions rather than nations, the French and Spanish Basques are feeling more united. This heavily industrialized region is enjoying a striking

21st-century renaissance. In France, long-ignored cities such as Bayonne and the surfing mecca of Biarritz are being revitalized. And in Spain, the dazzling new architecture of the Guggenheim Bilbao modern-art museum and the glittering resort of San Sebastián are drawing enthusiastic crowds. At the same time, traditional small towns—like France's St. Jean-de-Luz and nearby mountain villages, and Spain's Lekeitio and Hondarribia—are also thriving, making the entire region colorful, fun, welcoming... and unmistakably Basque.

Planning Your Time

One day is enough for a quick sample of the Basque Country, but two or three days lets you breathe deep and hold it in. Where you go depends on your interests: France or Spain? Cities (such as Bayonne or Bilbao) or resorts (such as St. Jean-de-Luz and San Sebastián)?

If you want to slow down and focus on Spain, spend one day relaxing in San Sebastián and the second side-tripping to Bilbao (and Guernica, if you have a car).

Better yet, sample Basque sights on both sides of the border. Sleep in one country, then side-trip into the other, devoting one day to France (St. Jean-de-Luz and Bayonne), and a second day to Spain (San Sebastián and maybe Bilbao).

Wherever you go, your Basque sightseeing should be a fun blend of urban, rural, cultural, and culinary activities.

Getting Around the Basque Country

The tourist's Basque Country—from Bayonne to Bilbao—stays close to the coastline. Fortunately, everything is connected by good roads and public transportation.

By Bus and Train: The three main French towns (St. Jean-de-Luz, Bayonne, Biarritz) are connected by bus (trains also zip between St. Jean-de-Luz and Bayonne). Even if you rent a car, do these three towns by public transit. To go between France and San Sebastián, a train—with a transfer in Hendaye—is your best bet (2/hour, about an hour between St. Jean-de-Luz and San Sebastián; less frequent by bus: Mon-Sat 2/day direct, 1 hour). Once is Spain, the bus is the best way to get from San Sebastián to Bilbao (and from there, Guernica). Specific connections are explained in each section.

Note that a few out-of-the-way areas—France's Basque villages of the interior, and Spain's Lekeitio and Bay of Biscay—are impractical by public transportation...but worth the trouble by car.

By Car: Bayonne, Biarritz, St. Jean-de-Luz, San Sebastián, and Bilbao are connected by a convenient expressway, called A-63 in France and A-8 in Spain (rough timings: St. Jean-de-Luz to

Basque Country

Biarritz or Bayonne—30 minutes; St. Jean-de-Luz to San Sebastián—45 minutes; San Sebastián to Bilbao—1.25 hours).

Language Warning: For the headers throughout this chapter, I've listed place names using the French or Spanish spelling first and the Euskara spelling second. In the text I use the spelling that prevails locally. And though most people refer to towns by their French or Spanish names, many road signs list places in Euskara. (In less separatist-minded France, signs are often only in French. In Spain, signs are usually posted in both Euskara and Spanish, either on the same sign or with dual signage on opposite sides of the street.) The French or Spanish version is sometimes scratched out by independence-minded locals, so you might have to navigate by Euskara names.

Also note that in terms of linguistic priority (e.g., museum information), Euskara comes first, French and Spanish second, and English a distant fourth...and it often doesn't make the cut.

The Basque Country's Cuisine Scene

Mixing influences from the mountains, sea, France, and Spain, Basque food is reason enough to visit the region. The local cuisine—dominated by seafood, tomatoes, and red peppers—offers some spicy dishes, unusual in most of Europe. Although you'll find similar specialties throughout the Basque lands, France is still France and Spain is still Spain. Here are some dishes you're most likely to find in each area.

French Basque Cuisine: The red peppers (called *piments d'espelette*) hanging from homes in small villages give foods a distinctive flavor and often end up in *piperade*, a dish that combines peppers, tomatoes, garlic, ham, and eggs. Peppers are also dried and used as condiments. Look for them with the terrific Basque dish *axoa* (a veal or lamb stew on mashed potatoes). Look also for anything "Basque-style" (*basquaise*)—cooked with tomato, eggplant, red pepper, and garlic. Don't leave without trying *ttoro* (tchoo-roh), a seafood stew that is the Basque Country's answer to bouillabaisse and cioppino. *Marmitako* is a hearty tuna stew. Local cheeses come from Pyrenean sheep's milk (*pur brebis*), and the local ham (*jambon de Bayonne*) is famous throughout France. After dinner, try a shot of *izarra* (herbal-flavored brandy). To satisfy your sweet tooth, look for *gâteau basque*, a local tart filled with cream or crème with cherries from Bayonne. Hard apple cider is a tasty and local beverage. The regional wine Irouléguy comes in red, white, and rosé, and is the only wine produced in the French part of Basque Country (locals like to say that it's made from the smallest vineyard in France, but the biggest in the Northern Basque Country).

Spanish Basque Cuisine: Hopping from bar to bar sampling *pintxos*—the local term for tapas—is a highlight of any trip (for details, see the sidebar on page 524). Local brews include *sidra* (hard apple cider) and *txakoli* (cha-koh-LEE, a local light, sparkling white wine—often theatrically poured from high above the glass for aeration). You'll want to sample the famous *pil-pil*, made from emulsifying the skin of *bacalao* (dried, salted cod) into a mayonnaise-like substance with chili and garlic. Another tasty dish is *kokotxas*, usually made from hake (*merluza*) fish cheeks, prepared like *pil-pil*, and cooked slowly over a low heat so the natural gelatin is released, turning it into a wonderful sauce—*qué bueno!* Look also for white asparagus from Navarra. Wine-wise, I prefer the reds and rosés from Navarra. Finish your dinner with a *membrillo*, a sweet and *muy* dense quince jelly. Try it with cheese for a light dessert, or look for it at breakfast.

French Basque Country (Le Pays Basque)

Compared to their Spanish cousins across the border, the French Basques seem French first and Basque second. You'll see less Euskara writing here than in Spain, but these destinations have their own special spice, mingling Basque and French influences with beautiful rolling countryside and gorgeous beaches.

My favorite home base here is the central, comfy, and manageable resort village of St. Jean-de-Luz. It's a stone's throw to Bayonne (with its big-city bustle and fine Basque museum) and the snazzy beach town of Biarritz. A drive inland rewards you with a panoply of adorable French Basque villages. And St. Jean-de-Luz is a relaxing place to "come home" to, with its mellow ambience, fine strolling atmosphere, and good restaurants.

St. Jean-de-Luz / Donibane Lohizune

St. Jean-de-Luz (san zhahn-duh-looz) sits happily off the beaten path, cradled between its small port and gentle bay. The days when whaling, cod fishing, and pirating made it wealthy are long gone, as tourism has become the economic mainstay. Pastry shops serve Basque specialties, and store windows proudly display berets (a Basque symbol). Ice-cream lickers stroll traffic-free streets, while soft, sandy beaches tempt travelers to toss their itineraries into the bay. The knobby little mountain La Rhune towers above the festive scene. Locals joke that if it's clear enough to see La Rhune's peak, it's going to rain, but if you can't see it, it's raining already.

The town has little of sightseeing importance, but it's a great base for exploring the Basque Country and a relaxing beach and port town that provides the most enjoyable dose of Basque culture in France. In July and August, the town fills with French tourists—especially the first two weeks of August, when it's practically impossible to find a room without a reservation made long in advance.

Orientation to St. Jean-de-Luz

St. Jean-de-Luz's old city lies between the train tracks, the Nivelle River, and the Atlantic. The main traffic-free street, rue Gambetta, channels walkers through the center, halfway between the train tracks and the ocean. The small town of Ciboure, across the river, holds nothing of interest.

Who Are the Basques?

To call the Basques "mysterious" is an understatement. Before most European nations had ever set sail, Basque whalers competed with the Vikings for control of the sea. During the Industrial Revolution and lean Franco years, Basque steel kept the Spanish economy alive. In the last few decades, the separatist army ETA has given the Basque people an unwarranted reputation for violence. And through it all, the Basques have spoken a unique language that to outsiders sounds like gibberish or a secret code.

So, just who are the Basques? Even for Basques, that's a difficult question. According to traditional stereotypes, Basques are thought of as having long noses, heavy eyebrows, floppy ears, stout bodies, and a penchant for wearing berets. But widespread Spanish and French immigration has made it difficult to know who actually has Basque ethnic roots. (In fact, some of the Basques' greatest patriots have had no Basque blood.) And so today, anyone who speaks the Basque language, Euskara, is considered a "Basque."

Euskara, related to no other surviving tongue, has been used since Neolithic times—making it, very likely, the oldest European language that's still spoken. With its seemingly impossible-to-pronounce words filled with k's, tx's, and z's (restrooms are *gizonak* for men and *emakumeak* for women), Euskara makes speaking French suddenly seem easy. (Some tips: *tx* is pronounced "ch," and *tz* is pronounced "ts." Other key words: *kalea* is "street," and *ostatua* is a cheap hotel.) Kept alive as a symbol of Basque cultural identity, Euskara is typically learned proudly as a second or third language. Many locals can switch effortlessly from Euskara to Spanish or French. Basques wave their language like a flag—look for Euskara street signs, menus, and signs in shops.

The Basque economy has historically been shaped by three factors: the sea, agriculture, and iron deposits.

Basque sailors were some of the first and finest in Europe, as they built ever-better boats to venture farther and farther into the Atlantic in search of whales. (These long journeys were made possible by the invention of *bacalao*—dried, salted cod that could be preserved for months to sustain whalers.) By the year 1000, Basque sailors were chasing whales a thousand miles from home, in the Norwegian fjords. Despite lack of physical evidence, many historians surmise that the Basques must have sailed to the Americas before Christopher Columbus.

When the "Spanish" era of exploration began, Basques continued to play a key role, as sailors and shipbuilders. Columbus' *Santa María* was likely Basque-built, and his crew included many

Basques. History books teach that Ferdinand Magellan was the first to circumnavigate the globe, with the footnote that he was killed partway around. Who took over the helm for the rest of the journey, completing the circle? The Basque sailor Juan Sebastián de Elcano. And a pair of well-traveled Catholic priests, known for their far-reaching missionary trips that led to founding the Jesuit order, were also Basques: St. Ignatius of Loyola and St. Francis Xavier.

Later, the Industrial Age swept Europe, gaining a foothold in Iberia when the Basques began using their rich iron deposits to make steel. Pioneering Basque industrialists set the tempo as they dragged Spain into the modern world. Cities such as Bilbao were heavily industrialized, sparking an influx of workers from around Spain (which gradually diluted Basque blood in the Basque Country).

The independence-minded Basques are notorious for their stubbornness. In truth, as a culturally and linguistically unique island surrounded by bigger and stronger nations, the Basques have learned to compromise. Historically Basques have remained on good terms with outsiders, so long as their traditional laws, the *Fueros*, were respected. Though outdated, the *Fueros* continue to symbolize a self-governance that the Basques hold dear. It is only when foreign law has been placed above the *Fueros*—as many of today's

Basques feel Spanish law is—that the people become agitated.

In recent years, most news of the Basques—especially in Spain—has been made by the terrorist organization ETA. (ETA stands for the Euskara phrase "Euskadi Ta Askatasuna," or "Basque Country and Freedom"; *eta* also means "and" in Euskara.) ETA has been blamed for more than 800 deaths since 1968. The violence ebbs and flows, but ETA tends to focus on political targets, and their activities go largely unnoticed by tourists. While many people in the Basque Country would like a greater degree of autonomy from Madrid, only a tiny minority of the population supports ETA, and the vast majority rejects violence.

Throughout the Basque Country—in both Spain and France—the Basque spirit remains strong. Basque nationalists with websites prefer the suffix .eh (for *Euskal Herria*) or the more generic .com to .es (for *España*).

This is only a first glimpse into the important, quirky, and fascinating Basque people. To better understand the Basques, there's no better book than Mark Kurlansky's *The Basque History of the World*—essential pre-trip reading for historians.

The only sight worth entering in St. Jean-de-Luz is the church where Louis XIV and Marie-Thérèse tied the royal knot (Eglise St. Jean-Baptiste, described later). St. Jean-de-Luz is best appreciated along its pedestrian streets, lively squares, and golden, sandy beaches. With nice views and walking trails, the park at the far eastern end of the beachfront promenade at Pointe Ste. Barbe makes a good walking destination.

Tourist Information

The helpful TI is next to the big market hall, along the busy boulevard Victor Hugo (July–Aug Mon–Sat 9:00–19:30, Sun 10:00–13:00 & 15:00–19:00; Sept–June Mon–Sat 9:00–12:30 & 14:00–19:00, Sun 10:00–13:00—except Jan–March, when it's closed Sun; 20 boulevard Victor Hugo, tel. 05 59 26 03 16, town info: www.saint-jean-de-luz.com, regional info: www.terreetcote basques.com).

Arrival in St. Jean-de-Luz

By Train or Bus: From the station, the pedestrian underpass leads toward the TI and the center of Old Town (just a few blocks away—see map).

By Car: Follow signs for *Centre-Ville*, then *Gare* and *Office de Tourisme*. The Old Town is not car-friendly. Your best bet may be paying to park in the big underground garage behind the TI (€1.20/hour, €11/day). Hotels or the TI can advise you.

By Plane: The nearest airport is in Biarritz, 10 miles to the northeast. The tiny airport is easy to navigate, with a useful TI desk (airport tel. 05 59 43 83 83, www.biarritz.aeroport.fr). To reach St. Jean-de-Luz, you can take a public bus (€3, 7/day, 30 minutes, tel. 05 59 26 06 99 for schedule) or a 20-minute taxi ride (about €30).

Helpful Hints

Market Days: Tuesday and Friday mornings (and summer Saturdays), the farmers' stands spill through the streets from Les Halles covered market on boulevard Victor Hugo, and seem to give everyone a rustic whiff of "life is good."

Supermarkets: A **Petit Casino** grocery is across from the market hall, next to the TI (Mon–Tue and Thu–Sat 8:30–13:00 & 15:30–19:30, Sun 9:00–13:00 & 16:30–19:30, closed Wed).

Internet Access: Run by friendly Irish expats Margaret and Peter, **Internet World** is best (daily 10:00–18:00, July–Aug Mon–Sat until 24:00, 7 rue Tourasse, tel. 05 59 26 86 92).

Laundry: Laverie Automatique du Port is at 4 boulevard Thiers (self-service daily 7:00–21:00, €4.80/load, machines accept bills; full-service available Tue–Fri 9:30–12:30 & 14:30–18:00).

Car Rental: Avis, at the train station, is handiest (Mon–Sat 8:00–12:00 & 14:00–18:00, closed Sun, tel. 05 59 26 76 66, fax 05 55 26 19 42).

Tours in St. Jean-de-Luz

Tourist Train—A little tourist train does a 30-minute trip around town (€5.50, departs every 45 minutes from the port, runs April–Nov 10:30–19:00, no train Dec–March). It's only worth the money if you are feeling particularly footsore.

Bus Excursions—Le Basque Bondissant runs popular day-trip excursions, including a handy one to the Guggenheim Bilbao (€35 round-trip, includes €13 museum admission, Wed only, departs 9:30 from green bus terminal across the street from train station, returns 19:30). Other itineraries include Ainhoa, Espelette, St. Jean-Pied-de-Port, Loyola and the Cantabrian coast, San Sebastián, and a trip to the *ventas* (see "*Ventas* Shops" sidebar on page 504). You can get information and buy tickets at the TI, or visit the Le Basque Bondissant office in the bus station (Mon–Fri 8:45–12:00 & 13:30–17:30 except closed Wed afternoon, closed Sat–Sun, tel. 05 59 26 30 74, www.basque-bondissant.com). Advance reservations are recommended in winter, when trips are cancelled if not enough people sign up.

Boat Trips—Le Passeur, at the port, offers mini-Atlantic cruises and fishing excursions (May–Sept, no guides; cruises-€9/45 minutes, €15/1.75 hours; fishing trips-€30; tickets sold on boat, tel. 06 11 69 56 93).

Self-Guided Walk

Welcome to St. Jean-de-Luz

To get a feel for the town, take this hour-long self-guided stroll. You'll start at the port and make your way to the historic church.

Port: Begin at the little working port (at place des Corsaires, just beyond the parking lot). Pleasure craft are in the next port over. While fishing boats used to catch lots of whales and anchovies, now they take in sardines and tuna, and take out tourists on joyrides. Anchovies, once a big part of the fishing business, were nearly overfished into extinction, so they've been protected by the EU for the last few years (though now some limited fishing is being permitted).

St. Jean-de-Luz feels cute and nonthreatening now, but in the 17th century it was home to the Basque Corsairs. With the French government's blessing, these pirates who worked the sea—and enriched the town—moored here.

• *After you walk the length of the port, on your right is the tree-lined...*

St. Jean-de-Luz

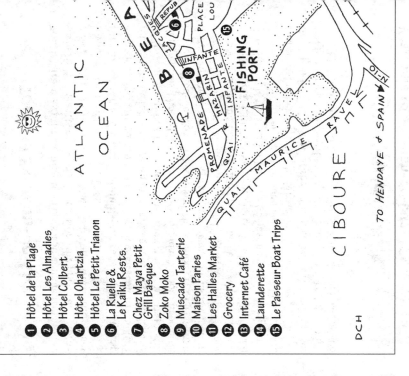

1. Hôtel de la Plage
2. Hôtel Les Almadies
3. Hôtel Colbert
4. Hôtel Ohartzia
5. Hôtel Le Petit Trianon
6. La Ruelle &
   Le Kaiku Rests.
7. Chez Maya Petit
   Grill Basque
8. Zoko Moko
9. Muscade Tarterie
10. Maison Pariès
11. Les Halles Market
12. Grocery
13. Internet Café
14. Launderette
15. Le Passeur Boat Trips

DCH

Place Louis XIV: The town's main square, named for the king who was married here, is a hub of action that serves as the town's communal living room. During the summer, the bandstand features traditional Basque folk music and dancing at 21:00 (almost nightly July–Aug; otherwise Sun and Wed). Facing the square is the City Hall (Herriko Etchea) and the "House of Louis XIV" (he lived here for 40 festive days in 1660). A visit to this house is worthwhile if you like period furniture, though it's only open for part of the year; the rest of the time, the privately owned mansion is occupied by the same family who've had it for over three centuries (€5, June–mid-Oct Wed–Mon, closed Tue and mid-Oct–July, visits by 40-minute guided tour only, 2–4/day, in French with English handouts, tel. 05 59 26 27 58, www.maison-louis-xiv.fr). The king's visit is memorialized by a small black equestrian statue at the entrance of the City Hall (a miniature of the huge one that marks the center of the Versailles courtyard). The plane trees, with truncated branches looking like fists, are cut back in the winter so in the summer they come back with thick, shady foliage.

- *Opposite the port on the far side of the square is...*

Rue de la République: From place Louis XIV, this historic lane leads to the beach. Once the home of fishermen, today it's lined with mostly edible temptations. Facing the square, the shop **Macarons Adam** (at #6; look for the gigantic display of plastic red peppers) still uses the family recipe to bake the *macarons* Louis XIV enjoyed during his visit. You can try one (€1), or sample a less historic but just as tasty *gâteau basque*, a baked tart with a cream or cherry filling.

Farther down rue de la République, you'll find the **Pierre Oteiza** shop, stacked with rustic Basque cheeses and meats from mountain villages (with a few samples generally out for the tasting,

Pelota

In keeping with their seafaring, shipbuilding, and metalworking heritage, Basque sports are often feats of strength: Who can lift the heaviest stone? Who can row the fastest and farthest?

But the most important Basque sport of all is *pelota*—similar to what you might know as jai alai. Players in white pants and red scarves or shirts use a long, hook-shaped wicker basket (called a *txistera* in Euskara) to whip a ball (smaller and far bouncier than a baseball) back and forth off walls at more than 150 miles per hour. This men's-only game can be played with a wall at one or both ends of the court. Most matches

are not professional, but betting on them is common. It can also be played without a racket—this slow-motion handball version is used as a starter game for kids.

It seems that every small Basque town has two things: a church and a *pelota* court (called *fronton*). And though some *frontons* are simple and in poor repair, others are freshly painted as a gleaming sign of local pride.

The TI in St. Jean-de-Luz sells tickets and has a schedule of matches throughout the area; you're more likely to find a match in summer (almost daily at 21:00 July-mid-Sept, afternoon matches sometimes on Sat-Sun). Matches are held throughout the year (except for winter) in the villages (ask for details at TI). The professional *cesta punta* matches on Tuesdays and Fridays often come with Basque folkloric halftime shows.

and handy €3.50 paper cones of salami slices perfect for munching during this walk).

You'll likely eat on this lane tonight. **Kaiku,** the town's top restaurant, fills the oldest building in St. Jean-de-Luz (with its characteristic stone lookout tower), dating from the 1500s. This was the only building on the street to survive a vicious 1558 Spanish attack. Each end of the street is flanked by cannon, which may be from Basque pirate ships. At the upper end of the street, notice the photo of fisherwomen with baskets on their heads, who would literally run to Bayonne to sell their fresh fish.

• *Continue to the...*

Beach: A high embankment protects the town from storm waters, but generally the Grande Plage—which is lovingly groomed daily—is the peaceful haunt of sun-seekers and happy children.

Walk the elevated promenade (to the right). Various tableaux tell history in French. Storms (including a particularly disastrous one in 1749) routinely knocked down buildings. Repeated flooding around 1800 drove the population down by two-thirds. Finally, in 1854, Napoleon III—who had visited here and appreciated the town—began building the three breakwaters you see today. After decades spent piling 8,000 fifty-ton blocks, by 1895 the town was protected. To develop their tourist trade, they built a casino and a fine hotel, and even organized a special getaway train from Paris. During those days there were as many visitors as residents (3,000).

• *Stroll through the seaside shopping mall fronting the late–Art Deco–style La Pergola, which houses a casino and the Helianthal spa center (entrance around back) and overlooks the beach. Anyone in a white robe strolling the beach is from the spa. Beyond La Pergola is the pink, Neo-Romantic Grand Hôtel (c. 1900), with an inviting terrace for an expensive coffee break (€7 cappuccino). From here, circle back into town along boulevard Thiers until you reach the bustling...*

Rue Gambetta: Turn right and circle back to your starting point, following the town's lively pedestrian shopping street. You'll notice many stores selling the renowned *linge Basque*—cotton linens such as tablecloths, napkins, and dishcloths, in the characteristic Basque red, white, and green.

• *Just before place Louis XIV, you'll see the town's main church.*

Eglise St. Jean-Baptiste: The marriage of Louis XIV and Marie-Thérèse put St. Jean-de-Luz on the map, and this church is where it all took place. The ultimate in political marriages, the knot tied between Louis XIV and Marie-Thérèse in 1660 also cinched a reconciliation deal between Europe's two most powerful countries. The king of Spain, Philip IV—who lived in El Escorial Palace—gave his daughter in marriage to the king of France, who lived in Versailles. This marriage united Europe's two largest palaces, which helped end a hundred years of hostility and forged an alliance that enabled both to focus attention on other matters (like England). Little St. Jean-de-Luz was selected for its 15 minutes of fame because it was roughly halfway between Madrid and Paris, and virtually on the France–Spain border. The wedding cleared out both Versailles and El Escorial palaces, as anyone who was anyone attended this glamorous event.

The church, centered on the pedestrian street rue Gambetta, seems modest enough from the exterior...but step inside (Mon–Sat 8:00–12:00 & 14:00–18:30, Sun 8:00–12:00 & 15:00–19:00). The local expertise was in shipbuilding, so the ceiling resembles the hull of a ship turned upside down. The dark wood balconies running along the nave segregated the men from the women and children (men went upstairs until the 1960s, as they still do in nearby villages) and were typical of Basque churches. The number of levels

depended on the importance of the church, and this church, with three levels, is the largest Basque church in France.

The three-foot-long paddle-wheel ship hanging in the center was a gift from Napoleon III's wife, Eugénie. It's a model of an ill-fated ship that had almost sunk just offshore when she was on it. The 1670 Baroque altar feels Franco-Spanish and features 20 French saints. Locals of this proud and rich town call it the finest in the Basque Country. The box across from the pulpit was reserved for leading citizens who were expected to be seen in church and set a good example. Today the mayor and city council members sit here on festival Sundays. The place has great acoustics, and the 17th-century organ is still used for concerts (around €10, mostly in summer, get schedule at TI or online at www.orgueluz.c.la, tickets available at door and possibly in advance at the TI).

As you leave the church, turn left to find the bricked-up doorway—the church's original entrance. According to a quaint but untrue legend, it was sealed after the royal marriage (shown on the wall to the right in a photo of a painting) to symbolize a permanent closing of the door on troubles between France and Spain.

Sleeping in St. Jean-de-Luz

Hotels are a good value here. The higher prices are for peak season (generally July–Sept). In winter, some prices drop below those I've listed. Most hoteliers speak English. Breakfast costs extra, except at my first listing. Those wanting to eat and sleep for less will do slightly better just over the border, in San Sebastián.

$$$ Hôtel de la Plage*** has the best location, right on the ocean. Its 22 rooms, 16 with ocean views, have a lively yellow-and-blue modern nautical decor (Db-€88–118, ocean view Db-€118–158, prices fluctuate with demand, family rooms for up to 5-€30 per extra person, breakfast-€10 but free for kids, air-con, elevator, free Wi-Fi, garage-€15, 33 rue Garat, tel. 05 59 51 03 44, fax 05 59 51 03 48, www.hoteldelaplage.com, reservation@hoteldelaplage.com, run by friendly Pierre, Laurent, and Frederic).

$$$ Hôtel Les Almadies***, on the main pedestrian street, is a bright boutique hotel with seven flawless rooms, comfy public spaces with clever modern touches, a pleasant breakfast room and lounge, an inviting sun deck, and a caring owner (Db-€80–130, higher prices are for rooms with tubs, buffet breakfast-€12, free

Sleep Code

(€1 = about $1.25, France country code: 33, Spain country code: 34, * = French hotel rating system, 0–4 stars)

S = Single, **D** = Double/Twin, **T** = Triple, **Q** = Quad, **b** = bathroom, **s** = shower only. Unless otherwise noted, credit cards are accepted and English is spoken, but breakfast is generally not included. This code applies to this chapter's listings in both France and Spain. The word *ostatua* (which you'll see throughout the Basque Country) means "pension."

To help you sort easily through these listings, I've divided the rooms into three categories based on the price for a standard double room with bath in peak season:

$$$ Higher Priced—Most rooms €90 or more.
$$ Moderately Priced—Most rooms between €60–90.
$ Lower Priced—Most rooms €60 or less.

Prices can change without notice: verify the hotel's current rates online or by email. For other updates, see www.ricksteves.com/update.

Wi-Fi, parking-€10, 58 rue Gambetta, tel. 05 59 85 34 48, fax 05 59 26 12 42, www.hotel-les-almadies.com, hotel.lesalmadies @wanadoo.fr, Monsieur and Madame Hargous will charm you with their Franglish).

$$$ Hôtel Colbert*, a Best Western, has 34 modern, tastefully appointed rooms across the street from the train station (Sb-€80–130, Db-€90–150, €10 extra for slightly bigger "superior" rooms, breakfast-€13, air-con, elevator, free Wi-Fi, 3 boulevard du Commandant Passicot, tel. 05 59 26 31 99, fax 05 59 51 05 61, www .hotelcolbertsaintjeandeluz.com, contact@hotelcolbertsaintjean deluz.com).

$$ Hôtel Ohartzia* ("Souvenir"), one block off the beach, is comfortable, clean, and peaceful, with the most charming facade I've seen. It comes with 17 simple but well-cared-for rooms, generous and homey public spaces, and a delightful garden. Higher prices are for the four rooms with tubs (mid-July–Sept Db-€79–89, April–mid-July Db-€69–74, Oct–March Db-€68–72, extra bed-€15, breakfast-€7, 28 rue Garat, tel. 05 59 26 00 06, fax 05 59 26 74 75, www.hotel-ohartzia.com, hotel.ohartzia@wanadoo.fr). Their front desk is technically open only 8:00–21:00, but owners Madame and Monsieur Audibert (who speak little English) live in the building; their son Benoît speaks English well.

$$ Hôtel Le Petit Trianon*, on a major street a couple of blocks above the Old Town's charm, is simple and traditional, with

26 decent rooms and an accommodating staff (July–Sept Db–€80; mid-March–June and Oct–mid-Nov Db–€65; even less off-season, air-con, free Wi-Fi, parking–€10, 56 boulevard Victor Hugo, tel. 05 59 26 11 90, fax 05 59 26 14 10, www.hotel-lepetittrianon.com, lepetittrianon@wanadoo.fr). To get a room over the quieter court-yard, ask for *côté cours* (coat-ay coor).

Eating in St. Jean-de-Luz

St. Jean-de-Luz restaurants are known for offering good-value, high-quality cuisine. You can find a wide variety of eateries in the old center. For forgettable food with unforgettable views, choose from several places overlooking the beach. Most places serve from 12:15 to 14:00, and from 19:15 on.

The traffic-free rue de la République, which runs from place Louis XIV to the ocean promenade, is lined with hardworking restaurants (two of which are recommended below). Places are empty at 19:30, but packed at 20:30. Making a reservation, especially on weekends or in summer, is wise. Consider a fun night of bar-hopping for dinner in San Sebastián instead (an hour away in Spain, described on page 521).

La Ruelle serves good, traditionally Basque cuisine—mostly seafood—in a convivial dining room packed with tables, happy eaters, and kitschy Basque decor. André and his playful staff obviously enjoy their work, which gives this popular spot a relaxed and fun ambience. They offer a free sangria to diners with this book. Portions are huge; their €18 *ttoro* (seafood stew) easily feeds two—splitting is OK if you order two starters (€19–24 *menus*, closed Tue–Wed Oct–May, 19 rue de la République, tel. 05 59 26 37 80).

Le Kaiku is *the* gastronomic experience in St. Jean-de-Luz. They serve modern, creatively presented cuisine, and specialize in wild seafood (rather than farmed). This dressy place is the most romantic in town, but manages not to be stuffy (€25 lunch *menus*, €30 dinner *menus*, closed Tue–Wed except July–Aug, 17 rue de la République, tel. 05 59 26 13 20, Serge and Julie). For the best experience, talk with Serge about what you like best and your price limits (about €45 will get you a three-course meal *à la carte*).

Chez Maya Petit Grill Basque serves hearty traditional Basque cuisine. Their €17 *ttoro* was a highlight of my day. They have €20 and €30 *menus*, but à la carte is more interesting. If you stick around in warm weather, you'll see the clever overhead fan system kick into action (closed Wed, 2 rue St. Jacques, tel. 05 59 26 80 76).

Zoko Moko offers Mediterranean nouveau cuisine, with small portions on big plates. Get an *amuse-bouche* (an appetizer chosen by the chef) and a *mignardise* (a fun bite-sized dessert) with each main plate ordered (€24 lunchtime *plats*, €40 evening *menu*,

It Happened at Hendaye

If taking the train between the Spanish and French Basque regions, you'll change trains at the nondescript little Hendaye Station. While it seems innocent enough, this was a site of a fateful meeting between two of Europe's most notorious 20th-century dictators.

In the days before World War II, Adolf Hitler and Francisco Franco maintained a diplomatic relationship. But after the fall of France, they decided to meet secretly in Hendaye to size each other up. On October 23, 1940, Hitler traveled through Nazi-occupied France, then waited impatiently on the platform for Franco's delayed train. The over-eager Franco hoped the Führer would invite him to join in a military alliance with Germany (and ultimately share in the expected war spoils).

According to reports of the meeting, Franco was greedy, boastful, and misguided, leading Hitler to dismiss him as a buffoon. Franco later spun the situation by claiming that he had cleverly avoided being pulled into World War II. In fact, his own incompetence is what saved Spain. Had Franco made a better impression on Hitler here at Hendaye, it's possible that Spain would have entered the war...which could have changed the course of Spanish, German, and European history.

closed Mon, Rue Mazarin 6, tel. 05 59 08 01 23, owner Charles).

Fast and Cheap: Consider the take-away crêpe stands on rue Gambetta. For a sit-down salad or a tart—either sweet or savory—consider **Muscade Tarterie** (€7–10 per slice; daily except June and Oct, when it's closed Mon; 20 rue Garat, tel. 05 59 26 96 73).

Sweets: Maison Paries is a favorite for its traditional sweets. Locals like their fine chocolates, *tartes*, *macarons*, fudge (*kanougas*), and *touron* (like marzipan, but firmer and made of sugar), which comes in a multitude of flavors—brought by Jews who stopped here just over the border in 1492 after being expelled from Spain. The delectable chocolate version of the *gâteau basque* is also worth a try (9 rue Gambetta, tel. 05 59 26 01 46).

St. Jean-de-Luz Connections

The train station in St. Jean-de-Luz is called St. Jean-de-Luz-Ciboure. Its handy departure board displays lights next to any trains leaving that day. Buses leave from the green building across the street. There is reduced bus and rail service on Sundays and off-season.

From St. Jean-de-Luz by Train to: Bayonne (hourly, 25 minutes), **St. Jean-Pied-de-Port** (4/day, 6/day in summer, 2 hours with transfer in Bayonne), **Paris** (4 TGV connections per day via

Bordeaux, 6–7 hours; more with bus transfer in Dax, 8 hours), **Bordeaux** (11/day, 2.5 hours), **Sarlat** (4/day, 6–8 hours, transfer in Bordeaux), **Carcassonne** (5/day, 6 hours, transfers likely in Bayonne and Toulouse).

By Train to San Sebastián: First, take the 10-minute train to the French border town of Hendaye (Gare SNCF stop, about 10/day). Or get to Hendaye by bus (3/day, 35 minutes); check the schedule to see which leaves first.

Leave the Hendaye station to the right, and look for the light-blue EuskoTren building, where you'll catch the commuter train into San Sebastián (2/hour, generally at :03 and :33 after the hour 7:00–22:33, 35 minutes). This slow, milk-run train is known as the Topo ("Mole"), because it goes underground part of the time.

By Bus: Buses leave from both sides of the road in front of the train station. Be sure you are on the correct side of the road for your bus (the road can only be crossed on the pedestrian underpass). All tickets are bought on the bus. Local bus #26 connects St. Jean-de-Luz either to **Bayonne** or **Biarritz** almost hourly. Confusingly, this one bus can run two different routes (one to Bayonne, the other to Biarritz Centre, 40 minutes to either one)—check the destination carefully. Another bus connects St. Jean-de-Luz to **Sare** (Mon–Fri 5/day, Sat 2/day, none Sun, 30 minutes). A Spanish bus runs to **San Sebastián** (Mon–Sat only, 2/day direct—likely at 12:45 and 19:15, none on Sun, 1 hour, only 1/week off-season, info in Spain toll tel. 902-101-210).

By Excursion: If you're without a car, consider using **Le Basque Bondissant**'s day-trip excursions to visit otherwise difficult-to-reach destinations, such as the Guggenheim Bilbao (see "Tours in St. Jean-de-Luz," earlier).

By Taxi to San Sebastián will cost you about €75 for up to four people, but it's convenient (tel. 05 59 26 10 11 or tel. 06 25 76 97 69).

Route Tips for Drivers

A one-day side-trip to both Bayonne and Biarritz is easy from St. Jean-de-Luz. These three towns form a sort of triangle (depending on traffic, each one is less than a 30-minute drive from the other). Hop on the autoroute to Bayonne, sightsee there, then take N-10 into Biarritz. Leaving Biarritz, continue on N-10 along the coast. In Bidart, watch (on the right) for the town's proud *frontón* (*pelota* court). Consider peeling off to go into the village center of Guéthary, with another *frontón*. If you're up for a walk on the beach, cross the little bridge in Guéthary, park by the train station, and hike down to the walkway along the surfing beach (lined with cafés and eateries). When you're ready to move on, you're a very short drive from St. Jean-de-Luz.

Bayonne / Baiona

To feel the urban pulse of French Basque Country, visit Bayonne—modestly but honestly nicknamed "your anchor in the Basque Country" by its tourist board. With frequent, fast connections with St. Jean-de-Luz (25 minutes by train, 40 minutes by bus), Bayonne makes an easy half-day side-trip.

Come here to browse through Bayonne's atmospheric and well-worn-yet-lively Old Town, and to admire its impressive Museum of

Basque Culture. Known for establishing Europe's first whaling industry and for inventing the bayonet, Bayonne is more famous today for its ham (*jambon de Bayonne*) and chocolate.

Get lost in Bayonne's Old Town. In pretty Grand Bayonne, tall, slender buildings, decorated in Basque fashion with green-and-red shutters, climb above cobbled streets. Be sure to stroll the streets around the cathedral and along the banks of the smaller Nive River, where you'll find the market (Les Halles).

Orientation to Bayonne

Bayonne's two rivers, the grand Adour and the petite Nive, divide the city into three parts. St. Esprit, with the train station; and the more interesting Grand Bayonne and Petit Bayonne, which together make up the Old Town.

Tourist Information

The TI is in a modern parking lot a block off the mighty Adour River, on the northeastern edge of Grand Bayonne. They have very little in English other than a map and a town brochure (Mon–Fri 9:00–18:30, Sat 10:00–18:00, closed Sun except 10:00–13:00 in July–Aug, place des Basques, tel. 08 20 42 64 64, www.bayonne-tourisme.com).

Arrival in Bayonne

By Train: The TI and Grand Bayonne are a 10-minute walk from the train station: Walk straight out of the station, cross the traffic circle, and then cross the imposing bridge (pont St. Esprit). Once past the big Adour River, continue across a smaller bridge (pont Mayou), which spans the smaller Nive River. Stop on pont Mayou to orient yourself: You just left Petit Bayonne (left side of Nive River. Ahead of you is Grand Bayonne (spires of cathedral straight ahead, TI a few blocks to the right). The Museum of

Basque Culture is in Petit Bayonne, facing the next bridge up the Nive River.

By Car and Bus: The handiest parking is also where buses arrive in Bayonne: next to the TI at the modern parking lot on the edge of Grand Bayonne. To reach the town center from here, first walk with the busy road on your left to the big park and the war memorial. Then turn right and walk with the park on your left-hand side. After a few blocks, you'll see atmospheric streets leading up to the cathedral on your right; if you continue straight, you'll reach the bridge over the Nive River called pont Mayou.

To reach this parking lot, **drivers** take the *Bayonne Sud* exit from the autoroute, then follow green *Bayonne Centre* signs, then white *Centre-Ville* signs (with an *i* for tourist information). You'll see the lot on your right. In high season, when this lot can be full, use one of the lots just outside the center (follow signs to *Glain* or *Porte d'Espagne* as you arrive in town), then catch the little orange *navette* (shuttle bus) to get into the center (free, find route maps posted at stops in town, every 7 minutes, Mon–Sat 7:30–19:30, closed Sun).

Sights in Bayonne

▲**Museum of Basque Culture (Musée Basque)**—This museum (in Petit Bayonne, facing the Nive River at pont Marengo) explains French Basque culture from cradle to grave—in French, Euskara, and Spanish. The only English you'll read is "do not touch" (unless you buy their informative €5 English booklet). Artifacts and videos take you into traditional Basque villages and sit you in the front row of time-honored festivals—letting you envision this otherwise hard-to-experience culture (€5.50; July–Aug daily 10:00–18:30, also open and free Wed evenings 18:30–20:30; Sept–June Tue–Sun 10:00–18:30, closed Mon; last entry one hour before closing, 37 quai des Corsaires, tel. 05 59 59 08 98, www.musee-basque.com).

On the ground floor, you'll begin by walking through some 16th-century gravestones, then see a display of carts and tools used in rural life. Look for the *laiak*—distinctive forked hoes used to work the ground. At the end of this section, you'll watch a grainy film on Basque rural lifestyles.

The next floor up begins by explaining that the house (*etxea*) is the building-block of Basque society. More than just a building, it's a social institution—Basques are named for their house, not vice versa. You'll see models and paintings of Basque houses, then domestic items, a giant door, kitchen equipment, and furniture (including a combination bench-table, near the fireplace). After an exhibit on Basque clothing, you'll move into the nautical life, with models, paintings, and actual boats. The little door leads to a model of the port of Bayonne in 1805, back when it was a strategic walled city.

Upstairs you'll learn that the religious life of the Basques was strongly influenced by the Camino de Santiago pilgrim trail, which passes through their territory. The section on social life explains Basque funeral traditions. One somber room shows off several types of *txistera* baskets (*chistera* in French), gloves, and balls used for the game, and videos show how these items are made. The museum wraps up with a brief lesson on the region's history from the 16th to the 20th centuries, including exhibits on the large Jewish population here (who had fled from a hostile Spain) and the renaissance of Basque culture in the 19th century.

Cathédrale Ste. Marie—Bankrolled by the whaling community, this cathedral sits dead-center in Grand Bayonne and is worth a peek (free, Mon–Sat 10:00–11:45 & 15:00–17:45, Sun 15:30–18:00). Find the unique keystones on the ceiling along the nave, then circle behind the church to find the peaceful 13th-century cloisters (free, daily 9:00–12:30 & 14:00–17:00, until 18:00 mid-May–mid-Sept).

Sweets Shops—With no more whales to catch, Bayonne turned to producing mouthwatering chocolates and marzipan; look for shops on the arcaded rue du Port Neuf (running between the cathedral and the Adour River). **Daranatz** is Bayonne's best chocolate shop, with bars of chocolate blended with all kinds of flavors—one with a general mix of spices (lots of cardamom), one with just cinnamon, and another with *piments d'Espelette* (15 Arceaux Port Neuf, tel. 05 59 59 03 55).

Ramparts—The ramparts around Grand Bayonne are open for walking and great for picnicking (access from park at far end of TI parking lot). However, the ramparts do not allow access to either of Bayonne's castles—both are closed to the public.

Eating in Bayonne

Le Bayonnais, next door to the Museum of Basque Culture, serves traditional Basque specialties à la carte. Sit in the blue-tiled interior or out along the river (€17 lunch and dinner *menu*, closed Sun–Mon, quai des Corsaires 38, tel. 05 59 25 61 19).

La Cidrerie Txotx (pronounced "choch") has a Spanish-bodega ambience under a chorus line of hams. You can also sit outside, along the river, just past the market hall (€8–10 Basque tapas or €12–16 *plats*, daily, 49 quai Jauréguiberry, tel. 05 59 59 16 80).

A la Bolée serves up inexpensive sweet and savory crêpes in a cozy atmosphere along the side of the cathedral (daily, 10 place Pasteur, tel. 05 59 59 18 75).

If the weather is good, consider gathering a **picnic** from shops along the pedestrian streets and heading for the park around the ramparts below the *Jardin Botanique* (benches galore).

Bayonne Connections

From Bayonne, you can reach **St. Jean-de-Luz** by bus #26, almost hourly, 40 minutes) or by train (hourly, 25 minutes). To **Biarritz**, the bus is best (take the unfortunately named "STAB" bus #1 to reach Biarritz Centre, departs every 10 minutes, takes 20 minutes). There's also a train from Bayonne up to **St. Jean-Pied-du-Port** (4/day, 6/day in summer, 1 hour). Buses to the inland Basque villages of Espelette and Ainhoa are impractical.

Biarritz / Biarritz

A glitzy resort town steeped in the belle époque, Biarritz (BEE-ah-ritz) is where the French Basques put on the ritz. In the 19th century, this simple whaling harbor became, almost overnight, a high-class aristocrat-magnet dubbed the "beach of kings." Although St. Jean-de-Luz and Bayonne are more fully French and more fully Basque, the made-for-international-tourists, jet-set scene of Biarritz is not without its charms. Perched over a popular surfing beach, anchored by grand

hotels and casinos, hemmed in by jagged and picturesque rocky islets at either end, and watched over by a lighthouse on a distant promontory, Biarritz is a striking beach resort. However, for sightseers with limited time, it's likely more trouble than it's worth.

Orientation to Biarritz

Biarritz feels much bigger than its population of 30,000. The town sprawls, but virtually everything we're interested in lines up along the waterfront: the beach, promenade, hotel and shopping zone, and TI.

Tourist Information

The TI is in a little pink castle two blocks up from the beach (just above the beach and casino, hiding behind the City Hall/*hôtel de ville*—look for signs). Pick up the free map and get details on any sightseeing that interests you (July–Aug daily 9:00–19:00; Sept–June Mon-Fri 9:00–18:00, Sat-Sun 10:00–17:00; Square d'Ixelles, tel. 05 59 22 37 00, www.biarritz.fr).

Arrival in Biarritz

By Car: Drivers follow signs for *Centre-Ville*, then carefully track signs for specific parking garages. The most central garages are called *Grande Plage*, *Casino*, *Bellevue*, and *St. Eugénie* (closest to the water). Signs in front of each tell you whether it's full (*complet*), in which case, move on to the next one.

By Bus: Buses stop at "Biarritz Centre," a parking lot next to the TI (STAB buses to/from Bayonne stop along the side of the lot; buses to/from St. Jean-de-Luz stop at the end of the lot). If you're taking a bus, be aware that some stops are at the outskirts of town—only take one to "Centre."

Don't bother taking the **train** to or from Biarritz, as the station is about two miles from the tourist area (buses #2 and #9 connect the train station to the city center).

There is no baggage storage in Biarritz.

Sights in Biarritz

There's little of "sightseeing" value in Biarritz. The TI can fill you in on the town's four museums (Marine Museum—described below; Chocolate Planet and Museum—intriguing, but a long walk from the center; Oriental Art Museum—large, diverse collection of art from across Asia; and Biarritz Historical Museum—really?).

Your time is best spent strolling along the various levels that climb up from the sea. From the TI, you can do a loop: First head west on the lively **pedestrian streets** that occupy the plateau above the water, which are lined with restaurants, cafés, and high-class, resorty "window-licking." (Place Georges Clemenceau is the grassy "main square" of this area.)

Work your way out to the point with the **Marine Museum** (Musée de la Mer). The most convenient of Biarritz's attractions, this pricey Art Deco museum/aquarium wins the "best rainy-day option" award, with a tank of seals and a chance to get face-to-teeth with live sharks (€8, daily 9:30–12:30 & 14:30–18:00, tel. 05 59 22 33 34, www.museedelamer.com).

Whether or not you're visiting the museum, it's worth hiking down to the entrance, then wandering out on the walkways that

connect the big offshore rocks. These lead to the so-called **Virgin Rock** (Rocher de la Vierge), topped by a statue of Mary. Spot any surfers?

From here, stick along the water as you head back toward the TI. After a bit of up and down over the rocks, don't miss the trail down to **Fishermen's Wharf** (Port des Pêcheurs), a little pocket of salty authenticity that clings like barnacles to the cliff below the hotels. The remnants of an aborted construction project from the town's glory days, this little fishing settlement of humble houses and rugged jetties seems to faintly echo the Basque culture that thrived here before the glitz hit. Many of the houses have been taken over by the tourist trade (gift shops and restaurants).

Continuing along the water (and briefly back up to street level), make your way back to the town's centerpiece, the **big beach** (Grande Plage). Dominating this inviting stretch of sand is the Art Deco casino, and the TI is just above that. If you haven't yet taken the time on your vacation to splash, wade, or stroll on the beach...now's your chance.

Biarritz Connections

Biarritz is connected by bus #26 to **St.-Jean-de-Luz** (nearly hourly, 40 minutes). STAB buses take you to **Bayonne** (#1, departs every 10 minutes, takes 20 minutes).

Villages in the French Basque Country

Traditional villages among the green hills, with buildings colored like the Basque flag, offer the best glimpse at Basque culture. Cheese, hard cider, and *pelota* players are the primary products of these villages, which attract few foreigners but many French summer visitors. Most of these villages have welcomed pilgrims bound for Santiago de Compostela since the Middle Ages. Today's hikers trek between local villages or head into the Pyrenees. The most appealing villages lie in the foothills of the Pyrenees, spared from beach-scene development.

Use St.-Jean-de-Luz as your base to visit the following Basque sights. You can reach some of these places by public transportation, but the hassle outweighs the rewards.

Do a circuit of these towns in the order they're listed here. Assuming you're driving, I've included route instructions as well.

- *From St. Jean-de-Luz, follow signs for Ascain, then Sare. On the road toward Sare, you'll pass the station for the train up to…*

La Rhune / Larrun

Between the villages of Ascain and Sare, near the border with Spain, a small cogwheel train takes tourists to the top of La Rhune, the region's highest peak (2,969 feet). You'll putt-putt up the hillside for 35 minutes in an open-air train car to reach panoramic views of land and sea (adults-€14 round-trip, kids-€8, all pay €3 more in summer, runs April–mid-Nov daily, March Sat–Sun only, closed mid-Nov–Feb, departures weather-dependent—the trip is worthless if it's not clear, goes every 35 minutes when busiest July–Aug, tel. 05 59 54 20 26, www.rhune.com).

- *Continue along the same road to…*

Sare / Sara

Sare, which sits at the base of the towering mountain La Rhune, is among the most picturesque villages—and the most touristed. It's easily reached from St. Jean-de-Luz by bus or car (see page 494). The small TI is on the main square (Mon–Fri 9:30–12:30 & 14:00–18:00, Sat 9:30–12:30, closed Sun, tel. 05 55 54 20 14). Nearby is a cluster of hotels and the town church (which has an impressive interior, with arches over the altar and Basque-style balconies lining the nave). At the far end of the square is the town's humble *fronton* (pelota court).

- *Leaving Sare, first follow signs for St. Pée, then watch for the turnoff to…*

Ainhoa / Ainhoa

Ainhoa is a colorful, tidy, picturesque one-street town that sees fewer tourists (which is a good thing). Its chunks of fortified walls and gates mingle with red-and-white, half-timbered buildings.

The 14th-century church—with a beautiful golden *retable* (screen behind the altar)—and the *fronton* share center stage.

Ainhoa is also a popular starting point for hikes into the hills. For a spectacular village-and-valleys view, drive five minutes (or walk 90 sweaty minutes)

up the steep dirt road to the Chapelle de Notre-Dame d'Aranazau ("d'Aubepine" in French). Start in the parking lot directly across the main street from the church, then head straight uphill. Follow signs for *oratoire*, then count the giant white crosses to the top.

- *As you leave Ainhoa, you'll have to backtrack the way you came in to find the road to…*

Espelette / Ezpeleta

Espelette won't let you forget that it's the capital of the region's AOC red peppers (*piments d'Espelette*), with strands of them dangling like good-luck charms from many houses and storefronts. After strolling the charming, cobbled center, wander downhill at the end of town to find the town church and the well-restored château and medieval tower, which now houses the town hall, an exhibition, and the TI (Mon–Fri 8:30–12:30 & 14:00–18:00, Sat 9:30–12:30, closed Sun, tel. 05 59 93 95 02).

Sleeping and Eating: For a good regional meal, consider the **$$ Hôtel Euzkadi** restaurant, with a *muy* Spanish

ambience (€26–33 *menus*, daily 12:30–14:00 & 19:30–21:00, July–Aug closed Mon, Sept–June closed Mon–Tue, 285 Karrika Nagusia, tel. 05 59 93 91 88). The hotel has 27 rooms with modern touches and a swimming pool (Sb-€41-43, Db-€52-65, €10 more in July–Aug, air-con, elevator, free Wi-Fi, www.hotel-restaurant-euzkadi.com).

• *From Espelette, if you have time, you can follow signs to* Cambo les Bains, *then* St. Jean-Pied-de-Port.

St. Jean-Pied-de-Port / Donibane Garazi

Just five miles from the Spanish border, the walled town of St. Jean-Pied-de-Port (sahn zhahn-pee-duh-por) is the most popular village in all the French Basque countryside. Traditionally, St. Jean-Pied-de-Port has been the final stopover in France for pilgrims undertaking the Camino de Santiago ("Way of Saint James")—the medieval pilgrimage route that runs from here 500 miles across the north of Spain to the city of Santiago de Compostela. After centuries of obscurity, the pilgrimage has become more popular again recently, as thousands of modern travelers each year follow that ancient trail on foot, bike, or horseback. From St. Jean-Pied-de-Port, Santiago-bound pilgrims cross the Pyrenees together and continue their march through Spain. The scallop shell of "St. Jacques" (French for "James") is etched on walls throughout the town.

Visitors to this town are equal parts pilgrims and French tourists. Gift shops sell a strange combination of pilgrim gear (such as quick-drying shirts and shorts) and Basque souvenirs. This place is packed in the summer (so come early or late).

Tourist Information: The TI, on the main road along the outside of the walled Old Town, can give you a town map (hours vary, generally July–Aug Mon–Sat 9:00–19:00, Sun 10:00–12:00; Sept–June Mon–Sat 9:00–12:00 & 14:00–18:00, Sun 10:00–12:00; maybe less in winter; tel. 08 10 75 36 71).

Arrival in St. Jean-Pied-de-Port: Parking is ample and well-signed from the main road. If arriving by **train**, exit the station to the left, then follow the busy road at the traffic circle toward the city wall.

Sights: There's little in the way of sightseeing here, other than pilgrim-spotting. Many modern pilgrims begin their Camino in this traditional spot because of its easy train connection to Bayonne, and because—as its name implies ("St. John at the Foot of the Pass")—it offers a very challenging but rewarding first leg: up, over, and into Spain.

Cross the old bridge over the Nive River (the same one that winds up in Bayonne) to the **Notre-Dame Gate,** which was once

a drawbridge. Then head up the main walking drag, **rue de la Citadelle.** With its rosy-pink buildings and ancient dates above its doorways, this lane simply feels old. Notice lots of signs for *chambres* (rooms) and *refuges*—humble, hostel-like pilgrim bunkhouses.

Partway up, on the left at #39, look for the **Pilgrim Friends Office** (Les Amis du Chemin de Saint-Jacques, daily 7:30–12:00 & 13:30–20:30 & 21:30–22:30, tel. 05 59 37 05 09). This is where pilgrims check in before their long journey to Santiago; 32,000 pilgrims started out here last year (compared to just 4,000 a decade ago). For €2 a pilgrim can buy the official credential (*credenciel*) that she'll get stamped at each stop between here and Santiago to prove she walked the whole way and earn her *compostela* certificate. Pilgrims also receive a warm welcome, lots of advice, and help finding a bunk (the well-traveled staff swears that no pilgrim ever goes without a bed in St. Jean-Pied-de-Port).

A few more steps up, you'll pass the skippable €3 Bishop's Prison (Prison des Evêques, on the left). Continue on up to the **citadel,** dating from the mid-17th century—when this was a highly strategic location, keeping an eye on the easiest road over the Pyrenees between Spain and France. Though not open to the public (as it houses a school), the grounds around this stout fortress offer sweeping views over the French Basque countryside.

Ventas Shops

Scattered between France and Spain and along the foothills of the Pyrenees, you'll see many signs for *ventas* (from the Spanish *vender*, "to sell"). Follow one of these signs to a cultural detour. Originally used as contraband outposts, a *ventas* shop operates as a café, a bar, a restaurant, a grocery store, a gas station, a cheap boutique, and more. Most are lost in the hills and hard to find, and many still don't have signs—locals just know where they are. Today, they are legal in a borderless Europe, and they still offer inexpensive products. Customers are mostly the French Basque, who cause traffic jams on weekends driving to the border to do border shopping or fill the gas tank. In most *ventas*, gas is cheaper by 25 percent, cigarettes and alcohol leave by the case, and the Spanish, French, and Euskara languages mingle as locals enjoy a coffee or beer among hanging garlands of cheap hams. You can take a bus tour to some *ventas* from St. Jean-de-Luz (see page 485).

Sleeping in St. Jean-Pied-de-Port: Lots of humble pilgrim dwellings line the main drag, rue de la Citadelle. If you're looking for a bit more comfort, consider these options.

$$ Hotel Ramuntcho** is the only real hotel option in the Old Town, located partway up rue de la Citadelle. Its 16 rooms above a restaurant are straightforward but modern (Db-€78–83, 1 rue de France, tel. 05 59 37 03 91, fax 05 59 37 35 17, http://perso.wanadoo.fr/hotel.ramuntcho, hotel.ramuntcho@wanadoo.fr).

$$ Itzalpea, a café and tea house, rents five rooms along the main road just outside the Old Town (Db-€64–80 depending on size, includes breakfast, closed Sat off-season, air-con, 5 place du Trinquet, tel. 05 59 37 03 66, fax 05 59 37 33 18, www.maisondhotes-itzalpea.com, itzalpea@wanadoo.fr).

$ Chambres Chez l'Habitant has five old-fashioned, pilgrim-perfect rooms along the main drag. Welcoming Maria and Jean Pierre speak limited English, but their daughter can help translate (€20–25/person in D, Db, Q, or Qb, includes breakfast, 15 rue de la Citadelle, tel. 05 59 37 05 83).

St. Jean-Pied-de-Port Connections: A scenic train conveniently links St. Jean-Pied-de-Port to **Bayonne** (4/day, 6/day in summer, 1 hour), and from there to **St. Jean-de-Luz** (about 30 minutes beyond Bayonne). It's about a 1.25-hour drive from St. Jean-de-Luz.

Spanish Basque Country (El País Vasco)

Four of the seven Basque territories lie within Spain. Many consider Spanish Basque culture to be feistier and more colorful than the relatively assimilated French Basques—you'll hear more Euskara spoken here than in France.

For 40 years, the figure of Generalísimo Franco loomed large over the Spanish Basques. Franco depended upon Basque industry to keep the floundering Spanish economy afloat. But even as he exploited the Basques economically, he so effectively blunted Basque culture that the language was primarily Spanish by default. Franco kicked off his regime by offering up the historic Basque town of Guernica as target practice to his ally Hitler's air force. The notorious result—the wholesale slaughter of innocent civilians—was immortalized by Pablo Picasso's mural *Guernica.*

But Franco is long gone, and today's Basques are looking to the future. The iron deposits have been depleted, prompting the Basques to re-imagine their rusting cities for the 21st century. True to form, they're rising to the challenge. Perhaps the best example is Bilbao, whose iconic Guggenheim Museum—built on the former site of an industrial wasteland—is the centerpiece of a bold new skyline.

San Sebastián is the heart of the tourist's *País Vasco,* with its sparkling beach picturesquely framed by looming green mountains and a charming Old Town with gourmet *pintxos* (tapas) spilling out of every bar. On-the-rise Bilbao is worth a look for its landmark Guggenheim and its atmospheric Old Town. For small-town fun, drop by the fishing village of Lekeitio (near Bilbao). And for history, Guernica has some intriguing museums.

San Sebastián / Donostia

Shimmering above the breathtaking Concha Bay, elegant and prosperous San Sebastián (Donostia in Euskara) has a favored location with golden beaches, capped by twin peaks at either end, and with a cute little island in the center. A delightful beachfront promenade runs the length of the bay, with an intriguing Old Town at one end and a smart shopping district in

Dipping into Spain

If you're heading from France to Spain, you don't have to worry about border stops or currency changes (both countries use the euro). But here are a few other practicalities:

Phones: Spain's telephone country code is 34. Remember that French phone cards and stamps will not work in Spain.

Hours: Most Spanish sights and stores close for a "siesta" from about 13:00 to 16:00, and dinner doesn't begin until 21:00 or 22:00 (though tapas are always available).

Eating Tips: Most Spaniards have their big meal at lunch, then build a light dinner out of appetizer portions called tapas (or, in Basque Country, *pintxos*). Rather than choosing one restaurant for the evening, eaters hop from bar to bar sampling these tasty snacks. For tips on this ritual, see "Do the *Txikiteo* Tango—Tapas Cheat Sheet" on page 524.

Spanish Survival Phrases: Although many Spanish Basques speak Euskara, most speak Spanish in everyday life. You'll find these phrases useful:

English	Spanish	Pronounced
Good day.	Buenos días.	**bway**-nohs **dee**-ahs
Mr. / Mrs.	Señor / Señora	sayn-**yor** / sayn-**yor**-ah
Please.	Por favor	por fah-**bor**
Thank you.	Muchas gracias.	**moo**-chahs **grah**-thee-ahs
You're welcome.	De nada.	day **nah**-dah
Excuse me.	Perdone.	pehr-**doh**-nay
Yes. / No.	Sí. / No	see / noh
Cheers!	¡Salud!	sah-**lood**
men	hombres, caballeros	**ohm**-brays, kah-bah-**yay**-rohs
women	mujeres, damas	moo-**hehr**-ays, **dah**-mahs
one / two / three	uno / dos / tres	**oo**-noh / dohs / trays
coffee with milk	café con leche	kah-**feh** kohn **lay**-chay
sandwich	bocadillo	boh-kah-**dee**-yoh
Where is...?	¿Donde está...?	**dohn**-day ay-**stah**
tourist office	turismo	too-**rees**-moh
city center	centro ciudad	**thehn**-troh thee-oo-**dahd**
Do you speak English?	¿Habla usted inglés?	**ah**-blah oo-**stehd** een-**glays**

the center. It has 180,000 residents and almost that many tourists in high season (July–Sept). With a romantic setting, a soaring statue of Christ gazing over the city, and a late-night lively Old Town, San Sebastián has a mini–Rio de Janeiro aura. While the actual "sightseeing" isn't much, the scenic city itself provides a pleasant introduction to Spain's Basque Country. And as a culinary capital of Spain, it dishes up some of the top tapas anywhere.

In 1845, Queen Isabel II's doctor recommended she treat her skin problems by bathing here in the sea. (For modesty's sake, she would go inside a giant cabana that could be wheeled into the surf—allowing her to swim far from prying eyes, never having to set foot on the beach.) Her visit mobilized Spain's aristocracy, and soon the city was on the map as a seaside resort. By the turn of the 20th century, San Sebastián was the toast of the belle époque, and a leading resort for Europe's beautiful people. Before World War I, Queen María Cristina summered here and held court in her Miramar Palace overlooking the crescent beach (the turreted, red-brick building partway around the bay). Hotels, casinos, and theaters flourished. Even Franco enjoyed 35 summers in a place he was sure to call San Sebastián, not Donostia.

Planning Your Time

San Sebastián's sights can be exhausted in a few hours, but it's a great place to be on vacation for a full, lazy day (or longer). Stroll the two-mile-long promenade and scout the place you'll grab to work on a tan. The promenade leads to a funicular that lifts you to the Monte Igueldo viewpoint. After exploring the Old Town and port, walk up to the hill of Monte Urgull. If you have more time, enjoy the delightful aquarium. Modern art-lovers can venture to the Chillida-Leku Museum on the outskirts. A key ingredient of any visit to San Sebastián is enjoying tapas in the Old Town bars.

Orientation to San Sebastián

The San Sebastián that we're interested in surrounds Concha Bay (Bahía de la Concha). It can be divided into three areas: Playa de la Concha (best beaches), the shopping district (called Centro), and the skinny streets of the grid-planned Old Town (called Parte Vieja, to the north of the shopping district). Centro, just east of Playa de la Concha, has beautiful turn-of-the-20th-century architecture, but no real sights. A busy drag called Alameda del

Boulevard (or just "Boulevard") stands where the city wall once ran, and separates the Centro from the Old Town.

It's all bookended by mini-mountains: Monte Urgull to the north and east, Monte Igueldo to the south and west. The river (Río Urumea) divides central San Sebastián from the district called Gros (which—contrary to its name—is actually quite nice, with a lively night scene and surfing beach).

Tourist Information

San Sebastián's TI, conveniently located right on the Boulevard, has information on city and regional sights, as well as bus and train schedules. Pick up the free map and the *Donostia/San Sebastián Holiday Guide* booklet, which has English descriptions of the three walking tours—the Old Town/Monte Urgull walk is best (July–Sept daily 9:00–20:00; Oct–June Mon–Thu 9:00–13:30 & 15:30–19:00, Fri–Sat 9:30–19:00, Sun 10:00–14:00; Boulevard 8, tel. 943-481-166, www.sansebastianturismo.com).

Arrival in San Sebastián

By Train: The town has two train stations (neither has luggage storage, but you can leave bags at Zarranet Internet café downtown—see "Helpful Hints," later).

If you're coming on a regional Topo train from Hendaye/Hendaia on the French border, get off at the **EuskoTren Station** (end of the line, called Amara). It's a level 15-minute walk to the center: Exit the station and walk across the long plaza, then veer right and walk eight blocks down Calle Easo (toward the statue of Christ hovering on the hill) to the beach. The Old Town will be ahead on your right, with Playa de la Concha to your left. To speed things up, catch bus #21, #26, or #28 along Calle Easo and take it to the Boulevard stop, near the TI at the bottom of the Old Town.

If you're arriving by train from elsewhere in Spain (or from France after transferring in Irún), you'll get off at the main **RENFE Station**. It's just across the river from the Centro shopping district. There are no convenient buses from the station—to get to the Old Town and most recommended hotels, catch a taxi (stand out front, €6 to downtown). Or just walk—cross the fancy dragon-decorated María Cristina Bridge, turn right onto the busy avenue called Paseo de los Fueros, and follow the Urumea River until the last bridge.

By Bus: A few buses—such as those from Hondarribia and the airport—can let you off at pretty Plaza de Gipuzkoa (first stop after crossing the river, in Centro shopping area, one block from the Boulevard, TI, and Old Town). But most buses—including those from Bilbao—take you instead to San Sebastián's makeshift "bus station" (dubbed Amara) at a big roundabout called Plaza Pío XII. It's basically a parking lot with a few bus shelters and a TI kiosk (open July–Aug only). At the end of the lot nearest the big roundabout, you'll see directional signs pointing you toward the town center (about a 30-minute walk). To save time and energy, catch local bus #21, #26, or #28 from the bus stop at the start of Avenida de Sancho el Sabio and get off at the Boulevard stop, near the TI at the start of the Old Town.

By Plane: San Sebastián Airport is beautifully situated along the harbor in the nearby town of Hondarribia, 12 miles east of the city (just across the bay from France). An easy bus (#1-2) connects the airport to San Sebastián's Plaza de Gipuzkoa, just a block south of the Boulevard and TI (€2.10, about hourly, 35 minutes, timetable at TI, runs daily 7:45–20:20). A taxi into town costs about €30. For flight information, call 943-668-500 (airport info: www.aena.es).

If you arrive at **Bilbao Airport,** go out front and take the Pesa bus directly to San Sebastián (€15.20, pay driver, runs hourly, 1 hour, drops off at Plaza Pío XII, www.pesa.net).

By Car: Take the Amara freeway exit, follow *centro ciudad* signs into the city center, and park in a pay lot (many are well-signed). If you're picking up or returning a rental car, you'll find **Europcar** at the RENFE train station (tel. 943-322-304). Not as centrally located are **Hertz** (Centro Comercial Garbera, Travesía de Garbera 1, bus #16 connects with downtown, tel. 943-392-223) and **Avis** (a taxi ride away at Hotel Barceló Costa Vasca, Pío Baroja 15, tel. 943-461-556).

Helpful Hints

Internet Access: A half-dozen Internet cafés are well-advertised throughout the Old Town, most offering fast access for about €2/hour; try **Zarranet** (Mon–Sat 10:00–22:00, Sun 16:00–22:00, Calle San Lorenzo 6, tel. 943-433-381, helpful Juan). These days, government-subsidized Wi-Fi access is available just about everywhere (including at most hotels).

Bookstore: Elkar, an advocate of Basque culture and literature, has two branches side-by-side in the Old Town. One focuses on Basque literature, and the other has a wide selection of guidebooks, maps, and books in English (Mon–Sat 10:00–14:00 & 16:00–20:00, Sun 11:00–14:00 & 16:30–20:30, Calle Fermín Calbetón 30, tel. 943-420-080).

Baggage Storage: There's no baggage storage at the train or bus stations. **Zarranet** Internet café, listed above, has space for about 80 bags (first-come, first-served; €0.50/hour, overnight–€5, 24 hours–€10).

Laundry: Wash & Dry is in the Gros neighborhood, across the river (self-service daily 8:00–22:00, drop-off service Mon-Fri 9:30–13:00 & 16:00–20:00, Iparragirre 6, tel. 943-293-150).

Bike Rental: Rare for Spain, the city has some great bike lanes and is a good place to enjoy on two wheels. Try **Bici Rent Donosti** (also rents scooters in summer, Avenida de Zurriola 22, 3 blocks across river from TI, mobile 639-016-013) or **Bicicletas Alai** (behind Amara bus station, Mon-Sat 11:00–13:00 & 17:00–20:00, Sun by appointment only, Avenida de Madrid 24, tel. 943-470-001).

Marijuana: Spain is famously liberal about marijuana laws, and the Basque Country is even more so. Walking around San Sebastián, you'll see "grow shops" sporting the famous green leaf (shopkeepers are helpful if you have questions). While the sale of marijuana is still illegal, the consumption of marijuana is decriminalized and people are allowed to grow enough for their personal use at home. With the town's mesmerizing aquarium and delightfully lit bars filled with enticing munchies, it just makes sense here.

Getting Around San Sebastián

By Bus: Along the Boulevard at the bottom edge of the Old Town, you'll find a line of public buses ready to take you anywhere in town; give any driver your destination, and he'll tell you the number of the bus to catch (€1.35, pay driver).

Some handy bus routes: #21, #26, and #28 connect the Amara bus and EuskoTren Stations to the TI (get off at the Boulevard stop); #16 begins at the Boulevard/TI stop, goes along Playa de la Concha and through residential areas, and eventually arrives at the base of the Monte Igueldo funicular. The TI has a bus-route map (or see www.ctss.es).

By Taxi: Taxis start at €6, which covers most rides in the center. You can't hail a taxi on the street—you must call one (tel. 943-404-040 or 943-464-646) or find a taxi stand (most convenient along the Boulevard).

By Metro: A new Metro system is currently under construction in San Sebastián, which will connect the main areas of the city and eventually extend to the airport.

Tours in San Sebastián

Walking Tours—The TI runs English-language walking tours. Options include Essential San Sebastián (€8, 1.5 hours), Flavors of San Sebastián (€16, 2 hours, includes three *pintxos* and three drinks), and San Sebastián—A Film City (€12, 2 hours, includes one *pintxo* and one drink). Schedules vary—ask at the TI. The TI may also rent **audioguides.**

Local Guides—Itsaso Petrikorena is good (mobile 647-973-231, betitsaso@yahoo.es). **Gabriella Ranelli**, an American who's lived in San Sebastián for 20 years, specializes in culinary tours. She can take you on a sightseeing spin around the Old Town, along with a walk through the market and best *pintxo* bars (€155/half-day, €195/day, more for driving into the countryside, mobile 609-467-381, www.tenedortours.com, info@tenedortours.com). Gabriella also organizes cooking classes—where you shop at the market, then join a local chef to cook up some tasty *pintxos* of your own (€120/person for a small group)—as well as wine-tastings (€50–130/person).

Gastronomic Tours—**Ramón Barea**, who owns the San Sebastián Gastronomic Club, offers travelers the opportunity to enter one of San Sebastián's exclusive "private eating clubs" (described on page 513) and even participate in preparing a gourmet dinner. Prices start around €80 per person, including ingredients but excluding wine. Ramón can also organize *pintxo* tours (mobile 650-862-202, www.bidainet.com, ramon@bidainet.com).

Tours on Wheels—Two tour options on wheels (following a similar route around the bay) are available, but most travelers won't find them necessary in this walkable city: the **"txu-txu"** tourist train (€4.50, daily 11:00–14:00 & 15:00–19:00, until 21:00 in summer, 40-minute round-trip, tel. 943-422-973); and the **Donosti Tours** hop-on, hop-off bus tour along the bay and around the city; €12, full loop takes about 1 hour, ticket good for 24 hours, leaves from Victoria Eugenia theater on the Boulevard, tel. 696-429-847, Raquel).

Basque Excursions—Based in San Sebastián, **Agustín Ciriza** leads minibus tours for up to eight people through the Spanish and French Basque Country, with destinations including Hondarribia, Biarritz, the Biscay Coast, Bayonne, or Pamplona. He also offers guided kayaking expeditions, pilgrimages, mountain treks, surf lessons, and surfing trips. Prices start at €65 per person for a half-day excursion (minimum two people, mobile 686-117-395, www.gorilla-trip.com, agus@gorilla-trip.com).

Sights in San Sebastián

▲▲Old Town (Parte Vieja)

Huddled in the shadow of its once-protective Monte Urgull, the Old Town is where San Sebastián was born about 1,000 years ago. Because the town burned down in 1813 (as Spain, Portugal, and England fought the French to get Napoleon's brother off the Spanish throne), the architecture you see is generally Neoclassical and uniform. Still, the grid plan of streets hides heavy Baroque and Gothic churches, surprise plazas, and fun little shops, including venerable pastry stores, rugged produce markets,

San Sebastián

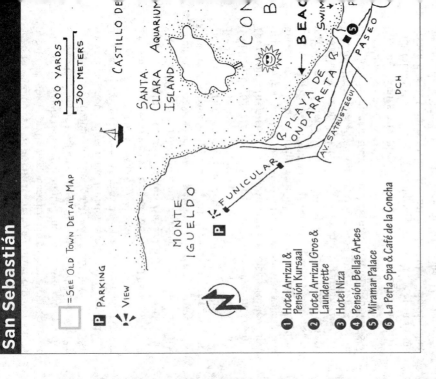

300 YARDS
300 METERS

= SEE OLD TOWN DETAIL MAP

P PARKING

🔆 VIEW

MONTE IGUELDO

FUNICULAR

SANTA CLARA ISLAND

CASTILLO DE

AQUARIUM

BEACH

Swim

PASEO

PLAYA DE ONDARRETA

AV. SATRUSTEGUI

DCH

❶ Hotel Arrizul & Pensión Kursaal
❷ Hotel Arrizul Gros & Launderette
❸ Hotel Niza
❹ Pensión Bellas Artes
❺ Miramar Palace
❻ La Perla Spa & Café de la Concha

Basque-independence souvenir shops, and seafood-to-go delis. The highlight of the Old Town is its array of incredibly lively tapas bars—though here, these snacks are called *pintxos* (PEEN-chohs; see "Eating in San Sebastián," later). To see the fishing industry in action, wander out to the port (described later).

The struggle for Basque independence is currently in a relatively calm stage, with most people opposing violent ETA tactics, but there are still underlying tensions between Spain and the Basque people. In the middle of the Old Town, **Calle Juan de Bilbao** is the political-action street. Here you'll find people more sympathetic to the struggle (while for others, it's a street to avoid). Pop into Bar Herria (marked by the Basque flag at #14) to see political art, posters, fliers for independence activities, and masked photos of (violent) political prisoners above the bar. While prisoners are generally incarcerated near their families in Spain, these were sent to jails all over the country, angering loved ones

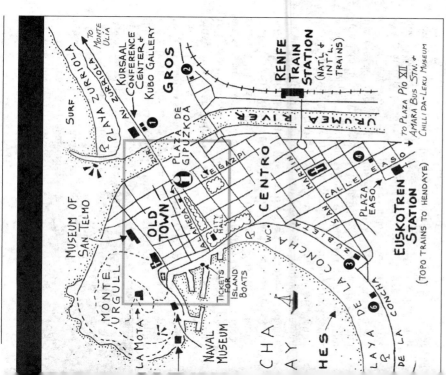

and creating a controversy. The bar used to list each prisoner's name and address under the photos, but a new law bans the posting of such information (although the barmaid can still tell you who's who). Speaking Basque is encouraged in this bar; taking photos is not.

Flagpoles mark **"private eating clubs"** throughout the Old Town (otherwise unmarked). Basque society is matrilineal and very female-oriented. A husband brings home his paycheck and hands it directly to his wife, who controls the house's purse strings (and everything else). Basque men felt they needed a place where they could congregate and play "king of the castle," so they formed these clubs where members could reserve a table and cook for their friends. While the clubs used to be exclusively male, women are now allowed as invited guests...but never in the kitchen, which remains the men's domain.

▲**Plaza de la Constitución**—The Old Town's main square is where bullfights used to be held. Notice the seat numbering on the

balconies: Even if you owned an apartment here, the city retained rights to the balconies, which it could sell as box seats. (Residents could peek over the paying customers' shoulders.) Above the clock, notice the seal of San Sebastián: A merchant ship with sails billowing in the wind. The city was granted trading rights by the crown—a reminder of the Basque Country's importance in Spanish seafaring. Inviting café tables spill into the square from all corners.

Museum of San Telmo—This museum, closed for renovation, will reopen soon as the Basque museum of anthropology. Rooms arranged around the peaceful cloister of a former Dominican monastery will hold artifacts telling the history of this region, dating back to ancient Roman times (Plaza Zuloaga 1, tel. 943-481-580).

▲**Bretxa Public Market (Mercado de la Bretxa)**—Wandering through the public market is a fun way to get in touch with San Sebastián and with Basque culture. Although the big, white market building facing the Boulevard has been converted into a modern shopping mall, the farmers produce market thrives here (lined up along the left side of the building), as well as the fish and meat market (behind it and underground). To get to the fish and meat market, walk past the produce vendors (look under the eaves of the modern building to see what the farmers are selling), and find a big glass cube in the square, where an escalator will take you down into the market (Mon–Fri 8:00–14:00 & 17:00–20:00, Sat 8:00–14:00, closed Sun, Plaza de Sarriegi).

At the bottom of the escalator, notice the **fish stall** on the left (marked *J. Ma. Mujika*). In the case you'll see different cuts of *bacalao* (cod). Entire books have been written about the importance of cod to the evolution of seafaring in Europe. The fish could be preserved in salt to feed sailors on ever-longer trips into the North Atlantic, allowing them to venture beyond the continental shelf (into deeper waters where they couldn't catch fresh fish). Cod was also popular among Catholic landlubbers on Fridays. Today cod remains a Basque staple. People still buy the salted version, which must be soaked for 48 hours (and the water changed three times) to become edible. If you're in a rush, you can buy de-salted cod...but at a cost in flavor. Stroll behind this stall to explore the fresh fish market—often with the catch of the day set up in cute little scenes. There's a free **WC** in the market—just ask "*¿Dónde está el servicio, por favor?*"

When you're done exploring, take the escalator up and cross the busy street to the **Aitor Lasa** cheese shop (Mon–Fri 8:30–14:00

& 17:15–20:00, Sat 8:30–14:30, closed Sun, Aldamar 12, tel. 943-430-354). Pass the fragrant piles of mushrooms at the entrance and head back to the display case, showing off the Basque specialty of *idiazabal*—raw sheep's milk cheese. Notice the wide variety, which depends on the specific region it came from, whether it's smoked or cured, and for how long it's been cured (*curación*). If you're planning a picnic, this is a very local (and expensive) ingredient. To try the cheese that won first prize a few years back in the Ordizia International Cheese Competition, ask for *"El queso con el premio de Ordizia, por favor."* The owners are evangelical about the magic of combining the local cheese with walnuts and *casero* (homemade) apple jam.

The Port

At the west end of the Old Town, protected by Monte Urgull, is the port. Take the passage through the wall at the appropriately named Calle Puerto, and jog right along the level, portside promenade, Paseo del Muelle. You'll pass fishing boats unloading the catch of the day (with hungry locals looking on), salty sailors' pubs, and fishermen mending nets. Also along this strip are the skippable

Naval Museum and the entertaining aquarium. Trails to the top of Monte Urgull are just above this scene, near Santa María Church (or climb the stairs next to the aquarium).

Cruises—Small boats cruise from the Old Town's port to the island in the bay (Isla Santa Clara), where you can hike the trails and have lunch at the lone café, or pack a picnic before setting sail (€3.60 round-trip, small ferry departs June–Sept only, on the hour from 10:00–20:00). The *City of San Sebastián* catamaran gives 30-minute tours of the bay for €8.

Naval Museum (Museo Naval)—This museum's two floors of exhibits describe the seafaring city's history, revealing the intimate link between the Basque culture and the sea (€1.20, free on Thu, borrow English description at entry, Tue-Sat 10:00–13:30 & 16:00–19:30, Sun 11:00–14:00, closed Mon, Paseo del Muelle 24, tel. 943-430-051).

▲▲**Aquarium**—San Sebastián's aquarium is surprisingly good. Exhibits are thoughtfully described in English and include a history of the sea, a collection of naval vessels, and models showing various drift-netting techniques. You'll see a petting tank filled with nervous fish; a huge whale skeleton; a trippy, illuminated, slowly tumbling tank of jellyfish; and a mesmerizing 45-foot-long tunnel that lets you look up into a wet world of floppy rays, menacing sharks, and local fish. The local section ends with a tank of shark fetuses safely incubating away from hungry predators. The tropical wing causes local kids to holler, "Nemo!" (€12, €6 for kids under 13; July–Aug daily 10:00–21:00; Sept–June Mon–Fri 10:00–19:00, Sat–Sun 10:00–20:00; at the end of Paseo del Muelle, tel. 943-440-099, www.aquariumss.com).

▲**Monte Urgull**—The once-mighty castle (Castillo de la Mota) atop the hill deterred most attackers, allowing the city to prosper in the Middle Ages. The free museum within the castle, featuring San Sebastián history, is mildly interesting. The best views from the hill are not from the statue of Christ, but from the ramparts on the left side (as you face the hill), just above the port's aquarium. **Café El Polvorín**, nestled in the park, is a free-spirited place with salads, sandwiches, and good sangria.

A walkway allows you to stroll the mountain's entire perimeter near sea level. This route is continuous from Hotel Parma to the aquarium, and offers an enjoyable after-dinner wander. You can also walk a bit higher up over the port (along the white railing)—called the *paseo de las curas*, or "priest's path," where the clergy could stroll unburdened by the rabble in the streets below. These paths are technically open only from sunrise to sunset (daily May–Sept 8:00–21:00, Oct–April 8:00–19:00), but you can often access them later.

The Beach and Beyond

▲▲**La Concha Beach and Promenade**—The shell-shaped Playa de la Concha, the pride of San Sebastián, has one of Europe's loveliest stretches of sand. Lined with a two-mile-long promenade, it allows even backpackers to feel aristocratic. Although it's pretty empty off-season, in summer, sunbathers pack its shores. But year-round, it's surprisingly devoid of eateries and money-grubbing businesses. There are

free showers, and *cabinas* provide lockers, showers, and shade for a fee. For a century, the lovingly painted wrought-iron balustrade that stretches the length of the promenade has been a symbol of the city; it shows up on everything from jewelry to headboards. It's shaded by tamarisk trees, with branches carefully pruned into knotty bulbs each winter that burst into leafy shade-giving canopies in the summer—another symbol of the city. **Café de la Concha**, while serving mediocre food, is reasonably priced, and you can't beat the location of its terrace overlooking the beach (€13 weekday lunch special, tel. 943-473-600).

The **Miramar palace and park**, which divides the crescent beach in the middle, was where Queen María Cristina held court when she summered here. Her royal changing rooms are used today as inviting cafés, restaurants, and a fancy spa. You can walk in the park, although the palace, used as a music school, is closed to the public.

La Perla Spa—The spa overlooking the beach attracts a less royal crowd today and appeals mostly to visitors interested in sampling "the curative properties of the sea." You can enjoy its Talasso Fitness Circuit, featuring a hydrotherapy pool, relaxation pool, panoramic Jacuzzi, cold-water pools, seawater steam sauna, dry sauna, and a relaxation area (€24 for 2-hour fitness circuit, €30 for 3-hour circuit, daily 8:00–22:00, €3 caps and €1 rental towels, bring a swimsuit or buy one for €33, on the beach at the center of the crescent, Paseo de la Concha, tel. 943-458-856, www.la-perla.net).

Monte Igueldo—For commanding city views (if you ignore the tacky amusements on top), ride the funicular up Monte Igueldo, a mirror image of Monte Urgull. The views over San Sebastián, along the coast, and into the distant green mountains are sensational day or night. The entrance to the funicular is on the

road behind the tennis club on the far western end of Playa de Ondarreta, which extends from Playa de la Concha to the west (funicular–€2.60 round-trip; July–mid-Sept daily 10:00–22:00; April–June and mid-Sept–Oct daily 11:00–20:00; Nov–March Mon–Tue and Thu–Fri 11:00–18:00, Sat–Sun 11:00–20:00, closed Wed). If you drive to the top, you'll pay €1.80 to enter. The #16 bus takes you from the Old Town to the base of the funicular in about 10 minutes.

In Gros

Gros and Zurriola Beach—The district of Gros, just east across the river from the Old Town, offers a distinct Californian vibe. Literally a dump a few years ago, today it has a surfing scene on Zurriola Beach (popular with students and German tourists) and a futuristic conference center (described next). Long-term plans call for a new promenade that someday will arc over the water and under Monte Ulía.

▲Kursaal Conference Center and Kubo Gallery—These two Lego-like boxes (just east and across the river from the Old Town, in Gros) mark the spot of what was once a grand casino, torn down by Franco to discourage gambling. Many locals wanted to rebuild it as it once was, in a similar style to the turn-of-the-20th-century buildings in the Centro. But, in an effort to keep up with the postmodern trends in Bilbao, city leaders opted instead for Rafael Moneo's striking contemporary design. The complex is supposed to resemble the angular rocks that make up the town's breakwater. The Kursaal houses a theater, conference facilities, some gift shops and travel agencies, a restaurant, and the Kubo Gallery. The gallery offers temporary exhibits by international artists and promotes contemporary Basque artists (free, daily 11:30–13:30 & 17:00–21:00). Each exhibit is complemented by a 10-minute video that plays continuously in the gallery theater.

Near San Sebastián

Chillida-Leku Museum—Eduardo Chillida (1924–2002), a popular Basque sculptor, is the focus of this enjoyable museum on the outskirts of town. Chillida worked rough, heavy materials (such as iron and marble) into huge but delicate-seeming abstract sculptures. You might not have heard of Chillida, but you've likely seen his big, blocky works, which decorate cities around Spain and throughout Europe. In San Sebastián, among the rocks at the west end of the beachfront promenade, you'll find one of Chillida's most famous works: the "wind combs" (peine del viento).

The museum has three parts: The entry area shows a 45-minute film loop of the artist at work; the grounds—with beautiful grassy rolling hills and trees—display his larger works, mostly of iron or rose marble; and a 16th-century farmhouse—which the artist renovated expressly for this purpose—shows off some of his smaller works (of bronze, felt, clay, alabaster, and so on).

As you explore, notice the way Chillida began with imposing chunks of media, then carved passages into them to allow light and air to penetrate an otherwise impenetrable block. This has the unexpected effect of making big, clumsy things seem light and graceful. Most of his works are carved from a single piece. The artist believed that works should be unique and evolve organically—he'd contemplate the medium and listen to what it had to say before carving it up. As you stroll the grounds surveying the works, imagine both the intense pressure and the delicate touch required to persuade these materials to become art.

Because it takes some effort to get here, the museum is best for people who know Chillida and appreciate his work. Art-lovers in the region to visit the Guggenheim might find this to be the perfect complement.

Cost and Hours: €8.50, €4.50 on Mon, good €5 audioguide; July–Aug Mon–Sat 10:30–20:00, Sun 10:30–15:00; Sept–June Wed–Mon 10:30–15:00, closed Tue; Barrio Jáuregui 66, Hernani, tel. 943-336-006, www.museochillidaleku.com.

Getting There: It's on the edge of San Sebastián, about a €10 taxi ride from the Old Town. You can also take bus #G-2 from near the Perla Spa along the beach or from Calle Okendo near the Boulevard (direction: Hernani; €1.35, 2/hour, departs on the hour and half-hour).

Sleeping in San Sebastián

(€1 = about $1.25, country code: 34)

Rates in San Sebastián fluctuate with the season. When you see a range of prices in these listings, the top end is for summer (roughly July–Sept), and the low end is for the shoulder season (May–June and Oct); outside of these times, you'll pay even less. Since breakfast is often not included, I've recommended some good options elsewhere in town (see "Eating in San Sebastián," later).

In or near the Old Town

$$$ Hotel Parma is a business-class place with 27 fine rooms and family-run attention to detail and service. It stands stately on the edge of the Old Town, away from the bar-scene noise, and overlooks the river and a surfing beach (Sb-€63–88, windowless interior Db-€92–133, view Db-€112–146, breakfast-€9, air-con, modern lounge, free Wi-Fi, Paseo de Salamanca 10, tel. 943-428-893, fax 943-424-082, www.hotelparma.com, hotelparma@hotelparma.com; Iñaki, Pino, Maria Eugenia, and Ana).

$$ Pensión Edorta ("Edward"), deep in the Old Town, elegantly mixes wood, brick, and color into 12 modern, stylish rooms (D-€40–60, Db-€60–80, extra bed-€20–25, elevator, Calle Puerto 15, tel. 943-423-773, fax 943-433-570, www.pensionedorta.com, info@pensionedorta.com, Javier).

$ Pensión Amaiur is a flowery place with long, skinny halls and great-value rooms within the Old Town. Kind Virginia gives the justifiably popular *pensión* a homey warmth. Her 13 colorful, cozy rooms share seven bathrooms (S-€24–45, quiet interior D-€35–54, exterior D-€42–64, T-€54–85, Q-€65–100, family room, kitchen facilities, pay Internet access, free Wi-Fi, next to Santa María Church at Calle 31 de Agosto 44, tel. 943-429-654, www.pensionamaiur.com, amaiur@telefonica.net).

Across the River, in Gros

The pleasant Gros district—San Sebastián's "uptown"—is marked by the super-modern, blocky Kursaal conference center. The nearby

Zurriola Beach is popular with surfers. These hotels are less than a five-minute walk from the Old Town. For locations, see the map on page 512.

$$$ Hotel Arrizul is bright and fresh, with mod and minimalist decor in each of its 12 rooms (Sb-€62-105, Db-€90-142, Db suite-€110-187, Qb-€84-138, breakfast-€6, air-con, elevator, free Wi-Fi, parking-€15, Peña y Goñi 1, tel. 943-322-804, fax 943-326-701, www.arrizul.com, info@arrizulhotel.com). Their sister hotel, **Hotel Arrizul Gros**, is a couple of blocks away and has 17 rooms with similar prices, plus 7 apartments (apartments: €99-169/2 people, €125-219/4 people, €159-319/6 people, Iparraguirre 3, same contact info as main Hotel Arrizul).

$$ Pensión Kursaal has 10 basic but colorful rooms in the original building, along with a new annex housing 8 rooms that are more modern, with white-and-beige decor (Db-€50-82, family room, elevator, pay Internet access, free Wi-Fi, parking-€12, Peña y Goñi 2, tel. 943-292-666, fax 943-297-536, www.pensiones conencanto.com, kursaal@pensionesconencanto.com).

On the Beach

$$$ Hotel Niza, set in the middle of Playa de la Concha, is often booked well in advance...even though it could do with a facelift. Half of its 40 rooms (some with balconies) overlook the bay. From its chandeliered and plush lounge, a classic elevator takes you to its comfortable, pastel rooms with wedding-cake molding (tiny interior Sb-€58-64, Db-€128-148, view rooms cost the same—requests with reservation considered...but no promises, extra bed-€22, only streetside rooms have air-con, fans on request, great buffet breakfast-€11, free Internet access and Wi-Fi, parking-€15/day—must reserve in advance, Zubieta 56, see map on page 512 for location, tel. 943-426-663, fax 943-441-251, www.hotelniza.com, niza@hotelniza.com). The breakfast room has a sea view and doubles as a bar with light snacks throughout the day (Bar Biarritz, daily 7:30-24:00). The cheap and cheery Italian restaurant downstairs, called La Pasta Gansa, serves good pizzas, pastas, and salads (closed Tue, tel. 943-426-663).

Between the Beach and EuskoTren Station

$$ Pensión Bellas Artes, while farther from the Old Town than my other listings, is worth the 15-minute walk. Lively Leire, who lived in New York and runs her *pensión* with pride, rents 10 small, well-appointed, tidy rooms with thoughtful extra touches like fresh flowers in each room and a loaner laptop. Leire loves to give her guests sightseeing and dining tips (Sb-€53-74, Db-€74-96, extra bed-€24, no breakfast, non-smoking, elevator, free Internet access and Wi-Fi, near EuskoTren Station at Urbieta 64, tel. 943-474-905, fax 943-463-111, www.pension-bellasartes.com, info@pension-bellasartes.com). For the location, see the map on page 512.

Eating in San Sebastián

Basque food is regarded as some of the best in Spain...and San Sebastián is the culinary capital of the Basque Country. What the city lacks in museums and sights, it more than makes up for in food. (For tips on Basque cuisine, see page 480.) San Sebastián is proud of its many Michelin-rated fine-dining establishments. But these require a big commitment of time and money. Most casual visitors will prefer to hop from pub to pub through the Old Town, following the crowds between Basque-font signs. I've listed a couple of solid traditional restaurants, but for the best value and memories, I'd order top-end dishes with top-end wine in top-end bars.

Pintxo Bar-Hopping

San Sebastián's Old Town provides the ideal backdrop for tapas-hopping; just wander the streets and straddle up to the bar in

the liveliest spot. Calle Fermín Calbetón has about the best concentration of bars; the streets San Jerónimo and 31 de Agosto are also good. I've listed these top-notch places in order as you progress deeper into the Old Town. Note that there are plenty of other options along the way. Before you

begin, study the "Tapas Cheat Sheet" sidebar, later.

Bar Goiz-Argi ("Morning Light"), every local's top recommendation, serves its tiny dishes with pride and attitude. Advertising *pintxos calientes*, they cook each treat for you, allowing you a montage of petite gourmet snacks. Try their *tartaleta de txangurro* (spider-crab spread on bread) or their signature shrimp kebab. A good selection of open wine bottles are clearly priced and displayed on the shelf (great prices, no chairs, congregate at bar, closed Mon-Tue, Calle Fermín Calbetón 4).

Bar Borda-Berri (loosely "Mountain Hut"), a couple doors down, features a more low-key ambience and top-quality €3 *pintxos*. There are only a few items at the bar; check out the chalkboard menu for today's options, order, and they'll cook it fresh. The specialty here is melt-in-your-mouth beef cheeks (*carrillera de ternera*) in a red-wine sauce, risotto with wild mushrooms, and foie gras (grilled goose liver) with apple jelly, which is even better

San Sebastián's Old Town

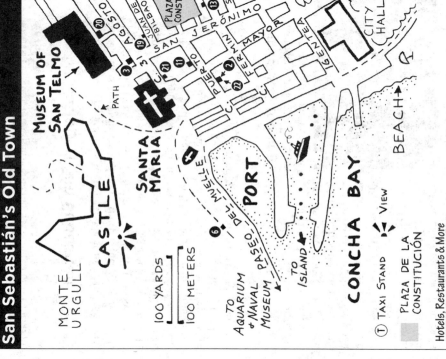

MONTE URGULL

CASTLE

MUSEUM OF SAN TELMO

SANTA MARIA

PORT

CONCHA BAY

BEACH

PATH

PASEO DEL MUELLE

PLAZA DE LA CONSTITUCIÓN

100 YARDS
100 METERS

TO AQUARIUM & NAVAL MUSEUM

TO ISLAND

CITY HALL

(T) Taxi Stand   **View**

Hotels, Restaurants & More
- ❶ Hotel Parma
- ❷ Pensión Edorta
- ❸ Pensión Amaiur
- ❹ Bodégon Alejandro
- ❺ Casa Urola
- ❻ La Rampa & Sebastián Rests.
- ❼ Bretxa Public Market
- ❽ Barrenetxe
- ❾ Kanpai Deli
- ❿ Bar Gorriti
- ⓫ Santa Lucía
- ⓬ Aitor Lasa Cheese Shop
- ⓭ Elkar Bookstore
- ⓮ Internet Café & Bag Storage

paired with a glass of their best red wine (closed Mon, Calle Fermín Calbetón 12).

Bar Txepetxa is *the* place for anchovies. A plastic circle displaying a variety of *antxoas* tapas makes choosing your anchovy treat easy. These fish are fresh—not cured and salted like those most Americans hate (€2.10/*pintxo*, Calle Pescadería 5).

Bar Tamboril is a traditional (but non-smoking) place right on the main square favored for its seafood, mushrooms (*txampis*

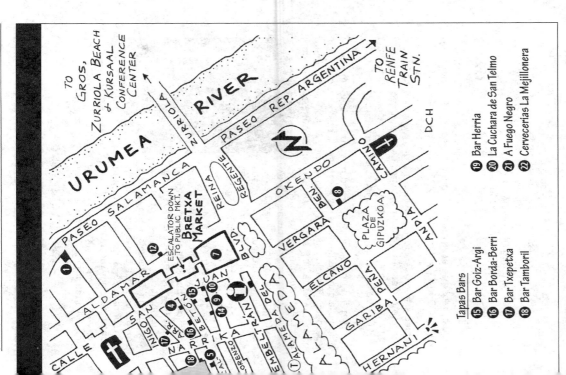

Tapas Bars

15 Bar Goiz-Argi
16 Bar Borda-Berri
17 Bar Txepetxa
18 Bar Tamboril
19 Bar Herria
20 La Cuchara de San Telmo
21 A Fuego Negro
22 Cervecerías La Mejillonera

tamboril), and anchovy tempura along with its good prices. Their list of hot *pintxos* (grab the little English menu on the bar) makes you want to break the one-tapa-per-stop rule (Calle Pescaderia 2).

Bar Herria, which flies the Basque flag above its door, is on a street avoided by many locals opposed to the violent tactics of the ETA. I'd just get a drink here, notices, and ponder the art, and propaganda of the independence movement. Photos of masked political prisoners hang in a thought-provoking line above the bar

Do the *Txikiteo* Tango—Tapas Cheat Sheet

Txikiteo (chih-kee-TAY-oh) is the Basque word for hopping from bar to bar, enjoying characteristically small sandwiches and tiny snacks (*pintxos*, PEEN-chohs) and glasses of wine. Local competition drives small bars to lay out the most appealing array of *pintxos*. The selection is amazing, but the key to eating well here is going for the *pintxos calientes*—the hot tapas advertised on blackboards and cooked to order. Tapas are best, freshest, and accompanied by the most vibrant crowd from 12:00 to 14:00 and from 20:00 to 22:30. Watch what's being served—the locals know each bar's specialty. No matter how much you like a place, just order one dish; you want to be mobile.

Later in the evening, bars get more crowded and challenging for tourists. To get service amid the din, speak loudly and direct (little sweet voices get ignored), with no extra words. Expect to share everything. Double-dipping is encouraged. It's rude to put a dirty napkin on the table; it belongs on the floor.

If you can't get the bartender's attention to serve you a particular *pintxo*, don't be shy—just grab it and a napkin, and munch away. You pay when you leave; just keep a mental note of the tapas you've eaten. There's a code of honor. Everyone is part of the extended Basque family.

If you want a meal instead of *pintxos*, some bars—even ones that look only like bars from the street—have attached dining rooms, usually in the back.

Pintxos

antxoas	anchovies (not the cured, heavily salted kind you always hated)
bocadillos	baguette sandwiches
bakalao	cod (served lots of ways)
txampis (CHAHM-pees)	mushrooms
gambas	shrimp
patatas bravas	crisp potato cubes served with a spicy sauce
tortilla	big round omelet pie served by the slice (many varieties)

| *txangurro*
(chang-GOO-roh) | spider crab, a delicacy, often mixed with onions, tomatoes, and wine, served hot or made into a spread to put on bread |

Descriptions

brocheta	anything on a stick
calientes	served hot and cooked to order (listed on chalkboard, not already on the bar)
cazuelas	hot meal-size servings (like *raciones* in Spanish)

Drinks

caña (KAHN-yah)	draft beer
mosto	non-alcoholic grape juice that comes in red or white (for when you've had enough beer and wine)
Rioja	a better wine
sidra	a dry cider that's a bit more alcoholic than beer
sin (seen)	non-alcoholic beer (literally means "without")
tinto	red house wine
txakoli (chah-koh-LEE)	fresh white wine, poured from high to "break against the glass" and aerate it to add sparkle. Good with seafood, and therefore fits the local cuisine well.
un crianza	a glass of nicely aged wine. It's smart to ask for this instead of "*un tinto*" to get better quality for nearly the same price.
vaso de agua	glass of tap water (they'll ask you "bottled?" and you say no)
zurito (thoo-REE-toh)	small beer

Paying the Bill

| *Zenbat da?* | "How much?" |
| *Me cobras?* | "What's the damage?" (a fun way to say "The bill, please") |

(Calle Juan de Bilbao 14). For more details on this bar's political leanings, see page 512.

La Cuchara de San Telmo, with cooks taught by a big-name Basque chef, Alex Mondiel, is a cramped place that devotes as much space to its thriving kitchen as its bar. It has nothing pre-cooked and set on the bar—order your mini-gourmet plates with a spirit of adventure from the constantly changing blackboard. Their foie gras with apple jelly is rightfully famous (€3 *pintxos*, closed Mon, tucked away on a lonely alley called Santa Corda behind Museum of San Telmo at 31 de Agosto #28).

A Fuego Negro is cool and upscale compared to the oth-ers, with a hip, slicker vibe and a blackboard menu of *pintxos* and drinks (there's an English translation sheet). They have a knack for mixing gourmet pretentiousness with whimsy here: Try their *txangurro* (crab), *aguacate* (avocado), and *regaliz* (licorice ice cream) trio for a unique taste-bud experience (€3). Enjoy their serious and extensive wine selection (closed Mon, 31 de Agosto #31). An invit-ing little section in the back makes this a sit-down dining oppor-tunity.

Cervecerías La Mejillonera is famous among students for its big cheap beers, *patatas bravas*, and mussels ("*tigres*" is the spicy favorite). A long, skinny stainless-steel bar and lots of photos make ordering easy—this is the only place in town where you pay when served (Puerto 15, tel. 943-428-465).

Restaurants

Bodégon Alejandro is a good spot for modern Basque cuisine in a dark and traditional setting (3-course fixed-price lunch–€15, Tue–Sun 13:00–15:30 & 20:00–22:30 except closed Sun night, closed Mon, in Old Town on Calle Fermín Calbetón 4, tel. 943-427-158).

Casa Urola, a block away, is a good option for a traditional, sit-down Basque meal (more expensive, €16–22 entrées, €42 tast-ing *menu*, Thu–Tue 13:00–16:00 & 20:00–23:30 except closed Sun night, closed Wed, reservations smart, Calle Fermín Calbetón 20, tel. 943-423-424).

Seafood Along the Port: For seafood with a salty sailor's view, check out the half-dozen hardworking, local-feeling restaurants that line the harbor on the way to the aquarium. **La Rampa** is an upscale eatery, specializing in crab (*txangurro*) and lobster dishes, and seafood *parillada* (€30–50 for dinner, closed Tue–Wed, Paseo Muelle/Kaiko Pasealekua 26-27, tel. 943-421-652). Also along here, locals like **Sebastián** (more traditional, closed Tue).

Picnics and Takeout

A picnic on the beach or atop Monte Urgull is a tempting option. You can assemble a bang-up spread at the **Bretxa Public Market** at Plaza de Sarriegi (described on page 514).

Upscale **Barrenetxe** has an amazing array of breads, prepared foods, and some of the best desserts in town. In business since 1699, their somewhat formal service is justified (daily 8:00–20:00, Plaza de Guipúzcoa 9, tel. 943-424-482).

Kanpai, a high-quality deli serving Basque and international cuisine, is run by David and his mother. Step up to the display case and get something "to go" for an easy and tasty picnic. David offers a fun tasting from his newfangled wine machine (€3 for 4 tastes, daily 10:00–15:00 & 17:00–20:30, Calle San Lorenzo 4, tel. 943-423-884).

Breakfast

If your hotel doesn't provide breakfast—or even if it does—consider one of these places. The first is a traditional stand-up bar, the second is a greasy spoon.

Bar Gorriti, delightfully local, is packed with market workers and shoppers starting their day. You'll stand at the bar and choose a hot-off-the-grill *francesca jamon* omelet (fluffy mini-omelet sandwich topped with a slice of ham) and other goodies (€2 each). This and a good cup of coffee makes for a very Basque breakfast (daily, breakfast served 7:00–10:00, facing the side of the big white market building at San Juan 3, tel. 943-428-353). By the time you get there for breakfast, many market workers will be taking their mid-morning break.

Santa Lucía, a 1950s-style diner, is ideal for a cheap Old Town breakfast or *churros* break (*churros* are like deep-fried doughnut sticks that can be dipped in pudding-like hot chocolate). Photos of two dozen different breakfasts decorate the walls, and plates of fresh *churros* keep patrons happy. Grease is liberally applied to the grill...from a squeeze bottle (daily 8:30–21:30, Calle Puerto 6, tel. 943-425-019).

San Sebastián Connections

By Train

San Sebastián has two train stations: RENFE and EuskoTren (described under "Arrival in San Sebastián" on page 508). The station you use depends on your destination.

EuskoTren Station: If you're going into France, take the regional Topo train (which leaves from the EuskoTren Station) over the French border into **Hendaye** (2/hour, 35 minutes, departs EuskoTren Station at :15 and :45 after the hour 6:15–21:45). From Hendaye, connect to France's SNCF network (www.sncf.com), where connections include **Paris** (4/day direct, 5.5–6 hours, or 8.5-hour night train, reservations required). Unfortunately, San

Sebastián's EuskoTren Station doesn't have information on Paris-bound trains from Hendaye. Don't buy the Spanish ticket too far in advance—EuskoTren tickets to Hendaye must be used within two hours of purchase (or else they expire).

Also leaving from San Sebastián's EuskoTren Station are slow regional trains to destinations in Spain's Basque region, including **Bilbao** (hourly, €8.15 round-trip ticket saves €2, 2.5 hours—the bus is faster; EuskoTren info: toll tel. 902-543-210, www.euskotren.es). Although the train ride from San Sebastián to Bilbao takes twice as long as the bus, it passes through more interesting countryside. The Basque Country shows off its trademark green and gray: lush green vegetation and gray clouds. It's an odd mix of heavy industrial factories, small homegrown veggie gardens, streams, and every kind of livestock you can imagine.

RENFE Station: This station handles long-distance destinations within Spain (most of which require reservations). Connections include **Irún** (9/day, 25 minutes), **Hendaye,** France (6/day, 30 minutes), **Madrid** (2/day, 5–6 hours), **Burgos** (6/day, 3 hours), **León** (1/day, 5 hours), **Pamplona** (2/day, 2 hours), **Barcelona Salamanca** (2/day, 6 hours), **Vitoria** (8/day, 1.75 hours), **Barcelona** (2/day, 5.5 hours on new Alvia train), and **Santiago de Compostela** (1/day direct, 11 hours, final destination A Coruña).

By Bus

San Sebastián's "bus station," called Amara, is a congregation of bus parking spots next to the big Hotel Amara Plaza, at the roundabout called Plaza Pío XII (on the river, four blocks south of EuskoTren Station). Some schedules are posted at various stops, but confirm departure times. You must buy your tickets in advance at the bus companies, with offices on either side of the block north of the station area (toward downtown, along Avenida de Sancho el Sabio and Paseo de Vizcaya). Bus tickets are not available from the driver. The Pesa office, which serves St. Jean-de-Luz and Bilbao, is located at Avenida de Sancho el Sabio 33 (toll tel. 902-101-210, www.pesa.net). The Alsa office—which serves Madrid, Burgos, and León—is just beyond Pesa at Sancho el Sabio 31 (toll tel. 902-422-242, www.alsa.es). The Roncalesa office is moving, and will probably be in the same office as Alsa (tel. 943-461-064, www.condasa.com). The Vibasa office—which serves Burgos, Pamplona, and Barcelona—is on the other side of the block, at Calle Vizcaya 15 (closed 13:30–15:00, toll tel. 902-101-363, www.vibasa.es).

From San Sebastián, buses go to **Bilbao** (get ticket from Pesa office, 2/hour, hourly on weekends, 6:30–22:00, 1.25 hours, €9.85, departs from Amara; morning buses fill with tourists, commuters, and students, so consider buying your ticket the day before; once in Bilbao, buses leave you at Termibús stop with easy tram connections to the Guggenheim modern-art museum); **Bilbao Airport** (a Pesa bus goes directly to the airport from San Sebastián's Plaza Pío XII, hourly, 1 hour, €15.20), **Pamplona** (Roncalesa office, 8/day, 1 hour, €7), **León** (Alsa office, 1/day, 6 hours, €29), **Madrid** (Alsa office, 8/day, 6 hours direct, otherwise 7 hours, €30–42), **Burgos** (Alsa or Vibasa office, 6/day, 3 hours, €15.50), and **Barcelona** (Vibasa office, 2/day and 1 at night, 7 hours, €29).

To visit **Hondarribia** (described next), you can catch bus #1-2 much closer to the center at Plaza Gipuzkoa (1 block south of TI; about 3/hour, 30 minutes, €2, same bus goes to airport en route to Hondarribia).

Buses to French Basque Country: A bus goes from San Sebastián's Amara bus station to **St-Jean-de-Luz** (Mon–Sat only, 2/day at 9:00 and 14:30, none on Sun, 1 hour, €4.40 each way, return trips at 12:45 and 19:15, get ticket from Pesa office, only 1/week off-season), then continues directly to **Biarritz** (1.25 hours from San Sebastián) and **Bayonne** (1.5 hours from San Sebastián).

Between San Sebastián and St. Jean-de-Luz: Hondarribia

Just 45 minutes apart by car, San Sebastián and St. Jean-de-Luz bridge the Spanish and French Basque regions. Between them you'll find the functional towns of Irún (Spain), Hendaye (France), and the delightful hill town of Hondarribia, which is worth a visit if you have time to spare.

Fuenterrabía / Hondarribia

For a taste of small-town *País Vasco*, dip into this enchanting, seldom-visited town (more commonly known by its Euskara name rather than the Spanish version, Fuenterrabía). Much smaller and easier to manage than San Sebastián, and also closer to France (across the picturesque Bay of Txingudi from Hendaye), Hondarribia allows travelers a stress-free opportunity to enjoy Basque culture. While it's easy to think of this as a border town (between France and Spain), culturally it's in the middle of the Basque Country.

The town comes in two parts: the lower port town and the historic, balcony-lined streets of the hilly and walled upper town. The upper town, which feels quite manicured, is a delightful place to poke around if you have time. The main square is fronted by Charles V's austere, oddly squat castle (now a parador inn—see below). You can follow the TI's self-guided tour of the Old Town (English brochure available) or just lose yourself within the walls to explore the plazas.

In the modern lower town, straight shopping streets serve a local clientele, and a pleasant walkway takes strollers along the beach.

Tourist Information: The TI is located where the lower town and the upper town meet, two blocks up from the port on Jabier Ugarte 6 (July–Sept daily 10:00–14:00 & 15:00–19:00; Oct–June Mon–Fri 9:00–13:30 & 16:00–18:30, Sat–Sun 10:00–14:00; tel. 943-645-458).

Arrival in Hondarribia: Drivers can use the metered parking by the port (marked with blue lines, prepay for parking at machine). Buses into town stop near the TI.

Sleeping in Hondarribia: Accommodations are pricey here, but it's a nice small-town alternative to San Sebastián.

$$$ Parador El Emperador, with 36 rooms housed in a former imperial fortress, is the town's splurge. Tourists are allowed to have sangria in the *muy* cool bar, though the terraces are for guests only (Sb–€168, Db–€225, elevator, free Wi-Fi, Plaza de Armas 14, tel. 943-645-500, fax 943-642-153, www.parador.es, hondarribia @parador.es).

$$$ Hotel San Nikolas, facing the parador from across the square, offers a more affordable alternative, with 17 nicely appointed rooms (many with views) above a local café (Sb–€60–85, Db–€70–105, higher price is for mid-July–mid-Sept, can be even cheaper Mon–Thu outside of summer, elevator, free Wi-Fi, Plaza de Armas 6, tel. 943-644-278, fax 943-646-217, www.hotelsan nikolas.com, info@hotelsannikolas.com).

Hondarribia Connections

From Hondarribia by Bus to: San Sebastián (about 3/hour, 30 minutes on express bus; departs from near TI—same bus also stops at airport; or twice as long on local public bus), **Hendaye** on the French border (2/hour, 20 minutes, June–Sept only). A bus stop in Hondarribia is across from the post office, one block below the TI.

By Boat to: Hendaye (4/hour in summer, 2/hour off-season, 10 minutes, runs about 11:00–19:00 or until dark).

Between San Sebastián and Bilbao: The Bay of Biscay

Between the two Spanish Basque cities of San Sebastián and Bilbao is a beautiful countryside of rolling green hills and a scenic, jagged coastline that looks almost Celtic. Aside from a scenic joyride, this area merits a visit for the cute fishing and resort town of Lekeitio.

Route Tips for Drivers

San Sebastián and Bilbao are connected in about an hour and a quarter by the A-8 expressway (€8 toll). Though speedy and scenic, this route is nothing compared to some of the free, but slower, back roads connecting the two towns.

If side-tripping from San Sebastián to Bilbao, you can drive directly there on A-8 in the morning. But coming home to San Sebastián, consider this more scenic route: Take A-8 until the turnoff for Guernica (look for *Gernika-Lumo* sign), then head up into the hills on BI-635. After visiting Guernica, follow signs along the very twisty road to Lekeitio (about 40 minutes). Leave Lekeitio on the road just above the beach; after crossing the bridge, take the left fork and follow BI-3428 to Ondarroa (with a striking modern bridge and nice views back into the steep town), Mutriku, and Deba to hug the coastline east to San Sebastián. There's a fine photo-op pull-out as you climb along the coast just after Deba. Soon after, you'll have two opportunities to get on the A-8 (blue signs) for a quicker approach to San Sebastián; but if you've enjoyed the scenery so far, stick with the coastal road (white signs), N-634) through Zumaia and Getaria, rejoining the expressway at Zarautz.

Lequeitio / Lekeitio

A small fishing port with an idyllic harbor and a fine beach, Lekeitio (leh-KAY-tee-oh) is just over an hour by bus from Bilbao and an easy stop for drivers. It's protected from the Bay of Biscay by a sand spit that leads to the lush and rugged

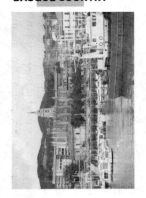

little San Nicolás Island. Hake boats fly their Basque flags and proud Basque locals black out the Spanish translations on street signs.

Lekeitio is a teeming resort during July and August (when its population of 7,000 triples as big-city Basque folks move into their vacation condos). Isolated from the modern rat race by its location down a long, windy little road, it's a backwater fishing village the rest of the year.

While sights are humble here, the 15th-century St. Mary's Parish Church is a good example of Basque Gothic, with an impressive altarpiece (Mon–Sat 8:00–12:00 & 17:00–19:30, closed Sun). The town's back lanes are reminiscent of old days when fishing was the only industry. Fisherwomen sell their husbands' catches each morning from about 10:30 along the port. The golden crescent beach is as inviting as the sandbar, which—at low tide—challenges you to join the seagulls out on San Nicolás Island.

The best beach in the area for surfers and sun-lovers is Playas Laga (follow signs off the road from Bilbao to Lekeitio). Relatively uncrowded, it's popular with body-boarders.

Getting There: Buses connect Lekeitio with **Bilbao** (hourly, 1.25 hours; same bus stops at **Guernica**, 40 minutes) and **San Sebastián** (4/day Mon–Fri, 2/day Sat–Sun, 1.25 hours). But this stop is most logical for those with a car. Drivers can park most easily in the lot near the bus station. Exit the station left, walk along the road, then take the first right (down the steep, cobbled street) to reach the harbor. There is no luggage storage in town.

Tourist Information: The TI faces the fish market next to the harbor (July–Aug daily 10:00–14:00 & 16:00–20:00; Sept–June Tue–Sat 10:30–13:30 & 16:00–19:00, Sun 10:00–14:00, closed Mon; tel. 946-844-017, www.lekeitio.com).

Sleeping in Lekeitio: **$$ Emperatriz Zita Hotel** is the obvious best bet for your beach-town break. It's named for Empress Zita (who lived here in exile after her Habsburg family lost World War I and was booted from Vienna). Zita's mansion burned down, but this 1930s rebuild still has a belle époque aristocratic charm, solid classy furniture in 42 spacious rooms, real hardwood floors, and an elegant spa in the basement. Located on the beach a few steps from the harbor, with handy free parking and a view restaurant, it's a fine value (Sb-€62-72, Db-€80-92, Db suite-€112-124, views— ask for *vistas del mar*—are worth the extra €6, high prices are for mid-June–mid-Sept and Fri–Sat all year, extra bed-€25, breakfast—€10, elevator, free Wi-Fi, Santa Elena Etorbidea, tel. 946-842-655, fax 946-243-500, www.aisiahoteles.com, lekeitio@aisia hoteles.com). The hotel also has a thermal seawater pool, Jacuzzi, and full-service spa (all available at reasonable prices).

Eating in Lekeitio: Although it's sleepy in the off-season, the harbor promenade is made to order in summer for a slow meal or a tapas crawl. **Restaurante Zapirain**, hiding in the narrow streets a few blocks up from the harbor, is a local favorite for fancy seafood. This cozy white-tablecloth eatery fills one small room with 10 tables of happy eaters (€15 starters, €20 main dishes, closed Tue, Igualdegi 3, tel. 946-840-255).

Guernica / Gernika

The workaday market town of Guernica (GEHR-nee-kah) is near and dear to Basques and pacifists alike. This is the site of the Gernikako Arbola (oak tree of Gernika), which marked the assembly point where the regional Basque leaders, the Lords of Bizkaia, met through the ages to assert their people's freedom. Long the symbolic heart of Basque separatism, it was also a natural target for Franco (and his ally Hitler) in the Spanish Civil War—resulting in an infamous bombing raid that left the town in ruins (see "The Bombing of Guernica" sidebar), as immortalized by Picasso in his epic work *Guernica*.

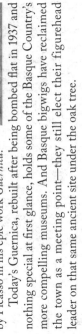

Today's Guernica, rebuilt after being bombed flat in 1937 and nothing special at first glance, holds some of the Basque Country's more compelling museums. And Basque bigwigs have reclaimed the town as a meeting point—they still elect their figurehead leader on that same ancient site under the oak tree.

Orientation to Guernica

Guernica is small (about 15,000 inhabitants) and compact, focused on its large market hall (Monday market 9:00–14:00).

Tourist Information: The TI is in the town center (Mon-Sat 10:00–14:00 & 16:00–19:00—no lunch break in summer, Sun 10:00–14:00, Artekalea 8, tel. 946-255-892, www.gernika -lumo.net). Pick up the good, free town map. If you'll be visiting both the Peace Museum and the Basque Country Museum, buy the €5.25 combo-ticket here (they'll also give you a voucher for a free *pintxo*).

Arrival in Guernica: Drivers will find a handy parking lot near the train tracks at the end of town. Buses drop off along the main road skirting the town center. No matter where you enter, the TI is well-signed (look for yellow *i* signs)—head there first to get your bearings.

Sights in Guernica

I've arranged Guernica's sights in the order of a handy sightseeing loop from the TI.

• *Exit the TI to the left, cross the street, and walk up the left side of the square, where you'll find the...*

▲**Gernika Peace Museum**—Because of the brutality of the Guernica bombing, and the powerful Picasso painting that documented the atrocities of war, the name "Guernica" has become synonymous with pacifism. This thoughtfully presented exhibit has taken a great tragedy of 20th-century history and turned it into a compelling cry for peace in our time. Borrow the English translations at the entry, request an English showing of the movie upstairs, and head up through the two-floor exhibit. The first floor begins by considering different ways of defining "peace." You'll then enter an apartment and hear Begoña describe her typical Guernica life in the 1930s...until the bombs dropped (a mirror effect shows you the devastating aftermath). You'll exit into an exhibit about the town's history, with a special emphasis on the bombing. Finally, a 10-minute movie shows grainy footage of the destruction, and ends with a collage of peaceful reconciliations in recent history—in Ireland, South Africa, Guatemala, Australia, and Berlin. On the second floor, Picasso's famous painting is superimposed on three transparent panels to highlight different themes. The exhibit concludes with a survey of the recent history of conflicts in the Basque Country (€4; July–Aug Tue–Sat 10:00–20:00, Sun 10:00–15:00, closed Mon; Sept–June Tue–Sat 10:00–14:00 & 16:00–19:00, Sun 10:00–14:00, closed Mon; Foru Plaza 1, tel. 946-270-213, www.peacemuseumguernica.org).

• *Continue uphill to the big church. At the road above the church, you can turn right and walk a block and a half to find an underwhelming tile replica of Picasso's Guernica (left-hand side of the street). Or you can head left to find the next two attractions.*

▲**Basque Country Museum (Euskal Herria Museoa)**—This well-presented, newly renovated exhibit offers a good overview of Basque culture and history. Start in the ground-floor theater and see the overview video (request English). Follow the suggested route and climb chronologically up through Basque history, with the necessary help of an included audioguide. You'll find exhibits

The Bombing of Guernica

During the Spanish Civil War, Guernica was the site of one of history's most reviled wartime acts.

Monday, April 26, 1937, was market day, when the town was filled with farmers and peasants from the countryside selling their wares. At about 16:40 in the afternoon, a German warplane appeared ominously on the horizon, and proceeded to bomb bridges and roads surrounding the town. Soon after, more planes arrived. Three hours of relentless saturation bombing followed, as the German and Italian air forces pummeled the city with incendiary firebombs. People running through the streets or along the green hillsides were strafed with machine-gun fire. As the sun fell low in the sky and the planes finally left, hundreds—or possibly thousands—had been killed, and many more wounded. (Because Guernica was filled with refugees from other besieged towns, nobody is sure how many perished.)

Hearing word of the attack in Paris, Pablo Picasso—who had been commissioned to paint a mural for the 1937 world's fair—was devastated at the news of what had gone on in Guernica. Inspired, he painted what many consider the greatest antiwar work of art, ever.

Why did the bombings happen? Reportedly, Adolf Hitler wanted an opportunity to try out his new saturation-bombing attack strategy. Francisco Franco, who was fed up with the independence-minded Basques, offered up their historic capital as a candidate for the experiment.

There's no doubt that Guernica, a gateway to Bilbao, was strategically located. But historians believe most of the targets here were far from strategic. Why attack so mercilessly, during the daytime, on market day, when innocent casualties would be maximized? Like the famous silent scream of Picasso's *Guernica* mother, this question haunts pacifists everywhere to this day.

---

about traditional Basque architecture and landscape, and a region-by-region rundown of the Basque Country's seven territories. One interesting map shows Basque emigration over the centuries—including to the US. The top floor is the most engaging, highlighting Basque culture: sports, dances, cuisine, myths and legends, music, and language, plus a wraparound movie featuring images of a proud people living the Basque lifestyle (€3; includes audioguide, Tue–Sat 10:00–14:00 & 16:00–19:00, Sun 10:00–14:30, closed Mon, Allendesalazar 5, tel. 946-255-451).

▲▲Gernika Assembly House and Oak Tree—

In the Middle Ages, the meeting point for the Basque general assembly was under the old oak tree on the gentle hillside above Guernica. The tradition continues today, as the tree stands at the center of a modest but interesting complex celebrating Basque culture and self-government (free, daily 10:00–14:00 & 16:00–18:00, June–Sept until 19:00, on Allendesalazar, tel. 946-251-138).

As you enter the grounds, you'll see an **old trunk** in the small colonnade dating from the 1700s. Basque traditions have lived much, much longer than a single tree's life span. When one dies, it's replaced with a new one. This is the oldest surviving trunk.

The exhibit has four parts: A stained-glass window room, the oak-tree courtyard, the assembly chamber, and a basement theater (request the 10-minute video in English that extols the virtues and beauties of the Basque Country).

Inside the first building, find the impressive **stained-glass window room.** The computer video here gives a good six-minute overview of the exhibit (plays in English when you click). The gorgeous stained-glass ceiling is rife with Basque symbolism. The elderly leader stands under the oak holding a book with the "Old Law" (*Lege Zarra*), which are the laws by which the Basques lived for centuries. Below him are groups representing the three traditional career groups of this industrious people: sailors and fishermen; miners and steelworkers; and farmers. Behind them all is a classic Basque landscape: on the left is the sea, and on the right are rolling green hills dotted with red-and-white homes.

Out back, a tribune surrounds the fateful **oak tree.** This little fella is from 2005, planted here when the earlier one "finished out its life cycle" after standing here for nearly a century and a half. This tree is a descendant of that one, and (supposedly) of all the trees here since ancient times. This location is where Basque leaders have met in solidarity across the centuries. In the Middle Ages, after Basque lands became part of Castile, Castilian kings came here to pledge respect to the old Basque laws. When Basque independence came under fire in the 19th century, patriots rallied by singing a song about this tree ("Ancient and holy symbol / Let thy fruit fall worldwide / While we gaze in adoration / Upon thee, our blessed tree"). After the 1937 bombing, in which this tree's predecessor was miraculously unscathed, hundreds of survivors sought refuge under its branches. Today, although official representatives in the Spanish government are elected at the polls, the Basques choose their figurehead leader, the Lehendakari ("First One"), in this same spot.

Step back inside and enter the **assembly chamber**—like a mini-parliament for the region of Bizkaia ("Vizcaya" in Spanish, "Biscay" in English; one of the seven Basque territories). Notice the holy water and the altar—a sign that there's no separation of church and state in Basque politics. The paintings show the Lords of Bizkaia swearing allegiance to the Old Law.

Guernica Connections

Guernica is well-connected to **Bilbao** (hourly trains to Bilbao's Atxuri Station, 40 minutes; also 4 buses/hour, 40 minutes) and to **Lekeitio** (hourly buses, 40 minutes). Connections are sparser on weekends. The easiest way to connect to San Sebastián is via Bilbao, though you can also get there on the slow Topo train (transfer in Lemoa).

Bilbao / Bilbo

In recent years, Bilbao (bil-BOW, rhymes with "cow") has seen a transformation like no other Spanish city. Entire sectors of the industrial city's long-depressed port have been cleared away to allow construction of a new opera house, convention center, and the stunning Guggenheim Museum.

Bilbao feels at once like a city of the grim industrial past...and of an exciting new future. It mingles beautiful but crumbling old buildings; eyesore high-rise apartment blocks; brand-new super-modern additions to the skyline (such as the Guggenheim); and, scattered in the lush green hillsides all around the horizon, typical whitewashed Basque homes with red roofs. Bilbao enjoys a vitality and well-worn charm befitting its status as a regional capital of culture and industry.

Planning Your Time

For most visitors, the Guggenheim is the main draw (and many could spend the entire day there). But with a little more time, it's also worth hopping on a tram to explore the atmospheric Old Town (Casco Viejo). Don't bother coming to Bilbao on Monday, when virtually all its museums—including the almighty Guggenheim— are closed (except in July–Aug).

Orientation to Bilbao

When you're in the center, Bilbao feels smaller than its popula-tion of 500,000. The city, nestled amidst green hillsides, hugs the Bilbao River as it curves through town. The Guggenheim is more

Bilbao

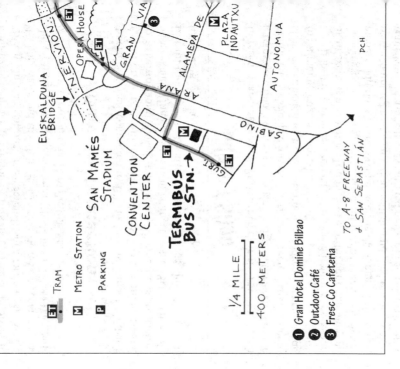

ET TRAM
M METRO STATION
P PARKING

1/4 MILE
400 METERS

1 Gran Hotel Domine Bilbao
2 Outdoor Café
3 Fresc Co Cafeteria

or less centrally located near the top of that curve; the bus station is to the west; the Old Town (Casco Viejo) and train stations are to the east; and a super-convenient and fun-to-ride green tram called the EuskoTran ties it all together.

Tourist Information

Bilbao's handiest TI is next to the Guggenheim (look for the *i* sign on top of a pole). Pick up a city map and the bimonthly *Bilbao Guide*. If you're interested in something beyond the Guggenheim, ask about walking tours in English (€4.50, Sat–Sun only) and grab the Bilbao museums brochure, describing museums dedicated to everything from bullfighting and seafaring to sports and Holy Week processionals (TI open July–Aug Mon–Sat 10:00–19:00,

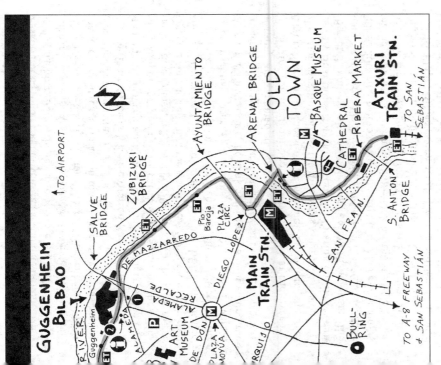

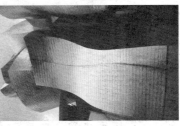

Sun 10:00–18:00; Sept–June Tue–Fri 11:00–18:00, Sat 11:00–19:00, Sun 11:00–15:00, closed Mon; tel. 944-795-760, www.bilbao.net). There are also TI branches at the airport and at Arriaga Theater (at Plaza de Arriaga, near the Old Town).

Arrival in Bilbao

Most travelers—whether arriving by train, bus, or car—will want to go straight to the Guggenheim. Thanks to a perfectly planned tram system (EuskoTran), this couldn't be easier. From any point of entry, simply buy a €1.25 single-ride ticket at a user-friendly green machine (€3.45 for an all-day pass), hop on a green-and-gray tram, enjoy the Muzak, and head for the Guggenheim stop (there's only one line, trams come every 10-15 minutes, www .euskotran.es). When you buy your ticket, validate it immediately at the machine (follow the red arrow), since you can't do it once onboard. If you get lost, ask: "¿Dónde está el museo Guggenheim?" (DOHN-day ay-STAH el moo-SAY-oh "Guggenheim"). Note that the only luggage storage in town is at the Termibús Station (not at either train station).

By Train: Bilbao's **RENFE Station** (serving most of Spain) is on the river in central Bilbao. The train station is on top of a small shopping mall (a Europcar rental office is by the train-station ticket office, tel. 944-239-390). To reach the tram to the Guggenheim, descend into the stores. Leave from the exit marked *Hurtado de Amézaga*, and go right to find the BBK bank. Enter, find the *Automatikoa* door on the right, and buy your ticket at the green machine marked *Abando* (the machine is mixed in with a bunch of ATMs). Leave the bank and continue right around the corner. Validate your ticket at the machines at the tram stop before boarding the tram marked *Basurto*.

Trains coming from San Sebastián arrive at the riverside **Atxuri Station,** southeast of the museum. From here, the tram (direction: Basurto) follows the river to the Guggenheim stop.

By Bus: Buses stop at the **Termibús Station** on the western edge of downtown, about a mile southwest of the museum. The station has luggage lockers and a left-luggage desk (€2/bag, daily 7:00–22:00, ring bell to enter). The tram (San Mamés Station) is on the road just below the station—look for the steel *CTB* sign or follow the *Tran* signs. Buy and validate a ticket at the machine, and hop on the tram (direction: Atxuri) to the Guggenheim.

By Plane: Bilbao's compact, modern, user-friendly airport is about six miles north of downtown. Everything branches off the light-and-air-filled main hall, designed by prominent architect Santiago Calatrava. A handy bus (#3247) takes you directly to the center (€1.30, pay driver, 3/hour, 20-minute trip, makes three stops downtown—the first one is closest to the Guggenheim—before ending at the Termibús Station). To find the Guggenheim, turn right out of the terminal. A taxi into town costs about €20. To get to San Sebastián, you can take a direct bus from Bilbao Airport (€15.20, pay driver, runs hourly, 1 hour, drops off at Plaza Pío XII, www.pesa.net). A taxi directly to San Sebastián will run you €150.

By Car: A big underground car park is near the museum; if you have a car, park it here and use the tram. From the freeway, take the exit marked *Centro* (with bull's-eye symbol), follow signs to *Guggenheim* (you'll see the museum), and look for the big "P" that marks the garage.

Sights in Bilbao

▲▲▲Guggenheim Bilbao

While the collection of art in this museum is no better than that in Europe's other great modern-art museums, the building itself—designed by Frank Gehry and opened in 1997—is the reason why so many travelers happily splice Bilbao into their itineraries.

Cost and Hours: €13, includes excellent audioguide; July–Aug daily 10:00–20:00; Sept–June Tue–Sun 10:00–20:00, closed Mon; same-day re-entry allowed—get bracelet on your way out; café, no photos inside, tram stop: Guggenheim, Metro stop: Moyua, Avenida Abandoibarra 2, tel. 944-359-080, www.guggenheim-bilbao.es.

Tours: Free guided tours in English generally run 4/day at 11:00, 12:30, 16:30, and 18:30. Show up at least 30 minutes early to put your name on the list at the tour desk (to the left as you enter).

Background: Frank Gehry's groundbreaking triumph offers a fascinating look at 21st-century architecture. Using cutting-edge technologies, unusual materials, and daring forms, he created a piece of sculpture that smoothly integrates with its environment and serves as the perfect stage for some of today's best art. Clad in limestone and titanium, the building connects the city with its river. Gehry meshed many visions.

To him, the building's multiple forms jostle like a loose crate of bottles. The building is inspired by a silvery fish...and also evokes wind-filled sails heading out to sea. Gehry keeps returning to his fish motif, reminding visitors that, as a boy, he was inspired by carp...even taking them into the bathtub with him.

⊙ Self-Guided Tour: The audioguide will lead you room-by-room through the collection, but this information will get you started.

Guarding the main entrance is artist Jeff Koons' 42-foot-tall **West Highland Terrier.** Its 60,000 plants and flowers, which blossom in concert, grow through steel mesh. A joyful structure, it brings viewers back to their childhood...perhaps evoking human-kind's relationship to God...or maybe it's just another notorious Koons hoax. One thing is clear: It answers to "Puppy." Although the sculpture was originally intended to be temporary, the people of Bilbao fell in love with Puppy—so they bought it.

Descend to the **main entrance.** After buying your ticket, be sure to pick up the free exhibit audioguide. At the information desk, pick up the small English brochure explaining the architecture and museum layout, and the seasonal *Guggenheim Bilbao* magazine that details the art currently on display.

After presenting your ticket, enter the **atrium.** This acts as the heart of the building, pumping visitors from various rooms on three levels out and back, always returning to this central area before moving on to the next. The architect invites you to caress the sensual curves of the walls. There are virtually no straight lines (except the floor). Notice the sheets of glass that make up the elevator shaft—overlapping one another like a fish's scales. Each glass and limestone panel is unique, designed by a computer and shaped by a robot…as will likely be standard in constructing the great buildings of the future.

From the atrium, step out onto the riverside **terrace.** The "water garden" lets the river symbolically lap at the base of the building. This pool is home to two unusual sculptures (which appear occasionally throughout the day): a five-part "fire fountain" (notice the squares in the pool to the right) and a "fog sculpture" that billows up from below.

Still out on the terrace, notice the museum's commitment to public spaces: On the right, a grand **staircase** leads under a big green bridge to a tower; the effect wraps the bridge into the museum's grand scheme. The 30-foot-tall **spider,** called *Maman* ("Mommy"), is French artist Louise Bourgeois' depiction of her mother: She spins a beautiful and delicate web of life…which is used to entrap her victims. (It makes a little more sense if you understand that the artist's mother was a weaver. Or maybe not.)

Gehry designed the vast **ground floor** mainly to house often-huge modern-art installations. Computer-controlled lighting adjusts for different exhibits. Surfaces are clean and bare, so you can focus on the art. While most of the collection comes and goes, Richard Serra's huge *Matter of Time* sculpture in the largest gallery is permanent (who would want to move those massive metal coils?). The intent is to have visitors walk among these metal walls—the "art" is experiencing this journey.

Because this museum is part of the Guggenheim "family" of museums, the **collection** perpetually rotates among the sister Guggenheim galleries in New York, Venice, and Berlin. The best approach to your visit is simply to immerse yourself in a modern-art happening, rather than to count on seeing a particular piece or a specific artist's works.

Twenty galleries occupy three floors. Use the handy touch-screens scattered throughout the museum to figure out exactly where you are and what's left to see, since the organic floor plan can be confusing.

Even if you're not turned on by this kind of art, the Guggenheim is a must-see experience. Full of surprises, it's well worth the entry fee just to appreciate the museum's structural design, which is a work of art in itself.

You can't fully enjoy the museum's architecture without taking a circular stroll up and down each side of the river along the handsome promenade and over the two modern **pedestrian bridges.** (After you tour the museum, you can borrow a free "outdoor audioguide" to learn more—ID required—but it doesn't say much or take you across the river.) The building's skin—shiny, metallic, with a scale-like texture—is made of thin titanium, carefully created to give just the desired color and reflective quality. The external appearance tells you what's inside: the blocky limestone parts contain square-shaped galleries, while the titanium sections hold nonlinear spaces.

As you look out over the rest of the city, think of this: Gehry designed his building to reflect what he saw here in Bilbao. Now other architects are, in turn, creating new buildings that complement his. It's an appealing synergy for this old city.

Leaving the Museum: To get to the Old Town from the Guggenheim, take the tram that leaves from the river level beside the museum, just past the kid-pleasing fountain. Hop off at the Arriaga stop, near the dripping-Baroque riverfront theater of the same name. From here it's a short walk into the twisty Old Town.

Old Town (Casco Viejo)

Bilbao's Old Town, with tall, narrow lanes lined with thriving shops and tapas bars, is worth a stroll. Because the weather is wetter here than in many other parts of Spain (hence the green hillsides), the little balconies that climb the outside walls of buildings are glassed in, creating cozy little breakfast nooks.

Whether you want to or not, you'll eventually wind up at Old Bilbao's centerpiece, the **Santiago Cathedral,** a 14th-century Gothic church with a tranquil interior that's recently been scrubbed clean inside and out (free, €1 to dip into cloister, Mon–Fri 10:00–13:00 & 17:00–19:30, closed Sat–Sun).

Various museums (including those dedicated to diocesan art and the Holy Week processions) are in or near the Old Town, but on a quick visit only one is worth considering....

Basque Museum (Euskal Museoa)—It's fitting that Bilbao, a leading city of Spain's Basque region, would have a museum dedicated to its unique culture. Unfortunately, the almost complete lack of English leaves the exhibits, much like the Basques themselves, shrouded in mystery. Around a ground-floor cloister, you'll see old stone monuments. The first floor delves into the Basque cultural heritage, displaying ceramics, guns, looms, and other tools. Special emphasis is given to nautical artifacts from this seafaring people; Basque settlers in the American West; and the pastoral lifestyles of rural Basques. The top floor is dedicated to archaeology, with exhibits about old tools and settlements (€3, Tue–Sat 11:00–17:00, Sun 12:00–14:00, closed Mon, Miguel de Unamuno Plaza 4, tel. 944-155-423, www.euskal-museoa.org).

Sleeping in Bilbao

(€1 = about $1.25, country code: 34)

Bilbao merits an overnight stay. Even those who are only interested in the Guggenheim find that there's much more to see in this historic yet quickly changing city. Unless otherwise noted, the 7 percent tax is not included in the prices listed in this section.

Near the Guggenheim Museum

$$$ Gran Hotel Domine Bilbao is *the* place for wealthy modern-art fans looking for a splurge close to the museum. It's right across the street from the main entrance to the Guggenheim and Jeff Koons' *Puppy*. The hotel is gathered around an atrium with a giant "stone tree" and other artsy flourishes, and its decor (by a prominent Spanish designer) was clearly inspired by Gehry's masterpiece. The 145 plush rooms are distinctly black, white, steel, and very postmodern (standard Db–€130–180, museum-view "executive" rooms for €20 more, rates vary widely with events and demand, breakfast–€19 or €12 if ordered when you reserve, non-smoking rooms, air-con, elevator, free Internet access and Wi-Fi, great museum-view breakfast terrace, free gym with wet and dry saunas, Alameda Mazarredo 61, tel. 944-253-300, fax 944-253-301, www .granhoteldominebilbao.com, recepcion.domine@hoteles-silken .com). If arriving by tram, take the main museum steps up by the fountains to reach the hotel.

In the Old Town

To reach the Old Town, take the tram to the Arriaga stop.

$$ Hotel Bilbao Jardines, a fresh new place buried in the Old Town, is the most hotelesque option, with 32 modern but basic rooms (Sb–€58, Db–€75, cheaper off-season, breakfast–€5, quieter rooms in back, air-con, elevator, free Wi-Fi, Calle Jardines 9, tel. 944-794-210, fax 944-794-211, www.hotelbilbao jardines.com, info@hotelbilbaojardines.com, Marta, Felix, and Monica).

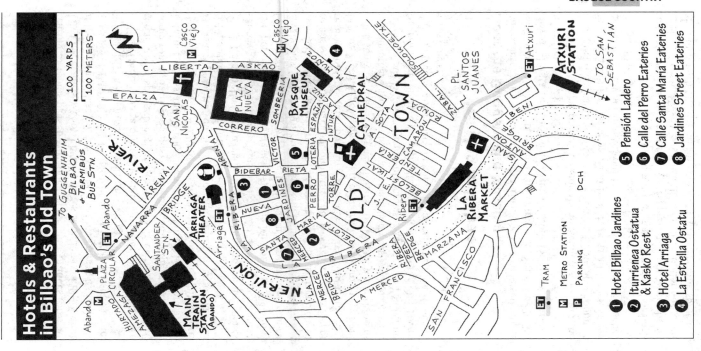

Hotels & Restaurants in Bilbao's Old Town

100 YARDS
100 METERS

TO GUGGENHEIM BILBAO + TERMIBÚS BUS STN.

Casco Viejo

Casco Viejo

C. LIBERTAD
ASKAO
EPALZA
CORRERO
PLAZA NUEVA
SAN NICOLAS
SOMBRERIA
Basque Museum
MUNOA

RIVER
NERVION
NAVARRA
ARENAL
SANTANDER STN.
Abando
Abando
PLAZA CIRCULAR
HURTADO
AMEZAGA
MAIN TRAIN STATION (ABANDO)

ARRIAGA THEATER
Arriaga
LA RIBERA
NUEVA
BIDEBAR-
RIETA
SANTA MARIA
LA MERCED
JARDINES
PERRO
VICTOR
LOTERIA
ESPAÑA
CINTUR.
TORRE
PELOTA
J.
E. TENDERIA
BELOSTIKAL
CAMARO
A SOTA
RONDA
ZABAL
ESPERIA

VIDEBAR
CATHEDRAL
OLD TOWN
PL. SANTOS JUANES

Ribera
LA RIBERA MARKET
RIBERA
RIBERA BRIDGE
PEDRO BRIDGE
LA MERCED
SAN FRANCISCO
MARZANA
DCH
SAN ANTON BRIDGE
BENI
IBENI
Atxuri

ATXURI STATION
TO SAN SEBASTIAN

1 Hotel Bilbao Jardines
2 Iturrienea Ostatua & Kasko Rest.
3 Hotel Arriaga
4 La Estrella Ostatu

5 Pensión Ladero
6 Calle del Perro Eateries
7 Calle Santa María Eateries
8 Jardines Street Eateries

ET TRAM
M METRO STATION
P PARKING

$ Iturrienea Ostatua, next door to the recommended Kasko restaurant on a pedestrian street in the Old Town, is a tidy pension renting 21 rooms packed with brick, stone, and antiques (Sb–€50, Db–€60, twin Db–€66, Tb–€80, prices include tax, €10–15 more July–Aug, breakfast–€6, free Wi-Fi, near the river at Santa Maria 14, tel. 944-161-500, fax 944-158-929, www.iturrieneaostatua.com, info@iturrieneaostatua.com, friendly Carlos).

$ Hotel Arriaga offers 21 traditional but well-maintained rooms and a spirited reception (Sb–€45, Db–€54, extra bed–€11, some rooms overlook a busy street—request a quiet back room, Internet access and Wi-Fi, lounge, parking–€11, Ribera 3, tel. 944-790-001, fax 944-790-516, www.hotelarriaga.es, info@hotel arriaga.es, Jon). As you cross the bridge from the station, it's just behind the big theater of the same name.

$ La Estrella Ostatu has 26 simple but neat rooms up a twisty staircase near the Basque Museum (Sb–€35, Db–€60 in summer, cheaper off-season, breakfast–€3–4, Maria Muñoz 6, tel. 944-164-066, fax 944-150-731, www.laestrellaostatu.com, laestrellabilbao @yahoo.es, just enough English spoken, Jesus and Begonia).

$ Pensión Ladero, renting 18 ramshackle but clean and cheap rooms, is a solid budget option in the Old Town. They don't accept reservations, so call upon arrival to check availability (S–€25, D–€37, T–€53, Q–€63, up 4 flights of stairs; 7 rooms up a very tight spiral staircase (watch your head) share 1 bathroom, while 11 rooms use the other 3 bathrooms on the main floor; cash only, Lotería 1, tel. 944-150-932, www.pensionladero.es, Margarita). You'll find the *pensión* just before the cathedral at the center of the Old Town. This is a better value than the more prominent Pensión Roquefer across the street.

Eating in Bilbao

Near the Guggenheim Museum

The easiest choice is the good **cafeteria** in the museum itself (upper level, separate entry above museum entry; Tue–Sun 9:00–20:30, closed Mon, €20 lunch deal offered 13:00–15:15, reservations smart, tel. 944-239-333).

The circular structure outside the museum just behind the fountains is a pleasant **outdoor café** serving €2.50 tapas (point at the ones you like on the bar) and fresh fruit salad for €3. If the tables are full, you can take your food to one of the stone benches nearby. Sometimes they have live music in the evenings.

The streets in front of the museum have a handful of both sit-down and carry-out eateries (cafés, pizzerias, sandwich shops) to choose from. **Fresc Co** is a healthy and cheap option for lunch or dinner, with an all-you-can-eat salad buffet including some hot dishes, dessert, and coffee for less than €10 (daily 12:30–24:00, 10-minute walk from the Guggenheim, three blocks to the left of Plaza Moyua at Gran Via 55).

In the Old Town

Bilbao has a thriving restaurant and tapas-bar scene. For pointers on Basque food, see page 480. You'll find plenty of options on the lanes near the cathedral. Most restaurants around the Old Town advertise a fixed-price lunch for around €10.

The street **Calle del Perro** (PEEN-chohs). **Xukela Bar** is my favorite, with its inviting atmosphere, good wines, and an addictive array of €1.60 tapas spread along its bar (tables only for clients eating hot dishes, Calle del Perro 2, tel. 944-159-772).

Calle del Perro is also good for sit-down restaurants. Browse the menus and interiors and choose your favorite. Well-regarded options include three places practically next door to one another: **Egiluz** (€10 meals served in small restaurant up steep spiral staircase in the back); **Rio-Oja** (€8 specialties, focus on shareable traditional dishes called *kazuelitas*); and **Rotterdam** (€10–15 meals, also has *kazuelitas*; try the *chipirones en su tinta*—squids in their ink, served with a glass of house red for €10).

Calle Santa María caters to a younger crowd, with softer lighting and a livelier atmosphere, and has three bars worth considering: Gatz, Santa María, and Kasko. **Kasko** is the most upscale option, with a pianist and an interesting dinner menu (starter, main course, dessert, and good wine for €32, served daily 20:30–23:00, Santa María 16, tel. 944-160-311).

Eateries also abound on **Jardines** street, including the popular **Breton** (meals and *pintxos*, at #11, closed Mon).

Bilbao Connections

For pointers on Basque food, see page 480.

From Bilbao by Bus to: San Sebastián (2/hour, hourly on weekends, 6:00–22:30, 1.25 hours, arrives at San Sebastián's Amara Station), **Guernica** (4/hour, 40 minutes), **Lekeitio** (hourly, 1.25 hours), **Pamplona** (6/day, 2 hours), **Burgos** (4/day, 2 hours), **Santander** (hourly, 1.5 hours, transfer there to bus to **Santillana del Mar** or **Comillas** in Cantabria). These buses depart from Bilbao's Termibús Station.

By EuskoTren to: San Sebastián (hourly, long and scenic 2.5-hour trip to San Sebastián's EuskoTren Station, €8.15 round-trip ticket saves €2, EuskoTren info: toll tel. 902-543-210, www.euskotren.es), **Guernica** (hourly, 40 minutes). These trains depart from Bilbao's Atxuri Station, just beyond the Old Town.

By RENFE Train to: Madrid (2/day, 6 hours), **Barcelona**

(2/day, 6.5–9 hours, €64), **Burgos** (4/day, 3 hours, €20), **Salamanca** (1/day, 5 hours), **León** (1/day, 5 hours), **Santiago de Compostela** (1/day direct, 11 hours). Remember, these trains leave from the RENFE Station, across the river from the Old Town (tram stop: Abando). A planned new train line (coming in 2017) will connect Bilbao to other cities in a snap (30 minutes to San Sebastián, 2.25 hours to Madrid, 5.5 hours to Paris)—but it's still slow trains for now.

LANGUEDOC

Albi • Carcassonne • Collioure

From the 10th to the 13th centuries, this mighty and independent region controlled most of southern France. The ultimate in mean-spirited crusades against the Cathars (or Albigensians) began here in 1208, igniting Languedoc's meltdown and eventual incorporation into the state of France.

The name *languedoc* comes from the *langue* (language) that its people spoke: *Langue d'oc* ("language of Oc," *Oc* for the way they said "yes") was the dialect of southern France; *langue d'oïl* was the dialect of northern France (where *oïl* later became *oui*, or "yes"). Languedoc's language faded with its power.

The Moors, Charlemagne, and the Spanish have all called this area home. The Spanish influence is still *muy* present in this region, particularly in the south, where restaurants serve paella and the siesta is still respected.

While sharing many of the same attributes as Provence (climate, wind, grapes, and sea), this sunny, intoxicating, southwesternmost region of France is allocated little time by most travelers. Lacking Provence's cachet and sophistication, Languedoc feels more real. Pay homage to Henri de Toulouse-Lautrec in Albi; spend a night in Europe's greatest fortress city, Carcassonne; scamper up to a remote Cathar castle; and sift through sand in Collioure. That wind you feel is called *la tramontane* (trah-mohn-tahn-yuh), Languedoc's version of Provence's mistral wind.

Planning Your Time

Albi makes a good day or overnight stop between the Dordogne region and Carcassonne (figure about 2 autoroute hours from Albi to either place). Plan your arrival in popular Carcassonne carefully:

Languedoc

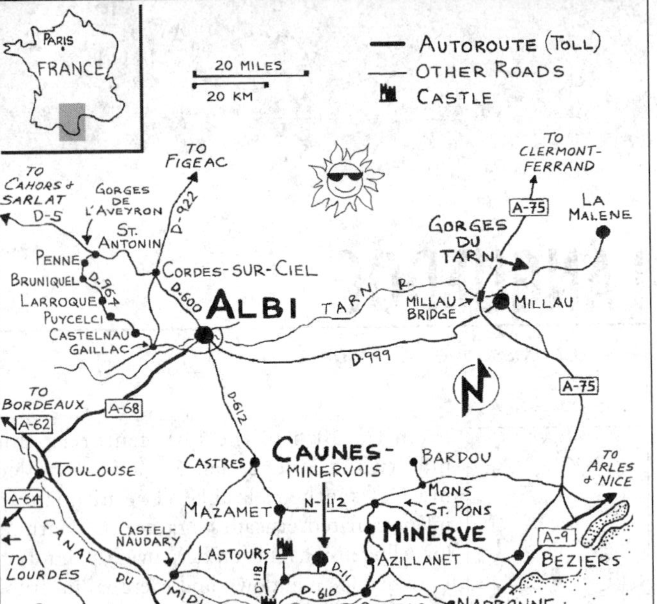

FRANCE
PARIS

—	AUTOROUTE (TOLL)
—	OTHER ROADS
⌂	CASTLE

20 MILES
20 KM

Get there late in the afternoon, spend the night, and leave by 11:00 the next morning to miss most day-trippers. Collioure lies a few hours from Carcassonne and is your Mediterranean beach-town vacation from your vacation, where you'll want two nights and a full day. To find the Cathar castle ruins and the village of Minerve, you'll need wheels of your own and a good map. If you're driving, the most exciting Cathar castles—Peyrepertuse and Quéribus—work well as day stops between Carcassonne and

Collioure. And if nature beckons, the Gorges du Tarn makes an idyllic joyride a few hours east of Albi. No matter what kind of transportation you use, Languedoc is a logical stop between the Dordogne and Provence—or on the way to Barcelona, which is just over the border.

Getting Around Languedoc

Albi, Carcassonne, and Collioure are all accessible by train, but a car is essential for seeing the remote sights. Pick up your rental car in Albi or Carcassonne, and buy Michelin Local maps #344 and #338. Roads can be pencil-thin, and traffic slow.

For a scenic one-hour detour route connecting Albi and points north (such as the Dordogne), take D-964 between Caussade (30 minutes south of Cahors), Bruniquel, Gaillac, and Albi. With a bit more time, link Caussade, Saint-Antonin-Noble-Val (D-5 and D-926), Bruniquel, Castelnau-de-Montmiral, Gaillac, and Albi (using D-115 and D-964; see "Route of the *Bastides*" on page 562). If you really want to joyride, take a half-day drive through the glorious Lot River Valley *via* Villefranche-de-Rouergue, Cajarc, and St. Cirq Lapopie (covered in the "Dordogne and Nearby" chapter—see page 472). If speed is of the essence, connect the Dordogne with Albi on the autoroute to Montauban.

Languedoc's Cuisine Scene

Hearty peasant cooking and full-bodied red wines are Languedoc's tasty trademarks. Be adventurous. Cassoulet, an old Roman concoction of goose, duck, pork, mutton, sausage, and white beans, is the main-course specialty. You'll also see *cargolade*, a satisfying stew of snail, lamb, and sausage. Local cheeses are Roquefort and Pelardon (a nutty-tasting goat cheese). Corbières, Minervois, and Côtes du Roussillon are the area's good-value red wines. The locals distill a fine brandy, Armagnac, which tastes just like cognac and costs less.

Remember, restaurants serve only during lunch (11:30–14:00) and dinner (19:00–21:00, later in bigger cities); some cafés serve food throughout the day.

Albi

Albi, an enjoyable river town of sienna-tone bricks and half-timbered buildings, is worth a stop for two world-class sights: its towering cathedral and the Toulouse-Lautrec Museum. Lost in the Dordogne-to-Carcassonne shuffle and overshadowed by its big brother Toulouse, unpretentious Albi rewards the stray tourist well.

Orientation to Albi

Albi's cathedral is home base. For our purposes, all sights, pedestrian streets, and hotels fan out from here and are less than a five-minute walk away. The Tarn River hides below and behind the cathedral. The best city view is from the 22 Août 1944 bridge. Albi is dead quiet on Sundays and Monday mornings.

Tourist Information

The TI is on the square in front of the cathedral, next to the Toulouse-Lautrec Museum (July-Aug Mon-Sat 9:00–19:00, Sun 10:30–12:30 & 14:30–18:30; Sept–June Mon–Sat 9:00–12:30 & 14:00–18:30, Sun 10:30–12:30 & 14:00–18:00; tel. 05 63 49 48 80, www.albi-tourisme.fr). They sell a "pass" that includes the museum and the cathedral choir for €6.50 (saves €1). Ask about concerts, pick up a map of the city center with the walking-tour brochure, and get the map of *La Route des Bastides Albigeoises* (hill towns near Albi).

Arrival in Albi

By Train: There are two stations in Albi; you want Albi-Ville (no baggage storage). It's a level 15-minute walk to the town center: Exit the station, take the second left onto avenue Maréchal Joffre, and then take another left on avenue du Général de Gaulle. Go straight across place Lapérouse and find the traffic-free street to the left that leads into the city center. This turns into rue Ste. Cécile, which takes you to my recommended hotels and the cathedral.

By Car: Follow *Centre-Ville* and *Cathédrale* signs (if you lose your way, follow the tall church tower). There's a big, free lot on avenue du Général de Gaulle, just before place Lapérouse. Metered parking is close to the old city along boulevard Général Sibille, also near place Lapérouse (free 12:00–14:00 & 19:00–8:00, and all day Sun).

Helpful Hints

Market Days: The Art Nouveau market hall, a block past the cathedral square, hosts a market daily except Monday

Albi

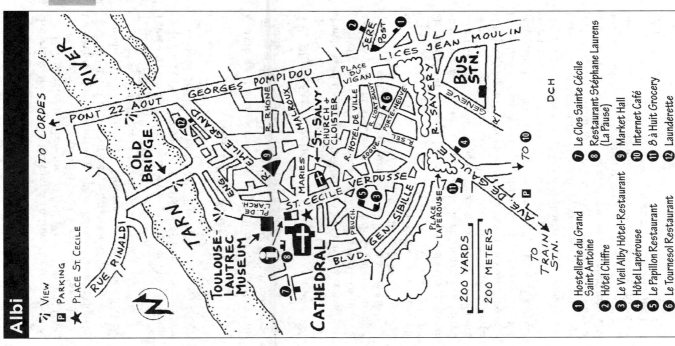

7i VIEW
P PARKING
★ PLACE ST. CECILE

1 Hostellerie du Grand Saint Antoine
2 Hôtel Chiffre
3 Le Vieil Alby Hôtel-Restaurant
4 Hôtel Lapérouse
5 Le Papillon Restaurant
6 Le Tournesol Restaurant
7 Le Clos Sainte Cécile
8 Restaurant Stéphane Laurens (La Pause)
9 Market Hall
10 Internet Café
11 8 à Huit Grocery
12 Launderette

DCH

(8:00–14:00). A farmers' market is held Saturdays outside the market hall.

Groceries: The store **8 à Huit** is across from the recommended Hôtel Lapérouse (Tue–Sat 10:00–12:30 & 15:00–19:00, plus Sun mornings and Mon afternoons, 14 place Lapérouse).

Internet Access: Internet is at 2 place Edmond Canet (Mon–Fri 10:00–19:00, closed Sat–Sun, tel. 05 63 38 47 68).

Laundry: Do your washing at **Lavotop-Lavomatique,** above the river at 10 rue Emile Grand (daily 7:00–21:00).

Taxi: Call **Albi Taxi Radio** at 05 63 54 85 03.

Tourist Train: Le Petit Train leaves from place Ste. Cécile (in front of the cathedral) and makes a 45-minute scenic loop around Albi (€6, buy tickets at TI, 6/day).

Sights in Albi

Everything of sightseeing interest is within a few blocks of the towering cathedral. (I've included walking directions to connect some of the key sights.) Get oriented in the main square.

▲▲▲Place Ste. Cécile

Grab a bench on the far side of place Ste. Cécile and face the church. With the church directly in front of you, the bishop's palace (along with the Toulouse-Lautrec Museum, river view, and TI) is a bit to the right. The market is a block behind you on your right. And the sleepy St. Salvy cloister is a block behind on your left.

Why the big church? At its peak, Albi was the administrative center for 465 churches. Back when tithes were essentially legally required taxes, everyone gave their 10 percent, or "*dime*" (dee-may), to the church. The local bishop was filthy rich, and with all those *dimes*, he had money to build a dandy church. In medieval times, there was no interest in making a space so people could step back and get a perspective on such a beautiful building. A clutter of houses snuggled right up to the church's stout walls, and only in the 19th century were things cleared away. Just in the last few years were the cars cleared out (another triumph for the European pedestrian).

Why so many bricks? Because there were no stone quarries nearby. Albi is part of a swath of red-brick towns from here to Toulouse (nicknamed "the pink city" for the way its bricks dominate that townscape). Notice on this square the buffed brick addresses next to the sluggish stucco ones. As late as the 1960s, the town's brickwork was considered low-class and was covered by stucco. Today, the stucco is being peeled away, and Albi has that brick pride again.

The Cathars

The Cathars were a heretical group of Christians who grew in numbers from the 11th through the 13th centuries under tolerant rule in Languedoc. They saw life as a battle between good (the spiritual) and bad (the material), and they considered material things evil and of the devil. Although others called them "Cathars" (from the Greek word for "pure") or "Albigensians" (for their main city, Albi), they called themselves simply "friends of God." Cathars focused on the teachings of St. John, and recognized only baptism as a sacrament. Because they believed in reincarnation, they were vegetarians.

Travelers encounter traces of the Cathars in their Languedoc sightseeing because of the Albigensian Crusades (1209–1240s). The king of France wanted to consolidate his grip on southern France. The pope needed to make a strong point that the only acceptable Christianity was Roman style. Both found self-serving reasons to wage a genocidal war against the Cathars, who never amounted to more than 10 percent of the local population and coexisted happily with their non-Cathar neighbors. After a terrible generation of torture and mass burnings, the Cathars were wiped out. The last Cathar was burned in 1321.

Today, tourists find haunting castle ruins (once Cathar strongholds) high in the Pyrenees, and eat hearty *salade Cathar*.

▲▲St. Cécile Cathedral (Cathédrale Ste. Cécile)

When the heretical Cathars were defeated in the 13th century, this massive cathedral was the final nail in their coffin. Big and bold, it made clear who was in charge. The imposing exterior and the stunning interior drive home the message of the Catholic (read: "universal") Church in a way that would have stuck with any medieval worshipper. This place oozes power—get on board, or get run over.

Cost and Hours: Free, daily June–Sept 9:00–18:00, Oct–May 9:00–12:00 & 14:00–18:30. Once inside, you'll pay €2 to enter the choir (worthwhile). The treasury (a single room of reliquaries and church art) is not worth the €2 fee or the climb (€3 for both with audioguide).

Organ Concerts: The cathedral hosts frequent concerts (the TI has a schedule); free organ concerts usually are offered in July and August (Sun at 16:00 and Wed at 17:00).

⊙ Self-Guided Tour: Visit the cathedral using the following self-guided commentary.

• *Begin facing the...*

Exterior: The cathedral looks less like a church and more like a fortress. In fact, it was a central feature of the town's defensive walls. Notice how high the windows are (out of stone-tossing range). The simple Gothic style was typical of this region—designed to be sensitive to the anti-materialistic tastes of the local Cathars.

The top (from the gargoyles and newer, brighter bricks upward) is a fanciful, 19th-century, Romantic-era renovation. The church was originally as plain and austere as the bishop's palace (the similar, bold brick building to the right, now housing the Toulouse-Lautrec Museum). Imagine the church with a rooftop more like that of the bishop's palace.

• *Climb up to the extravagant Flamboyant Gothic entry porch.*

Entry Porch: The entry was built about two centuries after the original plain church (1494), when concerns about Cathar sensitivities were long passé. Originally colorfully painted, it provided one fancy entry.

• *Head into the cathedral's...*

Interior: The inside of the church—also far from plain—looks essentially as it did in 1500. The highlights are the vast *Last Judgment* painting (west wall, under the organ) and the ornate choir (east end).

• *Walk to the front of the altar and face the...*

Last Judgment: The oldest art in the church (1474), this is also the biggest Last Judgment painting from the Middle Ages. The dead come out of the ground, then line up (above) with a printed accounting of their good and bad deeds displayed in ledgers on their chests. Judgment, here we come. Those on the left (God's right) look confident and comfortable. Those on the right—the hedonists—look edgy. Get closer. Below, on both sides of the arch, are seven frames illustrating a wonderland of gruesome punishments sinners could suffer through while attempting to earn a second chance at salvation. Those who fail end up in the black clouds of Hell (upper right). But where's Jesus—the key figure in any Judgment Day painting? The missing arch in the middle (cut out in late-Renaissance times to open the way to a new chapel) once featured Christ overseeing all the action. Close to the entry, near the last pew, find the black-and-white image on a small stand. The picture provides a good guess at how this painting would have looked—though no one knows for sure. The assembly above (on the left) shows the heavenly hierarchy: The pope and bishops sit closest to (the missing) Jesus; then more bishops and priests—before kings—followed by monks; and then, finally, commoners like you and me. To learn more about the *Last Judgment*, tour the choir (€2, described later), which includes an audioguide with commentary on the painting.

The **altar** is the newest art in the church. But this is not the front of the church at all—you're facing west. Turn 180 degrees and head east, for Jerusalem (where most medieval churches point).

• *Stop first at the choir—a fancy, more intimate room within the finely carved stone "screen."*

The Choir: In the Middle Ages, nearly all cathedrals had ornate Gothic choir screens like this one. These highly decorated walls divided the church into a private place for clergy and a general zone for the common rabble. The screen enclosed the altar and added mystery to the Mass. In the 16th century, with the success of the Protestant movement and the Catholic Church's Counter-Reformation, choir screens were removed. (In the 20th century, the Church took things one step further, and priests actually turned and faced their parishioners.) Later, French Revolutionary atheists destroyed most of the choir screens that remained—Albi's is a rare survivor.

Pay €2 to stroll around the choir (excellent audioguide included, follow the English diagram). You'll see Old Testament figures in the Dark Ages exterior and New Testament figures in the enlightened interior. Stepping inside, marvel at the fine limestone carving. Scan each of the 72 unique little angels just above the wood-paneled choir stalls. Check out the brilliant ceiling, which hasn't been touched or restored in 500 years. A bishop, impressed by the fresco technique of the Italian Renaissance, invited seven Florentine artists to do the work. Good call.

• *Exit through the side door, next to where you paid for the choir. You'll pass a WC on your way to the...*

▲▲Toulouse-Lautrec Museum (Musée Toulouse-Lautrec)

The Palais de la Berbie (once the fortified home of Albi's archbishop) has the world's largest collection of Henri de Toulouse-Lautrec's paintings, posters, and sketches.

Cost and Hours: €5.50, audioguide-€3.50 (for most, the printed English explanations are sufficient); July-Aug daily 9:00–18:00; June and Sept daily 9:00–12:00 & 14:00–18:00; April-May daily 10:00–12:00 & 14:00–18:00; Oct and March Wed-Mon 10:00–12:00 & 14:00–17:30, closed Tue; Nov-Feb Wed-Mon 10:00–12:00 & 14:00–17:00, closed Tue; tel. 05 63 49 48 70, www.musee-toulouse-lautrec.com.

Background: Henri de Toulouse-Lautrec, born here in 1864, was crippled from youth. After he broke both legs, the lower half of his body never grew correctly. His father, once very engaged in parenting, lost interest in his son. Henri moved to the fringe of society, and therefore had an affinity for people who didn't quite fit in. He later made his mark painting the dregs of the Parisian underclass with an intimacy only made possible by a man with his life experience.

⊙ **Self-Guided Tour:** The museum displays more than 1,000 of Toulouse-Lautrec's pieces, mostly in chronological order. As you tour, use the dates of the paintings (always indicated) to tie Henri's evolution as an artist to his work. *Suite de la Visite* signs guide you through the collection, and English information sheets—available in most rooms—give plenty of background for your visit.

Past the turnstile, find three rooms dedicated to his **early years.** Your visit begins with a small collection of portraits by Toulouse-Lautrec and various other artists. In the 1880s Henri was stuck in Albi, far from any artistic action. During these pre-Paris years, he found inspiration in nature, in the pages of magazines, and through observing people. This was his Impressionistic stage. Look for works from his youth (*jeunesse*) in a glass case—the impressive doodles of a kid just 11 to 15 years young (1870s).

From here his works are displayed more or less chronologically and around themes (e.g., close friends, family members, horses, and scenes from daily life). Here's an overview of Toulouse-Lautrec's life, tied to the art you'll see:

1882: Henri moved to the big city to pursue his passion. In his early Paris works, we see his trademark shocking colors; down-and-dirty, street-life scenes emerge. Compare his art-school work and his street work: Henri augmented his classical training with vivid life experience. His subjects were from bars, brothels, and cabarets...Toto, we're not in Albi anymore. Henri was particularly fascinated by cancan dancers (whose legs moved with an agility he'd never experience), and he captured them expertly.

1880–1889: These were his exploratory years—dabbling in any style he encountered. The naked body emerges as one of his fascinations.

1890s: Henri started making some money by illustrating for magazines and newspapers. Back then, the daily happy hour included brothel visits—1892-1894 was his prostitution period. He respected the ladies, feeling both fascination and empathy toward them. The prostitutes accepted him the way he was and let him into their world...and he sketched great portraits. Notice how he shows them as real humans—they are neither glorified nor vulgarized in his works.

The last (third) room in this section is dedicated to brothels. Find the big *Au Salon de la Rue des Moulins* (1894). There are two versions: the quick sketch, then the finished studio version. With this piece, Toulouse-Lautrec arrived—no more sampling. The artist has established his unique style: colors (garish), subject matter (hidden worlds), moralism (none), oblivious to society's norms. Henri's trademark use of cardboard was simply his quick, snapshot way of working: He'd capture these slice-of-life impressions on the fly on cheap, disposable material, intending to convert them to finer canvas paintings later, in his studio. But the cardboard quickies survive as Toulouse-Lautrec masterpieces.

• *Double back through the entry, then descend into the next part of the museum. (Note: The following section may move upstairs by late 2011.)*

Lithography: Toulouse-Lautrec's bread and butter were his advertising posters. He was an innovative advertiser, creating simple, bold, and powerful lithographic images for printing posters. Your visit to this part of the museum begins on a mezzanine, where you'll find displays of his original lithograph blocks (simply prepare the stone with a backward image, apply ink—which sticks chemically to the black points—and print posters).

• *Drop down a floor and find his advertising posters, the museum's highlight.*

Posters: Four-color posters meant creating four different blocks. The Moulin Rouge poster established his business reputation in Paris—strong symbols, bold and simple: just what, where, and when. Nearby, cabaret singer and club owner Aristide Bruant (*dans son cabaret—"in his cabaret"*) is portrayed as bold and dashing.

Toulouse-Lautrec's **cane** (in a glass case near the big glass door—if you can't find it, ask the clerk) offers additional insight into this tortured artistic genius. To protect him from his self-destructive lifestyle, loved ones had him locked up in a psychiatric hospital. But, with the help of this clever hollow cane, he still got his booze. Friends would drop by with hallucinogenic absinthe, his drink of choice—also popular among many other artists of the time. With these special deliveries, he'd restock his cane, which even came equipped with a fancy little glass.

In 1901, at age 37, alcoholic, paranoid, depressed, and syphilitic, Henri de Toulouse-Lautrec returned to his mother—the only woman who ever really loved him—and died in her arms. The art world didn't mourn. Obituaries, speaking for the art establishment, basically said good riddance to Toulouse-Lautrec and his ugly art. Although no one in the art world wanted Henri's pieces, his mother and best friend recognized his genius and saved his work. They first offered it to the Louvre, which refused. Finally, in 1922, the mayor of Albi accepted the collection and hung Toulouse-Lautrec's work here in what, for more than a century, had been a boring museum of archaeology.

• *Leave the Toulouse-Lautrec Museum courtyard and turn right, then follow the cobbled path to the gardens for a good city view over the Tarn River (described next).*

More Sights in Albi

▲Albi Town View—Albi was situated here because of its river access to Bordeaux (which connected the town to the rest of the trading world). In medieval times, the fastest, most economical way to transport goods was down rivers like this. The lower, older bridge (pont Vieux) was first built in 1020. Prior to its construction, the weir (which you can see just beyond this first bridge) provided a series of stepping stones that enabled people to cross the river. Look at the bishop's palace. The garden below dates from the 17th century (when the palace at Versailles was inspiring people all over France to create fancy gardens). The palace itself grew from the 13th century until 1789, when the French Revolution ended the power of the bishops and the state confiscated the building. Since 1905, it's been a museum.

• *The last two sights are right in the town center, roughly behind the cathedral.*

St. Salvy Church and Cloister (Eglise St. Salvi et Cloître)—

Although this church (the oldest in town) is nothing special, the cloister creates a delightful space. Delicate arches surround an enclosed courtyard (open all day), providing a peaceful interlude from the shoppers that fill the pedestrian streets. Notice the church wall from the courtyard. It was the only stone building in Albi in the 11th century; the taller parts, added later, are made of brick. This is one of many appealing little courtyards hiding throughout town. In the rough-and-tumble Middle Ages, many buildings faced inward. If doors are open, you're welcome to pop into courtyards. The Hôtel Décazes (8 rue Toulouse-Lautrec, across from La Viguière restaurant) is another good example.

Market Hall (Marché Couvert)—Albi's quiet Art Nouveau market, recently renovated, is good for picnic-gathering and people-watching (Tue–Sun 8:00–14:00, closed Mon, 2 blocks from cathedral). On Saturday, a farmer's market sets up outside the market hall.

Sleeping in Albi

$$$ Hostellerie du Grand Saint Antoine**** is Albi's oldest hotel (established in 1784), and the most comfortable and traditional place I list. Guests enter an inviting, spacious lobby that opens onto an enclosed garden. Rooms are Old World cozy, with all the comforts (Db-€125, big Db-€185, suites-€225, very pricey breakfast-€18, Wi-Fi, parking-€7, a block above big place du Vigan at 17 rue Sainte-Antoine, tel. 05 63 54 04 04, fax 05 63 47 10 47, www.hotel -saint-antoine-albi.com, courriel@hotel-saint-antoine-albi.com).

$$ Hôtel Chiffre*** is a safe bet, with 38 comfortable and well-appointed rooms (Db-€78, bigger Db-€115, family rooms-

Sleep Code

(€1 = about $1.25, country code: 33)

S = Single, **D** = Double/Twin, **T** = Triple, **Q** = Quad, **b** = bathroom, **s** = shower only, ***** = French hotel rating system (0–4 stars). Unless otherwise noted, credit cards are accepted and English is spoken.

To help you sort easily through these listings, I've divided the rooms into three categories based on the price for a standard double room with bath:

$$$ Higher Priced—Most rooms €90 or more.
$$ Moderately Priced—Most rooms between €60–90.
$ Lower Priced—Most rooms €60 or less.

Prices can change without notice; verify the hotel's current rates online or by email. For other updates, see www .ricksteves.com/update.

€136, some with queen-size beds, air-con, elevator, garage-€9/day, traditional restaurant, Wi-Fi in lobby, near place du Vigan at 50 rue Séré de Rivières, tel. 05 63 48 58 48, fax 05 63 47 20 61, www .hotelchiffre.com, hotel.chiffre@yahoo.fr).

$ Le Vieil Alby Hôtel-Restaurant**, in the heart of Albi's pedestrian area, has simple, well-maintained, non-smoking rooms, run by helpful Monsieur Sicard (Db-€49–66, Tb-€70, garage-€7/day, 25 rue Toulouse-Lautrec, tel. 05 63 54 14 69, fax 05 63 54 96 75, levieilalby@wanadoo.fr).

$ Hôtel Lapérouse** is a work in progress, one block from the old city and a 10-minute walk to the train station. The family-run hotel offers simple rooms; some are renovated and cheery, though I'd skip the rooms facing the busy street. There's easy parking, a quiet garden, a big pool, and *très* friendly English-speaking owners. Spring for a room with a balcony over the garden and pool (Sb/Db on street-€44, Sb/Db on garden-€57, Sb/Db on garden with deck-€65, Internet access and Wi-Fi, 21 place Lapérouse, tel. 05 63 54 69 22, fax 05 63 38 03 69, www.hotel-laperouse.com, hotel.laperouse@wanadoo.fr).

Eating in Albi

Albi is filled with reasonable restaurants that serve a rich local cuisine. Be warned: "Going local" here is likely to get you *tripe* (cow intestines), *andouillette* (sausages made from pig intestines), *foie de veau* (calf liver), and *tête de veau* (calf's head). Choose a restaurant or select one of the many cafés on the lively place du Vigan.

For a choice of traditional restaurants, survey the places along rue Toulouse-Lautrec (2 blocks from Hôtel St. Clair).

Le Papillon Restaurant, a jazzy, inviting, Cathar-cool eatery under medieval stones and timbers, fuses Californian and French cuisines. It's the dream come true for two guys from California—while Michael Gabel cooks, his partner, Rick Perry, serves. Seafood is their forte, though their meat dishes are tasty, too. There are also good vegetarian options, and the salads are tops. Reserve for both lunch and dinner (€19–29 *menus*, €15–20 evening *plats*, open Thu–Sat for dinner, Tue–Sat for lunch, 1 rue Toulouse-Lautrec, tel. 05 63 43 10 77).

Le Tournesol is a good lunch option for vegetarians, since that's all they do. The food is organic and delicious, the setting is bright with many windows, and the service is friendly (open Fri for lunch and dinner, Tue–Thu and Sat for lunch only, closed Sun–Mon, 11 rue de l'Ort en Salvy, tel. 05 63 38 38 14).

Le Clos Sainte Cécile, hidden behind the cathedral, is an old school transformed into a family-run restaurant. Friendly waiters serve delicious dishes in their large, shady garden (€16–23 *menus*, closed Tue–Wed, 3 rue du Castelviel, tel. 05 63 38 19 74).

Restaurant Stéphane Laurens (La Pause) sits alone in a quiet pedestrian area immediately north of the cathedral. It has a handsome interior along with a peaceful terrace offering point-blank views of the cathedral. The focus here is on wines (€9 lunch *plats*, €19–25 dinner *menus*, closed Sun–Mon, 10 place Monseigneur Mignot, tel. 05 63 43 62 41).

Albi Connections

You'll connect to just about any destination through Toulouse.

From Albi by Train to: Toulouse (11/day, 70 minutes), **Carcassonne** (10/day, 2–3 hours, change in Toulouse), **Sarlat** (6/day, 5–7 hours with 2–3 changes, some require bus from Souillac to Sarlat), **Paris** (6/day, 6–7.5 hours, change in Toulouse, also night train).

Near Albi

▲West of Albi: Route of the *Bastides* (La Route des Bastides Albigeoises)

The hilly terrain north of Albi was tailor-made for medieval villages to organize around for defensive purposes. Here, scores of fortified villages (*bastides*) spill over hilltops, above rivers, and between wheatfields, creating a worthwhile detour for drivers. These planned communities were the medieval product of community efforts organized by local religious or military leaders. Most

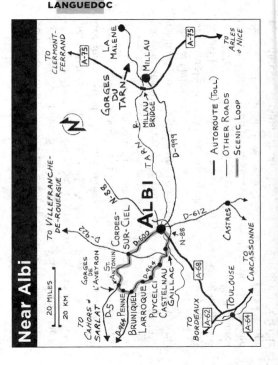

Near Albi

bastides were built during the Hundred Years' War (see sidebar on page 255) to establish a foothold for French or British rule in this hotly contested region, as well as to provide stability to benefit trade. Unlike other French hill towns, *bastides* were not the product of a safe haven provided by a castle. Instead, they were a premeditated effort by a community to collectively construct houses as a planned defensive unit, *sans* castle.

Connect these *bastides* as a day trip from Albi, or as you drive between Albi and the Dordogne. I've described the top *bastides* in the order you'll reach them on these driving routes.

Day Trip from Albi: For a good loop route from Albi, cross the 22 Août 1944 bridge and follow signs to *Cordes-sur-Ciel* (allow 30 minutes). The view of Cordes as you approach is memorable, but that's as close as I'd get to this overrun town (especially on weekends, or anytime July–Aug). From Cordes, follow signs to *Saint-Antonin-Noble-Val*, an appealing, flat "hill town" on the river, with few tourists. Then pass vertical little Penne, Bruniquel (signed from Saint-Antonin-Noble-Val), Larroque, Puycelci (my favorite), and, finally, Castelnau-de-Montmiral (with a lovely main square), before returning to Albi. Each of these places is worth exploring if you have the time.

On the Way to the Dordogne: For a one-way scenic route north to the Dordogne that includes many of the same *bastides*, leave Albi, head toward Toulouse, and make time on the free A-68. Exit at Gaillac, go to its center, and track D-964 to Castelnau-de-Montmiral, Puycelci, and on to Bruniquel. From here you can head directly to Caussade on D-118 and D-964, then to Cahors on A-20 or D-820 (and on to Sarlat if that or the river villages are your destination). Or, if you're into this scenic drive and not pushed for time, continue north on D-115 through the beautiful Gorges de l'Aveyron to Saint-Antonin-Noble-Val, making time to explore this fine town. From Saint-Antonin, you can follow D-5 and D-926 to Caussade, then take N-20 to Cahors.

Cordes-sur-Ciel—It's hard to resist this brilliantly situated hill town just 15 miles north of Albi, but I would (in high season, at least). Enjoy the fantastic view on the road from Albi, but go no closer. Cordes, once an important Cathar base, has slipped over the boutique-filled edge to the point where it's hard to find the medieval town. Plus, it's jammed on weekends and every day the summer (July–Aug).

Bruniquel—This overlooked, *très* photogenic, but less-tended village will test your thighs as you climb the lanes upward to the château (€2.50, April–Sept daily 10:00–12:30 & 14:00–18:00, closed Oct–March). Don't miss the dramatic view up to the village from the river below as you drive along D-964. The mellow **$$ L'Etape du Château** rents out cheap, big, and adequately comfortable rooms (Db-€60–70, Tb-€80–100, Qb-€100–120, includes breakfast, Wi-Fi, sauna, tel. 05 63 67 25 00, www.etapeduchateau.com, etapeduchateau@orange.fr). They also run a laid-back restaurant (€10 salads, €12–17 *plats, menus* from €17).

▲**Puycelci**—This town crowns a bluff surrounded only by green (20 minutes north of Gaillac). Drive to the top, where you'll find easy parking and an unspoiled, level village with a couple of cafés, one real restaurant, a small grocery, a happy bakery (selling great cookies and small cartons of the local sorbet), a few *chambres d'hôtes*, and one sharp little hotel.

Stroll through the village, starting at the parking lot. Enter the village, passing the recommended Puycelci Roc Café, and make your way through town. At the opposite side of the village, a rampart walk circles counterclockwise back to the parking lot, where an orientation table explains what's in the distance. The park-like ramparts come with picnic benches and grand vistas. It's a good place to listen to the birds and feel the wind.

As you wander, consider the recent history of an ancient town like this. In 1900, 2,000 people lived here with neither running water nor electricity. Then things changed. Half of all French men lost their lives in World War I; Puycelci didn't escape this fate, as the monument (by the parking lot) attests. By 1968 the village was down to three families. But then running water replaced the venerable cisterns, and things started looking up. Today, there is still almost no commercial activity, but the town has a stable population of 110, all marveling at how the value of their land has skyrocketed.

Eating and Sleeping in Puycelci: **Puycelci Roc Café**, at the parking lot, has café fare, a warm interior, and pleasant outdoor tables (daily for dinner, Sat–Wed for lunch, tel. 05 63 33 13 67).

A night in Puycelci is my idea of a vacation. **$$ L'Ancienne Auberge** is *the* place to eat and sleep, with eight surprisingly smart and comfortable rooms, a country-classy restaurant, a cozy *bistrot* with a fireplace you could walk into, and two outdoor patios (€11.50 lunch *menu*, dinner *plats* from €13, *menus* from €24). Owner/chef Dorothy moved here from New Jersey many years ago and is eager to share her cuisine and her passion for this region (Db–€70–125, air-con, free Wi-Fi, place de l'Eglise, tel. 05 63 33 65 90, fax 05 63 33 21 12, www.ancienne-auberge.com, caddack@aol.com).

$$ Delphine de Laveleye Chambres is another solid choice, with three homey rooms around a small garden and pool, and a three-room *gîte* (Db–€60–75, Tb–€90–125, *gîte*–€600/week, cash only, Wi-Fi, cooking classes, tel. 05 63 33 13 65, mobile 06 72 92 69 59, www.chezdelphine.com, delphine@chezdelphine.com).

Castelnau-de-Montmiral—This overlooked village has quiet lanes leading to a perfectly preserved *bastide* square surrounded by fine arcades and filled with brick half-timbered facades. Ditch your car below and wander up to the square, where a restaurant, a café, and a small *patisserie* await. Have a drink or lunch on the square at the simple **Auberge des Arcades** café (€10 salads, €12 lunch *menu*, open daily, tel. 05 63 33 20 88) or at the fancier **Restaurant des Consuls** (€12–15 *plats*, €29 *menus*, closed Wed and Sun, tel. 05 63 40 63 55).

East of Albi

Two hours east of Albi lies a hauntingly beautiful region unknown to most Americans. Mountains, rivers, and *Brigadoon*-like villages conspire to give the adventurous nature lover a true experience of *la France profonde.*

Gorges du Tarn—Adventure-lovers can canoe, hike, or drive the beautiful Tarn River Gorge by heading east from Albi to Millau, then following the gorge all the way to St. Enimie. Roads are slow but spectacular.

The best base for canoeing is from tiny La Malène (on the way to St. Enimie, 25 miles northeast of Millau). In La Malène, **Company Canoë 2000** rents what you need to run the mellow river (down the path to the right of bridge, tel. 04 66 48 57 71); the 8- or 11-kilometer trips (about 5 or 7 miles) have the best views (€28–33 per canoe). Take your lunch and picnic along the way. If you'd rather not paddle a canoe, you can take a Batelier boat (leaves from bridge, seats 5–6 people, ask for a boatman who speaks a leetle English).

Sleeping in La Malène: Stay at the simple but comfortable **$ Auberge de l'Embarcadère** (Db–€45, Tb–€52, tel. 04 66 48 51

03, fax 04 66 48 58 94, Aubergelembarcadere48@ornage.fr) or in the rustic-luxurious **$$$ Manoir de Montesquiou**, run entirely by one family. Dad manages the hotel, Mom is the head chef, and the three sisters serve your meals and run the bar (Db–€75–112, suites fit for a queen–€148, extra bed–€18, you'll be expected to dine at its great restaurant, *menus* from €24, tel. 04 66 48 51 12, fax 04 66 48 50 47, www.manoir-montesquiou.com, montesquiou@demeures -de-lozere.com).

Millau Bridge (Viaduc de Millau)—Completed in 2005, the sleek, futuristic 1.5-mile-long suspension bridge, which shoots across the Tarn River Valley, is the world's highest at 885 feet. A modern-day Pont du Gard, the Millau Bridge was built as a critical link in the A-75 autoroute, which connects Paris with the Mediterranean and Barcelona. A quarter-million tons of concrete were used to set the supporting pillars, with the tallest rising 1,125 feet—taller than the Eiffel Tower (in fact, it was built by the same construction company that erected the Eiffel Tower in 1889). The bridge's British architect, Lord Norman Foster, also designed London's egg-shaped City Hall, as well as Berlin's equally glassy Reichstag Parliament dome (bridge always open; current car toll about €6, or €7.50 in July–Aug; bridge is 70 miles northeast of Albi on A-75).

Carcassonne

Medieval Carcassonne is a 13th-century world of towers, turrets, and cobblestones. Europe's ultimate walled fortress city, it's also stuffed with too many tourists. At 10:00, salespeople stand at the doors of their main-street shops, a gauntlet of tacky temptations poised and ready for their daily ration of customers. But early, late, or off-season, a quieter Carcassonne is an evocative playground for any medievalist. Forget midday—spend the night.

Locals like to believe that Carcassonne got its name this way: 1,200 years ago, Charlemagne and his troops besieged this fortress-town (then called La Cité) for several years. A cunning townsperson named Madame Carcas saved the town. Just as food was running out, she fed the last few bits of grain to the last pig and tossed him over the wall. Splat. Charlemagne's bored and frustrated forces, amazed that the town still had enough food to throw fat party pigs over the wall, decided they would never succeed in starving the people out. They ended the siege, and the city was saved. Madame Carcas *sonne*-d (sounded) the long-awaited victory bells, and La Cité had a new name: Carcas-sonne. It's a cute story... but historians suspect that Carcassonne is a Frenchified version of the town's original name (Carcas).

As a teenager on my first visit to Carcassonne, I wrote this in my journal: 'Before me lies Carcassonne, the perfect medieval city. Like a fish that everyone thought was extinct, somehow Europe's greatest Romanesque fortress city has survived the centuries. I was supposed to be gone yesterday, but here I sit imprisoned by choice—curled in a cranny on top of the wall. The wind blows away the sounds of today, and my imagination 'medievals' me. The moat is one foot over and 100 feet down. Small plants and moss upholster my throne." Avoid the midday mobs and let this place make you a kid on a rampart.

Orientation to Carcassonne

Contemporary Carcassonne is neatly divided into two cities: The magnificent La Cité (the fortified old city, with 200 full-time residents taking care of lots more tourists) and the lively Ville Basse (modern lower city). Two bridges, the busy pont Neuf and the traffic-free pont Vieux, both with great views, connect the two parts.

Tourist Information

Carcassonne's TI has three locations. The main TI, in **Ville Basse,** is useful only if you're walking to La Cité (28 rue de Verdun). A far more convenient branch is in **La Cité,** to your right as you enter the main gate (Narbonne Gate—or porte Narbonnaise). Both TIs have the same hours and telephone number (daily July–Aug 9:00–19:00, until 18:00 April–June and Sept–Oct, until 17:00 Nov–March, tel. 04 68 10 24 30). The tower across from La Cité's TI (unpredictable hours) has information on walking tours of the walls, a good book selection, and an impressive wooden model of La Cité (notice that no house rises above the fortified walls). If you're arriving by train, the most convenient TI is the small kiosk across the canal from the **train station**—though its opening times are limited and variable (generally daily July–Aug 9:00–19:00, April–June and Sept–Oct 14:00–18:00, closed Nov–March, tel. 04 68 25 94 81).

At any of the TI locations, pick up the map of La Cité, which includes a fine self-guided tour. Also ask about festivals (www .carcassonne-tourisme.com) and guided excursions to sights near Carcassonne (described later, under "Helpful Hints").

Arrival in Carcassonne

By Train: The train station (no bag storage) is located in the Ville Basse, a 30-minute walk from La Cité. You have three basic options for reaching La Cité: taxi, various shuttles, or on foot.

Taxis charge €7 for the short but worthwhile trip to La Cité but cannot enter the city walls (taxis wait in front of the train station, or you can find the taxi stand one block after crossing the canal from the station).

A *navette* (which can be a bus or a tourist train) whisks you from boulevard Omer Sarraut (a block in front of the train station, across the canal to the right) to La Cité (€1.10 round-trip, 2/hour, mid-June–Sept daily 9:30–19:30, does not run off-season). **Public transit bus #4** provides access to la Cité from the same stop (hourly, Mon–Sat). An **airport bus** departs from in front of the station and runs about hourly to Carcassonne's airport, stopping at La Cité en route (€5).

The 30-minute **walk** through the new city to La Cité ends with a good uphill climb. Walk straight out of the station, cross the canal, then cross the busy ring road, and keep straight on rue Clémenceau for about seven blocks. After place Carnot (frequent markets), turn left on rue de Verdun, walk three blocks, and turn right on the vast square Gambetta. Angle across the square, turn right after Hôtel Ibis, then cross pont Vieux (great views). Signs will guide you up rue Trivalle and rue Nadaud to La Cité.

By Car: Follow signs to *Centre-Ville*, then *La Cité*. You'll come to a large parking lot at the entry to the walled city (first hour free, €5/1–6 hours, then €1/hour after that) and a drawbridge at the Narbonne Gate, at the walled city's entrance. If staying inside the walls, you can park for free in the castle moat (facing the Narbonne Gate, turn left, then right after the small cemetery). You must show your reservation (verbal assurances won't do; the recommended Hôtels le Donjon and de la Cité will pick you up). You are allowed to drive into the city after 18:00. Theft is common—leave nothing in your car at night.

Helpful Hints

Market Days: Pleasing place Carnot in Ville Basse hosts a non-touristy open market (Tue, Thu, and Sat mornings until 13:00; Sat is the biggest).

Summer Festivals: Carcassonne becomes colorfully medieval during many special events each July and August. Highlights are

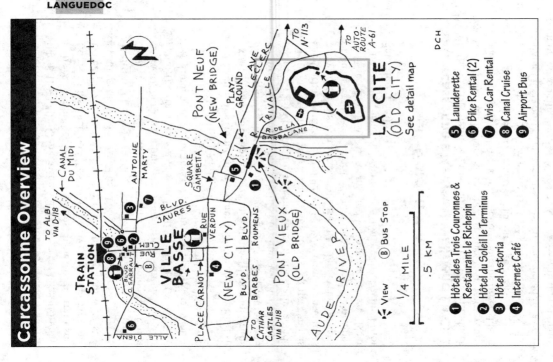

Carcassonne Overview

TO ALBI via D-118

TRAIN STATION

CANAL DU MIDI

PONT NEUF (NEW BRIDGE)

PLAY-GROUND

AVE LECLERC

TO N-113

TO AUTO-ROUTE A-61

R. TRIVALLE

R. DE LA BARBACANE

LA CITÉ (OLD CITY)
See detail map

DCH

ANTOINE MARTY

SQUARE GAMBETTA

BLVD. JAURES

RUE VERDUN

BLVD. VERDUN

BLVD. ROUMENS

VILLE BASSE (NEW CITY)

PLACE CARNOT

RUE CLEM

BLVD. O. SARRAUT

TO CATHAR CASTLES via D-118

BLVD. BARBES

PONT VIEUX (OLD BRIDGE)

AUDE RIVER

ALLE D'IENA

☀ VIEW   Ⓑ BUS STOP

0   1/4 MILE   .5 KM

1 Hôtel des Trois Couronnes & Restaurant le Richepin
2 Hôtel du Soleil le Terminus
3 Hôtel Astoria
4 Internet Café
5 Launderette
6 Bike Rental (2)
7 Avis Car Rental
8 Canal Cruise
9 Airport Bus

the *spectacle équestre* (jousting matches) and July 14 (Bastille Day) fireworks. The TI has details.

Internet Access: Most hotels have Internet access. In the Ville Basse, **Alerte Rouge** is best, with 25 computers, Wi-Fi, and a small bar (Mon–Sat 10:00–22:00, closed Sun, 73 rue de Verdun, tel. 04 68 25 20 39).

Laundry: Try **Laverie Express** (daily 8:00–22:00, 5 square Gambetta at Hôtel Ibis; from La Cité, cross pont Vieux and turn right).

Bike Rental: Evasion 2 Roues has bikes to go (€10/half-day, tandem—€20/half-day, closed Sun-Mon, 85 allée d'Iéna, tel. 04 68 11 90 40). **Génération VTT** also rents bikes (€16/day, daily 9:00–13:00 & 14:00–19:00, just beneath the train station TI kiosk, tel. 06 09 59 30 85, www.generation-vtt.com). Canalside rides are a fun and level way to spin your wheels.

Taxi: Call 04 68 71 50 50 or 04 68 71 36 36.

Car Rental: The **Avis** agency is at 52 rue A. Martyet (from train station, cross canal, then turn left on boulevard Omer Sarraut), but with a prior reservation, you can pick up your car at the train station (closed 12:00–14:00, tel. 04 68 25 05 84). Though the airport has other rental companies, it's a lousy place to pick up a car, as it's 30 minutes from Carcassonne and offices tend to be understaffed.

Guided Excursions from Carcassonne: Capable and fun English expat **Wendy Gedney**, based in Caunes-Minervois, runs day-long tours that mix sightseeing with wine-tasting and cultural experiences. She's thrilled to show you her adopted region (€75–95/person for full-day tours that usually include two wine-tastings, lunch, and visits to key sights, such as the Cathar castles; tel. 06 42 33 34 09, www.vinenvacances.com, info@vinenvacances.com). The **TI** offers excursion vans or buses each week from mid-June through mid-September to lesser-known sights, towns, and Cathar castles (see "Near Carcassonne," later; €35/half-day, €40/day, check with TI for dates and times).

Self-Guided Walk

▲▲▲Carcassonne's Medieval Walls and La Cité

While the tourists shuffle up the main street, this walk introduces you to the city with history and wonder, rather than tour groups and plastic swords. We'll sneak into the town on the other side of the wall...through the back door (see map on page 572).

Start on the asphalt outside La Cité's main entrance, the Narbonne Gate (porte Narbonnaise). You're welcomed by a contemporary-looking bust of Madame Carcas—which is actually modeled after a 16th-century original of the town's legendary first lady (for her story, see page 566).

• *Cross the bridge toward the...*

Narbonne Gate: Pause at the drawbridge and survey this immense fortification. When forces from northern France finally conquered Carcassonne, it was a strategic prize. Not taking any chances, they evicted the residents, whom they allowed to settle in the lower town (Ville Basse)—as long as they stayed across the river. (Though it's called "new," this lower town actually dates from the 13th century.) La Cité remained a French military garrison until the 18th century.

The drawbridge was made crooked to slow any attackers' rush to the main gate and has a similar effect on tourists today.

• *After crossing the drawbridge, lose the crowds and follow the cobbled path to the left and uphill, between the walls. At the first short set of stairs, climb to the outer-wall walkway and linger while facing the inner walls.*

Wall View: The Romans built Carcassonne's first wall, upon which the bigger medieval wall was constructed. Identify the ancient Roman bits by looking about two-thirds of the way up and finding the smaller rocks mixed with narrow stripes of red bricks (and no arrow slits). The outer wall that you're on was not built until the 1300s. The massive walls you see today—nearly two miles around, with 52 towers—defended an important site near the intersection of north-south and east-west trade routes.

Look over the wall and down at the moat below. Like most medieval moats, it was never filled with water (or even alligators). A ditch like this—which was originally even deeper—effectively stopped attacking forces from rolling up against the wall in their mobile towers and spilling into the city. Another enemy tactic was to "undermine" (tunnel underneath) the wall, causing a section to cave in. Notice the small, square holes at foot level along the ramparts. Wooden extensions of the rampart walkways (which we'll see later at the castle) once plugged into these holes so that townsfolk could drop nasty, sticky things on anyone tunneling in. In peacetime the area between the two walls (*les lices*) was used for medieval tournaments, jousting practice, and markets.

During La Cité's Golden Age, the 1100s, independent rulers with open minds allowed Jews and Cathars to live and prosper within the walls, while troubadours wrote poems of ideal love. This liberal attitude made for a rich intellectual life but also proved to be La Cité's downfall. The Crusades aimed to rid France of the dangerous Cathar movement (and their liberal sympathizers), which led to Carcassonne's defeat and eventual incorporation into the kingdom of France.

The walls of this majestic fortress were partially reconstructed in 1855 as part of a program to restore France's important monuments. The tidy crenellations and the pointy tower roofs are generally from the 19th-century. As you continue your wall walk to higher elevations, the lack of guardrails is striking. This would never happen in the US; in France, if you fall, it's your own fault (so be careful). Note the lights embedded in the walls. This fortress, like most important French monuments, is beautifully illuminated every night (for directions to a good nighttime view, see "Night Wall Walk to Pont Vieux" on page 575).

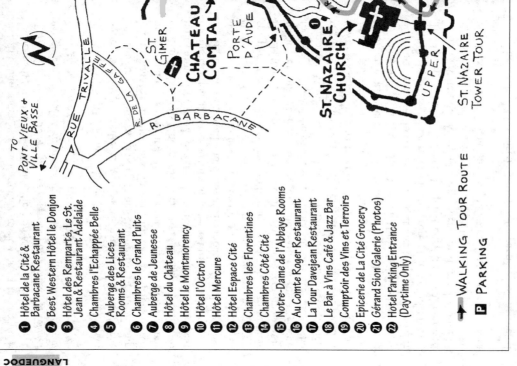

Carcassonne's La Cité

1. Hôtel de la Cité & Barbacane Restaurant
2. Best Western Hôtel le Donjon
3. Hôtel des Remparts, Le St. Jean & Restaurant Adelaide
4. Chambres l'Echappée Belle
5. Auberge des Lices Rooms & Restaurant
6. Chambres le Grand Puits
7. Auberge de Jeunesse
8. Hôtel du Château
9. Hôtel le Montmorency
10. Hôtel l'Octroi
11. Hôtel Mercure
12. Hôtel Espace Cité
13. Chambres les Florentines
14. Chambres Côté Cité
15. Notre-Dame de l'Abbaye Rooms
16. Au Comte Roger Restaurant
17. La Tour Davejean Restaurant
18. Le Bar à Vins Café & Jazz Bar
19. Comptoir des Vins et Terroirs
20. Epicerie de La Cité Grocery
21. Gérard Sion Galerie (Photos)
22. Hotel Parking Entrance (Daytime Only)

→ WALKING TOUR ROUTE

P PARKING

- You could keep working your way around the walls, and finish with the five Roman towers just before you return to the starting point. Walking the entire circle between the inner and outer gate is a terrific 20–30-minute stroll (and fantastic after dark).

But for this tour, we'll stop at the first entrance possible into La Cité, the...

Inner Wall Gate: The wall has the same four gates it had in Roman times. Before entering, notice the squat tower on the

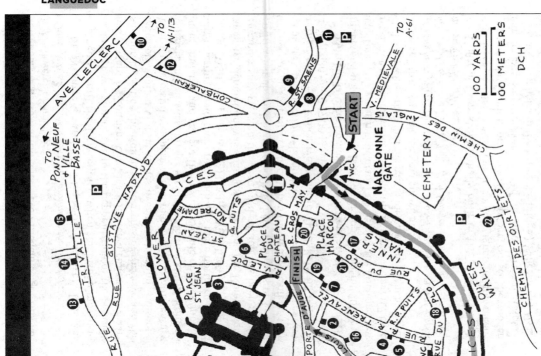

outer wall—this was a "barbican" (placed opposite each inner gate for extra protection). Barbicans were always semicircular—open on the inside to expose anyone who breached the outer defenses. Invading today is far easier than in the good old days. Make note of the holes in the barbican for supporting a wood catwalk (you'll see a good example soon). As you leave the square gate room to enter the town, look up to see a slot for the portcullis (the big iron grate), and the frame for a heavy wooden door.

Once safely inside, look back up at the inner wall tower to view *beaucoup* narrow arrow slits—even if enemies got this far, they still weren't home free.

• *Opposite the tower, work your way around to the entry of the...*

St. Nazaire Church (Basilique St. Nazaire): This was a cathedral until the 18th century, when the bishop moved to the lower town. Today, due to the depopulation of the basically dead-except-for-tourism Cité, it's not even a functioning parish church. Notice the Romanesque arches of the nave and the delicately vaulted Gothic arches over the altar and transepts. After its successful conquest of this region in the 13th-century Albigensian Crusades, France set out to destroy all the Romanesque churches and replace them with Gothic ones—symbolically asserting its northern rule with this more northern style of church. With the start of the Hundred Years' War in 1337, the expensive demolition was abandoned. Today, the Romanesque remainder survives, and the destroyed section has been rebuilt Gothic, which makes it one of the best examples of Gothic architecture in southern France. When the lights are off (as they often are), the interior—lit only by candles and 14th-century stained glass—is evocatively medieval (daily 9:00–11:45 & 14:00–18:30, until 17:00 in winter).

Hôtel de la Cité: Located 50 steps from St. Nazaire Church, this beyond-posh hotel sits where the Bishop's Palace did 700 years ago. Today, it's a worthwhile detour to see how the privileged few travel. You're free to wander, so find the library-cozy bar (€7 beer, €8 glass of wine), then find the rear garden and turn right for super wall views that you can't see from anywhere else.

• *From here, follow the main road (rue St. Louis) for several blocks, merge right onto rue Port d'Aude, then look for a small castle-view terrace on your left a block up.*

Château Comtal: Originally built in 1125, Carcassonne's third layer of defense was completely redesigned in later reconstructions. From this impressive viewpoint you can see the wooden rampart extensions that once circled the entire city wall. (Notice the empty peg holes to the left of the bridge.) When *Robin Hood: Prince of Thieves*, starring Kevin Costner, was filmed here in 1990, the entire city was turned into a film set. Locals enjoyed playing bit parts and seeing their château labeled "Nottingham Castle" in the fanciful film.

Château Comtal is open to the public and makes for a worthwhile visit. An intro film—well-done, with big sound—sets the table for your visit (sit on the left to read English subtitles). Next is a room-size model of La Cité, after which a self-guided tour leads you around the inner ramparts of Carcassonne's defenses, allowing you to see the underpinnings of towers and catwalks that hung from the walls. The views are terrific. Your visit ends with a museum showing bits of St. Nazaire Church and fragments from important homes (€8, €6 audioguide for two, daily April–Sept 10:00–18:30, Oct–March 9:30–17:00, last entry 45 minutes before closing, tel. 04 68 11 75 87).

Fifty yards away, opposite the entrance to the castle, is...

Place du Château: This busy little square sports a modest statue honoring the man who saved the city from deterioration and neglect in the 19th century. The bronze model circling the base of the statue shows Carcassonne's walls as they looked before the 1855 reconstruction by Eugène Viollet-le-Duc.

Facing the château entry, place du Grand Puits lies a block to your right. It's named for the oldest of Carcassonne's 22 wells that served the city in the Middle Ages. Behind you, the main drag leads down to the Narbonne Gate, where you began this walk.

Sights in Carcassonne

▲▲▲**Night Wall Walk to Pont Vieux**—Save some post-dinner energy for a don't-miss walk around the same walls you visited today (great dinner picnic sites as well). The effect at night is mesmerizing: The embedded lights become torches and unfamiliar voices become the enemy. End at pont Vieux for a floodlit fantasy, and you can do no better. The best route is a partial circumnavigation clockwise between the walls. Start at the Narbonne Gate, and follow my self-guided walk (described earlier) to the Inner Wall Gate. Don't enter through this gate; instead, continue your walk between the walls around La Cité (this section is occasionally closed; if so, you'll have to make your way through the village and out the rear along rue de la Porte d'Aude to meet up with the route described from here).

In about five minutes, you'll walk through a narrow passage behind Château Comtal and come to a ramp leading down; look for a hard left at the bottom of a cobbled decline, just before the path rises back up. This ramp leads all the way down past a church to rue de la Barbacane, where you'll turn right (follow *Centre–Ville* sign) to reach pont Vieux and exceptional views of floodlit Carcassonne. Return from pont Vieux the same way you came, then complete your clockwise walk between the walls back to the Narbonne Gate. For an easier return climb, cross the bridge and continue straight on rue Trivalle, then veer right up rue Nadaud and track the walls.

Gérard Sion Galerie—Duck into this impressive photo gallery before selecting which Cathar castles you want to visit (brilliant shots of many monuments in Languedoc, generally open daily 10:00–19:00, just up from place Marcou at 27 rue du Pló).

Canal du Midi—Completed in 1681, this sleepy 155-mile canal connects France's Mediterranean and Atlantic coasts and runs right by the train station in Carcassonne. Before railways, Canal du Midi was clogged with commercial traffic—today, it entertains only pleasure craft. Look for the slow-moving hotel barges strewn with tanned and well-fed vacationers. Small boats that ferry tourists along the canal leave from in front of the train station (€8/1.5 hours, €10/2.5 hours, 2–5/day, April–Oct, closed Mon, tel. 06 07 74 04 57). A better way to experience the canal is on a relaxed bike ride along the level towpath (for bike rental, see page 570).

Nightlife in Carcassonne

For relief from all the medieval kitsch, savor a drink in four-star, library-meets-bar ambience at the **Hôtel de la Cité** bar (€7 beer, €8 wine, place de l'Eglise). To taste the liveliest square, with loads of tourists and strolling musicians, sip a drink or nibble a dessert on **place Marcou.** To be a medieval poet, share a bottle of wine in your own private niche somewhere remote on the ramparts.

Le Bar à Vins (also recommended later, under "Eating in Carcassonne") offers jazz, good wines by the glass for €2.30, and a young crowd enjoying a garden in the moonshadow of the wall... without any tourists (open daily until 2:00 in the morning during high season).

Comptoir des Vins et Terroirs is a more "adult" place for a good glass of wine. Run by an English-speaking sommelier, this trendy wine bar serves a creative selection of local wines and tapas at reasonable prices (open daily 12:00–23:00, even later in summer, across from Auberge de Jeunesse hostel at 3 rue du Comte Roger, tel. 04 68 26 44 76).

For a fine before- or after-dinner drink and floodlit wall views, stop by the recommended **Hotel du Château's** broad terrace, below the porte Narbonnaise (2 rue Camille Saint-Saëns).

Sleeping in Carcassonne

(€1 = about $1.25, country code: 33)

Sleep within or near the old walls, in La Cité. I've also listed a pair of hotels near the train station. In the summer, when La Cité is jammed with tourists, think of sleeping in quieter Caunes-Minervois (you'll find my suggestions on page 580). Top prices listed are for July and August, when the town is packed. At other times of the year, prices drop and there are generally plenty of rooms.

In La Cité

Two pricey hotels, three good B&Bs, and an excellent youth hostel offer a full range of rooms inside the walls.

$$$ Hôtel de la Cité**** offers 61 rooms with deluxe everything in a beautiful building next to St. Nazaire Church. Peaceful gardens, a swimming pool, royal public spaces, an elegant restaurant, and reliable luxury are yours—for a price (deluxe Db-€450–575, suites-€750–1,400, extra adult-€80, breakfast-€28, air-con, garage-€21/day, place Auguste-Pierre Pont, tel. 04 68 71 98 71, fax 04 68 71 50 15, www.hoteldelacite.com, reservations@hoteldelacite.com).

$$$ Best Western Hôtel le Donjon**** has 62 pricey but well-appointed rooms, a polished lobby with a full bar, and a great location inside the walls. Rooms are split between two different buildings in La Cité (the main building and the cheaper Hôtel des Remparts annex a few blocks away). The main building is more appealing, and the rooms with terraces on the garden are delightful (main building Db-€125–145, Db suite-€160–220, Tb-€165–185, €20/extra person; annex Db-€105–125; look for Web deals, air-con, elevator, free Wi-Fi, Internet access, private parking-€8, 2 rue Comte Roger, tel. 04 68 11 23 00, fax 04 68 25 06 60, www.hotel-donjon.fr, info@bestwestern-donjon.com).

$$$ Chambres l'Echappée Belle is an oasis of peace in the center of La Cité. Three traditional, comfy rooms have wood floors, queen-size beds, jet showers, and air-conditioning. Serious owners Johanna and Bruce, originally from Scotland, take good care of their guests (Db-€85–125, includes breakfast, two-night minimum May–Sept, Wi-Fi, near St. Nazaire Church, just off rue du Plô at 5 rue Raymond Roger Trencavel, tel. 04 68 25 33 40, www.lechappeebelle.co.uk, info@lechappeebelle.co.uk). Call ahead to arrange check-in time (usually after 16:00).

$$ Auberge des Lices hides two lovely rooms above its restaurant, with high ceilings, exposed beams, and stone walls (Db with basilica views-€80, larger Db with rampart views-€140, €20/extra person up to five, air-con, 3 rue Raymond Roger Trencavel, tel. 04 68 72 34 07, fax 04 68 72 61 55, www.blasco.fr, leslices@blasco.fr).

$ Chambres le Grand Puits, across from Hôtel des Remparts, is a splendid value. It has one cute double room and two cavernous apartment-like rooms that could sleep five, with kitchenette, private terrace, and sweet personal touches. Inquire in the small boutique, and say *bonjour* to happy-go-lucky Nicole (Sb/Db-€50–70, Tb-€68–80, Qb-€78–90, includes self-serve breakfast, cash only, 8 place du Grand Puits, tel. 04 68 25 16 67, http://legrandpuits.free.fr, nicole.trucco@club-internet.fr).

$ The **Auberge de Jeunesse** (youth hostel) is big, clean, and well-run, with an outdoor garden courtyard, a self-service kitchen, a TV room, bar, a washer/dryer, bike rental, Internet access, Wi-Fi, and a welcoming ambience. If you ever wanted to bunk down in a hostel, do it here—all ages are welcome. Only summer is tight; reserve ahead. Non-members must purchase the €10 hostel card (bunk in 4- to 6-bed dorm-€22, first come, first served; includes sheets and breakfast, open all day, rue du Vicomte Trencavel, tel. 04 68 25 23 16, fax 04 68 71 14 84, www.fuaj.org or www.hihostels.com, carcassonne@fuaj.org).

Just Outside La Cité

Sleeping just outside La Cité offers the best of both worlds: quick access to the ramparts, less-claustrophobic surroundings, and easy parking.

The first three hotels are run by the same family and offer travelers a great range of price options. An easy walk to La Cité, they all have air-conditioning, offer free Internet access and Wi-Fi, and charge €10 for breakfast and €10 for parking. The first two come with a snazzy pool (heated all year), a Jacuzzi, and view terraces to the walls of Carcassonne (www.hotels-carcassonne.net, contact @hotels-carcassonne.net)

$$$ Hôtel du Château*** is the mothership, occupying the main building just across from La Cité's walls. It offers four-star comfort at three-star prices, with 15 over-the-top gorgeous rooms (standard Db-€140-160, superior Db-€180-200, Db with terrace on pool-€200-220, €20 less in winter, 2 rue Camille Saint-Saëns, tel. 04 68 11 38 38).

$$ Hôtel le Montmorency** is a block behind the Hôtel du Château (same reception) and has a split personality. Some rooms are razzle-dazzle (Db-€120-140) while others are more purely *Provençal* (Db-€75-95, Tb-€105-115). Several rooms have views to the ramparts, and some come with private decks (2 rue Camille Saint-Saëns, tel. 04 68 11 96 70).

$$ Hôtel l'Octroi* sits on the main drag, three blocks below its sister hotels. It's the most modest of the trio, but still delivers solid comfort at reasonable rates (Db-€70-80, Tb-€90, 106 avenue du Général Leclerc, tel. 04 68 25 29 08).

$$$ Hôtel Mercure*** hides a block behind the Hôtel le Montmorency, a five-minute walk to La Cité. It rents 80 over-priced, snug-but-comfy, air-conditioned rooms and has a refreshing garden, a good-sized pool, big elevators, and a warm bar-lounge. A few rooms have views of La Cité (small Db-€115-145, bigger Db-€145-185, pay Internet access and Wi-Fi, includes parking, 18 rue Camille Saint-Saëns, tel. 04 68 11 92 82, fax 04 68 71 11 45, www.mercure.com, h1622@accor.com).

$$$ Hôtel des Trois Couronnes*** offers 40 good rooms with terrific views up to La Cité (and 28 non-view rooms that you don't want), all trapped in an ugly concrete shell. It's a 15-minute walk below La Cité, and 20 minutes on foot from the train station (Db with view–€125-150, €25 less for no view, air-con, elevator, free Wi-Fi, indoor pool with views, garage–€9, 2 rue des Trois Couronnes—see map on page 569, tel. 04 68 25 36 10, fax 04 68 25 92 92, www.hotel-destroiscouronnes.com, hotel3couronnes @wanadoo.fr). The reasonably priced restaurant also has good views (see "Eating in Carcassonne," later).

On Rue Trivalle

These places are 10 minutes below La Cité and 20 minutes from the train station on foot.

$$ Hôtel Espace Cité**, two blocks downhill from Hôtel le Montmorency (described earlier), is a good value (though a bit soulless). With 48 small, modern, shiny rooms, this place is well-run and handy for drivers (Db–€62-85, Tb–€78-95, Qb–€93-120, air-con, free Internet access and Wi-Fi, includes parking, 132 rue Trivalle, tel. 04 68 25 24 24, fax 04 68 25 17 17, www.hotel espacecite.fr, infos@hotelespacecite.fr).

$$ Chambres les Florentines is a terrific five-room bed-and-breakfast run by welcoming Madame Mistler. The rooms are spacious, homey, and affordable. One room comes with a big deck and million-dollar views of La Cité (Db–€75-85, view Db–€115, includes breakfast, Wi-Fi, 71 rue Trivalle, tel. 04 68 71 51 97, www .lesflorentines.net, lesflorentines11@gmail.com).

$$ Chambres Côté Cité is a traditional place with canopy beds and big, high-ceilinged rooms off an interior courtyard. Parking is free and easy, and Madame Mayer is an elegant host (Db–€80-100, Wi-Fi, 81 rue Trivalle, tel. 04 68 71 09 65, www .cotecite.com, info@cotecite.com).

$ At Notre-Dame de l'Abbaye, you can sleep like a monk (with about the same level of comfort). This hostel-like abbey rents basic, spotless rooms—some with good views to the ramparts—that surround a quiet cloister. Lots of school groups stay here, but they're kept in the other wing (dorm bed–€17, S–€26-36, Sb–€38-46, D–€28-38, Db with tiny bathroom–€48-55, Tb/Qb–€64-72, breakfast–€4, credit cards OK, €10 dinners, 103 rue Trivalle, tel. 04 68 25 16 65, fax 04 68 11 47 01, www.abbaye-carcassonne.com, contact@abbaye-carcassonne.com).

Near the Train Station

$$$ Hôtel du Soleil le Terminus***, across from the train station, is turn-of-the-century faded-grand. The lobby reminds me of a train-station waiting hall. Rooms are big and comfortable, with high ceilings and prices (standard Db-€100-125, superior Db-€125-145, air-con, elevator, pay Internet access and Wi-Fi, basement pool, secure parking-€9, lots of groups, rental bikes, 2 avenue Maréchal Joffre, tel. 04 68 25 25 00, fax 04 68 72 53 09, www.hotels-du-soleil.com, reservation@soleilvacances.com).

$ Hôtel Astoria** offers some of the cheapest hotel beds that I list in town, divided between a main hotel and an annex across the street. The shiny tiled rooms are modern and clean, with foam mattresses. Call ahead; it's popular. From the train station, walk across the canal, turn left, and go two blocks (D-€35-46, Ds-€46-64, Db-€56-75, Tb/Qb-€68-93, free parking, free Wi-Fi, 18 rue Tourtel, tel. 04 68 25 31 38, fax 04 68 71 34 14, www.astoria carcassonne.com, hotel-astoria@wanadoo.fr).

Near Carcassonne, in Caunes-Minervois

To experience unspoiled, tranquil Languedoc, sleep surrounded by vineyards in the authentic-feeling village of Caunes-Minervois. Comfortably nestled in the foothills of the Montagne Noire, Caunes-Minervois—a 25-minute drive from Carcassonne—offers an eighth-century abbey (complete with Internet access), two cafés, a good pizzeria, a handful of wineries, and very few tourists. My two recommendations sit side by side in the heart of the village, and their owners are eager to help you explore their region.

$$ Hôtel d'Alibert**, in a 15th-century home with ambience galore, has a mix of nicely renovated Old World traditional rooms. It's managed with a relaxed *je ne sais quoi* by Frédéric "call me Fredo" Dalibert (small Db-€52, standard Db-€72, huge Db-€82, extra person-€10, free breakfast and 10 percent discount if staying 2 or more nights and booking on the Web, place de la Mairie, tel. 04 68 78 00 54, frederic.dalibert@wanadoo.fr). Eat lunch or dinner in his terrific restaurant (closed Sun-Mon).

$$ L'Ancienne Boulangerie is a relaxed place with thoughtfully appointed rooms and a breakfast terrace that will slow your pulse. Retired Irishmen Garreth and Roy run the joint while their wives work back home—these are two happy blokes (Sb-€50, Db-€65, lofty family room-€70/couple and €10/child, includes breakfast, Wi-Fi, rue St. Genes, tel. 04 68 78 01 32, www.ancienne boulangerie.com, ancienne.boulangerie@free.fr).

Eating in Carcassonne

For a social outing in La Cité, take your pick from a food circus of basic eateries on a leafy courtyard—often with strolling musicians in the summer—on lively **place Marcou** (just inside the front gate and up to the left). If rubbing elbows with too many tourists makes you edgy, go local and dine below in La Ville Basse (the new city).

Cassoulet (described on page 551) is the traditional must; big salads can provide a light yet rich alternative.

My favorite place for dinner in La Cité is on **place St. Jean,** where two good eateries sit side by side, each offering excellent value with view tables from their outside terraces to the floodlit Château Comtal. **Le St. Jean** attracts a lively and loyal following with its well-presented bistro fare at reasonable prices in a *très* warm interior. Come early or book ahead (€15–24 *menus,* €8 kid *menu,* daily, tel. 04 68 47 42 43). **Restaurant Adelaïde** serves a good €14, three-course *menu* with cassoulet, as well as tasty *plats* for €13–16. The interior blends orange walls and heavy beams (daily, tel. 04 68 47 66 61).

Hôtel de la Cité's **Barbacane Restaurant** owns Carcassonne's only Michelin star (€80 *menus;* see "Sleeping in Carcassonne," earlier).

Au Comte Roger's quiet elegance seems out of place in this touristy town. For half the price of the Barbacane, you can celebrate a special occasion. Chef Roger specializes in fresh products and Mediterranean cuisine. Ask for a table in the courtyard or dine inside with modern art, but book ahead (€35 and €45 *menus,* closed Sun–Mon, 14 rue St. Louis, tel. 04 68 11 93 40). Don't confuse this place with a part of the Hôtel le Donjon, called Le Comte Roger.

Auberge des Lices, a shy yet popular place hidden down a quiet lane, has a feminine interior and a peaceful courtyard. It manages a delicate balance of price and quality for traditional cuisine (€19–38 *menus,* closed Tue–Wed, 3 rue Raymond Roger Trencavel, tel. 04 68 72 34 07).

La Tour Davejean—surprisingly, not named for its owners (or a musical duo), but for the tower it hides—is a brown, wicker-warm, intimate escape. Diners climb one level to enjoy a decent meal at fair prices, either inside or on a quiet terrace (€13 lunch *menu,* dinner *menus* from €16, €2.50 wines by the glass, good cassoulet and desserts, closed Tue–Wed, 32 rue du Plô, tel. 04 68 71 60 63).

Restaurant le Richepin, just outside La Cité in Hôtel des Trois Couronnes (described earlier, under "Sleeping in Carcassonne"), gives you a panorama of Carcassonne—from the top floor of a concrete hotel (€19 or €25 *menus,* open daily for dinner only, call ahead, 2 rue des Trois Couronnes).

Le Bar à Vins, popular with the twenty- and thirty-some-thing set at night, is tucked away in a pleasant garden just inside the wall but away from the crowds. It serves an enticing selection of open wines (€2.30 a glass), €9–12 appetizers and tapas, and €6 sandwiches (daily 10:00–2:00 in the morning, closes earlier off-season, closed Nov–Jan, 6 rue du Plô, tel. 04 68 47 38 38).

Picnics: Basic supplies can be gathered at the shops along the main drag (generally open until at least 19:30). For your beggar's banquet, picnic on the city walls. For fast, cheap, hot food, look for places on the main drag that have quiche and pizza to go. Pick up limited groceries at **Epicerie de La Cité** (daily 10:00–19:00, shorter hours off-season).

Carcassonne Connections

From Carcassonne by Train to: Albi (10/day, 2–3 hours, change in Toulouse), **Collioure** (8/day, 2 hours, most require change in Narbonne), **Sarlat** (4/day, 5.5–7.5 hours, 1–2 changes, some require bus from Souillac to Sarlat), **Arles** (8/day, 3–4 hours, most with transfer in Narbonne or Nîmes), **Nice** (4/day, 6–7 hours), **Paris** (Gare Montparnasse or Gare de Lyon; 7/day, 5–6.5 hours, transfer in Toulouse, Narbonne, Montpellier, or Beziers; Gare d'Austerlitz: 1/day direct, 8.5 hours; 1 night train, 7.75 hours), **Toulouse** (hourly, 1 hour), **Barcelona** (5/day, 4–5 hours, change in Narbonne and Port Bou—the border town).

Near Carcassonne

The land around Carcassonne is carpeted with vineyards and littered with romantically ruined castles, ancient abbeys, and photogenic villages. The castle remains of Peyrepertuse and Quéribus make terrific stops between Carcassonne and Collioure (allow 1.5–2 hours from Carcassonne on narrow, winding roads). The gorge-sculpted village of Minerve, 40 minutes northeast of Carcassonne, works well for Provence-bound travelers.

Getting There: Public transportation is hopeless; taxis for up to six people cost €150–200 for a day-long excursion (taxi tel. 04 68 71 50 50). See page 570 for excursion bus and minivan tours to these places.

▲▲▲Châteaux of Hautes Corbières

About two hours south of Carcassonne, in the scenic foothills of the Pyrenees, lies a series of surreal, mountain-capping castle ruins. Like a Maginot Line of the 13th century, these sky-high castles were strategically located between France and the Spanish kingdom of Roussillon. As you can see by flipping through the picture books in Carcassonne tourist shops, these castles' crumbled ruins are an impressive contrast to the restored walls of La Cité. Bring a good map (lots of tiny roads) and sturdy walking shoes—prepare for a vigorous climb, and be wary of slick stones.

The most spectacular is the château of **Peyrepertuse,** where the ruins seem to grow right out from the narrow splinter of cliff. The views are sensational—you can almost reach out and touch

Near Carcassonne

Spain. Let your imagination soar, but watch your step as you try to reconstruct this eagle's nest (€5, daily July–Aug 9:00–20:30, April–June and Sept–Oct 10:00–18:30, Nov–Dec and Feb–March 10:00–17:00, closed Jan, tel. 06 71 58 63 36, www.chateau-peyrepertuse.com). Canyon-lovers will enjoy the detour to the nearby and narrow **Gorges de Galamus**, just north of St. Paul de Fenouillet. Closer to D-117, impressive **Quéribus** towers above the road and requires a steep hike. It's famous as the last Cathar castle to fall and was left useless after 1659, when the border between France and Spain was moved farther south into the high Pyrenees (same cost and hours as Peyrepertuse).

Sleeping and Eating near Peyrepertuse and Quéribus: To really get away (and I mean really), sleep in the lovely little village of Cucugnan, located between the castles. **$ L'Ecurie de Cucugnan** is a friendly bed-and-breakfast with five comfortable rooms at great rates, a view pool, and a shady garden (Sb-€54, Db-€60, includes breakfast, 10 rue Achille Mir, tel. 04 68 33 37 42, ecurie .cucugnan@wanadoo.fr). For a light meal, find the boulangerie at the 17th-century windmill, where they mill their own flour and prepare delicious breads and pasta (daily 8:00–19:00, closed Mon Nov–April, Moulin du Village de Cucugnan, tel. 04 68 33 55 03).

Near Caunes-Minervois

The next two Cathar sights tie in well with a visit to Caunes-Minervois (where I recommend some accommodations—see page 580) and provide an easy excursion from Carcassonne, offering you a taste of this area's appealing countryside.

Châteaux of Lastours

Ten miles north of Carcassonne, these four ruined castles cap a barren hilltop and give drivers a handy (if less dramatic) look at the region's Cathar castles. From Carcassonne, follow signs to *Mazamet*, then *Conques-sur-Orbiel*, then *Lastours*. In Lastours you can hike to the castle or drive to a viewpoint.

Hikers park at the lot as they enter the village, walk 10 minutes upriver to the glass entry (look for *Accueil* signs), then walk 20 minutes uphill to the castles (allow at least an hour for a reasonable tour). The castles, which once surrounded a fortified village, date from the 11th century. The village welcomed Cathars (becoming a bishop's seat at one point) but paid for this "tolerance" with destruction by French troops in 1227. Everyone should make the short drive to the belvedere for a smashing panorama over the castles (€5 for access to castles and belvedere viewpoint, €2 for belvedere viewpoint only, July–Aug daily 9:00–20:00, April–June and Sept daily 10:00–18:00, Oct daily 10:00–17:00, Nov–March Sat–Sun 10:00–17:00 only, tel. 04 68 77 56 02). An idyllic lunch awaits near the lower entry at **Le Moulin,** where a small bakery has arranged a few tables serenely overlooking the river (good quiche, sandwiches, drinks, closed Thu).

▲Minerve

A one-time Cathar hideout, the spectacular village of Minerve is sculpted out of a deep canyon that provided a natural defense. Strong as it was, it couldn't keep out the Pope's armies, and the village was razed during the vicious Albigensian Crusades. The view from the small parking lot alone (€2) justifies the detour. Cross the bridge on foot, then wander into the village to its upper end and a ruined tower. A worthwhile path leads across from the tower, around the village, and down to the river (watch your step as you descend); you can re-enter the village from the riverbed at its lower end.

Minerve has two cool cafés, one hotel, a nifty little bookshop, a few wine shops, and a smattering of art galleries. You'll also find two small museums: a prehistory museum and the compact **Hurepel de Minerve**, with models from the Cathar era that effectively describe this terrible time (€3, free under 14, excellent English explanations, interesting for kids, daily April–Oct 10:00–13:00 & 14:00–18:00, rue des Martyrs, tel. 04 68 91 12 26).

Getting to Minerve: Located between Carcassonne and Béziers, Minerve is nine miles north of Olonzac and 40 minutes by car from Carcassonne. It makes for a good stop between Provence and Carcassonne.

Sleeping and Eating in Minerve: Stay here and melt into southern France (almost literally, if it's summer). **$ Relais Chantovent's** unpretentious and spotless rooms are designed for those who came to get away from it all—no phones and no TV, but generous quiet (Db-€43–55, tel. 04 68 91 14 18, fax 04 68 91 81 99, www.relaischantovent-minerve.fr, sandra.bru@orange.fr). Its sharp restaurant deserves your business and is popular, so reserve ahead (*menus* from €20, closed Sun–Mon). The **Café de la Place** provides the perfect break with tranquil terrace tables (daily until about 19:00, tel. 04 68 91 22 94).

Collioure

Surrounded by less-appealing resorts, lovely Collioure is blessed with a privileged climate and a romantic setting. By Mediterranean standards, this seaside village should be slammed—it has everything. Like an ice-cream shop, Collioure offers 31 flavors of pastel houses and 6 petite, scooped-out, pebbled beaches sprinkled with visitors. This sweet scene, capped by a winking lighthouse, sits under a once-mighty castle in the shade of the Pyrenees.

Just 15 miles from the Spanish border, Collioure (Cotlliure in Catalan) shares a common history and independent attitude with its Catalan siblings across the border. Happily French yet proudly Catalan, it flies the yellow-and-red flag of Catalunya, displays street names in French and Catalan, and sports business names with *el* and *els*, rather than *le* and *les*. Sixty years ago, most villagers spoke Catalan; today the language is enjoying a resurgence as Collioure rediscovers its roots.

Come here to unwind and regroup. Even with its crowds of vacationers in peak season (July and Aug are jammed), Collioure is what many look for when they head to the Riviera—a sunny, relaxing splash in the Mediterranean.

Planning Your Time

Check your ambition at the station. Enjoy a slow coffee on *le Med*, lose yourself in the old town's streets, compare the *gelati* shops on rue Vauban, and relax on a pebble-sand beach (waterproof shoes are helpful). And if you have a car, don't miss a drive into the hills above Collioure.

Orientation to Collioure

Most of Collioure's shopping, sights, and hotels are in the old town, across the drainage channel from Château Royal. There are good views of the old town from across the bay near the recommended Hôtel Boramar and brilliant views from the hills above.

Tourist Information

The TI hides behind the main beachfront cafés at 5 place du 18 Juin (July–Aug Mon–Sat 9:00–20:00, Sun 10:00–18:00; April–June and Sept Mon–Sat 9:00–12:00 & 14:00–19:00, closed Sun; Oct–March Tue–Sat 9:00–12:00 & 14:00–18:00, closed Sun–Mon; tel. 04 68 82 15 47, www.collioure.com).

Arrival in Collioure

By Train: Walk out of the station (no baggage storage), turn right, and follow the road downhill for about 10 minutes until you see Hôtel Frégate (directions to hotels are listed from this reference point—see "Sleeping in Collioure," later). The station ticket office has irregular hours; if they're open, pick up a schedule for any Spain side-trips or for your next destination.

By Car: Collioure is 16 miles south of Perpignan. Take the *Perpignan-Sud Sortie* exit from the autoroute and follow signs to *Argelès-sur-Mer* (also called *Argelès*), then *Collioure* (*sortie* 14). Parking is a challenge and almost impossible in summer—arrive early or late. Follow *Collioure Centre-Ville* signs, turn left onto rue de la République when you see the *Garage Renault* sign, and look for any available spots. There's a big pay lot (Parking Glacis) off rue de la République (stay right at the bottom of rue de la République and pass through a metered lot, about €1.50/hour, €10/24 hours). In high season, it's easiest to park at the remote Parking Cap

Dourats (€6/24 hours) and take the free shuttle bus into town (3/hour, 10:00–midnight). You can also ask your hotelier for parking suggestions. Once parked, make sure to take everything of value out of the car.

Helpful Hints

Market Days: Markets are held on Wednesday and Sunday mornings on place Maréchal Leclerc, across from Hôtel Fregate.

Internet Access: Try the lighthearted **Café Sola,** next to the recommended Hôtel Casa Pairal (daily, about 7:00–21:00 or later, free Wi-Fi if you buy a drink, or use their computers, 2 avenue de la République, tel. 04 68 82 55 02).

Laundry: Laverie d'Ici will do your laundry for no extra fee while you do your relaxing (9:00–12:00, closed Wed and Sun; self-service launderette open daily-8:00–21:00; 28 rue de la République, tel. 06 33 14 30 99). Another **self-serve launderette** is a block away (daily 7:00–21:00, near 10 rue de Gaulle).

Taxi: Call 04 68 82 27 80 or 04 68 82 09 30.

Car Rental: National is pricey but central, located in Garage Renault, opposite the launderette on rue de la République (allow €110/day with 250 kilometers, tel. 04 68 82 08 34).

Sights in Collioure

There's no important sight here except what lies on the beach and the views over Collioure. Indulge in a long seaside lunch, inspect the colorful art galleries, catch up on your postcards, and maybe take a hike. Don't be surprised to see French Marines playing commando in their rafts; Collioure's bay caters to more than just sun-loving tourists. Sightseeing here is best in the evening, when the sky darkens, and yellow lamps reflect warm pastels and deep blues.

View from the Beach—Walk out to the jetty's end, past the church and the little chapel, and find a seat above the beach. Collioure has been a popular place since long before your visit. For more than 2,500 years, people have fought to control its enviable position on the Mediterranean at the foot of the Pyrenees. The mountains that rise behind Collioure provide a natural defense, and its port gives it a commercial edge, making Collioure an irresistible target. A string of forts defended Collioure's landlocked side. To the left, you can see the still-standing Fort St. Elme (built by powerful Spanish king Charles V, the same guy who built El Escorial near Madrid). The 2,100-foot-high observation tower of Madeloc rises way above, front and center, and scattered ruins crown several other hilltops. To the far right, the 18th-century *citadelle,* Fort Mirador, is now home to a French Marine base. Back

Collioure

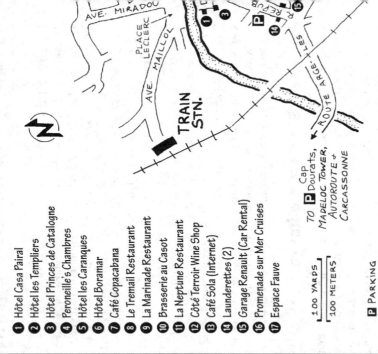

1. Hôtel Casa Pairal
2. Hôtel les Templiers
3. Hôtel Princes de Catalogne
4. Peroneille's Chambres
5. Hôtel les Caranques
6. Hôtel Boramar
7. Café Copacabana
8. Le Tremail Restaurant
9. La Marinade Restaurant
10. Brasserie au Casot
11. La Neptune Restaurant
12. Côté Terroir Wine Shop
13. Café Sola (Internet)
14. Launderettes (2)
15. Garage Renault (Car Rental)
16. Promenade sur Mer Cruises
17. Espace Fauve

100 YARDS
100 METERS

P PARKING
⋗ VIEW

to the left, that ancient windmill (1344) was originally used for grain; today it grinds out olive oil.

Collioure's medieval town gathers between its church and royal château, sandwiched defensively and spiritually between the two. The town was batted back and forth between the French and Spanish for centuries. Locals just wanted to be left alone—as Catalans, and most still do (notice the yellow-and-red Catalan flag flying above the château). It was Spanish for nearly 400 years before becoming definitively French in 1659 (*merci* to Louis XIV). After years of neglect, Collioure was rediscovered by artists drawn to its pastel houses and lovely setting. Henri Matisse, André Derain, Pablo Picasso, Georges Braque, Raoul Dufy, and Marc Chagall all parked their brushes here at one time or another. You're likely to recognize Collioure in paintings in many museums across Europe.

Château Royal (Royal Castle)—The 800-year-old castle, built over Roman ruins, served as home over the years to Majorcan kings, Crusaders, Dominican monks, and Louis XIV (who had the final say on the appearance we see now). Today it serves tourists, offering great rampart walks, views, and mildly interesting local history exhibits (€4, daily June–Sept 10:00–17:15, Oct–May 9:00–16:15, last entry 45 minutes before closing, tel. 04 68 82 06 43).

Notre-Dame des Anges (Our Lady of the Angels Church)— This waterfront church is worth a gander (daily 9:00–12:00 & 14:00–18:00). Find a pew and listen to the waves while searching your soul. Supporting a guiding light (in more than one way), the church's foundations are built into the sea, and its one-of-a-kind lighthouse–bell tower helped sailors return home safely. The highlight is its over-the-top golden altar, unusual in France but typical of Catalan churches across the border. Drop €1 in the box to the left of the altar: lights, cameras, reaction—ooh la la!

Path of Fauvism (Chemin du Fauvisme)—As you stroll Collioure's lanes, you'll occasionally see prints hanging on the walls. You're on the "Chemin du Fauvisme," where you'll find 20 copies of Derain's and Matisse's works, inspired by their stays in Collioure in 1905. The **Espace Fauve** office, across from the château at the foot of the footbridge, has fliers that identify where the copies are mounted in Collioure (June–Sept daily 9:30–12:00 & 15:00–18:00, Oct–May closed Mon and weekend mornings, quai de l'Amirauté, tel. 04 68 98 07 16). As with Arles and Vincent van Gogh, there are no original paintings by Derain or Matisse here for the public to enjoy. However, the museum in Céret has a good collection (see page 591), as does the recommended Hôtel les Templiers.

Beaches (Plages)—You'll usually find the best sand-to-stone ratio at plage St. Vincent and at plage de Port d'Avall (sporadically open paddleboat/kayak rental–€11/hour). The tiny plage de la Balette is quietest, with views of Collioure.

Wine-Tasting—Collioure and the surrounding area produce well-respected wines, and many shops offer informal tastings of the sweet Banyuls and Collioure reds and rosés. Try **Côté Terroir,** with a good selection from many wineries and fair prices (daily 10:00–13:00 & 15:00–20:00, July–Aug daily 10:00–24:00, next to Hôtel Fregate at 6 place Maréchal Leclerc, tel. 09 53 76 00 12).

Cruise—Mildly interesting **Promenade sur Mer** boat excursions provide views of Collioure from the Mediterranean as they cruise toward Spain and back (€10, 3–5/day, 1 hour, Easter–Sept weather permitting, leaves from breakwater near château, commentary in French only, tel. 06 15 06 56 25).

Hikes

The three views described here offer different perspectives of this splendid area.

▲**Stone Windmill**—Stone steps lead 10 minutes up behind Collioure's museum to a 13th-century windmill with magnificent views that are positively peachy at sunset. Find the museum behind Hôtel Triton, walk through its stony backyard, and follow the paved path marked with yellow dashes. Bring your own beverage.

▲**Hike to Fort St. Elme**—This vertical hike is best done early or late (there's no shade) and is worth the sweat, even if you don't make it to the top (trail starts from windmill described above, allow 30 minutes each way). You can't miss the square castle lurking high above Collioure, with a grand view from the top. The privately owned castle has medieval exhibits, but to see them you must take an hour-long tour in French (€6, daily 14:30–19:00, tel. 06 64 61 82 42, some English information available).

Cheaters can do it by car. Drive to Port Vendres, then find the small sign marked *Fort St. Elme* on your right just before leaving the port (the road also leads to the supermarket). Continue on the small road that leads up from the train station.

▲▲▲ **Drive/Hike Through Vineyards to Madeloc Tower (Tour de Madeloc)**—Check your vertigo at the hotel, fasten your seatbelt, and take this drive-and-hike combination high above Collioure. The narrow road, hairpin turns, and absence of guardrails only add to the experience, as Collioure shrinks to Lego-size and the clouds become your neighbors.

Leave Collioure, heading toward Perpignan, and look for signs reading *Tour de Madeloc* at the roundabout above the town. Climb through steep and rocky terraced vineyards, following *Tour* signs. After 10 kilometers (6 miles, or about 20 minutes), you'll come to a fork in the road with a paved path (marked by a "no entry" symbol that applies to cars) and a road leading downhill. Park at the fork in the road, and walk up the paved path. The views everywhere are magnificent—the Pyrenees on one side, and the beach towns of Port Vendres and Collioure on the other. Allow 30 minutes at a slow-yet-steady pace along the splintered ridgetop to reach the eagle's-nest setting of the ancient tower (La Tour), now fitted with communication devices. Here you can commune with the gods, but beware—there's no shade, so do this hike early or late in the day. Once you're back down among mortals, you can return to Collioure following *La Route des Vignobles* along a narrow road to Banyuls-sur-Mer, then take coastal N-114 to Collioure and your hotel (skip D-914 in July and Aug, when it's too crowded).

Near Collioure

Day Trip to Spain—The 15-mile, 40-minute coastal drive via the Col de Banyuls into Spain is beautiful and well worth the countless curves, even if you don't venture past the border. To visit the wild Salvador Dalí museum, take the autoroute to Figueres, which takes about an hour each way (museum: €11; July–Sept daily 9:00–20:00; Oct and March–June Tue–Sun 9:30–18:00, closed Mon; Nov–Feb Tue–Sun 10:30–18:00, closed Mon; last entry 45 minutes before closing, Spanish tel. 972-677-500, www.salvador-dali.org). Train travelers can day-trip to Spain, either to Barcelona (6/day, 3–4.5 hours one-way, most change in Port Bou) or to the closer Figueres (6/day, 1–2 hours one-way, most change in Port Bou). Get train schedules at the station.

Céret—To see the art that Collioure inspired, you'll have to drive 25 windy miles inland to this pleasing town, featuring fountains and mountains at its doorstep. Céret's claim to fame is its modern-art museum, with works by some of Collioure's more famous visitors, including Picasso, Joan Miró, Chagall, and Matisse

(€8, July–mid-Sept 10:00–19:00, mid-Sept–June 10:00–18:00, closed Tue Oct–March, tel. 04 68 87 27 76, www.musee-ceret .com). Allow 40 minutes to Céret by car, or take a train to nearby Perpignan and a bus from there—get details at TI.

Sleeping in Collioure

(€1 = about $1.25, country code: 33)

Collioure has a fair range of hotels at favorable rates. You have two good choices for your hotel's location: central, in the old town (closer to train station); or across the bay, with views of the old town (10-minute walk from the central zone, with easier parking).

In the Old Town

Directions to the following places are given from the big Hôtel Fregate, at the edge of the old town, a 10-minute walk down from the train station. Price ranges reflect low versus high season.

$$$ Hôtel Casa Pairal***, opposite Hôtel Fregate and hiding down a short alley (behind Café Sola), is Mediterranean-elegant and Collioure's best splurge. Enter to the sounds of a fountain gurgling in the flowery courtyard. Reclining lounges await in the garden and by the pool. The rooms are quiet, comfortable, and tastefully designed. "Medium" rooms, on the first floor, have high ceilings and small balconies over a courtyard (small Db–€105–125, medium Db–€158–197, big Db suite with terrace–€218–240, extra bed–€25, air-con, free Wi-Fi, parking–€14, impasse des Palmiers, tel. 04 68 82 05 81, fax 04 68 82 52 10, www.hotel-casa-pairal .com, contact@hotel-casa-pairal.com, reserve ahead for room and parking).

$$ Hôtel les Templiers**, in the heart of the old town, has wall-to-wall paintings squeezed in every available space, a perennially popular café-bar, and good-value rooms. The paintings are payments in kind and thank-yous from artists who have stayed here—find the black-and-white photo in the bar of the hotel's owner with Picasso. The rooms—some of which have views—are either new and modern, or older and charming (standard Db–€65–76, bigger Db–€90–130, ask about connecting family rooms, pass on the annex rooms unless they're next to main hotel block, air-con in some rooms, Wi-Fi, elevator, a block toward beach from Hôtel Fregate along drainage canal at 12 quai de l'Amirauté, tel. 04 68 98 31 10, fax 04 68 98 01 24, www.hotel-templiers.com, info@hotel -templiers.com).

$$ Hôtel Princes de Catalogne*** offers 30 comfortable, spacious, American-style rooms. Get a room on the mountain side, or *côté montagne* (koh-tay mon-tan-yah), for maximum quiet (Db–€66–86, family room–€126–150, air-con, next to Casa Pairal, rue

des Palmiers, tel. 04 68 98 30 00, fax 04 68 98 30 31, www.hotel
-princescatalogne.com, contact@hotel-princescatalogne.com).

$ Peroneille's Chambres, on the pedestrian street two blocks
past Hôtel Fregate, are the cheapest rooms in the old town. The
rooms are simple, clean, and mostly spacious. It's a family affair
that encompasses three generations, with friendly Véronique handling most of the details. Rooms in the main building *(la maison
principale)* are better than the cheaper rooms in the annex, but both
are acceptable. Ask to see the rooftop terrace (Sb-€32, D-€42,
Db-€47, Tb-€67, Qb-€75, cash only, 20 rue Pasteur, tel. 04 68 82
15 31, fax 04 68 82 35 94, www.collioure-chambre-peroneille.fr).

Across the Bay

$$$ Hôtel les Caranques**, a few curves toward Spain from
Collioure's center, tumbles down the cliffs and showcases million-
dollar sea views from each of its rooms (most with balconies). The
new owner is considering upgrades in coming years, so be pre-
pared for changes to these rates (Db-€95-115, Db with bigger
deck-€105-130, route de Port Vendres, 30-minute walk from train
station, tel. 04 68 82 06 68, fax 04 68 82 00 92, www.les-caranques
.com, contact@les-caranques.com). For a scenic walk to Collioure's
center, follow the sidewalk, then turn right down the steps just
after the *Relais des Trois Mas* sign.

$$ Hôtel Boramar**, across the bay from Collioure's center,
is understated and modest, but well-maintained. Get a room with
a terrace facing the sea and smile...or sleep elsewhere (Db without
view-€62, Db with view-€72, Tb with view-€77, rue Jean Bart, tel.
04 68 82 07 06, www.hotel-boramar.com).

Eating in Collioure

Test the local wine and eat anything Catalan, including the fish
and anchovies (hand-filleted, as no machine has ever been able to
accomplish this precise task). All of my recommended restaurants
have indoor and outdoor tables, and most are in the old town (the
first three are within 50 yards of each other). Your task is to decide
whether you want to eat well or with a view. Several delicious
gelati shops and a Grand Marnier crêpe stand next to the Café
Copacabana fuel after-dinner strollers with the perfect last course.
If you're traveling off-season, call ahead—many restaurants here
are closed December through February.

Café Copacabana, on the main beach (Boramar), offers big
salads and a few seafood dishes in its sandy café. Skip their side-
walk-bound restaurant (which has a bigger selection but smaller
view) and find a red sway-back chair beachside. The quality is good
enough, considering the view, and it's family-friendly—kids can

play on the beach while you dine (daily mid-March–mid-Dec, plage Boramar, tel. 04 68 82 24 11, best at sunset).

Le Tremail is *the* place to go for contemporary seafood and Catalan specialties served outside or in. It's a small, popular place one block from the bay, where rue Arago and rue Mailly meet. Reserve ahead if you can (€23–35 *menus*, open daily year-round, 16 bis rue Mailly, tel. 04 68 82 16 10).

La Marinade, across from the TI, is a consistently good bet for seafood served in a lively outdoor setting (€19–28 *menus*, daily, 14 place du 18 Juin, tel. 04 68 82 09 76).

Brasserie au Casot owns the best setting away from the crowds, past the church on plage St. Vincent, and serves salads and *plats* with views for a fair price. Matisse would dig the decor (€15 *plats*, June–Sept daily 11:00–20:00 weather permitting, lunch only Oct and May, closed Thu in winter, plage St. Vincent, tel. 04 68 22 42 46).

La Neptune, across the bay, dishes up top seafood and views of Collioure to discerning diners. Dress up a bit, cross the bay, and ask for a table with a view (*menus* from €40, closed Tue Nov–April, 9 route de Port Vendres, tel. 04 68 82 02 27).

Small places sell a variety of meals to go (*à emporter*; ah empohr-tay) for budget-minded romantics wanting to dine on the bay.

For post-dinner fun, head to one of the bayfront cafés on plage Boramar, or try the recommended **Hôtel les Templiers** and get down with the locals (daily, 12 quai de l'Amirauté, tel. 04 68 98 31 10).

Collioure Connections

From Collioure by Train to: Carcassonne (8/day, 2 hours, most require change in Narbonne), **Paris** (7/day, 6 hours, 1–2 changes, one direct night train to Gare d'Austerlitz in 10 hours), **Barcelona, Spain** (6/day, 3–4.5 hours, most change in Port Bou), **Figueres, Spain** (6/day, 1–2 hours, most change in Port Bou), **Avignon/Arles** (7/day, 3.5 hours, many transfer points possible). Consider handy night trains to Paris; key Italian destinations; and Geneva, Switzerland. The train station's ticket office has limited hours (tel. 04 68 82 05 89).

PROVENCE

Arles • Avignon • Pont du Gard • Les Baux •
Orange • Villages of the Côtes du Rhône •
Hill Towns of the Luberon

This magnificent region is shaped like a giant wedge of quiche. From its sunburned crust, fanning out along the Mediterranean coast from the Camargue to Marseille, it stretches north along the Rhône Valley to Orange. The Romans were here in force and left many ruins—some of the best anywhere. Seven popes, artists such as Vincent van Gogh and Paul Cézanne, and author Peter Mayle all enjoyed their years in Provence. This destination features a splendid recipe of arid climate, oceans of vineyards, dramatic scenery, captivating cities, and adorable hill-capping villages.

Explore the ghost town that is ancient Les Baux, and see France's greatest Roman ruins, the Pont du Gard aqueduct and the theater in Orange. Spend a few starry, starry nights with Van Gogh in Arles. Youthful but classy Avignon bustles in the shadow of its brooding Palace of the Popes. It's a short hop from Arles or Avignon into the splendid scenery and villages of the Côtes du Rhône and Luberon regions.

Planning Your Time

Make Arles or Avignon your sightseeing base—particularly if you have no car. Italophiles prefer smaller Arles, while poodles pick urban Avignon. Arles has a blue-collar quality; the entire city feels like Van Gogh's bedroom. Avignon—double the size of Arles—feels sophisticated, with more nightlife and shopping, and makes a good base for non-drivers thanks to its convenient public-transit options. To measure the pulse of rural Provence, spend at least one night in a smaller town (such as Vaison la Romaine or Roussillon), or in the countryside.

Provence

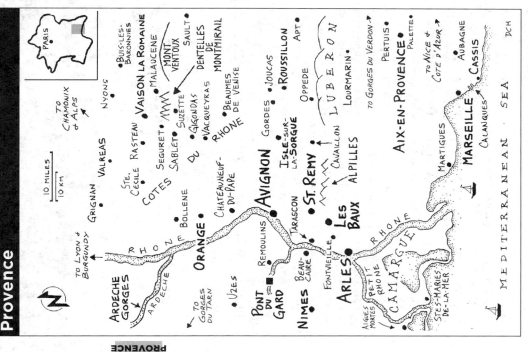

When budgeting your time, you'll want a full day for sightseeing in Arles and Les Baux (best on Wed or Sat, when it's market day); a half-day for Avignon; and a day or two for the villages and sights in the countryside.

Outside of Arles and Avignon, most destinations are accessible by public transit, though bus service can be sketchy. The Pont du Gard is a short hop west of Avignon and on the way to/from Languedoc for drivers. Les Baux works well by car from Avignon or Arles, and by bus from Arles from June to September. The town of Orange ties in tidily with a trip to the Côtes du Rhône villages. The Côtes du Rhône is ideal for wine connoisseurs and an easy stop for those heading to or from the north. Vaison la Romaine is ideal for those heading to/from the north, and Isle-sur-la-Sorgue (the most accessible small town) is centrally located between Avignon and the Luberon.

Getting Around Provence

By Bus or Train: Public transit is good between cities and decent to some towns, but marginal at best to the villages. Frequent trains link Avignon and Arles (about 30 minutes between each). Avignon has good train connections with Orange, and decent service to Isle-sur-la-Sorgue.

Buses connect many smaller towns, though service can be sporadic. From Avignon you can bus to Pont du Gard, St. Rémy, Uzès, Isle-sur-la-Sorgue (also by train), and, less easily, to Vaison la Romaine and some Côtes du Rhône villages. While a tour of the villages of the Côtes du Rhône or Luberon is best on your own by car, excellent minivan tours and basic bus excursions are available. (TIs in Arles and Avignon have information on bus excursions to regional sights that are hard to reach *sans* car; see "Tours of Provence," next.)

By Car: The region is made to order for a car. The yellow Michelin Local maps #332 and #340 are worth considering; the larger-scale orange Michelin map #527 also includes the Riviera. Arles (pop. 52,000) is easier, but still urban. Be wary of thieves: Park only in well-monitored spaces and leave nothing valuable in your car. If you're heading north from Provence, consider a three-hour detour through the spectacular Ardèche Gorges (see page 673).

Tours of Provence

Wine Safari—Dutchman Mike Rijken runs a one-man show, taking travelers through the region he adopted more than 20 years ago. Mike came to France to train as a chef, later became a wine steward, and has now found his calling as a driver/guide. His English is fluent, and though his focus is wine and wine villages, Mike knows the region thoroughly and is a good teacher of its history (€55/half-day, €100/day, priced per person, group size varies from 2 to 6; pickups possible in Arles, Avignon, Lyon, Marseille, or Aix-en-Provence; tel. 04 90 35 59 21, mobile 06 19 29 50 81, www.winesafari.net, mikeswinesafari@wanadoo.fr).

Avignon Wine Tour—For a playful, informative, and distinctly French perspective on wines of the Côtes du Rhône region, contact François Marcou, who runs his tours with passion and energy, offering different itineraries every day. Based in Avignon, François

Public Transportation in Provence

NOT TO SCALE

— RAIL
+ T.G.V. RAIL
-- BUS
··· BOAT
✚ AIRPORTS (NOT ALL) (SHOWN)

TO LYON & PARIS

P R O V E N C E

NYONS
BUIS
VAISON LA ROMAINE
MONTELIMAR
ORANGE
ROUSSILLON
ISLE-SUR-LA-SORGUE
CAV. ON
LUBERON
APT
LOUR-MARIN
AIX-EN-PROVENCE
AVIGNON
AVIGNON T.G.V.
UZES
PONT DU GARD
TARASCON
ST. REMY
LES BAUX
AIX T.G.V.
TO NICE
LA CIOTAT
CASSIS
TOULON
NIMES
ARLES
C A M A R G U E
MARSEILLE
LES CALANQUES
TO MONTPELLIER CARCASSONNE & BARCELONA (SPAIN)
STES MARIES
AIGUES MORTES
M E D I T E R R E N E A N   S E A

N

DCH

PROVENCE

can pick you up at your Avignon hotel, the TI, or at either of the city's train stations (€75/person for all-day wine tours that include 4–5 tastings, €350 for private groups, mobile 06 28 05 33 84, www .avignon-wine-tour.com, avignon.wine.tour@modulonet.fr).

Imagine Tours—Unlike most tour operators, this organization runs on a not-for-profit basis, with a focus on cultural excursions. It offers low-key, personalized tours that allow visitors to discover the "true heart of Provence." The itineraries adapt to your interests, and the volunteer guides will meet you at your hotel or the departure point of your choice (€150/half-day, €275/day, prices are for up to 4 people, mobile 06 89 22 19 87, fax 04 90 24 84 26, www .imagine-tours.net, imagine.tours@gmail.com). They also offer free assistance to travelers, should you want advice planning your itinerary, need help booking hotel rooms, or run into problems during your trip.

Wine Uncovered—Passionate Englishman (is that an oxymoron?) Olivier Hickman takes small groups on focused tours of selected wineries in Châteauneuf-du-Pape and in the villages near Vaison la Romaine. Olivier is serious about French wine, and knows his subject matter inside and out. His in-depth tastings include three wineries for €55 per person (his minimum half-day fee is €155; full-day is €195). If you need transportation, he can help arrange it (mobile 06 75 10 10 01, www.wine-uncovered.com, olivier.hickman@wine-uncovered.com).

Visit Provence—This company runs trips from Avignon (and a few from Arles) to most destinations covered in this chapter, and provides introductory commentary to what you'll see (but no guiding at the actual sights). They have eight-seat minivans (about €60/half-day, €100/day; they'll pick you up at your hotel in Avignon). Ask about their cheaper big-bus excursions, or consider hiring a van and driver for your own private use (plan on €210/half-day, €400/day, tel. 04 90 14 70 00, check website for current destinations, www.provence-reservation.com).

Madeleine's Culinary and Active Adventures—Madeleine Vedel, an effervescent American expat, plans small group tours from Avignon and Arles to visit food artisans and wineries. Madeleine also leads kid-friendly hikes in the countryside (€300/day, flat rate for 1-5 people, mobile 06 82 15 51 74, www.cuisine provencale.com).

Provence's Cuisine Scene

The almost extravagant use (by French standards) of garlic, olive oil, herbs, and tomatoes makes Provence's cuisine France's liveliest.

To sample it, order anything *à la provençal*. Among the area's spicy specialties are ratatouille (a mixture of vegetables in a thick, herbflavored tomato sauce), aioli (a rich, garlicky mayonnaise spread over vegetables, potatoes, fish, or whatever), tapenade (a paste of pureed olives, capers, anchovies, herbs, and sometimes tuna), *soupe au pistou* (thin yet flavorful vegetable soup with a sauce—called *pistou*—of basil, garlic, and cheese), and *soupe à l'ail* (garlic soup, called *aigo bouido* in the local dialect). Look for *riz de Camargue* (the reddish, chewy, nutty-tasting rice that has taken over the Camargue area) and *taureau* (bull's meat). *Banon de banon* or *banon à la feuille* (wrapped in chestnut leaves)

and spicy *picodon* are the native goat cheeses. Provence also produces some of France's great wines at relatively reasonable prices. Look for Gigondas, Sablet, Côtes du Rhône Villages, and Côte de Provence. If you like rosé, try the Tavel. This is the place to splurge for a bottle of Châteauneuf-du-Pape.

Remember, restaurants serve only during lunch (11:30–14:00) and dinner (19:00–21:00, later in bigger cities), but some cafés serve food throughout the day.

Provence Market Days

Provençal market days offer France's most colorful and tantalizing outdoor shopping. The best markets are on Monday in Cavaillon; Tuesday in Vaison la Romaine; Wednesday in St. Rémy; Thursday in Nyons; Friday in Lourmarin; Saturday in Arles, Uzès, and Apt; and, best of all, Sunday in Isle-sur-la-Sorgue. Crowds and parking problems abound at these popular events—arrive by 9:00, or, even better, sleep in the town the night before.

Monday:	Cavaillon, Bedoin (between Vaison la Romaine and Mont Ventoux)
Tuesday:	Vaison la Romaine, Gordes, and Lacoste
Wednesday:	St. Rémy, Arles, Uzès, Sault, and Malaucène (near Vaison la Romaine)
Thursday:	Nyons, Vacqueyras, Roussillon, and Isle-sur-la-Sorgue
Friday:	Lourmarin, Carpentras, Bonnieux, and Châteauneuf-du-Pape
Saturday:	Arles, Uzès, Apt, and Sainte-Cécile-les-Vignes, near Vaison la Romaine
Sunday:	Isle-sur-la-Sorgue, Coustellet

How About Them Romans?

Provence is littered with Roman ruins. Many scholars claim the best-preserved ancient Roman buildings are not in Italy, but in France. Since these ancient stones make up an important part of your sightseeing agenda in this region, it's worth learning about how they came to be.

Classical Rome endured from about 500 B.C. through A.D. 500—spending about 500 years growing, 200 years peaking, and 300 years declining. In 49 B.C., Julius Caesar defied the Republic by crossing the Rubicon River in northern Italy and conquering Provence (and ultimately all of France)—killing about a third of its population in the process. He erected a temple to Jupiter on the future site of Paris' Notre-Dame Cathedral.

The concept of one-man rule lived on with his grandnephew, Octavian (whom he had also adopted as his son). Octavian killed Brutus, eliminated his rivals (Mark Antony and Cleopatra), and

PROVENCE

Le Mistral

Provence lives with its vicious mistral winds, which blow 30–60 miles per hour, about 100 days out of the year. Locals say it blows in multiples of threes: three, six, or nine days in a row. The mistral clears people off the streets and turns lively cities into ghost towns. You'll likely spend a few hours or days taking refuge—or searching for cover. The winds are strongest between noon and 15:00.

When the mistral blows, it's everywhere, and you can't escape. Author Peter Mayle said it could blow the ears off a donkey (I'd include the tail). According to the natives, it ruins crops, shutters, and roofs (look for stones holding tiles in place on many homes). They'll also tell you that this pernicious wind has driven many people crazy (including young Vincent van Gogh). A weak version of the wind is called a *mistralet*.

The mistral starts above the Alps and Massif Central mountains and gathers steam as it heads south, gaining momentum as it screams over the Rhône Valley (which acts like a funnel between the Alps and the Cévennes mountains) before exhausting itself when it hits the Mediterranean. While this wind rattles shutters throughout the Riviera and Provence, it's strongest over the Rhône Valley...so Avignon, Arles, and the Côtes du Rhône villages bear its brunt. While wiping the dust from your eyes, remember the good news: The mistral brings clear skies.

united Rome's warring factions. He took the title "Augustus" and became the first in a line of emperors who would control Rome for the next 500 years—ruling like a king, with the backing of the army and the rubber-stamp approval of the Senate. Rome morphed from a Republic into an Empire: a collection of many diverse territories ruled by a single man.

Augustus' reign marked the start of 200 years of peace, prosperity, and expansion known as the *Pax Romana*. At its peak (c. A.D. 117), the Roman Empire had 54 million people and stretched from Scotland in the north to Egypt in the south, as far west as Spain and as far east as modern-day Iraq. To the northeast, Rome was bounded by the Rhine and Danube Rivers. On Roman maps, the Mediterranean was labeled *Mare Nostrum* ("Our Sea"). At its peak, "Rome" didn't just refer to the city, but to the entire civilized Western world.

The Romans were successful not only because they were good soldiers, but also because they were smart administrators and businessmen. People in conquered territories knew they had joined the winning team and that political stability would replace barbarian invasions. Trade thrived. Conquered peoples were welcomed into the fold of prosperity, linked by roads, education, common laws and gods, and the Latin language.

Provence, with its strategic location, benefited greatly from Rome's global economy and grew to become an important part of

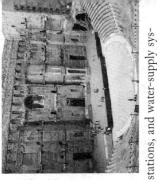

its worldwide empire. After Julius Caesar conquered Gaul, Emperor Augustus set out to Romanize it, building and renovating cities in the image of Rome. Most cities had a theater (some had several), baths, and aqueducts; the most important ones had sports arenas. The Romans also erected an infrastructure of roads, post offices, schools (teaching in Latin), police stations, and water-supply systems.

With a standard language and currency, Roman merchants were able to trade wine, salt, and olive oil for foreign goods. The empire invested heavily in cities that were strategic for trade. For example, the Roman-built city of Arles was a crucial link in the trade route from Italy to Spain, so they built a bridge across the Rhône River and fortified the town.

A typical Roman city (such as Nîmes, Arles, Orange, or Vaison la Romaine) was a garrison town, laid out on a grid plan with two main roads: one running north–south (the *cardus*), the other east–west (the *decumanus*). Approaching the city on your chariot, you'd pass through the cemetery, which was located outside of town for hygienic reasons. You'd enter the main gate and speed past warehouses and apartment houses to the town square (forum). Facing the square were the most important temples, dedicated to the patron gods of the city. Nearby, you'd find bathhouses; like today's fitness clubs, these served the almost sacred dedication to personal vigor. Also close by were businesses that catered to the citizens' needs: the marketplace, bakeries, banks, and brothels.

Aqueducts brought fresh water for drinking, filling the baths, and delighting the citizens with bubbling fountains. Men flocked

to the stadiums in Arles and Nîmes to bet on gladiator games, and eager couples attended elaborate plays at theaters in Orange, Arles, and Vaison la Romaine. Marketplaces brimmed with exotic fruits, vegetables, and animals from the far reaches of the empire. Some cities in Provence were more urban 2,000 years ago than they are today. For instance, Roman Arles had a population of 100,000—double today's size.

In these cities, you'll see many rounded arches. These were constructed by piling two stacks of heavy stone blocks, connecting them with an arch (supported with wooden scaffolding), then inserting an inverted keystone where the stacks met. *Voilà!* The heavy stones were able to support not only themselves, but also a great deal of weight above the arch. The Romans didn't actually invent the rounded arch, but they exploited it far better than their predecessors, stacking arches to build arenas and theaters, stringing them side by side for aqueducts, stretching out their legs to create barrel-vaulted ceilings, and building freestanding "triumphal" arches to celebrate conquering generals.

When it came to construction, the Romans' magic building ingredient was concrete. A mixture of volcanic ash, lime, water, and small rocks, concrete—easier to work than stone, longer-lasting than wood—served as flooring, roofing, filler, glue, and support. Builders would start with a foundation of brick, then fill it in with poured concrete. They would then cover important structures, such as basilicas, in sheets of expensive marble (held on with nails), or decorate floors and walls with mosaics—proving just how talented the Romans were at turning the functional into art.

Arles

By helping Julius Caesar defeat Marseille, Arles (pronounced "arl") earned the imperial nod and was made an important port city. With the first bridge over the Rhône River, Arles was a key stop on the Roman road from Italy to Spain, the Via Domitia. After reigning as the seat of an important archbishop and a trading center for centuries, the city became a sleepy backwater of little importance in the 1700s. Vincent van Gogh settled here in the late 1800s, but left only a chunk of his ear (now long gone). American bombers destroyed much of Arles in World War II as the townsfolk hid out in its underground Roman ruins. But today Arles thrives again, with its evocative Roman ruins, an eclectic assortment of museums, made-for-ice-cream pedestrian zones, and squares that play hide-and-seek with visitors.

The city's unpolished streets and squares are not to everyone's taste. This workaday city has not sold out to tourism, so you won't see dolled-up lanes and perfectly preserved buildings. But to me, that's part of its charm.

Orientation to Arles

Arles faces the Mediterranean, turning its back on Paris. And though the town is built along the Rhône, it largely ignores the river. Landmarks hide in Arles' medieval tangle of narrow, winding streets. Virtually everything is close—but first-timers can walk forever to get there. Hotels have good, free city maps, and Arles provides helpful street-corner signs that point you toward sights and hotels. Racing cars enjoy Arles' medieval lanes, turning sidewalks into tightropes and pedestrians into leaping targets.

Tourist Information

The **main TI** is on the ring road boulevard des Lices, at esplanade Charles de Gaulle (April-Sept daily 9:00–18:45; Oct-March Mon-Sat 9:00–16:45, Sun 10:00–13:00; tel. 04 90 18 41 20, www.arlestourisme.com). There's also a **train station TI** (Mon-Fri 9:00–13:30 & 14:30–16:45, closed Sat-Sun).

At either TI, pick up the city map, note the bus schedules (displayed in binders), and get English information on nearby destinations such as the Camargue wildlife area (described on page 616). Ask about "bullgames" (Provence's more humane version of bullfights—see page 618) and walking tours of Arles. Skip the useless €1 brochure describing several walks in Arles, including one that locates Van Gogh's "easels." Both TIs can help you reserve hotel rooms (credit card required for deposit).

Arrival in Arles

By Train: The train station is on the river, a 10-minute walk from the town center. Before heading into town, get what you need at the train station TI. There's no baggage storage at the station, but you can walk 10 minutes to stow it at Hôtel Régence (see "Helpful Hints," later).

To reach the town center, turn left out of the train station and walk 15 minutes; or wait for the free Starlette bus at the shelter across the street (3/hour, Mon–Sat only). Taxis usually wait in front of the station, but if you don't see any, call the posted telephone numbers, or dial 04 89 73 36 00. If the train station TI is open, you can ask them to call. Taxi rates are fixed—allow about €10 to any of my recommended hotels.

By Bus: The Centre-Ville bus station is a few blocks below the main TI, located on the ring road at 16–24 boulevard Georges Clemenceau.

By Car: Most hotels have parking nearby—ask for detailed directions (€1.50/hour at most meters, free 12:00–14:00 & 19:00–9:00). For most hotels, first follow signs to *Centre-Ville*, then *Gare SNCF* (train station). You'll come to a big roundabout (place

Lamartine) with a Monoprix department store to the right. You can park along the city wall and find your hotel on foot; the hotels I list are no more than a 10-minute walk away (best not to park here overnight due to theft concerns and markets on Wed and Sat). Fearless drivers can plunge into the narrow streets between the two stumpy towers via rue de la Calade, and follow signs to their hotel. Again, theft is a problem; leave nothing in your car, and trust your hotelier's advice on where to park.

If you can't find parking near your hotel, Parking des Lices (Arles' only parking garage), near the TI on boulevard des Lices, is a good fallback (€3/hour, €8/24 hours).

Helpful Hints

Market Days: The big markets are on Wednesdays and Saturdays. For all the details, see page 600.

Meetings and Festivals: An international photo event jams hotels in early July. The let-er-rip, twice-a-year Féria draws crowds over Easter and in mid-September (see www.arlestourisme .com for dates).

Internet Access: Internet cafés in Arles change with the wind. Ask your hotelier or at the TI.

Baggage Storage and Bike Rental: The recommended **Hôtel Régence** (see page 622) will store your bags for €3 (daily 7:30–22:00 mid-March–mid-Nov, closed in winter). They also rent bikes (€6/hour, €14/day, one-way rentals within Provence possible, same hours as baggage storage). Ask about their electric bikes—handy on windy days, but with limited power. From Arles you can ride to Les Baux (20 miles round-trip, very steep climb at the end) or into the Camargue (40 miles round-trip, forget it in the wind)—provided you're in great shape.

Laundry: There's a launderette at 12 rue Portagnel (daily 7:00–21:30, you can stay later to finish if you're already inside, English instructions).

Car Rental: Avis is at the train station (tel. 04 90 96 82 42), and **Europcar** and **Hertz** are downtown (Europcar is at 2 bis avenue Victor Hugo, tel. 04 90 93 23 24; Hertz is closer to place Lamartine at 10 boulevard Emile Combes, tel. 04 90 96 75 23).

Local Guide: Charming **Jacqueline Neujean**, an excellent guide, knows Arles and nearby sights intimately and loves her work (€90/2 hours, tel. & fax 04 90 98 47 51).

English Book Exchange: A small exchange is available at the recommended **Soleileïs** ice-cream shop (see page 626).

Cooking Courses: Food-lovers enjoy cooking classes and market tours offered by gentle Erick Vedel (tel. 04 90 49 69 20).

Arles

VAN GOGH WALKING TOUR

- → VAN GOGH WALKING TOUR
- **P** PARKING
- Ⓑ BUS STOP
- ⚠ VIEW
- ⊓ EASEL

100 YARDS
100 METERS

Ⓝ

Van Gogh Sights
1. The Yellow House (Easel)
2. Starry Night Over the Rhône (Easel)
3. Place du Forum & Café la Nuit (Easel)
4. Espace Van Gogh (Easel)
5. Fondation Van Gogh

Other
6. Baggage Storage & Bike Rental
7. Launderette
8. To Avis Car Rental
9. Europcar Car Rental
10. Hertz Car Rental
11. Le Petit Train Departure Point
12. Bus #1 (to Ancient History Museum)

TRINQUETAILLE BRIDGE

QUAI MARX

R. TRUCHET

DR. FANTON

ARLATEN FOLK MUSEUM
(CLOSED UNTIL 2013)

R. JOUVE. R. LIBERTÉ

RUE A. FRANCE

RUE GAMBETTA

ESPACE VAN GOGH

RUE MOLIÈRE

RUE REPUB.

BUS STN.

⑫ Ⓑ

④

BLVD.

TO ANCIENT HISTORY MUSEUM →

TO ANCIENT HISTORY MUSEUM

DCH

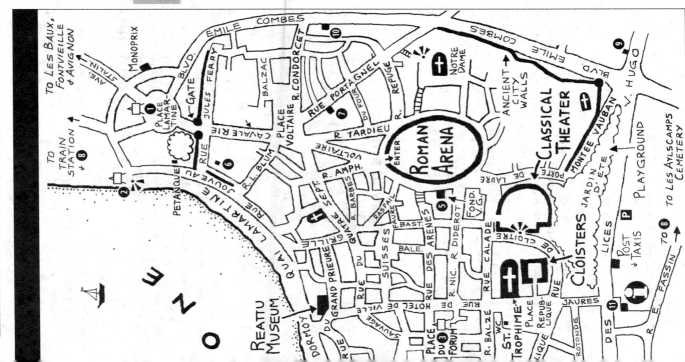

Public Pools: Arles has three public pools (indoor and outdoor). Ask at the TI or your hotel.

Boules: The local "*bowling alley*" is by the river on place Lamartine. After their afternoon naps, the old boys congregate here for a game of *pétanque* (see page 1033 for details on this popular local pastime).

Getting Around Arles

In this flat city, everything's within **walking** distance. Only the Ancient History Museum requires a healthy walk (or you can take a taxi or bus). The elevated riverside promenade provides Rhône views and a direct route to the Ancient History Museum (to the southwest) and the train station (to the northeast). Keep your head up for *Starry Night* memories, but eyes down for decorations by dogs with poorly trained owners.

Arles' **taxis** charge a set fee of about €10, but nothing except the Ancient History Museum is worth a taxi ride. To call a cab, dial 04 89 73 36 00 or 04 90 96 90 03.

The free **Starlette bus** circles the town (3/hour, Mon–Sat only), but is only useful for access to the train station.

Le Petit Train d'Arles provides a helpful orientation to the lay of the land—if you prefer sitting to walking (€6.50, 35 minutes, stops in front of the main TI and at the Arena).

Sights in Arles

Most sights cost €3.50–7, and while any sight warrants a few minutes, many aren't worth their individual admission price. The TI sells three different monument passes (called Passeports). **Le Passeport Avantage** covers almost all of Arles' sights (€13.50, under 18 for €12; Fondation Van Gogh discounted); the €9 **Le Passeport Arelate** covers Arles' four Roman sights and the Ancient History Museum; and the €9 **Le Passeport Liberté** lets you choose any five monuments (one must be a museum). Depending on your interests, one of the €9 Passeports is probably best.

Start at the Ancient History Museum for a helpful overview (drivers should try to do this museum on their way into Arles), then dive into the city-center sights. Remember, many sights stop selling tickets 30–60 minutes before closing (both before lunch and at the end of the day). To make the most of Arles' Roman history, see "How About Them Romans?" on page 600.

▲▲Ancient History Museum (Musée de l'Arles et de la Provence Antiques)

Begin your town visit here, for Roman Arles 101. Located on the site of the Roman chariot racecourse (the arc of which is built into

the parking lot), this air-conditioned, all-on-one-floor museum is just west of central Arles along the river. Models and original sculptures (with almost no posted English translations but a decent handout) re-create the Roman city, making workaday life and culture easier to imagine.

Cost and Hours: €6, Wed-Mon April–Oct 9:00–19:00, Nov-March 10:00–18:00, closed Tue year-round, presqu'île du Cirque Romain.

Information: Ask for the English booklet, which provides a helpful if not in-depth background on the collection, and inquire whether there are any free English tours (usually daily July–Sept at 17:00, 1.5 hours). Tel. 04 90 18 88 88, www.arles-antique.cg13.fr.

Getting There: To reach the museum on foot from the city center (a 20-minute **walk**), turn left at the river and take the riverside path to the big, blue, modern building. As you approach the museum, you'll pass the verdant Hortus Garden—designed to recall the Roman circus and chariot racecourse that were located here, and to give residents a place to gather and celebrate civic events. A **taxi** ride costs €10 (museum can call a taxi for your return). **Bus #1** gets you within a few minutes' walk (€0.80, 3/hour Mon-Sat, none Sun). Catch the bus in Arles (clockwise direction on boulevard des Lices), then get off at the Musée de l'Arles Antique stop (before the stop, you'll see the bright-blue museum ahead on the right). Turn left as you step off the bus, and follow the sidewalk. (To return to the center, the bus stop is across the street from where you got off.)

⊙ **Self-Guided Tour:** A huge map of the Roman Arles region greets visitors and shows the key Roman routes accessible to Arles. Find the impressive row of pagan and early-Christian **sarcophagi** (from the second to fifth centuries). These would have lined the Via Aurelia outside the town wall. In the early days of the Church,

Jesus was often portrayed beardless and as the good shepherd, with a lamb over his shoulder.

Next you'll see **models** of every Roman structure in (and near) Arles. These are the highlight for me, as they breathe life into the buildings as they looked 2,000 years ago. Start with the model of Roman Arles, and imagine the city's splendor. Find the

Forum—still the center of town today, though only two columns survive. Look at the space Romans devoted to their Arena and huge racecourse—a reminder that an emphasis on sports is not unique to modern civilizations. The model also illustrates how little Arles seems to have changed over two millennia, with its houses still clustered around the city center, and warehouses still located on the opposite side of the river.

Look for individual models of the major buildings shown in the city model: the elaborately elegant forum; the floating bridge that gave Arles a strategic advantage (over the widest, and therefore slowest, part of the river); the theater (with its magnificent stage wall); the Arena (with its movable stadium cover to shelter spectators from sun or rain); and the circus, or chariot racecourse. Part of the original racecourse was just outside the windows, and while long gone, it must have resembled Rome's Circus Maximus in its day—its obelisk is now the centerpiece of Arles' place de la République.

Finally, check out the **3-D model** of the hydraulic mill of Barbegal, with its 16 waterwheels and 8 grain mills cascading down a nearby hillside.

Other rooms in the museum display pottery, jewelry, fine metal and glass artifacts, and well-crafted mosaic floors that make it clear that Roman Arles was a city of art and culture. The many **statues** that you see are all original, except for the greatest—the *Venus of Arles*, which Louis XIV took a liking to and had moved to Versailles. It's now in the Louvre—and, as locals say, "When it's in Paris...bye-bye."

In Central Arles

Ideally, visit these sights in the order listed here. I've included some walking directions to connect the dots.

▲▲Forum Square (Place du Forum)—Named for the Roman forum that once stood here, place du Forum was the political and religious center of Roman Arles. Still lively, this café-crammed square is a local watering hole and popular for a pastis (anise-based apéritif). And though the bistros on the square are no place for a fine dinner, they can put together a decent salad or plat du jour—and when you sprinkle on the ambience, that's €10 well spent.

At the corner of Grand Hôtel Nord-Pinus (a favorite of Pablo Picasso), a plaque shows how the Romans built a foundation of galleries to compensate for Arles' slope down to the river. The two columns are all that survive from the upper story of the entry to the Forum. Steps leading to the entrance are buried—the Roman street level was about 20 feet below you (you can get a glimpse of it by peeking through the street-level openings under the Hôtel d'Arlatan, two blocks below place du Forum on rue Sauvage).

The statue on the square is of **Frédéric Mistral** (1830–1914). This popular poet, who wrote in the local dialect rather than in French, was a champion of Provençal culture. After receiving the Nobel Prize in Literature in 1904, Mistral used his prize money to preserve and display the folk identity of Provence. He founded the regional folk museum (the Arlaten Folk Museum, closed for renovation until 2013) at a time when France was rapidly centralizing. (The local mistral wind—literally "master"—has nothing to do with his name.)

The **bright-yellow café**—called Café la Nuit—was the subject of one of Vincent van Gogh's most famous works in Arles. While his painting showed the café in a brilliant yellow from the glow of gas lamps, the façade was bare limestone, just like the other cafés on this square. The café's current owners have painted it to match Van Gogh's version...and to cash in on the Vincent-crazed hordes who pay too much to eat or drink here.

• *Walk a block uphill (past Grand Hôtel Nord Pinus) and turn left. Walk through the Hôtel de Ville's vaulted entry (or take the next right if it's closed), and pop out onto the big...*

Republic Square (Place de la République)—This square used to be called "place Royale"...until the French Revolution. The obelisk was the former centerpiece of Arles' Roman Circus. The lions at its base are the symbol of the city, whose slogan is (roughly) "the gentle lion." Find a seat and watch the peasants—pilgrims, locals, and street musicians. There's nothing new about this scene.

• *Near the corner of the square where you entered, look for...*

▲▲St. Trophime Church—Named after a third-century bishop of Arles, this church sports the finest Romanesque main entrance (west portal) I've seen anywhere.

Like a Roman triumphal arch, the church façade trumpets the promise of Judgment Day. The tympanum (the semicircular area above the door) is filled with Christian symbolism. Christ sits in majesty, surrounded by symbols of the four evangelists: Matthew (the winged man), Mark (the winged lion), Luke (the ox), and John (the eagle). The 12 apostles are lined up below Jesus. It's Judgment Day... some are saved and others aren't. Notice the condemned (on the right)—a chain gang doing a sad bunny-hop over the fires of hell. For them, the tune trumpeted by the three angels above Christ is not a happy one. Below the chain gang, St. Stephen is being stoned to death, with his soul leaving through his mouth and instantly

being welcomed by angels. Ride the exquisite detail back to a simpler age. In an illiterate medieval world, long before the vivid images of our Technicolor time, this was a neon billboard over the town square.

Enter the church (free, daily April–Sept 9:00–12:00 & 14:00–18:30, Oct–March 9:00–12:00 & 14:00–17:00). Just inside the door on the right, a chart locates the interior highlights and helps explain the carvings you just saw on the tympanum.

Tour the church counterclockwise. The tall 12th-century Romanesque nave is decorated by a set of tapestries showing scenes from the life of Mary (17th century, from the French town of Aubusson). Amble around the Gothic apse. Just to the left of the high altar, check out the relic chapel—with its fine golden boxes that hold long-venerated bones of obscure saints. Farther down is a chapel built on an early-Christian sarcophagus from Roman Arles (dated about A.D. 300). The heads were lopped off during the French Revolution.

This church is a stop on the ancient pilgrimage route to Santiago de Compostela in northwest Spain. For 800 years pilgrims on their way to Santiago have paused here...and they still do today. As you leave, notice the modern-day pilgrimages advertised on the far right near the church's entry.

• *Leaving the church, turn left, then left again through a courtyard to enter the cloisters.*

The adjacent **cloisters** are worth a look only if you have a pass (big cleaning underway, enter at the far end of the courtyard). The many small columns were scavenged from the ancient Roman theater. Enjoy the sculpted capitals, the rounded 12th-century Romanesque arches, and the pointed 14th-century Gothic ones. The pretty vaulted hall exhibits 17th-century tapestries showing scenes from the First Crusade to the Holy Land. On the second floor, you'll walk along an angled rooftop designed to catch rainwater—notice the slanted gutter that channeled the water into a cistern and the heavy roof slabs covering the tapestry hall below (€3.50, daily March–Oct 9:00–18:00, Nov–Feb 10:00–17:00).

• *Turn right out of the cloisters, then take the first right on rue de la Calade to reach the...*

Classical Theater (Théâtre Antique)—This first-century B.C. Roman theater once seated 10,000...just like the theater in Orange. But unlike Orange, here in Arles there was no hillside to provide support. This theater was an elegant, three-level structure with 27 arches radiating out to the street level. From the outside, it looked much like a halved version of Arles' Roman Arena.

Start with the video outside, which provides helpful background information and images that make it easier to put the scattered stones back in place (crouch in front to make out the small

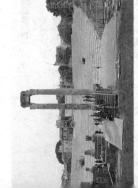

English subtitles). Next, walk to a center aisle and pull up a stone seat. To appreciate the theater's original size, look to the upper-left side of the tower and find the protrusion that supported the highest seating level. The structure required 33 rows of seats covering three levels to accommodate demand. During the Middle Ages, the old theater became a convenient town quarry—St. Trophime Church was built from theater rubble. Precious little of the original theater survives—though it still is used for events, with seating for 3,000 spectators.

Two lonely Corinthian columns are all that remain of a three-story stage wall that once featured more than 100 columns and statues painted in vibrant colors. The orchestra section is defined by a semicircular pattern in the stone in front of you. Stepping up onto the left side of the stage, look down to the slender channel that allowed the brilliant-red curtain to disappear below, like magic. The stage, which was built of wood, was about 160 feet across and 20 feet deep. Go backstage and browse through the actors' changing rooms, then loop back to the entry behind the grass (€3, daily May–Sept 9:00–19:00, March–April and Oct 9:00–12:00 & 14:00–18:00, Nov–Feb 10:00–12:00 & 14:00–17:00). Budget travelers can peek over the fence from rue du Cloître, and see just about everything for free.

• *A block uphill is the...*

▲▲▲**Roman Arena (Amphithéâtre)**—Nearly 2,000 years ago, gladiators fought wild animals here to the delight of 20,000 screaming fans. Today, local daredevils still fight wild animals here—"bullgame" posters around the Arena advertise upcoming spectacles (see page 618). A lengthy restoration process is well underway, giving the amphitheater an almost bleached-teeth whiteness.

In Roman times, games were free (sponsored by city bigwigs), and fans were seated according to social class. The many exits allowed for rapid dispersal after the games—fights would break out among frenzied fans if they couldn't leave quickly. Through medieval times and until the early 1800s, the arches were bricked up and the stadium became a fortified town—with 200 humble homes crammed within its circular defenses. Three of the medieval

Van Gogh in Arles

In the dead of winter in 1888, 35-year-old Dutch artist Vincent van Gogh left big-city Paris for Provence, hoping to jump-start his floundering career and personal life. He was inspired, and he was lonely. Coming from the gray skies and flat lands of the north, Vincent was bowled over by everything Provençal—the sun, bright colors, rugged landscape, and unspoiled people. For the next two years he painted furiously, cranking out a masterpiece every few days.

None of the 200-plus paintings that Van Gogh did in the south can be found today in the city that so moved him. But you can walk the same streets he knew and see places he painted, marked by about a dozen steel-and-concrete "**easels**," with photos of the final paintings for then-and-now comparisons. The TI has a €1 brochure that locates all the easels (the few described in this sidebar are easily found without the brochure—see the map on page 606). Small stone markers with yellow accents embedded in the pavement lead to the easels. Here's a quick summary of the places that inspired a few of his most famous paintings:

Vincent arrived in Arles on February 20, 1888, to a foot of snow. He rented a small house on the north side of **place Lamartine.** The house, painted yellow inside and out, had four rooms, including a small studio and the cramped trapezoid-shaped bedroom made famous in paintings. To see the house from the outside, find the stone easel across the grass from the Civette Arlesienne bistro. The house was destroyed in 1944 by an errant bridge-seeking bomb, but the four-story building behind it—where you see the Civette Arlesienne—still stands (look for it

towers survive (the one above the ticket booth is open and rewards those who climb it with terrific views). To see two still-sealed arches—complete with cute medieval window frames—turn right as you leave, walk to the Andaluz restaurant, and look back to the second floor (€6, daily May-Sept 9:00-19:00, March-April and Oct 9:00-18:00, Nov-Feb 10:00-17:00).

• Turn left out of the Arena and walk uphill to find the...

▲**Fondation Van Gogh**—A refreshing stop for modern-art-lovers and Van Gogh fans, this two-level gallery displays works by contemporary artists (including Roy Lichtenstein and Robert Rauschenberg) who pay homage to Vincent through thought-provoking interpretations of his works. The black-and-white photographs (both art and shots of places that Vincent painted) in the painting).

From place Lamartine, walk to the river (passing a monument in honor of two American pilots killed in action during the liberation of Arles) and find the easel in the wall where ramps lead down to the river. One night, Vincent set up along this river west of place Lamartine and painted the stars boiling above the city skyline—**Starry Night over the Rhône.** Come back at night to match his painting with today's scene. (Note: This painting is not the *Starry Night* you're thinking of, which Van Gogh painted at a hospital in nearby St. Rémy.)

Vincent—who dreamed of making Arles a magnet for fellow artists—persuaded his friend Paul Gauguin to come. At first, the two got along well. They spent days side by side, rendering the same subject in their two distinct styles. At night they hit the bars and brothels. Van Gogh's well-known *Café at Night* captures the glow of an absinthe buzz at Café la Nuit on **place du Forum** (look for the easel here).

After two months together, the two artists clashed over art and personality differences. On the night of December 23, they were drinking absinthe at the café when Vincent suddenly went ballistic. He threw his glass at Gauguin, who then left. Walking through place Victor Hugo, Gauguin heard footsteps behind him and turned to see Vincent coming at him, brandishing a razor. Gauguin quickly fled town. Later that night, Vincent sliced off his own earlobe and gave it to a prostitute.

Vincent was checked into the local hospital—today's **Espace Van Gogh** cultural center (the Espace is free, but only the courtyard is open to the public). It surrounds a flowery courtyard (with an easel) that the artist loved and painted during his month here.

In the spring of 1890, Vincent left Provence to be cared for by a doctor in Auvers-sur-Oise, north of Paris. On July 27 he wandered into a field and shot himself. He died two days later.

complement the paintings. (But be warned that the collection contains no Van Gogh originals.) Unfortunately, this collection is often on the road July through September, when non-Van Gogh material is displayed (€6, €4 with Le Passeport Avantage; good collection of Van Gogh souvenirs, prints, and postcards for sale in gift shop; April–June daily 10:00–18:00; July–Sept daily 10:00–19:00; Oct–March Tue–Sun 11:00–17:00, closed Mon; facing Arena at 24 bis rond-point des Arènes, tel. 04 90 49 94 04, www.fondationvangogh-arles.org). For more on Vincent, see the sidebar.

• *The next two attractions are back across town. The* Arlaten Folk Museum *(closed until 2013) is close to place du Forum, and the Réattu Museum is near the river.*

▲**Arlaten Folk Museum (Musée Arlaten/Museon Arlaten)**—This museum, which normally explains the ins and outs of daily Provençal life, is closed for renovation until 2013 (www.museon arlaten.fr).

Réattu Museum (Musée Réattu)—Housed in the former Grand Priory of the Knights of Malta, this mildly interesting, mostly modern art collection includes 57 Picasso drawings (some two-sided and all done in a flurry of creativity—I like the bullfights best), a room of Henri Rousseau's Camargue watercolors, and an unfinished painting by the Neoclassical artist Jacques Réattu... but none with English explanations. Occasional special exhibits show off the museum's impressive permanent collection, which is mostly in storage (€7, Tue–Sun July–Sept 10:00–19:00, Oct–June 10:00–12:30 & 14:00–18:30, closed Mon year-round, last entry 30 minutes before closing for lunch or at end of day, 10 rue du Grand Prieuré, tel. 04 90 96 37 68, www.museereattu.arles.fr).

Near Arles

The Camargue—Knocking on Arles' doorstep, this is one of the few truly "wild" areas of France, where pink flamingos, wild bulls, nasty boars, nastier mosquitoes (in every season but winter—come prepared), and the famous white horses wander freely through lagoons and tall grass. It's a ▲▲▲ sight for nature-lovers, but underwhelming for others. Barely possible by public transportation, it's ideal by car. The best route to follow is toward **Salin de Giraud:** Leave Arles on D-570 toward Stes-Maries-de-la-Mer, passing the D-36 turnoff to Salin de Giraud (you'll return along this route). After a stop at the Camarguais Museum, continue along D-570, then turn left on D-37 toward Salin de Giraud and follow it as it skirts the Étang de Vaccarès lagoon. The lagoon itself is off-limits, but this area has views and good opportunities to get out of the car and smell the marshes. Turn right off D-37 onto the tiny road at Villeneuve, following La Capelière and La Fiélouse.

The best part of the Camargue (particularly in spring) awaits at **La Digue de la Mer,** about 10 scenic kilometers (6 miles) past La Capelière. A rough dirt road rising above water on both sides greets travelers; it's time to get out of your car and stroll (though you can drive on for a few miles to Phare de la Gacholle). This is a critical reproduction area for flamingos (about 5,000 offspring annually), so it's your best chance to see groups of mamas and papas up close and personal.

Stes-Maries-de-la-Mer—At the western end of the Camargue lies this whitewashed, Spanish-feeling seafront town with acres of flamingos, bulls, and horses at its doorstep. The place is so popular that it's best avoided on weekends and during holidays. It's a French Coney Island—a trinket-selling, perennially windy place.

Near Arles

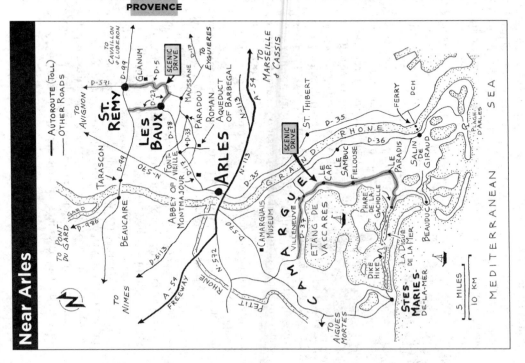

The town is also famous as a mecca for the Roma (also known as Gypsies). Every May, Roma from all over Europe pile in their caravans and migrate to Stes-Maries-de-la-Mer to venerate the statue of Saint Sarah. At other times, the town has little to offer except its beachfront promenade, bullring, and towering five-belled fortified church. Most tourists come to take a horse, jeep, or bike into the Camargue—and there's no lack of outfits ready to take you for a ride. The TIs in Arles and Stes-Maries-de-la-Mer have long lists (Stes-Maries-de-la-Mer TI open daily April-Sept 9:00–19:00, until 20:00 in summer, Oct–March 9:00–17:00, tel. 04 90 97 82 55, www.saintesmaries.com).

Events in Arles

▲▲Markets—On Wednesday and Saturday mornings, Arles' ring road erupts into an open-air festival of fish, flowers, produce, and you-name-it. The main event is on Saturday, with vendors jamming the ring road from boulevard Emile Combes to the east, along boulevard des Lices near the TI (the heart of the market), and continuing down boulevard Georges Clemenceau to the west. Wednesday's market runs only along boulevard Emile Combes, between place Lamartine and bis avenue Victor Hugo; the segment nearest place Lamartine is all about food, and the upper half features clothing, tablecloths, purses, and so on. On the first Wednesday of the month, a flea market doubles the size of the usual Wednesday market along boulevard des Lices near the main TI. Join in: Buy some flowers for your hotelier, try the olives, sample some wine, and swat a pickpocket. Both markets are open until 12.30.

▲▲Bullgames (Courses Camarguaises)—Occupy the same

seats that fans have used for nearly 2,000 years, and take in Arles' most memorable experience—the *courses camarguaises* in the ancient Arena. The nonviolent "bullgames" are more sporting than bloody bullfights (though traditional Spanish-style bullfights still take place on occasion). The bulls of Arles (who, locals stress, "die of old age") are promoted in posters even more boldly than their human foes. In the bullgame, a ribbon (*cocarde*) is laced between the bull's horns. The *razeteur*, with a special hook, has 15 minutes to snare the ribbon. Local businessmen encourage a *razeteur* (dressed in white with a red cummerbund) by shouting out how much money they'll pay for the *cocarde*. If the bull pulls a good stunt, the band plays the famous "Toreador" song from *Carmen*. The following day, newspapers report on the games, including how many *Carmens* the bull earned.

Three classes of bullgames—determined by the experience of the *razeteurs*—are advertised in posters: The *course de protection* is for rookies. The *trophée de l'Avenir* comes with more experience—and the *trophée des As* features top professionals. During Easter and the fall rice-harvest festival (*Féria du Riz*), the Arena hosts traditional Spanish bullfights (look for *corrida*) with outfits, swords, spikes, and the whole gory shebang. Bullgame tickets run €5–15, while bullfights are pricier (€14–80). Schedules change every year—ask at the TI or check online at www.arenes-arles.com.

Don't pass on a chance to see *Toro Piscine*, a silly spectacle for warm summer evenings where the bull ends up in a swimming pool (uh-huh...get more details at TI). Nearby villages stage *courses camargaises* in small wooden bullrings nearly every weekend; TIs have the latest schedule.

Sleeping in Arles

Hotels are a great value here; many are air-conditioned, though few have elevators. The Calendal, Musée, and Régence hotels offer exceptional value.

$$$ Hôtel le Calendal*** is a seductive place located between the Arena and Classical Theater. Enter an expertly run hotel with airy lounges and a lovely palm-shaded courtyard. Enjoy the elaborate €12 buffet breakfast, have lunch in the courtyard or at the inexpensive sandwich bar (daily 12:00–15:00), and take advantage of their four free laptops for guests. You'll also find a Jacuzzi and a "spa" with a Turkish bath, a hot pool, and massages at good rates. The comfortable rooms sport Provençal decor and come in all shapes and sizes (standard Db–€100–115, Db with balcony–€100–115, Tb–€120–170, Qb–€140–180, price depends on room size, air-con, Wi-Fi, reserve ahead for parking–€10, just above Arena at 5 rue Porte de Laure, tel. 04 90 96 11 89, fax 04 90 96 05 84, www.lecalendal.com, contact@lecalendal.com).

$$$ Hôtel d'Arlatan***, built on the site of a Roman basilica, is classy in every sense of the word. It has sumptuous public spaces, a tranquil terrace, a designer pond, a turtle pond, and antique-filled rooms, most with high, wood-beamed ceilings and

Arles Hotels & Restaurants

VAN GOGH WALKING TOUR

🅿 **PARKING**

Ⓑ **BUS STOP**

VIEW

100 YARDS
100 METERS

1 Hôtel/Rest. le Calendal
2 Hôtel d'Arlatan
3 Hôtel du Musée
4 Hôtel de la Muette
5 Hôtel Acacias
6 Hôtel Régence
7 Hôtel/Rest. Voltaire
8 To La Peiriero & Domaine de Laforest Hôtels
9 To Mas du Petit Grava Hôtel
10 Le 16, Le Gaboulet & Au Bryn du Thym Restaurants
11 Bistrot à Vins Restaurant
12 La Guele de Loup Restaurant
13 La Cuisine de Comptoir Rest.
14 Café de la Major (Coffee/Tea)
15 Le Grillon Restaurant
16 Le Criquet Restaurant
17 Media Luna Restaurant
18 L'Atelier & A Côté Restaurants
19 Soleileis Ice Cream

DCH

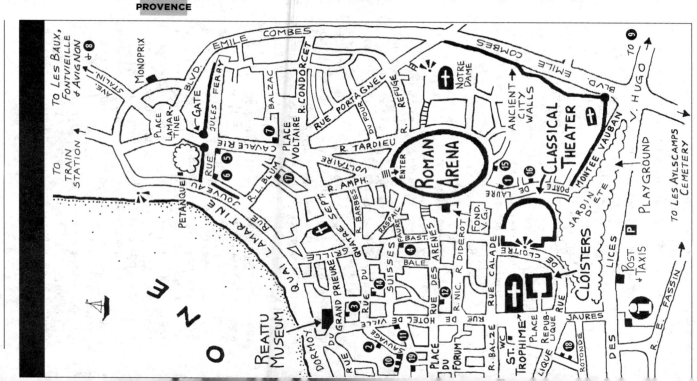

stone walls. In the lobby of this 15th-century building, a glass floor looks down into Roman ruins (standard Db-€137, bigger Db-€157, Db/Qb suites-€180, apartments-€200-250, excellent buffet breakfast-€15, air-con, bathrobes, ice machines, elevator, Wi-Fi, parking garage-€14, 1 block below place du Forum at 26 rue Sauvage—tricky by car, tel. 04 90 93 56 66, fax 04 90 49 68 45, www.hotel-arlatan.fr, hotel-arlatan@wanadoo.fr).

$$ Hôtel du Musée** is a quiet and affordable manor-home hideaway tucked deep in Arles (tough to find by car). This delightful refuge comes with 28 air-conditioned and wood-floored rooms, a flowery two-tiered courtyard, and comfortable lounges. Lighthearted Claude and English-speaking Laurence, the gracious owners, are eager to help (Sb-€50, Db-€60-70, Tb-€75-90, Qb-€95, Wi-Fi, laptop available for guests, garage-€10, follow signs to *Réattu Museum* to 11 rue du Grand Prieuré, tel. 04 90 93 88 88, fax 04 90 49 98 15, www.hoteldumusee.com, contact @hoteldumusee.com).

$$ Hôtel de la Muette**, with reserved owners Brigitte and Alain, is another good choice. Located in a quiet corner of Arles, this low-key hotel is well-kept, with stone walls, brown tones, and a small terrace in front. You'll pay a bit more for the upgraded rooms, but it's money well-spent (most Db-€66, bigger Db-€75, Tb-€77, Qb-€92, buffet breakfast-€8, air-con, Internet access and Wi-Fi, private garage-€8, 15 rue des Suisses, tel. 04 90 96 15 39, fax 04 90 49 73 16, www.hotel-muette.com, hotel .muette@wanadoo.fr).

$ Hôtel Régence**, a top budget deal, has a riverfront location, immaculate and comfortable Provençal rooms, safe parking, and easy access to the train station (Db-€50-60, Tb-€65-70, Qb-€75-80, good buffet breakfast-€6, choose river view or quieter courtyard rooms, most rooms have showers, air-con, no elevator but only two floors, Internet access and Wi-Fi; from place Lamartine, turn right immediately after passing between towers to reach 5 rue Marius Jouveau; tel. 04 90 96 39 85, fax 04 90 96 67 64, www.hotel-regence.com, contact@hotel-regence.com). The gentle Nouvions speak some English.

$ Hôtel Acacias**, just off place Lamartine and inside the old city walls, is a modern hotel with less personality. The pretty pastel rooms are on the small side, but they're reasonably priced (standard Sb or Db-€53, larger Db-€64-78, extra bed-€15, breakfast-€6, air-con, elevator, Wi-Fi, 2 rue de la Cavalerie, tel. 04 90 96 37 88, fax 04 90 96 32 51, www.hotel-acacias.com, contact@hotel-acacias .com).

$ Hôtel Voltaire* rents 12 small and questionably clean rooms with ceiling fans and nifty balconies overlooking a fun square. A block below the Arena, it's good for starving artists. Smiling owner "Mr." Ferran (fur-ran) loves the States (his dream is to travel there), and hopes you'll add to his postcard collection (D-€30, Ds-€35, Db-€40, 1 place Voltaire, tel. 04 90 96 49 18, fax 04 90 96 45 49, levoltaire13@aol.com). They also serve a good-value lunch and dinner in their recommended restaurant.

Near Arles

Many drivers, particularly those with families, prefer staying outside Arles in the peaceful countryside, with easy access to the area's sights. See also "Sleeping in Les Baux" on page 661.

$$$ La Peiriero*, 15 minutes from Arles in the town of Fontvieille, is a pooped parent's dream come true, with a grassy garden, a massive pool, table tennis, badminton, a massage parlor, an indoor children's play area, and even a few miniature golf holes. The spacious family-loft rooms, capable of sleeping up to five, have full bathrooms on both levels. This complete retreat also comes with a terrace café and a well-respected restaurant, and helpful owners the Levys (streetside Sb or Db-€100, gardenside Db-€120, Db with terrace-€144, loft-€218, dinner *menu*-€31, breakfast and dinner-€38, air-con, Wi-Fi, free parking, just east of Fontvieille on road to Les Baux, 34 avenue des Baux, tel. 04 90 54 76 10, fax 04 90 54 62 60, www.hotel-peiriero.com, info@hotel-peiriero.com). Just a short drive from Arles and Les Baux (and 20 minutes from Avignon), little Fontvieille slumbers in the shadows of its big-city cousins—though it has its share of restaurants and boutiques.

$$$ Mas du Petit Grava is a vintage Provençal farmhouse 15 tree-lined minutes east of Arles. Here California refugee Jim and Frenchman Ike offer four large and well-cared-for rooms with tubs, tiles, and memories of Vincent (Jim is an expert on Van Gogh's life and art—ask him anything). A lovely garden surrounds a generously sized pool, but what draws most here are Jim and Ike (Db-€110-130, includes good breakfast, no air-con, free Wi-Fi, tel. 04 90 98 35 66, www.masdupetitgrava.net, masdupetitgrava@masdupetitgrava.net). From Arles, drive east on D-453 toward St. Martin de Crau; 2.5 kilometers (about 1.5 miles) after passing through Raphèle, turn left on Route Saint Hippolite.

$$ Domaine de Laforest is ideally located a few minutes below Fontvieille, near the aqueduct of Barbegal. It's a big 320-acre spread engulfed by vineyards, rice fields, and swaying trees. The sweet owners (Sylvie and mama Mariette) have eight two-bedroom apartments with great weekly rates, though they may be rented for fewer days when available (€310, €400, or €700 per week, air-con, washing machines, Internet and Wi-Fi in all apartments, pool, big lawn, swings, mosquitoes can be a problem, 1000 route de l'Aqueduc Romain, tel. 04 90 54 70 25, fax 04 90 54 60 50, www.domaine-laforest.com, contact@domaine-laforest.com).

Eating in Arles

You can dine well in Arles on a modest budget—in fact, it's hard to blow a lot on dinner here (most of my listings have *menus* for €22 or less). The bad news is that restaurants here change regularly, so double-check my suggestions. Before dinner, go local on place du Forum and enjoy a *pastis*. This anise-based apéritif is served straight in a glass with ice, plus a carafe of water—dilute to taste. Sunday is a dead night for restaurants, though most eateries on place du Forum are open.

For **picnics**, a big, handy Monoprix supermarket/department store is on place Lamartine (Mon–Sat 8:30–19:25, closed Sun).

On or near Place du Forum

Great atmosphere and mediocre food at fair prices await on place du Forum. By all accounts, the garish yellow Café la Nuit is worth avoiding. Most other cafés on the square deliver acceptable quality and terrific ambience. A half-block below the Forum, on rue du Dr. Fanton, you'll find a lineup of more tempting restaurants. The first three are popular, and all have good indoor and outdoor seating.

Le 16 is a warm and affordable place to enjoy a fresh salad (€10)—though it's almost too popular for its own good (€13 *plats*, €21 three-course *menu*, closed Sat–Sun, 16 rue du Dr. Fanton, tel. 04 90 93 77 36).

Le Gaboulet has created a buzz in Arles by blending a cozy interior, classic French cuisine, and service with a smile (thanks to owner Frank). It's the most expensive of the places I list on this street, but it's still jammed every night—book ahead or come early (€27 *menu*, great fries, closed Sun–Mon, 18 rue du Dr. Fanton, tel. 04 90 93 18 11).

Au Bryn du Thym, next door, has long been reliable and specializes in traditional Provençal cuisine at fair prices—the bull steak is delicious. Arrive early for an outdoor table or call ahead, and let hardworking and sincere Monsieur and Madame Colombaud take care of you. Monsieur does *le cooking* while Madame does *le serving* (€19 three-course *menu*, closed Tue, 22 rue du Dr. Fanton, tel. 04 90 49 95 96).

Bistrot à Vins suits wine-lovers who enjoy pairing food and drink, and those in search of a good glass of *vin*. Sit at a convivial counter or at one of five tables while listening to light jazz (book ahead for a table). Affable Ariane speaks enough English and offers a limited selection of simple, tasty dishes. Her savory *tartes* and fresh green salad make a great meal (€10–16), and the wines— many available by the glass—are well-priced (indoor dining only from 18:30 to 22:00, closed Mon–Tue, 2 rue du Dr. Fanton, tel. 04 90 52 00 65).

La Guele de Loup is a small, traditional place with a loyal following (reserve ahead). Its good blend of Provençal and classic French cuisine is served in an intimate setting under wood beams in an upstairs room (€31 three-course *menu*, closed Wed, 39 rue des Arènes, tel. 04 90 96 96 69).

At **La Cuisine de Comptoir,** a cool little bistro, locals of all ages abandon Provençal decor. Welcoming owners Alexandre and Vincent offer light *tartine* dinners—a delicious cross between pizza and bruschetta, served with soup or salad for just €10 (a swinging deal). Sit at the counter and watch *le chef* at work (closed Sun, indoor dining only, just off place du Forum's lower end at 10 rue de la Liberté, tel. 04 90 96 86 28).

Café de la Major is the place to go to recharge with some serious coffee or tea (closed Sun, 7 bis rue Réattu, tel. 04 90 96 14 15).

Near the Roman Arena

For about the same price as on place du Forum, you can enjoy regional cuisine with a point-blank view of the Arena. Because

they change regularly, the handful of (mostly) outdoor eateries that overlook the Arena are pretty indistinguishable.

Le Grillon owns the best view above the Arena and serves good-enough salads, crêpes, and *plats du jour* for €9–12 (closed all day Wed and Sun nights, at the top of the Arena on rond-point des Arènes, tel. 04 90 96 70 97).

Le Criquet is a sweet little place serving Provençal classics at good prices two blocks above the Arena (€18 three-course *menu*, closed Mon, indoor dining only, 21 rue Porte de Laure, tel. 04 90 96 80 51).

Hôtel-le Calendal serves lunch in its lovely courtyard (€12–18, daily 12:00–15:00) or delicious little sandwiches for €2 each (three make a good meal) at its small café (also listed under "Sleeping in Arles," earlier).

Hôtel Voltaire, well-situated on a pleasing square, serves simple three-course lunches and dinners at honest prices to a loyal clientele (€13 *menus*; hearty *plats* and filling salads for €10—try the *salade fermière, salade Latine,* or the filling *assiette Provençale;* closed Sun evening, a few blocks below the Arena at 1 place Voltaire, tel. 04 90 96 49 18; also listed under "Sleeping in Arles," earlier).

Media Luna, a good choice for vegetarians, uses fresh, organic ingredients in its flavorful dishes. It's open on Sundays (rare in Arles) and welcomes guests with easygoing service (€14–16 *plats,* filling €15 vegetarian dish, organic wines, closed Tue, between the river and place Voltaire at 65 rue Amédée Pichot, tel. 04 90 97 81 89).

A Gastronomic Dining Experience

One of France's most recognized chefs, Jean-Luc Rabanel, has created a sensation with two different-as-night-and-day dining options 50 yards from place de la République (at 7 rue des Carmes). They sit side by side, both offering indoor and terrace seating.

L'Atelier is so intriguing that people travel great distances just for the experience. Diners fork over €90 (at lunch, you'll spoon out €50) and trust the chef to create a memorable meal...which he does. There is no menu, just an onslaught of delicious taste sensations served on artsy dishes. Don't plan on a quick dinner, and don't come for the setting—it's a contemporary, shoebox-shaped dining room, but several outdoor tables are also available. The get-to-know-your-neighbor atmosphere means you can't help but join the party. You'll probably spot the famous chef (hint: he has long brown hair), as he is very hands-on with his waitstaff (closed Mon-Tue, best to book ahead, friendly servers will hold your hand through this palate-widening experience, tel. 04 90 91 07 69, www .rabanel.com).

A Côté saddles up next door, offering a smart wine bar/bistro ambience and top-quality cuisine for far less. Here you can sample the famous chef's talents for as little as €16 (daily *plat*) or as much as €32 (three-course *menu*, smallish servings, reasonably priced wines, open daily, tel. 04 90 47 61 13).

And for Dessert...

Soleileis has Arles' best ice cream, with all-natural ingredients and unusual flavors such as *fadoli*—olive oil mixed with nougatine. There's also a shelf of English books for exchange (open daily 14:00–18:30, across from recommended Le 16 restaurant at 9 rue du Dr. Fanton).

Arles Connections

Some trains in and out of Arles require a reservation. These include connections with Nice to the east and Bordeaux to the west (including intermediary stops). Ask at the station.

From Arles by Train to: Paris (11/day, 2 direct TGVs—4 hours, 9 with transfer in Avignon—5 hours), Avignon Centre-Ville (11/day, 20 minutes, less frequent in the afternoon), Nîmes (9/day, 30 minutes), Orange (4/day direct, 35 minutes, more frequent with transfer in Avignon), Aix-en-Provence Centre-Ville (10/day, 2.25 hours, transfer in Marseille, train may separate midway—be sure you're in section going to Aix-en-Provence), Marseille (20/

PROVENCE

day, 1.5 hours), **Cassis** (7/day, 2 hours), **Carcassonne** (8/day, 3.5 hours, most with transfer in Nîmes or Narbonne, direct trains may require reservations), **Beaune** (10/day, 4.5 hours, 9 with transfer in Nîmes or Avignon and Lyon), **Nice** (11/day, 3.75–4.5 hours, most require transfer in Marseille), **Barcelona** (2/day, 6 hours, transfer in Montpellier), **Italy** (3/day, transfer in Marseille and Nice; from Arles it's 4.5 hours to Ventimiglia on the border, 8 hours to Milan, 9.5 hours to Cinque Terre, 11 hours to Florence, and 13 hours to Venice or Rome).

From Arles Train Station to Avignon TGV Station: If you're connecting from Arles to the TGV in Avignon, it's easiest to take the SNCF bus directly from Arles' train station to Avignon's TGV station (10/day, 1 hour). Another option—which takes the same amount of time, but adds more walking—is to take the regular train from Arles to Avignon's Centre-Ville Station, then catch the *navette* (shuttle bus) to the TGV station from there.

From Arles by Bus to: Nîmes (6/day, 1 hour), **St. Rémy** (bus #54, 3/day Mon–Sat, none on Sun, 50 minutes; bus #59/#57 also goes to St. Rémy—see below), **Fontvieille** (6/day, 10 minutes), **Camargue/Stes-Maries-de-la-Mer** (bus #20, 5/day Mon–Sat, 3/day Sun, 1 hour). The bus station is at 16–24 boulevard Georges Clemenceau (2 blocks below main TI, next to Café le Wilson). Bus info: tel. 04 90 49 38 01 (unlikely to speak English).

From Arles by Bus to Les Baux and St. Rémy: Bus #59/#57 connects Arles to **Les Baux** and **St. Rémy** (6/day daily July–Aug, Sat–Sun only in June and Sept; 35 minutes to Les Baux, 50 minutes to St. Rémy). Bus #54 (see above) also goes to St. Rémy, but not via Les Baux. For other ways to reach Les Baux and St. Rémy, see page 656.

Avignon

Famous for its nursery rhyme, medieval bridge, and brooding Palace of the Popes, contemporary Avignon (ahveen-yohn) bustles and prospers behind its mighty walls. During the 68 years (1309–1377) that Avignon starred as the *Franco Vaticano*, it grew from a quiet village into a thriving city. With its large student population and fashionable shops, today's Avignon is an intriguing blend of medieval history, youthful energy, and urban sophistication. Street performers entertain the international throngs who fill Avignon's ubiquitous cafés and trendy boutiques. If you're here in July, be prepared for big crowds and higher prices, thanks to the rollicking theater festival. (Reserve your hotel far in advance.) Clean, sharp, and popular with tourists, Avignon is more impressive for its outdoor ambience than for its museums and monuments.

Orientation to Avignon

The cours Jean Jaurès, which turns into rue de la République, runs straight from the Centre-Ville train station to place de l'Horloge and the Palace of the Popes, splitting Avignon in two. The larger eastern half is where the action is. Climb to Le Jardin du Rochers des Doms for the town's best view, consider touring the pope's immense palace, lose yourself in Avignon's back streets (you can follow my "Discovering Avignon's Back Streets" self-guided walk on page 638), and find a shady square to call home. Avignon's shopping district fills the traffic-free streets near where rue de la République meets place de l'Horloge.

Tourist Information

The main TI is between the Centre-Ville train station and the old town, at 41 cours Jean Jaurès (April–Oct Mon–Sat 9:00–18:00—until 19:00 in July, Sun 9:45–17:00; Nov–March Mon–Fri 9:00–18:00, Sat 9:00–17:00, Sun 10:00–12:00; tel. 04 32 74 32 74, www.avignon-tourisme.com). From April through mid-October, branch TI offices are open inside the St. Bénezet Bridge entrance (daily 10:00–13:00 & 14:00–18:00) and inside Les Halles market (Fri–Sun 10:00–13:00, closed Mon–Thu). At any TI, get the helpful map. If you're staying awhile, pick up the free *Guide Pratique* (info on bike rentals, hotels, apartment rentals, events, and museums).

Everyone should pick up the free **Avignon Passion Pass** (valid 15 days, for up to five family members). Get the pass stamped when you pay full price at your first sight, and then receive reductions at the others (for example, €2 less at the Palace of the Popes and €3 less at the Petit Palais). The discounts add up—always show your Passion Pass when buying a ticket. The pass comes with the Avignon "Passion" map and guide, which includes several good (but tricky-to-follow) walking tours.

Arrival in Avignon
By Train

Avignon has two train stations: TGV (linked to downtown by frequent shuttle buses) and Centre-Ville. While most TGV trains serve only the TGV train station, some serve Centre-Ville—verify your station in advance.

TGV Station (Gare TGV): This shiny new station, on the outskirts of town, has no baggage storage (bags can be stored only at Centre-Ville Station).

To get to the city center, take the *navette*/**shuttle bus** (marked *Navette/Avignon Centre*; €1.20, buy ticket from driver, 3/hour, 15 minutes). To find the bus stop, leave the station by the north exit (*sortie nord*), walk down the stairs, and find the long bus shelter to the left. In downtown Avignon, you'll arrive at a stop just inside the city walls, in front of the post office on cours Président Kennedy (see the map on page 632). From here you're three blocks from the city's main TI, and two blocks from Centre-Ville Station. A **taxi** ride between the TGV station and downtown Avignon costs about €16–20 (to find taxis, exit the TGV station via *sortie nord*).

To pick up a **rental car** at the TGV train station, walk out the south exit (*sortie sud*) to find the *location de voitures* in the parking lot. If you're driving directly to Arles, Les Baux, or the Luberon, leave the station following signs to *Avignon Sud*, then *La Rocade*. You'll soon see exits to Arles (best for Les Baux) and Cavaillon (for Luberon villages).

If you're heading from the Avignon TGV train station to the **Arles train station,** catch the direct SNCF bus from the TGV station's bus stop (10/day, 1 hour, schedule available at any information booth inside the TGV station).

Centre-Ville Station (Gare Avignon Centre-Ville): All non-TGV trains (and a few TGV trains) serve the central station. You can stash your bags here—exit the station to the left and look for the *consignes* sign (confirm closing time when you leave your bag). To reach the town center, cross the busy street in front of the station and walk through the city walls onto cours Jean Jaurès. The TI is three blocks down, at #41.

By Bus

The dingy bus station (*gare routière*) is 100 yards to the right as you leave the Centre-Ville train station (beyond and below Ibis Hôtel).

By Car

Drivers entering Avignon follow *Centre-Ville* and *Gare SNCF* (train station) signs. You'll find central pay lots (about €10/half-day, €14/day) in the garage next to Centre-Ville Station, at the Parking Jean Jaurès under the ramparts across from the train station; or at the Parking Palais des Papes (follow signs on the riverside road, boulevard St. Lazare, just past St. Bénezet Bridge). There are two free lots nearby with free shuttle buses to the center (follow *P Gratuit* signs): One is just across Daladier Bridge (pont Daladier), and the other is along the river past the Palace of the Popes, just northeast of the walls. Leave nothing in your car. Hotels have advice for smart overnight parking and can get you big discounts at pay lots.

Helpful Hints

Book Ahead for July: During the July theater festival, rooms are sparse—reserve very early, or stay in Arles.

Local Help: David at **Imagine Tours** (a nonprofit group whose goal is to promote this region) can help you with hotel emergencies or tickets to special events (mobile 06 89 22 19 87, www.imagine-tours.net, imagine.tours@gmail.com).

Internet Access: The TI has a current list of Internet cafés, or ask your hotelier.

English Bookstore: Try **Shakespeare Bookshop** (Tue–Sat 9:30–12:00 & 14:00–18:30, closed Sun–Mon, 155 rue Carreterie, in Avignon's northeast corner, tel. 04 90 27 38 50).

Baggage Storage: You can leave your bags at Centre-Ville train station (see "Arrival in Avignon," earlier).

Laundry: The launderette at 66 place des Corps-Saints, where rue Agricol Perdiguier ends, has English instructions and is handy to most hotels (daily 7:00–20:00).

Grocery Store: Carrefour City is central and has long hours (Mon–Sat 7:00–21:00, Sun 9:00–12:00, next to McDonald's, 2 blocks from the TI, toward place de l'Horloge on rue de la République).

Bike Rental: You'll see many **Velopop** city bikes stationed at key points in Avignon, making one-way and short-term rental a breeze. But note that the machines only accept American Express and chip-and-PIN credit cards (see page 17). You can also rent bikes and scooters at **Provence Bike** (52 boulevard St. Roch, tel. 04 90 27 92 61, www.provence-bike.com). You'll enjoy riding on the Ile de la Barthélasse, but biking is better in Isle-sur-la-Sorgue (see page 685) and Vaison la Romaine (see page 668).

Car Rental: The TGV train station has the car-rental agencies (open long hours daily).

Shuttle Boat: A free shuttle boat, the *Navette Fluviale*, plies back and forth across the river (as it did in the days when the town had no functioning bridge) from near St. Bénezet Bridge (daily July–Aug 11:00–21:00, Sept–June roughly 10:00–12:30 & 14:00–18:00, 3/hour). It drops you on the peaceful Ile de la Barthélasse, with its recommended riverside restaurant, grassy walks, and bike rides with terrific city views. If you stay on the island for dinner, check the schedule for the last return boat—or be prepared for a taxi ride or a pleasant 25-minute walk back to town.

Commanding City Views: For great views of Avignon and the river, walk or drive across Daladier Bridge, or ferry across the Rhône on the *Navette Fluviale* (described earlier). I'd take the boat across the river, walk the view path to Daladier Bridge, and then cross back over the bridge (45-minute walk over mostly level ground). You can enjoy other impressive vistas from the top of Le Jardin du Rochers des Doms, from the tower in the Palace of the Popes, and from the end of the famous, broken St. Bénezet Bridge.

Tours in Avignon

Walking Tours—The TI offers informative two-hour English walking tours of Avignon (€11, discounted with Avignon Passion Pass, April-Oct Wed and Fri-Sat at 10:00, depart from main TI; Nov-March on Sat only, depart from Palace of the Popes).

Tourist Trains—The little train leaves regularly from in front of the Palace of the Popes and gives a decent overview of the city, including Le Jardin du Rochers des Doms and St. Bénezet Bridge (€7, 2/hour, 40 minutes, mid-March–mid-Oct daily 10:00–19:00, English commentary).

Guided Excursions—Several minivan tour companies based in Avignon offer tours to destinations described in this chapter, including Pont du Gard, the Luberon, and the Camargue (about €65–75/person for all-day tours). See "Tours of Provence" on page 597 (note that guides Madeleine Vedel and François Marcou, as well as Imagine Tours, are all based in Avignon).

Self-Guided Walks

Combine these two walks—one ("Welcome to Avignon") covering the major sights, and the other ("Discovering Avignon's Back Streets") along the lanes less taken—to get beyond the surface of this historic city.

▲▲Welcome to Avignon

Before starting this walk—which connects the city's top sights—be sure to pick up the Avignon Passion Pass at the TI, then show it when entering each attraction to receive discounted admission (explained earlier, under "Tourist Information").

• *Start your tour where the Romans did, on place de l'Horloge, in front of City Hall (Hôtel de Ville).*

Avignon

1. Start of Welcome to Avignon Walk
2. Start of Discovering Back Streets Walk (Hôtel la Mirande)
3. Views & Orientation Table
4. Best View of Bridge & Stairs to Ramparts
5. City Hall
6. To Shakespeare Bookshop
7. Launderette
8. Carrefour City Grocery
9. Bike Rental
10. Shuttle Boat Stops (2)
11. Tourist Train Stop
12. TGV Shuttle Stop & Bus #11 Stop

200 YARDS
200 METERS

- VIEW
- PED. PATH
- P PARKING
- Ⓑ MAIN BUS STOP
- SELF-GUIDED WALKS

RHONE

ILE DE LA BARTHE

ST. BENEZET BRIDGE

DALADIER BRIDGE

TO VILLE-NEUVE, + P

BLVD. DE L'OULLE

ALLÉES DE L'OULLE

REMPART DE L'OULLE

RUE V. HUGO

PLACE CRILLON

PASSAGE L'ORAT.

CALVET-MUSEUM

BLVD. RASPAIL

BLVD.

TO NIMES VIA A-9

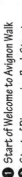

PROVENCE

PROVENCE

RIVER RHONE

TO LYON VIA D-225 & A-7

TO P.

LE JARDIN DU ROCHERS DES DOMS

PALACE OF THE POPES

ST. LAZARE BLVD.

R. BERTRAND

R. BANAS

R. INFIRM.

CARNOT

R. P. SAIN

THIERS

PETIT PALAIS MUSEUM

PALACE SQUARE

POND

R. N. LEGAT

PEYROL

R. CROIX

PLACE DE L'HORLOGE

R. BALANCE

GROTTES

FERRUCE

ST. ETIENNE

RUE JOSEPH

ST. AGRICOL

R. ST. PIERRE

MARCHANDS

SYNAGOGUE

PL. PIG.

RUE PIE

VIEUX

CARN.

ROUG.

R. FOUR

R. BONNETERIE

RUE RENE

R. ROI

ST. DIDIER

PLACE ST. DIDIER

FONDATION ANGLADON

MARKET

RUE DES TEINTURIERS

WATER-WHEEL

SORGUE RIVER

BON-MART.

PORT. MAG.

OLD WALLS

CITY BLVD.

ST. MICHEL

BUS STN.

TO ARLES & TGV TRAIN STN.

DCH

R. DE LA REPUBLIQUE

ST. FABRE

CONS.

FAU.

PLACE DES CORPS-SAINTS

RUE DES LICES

ST. MICHEL

PERP.

BOURSE

TASS.

R. JEAN JAURES

JAURES

COURS

R. ST. CHARLES

VERNET

RUE JEAN JAURES

COURS JFK

Post

VERN.

TRAIN STN. "CENTRE-VILLE"

ASSE

1 2 3 4 5 6 7 8 9 10 11 12

Place de l'Horloge

This café square was the town forum during Roman times and the market square through the Middle Ages. (Restaurants here offer good people-watching, but they also have less ambience and low-quality meals—you'll find better squares elsewhere to hang your beret in.) Named for a medieval clock tower that the City Hall now hides (find plaque in English), this square's present popularity arrived with the trains in 1854. Walk a few steps to the center of the square, and look down the main drag, rue de la République. When the trains came to Avignon, proud city fathers wanted a direct, impressive way to link the new station to the heart of the city (just like in Paris)—so they plowed over homes to create rue de la République and widened place de l'Horloge. This main drag's Parisian feel is intentional—it was built not in the Provençal manner, but in the Haussmann style that is so dominant in Paris (characterized by broad, straight boulevards lined with stately buildings).

• *Walk uphill past the carousel (public WCs behind). You'll see a golden statue of Mary, floating high above the buildings. Veer right at the street's end, and continue into...*

Palace Square (Place du Palais)

This grand square is lined with the Palace of the Popes, the Petit Palais, and the cathedral. In the 1300s, the entire headquarters of the Catholic Church was moved to Avignon. The Church bought Avignon and gave it a complete makeover. Along with clearing out vast spaces like this square and building this three-acre palace, the Church erected more than three miles of protective wall (with 39 towers), "appropriate" housing for cardinals (read: mansions), and residences for its entire bureaucracy. The city was Europe's largest construction zone. Avignon's population grew from 6,000 to 25,000 in short order. (Today, 13,000 people live within the walls.) The limits of pre-papal Avignon are outlined on city maps: Rues Joseph Vernet, Henri Fabre, des Lices, and Philonarde all follow the route of the city's earlier defensive wall.

The Petit Palais (Little Palace) seals the uphill end of the square and was built for a cardinal; today, it houses medieval paintings (museum described later). The church just to the left of the Palace of the Popes is Avignon's cathedral. It predates the Church's purchase of Avignon by 200 years. Its small size reflects Avignon's modest, pre-papal population. The gilded Mary was added in 1854, when the Vatican established the doctrine of her Immaculate Conception. Mary is taller than the Palace of the Popes by design: The Vatican never accepted what it called the "Babylonian Captivity" and had a bad attitude about Avignon long after the pope was definitively back in Rome. There hasn't been a French pope since the Holy See returned to Rome—over 600 years. That's what I call a grudge.

Directly across the square from the palace's main entry stands a cardinal's residence built in 1619 (now the Conservatoire National de Musique). Its fancy Baroque facade was a visual counterpoint to the stripped-down Huguenot aesthetic of the age. During this time, Provence was a hotbed of Protestantism—but, buried within this region, Avignon was a Catholic stronghold. Notice the stumps in front and nearby. Nicknamed *bites* (slang for the male anatomy), they effectively keep cars from double-parking in areas designed for people. Many of the metal ones slide up and down by remote control to let privileged cars come and go.

- *You can visit the massive Palace of the Popes (described on page 637)* *now, but it works better to visit that palace at the end of this walk, then continue directly to the "Back Streets" walk, described later.*

Now is a good time to take in the...

Petit Palace Museum (Musée du Petit Palais)

This former cardinal's palace now displays the Church's collection of mostly medieval Italian painting (including one delightful Botticelli) and sculpture. All 350 paintings deal with Christian themes. A visit here before going to the Palace of the Popes helps furnish and populate that otherwise barren building, and a quick peek into its courtyard shows the importance of cardinal housing (€6, €2 English brochure, some English explanations posted; June–Sept Wed–Mon 10:00–13:00 & 14:00–18:00, closed Tue; Oct–May Wed–Mon 9:30–13:00 & 14:00–17:30, closed Tue; at north end of Palace Square, tel. 04 90 86 44 58).

From Palace Square, we'll head up to the rocky hilltop where Avignon was first settled, then drop down to the river (park gates open daily April–Sept 7:30–20:00, Oct–March 7:30–18:00). With this short loop, you can enjoy a park, hike to a grand river view, and visit Avignon's beloved broken bridge—an experience worth ▲▲.

- *Start by climbing to the church level, then take the switchback ramps up to...*

▲▲Le Jardin du Rochers des Doms

While the park itself is a delight—with a sweet little café (good prices for food and drinks) and public WCs—don't miss the climax: a panoramic view of the Rhône River Valley and the broken bridge. For the best views (and the favorite

make-out spot for local teenagers later in the evening), find the terrace behind the odd zodiac display (across the grass from the pond-side park café, facing the statue of Jean Althen). On a clear day, the tallest peak you see, with its white limestone cap, is Mont Ventoux ("Windy Mountain"). Below and just to the right, you'll spot free passenger ferries shuttling across the river (great views from path on other side of the river), and—tucked amidst the trees on the far side of the river—a highly recommended restaurant, Le Bercail. The island in the river is the Ile de la Barthélasse, a nature preserve where Avignon can breathe.

St. André Fortress (across the river on the hill; see the info plaque to the left) was built by the French in 1360, shortly after the pope moved to Avignon, to counter the papal incursion into this part of Europe. The castle was across the border, in the kingdom of France. Avignon's famous bridge was a key border crossing, with towers on either end—one was French, and the other was the pope's. The French one, across the river, is the Tower of Philip the Fair (described on page 642).

• *From this viewpoint, take the stairs to the left (closed at night) down to the tower. As the stairs spiral down, just before St. Bénezet Bridge, catch a glimpse of the...*

Ramparts

The only bit of the rampart you can walk on is accessed from St. Bénezet Bridge (pay to enter—see next listing). When the pope came in the 1360s, small Avignon had no town wall...so he built one. What you see today was restored in the 19th century.

• *When you come out of the tower on street level, take the right-side exit and walk left along the river. Pass under the old bridge to find its entrance shortly after.*

▲▲St. Bénezet Bridge (Pont St. Bénezet)

This bridge, whose construction and location were inspired by a shepherd's religious vision, is the "pont d'Avignon" of nursery-rhyme fame. The ditty (which you've probably been humming all day) dates back to the 15th century: *Sur le pont d'Avignon, on y danse, on y danse, sur le pont d'Avignon, on y danse tous en rond* ("On the bridge of Avignon, we will dance, on the bridge of Avignon, we will dance all in a circle").

But the bridge was a big deal even outside of its kiddie-tune fame. Built between 1171 and 1185, it was the only bridge crossing the mighty Rhône in the Middle Ages.

It was damaged several times by floods and subsequently rebuilt, until 1668, when most of it was knocked down by a disastrous icy flood. Lacking a government stimulus package, the townsfolk decided not to rebuild this time, and for more than a century, Avignon had no bridge across the Rhône. And though only four arches survive today, the original bridge was huge: Imagine a 22-arch, 3,000-foot-long bridge extending from Vatican territory to the lonely Tower of Philip the Fair, which marked the beginning of France (see displays of the bridge's original length). A Romanesque chapel on the bridge is dedicated to St. Bénezet. While there's not much to see on the bridge, the audioguide included with your ticket tells a good enough story. It's also fun to be in the breezy middle of the river with a city view.

Cost and Hours: €4.50, €13 combo-ticket includes Palace of the Popes (see next listing), tel. 04 90 27 51 16. The ticket booth is housed in what was a medieval hospital for the poor (funded by bridge tolls). Admission includes a small room dedicated to the song of Avignon's bridge and your only chance to walk a bit of the ramparts (enter both from the tower).

• *To get to the Palace of the Popes from here, exit left, then turn left again back into the walls. Walk to the end of the short street, then turn right following signs to Palais des Papes. Look for the brown signs leading left under the passageway. After a block of uphill walking, find the stairs to the palace.*

▲Palace of the Popes (Palais des Papes)

In 1309, a French pope was elected (Pope Clément V). At the urging of the French king, His Holiness decided that dangerous Italy was no place for a pope, so he moved the whole operation to Avignon for a secure rule under a supportive king. The Catholic Church literally bought Avignon (then a two-bit town), and popes resided here until 1403. Meanwhile, Italians demanded a Roman pope, so from 1378 on, there were twin popes—one in Rome and one in Avignon—causing a schism in the Catholic Church that wasn't fully resolved until 1417.

A visit to the mighty yet barren papal palace comes with an audioguide that leads you along a one-way route and does a credible job of overcoming the complete lack of furnishings. It teaches the basic history while allowing you to tour at your own pace.

As you wander, ponder that this palace—the largest surviving

Gothic palace in Europe—was built to accommodate 500 people as the administrative center of the Holy See and home of the pope. This was the most fortified palace of the age (remember, the pope left Rome to be more secure). Nine popes ruled from here, making this the center of Christianity for 100 years. You'll walk through the pope's personal quarters (frescoed with happy hunting scenes), see many models of how the various popes added to the building, and learn about its state-of-the-art plumbing. The rooms are huge. The "pope's chapel" is twice the size of the adjacent Avignon cathedral.

Although the last pope checked out in 1403 (escaping a siege), the Church owned Avignon until the French Revolution in 1789. During this interim period, the pope's "legate" (official representative, normally a nephew) ruled Avignon from this palace. Avignon residents, many of whom had come from Rome, spoke Italian for a century after the pope left, making it a linguistic ghetto within France. In the Napoleonic age, the palace was a barracks, housing 1,800 soldiers. You can see cuts in the wall where high ceilings gave way to floor beams. Climb the tower (Tour de la Gâche) for grand views and a rooftop café with surprisingly good food at very fair prices.

A room at the end of the tour (called *la boutellerie*) is dedicated to the region's wines, of which they claim the pope was a fan. Sniff "Le Nez du Vin"—a black box with 54 tiny bottles designed to develop your "nose." (Blind-test your travel partner.) The nearby village of Châteauneuf-du-Pape is where the pope summered in the 1320s. Its famous wine is a direct descendant of his wine. You're welcome to taste here (€6 for three to five fine wines and souvenir tasting cup).

Cost and Hours: €10.50 (more during special exhibits), €13 combo-ticket includes St. Bénezet Bridge, daily mid-March–Oct 9:00–19:00, until 20:00 July and Sept, until 21:00 in Aug, Nov–mid-March 9:30–17:45, last entry one hour before closing, tel. 04 90 27 50 74, www.palais-des-papes.com.

• *You'll exit at the rear of the palace, where my "Back Streets" walking tour begins (described next). Or, to return to Palace Square, make two rights after exiting the palace.*

▲▲Discovering Avignon's Back Streets

Use the map on page 632 or the TI map to navigate this easy, level, 30-minute walk. This self-guided tour begins in the small square (place de la Mirande) behind the Palace of the Popes. If you've toured the palace, this is where you exit. Otherwise, from the front of the palace, follow the narrow, cobbled rue Peyrollerie—carved out of the rock—around the palace on the right side as you face it.

• *Our walk begins at the...*

Hotel la Mirande: Located on the square, Avignon's finest hotel welcomes visitors. Find the atrium lounge and consider a coffee break amid the understated luxury (€12 afternoon tea served daily 15:00–18:00, includes a generous selection of pastries). Inspect the royal lounge and dining room (recommended on page 649); cooking demos are offered in the basement below. Rooms start at about €400 in high season.

• *Turn left out of the hotel and left again on rue Peyrollerie ("Coppersmiths Street"), then take your first right on rue des Ciseaux d'Or. On the small square ahead you'll find the...*

Church of St. Pierre: The original chestnut doors were carved in 1551, when tales of New World discoveries raced across Europe. (Notice the Indian headdress, top center of left-side door.) The fine Annunciation (eye level on right-side door) shows Gabriel giving Mary the exciting news in impressive Renaissance 3-D. Now take 10 steps back from the door and look way up. The tiny statue breaking the skyline of the church is the pagan god Bacchus, with oodles of grapes. What's he doing sitting atop a Christian church? No one knows. The church's interior holds a beautiful Baroque altar. For recommended restaurants near the Church of St. Pierre, see "Eating in Avignon," later.

• *With your back to the church, follow the alley to the right, which was covered and turned into a tunnel during the town's population boom. It leads into...*

Place des Châtaignes: The cloister of St. Pierre is named for the chestnut (*châtaigne*) trees that once stood here (now replaced by plane trees). The practical atheists of the French Revolution destroyed the cloister, leaving only faint traces of the arches along the church side of the square.

• *Continue around the church and cross busy place Carnot to the Banque Chaix. Across the small lane to the right of the bank, find the classy...*

15th-Century Building: With its original beamed eaves showing, this is a rare vestige from the Middle Ages. Notice how this building widens the higher it gets. A medieval loophole based taxes on ground-floor square footage—everything above was tax-free. Walking down the pedestrian street, rue des Fourbisseurs ("Street of the Animal Furriers"), notice how the top floors almost meet. Fire was a constant danger in the Middle Ages, as flames leapt easily from one home to the next. In fact, the lookout guard's primary responsibility was watching for fires, not the enemy. Virtually all of Avignon's medieval homes have been replaced by safer structures.

• *Turn left from rue des Fourbisseurs onto the traffic-free rue du Vieux Sextier ("Street of the Balance," for weighing items); another left under the first arch leads 10 yards to Avignon's...*

Synagogue: Jews first arrived in Avignon with the Diaspora (exile) of the first century. Avignon's Jews were nicknamed "the

Pope's Jews" because of the protection that the Vatican offered to Jews expelled from France. This synagogue dates from the 1220s; in the mid-19th century it was completely rebuilt in a Neoclassical Greek-temple style by a non-Jewish architect. This is the only synagogue under a rotunda that you'll see anywhere. It's an intimate, classy place dressed with white colonnades and walnut furnishings. To visit the synagogue, press the buzzer (free, Mon–Fri 10:00–12:00 & 15:00–17:00, closed Sat–Sun, 2 place Jerusalem, tel. 04 90 55 21 24).

• *Retrace your steps to rue du Vieux Sextier and turn left, then continue to the big square and find the big, boxy...*

Market (Les Halles): In 1970, the town's open-air market was replaced by this modern one. The market's jungle-like green wall reflects the changes of seasons and helps mitigate its otherwise stark exterior (open Tue–Sun until 13:00, closed Mon, small TI inside open Fri–Sun). Step inside for a sensual experience of organic breads, olives, and festival-of-mold cheeses. The rue des Temptations cuts down the center. Cafés and cheese shops are on the right—as far as possible from the stinky fish stalls on the left. Follow your nose away from the fish and have a coffee with the locals.

• *Exit out the back door of Les Halles, turn left on rue de la Bonneterie ("Street of Hosiery"), and track the street for five minutes to the plane trees, where it becomes...*

Rue des Teinturiers: This "Street of the Dyers" is a tie-dyed, tree- and stream-lined lane, home to earthy cafés and galleries. This was the cloth industry's dyeing and textile center in the 1800s (a *teinturier* is a dyer). The stream is a branch of the Sorgue River. Those stylish Provençal fabrics and patterns you see for sale everywhere were first made here, modeled after a pattern imported from India.

About three small bridges down, you'll pass the Grey Penitents chapel on the right. The upper façade shows the GPs, who dressed up in robes and pointy hoods to do their anonymous good deeds back in the 13th century (long before the KKK dressed this way). As you stroll on, you'll see the work of amateur sculptors, who have carved whimsical car barriers out of limestone.

Trendy restaurants on this atmospheric street are recommended later, under "Eating in Avignon."

• *Farther down rue des Teinturiers, you'll come to the...*

Waterwheel: Standing here, imagine the Sorgue River—which hits the mighty Rhône in Avignon—being broken into several canals in order to turn 23 such wheels. In about 1800, waterwheels powered the town's industries. The little cogwheel above the big one could be shoved into place, kicking another machine into gear behind the wall.

• To return to the real world, double back on rue des Teinturiers and turn left on rue des Lices, which traces the first medieval wall. (Lice is the no-man's-land along a wall.) After a long block, you'll pass a striking four-story building that was a home for the poor in the 1600s, an army barracks in the 1800s, a fine-arts school in the 1900s, and is a deluxe condominium today (much of this neighborhood is going high-class residential). Eventually you'll return to rue de la République, Avignon's main drag.

More Sights in Avignon

Most of Avignon's top sights are covered by the walking tours, described earlier. With more time, consider these options.

Fondation Angladon-Dubrujeaud—Visiting this museum is like being invited into the elegant home of a rich and passionate art collector. It mixes a small but enjoyable collection of art from Postimpressionists (including Paul Cézanne, Vincent van Gogh, Honoré Daumier, Edgar Degas, and Pablo Picasso) with re-created art studios and furnishings from many periods. It's a quiet place with a few superb paintings (€6, Tue–Sun 13:00–18:00, closed Mon, 5 rue Laboureur, tel. 04 90 82 29 03, www.angladon.com).

Calvet Museum (Musée Calvet)—This fine-arts museum impressively displays its collection, highlighting French Baroque works. While the museum goes ignored by most, you'll find a few diamonds in the rough upstairs: Géricault, Soutine, and one painting each from Manet, Sisley, Bonnard, Dufy, and Vlaminck (€6, includes audioguide, Wed–Mon 10:00–13:00 & 14:00–18:00, closed Tue, in the quieter western half of town at 65 rue Joseph Vernet, antiquities collection a few blocks away at 27 rue de la République—same hours and ticket, tel. 04 90 86 33 84, www.musee-calvet.org).

Near Avignon

Villeneuve-lès-Avignon—For a refreshing village escape from Avignon, cross the Rhône River and explore Avignon's little sister city of Villeneuve-lès-Avignon (take bus #11 from in front of Avignon's post office on cours Président Kennedy, 2/hour Mon–Sat, none Sun—see map on page 632; or drive 5 minutes across

Daladier Bridge and follow signs).

As you approach Villeneuve, bus #11 stops near the **Tower of Philip the Fair** (Tour Philippe-le-Bel). Built in 1307 to protect access to St. Bénezet Bridge, this massive tower offers a terrific view over Avignon and the Rhône basin. It's best late in the day (€2.10; April–Sept daily 10:00–12:30 & 14:00–18:30; Oct–Nov Tue–Sat 10:00–12:30 & 14:00–17:00, closed Sun–Mon; closed Dec–March).

Once in Villeneuve, you'll find fewer tourists and a smattering of good restaurants and local cafés among its peaceful lanes and small squares. You'll also uncover a handful of worthwhile sights (the Avignon Passion Pass offers discounts for most). Climb to the monumental **Fort St. André** for film gobbling views from its ramparts and towers and roam the lovely **Abbey Gardens** inside the fort's walls with more views (fort–€5, daily Oct–March 10:00–17:00, April–Sept 9:30–18:00; abbey–€5, Tue–Sun 10:00–12:30 & 14:00–18:00, closed Mon). Or rattle around a romantic abbey at the **Chartreuse du Val de Bénédiction** (€7, same hours as fort, 58 rue de la République).

Sleeping in Avignon

(€1 = about $1.25, country code: 33)

Hotel values are better in Arles than in Avignon, though I've found some good values in Avignon and have listed them here. Avignon is particularly popular during its July festival, when you must book ahead (expect inflated prices). Drivers should ask about parking deals.

Near Avignon's Centre-Ville Station

The first five listings are a five- to ten-minute walk from the Centre-Ville train station. (For hotels Colbert, Parc, and Splendid, turn right off cours Jean Jaurès on rue Agricol Perdiguier.)

$$$ Hôtel Bristol*** is a big, professionally run place on the main drag, offering predictable "American" comforts, including spacious public spaces, large rooms decorated in neutral tones, duvets on the beds, a big elevator, air-conditioning, and a generous buffet breakfast (standard Db–€88–103, bigger Db–€126, Tb/Qb–€153, breakfast–€12, parking–€12, 44 cours Jean Jaurès, tel. 04 90 16 48 48, fax 04 90 66 22 72, www.bristol-hotel-avignon.com, contact@bristol-avignon.com).

$$$ Hôtel Colbert** is a solid two-star hotel and a good mid-range bet, with richly colored, comfortable rooms in many sizes. Your efficient hosts—Patrice, Annie, and *le chien* Brittany—care for this restored manor house, with its warm public spaces and sweet little patio. It's a popular place, so it's best to book well in advance (Sb–€65, small Db–€78, bigger Db–€84–100, some tight bathrooms, no triples available, creative homemade breakfast-€10, air-con, Wi-Fi, 7 rue Agricol Perdiguier, tel. 04 90 86 20 20, fax 04 90 85 97 00, www.lecolbert-hotel.com, contact@avignon-hotel -colbert.com).

$$ Hôtel du Parc* is a spotless value with white walls, some tiny bathrooms, and stone accents. Since it's likely to be under new ownership for 2011, these prices are *très* tentative (S-€32, Sb-€45, Ds-€65, Db-€70, Ts-€75; no TVs, phones, or air-con; tel. 04 90 82 71 55, fax 04 90 85 64 86, http://perso.modulonet.fr/hoduparc, hotel.parc@modulonet.fr). This place is homier than Hôtel le Splendid, across the street.

$$ At Hôtel Boquier*, engaging Madame Sendra offers 12 quiet, good-value, and homey rooms under wood beams in a central location (small Db-€58, bigger Db-€72, Tb-€80, Qb-€94, air-con, Internet access and Wi-Fi, steep and narrow stairways to some rooms, no elevator, parking-€7, near the TI at 6 rue du portail Boquier, tel. 04 90 82 34 43, fax 04 90 86 14 07, www.hotel -boquier.com, contact@hotel-boquier.com).

$ Hôtel le Splendid* rents 17 acceptable rooms with faux-wood floors, most of which could use a little attention (Sb-€48, Db-€62, bigger Db with air-con-€72, Tb with air-con-€82, three Db apartments-€92, Internet access and Wi-Fi, 17 rue Agricol Perdiguier, tel. 04 90 86 14 46, fax 04 90 85 38 55, www.avignon -splendid-hotel.com, splendidavignon@gmail.com).

In the Center, near Place de l'Horloge

$$$ Hôtel d'Europe**, with Avignon's most prestigious address, lets peasants sleep royally without losing their shirts—but only if you land one of the 10 surprisingly reasonable "standard" rooms. Enter a shady courtyard, linger in the lounges, and savor every comfort. The hotel is located on the handsome place Crillon, near the river (standard Db-€200, superior Db-€360, prestige Db-€495, breakfast-€17, elevator, Internet access, garage-€17, near Daladier Bridge at 12 place Crillon, tel. 04 90 14 76 76, fax 04 90 14 76 71, www.heurope.com, reservations@heurope.com). The hotel's restaurant is Michelin-rated (one star) and serves an upscale €48 *menu* in its formal dining room or front courtyard.

$$$ Hôtel Mercure Cité des Papes* is a modern chain hotel within spitting distance of the Palace of the Popes. It has 89 smartly designed, small rooms (Sb-€135, Db-€145-180, promotional deals best if booked 15 days ahead, many rooms have views over place de l'Horloge, air-con, elevator, 1 rue Jean Vilar, tel. 04 90 80 93 00, fax 04 90 80 93 01, www.mercure.com, h1952@accor.com).

$$$ Hôtel Pont d'Avignon*, just inside the walls near St. Bénezet Bridge, is part of the same chain as the Hôtel Mercure Cité des Papes, with the same prices for its 87 rooms (direct access

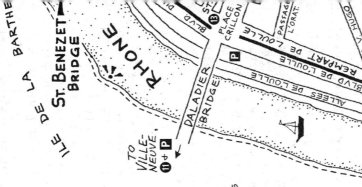

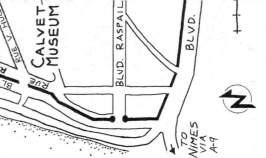

Avignon Hotels & Restaurants

1. Hôtel Bristol
2. Hôtel Colbert
3. Hôtel du Parc
4. Hôtel le Splendid
5. Hôtel Boquier
6. Hôtel d'Europe
7. Hôtel Mercure Cité des Papes
8. Hôtel Pont d'Avignon
9. Hôtel Médiéval
10. To Le Clos du Rempart & Lumani B&Bs
11. To Auberge Bagatelle (Hostel) & Jardin de Bacchus Rooms
12. Church of St. Pierre Eateries
13. Place Crillon Eateries
14. Place des Corps-Saints Eateries
15. Restaurant Françoise
16. La Cave des Passages Wine Bar
17. L'Empreinte Restaurant
18. To Restaurant Numéro 75
19. L'Isle Sonnante Restaurant
20. La Cantina Restaurant
21. Le Caveau du Théâtre Rest.
22. Hôtel la Mirande Restaurant
23. La Vache à Carreaux Rest.
24. L'Epice and Love Rest.
25. Le Bercail Rest.
26. Carrefour City Grocery

200 YARDS
200 METERS

☀ VIEW
- - - PED. PATH
P PARKING
Ⓑ MAIN BUS STOP

PROVENCE

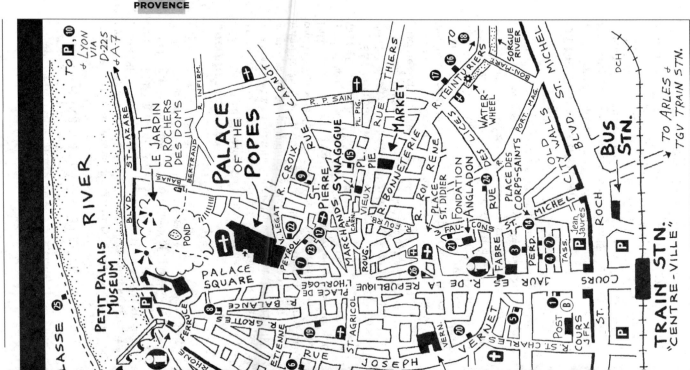

to a garage makes parking easier than at the other Mercure hotel, elevator, on rue Ferruce, tel. 04 90 80 93 93, fax 04 90 80 93 94, www.mercure.com, h0549@accor.com).

$$ Hôtel Médiéval** is burrowed deep a few blocks from the Church of St. Pierre. Built as a cardinal's home, this massive stone mansion has a small garden and friendly-as-they-get Mike at the helm. It has 35 wood-paneled, air-conditioned, unimaginative rooms (Sb-€49, Db-€62-77, bigger Db or Tb-€85-92, kitchenettes available but require 3-night minimum stay, Wi-Fi, 5 blocks east of place de l'Horloge, behind Church of St. Pierre at 15 rue Petite Saunerie, tel. 04 90 86 11 06, fax 04 90 82 08 64, www.hotel medieval.com, hotel.medieval@wanadoo.fr).

Chambres d'Hôte

$$$ At **Le Clos du Rempart**, a 10-minute walk from the center, Madame Assad rents two comfortable rooms and one apartment on a peaceful courtyard with Middle Eastern decor (Db-€120-150 depending on season and room size, 2-bedroom apartment for 4 with kitchen-€800-1,100/week, includes breakfast, cash only, aircon, Wi-Fi, one parking spot in garage, inside the walls east of the Palace of the Popes at 35-37 rue Crémade—call or check website for directions, tel. & fax 04 90 86 39 14, www.closdurempart.com, aida@closdurempart.com).

$$$ Lumani provides the ultimate urban refuge just inside the city walls, a 15-minute walk from the Palace of the Popes. In this graceful old manor house, gentle Elisabeth and Jean welcome guests to their art-gallery-cum-bed-and-breakfast that surrounds a fountain-filled courtyard with elbow room. She paints, he designs buildings, and both care about your experience in Avignon. The five rooms are decorated with flair—no two are alike, and all overlook the shady garden (small Db-€100, big Db-€140, Db suites-€170, extra person-€30, includes breakfast, credit cards OK except American Express, Internet access and Wi-Fi, music studio, parking-€10 or easy on street, 37 rue de Rempart St Lazare, tel. 04 90 82 94 11, www.avignon-lumani.com, lux@avignon-lumani.com).

On the Outskirts of Town

$ Auberge Bagatelle's hostel offers dirt-cheap beds, a lively atmosphere, a café, a grocery store, a launderette, great views of Avignon, and campers for neighbors (D-€44, Ds-€48, T-€60, Ts-€67, Tb-€82, Q-€73, Qb-€100, dorm bed-€18, includes breakfast, across Daladier Bridge on Ile de la Barthélasse, bus #10 from main post office, tel. 04 90 86 71 31, fax 04 90 27 16 23, www .aubergebagatelle.fr, auberge.bagatelle@wanadoo.fr).

Near Avignon

$$$ At **Jardin de Bacchus**, just 15 minutes northwest of Avignon and convenient to Pont du Gard, enthusiastic and English-speaking Christine and Erik offer three rooms in their rural farm-house overlooking little Tavel's famous vineyards (Db-€85–105, €30 extra for one-night stays, breakfast-€10, fine dinner possible, Wi-Fi, tel. 04 66 90 28 62, www.jardindebacchus.fr, jardinde bacchus@free.fr). To learn about their small-group food and wine tours, check their website.

Eating in Avignon

Skip the overpriced places on place de l'Horloge and find a more intimate location for your dinner. Avignon has many delightful squares filled with tables ready to seat you.

Near the Church of St. Pierre

The church divides two enchanting squares. One is quiet and intimate, the other is lively.

L'Epicerie, sitting alone on an intimate square, serves the highest-quality—and highest-priced—cuisine around the Church of St. Pierre, with a focus on products from the south of France. Expect lots of color and a dash of spice (€18–24 *plats*, closed Sun off-season, cozy interior good in bad weather, 10 place St. Pierre, tel. 04 90 82 74 22).

On Place des Châtaignes: Pass under the arch by L'Epicerie restaurant and enter enchanting place des Châtaignes, with a fun commotion of tables. Peruse your options. The **Crêperie du Cloître** makes mediocre dinner crêpes and salads (daily, cash only). **Restaurant Nem**, tucked in the corner, is Vietnamese and family-run (*menus* from €12, cash only). **Pause Gourmande** is a small, lunch-only eatery with €9 *plats du jour* and always a veggie option (closed Sun).

Place Crillon

This more refined square just off the river attracts a stylish crowd and houses a variety of dining choices. Traditional French **Restaurant les Artistes** and *italiano* **La Piazza** are both popular and owned by the same folks (good €11 lunch deals, €17 dinner *menus* with interesting choices, daily, tel. 04 90 82 23 54). **La Comédie** serves €9 crêpes and salads with mod seating (closed Sun).

Place des Corps-Saints

You'll find several youthful and reasonable eateries with tables sprawling under big plane trees on this locally popular square. **Bistrot à Tartines** specializes in—you guessed it—*tartines* (big slices of toast smothered with toppings), and has the coziest interior and best desserts on the square (€8 *tartines* and salads, daily, tel. 04 90 85 58 70). I also enjoy the €10 pizzas and friendly service at **Le Pili** (daily, tel. 04 90 27 39 53). **Zeste** is a friendly, modern deli offering fresh soups, pasta salads, wraps, smoothies, and more. Get it to go, or eat inside or on the scenic square—all at unbeatable prices (closed Sun, tel. 09 51 49 05 62).

By the Market (Les Halles)

Here you'll find a good selection of eateries with good prices. **Restaurant Françoise** is a pleasant café and tea salon, where fresh-baked tarts—savory and sweet—and a variety of salads and soups make a healthful meal, and vegetarian options are plentiful (€7-12 dishes, Mon-Sat 8:00-19:00, closed Sun, free Wi-Fi, 6 rue Général Leclerc, tel. 04 32 76 24 77).

Rue des Teinturiers

This "tie-dye" street has a wonderful concentration of eateries popular with the natives, and justifies the long walk. It's a youthful, trendy area, recently spiffed up with a canalside ambience and little hint of tourism. Survey the eateries listed here before choosing (all line up near the waterwheel).

La Cave des Passages makes a colorful pause before dinner. The owners enjoy serving you a fragrant €2.50 glass of regional wine. Choose from the blackboard by the bar that lists all the bottles open today, then join the gang outside by the canal. In the evening, this place is a hit with the young local crowd for its wine and weekend concerts (Mon-Sat 10:00-15:00 & 18:00-1:00 in the morning, closed Sun, no food in evening, across from waterwheel at 41 rue des Teinturiers).

L'Empreinte is good for North African cuisine. Choose a table in its tent-like interior, or sit canalside on the cobbles (copious couscous or *tajine* for €13-16, take-out and veggie options available, daily, 33 rue des Teinturiers, tel. 04 32 76 31 84).

Restaurant Numéro 75 is worth the walk (just where the cobbles end on rue des Teinturiers). It fills the Pernod mansion (of *pastis* liquor fame) and a large, romantic courtyard with outdoor tables. The menu is limited to Mediterranean cuisine, but everything's *très* tasty. It's best to go with the options offered by your young black-shirted server (€20 two-course lunch *menu* with wine and coffee, dinner *menus:* €27/appetizer and main course or main course and dessert, €33/3 courses; Mon-Sat

12:00–14:00 & 20:00–22:00, closed Sun, 75 rue Guillaume Puy, tel. 04 90 27 16 00).

Elsewhere in Avignon

At **L'Isle Sonnante**, join chef Boris and his wife, Anne, to dine intimately in their formal and charming one-room *bistrot*. You'll choose from a small menu offering only fresh products and be served by owners who care (*menus* from €30, closed Sun-Mon, 100 yards from the carousel on place de l'Horloge at 7 rue Racine, tel. 04 90 82 56 01, best to book ahead).

La Cantina delivers fine Italian cuisine in a beautiful courtyard (€15 pizzas, €20–30 *plats*, closed Sun evening, 83 rue Joseph Vernet, tel. 04 90 85 99 04).

Le Caveau du Théâtre is a welcoming place where Richard invites diners to have a glass of wine or dinner at a sidewalk table, or inside in one of two carefree rooms (€13 *plats*, €18 *menus*, fun ambience for free, closed for lunch Sat and all day Sun, 16 rue des Trois Faucons, tel. 04 90 82 60 91).

Hôtel la Mirande is the ultimate Avignon splurge. Reserve ahead here for understated elegance and Avignon's top cuisine (€35 lunch *menu*, €105 dinner tasting *menu*; closed Tue-Wed—but for a price break, dine in the kitchen with the chef on these "closed" days for €85–140 including wine; behind Palace of the Popes, 4 place de la Mirande, tel. 04 90 86 93 93, www.la-mirande.fr).

La Vache à Carreaux is a unique place with a passion for cheese in all its forms (non-cheese dishes are also available). The decor is as warm as the welcome, the wine list is extensive and reasonable, and it's a hit with the locals—so reserve ahead (€12–20 *plats*, daily, just behind Palace of the Popes at 14 rue Peyrollerie, tel. 04 90 80 09 05).

At **L'Epice and Love**, pronounced "lay peace and love" (the name is a fun French-English play on words), English-speaking owner Marie creates a playful atmosphere in her cozy, friendly restaurant. A few colorfully decorated tables and tasty meat, fish, and vegetarian dishes at good prices greet the hungry traveler (*menus* from €16, daily, 30 rue des Lices, tel. 04 90 82 45 96).

Across the River

Le Bercail offers a fun opportunity to get out of town (barely) and take in *le fresh air* with a terrific riverfront view of Avignon, all while enjoying inexpensive Provençal cooking served in big portions. Book ahead, as this restaurant is popular (*menus* from €17, serves late, daily April-Oct, tel. 04 90 82 20 22). To get there, take the free shuttle boat (located near St. Bénezet Bridge) to the Ile de la Barthélasse, turn right, and walk five minutes. As the boat usually stops running at about 18:00 (except in July-Aug, when it runs until 21:00), you can either taxi home or walk 25 minutes along the pleasant riverside path and over Daladier Bridge.

Avignon Connections

Trains

Remember, there are two train stations in Avignon: the suburban TGV Station, and the Centre-Ville Station in the city center (€1.20 shuttle buses connect to both stations, buy ticket from driver, 3/hour, 15 minutes). TGV trains usually serve the TGV train station only, though a few depart from Centre-Ville train station (check your station). Only Centre-Ville Station has baggage storage (see "Arrival in Avignon" on page 628). Car rental is available only at the TGV Station. Some cities are served by slower local trains from Centre-Ville Station as well as by faster TGV trains from the TGV Station; I've listed the most convenient stations for each trip.

From Avignon's Centre-Ville Station by Train to: Arles (11/day, 20 minutes, less frequent in the afternoon), **Orange** (15/day, 15 minutes), **Nîmes** (14/day, 30 minutes), **Isle-sur-la-Sorgue** (10/day on weekdays, 5/day on weekends, 30 minutes), **Lyon** (10/day, 2 hours, also from TGV Station—see below), **Carcassonne** (8/day, 7 hours, with transfer in Narbonne, 3 hours), **Barcelona** (2/day, 6–9 hours, transfer in Montpellier).

From Avignon's TGV Station to: Arles (by SNCF bus, 10/day, 1 hour), **Nice** (20/day, most via TGV, 4 hours, most require transfer in Marseille), **Marseille** (10/day, 1 hour), **Cassis** (7/day, 2 hours), **Aix-en-Provence TGV** (10/day, 25 minutes), **Lyon** (12/day, 1.5 hours, also from Centre-Ville Station—see above), **Paris'** Gare de Lyon (9/day direct, 2.5 hours; more connections with transfer, 3–4 hours), **Paris'** Charles de Gaulle airport (7/day, 3 hours).

Buses

The bus station (*gare routière*) is just past and below Ibis Hôtel, to the right as you exit the train station (info desk open Mon–Sat 8:00–19:30, closed Sun, tel. 04 90 82 07 35, staff speaks English). Nearly all buses leave from this station (buy tickets on bus, small bills only). The biggest exception is the SNCF bus service from the Avignon TGV train station to Arles (explained earlier). The Avignon TI has schedules. Service is reduced or nonexistent on Sundays and holidays. Check your departure time beforehand and make sure to verify your destination with the driver.

From Avignon to Pont du Gard: Buses go to this famous old aqueduct (3–5/day, 40–50 minutes, departs from bus station, usually from stall #11), but the schedule doesn't work well for day-trippers from Avignon; instead, consider a taxi one way and bus back.

By Bus to Other Regional Destinations: Uzès (3–5/day Mon–Sat, none Sun, 1 hour, stops at Pont du Gard); **St. Rémy-de-Provence** (6/day, 45 minutes, handy way to visit its Wed market); **Orange** (Mon–Sat hourly, none Sun, 45 minutes—take the train instead); **Isle-sur-la-Sorgue** (6–8/day Mon–Sat, 3–4/day Sun, 45 minutes). To reach the **Côtes du Rhône** area, the bus runs to **Vaison la Romaine, Nyons, Sablet,** and **Séguret** (5/day during the school year—called *période solaire*, 3/day otherwise, and 1/day from TGV station; 1.5 hours, all buses pass through Orange—faster to take train to Orange, and transfer to bus there). For the **Luberon** area—including **Lourmarin** and **Gordes**—first take the bus to Cavaillon (from there take bus #8 toward Pertuis for Lourmarin, or bus #15 for Gordes).

Pont du Gard

Throughout the ancient world, aqueducts were like flags of stone that heralded the greatness of Rome. A visit to this sight still works to proclaim the wonders of that age. This perfectly pre-served Roman aqueduct was built in about 19 B.C. as the critical link of a 30-mile canal that, by dropping one inch for every 350 feet, supplied nine million gallons of water per day (about 100 gal-lons per second) to Nîmes—one of ancient Europe's largest cities. Though most of the aqueduct is on or below the ground, at Pont du Gard it spans a canyon on a massive bridge—one of the most remarkable surviving Roman ruins anywhere. Wear sturdy shoes if you plan to climb around the aqueduct (footing is tricky), and bring swimwear and flip-flops if you plan to backstroke beneath the monument.

Getting to Pont du Gard

The famous aqueduct is between Remoulins and Vers-Pont du Gard on D-981, 13 miles from Avignon.

By Car: Pont du Gard is a 25-minute drive due west of Avignon (follow N-100 from Avignon, tracking signs to *Nîmes* and *Remoulins*, then *Pont du Gard* and *Rive Gauche*), and 45 minutes northwest of Arles (via Tarascon on D-15). Parking is available on the Rive Gauche (Right Bank), but it's farther away from the museum than parking on the Rive Gauche (Left Bank). If going to Arles from Pont du Gard, follow signs to *Nîmes* (not Avignon), then follow D-986 and D-15 to Arles.

By Bus: Buses run to Pont du Gard (on the Rive Gauche side) from Avignon (3/day, 50 minutes), Nîmes, and Uzès (confirm times locally). Consider this plan: Take the midday bus from Avignon to

Pont du Gard

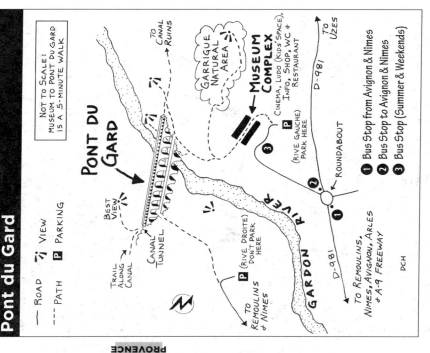

NOT TO SCALE:
MUSEUM TO PONT DU GARD
IS A 5-MINUTE WALK

— ROAD
--- PATH
🔭 VIEW
🅿 PARKING

PONT DU GARD

TO CANAL RUINS

GARRIGUE NATURAL AREA

MUSEUM COMPLEX

CINEMA, LUDO (KIDS SPACE), INFO, SHOP, WC + RESTAURANT

BEST VIEW

CANAL TUNNEL

TRAIL ALONG CANAL

🅿 (RIVE DROITE) DON'T PARK HERE

TO REMOULINS + NIMES

GARDON RIVER

🅿 (RIVE GAUCHE) PARK HERE

❸

D-981 TO UZES

ROUNDABOUT

❷

❶

D-981

TO REMOULINS, NIMES, AVIGNON, ARLES & A-9 FREEWAY

DCH

❶ Bus Stop from Avignon & Nimes
❷ Bus Stop to Avignon & Nimes
❸ Bus Stop (Summer & Weekends)

Pont du Gard (11:40 in 2010), then take the afternoon bus (16:15 in 2010) on to Nîmes (40 minutes), where trains run almost hourly back to Avignon. Or take a taxi back (see next page).

Buses stop at the traffic roundabout 300 yards from the aqueduct. In summer and on weekends, however, buses usually drive into the Pont du Gard site and stop at the parking lot's ticket booth. Confirm where the bus stops at the parking booth inside the Pont du Gard site.

At the roundabout, the stop for buses coming from Avignon and Nîmes (and going to Uzès) is on the side opposite Pont du Gard; the stop for buses to Nîmes and to Avignon is on the same side as Pont du Gard (a block to your left as you exit Pont du Gard onto the main road). Make sure you're waiting for the bus on the correct side of the traffic circle (stops have schedules posted), and wave your hand to signal the bus to stop for you (otherwise, it'll chug on by). Buy your ticket when you get on and verify your destination with the driver.

By Taxi: From Avignon it's about €42 for a taxi ride to Pont du Gard. If you're staying in Avignon and only want to see Pont du Gard, consider splurging on a taxi to the aqueduct in the morning, then take the early-afternoon bus back.

Orientation to Pont du Gard

There are two riversides to Pont du Gard: the Left Bank (Rive Gauche) and Right Bank (Rive Droite). Park on the Rive Gauche, where you'll find museums, ticket booth, ATM, cafeteria, WCs, and shops—all built into a modern plaza. You'll see the aqueduct in two parts: first the fine museum complex, then the actual river gorge spanned by the ancient bridge.

Cost and Hours: The aqueduct, museum, film, outdoor *garrigue* nature area, and related attractions are all free, but parking is €15 per car (those arriving by bus or bike pay nothing). The museum is open daily May–Sept 9:00–19:00, Oct–April 9:00–17:00, closed two weeks in Jan. The aqueduct itself is open until 1:00 in the morning, as is the parking lot. Toll tel. 08 20 90 33 30, www.pontdugard.fr. The *garrigue* is always open.

Tours and Information: For an extra €6, you can rent an **audioguide** with detailed explanations of the aqueduct in English. Call ahead or visit the website for information on **guided walks** on top of the aqueduct. Consider the helpful €4 English **booklet** about the *garrigue*—the extensive nature area featuring historic crops and landscapes of the Mediterranean.

Canoe Rental: Floating under Pont du Gard by canoe is an experience you won't soon forget. Collias Canoes will pick you up at Pont du Gard (or elsewhere, if pre-arranged) and shuttle you to the nearby town of Collias. You'll float down the river to the town of Remoulins, where they'll pick you up and take you back to Pont du Gard (€18/person, €9/child under 12, usually 2 hours, though you can take as long as you like, good idea to reserve the day before in July–Aug, tel. 04 66 22 85 54).

Plan Ahead for Swimming: Pont du Gard is perhaps best enjoyed on your back and in the water—bring along a swimsuit, and flip-flops for the rocks.

Sights at Pont du Gard

▲**Museum**—In this state-of-the-art museum (well-presented in English), you'll enter to the sound of water and understand the critical role fresh water played in the Roman "art of living." You'll see examples of lead pipes, faucets, and siphons; walk through a mock rock quarry; and learn how they moved those huge rocks into place and how those massive arches were made. While actual artifacts from the aqueduct are few, the exhibit shows the immensity of the undertaking as well as the payoff. Imagine the excitement as this extravagant supply of water finally tumbled into Nîmes. A relaxing highlight is the scenic video of a helicopter ride along the entire 30-mile course of the structure, from its start at Uzès all the way to the Castellum in Nîmes.

Other Activities—Several additional attractions are designed to give the sight more meaning—and they do (but for most visitors, the museum is sufficient). A corny, romancing-the-aqueduct 25-minute **film** plays in the same building as the museum and offers good information in a flirtatious French-Mediterranean style...and a cool, entertaining, and cushy break. The nearby **kids' museum**, called Ludo, offers a scratch-and-sniff teaching experience (in English) of various aspects of Roman life and the importance of water. The extensive outdoor *garrigue natural area*, closer to the aqueduct, features historic crops and landscapes of the Mediterranean.

▲▲▲Viewing the Aqueduct—A park-like path leads to the aqueduct. Until a few years ago, this was an actual road—adjacent to the aqueduct—that had spanned the river since 1743. Before you cross the bridge, pass under it and hike about 300 feet along the riverbank for a grand viewpoint from which to study the world's second-highest standing Roman structure. (Rome's Colosseum is only 6 feet taller.)

This was the biggest bridge in the whole 30-mile-long aqueduct. It seems exceptional because it is: The arches are twice the width of standard aqueducts, and the main arch is the largest the Romans ever built—80 feet (so it wouldn't get its feet wet). The bridge is about 160 feet high and was originally about 1,100 feet long. Today, 12 arches are missing, reducing the length to 790 feet.

Although the distance from the source (in Uzès) to Nîmes was only 12 miles as the eagle flew, engineers chose the most economical route, winding and zigzagging 30 miles. The water made the trip in 24 hours with a drop of only 40 feet. Ninety percent of the aqueduct is on or under the ground, but a few river canyons like this required bridges. A stone lid hides a four-foot-wide, six-foot-tall chamber lined with waterproof mortar that carried the stream for more than 400 years. For 150 years, this system provided Nîmes with good drinking water. Expert as the Romans were, they miscalculated the backup caused by a downstream corner, and had to add the thin extra layer you can see just under the lid to make the channel deeper.

The bridge and the river below provide great fun for holiday-goers. While parents suntan on rocks, kids splash into the gorge from under the aqueduct. Some daredevils actually jump from the aqueduct's lower bridge—not knowing that crazy winds scrambled by the structure cause painful belly flops (and sometimes even accidental deaths). For the most refreshing view, float flat on your back underneath the structure.

The appearance of the entire gorge changed in 2002, when a huge flood flushed lots of greenery downstream. Those floodwaters put Roman provisions to the test. Notice the triangular-shaped buttresses at the lower level—designed to split and divert the force of any flood *around* the feet of the arches rather than *into* them. The 2002 floodwaters reached the top of those buttresses. Anxious park rangers winced at the sounds of trees crashing onto the ancient stones...but the arches stood strong.

The stones that jut out—giving the aqueduct a rough, unfin-ished appearance—supported the original scaffolding. The pro-tuberances were left, rather than cut off, in anticipation of future repair needs. The lips under the arches supported wooden tem-plates that allowed the stones in the round arches to rest on some-thing until the all-important keystone was dropped into place. Each stone weighs four to six tons. The structure stands with no mortar—taking full advantage of the innovative Roman arch, made strong by gravity.

Hike over the bridge for a closer look and the best views. Steps lead up a high trail (marked *panorama*) to a superb viewpoint (go right at the top; best views are soon after the trail starts descending). You'll also see where the aqueduct meets a rock tunnel. Walk through the tunnel and continue for a bit, following a trail that meanders along the canal's path.

Back on the museum side, steps lead up to the Rive Gauche (parking lot) end of the aqueduct, where you can fol-low the canal path along a trail (marked with red-and-white horizontal lines) to find some remains of the Roman canal. You'll soon reach another *panorama* with great views of the aqueduct. Hikers can continue along the path, following the red-and-white markings that lead through a forest, after which you'll come across more remains of the canal (much of which are covered by vegetation). There's not much left to

see because of medieval cannibalization—frugal builders couldn't resist the precut stones as they constructed local churches (stones along the canal were easier to retrieve than those high up on the aqueduct). The path continues for about 15 miles, but there's little reason to go farther. However, there is talk of opening the ancient quarry...someday.

Les Baux

The hilltop town of Les Baux crowns the rugged Alpilles (ahl-pee) Mountains, evoking a tumultuous medieval history. Here, you can imagine the struggles of a strong community that lived a rough-and-tumble life—thankful more for their top-notch fortifications than for their dramatic views. It's mobbed with tourists most of the day, but Les Baux rewards those who arrive by 9:00 or after 17:30. (Though the hilltop citadel's entry closes at the end of the day, once you're inside, you're welcome to live out your medieval fantasies all night long.) Sunsets are dramatic, the castle is brilliantly illuminated after dark, and nights in Les Baux are pin-drop peaceful.

Getting to Les Baux

By Car: Les Baux is a 20-minute drive from Arles: Follow signs for *Avignon*, then *Les Baux*.

By Bus: From Arles, bus #59/#57 runs to Les Baux daily July through August and Saturday–Sunday in June and September (6/day, 35 minutes, via Abbey of Montmajour, Fontvieille, and Paradou). You can also get from Arles or Avignon to Les Baux via St. Rémy (this town is worth exploring, or use it as a transit point). From either city, take the bus to St. Rémy: It's a 50-minute ride from Arles (3–6/day, none on Sun off-season) and 45 minutes from Avignon (6/day). If buses aren't running to Les Baux, taxi there from St. Rémy, then take another one back to your home base).

By Taxi: Count on €37 for a taxi one-way from Arles to Les Baux (€45 after 19:00), and allow €15 one-way from St. Rémy (mobile 06 80 27 60 92).

By Minivan Tour: The best option for many is a minivan tour, which can be both efficient and economical (easiest from Avignon; see "Tours of Provence" on page 597).

Orientation to Les Baux

Les Baux is actually two visits in one: castle ruins perched on an almost lunar landscape, and a medieval town below. Savor the castle, then tour—or blitz—the lower streets on your way out. While the town, which lives entirely off tourism, is packed with shops, cafés, and tourist knickknacks, the castle above stays manageable since crowds are dispersed over a big area. The lower town's polished-stone gauntlet of boutiques is a Provençal dream-come-true for shoppers.

Tourist Information

The TI is immediately on the left as you enter the village (daily 9:00–17:30, later in summer, tel. 04 90 54 34 39, www.les bauxdeprovence.com). Ask about **combo-ticket** deals, such as the castle ruins and Cathédrale d'Images for €13 (saves €3), and the €15.50 **Les Baux Jours pass**, which covers the castle ruins, the Cathédrale d'Images, and the Yves Brayer Museum (saves €4.50). You'll also see deals combining Les Baux with other sights in the region (such as the theater in Orange). The TI can also call a cab for you.

Arrival in Les Baux

Drivers must pay €5 to park at the foot of the village, or €3 to park several blocks below (you'll pass the parking on your way in). Pay at the machine just below the town entry (next to telephone, WC, and bakery).

Walk up the cobbled street into town, where you're greeted first by the TI. From here, the main drag leads directly to the castle—just keep going uphill (a 10-minute walk).

Sights in Les Baux

▲▲▲The Castle Ruins (The "Dead City")

The sun-bleached ruins of the "dead city" of Les Baux are carved into, out of, and on top of a rock 650 feet above the valley floor. Many of the ancient walls of this striking castle still stand as a testament to the proud past of this once-feisty village.

Cost and Hours: €8 (ask about family rates), includes excellent audioguide, daily July–Aug 9:00–20:00, Easter–June and Sept–Oct 9:00–19:00, Nov–Easter 9:30–17:00. If you are inside the castle when the entry closes, you can stay as long as you like. From April to October, medieval pageantry, tournaments, or fun-for-kids demonstrations enliven the mountaintop. If you bring your lunch, enjoy the picnic tables.

History: Imagine the importance of this citadel in the Middle

Les Baux

1. Le Mas d'Aigret Hôtel
2. Le Mas de l'Esparou B&B
3. Hostellerie de la Reine Jeanne
4. To Le Mazet des Alpilles B&B

Ages, when the Lords of Baux were notorious warriors. (How many feudal lords could trace their lineage back to one of the "three kings" of Christmas-carol fame, Balthazar?) In the 11th century, Les Baux was a powerhouse in southern France, controlling about 80 towns. The Lords of Baux fought the counts of Barcelona for control of Provence...and eventually lost. But while in power, these guys were mean. One ruler enjoyed forcing unransomed prisoners to jump off his castle walls.

In 1426, Les Baux was incorporated into Provence and France. Not accustomed to subservience, Les Baux struggled with the French king, who responded by destroying the fortress in 1483. Later, Les Baux regained some importance and emerged as a center of Protestantism. Arguing with Rome was a high-stakes game in the 17th century, and Les Baux's association with the Huguenots brought destruction again in 1632 when Cardinal Richelieu (under King Louis XIII) demolished the castle. Louis rubbed salt in the wound by billing Les Baux's residents for his demolition expenses.

The once-powerful town of 4,000 was forever crushed.

Touring the Castle: Buy your ticket in the old olive mill, inspect the models of Les Baux before its 17th-century destruction, and then pick up your audioguide after entering the sight. The audioguide follows posted numbers counterclockwise around the rocky spur. Take full advantage of this tool—as you wander around, key in the number for any of the 30 narrated stops that interest you.

As you walk on the windblown spur (*baux* in French), you'll pass kid-thrilling medieval siege weaponry (go ahead, try the battering ram). Good displays in English and images help reconstruct the place. Try to imagine 4,000 people living up here. Notice the water-catchment system (a slanted field that caught rainwater and drained it into cisterns—necessary during a siege) and find the reservoir cut into the rock below the castle's highest point. Look for post holes throughout the stone walls that reveal where beams once supported floors.

For the most sensational views, climb to the blustery top of the citadel. Hang on. The mistral wind just might blow you away.

The St. Blaise chapel across from the entry/exit runs videos with Provençal themes (plays continuously; just images and music, no words).

▲Lower Town

After your castle visit, you can shop and eat your way back through the new town. Or you can escape some of the crowds by following my short tour, below, which covers these minor but worthwhile sights as you descend (all stay open at lunch except the Yves Brayer Museum).

• *On the main drag (grand rue Frédéric Mistral), a few blocks below the castle exit, is the...*

Manville Mansion City Hall—The 15th-century city hall flies the red-and-white flag of Monaco, a reminder that the Grimaldi family (which has long ruled the tiny principality of Monaco) owned Les Baux until the French Revolution (1789). In fact, in 1982, Princess Grace Kelly and her royal husband, Prince Rainier Grimaldi, came to Les Baux to receive the key to the city.

Twenty yards up rue Nueve, the impressive 1571 **Renaissance** window frame, marking the site of a future Calvinist museum, stands as a reminder of this town's Protestant history. This was probably a place of Huguenot worship—the words carved into the lintel, *Post tenebras lux*, were a popular Calvinist slogan: "After the shadow comes the light."

• *At the end of rue Nueve, head right on rue des Fours to get to the...*

Yves Brayer Museum (Musée Yves Brayer)—This enjoyable museum lets you peruse three floors of paintings (Van Gogh-like

Expressionism, without the tumult) by Yves Brayer (1907–1990), who spent his final years here in Les Baux. Like Van Gogh, Brayer was inspired by all that surrounded him. Brayer picked up inspiration from his travels through Morocco, Spain, and the rest of the Mediterranean world (€4, daily 10:00–12:30 & 14:00–18:30, tel. 04 90 54 36 99). Pick up the descriptive English sheet at the entry.

• Next door is…

St. Vincent Church—This 12th-century Romanesque church was built short and wide to fit the terrain. The center chapel on the right (partially carved out of the rock) houses the town's traditional Provençal processional chariot. Each Christmas Eve, a ram pulled this cart—holding a lamb, symbolizing Jesus, and surrounded by candles—through town to the church.

• *Around the corner (to the left as you leave the church) are public WCs. Directly in front of the church is a vast view, making clear the strategic value of this rocky bluff's natural fortifications. A few steps away is the…*

Chapel of Penitents—Notice the nativity scene painted by Yves Brayer, illustrating the local legend that says Jesus was born in Les Baux. On the opposite wall, find his version of a starry night. Leaving the church, turn left. Wash your shirt in the old-town "laundry"—with a pig-snout faucet and 14th-century stone washing surface designed for short women.

• *Heading downhill at the junction on rue de la Calade, you'll pass cafés with wonderful views, the town's fortified wall, and one of its two gates. After passing a free (and curiously evangelical) "museum of aromas and perfumes," you hit the…*

Museum of Santons—This free museum displays a collection of *santons* ("little saints"), popular folk figurines that decorate local Christmas mangers. Notice how the nativity scene "proves" once again that Jesus was born in Les Baux. These painted clay dolls show off local dress and traditions (with good English descriptions). Find the old couple leaning heroically into the mistral.

Near Les Baux

A half-mile beyond Les Baux, D-27 (toward Maillane) leads to dramatic views of the hill town. There are pullouts and walking trails at the pass, and two attractions that fill cool, cavernous caves in former limestone quarries dating back to the Middle Ages. (The limestone is easy to cut, but gets hard and nicely polished when exposed to the weather.) Speaking of quarries, in 1821, the rocks and soil of this area were found to contain an important mineral for making aluminum. It was named after the town: bauxite.

Caves de Sarragan—The best views of Les Baux are from this parking lot, occupied by the Sarragan Winery (which invites you in for a taste). Although this place looks like it's designed for groups, the friendly, English-speaking staff welcomes individuals (free, daily April–Sept 10:00–12:00 & 14:00–19:00, Oct–March until 18:00, tel. 04 90 54 33 58, www.caves-sarragan.com).

▲▲**Cathédrale d'Images**—This similar cave nearby offers a mesmerizing sound-and-slide show with a different program every year. In 2011, the remarkable life of Leonardo da Vinci will be highlighted. The show, which features 48 projectors flashing countless images on quarry walls, never fails to thrill wandering visitors (€8, March–Dec daily 10:00–18:00, closed Jan–Feb, www.cathedrale-images.com). Dress warmly, since the cave is cool.

Sleeping in Les Baux

(€1 = about $1.25, country code: 33)

Many of these accommodations are actually scattered around the countryside surrounding Les Baux.

$$$ Le Mas d'Aigret*, barely east of Les Baux on the road to St. Rémy, is a well-run, lovely refuge that crouches under Les Baux. Lie on your back and stare up at the castle walls rising beyond the swimming pool, or enjoy valley views from the groomed terraces (Db with no view-€115, larger Db with balcony and view-€155, Tb/Qb-€200–240, two cool troglodyte rooms-€200, half-pension option with big breakfast and good dinner for about €40/person more, air-con, rooms have some daytime road noise, tel. 04 90 54 20 00, fax 04 90 54 44 00, www.masdaigret.com, contact@masdaigret.com, Dutch Marieke and French Eric).

$$ Le Mas de l'Esparou *chambre d'hôte*, a few minutes below Les Baux toward Paradou, is welcoming and kid-friendly, with three spacious rooms, a big swimming pool, table tennis, and distant views of Les Baux. Sweet Jacqueline loves her job, and her lack of English only makes her more animated (Db-€68, extra bed-about €16, includes breakfast, cash only, between Les Baux and Maussane les Alpilles on D-5, look for white sign with green lettering, tel. & fax 04 90 54 41 32).

$ Hostellerie de la Reine Jeanne*, an exceptional value, is a good place to watch the sun rise and set from Les Baux. Warmly run by Gaelle and Marc, this place offers a handful of sufficiently comfy rooms above a busy (and good-value) restaurant (standard Ds-€52, standard Db-€58, Db with view deck-€62–72, Tb-€70–80, cavernous family suite-€105, air-con in half the rooms, ask for *chambre avec terrasse*, good *menus* from €16, 150 feet to your right after entry to the village of Les Baux, tel. 04 90 54 32 06, fax 04 90 54 32 33, www.la-reinejeanne.com, reine.jeanne@wanadoo.fr).

$ Le Mazet des Alpilles is a small home with three tidy, air-conditioned rooms just outside the unspoiled village of Paradou, five minutes below Les Baux. It may have rooms when others don't (Db–€56–60, ask for largest room, includes breakfast, cash only, air-con, child's bed available, pleasant garden, follow brown signs from D-17, in Paradou look for route de Brunelly, tel. 04 90 54 45 89, www.alpilles.com/mazet.htm, lemazet@wanadoo.fr). Sweet Annick speaks just enough English.

Eating in Les Baux

You'll find quieter cafés with views along my self-guided tour route. The recommended **Hostellerie de la Reine Jeanne** offers friendly service and good-value meals indoors or out (€12 salads, €16 *menus*, try the *salade Estivale*, open daily).

Orange

Orange is notable for its Roman arch and grand Roman Theater. Orange was a thriving city in ancient times—strategically situated on the *Via Agrippa*, connecting the important Roman cities of Lyon and Arles. It was actually founded as a comfortable place for Roman army officers to enjoy their retirement. Even in Roman times, professional military men retired with time for a second career. Does the emperor want thousands of well-trained, relatively young guys hanging around Rome? No way. What to do? "How about a nice place in the south of France...?"

Orientation to Orange

Tourist Information

The unnecessary TI is located next to the fountain and parking area at 5 cours Aristide Briand (April–Sept Mon–Sat 9:30–18:30, Sun 10:00–13:00 & 14:00–18:30; Oct–March Mon–Sat 10:00–13:00 & 14:00–17:30, closed Sun; tel. 04 90 34 70 88).

Arrival in Orange

By Train: Orange's **train station** is a level 20-minute walk from the Roman Theater (or an €8 taxi ride, mobile 06 09 51 32 25). The recommended Hôtel de Provence across from the station will keep your bags (see "Sleeping in Orange," later). To walk into town from the train station, head straight out of the station (down avenue Frédéric Mistral), merge left onto Orange's main shopping street (rue de la République), then turn left on rue Caristie; you'll run into the Roman Theater's massive stage wall.

Orange

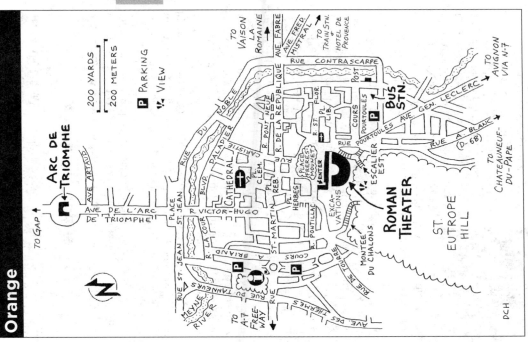

By Bus: Buses stop at the gare SNCF and at place Pourtoules, two blocks from the Roman Theater (walk to the hill and turn right to reach the theater, bus station tel. 04 90 34 15 59, www .vaucluse.fr/86-reseau-departemental.htm).

By Car: Follow *Centre-Ville* signs, then *Théâtre Antique* signs, and park as close to the Roman Theater's huge wall as possible; the easiest option is Parking Théâtre Antique (by the fountain and the TI). Those coming from the autoroute will land here by following

Centre-Ville signs; others should follow *Centre-Ville* signs, then *Office du Tourisme* signs, to find this parking. To reach the theater, walk to the hill and turn left.

Sights in Orange

▲▲**Roman Theater (Théâtre Antique)**—Orange's ancient theater is the best-preserved in existence, and the only one in Europe with its acoustic wall still standing. (Two others in Asia Minor also survive.)

Cost and Hours: €8, drops to €7 one hour before closing but doesn't include audioguide; daily April-Sept 9:00-18:00, until 19:00 in summer, Oct-March 9:30-17:30 except Nov-Feb until 16:30, tel. 04 90 51 17 60, www.theatre-antique.com. Your ticket includes an informative audioguide, a fun film covering 2,000 years of history (called *Phantom of the Theater*), and entrance to the small museum across the street (Musée d'Art et d'Histoire). Pop in to the museum to see a few theater details and a rare grid used as the official property-ownership registry—each square represented a 120-acre plot of land.

Cheap Trick: Vagabonds wanting to see the theater for free can hike up nearby stairs (called *escalier est*; off rue Pourtoules) to view it from the bluff high above.

Cafés: The café in the theater has reasonably priced snacks and lunches and great views. A shaded café-filled square (place de la République) is two blocks from the theater up rue Ségond Weber.

➲ **Self-Guided Tour:** After you enter (to the right of the actual theater), you'll see a huge dig—the site of the Temple to the Cult of the Emperor. Look for signs to the worthwhile movie (English subtitles) that gives you a good visual sense of how the theater looked to the Romans.

Enter the theater, then climb the steep stairs to find a seat high up to appreciate the acoustics (eavesdrop on people by the stage). Contemplate the idea that 2,000 years ago, Orange residents enjoyed grand spectacles with high-tech sound and lighting effects—such as simulated thunder, lightning, and rain.

A grandiose Caesar overlooks everything, reminding attendees who's in charge. If it seems like you've seen this statue before, you probably have. Countless sculptures identical to this one were mass-produced in Rome and shipped throughout the empire to grace buildings like this theater for propaganda purposes. To save money on shipping and handling, only the heads of these statues were changed with each new ruler. The permanent body wears a breastplate emblazoned with the imperial griffon (body of a lion, head and wings of an eagle) that only the emperor could wear. When a new emperor came to power, new heads were made in Rome and shipped off throughout the empire to replace the pop-off heads on all these statues. (Imagine Barack Obama's head on George W. Bush's body.)

Archaeologists believe that a puny, vanquished Celt was included at the knee of the emperor, touching his ruler's robe respectfully—a show of humble subservience to the emperor. It's interesting to consider how an effective propaganda machine can con the masses into being impressed by their leader.

The horn has blown. It's time to find your seat: row two, number 30. Sitting down, you're comforted by the "EQ GIII" carved into the seat (*Equitas Gradus #3*...three rows for the Equestrian order). You're not comforted by the hard limestone bench (thinking it'll probably last 2,000 years). The theater is filled with 10,000 people. Thankfully, you mix only with your class, the nouveau riche—merchants, tradesmen, and city big shots. The people seated above you are the working class, and way up in the "chicken roost" section is the scum of the earth—slaves, beggars, prostitutes, and youth hostellers. Scanning the orchestra section (where the superrich sit on real chairs), you notice the town dignitaries hosting some visiting VIPs.

OK, time to worship. They're parading a bust of the emperor from its sacred home in the adjacent temple around the stage. Next is the ritual animal sacrifice called *la pompa* (so fancy, future generations will use that word for anything full of such...pomp). Finally, you settle in for an all-day series of spectacles and dramatic entertainment. All eyes are on the big stage door in the middle—where the Julia Roberts and Brad Pitts of the day will appear. (Lesser actors come out of the side doors.)

The play is good, but many come for the halftime shows—jugglers, acrobats, and striptease dancers. In Roman times, the theater was a festival of immorality. An ancient writer commented, "The vanquished take their revenge on us by giving us their vices through the theater."

With an audience of 10,000 and no amplification, acoustics were critical. A roof originally covered the stage, somewhat like the glass-and-iron stage roof you see today (recently installed to protect the stage from the weather, but to project the voices of the actors into the crowd. For further help, actors wore masks with leather caricature mouths that functioned as megaphones. The side walls originally rose as high as the stage wall and supported a retractable roof that gave the audience some protection from the sun. After leaving the theater, look up to the stage wall from the outside and notice the supports for poles that held the roof in place.

The Roman Theater was all part of the "give them bread and circuses" approach to winning the support of the masses (not unlike today's philosophy of "give them tax cuts and *American Idol*"). The spectacle grew from 65 days of games per year when the theater was first built (and when Rome was at its height) to about 180 days each year by the time Rome finally fell.

▲**Roman "Arc de Triomphe"**—Technically the only real Roman arches of triumph are in Rome's Forum, built to commemorate various emperors' victories. The great Roman arch of Orange is actually a municipal arch erected (in about A.D. 19) to commemorate a general named Germanicus, who protected the town. The 60-foot-tall arch is on a noisy traffic circle (north of city center, on avenue Arc de Triomphe).

Sleeping in Orange

(€1 = about $1.25, country code: 33)

$$ Hôtel de Provence**, at the train station, is air-conditioned, quiet, comfortable, and affordable. Friendly Madame Verbe runs this traditional place with grace (Db-€60–75, Tb-€75–95, small rooftop pool, café, 60 avenue Frédéric Mistral, tel. 04 90 34 00 23, fax 04 90 34 91 72, www.hoteldeprovence84.com, hoteldeprovence84@orange.fr).

Orange Connections

From Orange by Train to: Avignon (15/day, 15 minutes), **Arles** (4/day direct, 35 minutes, more frequently with transfer in Avignon), **Lyon** (16/day, 2 hours).

By Bus to: Châteauneuf-du-Pape (1/day, none Sun, 30 minutes), **Vaison la Romaine** (3–5/day, 45 minutes—take the train instead), **Avignon** (Mon-Sat hourly, none Sun, 45 minutes). Buses to Vaison la Romaine and other wine villages depart from the gare SNCF and from place Pourtoules (turn right out of the Roman Theater, and right again onto rue Pourtoules).

Villages of the Côtes du Rhône

The sunny Côtes du Rhône wine road—one of France's best—starts at Avignon's doorstep. It winds north through a mountainous landscape carpeted with vines, peppered with warm stone villages, and presided over by the Vesuvius-like Mont Ventoux. The wines of the Côtes du Rhône (grown on the *côtes*, or hillsides, of the Rhône River Valley) are easy on the palate and on your budget. But this hospitable place offers more than famous wine—its hill-capping villages inspire travel posters, its Roman ruins inspire awe, and the people you'll meet are welcoming...and, often, as excited about their region as you are. Yes, you'll have good opportunities for enjoyable wine-tasting, but there is also a soul to this area...if you take the time to look.

Planning Your Time

Vaison la Romaine is the small hub of this region, offering limited bus connections with Avignon and Orange, bike rental, and a mini-Pompeii in the town center. Nearby, you can visit the impressive Roman Theater in Orange (described earlier), follow my self-guided "Côtes du Rhône Wine Road" driving tour, and pedal to nearby towns for a breath of fresh air. The vineyards' centerpiece, the Dentelles de Montmirail mountains, are laced with a variety of exciting trails ideal for hikers.

To explore this area, allow two nights for a good start. Drivers should head for the hills. Those without wheels find that Vaison la Romaine is the only practical home base (or, maybe better, consider a minivan tour for this area—see next page).

Getting Around the Côtes du Rhône

By Car: Pick up Michelin maps #332 or #527 to navigate your way around the Côtes du Rhône. (Landmarks like the Dentelles de Montmirail and Mont Ventoux make it easy to get your bearings.) I've described my favorite driving route on page 676. If your plan is to connect the Côtes du Rhône with the **Luberon,** you can do it scenically via Mont Ventoux (follow signs to *Malaucène,* then to *Mont Ventoux,* allowing 2 hours to Roussillon). This route is one of the most spectacular in Provence. If continuing north toward Lyon, consider the worthwhile detour via the Ardèche Gorges (described on page 673).

By Bus: Buses run to Vaison la Romaine from Orange and Avignon (3–5/day, 45 minutes from Orange, 1.5 hours from Avignon) and connect several wine villages (including Gigondas, Sablet, and Beaumes de Venise) with Vaison la Romaine and Nyons to the north. Another line runs from Vaison la Romaine to

Carpentras, serving Crestet (below Le Crestet), Malaucène, and Le Barroux (2/day, tel. 04 90 36 09 90). Both routes provide scenic rides through this area.

By Train: Trains get you as far as Orange (from Avignon: 10/day, 15 minutes); from there, buses make the 45-minute trip to Vaison la Romaine.

By Minivan Tour: Various all-day minivan excursions to this area leave from Avignon. For a wine-focused tour, I recommend several individuals who can expertly guide you through the region. For all tours to this area, see "Tours of Provence" on page 597.

Vaison la Romaine

With quick access to vineyards, villages, and Mont Ventoux, this lively little town of 6,000 makes a great base for exploring the Côtes du Rhône region by car or by bike. You get two villages for the price of one: Vaison la Romaine's "modern" lower city has worthwhile Roman ruins and a lone pedestrian street. (The big square, place Montfort, has great potential and is scheduled to be redone by 2011.) The car-free medieval hill town looms above,

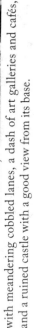

with meandering cobbled lanes, a dash of art galleries and cafés, and a ruined castle with a good view from its base.

Orientation to Vaison la Romaine

The city is split in two by the Ouvèze River. The Roman Bridge connects the more modern lower town (Ville-Basse) with the hill-capping medieval upper town (Ville-Haute).

Tourist Information

The superb TI is in the lower city, between the two Roman ruin sites, at place du Chanoine Sautel (July–Aug Mon–Sat 9:00–19:00, Sun 9:00–12:00; Sept–June Mon–Sat 9:00–12:00 & 14:00–17:45, Sun 9:00–12:00 & 14:00–19:00 except closed Sun Oct–April; tel. 04 90 36 02 11). Say *bonjour* to *char-mante* and ever-so-patient

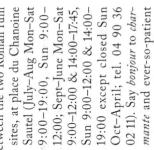

Vaison la Romaine

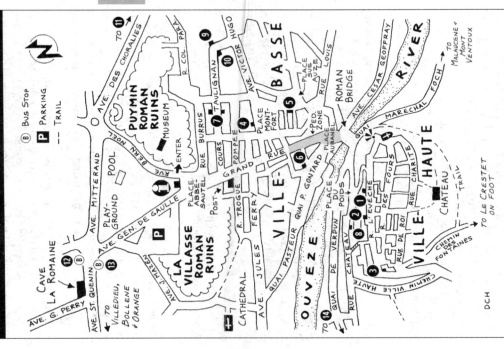

- ❶ Hôtel/Rest. le Beffroi
- ❷ L'Evêché Chambres
- ❸ Hôtel la Fête en Provence
- ❹ Hôtel Burrhus
- ❺ La Bartavelle Restaurant
- ❻ Le Brin d'Olivier Rest.
- ❼ Le Tournesol & La Lyriste Restaurants & Vaison 2 Mils Internet Café
- ❽ Bistro du 'O Restaurant
- ❾ Bike Rental
- ❿ Launderette
- ⓫ To Car Rental & Malaucène
- ⓬ To Avignon/Orange
- ⓭ Bus from Avignon/Orange
- ⓮ To Séguret by bike or car

Ⓑ Bus Stop
Ⓟ Parking
-- Trail

DCH

Valerie—get bus schedules, ask about festivals and evening programs, and pick up information on walks from Vaison la Romaine. Ask for the English pamphlets on biking and hiking—they have maps and instructions for several bike and walking loops, ranging from easy half-day trips to all-day affairs.

Arrival in Vaison la Romaine

By Bus: The unmarked bus stop to Orange and Avignon is in front of the Cave la Romaine winery. Buses from Orange or Avignon drop you across the street (3–5/day, 45 minutes from Orange, 1.5 hours from Avignon). Tell the driver you want the stop for the *Office de Tourisme*. When you get off the bus, walk five minutes down avenue Général de Gaulle to reach the TI and recommended hotels.

By Car: Follow signs to *Centre-Ville*, then *Office de Tourisme*; park for free across from the TI. Most parking is free in Vaison la Romaine.

Helpful Hints

Market Day: Sleep in Vaison la Romaine on Monday night, and you'll wake to an amazing Tuesday market. But be warned: Mondays are quiet during the day, as many shops close (but sights are open). If you spend a Monday night, avoid parking at market sites, or you won't find your car where you left it (if signs indicate *Stationnement Interdit le Mardi*, don't park there—ask your hotel where you can park).

Internet Access: Try **Vaison 2 Mils** at 51 cours Taulignan (tel. 04 90 36 23 24).

Laundry: The self-service **Laverie la Lavandière** is on cours Taulignan, near avenue Victor Hugo (daily 8:00–22:00). The friendly owners, who work next door at the dry cleaners, will do your laundry while you sightsee—when you pick up your laundry, thank them with a small tip (dry cleaners open Mon–Sat 9:00–12:00 & 15:00–19:00, closed Sun).

Bike Rental: Try **Mag 2 Roues,** in the lower town on cours Taulignan (tel. 04 90 28 80 46).

Taxi: To get a taxi, call 04 90 36 00 04 or 06 22 28 24 49.

Car Rental: Wallgreen has a few cars for rent at **Vaison Pneus** (closed Sun, avenue Marcel Pagnol, tel. 04 90 28 73 54). The TI has a list of other car rental agencies.

Local Guide: Let sincere and knowledgeable **Anna-Marie Melard** bring those Roman ruins to life for you (€55/80-minute tour, tel. 04 90 36 50 48).

Cooking Classes: Charming **Barbara Schuerenberg** offers reasonably priced, easygoing cooking classes from her home in Vaison la Romaine (€70, includes lunch, tel. 04 90 35 68 43, www.cuisinedeprovence.com, barbara@cuisinedeprovence.com).

PROVENCE

Sights in Vaison la Romaine

Roman Ruins—Ancient Vaison la Romaine had a treaty that gave it the preferred "federated" relationship with Rome (rather than simply being a colony). This, along with a healthy farming economy (olives and vineyards), made it a most prosperous place...as a close look at its sprawling ruins demonstrates. About 6,000 people called Vaison la Romaine home 2,000 years ago. When the barbarians arrived, the Romans were forced out, and the townspeople fled into the hills. Here's something to ponder: The town has only recently reached the same population it had during its Roman era.

Vaison la Romaine's Roman ruins are split by a modern road into two sites: Puymin and La Villasse. Each is well-presented with some English information panels (less necessary if you use the audioguide), offering a good look at life during the Roman Empire. The Roman town extended all the way to the river, and its forum lies under place Montfort. What you can see is only a small fraction of the Roman town's extent—most is still buried under today's city.

Visit **Puymin** first. Nearest the entry are the scant but impressive ruins of a sprawling mansion. Find the faint remains of a colorful frescoed wall. Climb the hill to the good little museum (pick up your audioguide here; exhibits also explained in English loaner booklet). Behind the museum is a 6,000-seat theater that is well used today, with just enough seats for the whole town (of yesterday and today). Back across the modern road in **La Villasse**, you'll explore a "street of shops" and the foundations of more houses. You'll also see a few wells, used before Vaison's two aqueducts were built.

Cost and Hours: €8 Roman ruins combo-ticket includes both ruins, helpful audioguide, and cloister at the Notre-Dame de Nazareth Cathedral (see next page); daily April–Sept 9:30–18:00, Oct–March 10:00–12:00 & 14:00–17:00.

Lower Town (Ville-Basse)—Vaison la Romaine's nondescript modern town stretches from its car-littered main square, place Montfort. Cafés grab the north side of the square, conveniently sheltered from the prevailing mistral wind, enjoying the generous shade of the ubiquitous plane (*platane*) trees (cut back each year to form a leafy canopy). Several blocks away, the stout **Notre-Dame de Nazareth Cathedral**—with an evocative cloister—is a good example of Provençal Romanesque (cloister entry–€1.50, or covered by €8 Roman ruins combo-ticket, daily 15:00–19:00). The pedestrian-only Grand Rue is a lively shopping street leading to the small river gorge and the Roman Bridge.

Roman Bridge—The Romans cut this sturdy, no-nonsense vault into the canyon rock 2,000 years ago, and it has survived ever since. Find the information panel at the new town end of the bridge. Until the 20th century, this was the only way to cross the Ouvèze River. The stone plaque on the wall (*Septembre 22–92...*) shows the high-water mark of the record flood that killed 30 people and washed away the valley's other bridges. The flood swept away the modern top of this bridge...but couldn't budge the 55-foot Roman arch.

Upper Town (Ville-Haute)—Although there's nothing of particular importance to see in the fortified medieval old town atop the hill, the cobbled lanes and enchanting fountains make you want to break out a sketchpad. Vaison la Romaine had a prince-bishop since the fourth century. He came under attack by the Count of Toulouse in the 12th century. Anticipating a struggle, the prince-bishop abandoned the lower town and built a château on this rocky outcrop (about 1195). Over time, the rest of the townspeople followed, vacating the lower town and building their homes at the base of the château behind the upper town's fortified wall.

To reach the upper town, hike up from the Roman Bridge (passing memorials for both world wars) through the medieval gate, under the lone tower crowned by an 18th-century wrought-iron bell cage. The château is closed, but a steep, uneven trail to it rewards hikers with a fine view.

▲▲Market Day—In the 16th century, the pope gave Vaison la Romaine market-town status. Ever since then, the town has hosted a farmers market. Today merchants gather with gusto, turning the entire place into a festival of produce and Provençal products. This Tuesday-morning market is one of France's best, but it can challenge claustrophobes. Be warned that parking is a real headache unless you arrive early (see

"Helpful Hints," earlier).

Wine-Tasting—Cave la Romaine, a five-minute walk up avenue Général de Gaulle from the TI, offers a variety of good-value wines from nearby villages in a pleasant, well-organized tasting room (daily 8:30–12:00 & 14:00–18:30, avenue St. Quenin, tel. 04 90 36 55 90, www.cave-la-romaine.com).

Hiking—The TI has good information on relatively easy hikes into the hills above Vaison la Romaine. It's about 1.25 hours to the tiny hill town of Le Crestet, though views begin immediately. To find this trail, drive or walk past the upper town (with the castle just on your left), find the *chemin des Fontaines*, and stay the course as far as you like (follow yellow *Crestet* signs). Cars are not allowed on the road after about a mile. I prefer taking a taxi to Le Crestet, and walking back (Le Crestet is described on page 678). The TI also has information on a loop hike from Vaison la Romaine to Crestet (a newer village below the older hillside town of Le Crestet)—it follows the same path to Le Crestet, with a different return route.

Biking—This area is not particularly flat, and if it's hot and windy, bike-riding is a dicey option. But if it's calm, the five-mile ride to cute little Villedieu (recommended restaurant listed on page 683) is a delight. The bike route is signed along small roads; you'll find signs from Vaison la Romaine to Villedieu at the roundabout past Cave La Romaine toward Orange (see map on page 669). With a bit more energy, you can pedal beyond Villedieu on the lovely road to Mirabel (from Villedieu, follow signs to *Nyons*). Or get a good map and connect the following villages for an enjoyable 11-mile loop ride: Vaison la Romaine, St. Romain-en-Viennois, Puyméras (with a recommended restaurant—see page 683), Faucon, and St. Marcellin-lès-Vaison. The TI and bike shop have good information on mountain-biking trails.

Near Vaison la Romaine

▲**Ardèche Gorges (Gorges de l'Ardèche)**—These gorges, which wow visitors with abrupt chalky-white cliffs, follow the Ardèche River through immense canyons and thick forests. To reach the gorges from Vaison la Romaine, drive west 45 minutes, passing through Bollène and Pont Saint-Esprit to Vallon Pont d'Arc (the tourist hub of the Ardèche Gorges). From Vallon Pont d'Arc you can canoe along the peaceful river through some of the canyon's most spectacular scenery and under the rock arch of Pont d'Arc (half-day, all-day, and 2-day trips possible; less appealing in summer, when the river is crowded and water levels are low), and learn about hiking trails that get you above it all (TI tel. 04 75 88 04 01, www.vallon-pont-darc.com, French only). If continuing north toward Lyon, connect Privas and Aubenas, then head back via the autoroute. Endearing little Balazuc—a village north of the gorges, with narrow lanes, flowers, views, and a smattering of cafés and shops—makes a good stop.

Sleeping in Vaison la Romaine

(€1 = about $1.25, country code: 33)

Hotels in Vaison la Romaine are a good value. Those in the medieval upper town (Ville-Haute) are quieter, cozier, and cooler, but require a 15-minute walk to the TI and Roman ruins. If staying at one of the first three places, follow signs to *Cité Médiévale* and park just outside the upper village entry (driving into the Cité Médiévale itself is a challenge, with tiny lanes and nearly impossible parking).

$$$ Hôtel le Beffroi* hides deep in the upper town, just above a demonstrative bell tower (you'll hear what I mean). It offers 16th-century red-tile-and-wood-beamed-cozy lodgings with nary a level surface. The rooms—split between two buildings a few doors apart—are Old World comfy, and some have views. You'll also find tasteful public spaces, a garden with view tables (light meals available in the summer), a small pool with more views, and animated Nathalie at the reception (standard Db-€95–120, superior Db-€150, Tb-€175, rue de l'Evêché, tel. 04 90 36 04 71, fax 04 90 36 24 78, www.le-beffroi.com, info@le-beffroi.com). The hotel's restaurant offers *menus* from €28.

$$$ L'Evêché Chambres, almost next door to le Beffroi in the upper town (look for the ivy), is a five-room melt-in-your-chair B&B. The owners (the Verdiers) own the art boutique across the street, have an exquisite sense of interior design, and are passionate about books, making this place feel like a cross between a library and an art gallery (Sb-€75–85, standard Db-€85–90, Db suite-€115–140, the *solanum* suite is worth every euro, Tb-€120–160, Internet access and Wi-Fi, rue de l'Evêché, tel. 04 90 36 13 46, fax 04 90 36 32 43, http://eveche.free.fr, eveche@aol.com).

$$ Hôtel la Fête en Provence, conveniently located for drivers at the entry to the medieval upper town, has a variety of room shapes and sizes. All the rooms are chiffon-comfortable, and several have small kitchenettes. Rooms are located around a calming courtyard, and there's a pool and Jacuzzi next door (standard Db-€80, bigger Db with king-size bed and bath-€110, extra person-€15, Cité Médiévale, tel. & fax 04 90 36 36 43, www.hotellafete-provence.com, fete-en-provence@wanadoo.fr). Their apartments (€155) sleep up to six people, and come with a kitchenette and sitting area.

$ Hôtel Burrhus** is part art gallery, part funky hotel—and the best value in the lower town. It's a central, laid-back, go-with-the-flow place, with a broad terrace over the raucous place Montfort (the double-paned windows are effective, but for maximum quiet, request a back room). Its floor plan will confound even the ablest navigator. The bigger, newer rooms—with contemporary decor, bigger bathrooms, and air-conditioning—are worth the extra euros for most travelers (Db-€55-61, newer Db-€71-88, Qb apartment-€140, extra bed-€15, air-con, free Internet access and Wi-Fi, 1 place Montfort, tel. 04 90 36 00 11, fax 04 90 36 39 05, www.burrhus.com, info@burrhus.com).

Eating in Vaison la Romaine

Vaison la Romaine offers a handful of excellent places—arrive by 19:30 or reserve ahead, particularly on weekends. And though you can eat very well on a moderate budget in Vaison, it's well worth venturing to nearby Côtes du Rhône villages to eat (see "Eating Along the Côtes du Rhône" on page 683). Wherever you dine, begin with a fresh glass of Muscat from the nearby village of Beaumes de Venise.

La Bartavelle is a lovely place to savor traditional French cuisine in the lower town. Owner Berangère (bear-ahn-zher) has put together a tourist-friendly mix-and-match menu of local options. You get access to the top-end selections even on the €22 bottom-end *menu*—just fewer courses. Be sure to reserve ahead (closed Mon, small terrace outside, air-con and pleasant interior, 12 place de Sus Auze, tel. 04 90 36 02 16).

Le Brin d'Olivier is the most romantic place I list, with soft lighting, hushed conversations, earth tones, and a menu that celebrates Provence (€29 *menu*, closed Wed, 4 rue du Ventoux, tel. 04 90 28 74 79).

Le Tournesol offers a good €18 dinner, with mostly Provençal dishes, rose walls, and friendly service. I love the *aubergine feuilleté* (eggplant puff pastry) and lamb with cheese. Show this book to get a free *kir* (daily, 30 cours Taulignan, tel. 04 90 36 09 18, owner Patrick speaks a little English).

La Lyriste, named for the loudest "singing" *cigale* (cicada), puts cuisine above decor. Marie serves what hubby Benoit cooks. Both are shy, yet proud of their restaurant. There's a fine *menu* for €19, but go for the slightly pricier *menus*, which are inventive and *très delectable* (closed Mon, indoor and outdoor seating, 45 cours Taulignan, tel. 04 90 36 04 67).

Bistro du'O, in the upper village, is the buzz of Vaison's yuppie crowd. Reserve ahead and you'll dine on soft leather chairs under soaring stone arches and enjoy mouthwatering cuisine that is creatively presented yet affordable (*menus from* €29, closed Sun, rue du Château, tel. 04 90 41 72 90).

Hôtel le Beffroi's garden is just right for a light dinner in the summer (*menus* from €28, hotel recommended earlier).

Vaison la Romaine Connections

The most central bus stop is at Cave Vinicole.

From Vaison la Romaine by Bus to: Avignon (5/day during school year—called *période scolaire*, otherwise 3/day, 1.5 hours; much faster to bus to Orange and train from there), **Orange** (3–5/day, 45 minutes), **Nyons** (2–3/day, 45 minutes), **Crestet** (lower village below Le Crestet, 2/day, 5 minutes), **Carpentras** (2/day, 45 minutes). Bus info: tel. 04 90 36 05 22.

Côtes du Rhône Sights near Vaison la Romaine

▲▲▲The Côtes du Rhône Wine Road

This tour introduces you to the characteristic best of the Côtes du Rhône wine road. While circling the rugged Dentelles de Montmirail mountain peaks, you'll experience all that's unique about this region: its natural beauty, glowing limestone villages, inviting wineries, and rolling hills of vineyards. As you drive, notice how some vineyards grow at angles—they're planted this way to compensate for the strong effect of the mistral wind.

The many fine restaurants along the way are another highlight of the route. I've mentioned some of my favorites; you'll find much more detail about these under "Eating Along the Côtes du Rhône" on page 683.

Our tour starts just south of Vaison la Romaine in little Séguret. This town is best for a visit early or late, when it's quieter. (If you get a late start or prefer ending your tour here, begin the tour in Le Crestet—stop #3—and save the first two stops for last.)

• *From Vaison la Romaine, the easiest way to reach Séguret is to follow signs for Orange, then look for the turnoff to Séguret in a few minutes.*

❶ Séguret

Blending into the hillside with a smattering of shops, two cafés, made-to-stroll lanes, and a natural spring, this hamlet is understandably popular. Séguret makes for a good coffee or dinner stop (restaurants recommended on page 683).

Séguret's name comes from the Latin word *securitas* (meaning "secure"). The bulky entry arch came with a massive gate, which drilled in the message of the village's name. In the Middle Ages, Séguret was patrolled 24/7—they never took their *securitas* for granted. Walk through the arch. To appreciate how the homes'

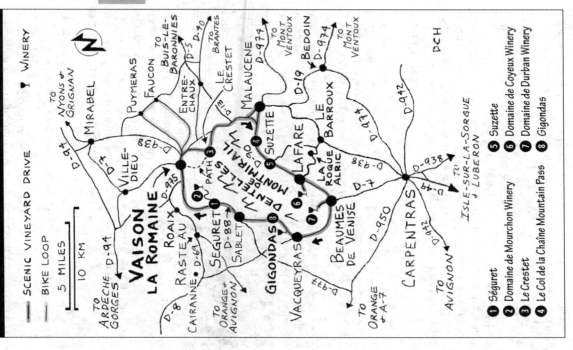

Côtes du Rhône Driving Tour

— SCENIC VINEYARD DRIVE
— BIKE LOOP
⚲ WINERY

1 Séguret
2 Domaine de Mourchon Winery
3 Le Crestet
4 Le Col de la Chaîne Mountain Pass
5 Suzette
6 Domaine de Coyeux Winery
7 Domaine de Durban Winery
8 Gigondas

outer walls provided security in those days, drop down the first passage on your right (near the fountain). These exit passages, or *poternes*, were needed in periods of peace to allow the town to expand below.

• *Signs near Séguret's parking will lead you up, up and away to our next stop, Domaine de Mourchon.*

❷ Domaine de Mourchon

This high-flying new winery has become the buzz of the Côtes du Rhône by blending state-of-the-art technology with traditional winemaking methods (a dazzling ring of stainless-steel vats holds wines grown on land plowed by horses). The wines are winning the respect of international critics, yet the (Scottish) owners seem eager to help anyone understand Rhône Valley wines. Language is not an issue here, nor is a lack of stunning views. Free, informative English tours of the vineyards are offered once a week (Easter–Sept Wed at 17:00, check website or call to verify; open Mon–Fri 10:00–12:00 & 14:00–18:00, plus April–Sept Sat 14:00–18:00, tel. 04 90 46 70 30, www.domainede mourchon.com).

• *Next, return to Vaison la Romaine and follow signs toward Carpentras/Malaucène. After passing through Crestet, you'll come to Le Crestet (on D-938). Look for signs leading up to Le Village and park at its entry.*

❸ Le Crestet

This village—founded after the fall of the Roman Empire, when people banded together in high places like this for protection from marauding barbarians—followed the usual hill-town evolution. The outer walls of the village did double duty as ramparts and house walls. The castle above (from about A.D. 850) provided a final safe haven when the village was attacked.

The Bishop of Vaison la Romaine was the first occupant, lending little Le Crestet a certain prestige. With about 500 residents in 1200, Le Crestet was a very important town in this region, reaching its zenith in the mid-1500s, when 660 people called it home. Le Crestet's gradual decline started when the bishop moved to Vaison la Romaine in the 1600s, though the population remained fairly stable until World War II. Today, about 35 people live within the walls year-round (about 55 during the summer).

The village's only business, the recommended café-restaurant **Le Panoramic**, has an upstairs terrace with a view that justifies the name...even if the food is overpriced and mediocre.

• *Reconnect with the road below, following signs to Malaucène. As you near Malaucène, look for the huge boules courts separated by logs (on your left). Entering Malaucène, turn right on D-90 (direction: Suzette) just before the gas station. As you climb to the mountain pass, look for signs on the left to Le Col de la Chaîne (Chain Pass). From this point on, the scenery gets better fast.*

❹ Le Col de la Chaîne Mountain Pass

Get out of your car at the pass (about 1,500 feet) and enjoy the breezy views. Wander around. The peaks in the distance—thrusting up like the back of a stegosaurus or a bad haircut (you decide)—are the Dentelles de Montmirail, a small range running just nine miles basically north to south and reaching 2,400 feet in elevation. This region's land is constantly shifting. Those rocky tops were the result of a gradual uplifting of the land, then were blown bald by the angry mistral wind. Below, pine and oak trees mix with scotch broom, which blooms brilliant yellow in May and June. The village below the peaks is Suzette (you'll be there soon). The yellow-signed hiking trail leads to the castle-topped village of Le Barroux (3.5 miles, mostly downhill).

Now turn around and face Mont Ventoux. Are there clouds in the horizon? You're looking into the eyes of the Alps (behind Ventoux), and those "foothills" help keep Provence sunny.

• *Time to push on. You'll pass countless yellow trail signs along this drive. (The Dentelles provide fertile ground for walking trails.) With the medieval castle of Le Barroux topping the horizon in the distance (off to the left), drive on to little...*

❺ Suzette

Tiny Suzette floats on its hilltop, with a small 12th-century chapel, one café, a handful of residents, and the gaggle of houses where they live. Park in Suzette's lot, below, then find the big orientation board above the lot (Rome is 620 kilometers—385 miles—away). Look out to the broad shoulders of Mont Ventoux. At 6,000 feet, it always seems to have some clouds hanging around. If it's clear, the top looks like it's snow-covered; if you drive up there, you'll see it's actually white stone. If it's very cloudy, the mountain takes on a dark, foreboding appearance.

Look to the village. A sign asks you to *Respectez son Calme* (respect its peace). Suzette's homes once lived in the shadow of an imposing castle, destroyed during the religious wars of the mid-1500s. The recommended **Les Coquelicots** café makes a good lunch or drink stop. Good picnic tables lie just past Suzette on our route. Back across the road from the orientation table is a tasting room for **Château Redortier** wines (English brochure and well-explained list of wines provided; skip their whites, but try the good rosés and reds).

- *Continue from Suzette in the direction of Beaumes de Venise. You'll drop down into the lush little village of La Fare. La Fare's best wine-tasting opportunity is just after leaving the village, at...*

❻ Domaine de Coyeux

The private road winds up and up to this impossibly beautiful setting, with the best views of the Dentelles I've found. Olive trees line the final approach, and *Le Caveau* signs lead to a modern tasting room (you may need to ring the buzzer). The owners and staff are formal and take your interest in their wines seriously—skip this stop if you only want a quick taste or are not interested in buying. These wines have earned their

excellent reputation (and are now available in the US). Start with their delectable Côtes du Rhône Villages red, and finish with their trademark dry and sweet Muscats (wines range from €7–13 per bottle, Mon–Sat 10:00–12:00 & 14:00–18:00, closed Sun except May–Aug, tel. 04 90 12 42 42, some English spoken). After tasting, take time to wander about the vineyards.

- *Drive on toward Beaumes de Venise. You'll soon pass the recommended* **Côté Vignes**, *a lovely place for lunch or dinner. Next you'll drop out of the hills as you approach Beaumes de Venise. To find the next winery, keep right at the first Centre-Ville sign as the road bends left, then carefully track Domaine de Durban signs for three scenic miles to...*

❼ Domaine de Durban

Find the small tasting room and let your young hostess take your taste buds on a tour. This *domaine* produces appealing whites, reds, and Muscats. Start with the 100 percent Viognier (€4.50 a bottle), then try their Viognier–Chardonnay blend. Their rosé is light and refreshing (and cheap). Their three reds are very different from one another: One is fruity, one is tannic (aged in oak), and one has some fruit and tannin. Finish with their popular Muscat de Venise (wines are €4–10/bottle, Mon–Sat 9:00–12:00 & 14:00–18:30, closed Sun, tel. 04 90 62 94 26). Picnics are not allowed,

and the grass is off-limits, though strolling amid the gorgeous vineyards is OK.

• *Retrace your route to Beaumes de Venise, turn left at the bottom, then make a quick right and navigate through Beaumes de Venise, following signs for Gigondas and Vaison par la route touristique. As you enter Gigondas, follow signs to the TI and park on or near the tree-shaded square.*

❽ Gigondas

This town produces some of the region's best reds and is ideally situated for hiking, mountain-biking, and driving into the mountains. The **TI** has a list of wineries, *chambres d'hôte*, and good hikes or drives (Mon–Sat 10:00–12:30 & 14:00–18:00, likely closed Sun, place du Portail, tel. 04 90 65 85 46, www.gigondas-dm.fr). Take a short walk through the village lanes above the TI—the church is an easy destination with good views over the heart of the Côtes du Rhône vineyards.

Several good tasting opportunities can be found on the main square. **Le Caveau de Gigondas** is best, where Sandra and Barbara await your visit with a large, free selection of tiny bottles for sampling, filled directly from the barrel (daily 10:00–12:00 & 14:00–18:30, 2 doors down from TI, tel. 04 90 65 82 29). Here you can compare wines from a variety of private producers in an intimate, low-key surrounding. You'll find a small grocery store and several eating options in the village. Diagonally across from the TI, the shaded red tables of **Du Verre à l'Assiette** ("From Glass to Plate") entice lunchtime eaters (also good interior ambience, €10 salads, €14 *plats*, daily, place du Village, tel. 04 90 12 36 64). To dine very well or sleep nearby, find the recommended **Hôtel les Florets**, a half-mile above town (closed Wed).

• *From Gigondas, follow signs to the circular wine village of Sablet—with generally inexpensive yet tasty wines (the TI and wine cooperative share a space in the town center)—then past Séguret and back to Vaison la Romaine, where our tour ends.*

Sleeping Along the Côtes du Rhône

(€1 = about $1.25, country code: 33)

These accommodations are along the self-guided driving tour route described earlier. They offer a great opportunity for drivers who want to experience rural France and get better values.

Near Vaison la Romaine

These accommodations are within a 10-minute drive of Vaison la Romaine.

$$$ Domaine de Cabasse*** is a lovely spread flanked by vineyards at the foot of Séguret (with a walking path to the village). Winemaking is their primary business (tastings possible), though the hotel is well-run by its relaxed staff. The 13 rooms have retained a simple Old World feel. All the rooms have decks, and a big pool is at your disposal. From the entry gate—which opens automatically...and slowly—the place appears more formal than it is (Db-€125-140, Wi-Fi in lobby, on D-23 between Sablet and Séguret, tel. 04 90 46 91 12, fax 04 90 46 94 01, www.cabasse.fr, info@cabasse.fr). The restaurant offers a satisfying, though limited, €28 dinner *menu* served inside or out.

$$$ Hôtel les Florets**, a half-mile above Gigondas, is surrounded by pine trees at the foothills of the Dentelles de Montmirail. It comes with a huge terrace that Van Gogh would have loved, thoughtfully designed rooms, and an excellent restaurant (standard Db-€100-110, superior Db-€125-160, annex rooms are best, tel. 04 90 65 85 01, fax 04 90 65 83 80, www.hotel-lesflorets.com, accueil@hotel-lesflorets.com). See more details about the hotel's restaurant on the next page.

$$$ La Table du Comtat is ideal if you want to sleep in adorable little Séguret. Rooms are simple and traditional and a fair value. Some have views; the terrace and restaurant (described later) are a serious draw. The hotel is closed Wednesday, except in July and August—start your stay on a different day of the week (Db-€90-110, no air-con, tel. 04 90 46 91 49, www.table-comtat .fr, direction@table-comtat.fr).

$ L'Ecole Buissonnière Chambres is run by an engaging Anglo-French team, Monique and John, who share their peace and quiet 10 minutes from Vaison la Romaine. This creatively restored farmhouse has three character-filled half-timbered rooms and convivial public spaces. Getting to know John, who has lived all over the south of France and even worked as a *gardian* (cowboy) in the Camargue, is worth the price of the room; he's also generous with his knowledge of the area. The outdoor kitchen allows guests to picnic in high fashion in the tranquil garden (Db-€56-65, Tb-€75-79, Qb-€90-97, includes breakfast, cash only, Wi-Fi; between Villedieu and Buisson on D-75—leave Vaison following signs to *Villedieu*, then follow D-51 toward *Buisson* and turn left onto D-75, tel. 04 90 28 95 19, ecole .buissonniere@wanadoo.fr). Ask about their all-inclusive stay for groups of four to seven people (includes pickup at airport or train station, winery and region tour).

Near Suzette

$$ La Ferme Dégoutaud, a 20-minute drive from *Vaison la Romaine*, is a splendidly situated, roomy, and utterly isolated *chambre d'hôte* about halfway between Malaucène and Suzette (well-signed, a mile down a dirt road). Animated *Véronique* (minimal English) rents three country-cozy rooms with many thoughtful touches, a view pool, table tennis, picnic-perfect tables, and a barbecue at your disposal (Db-€72, Tb-€82, Qb-€92, includes breakfast, tel. & fax 04 90 62 99 29, www.degoutaud.fr, le.degoutaud @wanadoo.fr).

Eating Along the Côtes du Rhône

Many of these eateries are described in my self-guided driving tour route (earlier); I've listed them by distance from Vaison la Romaine (nearest to farthest). Most are within a 10-minute drive of Vaison la Romaine. All have some outdoor seating and should be considered for lunch or dinner.

La Girocedre is an enchanting place to eat lunch or dinner if you have a car and it's nice outside. Just three picturesque miles from Vaison la Romaine in adorable Puyméras, this place offers you a complete country-Provençal package: outdoor tables placed just so in a lush garden, warm interior decor, and real Provençal cuisine (€18 three-course lunch *menus*, €26 dinner *menus*, closed Mon, tel. 04 90 46 50 67).

Le Panoramic, in hill-capping Le Crestet, serves average salads, pizzas, and *plats* for more than you should spend at what must be Provence's greatest view tables. Come for a drink and view, but if you're really hungry, eat elsewhere (open daily for lunch and dinner, €28 *menus*, tel. 04 90 28 76 42). Drivers should pass on the first parking lot in Le Crestet and keep climbing to park at place du Château. The restaurant is to your right as you face the view.

La Table du Comtat, in charming little Séguret, allows you to combine a village visit with a fine meal and finer views over vineyards and villages. Book a window table in advance, and come while there's still light (€20 lunch *menu*, €38 dinner *menu*, classic French cuisine, closed Wed-Thu, tel. 04 90 46 91 49). See hotel listing, earlier.

Hôtel les Florets, in Gigondas, is a traditional, family-run place that's worth the drive. Dinners are a sumptuous blend of classic French cuisine and Provençal accents, served with class by English-speaking Thierry. The marvelous terrace makes your meal even more memorable (*menus* from €30, restaurant closed Wed, service can be slow). See hotel listing, earlier.

La Maison Bleue, on Villedieu's adorable little square, is a pizza-and-salad place with great outdoor ambience. Skip it if the weather forces you inside (open for lunch and dinner, closed Mon, tel. 04 90 28 97 02).

Les Coquelicots, a tiny eatery surrounded by vines and views in minuscule Suzette, is a sweet spot. The food is scrumptious (owner/chef Frankie insists on fresh products), and the setting is memorable. Try the *Assiette Provençale*, his omelets with herbs, or any of his grilled meats and fish (May-Sept usually closed Tue evening and all day Wed, Oct-April open weekends only, tel. 04 90 65 06 94).

Côté Vignes, off a short dirt road between Suzette and Beaumes de Venise, is a lighthearted wood-fired-everything place with outdoor tables flanked by fun interior dining. Young Corinne runs the restaurant with enthusiasm; try the Camembert cheese flambé with lettuce, potatoes, and ham (€9 salads and good pizza, *menus* from €18, closed Tue evening and Wed, tel. 04 90 65 07 16).

Hill Towns of the Luberon

Just 30 miles east of Avignon, the Luberon region hides some of France's most captivating hill towns and sensuous landscapes. Those intrigued by Peter Mayle's books love joyriding through the region, connecting I-could-live-here villages, crumbled castles, and meditative abbeys. Mayle's bestselling *A Year in Provence* marked its 20th anniversary in 2010. The book describes the ruddy local culture from an Englishman's perspective as he buys a stone farmhouse, fixes it up, and adopts the region as his new home. *A Year in Provence* is a great read while you're here—or, better yet, get it as an audio book and listen as you drive.

The Luberon terrain in general (much of which is a French regional natural park) is as enticing as its villages. Gnarled vineyards and wind-sculpted trees separate tidy stone structures from abandoned buildings—little more than rock piles—that seem to challenge city slickers to fix them up. Mountains of limestone bend along vast ridges, while colorful hot-air balloons survey the sun-drenched scene from above.

Getting Around the Luberon

By Car: Luberon roads are scenic and narrow. With no major landmarks, it's easy to get lost in this area—and you will get lost,

trust me—but getting lost is the point. Pick up Michelin map #332 or #527 to navigate.

By Bus: Isle-sur-la-Sorgue is accessible by bus from Avignon, with several daily trips and a central stop at the post office (6–8/day Mon–Sat, 3–4/day Sun, 45 minutes). Without a car or minivan tour, I'd skip the more famous hill towns of the Luberon.

By Train: Trains get you to Isle-sur-la-Sorgue (station called "L'Isle-Fontaine de Vaucluse" from Avignon (10/day on weekdays, 5/day on weekends, 30 minutes). If you're day-tripping by train, check return times before leaving the station.

By Minivan Tour: Dutchman Mike Rijken, who runs **Wine Safari**, offers tours of this area, as do several other Avignon-based companies (see "Tours of Provence" on page 597).

By Taxi: Contact **Luberon Taxi** (based in Maubec off D-3, mobile 06 08 49 40 57, www.luberontaxi.com, contact@luberontaxi.com).

By Bike: Hardy cyclists can ride from Isle-sur-la-Sorgue to Gordes, then to Roussillon, connecting other villages in a full-day loop ride (30 miles round-trip to Roussillon and back, with lots of hills). Many appealing villages are closer to Isle-sur-la-Sorgue and offer easier biking options (see "Biking" on page 689).

Isle-sur-la-Sorgue

This sturdy market town—literally, "Island on the Sorgue River"—sits within a split in its crisp, happy little river. It's a workaday town, with a gritty charm that feels refreshingly real after so many adorable villages. It also makes a good base for exploring the Luberon (15 minutes by car, doable by hardy cyclists) and Avignon (30 minutes by car or train) and can work for exploring the Côtes du Rhône by car (allow an hour to Vaison la Romaine).

After the arid cities and villages elsewhere in Provence, the presence of water at every turn is a welcome change. In Isle-sur-la-Sorgue—called the "Venice of Provence"—the Sorgue River's extraordinarily clear and shallow flow divides like cells, producing water, water everywhere. The river has long nourished the region's economy. The fresh spring water of the Sorgue's many branches has provided ample fish, irrigation for crops, and power for local industries for centuries. Today, antiques shops power the town's economy—every other shop seems to sell some kind of antique.

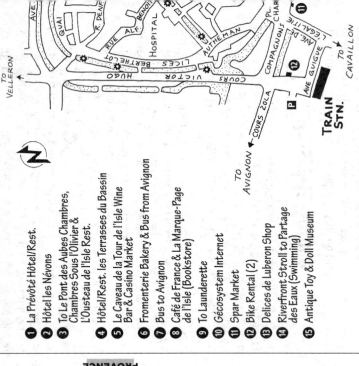

Isle-sur-la-Sorgue

1. La Prévôté Hôtel/Rest.
2. Hôtel les Névons
3. To Le Pont des Aubes Chambres, Chambres Sous l'Olivier & L'Ousteau de l'Isle Rest.
4. Hôtel/Rest. les Terrasses du Bassin
5. Le Caveau de la Tour de l'Isle Wine Bar & Casino Market
6. Fromenterie Bakery & Bus from Avignon
7. Bus to Avignon
8. Café de France & La Marque-Page de l'Isle (Bookstore)
9. To Launderette
10. Gécosystem Internet
11. Spar Market
12. Bike Rental (2)
13. Delices de Luberon Shop
14. Riverfront Stroll to Partage des Eaux (Swimming)
15. Antique Toy & Doll Museum

Orientation to Isle-sur-la-Sorgue

Isle-sur-la-Sorgue is renowned for its market days (Sun and Thu), it's otherwise a pleasantly average town with no important sights and a steady trickle of tourism. It's calm at night and dead on Mondays. The town revolves around its river, the church square, and two pedestrian-only streets, rue de la République and rue Carnot.

Tourist Information

The TI has information on hiking, biking itineraries, and a line on rooms in private homes, all of which are outside of town (Mon–Sat 9:00–12:30 & 14:30–18:00, Sun 9:00–12:30, in town center next to church, tel. 04 90 38 04 78, www.oti-delasorgue.fr).

Arrival in Isle-sur-la-Sorgue

By Car: Traffic is a mess and parking is a headache on market days (all day Sunday and Thursday mornings). Circle the ring road and

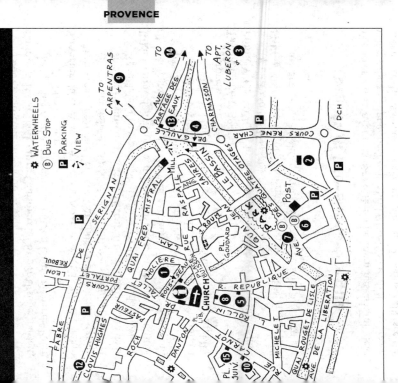

look for parking signs, or give up and find the pay lot behind the post office (PTT). There are several lots just west of the roundabout at Le Bassin. You'll also pass freestyle parking on roads leaving the city. Don't leave anything visible in your car.

By Train: Remember that the train station is called "L'Isle–Fontaine de Vaucluse." To reach my recommended hotels, walk straight out of the station and turn right on the ring road.

By Bus: The bus from Avignon drops you near the post office (PTT, ask driver for "*lub pay-tay-tay*"), a block from the recommended Hôtel les Névons.

Helpful Hints

Shop Hours: The antiques shops this town is famous for are open Saturday to Monday only.

Internet Access: Your best option is the centrally located **Gécosystem** (rue Carnot 40, tel. 04 90 15 40 16).

Bookstore: You'll find a handful of English novels at **La Marque-Page de l'Isle**, where the pedestrian street rue de la République meets Notre-Dame des Anges church (Tue–Sat 7:00–12:30 & 15:00–19:00, Sun–Mon 7:00–12:30).

Laundry: It's at the **Centre Commercial Super U** supermarket, on the ring road at the roundabout, on Cours Fernande Peyre (daily 9:00–19:00).

Supermarket: A well-stocked **Spar** market is on the main ring road, near the Peugeot Car shop and the train station (Mon–Sat 8:30–12:30 & 15:00–19:00, Sun 15:00–19:00). A smaller **Casino** market is more central on pedestrian rue de la République (Tue–Sun 7:30–12:30 & 15:30–19:30, closed Mon).

Bike Rental: Christophe at **Isles 2 Roues,** by the train station, rents good bikes (€15/day, closed Sun–Mon, must show your passport, 10 avenue de la Gare, tel. 04 90 38 19 12). **Vélo Services** is also fine (on the northern side of ring road at 1 quai Clovis Hugues, mobile 06 82 58 35 02, www.europbike-provence.fr).

Taxi: Call 06 13 38 32 11.

Public WC: A WC is in the parking lot between the post office (PTT) and the Hôtel les Névons.

Hiking: The TI has good information on area hikes; most trails are accessible by short drives, and you can use a taxi to get there.

Sights in Isle-sur-la-Sorgue

Wandering Isle-sur-la-Sorgue—The town has crystal-clear water babbling under pedestrian bridges stuffed with flower boxes, and its old-time carousel is always spinning. For this walk, see the map on the previous page and navigate by the town's splintered streams and nine mossy waterwheels, which, while still turning, power only memories of the town's wool and silk industries. Here are a few landmarks to look for:

Notre-Dame des Anges: This 12th-century church has a festive Baroque interior and feels too big for today's town. Walk in. The curls and swirls and gilded statues date from an era that was all about Louis XIV, the Sun King. This is propagandist architecture, designed to wow the faithful into compliance. (It was made possible thanks to profits generated from the town's river-powered industries.) When you enter a church like this, the heavens should open up and assure you that whoever built it had celestial connections (daily 10:00–12:00 & 15:15–17:00, Mass on Sun at 10:30).

Three Waterwheels: A block down rue Orleans across from the church, these high, forgotten waterwheels have been in business here since the 1200s, when they were first used for grinding flour. Paper, textile, silk, and woolen mills would later find their power from this river. At its peak, Isle-sur-la-Sorgue had 70 waterwheels like this, and in the 1800s, the town competed with Avignon as Provence's cloth-dyeing and textile center. Those stylish Provençal fabrics and patterns you see for sale everywhere were made possible by this river.

Le Bassin: At the town's east end and literally translated as a "pond," this is where the Sorgue River crashes into the town. Track as many branches as you can see (Frank Provost hides a big one), and then find the round lookout point for the best perspective (carefully placed lights make this a beautiful sight after dark). Fishing was the town's main industry until the waterwheels took over. In the 1300s, local fishermen provided the pope with his fresh-fish quota. They trapped them in nets and speared them while standing on skinny, flat-bottomed boats. Several streets are named after the fish they caught—including rue de l'Aiguille ("Eel Street") and rue des Ecrevisses ("Crayfish Street").

The sound of the rushing water reminds us of the power that rivers can generate. With its source (a spring) a mere five miles away, the Sorgue River never floods and has a constant flow and temperature in all seasons. Despite its exposed (flat) location, Isle-sur-la-Sorgue prospered in the Middle Ages, thanks to the natural protection this river provided. Walls with big moats once ran along the river, but they were destroyed during the French Revolution.

▲▲**Market Days**—The town erupts into a carnival-like market frenzy each Sunday and Thursday, with hardy crafts and local produce. The Sunday market is astounding and famous for its antiques; the Thursday market is more intimate. Find a table across from the church at the Café de France and enjoy the scene.

Antique Toy and Doll Museum (Musée du Jouet et de la Poupée Ancienne)—The town's lone sight is a fun and funky toy museum with more than 300 dolls displayed in three small rooms (€3.50, kids–€1.50; July-Sept Mon–Sat 10:30–18:30, Sun 11:00–18:00; Oct-June Tue–Fri 13:00–18:00, Sat–Sun 11:00–17:00, closed Mon; call ahead to reconfirm opening times, 26 rue Carnot, mobile 06 09 10 32 66).

Biking—Isle-sur-la-Sorgue is ideally situated for short biking forays into the mostly level terrain. Pick up a biking itinerary at the TI. These towns make easy biking destinations from Isle-sur-la-Sorgue: Velleron (5 miles north, flat, a tiny version of Isle-sur-la-Sorgue with waterwheels, fountains, and an evening farmer's market Mon–Sat 18:00–20:00); Lagnes (3 miles east, a pretty and well-restored hill town with views from its ruined château); and Fontaine-de-Vaucluse (5 miles northeast, a touristy village at the source of the Sorgue River, gently uphill). Allow 30 miles and many hills for the round-trip ride to Roussillon. (A bike-rental company in Isle-sur-la-Sorgue is listed under "Helpful Hints," earlier.)

Sleeping in Isle-sur-la-Sorgue

(€1 = about $1.25, country code: 33)

Pickings are slim for good sleeps in Isle-sur-la-Sorgue, though the few I've listed provide solid values.

$$$ La Prévôte*** has the town's highest-priced digs. Each of its five meticulously decorated rooms—located above a classy restaurant—is decorated in earth tones, with high ceilings, a few exposed beams, and beautiful furnishings. Helpful Séverine manages the hotel while chef-hubby Jean-Marie controls the kitchen (standard Db-€135, larger Db-€160, suite Db-€180, no air-con or elevator, Internet access and Wi-Fi, rooftop deck with Jacuzzi, no parking, one block from the church at 4 rue J. J. Rousseau, tel. & fax 04 90 38 57 29, www.la-prevote.fr, contact@la-prevote.fr).

$$ Hôtel les Névons**, two blocks from the center (behind the post office), is concrete motel-modern outside, but a fair value within. The staff is eager to please, and you have two wings to choose from: the new wing, with cavernous (by local standards) and well-appointed rooms; or the old wing, with humble, but cheaper rooms. There are several family suites and a roof deck with 360-degree views around a small pool (old wing—Db-€61; new wing—huge Db-€70, Tb-€90, Qb-€95; good but pricey breakfast, air-con, Internet access, Wi-Fi in lobby, easy parking, 205 chemin des Névons, push and hold the gate button a bit on entry, tel. 04 90 20 72 00, fax 04 90 20 56 20, www.hotel-les-nevons.com, info@hotel-les-nevons.com).

$$ Le Pont des Aubes Chambres has two huggable rooms in an old green-shuttered farmhouse right on the river a mile from town. Borrow a bike or a canoe. From here you can cross a tiny bridge and walk 15 minutes along the river into Isle-sur-la-Sorgue, or cross the street to the recommended L'Ousteau de l'Isle restaurant. Charming Martine speaks English, while husband Patrice speaks smiles (Db-€75, Tb-€90, 1-room apartments-€380–450/week, cash only, a mile from town toward Apt, next to Pain d'Antan Boulangerie at 189 route d'Apt, tel. & fax 04 90 38 13 75, http://perso.wanadoo.fr/lepontdesaubes, patriceaubert@wanadoo.fr).

$ Hôtel les Terrasses du Bassin rents eight spotless rooms with designer touches over a good restaurant on Le Bassin, where the river waters separate before running through town. Several rooms look out over Le Bassin, a few have queen-size beds, and there's some traffic noise (Db-€64, extra bed-€10, air-con, Wi-Fi, 2 avenue Charles de Gaulle, tel. 04 90 38 03 16, fax 04 90 38 65 61, www.lesterrassesdubassin.com, corinne@lesterrassesdu bassin.com).

Near Isle-sur-la-Sorgue

$$$ Chambres Sous l'Olivier, located five minutes east of Isle-sur-la-Sorgue, is well-situated for exploring the hill towns of the Luberon and Isle-sur-la-Sorgue. Its six lovely rooms are housed in a massive 150-year-old farmhouse with lounges that you and your entire soccer team could spread out in. Julien and Carole take care of your every need, and will cook you a full-blown dinner with wine for €30 per person (Db-€90–135, Tb-€120, two-room Tb-€180, three-room suite for up to six people-€220, prices include breakfast; credit cards not accepted—pay with cash, euro travelers checks, or bank transfer; pool; route d'Apt, tel. 04 90 20 33 90, www.chambresdhotesprovence.com, souslolivier@orange.fr). It's below Isle-sur-la-Sorgue, about 25 minutes from Avignon toward Apt on D-900 (near Petit Palais—don't go to Lagnes by mistake). Look for signs 200 yards after the big sign to *le Mas du Grand Jonquier*, on the right.

Eating in Isle-sur-la-Sorgue

Inexpensive restaurants are easy to find in Isle-sur-la-Sorgue, but consistent quality is another story. The restaurants I list offer good value, but none of them is really "cheap." For inexpensive meals, troll the riverside cafés for today's catch. Dining on the river is a unique experience in this arid land famous for its hill towns, and shopping for the perfect table is half the fun. Riverside picnics work well here (the Fromenterie bakery, listed on the next page, stocks mouthwatering quiche and more).

Begin your dinner with a glass of wine at the cozy **Le Caveau de la Tour de l'Isle** (the wine bar hides in the rear, Tue–Sun 9:30–12:30 & 15:30–20:00, closed Mon, 12 rue de la République, tel. 04 90 20 70 25).

Les Terrasses du Bassin has moderate prices, good choices, and a cool riverfront location (terrace dining available). The hardworking owners are dedicated to providing a good value and welcoming service. Come for a full meal or just a *plat* (€10 lunch salads and starters, €16 dinner *plats*, €24-34 dinner *menu*, closed Tue–Wed Oct–May, 2 avenue Charles de Gaulle, tel. 04 90 38 03 16).

La Prévôté is a place to really do it up. Its dining room is covered in wood beams, the outdoor patio is peaceful, and the ambience is country-classy but not stuffy. A branch of the Sorgue runs under the restaurant, visible through glass windows (*menus* from €50, save room for amazing cheese platter, closed Tue–Wed, 4 rue J. J. Rousseau, on narrow street that runs along left side of church as you face it, tel. 04 90 38 57 29).

L'Oustau de l'Isle, a mile from the town center, dishes up regional cuisine with a modern twist and a friendly welcome. Skip the modern interior and ask for a table *sur la terrasse* (dinner *menus* from €27, lunch *menu* for €17, closed Tue–Wed, 147 chemin de Bosquet, tel. 04 90 20 81 36). From Isle-sur-la-Sorgue's center, follow signs toward *Apt*, and turn right at Pain d'Antan Boulangerie; or walk 20 minutes along the river and cross the small bridge to chemin de Bosquet.

The **Fromenterie** bakery next to the post office (PTT) sells decadent quiche, monster sandwiches, desserts, wine, and other drinks—in other words, everything you need to picnic (open daily until 20:00).

Roussillon

With all the trendy charm of Santa Fe on a hilltop, photogenic Roussillon requires serious camera and café time (and €3 for parking). Roussillon has been a protected village since 1943 and has benefited from a complete absence of modern development. An enormous deposit of ochre gives the earth and its buildings that distinctive red color and provided this village with its economic base until shortly after World War II. This place is popular, so it's best to visit early or late in the day.

Orientation to Roussillon

Roussillon sits atop Mont Rouge (Red Mountain) at about 1,000 feet above sea level, and requires some uphill walking to reach. Exposed ochre cliffs form the village's southern limit.

Tourist Information

The little TI is in the center, across from the David restaurant. If in need of accommodations, leaf through their good binders describing area hotels and *chambres d'hôte*. Walkers should get info on trails from Roussillon to nearby villages (TI open April–Oct Mon–Sat 9:30–12:00 & 13:30–18:00, closed Sun except in summer; Nov–March Mon–Sat 14:00–17:30, closed Sun; tel. 04 90 05 60 25).

Arrival in Roussillon

Parking lots are available at every entry to the village. The closest two lots are on the northern edge (Parking Sablons, by the recommended Hôtel Rêves d'Ocres) and on the southern flank, closer to

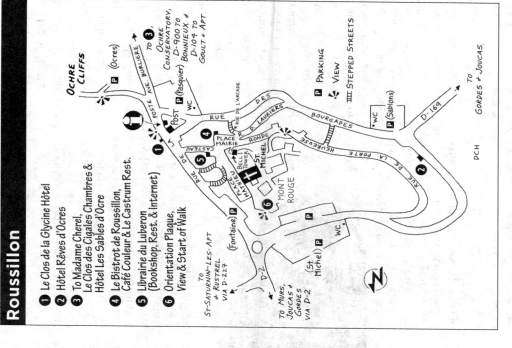

Roussillon

1. Le Clos de la Glycine Hôtel
2. Hôtel Rêves d'Ocres
3. To Madame Cherel, Le Clos des Cigales Chambres & Hôtel Les Sables d'Ocre
4. Le Bistrot de Roussillon, Café Couleur & Le Castrum Rest.
5. Librairie du Luberon (Bookshop, Rest. & Internet)
6. Orientation Plaque, View & Start of Walk

the ochre cliffs (Parking Pasquier). If you approach from Gordes or Joucas, you'll park at Sablons. If you're coming from D-900 and the south, you'll land at Pasquier (but don't park there on Wednesday night, because Thursday is Roussillon's market day). Leave nothing valuable showing in your car.

Helpful Hints

An ATM is next to the TI. Internet access and a modest selection of English books are available at the delightful **Librairie du Luberon** on the main square (daily 10:00–18:00, tel. 04 90 71 55 72; its restaurant is described later, under "Eating in Roussillon").

Sights in Roussillon

▲The Village

Climb a few minutes from either parking lot (passing the Hollywood set-like square under the bell tower and the church) and find the orientation plaque and the dramatic **viewpoint,** often complete with a howling mistral. During the Middle Ages, a castle stood where you are, on the top of Red Mountain (Mont Rouge), and watched over the village below. While nothing remains of the castle today, the strategic advantage of this site is clear. Count how many villages you can identify, and then notice how little sprawl there is in the valley below. Because the Luberon is a natural reserve (Parc Naturel Régional du Luberon), development is strictly controlled.

A short stroll down leads to the church. Duck into the pretty 11th-century **Church of St. Michel,** and appreciate the natural air-conditioning and the well-worn center aisle. The white interior tells you that the stone came from elsewhere, and the WWI memorial plaque over the side door suggests a village devastated by the war (over 40 died from little Roussillon).

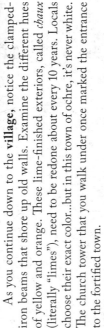

As you continue down to the **village,** notice the clamped-iron beams that shore up old walls. Examine the different hues of yellow and orange. These lime-finished exteriors, called *chaux* (literally "limes"), need to be redone about every 10 years. Locals choose their exact color...but in this town of ochre, it's never white. The church tower that you walk under once marked the entrance to the fortified town.

Linger over *un café,* or—if it's later in the day—*un pastis,* in what must be the most picturesque village **square** in Provence (place de la Mairie). Watch the stream of shoppers. Is anyone playing *boules* at the opposite end? You could paint the entire town without ever leaving the red-and-orange corner of your palette. Many do. While Roussillon receives its share of day-trippers, mornings and evenings are romantically peaceful on this square. The

Librairie du Luberon bookshop on the square's corner deserves a visit (nice top-floor restaurant).

▲▲Ochre Cliffs

Roussillon was Europe's capital for ochre production until World War II. A stroll to the south end of town, beyond the upper parking lot, shows you why: Roussillon sits on the world's largest known ochre deposit. A radiant orange path leads through the richly colored ochre canyon, explaining the hue of this village (€2.50, daily 9:00–17:00, until 19:00 in summer; beware—light-colored clothing and orange powder don't mix).

The value of Roussillon's ochre cliffs was known even in Roman times. Once excavated, the clay ochre was rinsed with water to separate it from sand, then bricks of the stuff were dried and baked for deeper hues. The procedure for extracting the ochre did not change much over 2,000 years, until ochre mining became industrialized in the late 1700s. Used primarily for wallpaper and linoleum, ochre use reached its zenith just before World War II. (After that, cheaper substitutes took over.)

Sleeping in Roussillon

(€1 = about $1.25, country code: 33)

The TI posts a list of hotels and *chambres d'hôte*. Parking is free if you sleep in Roussillon—ask your hotelier where to park. The village offers three good-value accommodations—conveniently, one for each price range.

$$$ Le Clos de la Glycine*** provides Roussillon's plushest accommodations, with nine gorgeous rooms located dead-center in the village (Db-€140-160, big Db-€180, loft suite with deck and view-€275, Wi-Fi, located at the refined restaurant David—so they prefer you pay for half-pension, across from the TI on place de la Poste, tel. 04 90 05 60 13, fax 04 90 05 75 80, www.luberon-hotel.com, le.clos.de.la.glycine@wanadoo.fr).

$$ Hôtel Rêves d'Ocres** is a solid two-star value, run by eager-to-help Sandrine and Yvan. It's ochre-colored, warm, and comfortable, with 16 mostly spacious and tastefully designed rooms—some with musty bathrooms. Eight smaller rooms have view terraces, but are *très* cozy. There's also a lovely lounge where you can stretch out (Sb-€60, Db without balcony-€76, Db with balcony-€80, Tb-€95, Qb-€115, meek air-con, Internet access, Wi-Fi, route de Gordes, tel. 04 90 05 60 50, fax 04 90 05 79 74, www.hotel-revesdocres.com, hotelrevesdocres@wanadoo.fr). Coming from Gordes and Joucas, it's the first building you pass in Roussillon.

$ Madame Cherel rents ramshackle rooms that are barely this side of a youth hostel. A shared view terrace and good reading materials are available, and the beds have firm mattresses (D-€45-49, family suite available, includes breakfast, cash only, 3 blocks from upper parking lot, between the gas station and school, La Burlière, tel. 04 90 05 71 71, mulhane@hotmail.com). Chatty and sincere Cherel speaks English and is a wealth of regional travel tips.

Near Roussillon, in or near Joucas

The tiny village of Joucas lies a few minutes below Roussillon and hides a handful of good-value accommodations. Each of the three hotels listed below comes with a good restaurant.

$$$ La Ferme de la Huppe*** has a Gordes address, but it's closer physically and spiritually to Joucas. This small farmhouse-elegant hacienda makes an excellent mini-splurge. Ten low-slung rooms gather on two levels behind the stylish pool. The decor is tasteful, understated, and rustic (small Db-€140, bigger Db-€170, much bigger Db-€200, includes good breakfast, small fridges, air-con, Wi-Fi; between Joucas and Gordes on D-156 road to Goult, just off D-2; tel. 04 90 72 12 25, fax 04 90 72 25 39, www.lafermedelahuppe.com, info@lafermedelahuppe.com). Dine poolside or in the smart dining room (€46 three-course *menu* or €62 six-course tasting *menu*).

$$$ Le Mas du Loriot is another worthwhile almost-in-Joucas value. Gentle owners Alain and Christine have carved the ideal escape out of an olive grove, with eight soothing rooms, private terraces, a generous pool, and home-cooked dinners—all at fair prices and with a view to remember (Db-€105-135, extra bed-€20, €32 four-course dinners available four nights a week—when half-pension is a smart idea, Internet access, on D-102 between Joucas and Murs, tel. 04 90 72 62 62, Wi-Fi, fax 04 90 72 62 54, www.masduloriot.com, hotel@masduloriot.com).

$$ Hostellerie des Commandeurs**, run by soft Sophie, has modern, comfortable, and clean rooms in the village of Joucas. It's kid-friendly, with a big pool and a sports field/play area next door. Ask for a south-facing room (*coté sud*) for the best views, or a north-facing room (*coté nord*) if it's hot. All rooms have showers (Db-€64-68, extra bed-€16, small fridges, above park at village entrance, tel. 04 90 05 78 01, fax 04 90 05 74 47, www.lescommandeurs.com, hostellerie@lescommandeurs.com). The simple restaurant offers tasty cuisine at fair prices (three-course *menus* from €20, succulent lamb, memorable crème brûlée with lavender, restaurant closed Wed).

Eating in Roussillon

Choose ambience over cuisine if dining in Roussillon, and enjoy any of the eateries on the main square. It's a festive place, where children twirl while parents dine, and dogs and cats look longingly for leftovers. Restaurants change with the mistral here—what's good one year disappoints the next. Consider my suggestions and go with what looks best. The first three places listed next share the same square and offer similar values. One should always be open.

At **Le Bistrot de Roussillon**, Johan offers the most consistent value on the square, with excellent salads (try the *salad du bistrot*) and *plats* for the right price. There's a breezy terrace in back and a comfy interior (€15 for a filling salad and dessert, €13 *plats*, daily, tel. 04 90 05 74 45).

Café Couleur and **Le Castrum** flank Le Bistrot de Roussillon, offering similar atmosphere and prices, but less-steady quality.

Librairie du Luberon, opposite the above-listed restaurants on the square, hides a slick top-floor restaurant/*salon de thé* above its bookstore. Have lunch or a drink outside on the splendid terrace, or inside surrounded by books—for a price (€19 *plats*, restaurant closed Mon).

More Luberon Hill Towns and Sights

Le Luberon is packed with appealing villages and beautiful scenery, but it has only a handful of must-see sights. The more popular section lies above D-900 (with Roussillon and Gordes), whereas the villages to the south seem a bit less trampled. Rambling the Luberon's spaghetti network of small roads is a joy, and getting lost comes with the territory—go with it. Pick up a good map (Michelin Local map #332 works for me).

Gordes

For the last 40 years, Gordes has been the most touristy and trendy town in the Luberon—creating gridlock and parking headaches (come early). In the 1960s, Gordes was a virtual ghost town of derelict buildings, but now it's thoroughly renovated and filled with people who live in a world without calluses. Many Parisian big shots and wealthy foreigners have purchased and restored older homes here, putting property values out of sight for locals. As you approach Gordes,

make a hard right at the impressive view of the place (you'll find some parking along the small road). Beyond here, the village has little of interest, except its Tuesday market (which ends at 13:00). The town's 11th-century castle houses a mildly interesting collection of contemporary art.

The more interesting Abbey Notre-Dame de Sénanque (listed next) is nearby and well-marked from Gordes.

Abbey Notre-Dame de Sénanque

This still-functioning and beautifully situated Cistercian abbey was built in 1148 as a back-to-basics reaction to the excesses of Benedictine abbeys. The Cistercians strove to be separate from the world, and to recapture the simplicity, solitude, and poverty of the early Church. To succeed required industrious self-sufficiency—a skill that these monks had. Their movement spread and colonized Europe with a new form of Christianity. By 1200 there were more than 500 such monasteries and abbeys in Europe.

The abbey is best appreciated from the outside, and is worth the trip for its splendid and remote setting alone. Come early or late, stop at a pullout for a bird's-eye view as you descend, then wander the abbey's perimeter with fewer tourists. The abbey church (Eglise Abbatiale) is open and highlights the utter simplicity sought by these monks. The beautiful bookshop is worth a look as well (Cistercians know how to turn a profit). In late June through much of July, the lavender fields that surround the abbey make for breathtaking pictures and draw loads of visitors, making it more important to arrive early or late.

The abbey itself can only be visited on a 50-minute, French-only tour with an English handout. The interior, which doesn't

measure up to the abbey's spectacular setting, is not worth it for most people. The tour covers Sénanque's church, the small cloisters, the refectory, and a *chauffoir*, a small heated room where monks could copy books year-round (€7, includes tour—about 6/day Mon–Sat; Mon–Sat 10:00–12:00 & 13:30–18:00, Sun 14:00–18:00, tel. 04 90 72 05 72, www.senanque.fr).

Museum of Lavender (Musée de la Lavande)

Located halfway between Gordes and Isle-sur-la-Sorgue in Coustellet, this surprisingly interesting museum does a good job explaining the process of lavender production with interesting exhibits and good English information (with an audioguide, a film, and posted explanations at the exhibits). It's popular with tour groups, smells great inside, and offers the ultimate "if they made it with lavender, we sell it" gift shop (€6, daily May–Sept 9:00–19:00, Oct–April 9:00–13:00 & 14:00–18:00, in Coustellet just off D-900 toward Gordes, tel. 04 90 76 91 23).

The next three stops are all located just below D-900, near the hill town of Bonnieux.

St. Julien Bridge (Pont St. Julien)

This delicate three-arched bridge survives as a testimony to Roman engineers—and to the importance of this rural area 2,000 years ago. It's the only surviving bridge on what was the main road from northern Italy to Provence—the primary route used by Roman armies. The 215-foot-long Roman bridge was built from 27 B.C. to A.D. 14. Mortar had not yet been invented, so (as with Pont du Gard) stones were carefully set in place. Amazingly, the bridge survives today, having outlived Roman marches, hundreds of floods, and decades of automobile traffic. A new bridge finally rerouted traffic from this beautiful structure in 2005.

Bonnieux

Spectacular from a distance, this town disappoints me up close. It lacks a pedestrian center, though the Friday-morning market briefly creates one. The main reason to visit here is to enjoy its excellent restaurants and views.

Eating in Bonnieux: **Le Fournil** has marvelous food, a postcard-perfect terrace, and outdoor tables around a tranquil fountain. The interior is uninviting (unless you dig caves and modern decor), so book an out-

door table or skip it (€15 lunch *plats*, €42 dinner *menus*, closed for dinner Mon, closed for lunch Mon–Tue and Sat, next to TI, tel. 04 90 75 83 62).

Lacoste

Little Lacoste slumbers across the valley from Bonnieux in the shadow of its looming castle. Climb through this photogenic village of arches and stone paths, passing American art students (from the Savannah College of Art and Design) showing their work. Support an American artist, learn about his or her art, and then keep climbing and climbing to the ruined castle base. The view of Bonnieux from the base of Lacoste's castle is as good as it gets.

The Marquis de Sade (1740–1814) lived in this castle for more than 30 years. Author of dirty novels, he was notorious for hosting orgies behind these walls, and for kidnapping peasants for scandalous purposes. He was eventually arrested and imprisoned for 30 years—thanks to him, we have a word to describe his favorite hobby: sadism. Today, clothing designer Pierre Cardin is spending a fortune renovating the castle in lavish fashion, complete with a concert hall that now hosts a summer theater and opera festival. Some locals are critical of Cardin, who they say is buying up the town to create his own "faux-Provence." Could "Cardism" be next?

Eating in Lacoste: If it's time for lunch, find the **Bar/ Restaurant de France**'s outdoor tables overlooking Bonnieux and savor the view (inexpensive, good omelets, daily, lunch only off-season, tel. 04 90 75 82 25).

THE FRENCH RIVIERA

La Côte d'Azur: Nice • Villefranche-sur-Mer •
The Three Corniches • Monaco • Antibes • Inland Riviera

A hundred years ago, celebrities flocked from London to Moscow flocked to the French Riviera to socialize, gamble, and escape the dreary weather at home. Today, budget vacationers and heat-seeking Europeans fill belle époque resorts at France's most sought-after fun-in-the-sun destination.

Some of the Continent's most stunning scenery and intriguing museums lie along this strip of land—as do millions of sun-worshipping tourists. Nice has world-class museums, a splendid beachfront promenade, a seductive old town, and all the drawbacks of a major city (traffic, crime, pollution, and so on). But the day-trip possibilities are easy and exciting: Monte Carlo welcomes everyone and will happily take your cash; Antibes has a thriving port and silky sand beaches; and the hill towns present a breezy and photogenic alternative to the beach scene. Evenings on the Riviera, a.k.a. La Côte d'Azur, were made for a promenade and outdoor dining.

Choose a Home Base

My favorite home bases are Nice, Antibes, and Villefranche-sur-Mer.

Nice is the region's capital and France's fifth-largest city. With convenient train and bus connections to most regional sights, this is the most practical base for train travelers. Urban Nice also has a full palette of museums (most of which are free), a beach scene that rocks, the best selection of hotels in all price ranges, and good nightlife options. A car is a headache in Nice, though it's easily stored at one of the many pricey parking garages or for free at an outer tram station.

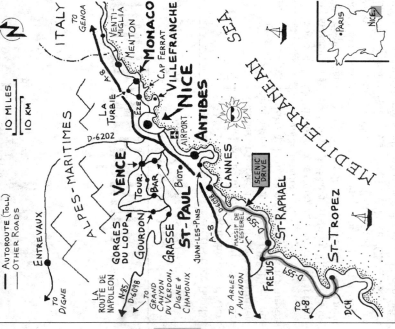

The French Riviera

Nearby **Antibes** is smaller, with a bustling center, a lively night scene, great sandy beaches, grand vistas, good walking trails, and a much-admired Picasso Museum. Antibes has frequent train service to Nice and Monaco, and it's easy for drivers.

Villefranche-sur-Mer is the romantic's choice, with a serene setting and small-town warmth. It has finely ground pebble beaches, quick public transportation to Nice and Monaco, easy parking, and a smaller selection of hotels in most price ranges.

Planning Your Time

Ideally, allow a full day for Nice, a full day for Monaco and the Corniche route that connects it with Nice, and a half-day for Villefranche-sur-Mer or Antibes. Monaco and Villefranche-sur-Mer have good energy at night (sights are closed, but crowds are few; consider dinner there), and Antibes works well by day (good

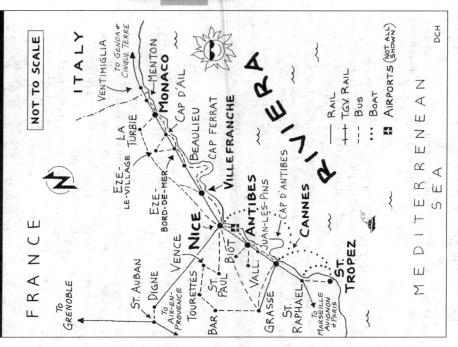

Public Transportation on the French Riviera

NOT TO SCALE

FRANCE

ITALY

MEDITERRANEAN SEA

RIVIERA

TO GENOA + CINQUE TERRE

VENTIMIGLIA
MENTON
MONACO
CAP D'AIL
LA TURBIE
EZE-LE-VILLAGE
BEAULIEU
CAP FERRAT
EZE-BORD-DE-MER
VILLEFRANCHE
NICE
VENCE
ST. AUBAN
DIGNE
TOURETTES
ST. PAUL
BIOT
VALL.
ANTIBES
JUAN-LES-PINS
CAP D'ANTIBES
CANNES
BAR.
GRASSE
ST. RAPHAEL
ST. TROPEZ

TO GRENOBLE
TO AIX-EN-PROVENCE
TO MARSEILLE AVIGNON + PARIS

RAIL
T.G.V. RAIL
BUS
BOAT
AIRPORTS (NOT ALL SHOWN)

DCH

beaches and hiking) and by night (good choice of restaurants and a lively after-hours scene). Hill town–loving naturalists should allow a day to explore the hill-capping hamlets near Vence (but these are a lower priority for most).

Helpful Hints

Medical Help: Riviera Medical Services has a list of English-speaking physicians all along the Riviera. They can help you make an appointment or call an ambulance (tel. 04 93 26 12 70, www.rivieramedical.com).

Closed Days: The following sights are closed on Mondays—the Modern and Contemporary Art Museum, the Fine Arts

Museum, and cours Saleya market in Nice, along with Antibes' Marché Provençal market from September through May. The Chagall, Matisse, and Archaeological museums in Nice are closed on Tuesdays.

Events: The Riviera is famous for staging major events. Unless you're actually taking part in the festivities, these events give you only room shortages and traffic jams. Here are the three biggies in 2011: **Nice Carnival** (Feb 18–March 8, www .nicecarnaval.com), **Grand Prix of Monaco** (May 26–29, www.grand-prix-monaco.com), and Festival de Cannes, better known as the **Cannes Film Festival** (May 11–22, www .festival-cannes.com).

Getting Around the Riviera

Nice is perfectly situated for exploring the Riviera by public transport. Monaco, Eze-le-Village, Villefranche-sur-Mer, Antibes, and St-Paul-de-Vence are all within about a one-hour bus or train ride. Boats go from Nice to Monaco and St-Tropez.

By Train and Bus: All trains serving Nice arrive at and depart from the Nice-Ville station. Many key Riviera destinations are connected by direct bus or train service from Nice, and some are served by both. Since bus fare is only €1 (except on express airport buses), the pricier train is only a better choice when it saves you time (which it generally does—there is no faster way to move about the Riviera than by train).

You make the call—both modes of transportation work well. Unless otherwise noted, the following bus frequencies are for Monday–Saturday (Sunday often has limited or no service). All prices are one-way.

Destination	Bus from Nice	Train from Nice
Villefranche-sur-Mer	4/hr daily, 15 min	2/hr, 10 min, €1.90
Monaco	4/hr Mon–Sat, 3/hr Sun, 45 min	2/hr, 20 min, €3.60
Antibes	2–4/hr, 1–1.5 hrs	2/hr, 15–30 min, €4
St-Paul-de-Vence	every 40 min, 45 min	none
Vence	every 40 min, 50 min	none
Eze-le-Village	16/day, 25 min	none
La Turbie	4/day, 45 min	none

Buses also run from Monaco to Eze-le-Village and to La Turbie, allowing travelers to triangulate Nice, Monaco, and Eze-le-Village or La Turbie for a good all-day excursion—ending up back in Nice (see page 770 for details).

By Minivan Excursion: Sylvie Di Cristo offers terrific full-day tours throughout the French Riviera in a car or minivan. She adores educating people about this area's culture and history, and loves adapting her tour to your interests, from overlooked hill towns to wine, cuisine, art, or perfume (€170/person for 2–3 people, €120/person for 4–6 people, €100/person for 7–8 people, 2-person minimum, mobile 06 09 88 83 83, www.frenchrivieraguides.net, sylvie.di.cristo@wanadoo.fr).

The TI and most hotels have information on other minivan excursions from Nice (roughly €50–60/half-day, €80–110/day). **Med-Tour** is one of many (tel. 04 93 82 92 58, mobile 06 73 82 04 10, www.med-tour.com); **Tour Azur** is another (tel. 04 93 44 88 77, www.tourazur.com). **Revelation Tours** specializes in English-language excursions (tel. 04 93 53 69 85, www.revelation-tours .com). All also offer private tours by the day or half-day (check with them for their outrageous prices, about €90/hour).

By Boat: From June to mid-September, **Trans Côte d'Azur** offers scenic trips from Nice to Monaco and Nice to St-Tropez. Boats leave in the morning and return in the evening, giving you all day to explore your destination. Drinks and WCs are available on board. Boats to **Monaco** depart at 9:30 and 16:00, and return at 11:00 and 18:00 (€32 round-trip, €27 if you don't get off in Monaco, 45 minutes each way, June–Sept Tue, Thu, and Sat only). Boats to **St-Tropez** depart at 9:00 and return at 19:00 (€55 round-trip, 2.5 hours each way; July–Aug Tue–Sun, no boats Mon; late June and early Sept Tue, Thu, and Sun only). Reservations are required for both boats, and tickets for St-Tropez often sell out, so book a few days ahead (tel. 04 92 98 71 30 or 04 92 00 42 30, www.trans-cote -azur.com, croisieres@trans-cote-azur.com). The boats leave from Nice's port, bassin des Amiraux, just below Castle Hill—look for the blue ticket booth (*billeterie*) on quai de Lunel (see map on page 708). The same company also runs one-hour round-trip cruises along the coast to Cap Ferrat (see "Tours in Nice," later).

The Riviera's Art Scene

The list of artists who have painted the Riviera reads like a Who's Who of 20th-century art: Pierre-Auguste Renoir, Henri Matisse, Marc Chagall, Georges Braque, Raoul Dufy, Fernand Léger, and Pablo Picasso all lived and worked here—and raved about the region's wonderful light. Their simple, semi-abstract, and—most importantly—colorful works reflect the Riviera. You'll experience the same land-scapes they painted in this bright, sun-drenched region, punctuated with views of the "azure sea." Try to imagine the Riviera with a fraction of the people and the development you see today.

But the artists were mostly drawn to the uncomplicated lifestyle of fishermen and farmers that has reigned here since time began. As the artists grew older, they retired in the sun, turned their backs on modern art's "isms," and painted with the wide-eyed wonder of children, using bright primary colors, basic outlines, and simple subjects.

A dynamic concentration of well-organized modern- and contemporary-art museums (many described in this chapter) litter the Riviera, allowing art-lovers to appreciate these masters' works while immersed in the same sun and culture that inspired them. Many of the museums were designed to blend pieces with the surrounding views, gardens, and fountains, thus highlighting that modern art is not only stimulating, but sometimes simply beautiful.

The Riviera's Cuisine Scene

The Riviera adds a Mediterranean flair to the food of Provence. And though many of the same dishes served in Provence are available throughout the Riviera (see "Provence's Cuisine Scene" on page 599), there are differences, especially if you look for anything Italian or from the sea.

Local specialties are bouillabaisse (the spicy seafood stew that seems worth the cost only for those with a seafood fetish), *bour-ride* (a creamy fish soup thickened with aioli, a garlic sauce), and *salade niçoise* (nee-swaz). This salad has many variations, though most include a base of green salad topped with green beans, boiled potatoes (sometimes rice), tomatoes (sometimes corn), anchovies, olives, hard-boiled eggs, and lots of tuna. You'll also find these tasty bread treats: *pissaladière* (bread dough topped with onions, olives, and anchovies), *fougasse* (a spindly, lace-like bread sometimes flavored with nuts, herbs, olives, or ham), and *socca* (a thin chickpea crêpe, seasoned with pepper and olive oil and often served in a paper cone by street vendors). Italian cuisine is native (ravioli was first made in Nice), easy to find, and generally a good value (*pâtes fraîches* means "fresh pasta"). For wine, Bandol (red) and Cassis (white) are popular, and from a region nearly on the Riviera. The only wines made in the Riviera are Bellet rosé and white.

Remember, restaurants serve only during lunch (11:30–14:00) and dinner (19:00–21:00, later in bigger cities); cafés—except for the smaller ones—serve food throughout the day.

Nice

Nice (sounds like "niece"), with its spectacular Alps-to-Mediterranean surroundings, is an enjoyable big-city highlight of the Riviera. Its traffic-free old city mixes Italian and French flavors to create a spicy Mediterranean dressing, while its broad seaside walkways invite lounging and people-watching. Nice may be nice, but it's hot and jammed in July and August—reserve ahead and get a room with air-conditioning (*une chambre avec climatisation*). Everything you'll want to see in Nice is either within walking distance, or a short bus or tram ride away.

Orientation to Nice

Everything of interest lies between the beach and the train tracks (about 15 blocks apart—see map on page 708). The city revolves around its grand place Masséna, where pedestrian-friendly avenue Jean Médecin meets Old Nice and the Albert 1er parkway (with quick access to the beaches). It's a 20-minute walk (or a €10 taxi ride) from the train station to the beach, and a 20-minute walk along the promenade from the fancy Hôtel Negresco to the heart of Old Nice.

A 10-minute ride on the smooth-as-silk tramway takes you through the center of the city, connecting the train station, place Masséna, Old Nice, the bus station, and the port (from nearby place Garibaldi). The tram and all city and regional buses cost only €1 per trip, making this one of the cheapest and easiest cities in France to get around in (see "Getting Around Nice," later).

Tourist Information

Nice's helpful TI has three locations: at the **airport** (in Terminal 1, daily 8:00–21:00, closed Sun off-season), next to the **train station** (usually busy; summer Mon–Sat 8:00–20:00, Sun 9:00–18:00; rest of year Mon–Sat 9:00–19:00, Sun 10:00–17:00), and facing the **beach** at 5 promenade des Anglais (usually quiet, daily 9:00–18:00,

Nice

N (compass)

1/4 MILE
400 METERS

1 To High Corniche (sky-high route to Monaco)
2 To Middle Corniche (middle route, best for Monaco & Eze-le-Village)
3 To Low Corniche (low route to Villefranche-sur-Mer & Cap Ferrat)
4 To Fine Arts Museum
5 War Memorial
6 US Consulate
7 Trans Côte d'Azur Cruises
8 Le Grand Tour Bus Departure Point & Albert 1er Park
9 Buses #15 & #22 Stops (3)
10 Bus #17 Stops (2)

TRAM
P PARKING

TO LAS PLANAS TRAM STOP, P & A-8 AUTOROUTE

AVE. MALAUSSENA

GARE DE SUD TRAIN STN.

TO ENTRE-VAUX

RUSSIAN CATH.

DURANTE

CONGRES

AVE. THIERS

TRAIN STN.

MASSENA MUSEUM

BLVD.

GAMBETTA

ELE-VATED

R. DE FRANCE

HOTEL NEGRESCO

TO 4

PROMENADE DES ANG

BEACH

MED

TO AIRPORT

TO ANTIBES, CANNES & VENCE

THE FRENCH RIVIERA

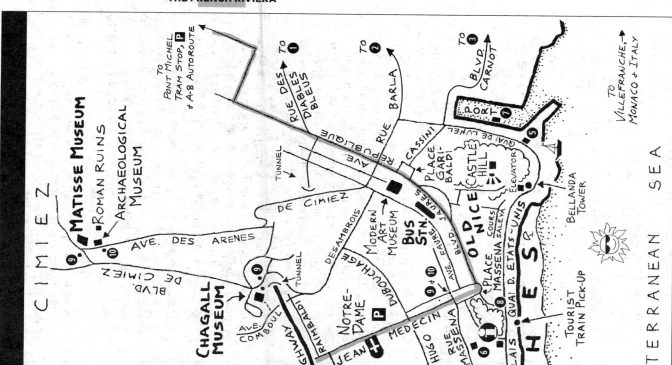

until 20:00 July–Aug, closed Sun off-season, toll tel. 08 92 70 74 07—€0.34/minute, www.nicetourisme.com). Pick up the thorough *Practical Guide to Nice* and a free Nice map (or find a better one at your hotel). You can also get information here on day trips (including maps of Monaco or Antibes, details on boat excursions, and bus schedules to Eze-le-Village, La Turbie, or Vence).

Arrival in Nice

By Train: All trains stop at Nice's main station, Nice-Ville (baggage storage at the far right with your back to the tracks, lockers open daily 8:00–21:00). The station area is gritty and busy: Never leave your bags unattended and don't linger here longer than necessary.

Turn left out of the station to find a **TI** next door. Continue a few more blocks down for the Gare Thiers **tram stop** (this will take you to place Masséna, the old city, bus station, and port). Board the tram heading toward the right, direction Pont Michel (see "Getting Around Nice," later). You'll find many recommended hotels a 10- to 20-minute walk down the same street (those listed under "Between Nice Etoile and the Sea," on page 729), though it's easier taking the tram to place Masséna and walking from there.

To walk to other recommended hotels (those listed under "Between the Train Station and Nice Etoile" on page 728 and "Between Boulevard Victor Hugo and the Sea" on page 733), cross avenue Thiers in front of the station, go down the steps by Hôtel Interlaken, and continue walking down avenue Durante. Follow this same route for the fastest path from the station to the beach—avenue Durante turns into rue des Congrés. You'll soon reach the heart of Nice's beachfront promenade.

Taxis and **buses to the airport** (#23 and #99) wait in front of the train station. **Car rental** offices are to the right as you exit the station.

By Bus: Nice's bus station *(gare routière)* is sandwiched between boulevard Jean Jaurès and avenue Félix Faure, next to the old city. Cross boulevard Jean Jaurès to enter Old Nice, or cross avenue Félix Faure to get to my recommended hotels near Nice Etoile. Trams run along boulevard Jean Jaurès; take the tram in the direction of Las Planas to reach place Masséna and the train station.

By Car: To reach the city center on the autoroute from the west, take the first Nice exit (for the airport—called Côte d'Azur, Central) and follow signs for *Nice Centre* and *Promenade des Anglais*. (Be ready to cross three left lanes of traffic as soon as you get off the autoroute.) Try to avoid arriving at rush hour (usually Mon–Fri 8:00–9:30 & 17:00–19:30), when promenade des Anglais grinds to a halt. Hoteliers know where to park (allow €15–26/day).

The parking garage at the Nice Etoile shopping center on avenue Jean Médecin is pricey but near many of my recommended hotels (ticket booth on third floor, about €20/day, €11 from 20:00–8:00). The garage next to the recommended Hôtel Ibis at the train station has better rates. All on-street parking is metered (9:00–18:00 or 19:00), but usually free all day on Sunday.

You can avoid driving in the center—and park for free—by ditching your car at a parking lot at a remote tram stop (Las Planas is best) and taking the tram into town (€1, 15 minutes, 10/hour, don't leave anything in your car, tramway described later under "Getting Around Nice"). From the A-8 autoroute, take the *Nice Nord* exit and find the Las Planas tram station (see map on page 708).

By Plane: For information on Nice's handy airport, see page 743.

Helpful Hints

Theft Alert: Nice has its share of pickpockets. Thieves target fanny packs: Have nothing important on or around your waist, unless it's in a money belt tucked out of sight. Don't leave anything visible in your car; be wary of scooters when standing at intersections; don't leave things unattended on the beach while swimming; and stick to main streets in Old Nice after dark.

US Consulate: You'll find it at 7 avenue Gustave V (tel. 04 93 88 89 55, fax 04 93 87 07 38, http://france.usembassy.gov/nice .html, usca.nice@orange.fr).

Canadian Consulate: It's at 2 place Franklin (tel. 04 93 92 93 22, fax 04 93 92 55 51).

Museums: Some Nice museums (Chagall, Matisse, Archaeological) are closed Tuesdays, while others (Modern and Contemporary Art, Fine Arts) close on Mondays. City museums are free of charge—so all of the sights in Nice (except the Chagall Museum and the Russian Cathedral) cost zilch to enter, making rainy-day options a swinging deal here.

Internet Access: There's no shortage of places to get online in Nice—they're everywhere. Ask at your hotel, or just look up as you walk (keep your eye out for the @ symbol).

English Bookstore: **The Cat's Whiskers** has an eclectic selection of novels and regional travel books, including mine (Tue–Sat 10:00–12:00 & 14:00–19:00, closed Sun–Mon, 26–30 rue Lamartine—see map on page 730, tel. 04 93 80 02 66).

Laundry: You'll find launderettes everywhere in Nice—ask your hotelier for the nearest one. The self-service **Point Laverie** is centrally located (daily 8:00–20:00, at the corner of rue Alberti and rue Pastorelli, next to Hôtel Vendôme—see map on page 730).

Grocery Store: The big **Monoprix** on avenue Jean Médecin and rue Biscarra has it all, including a deli counter, a bakery, and cold drinks (Mon–Sat 8:30–21:00, closed Sun, see map on page 738). You'll also find many small grocery stores (some open Sun and/or until late hours) near my recommended hotels.

Renting a Bike (and Other Wheels): Roller Station rents bikes (*vélos*, €5/hour, €10/half-day, €15/day), rollerblades (*rollers*, €6/day), Razor-type scooters (*trotinettes*, €6/half-day, €9/day), and skateboards (€6/half-day, €9/day). You'll need to leave your ID as a deposit (daily 9:30–19:00, July–Aug until 20:00, next to yellow awnings of Pailin's Asian restaurant at 49 quai des Etats-Unis—see map on page 734, another location at 10 rue Cassini near place Garibaldi, tel. 04 93 62 99 05, owner Eric). If you need more power, try the electric-assisted bikes or scooters at **Energy Scoot** (2 rue St. Philippe, near the promenade des Anglais and avenue Gambetta, tel. 04 97 07 12 64).

Car Rental: Renting a car is easiest at Nice's airport, which has offices for all the major companies. You'll also find most companies represented at Nice's train station and near Albert 1er Park.

English Radio: Tune in to Riviera-Radio at FM 106.5.

Views: For panoramic views, climb Castle Hill (see page 720), or take a one-hour boat trip (described later, under "Tours in Nice").

Beach Gear: To make life tolerable on the rocks, swimmers should buy a pair of the cheap plastic beach shoes sold at many shops (flip-flops fall off in the water). **Go Sport** at #13 on place Masséna sells beach shoes, flip-flops, and cheap sunglasses (daily 10:00–19:00—see map on page 734).

Getting Around Nice

Although you can walk to most attractions in Nice, smart travelers make good use of the buses and tram. Both are covered by the same single-ride €1 ticket (good for 74 minutes in one direction, including transfers between bus and tram; can't be used for a round-trip). An all-day pass is €4 (valid on local buses and trams, as well as buses to nearby destinations—see "Getting Around the Riviera" on page 704).

The **bus** is handy to reach the Chagall and Matisse museums and the Russian Cathedral. Make sure to validate your ticket in the machine just behind the driver—watch locals do it and imitate.

Nice's new **tramway** makes an "L" along avenue Jean Médecin and boulevard Jean Jaurès, and connects the main train station (Gare Thiers stop), place Masséna (Masséna stop, a few blocks' walk from the sea), Old Nice (Opéra-Vieille Ville), the bus station

(Cathédrale-Vieille Ville), and the Modern and Contemporary Art Museum and port (Place Garibaldi). It also comes within a few blocks of the Gare du Sud train station (Libération stop)—the departure point for the scenic Chemins de Fer de Provence trains (see page 789).

Taking the tram in the direction of Pont Michel takes you from the train station toward the beach and bus station (direction Las Planas goes the other way). Buy tickets at the machines on the platforms (coins only, no credit cards). Choose the English flag to change the display language, turn the round knob and push the green button to select your ticket, press it twice at the end to get your ticket, or press the red button to cancel. Once you're on the tram, validate your ticket by inserting it into the top of the white box, then reclaiming it.

Taxis are useful for getting to Nice's outlying sights, and worth it if you're nowhere near a bus or tram stop (figure €15 from promenade des Anglais). They normally only pick up at taxi stands (*tête de station*), or you can call 04 93 13 78 78.

The hokey **tourist train** gets you up Castle Hill (see "Tours in Nice," below).

Tours in Nice

Bus Tour—Le Grand Tour Bus provides a 12-stop, hop-on, hop-off service on an open-deck bus with headphone commentary (2/hour, 1.5-hour loop) that includes the promenade des Anglais, old port, Cap de Nice, and the Chagall and Matisse museums on Cimiez Hill (€20/1-day pass, €23/2-day pass, cheaper for seniors and students, €10 for last tour of the day at about 18:00, some hotels offer €3 discounts, buy tickets on bus, main stop is near where promenade des Anglais and quai des Etats-Unis meet, across from plage Beau Rivage, tel. 04 92 29 17 00). This tour is a pricey way to get to the Chagall and Matisse museums, but it's an acceptable option if you also want a city overview. Check the schedule if you plan to use this bus to visit the Russian Cathedral, as it may be faster to walk there.

Tourist Train—For €7 (or €3 for children under 9), you can spend 40 embarrassing minutes on the tourist train tooting along the promenade, through the old city, and up to Castle Hill. This is a sweat-free way to get to Castle Hill..but so is the elevator, which is much cheaper (every 30 minutes, daily 10:00–18:00, June–Aug until 19:00, recorded English commentary, meet train near Le Grand Tour Bus stop on quai des Etats-Unis, tel. 04 93 62 85 48).

▲**Boat Cruise**—Here's your chance to join the boat parade and see Nice from the water. On this one-hour, star-studded tour, you'll cruise in a comfortable yacht-size vessel to Cap Ferrat and

Nice at a Glance

▲▲▲**Chagall Museum** The world's largest collection of Chagall's work, popular even with people who don't like modern art. **Hours:** Wed-Mon 10:00-17:00, May-Oct until 18:00, closed Tue. See page 721.

▲▲▲**Promenade des Anglais** Nice's four-mile sun-struck seafront promenade. **Hours:** Always open. See page 717.

▲▲**Old Nice** Charming old city offering enjoyable atmosphere and a look at Nice's French-Italian cultural blend. **Hours:** Always open. See page 715.

▲**Matisse Museum** A worthwhile collection of Henri Matisse's paintings. **Hours:** Wed-Mon 10:00-18:00, closed Tue. See page 723.

▲**Modern and Contemporary Art Museum** Ultramodern museum with enjoyable collection from the 1960s-1970s, including Warhol and Lichtenstein. **Hours:** Tue-Sun 10:00-18:00, closed Mon. See page 724.

▲**Russian Cathedral** Finest Orthodox church outside of Russia. **Hours:** Mon-Sat 9:00-12:00 & 14:30-18:00, Sun 14:30-18:00, until 17:00 off-season. See page 726.

Fine Arts Museum Lush villa shows off impressive paintings by Monet, Sisley, Bonnard, and Raoul Dufy. **Hours:** Tue-Sun 10:00-18:00, closed Mon. See page 724.

Molinard Perfume Museum Small museum tracing the history of perfume. **Hours:** Daily July-Aug 10:00-19:00, Sept-June 10:00-13:00 & 14:00-18:30, sometimes closed Mon off-season. See page 724.

Castle Hill Site of an ancient fort boasting great views—especially in early mornings and evenings. **Hours:** Park closes at 20:00 in summer, earlier off-season. Elevator runs daily 10:00-19:00, until 20:00 in summer. See page 720.

past Villefranche-sur-Mer, then return to Nice with a final lap along promenade des Anglais. It's a scenic trip (the best views are from the seats on top), and worthwhile if you won't be hiking along the Cap Ferrat trails that provide similar views.

French (and sometimes English-speaking) guides play Robin Leach, pointing out mansions owned by some pretty famous people, including Elton John (just as you leave Nice, it's the soft-yellow square-shaped place right on the water), Sean Connery (on the hill above Elton, with rounded arches and tower), and Microsoft co-founder Paul Allen (in saddle of Cap Ferrat hill, above yellow-umbrella beach with sloping red-tile roof). Guides also like to point out the mansion where the Rolling Stones recorded *Exile on Main Street* (between Villefranche-sur-Mer and Cap Ferrat). I wonder if this gang ever hangs out together (€15; May–Oct Tue–Sun 2/day, usually at 11:00 and 15:00, no boats Mon; March–April Tue–Wed, Fri, and Sun at 15:00; no boats Nov–Feb; call ahead to verify schedule, arrive 30 minute early to get best seats, drinks and WCs available). For directions to the dock and contact information, see "Getting Around the Riviera—By Boat" on page 705.

Walking Tours—The TI on promenade des Anglais organizes weekly walking tours of Old Nice in French and English (€12, May–Oct only, usually Sat morning at 9:30, 2.5 hours, reservations necessary, depart from TI, tel. 08 92 70 74 07). They also have evening art walks on Fridays at 19:00.

Nice's cultural association (Centre du Patrimoine) offers incredibly cheap €5 walks on varying themes (in English, minimum 5 people). Call 04 92 00 41 90 a few days ahead to make a reservation. Most tours start at their office near the beach at 75 quai des Etats-Unis; look for the red plaque next to Musée des Ponchettes.

Local Guides—**Sylvie Di Cristo** gives expert tours of Nice (for contact info, see page 704). **Sofia Villavicencio** can guide you expertly in Nice and around the Riviera. Her English is flawless, and her passion is art (€135/half-day, €200/full-day, tel. 04 93 32 45 92, mobile 06 68 51 55 52, sofia.villavicencio@laposte.net). Lovely **Pascale Rucker** tailors her tours in Nice to your interests. Book in advance, though it's also worth a try on short notice (€140/half-day, €230/day, tel. & fax 04 93 87 77 89, mobile 06 16 24 29 52).

Les Petits Farcis Cooking Tour and Classes—Charming Canadian Francophile Rosa Jackson, a food journalist and Cordon Bleu-trained cook, offers popular cooking classes in Old Nice. Her single-day classes include a morning trip to the open-air market on cours Saleya to pick up ingredients, and an afternoon session spent creating an authentic Niçois meal from your purchases (€195/person, mobile 06 81 67 41 22, www.petitsfarcis.com).

Self-Guided Walk

▲▲▲ Scratch-and-Sniff Walk Through Old Nice

• *See the map on page 734, and start at Nice's main market square...*

Cours Saleya (koor sah-lay-yuh): Named for its broad exposure to the sun (*soleil*), this commotion of color, sights, smells, and people has been Nice's main market square since the Middle Ages (produce market held Tue–Sun until 13:00—on Mon, an antiques market takes center stage). Amazingly, part of this square was a parking lot until 1980, when the mayor of Nice had an underground garage built.

The first section is devoted to the Riviera's largest flower market (all day Tue–Sun and in operation since the 19th century). Here you'll find the ubiquitous plants and flowers that grow effortlessly in this climate, including the local favorites: carnations, roses, and jasmine. Fresh flowers are perhaps the best value in this otherwise pricey city.

The boisterous produce section trumpets the season with mushrooms, strawberries, white asparagus, zucchini flowers, and more—whatever's fresh gets top billing.

Place Pierre Gautier (also called Plassa dou Gouvernou—bilingual street signs include the old Niçoise language, an Italian dialect) is where farmers set up stalls to sell their produce and herbs directly.

Continue down the center of cours Saleya, stopping when you see La Cambuse restaurant on your left. In front, hovering over the black-barrel fire with the paella-like pan on top, is the self-proclaimed **Queen of the Market,** Thérèse (tehr-ehz). When she's not looking for a husband, Thérèse is cooking *socca,* Nice's chickpea crêpe specialty (until about 13:00). Spend €3 for a wad of *socca* (careful—it's hot, but good). If she doesn't have a pan out, that means it's on its way (watch for the frequent scooter deliveries). Wait in line...or else it'll be gone when you return.

• *Continue down cours Saleya. The golden building that seals the end of the square is where Henri Matisse spent 17 years with a brilliant view onto Nice's world. Turn left a block before the end of the square and head down...*

Rue de la Poissonnerie: Look up at the first floor of the first building on your right. **Adam and Eve** are squaring off, each holding a zucchini-like gourd. This scene (post-apple) represents the annual rapprochement in Nice to make up for the sins of a too-much-fun Carnival (Mardi Gras). Residents of Nice have partied hard during Carnival for more than 700 years (Feb 18–March 8 in 2011).

A few steps away, check out the small **Baroque church** (Notre-Dame-de-l'Annonciation) dedicated to St. Rita, the patron saint of desperate causes. She holds a special place in locals' hearts, making this the most popular church in Nice.

• *Turn right on the next street, where you'll pass Old Nice's most happening café/bar (**Distilleries Ideales**), with a lively happy hour (18:00–20:00) and a Pirates-of-the-Caribbean–style interior. Now turn left on "Right" Street (rue Droite), and enter an area that feels like a Little Naples.*

Rue Droite: In the Middle Ages, this straight, skinny street provided the most direct route from wall to wall, or river to sea. Stop at **Esipuno's bakery** (at place du Jésus, closed Mon–Tue) and say *bonjour* to the friendly folks. Thirty years ago, this baker was voted the best in France—the trophies you see were earned for bread-making, not bowling. His son now runs the place. Notice the firewood stacked by the oven. Try the house specialty, *tourte aux blettes* (pastry stuffed with pine nuts, raisins, and white beets).

Farther along, at #28, Thérèse (whom you met earlier) cooks her *socca* in the wood-fired oven here before she carts it to her barrel on cours Saleya. The balconies of the mansion in the next block mark the **Palais Lascaris** (1647, gorgeous at night), a rare souvenir from one of Nice's most prestigious families. It's worth popping inside for its Baroque Italian architecture, antique musical instruments, tapestries, and furniture (free, Wed–Mon 10:00–18:00, closed Tue). Look up and make faces back at the guys under the balconies.

• *Turn left on rue de la Loge, then left again on rue Centrale, to reach...*

Place Rossetti: The most Italian of Nice's piazzas, place Rossetti feels more like Roma than Nice. This square comes alive after dark. Fenocchio is popular for its many gelato flavors, ranging from classic to innovative (daily March–Nov 9:00–24:00; mouthwatering preview at www.fenocchio.fr). Walk to the fountain and stare back at the church. This is the **Cathedral of St. Réparate**—an unassuming building for a major city's cathedral. It was relocated here in the 1500s, when Castle Hill was temporarily converted to military-only. The name comes from Nice's patron saint, a teenage virgin named Réparate whose martyred body floated to Nice in the fourth century accompanied by angels. The interior of the cathedral gushes Baroque, a response to the Protestant Reformation. With the Catholic Church's Counter-Reformation, the theatrical energy of churches was cranked up—with re-energized, high-powered saints and eye-popping decor.

• *Our walk is over. Castle Hill is straight up the stepped lane opposite the cathedral.*

Sights in Nice

Walks and Beach Time

▲▲▲**Promenade des Anglais**—Welcome to the Riviera. There's something for everyone along this four-mile-long seafront circus.

Watch the Europeans at play, admire the azure Mediterranean, anchor yourself on a blue seat, and prop your feet up on the made-to-order guardrail. Later in the day, come back to join the evening parade of tans along the promenade.

The broad sidewalks of the promenade des Anglais ("walkway of the English") were financed by upper-crust English tourists who wanted a safe place to stroll and admire the view. The walk was done in marble in 1822 for aristocrats who didn't want to dirty their shoes or smell the fishy gravel. For now, stroll like the belle époque English aristocrats for whom the promenade was built.

Start at the pink-domed Hôtel Negresco, then cross to the sea and end your promenade at Castle Hill. The following sights are listed in the order you'll pass them. This walk is ideally done at sunset (as a pre-dinner stroll).

Hôtel Negresco—Nice's finest hotel is also a historic monument, offering up the city's most expensive beds (see "Sleeping in Nice," later) and a free "museum" interior (always open—provided you're dressed decently, absolutely no beach attire). The hotel underwent a massive renovation in 2010, so expect some changes to the following description.

March straight through the lobby (as if you're staying here) into the exquisite **Salon Royal**, a cozy place for a drink and a frequent host to art exhibits (opens at 11:00). The chandelier hanging from the Eiffel-built dome is made of 16,000 pieces of crystal. It was built in France for the Russian czar's Moscow palace...but because of the Bolshevik Revolution in 1917, he couldn't take delivery. Read the explanation of the bucolic dome scene, painted in 1913 for the hotel, then saunter around the perimeter counterclockwise. If the bar door is open (after about 15:00), wander up the marble steps for a look. Farther along, nip into the toilets for either an early 20th-century powder room or a Battle of Waterloo experience. The chairs nearby were typical of the age (cones of silence for an afternoon nap sitting up).

Bay of Angels (Baie des Anges)—Grab a blue chair and face the sea. The body of Nice's patron saint, Réparate, was supposedly escorted into this bay by angels in the fourth century. To your right is where you might have been escorted into France—Nice's airport, built on a massive landfill. On that tip of land way beyond the runway is Cap d'Antibes. Until 1860, Antibes and Nice were in different countries—Antibes was French, but Nice was a protectorate of the Italian kingdom of Savoy-Piedmont, a.k.a. the Kingdom of Sardinia. (During that period, the Var River—just west of Nice—was the geographic border between these two peoples.) In 1850, the people here spoke Italian and ate pasta. As Italy was uniting, the region was given a choice: Join the new country of Italy or join good old France (which was enjoying good times under the rule of Napoleon III). The vast majority voted in 1860 to go French...and voilà!

The first green hill to your left (Castle Hill) marks the end of this walk. Farther left lies Villefranche-sur-Mer (marked by the tower at land's end, and home to lots of millionaires), then Monaco (which you can't see, with more millionaires), then Italy (with lots of, uh, Italians). Behind you are the foothills of the Alps (Alpes Maritimes), which trap threatening clouds, ensuring that the Côte d'Azur enjoys sunshine more than 300 days each year. Though half a million people live here, pollution is carefully treated—the water is routinely tested and very clean.

Stroll the promenade with the sea starboard, and contemplate beach time (see next) on your way to the Albert 1er Park.

Beaches—Dig your feet into the smooth pebbles and consider your options: you can play beach volleyball, table tennis, or *boules*; rent paddleboats, personal watercraft, or windsurfing equipment; explore ways to use your zoom lens and pretend you're a paparazzo; or snooze on a comfy beach bed.

To rent a spot on the beach, compare rates, as prices vary—beaches on the east end of the bay are usually cheaper (chair and mattress—*chaise longue* and

transat–€12–18, umbrella–€3–5, towel–€4). Some hotels have special deals with certain beaches for discounted rentals (check with your hotel for details). Consider having lunch in your bathing suit (€12 salads and pizzas in bars and restaurants all along the beach). Or, for a peaceful café au lait on the Mediterranean, stop here first thing in the morning before the crowds hit. *Plage Publique* signs explain the 15 beach no-nos (translated into English).

Albert 1er Park—The park is named for the Belgian king who enjoyed wintering here. While the English came first, the Belgians and Russians were also big fans of 19th-century Nice. That tall statue at the edge of the park commemorates the 100-year anniversary of Nice's union with France.

If you detour from the promenade into the park and continue down the center of the grassy strip, you'll be walking over Nice's river, the Paillon (covered since the 1800s). For centuries this river was Nice's natural defense to the north and west (the sea protected the south, and Castle Hill defended the east). Imagine the fortified wall that ran along its length from the hills to the sea. With the arrival of tourism in the 1800s, Nice expanded over and beyond the river (toward the train station).

▲**Castle Hill (Colline du Château)**—This hill—in an otherwise flat city center—offers sensational views over Nice, the port (to the east), the foothills of the Alps, and the Mediterranean. The views are best early or at sunset, or whenever the weather's really clear (park closes at 20:00 in summer, earlier off-season). The city of Nice was first settled here by Greeks circa 400 B.C. In the Middle Ages, a massive castle stood there, with turrets, high walls, and soldiers at the ready. Nice's medieval seawall ran between cours Saleya and quai des Etats Unis. With the river guarding one side and the sea the other, this mountain fortress seemed strong—until Louis XIV leveled it in 1706. Today, you'll find a waterfall, a playground, two cafés (with fair prices), and a cemetery—but no castle—on Castle Hill. You can get to the top by foot, by elevator (€0.70 one-way, €1.10 round-trip, runs daily 10:00–19:00, until 20:00 in summer, next to beachfront Hôtel Suisse), or by pricey tourist train (described under "Tours in Nice," earlier).

Nice's port, where you'll find Trans Côte d'Azur's boat cruises (also described in "Tours in Nice"), is just below on the east edge of Castle Hill.

Bike Routes—Meandering along Nice's seafront on foot or by bike is a must. To rev up the pace of your saunter, rent a bike and glide along the coast in both directions (about 30 minutes each way; for rental info see "Helpful Hints," earlier). Both of the following paths start along promenade des Anglais.

The path to the **west** stops just before the airport, at perhaps the most scenic *boules* courts in France. Pause here to watch the old-timers tossing shiny metal balls (see page 1033). If you take the path heading **east,** you'll curve below Castle Hill—passing a scenic cape and the town's memorial to both world wars—to the harbor of Nice, with a chance to survey some fancy yachts. Pedal around the harbor and follow the coast past the Corsica ferry terminal (you'll need to carry your bike up a flight of steps). From there the path leads you to an appealing tree-lined residential district.

Museums and Monuments

To bring culture to the masses, the city of Nice has nixed the entry fee to all municipal museums—so it's free to enter all of the following sights except the Chagall Museum and the Russian Cathedral. Cool.

The first two museums (Chagall and Matisse) are a long walk

northeast of Nice's city center. Because they're in the same direction and served by the same bus line (buses #15 and #22 stop at both museums), it makes sense to visit them on the same trip. From place Masséna, the Chagall Museum is a 10-minute bus ride or 30-minute walk, and the Matisse Museum is a 20-minute bus ride or one-hour walk.

▲▲▲Chagall Museum (Musée National Marc Chagall)—

Even if you're suspicious of modern art, this museum—with the world's largest collection of Marc Chagall's work in captivity—is a delight. After World War II, Chagall returned from the United States to settle in Vence, not far from Nice. Between 1954 and 1967, he painted a cycle of 17 large murals designed for, and donated to, this museum. These paintings, inspired by the biblical books of Genesis, Exodus, and the Song of Songs, make up the "nave," or core, of what Chagall called the "House of Brotherhood."

Each painting is a lighter-than-air collage of images that draw from Chagall's Russian folk-village youth, his Jewish heritage, biblical themes, and his feeling that he existed somewhere between heaven and earth. He believed that the Bible was a synonym for nature, and that color and biblical themes were key ingredients for understanding God's love for his creation. Chagall's brilliant blues and reds celebrate nature, as do his spiritual and folk themes. Notice the focus on couples. To Chagall, humans loving one another mirrored God's love of creation.

Cost and Hours: €7.50, free first Sun of the month (but crowded), open Wed–Mon 10:00–17:00, May–Oct until 18:00, closed Tue year-round, avenue Docteur Ménard, tel. 04 93 53 87 20, www.musee-chagall.fr.

Getting to the Chagall Museum: You can reach the museum, located on avenue Docteur Ménard, by bus or on foot.

Buses #15 and #22 serve the Chagall Museum from the Masséna Guitry stop, near place Masséna (5/hour Mon–Sat, 3/hour Sun, €1; stop faces eastbound on rue Sacha Guitry, a block east of Galeries Lafayette department store—see map on page 734). The museum's bus stop (called Musée Chagall, shown on the bus shelter) is on boulevard de Cimiez (walk uphill from the stop to find the museum).

To **walk** from central Nice to the Chagall Museum (30 minutes), go to the train-station end of avenue Jean Médecin and turn right onto boulevard Raimbaldi. Walk four long blocks along the

Chagall's Style

Chagall uses a deceptively simple, almost childlike style to paint a world that's hidden to the eye—the magical, mystical world below the surface. Here are some of his techniques:

- **Deep, radiant colors,** inspired by Expressionism and Fauvism (an art movement pioneered by Matisse and other French painters).

- **Personal imagery,** particularly from his childhood in Russia—smiling barnyard animals, fiddlers on the roof, flower bouquets, huts, and blissful sweethearts.

- **A Hasidic Jewish perspective,** the idea that God is everywhere, appearing in everyday things like nature, animals, and humdrum activities.

- **A fragmented Cubist style,** multifaceted and multidimensional, a perfect style to capture the multifaceted, multidimensional complexity of God's creation.

- **Overlapping images,** like double-exposure photography, with faint imagery that bleeds through, suggesting there's more to life under the surface.

- **Stained-glass-esque technique** of dark, deep, earthy, "potent" colors and simplified, iconic, symbolic figures.

- **Gravity-defying compositions,** with lovers, animals, and angels twirling blissfully in midair.

- **Happy (not tragic) moods** depicting a world of personal joy, despite the violence and turmoil of world wars and revolution.

- **Childlike simplicity,** drawn with simple, heavy outlines, filled in with Crayola colors that often spill over the lines. Major characters in a scene are bigger than the lesser characters. The grinning barnyard animals, the bright colors, the magical events presented as literal truth...Was Chagall a lightweight? Or a lighter-than-air-weight?

elevated road, then turn left onto avenue Raymond Comboul, and follow *Musée Chagall* signs.

Leaving the Museum: To take **buses** #15 or #22 back to downtown Nice, turn right out of the museum, then make another right down boulevard de Cimiez, and catch the bus heading downhill. To continue on to the Matisse Museum, catch buses #15 or #22 using the uphill stop located across the street. **Taxis** usually wait in front of the museum. It's about €12 for a ride to the city center.

To **walk** to the train station area from the museum (20 minutes), turn left out of the museum grounds, then left again on the street behind it (avenue Docteur Ménard). As the street bends right, take the ramps and staircases down on your left, turn left at the bottom, cross under the freeway and the train tracks, then turn right onto boulevard Raimbaldi to reach the station.

Cuisine Art and WCs: An idyllic café (€10 salads and *plats*) awaits in the corner of the garden. A spick-and-span WC is next to the ticket desk (there's one inside, too).

▲**Matisse Museum (Musée Matisse)**—This small museum contains the world's largest collection of Henri Matisse paintings. It offers a painless introduction to the artist, whose style was shaped by Mediterranean light and by fellow Côte d'Azur artists Pablo Picasso and Pierre-Auguste Renoir. The collection—which includes several early paintings, models of his famous Rosary Chapel, paper mâché cut-outs, and personal objects—lacks a certain *je ne sais quoi* when compared to the Chagall Museum.

Matisse, the master of leaving things out, could suggest a woman's body with a single curvy line—letting the viewer's mind fill in the rest. Ignoring traditional 3-D perspective, he used simple dark outlines saturated with bright blocks of color to create recognizable but simplified scenes composed into a decorative pattern to express nature's serene beauty. You don't look "through" a Matisse canvas, like a window; you look "at" it, like wallpaper.

Matisse understood how colors and shapes affect us emotionally. He could create either shocking, clashing works (Fauvism) or geometrical, balanced, harmonious ones (later pieces). While other modern artists reveled in purely abstract design, Matisse (almost) always kept the subject matter at least vaguely recognizable. He used unreal colors and distorted lines not just to portray what an object looks like, but to express its inner nature (even inanimate objects). Meditating on his paintings helps you connect with nature—or so Matisse hoped.

Cost and Hours: Free, Wed-Mon 10:00-18:00, closed Tue, 164 avenue des Arènes de Cimiez, tel. 04 93 81 08 08, www.musee-matisse-nice.org. The museum is housed in a beautiful Mediterranean mansion set in an olive grove amid the ruins of the Roman city of Cemenelum.

Getting to the Matisse Museum: It's a long uphill walk from the city center. Take the bus (details follow) or a cab (about €15 from promenade des Anglais). Once here, walk into the park to find the pink villa. Buses **#15, #17,** and **#22** offer regular service to the Matisse Museum from just off place Masséna on rue Sacha Guitry (Masséna Guitry stop, a block east of the Galeries Lafayette department store—see map on page 734; 20 minutes; note that bus #17 does not stop at the Chagall Museum). **Bus #20** connects the port to the museum. On any bus, get off at the Arènes–Matisse bus stop.

Leaving the Museum: When leaving the museum, find the stop for buses #15 and #22 (frequent service downtown and stops en route at the Chagall Museum): Turn left out of the Matisse Museum into the park and keep straight, exiting the park at the Archeological Museum, then turn right. Pass the bus stop across the street (#17 goes to the city center but not the Chagall Museum, and #20 goes to the port), and walk to the small roundabout. Cross the roundabout to find the shelter (facing downhill) for buses #15 and #22 by the apartment building with the oval portico (see map on page 708).

▲Modern and Contemporary Art Museum (Musée d'Art Moderne et d'Art Contemporain)—This ultramodern museum features an explosively colorful, far-out, yet manageable collection focused on American and European-American artists from the 1960s and 1970s (Pop Art and New Realism styles are highlighted). The exhibits cover three floors and include a few works by Andy Warhol, Roy Lichtenstein, and Jean Tinguely, and small models of Christo's famous wrappings. You'll find rooms dedicated to Robert Indiana, Yves Klein, and Niki de Saint Phalle (my favorite). The temporary exhibits can be as appealing to modern-art-lovers as the permanent collection: Check the museum website for what's playing. And don't leave without exploring the rooftop terrace.

Cost and Hours: Free, Tue–Sun 10:00–18:00, closed Mon, about a 15-minute walk from place Masséna, near bus station on promenade des Arts, tel. 04 93 62 61 62, www.mamac-nice.org.

Fine Arts Museum (Musée des Beaux-Arts)—Housed in a sumptuous Riviera villa with lovely gardens, this museum holds 6,000 works from the 17th to 20th centuries. Start on the first floor and work your way up to experience an appealing array of paintings by Monet, Sisley, Bonnard, and Raoul Dufy, as well as a few sculptures by Rodin and Carpeaux (free, Tue–Sun 10:00–18:00, closed Mon, 3 avenue des Baumettes, inconveniently located at the western end of Nice, take buses #12 or #23 from the train station or bus #38 from the bus station to the Rosa Bonheur stop, tel. 04 92 15 28 28, www.musee-beaux-arts-nice.org).

Molinard Perfume Museum—The Molinard family has been making perfume in Grasse (about an hour's drive from Nice) since 1849. Their Nice store has a small museum in the rear that illustrates the story of their industry. Back when people believed water spread the plague (Louis XIV supposedly bathed less than once a year), doctors advised people to rub fragrances into their skin and then powder their body. At that time, perfume was a necessity of everyday life.

Tiny Room 1 shows photos of the local flowers, roots, and other parts of plants used in perfume production. Room 2 explains the earliest (18th-century) production method. Petals would be laid out in the sun on a bed of animal fat, which would absorb the essence of the flowers as they baked. Petals were replaced daily for two months until the fat was saturated. Models and old photos show the later distillation process (660 pounds of lavender produced only a quarter-gallon of essence). Perfume is "distilled like cognac and then aged like wine." The small bottles on the table in the corner demonstrate the role of the "blender" and the perfume mastermind called the "nose" (who knows best). Notice the photos of these lab-coat-wearing perfectionists. Of the 150 real "noses" in the world, more than 100 are French. You are welcome to enjoy the testing bottles.

Cost and Hours: Free, daily July–Aug 10:00–19:00, Sept–June 10:00–13:00 & 14:00–18:30, sometimes closed Mon off-season, just between beach and place Masséna at 20 rue St. François de Paule, see map on page 734, tel. 04 93 62 90 50, www.molinard.com.

Other Nice Museums—Both of these museums are acceptable rainy-day options, and free of charge.

The **Archaeological Museum** (Musée Archéologique) displays various objects from the Romans' occupation of this region. It's convenient—just below the Matisse Museum—but has little of interest to anyone but ancient Rome aficionados. You also get access to the Roman bath ruins...which are, sadly, overgrown with weeds (free, very limited information in English, Wed–Mon 10:00–18:00, closed Tue, near Matisse Museum at 160 avenue des Arènes de Cimiez, tel. 04 93 81 59 57, www.musee-archeologique -nice.org).

The **Masséna Museum** (Musée Masséna), like Nice's main square, is named in honor of Jean-André Masséna, a commander during France's Revolutionary and Napoleonic Wars. This beach-front mansion is worth a gander for its lavish decor and lovely gardens alone (pick up your free ticket at the boutique just outside).

The ground floor shows rotating exhibits, and the upstairs floors offer a folk-museum-like look at Nice through the years, with antique posters, models of the old casino destroyed in World War II, many 18th- and 19th-century paintings (mostly by artists from Nice), and other collections relevant to the city's tumultuous history. Find the images of Nice before they covered the river that runs under place Masséna. You'll also come across some Napoleon paraphernalia; Josephine's cape and tiara are impressive, and I'd look good in Napoleon's vest. Check out the paintings of the Italian patriot and Nice favorite Giuseppe Garibaldi, as well as his burial sheet (free, daily 10:00–18:00, 35 promenade des Anglais, tel. 04 93 91 19 10).

▲**Russian Cathedral (Cathédrale Russe)**—Nice's Russian Orthodox church—claimed to be the finest outside Russia—is worth a visit. Five hundred rich Russian families wintered in Nice in the late 19th century. Since they couldn't pray in a Catholic church, the community needed a worthy Orthodox house of worship. Czar Nicholas I's widow provided the land (which required tearing down her house), and Czar Nicholas II gave this church to the Russian community in 1912. (A few years later, Russian comrades who *didn't* winter on the Riviera assassinated him.) Here in the land of olives and anchovies, these proud onion domes seem odd. But, I imagine, so did those old Russians.

Step inside (pick up English info sheet). The one-room interior is filled with icons and candles, and the old Russian music adds to the ambience. The wall of icons (iconostasis) divides things between the spiritual world and the temporal world of the worshippers. Only the priest can walk between the two worlds, by using the "Royal Door." Take a close look at items lining the front (starting in the left corner). The angel with red boots and wings—the protector of the Romanov family—stands over a symbolic tomb of Christ. The tall black hammered-copper cross commemorates the massacre of Nicholas II and his family in 1918. Notice the Jesus icon to the right of the Royal Door. According to a priest here, as worshippers meditate, staring deep into the eyes of Jesus, they enter a lake where they find their soul. Surrounded by incense, chanting, and your entire community...it could happen. Farther to the right, the icon of the unhappy-looking Virgin and Child is decorated with semiprecious stones from the Ural Mountains. Artists worked a triangle into each iconic face—symbolic of the Trinity.

Cost and Hours: €3, Mon–Sat 9:00–12:00 & 14:30–18:00, Sun 14:30–18:00, until 17:00 off-season, chanted services Sat at 17:30 or 18:00, Sun at 10:00, no tourist visits during services, no short shorts, 17 boulevard du Tzarewitch, tel. 04 93 96 88 02, www.acor-nice.com. The park around the church stays open at lunch and makes a nice setting for picnics.

Getting to the Russian Cathedral: It's a 10-minute walk from the train station. Exit the station to the right onto avenue Thiers, turn right on avenue Gambetta, go under the freeway, and turn left following *Eglise Russe* signs. Or, from the station, take any bus heading west on avenue Thiers and get off at avenue Gambetta (then follow the previous directions).

Nightlife in Nice

Promenade des Anglais, cours Saleya, and rue Masséna are all worth an evening walk. Nice's bars play host to a happening late-night scene, filled with jazz, rock, and trolling singles. Most activity focuses on Old Nice. Rue de la Préfecture is ground zero for bar life, though place Rossetti and rue Droite are also good targets. **Distilleries Ideales** is a good place to start or end your evening, with a lively international crowd and a fun interior (where rues de la Poissonnerie and Barillerie meet, happy hour 18:00–20:00). **Wayne's Bar** is a happening spot for the younger, English-speaking backpacker crowd (15 rue Préfecture). Along the promenade des Anglais, the plush bar at **Hôtel Negresco** is fancy-cigar old English.

Plan on a cover charge or expensive drinks where music is involved. If you're out very late, avoid walking alone. Nice is well-known for its lively after-dark action; if Nice's nightlife doesn't meet your needs, head for the town of Juan-les-Pins (page 780). For more relaxed and accessible nightlife, consider nearby Antibes (page 771).

Sleeping in Nice

Don't look for charm in Nice. Go for modern and clean, with a central location and, in summer, air-conditioning. The rates listed here are for April through October. Prices generally drop €15–30 from November through March but go sky-high in 2011 during the Nice Carnival (Feb 18–March 8), the Cannes Film Festival (May 11–22), and Monaco's Grand Prix (May 26–29). Between the film festival and the Grand Prix, the second half of May is very tight every year. Nice is also one of Europe's top convention cities, and June is convention month here. Reserve early if visiting May through August, especially during these times. For parking, ask your hotelier (several hotels have limited private parking), or see "Arrival in Nice—By Car" on page 710.

I've divided my sleeping recommendations into three areas: between the train station and Nice Etoile shopping center (easy access to the train station and Nice Etoile on the sleek new tramway, 20-minute walk to promenade des Anglais); between Nice Etoile and the sea (east of avenue Jean Médecin, good access to Old Nice and the sea at quai des Etats-Unis); and between boulevard Victor Hugo and the sea (a somewhat classier area, offering better access to the promenade des Anglais but longer walks to the train station and Old Nice). I've also listed a hotel near the airport and a hostel on the outskirts.

Check hotel websites for deals (which are more common at larger hotels).

Between the Train Station and Nice Etoile

This area offers Nice's cheapest sleeps, though most hotels near the station ghetto are overrun, overpriced, and loud. The following hotels are the pleasant exceptions (most are near avenue Jean Médecin), and are listed in order of proximity to the train station, going toward the beach.

$$ Hôtel Ibis Nice Centre Gare**, 100 yards to the right as you leave the station, gives those in need of train station access a secure refuge in this seedy area. It's modern, with two-star business comfort (Db-€90–105, air-con, Wi-Fi, bar, café, 14 avenue Thiers, tel. 04 93 88 85 85, fax 04 93 88 58 00, www.ibishotel.com, h1396@accor.com).

$$ At Hôtel Durante**, you know you're on the Mediterranean as soon as you enter this cheery, way-orange building with its rooms wrapped around a flowery courtyard. Every one of its quiet rooms overlooks a spacious and well-maintained patio/garden with an American-style Jacuzzi. The rooms are good enough (mostly big beds) and the price is right enough (Ds-€72–80, bigger Db-€100–150, Tb-€130–170, air-con, Wi-Fi, 16 avenue Durante, tel. 04 93 88 84 40, fax 04 93 87 77 76, www.hotel-durante.com, info@hotel-durante.com).

$$ Hôtel St. Georges**, five blocks from the station toward the sea, has a backyard garden, reasonably clean and comfortable high-ceilinged rooms, orange tones, blue halls, fair rates, and friendly Houssein at the reception (Sb-€85, Db-€85–100, Tb with

3 beds–€120, extra bed–€20, air-con, Wi-Fi, 7 avenue Georges Clemenceau, tel. 04 93 88 79 21, fax 04 93 16 22 85, www.hotel saintgeorges.fr, contact@hotelsaintgeorges.fr).

$ Hôtel Belle Meunière*, in a fine old mansion built for Napoleon III's mistress, offers cheap beds and private rooms a block below the train station. Lively and youth hostel–esque, this simple but well-kept place attracts budget-minded travelers of all ages with basic-but-adequate rooms and charismatic Mademoiselle Marie-Pierre presiding (with perfect English). Tables in the front yard greet guests and provide opportunities to meet other travelers (bunk in 4-bed dorm–€23 with private bath, €18 with shared bath, Db–€60, includes breakfast, Wi-Fi, laundry service, 21 avenue Durante, tel. 04 93 88 66 15, fax 04 93 82 51 76, www.belle meuniere.com, hotel.belle.meuniere@cegetel.net).

$ Auberge de Jeunesse les Camélias is a laid-back youth hostel with a great location and modern facilities. Rooms accommodate between four and eight people in bunk beds (136 beds in all) and come with showers and sinks—WCs are down the hall. Reservations must be made on the website in advance or on the same day by phone. If you don't have a reservation, call by 10:00 or, better, try to snag a bunk in person. The place is popular but worth a try for last-minute availability (€23/bed, one-time €15 extra charge without hostel membership, includes breakfast, rooms closed 11:00–15:00 but can leave bags, Internet access, laundry, kitchen, safes, bar, 3 rue Spitalieri, tel. 04 93 62 15 54, www.hi hostels.com, nice-camelias@fuaj.org).

$ B&B Nice Home Sweet Home is a great value. Gentle Geneviève (a.k.a. Jennifer) Levert rents out three large rooms and one small single in her home. Her rooms are simply decorated, with high ceilings, big windows, lots of light, and space to spread out. One room comes with private bath; otherwise, it's just like at home...down the hall (S–€31–38, D–€61–70, Db–€65–75, Tb–€74–84, Q–€80–90, includes breakfast, air-con units available in summer, no elevator, two floors up, washer/dryer–€5, kitchen access, 35 rue Rossini at intersection with rue Auber, mobile 06 19 66 03 63, www.nicehomesweethome.com, glevert@free.fr).

Between Nice Etoile and the Sea

These hotels are either on the sea or within an easy walk of it, and are the closest to Old Nice.

$$$ Hôtel Masséna**, in a classy building a few blocks from place Masséna, is a "professional" hotel (popular with tour groups) with 100 rooms at almost-reasonable rates and mod public spaces (5 small Db–€160, larger Db–€200, still larger Db–€295, extra bed–€30, skip the €20 breakfast, call same day for special rates—prices drop big time when hotel is not full, sixth-floor rooms have

Nice Hotels

THE FRENCH RIVIERA

TRAIN STATION →

TO 19, Las Planas Tram Stop & A-8 Autoroute

TO CHAGALL MUSEUM ON FOOT

TO RUSSIAN CHURCH

Nice ÉTOILE SHOPPING MALL

PLACE MASSENA

ALBERT 1er PARK

TOURIST TRAIN PICK-UP

MEDITERRANEAN

BEACH

PROMENADE DES ANGLAIS

1 Hôtel Ibis Nice Centre Gare
2 Hôtel Belle Meunière
3 Hôtel Durante
4 Hôtel St. Georges
5 Auberge de Jeunesse les Camélias
6 B&B Nice Home Sweet Home
7 Hôtel Masséna
8 Hôtel Suisse
9 Hôtel Mercure Marché aux Fleurs
10 Hôtel Vendôme & Launderette
11 Hôtel Lafayette

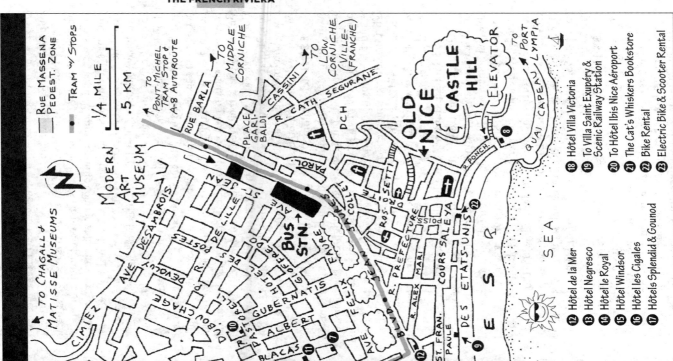

RUE MASSENA PEDEST. ZONE

TRAM W/ STOPS

1/4 MILE
.5 KM

12 Hôtel Villa Victoria
13 Hôtel Negresco
14 Hôtel le Royal
15 Hôtel Windsor
16 Hôtel les Cigales
17 Hôtels Splendid & Gounod
18 Hôtel de la Mer
19 To Villa Saint Exupéry & Scenic Railway Station
20 To Hôtel Ibis Nice Aéroport
21 The Cat's Whiskers Bookstore
22 Bike Rental
23 Electric Bike & Scooter Rental

TO CHAGALL & MATISSE MUSEUMS

MODERN ART MUSEUM

BUS STN.

PLACE GARIBALDI

OLD NICE

CASTLE HILL

ELEVATOR

TO PORT LYMPIA

SEA

TO MIDDLE CORNICHE

TO LOW CORNICHE (VILLE-FRANCHE)

TO PONT MICHEL TRAM STOP & A-8 AUTOROUTE

balconies, reserve parking ahead-€25/day, 58 rue Gioffredo, tel. 04 92 47 88 88, fax 04 92 47 88 89, www.hotel-massena-nice.com, info@hotel-massena-nice.com).

$$$ Hôtel Suisse***, below Castle Hill, has Nice's best ocean and city views for the money, and is surprisingly quiet given the busy street below. Rooms are quite comfortable, the decor is classy, and the staff is professional. There's no reason to sleep here if you don't land a view, so I've listed prices only for view rooms—many of which have balconies (Db-€170–205, extra bed-€36, breakfast-€15, 15 quai Rauba Capeu, tel. 04 92 17 39 00, fax 04 93 85 30 70, www .hotels-ocre-azur.com, hotel.suisse@hotels-ocre-azur.com).

$$$ Hôtel Mercure Marché aux Fleurs*** is ideally situated across from the sea and behind cours Saleya. Rooms are tastefully designed and well-maintained (some with beds in a loft). Prices are reasonable, though rates vary dramatically depending on demand: Be sure to check their website for deals (standard Db-€135, superior Db-€165 and worth the extra euros, sea view-€50 extra, air-con, 91 quai des Etats-Unis, tel. 04 93 85 74 19, fax 04 93 13 90 94, www.hotelmercure.com, h0962@accor.com). Don't confuse this Mercure with the four others in Nice.

$$$ Hôtel Vendôme*** gives you a whiff of the belle époque, with pink pastels, high ceilings, and grand staircases in a mansion set off the street. Its public spaces are delightful. The rooms are modern and come in all sizes; the best have balconies (on floors 4 and 5)—request *une chambre avec balcon* (Sb-€115, Db-€150, Tb-€165, air-con, Internet access and Wi-Fi, book ahead for limited parking-€12/day, 26 rue Pastorelli, tel. 04 93 62 00 77, fax 04 93 13 40 78, www.vendome-hotel-nice.com, contact@vendome -hotel-nice.com).

$$$ Hôtel Lafayette***, in a handy location a block behind the Galeries Lafayette department store, is a great value. The hotel may look average from the outside, but inside it's comfortable and homey, with 18 well-designed, mostly spacious rooms, all one floor up from the street. It's family-run by Kirill, Tina, and little Victor. Rooms not overlooking rue de l'Hôtel des Postes are quieter and worth requesting (standard Db-€105–120, spacious Db-€115–130, extra bed-€24, coffee service in rooms, air-con, no elevator, 32 rue de l'Hôtel des Postes, tel. 04 93 85 17 84, fax 04 93 80 47 56, www.hotellafayettenice.com, info@hotellafayette nice.com).

$$ Hôtel de la Mer** is a humble place with an enviable position overlooking place Masséna, just steps from Old Nice (of my listings, it's among the closest to the old town). Although this small hotel has a few rough edges, new (and very helpful) owner Pierre seems to be on top of things, the beds are firm, and it's quiet (small Db-€100, bigger Db facing place Masséna-€130, Tb-€145,

air-con, Wi-Fi, 4 place Masséna, tel. 04 93 92 09 10, fax 04 93 85 00 64, www.hoteldelamernice.com, hotel.mer@wanadoo.fr).

Between Boulevard Victor Hugo and the Sea

These hotels are either on the beach or within walking distance, and closest to promenade des Anglais.

$$$ Hôtel Negresco**** owns Nice's most prestigious address on promenade des Anglais and knows it. Still, it's the kind of place that, if you were to splurge just once in your life... Rooms are opulent (see page 718 for more description), and tips are expected (viewless Db-€360, Db with sea view-€460–580, view suite-€770–1,900, breakfast-€30, Old World bar, 37 promenade des Anglais, tel. 04 93 16 64 00, fax 04 93 88 35 68, www.hotel-negresco-nice.com, reservations@hotel-negresco.com).

$$$ Hôtel le Royal*** stands shoulder-to-shoulder on promenade des Anglais with the big boys (the Negresco, Palais, and Westminster hotels). With 140 rooms, big lounges, and hallways that stretch forever, it feels a bit institutional. But the prices are reasonable considering the solid air-conditioned comfort and terrific location—and sometimes they have rooms when others don't (viewless Db-€125, Db with sea view-€155–175, bigger view room-€175–195 and worth it, extra person-€25, 23 promenade des Anglais, tel. 04 93 16 43 00, fax 04 93 16 43 02, www.hotel-royal-nice.cote.azur.fr, royal@vacancesbleues.com).

$$$ Hôtel Windsor*** is a snazzy garden retreat that feels like a cross between a modern-art museum and a health spa. Some of the contemporary rooms, designed by modern artists, defy explanation. It has a full-service bar, a small outdoor swimming pool and gym (both free for guests), an €11 sauna, €55 massages, and full meal service in the cool, shaded garden area (standard Db-€125, bigger Db-€155, big Db with balcony-€180, extra bed-€20, rooms over garden worth the higher price, air-con, Internet access and Wi-Fi, 11 rue Dalpozzo, tel. 04 93 88 59 35, fax 04 93 88 94 57, www.hotelwindsornice.com, reservation@hotelwindsornice.com).

$$$ Hôtel les Cigales*** is one of my favorites. It's a smart little pastel place with tasteful decor, 19 plush rooms (most with tub-showers), air-conditioning, and a nifty upstairs terrace, all well-managed by friendly Mr. Valentino, with Veronique and Elaine. Book directly through the hotel and show this book for a surprise treat on arrival (standard Db-€135–160, Tb-€160–180, free Wi-Fi, 16 rue Dalpozzo, tel. 04 97 03 10 70, fax 04 97 03 10 71, www.hotel-lescigales.com, info@hotel-lescigales.com).

$$$ Hôtel Splendid**** is a worthwhile splurge if you miss your Marriott. The panoramic rooftop pool, Jacuzzi, bar, restaurant, and breakfast room almost justify the cost...but throw in

Old Nice Hotels & Restaurants

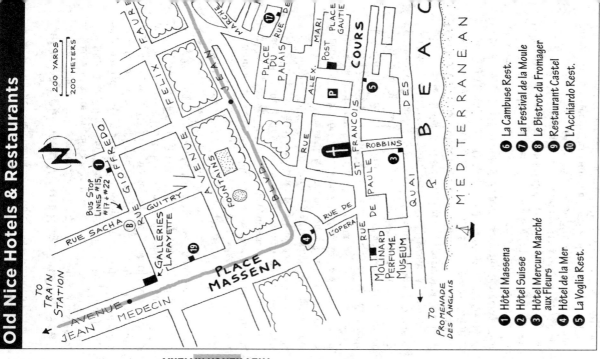

- 200 YARDS
- 200 METERS

N

Bus Stop Lines #15, #17 & #22

RUE SACHA GIOFFREDO

RUE GUITRY

GALLERIES LAFAYETTE

RUE SACHA

AVENUE JEAN

FELIX FAURE

AVENUE JEAN MEDECIN

TO TRAIN STATION

PLACE MASSENA

BLVD.

FOUNTAINS

RUE DE L'OPERA

MOLINARD PERFUME MUSEUM

RUE DE PAULE

RUE ST. FRANCOIS

ROBBINS

PLACE DU PALAIS

ALEX. MARI

POST PLACE GAUTIE

RUE DE MARCHÉ

COURS

QUAI DES

R DES BEA C

MEDITERRANEAN

TO PROMENADE DES ANGLAIS

- 1 Hôtel Massena
- 2 Hôtel Suisse
- 3 Hôtel Mercure Marché aux Fleurs
- 4 Hôtel de la Mer
- 5 La Voglia Rest.
- 6 La Cambuse Rest.
- 7 La Festival de la Moule
- 8 Le Bistrot du Fromager
- 9 Restaurant Castel
- 10 L'Acchiardo Rest.

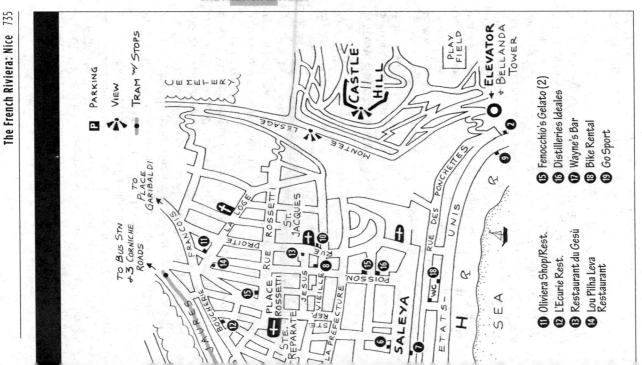

PARKING

VIEW

TRAM w/ Stops

P PARKING

⋏ VIEW

● TRAM w/ STOPS

CEMETERY

CASTLE HILL

PLAY FIELD

MONTEE LESAGE

ELEVATOR

⊕ BELLANDA TOWER

TO PLACE GARIBALDI

TO BUS STN
& 3 CORNICHE ROADS

LA LOGE

FRANCOIS

RUE DROITE

RUE ROSSETTI

ST. JACQUES

RUE DES PONCHETTES

HIR R UNIS

RUE DES PONCHETTES

ETATS-UNIS

SEA

BOUCHERE

PLACE ROSSETTI

RUE JESUS

RUE VIEILLE

STE. REPARATE

ST REPARATE

LA PREFECTURE

RUE POISSONNERIE

SALEYA

WC

⑥

⑦

⑧

⑩

⑬

⑭

⑮

⑮

⑯

⑪

⑫

⑱

❶❶ Oliviera Shop/Rest.
❶❷ L'Ecurie Rest.
❶❸ Restaurant du Gesù
❶❹ Lou Pilha Leva Restaurant

❶❺ Fenocchio's Gelato (2)
❶❻ Distilleries Ideales
❶❼ Wayne's Bar
❶❽ Bike Rental
❶❾ Go Sport

solid rooms (four of the six floors are non-smoking), a free gym, spa services, and air-conditioning, and you're as good as home (Db-€235, deluxe Db with terrace-€280, suites-€360–410, breakfast-€16, check website for special deals, parking-€24/day, 50 boulevard Victor Hugo, tel. 04 93 16 41 00, fax 04 93 16 42 70, www.splendid-nice.com, info@splendid-nice.com).

$$$ Hôtel Gounod*** is behind Hôtel Splendid, and because the two share the same owners, Gounod's guests are allowed free access to Splendid's pool, Jacuzzi, and other amenities. Don't let the lackluster lobby fool you—most rooms are richly decorated, with high ceilings and air-conditioning (Db-€170, palatial 4-person suites-€270, parking-€15/day, 3 rue Gounod, tel. 04 93 16 42 00, fax 04 93 88 23 84, www.gounod-nice.com, info@gounod-nice.com).

$$$ Hôtel Villa Victoria*** is managed by cheery Marlena, who welcomes travelers into this spotless, classy old building with a green awning and an open, attractive lobby overlooking a generous garden. Rooms are traditional and well-kept, with space to stretch out (streetside Db-€150, garden-side Db-€180, Tb-€160–185, suites-€210–235, breakfast-€15, air-con, minibar, Wi-Fi, parking-€18, 33 boulevard Victor Hugo, tel. 04 93 88 39 60, fax 04 93 88 07 98, www.villa-victoria.com, contact@villa-victoria.com).

Barely Beyond Nice

$ Villa Saint Exupéry, a service-oriented hostel, is a haven two miles north of the city center. Its amenities and 60 comfortable, spick-and-span rooms create a friendly climate for budget-minded travelers of any age. Often filled with energetic youth, the place can be noisy. There are units for one, two, and up to six people. Many have private bathrooms and views of the Mediterranean—some come with balconies. You'll also find a laundry room, complete kitchen facilities, and a lively bar. There's easy Internet access with a wall of computers in the lobby and Wi-Fi in all the rooms (bed in dorm-€30/person, S-€50–70, Db-€60–90, Tb-€115, includes big breakfast, no curfew; take bus #23 from the airport or train station, or take the tram—direction: Las Planas—to the Compte de Falicon stop and walk 10 minutes; ask about free pickup at train station, 22 avenue Gravier, toll-free tel. 08 00 30 74 09, fax 04 92 09 82 94, www.vsaint.com, reservations@vsaint.com).

Closer to the Airport

$$ Hôtel Ibis Nice Aéroport** offers a handy port in the storm for those with early flights or just stopping in for a single night (Db-€78–98 when no special events in town, parking-€7, 359 promenade des Anglais, tel. 04 93 83 30 30, fax 04 93 21 19 43, www.ibisnice.com, reception@ibisnice.com). Hotel chains Etap, Campanile, and Novotel also have hotels at the airport.

Eating in Nice

Remember, you're in a resort. Seek ambience and fun, and lower your palate's standards. Italian is a low-risk and regional cuisine. The listed restaurants are concentrated in neighborhoods close to my recommended hotels. Promenade des Anglais is ideal for picnic dinners on warm, languid evenings. Old Nice has the best and busiest dining atmosphere (and best range of choices), while the Nice Etoile area is more local, convenient, and also offers a good range of choices. To feast cheaply, eat on rue Droite in Old Nice, or explore the area around the train station. For a more peaceful meal, head for nearby Villefranche-sur-Mer (see page 753). Allow yourself one dinner at a beachfront restaurant in Nice, and for terribly touristy trolling, wander the wall-to-wall eateries lining rue Masséna. Yuck.

In Old Nice

Nice's dinner scene converges on cours Saleya, which is entertaining enough in itself to make the generally mediocre food a good deal. It's a fun, festive spot to compare tans and mussels. Even if you're eating elsewhere, wander through here in the evening. For locations, see the map on page 734.

La Voglia is all about good Italian food at fair prices. It's popular with locals, lively, and offers fun inside and outside seating (€14 pizza and pasta, open daily, at the western edge of cours Saleya at 2 rue St Francois de Paule, tel. 04 93 80 99 16).

La Cambuse is a classy place by cours Saleya standards, and may be the only restaurant along here that doesn't try to reel in passersby. The cuisine is Franco-Italian with an emphasis on Italy. There's attentive service and good seating indoors and out (€14 starters, €18–24 *plats*, 5 cours Saleya, tel. 04 93 80 82 40).

La Festival de la Moule is a simple, touristy place for lovers of mussels (or for just plain hungry folks). For €14 you get all-you-can-eat mussels (11 sauces possible) and fries in a youthful outdoor setting. Let twins Alex and Marc tempt you with their spicy and cream sauces—be daring and try several (other bistro fare available, across the square from la Cambuse, 20 cours Saleya, tel. 04 93 62 02 12).

Le Bistrot du Fromager's owner is crazy about cheese and wine. Come here to escape the heat and dine in cool vaulted cellars surrounded by shelves of wine. All dishes use cheese as their base ingredient, although you'll also find pasta, ham, and salmon (with cheese, of course). This is a good choice for vegetarians (€10 entrées, €12–14 *plats*, €6 desserts, closed Sun, just off place de Gésu at 29 rue Benoit Bunico, tel. 04 93 13 07 83).

Restaurant Castel is a fun eat-on-the-beach option, thanks

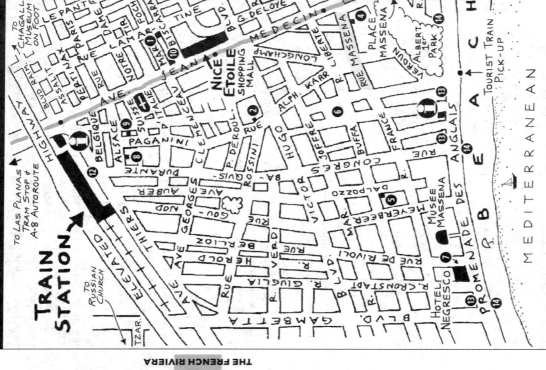

Nice Restaurants

TRAIN
STATION

THE FRENCH RIVIERA

1 Rue Biscarra Eateries
2 Bistrot les Viviers
3 L'Ovale Restaurant
4 La Maison de Marie Rest.
5 Cave de l'Origine Wine Bar

6 Place Grimaldi Eateries
7 Chantecler Restaurant
8 Voyageur Nissart Rest.
9 Zen Restaurant
10 Monoprix Grocery Store

THE FRENCH RIVIERA

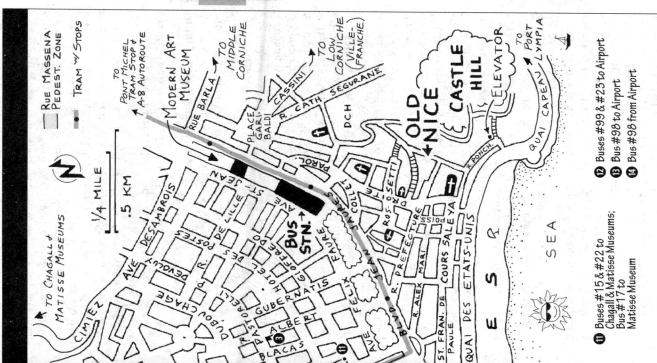

Legend:
- Rue Massena Pedestrian Zone
- ● Tram w/ Stops

To Chagall & Matisse Museums

¼ MILE
.5 KM

MODERN ART MUSEUM

To Pont Michel Tram Stop & A-8 Autoroute

To Middle Corniche

RUE BARLA

To Low Corniche (Villefranche)

R. CASSINI

PLACE GARIBALDI

R. CATH. SEGURANE

RUE BARLA

To Port Lympia

OLD NICE

CASTLE HILL

ELEVATOR

QUAI CAPEAU LYMPIA

AVE. DESAMBROIS

CIMIEZ

AVE. DUBOUCHAGE

R. DEVOUT

R. PASTORELLI

HOTEL DES POSTES

R. DE L'HOTEL

AVE. FELIX FAURE

BUS STN.

BLVD. JEAN JAURES

DCH

PAROI

ROSSETTI

PREFECTURE

R. ALEX MARI

COURS SALEYA

R. PONCH.

ST. FRAN. DE PAULE

QUAI DES ETATS-UNIS

ALBERT

BLACAS

GUBERNATIS

AVE. ST-JEAN

R. COLLET

SEA

⓫ Buses #15 & #22 to Chagall & Matisse Museums; Bus #17 to Matisse Museum

⓬ Buses #99 & #23 to Airport

⓭ Bus #98 to Airport

⓮ Bus #98 from Airport

to its location at the very east end of Nice looking over the bay. Dining here, you almost expect Don Ho to step up and grab a mic. Lose the city hustle and bustle by dropping down the steps below Castle Hill. The views are unforgettable even if the cuisine is not; you can even have lunch at your beach chair if you've rented one here (€10/half-day, €14/day). Dinner here is best: Arrive before sunset and find a waterfront table perfectly positioned to watch evening swimmers get in their last laps as the sky turns pink and city lights flicker on. Linger long enough to merit the few extra euros the place charges (€16 salads and pastas, €20–26 main courses, 8 quai des Etats-Unis, tel. 04 93 85 22 66).

Dining Cheap à la Niçoise

Try at least one of these five places—not just because they're terrific budget options, but primarily because they offer authentic *niçoise* cuisine.

L'Acchiardo, hidden away in the heart of Old Nice, is a dark and homey eatery that does a good job mixing a loyal clientele with hungry tourists. Its simple, hearty *niçoise* cuisine is served for fair prices by gentle Monsieur Acchiardo. The small plaque under the menu outside says it's been run by father and son since 1927 (€7 starters, €14 *plats*, €5 desserts, cash only, closed Sat–Sun, indoor seating only, 38 rue Droite, tel. 04 93 85 51 16).

Oliviera venerates the French olive. This shop/restaurant sells a variety of oils, offers free tastings, and serves a menu of dishes paired with specific oils (think of a wine pairing). Welcoming owner Nadim, who speaks excellent English, knows all of his producers personally and provides "Olive Oil 101" explanations with his tastings (best if you buy something afterward or have a meal). You'll learn how passionate he is about his products, and once you come to taste, you'll want to stay and eat (€14–22 main dishes, Tue–Sat 10:00–22:00, closed Sun–Mon, indoor seating only, 8 bis rue du Collet, tel. 04 93 13 06 45).

L'Ecurie, a favorite for Nice residents, is off the beaten path in Old Nice. The cuisine is a mix of traditional *niçoise* and Italian specialties, and the ambience is warm inside and out (€23 three-course *menu,* €11 wood-fired pizza, open daily, 4 rue du Marché, tel. 04 93 62 32 62).

Restaurant du Gesù, a happy-go-lucky greasy spoon, squeezes plastic tables into a slanting square deep in the old city (sailors accustomed to dining off-balance will feel right at home). Arrive early or join the mobs waiting for an outside table; better yet, have fun in the soccer-banner-draped interior. The *raviolis sauce daube* is popular (€10 pizzas and pastas, closed Sun, 1 place du Jésus, tel. 04 93 62 26 46).

Lou Pilha Leva delivers fun, cheap lunch or dinner options with *niçoise* specialties and outdoor-only benches that are swimming in pedestrians (open daily, located where rues de la Loge and Centrale meet in Old Nice).

And for Dessert...

Gelato-lovers should save room for the tempting ice-cream stands in Old Nice. **Fenocchio** is the city's favorite, with mouthwatering displays of 86 flavors ranging from tomato to lavender to avocado—all of which are surprisingly good (daily March-Nov until 24:00, two locations: 2 place Rossetti and 6 rue de la Poissonnerie).

Near Nice Etoile

If you're not up for eating in Old Nice, try one of these spots around the Nice Etoile shopping mall.

On rue Biscarra: An appealing lineup of bistros overflowing with outdoor tables stretches along the broad sidewalk on traffic-free rue Biscarra (just east of avenue Jean Médecin behind Nice Etoile, all closed Sun). Come here to dine with area residents away from the tourists. These three places are all good choices, with good interior and exterior seating; **Le Cenac** seems most popular and features cuisine from southwest France (such as duck, foie gras, and omelets with cep mushrooms, €14–23 *plats*). **L'Authentic** has the most creative cuisine and comes with two memorable owners: burly Philippe and sleek Laurent (€25 two-course *menus*, €25 three-course *menus*, reasonable pasta dishes, tel. 04 93 62 48 88). **Le 20 sur Vin** is a neighborhood favorite with a cozy, wine-bar-meets-café ambience. It offers *(bien sûr)* good wines at fair prices, and basic bistro fare (tel. 04 93 92 93 20).

Bistrot les Viviers attracts those who require attentive service and authentic *niçoise* cuisine with a big emphasis on fish. This classy splurge offers two intimate settings as different as night and day: a soft, formal restaurant (€50 *menu*, €28–35 *plats*), and a relaxed *bistrot* next door (€35 weekday *menu*, €25–32 *plats*, bouillabaisse-€41, bourride-€25). I'd reserve a table in the atmospheric *bistrot*, where some outdoor seating is available (restaurant closed Sun, *bistrot* open daily, 5-minute walk west of avenue Jean Médecin at 22 rue Alphonse Karr, tel. 04 93 16 00 48).

L'Ovale is a find. Named for the shape of a rugby ball, how this ever-so-local and rugby-loving café survives in a tourist mecca, I'll never know. It's a well-run, welcoming bistro with quality food at respectable prices. Dine inside on big *plats* for €13; consider their specialty, *cassoulet* (€35 for two people, though it's enough for three); or enjoy *la planche de charcuterie* as a meaty, filling first course. The *salade de manchons* with duck and walnuts is incredible (excellent €17 three-course *menu*, €12 monster salads, closed

Sun, air-con, 29 rue Pastorelli, tel. 04 93 80 31 65). Effervescent Johanna ensures good service.

La Maison de Marie is a surprisingly good-quality refuge off touristy rue Masséna, where most other restaurants serve mediocre food to tired travelers. Enter through a deep-red arch to a bougainvillea-draped courtyard, and enjoy the fair prices and good food that draw neighborhood regulars and out-of-towners alike. The interior tables are as appealing as those in the courtyard (*menus* from €22, open daily, look for the square red sign at 5 rue Masséna, tel. 04 93 82 15 93).

Near Promenade des Anglais

Cave de l'Origine is a warm, local spot run by kind Isabelle and Carlo, where you'll find a quality food shop (*épicerie*) and wine bar/ *bistrot* serving a small selection. Carlo loves talking about his all-natural wines and other products. Stop by for a glass of wine, to peruse the shop, or, better, to reserve a table for a meal (€10 starters, €19 *plats*, open Tue–Sat for lunch, Thu–Sat for dinner, reservations smart, indoor seating only; shop open Tue–Sat 10:00–20:00, closed Sun–Mon; 3 rue Dalpozzo, tel. 04 83 50 09 60).

Place Grimaldi nurtures several appealing restaurants with good indoor and outdoor seating along a broad sidewalk and under tall sycamore trees. **Crêperie Bretonne** is the only crêperie I list in Nice (€8 dinner crêpes, closed Sun, 3 place Grimaldi, tel. 04 93 82 28 47). **Le Grimaldi** is popular for its café fare (€12 pasta and pizza, €15–19 *plats*, closed Sun, 1 place Grimaldi, tel. 04 93 87 98 13).

Chantecler has Nice's most prestigious address—inside the Hôtel Negresco. This is everything a luxury restaurant should be: elegant, soft, and top-quality. If your trip is ending in Nice, call or email for reservations—you've earned this splurge (*menus* from €90, closed Mon–Tue, 37 promenade des Anglais, tel. 04 93 16 64 00, chantecler@hotel-negresco.com).

Near the Train Station

Both of the following restaurants provide good indoor and outdoor seating.

Voyageur Nissart has blended good-value cuisine with cool Mediterranean ambience and friendly service since 1908. Alexis and Max could not be kinder hosts, making this a top option for those on a budget (€16 three-course *menus*, €7 fine *salade niçoise*, €10 *plats*, closed Mon, 19 rue d'Alsace-Lorraine, tel. 04 93 82 19 60).

Zen provides a Japanese break from French cuisine. Its friendly staff, pleasing contemplative decor, and tasty specialties draw a strong following (€16 three-course *menu*, €8–13 sushi, open daily, 27 rue d'Angleterre, tel. 04 93 82 41 20).

Nice Connections

For rough train, bus, and boat schedules from Nice to nearby towns, see "Getting Around the Riviera" on page 704. Note that most long-distance train connections to other French cities require a change in Marseille. The Grande Ligne train to Bordeaux (serving Antibes, Cannes, Toulon, Arles, Carcassonne, and other stops en route) requires a reservation.

From Nice by Train to: Marseille (18/day, 2.5 hours), **Cassis** (14/day, 3 hours, transfer in Toulon or Marseille), **Arles** (11/day, 3.75–4.5 hours, most require transfer in Marseille or Avignon), **Avignon** (20/day, most of which are via TGV, 4 hours, most require transfer in Marseille), **Paris'** Gare de Lyon (10/day, 6 hours, may require change; 11-hour night train goes to Paris' Gare d'Austerlitz), **Aix-en-Provence** TGV station (10/day, 3.5 hours, may require transfer in Marseille or Toulon), **Chamonix** (4/day, 10 hours, 3 transfers), **Beaune** (7/day, 7 hours, 1–2 changes), **Munich** (4/day, 12–13 hours with 2–4 transfers, night trains possible via Italy), **Interlaken** (6/day, 9–11 hours, 2–5 transfers), **Florence** (6/day, 7–9 hours, 1–3 transfers), **Milan** (7/day, 5–5.5 hours, all require transfers), **Venice** (5/day, 8–9 hours, all require transfers), **Barcelona** (1/day via Montpelier, 10.5 hours, more with multiple changes).

Nice's Airport

Nice's easy-to-navigate airport (Aéroport de Nice Côte d'Azur) is on the Mediterranean, a 20- to 30-minute drive west of the city center. Planes leave about hourly to Paris (one-hour flight, about the same price as a train ticket; check www.easyjet.com for the cheapest flights to Paris' Orly airport). The two terminals (Terminal 1 and Terminal 2) are connected by frequent shuttle buses (navettes). Both terminals have banks, ATMs, taxis, baggage storage (open daily 6:00–23:00), and buses to Nice. The TIs for Nice and Monaco are in Terminal 1 (tel. 08 20 42 33 33 or 04 89 88 98 28, www.nice.aeroport.fr).

Taxis into the center are expensive considering the short distance (figure €35 to Nice hotels and €55 to Villefranche-sur-Mer, 10 percent more from 19:00–7:00, and all day Sun). Taxis stop outside door (Porte) A-1 at Terminal 1 and outside Porte A-3 at Terminal 2. Notorious for overcharging, Nice taxis are not always so nice. If your fare for a ride into town is much higher than €35 (or €40 at night or on Sun), refuse to pay the overage. If this doesn't work, tell the cabbie to call a gendarme (police officer). It's always a good idea to ask for a receipt (reçu).

Airport shuttle vans work with some of my recommended hotels, but they only make sense when going to the airport, not when arriving on an international flight. Unlike taxis, shuttle vans offer a fixed price that doesn't rise on Sundays, early mornings, or evenings. Prices are best for groups (figure €25 for one person, and only a little more for additional people). **Nice Airport Shuttle** is one option (€25/one person, €32/two people, mobile 06 60 33 20 54, www.nice-airport-shuttle.com), or ask your hotelier for recommendations.

Three bus lines connect the airport with the city center, offering good alternatives to high-priced taxis. **Bus #99** (airport express) runs from both terminals to Nice's main train station (€4, 2/hour, 8:00–21:00, 30 minutes, drops you within a 10-minute walk of many recommended hotels). To take this bus *to* the airport, catch it right in front of the train station (departs on the half-hour). If your hotel is within walking distance of the station, #99 is a breeze.

Bus #98 serves both terminals, and runs along promenade des Anglais to Nice's main bus station (*gare routière*), which is near Old Nice (€4, 3/hour, from the airport 6:00–23:00, to the airport until 21:00, 30 minutes, see map on page 738 for stops). The slower, cheaper local **bus #23** serves only Terminal 1, and makes every stop between the airport and train station (€1, 5/hour, 6:00–20:00, 40 minutes, direction: St. Maurice).

For all buses, buy tickets in the information office just outside either terminal, or from the driver. To reach the bus information office and stops at Terminal 1, turn left after passing customs and exit the doors at the far end. Buses serving Terminal 2 stop across the street from the airport exit (information kiosk and ticket sales to the right as you exit).

If you take bus #98 or #99, hang on to your €4 ticket—it's good all day on any public bus and the tramway in Nice, and for buses between Nice and nearby towns (see page 704 for details). Note that if you take your big bag onto any non-airport bus, you may be charged an extra €5.

To get to **Villefranche-sur-Mer** from the airport, take bus #98 to Nice's bus station (*gare routière*), then transfer to the Villefranche-sur-Mer bus (bus #100, use same ticket).

To reach **Antibes**, take bus #250 from Terminal 1 (€8, about 2/hour, 40 minutes). For **Cannes**, take bus #210 from either terminal (2/hour, 30 minutes by freeway). Pricey express buses (line #110) run directly to **Monaco** from the airport (€18, hourly, 50 minutes), but you'll save money by transferring in Nice to a Monaco-bound bus.

Villefranche-sur-Mer

In the glitzy world of the Riviera, Villefranche-sur-Mer offers travelers an easygoing slice of small-town Mediterranean life. From here, convenient day trips allow you to gamble in style in Monaco, saunter the promenade des Anglais in Nice, or drink in immense views from Eze-le-Village. Villefranche-sur-Mer feels Italian, with soft-orange buildings; steep, narrow streets spilling into the sea; and pasta on most menus. Luxury sailing yachts glisten in the bay—an inspiration to those lazing along the harborfront to start saving when their trips are over. Cruise ships make occasional calls to Villefranche-sur-Mer's famously deep harbor, creating periodic rush hours of frenetic shoppers and happy boutique owners. Sand-pebble beaches and a handful of interesting sights keep other visitors just busy enough.

Orientation to Villefranche-sur-Mer

Tourist Information

The TI is in the park named jardin François Binon, below the main bus stop, labeled Octroi (July-Aug daily 9:00-19:00; Sept-June Mon-Sat 9:00-12:00 & 14:00-18:00, closed Sun; 20-minute walk or €10 taxi ride from train station, tel. 04 93 01 73 68, www.villefranche-sur-mer.com). Pick up schedules for bus #83 to Eze-le-Village (with an easy transfer). Also ask for the brochure detailing a self-guided walking tour of Villefranche-sur-Mer and information on boat rides (usually mid-June–Sept).

Arrival in Villefranche-sur-Mer

By Bus: Take bus #100 or #81 from Nice (the bus bays are adjacent at Nice's *gare routière*), or bus #100 from Monaco, to the Octroi stop in Villefranche-sur-Mer (see "Villefranche-sur-Mer Connections," on page 754). The Octroi stop is at the jardin François Binon, just above the TI. To reach the old town, walk past the TI down avenue Général de Gaulle, take the first stairway on the left, then make a right at the street's end.

By Plane: Allow an hour from Nice's airport to Villefranche-sur-Mer. Take express bus #98 from Nice's airport to its bus station (€4, 3/hour, 30 minutes), then transfer to bus #100 or #81 to Villefranche-sur-Mer (4/hour on #100, 3/hour Sun; about 2/hour on #81; 15 minutes). One €4 ticket covers the whole trip.

Villefranche-sur-Mer

1 Hôtel Welcome & Souris Gourmande Rest.
2 Hôtel Villa Vauban
3 Hôtel la Flore
4 To Hôtel la Fiancée du Pirate & Minibus Route
5 Hôtel de la Darse
6 Le Cosmo Bistrot/Brasserie
7 La Grignotière Restaurant
8 La Serre Restaurant
9 La Mère Germaine Rest.
10 Casino Grocery
11 Internet: Chez Net Bar & L'Ex Café
12 Boat Rides & Electric Bike Rental
13 Launderette
14 Octroi Bus Stop (from Nice; to Monaco & Cap Ferrat)
15 Octroi Bus Stop (to Nice; from Monaco & Cap Ferrat)

200 YARDS
200 METERS

P PARKING
T TAXI STAND
STEPPED STREETS

TO 4, EZE-LE VILLAGE & MONACO VIA MIDDLE CORNICHE ROAD

TO MONT-ALBAN FORT & NICE

AVE. PRINCESSE GRACE

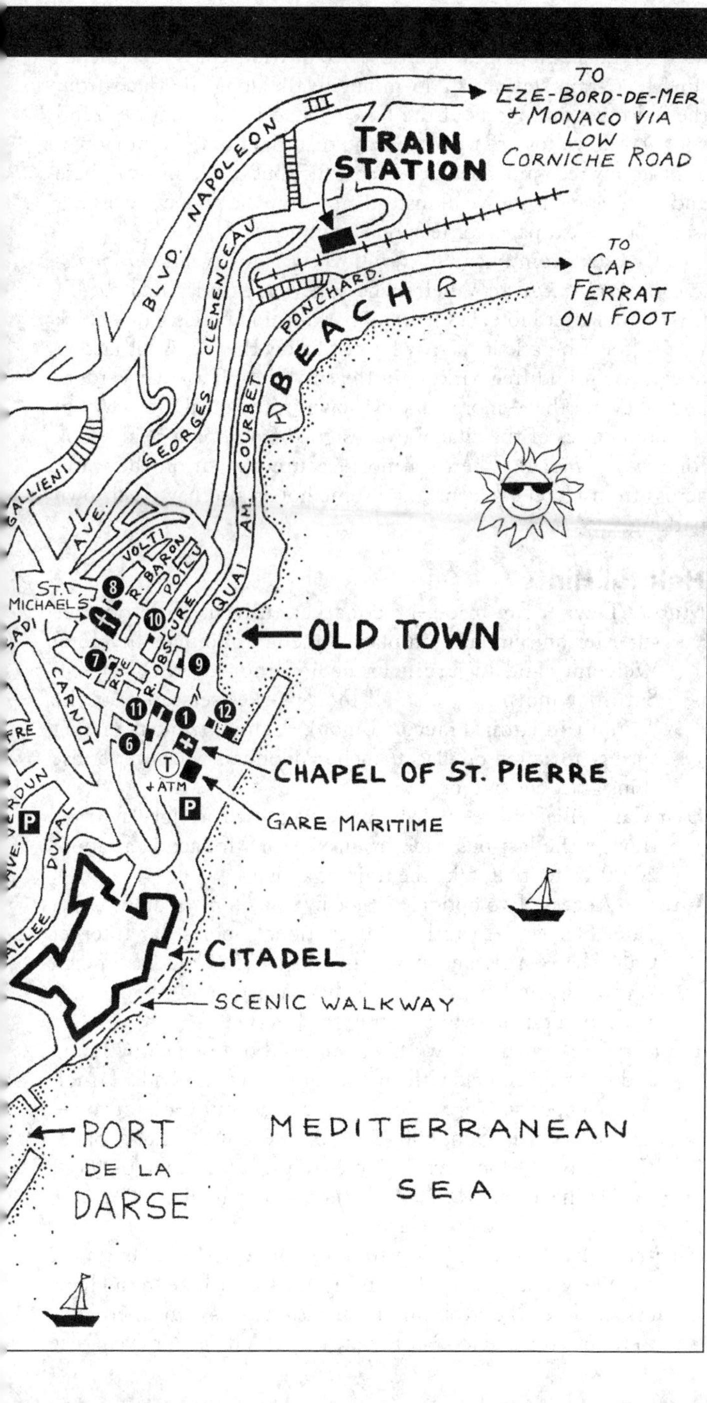

TO EZE-BORD-DE-MER + MONACO VIA LOW CORNICHE ROAD
TRAIN STATION
TO CAP FERRAT ON FOOT
BLVD. NAPOLEON
CLEMENCEAU
GEORGES
PONCHARD.
BEACH
AM. COURBET
QUAI
GALLIENI
AVE.
VOLTI
R. BARON
POILU
OBSCURE
R.
RUE
ST. MICHAEL'S
SADI
CARNOT
FRE
AVE. VERDUN
DUVAL
ALLEE
OLD TOWN
CHAPEL OF ST. PIERRE
+ ATM
GARE MARITIME
CITADEL
SCENIC WALKWAY
PORT DE LA DARSE
MEDITERRANEAN SEA

By Train: Not all trains stop in Villefranche-sur-Mer (you may need to transfer to a local train in Nice or Monaco). Villefranche-sur-Mer's train station is a 15-minute walk along the water from the old town and many of the hotels listed in this section. Find your way down toward the water, and turn right to walk into town. Taxis to my recommended hotels cost €15, but they don't wait here and prefer longer rides; call instead, and pray the phone is working (see "Taxi," next page, for telephone numbers).

By Car: From Nice's port, follow signs for *Menton, Monaco,* and *Basse Corniche.* In Villefranche-sur-Mer, turn right at the TI (first signal after Hôtel la Flore) for parking and hotels. For a quick visit to the TI, park at the pay lot just below the TI. A bit farther down, you'll find free parking in the small lot off avenue Verdun, and—beyond that—more parking down in the moat areas within the boundaries of the citadel (well-signed from main road—look for *Parking Fossés*). There's a more-secure pay lot on the water across from Hôtel Welcome, and some hotels also have their own parking.

Helpful Hints

Market Day: A fun bric-a-brac market enlivens Villefranche-sur-Mer on Sundays (on place Amélie Pollonnais by Hôtel Welcome, and in jardin François Binon by the TI). On Saturday mornings, a small food market sets up near the TI (only in jardin François Binon). A small trinkets market springs to action on place Amélie Pollonnais whenever cruise ships grace the harbor.

Last Call: Villefranche-sur-Mer makes a great base for day trips, though the last bus back from Nice or Monaco is at about 20:00. After that, take the train or a cab.

Internet Access: Two options sit side by side on place du Marché. **Chez Net,** an "Australian International Sports Bar Internet Café," has American keyboards, while **L'Ex Café** has French keyboards. Both are open daily, have Wi-Fi, and let you enjoy a late-night drink while surfing the Internet.

Laundry: The town has two launderettes, both owned by Laura and located just below the main road on avenue Sadi Carnot. At the upper *pressing moderne,* Laura does your wash for you—for a price (Tue–Sun 9:00–12:30 & 15:00–18:30, closes Sat at 17:00, closed Mon, next to Hôtel Royal Riviera, tel. 04 93 01 73 71). The lower *laverie* is self-service only (daily 7:00–20:00, opposite 6 avenue Sadi Carnot).

Electric Bike Rental: If you plan to explore Cap Ferrat but don't feel like walking, consider renting an electric bike from Henri at **Eco-Loc.** The adventurous can also try this as an alternative to taking the bus to Cap Ferrat, Eze-le-Village, or even Nice (although the road to Nice is awfully busy). You get about 25 miles on a fully charged battery (less on hilly terrain—after that you're pedaling; €5/hour, €20/day, April-Sept daily 9:00–17:30, deposit and ID required, best to call for reservations 24 hours in advance; helmets, locks, baskets, and child seats available; find the small tent on the port next to Café Calypso, mobile 06 66 92 72 41).

Taxi: For a reliable taxi in Villefranche-sur-Mer, call or email **Didier** (mobile 06 15 15 39 15, taxididier.villefranchesurmer @orange.fr). If he's busy, beware of taxi drivers who overcharge—the normal weekday, daytime rate to central Nice is about €35; to the airport, figure €50–60; one-way to Cap Ferrat is about €20 and to Eze-le-Village is about €35. The five-minute trip from the waterfront up to the main street level (to bus stops on the Low Corniche) should be less than €10. Ask your driver to write down the price before you get in, and get a receipt when you pay (mobile 06 09 33 36 12 or 06 39 32 54 09).

Minibus: Little **minibus #80** will save you the sweat of going from the harbor up the hill, but it only runs once per hour (daily 7:00–19:00, €1). It travels from the port to the top of the hill, stopping near Hôtel la Fiancée du Pirate and the stop for buses #82 and #112 to Eze-le-Village, before going to the outlying suburban Nice Riquier train station (only convenient if you're already on minibus, must transfer to train to downtown Nice).

Tourist Train: Skip the useless white **Petit Train**, which goes nowhere interesting (€6, 20-minute ride).

Sports Fans: Lively *boules* action takes place each evening just below the TI and the huge soccer field (see page 1033).

Sights in Villefranche-sur-Mer

The Harbor—Browse Villefranche-sur-Mer's minuscule harbor. The town was once an important fishing community, but only eight families still fish here to make money. Find the footpath that leads below the citadel to the sea (by the port parking lot). Stop where the path hits the sea and marvel at the scene: a bay filled with beautiful sailing yachts. (You might see well-coiffed captains being ferried in by dutiful mates to pick up their statuesque call girls.) Local guides keep a list of the world's 100 biggest yachts and talk about some of them as if they're part of the neighborhood.

Looking far to the right, that last apartment building on the sea was the headquarters for the US Navy's Sixth Fleet following World War II and remained so until 1966, when de Gaulle pulled France out of the military wing of NATO. (The Sixth Fleet has been based in Naples ever since.) A wall plaque at the bottom of rue de l'Eglise commemorates the US Navy's presence in Villefranche.

Citadel—The town's mammoth castle was built in the 1500s by the Duke of Savoy to defend against the French. When the region joined France in 1860, it became just a barracks. In the 20th century, the city had no military use for the space, and started using the citadel to house its police station, city hall, summer outdoor theater, and two art galleries. There's still only one, fortified entry to this huge complex.

Chapel of St. Pierre (Chapelle Cocteau)—This chapel, decorated by artist Jean Cocteau, is the town's cultural highlight. Cocteau was a Parisian transplant who adored little Villefranche-sur-Mer and whose career was distinguished by his work as an artist, poet, novelist, playwright, and filmmaker. Influenced by his pals Marcel Proust, André Gide, Edith Piaf, and Pablo Picasso, Cocteau was a leader among 20th-century avant-garde intellectuals. At the door, Marie-France—who is passionate about Cocteau's art—collects a €2.50 donation for a fishermen's charity. She then sets you free to enjoy the chapel's small but intriguing interior. She's happy to give some explanations if you ask.

In 1955, Jean Cocteau covered the barrel-vaulted chapel with heavy black lines and pastels. Each of Cocteau's surrealist works—the Roma (Gypsies) of Stes-Maries-de-la-Mer who dance and sing to honor the Virgin, girls wearing traditional outfits, and three scenes from the life of St. Peter—is explained in English. Is that Villefranche-sur-Mer's citadel in the scene above the altar (Tue-Sun 10:00–12:00 & 15:00–19:00, closed Mon and when Marie-France is tired, below Hôtel Welcome)?

A few blocks north along the harbor (past Hôtel Welcome), rue de May leads to the mysterious **rue Obscura**—a covered lane running 400 feet along the medieval rampart. This street served as an air-raid shelter during World War II. Much of the lane is closed indefinitely for repair.

Boat Rides (Promenades en Mer)—These little cruises provide a seaborne perspective of this beautiful area (€11 for 1-hour cruise around Cap Ferrat, departs Wed at 17:00 July–Aug only; €17 for 2-hour cruise as far as Monaco—but doesn't actually stop there, departs Wed and Sat at 15:00 June–Sept; no trips Oct–May, boats depart from the harbor across from Hôtel Welcome, call to confirm the ever-changing schedule, reservations a must, tel. 04 93 76 65 65, www.amv-sirenes.com).

You can be your own skipper and rent a motor boat at **Dark Pelican** (€75–90/half-day, €130/day, deposit required, on the harbor at the Gare Maritime, tel. 04 93 01 76 54, www.darkpelican.com).

St. Michael's Church—The town church, a few blocks up rue de l'Eglise from the harbor, features an 18th-century organ and a fine statue of a recumbent Christ—carved, they say, from a fig tree by a galley slave in the 1600s.

Seafront Walks—A seaside walkway originally used by customs agents to patrol the harbor leads under the citadel and connects the old town with the interesting workaday harbor (port de la Darse). At the port, you'll find a few cafés, France's Institute of Oceanography (an outpost for the University of Paris oceanographic studies), and an 18th-century dry dock. This scenic walk turns downright romantic after dark—if you're sleeping elsewhere, take an ice-cream-licking stroll here. You can also wander along Villefranche-sur-Mer's waterfront and continue beyond the train station for postcard-perfect views back to Villefranche-sur-Mer (ideal in the morning—go before breakfast). You can even extend your walk to Cap Ferrat (the wooded peninsula across the bay from Villefranche).

Sleeping in Villefranche-sur-Mer

(€1 = about $1.25, country code: 33)

You have a handful of good hotels to choose from in Villefranche-sur-Mer. The ones I list have sea views from at least half of their rooms—well worth paying extra for.

$$$ Hôtel Welcome*** easily has the best location in Villefranche-sur-Mer, anchored right on the water in the old town, with all 32 balconied rooms overlooking the harbor. The lobby opens to the water, and the mellow wine bar lowers my pulse. You'll pay top price for all the comforts in this smart hotel (Sb–€99, "comfort" Db–€196, bigger "superior" Db–€230, suites–€340–380, extra bed–€35, air-con, elevator, parking garage–€17–25/day, 3 quai Amiral Courbet, tel. 04 93 76 27 62, fax 04 93 76 27 66, www.welcomehotel.com, resa@welcomehotel.com).

$$$ Hôtel Villa Vauban*** is a small villa two blocks below the TI, with nine simple and huggable rooms. Many have balconies and sea views, and most come with Old World bathrooms. The cheaper rooms on the lower level are a tad musty. Amiable British expat Alan Powers adds a personal touch that's rare in this area, making the place feel more like an intimate B&B (Db with small view–€95–130, Db with big sea view–€125–170, Db suite with sea view–€140–190, air-con, Wi-Fi, 11 avenue Général de Gaulle, tel. & fax 04 93 55 94 51, www.hotelvillavauban.com, info@hotel villavauban.com).

$$$ Hôtel la Flore* ** is a good Villefranche value if your idea of sightseeing is to enjoy the view from your spacious bedroom deck (most rooms have one) or the pool. It's a 15-minute uphill walk from the old town, but the parking is free, and the bus stops for Nice and Monaco are close (Db with no view-€100–135, Db with view and deck-€140–160, larger Db with even better view and bigger deck-€170–210, Db mini-suite-€220, Qb loft with huge terrace-€220, extra bed-€34, 15 percent cheaper Oct–March, online deals, air-con, elevator; just off main road high above harbor—go 2 blocks from TI toward Nice, at 5 boulevard Princesse Grace de Monaco; tel. 04 93 76 30 30, fax 04 93 76 99 99, www.hotel-la -flore.fr, hotel-la-flore@wanadoo.fr).

$$$ Hôtel la Fiancée du Pirate is a family-friendly refuge that's best suited for drivers, as it's high above Villefranche-sur-Mer on the Middle Corniche (although it is on bus lines #82 and #112 to Eze-le-Village and Monaco). Don't let the streetside appearance deter you: Eager-to-please Eric and Laurence offer 15 bright and comfortable rooms, along with a generous-size pool, a pleasant garden, a roomy lounge area (with board games), and a breakfast terrace with partial views of Cap Ferrat and the sea. Choose between rooms in the main building or below on the garden patio. Parking and Wi-Fi are free, the beds are firm, all rooms are air-conditioned, and the big breakfast features homemade crêpes. Light lunches, salads, and snacks are available during the day (Db-€120–140, Tb-€155, Qb-€185, 8 boulevard de la Corne d'Or, Moyenne Corniche N7, tel. 04 93 76 67 40, fax 04 93 76 91 04, www.fianceedupirate.com, info@fiancee dupirate.com).

$ Hôtel de la Darse ** is a shy and unassuming little hotel burrowed in the shadow of its highbrow neighbors. This low-profile alternative on the water at Villefranche-sur-Mer's old port is a great budget option. It's central—figure 10 minutes of level walking to the harbor, but a steep 15-minute walk up to the main road and buses. The rooms facing the sea are worth the extra few euros for their million-dollar-view balconies (view Db-€87, view Tb-€100, Qb-€113, most with air-con and some noise on weekend nights, book well ahead for these). Rooms on the quieter garden side are sharp and have air-con but no view (Sb-€63, Db-€72; extra bed-€10, up to 4 floors, no elevator, good-value breakfast; from TI walk or drive down avenue Général de Gaulle; walkers should turn left shortly after Hôtel Villa Vauban into the jardins de Narvik and follow steps to bottom, then turn right at the old Port de la Darse; parking usually available nearby, tel. 04 93 01 72 54, fax 04 93 01 84 37, www.hotel-dela-darse-villefranche-sur-mer .cote.azur.fr, hoteldeladarse@wanadoo.fr).

Eating in Villefranche-sur-Mer

Comparison-shopping is half the fun of dining in Villefranche-sur-Mer. Make an event out of a pre-dinner stroll through the old city. Check what looks good on the lively place Amélie Pollonnais (next to Hôtel Welcome), where the whole village seems to converge at night; saunter the string of pricey candlelit places lining the waterfront; and consider the smaller, wallet-friendlier eateries embedded in the old city's walking streets. Arm yourself with a gelato from any ice-cream shop and enjoy a floodlit, post-dinner stroll along the sea.

Le Cosmo Bistrot/Brasserie takes center stage on place Amélie Pollonnais with a great setting—a few tables have views to the harbor and to Cocteau chapel's facade (after some wine, Cocteau pops). Manager Arnaud runs a tight-but-friendly ship and offers well-presented and tasty meals with good wines (I love their red Bandol). Ask for the daily suggestions and consider the €12 *omelette niçoise* (€13–16 fine salads and pastas, €15–27 *plats*, open daily, place Amélie Pollonnais, tel. 04 93 01 84 05).

Disappear into Villefranche-sur-Mer's walking streets and find cute little **La Grignotière,** serving generous and delicious €18 *plats,* and plenty of other options. The mixed seafood grill is a smart order, as is the spaghetti and *gambas* (shrimp). They also offer a hearty €30 *menu,* but good luck finding room for it. Gregarious Michel speaks English fluently and runs the place with his sidekick Bridget. Dining is primarily inside, making this a good choice for cooler days (daily May–Oct, closed Wed Nov–April, 3 rue Poilu, tel. 04 93 76 79 83).

La Serre, nestled beneath the church in the old town, is a simple place with a hardworking owner. Sylvie serves well-priced meals to a loyal local clientele, always with a smile. Choose from the many pizzas (all named after US states and €10 or less), salads, and meats; or try the good-value, €17 three-course *menu* (open daily, cheap house wine, 16 rue du May, tel. 04 93 76 79 91).

La Mère Germaine, right on the harbor, is the only place in town classy enough to lure a yachter ashore. It's dressy, with formal service and a price list to match. The name commemorates the current owner's grandmother, who fed hungry GIs during World War II. Try the bouillabaisse, served with panache (€72/person with 2-person minimum, €45 mini-version for one, €41 *menu,* open daily, reserve harborfront table, tel. 04 93 01 71 39).

Souris Gourmande ("Gourmet Mouse") is handy for a made-to-order sandwich, either to take away or to eat there (€5 sandwiches, daily 11:00–22:00, closed Fri in winter, at base of steps behind Hôtel Welcome). Sandwich in hand, you'll find plenty of great places to enjoy a harborside sit.

There's a handy **Casino market/grocery store** a few blocks above Hôtel Welcome at 12 rue Poilu (Thu–Tue 7:30–12:30 & 15:00–19:30, Wed 7:30–13:00 only).

For Drivers: If you have a car and are staying a few nights, take the short drive up to Eze-le-Village or, better still, La Turbie (recommendations are listed under each destination, later in this chapter).

If it's summer (June–Sept), the best option of all is to go across to Cap Ferrat's **Restaurant de la Plage Passable** for a before-dinner drink or a dinner you won't soon forget (50-minute walk, 10-minute drive, follow signs from near Villa Rothschild). Enjoy a surprisingly elegant dining experience to the sounds of children still at play on the beach (€12–16 starters, €18–27 *plats*, open daily late May–mid-Sept, until 20:00 in good weather April–late May and mid-Sept–Oct, tel. 04 93 76 06 17).

Villefranche-sur-Mer Connections

The last bus leaves Nice for Villefranche-sur-Mer at about 19:45; the last bus from Villefranche-sur-Mer to Nice departs at about 20:50; and trains runs later (until 24:00). Never board a train without a ticket or valid pass—inspectors don't accept excuses. The minimum fine is €70.

From Villefranche-sur-Mer by Bus to: Monaco (#100, 4/hour Mon–Sat, 3/hour Sun, 25 minutes), **Nice** (#100, 4/hour Mon–Sat, 3/hour Sun, 15 minutes; or #81, 2/hour daily, 15 minutes). In Villefranche-sur-Mer, all bus stops are along the main drag; the most convenient is the Octroi stop, just above the TI.

By Train to: Monaco (2/hour, 10 minutes), **Nice** (2/hour, 10 minutes), **Antibes** (2/hour, 40 minutes).

The Three Corniches: Villefranche to Monaco

Nice, Villefranche-sur-Mer, and Monaco are linked by three coastal routes: the Low, Middle, and High Corniches. The roads are nicknamed after the decorative frieze that runs along the top of a building (cornice). Each Corniche (kor-neesh) offers sensational views and a different perspective. You can find the three routes from Nice by driving up boulevard Jean Jaurès past the bus station (*gare routière*). For the Low Corniche, follow signs to

N-98 (*Monaco par la Basse Corniche*), which leads past Nice's port. Shortly after the turnoff to the Low Corniche, you'll see signs for N-7 (*Moyenne Corniche*) leading to the Middle Corniche. Signs for the High (*Grande*) Corniche appear a bit after that; follow D-2564 to *Col des 4 Chemins* and the *Grande Corniche*.

Low Corniche: The Basse Corniche (also called "Corniche Inférieure") strings ports, beaches, and seaside villages together for a traffic-filled ground-floor view. It was built in the 1860s (along with the train line) to bring people to the casino in Monte Carlo. When this Low Corniche was finished, many hill-town villagers descended to the shore and started the communities that line the sea today. Before 1860, the population of the coast between Villefranche-sur-Mer and Monte Carlo was zero. Think about that as you make the trip today.

Middle Corniche: The Moyenne Corniche is higher, quieter, and far more impressive. It runs through Eze-le-Village and provides breathtaking views over the Mediterranean, with several scenic pullouts. (The ones above Villefranche-sur-Mer are the best.)

High Corniche: Napoleon's crowning road-construction achievement, the Grande Corniche caps the cliffs with staggering views from almost 1,600 feet above the sea. It is actually the Via Aurelia, used by the Romans to conquer the West.

Villas: Driving from Villefranche-sur-Mer to Monaco, you'll come upon impressive villas. A particularly grand entry leads to the sprawling estate built by King Leopold II of Belgium in the 1920s. Those driving up to the Middle Corniche from Villefranche-sur-Mer can look down on this yellow mansion and its lush garden, which fill an entire hilltop. This estate was later owned by the Agnelli family (of Fiat fame and fortune), and then by the Safra family (American bankers).

The Best Route: For a ▲▲▲ route, **drivers** should take the Middle Corniche from Nice or Villefranche-sur-Mer to Eze-le-Village; from there, follow signs to the *Grande Corniche* and *La Turbie* (*La Trophée des Alpes*), then finish by dropping down into Monaco. **Buses** travel each route; the higher the Corniche, the less frequent the buses (4/hour on Low, 12/day on Middle, and 5/day on High). There are no buses between Eze-le-Village and La Turbie (45-minute walk), though buses do connect Nice and Monaco with La Turbie.

Sights Along the Three Corniches

The following two sights—Eze-le-Village and La Trophée des Alpes monument—are listed in the order you'll reach them, traveling from Villefranche-sur-Mer to Monaco.

Villefranche, Monaco & the Corniches

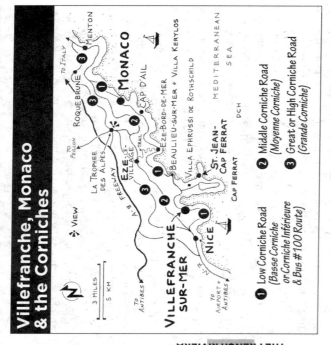

N

3 MILES

5 KM

TO ANTIBES

VILLEFRANCHE-SUR-MER

NICE

TO AIRPORT + ANTIBES

LA TROPHÉE DES ALPES

FREEWAY

A-8 FREEWAY

ÉZE-VILLAGE

TO PEILLON

TRAIL

ÉZE-BORD-DE-MER

BEAULIEU-SUR-MER + VILLA KERYLOS

VILLA EPHRUSSI DE ROTHSCHILD

ST. JEAN-CAP FERRAT

CAP FERRAT

CAP D'AIL

MONACO

ROQUEBRUNE

MENTON

TO ITALY

MEDITERRANEAN SEA

DCH

VIEW

① Low Corniche Road
(Basse Corniche or Corniche Inférieure & Bus #100 Route)

② Middle Corniche Road
(Moyenne Corniche)

③ Great or High Corniche Road
(Grande Corniche)

▲Eze-le-Village

Floating high above the sea, flowery and flawless Eze-le-Village (don't confuse it with the seafront town of Eze-Bord-de-Mer) is entirely consumed by tourism. This *village d'art et de gastronomie* (as it calls itself) nurtures perfume outlets, upscale boutiques, steep cobbled lanes, and magnificent views (best from the terrace at Château Eza). Touristy as this place certainly is Eze, its stony state of preservation and magnificent hilltop setting over the Mediterranean may draw you away from the beaches. Day-tripping by bus to Eze-le-Village from Nice, Monaco, or Villefranche-sur-Mer works well, provided you know the bus schedules (ask at TIs or check www.lignedazur .com; Villefranche-sur-Mer requires a transfer).

Bus stops and parking lots weld the town to the highway (Middle Corniche) that passes under its lowest wall. Eze-le-Village's main parking lot is a block below the town's entry. The stop for buses to Nice is across the road by the Avia gas station, and the stops for buses to Eze-Bord-de-Mer and Monaco are on the village side of the main road, near the Casino Market. The helpful **TI**, in the lot's far corner, has bus schedules (April-Oct daily 9:00–18:00, July–Aug until 19:00; Nov–March Mon–Sat 9:00–18:30, closed Sun; place de Gaulle, tel. 04 93 41 26 00, www.eze-riviera.com). English-language tours of the village and gardens are available for €8 (call to arrange in advance). Public WCs are located just behind the TI and in the village behind the church, though the cleanest and best-smelling are at either perfume showroom.

At the **Jardins d'Eze** you'll find a prickly festival of cactus. Since 1949 these ruins have been home to 400 different plants 1,300 feet above the sea (€5, open daily, hours change frequently but usually May–Sept 9:00–19:00, Oct–April until dusk, well-described in English, tel. 04 93 41 10 30). At the top, you'll be treated to a commanding 360-degree view, with a helpful *table d'orientation*. On a crystal-clear day (they say...), you can see Corsica.

The **Perfume Factory Fragonard**, 350 feet below Eze-le-Village, is designed for tour groups—it cranks them through all day long. Drop in for an informative and free tour, which can last anywhere from 20 to 40 minutes depending on the walking ability of the group (daily 9:00–18:00, but best Mon–Fri 9:00–11:00 & 14:00–15:30, when the "factory" actually has people working, tel. 04 93 41 05 05). You'll see how the perfume and scented soaps are made and bottled before you're herded into the gift shop. For a more personal and intimate (but unguided) look at perfume, cross the main road in Eze-le-Village to visit the **Gallimard** shop.

Eating in Eze-le-Village: To enjoy Eze-le-Village in relative peace, visit at sunset and stay for dinner. **Le Cactus** serves cheap crêpes, salads, and sandwiches at outdoor tables near the entry to the old town (daily, tel. 04 93 41 19 02). For a real splurge, dine at **Château Eza**. Its sensational view terrace is also home to an expensive-but-sensational restaurant. Reserve well ahead for dinner (€7 beer, €50 lunch *menus*, allow €110 for dinner, open daily, tel. 04 93 41 12 24, www.chateaueza.com, info@chateaueza.com).

Getting to Eze-le-Village: There are two Ezes: Eze-le-Village (the spectacular hill town) and Eze-Bord-de-Mer (a modern beach resort far below Eze-le-Village). Eze-le-Village is about 20 minutes east of Villefranche-sur-Mer on the Middle Corniche.

From Nice and upper Villefranche-sur-Mer, buses #82 and #112 provide 16 buses per day to Eze-le-Village (eight on Sun, 25 minutes). Take bus #80 from the center of Villefranche-sur-Mer uphill to the stop in front of Hôtel la Fiancée du Pirate to make this connection.

From Nice, Villefranche, or Monaco,

you can also take the train or the Nice–Monaco bus to Eze-Bord-de-Mer, getting off at the Gare d'Eze stop. From here, take the #83 shuttle bus straight up to Eze-le-Village (8/day, daily 9:45–18:00, schedule is posted at the stop but it's best to know schedule before you go).

To connect Eze-le-Village directly with Monte Carlo in Monaco, take bus #112 (7/day Mon–Sat, none on Sun, 25 minutes). There are no direct buses from Villefranche-sur-Mer to Eze-le-Village, and there are no buses between La Turbie (La Trophée des Alpes) and Eze-le-Village (40-minute walk).

You could take a pricey taxi between the two Ezes or from Eze-le-Village to La Turbie (allow €25 one-way, mobile 06 09 84 17 84).

▲▲La Trophée des Alpes (in La Turbie)

High above Monaco, on the Grande (High) Corniche in the over-looked village of La Turbie, lies one of this region's most evoca-tive historic sights (with dramatic views over the entire country of Monaco as a bonus). Rising well above all other buildings, this massive Roman monument commemorates Augustus Caesar's conquest of the Alps and its 44 hostile tribes. It's exciting to think that, in a way, La Trophée des Alpes celebrates a victory that kicked off the Pax Romana—joining Gaul and Germania, freeing up the main artery of the Roman Empire, and linking Spain and Italy. (It's depressing to think that it's closed on Mondays, if that's your only chance to visit.)

Walk around the monument and notice how the Romans built a fine, quarried-stone exterior, filled in with rubble and coarse con-crete. Flanked by the vanquished in chains, the towering inscrip-tion tells the story: It was erected "by the senate and the people to honor the emperor." The monument later became a quarry before being restored in the 1930s and 1940s with money from the Tuck family of New Hampshire.

The one-room **museum** shows a reconstruction and transla-tion of the dramatic inscription, which lists all the feisty alpine tribes that put up such a fight. Escorts from the museum take people up to the monument, but it's not worth waiting for.

Cost and Hours: €5, Tue–Sun mid-May–mid-Sept 9:30–13:00 & 14:30–17:30, off-season 10:00–13:00 & 14:30–17:00, closed Mon year-round, tel. 04 93 41 20 84.

La Turbie: The sweet old village of La Turbie sees almost no tourists, but it has plenty of cafés and restaurants. To stroll the old village, park in the main lot on place Neuve (follow *Monaco* signs one block from the main road to find it); then walk behind the post office and find brick footpaths—they lead through a village with nary a shop. To eat very well, find **La Terrasse,** the Riviera's most welcoming restaurant (I'm not kidding—free calls are encouraged from their phone anywhere, anytime; there's a computer at your disposal; and the Wi-Fi is free). Here, tables gather under sun shades and everyone seems to be on a first-name basis. Let Helen, Jacques, and Annette tempt you to return for dinner at sunset, and book ahead for a table with a view (€8–11 salads, great €12.50 *plats du jour*, €19.50 three-course *menu* includes glass of wine, steak tartare is a specialty, daily, near the PTT/post office at the main parking lot, 17 place Neuve, tel. 04 93 41 21 84).

Getting to and from La Trophée des Alpes (in La Turbie): By **car**, take the High Corniche to La Turbie, ideally from Eze-le-Village (La Turbie is 10 minutes east of, and above, Eze-le-Village), then look for signs to *La Trophée des Alpes*. Once in La Turbie, you can park in the lot in the center of town (place Neuve, follow *Monaco* signs for a short block) and walk from there (walk 5 minutes around the old village, with the village on your right); or drive to the site by turning right in front of La Régence Café. Those coming from farther afield can take the efficient A-8 to the La Turbie exit. To reach Eze-le-Village from La Turbie, follow signs to *Nice*, and then look for signs to *Eze-le-Village*.

You can also get here on **bus #16** from Nice (5/day, 45 minutes, last bus returns to Nice at about 18:00), or on bus #114 from Monaco (6/day, 3/day Sat morning only, none on Sun, 20 minutes). La Turbie's bus stop is across from the PTT/post office on place Neuve (to reach La Trophée des Alps, walk around the old village, with the village on your right—5 minutes).

Monaco

Despite high prices, wall-to-wall daytime tourists, and a Disney-esque atmosphere, Monaco is a Riviera must. Monaco is on the go. Since 1929, cars have raced around the port and in front of the casino in one of the world's most famous auto races, the Grand Prix de Monaco (May 26–29 in 2011). The modern breakwater—constructed elsewhere and towed in by sea—enables big cruise ships to dock here. The district of Fontvieille, reclaimed from the sea, bristles with luxury high-rise condos. But don't look for anything too deep in this glittering tax haven. Two-thirds of its 30,000 residents live here because there's no income tax—leaving fewer than 10,000 true Monegasques.

This minuscule principality (0.75 square mile) borders only France and the Mediterranean. The country has always been tiny, but it used to be...less tiny. In an 1860 plebiscite, Monaco lost two-thirds of its territory when the region of Menton voted to join France. To compensate, France suggested that Monaco build a fancy casino and promised to connect it to the world with a road (the Low Corniche) and a train line. This started a high-class tourist boom that has yet to let up.

While "independent," Monaco is run as a piece of France. A French civil servant appointed by the French president—with the blessing of Monaco's prince—serves as state minister and manages the place. Monaco's phone system, electricity, water, and so on, are all French.

The death of Prince Rainier in 2005 ended his 56-year career of enlightened rule. Today, Monaco is ruled by Prince Rainier's unassuming son, Prince Albert Alexandre Louis Pierre, Marquis of Baux. At 50-some years old, Prince Albert had long been considered Europe's most eligible bachelor—though he has admitted to fathering two children out of wedlock—but finally got engaged in 2010. A graduate of Amherst College, Albert is a bobsled enthusiast who raced in several Olympics, and an avid environmentalist who seems determined to clean up Monaco's tarnished tax-haven, money-laundering image. (Monaco is infamously known as a "sunny place for shady people.")

Monaco is big business, and Prince Albert is its CEO. While its famous casino contributes only 5 percent of the state's revenue, its 43 banks—which offer an attractive way to hide your money—are hugely profitable. The prince also makes money with a value-added tax (19.6 percent, the same as in France), plus real estate and corporate taxes.

The glamorous romance and marriage of the American actress Grace Kelly to Prince Rainier added to Monaco's fairy-tale mystique. Grace Kelly (Prince Albert's mother) first came to Monaco to star in the 1955 Hitchcock movie *To Catch a Thief*, in which she was filmed racing along the Corniches. Later, she married the prince and adopted the country. Tragically, Monaco's much-loved Princess Grace died in a car wreck on that same Corniche in 1982. She was just 52 years old.

Monaco is a special place: There are more people in Monaco's philharmonic orchestra (about 100) than in its army (about 80 guards). The princedom is well-guarded, with police and cameras on every corner. (They say you could win a million dollars at the casino and walk to the train station in the wee hours without a worry...and I believe it.) Stamps are so few that they increase in value almost as soon as they're printed. And collectors snapped up the rare Monaco versions of euro coins (with Prince Rainier's portrait) so quickly that many Monegasques have never even seen one.

Orientation to Monaco

The principality of Monaco consists of three distinct tourist areas: Monaco-Ville, Monte Carlo, and La Condamine. Monaco-Ville fills the rock high above everything else and is referred to by locals as Le Rocher ("The Rock"). This is the oldest section, home to the Prince's Palace and all the sights except the casino. Monte Carlo is the area around the casino. La Condamine is the port (which divides Monaco-Ville and Monte Carlo). From here

it's a 25-minute walk up to the Prince's Palace or to the casino, or three minutes by local bus (see "Getting Around Monaco," later). A fourth, less-interesting area, Fontvieille, forms the west end of Monaco and was reclaimed from the sea by Prince Rainier in the 1970s.

Tourist Information

The main TI is at the top of the **park**, above the casino (Mon–Sat 9:00–19:00, Sun 10:00–12:00, 2 boulevard des Moulins, tel. 00-377/92 16 61 16 or 00-377/92 16 61 66, www.visitmonaco.com). A branch TI is in the **train station** (Tue–Sat 9:00–17:00, closed Sun–Mon except July–Aug). From June to September, you might find information kiosks in the Monaco-Ville parking garage and on the port. There is also a TI desk for Monaco in Terminal 1 of Nice's airport.

Arrival in Monaco

By Bus from Nice and Villefranche-sur-Mer: Bus riders need to pay attention, since stops are not announced. Cap d'Ail is the town before Monaco, so be on the lookout after that (the last stop before Monaco is called Cimitière). You'll enter Monaco through the modern cityscape of high-rises of the Fontvieille district. When you see the rocky outcrop of old Monaco, be ready to get off.

There are three stops in Monaco. Listed in order from Nice, they are Place d'Armes (in front of a tunnel at the base of Monaco-Ville's rock), Stade Nautique (center on the port), and Casino (near the casino on avenue d'Ostende). The Place d'Armes stop is the best starting point. From there you can walk up to Monaco-Ville and the palace (10 minutes straight up), or catch a quick local bus (line #1 or #2, details follow). To reach the bus stop and steps up

Monaco

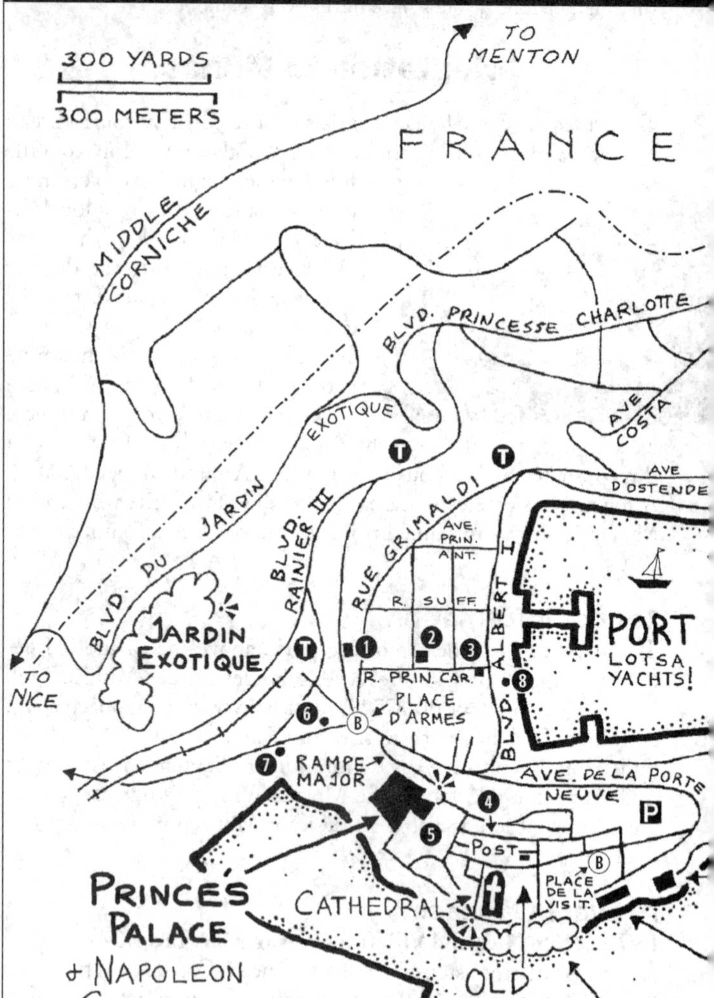

300 YARDS
300 METERS

FRANCE

TO MENTON

BLVD. PRINCESSE CHARLOTTE

AVE. COSTA

AVE. D'OSTENDE

PORT
LOTSA YACHTS!

AVE. DE LA PORTE NEUVE

P

PLACE DE LA VISIT.

JARDIN BOTANIQUE

OLD TOWN

BLVD. ALBERT I

AVE. PRIN. ANT.

R. SUFF.

RUE GRIMALDI

R. PRIN. CAR.

PLACE D'ARMES

Post

MIDDLE CORNICHE

BLVD. RAINIER III

BLVD. DU JARDIN EXOTIQUE

JARDIN EXOTIQUE

RAMPE MAJOR

CATHEDRAL

PRINCE'S PALACE
+ NAPOLEON COLLECTION

FONTVIEILLE

TO NICE

THE FRENCH RIVIERA

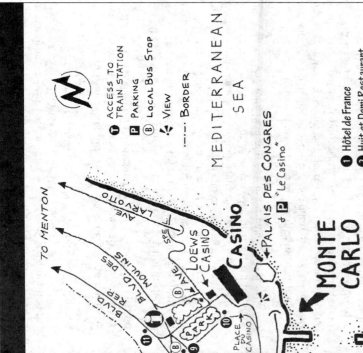

Legend:

- **T** ACCESS TO TRAIN STATION
- **P** PARKING
- **B** LOCAL BUS STOP
- **✦** VIEW
- --- BORDER

MEDITERRANEAN SEA

1. Hôtel de France
2. Huit et Demi Restaurant
3. Crock'in Café
4. Boulangerie
5. Palace Square: Start of Self-Guided Walk
6. Bus #100 to Nice: Place d'Armes Stop
7. Bus #100 from Nice: Place d'Armes Stop
8. Bus #100 to/from Nice: Stade Nautique Stop
9. Bus #100 to Nice: Casino Stop
10. Bus #100 from Nice: Casino Stop
11. Bus #112 to Eze-le-Village & #114 to La Turbie

TO MENTON

BLVD DU REP
BLVD DES MOULINS
AVE DES SPE
AVE LARVOTTO

LOEWS CASINO

CASINO

PALAIS DES CONGRES
& P "Le Casino"

MONTE CARLO STORY
& P "Le Palais"

MONTE CARLO

MONACO-VILLE

PLACE DU CASINO

COUSTEAU AQUARIUM

to Monaco-Ville, cross the street right in front of the tunnel and walk with the rock on your right for about 200 feet (good WCs at the local-bus stop). To begin at the Casino stop, walk uphill to the Häagen-Dazs and turn right to find the casino.

For directions on returning to Nice by bus, see "Monaco Connections," later.

By Train from Nice: This l-o-o-ong underground train station is in central Monaco, about a 15-minute walk to the casino or to the port, and about 25 minutes to the palace. The station has no baggage storage.

The TI and ticket windows are up the escalator at the Italy end of the station. There are three exits from the train platform level (one at each end and one in the middle).

To reach Monaco-Ville and the palace from the station, take the platform-level exit at the Nice end of the tracks (signed *Sortie Fontvieille/Monaco Ville*), which leads through a long tunnel (TI annex at end) to the foot of Monaco-Ville; turn left at the end of the walkway and hike 15 minutes up to the palace, or take the bus (#1 or #2).

To reach Monaco's port and the casino, take the mid-platform exit, closer to the Italy end of the tracks. Follow *Sortie la Condamine* signs down the steps and escalators, then follow *Accès Port* signs until you pop out at the port, where you'll see the stop for buses #1 and #2. It's a 25-minute walk from the port to the palace (to your right) or 20 minutes to the casino (up avenue d'Ostende to your left), or a short trip on buses #1 or #2 to either.

If you plan to return to Nice by train after 20:30, when ticket windows close, buy your return tickets now or be sure to have about €4 in coins (the ticket machines only take coins).

To take the short-but-sweet coastal **walking path** into Monaco's Fontvieille district, get off the train at Cap d'Ail, which is one stop before Monaco. Turn left out of the little station and walk 50 yards up the road, then turn left again, going downstairs and under the tracks. Turn left onto the coastal trail, and hike the 20 minutes to Fontvieille. You'll end up at Pointe des Douaniers. Once there, it's a 20-minute uphill hike to Monaco's sights (or hop on bus #100).

By Car: Follow *Centre-Ville* signs into Monaco (warning: traffic can be a problem), then watch for the red-letter signs to parking garages at *Le Casino* (for Monte Carlo) or *Le Palais* (for Monaco-Ville). You'll pay about €10 for four hours.

Helpful Hints

Telephone Tip: To call Monaco from France, dial 00, then 377 (Monaco's country code) and the eight-digit number. Within Monaco, simply dial the eight-digit number.

Minivan Tours from Nice: Several companies offer daytime and nighttime tours of Monaco, allowing you freedom to gamble without worrying about catching the last train or bus home (see "Getting Around the Riviera" on page 704).

Loop Trip by Bus: You can visit Monaco by bus, then take a bus from Monaco directly to Eze-le-Village (#112, no Sun bus) or La Turbie (#114, no Sun bus), then return to Nice by bus from there. For details, see "Monaco Connections," later.

Getting Around Monaco

By Local Bus: Buses #1 and #2 link all areas with fast and frequent service (single ticket-€1, 10 tickets-€6, day pass-€3, pay driver, 10/hour, fewer on Sun, buses run until 21:00). You can split a 10-ride ticket with your travel partners, since you're unlikely to take more than two or three rides in Monaco.

By Open Bus Tour: You could pay €17 for a hop-on, hop-off open-deck bus tour that makes 12 stops in Monaco, but I wouldn't. This tour doesn't go to the best view spot in the Jardin Exotique (described on page 768) and, besides, most of Monaco is walkable. If you want a scenic tour of the principality that includes its best views, pay €1 to take local bus #2, and stay on board for a full loop (or hop on and off as you please).

By Tourist Train: "Monaco Tour" tourist trains begin at the aquarium and pass by the port, casino, and palace (€7, 2/hour, 10:30–18:00 in summer, 11:00–17:00 in winter depending on weather, 30 minutes, recorded English commentary).

By Taxi: If you've lost track of time at the casino, you can call the 24-hour taxi service (tel. 08 20 20 98 98)...provided you still have enough money to pay for the cab home.

Self-Guided Walk

Welcome to Monaco-Ville

All of Monaco's sights (except the casino) are in Monaco-Ville, packed within a few cheerfully tidy blocks. This walk makes a tidy loop around Monaco-Ville.

• *To get from anywhere in Monaco to the palace square (Monaco-Ville's sightseeing center, home of the palace and the Napoleon Collection), take bus #1 or #2 to place de la Visitation (end of the line). Turn right as you step off the bus and walk five minutes straight down the street leading from the left corner of the little square (the one on the left goes right past the post office, if you want Monaco stamps). If you're walking up from the port, the well-marked lane leads directly to the palace.*

Palace Square (Place du Palais): This square is the best place to get oriented to Monaco. Facing the palace, go to the right and look out over the city (er...principality). This rock gave birth to the little pastel Hong Kong look-alike in 1215, and it's managed to remain an independent country for most of its nearly 800 years. Looking beyond the glitzy port, notice the faded green roof above and to the right: It belongs to the casino that put Monaco on the map. The famous Grand Prix runs along the port, and then up the ramp to the casino. And Italy is so close, you can almost smell the pesto. Just beyond the casino is France again (which flanks Monaco on both sides)—you could walk one-way from France to France, passing through Monaco in about 60 minutes.

The odd statue of a woman with a fishing net is dedicated to **Prince Albert I**'s glorious reign (1889–1922). Albert was a Renaissance man with varied skills and interests. He had a Jacques Cousteau–like fascination with the sea (and built Monaco's famous aquarium), and was a determined pacifist who made many attempts to dissuade Germany's Kaiser Wilhelm II from becoming involved in World War I. It was Albert I's dad, Charles III, who built the casino.

• *Now walk toward the palace and find the statue of the monk grasping a sword.*

Meet **François Grimaldi**, a renegade Italian dressed as a monk, who captured Monaco in 1297 and began the dynasty that still rules the principality. Prince Albert is his great-great-great-grandson, which gives Monaco's royal family the distinction of being the longest-lasting dynasty in Europe.

• *Make your way to the...*

Prince's Palace (Palais Princier): A medieval castle sat where Monaco's palace is today. Its strategic setting has had a lot to do with Monaco's ability to resist attackers. Today, Prince Albert lives in the palace, while Princesses Stephanie and Caroline live down the street a few blocks. The palace guards protect the prince 24/7 and still stage a **Changing of the Guard** ceremony with all the pageantry of an important nation (daily at 11:55, fun to watch but jam-packed). Audioguide tours take you through part of the prince's lavish palace in 30 minutes. The rooms are well-furnished and impressive, but interesting only if you haven't seen a château lately (€8 combo-ticket includes audioguide and the Napoleon Collection, April–Oct daily 10:00–18:00, last entry 30 minutes before closing, closed Nov–March, tel. 00-377/93 25 18 31).

• *Next to the palace entry is the...*

Napoleon Collection: Napoleon occupied Monaco after the

French Revolution. This is the prince's private collection of items Napoleon left behind: military medals, swords, guns, letters, and, best, his hat. I found this collection more interesting than the palace (€4 includes audioguide, €8 combo-ticket includes Prince's Palace, same hours as palace).

• *With your back to the palace, leave the square through the arch to the right (under the most beautiful police station I've ever seen) and find the...*

Cathedral of Monaco (Cathédrale de Monaco): The somber but beautifully lit cathedral, rebuilt in 1878, shows that Monaco cared for more than just its new casino. It's where centuries of Grimaldis are buried, and where Princess Grace and Prince Rainier were married. Circle slowly behind the altar (counterclockwise). The second tomb is that of Albert I, who did much to put Monaco on the world stage. The second-to-last tomb—inscribed "*Gratia Patricia, MCMLXXXII*"—is where Princess Grace was buried in 1982. Prince Rainier's tomb lies next to Princess Grace's (daily 8:30–18:45, until 18:00 in winter).

• *As you leave the cathedral, find the 1956 wedding photo of Princess Grace and Prince Rainier (keep an eye out for other photos of the couple as you walk), then walk left through the immaculately maintained Jardin Botanique, with more fine views. Find the...*

Cousteau Aquarium (Musée Océanographique): Prince Albert I built this impressive, cliff-hanging aquarium in 1910 as a monument to his enthusiasm for things from the sea. The aquarium, which Captain Jacques Cousteau directed for 32 years, has 2,000 different specimens, representing 250 species. The bottom floor features Mediterranean fish and colorful tropical species (all nicely described in English). My favorite is the zebra lionfish, though I'm keen on eels too. Rotating exhibits occupy the entry floor. Upstairs, the fancy Albert I Hall houses a museum (included in entry fee, very little English information) and features ship models, whale skeletons, oceanographic instruments and tools, and scenes of Albert and his beachcombers hard at work. Find the display on Christopher Columbus with English explanations. Don't miss the elevator to the rooftop terrace view, where you'll also find convenient WCs and a reasonable café (€13, kids–€7, daily July–Aug 9:30–19:30, April–June and Sept 9:30–19:00, Oct–March 10:00–18:00; down the steps from Monaco-Ville bus stop, at the opposite end of Monaco-Ville from the palace; tel. 00-377/93 15 36 00, www.oceano.mc).

• *The red-brick steps, across from the aquarium to the right, lead up to buses #1 and #2, both of which run to the port, the casino, and the train station. To walk back to the palace and through the old city, turn left at the top of the brick steps. For a brief movie break, take the escalator to the right of the aquarium as you leave it and drop into the parking garage, then take the elevator down and find the...*

Monte Carlo Story: This informative 35-minute film gives an entertaining and informative account of Monaco's fairytale history, from fishing village to jet-set principality, and offers a comfortable, soft-chair break from all that walking. The last part of the film was added to the original version after the death of Prince Rainier, which is why your sound stops early (€7, headphone commentary in English; daily showings usually on the hour at 14:00, 15:00, 16:00, and 17:00; there may be a morning showing for groups that you can join—ask, tel. 00-377/93 25 32 33).

Sights in Monaco

Above Monaco-Ville

Jardin Exotique—This cliffside municipal garden, located above Monaco-Ville, has eye-popping views from France to Italy. It's a fascinating home to more than a thousand species of cacti (some giant) and other succulent plants, but probably worth the entry only for view-loving botanists (some posted English explanations provided). Your ticket includes entry to a skippable natural cave and an anthropological museum, as well as a not-to-be-missed view snack bar/café (€7, daily mid-May–mid-Sept 9:00–19:00, mid-Sept–mid-May 9:00–18:00 or until dusk, tel. 00-377/93 15 29 80). Bus #2 runs here from any stop in Monaco, and makes for a worthwhile mini tour of the country, even if you don't visit the gardens. You can get similar views over Monaco for free from behind the souvenir stand at the Jardin's bus stop; or, for even grander vistas, cross the street and hike toward La Turbie.

In Monte Carlo

▲**Casino**—Monte Carlo, which means "Charles' Hill" in Spanish, is named for the prince who presided over Monaco's 19th-century makeover. Begin your visit opposite Europe's most famous casino, in the park above the pedestrian-unfriendly traffic circle. In the mid-1800s, olive groves stood here. Then, with the construction of the casino, spas, and easy road and train access, one of Europe's poorest countries was on the Grand Tour map—*the* place for the vacationing aristocracy to play. Today, Monaco has the world's highest per-capita income.

The casino is intended to make you feel comfortable while losing money. Charles Garnier designed the place (with an opera house inside) in 1878, in part to thank the prince for his financial help in completing

Paris' Opéra Garnier (which the architect also designed). The central doors provide access to slot machines, private gaming rooms, and the opera house. The private gaming rooms occupy the left wing of the building.

If you're over 21, you can try your luck at the one-armed bandits (push button on slot machines to claim your winnings). If it's before 20:00, shorts are allowed at the slots, though you'll need decent attire to go any farther. After 20:00, shorts are off-limits everywhere. The scene, flooded with camera-toting tourists during the day, is great at night—and downright James Bond–like in the private rooms.

If paying an entrance fee to lose money is not your idea of fun, you can access all games for free in the plebeian, American-style Loews Casino, adjacent to the old casino.

Cost and Hours: The slot machines and the first gaming rooms (*salons européens*) open daily at 14:00. Slots are free, but you'll pay €10 to enter *les salons européens*. Most of the glamorous private game rooms open Mon-Fri at 16:00 and Sat-Sun at 15:00, though some don't open until 21:00 or 22:00. Here you can rub elbows with high rollers—provided you're 18 or older (bring your passport for proof) and properly attired (tie and jacket for men, dress standards for women are far more relaxed—only tennis shoes are a definite no-no). Men might be able to rent a tie and jacket at a nearby store (ask at the TI or casino before you go, casino tel. 00-377/92 16 20 00, www.montecarlocasinos.com).

Take the Money and Run: The stop for buses returning to Nice and Villefranche-sur-Mer, and for local buses #1 and #2, is at the top of the park, above the casino on avenue de la Costa (under the arcade to the left). To get back to the train station from the casino, take bus #1 or #2 from this stop, or walk about 15 minutes down avenue d'Ostende (just outside the casino) toward the port, and follow signs to *Gare SNCF* (see map).

Sleeping and Eating in Monaco

(€1 = about $1.25, country code: 377)

$$ Hôtel de France**, run by friendly Sylvie, is centrally located, spotlessly maintained, reasonably priced, and perfectly pleasant. Its extensive renovation should be complete in time for your visit; expect air-conditioning and higher prices than those printed here—check their site for updated rates (Db-€90-125, Tb-€110-155, includes breakfast, Wi-Fi, 6 rue de la Turbie, near west exit from train station, tel. 00-377/93 30 24 64, fax 00-377/92 16 13 34, www.monte-carlo.mc/france, hotel-france@monte-carlo.mc).

Several cafés serve basic, inexpensive fare (day and night) on the port. I prefer the eateries that line the flowery, traffic-free rue de la Princesse Caroline, which runs between rue Grimaldi and the port. The best this street has to offer is **Huit et Demi.** It has a white-tablecloth-meets-director's-chair ambience, mostly outdoor tables, and cuisine worth returning for (€13 salads, €14 pizzas, €18–24 *plats*, closed Sat for lunch and all day Sun, 7 rue de la Princesse Caroline, tel. 00-377/93 50 97 02). For a simple and cheap salad or sandwich, find the **Crock'in** café farther down at 2 rue de la Princesse (closed Sun, tel. 04 93 15 02 78).

In Monaco-Ville you'll find incredible *pan bagnat* (*salade niçoise* sandwich), quiche, and sandwiches at the yellow-bannered **Boulangerie,** a block off Palace Square (open daily until 19:00, 8 rue Basse). Try a *barbajuan* (a spring roll–size beignet with wheat, rice, and parmesan), the *tourta de bléa* (pastry stuffed with pine nuts, raisins, and white beets), or the focaccia sandwich (salted bread with herbs, mozzarella, basil, and tomatoes, all drenched in olive oil). For dessert, order the *fougasse monégasque* (a soft-bread pastry topped with sliced almonds and anise candies). Monaco-Ville has many pizzerias, *crêperies,* and sandwich stands, but the neighborhood is dead at night. If you're here in the evening, eat near the port.

Monaco Connections

From Monaco by Train to: Nice (2/hour, 20 minutes, €3.60), **Villefranche-sur-Mer** (2/hour, 10 minutes), **Antibes** (2/hour, 45–60 minutes).

By Bus to: Nice (#100, 4/hour Mon–Sat, 3/hour Sun, 45 minutes, €1), **Nice Airport** (#110 express on the freeway, hourly, 50 minutes, €18), **Villefranche-sur-Mer** (#100, 4/hour Mon–Sat, 3/hour Sun, 25 minutes, €1), **Eze-le-Village** (#112, 7/day Mon–Sat, none on Sun, 25 minutes), **La Turbie** (#114, 6/day Mon–Fri, 3/day Sat morning only, none on Sun, 20 minutes).

The Monaco-to-Nice bus (#100) is not identified at every stop—verify with a local by asking, *"Direction Nice?"* There's a handy stop below Monaco-Ville at place d'Armes (on the main road to Nice in front of the Brasserie Monte Carlo). Another is a few blocks above the casino on avenue de la Costa (under the arcade to the left of Barclays Bank).

Buses #112 (to Eze-le-Village) and #114 (to La Turbie) depart Monaco from place de la Crémaillère, one block above the main TI and casino park. Walk up rue Iris with Barclays Bank to your left, curve right, and find the bus shelter across the street by the green Costa à la Crémaillère café. Bus numbers for these routes are not posted, but this is the stop.

Last Call: The last bus leaves Monaco for Villefranche-sur-

Mer and Nice at about 20:00; the last train leaves Monaco for Villefranche-sur-Mer and Nice at about 23:30. If you plan to leave Monaco by train after 20:30, buy your tickets in advance (since the window will be closed), or bring enough coins for the machines.

Antibes

Antibes has a down-to-earth, easygoing ambience that's rare in this area. Its old town is a maze of narrow streets and red-tile roofs rising above the blue Med, protected by twin medieval towers and wrapped in extensive ramparts. Visitors making the short trip from Nice can browse Europe's biggest yacht harbor, snooze on a sandy beach, loiter through an enjoyable old town, and hike along a sea-swept trail. The town's cultural claim to fame, the Picasso Museum, shows off its great collection in a fine old building.

Though much smaller than Nice, Antibes has a history that dates back just as far. Both towns were founded by Greek traders in the fifth century B.C. To the Greeks, Antibes was "Antipolis"—the town (*polis*) opposite (*anti*) Nice. For the next several centuries, Antibes remained in the shadow of its neighbor. By the turn of the 20th century, the town was a military base—so the rich and famous partied elsewhere. But when the army checked out after World War I, Antibes was "discovered" and enjoyed a particularly roaring '20s—with the help of party animals like Rudolph Valentino and the rowdy (yet silent) Charlie Chaplin. Fun-seekers even invented water-skiing right here in the 1920s.

Orientation to Antibes

Antibes' old town lies between the port and boulevard Albert 1er and avenue Robert Soleau. Place Nationale is the old town's hub of activity. The restaurant-lined rue Aubernon connects the port and the old town. Stroll along the sea between the old port and place Albert 1er (where boulevard Albert 1er meets the water). The best beaches lie just beyond place Albert 1er, and the walk is beautiful. Good play areas

for children are along this path and on place des Martyrs de la Résistance (close to recommended Hôtel Relais du Postillon).

Tourist Information

Antibes has three TIs: one in a kiosk at the **train station** (April–Sept only, Mon–Sat 9:00–18:00, closed Sun), one near the **port** at 32 boulevard d'Aguillon (Mon–Sat 10:00–12:00 & 13:30–18:00, closed Sun), and the main TI on **place Général de Gaulle** where the fountains squirt (July–Aug daily 9:00–19:00; Sept–June Mon–Sat 9:00–12:30 & 13:30–18:00, Sun 9:00–12:00; tel. 04 97 23 11 11, www.antibesjuanlespins.com). At any TI, pick up the excellent city map and the self-guided walking tour of old Antibes. The Nice TI has Antibes maps and the Antibes TI has Nice maps—plan ahead.

Arrival in Antibes

By Train: Bus #14 runs every 20 minutes from the train station (bus stop 50 yards to right as you exit station) to the *gare routière* (bus station; near the main TI and old town), and continues to the fine *plage de la Salis* with quick access to the Phare de la Garoupe trail. **Taxis** usually are waiting in front of the train station.

To **walk** to the port, the old town, and the Picasso Museum (15–20-minute walk), cross the street in front of the station, skirting left of the Piranha Café, and follow avenue de la Libération downhill as it bends left. At the end of the street, the port will be in front of you and the old town to the right.

To walk directly to my recommended hotels and to the main TI (15-minute walk to TI), cross the street to the Piranha Café, turn right, and stay the course for about eight blocks on avenue Robert Soleau until you reach the fountain-soaked place Général de Gaulle.

The last train back to Nice leaves at about midnight.

By Bus: Slow bus #200 stops a few blocks from the TI (turn right as you leave the TI to find the stops just off boulevard Dugommier: buses from Nice and to Cannes stop on avenue Aristide Briand—second shelter down; buses to Nice and from Cannes stop on boulevard Gustave Chancel). The airport bus (#250) drops you behind the train station (see "Helpful Hints," later). Buses from other destinations use the **bus station** at the edge of the old town on place Guynemer, a block below the main TI on place Général de Gaulle (info desk open Mon–Sat 7:30–19:00, closed Sun, www.envibus.fr).

By Car: Day-trippers follow signs to *Centre-Ville*, then *Port Vauban*, and park near the old town walls (first 30 minutes free, then about €2.50/hour). Walk into the old town through the last arch on the right.

If you're sleeping here, follow *Centre-Ville* signs, then signs to your hotel, and get advice from your hotelier on where to park. (Most hotels have free parking.) The most appealing hotels in

Antibes are easiest by car. Antibes works well for drivers; compared to Nice, parking is easy, it's a breeze to navigate, and it's a convenient springboard for the Inland Riviera. Pay parking is usually available at Antibes' train station, so drivers can ditch their cars here and day-trip from Antibes by train.

Helpful Hints

Monday, Monday: Avoid Antibes on Mondays, when all sights are closed.

Internet Access: Centrally located **l'Outil du Web** is two blocks from place Général de Gaulle TI—walk toward the train station (Mon–Fri 9:30–18:00, Sat 9:30–13:00, closed Sun, 11 avenue Robert Soleau, tel. 04 93 74 11 86).

English Bookstore: Heidi's English Bookshop has a welcoming vibe and a great selection of new and used books, with many guidebooks—including mine (Mon–Fri 10:00–19:00, Sat–Sun 11:00–18:00, 24 rue Aubernon).

Laundry: Smiling **Madame Hallepau** will do your laundry while you swim. Her launderette is above the market hall on rue de la Pompe (Mon–Fri 8:30–12:00 & 15:00–18:30, closed Sat–Sun).

Grocery Store: Picnickers will appreciate Casino's **Epicerie de la Place market** (daily until 22:00 in summer, until 21:00 off-season, where rue Sade meets place Nationale).

Bike and Scooter Rental: Centrally located **CityZen Bikes** rents scooters and bikes—electric or pedal (clever name, near the main TI at 22 boulevard Dugommier, tel. 04 93 74 56 46, www.cityzenbikes.fr). The TI can give you more bike-rental options. See "Walks and Hikes" on page 779 for possible biking destinations.

Taxi: For a taxi, call 08 25 56 07 07 or 04 93 67 67 67.

Car Rental: The big-name agencies have offices in Antibes. The most central are **Avis** (32 boulevard Albert 1er, tel. 04 93 34 65 15) and **Hertz** (across from the train station at 52 avenue Robert Soleau, tel. 04 93 61 18 15). **Europcar** is less central, at 106 route de Grasse (tel. 04 93 34 79 79). These offices are closed Mon–Sat 12:00–14:00 and Sundays.

Boat Rental: You can motor your own seven-person yacht thanks to **Antibes Bateaux Services** (€300/half-day, at the small fish market on the port, mobile 06 15 75 44 36, www.antibes-bateaux.com).

Airport Bus: Bus #250 runs from near the train station to Nice's airport (€8, 2/hour, 40 minutes; cross over the tracks on the pedestrian bridge—it's the last shelter to the right, stop from the airport is labeled *Vautrin*, stop going to the airport is labeled *Passerelle*).

Antibes

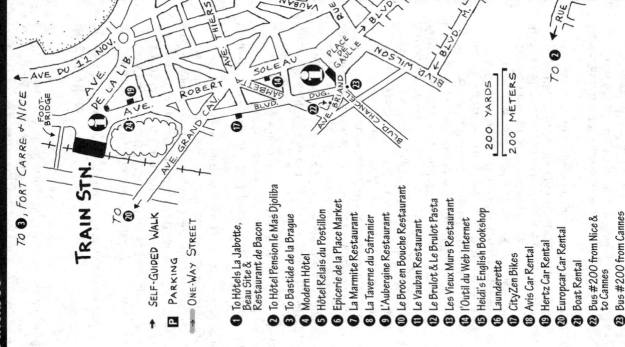

TO ❸, FORT CARRÉ & NICE

TRAIN STN.

↑ SELF-GUIDED WALK

P PARKING

↑ ONE-WAY STREET

1. To Hôtels La Jabotte, Beau Site & Restaurant de Bacon
2. To Hôtel Pension le Mas Djoliba
3. To Bastide de la Brague
4. Modern Hôtel
5. Hôtel Relais du Postillon
6. Epicerie de la Place Market
7. La Marmite Restaurant
8. La Taverne du Safranier
9. L'Aubergine Restaurant
10. Le Broc en Bouche Restaurant
11. Le Vauban Restaurant
12. Le Brulot & Le Brulot Pasta
13. Les Vieux Murs Restaurant
14. l'Outil du Web Internet
15. Heidi's English Bookshop
16. Launderette
17. CityZen Bikes
18. Avis Car Rental
19. Hertz Car Rental
20. Europcar Car Rental
21. Boat Rental
22. Bus #200 from Nice & to Cannes
23. Bus #200 from Cannes
24. Bus #14 Stop

THE FRENCH RIVIERA

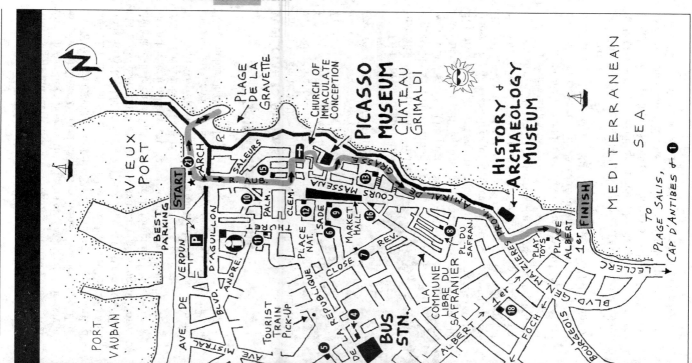

Getting Around Antibes

Most sights and activities are walkable, but buses are a great value in Antibes, allowing three hours of travel for €1 (one-way or round-trip). **Bus #2** provides access to the best beaches, the path to La Phare de la Garoupe, and the Cap d'Antibes trail (all described later). It runs from the bus station down boulevard Albert 1er, with stops every few blocks (daily 7:00–19:00, every 40 minutes). **Bus #14** is also useful, linking the train station, bus station, old town, and plage de la Salis. Pick up a schedule for return times for these and other regional buses at the bus station (for more on buses, see "Arrival in Antibes," earlier).

A **tourist train** offers circuits around old Antibes, the port, the ramparts, and to Juan-les-Pins (€7, departs from place de la Poste, mobile 06 03 35 61 35).

Self-Guided Walk

Welcome to Antibes

This 40-minute walk will help you get your bearings, and works well day or night.

• *Begin at the old port (Vieux Port) at the southern end of avenue de Verdun. Stand across from the archway with the clock (parking right there).*

Old Port: Locals claim that this is Europe's first and biggest pleasure-boat harbor, with 1,600 stalls. The port was enlarged in the 1970s to accommodate ever-expanding yacht dimensions. The work was financed by wealthy yacht owners (mostly Saudi Arabian) eager for a place to park their aircraft carriers. That old four-pointed structure crowning the opposite end of the port is **Fort Carré,** which protected Antibes from foreigners for more than 500 years. (For information on visiting the fort, see "Sights in Antibes," later.)

The pathetic remains of a once-hearty **fishing fleet** are moored in front of you. The Mediterranean is pretty much fished out. Most of the seafood you'll eat here comes from fish farms or the Atlantic.

Pass the sorry fleet and find the entry to the shell-shaped **plage de la Gravette,** a normally quiet public beach tucked right in the middle of old Antibes. Wander up the ramp to the round lookout to better appreciate the scale of the ramparts that protected this town. Because Antibes was the last fort before the Italian border, the French king made sure the ramparts were top-notch. Those twin towers crowning the old town are the church's bell tower and the tower topping Château Grimaldi (today's Picasso Museum). Forested Cap d'Antibes is the point of land in the distance to the left.

Backtrack and enter Antibes' **old town** through the arch under the rampart. Today, the town is the haunt of a large community of English, Irish, and Aussie boaters who help crew those giant yachts in Antibes' port. (That helps explain the Irish pubs and English bookstores.)

Continue straight and uphill (halfway up on the right, you'll pass rue Clemenceau, which leads to the heart of the old town), and you'll arrive at Antibes' **market hall** (Tue–Sun until 13:00, closed Mon except June–Aug). This hall does double duty—market by day, restaurants by night (a fun place for dinner).

Go left where the market starts (rue Chessel) and find Antibes' pretty pastel **Church of the Immaculate Conception,** built on the site of a Greek temple (worth a peek inside). A church has stood on this site since the 12th century. This one served as the area's cathedral until the mid-1200s.

Looming above the church on prime real estate is the white-stone **Château Grimaldi,** where you'll find Antibes' prized **Picasso Museum** (described later). This site has been home to the acropolis of the Greek city of Antipolis, a Roman fort, and a medieval bishop's palace (once connected to the cathedral below). Later still, the château was the residence of the Grimaldi family (who still rule Monaco). Its proximity to the cathedral symbolized the sometimes too-cozy relationship between society's two dominant landowning classes: the Church and the nobility. (In 1789, the French Revolution changed all that.)

Find your way to the water and—heading right—follow the ramparts and views to the **History and Archaeology Museum.** From the terrace above the museum, you'll get a clear view of **Cap d'Antibes,** crowned by its lighthouse and studded with mansions (a good place for a hike, described under "Walks and Hikes," later). The Cap was long the refuge of Antibes' rich and famous, and a favorite haunt of F. Scott Fitzgerald and Ernest Hemingway.

After taking a quick spin through the museum, continue hugging the shore past place Albert 1er until you see the views back to old Antibes. Benches and soft sand await (a few copies of famous artists' paintings of Antibes are placed on bronze displays along the beach walkway). You're on your own from here—energetic walkers can continue to the view from the Phare de la Garoupe (see page 780); others can return to old Antibes and poke around in its peaceful back lanes.

Sights in Antibes

▲▲**Picasso Museum (Musée Picasso)**—Sitting serenely where the old town meets the sea, this compact three-floor museum offers art-lovers a manageable collection of Picasso's paintings, sketches, and ceramics. Picasso lived in this castle for four months in 1946, when he cranked out an amazing amount of art. Elated by the end of World War II, his works show a celebration of color and a rediscovery of light after France's long nightmare of war. Picasso was also reenergized by his young and lovely companion, Françoise Gilot (with whom he

would father two children). The resulting collection (donated by Picasso) put Antibes on the tourist map. You'll see many of his ceramics: plates with faces, bird-shaped vases, woman-shaped bottles, bull-shaped statues, and colorful tiles. But the highlight is his lively, frolicking, and big-breasted *La Joie de Vivre* painting (from 1946). This Greek bacchanal sums up the newfound freedom in a newly liberated France and sets the tone for the rest of the collection. You'll also see the colorless three-paneled *Satyr, Faun and Centaur with Trident*. Find a room filled with ink sketches labeled *Figures Feminines* that challenge the imagination—these show off Picasso's skill as a cartoonist and caricaturist. Then look for the Basque fishermen and several Cubist-style nudes (*nus couchés*), one painted on plywood—Picasso loved experimenting with materials and different surfaces (I particularly like the crayon sketches).

Cost and Hours: €6; mid-June–mid-Sept Tue–Sun 10:00–18:00, July–Aug Wed and Fri until 20:00; mid-Sept–mid-June Tue–Sun 10:00–12:00 & 14:00–18:00; closed Mon year-round, last entry 30 minutes before closing, tel. 04 92 90 54 20, www.antibes-juanlespins.com/eng/culture/musees.

History and Archaeology Museum (Musée d'Histoire et d'Archéologie)—More than 2,000 years ago, Antibes was the center of a thriving maritime culture. It was an important Roman city with aqueducts, theaters, baths, and so on. This museum—the only place to get a sense of the city's ancient roots—displays Greek, Roman, and Etruscan odds and ends in two easy-to-visit halls (no English descriptions, though the small museum brochure offers some background in English). Your visit starts at an 1894 model of Antibes and continues past displays of Roman coins, cups, plates, and scads of amphorae. The lanky lead pipe connected to a center box was used as a bilge pump; nearby is a good display of Roman anchors (€3, Tue–Sun 10:00–13:00 & 14:00–17:00, closed Mon, on the water between Picasso Museum and place Albert 1er, tel. 04 93 34 00 39.

▲**Market Hall (Marché Provençal)**—The daily market bustles under a 19th-century canopy, with flowers, produce, Provençal products, and beach accessories (in the old town, behind Picasso Museum on cours Masséna). The market wears many hats: produce daily until 13:00, handicrafts Thursday through Sunday in the afternoon, and fun outdoor dining in the evenings (market closed Mon Sept–May).

Other Markets and Squares—Antibes' lively antiques/flea market fills place Nationale and place Audiberti (next to the port) on Thursdays and Saturdays (7:00–18:00). Its clothing market winds through the streets around the post office (rue Lacan) on Thursdays (9:00–18:00). Place Général de Gaulle, a pleasing, palm-studded, and fountain-flowing square in Antibes' modern city, is the trendy place to be seen.

Fort Carré—This impressively situated citadel, dating from 1487, was the last fort inside France. It protected Antibes from Nice, which until 1860 was part of Italy. You can tour this unusual four-pointed fort for the fantastic views over Antibes, but there's little to see inside (€3, includes tour in French, Tue–Sun June–Sept 10:00–18:00, Oct–May 10:00–16:30, closed Mon, 30-minute walk from Antibes along avenue 11 Novembre, easy parking nearby).

▲**Beaches (Plages)**—The best beaches stretch between Antibes' port and Cap d'Antibes. The first you'll cross is the plage Publique (no rentals required). Next are the groomed plages de la Salis and du Ponteil, with mattress, umbrella, and towel rental. All are busy but manageable in summer and on weekends, with cheap snack stands and exceptional views of the old town. The closest beach to the old town is at the port (plage

de la Gravette), which seems calm in any season.

Walks and Hikes

From place Albert 1er (where boulevard Albert 1er meets the beach), you get a good view of plage de la Salis and Cap d'Antibes. That tower on the hill is your destination for the first walk I describe. The longer "Cap d'Antibes Hike" begins on the next beach, just over that hill. The two hikes are easy to combine by bus, bike, or car.

▲▲Chapelle et Phare de la Garoupe—The territorial views—best in the morning, skippable if hazy—from this viewpoint merit more than merit the 20-minute uphill climb from the plage de la Salis (a few blocks after Maupassant Apartments, where the road curves left, follow signs and the rough, cobbled chemin du Calvaire up to lighthouse tower). An orientation table explains that you can see from Nice to Cannes and up to the Alps. Take buses #2 or #14 to the plage de la Salis stop and find the trail a block ahead. By car or bike, follow signs for *Cap d'Antibes*, then look for *Chapelle et Phare de la Garoupe* signs.

▲Cap d'Antibes Hike (Sentier Touristique Piétonnier de Tirepoil)—At the end of the mattress-ridden plage de la Garoupe (over the hill from Phare de la Garoupe lighthouse) lies a terrific trail around the tip of Cap d'Antibes. The beautiful path undulates above a splintered coastline splashed by turquoise water and peppered with exclusive mansions. You'll walk for two miles, then head inland

along small streets, ending at the recommended Hôtel Beau-Site (and bus stop). You can walk as far as you'd like and then double back, or do the whole loop (allow 2.5 hours at most, use the TI's Antibes map). Bring good shoes, as the walkway is uneven and slippery in places. Sundays are busiest.

To get to the trail from Antibes, take bus #2 (catch it at the bus station, along boulevard Albert 1er, or at plage de la Salis) for about 15 minutes to the La Fontaine stop at Hôtel Beau-Site (return stop is 50 yards away on opposite side, get return times at station). Walk 10 minutes down to plage de la Garoupe and start from there.

By car or bike, follow signs to *Cap d'Antibes*, then *plage de la Garoupe*, and park there.

The trail begins at the far-right end of plage de la Garoupe.

Near Antibes

Juan-les-Pins—This village, across the Cap d'Antibes isthmus from Antibes, is where the action is...after hours. It's a modern seaside resort with good beaches, plenty of lively bars and restaurants, and a popular jazz festival in July. Buses, trains, and even a tourist train (see "Getting Around Antibes," earlier) make the 10-minute trip to and from Antibes constantly.

Sleeping in Antibes

(€1 = about $1.25, country code: 33)

My favorite Antibes hotels are best by car or taxi, though walkers and bus users can manage as well. Pickings are slim when it comes to centrally located hotels in this city, where restaurants are a dime a dozen but hotels play hard to get. Air-conditioning is rare.

Outside the Town Center

$$$ Hôtel la Jabotte, hidden along an ignored alley a block from the famous beaches and a 15-minute walk from the old town, is a cozy place that defies the rules. Yves, Claude, and dog Tommy have turned a small beach villa into a boutique hotel with personality: The colors are rich, the decor shows a personal touch, and most rooms have individual terraces facing a small, central garden where you'll get to know your neighbor. Rooms are not air-conditioned, but fans are provided (Db-€115–130, includes good breakfast and a few parking spots, Wi-Fi, 13 avenue Max Maurey, take the third right after passing the big Hôtel Josse, tel. 04 93 61 45 89, fax 04 93 61 07 04, www.jabotte.com, info@jabotte.com).

$$$ Hôtel Pension le Mas Djoliba* is a fair splurge that's better for drivers but also workable for walkers (10-minute walk from plage de la Salis, 15 minutes to old Antibes, and 30 minutes to the train station). Reserve early for this traditional, bird-chirping, flower-filled manor house where no two rooms are the same. From May to September, they definitely prefer (but won't insist) that you dine here. It's hard to pass up once you see the setting: After a busy day of sightseeing, dinner by the pool is a treat. The cuisine is average but copious. Some rooms are small, but the bigger rooms are well worth the additional cost and several come with small decks (Sb-€130, Db-€120–200, several good family rooms-€200–280, figure €100–115/person with breakfast and dinner; air-con, Wi-Fi, cool *boules* court and loaner balls, avenue de Provence; from boulevard Albert 1er, look for gray signs as you approach the beach and turn right up avenue Gaston Bourgeois; tel. 04 93 34 02 48, fax 04 93 34 05 81, www.hotel-djoliba.com, contact@hotel-djoliba.com).

$$ Hôtel Beau Site*** is my only listing on Cap d'Antibes, a 10-minute drive from the old town. It's a terrific value if you want to get away...but not *too* far away. (But if you don't have a car, you may feel isolated.) This place is a sanctuary, with sweet Nathalie in charge, a pool, a comfy patio garden, and free parking. Rooms are spacious and comfortable, and several have balconies (standard Db-€90, bigger Db-€125, even bigger Db-€160, family rooms-€175–230, extra bed-€25; huge breakfast-€13, continental breakfast-€7.50, air-con, Wi-Fi, bikes available, 141 boulevard Kennedy, tel. 04 93 61 53 43, fax 04 93 67 78 16, www.hotelbeausite.net, hbeausit@club-internet.fr). From the hotel, it's a 10-minute walk down to the plage de la Garoupe and a nearby hiking trail (see "Walks and Hikes," earlier).

$$ Bastide de la Brague is an easygoing seven-room bed-and-breakfast hacienda up a dirt road above Marineland (10-minute drive east of Antibes). It's run by a fun-loving family (wife Isabelle, who speaks English, hubby Franck, and Mama). Rooms are quite comfortable, air-conditioned, and affordable; several are made for families. Request the tasty €22 home-cooked dinner (includes apéritif, wine, and coffee) and enjoy a family dining experience. There's enough space to stretch out, and they adore kids (Db-€80–100, Tb/Qb-€100–120, includes breakfast, free Wi-Fi and computer with printer for guests, 55 avenue No. 6, Antibes 06600, tel. 04 93 65 73 78, www.bbchambreantibes.com, bastidebb06@gmail .com). Franck is happy to take guests on a private boat tour of the coast (allow €40/person for all afternoon, 4-person minimum). From Antibes, follow signs that read *Nice par Bord de la Mer*, turn left toward Brague and Marineland, then right at the roundabout (toward Groules), then take the first left and follow signs. Antibes bus #10 drops you five minutes away, and the Biot train station and bus #200 are a 15-minute walk (ask for details when you book). If you arrange it in advance, they'll pick you up at the train station in Antibes or Biot.

In the Town Center

$$ Modern Hôtel**, in the pedestrian zone near the bus station, is a solid value for budget-conscious travelers. The 17 standard-size rooms—each with air-conditioning, bright decor, and Wi-Fi—are simple, spick-and-span, and well-run by Laurence (Sb-€60–70, Db-€68–88, 1 rue Fourmillière, tel. 04 92 90 59 05, fax 04 92 90 59 06, www.modernhotel06.com, modern-hotel@wanadoo.fr).

$$ Hôtel Relais du Postillon** is a mellow place on a central square above a peaceful café. There are a few cheap true singles and 12 well-designed doubles with small balconies, but no air-conditioning (Sb-€50, Db-€69–98, price varies by room size, most have tight bathrooms, Wi-Fi, 8 rue Championnet, tel. 04 93 34 20 77, fax 04 93 34 61 24, www.relaisdupostillon.com, relais@relais dupostillon.com).

Eating in Antibes

Antibes is a fun place to dine out. You can eat on a budget, enjoy a fine meal at an acceptable price, or join the party just inside the walls on boulevard d'Aguillon, on place Nationale, or—my favorite—under the festive Marché Provençal (all are filled with tables and tourists). The options are endless. Take a walk and judge for yourself, and be tempted by these suggestions. Romantics should picnic at the beach (the **Epicerie de la Place market** is open late; see "Helpful Hints" on page 773). Everyone should stroll along the ramparts after dinner.

La Marmite owner Patrick offers diners an honest, unpretentious budget value in old Antibes, with eight tables, helpful service, and delicious seafood choices but no air-conditioning (*menus* from €16, closed Mon, 20 rue James Close, tel. 04 93 34 56 79).

La Taverne du Safranier, hiding in a small square a block from the sea, feels right out of a movie. It's a cheery place away from the rest, where you'll order from colorful chalkboard menus and dine under grapevines and happy lights (seafood is their forte, €11 pasta, €14-24 *plats*, €28 three-course *menu*, closed Mon, place du Safranier, tel. 04 93 34 80 50).

L'Aubergine delivers fine cuisine at fair prices—including good vegetarian options—served with no hurry in an intimate room rich with color. Arrive early to get a table (€32 bouillabaisse, *menus* from €23, opens at 18:30, closed Wed, 7 rue Sade, tel. 04 93 34 55 93).

Le Broc en Bouche is part cozy wine bar, part bistro, and part collector's shop. Come early to get a seat at this cool little place and enjoy well-prepared dishes from a selective list (€23 *plats*, closed Tue-Wed, 8 rue des Palmiers, tel. 04 93 34 75 60).

Le Vauban is run by a young couple who draw a local following with their handsome interior, smart tableware, and reliable cuisine at fair prices (€29 three-course *menu*, closed Tue, opposite 4 rue Thuret, tel. 04 93 34 33 05).

Le Brulot is an Antibes institution with two restaurants— Le Brulot and Le Brulot Pasta—that sit almost side-by-side a short block below Marché Provençal on rue Frédéric Isnard. Join Antibes residents at the very popular **Le Brulot,** known for its Provençal cuisine and meats cooked on an open fire. It's a small place, overflowing onto the street, with a few outside tables and a dining room below. Try the aioli (€19 *menus*, closed Sun, at #2, tel. 04 93 34 17 76). **Le Brulot Pasta** is family-friendly and goes Italian with excellent pizza (the €11 *printanière* is tasty and huge) and big portions of pasta, served in air-conditioned comfort under stone arches (daily, at #3, tel. 04 93 34 19 19).

Les Vieux Murs is a romantic splurge with a candlelit, red-toned interior overlooking the sea. The outside tables are worth booking ahead—but pass on the upstairs room (€46 dinner *menu*, €30 lunch *menu*, open daily June-mid-Sept, closed Mon off-season, valet parking available, along ramparts beyond Picasso Museum at 25 promenade de l'Amiral de Grasse, tel. 04 93 34 06 73).

Restaurant de Bacon is often picked as Antibes' best restaurant, thanks to its top-notch bouillabaisse and views of Antibes.

Located on Cap d'Antibes, past the plage de la Salis, it's simple from the outside (no sign), but lovely on the inside, and made for seafood-lovers (*menus* from €50, allow €70 for bouillabaisse, closed Mon–Tue and Oct–Feb, boulevard de Bacon, tel. 04 93 61 50 02).

Antibes Connections

From Antibes by Train: TGV and local trains serve Antibes' little station. Trains go to **Cannes** (2/hour, 15 minutes), **Nice** (2/hour, 15–30 minutes, €4), **Grasse** (1/hour, 40 minutes), **Villefranche-sur-Mer** (2/hour, 40 minutes), **Monaco** (2/hour, 45–60 minutes), and **Marseille** (16/day, 2.5 hours).

By Bus: Handy bus #200 ties everything together, but runs at a snail's pace when traffic is bad (Mon–Sat 4/hour, Sun 2–3/hour, any ride costs €1). This bus goes west to **Cannes** (35 minutes) and east to **Nice** (1–1.5 hours). Bus #250 links to **Nice Airport** (2/hour, 40 minutes).

Inland Riviera

For a verdant, rocky, fresh escape from the beaches, head inland and upward. Some of France's most perfectly perched hill towns and splendid scenery hang overlooked in this region that's more famous for beaches and bikinis. Driving is the easiest way to get around, though the bus gets you to many of the places described. Vence and St-Paul-de-Vence are well-served by bus from Nice every 40 minutes (see "Getting Around the Riviera" on page 704).

Vence

Vence is a well-discovered yet appealing town set high above the Riviera. While growth has sprawled beyond Vence's old walls, and cars jam its roundabouts, the mountains are front and center and the breeze is fresh. Vence bubbles with workaday life and ample tourist activity in the day but is quiet at night, with few tourists and cooler temperatures than along the coast. Vence makes a handy base for travelers wanting the best of both worlds: a hill-town refuge near the sea.

Orientation to Vence

Tourist Information

Vence's fully loaded and eager-to-help TI faces the main square at 8 place du Grand Jardin. They have bus schedules, brochures on the cathedral, and a city map with a well-devised self-guided walking tour (25 stops), incorporates informative wall plaques). They also publish a list of Vence art galleries with English descriptions of the collections. To properly engage you in French culture, the TI has information on French-language classes, and—even better—*pétanque* instructions with *boules* to rent for €3 per person (TI open July-Aug Mon-Sat 9:00-19:00, Sun 10:00-18:00; Sept-June Mon-Sat 9:00-18:00 but 10:00-17:00 in winter, Sun 10:00-17:00; tel. 04 93 58 06 38, www.ville-vence.fr).

Market day in the *cité historique* (old town) is on Tuesday and Friday mornings on place Clemenceau. There's a big all-day antiques market on place du Grand Jardin every Wednesday.

Arrival in Vence

By Bus: The bus stop (labeled *l'Ara*) is on a roundabout. It's a 10-minute walk to the town center along avenue Henri Isnard.

By Car: Follow signs to *cité historique*, and park where you can. A central pay lot is under place du Grand Jardin, across from the TI.

Sights in Vence

Explore the narrow lanes of the old town using the TI's worth-while self-guided tour map. Connect the picturesque streets, enjoy a drink on a quiet square, inspect an art gallery, and find the small 11th-century cathedral with its colorful Chagall mosaic of Moses. If you're here later in the day, enjoy the *boules* action across from the TI (rent a set from the TI and join in).

Château de Villeneuve—This 17th-century mansion, adjoining an imposing 12th-century watchtower, bills itself as "one of the Riviera's high temples of modern art," with a rotating collection. Check with the TI to see what's playing in the temple (€5, Tue-Sun 10:00-12:30 & 14:00-18:00, closed Mon, tel. 04 93 58 15 78).

▲**Chapel of the Rosary (Chapelle du Rosaire)**—The chapel, a short drive or 20-minute walk from town, was designed by an elderly and ailing Henri Matisse as thanks to the Dominican sister who had taken care of him (he was 81 when the chapel was completed). The modest chapel is a simple collection of white walls laced with yellow, green, and blue stained-glass windows and charcoal black-on-white tile sketches. The sunlight filters through the glass and does

a cheery dance across the sketches. And though the chapel is the ultimate pilgrimage for serious Matisse fans, the experience may underwhelm others. (If you've visited the Matisse Museum in Nice, you'll remember that he was the master of leaving things out.) Decide for yourself whether Matisse met the goal he set himself: "Creating a religious space in an enclosed area of reduced proportions and to give it, solely by the play of colors and lines, the dimension of infinity."

Cost and Hours: €3; Mon, Wed, and Sat 14:00–17:30; Tue and Thu 10:00–11:30 & 14:00–17:30, Sun only open for Mass at 10:00 followed by tour of chapel, closed Fri and mid-Nov–mid-Dec, 466 avenue Henri Matisse, tel. 04 93 58 03 26, http://pagesperso-orange.fr/maison.lacordaire.

Getting There: To reach the chapel from the Vence TI, turn right out of the TI and walk or drive down avenue Henri Isnard, then right on avenue Henri Matisse, following signs to *St-Jeannet* (allow 20 minutes).

Sleeping in Vence

(€1 = about $1.25, country code: 33)

Hôtel Miramar is a 10-minute walk above the old town. La Maison du Frêne and L'Auberge des Seigneurs are a short walk from the TI, next to the Château de Villeneuve; to reach them, turn right out of the TI, then right again, then left. Maison Lacordaire is next to Matisse's chapel, a 20-minute walk from the TI.

$$$ La Maison du Frêne is an art-packed B&B with four sumptuous rooms located behind the TI. Energetic Thierry combines his passion for contemporary art and hosting travelers in his lovingly restored manor house (Db–€150–185, higher price is for peak times, includes breakfast, air-con, Wi-Fi, 1 place du Frêne, tel. 04 93 24 37 83, www.lamaisondufrene.com, contact@lamaison dufrene.com).

$$ Hôtel Miramar*** is a laid-back, 18-room Mediterranean villa perched on a ledge with grand panoramas. Friendly owner Daniel welcomes you into this refuge, which he's filled with many personal touches. The Old World rooms come in soothing colors, with firm beds and worn furnishings. The pool and view terrace could make you late for dinner, or seduce you into skipping it altogether—picnics are allowed (standard Db–€90–125, Db with balcony–€120–135, Db with great view and balcony–€160, family suite–€185, some rooms have air-con, most don't need it, bar, table tennis, parking, turn left out of the TI and follow the brown signs to 167 avenue Bougearel, tel. 04 93 58 01 32, fax 04 93 58 20 22, www.hotel-miramar-vence.com, contact@hotel-miramar-vence.com).

\$\$ L'Auberge des Seigneurs** is a shy little place just inside the old town. Its six simple yet character-filled rooms—above a cozy restaurant—have wood furnishings, red-tile floors, and adequate bathrooms (spacious Sb–€65, Db–€85-100, place du Frêne, tel. 04 93 58 04 24, fax 04 93 24 08 01, www.auberge-seigneurs.com, sandrine.rodi@wanadoo.fr).

\$\$ Maison Lacordaire, adjacent to Matisse's Chapel of the Rosary, lets you sleep like a nun. This simple place has 24 rooms in 2 restored villas, with a sweet garden and view terrace. It's run by Dominican nuns, so be on your best behavior (Db–€43/person for required half-board, 466 avenue Henri Matisse, tel. 04 93 58 03 26, http://pagesperso-orange.fr/maison.lacordaire, dominicaines @wanadoo.fr).

Eating in Vence

Tempting outdoor eateries litter the old town; they all look good to me. Lights embedded in the old-town cobbles illuminate the way after dark.

On place Clemenceau: These two restaurants serve tasty Provençal cuisine a few doors apart on the charming place Clemenceau: **La Cassolette,** at #10, is an intimate place with reasonable prices and a romantic terrace across from the floodlit church (€28 *menus,* €14-17 *plats,* closed Thu, tel. 04 93 58 84 15). **Les Agapes,** at #4, offers limited outdoor seating, a lovely upstairs dining room, and a menu that stays fresh with each season (€24 and €30 *menus,* closed Sun–Mon, tel. 04 93 58 50 64).

At nearby **La Peyra,** relax with a dinner salad or pasta dish outdoors to the sound of the town's main fountain (€15 "maxi salads" and *plats,* daily, 13 place du Peyra, tel. 04 93 58 67 63).

L'Auberge des Seigneurs feels more alpine than Mediterranean, and is good for a cooler day, when you can sit by the fire and watch your meat being cooked. The choices are limited and filling. Sandrine will help you decide (*menus* from €32, closed Sun–Mon; also recommended under "Sleeping in Vence," earlier).

Near Vence

St-Paul-de-Vence

The most famous of Riviera hill towns is also the most-visited village in France. And it feels that way—like an overrun and over-restored artist-shopping-mall. Its attraction is understandable, as every cobble and flower seems *just-so*, and the setting is memorable. Avoid visiting between 11:00 and 18:00, particularly on weekends. Arriving early makes it easier to park near the village (cars are not allowed inside St-Paul). Consider skipping breakfast at your hotel and instead eating at the local hangout, **Café de la Place,** where you can watch as waves of tourists crash into town.

The **TI,** just through the gate into the old city on rue Grande, has maps with minimal explanations of key buildings (daily 10:00–18:00, tel. 04 93 32 86 95, www.saint-pauldevence.com). If the traffic-free lane leading to the old city is jammed, take the road that veers up and left just after Café de la Place, and enter the town through its side door. Meander deep into St-Paul-de-Vence's quieter streets to find panoramic views. See if you can locate the hill town of Vence at the foot of an impressive mountain.

▲**Fondation Maeght**—This inviting, pricey, and far-out private museum is situated a steep walk or short drive above St-Paul-de-Vence. Fondation Maeght (fohn-dah-shown mahg) offers an excellent introduction to modern Mediterranean art by gathering many of the Riviera's most famous artists under one roof. The founder, Aimé Maeght, long envisioned the perfect exhibition space for the artists he supported and befriended as an art dealer. He purchased this arid hilltop, planted more than 35,000 plants, and hired an architect (José Luis Sert) with the same vision.

A sweeping lawn laced with amusing sculptures and bending pine trees greets visitors. On the right, a chapel designed by Georges Braque—in memory of the Maeghts' young son, who died of leukemia—features a moving purple stained-glass work over the altar. The unusual museum building is purposefully low-profile, to let its world-class modern-art collection take center stage. Works by Fernand Léger, Joan Miró, Alexander Calder, Georges Braque, and Marc Chagall are thoughtfully arranged in well-lit rooms. The backyard of the museum has views, a Gaudí-esque sculpture labyrinth by Miró, and a courtyard filled with the wispy works of Alberto Giacometti. The only permanent collection in the museum consists of the sculptures, though the museum tries to keep a good selection of paintings by the famous artists here year-round. For a review of modern art, see "The Riviera's Art Scene" on page 705. There's also a great gift shop and cafeteria.

Cost and Hours: €14, €5 to take photos, daily July–Sept 10:00–19:00, Oct–June 10:00–18:00, tel. 04 93 32 81 63, www.fondation-maeght.com.

Getting There: The museum is a steep uphill-but-doable 20-minute walk from St-Paul-de-Vence and the bus stop. Blue signs indicate the way (parking is usually available at the top).

La Route Napoléon: North to the Alps

After getting bored in his toy Elba empire, Napoleon gathered his entourage, landed on the Riviera, bared his breast, and told his fellow Frenchmen, "Strike me down or follow me." France followed. But just in case, he took the high road, returning to Paris along the route known today as La Route Napoléon. (Waterloo followed shortly afterward.)

By Car: The route between the Riviera and the Alps is beautiful (from south to north, follow signs: Digne, Sisteron, and Grenoble). An assortment of pleasant villages with inexpensive hotels lies along this route, making an overnight easy. Little Entrevaux feels forgotten and still stuck in its medieval shell. Cross the bridge, meet someone friendly, and consider the steep hike up to the citadel (€3, TI tel. 04 93 05 46 73). Sisteron's Romanesque church and view from the citadel above make this town worth a quick leg-stretch.

By Narrow-Gauge Train (Chemins de Fer de Provence): Leave the tourists behind and take your kids (or just yourselves) on the scenic train-bus-train combination that runs between Nice and Digne through canyons, along whitewater rivers, and through many tempting villages (Nice to Digne: 4/day, 3.5 hours, about €19, 25 percent discount with railpass, departs Nice from the South Station—Gare du Sud—about 10 blocks behind the main train station, two blocks from the Libération tram stop, 4 rue Alfred Binet, tel. 04 97 03 80 80, www.trainprovence.com).

Start with an 8:50 departure and go as far as you want. Little **Entrevaux** is a good destination that feels forgotten and still stuck in its medieval shell (1.5 scenic hours from Nice, about €10). Climb high to the citadel for great views.

The train ends in **Digne-les-Bains,** where you can catch a main-line train (covered by railpasses) to other destinations—or better, continue scenically to **Annecy** following this plan (assuming you've taken the 8:50 train from Nice): take the bus (quick transfer if you get the 8:50 train from Nice, free with railpass) to **Veynes** (4/day, 1.5 hours). From there you can catch the most scenic two-car train to **Grenoble** (5/day, 2 hours), then take a train to Annecy (arriving about 18:50).

To do the entire trip from Nice to Annecy in one day, you must start with the 8:50 departure, but I'd rather spend a night in one of the tiny villages en route. **$ Hôtel Beauséjour*** in little Annot, about two hours from Nice, makes a great reasonable get-away (Db–€55–65, tel. 04 92 83 21 08, www.francebeausejour.com). Farther along, in remote Clelles, you'll find the **$ Hôtel Ferrat****, a basic family-run mountain hacienda at the base of Mont Aiguille, with a swimming pool and a good restaurant (Db–€56–65, tel. 04 76 34 42 70, fax 04 76 34 47 47, hotel.ferrat@wanadoo.fr).

THE FRENCH ALPS

Annecy • Chamonix

The Savoie region grows Europe's highest mountains and is the top floor of the French Alps (the lower Alpes-Dauphiné lie to the south). More than just a pretty-peaked face, stubborn Savoie maintained its independence from France until 1860, when mountains became targets, rather than obstacles, for travelers. Savoie's borders once extended south to the Riviera and far west across the Rhône River Valley. Home to skier Jean-Claude Killy and the first winter Olympics (1924 in Chamonix), today's Savoie is France's mountain-sports capital, featuring 15,771-foot Mont Blanc as its centerpiece. With wood chalets overflowing with geraniums and cheese fondue in every restaurant, Savoie feels more Swiss than French.

The scenery is drop-dead spectacular. Serenely self-confident Annecy is a postcard-perfect blend of natural and man-made beauty. In Chamonix, it's just you and Madame Nature—there's not a museum or important building in sight. If the weather's right, take Europe's ultimate cable-car ride to the 12,600-foot Aiguille du Midi in Chamonix.

Planning Your Time

Lakefront Annecy has boats, bikes, and hikes with mountain views for all tastes and abilities. Its trademark arcaded walking streets and good transportation connections (most trains to Chamonix pass through Annecy) make it a convenient stopover, but if you're pressed for time and antsy for Alps, get your sled to Chamonix. There you can skip along alpine ridges, glide over mountain meadows, zip down the mountain on a luge (wheeled bobsled), or meander along riverside paths on a mountain bike. Plan a minimum

The French Alps

of two nights and one day in Chamonix, and try to work in a night in Annecy. Because weather is everything in this area, get the forecast by calling Chamonix's TI (tel. 04 50 53 00 24) or the weather-report line (in English, dial from anywhere in France, tel. 08 92 68 02 74). If it looks good, make haste to Chamonix; if it's gloomy, Annecy offers more distraction. (If you're driving or taking the train from here to the Riviera, see tips in "La Route Napoléon: North to the Alps" on page 789.) Both towns are mobbed with tourists in summer.

The Alps have twin peaks: the summer and winter seasons, when hotels and trails or slopes are slammed. June and November are dead-quiet in Chamonix (many hotels and restaurants close) as locals recover from one high season and prepare for the next.

Getting Around the Alps

Annecy and Chamonix are well-connected by trains. Buses run from Chamonix to nearby villages, and the Aiguille du Midi lift takes travelers from Chamonix to Italy over Europe's most scenic border crossing.

Savoie's Cuisine Scene

Savoie cuisine is mountain-hearty. Its Swiss-similar specialties include *fondue savoyarde* (melted Beaufort and Comté cheeses and local white wine, sometimes with a dash of Cognac), raclette (chunks of semi-melted cheese served with potatoes, pickles, sausage, and bread), *tartiflettes* (hearty scalloped potatoes with melted cheese), *poulet de Bresse* (the best chicken in France), *Morteau* (smoked pork sausage), *gratin savoyard* (a potato dish with cream, cheese, and garlic), and fresh fish. Local cheeses are Morbier (look for a charcoal streak down the middle), Comté (like Gruyère), Beaufort (aged for two years, hard and strong), Reblochon (mild and creamy), and Tomme de Savoie (mild and semi-hard). Evian water comes from Savoie, as does Chartreuse liqueur. Apremont and Crépy are two of the area's surprisingly good white wines. The local beer, Baton de Feu, is more robust than other French beers.

Remember, restaurants serve only during lunch (11:30–14:00) and dinner (19:00–21:00, later in bigger cities); some cafés serve food throughout the day.

Annecy

There's something for everyone in this lakefront city that knows how to be popular: mountain views, flowery lanes, romantic canals, a hovering château, and swimming in—or boating on, or biking around—the translucent lake. Sophisticated yet outdoors-oriented and bike-crazy, Annecy (ahn-see) is France's answer to Switzerland's Luzern, and, though you may not have glaciers knocking at your door as in nearby Chamonix, the distant peaks paint

a darn pretty picture with Annecy's lakefront setting. Annecy has a few museums, but none worth your time: You're here to enjoy its stunning setting and outdoor sights. Annecy is also fun during the winter holidays, as Christmas markets and festive decorations animate the city throughout December. But the buzz is all about Annecy's bid to host the 2018 Winter Olympics. The host city will be selected on July 6, 2011.

Orientation to Annecy

Modern Annecy (pop. 50,000) sprawls for miles, but we're interested only in its compact old town, hunkered down on the northwest corner of the lake. The old town is split by the Thiou River and bounded by the château to the south, the TI and rue Royale to the north, rue de la Gare to the west, and the lake to the east.

Tourist Information

The TI is a few blocks from the old town, across from the big grass field, inside the brown-and-glass Bonlieu shopping center (mid-May–mid-Sept daily 9:00–18:30 except closed Sun 12:30–13:45; mid-Sept–mid-May Mon–Sat 9:00–12:30 & 13:45–18:00, Sun 10:00–13:00 except closed Sun mid-Nov–March, 1 rue Jean Jaurès, tel. 04 50 45 00 33, www.lac-annecy.com). Get a city map, the *Town Walks* walking-tour brochure (describes four mildly interesting walks), the map of the lake showing the bike trail, and, if you're staying a few days, the helpful *Annecy Guide*, with everything a traveler needs to know. Ask about walking tours in English (€6, July–Aug only, normally Tue and Fri at 16:00). You'll also find TIs in most villages on the lake.

Arrival in Annecy

By Train: To reach the old town and TI, leave the station, veer left at street level, and cross the big road to the pinkish Hôtel des Alpes. Continue a few blocks down rue de la Poste, then turn left on rue Royale for the TI and some hotels, or continue straight to more recommended hotels. There is no baggage storage in Annecy, but day-trippers who rent bikes can leave their bags at the Roul' ma Poule bike-rental shop while they ride (see listing under "Helpful Hints," later).

By Car: Annecy is a traffic mess; in high season (July–Aug), try to arrive very early, during lunch, or late. Avoid most of the snarls by taking the Annecy Sud exit (#16) from the autoroute and following *Annecy/Albertville* signs. Upon entering Annecy, follow signs to *Le Lac*, and when you reach the lake, turn left at the roundabout for the city center. (Don't follow signs for *Annecy-le-Vieux*, which is another town entirely.)

Refer to the map on page 796 to find these pay parking lots: You can park right on the lake with the buses opposite the boat dock at Parking Stade Nautique (few spaces for cars, but this might be your lucky day), or follow signs to the big underground Parking du Château (under the Hôpital-Clinique), where you should find a spot. There are also handy lots near the train station. If you're staying at a hotel in town, you can park overnight for free at a public lot—but only if you ask at your hotel. If you're staying at the Hôtel du Château or Maison d'Hôtes Les Jardins du Château, see the parking tips on page 801.

Helpful Hints

Market Days: The biggest market in Annecy is on Saturday, with food, clothes, and crafts (until 12.30), around boulevard Taine—several blocks behind the TI). A thriving outdoor food market occupies much of the old town center on Tuesday, Friday, and Sunday mornings until about 12.30.

Department Store: The Monoprix is at the corner of rue du Lac and rue Notre-Dame (Mon–Sat 8:30–19:50, closed Sun, supermarket upstairs).

Internet Access: Planete Telcom is near the TI with long hours, lots of services (including fax), and helpful staff (daily 9:30–20:20, 4 rue Jean Jaurès, tel. 04 40 33 92 60).

Laundry: The launderette is at the western edge of the old town near where rue de la Gare meets rue Ste. Claire (daily 7:00–21:00, 6 rue de la Gare).

Bike Rental: Across from the lake steamers, **Roul' ma Poule** rents all kinds of bikes—standard, tandem, and electric—and is near the lakefront bike path (€11/half-day, €16/day, includes helmet and basket, leave ID as deposit, mid-May–mid-Oct daily 9:00–12:00 & 13:30–19:00, closed mid-Oct–mid-May, 4 rue Marquisats, tel. & fax 04 50 27 86 83, www.annecy-location-velo.com, helpful owner Stefan). You can also rent a bike at **Veloncey** at the train station (€10/half-day, €15/day; less for students, seniors, and train travelers; includes helmet and basket, requires credit-card deposit, Mon–Sat 9:00–12:00 & 13:00–18:30, closed Sun, tel. 04 50 51 38 90).

Bad Weather: If it's raining, consider a day trip to Lyon (7 trains/day, 2 hours; see Lyon chapter). The last train back to Annecy usually leaves Lyon at about 20:00, allowing a full day in the big city.

Sights in Annecy

Strolling—Most of the old city is wonderfully traffic-free. The river, canals, and arcaded streets are made for ambling. The TI's *Town Walks* brochure describes Annecy with basic historical information. Get lost—the water is your boundary. Surrender to the luscious ice-cream shops and waterfront cafés.

Museum of Annecy (Palais de l'Isle)—This serenely situated 13th-century building cuts like the prow of a ship through the heart of the Thiou River. Once a prison, it held French Resistance fighters during World War II. Today it's a boring museum that holds rotating exhibits and a small section on local architecture

Annecy

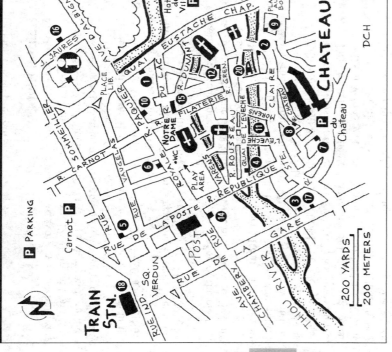

(€4, June–Sept Wed–Mon 10:30–18:00, Oct–May Wed–Mon 10:00–12:00 & 14:00–18:00, closed Tue, free English leaflet).

Château Museum (Musée-Château d'Annecy)—The castle was built in the late 1100s by aristocrats from nearby Geneva, and cuts an impressive figure as it hangs above the lake in the old city. But inside the château has little to offer. Many rooms house modern-art collections that rotate regularly, with a few rooms devoted to local folklore, anthropology, and natural history. Skip it (€5, same hours as Museum of Annecy).

▲**Boating**—This is one of Europe's cleanest, clearest lakes, and the water is warmer than you'd think (average summer water temperature is 72 degrees Fahrenheit). To tool around the lake, rent a paddleboat (*pédalos*), some equipped with a slide, about €10/30 minutes, €14/hour) or a motorboat (*bors-bord*, no license needed, for 2 people about €28/30 minutes, €46/hour, each extra person about €1, up to 7 people, several companies all have the same rates). Traditional open-air wood-hulled motorboats offer 35-minute

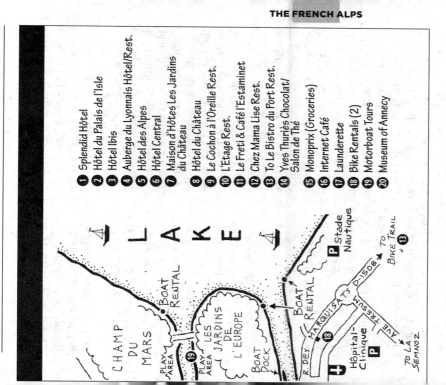

1 Splendid Hôtel
2 Hôtel du Palais de l'Isle
3 Hôtel Ibis
4 Auberge du Lyonnais Hôtel/Rest.
5 Hôtel des Alpes
6 Hôtel Central
7 Maison d'Hôtes Les Jardins du Château
8 Hôtel du Château
9 Le Cochon à l'Oreille Rest.
10 L'Etage Rest.
11 Le Freti & Café l'Estaminet
12 Chez Mama Lise Rest.
13 To Le Bistro du Port Rest.
14 Yves Thuriès Chocolat/ Salon de Thé
15 Monoprix (Groceries)
16 Internet Café
17 Launderette
18 Bike Rentals (2)
19 Motorboat Tours
20 Museum of Annecy

loops around the lake (€9, up to about 10 people per boat).

Compagnie des Bateaux du Lac d'Annecy offers worthwhile lake cruises. The one-hour cruise makes no stops but has frequent departures (€13, 8–10/day May–Aug, 6–8/day April and Sept). The two-hour cruises, called Circuit Omnibus, make stops at several villages on a clockwise loop around the lake (€16 for the entire loop, 3–5/day); these are ideal for hikers and cyclists (see next two listings). The elaborate dinner (€50–75) and dancing cruises look like fun. Get schedules and prices for all boat trips at the TI or on the lake behind Hôtel de Ville (tel. 04 50 51 08 40, www.annecy-croisieres.com).

Scenic Walks—Get details on these walks from the TI. For a picturesque workout and a rewarding full-day excursion, take the 10:30 Omnibus boat to Menthon–St. Bernard (€5.30), hike 2.5 hours to lovely Talloires, then catch the boat back to Annecy (€9). From the boat dock in Menthon–St. Bernard, walk to the right along the shore toward the large palace, and follow the signposts for *Roc de Chère*. The path leads up and over the Roc, passing the Golf de Talloires. The last stretch into Talloires is a steep drop—wear good shoes. Cross Talloires to the port and beach (swim and lunch there), then catch the 15:00 boat back to Annecy to arrive at about 16:15 (the last boat for Annecy from Talloires leaves at 17:30).

For an easy lakeside amble, take the Omnibus boat to Duingt (about €9, 1.25 hours), then take the one-hour walk to St. Jorioz and return by boat to Annecy from there. The walk is mostly along a lakefront path called the *sentier Roselières*. To reach the path from Duingt's boat dock, follow the *piste cyclable* (bike path) to the right from the dock through the village, cross the main road, and find the foot trail near the lake. In St. Jorioz, catch the next boat back to Annecy (€5.50, 30 minutes). The 14:15 departure from Annecy leaves you in Duingt at 15:30, with 2.75 hours before the 18:15 boat from St. Jorioz back to Annecy (the first boat from Annecy gives you 4 hours for your walk to St. Jorioz).

▲▲**Biking**—Annecy was made for biking; it's an ain't-it-great-to-be-alive way to poke around the lake and test waterfront cafés and grassy parks. A popular bike trail runs along the west side of the lake (look for the green bike icon on white signs); it's smart to wear sunglasses and bring water. Even a short ride on the bike path is worth the effort. Ride as far as your legs take you, break for a lakefront café, then return to Annecy (the path is best after the town of Sévrier, where it leaves the roadside).

The small village of Duingt is seven level miles away and makes a terrific destination. Steady pedalers make it in 45 minutes; smell-the-roses cyclists need at least an hour. You can ride to Duingt and take the Omnibus boat back to Annecy (€7, 3 departures per day from Duingt; normally at 11:45, 15:30, and 18:00; more in summer, verify at boat dock or TI, bikes allowed).

To get to Duingt, leave Annecy on the main road toward Albertville (D-1508). Don't worry—you'll join the bike trail before long. Once the painted bike lane ends, you'll see a sign for the trail (*piste cyclable*) to the left. Follow it to Duingt (to reach the boat dock, exit the trail just before the tunnel for Duingt, ride down to the main road and turn right, then find the small, green boat-dock shelter just after the castle). The trail beyond Duingt is beautiful. Hardy cyclists can make it all the way around the lake in about three hours (no bike path on opposite side of lake, just narrow roads, with one good hill). The bike path leaves the lake at its southern end and continues south for another seven miles, paralleling D-1508.

This route also works well in reverse: Take the Omnibus boat to Duingt and pedal back (turn right when you get off the boat and join the bike trail behind Duingt's tall church).

Driving Around the Lake—The road that links villages along the lake (D-1508) is busy, with little reward for drivers. However, it does lead to a scenic route to Chamonix and to fantastic mountaintop views (described next).

Nearby Views—Several routes lead to remarkable views of this beautiful area. Go early for clearest skies, and skip it if it's hazy. For lovely mountain panoramas near Annecy that include Mont Blanc, take the summer-only bus or drive up...and up...and up to **Le Semnoz** (about 5,000 feet). Here you'll find cafés, a summer luge, and easy mountain walks (one leads to a cheese farm). Ligne d'été buses to Le Semnoz leave from the Annecy train station (6/day, 40 minutes, daily July-Aug, Sat-Sun only in June, none Sept-May, the TI has details). To drive, follow D-41 from near the Hôpital-Clinique parking lot and allow 25 minutes (see map on page 796).

For drop-dead gorgeous views that take in the entire lake, drive 18 miles from Annecy (allow 45 minutes one-way) to **Col de la Forclaz**. Start by taking D-1508 south along the lake past Duingt. A few miles after leaving the lake, turn left on D-42 (signed *Col de la Forclaz*), then wind your way up a narrow, windy lane for five miles past meadows and lovely scenery to the Col de la Forclaz (3,600 feet). Watch for cyclists on this climb. At the top you'll find a sensational viewpoint, cafés and restaurants, and paragliders galore. Several outfits offer a chance to jump off a cliff and sail over the lake, including the appropriately named Adrenaline Parapente (www.annecy-parapente.com). This trip ties in very well with the scenic route to Chamonix via D-1508.

Sleeping in Annecy

Annecy is popular, particularly on weekends and during the summer. Hotel rates drop from about mid-October through late April and generally increase in summer. Most hotels can help you find free overnight parking (in lots, usually after 19:00 until 9:00 in the morning). Unless otherwise noted, these hotels do not have elevators. For more hotel listings, try the site for Annecy's TI: www.lac-annecy.com.

In the Town Center

This part of town is pedestrian-friendly and comes with some noise.

$$$ Splendid Hôtel*** makes an impression with its grand facade. This business hotel offers every comfort, and sits on Annecy's busiest street across from the park and the TI. Rooms are handsome and well-appointed (Db-€125-138, suites-€165, extra person-€15, breakfast buffet-€14, air-con, elevators, big beds, free

Sleep Code

(€1 = about $1.25, country code: 33)

S = Single, **D** = Double/Twin, **T** = Triple, **Q** = Quad, **b** = bathroom, **s** = shower only, * = French hotel rating system (0–4 stars). Unless otherwise noted, credit cards are accepted and English is spoken.

To help you sort easily through these listings, I've divided the rooms into three categories based on the price for a standard double room with bath:

$$$ **Higher Priced**—Most rooms €95 or more.
$$ **Moderately Priced**—Most rooms between €70–95.
$ **Lower Priced**—Most rooms €70 or less.

Prices can change without notice; verify the hotel's current rates online or by email. For other updates, see www.ricksteves.com/update.

Internet access and Wi-Fi, bar, terrace, 4 quai Eustache Chappuis, tel. 04 50 45 20 00, fax 04 50 45 52 23, www.splendidhotel.fr, info@splendidhotel.fr).

$$$ Hôtel du Palais de l'Isle*** offers a romantic and pricey canalside location in the thick of the old town, and 33 contemporary and well-maintained rooms—several with canal or rooftop views, all with minibars. The wine bar/TV room doubles as a nice lounge (Sb-€107–130, Db-€118–140, magnificent suites-€220–280, air-con, elevator, Internet access and Wi-Fi, 13 rue Perrière, tel. 04 50 45 86 87, fax 04 50 51 87 15, www.hoteldupalaisdelisle.com, palisle@wanadoo.fr).

$$ Hôtel Ibis** is a cheery place and a good option in Annecy, with narrow rooms, a canalside lounge, and easy underground parking. It's well-situated on a modern courtyard on the edge of the old town, a few blocks from the train station (Sb/Db-€92, extra bed-€10, buffet breakfast-€8, air-con, elevator, free Internet access and Wi-Fi, 12 rue de la Gare, tel. 04 50 45 43 21, fax 04 50 52 81 08, www.ibishotel.com, H0538@accor.com).

$$ Auberge du Lyonnais** has 10 good-value, alpine-decorated rooms that play second fiddle to its bustling restaurant (recommended under "Eating in Annecy," later). It's as central as you can get, with adequately comfortable rooms—the rooms on the canal are worth the few extra euros (Db-€68, canalside Db-€78, big Tb or Qb with deck over canal-€125, 9 rue de la République, walk through the restaurant to the small reception, tel. 04 50 51 26 10, fax 04 50 51 05 04, www.auberge-du-lyonnais.com).

$$ Hôtel des Alpes, a top value, has 32 immaculate, comfortable, and attractive rooms at a busy intersection just across from the train station. Rooms on the courtyard are quieter but darker; those on the street have effective double-pane windows (Sb-€58–65, Db-€70–90, Tb-€85–96, Qb-€98–108, free Wi-Fi, 12 rue de la Poste, tel. 04 50 45 04 56, fax 04 50 45 12 38, www .hotelannecy.com, info@hotelannecy.com).

$ Hôtel Central* is just that. This modest and homey place, behind an ivy-covered courtyard and dirty stairway off a big pedestrian street, makes a good, bare-bones budget option (D-€44, Db-€56, Tb-€64, Qb-€77, breakfast-€6, Wi-Fi, 6 bis rue Royale, tel. 04 50 45 05 37, fax 04 50 51 80 19, www.hotelcentralannecy .com, contact@hotelcentralannecy.com).

At the Foot of the Château

These places are in a quiet area on rampe du Château. Drivers can pull up to the barrier at the Parking du Château, press the little button, and tell whoever answers that you are a hotel guest. They will raise the bar to let you drive in (staffed 24/7).

At **$$ Maison d'Hôtes Les Jardins du Château**, welcoming Anne-Marie and Jean-Paul have created Annecy's highest urban refuge (near the château entry). Their chalet *chambre d'hôte* comes with a small garden and eight modern yet comfy rooms, all with kitchenettes and some with views and balconies. Jean-Paul doubles as a mountain guide and offers a wealth of information (small Db-€70, bigger Db-€90–140—most about €90, good family rooms-€82–124, includes breakfast except Nov–March when rooms are cheaper, cash only, no refunds, Wi-Fi, bike rental, 1 place du Château, tel. 04 50 45 72 28, http://annecy-chambre -dhote.monsite.wanadoo.fr, jardinduchateau@wanadoo.fr).

$ Hôtel du Château*, an unpretentious place barely below the château, comes with a view terrace and 15 simple, spotless rooms; about half have views. It's first-come, first-get for the precious few free parking spots (Db-€60–70, Tb-€70–77, Qb-€80–88, breakfast-€7, Internet access and Wi-Fi, 16 rampe du Château, tel. 04 50 45 27 66, fax 04 50 52 75 26, www.annecy-hotel.com, hotel duchateau@noos.fr).

Eating in Annecy

Although the touristy old city is well-stocked with forgettable restaurants, I've found a few worthy places. And though you'll pay more to eat with views of the river or canal, the experience is uniquely Annecy. The ubiquitous and sumptuous *gelati* shops remind you how close Italy is. If it's sunny, assemble a gourmet picnic at the arcaded stores and dine lakeside. Annecy's coolest café tables hang opposite the entrance to the Palais de l'Isle Museum.

Le Cochon à l'Oreille ("The Pig's Ear") is a meat-lover's nirvana. Just off the Thiou canal, it welcomes you with a leafy courtyard and a raucous, higgledy-piggledy interior. Amicable owners "Fred" and Jean speak enough English (and fluent pig) and are serious about their cooking. The accent is on fresh products and meat dishes (particularly ham and pork). Melted cheese is not their thing (€18 *menu* changes weekly, open daily for lunch and dinner, quai du Perriere, tel. 04 50 45 92 51).

L'Etage is a good choice if you can't decide what you want. Regional specialties and a good range of standard brasserie fare are served at fair prices. Dine along the pedestrian street terrace or upstairs under wood beams around a big fireplace (€14 fondue, €18 three-course *menus*, open daily, 13 rue du Paquier, tel. 04 50 51 03 28).

Le Freti, with a lighthearted waitstaff, is the most reliable restaurant for local cuisine I've found in Annecy. It's *the* place to go for mouthwatering fondue, raclette, or anything with cheese. Each booth comes with its own outlet for melting raclette (€12–14 fondue, good salads and onion soup and cheap wine, open daily; walk through door at 12 rue Ste. Claire, it's upstairs; tel. 04 50 51 29 52).

If Le Freti sounds too cheesy, go next door to **Café l'Estaminet** for some pub grub. You'll get salads, omelets, pasta, mussels, fries, and more for fair prices. A sliver of a backyard deck hangs over the river (open daily in summer, closed Sun off-season, 8 rue Ste. Claire, tel. 04 50 45 88 83).

Chez Mama Lise is like eating in an alpine folk museum, with stuffed mountain animals, rusted tools, tourists, and knick-knacks everywhere. The cuisine—fondue, raclette, and other cheese dishes—is as alpine as the decor (€20 three-course *menu*, open daily, 11 rue Grenette, tel. 04 50 45 41 18).

Auberge du Lyonnais is a classy, well-respected riverfront eatery that specializes in seafood (indoor and outdoor seating). The outgoing owners love Americans; ask Dominique about his many trips to the States, and about his Ford pickup (€26–44 *menus*, cheaper on weeknights, open daily, 9 rue de la République, tel. 04 50 51 26 10).

Many cafés and restaurants ring Annecy's postcard-perfect lake. If you have a car and want views, prowl the many lakefront villages. **Le Bistro du Port**, a nautical place five minutes from Annecy by car, is beautifully situated at the boat dock at the southern end of Sévrier (€12 salads, €17–24 *plats*, open daily, Port de Sévrier, tel. 04 50 52 45 00).

Dessert: Wherever you eat, don't miss an ice-cream-licking stroll along the lake after dark. But if it's chocolate you crave, head for **Yves Thuriès Chocolat/Salon de Thé,** where you'll be warmly welcomed. You won't be disappointed (closed Sun, 13 rue Royale, tel. 04 50 52 28 58).

Annecy Connections

From Annecy by Train to: Chamonix (8/day, 2.5 hours, change in St. Gervais), **Lyon** (7/day, 2 hours, most change in Aix-les-Bains, some by bus), **Beaune** (7/day, 4–6 hours, change in Lyon), **Nice** (8/day, 7–9 hours, at least 3 changes), **Paris'** Gare de Lyon (13/day, 4–5 hours, many with change in Lyon).

Chamonix

Bullied by snow-dipped peaks, churning with mountain lifts, and littered with hiking trails, the resort of Chamonix (shah-moh-nee) is France's best base for alpine exploration. Officially called Chamonix–Mont Blanc, it's the largest of five villages at the base of Mont Blanc, with about 8,000 residents. Chamonix's purpose in life has always been to accommodate visitors with some of Europe's top alpine thrills—it's slammed from early July through mid-August

and on winter holidays, but it's plenty peaceful at other times. Appropriately, Chamonix's sister city is Aspen, Colorado.

Planning Your Time

Summers bring huge crowds and long lift lines. You won't regret planning your trip to avoid the summer school break (*vacances scolaires*), usually early July to late August. Ride the lifts early (crowds and clouds roll in later in the morning) and save your afternoons for lower altitudes. If you have one sunny day, spend it this way: Start with the Aiguille du Midi lift (go early, reservations possible and recommended July–Aug), take it all the way to Helbronner (linger around the rock needle longer if you can't get to Helbronner), double back to Plan de l'Aiguille, hike to Montenvers and the Mer de Glace (only with good shoes and snow level permitting), explore there, then take the train down. End your day with a well-deserved drink at a view café in Chamonix. If the weather disappoints or the snow line's too low, hike the Petit Balcon Sud or Arve River trails.

Orientation to Chamonix

Eternally white Mont Blanc is Chamonix's southeastern limit; the Aiguilles Rouges mountains form the northwestern border. The frothy Arve River splits linear Chamonix in two. The thriving pedestrian zone, just west of the river along rues du Docteur Paccard and Joseph Vallot, is Chamonix's core. The TI is just above the pedestrian zone, and the train station is two long blocks east of the river. To get your bearings, head to the TI and find the big photo in front. With Switzerland and Italy as next-door neighbors, this town has always drawn an international crowd. Today about 50 percent of its foreign visitors are British—many have stayed and found jobs in hotels and restaurants.

Tourist Information

Visit the TI to prepare your attack. Get the weather forecast, pick up the free town and valley map and the "panorama" map of all the valley lifts, and consider the €4 hiking map called *Carte des Sentiers* (see "Chamonix Area Hikes" on page 814). Ask about hours of lifts and trains (critical), the Multipass for lifts (described under "Getting Around (and Up and Down) the Valley" on page 806), biking information, and help with hotel reservations. Their helpful website has updated sightseeing info, weather forecasts, and more (July–Aug daily 9:00–19:00; Sept–June Mon–Sat 9:00–12:30 & 14:00–18:30, Sun 9:00–12:00; hours may vary—call ahead, tel. 04 50 53 00 24, fax 04 50 53 58 90, www.chamonix .com, info@chamonix.com). Pull up a beachy sling chair outside the TI and plan your hike, or check your email using their 24-hour Wi-Fi (free outside access plus small cubicles inside to hole up in).

Arrival in Chamonix

By Train: Walk straight out of the station (no baggage check or WCs available) and up avenue Michel Croz. In three blocks, you'll reach the town center; turn left at the big clock, then right for the TI.

By Bus: The long-distance bus station is at the train station.

By Car: For most of my recommended hotels and the TI, take the Chamonix Nord turnoff—coming from Annecy, it's the second exit after you pass under the Aiguille du Midi cable car—and follow signs to *Centre-Ville*. Most parking is metered and well-signed, though your hotel can direct you to free parking.

The Mont Blanc tunnel (7.2 miles long, about a 12-minute drive) allows quick access between Chamonix and Italy (one-way-€37, round-trip-€46 with return valid for 1 week, about €400 if you're driving a truck, www.tunnelmb.com).

Chamonix: A Quick History

1786 Jacques Balmat and Michel-Gabriel Paccard are the first to climb Mont Blanc (find the statue in Chamonix's pedestrian zone).

1818 First ascent of Aiguille du Midi.

1860 The Savoie region (including Chamonix) becomes part of France. After a visit by Napoleon III, the trickle of nature-loving visitors to Chamonix turns to a gush.

1901 Train service reaches Chamonix, unleashing its tourist appeal forever.

1908 The cogwheel train to Montenvers is completed.

1924 First Winter Olympics held in Chamonix.

1930 Le Brévent *téléphérique* (gondola lift) opens to tourists.

1955 Aiguille du Midi *téléphérique* opens to tourists.

2011 You visit Chamonix.

By Plane: The nearest international airports are in Lyon (linked by 10 trains/day, 4 hours; 3 hours by car) and in Geneva, Switzerland (hourly trains, 3.5 hours; 3/day, 2 hours by shuttle van—see "Chamonix Connections" on page 831; 1.5 hours by car).

Helpful Hints

Crowd-Beating Tips: In high season, take the first lift to beat the crowds and afternoon clouds. Consider breakfast at *le* top.

Plan Ahead: Snow abounds up high, making the glare unbearable, so bring your sunglasses. Be sure your camera has enough battery power and memory space for those perfect alpine shots. For Chamonix's weather, check at your hotel, the TI, or at www.chamonix.com. For a five-day weather forecast in English, call 08 92 68 02 74 from anywhere in France (there's a small charge). Check the Compagnie du Mont Blanc website (www.compagniedumontblanc.com) for current lift information and to book the Aiguille du Midi lift.

Open-Air Market: Chamonix's market is held Saturdays at place Mont Blanc.

Supermarkets: Little **Casino** markets are omnipresent in Chamonix, though the **Super U** market is big and central (Mon–Sat 8:15–19:30, Sun 8:30–12:00, rue Joseph Vallot). Supplement your run-of-the-mill groceries with gourmet local specialties from **Le Refuge Payot** (two locations: 166 rue Joseph Vallot and 255 rue du Docteur Paccard).

Inexpensive Mountain Gear: The best deals on sunglasses, day-packs, and the like are at **Technique Extrême** (204 avenue de l'Aiguille du Midi).

Internet Access: The TI has free Wi-Fi and a good list of Internet cafés. **Mojo's** has three terminals tucked in a small café selling good sandwiches, quiche, and wraps for fair prices with great view tables out front (daily, 31 place du Joseph Balmat, tel. 04 50 21 99 45).

English Books: A small collection is kept at **Maison de la Presse** (101 rue du Docteur Paccard).

Laundry: Laverie Alpina (look for *Pressing* sign) is in the rear of Galerie Commerciale shopping center (where avenue du Mont Blanc crosses the river). Marie-Paule will do your laundry for the cost of the washer and dryer (allow €9 for a load, leave a small tip and fold your clothes yourself, Mon-Sat 8:00–18:00, closed Sun, tel. 04 50 53 30 67). Another *laverie* is one block up from the Aiguille du Midi lift at 174 avenue de l'Aiguille du Midi (daily 9:00–20:00, instructions in English).

Taxis: There's usually one at the train station (tel. 04 50 53 13 94 or 06 07 26 36 62).

Car Rental: Europcar, the only game in town, is across from the train station and offers free airport pickup (36 place de la Gare, tel. 04 50 53 63 40).

Getting Around (and Up and Down) the Valley

Lifts and cogwheel trains are named for their highest destination (e.g., Aiguille du Midi, Montenvers, and Le Brévent). More details on individual lifts are described under "Sights in Chamonix," later. You can find current lift information and book the Aiguille du Midi lift on the Compagnie du Mont Blanc website (www .compagniedumontblanc.com).

By Lift: Gondolas *(téléphériques)* climb mountains all along the valley, but the best one—Aiguille du Midi—leaves from Chamonix. And though sightseeing is optimal from the Aiguille du Midi gondola, there are more hiking options from the Le Brévent and La Flégère gondolas.

The lift to Aiguille du Midi is open summer and winter (closures possible in May and late Oct–early Dec). The *télécabines* on the Panoramic Mont Blanc lift to Helbronner (Italy) run only from May to late September, and even then only in good weather (call the TI to confirm). Other area lifts are generally open from January to mid-April and from mid-June to late September. For all lifts, because maintenance closures can occur anytime, it's always smart to verify schedules at the TI.

The **Multipass** ticket option saves time and money for most

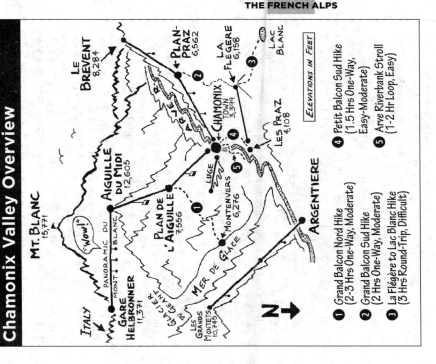

Chamonix Valley Overview

ELEVATIONS IN FEET

Mt. Blanc 15,771

"wow!"

Le Brevent 8,284

Aiguille du Midi 12,605

Panoramic du Mont Blanc

Gare Helbronner 11,371

Italy

Plan de l'Aiguille 7,556

Mer de Glace Glacier

Les Grands Montets 10,745

Plan-Praz 6,562

La Flégère 6,158

Lac Blanc

Chamonix Town 3,399

Luge

Montenvers 6,276

Les Praz 4,108

Argentière

N →

1 **Grand Balcon Nord Hike** (2-3 Hrs One-Way, Moderate)

2 **Grand Balcon Sud Hike** (2 Hrs One-Way, Moderate)

3 **La Flégère to Lac Blanc Hike** (3 Hrs Round-Trip, Difficult)

4 **Petit Balcon Sud Hike** (1.5 Hrs One-Way, Easy-Moderate)

5 **Arve Riverbank Stroll** (1-2 Hr Loop, Easy)

visitors, particularly if you're spending two or more days in the Chamonix valley. It allows unlimited access to all the lifts and trains (except the Helbronner gondola to Italy), and includes all reservation fees (both Aiguille du Midi and Montenvers) and the elevator at the top of the Aiguille du Midi. You also get discounts for various activities in Chamonix, such as the Parc de Loisirs des Planards.

Best of all, it allows you to bypass lift-ticket lines after your first purchase. Your pass is a "smart card," valid all day, that allows you to scan your way to the top, letting you ride lifts you'd otherwise skip—hop on a lift just to have a drink from a view café at the top (€51/1 day, €57/2 days, €72/3 days, €90/4 days, €97/5 days, available for up to 15 days; days are consecutive, though you can also buy a more expensive pass for nonconsecutive days; kids age 4-15 and adults over 64 pay about 20 percent less, kids under 4 may not be allowed, kids 16 and over pay adult fare,

Chamonix Activities at a Glance

▲▲▲**Aiguille du Midi Gondola** The valley's most spectacular and popular lift, taking you to magnificent views at 12,600 feet. From here you can ride the cute *télécabines* over the Alps to Italy and back, take Chamonix's greatest hike to the Mer de Glace (from the halfway-up stop at Plan de l'Aiguille), or just enjoy the views.

▲▲▲**Train to Montenvers** Cogwheel train to the Mer de Glace, an eight-mile-long glacier where you can walk inside the glacier, admire jagged mountain peaks, have lunch with a view (or sleep) at the Montenvers hotel, and hike to the Aiguille du Midi lift (though the hike is best done in the other direction).

▲▲▲**Le Brévent Gondola** Second-most-spectacular lift from Chamonix, allowing access to the mountain range on the opposite side of the valley from Mont Blanc. Get off halfway at the Planpraz station for the Grand Balcon Sud hike to the La Flégère lift, or go all the way to Le Brévent for sky-high views and a restaurant.

▲▲▲**La Flégère Lift** Starting point for hikes to Lac Blanc and to the Grand Balcon Sud trail back to Planpraz (on the Le Brévent gondola). Refuge-Hôtel La Flégère, at the station, offers drinks, snacks, and accommodations, all with a view (details under "Refuges and Refuge-Hotels near Chamonix," later).

Arve River Valley Stroll Several trails allow a level walk or bike ride in the woods between Chamonix and Les Praz. See paragliders make dramatic landings and enjoy mountain views outside Chamonix to the sound of the Arve River.

---

www.compagniedumontblanc.com). The one-day price is a good savings if you plan to ride round-trip from Chamonix to Aiguille du Midi and the train to Montenvers (and not hike between the two). Notice that a two-day pass costs only €6 more than a one-day pass.

Families can benefit from reduced fares by asking for family tickets (2 adults and 2 children age 15 and under).

By Foot: See "Chamonix Area Hikes" on page 814.

By Bike: The peaceful river valley trail is ideal for bikes (and pedestrians). The TI has a brochure showing bike-rental shops and the best biking routes.

By Bus or Train: One road and one scenic rail line lace together the valley's towns and lifts. To help reduce traffic and pollution, your hotel will give you a free Chamonix Guest Card good for free travel during your stay. The cards are valid on all Chamonix-area buses (except the night bus) and the scenic valley train between Serves and Vallorcine, and also give small discounts on a handful of area sights. This is a great value for those with time to explore the valley.

Local buses #1 and #2 run to valley villages (1–2/hour, main stops are 200 yards to the right when you leave the TI—past Hôtel Mont Blanc—look for the bus shelters, and on rue Joseph Vallot where it crosses avenue du Mont Blanc). Direction "Le Tour" on bus #1 and "Les Praz/Flégère" on bus #2 takes you toward Les Praz (for Hike #2) and Switzerland; direction "Les Houches" on bus #1 takes you in the opposite direction.

Le Mulet minibuses circulate around Chamonix village and are lifesavers for pooped hikers; they're especially handy to or from the Aiguille du Midi lift, which is a 15-minute walk from many hotels (free, runs every 10 minutes 8:30–18:30).

The train ride toward **Martigny** in Switzerland is gorgeous, and villages such as Les Praz and Tines (10 minutes by bus) offer quiet village escapes from busy Chamonix. The Chamonix Guest Card also gives small discounts at the Alpine Museum and the Espace Tairraz.

By Excursion Tour: British-run **Chamexcursions** offers trips in English to top area sights, including a half-day tour of Chamonix or the Parc de Merlet animal park, and day trips to Annecy or Geneva (€29–39/half-day, €49–79/day, tel. 04 50 54 73 72, http://chamexcursions.com).

Sights in Chamonix

▲▲▲Aiguille du Midi

This is easily the valley's (and, arguably, Europe's) most spectacular and popular lift. If the weather's clear, the price doesn't matter. Pile into the *téléphérique* (gondola) and soar to the tip of a rock needle 12,600 feet above sea level (you'll be packed into the gondola like sardines). Chamonix shrinks as trees fly by, soon replaced by whizzing rocks, ice, and snow. Change gondolas at plan de l'Aiguille to reach the top. No matter how sunny it is, it's cold and the air is thin. People are giddy with delight (those prone to altitude sickness or agoraphobia are less so). Fun things can happen at Aiguille du Midi (ay-gwee doo mee-dee) if you're not too winded to join the locals in the halfway-to-heaven tango.

From the top of the lift station, you have several options. Follow *ascenseur* signs through a tunnel, then ride the elevator through the rock to the summit of this pinnacle (€3 in high season, free off-season and when the *télécabines* to Helbronner are not

Over the Alps—France to Italy

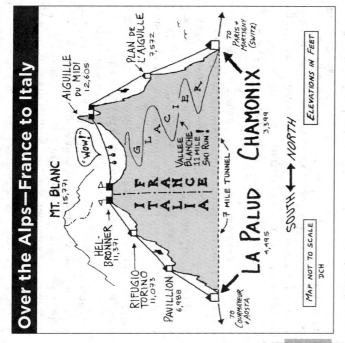

MT. BLANC
15,771

AIGUILLE
DU MIDI
12,605

PLAN DE
L'AIGUILLE
7,572

"Wow!"

GLACIER

VALLEE
BLANCHE
11 MILE
SKI RUN!

I F T R A N C E
I T A L I A

HEL-
BRONNER
11,371

RIFUGIO
TORINO
11,073

PAVILLON
6,988

TO
COURMAYEUR
& AOSTA

LA PALUD
4,495

7 MILE TUNNEL

CHAMONIX
3,399

TO
PARIS &
MARTIGNY
(SWITZ)

SOUTH ← → NORTH

MAP NOT TO SCALE

ELEVATIONS IN FEET

DCH

running). Missing the elevator is a kind of Alpus-Interruptus I'd rather not experience. The Alps spread out before you. Find the orientation posters to identify key peaks. If it's really clear, you can see the bent little Matterhorn—the tall, shady pyramid listed in French on the observation table as "Cervin—4,505 meters" (14,775 feet). And looming on the other side is **Mont Blanc**, the Alps' highest point, at 4,810 meters (15,771 feet). Use the telescopes to spot mountain climbers; more than 2,000 scale this mountain each year. That rusty tin-can needle above you serves as a communications tower. Check the temperature next to the elevator. Plan on 32 degrees Fahrenheit, even on a sunny day. Sunglasses are essential.

Back down, explore Europe's tallest lift station. More than 150 yards of tunnels (galeries) lead to various view terrasses, a cafeteria (fair prices—have lunch or coffee with a view), a restaurant (not such fair prices), toilets, a gift shop, and an icicle-covered gateway to the glacial world. A right turn out of the elevator leads you through a tunnel to Les Terraces, a small deck with more views.

Follow la Vallée Blanche signs to a drippy "ice tunnel" where skiers and mountain climbers make their exit. The views are sensational; merely observing is exhilarating. Peek down the icy cliff and ponder the value of an ice ax. Skiers make the 11-mile run to the Mer de Glace (described later) in about half a day (in winter they can ski 13 miles all the way back to the valley at Argentière).

The Belvedere Rébuffet walkway leads to bird's-eye views of the *télécabines* to Helbronner and to more amazing mountain views.

Go back through the tunnel to the main building, where gondolas return to Chamonix and climb metal stairs to more great view terraces, WCs, and the cafeteria/gift shop. Inside you'll see posters describing the 1950s construction of the lift station and the gondola line (the first cable was destroyed during construction by an avalanche). The photos are fascinating.

For your own private glacial dream world, get into the little red *télécabine* (called Panoramic Mont Blanc) and sail south to **Helbronner Point,** the Italian border station. This line stretches three miles with no solid pylon. (It's propped by a "suspended pylon," a line stretched between two peaks 1,300 feet from the Italian end.) In a gondola for four, you'll dangle silently for 40 minutes as you glide over glaciers and past a forest of peaks to Italy. Hang your head out the window and explore every corner of your view. From Helbronner Point, you can continue down into Italy (see "Day Trips near Chamonix" on page 823), but there's really no point unless you're traveling that way.

From Aiguille du Midi, you can ride all the way back to Chamonix; or—way, way better, get off halfway down at **Plan de l'Aiguille,** where you'll find a scenic café with sandwiches, drinks, and outdoor tables, paragliders jumping off cliffs (except in July–Aug), and hiking trails. But the best reason to get off here is to follow the wonderful trail to the Mer de Glace, then catch the train back into Chamonix (for details, see "Chamonix Area Hikes—Hike #1" on page 817).

Even if you don't do the hike, take a 15-minute walk below the lift station to the ignored and peaceful **Plan de l'Aiguille Refuge** for reasonable meals (good omelets) and drinks inside or out (open daily June–Sept, may be open off-season—ask, tel. 06 55 54 27 53). This makes an easy mini-hike for hurried travelers. The short but steep climb back up to the lift will be your exercise for the day.

Whatever you do, don't hike all the way down to Chamonix from Plan de l'Aiguille or Montenvers-Mer de Glace; it's a long, steep walk through thick forests with few views.

Hours: Lift hours are weather- and crowd-dependent, but lifts generally run daily July–Aug 6:00 or 7:00–16:30, late May–June and Sept 7:00 or 8:00–16:30, and Oct–late May 8:00–15:30. Gondolas run every 10 minutes during busy times; the last return from Aiguille du Midi is generally one hour after the last ascent. The last *télécabine* departure to Helbronner Point is about 14:00–15:00, and the last train down from Montenvers (for hikers) is about 17:00–18:00.

Strategy: To beat the hordes and clouds, ride the Aiguille du Midi lift (up and down) as early as you can. To beat major delays in summer, leave no later than 7:00 or reserve ahead (first lift departs at 6:00 or 7:00, easy to verify in advance). If the weather has been bad and turns good, expect big crowds in any season (even worse on weekends). If it's clear, don't dillydally.

In peak season, smart travelers reserve the Aiguille du Midi lift in advance (€2 fee). You can reserve at the information booth next to the lift (open mid-June–mid-Sept), online at www .compagniedumontblanc.com, or by phone (year-round, tel. 04 50 53 22 75, automated reservations in English). Reservations are taken up to 10 days in advance (6 days in winter); pick tickets up at the lift station at least 30 minutes before departure (the information booth at the Aiguille du Midi lift tells you which window to use). Reservations are free with a Multipass (described on page 807) and are not possible for the *télécabines* to Helbronner.

Costs: From Chamonix to: Plan de l'Aiguille—round-trip—€25 (one-way—€20), Aiguille du Midi—round-trip—€42 (one-way—€38, not including parachute); the Panoramic Mont Blanc *télécabine* to Helbronner—round-trip—€66 (one-way—€55). If you are planning to stop at Plan de l'Aiguille on the way back down and hike to Montenvers, ask about a "*spécial randonée*" ticket for about €39. Tickets just for the stretch from Aiguille du Midi to Helbronner are sold at both base and summit lift stations with no difference in price (round-trip—€21, one-way—€15). It's €29 to drop into Italy (sold at Helbronner). *Oui* and *si*, you can bring your luggage—but pack light.

Discounts: The prices listed above are for ages 16–60; kids age 4–11 are 30 percent less, and kids age 12–15 and adults over 60 are 15 percent less (family rates for 2 adults and 2 children age 15 and under are also available).

Time to Allow: Chamonix to Aiguille du Midi—20 minutes one-way, two hours round-trip, three to four hours in peak season; Chamonix to Helbronner—1.5 hours one-way, three to four hours round-trip, longer in peak season. On busy days, minimize delays by making a reservation for your return lift time upon arrival at the top. (For information on Aiguille du Midi, call 04 50 53 30 80.)

▲▲▲Mer de Glace (Montenvers)

From Gare de Montenvers (the little station over the tracks from Chamonix's main train station), the cute cogwheel Train du Montenvers toots you up to tiny Montenvers (mohn-tuh-vehr). There you'll see a dirty, rapidly receding glacier called the Mer de Glace (mayr duh glahs, "Sea of Ice") and fantastic views up the white valley (Vallée Blanche) of splintered, snow-capped peaks (2–3/hour, 20 minutes, round-trip—€25, one-way—€19, family rates available, prices include gondola and ice caves entry, daily 8:30–17:00, July–Aug 8:00–18:00, confirm times with TI or call 04 50 53 12 54).

Find the **view deck** across from the train station. France's largest glacier, at eight miles long, is impressive from above and below. The swirling glacier extends under the dirt about a half-mile downhill to the left. Imagine that it recently reached as high as the vegetation below (see the dirt cliffs—called moraines—left in its retreat). In 1860, this glacier stretched all the way down to the valley floor. They say this fast-moving glacier is just doing its cycle thing, growing and shrinking—a thousand years ago, cows grazed on grassy fields here. Al Gore thinks people are speeding up the process.

Use the **orientation table** as you look up to the peaks. **Monsieur Dru**'s powerful spire, at about 11,700 feet, makes an irresistible target for climbers. It was first scaled in 1860 (long before the train you took here was built) and was recently free-climbed (no ropes, belays, etc.); see the colored lines indicating different routes taken—one by an *Américain*. Those guys are nuts. The smooth snow field to the left of Dru's spire (Les Grands Montets) is the top of Chamonix's most challenging ski run, with a vertical drop of about 6,500 feet (down the opposite side).

The glacier's **ice caves** are beneath you. Take the small gondola down and prepare to walk 400 steps each way. (Several years ago, it was 280 steps; this glacier is beating a hasty retreat.) If you've already seen a glacier up close, you might skip this one, though I found it a relevant trip given the attention being paid to global warming (*le rechauffement climatique*). This is also where skiers end their run from the Aiguille du Midi (you might recognize someone if you rode that lift earlier). The path to the right (as you face the glacier) leads to a fine view café and a reconstruction of a crystal cave.

The **Refuge-Hôtel du Montenvers**, a few minutes walk toward Chamonix, offers a full-service restaurant, view tables (fair prices, limited selection), and a warm interior (for more on bunking here, see "Refuges and Refuge-Hotels near Chamonix," page 828). The five-room museum upstairs describes the history of the Montenvers train (no English but good exhibits). The hotel was built in 1880, when "tourists" arrived on foot or by mule.

The three-hour trail to **Plan de l'Aiguille** begins from above the hotel. For terrific views, hike toward Plan de l'Aiguille—via the trail that veers left—even just a short distance. The views get better fast, and the higher you climb, the better the view (follow signs on the stone building opposite the hotel; you want *sentier gauche* to *Signal Montenvers*). Bring a picnic and join the locals.

▲▲▲Gondola Lifts (Téléphériques) to Le Brévent and La Flégère

Though Aiguille du Midi gives a more spectacular ride, the Le Brévent and La Flégère lifts offer worthwhile hiking and viewing options, with unobstructed panoramas across to the Mont Blanc range. Le Brévent (luh bray-vahn) lift is in Chamonix; La Flégère (lah flay-zhair) lift is in nearby Les Praz (lay prah). The lifts are connected by a scenic hike or by bus along the valley floor (free with Chamonix Guest Card, see "Chamonix Area Hikes—Hike #2" on page 818); both have sensational view cafés.

Le Brévent lift is a steep 10-minute walk up the road above Chamonix's TI. It takes two lifts to reach **Le Brévent's** top. The first lift to Planpraz, with automated eight-person *télécabines*, runs every minute. Sit backward and watch Chamonix shrink below. Notice supports for the old lift, which recently was replaced with this *très moderne* one (round-trip to Planpraz-€14, one-way-€11, nice restaurant, great views and good hiking options, see "Chamonix Area Hikes—Hike #2" on page 818). The less impressive gondola to Le Brévent station needs a facelift. It leaves from Planpraz and runs less often (about 2-3/hour). At the top you get 360-degree views, more hikes, and a good view restaurant, but few visitor services. For most, Planpraz is high enough (round-trip to Le Brévent-€25, one-way from Chamonix-€19, mid-June–Sept and Nov-late April daily 9:00–16:00, July–Aug 8:00–17:00, last return from Planpraz one hour after last ascent, closed late April–mid-June and Oct, tel. 04 50 53 13 18).

La Flégère lift runs from the neighboring village of Les Praz, with just one stop at La Flégère station (round-trip-€14, one-way-€11, mid-June–mid-Sept and Nov-late April daily 8:40–16:00, summer 7:40–17:00, last return from La Flégère 50 minutes after last ascent, closed late April–mid-June and mid-Sept–Oct, tel. 04 50 53 22 08). Hikes to Planpraz and Lac Blanc leave from the top of this station (see Hikes #2 and #3 in the next section).

Chamonix Area Hikes

A good first stop is the full-service **Maison de la Montagne**, across from the TI. On the third floor, the **Office of the High Mountain** (Office de Haute-Montagne) can help you plan your hikes and tell you about trail and snow conditions (daily 9:00–12:00 & 15:00–18:00, tel. 04 50 53 22 08, www.ohm-chamonix.com). The staff speaks enough English and has vital weather reports and maps, as well as some English hiking guidebooks (you can photocopy key pages). Ask to look at the trail guidebook (sold in many stores and at the TI but not here, includes the helpful €4 *Carte des Sentiers*, the region's hiking map). You can also use the handy restroom here on the second floor.

Kid Activities

Chamonix provides a wealth of fun opportunities for kids. The TI can suggest family-friendly hikes and activities (such as mini-golf, swimming pools with big slides, and more). Here are a few kid-friendly activities to consider.

Parc de Loisirs des Planards Chamonix's fun-park for kids of all ages. It includes a luge (summer only—see page 822) and a Parc d'Aventure with tree courses, Tarzan swings, trampolines, electric motorbikes, Jet Skis, and more (€14, daily July–Aug 10:00–19:00, April–June and Sept–Oct 11:00–18:00; 15-minute walk from town center, over the tracks from train station and past Montenvers train station; tel. 04 50 53 08 97, www.planards.com).

Le Paradis des Praz Pleasant Activity park ideal for 4- to 10-year-olds, with pony rides, zip-wire rides, and more. It's in the small village of Les Praz, by the lift to Flégère (pony rides–€4, otherwise free, July–Aug daily 10:00–16:00, otherwise Wed and weekend afternoons and holidays only, tel. 06 61 73 23 00). Rent a bike in Chamonix and ride along the level Arve River trail to this park, or take the free bus (described on page 808).

Parc de Merlet Animal sanctuary with trails that let you discover mountain animals (marmots, mountain goats, llamas, deer, and more). It's located in Coupeau above Les Houches, and comes with exceptional views (so parents get some scenery while kids get to see animals). You can get there by car (20-minute drive) or hike for two beautiful hours from Chamonix (too much for most kids). If you drive, head to the very top parking lot, as you'll be hiking uphill for 20–30 minutes just to reach the entry. There's a lot more walking inside the park to find the animals—bring good shoes and water (€6, age 4-12–€4, view café with salads and regional dishes, no picnics allowed, May-Sept daily 10:00–18:00, July–Aug until 19:30, tel. 04 50 53 47 89, www.parcdemerlet.com).

At **Compagnie des Guides de Chamonix** on the ground floor, you can hire a guide to take you hiking for the day (about €300/day, €170/half-day), help you scale Mont Blanc, or hike to the Matterhorn and Zermatt (about €850 for the 2-day climb up Mont Blanc; open daily 9:00–12:00 & 15:30–19:00, closed Sun–Mon off-season, tel. 04 50 53 00 88, fax 04 50 53 48 04, www.chamonix-guides.com).

I describe three big hikes (Hikes #1, #2, and #3) and two easier walks (Hikes #4 and #5); see the map on the next page. These hikes give nature-lovers of any ability good options for enjoying the valley in most seasons. Start early, when the weather's generally best. This is critical in summer—if you don't get to the lifts

Chamonix Area Hikes & Lifts

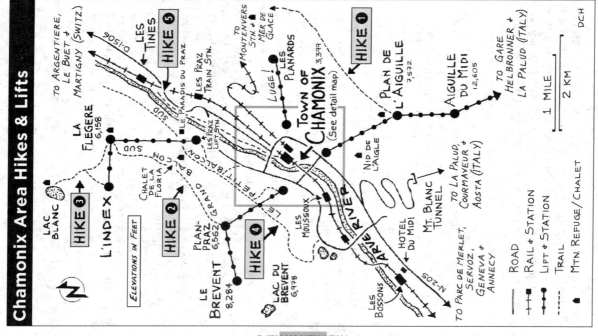

by 8:30, you'll meet a conveyor belt of hikers. If starting later or walking longer, confirm lift closing hours, or prepare for a long, steep hike down. No matter when you're here, come ready for a lot of hikers on the trails and be prepared to wait it out if the weather gets rough—lifts don't run during electrical storms.

For your hike, pack sunglasses, sunscreen, rain gear, water, and snacks. Bring warm layers (mountain weather can change in a moment) and good shoes (trails are rocky and uneven). Take your time, watch your footing, don't take shortcuts, and say *"Bonjour!"* to your fellow hikers. Note that there's no shade on Hikes #1, #2, and #3.

▲▲▲Hike #1: Plan de l'Aiguille to Montenvers–Mer de Glace (Grand Balcon Nord)—

This is the most efficient way to

incorporate a high-country hike into your ride down from the valley's greatest lift, and check out a world-class glacier to boot. The well-used trail rises some but mostly falls (dropping 1,500 feet from Plan de l'Aiguille to Montenvers and the Mer de Glace) and is moderately difficult, provided the snow is melted (generally covered by snow until June; get trail details at the Office of the High Mountain, see page 814). Some stretches are steep and strenuous, with uneven footing and slippery rocks. Take your time. Note the last train time from Montenvers–Mer de Glace back to Chamonix, or you'll be hiking another hour and a half straight down.

Here is an overview of this 2.5-hour hike: From the Aiguille du Midi lift, get off halfway down at Plan de l'Aiguille, *sortie* to the café, then find signs leading down to *Montenvers–Mer de Glace*. You'll drop steadily for 15 minutes down to a small refuge (good prices for meals and drinks), then go right, hiking the spectacularly scenic, undulating, and (for short periods) strenuous trail to Montenvers (overlooking the Mer de Glace glacier). You'll do lots of boulder-stepping and cross occasional streams that can dampen your shoes and make the rocks very slippery. Pay attention.

After about an hour at a steady pace, the trail splits. Follow signs up the steep trail to *Le Signal* (more scenic and easier), rather than to the left toward Montenvers (looks easier, but becomes very difficult). At this point you'll grind it out up switchbacks for about 30 minutes to the best views of the trail at Le Signal. Take time to savor the views you worked so hard to reach. Scramble about the rocks and create your own rock pile. From here it's a long, sometimes steep, but always memorable drop to Montenvers and

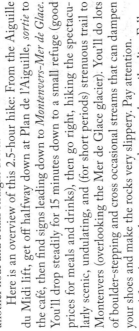

the Mer de Glace. As you drop, notice the dirt path the receding glacier left in its wake. In Montenvers, take the train back to Chamonix. Don't walk the rest of the trail down from Montenvers (long, steep, disappointing views).

▲▲**Hike #2: La Flégère to Planpraz (Grand Balcon Sud)**—This lovely hike undulates for two hours above Chamonix Valley, with staggering views of Mont Blanc and countless other peaks, glaciers, and wildflowers. There's just 370 feet of difference in elevation between the La Flégère and Planpraz lift stations—so this hike, though not without its ups and downs, is manageable (but still requires serious stamina and appropriate shoes). The trail is a mix of dirt paths, ankle-twisting rocky sections, and short stretches of service roads. You'll pass by winter lifts, and walk through meadows and along small sections of forest. Watch for signs to *La Flégère* or *Planpraz*, depending on your direction; red-and-white markers also help identify the trail.

You can hike the trail in either direction, but I prefer starting at La Flégère, as Mont Blanc stays in your sights the entire walk. You decide. Ask for the round-trip rate allowed with La Flégère and Planpraz (Le Brévent) lifts, available at either lift (saves about €6).

To start at La Flégère, take free bus #1 or #2 (get departure times to Les Praz/La Flégère at TI; see "Getting Around (and Up and Down) the Valley" on page 806)—or walk 40 minutes along the Arve River to Les Praz (see Hike #5, described later). In Les Praz, take the lift to La Flégère, and exit following signs down to *Planpraz* (you don't want Les Praz–Chamonix—that's straight down). Hike the rolling Grand Balcon Sud to Planpraz station, the midway stop on the Le Brévent lift line, and return to Chamonix from there.

If starting from the Le Brévent lift, take the *télécabine* up to Planpraz (automated cars leave every minute). As you ride up with your back to Mont Blanc, your destination lift station (La Flégère) is visible to the right. From the Planpraz lift station, don't take what appears to be the direct way there down the big dirt road. Instead, leave the station, walking behind it (not past La Bergerie Restaurant), then climb above, following signs to *La Flégère*. When you reach the La Flégère lift, ride it down to Les Praz (the hike down is not worth the trouble), then walk back to Chamonix following Hike #5 (described later), or take the free Chamonix bus (about 2/hour, 10-minute ride). Bus #1 stops at the shelter on the road in front of the lift station; bus #2 stops in the lift station parking lot, near the main road.

▲▲**Hike #3: La Flégère to Lac Blanc**—This is the most demanding hiking trail of those I list; it climbs steeply and steadily over a rough, boulder-strewn trail for 1.5 hours to snowy Lac Blanc (pronounced "lock blah"). Some footing is tricky, and good shoes or boots are a must. I like this trail, as it gets you away from the valley edge and opens views to peaks you don't see from other hikes. The destination is a snow-white lake surrounded by peaks and a nifty chalet-refuge offering good lunches (and dinners, if you stay the night). The views on the return trip are breathtaking. Check for snow conditions on the trail (often a problem until July) and go early (particularly in summer), as there is no shade and this trail is popular.

Follow the directions for Hike #2 to La Flégère station, then walk out the station's rear door past the snack stand and view area, and follow signs to *Lac Blanc*. The trail is well-signed and its surface improves as you climb. You can eliminate a good part of the uphill hiking by riding the lift from La Flégère to L'Index (€6 one-way, €8 round-trip), but make sure the trail from L'Index is free of snow as this short-cut can be dicey, especially for kids.

▲Hike #4: Petit Balcon Sud to Chalet de la Floria and Les Praz

—This trail runs above the valley on the Brévent side from the village of Servoz to Argentière, passing Chamonix about halfway, and is handy when snow or poor weather make other hikes problematic. No lifts are required—just firm thighs to climb up to and down from the trail. Access paths link the trail to villages below. Once you're up, the trail rises and falls with some steep segments and uneven footing, but is generally easy to walk. The highlight of the trail is Chalet de la Floria, where you can get drinks and snacks with views (allow 1 hour each way from Chamonix).

Reach the trail from Chamonix by starting at the Le Brévent lift station (find signs to *Le Petit Balcon Sud*). You'll begin by walking along an asphalt road to the left of the lift leading uphill (on chemin de la Pierre à Ruskin), which turns into a dirt road marked as the *Petit Balcon Sud* trail. After about 20 minutes on the dirt road, you'll see a sign for the *Petit Balcon Sud* pointing left and up a smaller trail. Bypass this turnoff (which doubles back above Chamonix with great views) and continue along the dirt road.

After about 30 more minutes, follow *la Floria* signs on a 20-minute round-trip detour to Chalet de la Floria, which has drinks, snacks, flowers, and magnificent views (daily mid-June-early Nov). From here, trails lead back down to Chamonix or to Les Praz village. Following signs to *Les Praz* eventually lands you on the main road; turn left to explore the village and to connect with the river trail back to Chamonix (the trail is immediately to the right after the bridge), or turn right on the road to reach the bus stop back to Chamonix (it takes bus #1 about 20 minutes to reach Les Praz from the time point posted in Le Tour; bus #2 starts a minute away at the Les Praz/La Flégère lift).

Winter Sports in Chamonix

Chamonix offers some of the best expert-level skiing in the world, a huge choice of terrain at reasonable prices (cheaper than Switzerland), access to lots of high-elevation runs (which means good snow and views), and great nightlife. Ski here for jaw-dropping views and a good balance between true mountaineer culture and touristy glitz.

The slopes are strung out along the valley for about 10 miles, so you must drive or catch the often-crowded shuttle buses to ski more than one area. There's also limitless *off-piste* (un-groomed) skiing, but first you'll need an experienced guide due to hidden crevasses, deadly patches of ice, and avalanche danger.

Non-skiers won't be bored. The lifts described in this chapter lead to top-notch views. Swimming, saunas, tennis, skating, and climbing are available at Chamonix's Centre Sportif. You can also relax in a spa, go bowling or dog-sledding, and hike along groomed winter footpaths.

When to Go

High season is usually from December to mid-May. Chamonix is packed from Christmas through New Year's Day and busy in February and March (during European winter and spring breaks). It's quieter in early December, in January after New Year's, the second half of March, and in April (but Easter can be busy). Thanks to easy access to high-elevation runs, you'll usually find good powder in April and May, when it's less crowded. Chamonix is one of the great resorts for spring skiing, and you can usually find special spring package deals. Whenever you go, get an early start to avoid the late-morning (après-ski-party-recovery) crowds.

Tickets

Adult lift tickets covering Chamonix's three main areas, including the lower-elevation beginner areas, are €42/1 day, €77/2 days, €115/3 days, €150/4 days, €190/5 days (about 20 percent less for those ages 65 and up and kids ages 4-15). For lift-ticket information on specific areas and the Mont Blanc Unlimited pass (covering all the areas in the Chamonix Valley), see www.chamonix .com, www.compagniedumontblanc.fr, and www.leshouches .com.

Ski Rentals

Prices don't vary much, so go with something convenient to where you're staying and ask your hotel for deals with nearby shops. You'll pay about €12-20/day for skis and about €6-12/ day for boots. **Technique Extrême** has the best deals on rentals and gear (tel. 04 50 53 38 25, 200 avenue de l'Aiguille du Midi, www.technique-extreme.com). **Snell Sports** is a respected shop that's been around for many years (tel. 04 50 53 02 17, 104 rue du Docteur Paccard, www.cham3s.com). **Sports Alpins** provides great service (tel. 04 50 53 13 60, 7 place Edmond Désailloud, Chamonix Sud, www.cham3s.com).

Information

For general information about Chamonix and lift rates, check www.chamonix.com and www.compagniedumontblanc.fr, or contact the Chamonix TI. To hire a guide, see www.chamonix-guides.com (info@chamonix-guides.com).

Where to Go

It's tough to find one area in Chamonix that offers a perfect mix of terrain for every level of skier, but here's a rundown of Chamonix's key ski areas:

Le Brévent/La Flégère—A 10-minute walk from Chamonix's center, this area has one of the valley's better mixes of terrain. If you're staying in Chamonix and have just a day, ski Le Brévent/La Flégère. Runs are good for intermediates, with some expert options, but not great for beginners. You'll enjoy fantastic views of Mont Blanc.

Les Grands Montets—Above the village of Argentière (about 10 minutes from Chamonix by bus), this area is internationally renowned for its expert terrain (and killer views from the observation deck). Part of Les Grands Montets lies on the Argentière glacier, and there's lots of vertical. Hire a local guide to explore the off-piste options.

Les Houches—A five-minute bus or train ride from Chamonix, Les Houches covers a large area with a variety of runs for most skill levels (good for families), but it has fewer expert options. This area is less crowded than other Chamonix Valley areas and there is good tree skiing.

Domaine de Balme—The area above the nearby town of Le Tour offers good options for beginners, intermediates, and those looking for mellow cruising runs.

Lower Areas Good for Beginners—Le Savoy is at the bottom of Le Brévent, near Chamonix's center, with scads of kids and a few rope-tows. Les Planards is a short walk from the town center and the largest area for kids and beginners. These areas depend on good snow conditions.

The Vallée Blanche—This unique-to-Chamonix run starts on the sky-high Aiguille du Midi lift and takes you 13 miles down a glacier past astounding views and terrain to Montenvers (easy train back to Chamonix). It requires a lift ticket and hiring a guide or joining a group tour (figure about €300 for a private tour of up to 4 people, €25/additional person, maximum of 6 people).

Driver Shortcut: If you have a car, ask the TI about a shortcut to Chalet de la Floria, where you park at the base of the chemin de la Floriaz road (shown on the upper-right of the TI's Chamonix town map). This way, you can shave considerable time off the hike but still get great views from the chalet.

Hike #5: Arve Riverbank Stroll and Paragliding Landing Field

For a level, forested-valley stroll, follow the Arve River toward Les Praz. At Chamonix's Hôtel Alpina, follow the path upstream past red-clay tennis courts and find the green arrow to *Les Praz.* Cross two bridges to the left and turn right along the rushing Arve River, and then follow Promenade des Econtres. Several trails loop through these woods; if you continue walking straight, you'll reach Les Praz—an appealing destination with several cafés and a pleasing village green.

If you keep right after the tennis courts (passing piles of river sediment dredged to keep the river from flooding), you'll come to a grassy landing field, signed *Parapente,* where paragliders hope to touch down. Walk to the top of the little grassy hill for fine Mont Blanc views and a great picnic spot. The recommended Micro Brasserie de Chamonix is nearby.

Other Activities

▲**Luge (Luge d'Eté)**—Here's something for thrill-seekers: Ride a chairlift up the mountain and then scream down a twisty, banked, concrete slalom course on a wheeled sled. Chamonix has two roughly parallel luge courses: While each course is just longer than a half-mile and about the same speed, one is marked for slower sledders, the other for speed demons. Young or old, hare or tortoise, any fit person can manage a luge. *Freinez* signs tell you when to brake. Don't take your hands off your stick; the course is fast and slippery. The luge courses are set in a grassy park with kids' play areas (€6 for one ride, €14 for all the luge-ing you can stomach, entry includes all activities in Parc de Loisirs des Planards—see "Kid Activities" sidebar, earlier; generally early April–Oct daily 13:30–17:30 though often closed Thu–Fri; July–Aug daily 10:00–19:00; 15-minute walk from town center, over the tracks from train station and past Montenvers train station; tel. 04 50 53 08 97, www.planards.com).

▲▲▲**Paragliding (Parapente)**—When it's sunny and clear, the skies above Chamonix sparkle with colorful parachute-like sails that circle the valley like birds of prey. For about €90, launch yourself off a mountain in a tandem paraglider with a trained, experienced pilot and fly like a bird for about 20 minutes. Try **Summits Parapente** (smart to reserve a day ahead, open year-round, tel. 04 50 53 50 14, mobile 06 84 01 26 00, fax 04 50 55 94 16, www .summits.fr).

For a sneak preview, walk to the main landing area and watch paragliders perfect their landings (see "Chamonix Area Hikes—Hike #5," earlier).

Rainy-Day Options

If the weather disagrees with your plans, stay cool and check out the following options, which are both included in one €5.50 ticket (€1 off with Chamonix Guest Card). Although neither offers a word of English, the exhibits are fairly straightforward.

Alpine Museum (Musée Alpin)—Situated in one of Chamonix's oldest "palaces," this place has good exhibits about Chamonix's evolution from a farming area to one focused on skiing. The museum shows off Chamonix's mountaineering, skiing, and mineralogical history (explanations in French only) and has exhibits on the first Winter Olympics, held right here (€5.50, includes Espace Tairraz, daily 15:00–19:00 plus 10:00–12:00 in summer, 89 avenue Michel Croz, tel. 04 50 53 25 93).

Espace Tairraz—This fascinating collection features crystals from the region in every color, shape, and size. My kids loved it. Pick up the basic brochure in English for some background (€5.50, includes Alpine Museum, daily 14:00–19:00 plus 10:00–12:00 in summer).

Day Trips near Chamonix

A Day in French-Speaking Switzerland—Plenty of tempting alpine and cultural thrills await just an hour or two away in Switzerland. A scenic road-and-train line sneaks you from Chamonix to the Swiss town of Martigny. Whereas train travelers cross without formalities, drivers are charged a one-time fee of 40 Swiss francs (about €29) for a permit to use Swiss autobahns (valid for one calendar year).

A Little Italy—The remote Valle d'Aosta and its historic capital city of Aosta are the finale to a spectacular gondola ride over the Mont Blanc range. The side-trip is worthwhile if you'd like to taste Italy (spaghetti, gelato, and cappuccino), enjoy the town's great evening ambience, or view the ancient ruins in Aosta (often called the "Rome of the North").

Take the spectacular lift (Aiguille du Midi–Helbronner) to Italy, described on page 811. From Helbronner, catch the lift down to La Palud and take the bus to Aosta (hourly, change in Courmayeur). Aosta's train station has connections to anywhere in Italy (about every 2 hours, usually on slow trains via Turin).

For a more down-to-earth experience, you can take the two-hour bus from Chamonix to Aosta (about €16 one-way, €26 round-trip, reservation required in summer, 4/day July–mid-Sept, 2/day mid-Sept–June). Get schedules at Chamonix's bus station (located at train station, tel. 04 50 53 01 15, www.sat-montblanc.com—click "download timetables" on the right). For buses using the Mont Blanc tunnel, it's a two-hour trip to Aosta (otherwise it's at least three hours via Martigny). Drivers can drive straight through the Mont Blanc tunnel (€37 one-way, €46 round-trip, www.tunnelmb.com).

Sleeping in Chamonix

(€1 = about $1.25, country code: 33)

Reasonable hotels and dorm-like chalets abound in Chamonix, with easy parking and quick access from the train station. The TI can help you find budget accommodations anytime—either in person or by email (reservation@chamonix.com). Outside winter, mid-July to mid-August is most difficult, when some hotels have five-day minimum-stay requirements. Prices tumble off-season (outside July–Aug and Dec–Jan). Many hotels and restaurants are closed in April, June, and November, but you'll still find a room and a meal. If you want a view of Mont Blanc, ask for *côté Mont Blanc* (coat-ay mohn blah). Travelers who visit June through September should contemplate a night high above in a refuge-hotel.

All hoteliers speak English. Price ranges usually reflect low-to-high season rates (low season is roughly March–June and Sept–Dec). Ask at your hotel about the free Chamonix Guest Card, which provides free use of most buses and trains during your stay (described on page 808).

Hotels in the City Center

$$$ Hôtel l'Oustalet*** is a modern chalet hotel that makes me feel like I'm in Austria. It's warmly run by two sisters (Véronique and Agnes), who understand the importance of good service. The place is family-friendly, with lots of grass, a pool, and six family suites. All rooms are sharp, with views and balconies (Sb-€85–140, standard Db-€110–125, bigger Db with terrace-€120–150, Qb family rooms-€150–210, buffet breakfast-€13, Wi-Fi in lobby, free parking, near Aiguille du Midi lift at 330 rue du Lyret, tel. 04 50 55 54 99, fax 04 50 55 54 98, www.hotel-oustalet.com, infos@hotel-oustalet.com).

$$$ Hôtel Hermitage*** , a 10-minute walk from the town center, is a beautiful and well-run chalet with the coziest lounges in Chamonix and a lovely garden with good kids' toys (swings, slides, ping-pong). It has a fun bar and 30 immaculate, rustic-elegant rooms, all with balconies. Rooms facing Mont Blanc have incredible views (Db-€100–115, Db with king-size bed and Mont Blanc view-€115–150, Tb-€145–165, family rooms-€175–195,

THE FRENCH ALPS

breakfast-€14, Internet access and Wi-Fi, near train station at 63 chemin du Cé, tel. 04 50 53 13 87, fax 04 50 55 98 14, www .hermitage-paccard.com, info@hermitage-paccard.com).

$$ Hôtel Gourmets et Italy*** is a 40-room place with cozy public spaces, a cool riverfront terrace, balcony views from many of its appealing rooms, and a small pool (standard Db with shower-€90–110, larger Db with bath and Mont Blanc view-€95–140, extra person-€16, closed late April–early June, pay Internet access and Wi-Fi, 2 blocks from casino on Mont Blanc side of river, 96 rue du Lyret, tel. 04 50 53 01 38, fax 04 50 53 46 74, www .hotelgourmets-chamonix.com, hgicham@aol.com).

$$$ Hôtel Richemond** has a retirement-home feel in its well-worn public spaces. The same family has run this grand old hotel since it was built in 1914, and I don't think the rooms have changed much since then. Hallways are broad, and rooms are Old World comfortable and relatively spacious, though bathrooms are rustic. There's also an outdoor terrace and a game room with a pool table, "flipper" (pinball), and table tennis (Sb-€62–70, Db-€95–110, Tb-€115–138, Qb-€128–152, includes buffet breakfast, Wi-Fi, free parking, 228 rue du Docteur Paccard, tel. 04 50 53 08 85, fax 04 50 55 91 69, www.richemond.fr, richemond@wanadoo.fr). Helpful Evelyn runs the day reception and speaks impeccable English.

$$ Hôtel Faucigny** is a quiet and well-run little refuge set back from the street, near the TI. Tasteful wood paneling gives the rooms an alpine feel, the lounge is mountain-homey, and the front terrace provides a peaceful retreat with sensational views (Db-€84–96, Tb-€105, family rooms-€130, Internet access and Wi-Fi, 118 place de l'Eglise, tel. 04 50 53 01 17, fax 04 50 53 73 23, www.hotelfaucigny-chamonix.com, hotel.faucigny@wanadoo.fr).

$$ Hôtel de l'Arve** offers solid two-star comfort with a contemporary alpine feel in its 37 comfortable rooms, some right on the Arve River looking up at Mont Blanc. Owners Isabelle and Beatrice run a tight ship at this hotel that comes with a fireplace lounge, a pool room, a pleasant garden, a sauna, a climbing wall, and easy parking (standard Db-€70–96, larger or view Db-€80–115, big view room-€90–128, extra person-€15, great breakfast-€11, Internet access and free Wi-Fi, nice restaurant, around the corner from huge Hôtel Alpina, 60 impasse des Anémones, tel. 04 50 53 02 31, fax 04 50 53 56 92, www.hotelarve-chamonix.com, contact @hotelarve-chamonix.com).

$$ Hôtel les Crêtes Blanches** is a central and sweet little place wrapped around a peaceful courtyard (with outdoor tables) just off rue Joseph Vallot (next to the Super U grocery). Rooms are well-designed with appealing wood paneling; all come with views of Mont Blanc and most have small balconies. A ceramic woodstove and stylish couches anchor the comfy lounge area

Chamonix Town

Ⓑ Bus Stop

🅿 Parking

N

¼ MILE

400 METERS

TO HIKE #2 + #3

LE BREVENT LIFT

HIKE #4

MAISON DE LA MONTAGNE

RUE MOUSSOUX

LA MOLLARD

ALLÉE

RECTEUR-PAYOT

PAYOT

ROUTES PECLEY

TO LES BOSSONS + 9

ARVE RIVER

TO MT BLANC TUNNEL

TO MT BLANC + 9

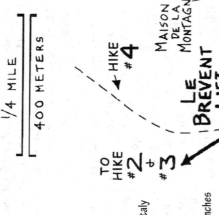

1 Hôtel l'Oustalet
2 Hôtel Hermitage
3 Hôtel Gourmets et Italy
4 Hôtel Richemond
5 Hôtel Faucigny
6 Hôtel/Café de l'Arve
7 Hôtel les Crêtes Blanches
8 Hôtel le Chamonix & Le Chamonix Café
9 To Hôtel l'Aiguille du Midi
10 Le Lapin Agile Wine Bar
11 La Calèche, Brasserie le National, Midnight Express Rest., Le Pub & Maison de la Presse
12 Le Boccalatte Brasserie
13 Le Bivouac, Le Panier des 4 Saisons & Le Refuge Payot
14 Elevation 1904 & Europcar
15 L'Impossible Restaurant
16 Bistro des Sports
17 Micro Brasserie de Chamonix (MBC)
18 Café les Terraces
19 Mojo's
20 Le Refuge Payot
21 Super U Grocery
22 Launderette & Casino Market
23 Launderette & Technique Extrême
24 Alpine Museum
25 Espace Tairraz (Crystals)

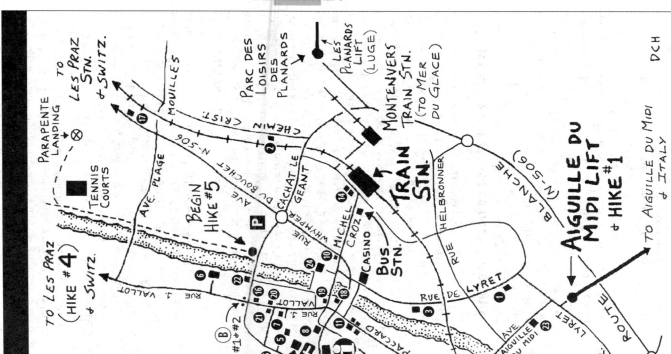

(Db–€68–94, Tb–€95–118, Qb–€110–136, highest prices are mid-July–Aug, adorable dollhouse-sized chalet with kitchen sleeps five–€130–155, Wi-Fi, 6 impasse du Génépy, tel. 04 50 53 05 62, fax 04 50 53 67 25, www.cretes-blanches.com, cretes-blanches @wanadoo.fr).

$$ Hôtel le Chamonix**, across from the TI and above a café, is simple, with 16 paneled rooms at fair rates and no elevator. The rooms facing Mont Blanc have great views, are larger and brighter, and have little balconies...but also attract noise from *le café* below, which closes at 20:00 (standard Db–€64–84, standard Db with Mont Blanc view–€66–92, Tb–€90–120, Qb–€105–140, Wi-Fi, 11 rue de l'Hôtel de Ville, tel. 04 50 53 11 07, fax 04 50 53 64 78, www .hotel-le-chamonix.com, hotel-le-chamonix@wanadoo.fr).

Near Chamonix

If Chamonix overwhelms you, spend the night in one of the valley's often-overlooked, lower-profile villages.

$$ Hôtel l'Aiguille du Midi***, a mountain retreat, lies in the village of Les Bossons, about two miles from Chamonix toward Annecy. It's run by the English-speaking Farini family in a park-like setting with point-blank views of Mont Blanc and the Bossons Glacier. This family-friendly place has a swimming pool, a clay tennis court, table tennis, a massage room, and a laundry room to boot. The alpine-comfortable rooms come with Old World bathrooms, many have decks with views, and several are good for families. The classy restaurant offers à la carte and *menu* options, with *menus* from €31 (Db–€90–98, Tb–€120, Qb–€142, ask for these special Rick Steves rates for 2011 when you reserve, elevator, Internet access and Wi-Fi, easy by train, get off at Les Bossons, tel. 04 50 53 00 65, fax 04 50 55 93 69, www.hotel-aiguilledumidi .com, hotel-aiguille-du-midi@wanadoo.fr).

Refuges and Refuge-Hotels near Chamonix

Chamonix has the answer for hikers who want to sleep high above, but aren't into packing it all in: refuge-hotels (generally open mid-June to mid- or late September, depending on snow levels). Refuge-hotels usually have some private rooms (along with dorm rooms), hot showers down the hall, and restaurants. Most expect you to take dinner and breakfast there (which is a good value—about €45/person). Reserve in advance (a few days is generally enough), then pack a small bag for a memorable night among new international friends. The **Office of the High Mountain** in Chamonix can explain your options (see page 814).

$ Refuge-Hôtel du Montenvers, Chamonix's oldest refuge, is a cool experience at the Montenvers train stop. It was built in

1880 as a climbing base for mountain guides before the train went there, so materials had to be gathered from nearby. The five simple wood-cozy rooms and dining room feel as though they haven't been modified since then (half-pension in a double room about €56/person, €40/person in dorm room, good showers down the hall, tel. 04 50 53 14 14, fax 04 50 55 38 55). For directions, see "Chamonix Area Hikes—Hike #1" on page 817.

$ Refuge-Plan de l'Aiguille is a small, easy-to-reach refuge a 15-minute walk below the plan de l'Aiguille lift, right on the trail between the Aiguille du Midi and Montenvers-Mer de Glace. It has a cozy interior and a view café. The cook is a retired pastry chef, so the meals are good and the desserts heavenly (€18/bed, half-pension-€41/person, tel. 06 65 64 27 53).

$ Refuge Nid de l'Aigle is a 15-minute walk from the base of the Aiguille du Midi lift (so no need to take a lift), and it's where Mont Blanc climbers start, so the atmosphere is fun (€18/bed, half-pension-€42/person, tel. 04 50 47 76 23).

$ Refuge-Hôtel La Flégère hangs on the edge right at the La Flégère lift station. It's simple, but ideally located for hiking to Lac Blanc or Planpraz (3 private rooms with 5 beds, many dorm beds, half-pension required-€48/person, fireplace, cozy bar-café, tel. 06 03 58 28 14). For directions, see "Chamonix Area Hikes—Hike #2" on page 818.

Eating in Chamonix

You have two basic dining options in Chamonix—cozy, traditional *savoyarde* restaurants serving fondue, raclette, and the like, or big cafés in central locations serving a wide variety of dishes (including regional specialties) that allow you to watch rivers of hikers return from a full day in the mountains. Prices are roughly the same—you choose. If it's a beautiful day, take an outdoor table at a central café (see "View Cafés" on page 831); if you're dining inside, go local and consider a place in or near the town center (most are closed between lunch and dinner).

If a pre-dinner glass of wine from anywhere in the world sounds appealing, hop on into little **Le Lapin Agile** for cozy ambience and a happy-hour buffet of finger foods—free if you purchase a drink (closed Mon, a block from the train station at 11 rue Whymper, tel. 04 50 53 33 25).

In the Town Center

La Calèche presents delectable regional dishes in a warm, hyper-decorated alpine setting (pass on the outside seating). You'll dine amid antique dolls, cuckoo clocks, copper pots, animal trophies, and more (see if you can find the luge sled from the 1924 Olympic Games). Try the *croziflette*—buckwheat pasta cut into tiny flat squares, baked with cream, onion, and cheese, then topped with cured ham (€17); or the *tartiflette*—tasty scalloped potatoes with melted cheese (€22 *menu*, the €28 *menu* is much better, open daily, centrally located just off place Balmat at 18 rue du Docteur Paccard, tel. 04 50 55 94 68). Don't leave without a visit to the WCs.

Le Boccalatte Brasserie, with a convivial atmosphere inside and out, serves a simple but good-value lunch or dinner a few blocks above the Aiguille du Midi lift. The place is family-friendly, with a playful waitstaff. Try the €18 or €28 *menus*, or choose from a large selection of local specialties, big €10 salads, good pizzas, and 20 kinds of beer. It's run by English-speaking Thierry, a friendly Alsatian (daily 12:00–22:00, 59 avenue de l'Aiguille du Midi, tel. 04 50 53 52 14).

Le Bivouac is an unassuming but lively shoebox-sized place where you'll eat cheap and well in an informal setting. It's a youthful family affair run by son Chris, who speaks English, loves Colorado, and is monitored by gregarious owner-chef Jean-Guy (who should sing opera). Salads are good, the *plats* are tasty, and the selection is big (good kid options). Ask *le chef's* opinion—he likes his souvlaki and *roulée savoyarde* (266 rue du Docteur Paccard, tel. 04 50 53 34 08).

Café de l'Arve, at the recommended Hôtel de l'Arve, serves an appealing but limited selection of alpine and Italian fare at fair prices. Dine above the Arve river inside or out (€15 *plats*, *menus* from €25, closed Sun–Mon, tel. 04 50 53 58 57).

Le Panier des 4 Saisons is where locals go for traditional French (not local) cuisine like *Grand-mère* used to make. In spite of its mini-mall location, the place is charmingly elegant and merits its good reputation (€16–22 *plats*, closed Sun–Mon, located on the first floor in Galerie Blanc Neige at 266 rue du Docteur Paccard, tel. & fax 04 50 53 98 77).

Brasserie le National is a fair choice for outdoor dining in the thick of the traffic-free center. The cuisine highlights local specialties, though you'll find a good selection of noncheesy options as well (*menus* from €19, nonstop service daily 8:30–22:00, 3 rue du Docteur Paccard, tel. 04 50 53 02 23).

Budget Meals: **Midnight Express** serves good sandwiches until late and has a few outside tables across from the recommended La Calèche restaurant. Try a *pain rond-rustique* (round-bread rustic sandwich), served hot (*chaud*) or cold (*froid*). **Elevation 1904** is a down-and-dirty climbers' haunt across from the train station, serving cheap and tasty sandwiches, burgers, pasta, and salads (daily until about 20:00, Wi-Fi, 263 rue Michel Croz).

Away from the Pedestrian Center

L'Impossible, housed in a beautiful farmhouse a 10–20-minute walk from most recommended hotels, is *the* place to go for refined organic cuisine with an Italian bias. Even if eating organic doesn't matter, you'll appreciate the exquisite meals and attention to detail. Papa (who hails from Tuscany) cooks, while Mama and daughter Martha serve (€16–24 *plats*, *menus* from €30, open daily, 5-minute walk from Aiguille du Midi lift on route des Pèlerins, tel. 04 50 53 20 36).

Après Hike: The **Bistro des Sports** is where locals hang their ice picks after a hard day in the mountains. Drinks are cheap, the crowd is loud, and the ambience works (daily until late, 176 rue Joseph Vallot). **Le Pub** is a good spot to raise a glass with the British crowd (225 rue du Docteur Paccard, tel. 04 50 55 92 88) and **Micro Brasserie de Chamonix (MBC),** a knockoff of microbrew pubs back home, is a cool place to hang out after a day of paragliding or rappelling. It's not central, across from the *parapente* landing strip (see "Chamonix Area Hikes—Hike #5" on page 822), but it's reasonable and lively. Come here for a homemade brew, a glass of wine, or a pub dinner, and expect crowds of twenty- and thirtysomethings (daily 16:00–1:00 in the morning, 350 route du Bouchet, look for *MBC* sign, tel. 04 50 53 61 59).

View Cafés: Chamonix excels in outdoor café views, but here are several I think stand above the rest. Facing the TI a block off the action-packed pedestrian core, scenic **Le Chamonix Café** sits below Chamonix's pretty little church and has terrific views of both mountain ranges (daily until 20:00, place de l'Eglise). **Café Les Terraces** has a cool location (literally) above the rush of the Arve River and is well-positioned for Mont Blanc views (daily until late, across from the casino on place Balmat). **Mojo's** is a relaxed place for cheap food, Internet access, and lovely views of the main square and mountains (daily, 31 place du Joseph Balmat, tel. 04 50 21 99 45).

Chamonix Connections

Bus and train service to Chamonix is surprisingly good. You'll find bus and train information desks at the train station. Some train routes pass through Switzerland to reach Chamonix (such as from Paris and Colmar) and require additional tickets if you have a France-only railpass. You can avoid passing through Switzerland if you plan ahead, but it usually takes longer, and you miss some great scenery. The **route to Colmar** (via Bern and Basel) is beautiful and costs €60 for the Swiss segment. You'll get a fun taste of Switzerland's charms and, though you'll make many changes en route, they all work like a Swiss clock.

From Chamonix by Train to: Annecy (8/day, 2.5 hours, change in St. Gervais), **Beaune** and **Dijon** (7/day, 6–7 hours, change in St. Gervais and Lyon), **Nice** (4/day, 10 hours, change in St. Gervais and Lyon), **Arles** (5/day, 7–8 hours, change in St. Gervais and Lyon), **Paris'** Gare de Lyon (8/day, daily July–Aug and Dec–April, Fri–Sun only May–June and Sept–Nov, may be more frequent in May, 6–8 hours, some change in Switzerland), **Colmar** (hourly, 6 hours via Switzerland with 3–4 changes), **Martigny**, Switzerland (nearly hourly, 2 hours, scenic trip), **Geneva**, Switzerland, and its airport (roughly hourly, 3–4 hours, two changes).

From Chamonix by Bus to: Geneva Airport, Switzerland (3/day, 4/day, 45 minutes), **Aosta**, Italy (4/day mid-Sept–June, 2/day mid-Sept–June, 2–3 hours). Long-distance buses depart from the train station—get information at the TI or at the bus station (tel. 04 50 53 01 15, www.sat-montblanc.com). For more on buses to Italy, see "Day Trips near Chamonix" on page 823.

Airport shuttles provide fast service from €25 per person between Chamonix's city center and the airport in **Geneva**, Switzerland (3–7/day, 2 hours. **Chamexpress** is British-run and easy to work with (www.chamexpress.com). Also try www.chamonix-transfer.com or www.cham-van.com.

BURGUNDY

*Beaune • Châteauneuf-en-Auxois • Semur-en-Auxois •
Abbey of Fontenay • Flavigny-sur-Ozerain • Alise Ste.
Reine • Vézelay • Château de Guédelon • Cluny • Taizé*

The rolling hills of Burgundy gave birth to superior wine, fine cuisine, spicy mustard, and sleepy villages smothered in luscious landscapes. This deceptively peaceful region witnessed Julius Caesar's defeat of the Gauls, then saw the Abbey of Cluny rise from the ashes of the Roman Empire to vie with Rome for religious influence in the 12th century. Burgundy's last hurrah came in the 15th century, when its powerful dukes controlled an immense area stretching north to Holland.

Today, bucolic Burgundy runs from about Auxerre in the north to near Lyon in the south, and it's crisscrossed with canals and dotted with quiet farming villages. It's also the transportation funnel for eastern France and makes a convenient stopover for travelers (car or train), with easy access north to Paris or Alsace, east to the Alps, and south to Provence.

Traditions are strong. In Burgundy, both the soil and the farmers who work it are venerated. Although many of the farms you see are growing grapes, only a small part of Burgundy is actually covered by vineyards. The white cows grazing amid green meadows are Charolais, producing France's best beef (*bœuf bourguignon* and steak are good choices here).

This is a calm, cultivated, and serene region, where nature is as sophisticated as the people. If you're looking for quintessential French culture, you'll find it in Burgundy.

Planning Your Time

With limited time, stay in or near Beaune. Plan on a half-day in Beaune and a half-day for the vineyards and countryside at its

doorstep. With a full day, spend the morning in Beaune and the afternoon exploring the surrounding vineyards and wine villages (good by bike, car, or minibus tour). If you have a car (cheap rentals are available), or good legs and a bike, the best way to spend your afternoon is by following my scenic vineyard drive to La Rochepot Castle (see page 860).

To explore off-the-beaten-path Burgundy, visit unspoiled Semur-en-Auxois and France's best-preserved medieval abbey complex at Fontenay (they're on the way to Paris, or double as a long day trip from Beaune). The magnificent church at Vézelay is more famous but harder to reach, and is best done as an overnight trip, or en route to Paris or the Loire Valley. If you're connecting Burgundy with the Loire, don't miss the medieval castle construction at Guédelon (works well with Vézelay). And if you're driving between Beaune and Lyon, take the detour to adorable Brancion and once-powerful Cluny.

For up-to-date information on accommodations, restaurants, events, and shopping, see www.burgundyeye.com.

Getting Around Burgundy

Trains link Beaune with Dijon to the north and Lyon to the south; some stop in the wine villages of Meursault, Ladoix-Serrigny, and Santenay. Several buses per day cruise between vineyards north of Beaune on D-974, though precious few buses connect Beaune with villages to its south (see page 859). Bikes, minibus tours, and short taxi rides get non-drivers from Beaune into the countryside. Buses connect Semur-en-Auxois with the Dijon and Montbard train stations. Drivers enjoy motoring on Burgundy's lovely roads; you'll cruise along canals, past rolling hills of vineyards, and on tree-lined lanes. Drivers can navigate by the excellent (and free) map of the Côte d'Or available at all TIs.

Burgundy's Cuisine Scene

Arrive hungry. Considered by many to be France's best, Burgundian cuisine is peasant cooking elevated to an art. Entire lives are spent debating the best restaurants and bistros.

Several classic dishes were born in Burgundy: *escargots de Bourgogne* (snails served sizzling hot in garlic butter), *bœuf bourguignon* (beef simmered for hours in red wine with onions and mushrooms), coq au vin (rooster stewed in red wine), and *œufs en meurette* (poached eggs in a red wine sauce, often served on a large

Burgundy

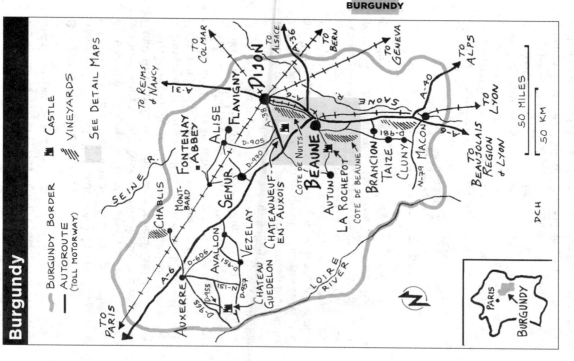

Legend:
- BURGUNDY BORDER
- AUTOROUTE (TOLL MOTORWAY)
- SEE DETAIL MAPS
- CASTLE
- VINEYARDS

Map labels: TO PARIS, TO REIMS & NANCY, TO COLMAR, TO ALSACE, A-36, TO BERN, TO GENEVA, TO ALPS, DIJON, FLAVIGNY, ALISE, FONTENAY ABBEY, SEMUR, CHABLIS, MONTBARD, SEINE R., D-905, D-970, A-38, A-6, COTE DE NUITS, BEAUNE, COTE DE BEAUNE, SAONE, A-31, N-6, A-40, TO LYON, BEAUJOLAIS REGION & LYON, N-79 MACON, CLUNY, TAIZE, D-981, BRANCION, AUTUN, LA ROCHEPOT, CHATEAUNEUF-EN-AUXOIS, VEZELAY, AVALLON, D-606, N-6, D-957, CHATEAU GUEDELON, D-955, 151-N, D-965, AUXERRE, LOIRE RIVER, 50 MILES, 50 KM, DCH, PARIS, BURGUNDY

crouton), as well as the famous Dijon mustards. Look also for delicious *jambon persillé* (cold ham layered in a garlic-parsley gelatin), *pain d'épices* (spice bread), and *gougères* (light, puffy cheese pastries). Native cheeses are Époisses and Langres (both mushy and great) and my favorite, Montrachet (a tasty goat cheese). Crème de cassis (black currant liqueur) is another Burgundian specialty; look for it in desserts and snazzy drinks (try a *kir*).

Remember, restaurants serve only during lunch (11:30–14:00) and dinner (19:00–21:00, later in bigger cities); some cafés serve food throughout the day.

Burgundy's Wines

Along with Bordeaux, Burgundy is why France is famous for wine. From Chablis to Beaujolais, you'll find great fruity reds, dry whites, and crisp rosés. The three key grapes are Chardonnay (dry white wines), Pinot Noir (medium-bodied red wines), and Gamay (light, fruity red wines, such as Beaujolais). Every village produces its own distinctive wine, from Chablis to Meursault to Chassagne-Montrachet. Road maps read like fine-wine lists. If the wine village has a hyphenated name, the latter half of its name usually comes from the town's most important vineyard (e.g., Gevrey-Chambertin, Aloxe-Corton, and Vosne-Romanée). Look for *Dégustation Gratuite* (free tasting) signs, and prepare for serious wine-tasting—and steep prices, if you're not careful. For a more easygoing tasting, head for the hills: The less prestigious Hautes-Côtes (upper slopes) produce some terrific, inexpensive, and overlooked wines. The least expensive (but still tasty) wines are Bourgogne and Passetoutgrain (both red) and whites from the Mâcon and Chalon areas (St. Véran whites are a good value). If you like rosé, try Marsannay, considered one of France's best. And *les famous* Pouilly-Fuissé grapes are grown near the city of Mâcon. For tips on tasting, see "French Wine-Tasting 101" on page 40.

Beaune

You'll feel comfortable right away in this prosperous, popular, and quintessentially French little wine capital, where life centers on the production and consumption of the prestigious Côte d'Or wines. *Côte d'Or* means "Golden Hillside," and the slopes here are a spectacle to enjoy in late October as the leaves turn.

Medieval monks and powerful dukes of Burgundy laid the groundwork that established this town's prosperity. The monks cultivated wine and cheese, whereas the dukes cultivated wealth. A ring road (with a bike path) follows the foundations of the medieval walls, and parking lots just outside keep most traffic from seeping into the historic center. One of the world's most important wine auctions takes place here every year on the third weekend of November.

Beaune's Best Wine and Food Stores

Beaune overflows with wine boutiques eager to convince you that their food products or wines are best. Here are a few to look for.

The wine shop **Denis Perret** has a good selection in all price ranges and a helpful, English-speaking staff managed by friendly owner Alain. If you've tasted a wine elsewhere that you like, they can usually find a less costly bottle with similar qualities. They can chill a white for your picnic (Mon-Sat 9:00–12:00 & 14:00–19:00, Sun 9:00–12:00, 40 place Carnot, tel. 03 80 22 35 47, www.denisperret.fr).

For an exquisite selection of fruit liqueurs (such as crème de cassis—a Burgundian treat), fruit syrups, and Burgundian brandy, find **Védrenne** at 28 rue Carnot (closed Sun).

For food, **Alain Hess** has a beautiful display of local cheeses, mustards, and other gourmet food products (7 place Carnot). A few doors down, welcoming **Mulot-Petitjean Pain d'Épices** shows off exquisite packages of this tasty local spice bread, also handy as gifts (1 place Carnot).

Orientation to Beaune

Beaune is compact (pop. 25,000), with a handful of interesting monuments and vineyards knocking at its door. Limit your Beaune ramblings to the town center, lassoed within its medieval walls and circled by a one-way ring road, and leave time to stroll into the vineyards. All roads and activities converge on the perfectly French squares, place Carnot and place de la Halle. Beaune is quiet on Sundays and Monday mornings.

Tourist Information

The main TI is located across from the post office on the ring road's southeastern corner (look for *Porte Marie de Bourgogne* on the banner; daily 9:00–18:30, tel. 03 80 26 21 30, www.beaune -tourisme.fr). A small TI annex is housed in the market hall, across from Hôtel Dieu. Either TI has extensive information on wine-tasting in and near Beaune, a room-finding service, a list of *chambres d'hôtes*, bus schedules, and an excellent, free road map of the region. They can also arrange a local guide (€130/2 hours, €180/4 hours). The town model in the room outside the main TI can help you get your Beaune bearings.

Ambitious sightseers can benefit by buying the **Pass Beaune**, which gets you a discount at most attractions in Beaune (including Hôtel Dieu, Wine Museum, Abbey of Fontenay, the site of the Cluny Abbey, and most major wine cellars). The catch: You have

Beaune

BURGUNDY

to decide what you're going to see when you buy the pass, so you're committed to visiting those attractions. Buy this pass only if your plans are set in stone (5 percent off 2 sights, 10 percent off 3 sights, 15 percent off 4 or more sights; buy at the TI).

Arrival in Beaune

By Train: To reach the city center from the train station (no baggage storage), walk straight out of the station up avenue du

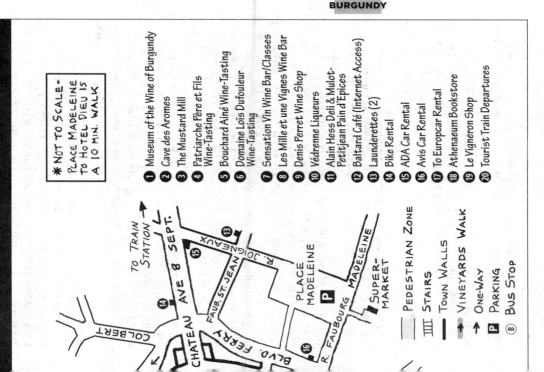

NOT TO SCALE—PLACE MADELEINE TO HOTEL DIEU IS A 10 MIN. WALK

1. Museum of the Wine of Burgundy
2. Cave des Aromes
3. The Mustard Mill
4. Patriarche Père et Fils Wine-Tasting
5. Bouchard Aîné Wine-Tasting
6. Domaine Loïs Dufouleur Wine-Tasting
7. Sensation Vin Wine Bar/Classes
8. Les Mille et une Vignes Wine Bar
9. Denis Perret Wine Shop
10. Védrenne Liqueurs
11. Alain Hess Deli & Mulot-Petitjean Pain d'Epices
12. Baltard Café (Internet Access)
13. Launderettes (2)
14. Bike Rental
15. ADA Car Rental
16. Avis Car Rental
17. To Europcar Rental
18. Athenaeum Bookstore
19. Le Vigneron Shop
20. Tourist Train Departures

Legend:

- Pedestrian Zone
- Stairs
- Town Walls
- Vineyards Walk
- ↑ One-Way
- P Parking
- Ⓑ Bus Stop

8 Septembre, cross the busy ring road, and continue up rue du Château. Follow it as it angles left and pass the mural, veering right onto rue des Tonneliers. A left on rue de l'Enfant leads to Beaune's pedestrian zone and place Carnot.

By Bus: Beaune has no bus station—only several stops along the ring road. Ask the driver for *le Centre-Ville*. The Jules Ferry (zhul fair-ee) stop is closest to the train station. (For details on bus service, see "Getting Around the Beaune Region" on page 859.)

By Car: Follow *Centre-Ville* signs to the ring road. Once on the ring road, turn right at the first signal after the modern post office (rue d'Alsace), and park for free a block away in place Madeleine. If the lot is full—which it often is on market days—look for spaces on surrounding streets or in other lots along the ring road. Most parking inside Beaune's ring road is metered.

Helpful Hints

Market Days: Beaune hosts a smashing Saturday market and a modest Wednesday market. Both are centered on place de la Halle and open until 12:30. The Saturday market animates much of the old town and is worth planning ahead for. For either market, watch the action from the **Baltard Café** on place de la Halle, then do as the locals do and have lunch at an outdoor café (many good choices—see "Eating in Beaune," later, for ideas; sit down by 12:30 or forget it).

Supermarket: Supermarché Casino has a great selection, a deli, and fair prices (Mon–Sat 8:30–20:00, closed Sun, through the arch off place Madeleine).

Internet Access: The **Baltard Café,** across from the main TI, has pricey Internet access and Wi-Fi (€1/15 minutes, computer terminals upstairs, daily, 14 place de la Halle, tel. 03 80 24 21 86). The recommended **Bistrot Bourguignon** has Wi-Fi with wine.

Laundry: Beaune's two launderettes are both open daily 7:00–21:00. One is in the town center at 65 rue Lorraine; the other is between the train station and place Madeleine at 17–19 rue du Faubourg St. Jean.

Bike Rental: See "Getting Around the Beaune Region—By Bike" on page 859.

Taxi: Call **Gerard Rebillard** for Beaune's friendliest taxi (cabbies speak English, mobile 06 11 83 06 10, allo-beaune.taxi @libertysurf.fr). For other taxis, call 06 09 35 63 12 or 03 80 24 21 73.

Post Office: A handy PTT annex sells stamps and Colissimo boxes for international shipping (see page 1012), and can recharge any mobile phone (Mon–Fri 10:00–12:00 & 14:00–18:00, Sat 10:00–12:00 & 14:00–17:00, closed Sun, 37 rue Carnot).

Car Rental: ADA is cheap and closest to the train station (allow €50/day for a small car with 100 kilometers/62 miles free, Mon–Sat 8:00–12:00 & 14:00–18:00, closed Sun, 26 avenue 8 Septembre, tel. 03 80 22 72 90). **Avis** is five blocks away on the ring road, near place Madeleine (hours vary, but generally Mon–Sat 9:00–13:00 & 14:00–17:30, closed Sun, 48 bis Jules Ferry, tel. 03 80 24 96 46). **Europcar** is less centrally located (53 route de Pommard, tel. 03 80 22 32 24).

Cooking Classes: Enthusiastic American **Marjorie Taylor** combines market-day tours with cooking classes and a full, five-course lunch with wine (€200/person)—or offers cooking classes followed by a traditional dinner (you eat what you make) in her elegant apartment (€125/person, 12 people max). Ask about her weekend and longer programs (mobile 06 17 36 46 60, www.thecooksatelier.com, marjorieleetaylor@mac.com).

Best Souvenir Shopping: The **Athenaeum** has a great variety of souvenirs, including wine and cooking books in English, with a good children's section upstairs (daily 10:00–19:00, across from Hôtel Dieu at 7 rue de l'Hôtel Dieu). And you won't find a bookstore with a better wine bar. **Le Vigneron**, at #6 rue d'Alsace, has a great selection of wine-related souvenirs, French knives, and more.

Tours in Beaune

Tourist Train—A TGV-esque little train will show you Beaune and nearby vineyards (€5, runs April–Oct 11:00–17:00, almost hourly departures from Hôtel Dieu, no morning trips on Wed and Sat market days, 45 minutes).

Local Guides—You have three great choices. For Beaune and nearby, consider animated, athletic, and smart Canadian **Sarah Bird**—she's married to a local and knows Beaune thoroughly. She can do tours of Beaune only, or include a sample of the vineyards and countryside by bike, foot, or car (€100/1.5 hours, €250/half-day). She and her brother-in-law also rent bikes (see "Bourgogne Randonnées" on page 859).

For tours that focus on vineyards and Burgundian history, **Colette Barbier,** a professor of gastronomy and wines at the University of Dijon, is an engaging guide who is fluent in English and passionate about her region. She knows Burgundy like a local—because she is one (her family has lived in the region for 250 years). Book well in advance, though last-minute requests sometimes work (€230/half-day, €390/day, tel. & fax 03 80 23 94 34, mobile 06 80 57 47 40, www.burgundy-guide.com, cobatour @aol.com).

Delightful and wine-smart **Stephanie Jones** is British and came to Burgundy to learn its wines—which she has, getting her degree in oenology and working in Burgundian wine cellars for years. Today she leads informative, enjoyable tours of the vineyards while also running a B&B (tours: €165/person, 2-person minimum, mobile 06 10 18 04 12, www.aux-quatre-saisons.net, stephnwine@aol.com).

Minibus and Walking Tours of Vineyards—Safari Wine Tours offers two-hour van tours of the villages and vineyards around Beaune. Friendly Loïck leads these English-speaking tours that get you into the countryside and smaller wineries (though you won't do much tasting—generally one tasting per tour). There are three itineraries (€35–45, tour #2 is best for beginners; tours depart from TI generally at 12:00, 14:30, and 17:00; tel. 03 80 24 79 12, www.burgundy-tourism-safaritours.com, or call TI to reserve). **Vinéa Tours** is more formal and upscale, with three different itineraries that last two and a half hours each (€48, tel. 03 80 22 51 70, www.vineatours.com).

Sights in Beaune

▲▲▲Hôtel Dieu

This medieval charity hospital is now a museum. The Hundred Years' War and the plague (a.k.a. the Black Death) devastated Beaune, leaving three-quarters of its population destitute. Nicholas Rolin, chancellor of Burgundy (enriched, in part, by his power to collect taxes), had to do something for "his people" (or, more likely, was getting old and wanted to close out his life on a philanthropic, rather than a greedy, note). So, in 1443 Rolin paid to build this hospital. It was completed in just eight years and served as a hospital until 1971, when the last patient checked out. The Hospices de Beaune began opening its doors to visitors in the 1950s, although it wasn't fully open to tourists until the early 1980s.

Cost and Hours: €6.70, daily April–mid-Nov 9:00–18:30, mid-Nov–March 9:00–11:30 & 14:00–17:30, last ticket sold one hour before closing. It's dead-center in Beaune, dominating place de la Halle.

◉ Self-Guided Tour: Although the English flier and the scant posted English descriptions are helpful, this self-guided tour gives your visit more meaning. Tour the rooms, which circle the courtyard, in a clockwise direction.

Courtyard of Honor: Honor meant power, and this was all about showing off. The exterior of the hospital and the town side of the courtyard are intentionally solemn, so as not to attract pesky 15th-century brigands who looted whatever looked most rewarding. The dazzling inner courtyard features a colorful glazed tile roof, establishing what became a style recognized in France as typically "Burgundian." The tiles, which last 300 years, are fired three times; once to harden, again to burn in the color, and finally for the glaze. They were redone in 1902. The building is lacy Flamboyant Gothic with lots of decor—and boasts more weathervanes than any other building in France.

Paupers' Ward: Enter the hospice halfway down the courtyard on the left. This grandest room of the hospital was the ward for the poorest patients. The vault, typical of big medieval rooms, was constructed like the hull of a ship. The screen separates the ward from the chapel at the front. Every three hours, the door was opened, and patients could experience Mass from their beds. Study the ceiling. Crossbeams are held by the mouths of creatively carved monsters—each mouth is stretched realistically, and each face has individual characteristics. Between the crossbars are busts of real 15th-century townsfolk—leading citizens, with animals humorously indicating their foibles (e.g., a round-faced glutton next to a pig).

The carved wooden statue over the door you just entered shows a bound Christ—demonstrating graphically to patients that their Savior suffered and was able to empathize with their ordeal. Its realism shows that Gothic art had moved beyond the stiff formality of Romanesque carving. Behind the little window, next to the statue, was the nuns' dorm. The sisters (who were the first nurses) would check on patients from here. Notice the scrawny candleholder; if a patient died in the night, the candle was extinguished.

A painting halfway up on the left shows patients being treated in this room in 1949, 500 years after its founding. During epidemics, there were two to a bed. Study the glass display cases near the beds. Rolin, who believed every patient deserved dignity, provided each patient with a pewter jug, mug, bowl, and plate. But the ward didn't get heat until the 19th century (notice the heating grates on the floor), and the staff didn't get the concept of infection (and the basic practices of hand-washing and covering your mouth when coughing) until the late 19th century (thanks to Louis Pasteur). Most patients would have been better off left in a ditch outside.

Chapel: The hospice was not a place of hope. People came here to die. Care was more for the soul than the body. (Local guides are routinely instructed in writing by American tour companies not to use the word "hospice," because it turns off their clients. But this was a hospice, plain and simple, and back then, death was apparently less disturbing.) The stained glass shows Nicolas Rolin (lower left) and

his wife, Guigone (lower right), dressed as a nun to show her devotion. Nicolas' feudal superior, the Duke of Burgundy, is portrayed above him. Notice the action on Golgotha. As Jesus is crucified, the souls of the two criminals crucified with him (portrayed as miniature naked humans) are being snatched up—one by an angel and the other by a red devil. At the bottom, Mary cradles the dead body of Christ. You're standing on tiles with the love symbol (or "gallant device") designed by Nicolas and Guigone to celebrate their love (as noble couples often did). The letters *N* and *G* are entwined in an oak branch, meaning that their love was strong. The word *seule* ("only one") and the lone star declare that Guigone is the only star in Nicolas' cosmos.

St. Hugue Ward: In the 17th century, this smaller ward was established for wealthy patients (who could afford better health care). They were more likely to survive, rather than resignation: The series of Baroque themes of hope, rather than resignation: The series of Baroque paintings lining the walls show the biblical miracles that Jesus performed. As the wealthy would lie in their beds, they'd stare at the ceiling—a painting with the bottom of an angel's foot, surrounded by the sick waiting to be healed by Jesus in his scarlet robe. The syringes in the display cases with English descriptions are as delicate as caulking guns. Ouch.

St. Nicolas Room: Originally divided into smaller rooms—one used for "surgery" (a.k.a. bloodletting and amputation), the other as an extension of the kitchen that you'll see next—this room now holds a model of the steep roof support and more tools of the doctoring trade (amputation saws, pans for bloodletting, and so on). The glass panel in the floor's center shows the stream running below; the hole provided a primitive but convenient disposal system after dinner or surgery. Living downstream from the hospital was a bad idea. Notice the display case showing the *Vente aux Enchères des Hospices de Beaune*. Operation of the hospice was primarily funded through auctioning its great wines (made from land donated by grateful patients over the years). Today, the auction of Hospices de Beaune wines is an internationally followed event, and gives the first indication of prices for the last year's wines. Proceeds from the auction still support the hospital at its current location in a Beaune suburb.

Kitchen: The kitchen display shows a 16th-century rotisserie. When fully wound, the cute robot would crank away, and the spit would spin slowly for 45 minutes. The 19th-century stove provided running hot water, which spewed from the beaks of swans. A five-minute, French-only sound-and-light show runs every 15 minutes.

Pharmacy: The nuns grew herbs out back, and strange and wondrous concoctions were stored in pottery jars. The biggest jar (by the window) was for *theriaca* ("panacea," or cure-all). The most commonly used medicine back then, it was a syrup of herbs, wine, and opium.

St. Louis Ward: A maternity ward until 1969, this room is lined with fine 16th- and 17th-century tapestries illustrating mostly Old Testament stories. Dukes traveled with tapestries to cozy up the humble places they stayed in while on the road. The 16th-century pieces have better colors but inferior perspective. (The most precious 15th-century tapestries are displayed in the next room, where everyone is enthralled by the great van der Weyden painting.)

Roger van der Weyden's *Last Judgment*: This exquisite painting, the treasure of the Hôtel Dieu, was commissioned by Rolin in 1450 for the altar of the Paupers' Ward. He spared no cost, hiring the leading Flemish artist of his time. The entire altarpiece survives. The back side (on right wall) was sliced off so everything could be viewed at the same time. The painting is full of symbolism. Christ presides over Judgment Day. The lily is mercy, the sword is judgment, the rainbow promises salvation, and the jeweled globe at Jesus' feet symbolizes the universality of Christianity's message. As four angels blow their trumpets, St. Michael the archangel—very much in control—determines which souls are heavy with sin. Mary and the apostles pray for the souls of the dead as they emerge from their graves. But notice how both Michael and Jesus are expressionless—at this point, the cries of the damned and their loved ones are useless. In the back row are real people of the day.

The intricate detail, painted with a three-haired brush, is typical of Flemish art from this period. While Renaissance artists employed mathematical tricks of perspective, these artists captured a sense of reality by painting minute detail upon detail. (The attendant is dying to be asked to move the magnifying glass—*le loup*—into position to help you appreciate the exquisite detail in the painting.) Stare at Michael's robe and wings. Check out John's delicate feet and hands. Study the faces of the damned; you can almost hear the gnashing of teeth. The feet of the damned show the pull of a terrible force. On the far left, notice those happily entering the pearly gates. On the far right, it's the flames of hell (no, this has nothing to do with politics).

Except for Sundays and holidays, the painting was kept closed and people saw only the panels that now hang on the right wall: Nicolas and Guigone—invoked to fight the plague—and St. Sebastian—invoked to fight the plague—and St. Anthony, whom patients called upon for help in combating burning skin diseases.

The unusual 15th-century tapestry *A Thousand Flowers*, hanging on the left wall, tells the medieval story of St. Eligius.

More Sights in Beaune

Collégiale Notre-Dame—Built in the 12th and 13th centuries, Beaune's cathedral was a "daughter of Cluny" (built in the style of the Cluny Abbey, described on page 887). Except for the 14th-century Gothic front porch addition, it's a good example of Cluny-style Romanesque architecture. Enter to see the 15th-century tapestries (behind the altar), a variety of stained glass, and what's left of frescoes depicting the life of Lazarus (tapestry open daily

9:30–12:30 & 14:00–17:00, until 19:00 during high season).

To get to the Museum of Wine (listed next), turn left down a cobbled alley (rue d'Enfer, or "Hell Street," named for the fires of the Duke's kitchens once located on this street), keep left, and enter the courtyard of Hôtel des Ducs.

Museum of the Wine of Burgundy (Musée du Vin de Bourgogne)—From this well-organized folk-wine museum, which fills the old residence of the Dukes of Burgundy, it's clear that the history and culture of Burgundy and its wine were fermented in the same bottle. Wander into the free courtyard for a look at the striking palace, antique wine presses (in the *cuverie*, or vatting shed; good English explanations), and a concrete model of Beaune's 15th-century street plan (a good chance to appreciate the town's once-impressive fortified wall). Inside the museum, you'll see a model of the region's topography, along with tools, costumes, and scenes of Burgundian wine history—but no tasting. Each room has helpful handheld English explanations (€5.60, €11 with the Hôtel Dieu, ticket also includes the Musée des Beaux-Arts et Musée Marey art museum; April–Nov daily 9:30–18:00; Dec–March Wed–Mon 9:30–17:00, closed Tue; tel. 03 80 22 08 19).

Cave des Aromes—An engaging exhibit on the sense of smell is usually set up during the summer months at Beaune's Chambre de Commerce. You'll sniff glass containers holding a great range of aromas and try to associate them with those you find in wine. It's pricey yet informative—you'll learn why Burgundy was the birthplace of mustard (it's about wine juice), and where they get their grains today (Canada)—but it takes over an hour to explain what could be explained in half that time. Still, for mustard enthusiasts, it's well-presented—you'll see a short film, learn about the key machines used in processing mustard (with the help of audioguides), and finish with a mustard tasting (€10, open Mon–Sat with tours at 10:00 and 11:30, additional tours mid-June–mid-Sept at 15:30 and 17:00, closed Sun, call TI to reserve or book online, across ring road in the appropriately yellow building at 31 rue du Faubourg Bretonnière, www.fallot.com).

The Mustard Mill (La Moutarderie Fallot)—The last of the independent mustard mills in Burgundy opens its doors for bilingual guided tours in French and English. The tour is pricey (€10) a fun place to drop in and sniff (free, usually July–mid-Sept daily 10:00–12:30 & 14:00–18:00, 2 rue Tribunal).

Walk to Parc de la Bouzaise and into the Vineyards—Stroll across the ring road, through a pleasant park, and into Beaune's beautiful vineyards. This walk is ideal for picnickers, families (good play toys in park), and vine enthusiasts.

Follow avenue de la République west from the center, cross the ring road, and follow the stream (which also runs under the Hôtel Dieu) along a few grassy blocks for about five minutes, then turn right to reach the park. Pop out at the rear of the park, turn left on the small road, and enter the Côte de Beaune vineyards (walkers need 15 minutes from Beaune's center to reach the vineyards; drivers need about two minutes—parking available at park). A big duck pond fills the park, and vineyards fill the hillsides behind it. The vine-covered landscape is crisscrossed with narrow lanes and stubby stone walls (good for picnics, but no shade) and provides terrific early-morning and sunset views.

Find the big poster showing how the land is sliced and diced among different plots (called *clos*, for "enclosure"). Wander among the enclosures, noticing the rocky soil (wine grapes need to struggle). The highest areas of the hills far above you grow grapes that end up in wines labeled *Haute Côte de Beaune*, and are cheaper and generally less intense than those made from the grapes in front of you. As you wander about, keep in mind that subtle differences of soil and drainage between adjacent plots of land can be enough to create very different-tasting wines—from grapes grown only feet apart. *Vive la différence.*

Wine-Tasting in and near Beaune

Countless opportunities exist for you to learn about the finer points of Burgundy's wines. Shops everywhere offer free, informal, and informative tastings (with the expectation that you'll buy at least one bottle), but everyone understands the limits on our ability to bring wines back to North America. Burgundy's winemakers hope you'll like their wines and ask for them at your shop back home. Many can arrange shipping (about €12 per bottle to ship a case, though you save about 20 percent on the VAT tax when shipping—so expensive wines are worth the shipping cost). For tips on wine-tasting, see "French Wine-Tasting 101" on page 40.

A few large cellars (*caves*) charge an entry fee, allowing you to taste a variety of wines (with less expectation that you'll buy). Most of these *caves* offer some form of introduction or self-guided tour. Don't mind the mossy ceilings. Many cellars have spent centuries growing this "angel's hair"—the result of humidity created by the evaporation of the wines stored there.

In Beaune

Here are a few good places to learn about Burgundy wines in Beaune.

Patriarche Père et Fils—With Burgundy's largest and most impressive wine cellar, this is the best of the major wineries to visit

Burgundian Wine Quality, 2001–2009

2001 A difficult growing season, with rain and a late frost, producing reds that are thinner, less consistent, and more tannic than in previous years. Whites fared much better.

2002 Called the "vintage of the decade" by some, the reds have now been released. The whites are excellent, with good structure, balance, and pure, clean fruit flavors.

2003 A most unusual year due to the extreme summer heat. The harvest was a month early, so the grapes were small, with thick skins, and produced only about half the usual yield. The reds are deeper in color and taste very different from usual Pinot Noirs. All wines need to be drunk sooner—the average time you can keep this year's vintage is about half the normal (10 years at most for reds; whites should be consumed right away).

2004 A lousy summer (rain, hail, and wind) but a brilliant September (three weeks of bright sunshine). The good *domaines* produced reds that are very fruity, clean, supple, and "flattering" (according to my friend). They can be drunk and appreciated early, though they will last a long time. The whites are excellent, with a precise acidity giving them the freshness and pure fruitiness of a great vintage.

2005 Has the makings of a great vintage: The harvest was healthy and balanced, with great natural sugar. A local magazine called 2005 "the vintage of dreams." The reds

in the city. Listening to a helpful audioguide, you'll tour some of their three miles of underground passages. Then you'll enter the atmospheric tasting room, where you'll taste 13 Burgundian classics (3 whites and 10 reds); each bottle sits on top of its own wine barrel. The long walk back to *la sortie* helps sober you up (€10, daily 9:30–11:30 & 14:00–17:30, last entry 30 minutes before closing, 5 rue du Collège, tel. 03 80 24 53 78, www.patriarche.com).

Bouchard Aîné—This venerable place has been in business since 1753, and it offers a traditional cellar tour and an introduction to wine-tasting while highlighting the five senses. You'll stop at several stations to taste as you visit the cellars, and learn why each sense matters when it comes to wine (€9.50; daily bilingual tours usually at 10:30, 11:30, 14:30, 15:30, 16:30, and 17:30; on the ring road at 4 boulevard Maréchal Foch, tel. 03 80 24 06 66, www.bouchard-aine.fr).

Domaine Loïs Dufouleur—Welcoming Philippe and Anne-Marie add a personal touch at this beautiful, family-run cellar, and are superb—rich, plain, concentrated, full-bodied, and intense. They will age magnificently. The whites may be a little less impressive, but they are still good.

2006 Challenged even the most experienced winemakers with capricious weather that didn't allow an idle moment in the vineyards or the cellar. The whites look to be of high quality with good consistency from Chablis to Mâcon. Supple and fresh, they are already fruity with considerable richness. The reds are excellent across the board, with beautiful, intense color. Some are delicate and elegant; others are robust and full-bodied. Their aromas vary from red fruits to cherry, spices, and cocoa.

2007 A hot spring, combined with the worst Burgundian summer in 30 years, meant a light vintage for the reds—so drink them sooner rather than later. Whites will probably be subpar as well, so you may want to skip this vintage.

2008 Another tricky year for grapes, but shows promise. Those who waited longest to harvest will make the best wines, as September was a warm, dry month. The wines of Chablis are likely to be excellent, but the word is still out on other wines.

2009 This looks to be a banner year for Burgundies. The harvest provided beautiful grapes, so the expectations are sky-high after two tough years. And though the wines may not be as full-bodied as the great 2005 vintage, they should be more supple and ready to drink sooner (but won't keep as long).

they are happy to teach you about their wines (€8 for 4 wines, call ahead for an appointment, 8 boulevard Bretonnière, tel. 03 80 22 04 62, mobile 06 73 85 11 06, www.jardinsdelois.com; their B&B, Les Jardins de Loïs, is listed under "Sleeping in Beaune," later).

Sensation Vin—For a good introduction to Burgundy wines, try these short, easygoing, and informative wine classes. You'll gather around a small counter in the comfortable wine bar/classroom and learn while you taste. Since the owners do not make wine, you'll get an objective education (with blind tastings) and sample from a variety of producers. Call or email ahead to arrange a class/tasting (€11 for 4 wines in a 30-minute class, €21 for 6 wines and more info in a 1-hour class, €39 for 12 wines in a 2-hour class—aspirin and pillow provided; 2-person minimum, daily 10:00–19:00, near Collégiale Notre-Dame at 1 rue d'Enfer, tel. 03 80 22 17 57, www.sensation-vin.com, contact@sensation-vin.com).

Les Mille et une Vignes—Escape the tourists at this wine bar, which reeks with old-time ambience and local characters. Young

> ## Savoring Burgundy:
> ## Wine-Tasting Tactics
>
> **If you don't want to leave Beaune:** Visit one (or more) of the wine cellars listed under "In Beaune" on page 847.
>
> **Visiting vineyards without wheels:** Take a taxi to wine villages just a short drive from Beaune (see "Outside of Beaune," below), book a minibus tour or a recommended local guide (see page 841), or try Transco bus #44 for villages on La Route des Grand Crus (see page 859).
>
> **Visiting vineyards by car:** Follow one of my three self-guided routes, described on page 860. The first two routes also work well for bikes.

owner Marine serves a good selection of wines by the glass at fair prices (Tue–Sat 11:00 until late, closed Sun–Mon, 61 rue de Lorraine, tel. 03 80 22 03 02).

Outside of Beaune

A handy way to sample village life—and prowl the vineyards—is to hop on a bike or take a taxi. These wineries are a short jaunt from Beaune (just a 10- to 20-minute drive). Remember that at free tastings, you're expected to buy a bottle or two, unless you're with a group tour. All of these places can ship overseas. For wine-tasting suggestions along La Route des Grands Crus, see page 866.

In Puligny-Montrachet and Chassagne-Montrachet

These two villages are situated about a 10-minute drive (or 45-minute bike ride) south of Beaune, on the scenic route to the Rochepot Castle (see page 860).

Caveau de Puligny-Montrachet—Located on the village's central roundabout, this convivial wine-bar–like tasting room represents many top-quality Burgundian vintners and has a good selection from Puligny-Montrachet. There's a smart outdoor terrace where you can taste, as well. Knowledgeable Julien is happy to answer your every question (€10 for 5 wines, free if you buy 6 bottles; March–Oct daily 9:30–12:00 & 14:00–19:00, sometimes open later; Nov–Feb Tue–Sat 10:00–12:00 & 15:00–18:00, closed Mon; tel. 03 80 21 96 78).

Château de Chassagne-Montrachet—If you're looking for a grand wine château experience, come here. Signs in Chassagne-Montrachet lead to an elegant mansion where an informative tour takes you through gorgeous cellars—some dating to the 11th century. You'll taste five of Michel Picard's impressive wines from throughout Burgundy (€12, allow at least an hour). They also offer a well-designed wine-tasting lunch (*table dégustation*) for €40 with six wines or €50 with 12 wines...cots are provided (daily 10:00–18:00, best to call ahead, tel. 03 80 21 98 57, www .michelpicard.com).

In Aloxe-Corton

This village is about a 10-minute drive north of Beaune.

Domaines d'Aloxe-Corton—You can sample seven makers of the famous Aloxe-Corton wines in this comfortable and relaxed setting. Prices are affordable, and the easygoing staff speaks enough English (small fee for tasting, free if you buy 2 bottles, Thu–Mon 10:00–13:00 & 15:00–19:00, usually closed Tue–Wed, tel. 03 80 26 49 85). You'll find the *caveau* a few steps from the church on the little square in Aloxe-Corton.

Château Corton-André—A block farther into Aloxe-Corton, this château winery offers a tour of its cellars with wine-tastings (daily 10:00–13:00 & 14:00–19:00, rue des Cortons, tel. 03 80 26 44 25, www.pierre-andre.com).

In Magny-les-Villers

Domaine Naudin-Ferrand—Located 15 minutes north of Beaune (beyond Aloxe-Corton), in the Hautes-Côtes village of Magny-les-Villers, this *domaine* is overlooked by most, but makes terrific reds and whites. Its best values are wines from the Hautes-Côtes vineyards. As it's a small enterprise, call or email to let them know you are coming (tel. 03 80 62 91 50, www.naudin-ferrand .com, info@naudin-ferrand.com).

Sleeping in Beaune

In the Center of Beaune

$$$ Hôtel le Cep***** is *the* venerable place to stay in Beaune, if you have the means. Buried in the town center, this historic building comes with fine public spaces inside and out, and 64 gorgeous wood-beamed, traditionally decorated rooms in all sizes (standard Sb–€140, Db–€175, deluxe Db–€215, suites–€255–500, continental breakfast–€20, air-con, king-size beds, Internet access and Wi-Fi, fitness center, parking–€15/day, 27 rue Maufoux, tel. 03 80 22 35 48, fax 03 80 22 76 80, www.hotel-cep-beaune.com, resa@hotel -cep-beaune.com).

$$$ Hôtel des Remparts***, a peaceful oasis in a manor house built around a calming courtyard, features traditional comfort, rooms with beamed ceilings, big beds, and a few good family suites (standard Db–€90–115, bigger Db–€135–153, Tb–€100–130, Qb–€160, ask for Rick Steves discount when booking, top-floor rooms have air-con, Internet access, pay Wi-Fi, laundry service,

Sleep Code

(€1 = about $1.25, country code: 33)

S = Single, **D** = Double/Twin, **T** = Triple, **Q** = Quad, **b** = bathroom, **s** = shower only, * = French hotel rating system (0-4 stars). Unless otherwise noted, credit cards are accepted and English is spoken.

To help you easily sort through these listings, I've divided the rooms into three categories based on the price for a standard double room with bath:

$$$ Higher Priced—Most rooms €90 or more.
$$ Moderately Priced—Most rooms between €60-90.
$ Lower Priced—Most rooms €60 or less.

Prices can change without notice: verify the hotel's current rates online or by email. For other updates, see www.ricksteves.com/update.

bike rental, garage–€10/day, just inside ring road between train station and main square at 48 rue Thiers, tel. 03 80 24 94 94, fax 03 80 24 97 08, www.hotel-remparts-beaune.com, hotel.des .remparts@wanadoo.fr, run by the formal Epaillys).

$$$ Les Jardins de Loïs****, run by welcoming winemakers Philippe and Anne-Marie, is a four-star B&B. The four big rooms all overlook gargantuan gardens lined with fruit trees, and show a no-expense-spared attention to detail and comfort. There's also a nice lounge area and a Turkish bath (Db–€135, big Db–€160-180, Tb–€180, includes breakfast, air-con, Wi-Fi, on the ring road a block after Hôtel de la Poste at 8 boulevard Bretonnière, tel. 03 80 22 41 97, mobile 06 73 85 11 06, www.jardinsdelois.com, contact @jardinsdelois.com). Their atmospheric wine cellar, Domaine Loïs Dufouleur, also offers tastings (€8 for 4 wines, free for guests, arrange ahead, see page 848).

$$$ Hôtel Athanor*** enjoys a privileged location a block from the cathedral, and mixes modern comfort with a touch of old Beaune. The atmospheric lounge sports a pool table—free for guests—and a full-service bar (standard Db without air-con–€99, *supérieure* Db with air-con–€135, deluxe Db–€155, extra bed–€20, ask for Rick Steves discount when booking, elevator, Wi-Fi, 9-11 avenue de la République, tel. 03 80 24 09 20, fax 03 80 24 09 15, www.hotel-athanor.com, hotel.athanor@wanadoo.fr, helpful Caroline).

$$ Hôtel Ibis**, centrally located with free and easy parking, has 73 efficient rooms. It's a good value—even better if you have kids and want a pool. The bigger and better-appointed "Club" rooms are worth the extra euros (standard Db–€82–92, "Club" Db–€90–105, extra person–€10, lower rates on website, non-smoking floor, air-con, free Wi-Fi, free parking, 5-minute walk to town center, you'll pass it as you enter Beaune from the autoroute, tel. 03 80 22 75 67, fax 03 80 22 77 17, www.hotelibis.com, h1363 @accor.com). There's another (cheaper) Ibis Hôtel—along with a gaggle of Motel 6–type places—closer to the autoroute.

$$ Hôtel de France** is a well-run place and easy for train travelers (parking across from the train station). It comes with clean rooms and outgoing owners Tita and Eric (Sb–€63–98—most are about €63, Db–€68–100—most are about €68, Tb–€78–105, Qb–€88–100, air-con, Internet access and Wi-Fi, garage–€9/day, 35 avenue du 8 Septembre, tel. 03 80 24 10 34, fax 03 80 24 96 78, www.hoteldefrance-beaune.com, hoteldefrance .beaune@wanadoo.fr).

$$ Hôtel La Villa Fleurie*** , an adorable 10-room refuge, is run by affable Madame Chartier on a plain street a few blocks out-side the ring road (15-minute walk from the center). Most rooms are wood-floored, plush, and *très* traditional and come with big bathrooms and air-conditioning (small Db–€70, bigger Db–€80– 100, nifty Tb/Qb loft–€110–130, Wi-Fi, easy and free parking, cute garden, 19 place Colbert, tel. 03 80 22 66 00, fax 03 80 22 45 46, www.lavillafleurie.fr, la.villa.fleurie@wanadoo.fr). From Beaune's ring road, turn right in front of the Bichot winery.

Place Madeleine

These hotels are a few blocks from the city center and train station, with easy parking.

$$$ Hôtel de la Paix*** , a few steps off place Madeleine, is a top choice, with 24 handsome, well-appointed rooms (the suites are four-star quality), several good family rooms, and snazzy pub-lic spaces. The unsmiling owner is serious, but runs a tight ship (Db–€78–95, Db suite–€160, loft Tb–€118, Qb–€130–170, air-con, Internet access and Wi-Fi, private parking, 45 rue du Faubourg Madeleine, tel. 03 80 24 78 08, fax 03 80 24 10 18, www.hotelpaix .com, contact@hotelpaix.com).

$$ L'Auberge Bourguignonne's restaurant hides 10 comfort-able, well-priced rooms with no public spaces (Db–€59–69, big-ger Db with air-con–€78, Tb–€78, check in at restaurant, 4 place Madeleine, tel. 03 80 22 23 53, fax 03 80 22 51 64, www.auberge -bourguignonne.fr, contact@auberge-bourguignonne.fr).

$$ Hôtel Rousseau is a good-value, no-frills, frumpy manor house that turns its back on Beaune's sophistication. Cheerful, quirky, and elusive owner Madame Rousseau, her pet birds, and the quiet garden will make you smile, and the tran-quility will help you sleep. The cheapest rooms are a godsend for

Beaune Hotels & Restaurants

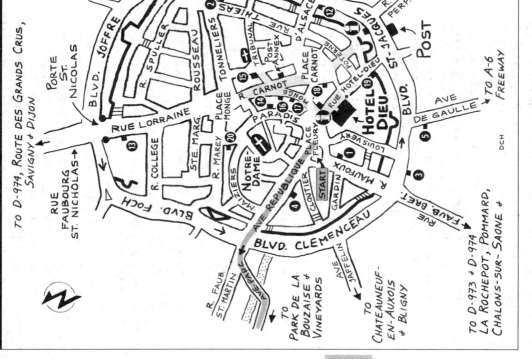

budget travelers. The rooms with showers are like Grandma's, with enough comfort (S-€32, D-€42, D with toilet-€52, Db-€63, T with toilet-€60, Tb-€70, Q-€64, Qb-€76, showers down the hall-€3, includes breakfast, cash only, reservations preferred by email, free and easy parking, 11 place Madeleine, tel. 03 80 22 13 59, fax 03 80 22 67 55, hotelrousseaubeaune@orange.fr). Check-ins after 19:00 and morning departures before 7:30 must be arranged in advance.

BURGUNDY

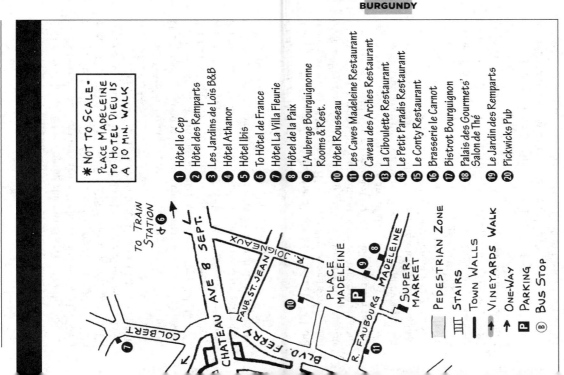

* NOT TO SCALE.
PLACE MADELEINE
TO HOTEL DIEU IS
A 10 MIN. WALK

1. Hôtel le Cep
2. Hôtel des Remparts
3. Les Jardins de Loïs B&B
4. Hôtel Athanor
5. Hôtel Ibis
6. To Hôtel de France
7. Hôtel La Villa Fleurie
8. Hôtel de la Paix
9. L'Auberge Bourguignonne Rooms & Rest.
10. Hôtel Rousseau
11. Les Caves Madeleine Restaurant
12. Caveau des Arches Restaurant
13. La Ciboulette Restaurant
14. Le Petit Paradis Restaurant
15. Le Conty Restaurant
16. Brasserie le Carnot
17. Bistrot Bourguignon
18. Palais des Gourmets' Salon de Thé
19. Le Jardin des Remparts
20. Pickwicks Pub

TO TRAIN STATION & 6

AVE 8 SEPT.

R. JOIGNEAUX

FAUB. ST. JEAN

CHATEAU

BLVD. FERRY

COLBERT

PLACE MADELEINE

R. FAUBOURG MADELEINE

SUPER-MARKET

▮▮▮ PEDESTRIAN ZONE
▮▮▮ STAIRS
▬ TOWN WALLS
↟ VINEYARDS WALK
↑ ONE-WAY
🅿 PARKING
Ⓑ BUS STOP

Outside of Beaune

You'll find some exceptional family-friendly values within a short drive of Beaune. Also see the suggestions along the Route des Grands Crus (page 866).

Hotels

$$$ Hôtel Villa Louise*** is a romantic place burrowed in the prestigious wine hamlet of Aloxe-Corton, five minutes north of

Beaune. Many of its 13 *très* cozy and tastefully decorated rooms overlook the backyard vineyards, a small covered pool, and a large, grassy garden made for sipping the owner's wine (sadly, no picnics allowed). The serious owners—the Perrins—will show you their vaulted cellars (Db-€110-152—most are about €110-130, Db suite-€150-200, buffet breakfast-€15, Internet access and Wi-Fi, covered pool, sauna, near the château at 9 rue Franche, tel. 03 80 26 46 70, fax 03 80 26 47 16, www.hotel-villa-louise.fr, hotel-villa-louise@wanadoo.fr).

$$ Hôtel le Home**, just off busy D-974 a half-mile north of Beaune, is a good value, with comfy rooms in an old mansion. The rooms in the main building come in soft pastels (Db-€70-77, Tb-€75-85, Qb-€98, top-floor rooms have the most character). Rooms on the parking courtyard (only Db-€66) come with stone floors, small terraces, and bright colors, but can be dark and musty (free parking and Wi-Fi, 138 route de Dijon, tel. 03 80 22 16 43, fax 03 80 24 90 74, www.lehome.fr, info@lehome.fr).

Chambres d'Hôtes

The Côte d'Or has scads of *chambres d'hôtes*; get a list at the TI and reserve ahead in the summer. The wine villages south of Beaune (such as Puligny-Montrachet) and the cliff-dwelling villages near La Rochepot (such as St. Romain and Orches) make great non-Beaune bases, with several *chambres d'hôtes* (well-signed in the villages). You'll need a car to get to any of these places.

$$$ Domaine des Anges is a lovely place run by a British couple who spoil their fortunate guests with the Queen's English, sumptuous rooms (a few with views), linger-longer lounges inside and out, a laundry room, fine dinners with drinks (€35, book ahead), and high tea every afternoon. It's also ideally located in the center of Puligny-Montrachet (Db-€75-130, includes a smashing breakfast, no children under 16, place des Marronniers, tel. 03 80 21 38 28, mobile 06 23 86 63 91, www.domainedesangespuligny.com, domainedesanges@yahoo.fr).

$$$ Château de Melin, run by friendly Hélène, is a semi-restored château that offers comfort, though no interior public spaces. Four huge rooms play second fiddle to their winery (don't expect prompt service). Outside you can enjoy a small pond, vineyards (tastings available), and gardens to stretch out in (Db-€100-125, Tb-€135, Qb-€155, includes good breakfast, cash only, 10 minutes from Beaune toward La Rochepot, between villages of Auxey-Duresses and La Rochepot, tel. 03 80 21 21 19, fax 03 80 21 21 72, www.chateaudemelin.com, derats@chateaudemelin.com).

$$ La Domaine de Corgette is hunkered beneath a hillside in lovely little St. Romain. Welcoming Véronique has restored an old vintner's home with style. A stay-awhile terrace, private parking, cozy common rooms, and wine-tastings are at your disposal (Db–€80–100, Tb–€125, Qb–€150, includes breakfast, cash only, follow signs from Auxey-Duresses, on rue de la Perrière, tel. & fax 03 80 21 68 08, www.domainecorgette.com, accueil@domaine corgette.com).

Eating in Beaune

For a small town, Beaune offers a wide range of reasonably priced restaurants. Review my suggestions carefully before setting out, and reserve ahead to avoid frustration (especially on weekends). Many places are closed Sunday and Monday. The first three listings are on or very near big place Madeleine; the rest are scattered about the old town.

At **Les Caves Madeleine**, step down into the warm and enchanting little dining room that doubles as a wine shop. Choose a private table—or, better, join the convivial communal table, where good food and wine kindle conversation, then lubricate new friendships (this is a boon for solo travelers). The sincere young owner, Monsieur Lo-Lo, speaks English and enjoys sharing his love of food and wine. Because he's also a wine merchant, he can pass his savings on to you by selling bottles at store prices plus €5 to drink them here, making top-end wines almost affordable. Lo-Lo also runs the kitchen; his *cassolette d'escargot* will melt your taste buds, and his *jambon persillé* and *bœuf bourguignon* are excellent (€14 and €24 *menus*, closed Thu and Sun, 8 rue du Faubourg Madeleine, tel. 03 80 22 93 30).

Caveau des Arches is a smart choice if you want to dine on delicious Burgundian specialties at fair prices in atmospheric stone cellars (€22 *menu* with the classics, closed Sun–Mon, where the ring road crosses rue d'Alsace—which leads to place Madeleine—at 10 boulevard Perpreuil, tel. 03 80 22 10 37).

La Ciboulette, intimate and family-run with petite Hélène as your hostess, offers good cuisine that mixes traditional Burgundian flavors with creative dishes and lovely presentation. It's worth the longer walk—and you can do your laundry next door while you dine (€20 and €32 *menus*, closed Mon–Tue; from place Carnot, walk out rue Carnot to 69 rue Lorraine, tel. 03 80 24 70 72).

Le Petit Paradis does its name justice, with 10 tables crowding a sharp little room. The chef's menu is inventive and ever-changing (*menus* from €29, closed Sun–Mon, 25 rue de Paradis, tel. 03 80 24 91 00).

Le Conty owns a privileged position at the junction of two pedestrian lanes. With its great outdoor seating, it's ideal for a big salad or good brasserie fare (*menus* from €22, closed Sun–Mon, 5 rue Ziem, tel. 03 80 22 63 94).

Brasserie le Carnot is a locally popular café with good interior seating and better exterior tables in the thick of the pedestrian zone. It serves excellent pizza, good salads, pasta dishes, and the usual café offerings (open daily, where rue Carnot and rue Monge meet).

Bistrot Bourguignon is a relaxed wine bar-bistro with a lengthy wine list and 15 wines available by the glass (order by number from display behind bar). The bon vivant owner, Jean-Jacques, and son Virgil offer the same affordable prices at either bar or table. Come for a glass of wine or to enjoy a light dinner. Dine at the counter, the sidewalk tables, or in the casually comfortable interior (€10 starters, €18 *plats*, €12 lunch *menu*, closed Sun-Mon, on a pedestrian-only street at 8 rue Monge, tel. 03 80 22 23 24).

L'Auberge Bourguignonne is decidedly Burgundian, with serious service and proudly displayed awards. Choose from two traditional dining rooms, or eat outside on the square (*menus* from €21, some seafood, air-con, reservations smart, 4 place Madeleine, tel. 03 80 22 23 53).

Palais des Gourmets' Salon de Thé provides the best-value outdoor lunch on place Carnot, with delicious quiche, omelets, crêpes, and memorable desserts (open daily until 18:30, next to The Athenaeum's back door entrance at 14 place Carnot, tel. 03 80 22 13 39).

Le Jardin des Remparts is a Burgundian splurge. This dressy stone manor house is elegant inside and out (leafy terrace dining in summer), yet the service is casual and attentive. The excellent nouvelle cuisine proudly works with regional products. Always reserve ahead (€70-90 *menus*, €35 at lunch, closed Sun-Mon, just past Hôtel Dieu on ring road at 10 rue de l'Hôtel Dieu, tel. 03 80 24 79 41, lejardin@club-internet.fr).

After Dinner

If you're tired of speaking French, pop into the late-night-lively **Pickwicks Pub** (Mon-Sat 17:00-05:00, closed Sun, behind church at 2 rue Notre-Dame).

Near Beaune, in Puligny-Montrachet

This wine village is a 10-minute drive away from Beaune.

At **Le Montrachet**, settle in for a truly traditional Burgundian experience—a justifiable splurge if you want a refined and classy dining experience without the stuffiness, and a remarkable choice for a gourmet lunch on a lovely terrace at affordable prices (€28 lunch *menu*, €60 dinner *menu*, on Puligny-Montrachet's main square at 19 place des Marronniers, tel. 03 80 21 30 06). Come early for a glass of wine before dinner with Julien at the Caveau de Puligny-Montrachet (see page 850).

L'Estaminet de Meix delivers good brasserie fare in the heart of the village with sharp indoor and outdoor seating (place des Marronniers, tel. 03 80 21 33 01).

Beaune Connections

From Beaune by Train to: Dijon (15/day, 25 minutes), **Paris'** Gare de Lyon (15/day, 2.5 hours, most require reservation and easy change in Dijon; more via Dijon to Paris' Gare de Bercy, no reservation required, 4 hours), **Colmar** (6/day, 4–5 hours, changes in Dijon and in Besançon, Mulhouse, or Belfort), **Arles** (10/day, 4.5 hours, 9 with transfer in Lyon and Nîmes or Avignon), **Chamonix** (7/day, 7 hours, change in Lyon and St. Gervais, some require additional changes), **Annecy** (7/day, 4–6 hours, change in Lyon), **Amboise** (2/day, 5 hours, via Dijon and Tours, plus 12/day, 6 hours, most with changes in Dijon and in Paris, arrive at Paris' Gare de Lyon, then Métro to Austerlitz or Montparnasse stations to catch the connection to Amboise).

The Beaune Region

Getting Around the Beaune Region

By Bus: Transco bus #44 links Beaune with other wine villages to the north along the famous Route des Grands Crus, and runs to Dijon's train station (7/day, toll-free tel. 08 00 10 20 04, www.mobigo-bourgogne.com). Find bus stops along Beaune's ring road. Bus service south of Beaune to villages like Meursault and Puligny-Montrachet is hopeless—take a taxi, hop a train (limited options), or rent a bike.

By Train: Hourly trains stop in the wine villages of Meursault and Santenay to the south of Beaune, and Ladoix-Serrigny to the north. Meursault's station is a 25-minute walk through vineyards to the town center.

By Minibus Tour: Try **Safari Wine Tours** or **Vinéa Tours** (see page 841).

By Taxi: Call **Gerard Rebillard** (mobile 06 11 83 06 10); for other taxis, see page 840.

By Bike: Well-organized, English-speaking Florent and Canadian Sarah at **Bourgogne Randonnées** offer good bikes, bike racks, maps, and detailed itineraries (their advice inspired some of the trips described next). Ask about their favorite routes that follow only small roads and dedicated bike paths. I like the *Discovering the Chardonnay Kingdom* tour. It departs from Beaune's parc de la Bouzaise and connects the wine villages of Pommard, Meursault, and Volnay in a scenic, mostly level, 14-mile loop ride (can be extended to Puligny-Montrachet for a level, 22-mile loop). They can deliver your bike to your hotel anywhere in France (bikes–€4/hour, €18/day, Mon–Sat 9:00–12:00 & 13:30–19:00, Sun 10:00–12:00 & 14:00–19:00, near train station at 7 avenue du 8 Septembre, tel. 03 80 22 06 03, fax 03 80 22 15 58, www.detours -in-france.com, info@bourgogne-randonnees.com).

Sights in the Beaune Region

Cars provide the ultimate flexibility for touring the vineyards, though drivers need to sip small samples (use the handy buckets to spit back after tasting). If you hop on a bike in Beaune, within minutes you'll be immersed in the lush countryside and immaculate vineyards of the Côte d'Or. The bike lane that circles Beaune's ring road—and the many quiet service roads—make this area wonderful for biking. (Beware of loose gravel on the shoulders and along the small roads.) A bike route runs south from Beaune all the way to Cluny, and a new route from Beaune north to Dijon should be in place by your visit.

In the following section, you'll find three vineyard routes that combine great scenery with some of my favorite wine destinations. I prefer the beautiful route connecting villages **between Beaune and La Rochepot Castle** (villages such as Monthelie, Nantoux, St. Romain, and St. Aubin are off the beaten path and offer ample tastings). Most bikers will prefer doing a section of this route, or should consider my **"Vineyard Loop,"** near Beaune. I also cover the famous **Route des Grands Crus,** connecting Burgundy's most prestigious wine villages, but this is less than ideal for bikes. The first part, between Aloxe-Corton and Nuits St. Georges, is disappointing, as you're forced onto an unappealing highway (D-974). But from Vougeot north, the route improves—locals call this section the "Champs-Élysées of Burgundy."

In most cases, I avoid the famous wine châteaux (like in Pommard and Meursault), which I find overpriced and impersonal. Although you can drop in unannounced at most wineries (*comme un cheveux sur la soupe*—"like a hair on the soup"), you'll get better service by calling ahead and letting them know you're coming. Remember that at free tastings, you're expected to buy a bottle or two, unless you're on a group tour.

▲▲Scenic Vineyard Route to/from La Rochepot Castle

Take this pretty, peaceful route for the best approach to La Rochepot's romantic castle, and to glide through several of

La Rochepot Scenic Vineyard Route

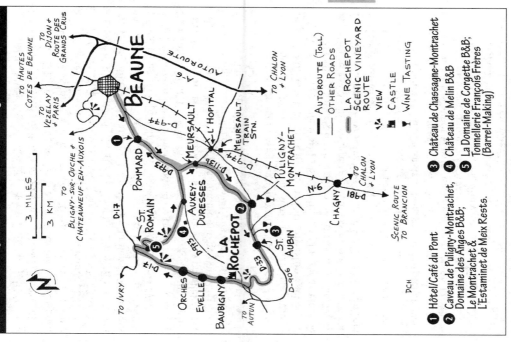

3 MILES
3 KM

TO HAUTES CÔTES DE BEAUNE
TO DIJON + ROUTE DES GRANDS CRUS
TO VEZELAY + PARIS
TO BLIGNY-SUR-OUCHE + CHATEAUNEUF-EN-AUXOIS
TO CHALON + LYON

BEAUNE

A-6 AUTOROUTE

L'HOPITAL
D-974
MEURSAULT
D-973
MEURSAULT TRAIN STN.
POMMARD
ST. ROMAIN
AUXEY-DURESSES
PULIGNY-MONTRACHET
D-113B
N-6
TO CHALON + LYON
D-17
D-973
CHAGNY
186a
SCENIC ROUTE TO BRANCION
D-973
LA ROCHEPOT
ST. AUBIN
D-33
ORCHES
EVELLE
BAUBIGNY
D-17
D-906
TO IVRY
TO AUTUN
DCH

Legend:
- ▬ AUTOROUTE (TOLL)
- — OTHER ROADS
- LA ROCHEPOT SCENIC VINEYARD ROUTE
- VIEW
- CASTLE
- ¶ WINE TASTING

❶ Hôtel/Café du Pont
❷ Caveau de Puligny-Montrachet, Domaine des Anges B&B; Le Montrachet & L'Estaminet de Meix Rests.
❸ Château de Chassagne-Montrachet
❹ Château de Melin B&B
❺ La Domaine de Corgette B&B; Tonnellerie François Frères (Barrel-Making)

Burgundy's most reputed vineyards. Read ahead and note that if you want to see the wine-barrel-makers at work, you need to get there by 15:00—if that's a push, reverse this loop. Bikers can short-cut this ride by following Bourgogne Randonnées' *Discovering the Chardonnay Kingdom* itinerary (see page 859), or by doubling back to Beaune after visiting Puligny-Montrachet (figure an hour of level riding each way), though the bike route continues on a mix of small roads and paths all the way to Cluny (eventually signed as *la Voie Verte*).

Self-Guided Tour: Drivers leave Beaune's ring road, following signs for *Chalon-sur-Saône* and *Autun*, then follow signs to *Pommard*. Cyclists take the lovely vineyard bike path by leaving the ring road toward *Auxerre* and *Bligny-sur-Ouche*, and turning left just after Lycée Viticole de Beaune—look for bike route signs.

When you come to Pommard, you'll pass many wine-tasting opportunities and a cool lunch café, **Hôtel du Pont** (€13 lunch menus, €8 salads, good terrace, closed Sun, tel. 03 80 22 03 41).

South of Pommard, the road gradually climbs through terrific views (bikers take their own path). From here, follow signs into *Meursault*, then carefully work your way through this world-famous wine town by following small signs to *Centre-Ville* (not D-974). When you reach the main square (look for a big church), stay right and find the bike-route signs (to the right of the Casino store). Leave Meursault, following bike route signs paralleling the hills to your right, then keep straight and merge onto D-113b to Puligny-Montrachet (bikers will follow signs onto smaller roads). If you end up on D-974, head west toward the hills, and you'll soon cross D-113b.

You'll pass through low-slung vineyards, then enter Puligny-Montrachet. At the big roundabout with a bronze sculpture of vineyard workers, find the **Caveau de Puligny-Montrachet** and a chance to sample the world's best whites and a good selection of reds (see page 850). A block straight out the door of the *caveau* leads to the town's big square (place des Marronniers) and the **Hôtel-Restaurant Le Montrachet** and the **Café de l'Estaminet de Meix** (both described on page 858).

Go back to the roundabout and follow signs *to Chassagne-Montrachet* and *St. Aubin*, leading you through more manicured vineyards. To tour the **Château de Chassagne-Montrachet** (well-signed, see page 850), head into Chassagne-Montrachet. To continue on to La Rochepot Castle, make a hard right on D-906 to St. Aubin, where you'll follow *La Rochepot* signs onto D-33. As you head over the hills and through the vineyards of the Hautes-Côtes (upper slopes), you'll come to a drop-dead view of the castle (stop mandatory). Turn right when you reach La Rochepot, and follow *Le Château* signs to the castle (described next).

After visiting the castle, turn right out of its parking lot and mosey through Baubigny, Evelles, and rock-solid Orches. After Orches, climb to the top of Burgundy's world—keeping straight on D-17, you'll pass several exceptional lookouts (the village of St. Romain swirls below, and if it's really clear, look for Mont Blanc on the eastern horizon).

Then drive down to St. Romain, stopping at Burgundy's most important wine-barrel-maker, **Tonnellerie François Frères.** Park in their lot just above the village and walk to the left end of the modern building, then follow the hammer noises up a few steps and take in the medieval scene. Well-stoked fires heat the oak staves to make them flexible, and sweaty workers pound iron rings around the barrels just the way they've always done. No one slacks in this hardworking factory, where demand seems strong. Work starts early and ends by about 15:00 (open Mon-Fri, closed Sat-Sun, tel. 03 80 21 23 33, www.francoisfreres.com).

Next, follow signs for *Auxey-Duresses*, and then *Beaume* for a pretty finale to your journey.

▲Château de la Rochepot

This very Burgundian castle rises above the trees and its village, eight miles from Beaune. It's accessible by car, bike (hilly), or infrequent bus. Cross the drawbridge under the Pot family coat of arms and knock three times with the ancient knocker to enter. If no one comes, knock harder, or find a log and ram the gate. This pint-size castle is splendid inside and out. Tour half on your own and the other half with a French guide (get the English handout, some English tours in English—call ahead, most guides speak some English and can answer questions). This castle's construction began during the end of the Middle Ages (when castles were built to defend) and was completed during the Renaissance (when castles were transformed into luxury homes). So it's neither a purely defensive structure (as in the Dordogne) nor a palace (as in the Loire)—it's a blend of both.

The furnishings are surprisingly elaborate given the military look of the exterior. I could sleep like a baby in the Captain's Room, surrounded by nine-foot-thick walls. Don't miss the 15th-century alarmed safe. Notice the colorful doorjamb. These same colors were used to paint many buildings (including castles and churches) and remind us that medieval life went beyond beige and stone. The kitchen will bowl you over; the dining room sports a 15th-century walnut high-chair. Climb the tower and see the Chinese room, sing chants in the resonant chapel, and make ripples in the 240-foot-deep well. (Can you spit a bull's-eye?) Paths outside lead you on a worthwhile walk around the castle. Don't leave without driving, walking, or pedaling up D-33 a few hundred yards toward St. Aubin (behind Hôtel Relais du Château) for a romantic view.

Cost and Hours: €7.50, €9.50 if you add tour of exterior offered Sundays at 11:30, private tours in English-€60, call to confirm times, open Wed-Mon June-mid-Sept 10:00–18:00, April-May 10:00–11:45 & 14:00–17:30, mid-Sept-Oct 10:00–11:45 & 14:00–16:45, closed Tue and Nov-March, tel. 03 80 21 71 37, www.larochepot.com.

Getting There: The highly recommended scenic route from Beaune to the château is described earlier. Or, to reach the château more directly from Beaune, follow signs for *Chalon-sur-Saône* from Beaune's ring road, then follow signs to *Autun* along a lovely 15-minute drive to La Rochepot. Once in the town, turn right a block before the Relais du Château Hôtel to reach the castle.

▲Vineyard Loop near Beaune

For an easy and rewarding spin (by car or ideally by bike) through wine paradise, follow this relatively level 10-mile loop from Beaune (with tastings, allow a half-day by bike or 1.5 hours by car). It laces together three renowned wine villages—Aloxe-Corton, Pernand Vergelesses, and Savigny-les-Beaune—connecting you with Burgundian nature and village wine culture. Bring water and snacks, as there is precious little available until the end of this route. Your tour concludes in Savigny-les-Beaune, where you'll find several attractions, including a café-pizzeria, plenty of wine-tastings, a small grocery, and a unique château.

Drivers can extend the loop into the Hautes-Côtes and visit the recommended winery **Domaine Naudin-Ferrand** in Magny-les-Villers (see page 851). They can also combine this loop with the Route des Grands Crus, described next.

⦿ Self-Guided Tour: From Beaune's ring road bike lane, take D-974 north toward Dijon; soon after, follow signs leading left to *Savigny-les-Beaune.* Cross over the freeway, then follow signs to *Pernand Vergelesses* on D-18 (at the roundabout). Turn right at signs to *Aloxe-Corton,* and pedal or drive into **Aloxe-Corton** (aim for its church spire; drivers can stop at the small parking area near the church). This tiny town, with a world-class reputation among wine enthusiasts, has several tasting opportunities (but no cafés). The easygoing **Domaines d'Aloxe Corton** and grand **Château Corton-André** offer tastings (see page 851).

Back on your bike, leave Aloxe's little square and head up the hill to **Pernand Vergelesses.** There's a cute little café to the right as you enter the village. **La Grappe,** with cheap food and drink (look for colorful umbrellas, closed Mon, tel. 03 80 21 59 46). Drivers (and steel-legged bikers) should climb well above the village to a fantastic vineyard panorama: Enter Pernand Vergelesses at the small roundabout and climb, turning right on rue du Creux St. Germain, and then right again up rue Copeau. Continue up past the church until you see small *Panorama* signs. Most bikers will want to skip Pernand Vergelesses and continue on to Savigny-les-Beaune. Drivers can continue past Pernand Vergelesses a few minutes to the recommended winery Domaine Naudin-Ferrand, mentioned above.

Follow the main road (D-18) back toward Beaune, and turn right into the vineyards on the first lane (about 400 yards from Pernand Vergelesses). Keep left as it curves and rises gently to

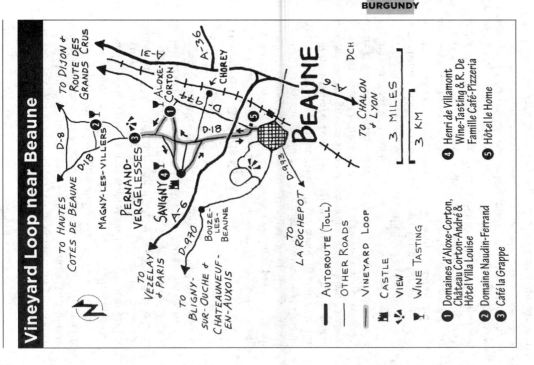

Vineyard Loop near Beaune

TO HAUTES CÔTES DE BEAUNE — D-8

TO DIJON + ROUTE DES GRANDS CRUS

TO VÉZELAY + PARIS

MAGNY-LES-VILLERS

D.18

PERNAND-VERGELESSES

D.18

ALOXE-CORTON

TO BLIGNY-SUR-OUCHE & CHÂTEAUNEUF-EN-AUXOIS

D-970

A-6

SAVIGNY

BOUZE-LES-BEAUNE

D-973

CHOREY

A-36

A-31

D.974

BEAUNE

TO LA ROCHEPOT

TO CHALON + LYON

A-6

DCH

3 MILES

3 KM

▬	AUTOROUTE (TOLL)
—	OTHER ROADS
▬	VINEYARD LOOP
⌂	CASTLE
✶	VIEW
▼	WINE TASTING

1 Domaines d'Aloxe-Corton, Château Corton-André & Hôtel Villa Louise
2 Domaine Naudin-Ferrand
3 Café la Grappe
4 Henri de Villamont, Wine-Tasting & R. De Famille Café-Pizzeria
5 Hôtel le Home

lovely views. Drop down and turn right when you come to a T and keep going until you see a *5T* sign (bikers should watch for loose gravel on this section). Turn left before the sign, then a quick right, and right again, and ride into **Savigny-les-Beaune.**

You'll come to a three-way intersection. The left fork leads back to Beaune. The middle fork leads to *Centre-Ville,* and the road to the right leads to wine-tasting at **Henri de Villamont,** a big enterprise with a reasonable range of wines from nearby vineyards and a welcoming tasting room (daily 10:00–18:00, rue du Dr. Guyot, tel. 03 80 21 52 13, www.hdv.fr).

Follow the middle fork to reach the town center and find

the **R. De Famille** café-pizzeria facing a little square (daily, tel. 03 80 21 50 00); a grocery shop a few blocks past the café (closed 12:30–15:00); and a four-towered collectors' château, **Le Château de Savigny.** This medieval castle comes with a moat, 80 fighter jets parked in the side yard, Abarth antique racing cars, fun tractor and fire-engine collections, 300 motorcycles, 2,000 airplane models, and vineyards (the owner's wine is available for tasting). The collection fills most of the interior, so don't look for the traditional château furnishings (€9, daily April–Oct 9:00–18:30, Nov–March 9:00–12:00 & 14:00–17:30, last entry 1.5 hours before closing, English handout, tel. 03 80 21 55 03, www.chateau-savigny.com).

From Savigny-les-Beaune, it's a short pedal back into Beaune. Or you can continue along...

▲Route des Grands Crus

While I prefer the areas south and east of Beaune, this route is a must for wine connoisseurs with a car, as it passes through Burgundy's most fabled vineyards. Between Vosne-Romanée and Gevrey-Chambertin, you'll pass 24 grand cru wineries of Côte de Nuits—Pinot Noir paradise, where 95 percent of the wines are red.

○ **Self-Guided Tour:** Those taking the "Vineyard Loop near Beaune" to Savigny-les-Beaune (described earlier) can continue along this route. Or from Beaune, take D-974 toward Vougeot, where the most appealing section begins (skip the area between Beaune and Nuits St. George).

A few minutes beyond the wine village of Vosne-Romanée, in the hamlet of Concoeur, you'll uncover **Ferme Fruirouge**—the ultimate Back Door stop, where cassis liqueur, mustards, and jams are made with passion. After passing fields growing red fruits (*fruits rouges*), you'll come to the Fruirouge barn, dripping with ambience. Adorable owners Sylvain and Isabelle will explain their time-honored process for making the famous crème de cassis, vinegars, and mustards, as well as jams made from cherries, raspberries, and black currants. You can sample everything—including their one-of-a-kind cassis-ketchup—and get free recipe cards in French (Thu–Mon 9:00–12:00 & 14:00–19:00, closed Tue–Wed, tel. 03 80 62 36 25, www.fruirouge.fr, call ahead to arrange for a detailed explanation of their operation).

In the nearby village of Vougeot, you'll find the **Château de Clos Vougeot.** In many ways, this is the birthplace of great Burgundian wines. In the 12th century, monks from the abbey of Cîteaux (8 miles southeast from here) created this beautiful stone structure to store equipment and make their wines. Their careful study of winemaking was the foundation for the world-famous reputation of Burgundian wines. There's little to see inside except for the fine stone construction, four ancient and massive

Route des Grands Crus

Legend:
- Autoroute (Toll)
- Other Roads
- Grands Crus Vineyard Route
- Wine Tasting
- Castle
- View

1. Ferme Fruirouge
2. Château de Clos Vougeot & Château de la Tour
3. Caveau des Musignys & Le Millésime Restaurant
4. Le Castel des Très Girard
5. Hôtelles Grands Crus & Chez Guy

DCH

wine presses, and the room where the Confrérie des Chevaliers Tastevin (a Burgundian brotherhood of wine-tasters) meets to celebrate their legacy—and to apply their label of quality to area wines, called *le Tastevinage.* There is a good English handout and posted information, but there's no tasting in the château (€4, daily April–Sept 9:00–18:30, Oct–March 9:00–11:30 & 14:00–17:30, tel. 03 80 62 86 09).

A few vines below the famous château, you can visit the largest producer of Vougeot wines at the welcoming **Château de la**

Tour winery. Hip, charming, and English-fluent Claire will show you the winery's fine cellars, then take your taste buds on a tour of their prestigious varieties. (If you're planning to buy, prices range from €13 to €110 per bottle, most at about €27.) Learn about their traditional approach to winemaking, and why you won't find last year's wines on their list. While it's best to call ahead and let her know you're coming, dropping in is OK, too (€5 for tasting, free if you buy, Wed–Mon 10:00–18:00, closed Tue, tel. 03 80 62 86 13, www.chateaudelatour.com).

Just northwest of Vougeot is the wine-soaked little village of **Chambolle-Musigny**, with a lovely restaurant offering good-value lunch *menus* and what may be the single best place to sample Burgundy's rich variety of wines, the **Caveau des Musignys.** Say *bonjour* to baritone Paulo, who will introduce you to the region's wines in his vaulted tasting room. He represents more than 40 producers making wines from Gevery-Chambertin to south of Beaune, selling excellent wines in all price ranges. His whites from the Côte Challonaise are a great value, as are his mid-range reds from Chambolle-Musigny and Vosne-Romanée (Wed–Sun 9:00–18:00, closed Mon–Tue, tel. 03 80 62 84 01, www.caveaudes musignys.com). Then dine upstairs in an elegant setting, where modern blends with tradition at **Le Millesime** (€18 lunch *menus*, €28–40 dinner *menus*, indoor seating only, closed all day Sun and Mon evening, 1 rue Traversière, tel. 03 80 62 80 37, www.caveau desmusignys.com).

The next village north is **Morey St. Denis**, which houses more vineyards and a very sharp and intimate upscale hotel-restaurant, **$$$ Le Castel des Très Girard*****. Located in the heart of the Route des Grands Crus, this eight-room hotel delivers top service and classy comfort, including a pool, and a restaurant that locals go out of their way for (Db–€130–170; lunch *menus* from €20, dinner *menus* from €37; poolside tables, tel. 03 80 34 33 09, fax 03 80 51 81 92, www.castel-tres-girard.com, info@castel-tres-girard .com).

Finally, you reach **Gevrey-Chambertin.** For many Pinot Noir-lovers, a visit to this flowery village is the ultimate Burgundian pilgrimage. Gevrey-Chambertin produces nine out of the 32 grand cru wines from Burgundy. All are Pinot Noirs (no whites in sight), and all use the suffix "Chambertin" ("Gevrey" is the historic name of the village; "Chambertin" is its most important vineyard). While you drive through the countryside south of the village, look for signs identifying the famous vineyards.

You can sleep well for a steal at the **$$ Hôtel les Grands Crus*****, with traditional rooms overlooking vineyards, cozy lounges, and a nice backyard terrace (Db–€80–90; air-con, Wi-Fi, at the northwest edge of the town on rue de Lavaux, tel. 03 80

34 34 15, fax 03 80 51 89 07, www.hoteldesgrandscrus.com, hotel .lesgrandscrus@nerim.net). To dine well in stylish surroundings inside or out, find **Chez Guy** in the center of the village (daily, 3 place de la Mairie, tel. 03 80 58 51 51).

Between Beaune and Paris

North of Beaune, you'll find a handful of appealing places that string together well for a full-day excursion: towering Châteauneuf-en-Auxois, sleepy Semur-en-Auxois, remote Fontenay's abbey, pretty little Flavigny-sur-Ozerain, and Julius Caesar's victorious battlefield at Alise Ste. Reine.

As a bonus, following my self-guided driving tour of this area (below) takes you along several stretches of the **Burgundy Canal** (Canal de Bourgogne). Like much of France, Burgundy is laced by canals dug in the early Industrial Age. Two hundred years ago, canals like these provided the cheapest way to transport cargo. The Burgundy canal was among the most important of France's canals, linking Paris with the Mediterranean Sea. The canal is 145 miles long, with 209 locks, and rises over Châteauneuf-en-Auxois (where the canal runs underground for about two miles). Digging began on the canal in 1727 and was not completed until 1832—ironically, just in time for the invention of steam engines on rails that would soon replace the need for canals.

Self-Guided Driving Tour

Back Door Burgundy

This all-day loop links Châteauneuf-en-Auxois, Semur-en-Auxois, Fontenay, Flavigny-sur-Ozerain, and Alise Ste. Reine. The trip trades vineyards for wheat fields and pastoral landscapes. You'll drive along the Burgundy canal and visit a Cistercian abbey, two medieval villages, and the site of Gaul's last stand against the Romans. If you're heading to/from Paris, this tour works well en route or as an overnight stop; accommodations are listed. It requires a car, Michelin map #320 or #519, and navigational patience. Stops that are bolded are described in greater detail later in this chapter.

⊙ Self-Guided Tour: Here's your itinerary for a full day in Back Door Burgundy. Leave Beaune following signs for *Auxerre* and *Bligny-sur-Ouche;* from Bligny-sur-Ouche, take D-33 to Pont d'Ouche (following signs to *Pont du Pany* and *Dijon*), where you'll turn left along the canal (D-18), following signs to *Château de Châteauneuf.* In five minutes, you'll see **Châteauneuf-en-Auxois**

castle looming above. Cross the canal and the freeway for great views of the hill town, even if you're not visiting it. A right on the small lane at the second farm, one kilometer (about a half-mile) after leaving D-18, leads to the best views.

After visiting Châteauneuf, drop back down to the canal at Vandenesse and turn right toward Créancy (still on D-18). There's a nice picnic spot on its "port," with water views of Châteauneuf. From Créancy drive to Pouilly-en-Auxois and pop out the other end (following D-970) to **Semur-en-Auxois.**

From Semur-en-Auxois, follow *Montbard,* then *Fontenay* signs to reach the **Abbey of Fontenay.** The abbey is your goal today; allow at least an hour to tour it. With no stops, this one-way drive from Beaune to Fontenay should take about an hour and a quarter. But you should be stopping—a lot.

Return to Beaune along D-905, following signs for *Venary les Laumes,* and contemplate short detours to **Alise Ste. Reine** (the "Alésia" battlefield where Caesar defeated the Gauls) and lovely little **Flavigny-sur-Ozerain** (of *Chocolat* film fame). If you're doing this trip on your way to or from Paris, fit in Flavigny and Alise Ste. Reine between Semur-en-Auxois and Fontenay, or skip them. Better yet, sleep in Semur-en-Auxois or Châteauneuf-en-Auxois, and do it all at a sane pace.

Non-drivers can get as far as Semur-en-Auxois by bus (3/day Mon-Sat, 1/day Sun, from Montbard or Dijon—runs early morning, noon, and evening; railpass gets you a free ticket; ask TI in Semur about where to get bus ticket). There are no trains to Semur.

Châteauneuf-en-Auxois

This perfectly medieval castle monitored passage between Burgundy and Paris, with hawk's-eye views from its 2,000-foot setting. *Châteauneuf* means "new castle," so you'll see many in France. This one is in the Auxois area, so it's Châteauneuf-en-Auxois (not to be confused with the famous Châteauneuf-du-Pape in Provence). The living hill town hunkers in the shadow of its pit-bull château and merits exploring. Park at the lot in the upper end of the village, and don't miss the **panoramic viewpoint** nearby. The military value of this site is powerfully clear from here. Find the Burgundy Canal and the three reservoirs that have maintained the canal's flow for more than 300 years. The small village below is Châteauneuf's port, Vandenesse-en-Auxois—you'll be there shortly. If not for phylloxera—the vine-loving insect that ravaged France in the early 1900s, killing all of its vineyards—you'd see more vineyards than wheat fields.

Saunter into the village, where every building feels historic and stocky farmers live side-by-side with slender artists. Walk into the courtyard, but skip the château's interior (€5, Tue–Sun 10:00–12:00 & 14:00–18:00, closed Mon, get English handout). You'll get better moat views and see the more important castle entry by walking beneath the Hôstellerie du Château, and then turning right, following *Eglise* signs. If you're hungry, Châteauneuf has several affordable cafés and restaurants along its main drag (the **Grill du Castel**, across from the Hôstellerie du Château, offers the best value).

Sleeping in Châteauneuf-en-Auxois

(€1 = about $1.25, country code: 33)

$$ Lady A Barge, in the canalside village of Vandenesse-en-Auxois, has tight but sufficiently comfortable rooms on a handsome hotel barge at two-star prices, with views of Châteauneuf's castle. The barge is for sale, so these rates could change for 2011 (Db-€80, €70 for second night, includes breakfast, book ahead in summer, ask about cruises on the canal—although the barge usually stays put, open all year, cash only, bikes available, Lady A, Bord du Canal, tel. 03 80 49 26 96, fax 03 80 49 27 00, www .peniche-lady-a.com, ladyabarge@yahoo.fr). From the freeway exit in Pouilly-en-Auxois, take D-18 to Vandenesse-en-Auxois to find the canal.

$ Hôstellerie du Château** is a modest but cozy place for a good night's sleep in Châteauneuf. It houses an enticing budget-vacation ensemble: nine homey, inexpensive rooms with a rear garden overlooking a brooding castle (floodlit at night). The restaurant offers a good selection, featuring regional cuisine and *menus* from €29; outdoor seating is available (Db-€60 for tight bathrooms with showers, Db-€75 for larger rooms with tubs, Tb-€90, Wi-Fi, closed Nov–Feb, tel. 03 80 49 22 00, fax 03 80 49 21 27, www .hostellerie-chateauneuf.com, infos@hostellerie-chateauneuf.com).

Semur-en-Auxois

This happy town feels real. There are few tourists and no important sights to digest—just a pleasing jumble of Burgundian alleys perched above the meandering Armançon River and behind the town's four massive towers, all beautifully illuminated after dark.

Semur-en-Auxois (suh-moor-ahn-ohx-wah) works as a base to visit the sights described in this area, or as

a handy lunch or dinner stop. Semur is also about 45 minutes from the famous church in *Vézelay* and two hours from Paris, making it an easy first- or last-night stop on your trip. Don't miss the smashing panorama of Semur from the viewpoint by the Citroën shop where D-980 and D-954 intersect (best at night and explained on page 873).

Tourist Information

The TI is across from Hôtel Côte d'Or, at Semur's medieval entry (Tue–Sat 9:00–12:30 & 13:30–18:00, closed Sun–Mon except July–Aug, 2 place Gaveau, tel. 03 80 97 05 96, www.ville-semur-en-auxois.fr). Pick up their city-walking brochure, information on the regional sights, and bike-rental information and suggested routes (hilly terrain).

Arrival in Semur-en-Auxois

To reach the town center from the "Back Door Burgundy" driving tour described earlier, follow *Autres Directions* from D-970, then *Centre-Ville*, and park when you see the old town gate.

Sights in Semur-en-Auxois

Connect the following sights (and see everything of importance in Semur) with a short stroll. Begin at the TI, then stop under the Sauvigny gate.

Sauvigny and Guiller Gates—These connected gates provided safe entry to Semur in the Middle Ages. Look up at the Sauvigny gate and see the indentations for posts that held a drawbridge in place, then find a stone hinge for the original gate on the right. The Guiller gate, 100 years older, marked the town's limit in the 1300s.

• *From here, enter charming rue Buffon, Semur's oldest commercial street. At the end of this street is the...*

Church of Notre-Dame—The town's main sight, the 13th-century church that dominates its small square, is worth a quick look. Walk counterclockwise around the ambulatory behind the altar. The first chapel on the right has unusual stained-glass windows honoring Semur's WWI soldiers. Then notice the rich colors in the next chapel. Gothic churches were usually brightly painted, not somber and gray, as you see them today. The stained-glass windows around Mary's statue date from the 13th century and are the only originals left. Before leaving the church, glance at the second-to-last chapel on your right, with a large plaque honoring American soldiers who lost their lives in World War I (free, Mon–Sat 9:00–12:00 & 14:00–18:30, Sun 14:00–18:30, decent English handout).

- *Leave with the church to your back and walk down the square past the half-timbered charcuterie, turn left at the bottom on rue du Rempart, then take another left down cobbled rue du Fourneau to the river to see...*

Semur's Towers—In the Middle Ages, 18 towers were connected by defensive ramparts to protect the center city. Caught in the crossfire between the powerful Dukes of Burgundy and the king of France, Semur's defenses were first destroyed by Louis XI in 1478, then finished off during the wars of religion in 1602.

- *For postcard-perfect views, continue your stroll for a few blocks in either direction along the Armançon River, then return back up rue du Fourneau. Then you can head out to see a sweeping...*

▲▲**View over Semur-en-Auxois**—Drive or hike downhill from the TI along rue du Pont Joly, cross the river, then head uphill and turn left at the top roundabout (walkers can veer left a block after the bridge for a shortcut). Across from the Citroën dealership, find the lookout with an orientation table and a memorable view of the red roofs, spires, and towers—especially striking at night. If the climb uphill feels like too much, walkers will find great views just after crossing the bridge.

Sleeping and Eating in Semur-en-Auxois

(€1 = about $1.25, country code: 33)

If Semur-en-Auxois seduces you into spending a night, try $$ **Hôtel les Cymaises**★★, with comfortable rooms and big beds in a manor house with a quiet courtyard (Db–€70, Tb–€80, 2-room Qb–€100, private parking, 7 rue du Renaudot, tel. 03 80 97 21 44, fax 03 80 97 18 23, www.hotelcymaises.com, hotel.cymaises @wanadoo.fr).

The various cafés along rue du Buffon offer ambience and average quality. **L'Entract** is where everybody goes for pizza, pasta, salads, and more in a relaxed atmosphere (daily, below the church on 4 rue du Fevret, tel. 03 80 96 60 10). The historic **charcuterie** (delicatessen) across from the church can supply your picnic needs (Tue–Sat 9:00–19:30, Sun 9:00–12:00, closed Mon). **Le Coin du Monde** is a laid-back café with cheap meals, Wi-Fi, and a computer (a block below rue du Buffon at 3 rue du Vieux Marché, closed Mon, tel. 03 80 97 00 35).

Abbey of Fontenay

The entire ensemble of buildings comprising this isolated Cistercian abbey, rated ▲▲, has survived, giving visitors perhaps the best picture of medieval abbey life in France. In the Middle Ages, it was written, "To fully grasp the meaning of Fontenay and the

power of its beauty, you must approach it trudging through the forest footpaths...through the brambles and bogs...in an October rain." But even if you use the parking lot, Fontenay's secluded setting—blanketed in birdsong, and with a garden lovingly used "as a stage set"—is truly magical.

Cost and Hours: €9.50, daily 10:00–18:00, until 19:00 July–Aug, tel. 03 80 92 15 00, www.abbayedefontenay.com.

Getting There: The abbey is a 20-minute drive from Semur via Montbard. There's no bus service—allow about €25 round-trip for a taxi from Montbard's train station (taxi mobile 06 08 26 61 55 or 06 08 99 21 13), or rent a bike at Montbard's TI and ride 45 minutes each way (Montbard TI tel. 03 80 92 53 81).

Background: This abbey—one of the oldest Cistercian abbeys in France—was founded in 1118 by St. Bernard as a back-to-basics reaction to the excesses of Benedictine abbeys, such as Cluny. The Cistercians worked to recapture the simplicity, solitude, and poverty of the early Church. Bernard created "a horrible vast solitude" in the forest, where his monks could live like the desert fathers of the Old Testament. They chose marshland ("Cistercian" is derived from "marshy bogs") and strove to be separate from the world (which required the industrious self-sufficiency these abbeys were so adept at). The movement spread, essentially colonizing Europe religiously. In 1200, there were more than 500 such monasteries and abbeys in Europe.

Like the Cistercian movement in general, Fontenay flourished through the 13th–15th centuries. A 14th-century proverb said, "Wherever the wind blows, to Fontenay money flows." Fontenay thrived as a prosperous "mini-city" for nearly 700 years, until the French Revolution, when it became the property of the nation and was eventually sold.

⊙ Self-Guided Tour: Like visitors centuries ago, you'll enter through the abbey's **gatehouse.** The main difference: Anyone with a ticket gets in, and there's no watchdog barking angrily at you (through the small hole on the right). Pick up the English self-guided tour flier with your ticket. Your visit follows the route below (generally clockwise). Arrows keep you on course, and signs tell you which sections of the abbey are private (as its owners still live here).

The **abbey church** is pure Romanesque and built to St. Bernard's specs: Latin cross plan, no fancy stained glass, unadorned columns, nothing to distract from prayer. The lone statue is the 13th-century *Virgin of Fontenay*, a reminder that the church was dedicated to Mary. Enjoy the ethereal light. You can almost hear the brothers chanting.

Stairs lead from the front of the church to a vast 16th-century, oak-beamed **dormitory** where the monks slept—together, fully dressed, on thin mats. Monastic life was pretty simple: prayer, reading, work, seven services a day, one meal in the winter, two in the summer. Daily rations: a loaf of bread and a quarter-liter of wine.

Back down the stairs, enter the **cloister**, beautiful in its starkness. This was the heart of the community, where monks read, exercised, washed, did small projects—and, I imagine, gave each other those silly haircuts. The shallow alcove (next to the church door) once stored prayer books; notice the slots for shelves. Next to that, the chapter room was where the abbot led discussions and community business was discussed. The adjacent monks' hall was a general-purpose room, likely busy with monks hunched over tables copying sacred texts (a major work of abbeys). The dining hall, or refectory, also faced the cloister (closed to the public).

Across the garden stands the huge abbey **forge.** In the 13th century, the monks at Fontenay ran what many consider Europe's first metalworking plant. Iron ore was melted down in ovens with big bellows. Tools were made and sold for a profit. The hydraulic hammer, which became the basis of industrial manufacturing of iron throughout Europe, was first used here. Leaving the building, walk left around the back to see the stream, which was diverted to power the wheels that operated the forge. Water was vital to abbey life. The pond—originally practical, rather than decorative—was a fish farm (some whopper descendants still swim here). Leave through the gift shop, which was the public chapel in the days when visitors were not allowed inside the abbey grounds.

Flavigny-sur-Ozerain

Ten minutes from Semur and five minutes from Alise Ste. Reine, little Flavigny-sur-Ozerain (flah-veen-yee sur oh-zuh-rain) had its 15 minutes of fame in 2000, when the movie *Chocolat* was filmed here. Taking its *chocolat*-covered image in stride, this unassuming and serenely situated village feels permanently stuck in the past, with one café-restaurant, one *crêperie*, a tiny grocery shop—but no counts and, alas, no Juliette Binoche.

Flavigny has been home to an abbey since 719, when the first abbey of St. Pierre was built, and recently has been reinvigorated by the return of 50 Benedictine monks at the abbey of St. Joseph.

Getting There

To reach Flavigny-sur-Ozerain by car, leave Semur-en-Auxois, following *Venarey les Laumes* signs, and look for the turnoff to Flavigny in a few minutes. The approach to Flavigny from Pouillenay via D-9 is picture-perfect. Park at the gate or in the lot just below. From this lot, signs lead to *Alise Ste. Reine*, described next (great views back to Flavigny after a few miles).

Sights in Flavigny-sur-Ozerain

There's little to do here other than appreciate the setting (best from the grassy ramparts) and try the little *anis* (anise) candies. Pick up a map at the **TI** (called "La Maison du Notaire") and ask to see the photos of buildings used in *Chocolat* (hours vary, but generally April–Oct Wed–Mon 10:00–12:30 & 13:30–18:30, closed Tue and Nov–March, down rue de l'Église in front of church, tel. 03 80 96 25 34).

Chocolat-lovers will have to be satisfied with a few of the building facades featured in the film; there are no souvenirs or posters to be found, and nary a chocolate shop (locals, who prefer their homemade *anis* candies, weren't wowed by the movie). There are five buildings that fans should recognize. The evocative **Church of St. Genest** is the only one you can enter—stand where the preacher did and feel the gaze of the congregation, then find the upstairs seating (daily 10:30–12:00 & 14:00–18:30). The movie's *chocolaterie* lies across the square from the church entry, below La Grange restaurant, on rue du Four (look for the arched window with the brown frame). The **count's home** is today's *mairie* (city hall), next to the church entry. The *coiffure* (hairdresser) is one door down from the TI—look for the white shutters. And what was the **Café de la République** is three doors up from the TI, with an austere facade and metal shutters. Johnny Depp never visited Flavigny (his loss), and there is no river here (the river scenes were filmed in the Dordogne, near Beynac).

Elsewhere in Flavigny, you can buy the locally produced **anis candies** in pretty tins. They make great souvenirs (see them being made Mon–Fri 9:00–11:00 in the Abbey of St. Pierre).

The grassy **ramparts** are worth a stroll for the view (behind the church, walk down rue de la Poterne, turn right at the fork, then look for *Petite Ruelle des Remparts* and walk to the next gate).

Sleeping and Eating in Flavigny-sur-Ozerain

(€1 = about $1.25, country code: 33)

$$ L'Ange Souriant Chambre d'Hôte is comfortable and intimate (Sb–€50, Db–€65, Tb–€90, Qb–€98, includes breakfast, a block below the TI on rue Voltaire, tel. & fax 03 80 96 24 93, http://ange-souriant.fr, a.souriant@wanadoo.fr).

$ Le Relais de Flavigny, next door, has a little restaurant with seven basic bargain rooms above (Ss/Ds-€35, *menus* from €17, €10 hearty summertime lunch salads, open daily, at bottom of rue de l'Église from church, tel. 03 80 96 27 77, www.le-relais.fr, relais-de-flavigny@wanadoo.fr).

La Grange ("The Barn") serves dirt-cheap, farm-fresh fare, including luscious quiche, salads, fresh cheeses, pâtés, and fruit pies (July–mid-Sept Tue–Sun 12:30–18:00, closed Mon; April–June and mid-Sept–Nov open only on Sun, closed Dec–March; across from church, look for brown doors and listen for lunchtime dining, tel. 03 80 35 81 78).

Alise Ste. Reine

A united Gaul forming a single nation animated by the same spirit could defy the universe.

—Julius Caesar, *The Gallic Wars*

A five-minute drive from Venary les Laumes or Flavigny-sur-Ozerain, above the vertical little village of Alise Ste. Reine, is where historians think Julius Caesar defeated the Gallic leader Vercingétorix in 52 B.C., thus winning Gaul for the Roman Empire and forever changing France's destiny.

Follow the *Statue de Vercingétorix* signs leading up through Alise Ste. Reine (skip the archaeological site and small museum) to the park with the huge statue of the Gallic warrior overlooking his Waterloo. Stand as he did, imagine yourself trapped on this hilltop, then find the orientation table under the gazebo, and read about...

The Dying Gauls

In 52 B.C., General Julius Caesar and his 60,000 soldiers surrounded Alésia (today's Alise Ste. Reine), hoping to finally end the uprising of free Gaul and establish Roman civilization in France. Holed up inside the hilltop fortress were 80,000 die-hard (long-haired, tattooed) Gauls under their rebel chief, Vercingétorix (pronounced something like "verse in Genesis"). Having harassed Caesar for months with guerrilla-war attacks, they now called on their fellow Gauls to converge on Alésia to wipe out the Romans.

Rather than attack the fierce-fighting Gauls, Caesar's soldiers patiently camped at the base of the hill and began building a wall. In 6 weeks they completed a 12-foot-tall stone wall all the way around Alésia (11 miles around—blue line on the orientation table), and then a second, larger one (13 miles around—red line on the orientation table), trapping the rebel leaders and hoping to starve them out. If the Gauls tried to escape, not only would they have to breach the two walls, they'd first have to cross a steep no-man's-land dotted with a ditch, a moat, and booby traps (like sharp stakes in pits and buried iron spikes).

The starving Gauls inside Alésia sent their women and children out to beg mercy from the Romans. The Romans (with little food themselves) refused. For days, the women and children wandered the unoccupied land, in full view of both armies, until they starved to death.

After months of siege, Vercingétorix's reinforcements finally came riding to save him. With 90,000 screaming Gallic warriors (Caesar says 250,000) converging on Alésia, and 80,000 more atop the hill, Caesar ordered his men to move between the two walls to fight a two-front battle. The Battle of Alésia raged for five days—a classic struggle between the methodical Romans and the impetuous "barbarians." When it became clear the Romans would not budge, the Gauls retreated.

Vercingétorix surrendered, and Gallic culture was finished in France. During the three-year rebellion, one in five Gauls had been killed, enslaved, or driven out. Roman rule was established for the next 500 years, strangling the Gallic/Celtic heritage. Vercingétorix spent his last years as a prisoner, paraded around as a war trophy. In 46 B.C., he was brought to Rome for Caesar's triumphal ascension to power, where he was strangled to death in a public ritual.

Between Burgundy and the Loire

These two sights—Vézelay and its Romanesque Basilica of Ste. Madeleine, and the under-construction Château de Guédelon—make good stops for drivers connecting Burgundy and the Loire Valley, or linking Burgundy and Paris, though you'll want to leave by 9:00 to fit in both. (Allow six hours of driving from Beaune to Paris or the Loire, plus time to visit each sight; see map on page 835.)

Vézelay and the Basilica of Ste. Madeleine

For more than eight centuries, travelers have hoofed it up through this pretty little town to get to the famous hilltop church, the Basilica of Ste. Madeleine. In its 12th-century prime, Vézelay welcomed the medieval masses. Cultists of Mary Magdalene came to file past her (supposed) body. Pilgrims rendezvoused here to march to Spain to venerate St. James' (supposed) relics in Santiago de Compostela. Three Crusades were launched from this hill: the Second Crusade (1146), announced by Bernard of Clairveaux; the Third Crusade (1190), under Richard the Lionhearted and King Philippe Auguste; and the Seventh Crusade (1248), by King (and Saint) Louis IX. Today, tourists flock to Vézelay's basilica, famous for its place in history, its soul-stirring Romanesque architecture—reproduced in countless art books—and for the relics of Mary Magdalene.

Tourist Information: Vézelay's TI is at the lower end of the village (on rue St. Etienne, which turns into rue St. Pierre; June-Sept daily 10:00–13:00 & 14:00–18:00; Oct–May Fri–Wed 10:00–13:00 & 14:00–18:00, closed Thu, also closed Sun Nov–March; tel. 03 86 33 23 69). The TI provides Internet access.

Sights in Vézelay

▲Basilica of Ste. Madeleine

To accommodate the growing crowds of medieval pilgrims, the abbots of Vézelay enlarged their original church (1104), then rebuilt it after a disastrous 1120 fire. The building we see today—one of the largest and best-preserved Romanesque churches anywhere—was built in stages: nave (1120–1140), narthex (1132–1145), and choir (1215). The construction spanned the century-long transition from the Romanesque style (round barrel arches like the ancient Romans', thick walls, small windows) to Gothic (pointed arches, flying buttresses, high nave, lots of stained glass). Vézelay blends elements of both styles.

Cost and Hours: Free entry, daily 7:00–20:00, tel. 03 86 33 39 50, http://vezelay.cef.fr.

Tours and Information: Eager volunteers offer one-hour English guided tours that depart from inside the narthex in summer (donation requested, no tours 12:00–14:00). Other tours can be arranged by contacting the volunteer coordinator (tel. 03 86 33 39 50, recteur.madeleine@vezelay.cef.fr). For extra credit, buy the €6 guidebook as you enter. The view from the park behind the church is sublime.

⊕ Self-Guided Tour: The **facade**—with one tower missing its original steeple, another that's unfinished, and an inauthentic tympanum—isn't why you came. Step inside.

The **narthex**, or entrance hall, served several functions. Religiously, it was a place to cross from the profane to the sacred. Practically, it gave shelter to overflow pilgrim crowds (even overnight, if necessary) as they shuffled through one of the three doorways. And aesthetically, the dark narthex prepares the visitor for the radiant nave.

The **tympanum** (carved relief) over the central doorway is one of Romanesque's signature pieces. It shows the risen Christ, ascending to heaven in an almond-shaped cloud, shooting Holy Ghost rays at his apostles and telling them to preach the Good News to the ends of the Earth. The whole diversity of humanity (appropriate, considering Vézelay's function as a gathering place) appears beneath: hunters, fishermen, farmers, pygmies, and men with long ears, feathers, and dog heads. The signs of the zodiac arch over the scene.

Gaze through the central doorway into the **nave** at the rows and rows of arches that seem to recede into a luminous infinity—the effect is mesmerizing. The nave is long, high, and narrow (200' x 60' x 35'), creating a tunnel effect formed by 10 columns and arches on each side. Overhead is the church's most famous feature—barrel vaults (wide arches) built of stones alternating between creamy-white and pink-brown. The side aisles have low ceilings, whereas the nave rises up between them, lined with slender floor-to-ceiling columns that unite both stories. The interior glows with an even light from the unstained glass of the clerestory windows. The absence of distractions or bright colors makes this simple church perfect for meditation.

The capitals of the nave's columns are carved masterpieces by several sculptors of saints and Bible scenes. All are worth studying (the guidebook sold at the entry identifies each scene, starting in the narthex), but some you might easily recognize are David and Goliath (fourth column on left), Moses and the Golden Calf (sixth column), Adam and Eve (ninth column), Peter Freed from Prison (10th and final column on the left), and the well-known "Mystical Mill" (fourth column on right), showing Old Testament Moses and New Testament Paul working together to fill sacks with grain (and, metaphorically, the Bible with words).

The light at the end of the tunnel-like nave is the **choir** (altar area), radiating a brighter, blue-gray light. Constructed when Gothic was the rage, the choir has pointed arches and improved engineering, but the feel is monotone and sterile.

In the right transept stands a statue of the woman this church was dedicated to—not the Virgin Mary (Jesus' mother) but one

Mary Magdalene

France has a special affection for Mary Magdalene (*La Madeleine*), and Vézelay is one of several churches dedicated to her—a rarity in Europe, where most churches honor Jesus' mother, the Virgin Mary.

The Bible says that Mary Magdalene, one of Jesus' followers, was exorcised of seven demons (Luke 8:2), witnessed the Crucifixion (Matthew 27:56), and was the first mortal to see the resurrected Jesus (Mark 16:9-11)—the other disciples didn't believe her.

Some theologians have fleshed out Mary's reputation by associating her with biblical passages that don't specifically name her—e.g., the sinner who washed Jesus' feet with her hair (Luke 7:36-50), the forgiven adulteress (John 8), or the woman with the alabaster jar who anointed Jesus (Matthew 26:7-13).

In medieval times, legends appeared (especially in France) that, after the Crucifixion, Mary Magdalene fled to southern France, lived in a cave, converted locals, performed miracles, and died in Provence. Renaissance artists portrayed her as a fanciful blend of Bible and legend: a red-headed, long-haired prostitute who was rescued by Jesus, symbolizing the sin of those who love too much.

In recent times, feminists have claimed Mary Magdalene a victim of male-dominated Catholic suppression. Bible scholars cite passages in two ancient (but noncanonical) gospels that cryptically allude to Mary as Jesus' special "companion." *The Da Vinci Code*—a popular if unhistorical novel—seizes on this, slathers it with medieval legend, and asserts that Mary Magdalene was actually Jesus' wife who bore him descendants, and that her relics lie not in Vézelay but in a shopping mall in Paris.

of Jesus' disciples, Mary Magdalene. She cradles an alabaster jar of ointment she used (according to some Bible interpretations) to anoint Jesus.

Drop into the **crypt** for the ultimate medieval experience in one of Europe's greatest medieval churches. You're entering the foundations of the earlier ninth-century church that monks built here on the hilltop after Vikings had twice pillaged their church at the base of the hill.

File past the small container with the **relics of Mary Magdalene**. In medieval times, Vézelay claimed to possess Mary's entire body, but the relics were later damaged and scattered by anti-Catholic Huguenots (16th century) and Revolutionaries (18th century), leaving only a few pieces.

Are they really her mortal remains? We only have legends—

many different versions—that first appeared in the historical record around A.D. 1000. The most popular legends say that Mary Magdalene traveled to Provence, where she died, and that her bones were brought from there by a monk to save them from Muslim pirates. In the 11th century, the abbots of Vézelay heavily marketed the notion that these were Mary's relics, and when the pope authenticated it in 1058, tourism boomed.

Vézelay prospered until the mid-13th century, when King Charles of Anjou announced that Mary's body was not in Vézelay, but had been found in another town. Vézelay's relics suddenly looked bogus, and pilgrims stopped coming. For the next five centuries, the church fell into disrepair and then was vandalized by secularists in the Revolution. The church was restored (1840–1860) by a young architect named Eugene Viollet-le-Duc, who would later revamp Notre-Dame in Paris (and build the base of the Statue of Liberty).

After visiting the chapter house and cloisters (out the right transept), don't pass on the view from behind the church of the Cure River Valley.

Sleeping and Eating in Vézelay

(€1 = about \$1.25, country code: 33)

You'll find pleasant cafés with reasonable food all along the street leading to the church.

\$\$ Hôtel de la Poste et du Lion d'Or has the best moderate, country-classy rooms in Vézelay (good Db-€84, bigger Db-€95–115, extra bed-€18, Wi-Fi, easy parking, garage-€6, at the foot of the village, place du Champ-de-Foire, tel. 03 86 33 21 23, fax 03 86 32 30 92, www.laposte-liondor.com). Dinner in the hotel's country-elegant **restaurant**—indoors or *en plein air*—is a treat (*menus* from €23, closed Mon).

La Dent Creuse has the best terrace tables at the lower end of the village (left side), with salads, pizza, and more (daily until 21:30, place du Champ-de-Foire, tel. 03 86 33 36 33).

Auberge de la Coquille is a cozy place to eat inside and out, with reasonable prices (daily until 21:30, halfway up to the church at 81 rue St. Pierre, tel. 03 86 33 35 57).

Vézelay Connections

Vézelay is about 45 minutes northwest of **Semur-en-Auxois** (20 minutes off the autoroute to Paris). Train travelers go to **Sermizelles** (via Auxerre or Avallon, 5/day) and taxi from there (6 miles, allow €17 one-way, taxi tel. 03 86 32 31 88 or mobile 06 85 77 89 36). Buses also run from Montbard to Avallon (with train connections to Sermizelles).

BURGUNDY

Château de Guédelon

A historian's dream (worth ▲▲, or ▲▲▲ for kids), this castle is being built by 35 enthusiasts using only the tools, techniques, and materials available in the 13th century. The project is the dream of two individuals who wanted to build a medieval castle (this one is based on plans drafted in 1228). Started in 1997, it will ultimately include four towers surrounding a central courtyard with a bridge and a moat. The goal of this exciting project is to give visitors a better appreciation of medieval construction, and for the builders to learn about medieval techniques while they work. The castle won't be complete for another 13 years, so you still have time to watch the process. (It's currently about 15–50 feet tall, and the great hall is just about complete.) When the castle is done, the ambitious owners plan to build a medieval abbey.

Enter the project to the sound of chisels chipping rock and the sight of people dressed as if it were 800 years ago. A human-powered hamster wheel hoists carefully dressed stone up tower walls (the largest tower will reach six stories when completed). Carpenters whack away at massive beams, creating supports for stone arches, while weavers demonstrate how clothing was made (a sheep's pen provides the raw material). Thirteen workstations help visitors learn about castle construction, from medieval rope-making to blacksmithing. Feel free to ask the workers questions—some speak English.

Kids can't get enough of Guédelon. It's a favorite for local school field trips, so expect lots of kids. And if it's been raining, expect a muddy mess—you are, after all, in a construction site.

Cost and Hours: €9, kids 5–17–€7, under 5–free, excellent English handout, picnic area and lunch café inside; castle open July–Aug daily 10:00–19:00; mid-March–June Thu–Tue 10:00–18:00, Sun until 19:00, closed Wed; Sept Thu–Tue 10:00–17:30, Sat–Sun until 18:00, closed Wed; Oct Thu–Tue 10:00–17:30, closed Wed; closed Nov–mid-March; tel. 03 86 45 66 66, www.guedelon.fr.

Getting There: Guédelon is an hour west of Vézelay on D-955, between St. Amand-en-Puisaye and St. Saveur-en-Puisaye.

Sleeping near Guédelon: Guédelon is remote. If you need to sleep nearby, try **$$ Hôtel Les Grands Chênes,** where British Rachael and French Alain have restored a pretty manor home among trees, lakes, and waves of grass (Db–€76, Tb–€89, Qb–€100–115, Wi-Fi, on D-18 between St. Fargeau and St. Amand-en-Puisaye, tel. 03 86 74 04 05, fax 03 86 74 11 41, www.hotel-de-puisaye.com, contact@hotel-de-puisaye.com).

Between Burgundy and Lyon

Drivers traveling south from Beaune should think about detouring into the lovely, unspoiled Mâconnais countryside. Brancion, Chapaize, Cluny, and Taizé gather a few minutes from one another, about 25 minutes west of the autoroute between Mâcon and Tournus (see map on page 835). For a lovely romp through vineyards and unspoiled villages, drive south of Beaune on D-974 to Chagny, then hook up with D-981 to Cluny (via Givry, Buxy, and Cormatin). South of Buxy, be on the lookout for a surprising château on the west side of road in cute little Sercy. D-14 heading east to Brancion meets D-981 at Cormatin.

Brancion and Chapaize

An hour south of Beaune by car (12 miles west of Tournus on D-14) are two tiny villages, each with "daughters of Cluny"—churches that owe their existence and architectural design to the nearby and once-powerful Cluny Abbey. Between the villages you'll pass a Stonehenge-era menhir (standing stone) with a cross added on top at a later point—evidence that this was sacred ground long before Christianity (from Brancion, it's on the right just after passing the bulky Château de Nobles).

Brancion

This is a classic feudal village. Back when there were no nations in Europe, control of land was delegated from lord to vassal. The Duke of Burgundy ruled here through his vassal, the Lord of Brancion. His vast domain—much of south Burgundy—was administered from this tiny fortified town.

Within the town's walls, the feudal lord had a castle, a church, and all the necessary administrative buildings to provide justice, collect taxes, and so on. Strategically perched on a hill between two river valleys, he enjoyed a complete view of his domain. Brancion's population peaked centuries ago at 60. Today, it's home to only four full-time residents.

The castle, part of a network of 17 castles in the region, was destroyed in 1576 by Protestant Huguenots. After the French Revolution, it was sold to be used as a quarry and spent most of the 19th century being picked apart. Though the flier gives a brief tour and the audioguide a longer one, the small castle is most enjoyable for its evocative angles and the lush views from the top of its keep (€5, audioguide-€2, daily 10:00–13:00 & 14:00–18:30).

Wandering from the castle to the church, you'll pass the town's lone business (l'Auberge du Vieux Brancion), a 15th-century market hall demonstrating France's boundless love affair with market day (used by farmers from the surrounding countryside until 1900), plus a handful of other buildings from that period.

The 12th-century warm-stone church (with faint paintings surviving from 1330) is the town's highlight. Circumnavigate the small building—this is Romanesque at its pure, unadulterated, fortress-of-God best (thick walls, small windows, once colorfully painted interior, no-frills exterior). Notice the stone roof; inside, find the English explanations of the paintings. From its front door, enjoy a lord's view over one glorious Burgundian estate.

Sleeping and Eating in or near Brancion: You have two good choices. In the center of the village, **$ L'Auberge du Vieux Brancion** serves traditional Burgundian fare (€14 lunch *menu*, €22 dinner *menu*) and also offers a perfectly tranquil place to spend the night (very simple and frumpy rooms, Ds-€38, Db-€50–56, family rooms-€55–72, tel. & fax 03 85 51 03 83, www.brancion.fr, josserand@brancion.fr).

For a much more upscale experience, including the best Burgundian view rooms I've found, drive a mile south of the village, following the sign to **$$$ Hôtel la Montagne de Brancion*****. A vine-covered paradise awaits...for a price. Every one of the 19 sharp, deck-equipped rooms faces a territorial view over vineyards, hills, and pastures. The garden comes with sway-back view chairs, and a pool lies below. The owners pride them-selves on their "gourmet restaurant" and expect you to dine there (Db-€105, Db suite-€150, extra bed €18, pricey breakfast-€18, *menus* from €48 or à la carte, tel. 03 85 51 12 40, fax 03 85 51 18 64, www.brancion.com, reservation@brancion.com).

Chapaize

This hamlet, a few miles closer to Beaune, grew up around its Benedictine monastery—only its 11th-century church survives. It's a pristine place (cars park at the edge of town), peppered with flowers and rustic decay, and surrounded by grassy fields. A ghost-town café faces the village's classic Romanesque church—study the fine stonework by Lombard masons. (Its lean seems designed to challenge the faith of parishioners.) The WWI monument near the entry—with so many names from such a tiny hamlet—is a reminder that about 4.2 million young French men were wounded or died in the war that *didn't* end all wars. Wander around the back for a view of the belfry, and then ponder Chapaize across the street while sipping a café au lait.

Cluny

People come from great distances to admire Cluny's great abbey that is no more. This mother of all abbeys once vied with the Vatican as the most important power center in Christendom (Cluny's abbot often served as mediator between Europe's kings and the pope). The building was destroyed during the French Revolution, and, frankly, there's not a lot to see today. Still, the abbey makes a worthwhile visit for history buffs looking to get some idea of the scale of this vast complex. Big plans are underfoot to improve the sight, making it easier for tourists to reconstruct its glory days.

The pleasant little town that grew up around the abbey maintains its street plan, with plenty of original buildings, and even the same population it had in its 12th-century heyday (4,500). As you wander the town, which claims to be the finest surviving Romanesque town in France, enjoy the architectural details on everyday buildings. Much of the town's fortified walls, gates, and towers survive.

Orientation to Cluny

Everything of interest is within a few minutes' walk of the **TI** (daily June–Sept 10:00–12:30 & 14:30–18:45, no midday closure July–Aug, May and Oct closes at 18:00, Nov–April closes at 17:00, pick up the "helpful practical guide," 6 rue Mercière, tel. 03 85 59 05 34).

The TI is at the base of the **"Cheese Tower,"** so named because it was used to age cheese (or perhaps for the way tourists smell after climbing to the top). The tower offers a sweeping city view (€2, same hours as TI). Facing the abbey's entrance, the TI is 100 yards to the right.

A **farmers' market** animates the old town each Saturday.

Arrival in Cluny

Drivers park at designated lots and follow *Centre-Ville* signs on foot. Bus Céphale provides a few trips to Cluny (4/day from Chalon-sur-Saône, 1.25 hours; 6/day from Mâcon, 50 minutes; toll-free tel. 08 00 07 17 10). There is no train station in Cluny.

Sights in Cluny

Cluny has two sights—a museum and the abbey (€7 ticket covers museum and abbey entrance, both open daily May–Aug 9:30–18:30, Sept–April 9:30–12:00 & 13:30–17:00, tel. 03 85 59 15 93). Historians should invest in the €7 *The Abbey of Cluny* guidebook,

History of Cluny and Its (Scant) Abbey

In 1964, St. Benedict (480-547), founder of the first monastery (Montecassino, south of Rome) from which a great monastic movement sprang, was named the patron saint of Europe. Christians and non-Christians alike recognize the impact that monasteries had in establishing a European civilization out of the dark chaos that followed the fall of Rome.

The Abbey of Cluny was the ruling center of the first great international franchise, or chain, of monasteries in Europe. It was the heart of an upsurge in monasticism, of church reform, and an evangelical revival that spread throughout Europe—a phenomenon historians call the Age of Faith (11th and 12th centuries). From this springboard came a vast network of abbeys, priories, and other monastic orders that kindled the establishment of modern Europe.

In 910, 12 monks founded a house of prayer at Cluny, vowing to follow the rules of St. Benedict. The cult of saints and relics was enthusiastically promoted, and the order was independent and powerful. From the start, the Abbot of Cluny answered only to the pope (not to the local bishop or secular leader). The abbots of the other Cluniac monasteries were answerable only to the Abbot of Cluny (not to their local bishop or prince). This made the Abbot of Cluny arguably the most powerful person in Europe.

The abbey's success has been attributed to a series of wise leaders, or abbots. In fact, four of the first six abbots actually became saints. They preached the principles of piety and the art of shrewd fundraising. Concerning piety, the abbots got people to stop looting the monasteries. Regarding shrewd fundraising, they convinced Europe's wealthy landowners to will their estates to the monasteries in return for perpetual prayers for the benefit of their needy and frightened souls.

From all this grew the greatest monastic movement of the High Middle Ages. A huge church was built at Cluny, and by 1100 it was the headquarters of 10,000 monks who ran nearly a thousand monasteries and priories across Europe. Cluny peaked in the 12th century, then faded in influence (though monasteries continued to increase in numbers and remain a force until 1789).

sold in the museum. English tours should be available Tuesday, Thursday, and Saturday in July and August at 10:15 and 15:15.

Museum of Art and Archaeology (Musée Ochier)—The small abbey museum fills the Palace of the Abbot with bits from medieval Cluny and a terrific model of the abbey complex (visit this before you explore the ruins). I like seeing the stone carvings eye-to-eye, though the museum holds little else of interest.

Site of Cluny Abbey—Much of today's old town stands on the site of what was the largest church in Christendom. It was almost two football fields long (555 feet), and was crowned with five soaring naves. The whole complex (church plus monastery) covered 25 acres. Revolutionaries destroyed it in 1790, and today the National Stud Farm and a big school obliterate much of the floor plan of the abbey. Only one tower and part of the transept still stand. The visitor's challenge: visualize it. Get a sense of its grandeur.

The best point from which to appreciate the abbey's awesome dimensions is atop the steps across from the museum. Look out to the remaining tower (there used to be three). You're standing above the end of the nave that stretched all the way to those towers. Down the steps, a marble table shows the original floor plan (*vous êtes ici* means "you are here"). Walk past the nubs that remain of the once-massive columns.

The abbey entrance lies between the Hôtel de Bourgogne and the Brasserie du Nord. Elaborate information displays designed to introduce the abbey and put it in its historical context should be in place by your visit. You'll also see a new 12-minute 3-D film, giving a virtual tour of the 1,100-year-old church that helps you grasp the tragedy of its destruction (almost worth the price of entry alone, English headphones). Use the English flier to tour what little of the abbey still stands. Along the way, you'll find helpful English information posted, and several backlit panels that swivel, allowing visitors to see that section of the abbey at its zenith in three dimensions. Very cool. You'll exit at the flour mill (Tour de Farine), where you can loop back along the town's pleasing main drag, rue de Mercière (cafés, shops, and the TI line this pedestrian-friendly street).

National Stud Farm (Les Haras Nationaux)—Napoleon (who needed *beaucoup de* horses for his army of 600,000) established this horse farm in 1806. Today, 50 thoroughbred stallions kill time in their stables. If the stalls are empty, they're out doing their current study duty...creating strapping racehorses. The gate is next to Hôtel de Bourgogne (€5, visits only by guided tour, usually in the afternoon, guides speak some English, get schedule from TI).

Sleeping in Cluny

(€1 = about $1.25, country code: 33)

If you're spending the night, bed down at the cushy, traditional **$$$ Hôtel de Bourgogne*****, which is built into the wall of the abbey's right transept and is as central as can be for enjoying the town (standard Db–€90–100, bigger Db–€130, parking–€9, place de l'Abbaye, tel. 03 85 59 00 58, fax 03 85 59 03 73, www.hotel-cluny.com, contact@hotel-cluny.com). It also has a fine restaurant (*menus* from €26).

Taizé

To experience the latest in European monasticism, drop by the booming Christian community of Taizé (teh-zay), a few miles north of Cluny on the road to Brancion. The normal, uncultlike ambience of this place—with thousands of mostly young, European pilgrims asking each other, "How's your soul today?"—is remarkable. Even if this sounds a tad airy, you might find the 30 minutes it takes to stroll from one end of the compound to the other—amid ancient abbeys and noble Romanesque churches—a worthwhile detour. A visit to Taizé can be a thought-provoking experience, particularly after a visit to Cluny. A thousand years ago, Cluny had a similar power to draw the faithful in search of direction and meaning in life.

The Taizé community welcomes visitors who'd like to spend a few days getting close to God through meditation, singing, and simple living. Although designed primarily for youthful pilgrims in meditative retreat (there are about 5,000 here in a typical week), people of any age are welcome to pop in for a meal or church service.

Taizé is an ecumenical movement—prayer, silence, simplicity—welcoming Protestant as well as Catholic Christians. Though it feels Catholic, it isn't. (But, as some of the brothers are actually Catholic priests, Catholics may take the Eucharist here.) The Taizé style of worship is well-known among American Christians for its hauntingly beautiful chants—songbooks and CDs are the most popular souvenirs from here.

Three times a day, the bells ring and worshippers file into the long, low, simple, and modern Church of Reconciliation. It's dim—candlelit with glowing icons—as the white-robed brothers enter. The service features responsive singing of chants (from well-worn songbooks that list lyrics in 19 languages), reading of biblical passages, and silence, as worshippers on crude kneelers stare into icons. The aim: "Entering together into the mystery of God's presence." (Secondary aim: Helping Lutherans get over their fear of icons.)

Getting There: Drivers follow *La Communauté* signs and park in a dirt lot. SNCF buses (free with railpass) serve Taizé from Chalon-sur-Saône to the north (4/day, 1 hour) and from Mâcon to the south (6/day, 1 hour).

Orientation: At the southern (Cluny) end, the Welcome Office provides an orientation and daily schedule, and makes a good first stop (pick up a copy of the bimonthly *Letter from Taizé* and the single-page information leaflet, *The Taizé Community*). Time your visit for a church service (Mon–Sat 8:15, 12:20, and 20:30; Sun 10:00 and 20:30; Catholic and Protestant communion available daily). The Exposition (next to the church) is the thriving community shop, with books, CDs, sheet music, handicrafts, and other souvenirs. The Oyak (near the parking lot) is where those in a less monastic mood can get a beer or burger.

Staying at Taizé: Those on retreat fill their days with worship services; workshops; simple, relaxed meals; and hanging out in an international festival of people searching for meaning in their lives. Visitors are welcome for free. The cost for a real stay is about €10–25 per day (based on a sliding scale; those under 18 stay for less) for monastic-style room and board. Adults (over age 30) are accommodated in a more comfortable zone, but count on simple dorms. Call or email first if you plan to stay overnight (reception open Mon–Fri 10:00–12:00 & 18:00–19:00, tel. 03 85 50 30 02). The Taizé community website explains everything—in 29 languages (www.taize.fr).

LYON

Straddling the Rhône and Saône rivers between Burgundy and Provence, Lyon has been among France's leading cities since Roman times. In spite of its workaday, business-first facade, Lyon is France's most historic and culturally important city after Paris. You'll experience two different-as-night-and-day cities: the Old World cobbled alleys, Renaissance mansions, and colorful facades of Vieux Lyon; and the more staid but classy, Parisian-feeling shopping streets of Presqu'île. Once you're settled, this big city feels small, welcoming, and surprisingly untouristy. It seems everyone's enjoying the place—and they're all French.

Planning Your Time

Just 70 minutes south of Beaune, two hours north of Avignon, and 90 minutes west of Annecy, Lyon is France's best-kept urban secret. Lyon deserves at least one night and a full day. The city makes a handy day visit for train travelers, as many trains pass through here, and both stations have baggage storage and easy connections to the city center. But those who spend the night can experience the most renowned cuisine in France at appetizing prices, and enjoy one of Europe's most beautifully floodlit cities.

For a full day of sightseeing, take the funicular up to Fourvière Hill, visit the Notre-Dame Basilica, and tour the Roman Theaters and Gallo-Roman Museum. Ride the funicular back down to Vieux Lyon and have lunch, then explore the old town and its hidden passageways. Finish your day touring the Museum of Fine Arts, Resistance Center, or Lumière Museum (on early films). Most of Lyon's important sights are closed on Mondays or Tuesdays, or both. Dine well in the evening and cap your day enjoying a stroll through the best-lit city in France.

Drivers connecting Lyon with southern destinations should consider the scenic detour via the Ardèche Gorges (described on page 673), and those connecting to Burgundy should consider taking the Beaujolais Wine Route (page 916), then visiting Brancion and Cluny (in the Burgundy chapter).

Lyon's Cuisine Scene

In Lyon, how well you eat determines how well you live. The best restaurants are all the buzz—a favorite conversation topic likely to generate heated debate. Here, great chefs are more famous than professional soccer players. (Paul Bocuse is the most famous chef.) Restaurants seem to outnumber cars, and all seem busy. With an abundance of cozy, excellent restaurants in every price range, it's hard to go wrong—unless you order *tripes* (cow intestines, also known as *tablier de sapeur*), *foie de veau* (calf's liver), or *tête de veau* (calf's head). Beware: These questionable dishes are very common in small bistros (*bouchons*) and can be the only choices on cheaper *menus*. Look instead for these classics: St. Marcellin cheese, *salade lyonnaise* (croutons, fried bits of ham, and a poached egg on a bed of lettuce), green lentils (*lentilles*) served on a salad or with sausages, *quenelles de brochet* (fish dumplings in a creamy sauce), and *filet de sandre* (local whitefish).

Orientation to Lyon

Despite being France's third-largest city (after Paris and Marseille), Lyon is peaceful and manageable. Traffic noise is replaced by pedestrian friendliness in the old center—listen to how quiet this big city is. Notice the emphasis on environmentally friendly transport: Electric buses have replaced diesel buses in the historic core, and pedal taxis (called "*cyclopolitains*," seek-loh-poh-lee-tan) are used instead of traditional taxis for short trips for a cost of just €1 per kilometer (short pedal-taxi tours are available, too). Lyon's network of more than 1,000 city-owned bikes was in place years before Paris' (available for locals' use only, unless you have a smart chip in your credit card).

Lyon provides the organized traveler with a full day of activities. Sightseeing can be enjoyed on foot from any of the recommended hotels, though it's smart to make use of the funiculars, trams, and Métro. Most of the town's attractions can be conveniently linked in an easy walking-tour route. Lyon's sights are concentrated in three areas: **Fourvière Hill**, with its white Notre-Dame Basilica glimmering over the city; historic **Vieux Lyon**, which hunkers below on the bank of the Saône River; and the **Presqu'île** (home to my recommended hotels), lassoed by the Saône and Rhone rivers. Huge and curiously empty place Bellecour, which lies in the middle of the Presqu'île, always seems to be hosting an event.

Tourist Information

The well-equipped TI is generous with helpful, free information, and can reserve a hotel for you at no charge (daily 9:00–18:00, tel. 04 72 77 69 69, www.lyon-france.com, corner of place Bellecour, free public WCs behind the TI building). Pick up the city map (with good enlargements of central Lyon and Vieux Lyon, a handy Métro and tramway map insert, and all public parking lots; hotels have similar maps), an event schedule (ask about concerts in the Roman Theaters during *Les Nuits de Fourvière*—early June–early Aug—and events at the Opera House), and the *Only Lyon* booklet (with a directory of shopping and eateries, as well as articles on special aspects of the city).

The TI's **audioguide** (€10/half-day) offers good, self-guided walking tours of Vieux Lyon. Live **guided walks** of Vieux Lyon are offered at 14:30 on weekends and on most days July through early September (€9, 2 hours, usually in French but in English if enough demand, depart from the TI, verify days and times with TI). Other, less-frequent English-language walks include tours of the Opera House, the La Croix-Rousse district, and the silk workshops.

The TI sells a good-value **Lyon City Card** for serious sightseers (€20/1 day, €30/2 consecutive days, €40/3 consecutive days, under 18 half-price). This pass includes all Lyon museums, free use of the Métro/bus system, a river cruise (April–Oct), a walking tour of Lyon with a live guide, and a 50 percent discount on the TI's audioguide. The one-day pass pays for itself if you visit the Gallo-Roman Museum and the Resistance and Deportation History Center, plus take a guided walking tour and use public transit.

Arrival in Lyon

By Train: Lyon has two train stations—Lyon-Perrache and Part-Dieu. Many trains stop at both, and through-trains connect the two stations every 10 minutes. Both stations have baggage storage (daily 6:00–23:00) and are well-served by Métro, bus, airport shuttle, and taxi.

The **Perrache station** is more central and within a 20-minute walk of place Bellecour (follow *Place Carnot* signs out of the station, then cross place Carnot and walk up pedestrian rue Victor Hugo). Or take the Métro (direction: Laurent Bonnevay) two stops to Bellecour and follow *sortie rue République* signs.

The **Part-Dieu station**, with the same services as Perrache, is where most visitors arrive. To get to the **city center**, follow *sortie Vivier Merle* signs outside the station to the Métro. (If you'll be doing a lot of sightseeing around the city, buy the great-value all-day transit ticket here, or wait to pick up a Lyon City Card—which covers transit—at the TI; for more tips on the Métro, see "Getting Around Lyon," later.) Take the Métro toward Stade de Gerland, transfer at Saxe-Gambetta to the Gare de Vaise route, and get off at Bellecour. Follow signs reading *sortie rue République*. A new **airport tram** (described under "By Plane," below) leaves from the east end of the station (opposite from the Vivier Mere exit). Follow airplane icon and *gare routière* signs to find the T3 tram to the airport, and SNCF buses to Annecy and Grenoble (most trips are by train).

Figure €13 for a **taxi** from either train station to the hotels listed near place Bellecour.

By Car: The city center has good signage and is manageable to navigate, though you'll encounter traffic on the surrounding freeways. If autoroute A-6 is jammed (not unusual), you'll be directed to bypass freeways (such as A-46) that work well. Either way, follow *Centre-Ville* and *Presqu'île* signs, and then follow *Office de Tourisme* and *place Bellecour* signs. Park in the lots under place Bellecour or place des Célestins (yellow *P* means "parking lot") or get advice from your hotel. The TI's map identifies all public parking lots. Overnight parking (generally 19:00–8:00) is only €4, but day rates are nearly €2 per hour (€25/24 hours).

By Plane: Lyon's sleek little airport, Saint-Exupéry—15 miles from the city center—is a breeze to navigate (ATMs, English information booths, tel. 08 26 80 08 26, www.lyon.aeroport.fr). It has connections to most major European cities, including two flights per hour to Paris' Charles de Gaulle Airport and a TGV station (9 trains/day from downtown Paris, 2 hours). Car rental is a snap. Six trams per hour on line T3 make the 30-minute trip from the airport to the Part-Dieu station (€14 one-way, €25 round-trip). Allow €50–60 for a taxi if you have baggage.

Helpful Hints

Consulates: The **US Consulate** is near the Rhône River, east of the Cordeliers Métro stop at 1 quai Jules Courmant. It provides limited consular services for American citizens—visa questions should be referred to the American Embassy Consular Services in Paris (open Mon-Fri 10:00–12:00 & 14:00–17:00,

Illuminated Lyon

The golden statue of Mary above Notre-Dame Basilica was placed atop a 16th-century chapel on December 8, 1852. Spontaneously, the entire city welcomed her with candles in their windows. Each December 8 ever since, the city glows softly with countless candles.

This tradition has spawned an actual industry. Lyon is famous as a model of state-of-the-art floodlighting, and the city hosts conventions on the topic. Each night more than 200 buildings, sites, and public spaces are gloriously flood-lit. Go for an after-dinner stroll and enjoy the view from the Bonaparte Bridge after dark. Paris calls itself the City of Light—but actually Lyon is.

closed Sat–Sun, tel. 04 78 38 33 03, usalyon@state.gov). The **Canadian Consulate** is at 17 rue Bourgelat (tel. 04 72 77 64 07, consulat.canada-lyon@amb-canada.fr).

Market Days: A small market stretches along the Saône River between pont Bonaparte and passerelle du Palais de Justice (daily until 12:30). Tuesday through Saturday, it's produce; Sunday morning, it's crafts and contemporary art on the other side of the bridge near the Court of Justice; and Monday, it's textiles. There's another bustling morning produce market on boulevard de la Croix-Rousse every day except Monday until 12:30 (see "La Croix-Rousse" on page 905).

Festivals: Lyon celebrates the Virgin Mary with candlelit windows during the Festival of Lights each year on December 8 (www.lumieres.lyon.fr). Les Nuits de Fourvière (dance, music, and theater) takes place from early June to early August in the Roman theaters (www.nuitsdefourviere.com).

Internet Access: Raconte Moi La Terre is a cool place to check your email (Mon–Sat 10:00–19:30, closed Sun, free Wi-Fi, air-con, drinks and snacks, 14 rue du Plat, tel. 04 78 92 60 22).

Laundry: A launderette is at 7 rue Mercière on the Presqu'île near the Alphonse Juin bridge (daily 6:00–21:00); another is between place Bellecour and Perrache station, a few steps off rue Victor Hugo (daily 7:30–20:30, 19 rue Ste. Helene).

SNCF Train Office: The **SNCF Boutique** at 2 place Bellecour is handy for train info, reservations, and tickets (Mon–Fri 9:00–18:45, Sat 10:00–18:30, closed Sun).

Chauffeur Hire: Design your own half-day or full-day tour with a car and driver (tel. 06 65 38 75 08, www.lugdunum-ips.com, contact@lugdunum-ips.com).

Children's Activities: The Parc de la Tête d'Or is vast, with rental rowboats, a miniature golf course, and ponies to ride (across

Rhône River from La Croix-Rousse neighborhood, Métro: Masséna, tel. 0472 69 47 60).

Getting Around Lyon

Lyon has a user-friendly public transit system, with four sleek streetcar lines (tramways T1–T4), four underground Métro lines (A–D), an extensive bus system, and two funiculars (there are two directions heading uphill: *Fourvière* for the basilica and *Saint-Just* for the Roman Theaters). The subway is similar to Paris' Métro in many ways (e.g., routes are signed by *direction* for the last stop on the line) but is more automated (you buy tickets at coin-op machines), cleaner, and less crowded. You can transfer between Métro and tramway lines with the same ticket (valid one hour), but you can't do round-trips and must revalidate your ticket whenever boarding a tram (€1.60/1 hour, €2.40/2 hours, €4.70/1 day, €13.20/10 rides, all tickets cover funicular). The €4.40 one-day ticket is a great deal even if you only use the funicular and visit one of the outlying museums (Resistance Center or Lumière Museum). Also remember that the Lyon City Card (described on page 893, under "Tourist Information") covers transit.

To use the ticket machines, change the display language to English. Then use the black roller to *selectionner* your ticket, firmly push the top button twice to *confirmer* your request, and then insert coins. In the Métro, insert your ticket in the turnstile, then reclaim it. If the stop has no turnstile, you must validate your ticket by punching it in a nearby machine (tramway users always validate on the trams). Study the wall maps to be sure of your direction; ask a local if you're not certain. Yellow signs lead to transfers, and green signs lead to exits (*Sortie*).

Self-Guided Spin-Tour

Bonaparte Bridge (Pont Bonaparte)

This central bridge, just a block from place Bellecour, is made to order for a day-or-night spin-tour.

• *Stand on the bridge and face the golden statue of the Virgin Mary marking the Notre-Dame Basilica on Fourvière Hill. (It's actually capping the smaller chapel, which predates the church by 500 years.) The basilica is named for the Roman Forum (*Fourvière*) upon which it sits. Now begin to look clockwise.*

The Metallic Tower (called La Tour Métallique—not La Tour Eiffel), like the basilica, was finished just before World War I. It was originally an observation tower but today functions only as a TV tower. The husky church on the riverbank below (St. Jean Cathedral) marks the center of the old town. Upstream, the Neoclassical columns are part of the Court of Justice (where Klaus

Lyon at a Glance

▲▲**Roman Theaters and Gallo-Roman Museum** Terrific museum covering Roman Lyon. **Hours:** Tue–Sun 10:00–18:00, closed Mon. See page 901.

▲**Resistance and Deportation History Center** Displays and videos telling the inspirational story of the French Resistance. **Hours:** Wed–Fri 9:00–17:30, Sat–Sun 9:30–18:00, closed Mon–Tue. See page 907.

▲**Museum of Fine Arts** France's second-most-important fine-arts museum (after the Louvre). **Hours:** Wed–Thu and Sat–Mon 10:00–18:00, Fri 10:30–18:00, closed Tue. See page 906.

▲**Lumière Museum** Museum of film, dedicated to the Lumière brothers' pivotal contribution. **Hours:** Tue–Sun 11:00–18:30, closed Mon. See page 910.

▲**Notre-Dame Basilica** Lyon's ornate version of Paris' Sacré-Cœur. **Hours:** Daily 8:00–19:00; weekday Mass usually at 7:15, 11:00, and 17:00; Sun Mass at 7:30, 9:30, 11:00, and 17:00. See page 898.

▲**Traboules** Cool covered passageways in Vieux Lyon. **Hours:** Daily 8:00–19:30. See page 904.

St. Jean Cathedral Gothic church with 700-year-old astronomical clock. **Hours:** Mon–Fri 8:00–12:00 & 14:00–19:30, Sat–Sun 14:00–17:00. See page 902.

Atelier de la Soierie Workshop demonstrating handmade silk printing and screen painting. **Hours:** Mon–Fri 9:00–12:00 & 14:00–19:00, Sat 9:00–13:00 & 14:00–18:00, closed Sun. See page 905.

Museums of Fabrics and Decorative Arts Museum of Fabrics tracing development of textile weaving over 2,000 years; Museum of Decorative Arts featuring 18th-century decor in a mansion. **Hours:** Tue–Sun 10:00–17:30, closed Mon, Museum of Decorative Arts closes 12:00–14:00. See page 906.

Barbie, head of the local Gestapo—a.k.a. "the Butcher of Lyon"—was sentenced to life in prison). Farther upstream, the hill covered with tall, pastel-colored houses is the La Croix-Rousse district, former home of the city's huge silk industry. With the invention of the "Jacquard looms," which required 12-foot-tall ceilings, new factory buildings were needed and the new weaving center grew up on this hill. In 1850, it was thriving, with 30,000 looms.

The place Bellecour side of the river is the district of Presqu'île. This strip of land is sandwiched by the Saône and Rhône rivers, and is home to Lyon's Opera House, City Hall, theater, top-end shopping, banks, and all of my recommended hotels. A morning market sets up daily under the trees (upriver, just beyond the red bridge). The simple riverfront café at the foot of the bridge, La Buvette des Célestins, is ideal for a drink with a view (best at night).

Speaking of bridges, all of Lyon's bridges—including the one you're standing on—were destroyed by the Nazis as they checked out in 1944. Looking downstream, you can see the stately mansions of Lyon's well-established families. Across the river again, the Neo-Gothic St. Georges church marks the neighborhood of the first silk-weavers. The ridge behind St. Georges is dominated by a big building—once a seminary for priests, now a state high school—and leads us back to Mary.

• Walk across the bridge and continue toward the hill two blocks to find the funicular station (a bit to the left), where you can ride up Fourvière Hill to the basilica (catch the train marked Fourvière, not St. Just); sit up front and admire the funicular's funky old technology (€2.40 round-trip, Metro/tramway tickets valid). From there you can tour the basilica, enjoy the city view, and visit the Roman Theaters and Gallo-Roman Museum, then catch another funicular back down and explore the old town (Vieux Lyon). I've listed key sights (next) in this order. Otherwise, it's a 20-minute walk upriver to place des Terreaux, where you'll find the City Hall (Hôtel de Ville) and Museum of Fine Arts.

Sights in Lyon

Fourvière Hill

▲Notre-Dame Basilica
(Basilique Notre-Dame de Fourvière)

Bam!—this ornate church fills your field of view as you exit the funicular. About the year 1870, the bishop of Lyon vowed to build a magnificent tribute to the Virgin Mary if the Prussians spared his city. (Similar deal-making led to the construction of the basilica of Sacré-Cœur in Paris.) Building began in 1872, and the church was ready for worship by World War I.

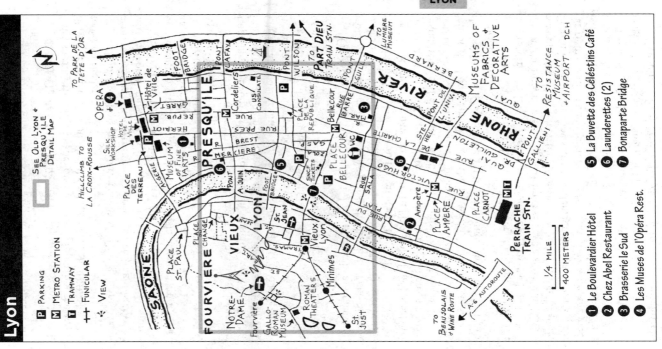

Lyon

LYON

P Parking
M Metro Station
T Tramway
+ + Funicular
* View

☐ See Old Lyon + Presqu'île Detail Map

Ⓝ

1 Le Boulevardier Hôtel
2 Chez Abel Restaurant
3 Brasserie le Sud
4 Les Muses de l'Opéra Rest.
5 La Buvette des Célestins Café
6 Launderettes (2)
7 Bonaparte Bridge

1/4 MILE
400 METERS

Cost and Hours: Free, daily 8:00-19:00; weekday Mass usually at 7:15, 11:00, and 17:00; Sun Mass at 7:30, 9:30, 11:00, and 17:00.

Self-Guided Tour: Before entering, step back to view the fancy facade, the older chapel on the right (supporting the statue of Mary), and the top of the Eiffel-like TV tower on the left.

Climb the steps to enter. You won't find a more Mary-centered church. Everything—floor, walls, ceiling—is covered with elaborate **mosaics**. Scenes glittering on the walls tell stories of the Virgin (in Church history on the left, and in French history on the right). Amble down the center aisle at an escargot's pace and examine some of these scenes:

First scene on the left: In 431, the Council of Ephesus declared Mary to be the "Mother of God."

Across the nave, first on the right: The artist imagines Lugdunum (Lyon)—the biggest city in Roman Gaul, with 50,000 inhabitants—as the first Christian missionaries arrive. The first Christian martyrs in France (killed in A.D. 177) dance across heaven with palm branches.

Next left: In 1571, at the pivotal sea battle of Lepanto, Mary provides the necessary miracle as the outnumbered Christian forces beat the Turks.

Opposite (from right to left): Joan of Arc hears messages from Mary, rallies the French against the English at the Siege of Orléans in 1429 (find the Orléans coat of arms above), and is ultimately burned at the stake in Rouen at age 19 (1431).

Back across the nave on the left: In 1854, Pope Pius I proclaims the dogma of the Immaculate Conception in St. Peter's Square (establishing the belief among Catholics that Mary was born without the "Original Sin" of apple-eating Adam and Eve). To the left of the Pope, angels carry the tower of Fourvière Church; to the right is the image of the Virgin of Lourdes (who miraculously appeared in 1858).

Finally, on the right: Louis XIII offers the crown of France to the Virgin Mary. (The empty cradle hints that while he had her on the line, he asked, "Could I please have a son?" Louis XIV was born shortly thereafter.) Above marches a parade of pious French kings, from Clovis and Charlemagne to Napoleon (on the far right—with the white cross and red coat). Below are the great Marian churches of France (left to right)—Chartres, Paris' Sacré-Cœur and Notre-Dame, Reims (where most royalty was crowned), and this church. These six scenes in mosaic all lead to the altar where Mary reigns as Queen of Heaven.

Exit under Joan of Arc and descend to the **lower church,** dedicated to Mary's earthly husband, Joseph. Priorities here are painfully clear, as money ran out for Joseph's church. Today, it's used as a concert venue (notice the spongy-yellow acoustic material covering the vaulting). Return on the same stairs to the humble 16th-century chapel to the Virgin (push the door); outside, look up to see the glorious statue of Mary that overlooks Lyon.

Just around this chapel (past the church museum and the recommended Restaurant Panoramique) is a commanding **view** of Lyon. You can see parts of both rivers and north from La Croix-Rousse district south to the Bonaparte Bridge, with greater Lyon (pop. 1.3 million) spread out before you in the distance. The black barrel-vaulted structure to the left is the Opera House, and the rose-colored skyscraper in the distance is called, appropriately, "Le Crayon" (the pencil). On a clear afternoon you'll get a glimpse of Mont Blanc (the highest point in Europe, just left of the pencil-shaped skyscraper).

• *To get to the Roman Theaters and Gallo-Roman Museum (described next), walk back toward the funicular station and turn left down rue Roger Radisson. The museum hides down the steps where rue Roger Radisson meets rue Cléberg. Before entering the museum, get the best overview of the site by taking a few steps left on the road leading downhill (rue Cléberg). Then find the ramp that leads to the museum's rooftop (open the gate). A red banner marks the museum entry.*

▲▲Roman Theaters and Gallo-Roman Museum (Musée de la Civilisation Gallo-Romaine)

Constructed in the hillside with views of the two Roman Theaters, this museum makes clear Lyon's importance in Roman times. Lyon (founded in A.D. 43) was an important transportation hub for the administration of Roman Gaul (and much of modern-day France). Emperors Claudius and Caracalla were both born in Lugdunum (Roman Lyon). For more on the Romans, see "How About Them Romans?" on page 600.

The fascinating **Gallo-Roman Museum** is wonderfully explained in English, and takes you on a chronological stroll down several floors through ancient Lyon. The displays are well-organized and easy to follow (small beige plaques posted in each room give a good overview of that room's collection).

After a brief glimpse at prehistoric objects, dive into the Gallo-Roman rooms. The artifacts you'll see were found locally. The unusual bronze chariot dates from the seventh century B.C. The model of Roman Lyon shows a town of 50,000 in its second-century A.D. glory days. (In the model, the forum stands where the basilica does today, hanging on the cliff edge.) Notice the white bits of the actual ruins nearby) and the network of grey roads leading to Lyon. The stone Roman pump behind the city model looks like an engine block.

Next, a speech by Emperor Claudius carved into a big, black-bronze tablet recalls how, in A.D. 48, he worked to integrate Gauls into the empire by declaring that they were eligible to sit in the Roman Senate (English translation on the wall). Those curved stones you pass were actual seats in an arena—inscribed with the names of big shots who sat there. Farther on, a mosaic shows a *Ben Hur*-type chariot race, a glass case displays Roman coins, and, with the push of a button, you can see the mechanics of a Roman theater stage curtain in action...raised instead of lowered (€4, €6 if special exhibits, free on Thu, open Tue–Sun 10:00–18:00, closed Mon, tel. 04 72 38 49 30, www.musees-gallo-romains.com).

• *Exit the museum into the theaters.*

The closer, **big theater** (which originally held 10,000) today seats 3,000 for concerts. The **smaller theater,** an "odeon" (from the Greek "ode" for song), was acoustically designed for speeches and songs (both free and open daily until 19:00). The grounds are peppered with gravestones and sarcophagi. Find a seat in the big theater and read up on Roman theaters (see page 664 in the Provence chapter).

From early June through early August, the theaters host *Les Nuits de Fourvière,* an open-air festival of concerts, theater, dance, and film. Check programs at the TI and purchase tickets here at the theaters (box office at gate exit toward the Minimes funicular station, Mon–Sat 11:00–18:00, closed Sun), or online at www .nuitsdefourviere.com.

• *The ancient road between the Roman Theaters leads down and out, where you'll find the Minimes funicular station (to the right as you leave). Take the funicular to Vieux Lyon (not St. Just), where it deposits you only a few steps from St. Jean Cathedral. Take some time to explore Vieux Lyon (described next). Or, from the Vieux Lyon funicular stop, Métro line D makes a direct run to the Lumière Museum, and an easy transfer to the Resistance and Deportation History Center (both described later).*

Vieux Lyon (Old Lyon)

St. Jean Cathedral—Stand back in the square for the best view of the cathedral (brilliant at night and worth returning for). This mostly Gothic cathedral took 200 years to build. It doesn't soar as high as its northern French counterparts; influenced by their Italian neighbors, churches in southern France are less vertical than those in the north. This cathedral, though unremarkable inside (except for its 700-year-old astronomical clock that performs several times a day), is the "primate cathedral of Gaul," serving what's considered the oldest Christian city in France (Mon–Fri 8:00–12:00 & 14:00–19:30, Sat–Sun 14:00–17:00).

Outside (make two right turns as you leave) are the ruins

Old Lyon

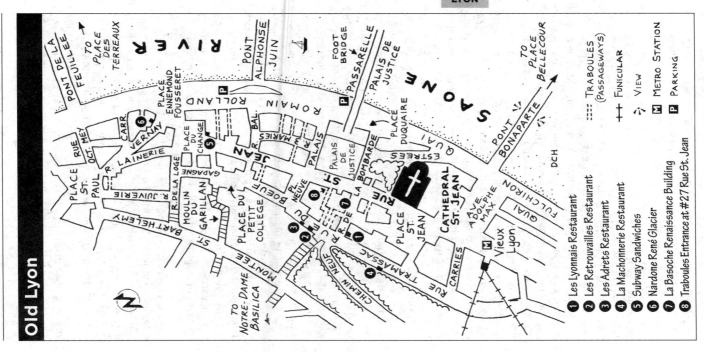

1 Les Lyonnais Restaurant
2 Les Retrouvailles Restaurant
3 Les Adrets Restaurant
4 La Machonnerie Restaurant
5 Subway Sandwiches
6 Nardone René Glacier
7 La Basoche Renaissance Building
8 Traboules Entrance at #27 Rue St. Jean

::: TRABOULES (PASSAGEWAYS)
++ FUNICULAR
View
M METRO STATION
P PARKING

of a mostly 11th-century church, destroyed during the French Revolution (the cathedral was turned into a "temple of reason"). What's left of a baptistery from an early Christian church (c. A.D. 400) is under glass.

▲**Old Lyon and Covered Passageways (Traboules)**—Lyon offers the best concentration of well-preserved Renaissance buildings in the country (see map on page 903). The city grew rich from its trade fairs and banking, and was the king of Europe's silk industry from the 16th to 19th centuries, humming with some 30,000 looms. The grand buildings of the old center were inspired by Italy and financed by the silk industry.

Rue St. Jean, leading north from the cathedral to place du Change, is the main drag, flanked by parallel pedestrian streets. (The rue de Bœuf is quieter and more appealing than touristy rue St. Jean.) The old city's serpentine passageways (*traboules*) were essentially shortcuts linking the old town's three main streets. These hidden paths give visitors a hide-and-seek opportunity to discover pastel courtyards, lovely loggias, and delicate arches. Spiral staircases were often shared by several houses. The *traboules* provided shelter when silk was being moved from one stage to the next.

Detour a few steps from rue St. Jean and make a left up rue de la Bombarde. You'll find a well-restored Renaissance building (La Basoche) that gives you a good idea of what hides behind many facades in old Lyon. Note the black-and-white photos showing this structure before its 1968 renovation, and imagine most of Vieux Lyon in this state.

As you stroll along rue St. Jean, notice the heavy doors leading to the *traboules*. Though several short *traboules* leading to courtyards are accessible (if a doorway is open, you can wander in), only three of Vieux Lyon's numerous *traboules* that connect different streets are open to the public. The longest *traboule* is between #27 rue St. Jean and #54 rue du Bœuf; another leads from #27 St. Jean to #6 rue de Trois Maries; and the third is at #42 Montée St Barthélemy. *Traboules* are accessible until 19:30. Press the top button next to the street-front door to release the door when entering, push the lit buttons to illuminate dark walkways, and slide the door-handle levers when leaving. You're welcome to explore—but please be respectful of the residents, and don't go up any stairs.

While you wander Vieux Lyon, look for door plaques giving a history of each building and *traboule*. After walking through a *traboule*, you'll understand why Lyon's old town was an ideal center for the Resistance fighters to slip in and out of as they confounded the Nazis.

The place du Change, at the north end of rue St. Jean, was the banking center of medieval Lyon. This money scene developed after the city was allowed to host trade fairs in 1420. Its centerpiece is France's first stock exchange.

• *From here it's a short walk across the river to place des Terreaux and the Museum of Fine Arts (cross pont de la Feuillée and continue straight four blocks). Ice-cream connoisseurs must stop at **Nardone René Glacier** before crossing the river (daily 10:00–24:00, on river near place du Change, 3 place Ennemond Fousseret).*

Presqu'île

This bit of land (French for "peninsula," and literally meaning "almost-an-island") between the two rivers is Lyon's shopping spine, with thriving pedestrian streets. The neighborhood's northern focal point is the...

Place des Terreaux—This grand square hosts the City Hall (Hôtel de Ville), the Museum of Fine Arts, and a grand fountain by Frédéric-Auguste Bartholdi (the French sculptor who designed America's Statue of Liberty). Its most important function for locals is allowing the last rays of sun to penetrate the café tables near the City Hall. Join the crowd for a late-afternoon sip.

The fountain features Marianne (the Lady of the Republic) riding a four-horse-powered chariot. The square itself is usually wet, with 69 fountains spurting playfully in a vast grid.

Atelier de la Soierie—This silk workshop, just off place des Terreaux on rue Romarin (behind Café le Moulin Joli, a Resistance hangout during World War II), welcomes the public to drop in to see silk printing and screen painting by hand. Keep in mind that this is a lost art that today has mostly been replaced by machines. Within the shop you'll see stretched silk canvases, buckets of dye, and artists in action. Climb the staircase to visit a boutique selling handmade silk creations. Prices range from €25 to €250 (free entry, Mon-Fri 9:00–12:00 & 14:00–19:00, Sat 9:00–13:00 & 14:00–18:00, closed Sun, tel. 04 72 07 97 83).

La Croix-Rousse—Hilly, untouristy, and SoHo-esque, this neighborhood was home to 30,000 silk looms in the 1800s. Today this part of town is popular with Lyon's tie-dye types.

The smartest way to visit is to take the Métro to the top, then follow a series of scenic slopes and stairs back down—past bohemian cafés, art galleries, creative graffiti, and used-clothing shops—to the Presqu'île. (Or—to burn off last night's *Lyonnaise* feast—follow this suggested route in reverse.)

Begin by exiting Métro line C at the La Croix-Rousse stop. Every day but Monday until about 12:30, a lively, local produce market stretches across the square and down boulevard de la Croix-Rousse. Start your downhill stroll from behind the Métro stop along rue des Pierres Plantées. Pause to appreciate the views from the Jardin de la Grande Côte, and notice how the concrete square is used as a soccer field, a tricycle track, an outdoor café, and any other use that the neighbors can find for it. Continue down the stairs and follow the main drag, montée de la Grande Côte. Detour a block to the right on rue des Tables Claudiennes for a view over the Roman Amphitheater of the Three Gauls (which in most other cities would be big news, but in Lyon feels ignored). Backpedal to the hill climb and continue your descent, working your way down to place des Terreaux.

▲**Museum of Fine Arts (Musée des Beaux-Arts)**—Located in a former abbey, which was secularized by Napoleon in 1803 and made into a public museum, this fine-arts museum has an impressive collection, ranging from Egyptian antiquities to Impressionist paintings.

The first floor offers a stroll through a fine collection of ancient (especially Egyptian) art, medieval art, and Art Nouveau (furniture). The adjacent chapel is a dreamy Orsay-like display of 19th- and 20th-century statues (including work by Auguste Rodin and Bartholdi).

The second floor displays a pretty selection of paintings from many ages and countries (with no famous works, but a good Impressionist collection). The highlight is a series of pre-Raphaelite-type works called *Le Poème de l'Âme* ("The Poem of the Soul"), by Louis Janmot. This cycle of 18 paintings and 16 charcoal drawings traces the story of the souls of a boy and a girl as they journey through childhood, adolescence, and into adulthood. They struggle with fears and secular temptations before gaining spiritual enlightenment on the way to heaven. The boy loses his faith and enjoys a short but delicious hedonistic fling that leads to misery in hell. But a mother's prayers intercede, and he reunites with the girl to enjoy heavenly redemption.

Cost and Hours: €7, Wed–Thu and Sat–Mon 10:00–18:00, Fri 10:30–18:00, closed Tue, first floor closes 11:55–13:05, second floor closes 13:05–14:15, pick up museum map on entering, picnic-perfect courtyard, 20 place des Terreaux, Métro: Hôtel de Ville, tel. 04 72 10 17 40, www.mba-lyon.fr. A bar/café with calming terrace seating is on the first floor, next to the bookstore.

Museums of Fabrics and Decorative Arts (Musées des Tissus et des Arts Décoratifs)—These museums, south of place Bellecour, fill two buildings (sharing a courtyard and connected with an interior hallway). Though packed with exquisite exhibits, the museums offer little information in English (some English information posted in the Museum of Fabrics, nothing in Museum of Decorative Arts). The Museum of Fabrics traces the development of textile weaving over the course of 2,000 years and shows off some breathtaking silk work. The Museum of Decorative Arts, billed as "an ambience museum," is a luxurious mansion decorated to the hilt with 18th-century furniture, textiles, and tapestries in a plush domestic setting (€5, €9 covers both museums, Tue–Sun 10:00–17:30, closed Mon, Museum of Decorative Arts closes 12:00–14:00, 34 rue de la Charité, Métro: Bellecour, tel. 04 78 38 42 00, www.musee-des-tissus.com).

Enjoying Presqu'île—There's more to this "almost-an-island" than the sights listed here. Join the treadmill of shoppers on sprawling rue de la République (north of place Bellecour) and the teeming rue Victor Hugo pedestrian mall (south of place Bellecour). Peruse the *bouchons* (characteristic bistros—especially characteristic in the evening) of rue Mercière.

Passage de l'Arque is a classy, covered shopping passage from the 1800s that predates shopping malls (78 rue Président Edouard Herriot).

Grand Café des Négociants is ideal for an indoor break (skip the outside terrace). This *grand café*, which has been in business since 1864, feels like it hasn't changed since then, with its soft leather chairs, painted ceilings, and glass chandeliers (daily, 1 place Francisque Régaud, near Cordeliers Métro stop, tel. 04 78 42 50 05).

Away from the Center

▲Resistance and Deportation History Center (Centre d'Histoire de la Résistance et de la Déportation)—Located near Vichy (capital of the French puppet state) and neutral Switzerland, Lyon was the center of the French Resistance from 1942 to 1945. These "underground" Resistance heroes fought the Nazis tooth and nail. Bakers hid radios inside loaves of bread to secretly contact London. Barmaids passed along tips from tipsy Nazis. Communists in black berets cut telephone lines. Farmers hid downed airmen in haystacks. Housewives spread news from the front with their gossip. Printers countered Nazi propaganda with anonymous pamphlets.

This center served as a Nazi torture chamber and Gestapo headquarters under Klaus Barbie (who was finally tried and convicted in 1987 after extradition from Bolivia). Over 11,000 people were killed or deported to concentration camps during his reign.

The excellent museum uses audioguides, videos, reconstructed rooms, small theaters, and numerous photos with detailed English descriptions to tell the inspirational story of the French Resistance. The portraits in the entry are of witnesses who return to the center to speak about their experiences. To use the free audioguide, press "C" when done with an exhibit; don't move too quickly or it won't work. Some displays only have audio of French music and speeches (€4, Wed–Fri 9:00–17:30, Sat–Sun 9:30–18:00, closed Mon–Tue, 14 avenue Berthelot, tel. 04 78 72 23 11, www.chrd.lyon.fr).

Getting There: You have several good options: Ride the **Métro** line B to Jean Macé, exit toward the elevated train line,

Old Lyon & Presqu'île

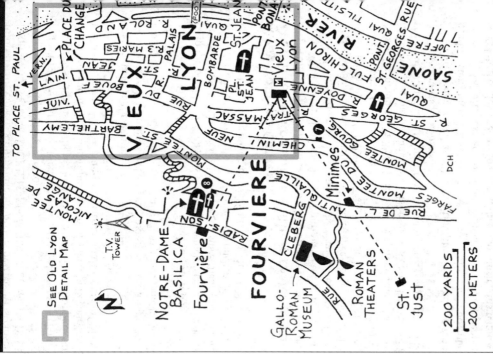

SEE OLD LYON DETAIL MAP

TO PLACE ST. PAUL

PLACE DU CHANGE

VERN.

LAIN.

R. 3 MARIES

JEAN

ST. JEAN

R. PALAIS BOUEF

JUIV.

BARTHELEMY

VIEUX LYON

R. ROLAND

BOMBARDE

PL. ST. JEAN

RUE DU BOEUF

ST. JEAN

RUE NEUVE ST. JEAN

MONTEE ST.

CHEMINI

FOO

QUAI

PONT BONA

R. FULCHIRON

R. DOYENNE

TRA MASSAC

Vieux Lyon

R. ST. GEORGES

ST. GEORGES

Vieux Lyon

QUAI

RIVER

SAÔNE

QUAI TILSIT

JOFFRE RUE

ST. GEORGES PONT

PONT

DCH

MONTEE NICOLAS DE LANGE

T.V. TOWER

N

NOTRE-DAME BASILICA

Fourvière

Fourvière-Radisson

FOURVIÈRE

GALLO-ROMAN MUSEUM

CLEBERG

RUE DE L' ANTIQUAILLE

Minimes

MONTEE DES

FARGES MONTEE

ROMAN THEATERS

RUE

ST. JUST

200 YARDS

200 METERS

① Hôtel Globe et Cecil
② Hôtel des Artistes
③ Hôtel des Célestins
④ Hôtel du Théâtre

⑤ To Le Boulevardier Hôtel
⑥ Hôtel la Residence
⑦ Vieux Lyon Youth Hostel
⑧ Rest. Panoramique de la Fourvière

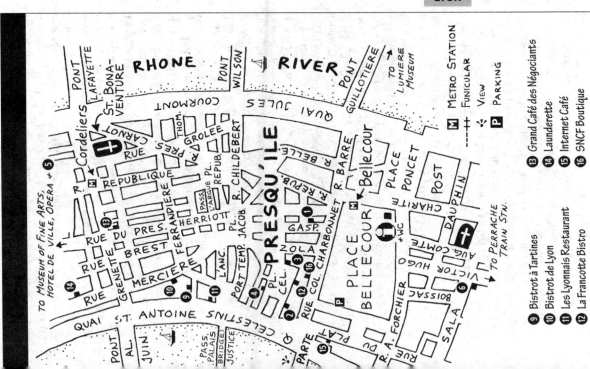

9 Bistrot à Tartines
10 Bistrot de Lyon
11 Les Lyonnais Restaurant
12 La Francotte Bistro

13 Grand Café des Négociants
14 Launderette
15 Internet Café
16 SNCF Boutique

M Metro Station
Funicular
View
P Parking

and transfer to the T2 tramway (going right) or turn right on avenue Berthelot and walk five blocks; **walk** from Perrache station across pont Gallieni, then three blocks to 14 avenue Berthelot (15 minutes); or take the T2 tramway from below Perrache station to Centre Berthelot.

▲**Lumière Museum (Musée Lumière)**—Antoine Lumière and his two sons Louis and Auguste—the Eastman-Kodaks of France—ran a huge factory with 200 workers in the 1880s, producing four million glass photographic plates a day. Then, in 1895, they made the first *cinématographe*, or movie. In 1903 they pioneered the "autochrome" process of painting frames to make "color photos." This museum tells their story.

This museum does a great job of explaining the history of filmmaking, thanks to many interesting displays and the essential audioguide. After leaving this place, where the laborious, yet fascinating process of creating moving images is driven home, you'll never take the quality of today's movies for granted. The museum's highlights are the many antique cameras and the screens playing the earliest "movies." The first film reels held about 950 frames, which played at 19 per second, so these first movies were only 50 seconds long. About 1,500 Lumière films are catalogued between 1895 and 1907. (Notice that each movie is tagged with its "Catalog Lumière" number.) The very first movie ever made features workers piling out of the Lumière factory at the end of a work day. People attended movies at first not for the plot or the action, but rather to be mesmerized by the technology that allowed them to see moving images.

The museum fills the Villa Lumière, the family's belle époque mansion, built in 1902. The ground floor shows movies and the earliest cameras and projectors. Upstairs are exhibits on still photography and the Lumière living quarters (furnished c. 1900). Across the park from the mansion is a shrine of what's left of the warehouse where the first movie was actually shot. In a wonderful coincidence, *lumière* is the French word for "light."

En route to the museum, enjoy your ride on the futuristic (and driverless) Métro line D. Sit in the front and command your own underground starship. The unsigned museum is in the large mansion on the square, kitty-corner from the Métro stop (€6, €3 audioguide, Tue–Sun 11:00–18:30, closed Mon, half a block from the Monplaisir-Lumière Métro stop at 25 rue du Premier-Film, tel. 04 78 78 18 95, www.institut-lumiere.org).

Nightlife in Lyon

Lyon has France's second-largest cultural budget after Paris, so there are always plenty of theatrical productions and concerts to attend (in French, of course). The TI has the latest information and schedules. From mid-June through mid-September, the terrace-café at the Opera House hosts an outdoor jazz café with free concerts (usually Mon–Sat at 19:00, 20:00, and 22:00; no Sun concerts, www.opera-lyon.com).

After dinner, a stroll through Lyon's old town, then along the river (the view from the pedestrian bridge—*paserelle*—that leads to the Palais de la Justice is sensational), and along key streets past the main monuments of Presqu'île affords a chance to savor the city's famous illuminations (see sidebar on page 895).

For lively bar and people-watching scenes, prowl rue de la Monnaie (angles off "restaurant row," rue Mercière to the south) and the streets between place des Terreaux and the Opera House.

Sleeping in Lyon

Hotels in Lyon are a steal compared with those in Paris. Weekends are generally discounted in this city that lives off business travelers (some hotels even offer 2-for-1 deals if booked ahead—ask about weekend packages). Prices rise and rooms disappear when trade fairs are in town, so it's smart to reserve your room in advance. If you have trouble, the TI can help for free in person or by email (resa@lyon-france.com). All hotels listed here are on the Presqu'île. Hotels have elevators unless otherwise noted, and air-conditioning is a godsend when it's hot (hottest June–mid-Sept). Expect to push buttons to gain access to many hotels.

On or near Place des Célestins

It's well worth booking ahead to sleep in this classy yet unpretentious neighborhood (Métro: Bellecour). Just a block off the central place Bellecour and a block to the Saône River, travelers have easy access to Lyon's sights, can join shoppers perusing the upscale boutiques, or can watch children playing in the small square fronting the Théâtre des Célestins. Warning: Weekend nights can be noisy if you score a room facing place des Célestins.

$$$ Hôtel Globe et Cecil***, the most elegant of my listings, offers refined comfort on a refined street with traditionally decorated and generously sized rooms. The lounge areas are spaciously classy (Sb-€145, Db-€180, includes breakfast, air-con, pay Wi-Fi, 21 rue Gasparin, tel. 04 78 42 58 95, fax 04 72 41 99 06, www .globeetcecilhotel.com, accueil@globeetcecilhotel.com).

$$$ Hôtel des Artistes**, ideally located on place des Célestins, is comfortable, professional, and a fair value (Sb-€95–115, standard Db-€125, larger Db-€140, extra bed-€10, breakfast-€11, standard rooms are comfortable but a bit tight, air-con, pay Wi-Fi, 8 rue Gaspard-André, tel. 04 78 42 04 88, fax 04 78 42 93 76, www.hoteldesartistes.fr, reservation@hotel-des-artistes.fr).

Sleep Code

(€1 = about $1.25, country code: 33)

S = Single, **D** = Double/Twin, **T** = Triple, **Q** = Quad, **b** = bathroom, **s** = shower only, ***** = French hotel rating system (0–4 stars). Unless otherwise noted, credit cards are accepted and English is spoken.

To help you sort easily through these listings, I've divided the rooms into three categories based on the price for a standard double room with bath:

$$$ Higher Priced—Most rooms €95 or more.
$$ Moderately Priced—Most rooms between €65–95.
$ Lower Priced—Most rooms €65 or less.

Prices can change without notice; verify the hotel's current rates online or by email. For other updates, see www .ricksteves.com/update.

$$$ Hôtel des Célestins**, just off place des Célestins, is warmly run by Cornell-grad Laurent. Its cheery, immaculate rooms are filled with thoughtful touches. Streetside rooms have more light and weekend noise (Sb–€79–129, Db–€79–105, bigger Db–€109–139 and worth the extra euros, Tb–€115–155, apartments–€120–170, €9 buffet breakfast served 7:00–12:00, completely non-smoking, air-con, Internet access, pay Wi-Fi, 4 rue des Archers, tel. 04 72 56 08 98, fax 04 72 56 08 65, www.hotel celestins.com, info@hotelcelestins.com).

$$ Hôtel du Théâtre** requires a romp up two flights of stairs to reach the lobby and does not have air-conditioning, but it's well-located on place des Célestins and offers the best deal at moderate prices that I've found (enter from the hotel's rear). Owner Monsieur Kuhn runs a tight ship, most of the rooms and bathrooms are spacious, and the beds are firm (Db–€66–72, Tb–€90, free Wi-Fi, place des Célestins, tel. 04 78 42 33 32, fax 04 72 40 00 61, www .hotel-du-theatre.fr, contact@hotel-du-theatre.fr).

$ Le Boulevardier** is a fun budget option—particularly for jazz-lovers, as the 11 rooms sit above a jazz café. Rooms are whimsically decorated, reflecting the personality of the happy-go-lucky owner (Db–€49–55, 5 rue de la Fromagerie, tel. 04 78 28 48 22, http://leboulevardier.fr, ccgbernard@free.fr).

South of Place Bellecour

$$ Hôtel la Residence***, my closest listing to the Perrache train station, feels big and institutional. The lobby is spartan, but its 67 rooms are air-conditioned, well cared for, and a solid value. Most are spacious and have high ceilings and bathtubs (Sb/Db-€85, Tb-€90, Qb-€109, Internet access, free Wi-Fi, 18 Victor Hugo, tel. 04 78 42 63 28, fax 04 78 42 85 76, www.hotel-la-residence .com, hotel-la-residence@wanadoo.fr).

$ Vieux Lyon Youth Hostel is impressively situated a 10-minute walk above Vieux Lyon. Open 24 hours daily, it has a lively common area with kitchen access and cheap meals (bed in 4- to 6-bed room-€19, includes sheets and breakfast, small safes available, 45 montée du Chemin, Métro: Hôtel de Ville, tel. 04 78 15 05 50, fax 04 78 15 05 51, www.fuaj.org, lyon@fuaj.org). Book only by email. Take the funicular to Minimes, exit the station and make a left U-turn, and follow the station wall downhill to montée du Chemin.

Eating in Lyon

Dining is a ▲▲▲ attraction in Lyon, and it comes at a bearable price. Half the fun is joining the procession of window-shoppers mulling over where they'll *dîner ce soir*. In the evening, the city's population seems to double as locals emerge to stretch their stomachs. The tried-and-true *salade lyonnaise* (usually filling) followed by *quenelles* are one of my favorite one-two punches in France. You won't want dessert.

Lyon's characteristic *bouchons* are small bistros that evolved from the days when Mama would feed the silk workers after a long day. True *bouchons* are simple places with limited selection and seating (just like Mama's), serving only traditional fare and special 46-centiliter *pot* (pronounced "poh") wine pitchers. The lively pedestrian streets of Vieux Lyon and rue Mercière on the Presqu'île are *bouchon* bazaars, worth strolling even if you dine elsewhere. Though food quality may be better away from these popular restaurant rows, you can't beat the atmosphere. Many of Lyon's restaurants close on Sunday and Monday and during August, except along rue Mercière. If you plan to dine somewhere special, reserve ahead.

Vieux Lyon

Come to Old Lyon for an ideal blend of ambience and quality (if you choose carefully). For the epicenter of restaurant activity, go to place Neuve St. Jean, and survey the scene and menus before sitting down. The first four places below, near the place Neuve St. Jean, have proven reliable.

Les Lyonnais, barely a block off the rue du Boeuf action, so a bit quieter, is lighthearted, with rich colors, wood tables, and a photo gallery of loyal customers. Sincere Stephane runs the place with grace (€22–25 *menus*, good *salade lyonnaise* and *quenelles*, €15 *salade Gourmande* is dinner in itself, closed Sun, small terrace, 1 rue Tramassac, tel. 04 78 37 64 82). A second location (described later, under "On or near rue Mercière") faces the Saône River.

Les Retrouvailles serves tasty but less traditional Lyonnaise cuisine in a charming setting under wood-beam ceilings. Here your dining experience is carefully managed by adorable owners Pierre (*le chef*) and Odile (€23 and €29 *menus*, inside dining only, closed Sun, 38 rue du Bœuf, tel. 04 78 42 68 84).

Les Adrets is where *bouchon* meets beer hall. This long, heavy-beamed place is crammed with a lively crowd and good-value Lyonnaise cuisine (€23–30 *menus*, inside dining only, closed Sat–Sun and Aug, 30 rue du Bœuf, tel. 04 78 38 24 30).

La Machonnerie serves tasty traditional cuisine by gregarious owner-chef Félix that draws in the locals—try to reserve in advance (€29–39 *menus*, inside dining only, closed Sun, air-con, 36 rue Tramassac, a block opposite the cathedral, tel. 04 78 42 24 62).

Restaurant Panoramique de la Fourvière, atop Fourvière Hill with a spectacular view overlooking Lyon, serves fine traditional cuisine in a superb setting. Choose from the non-smoking interior or the leafy terrace, both with views (*menus* from €26, €14 lunch *plat du jour*, daily until 22:00, 9 place de Fourvière, near Notre-Dame Basilica, tel. 04 78 25 21 15).

Subway Sandwiches...*mais oui*, even gourmet diners need a slimming lunch now and then (5 rue St. Jean, just before place du Change).

Ice Cream: **Nardone René Glacier**, on the river near place du Change, with pleasant outdoor seating, serves up Lyon's best ice cream (daily 10:00–24:00, 3 place Ennemond Fousseret).

On the Presqu'île

The pedestrian rue Mercière is the epicenter of *bouchons* on the Presqu'île. Along this street, an entertaining cancan of restaurants stretches four blocks from place des Jacobins to rue Grenette. Enjoy surveying the scene and choose whichever eatery appeals.

On or near rue Mercière

Bistrot à Tartines is an adorable, cheap, light, young, and fun place for nontraditional cuisine (€7 *tartines*, €5–6 salads, €4 desserts, daily, 2 rue de la Monnaie, tel. 04 78 377 85).

Bistrot de Lyon bustles with authentic Lyonnaise atmosphere and good meals at fair prices. It must be famed chef-owner Jean-Paul Lacombe's least expensive establishment (€14 *quenelles*, €10 *salade lyonnaise*, *menus* from €25, open daily, 64 rue Mercière, tel. 04 78 38 47).

Les Lyonnais (recommended earlier) has a second location facing the Saône River, with a spacious terrace and stellar views up to the basilica—particularly at night (closed Sun-Mon, 1 quai des Célestins, tel. 04 78 37 41 80).

On Place des Célestins

La Francotte is a top choice with a warm interior and a solid zinc-topped bar. Try the excellent fish dishes or anything served with their mouthwatering roasted garlic potatoes (*menus* from €23–31, closed Sun-Mon, near many recommended hotels at 8 place des Célestins, tel. 04 78 37 38 64).

Worth a Detour

Chez Abel is the ultimate local *bouchon*, far away from restaurant rows and tourists, and catering to one kind of client only: Lyon residents. It has a warm, chalet-like interior and a welcoming red-cheeked owner. Servings are generous; the *quenelle de brochet* is downright massive. Consider a *plat du jour* and maybe a salad. Reserve ahead (€23–39 *menus*, closed Sat–Sun and Aug, about a 15-minute walk south of place Bellecour, Métro: Ampère, a short block from Saône River, 25 rue Guynemer, tel. 04 78 37 46 18).

Brasserie le Sud is one of the places in Lyon where you can sample legendary chef Paul Bocuse's cuisine at affordable prices. His four brasseries feature international cuisine from different corners of the world (each named for the corner it represents—north, south, east, and west). Le Sud ("The South") is the most accessible, with a Mediterranean feel inside and out (€19–35 *menus*, reasonably priced *plats*, daily, 11 place St Antonin Poncet, a few blocks off place Bellecour, tel. 04 72 77 80 00).

Les Muses de l'Opéra is an intriguing option for lunch or dinner (after 19:00) with a great view (and average quality). Ride the elevator to the seventh floor of the Opera House (€31 dinner *menu*, closed Sun, tel. 04 72 00 45 58).

Lyon Connections

After Paris, Lyon is France's most important rail hub. Train travelers find this gateway to the Alps, Provence, the Riviera, and Burgundy an easy stopover. Two main train stations serve Lyon: Part-Dieu and Perrache. Most trains officially depart from Part-Dieu, though many also stop at Perrache, and trains run between the stations every 10 minutes. Double-check which station your train departs from.

From Lyon by Train to: Paris (9/day, 2 hours), **Annecy** (7/day, 2 hours, most change in Aix-les-Bains, some by bus), **Chamonix** (8/day July-Aug and Dec-April, Fri-Sun only May–June and Sept-Nov, can be more frequent in May, 6–8 hours, some change in Switzerland), **Strasbourg** (5/day, 5 hours), **Dijon** (12/day,

2 hours), **Beaune** (10/day, 2 hours, many change in Mâcon), **Avignon** (22/day; 12 to TGV station in 1.5 hours, 10 to main station in 2 hours), **Arles** (14/day, 2.5 hours, most change in Avignon, Marseille, or Nîmes), **Nice** (6/day, 5 hours), **Carcassonne** (6/day, 4 hours), **Venice** (6/day, 11–13 hours, most change in Geneva and Milan, night train), **Rome** (4/day, 10–12 hours, at least one change in Milan, night train), **Florence** (3/day, 10 hours), **Geneva** (8/day, 2 hours), **Barcelona** (1 day train, 7 hours, change in Perpignan; 2 night trains with transfers).

Route Tips for Drivers: En route to Provence, consider a three-hour detour through the spectacular Ardèche Gorges: Exit the A-6 autoroute at Privas and follow the villages of Aubenas, Vallon Pont d'Arc (offers kayak trips), and Pont Saint-Esprit (for more on this route, see page 673). En route to Burgundy, consider a Beaujolais detour (see below).

Near Lyon: The Rhône Valley

The Rhône Valley is the narrow part of the hourglass that links the areas of Provence and Burgundy. The region is bordered to the west by the soft hills of the Massif Central, and with the rolling foothills of the Alps just to the east, it's the gateway to the high Alps (the region is called "Rhône-Alpes"). The mighty Rhône River rumbles through the valley from its origin in Lake Geneva to its outlet 500 miles away in the Mediterranean near Arles.

Vineyards blanket the western side of the Rhône Valley, from those of the Beaujolais just north of Lyon, to the steep slopes of Tain-l'Hermitage below Lyon. On the eastern side of the river and closer to Avignon are the vineyards of the famous Côtes du Rhône.

The Rhône Valley has always provided the path of least resistance for access from the Mediterranean to northern Europe, and today, Roman ruins litter the valley between Lyon and Orange.

Beaujolais Wine Route

Between Cluny and Lyon, the beautiful vineyards and villages and easygoing wine-tastings of the Beaujolais region make for an appealing detour. The most scenic and interesting section lies between Mâcon and Villefranche-sur-Saône, a few minutes west of A-6 on D-306 (old N-6). The route runs from the Mâconnais wine region and the famous village of Pouilly-Fuissé south through Beaujolais' most important villages: Chiroubles, Fleurie, and Juliénas. Look for *Route de Beaujolais* signs, and expect to get lost a few times. Trains running between Lyon and Macon stop at several wine villages, including Romanèche-Thorins (described next; 6 trains/day from Lyon).

For a pricey but thorough introduction to this region's wines, visit **Le Hameau du Vin** in Romanèche-Thorins. The king of Beaujolais, Georges Duboeuf has constructed a Disney-esque introduction to wine at his wine museum, which immerses you into the life of a winemaker and features impressive models, exhibits, films, and videos. You'll be escorted from the beginning of the vine to present-day winemaking, with a focus on Beaujolais wines. It also has a lovely garden with fragrant flowers, fruits, herbs, and spices that represent the rich aromas present in wine (€18, includes a small tasting and free English headphones, daily April–Oct 9:00–19:00, Nov–March 10:00–18:00; in Romanèche-Thorins, look for signs labeled *Le Hameau du Vin* from D-306—the old N-6, then *La Gare* signs, and look for the old train-station-turned-winery; tel. 03 85 35 22 22, www.hameauduvin.com).

ALSACE

The province of Alsace stands like a flower-child referee between Germany and France. Bounded by the Rhine River on the east and the Vosges Mountains on the west, this is a green region of Hansel-and-Gretel villages, ambitious vineyards, and vibrant cities. Food and wine are the primary industry, topic of conversation, and perfect excuse for countless festivals.

Alsace has changed hands several times between Germany and France because of its location, natural wealth, naked vulnerability—and the fact that Germany considered the mountains as the natural border, whereas the French saw the Rhine as the dividing line.

Having been a political pawn for 1,000 years, Alsace has a hybrid culture: Natives who curse do so bilingually, and the local cuisine features sauerkraut with fine wine sauces. If you're traveling in December, come here for France's most celebrated Christmas markets and festivals.

Colmar is one of Europe's most enchanting cities—with a small-town warmth and world-class art. Strasbourg is a big-city version of Colmar, worth a stop for its remarkable cathedral and to feel its high-powered and trendy bustle. The small villages that dot the wine road between them are like petite Colmars, and provide a refreshing escape from the cities.

Planning Your Time

Set up for two nights in or near Colmar. Allow one day for Colmar and another for Strasbourg and the Route du Vin (Wine Road). If you have only one day, spend your morning in Colmar and your

Alsace

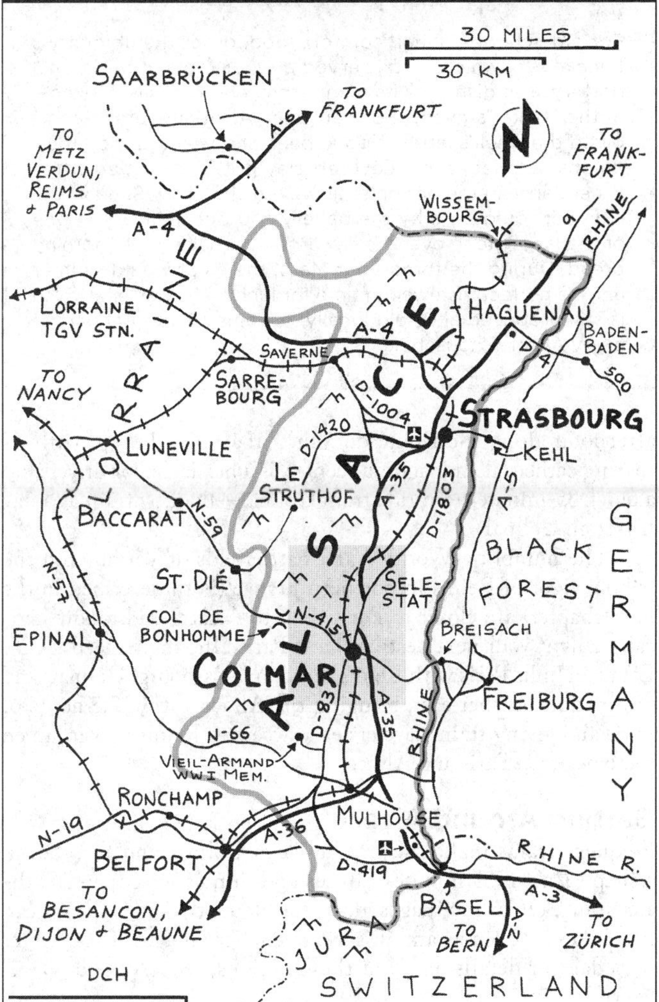

ALSACE

Map legend:
- AUTOROUTE (TOLL MOTORWAY)
- OTHER ROADS
- AIRPORTS
- ALSACE BORDER
- ROUTE DU VIN (SEE DETAIL MAP)

Scale: 30 MILES / 30 KM

Labeled places and routes include: STRASBOURG, COLMAR, MULHOUSE, HAGUENAU, WISSEMBOURG, SAVERNE, SARREBOURG, LUNEVILLE, BACCARAT, ST. DIÉ, COL DE BONHOMME, LE STRUTHOF, SELESTAT, RONCHAMP, BELFORT, EPINAL, VIEIL-ARMAND WWI MEM., SAARBRÜCKEN, BADEN-BADEN, KEHL, BREISACH, FREIBURG, BASEL, LORRAINE TGV STN.

Regions: GERMANY, BLACK FOREST, SWITZERLAND, JURA, ALSACE, LORRAINE, RHINE R.

Directional references: TO FRANKFURT, TO METZ VERDUN, REIMS + PARIS, TO NANCY, TO BESANCON, DIJON + BEAUNE, TO ZÜRICH, TO BERN

Roads: A-4, A-6, A-35, A-36, A-5, A-3, A-2, D-1004, D-1803, D-420, D-419, D-83, N-415, N-59, N-66, N-57, N-19, P-4, 500

Inset: FRANCE with PARIS and ALSACE marked

Early Crockpots

For old-school Alsatian comfort food, order the ubiquitous *baeckeoffe*, which is still served at your table in traditional pottery. The dish gets its name from where it was cooked—in the "baker's oven." For centuries Alsatian women combined the week's leftover pork, beef, and veal with potatoes, onions, and leeks in a covered clay pot, then added white wine. Carrying the pot on their way to church on Sunday, the women would pass by the bakery and put their pot in one of the large stone ovens, still warm from baking the morning bread. During the three-hour Mass, the meat would simmer and be perfectly stewed in time for lunch. The pottery, which is still produced and sold locally, remains an integral part of every Alsatian household.

---

afternoon along the Route du Vin. Urban Strasbourg, with its soaring cathedral and vigorous center, is a headache for drivers but a quick 35-minute train ride from Colmar—do it by train as a day trip from Colmar.

The humbling World War I battlefields of Verdun and the bubbly vigor of Reims in northern France (both described in the next chapter) are closer to Paris than to Alsace, and follow logically only if your next destination is Paris. The high-speed TGV-Est train links Paris with Reims, Verdun, Strasbourg, Colmar, and destinations farther east, bringing the Alsace within 2.5 hours of Paris and giving train travelers easy access to Reims or Verdun en route between Paris and Alsace.

Getting Around Alsace

Frequent trains make the trip between Colmar and Strasbourg a snap (2/hour, 35 minutes). Buses and minivan excursions radiate from Colmar to villages along the Route du Vin, and you can rent bikes in Colmar and in several smaller villages if you prefer to pedal (for details on all of these options, see "Route du Vin," later).

Alsace's Cuisine Scene

Alsatian cuisine is a major tourist attraction in itself. You can't mistake the German influence: sausages, potatoes, onions, and sauerkraut. Look for *choucroute garnie* (sauerkraut and sausage—although it seems a shame to eat it in a fancy restaurant), the more traditionally Alsatian *baeckeoffe* (see sidebar), *rösti* (an oven-baked potato-and-cheese dish), fresh trout, and foie gras. For lighter fare, try the *poulet au Riesling*, chicken cooked ever-so-slowly in Riesling wine (*coq au Riesling* is the same dish done with rooster). At lunch,

or for a lighter dinner, try a *tarte à l'oignon* (like an onion quiche, but better) or *tarte flambée* (like a thin-crust pizza with onion and bacon bits). If you're picnicking, buy some stinky Munster cheese. Dessert specialties are *tarte alsacienne* (fruit tart) and *glace kugelhopf* (a light cake mixed with raisins, almonds, dried fruit, and cherry liqueur).

Remember, restaurants serve only during lunch (11:30–14:00) and dinner (19:00–21:00, later in bigger cities), but some cafés serve food throughout the day.

Alsatian Wines

Thanks to Alsace's Franco-Germanic culture, its wines are a kind of hybrid. The bottle shape, grapes, and much of the wine terminology are inherited from its German past, though wines made today are distinctly French in style (and generally drier than their German sisters). Alsatian wines are named for their grapes—unlike in Burgundy or Provence, where wines are commonly named after villages, or in Bordeaux, where wines are often named after châteaux. White wines rule in Alsace. The following wines are made entirely of their namesake grape variety: Sylvaner (fairly light, fruity, and inexpensive), Riesling (more robust than Sylvaner, but drier than the German style you're probably used to), Gewürztraminer (spicy, with a powerful bouquet; good with pâtés and local cheeses), Muscat (very dry, with a distinctive bouquet and taste; best as a before-dinner wine), Tokay Pinot Gris (more full-bodied than Riesling, but fine with many local main courses), Pinot Noir (the local red is very light and fruity, generally served chilled), and the tasty Crémant d'Alsace (the region's good, inexpensive sparkling wine). You'll also see *eaux-de-vie*, powerful fruit-flavored brandies—try the *framboise* (raspberry) flavor.

For more details, see "Route du Vin Wines" on page 944.

Colmar

Colmar is a well-pickled old place of 65,000 residents, offering a few heavyweight sights in a comfortable, midsize-town package. Historic beauty was usually a poor excuse for being spared the ravages of World War II, but it worked for Colmar. The American and British military were careful not to bomb the half-timbered old burghers' houses, characteristic red- and green-tiled roofs, and cobbled lanes of Alsace's most beautiful city. The town's distinctly French shutters combined with the ye-olde German half-timbering give Colmar an intriguing ambience.

Today, Colmar is alive with colorful buildings, impressive art treasures, and German tourists. Schoolgirls park their rickety horse carriages in front of City Hall and are ready to give visitors a clip-clop tour of the old town. Antiques shops welcome browsers, and hoteliers hurry down the sleepy streets to pick up fresh croissants in time for breakfast.

Orientation to Colmar

There isn't a straight street in Colmar—count on getting lost. Thankfully, most streets are pedestrian-only, and it's a lovely town to be lost in. Navigate by the high church steeples and the helpful signs that seem to pop up whenever you need them (directing visitors to the various sights). For tourists, the town center is place Unterlinden (a 20-minute walk from the train station), where you'll find the TI, Colmar's most important museum, and a big Monoprix supermarket/department store. Every city bus starts or finishes on place Unterlinden.

Colmar is most crowded from May through September and during its festive Christmas season (www.noel-colmar.com). Weekends are busy all year (reserve ahead). The impressive music festival fills hotels the first two weeks of July (www.festival-colmar .com), and the local wine festival rages for 10 days in early August. Open-air markets bustle next to the Dominican Church and St. Martin Cathedral on Thursdays and Saturdays.

Tourist Information

The TI, next to the Unterlinden Museum on place Unterlinden, is generous with printed material (April–Oct Mon–Sat 9:00–18:00 except July–Aug until 19:00, Sun 10:00–13:00; Nov–March Mon–

Sat 9:00–12:00 & 14:00–18:00, Sun 10:00–13:00; tel. 03 89 20 68 92, www.ot-colmar.fr). Pick up the city map, a map of the Route du Vin (Wine Road), information on bike rental, and bus schedules (and ask where the bus stops for your trip). Get information about concerts and festivals in Colmar and in nearby villages, and ask about Colmar's Folklore Tuesdays (with folk dancing on place de l'Ancienne Douane at 20:30 every Tue mid-May–mid-Sept, except during the July music festival). Drivers exploring the Route du Vin can buy the *Blay Foldex Alsace* map (€5.50). The TI also reserves hotel rooms and has *chambre d'hôte* listings for Colmar and the region. A public WC is 20 yards left of the TI.

Arrival in Colmar

By Train and Bus: Colmar's old train station and new TGV station have been fused into one station, with entrances connected by an underground passageway. There is no baggage check.

The old train station was built during Prussian rule using the same plans as the station in Danzig (now Gdańsk, Poland). Check out the charming 1991 window that shows two local maidens about to be run over by a train and rescued by an artist. Opposite, he's shown painting their portraits.

Most buses to Route du Vin villages arrive and depart from stops as you leave the old station, as well as from stops closer to the city center (ask at the TI and see "Route du Vin," later).

To reach the town center (15-minute walk), you can **walk** straight out past Hôtel Bristol, turn left on avenue de la République, and keep walking. For a faster trip, **buses** #1, #2, and #3 (to the left outside of the old station) all go to the TI (€1.20, pay driver). Allow €8 for a **taxi** to any hotel in central Colmar (the taxi stand is on the left as you leave the station).

By Car: Follow signs for *Centre-Ville*, then *place Rapp*. There's a 900-space pay-parking garage under place Rapp, and free lots at place Scheurer-Kestner (across from Hôtel Primo) and off the ring road near Hôtel St. Martin (follow signs from the ring road to *Parking de la Vieille Ville*). Several hotels have private parking, and those that don't can advise you where to park (many get deals at pay lots for their guests—ask). When entering or leaving on the Strasbourg side of town, look for the big Statue of Liberty replica erected on July 4, 2004, to commemorate the 100th anniversary of the death of sculptor Frédéric-Auguste Bartholdi.

Helpful Hints

Market Days: Markets take place Thursdays mornings at the market hall (*marché couvert*). The Saturday morning market on place St. Joseph is where locals go to find fresh produce and cheese (over the train tracks, 15 minutes on foot from the center, no tourists). Textiles are on sale Thursdays on place de la Cathédrale (all day) and Saturdays on place des Dominicains (afternoons only), and fish and produce are featured in the old market hall in the Tanners' Quarter on Thursday mornings. There's also a flea market every Friday from June to August on place des Dominicains.

Department/Grocery Store: The big **Monoprix,** with a supermarket, is across from the TI and Unterlinden Museum (Mon–Sat 8:00–20:00, closed Sun). The **Super U** at the TGV side of the train station is open on Sunday.

Internet Access: Try **Cyber Didim,** near the TI at 9 rue du Rempart (no Wi-Fi; Mon–Sat 10:00–23:00, Sun 14:00–22:00, tel. 03 89 23 90 45).

Laundry: There's a launderette near the recommended Maison Jund *chambre d'hôte* at 1 rue Ruest, just off the pedestrian street rue Vauban (usually open daily 7:00–21:00). The TI has more suggestions.

Bike Rental: The TI has a list. **Kiosque Colmarvélo** is the cheapest, with the most extensive hours. Their bikes are designed for city use (€5/half-day, €6/day; bikes have 5 speeds, medium-width tires, basket, and lock; baby seats and helmets on request, €50 cash deposit and passport required, April–Oct daily 8:30–12:15 & 13:15–19:15, closed Nov–March, look for the orange kiosk in the park at place Rapp—near the carousel, tel. 03 89 41 37 90). Before you head out, buy a biking map either at the TI or a *librairie* (bookstore).

Taxis: You can find one at the train station, or call 03 89 23 10 33 or 06 72 94 65 55.

Car Rental: The least expensive is **ADA** (Mon–Fri 8:00–12:00 & 14:00–18:30, Sat 8:00–12:00, closed Sun, 22 rue Stanislas, tel. 03 89 23 90 30, www.ada.fr). **Avis** is at the train station (Mon–Fri 8:00–12:00 & 14:00–19:00, Sat until 17:00, closed Sun, tel. 03 89 23 16 89). The TI has a long list of other options.

Poodle Care: To give your poodle a shampoo and a haircut (or just watch the action), drop by **Quatt Pattes** (near Hôtel Rapp at 8 rue Berthe Molly).

Tours in Colmar

There are no scheduled city tours in English, but private English-speaking **guides** are available through the TI (about €120/3 hours).

Colmar has two competing **tourist trains.** Le Petit Train Blanc, the better of the two, departs across from the Monoprix, near the Dominican church (€6, 45-minute tours, departs every 30 minutes 9:00–18:00, recorded commentary, hop on or off as you please). In the summer, **horse-drawn carriages** do a similar route (€6, 30-minute tours).

For **minivan tours** of the Route du Vin, see page 943.

Self-Guided Walk

Welcome to Colmar's Old Town

This walk—good by day, romantic by night—is a handy way to link the city's three worthwhile sights (see the map on page 926 to help navigate). Supplement my commentary by reading the sidewalk information plaques that describe points of interest in town. Allow an hour for this walk at a peaceful pace (more if you enter sights). Colmar is wonderfully floodlit after dark. The lights can be changed to give different intensities and colors, keeping Colmar fresh and inviting.

The importance of 15th- to 17th-century Colmar is clear as you wander its pedestrian-friendly old center. It's decorated with 45 buildings classified as historic monuments. In the Middle Ages, most of Europe was fragmented into chaotic little princedoms and dukedoms. Merchant-dominated cities, natural proponents of the formation of large nation-states (a.k.a. globalization), banded together to form "trading leagues" (the World Trade Organizations of their day). The Hanseatic League was the super-league of northern Europe. Prosperous Colmar was the leading member of a smaller league of 10 Alsatian cities, called the Decapolis (founded 1354). The names of the streets you'll walk along bear witness to the merchants' historic importance to Colmar.

• *Start your tour on Grand Rue, where it meets rue des Marchands, and face the old...*

Customs House (Koifhus): Here, delegates of the Decapolis would meet to sort out trade issues, much like the European Union does in nearby Strasbourg today. In Colmar's heyday, this was where the action was. Notice the fancy green roof tiles and the intricate railing at the base of the roof. The Dutch-looking gabled building on the left was the birthplace of Colmar's most famous son, General Jean Rapp, who distinguished himself during France's Revolutionary Wars to become one of Napoleon's most trusted generals.

Walk under the archway to place de l'Ancienne Douane and face the Frédéric-Auguste Bartholdi statue—arm raised, à la Statue of Liberty—and do a 360-degree spin to appreciate a gaggle of gables. This was the center of business activity in Colmar, with goods and trade routes radiating to several major European cities. All goods that entered the city were taxed here. Today, it's the festive site of

Colmar

1. Hôtel St. Martin
2. Hostellerie le Maréchal
3. Hôtel/Restaurant le Rapp
4. Hôtel Turenne
5. Hôtel Ibis Colmar Centre
6. Maison Martin Jund Rooms
7. Hôtel Primo
8. To Grand Hôtel Bristol; B&B Chez Leslie
9. L'un des Sens Wine Bar
10. Sorbetière d'Isabelle
11. Wistub de la Petite Venise, JY's & La Krutenau Rests.
12. Le Comptoir de Georges Rest.
13. La Venezia Sandwiches
14. Winstub Schwendi Rest.
15. Chez Hansi Restaurant
16. La Maison Rouge Restaurant
17. Le Bartholdi Restaurant
18. Internet Café
19. Launderette
20. Bike Rental
21. ADA Car Rental
22. Quatt Pattes Dog Grooming
23. Maison Pfister
24. Le Petit Train Blanc Departure Point

|||| PEDESTRIAN ZONE

➤ VIEW

P PARKING

→ ONE-WAY STREET

➤ WALKING TOUR ROUTE (START AT STAR)

TRAIN STATION

BEST ROUTE TO KAYSERSBERG + RIQUEWIHR VIA N-415

To EGUISHEIM BY BIKE

POST

RUE

RUE

AVE DE GAULLE

R. PREISS

AVE BRUAT

PLAY AREA

CHAMP MA

D-30 ROUTE DE ROUFFACH

TO 8, EGUISHEIM, + D-83 TO BURGUNDY + ALPS

ALSACE

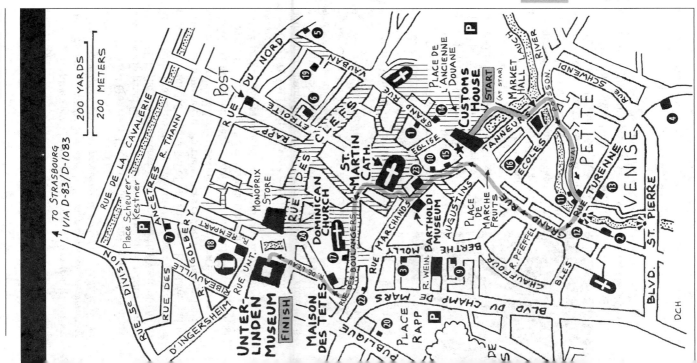

TO STRASBOURG VIA D-83/D-1083

200 YARDS
200 METERS

UNTERLINDEN MUSEUM **FINISH**

MAISON DES TÊTES

DOMINICAN CHURCH

ST. MARTIN CATH.

BARTHOLDI MUSEUM

Customs House **START** (at star)

MARKET HALL

PETITE VENISE

LAUCH RIVER

POST

DCH

outdoor cafés and, on many summer evenings, wine-tastings (open to everyone).

• *Follow the statue's left elbow and walk down petite rue des Tanneurs (not the larger "rue des Tanneurs"). The half-timbered commotion of biggledy-piggledy rooftops on the downhill side of the fountain marks the...*

Tanners' Quarter: These vertical 17th- and 18th-century rooftops competed for space in the sun to dry their freshly tanned hides, while the nearby river channel flushed the waste products. This neighborhood, restored in about 1970, was a pioneer in the government-funded renovation of old quarters. Residents had to play along or move out. At the street's end, enter the small parkway, then turn back. You're looking at the city's first defensive wall. The oldest stones you see are from 1230, now built into the row of houses; later walls encircled the city farther out.

• *Walk with the old walls on your right, then take the first left along the stream.*

Old Market Hall: On your right is Colmar's historic market hall, which should be freshly renovated by your visit. Here locals buy fish, produce, and other products (originally brought here by flat-bottom boat).

• *Take a spin through the market, then cross the canal and turn right on quai de la Poissonnerie ("Wharf of the Fish Market"), and you'll enter...*

Petite Venise: This neighborhood, a collection of Colmar's most colorful houses lining the small canal, is popular with tourists during the day. But at night it's romantic, with fewer crowds. It lies between the town's first wall (built to defend against arrows) and its later wall (built in the age of gunpowder). The river was canalized for medieval industry—to provide water for the tanners, to allow farmers to barge their goods into town, to power mills, and so on. Walk several blocks along the flower-box-lined canal to the end of rue de la Poissonnerie. Turn right, walk to the center of the bridge, and enjoy the view. To the right you'll see examples of the flat-bottom gondolas used to transport goods on the small river. Today, they give tourists sleepy, scenic 30-minute, €6 canal tours (departure on demand, buy tickets at the bar/restaurant La Krutenau).

• *Cross the bridge and take the second right on Grande Rue. Walk for several blocks back to the Customs House (green-tiled roof). With your back to the Customs House, look uphill along rue des Marchands*

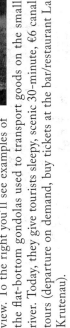

("Merchants' Street")—one of the most scenic intersections in town. (The ruler of Malaysia was so charmed by this street that he had it re-created in Kuala Lumpur.)

Walk up rue des Marchands, and you'll soon come face-to-face with the...

Maison Pfister (Pfister House): This richly decorated merchant's house dates from 1537. Here the owner displayed his wealth for all to enjoy (and to envy). The external spiral-staircase turret, a fine loggia on the top floor, and the bay windows (called oriels) were pricey add-ons. The painted walls illustrate the city folks' taste for Renaissance humanism (a nice little wine shop fills the ground floor). The man carved into the side of the building next door (at #9) was a drape-maker; he's shown holding a bar, Colmar's measure of about one meter. In the Middle Ages, it was common for cities to have their own units of length; one reason merchants supported the "globalization" efforts of their time was to standardize measuring systems.

• Look closely at the architecture of the house next door.

Half-Timbered Houses: The building with the guy holding the bar shows off the classic half-timbered design—the beams (upright, cross, angular supports) are grouped in what's called (and looks like) "a man." Typical houses are built with a man in the middle flanked by two "half men." Whereas houses of the rich were made of stone, anyone on a budget built half-timbered structures (though all homes here sit on a stone base to prevent them from sinking into the marshy ground). Originally, proud townsfolk would plaster over their cheap half-timbered walls to create the illusion of a stone house. Then, in the 20th century, half-timbered became charming, so they peeled away the plaster to reveal the old beams. You can identify true stone homes by their windowsills: Wooden sills mean they're half-timbered (like this one), whereas stone sills indicate the entire building is built of stone (like the Pfister House).

As you explore the town, notice how upper floors are cantilevered out. This was both a structural support trick and a tax dodge, as real-estate taxes were based on the square footage of the ground floor.

A short block along on the left is the **Bartholdi Museum** (described later, under "Sights in Colmar"), located in the home where the famous sculptor Frédéric-Auguste Bartholdi was raised. Next door (at #28) is Au Pain Dorée, with its charming Art Nouveau facade and interior. Art Nouveau was rare in Colmar. During the style's heyday in the early 20th century—which was also just after this region was taken from France by Germany—Art Nouveau was considered an anti-German statement, and therefore controversial.

• A passage to the right before the Bartholdi entrance leads you through the old guards' house to...

St. Martin Cathedral: The city's golden cathedral (erected in 1235), with its lone tower (two were planned) and gleaming tiles, was inspired by the Hôtel Dieu in Beaune. Walk left, to the front of the cathedral. Notice that the relief over the main door depicts not your typical Last Judgment scene, but the Three Kings who visited Baby Jesus. The Magi, whose remains are in the Rhine city of Köln, Germany, are popular in this region. The interior is dark, but it holds a few finely carved and beautifully painted altarpieces. The cathedral's beautiful Vosges-stone exterior radiates color in the late afternoon.

• Walk past the cathedral, go left around Café Jupiler, and wander up the pedestrian-only rue des Serruriers ("Locksmiths' Street") to the...

Dominican Church: Compare St. Martin Cathedral's impressive exterior with this low-slung, sober structure that perfectly symbolizes Dominican austerity. These two very different houses of worship were built at the same time. Dominican churches were intentionally plain, symbolic of their zeal to purify their faith and compete with the growing popularity of 13th-century heretical movements, such as Catharism, which preached a simpler faith. This church is well worth entering (and described later, under "Sights in Colmar").

• Continuing past the Dominican Church, rue des Serruriers becomes rue des Boulangers—"Bakers' Street." Turn right on rue des Têtes (notice the beautiful swan sign over the pharmacie at the corner). Walk a block to the fancy old house festooned with heads (on the right).

Maison des Têtes ("House of Heads"): Colmar's other famous merchant's house, built in 1609 by a big-shot winemaker (see the grapes hanging from the wrought-iron sign and the happy man at the tip-top), is playfully decorated with 105 faces and masks. On the ground floor, the guy in the window's center has pig's feet. Look four houses to the right to see a 1947 bakery sign (above the big pretzel), which shows the boulangerie basics in Alsace: croissant, kugelhopf, and baguette. Across from the Maison des Têtes (above Esprit boutique), study the early-20th-century store sign trumpeting the wonders of a butcher who once occupied these premises (with the traditional maiden chasing a goose about to be force-fed, all hung from the beak of a chicken). Before leaving, wander into the Maison des Têtes' pretty courtyard, now home to a gourmet restaurant and a four-star hotel.

• Angle down rue de l'Eau ("Water Street") opposite Maison des Têtes for a shortcut to the TI and the Unterlinden Museum, with its name-sake linden trees lining the front yard (popular locally for making the calming "Tilleul" tea).

Sights in Colmar

▲▲▲Unterlinden Museum

Colmar's touristic claim to fame is one of my favorite museums in Europe. Its extensive yet manageable collection ranges from Roman Colmar to medieval winemaking exhibits, and from traditional wedding dresses to paintings that give vivid insight into the High Middle Ages. Make sure to allocate sufficient time for this museum, as its collection is so unique and varied, and the excellent audioguide makes the curator your best friend. The museum is one of the most visited in all of France for its devastatingly beautiful *Isenheim Altarpiece*, so it can be crowded and loud. (The best time to visit is about 12:00–14:00—when most are lunching—or at the end of the day.) Big plans are afoot to expand the museum over the next few years, so be ready for construction-related changes.

Cost and Hours: €7, €6 for seniors, price includes indispensable audioguide; May–Oct daily 9:00–18:00; Nov–April Wed–Mon 9:00–12:00 & 14:00–17:00, closed Tue; 1 rue d'Unterlinden, tel. 03 89 20 15 58, www.musee-unterlinden.com.

⊖ **Self-Guided Tour:** Use this commentary to supplement the information provided by the included audioguide (which doesn't start until the painting gallery).

Gothic Statues (Room 1): Room 1 features 14th-century Gothic statues from nearby St. Martin Cathedral's facade and other area churches. Study the Romanesque detail of the capitals and the faces of the statues. Even though they endured the elements outdoors for more than 500 years, it's still clear that they were sculpted carefully. The reddish stone is quarried from the Vosges Mountains, giving these works their unusual coloring. Notice the faint remnants of paint still visible on some statues—then imagine all of these works brightly painted. At the far end of the room, gaze into the medieval eyes of the Byzantine-looking Magi (*un roi Mage*) and take a close look at the 15th-century stained glass; fine details are painted into the glass that no one would ever see (these windows were made 300 years after those of Paris' Sainte-Chapelle). The glass is essentially a jigsaw puzzle connected by lead. Around here, glass this old is rare—most of it was destroyed by rampaging Protestants in the Reformation wars.

Cloister: Step into the soothing cloister (the largest 13th-century cloister in Alsace) and walk right, passing the WCs in the corner. This was a Dominican convent founded for noblewomen in 1230. It functioned until the French Revolution, when the building became a garrison. Rooms with museum exhibits branch off from here. Don't miss the wine room (next corner) with its 17th-century oak presses and finely decorated casks. Those huge presses were turned by animals. Wine revenue was used to care for Colmar's poor. The nuns owned many of the best vineyards around, and production was excellent. So was consumption. Notice (on the first cask on left) the Bacchus with the distended tummy straddling a keg. The quote from 1781 reads: "My belly's full of juice. It makes me strong. But drink too much and you lose dignity and health."

Painting Gallery (the museum audioguide begins here): To the left of the wine-press room, enter the painting gallery marked *art médiéval*. Find the spinning case of engravings by Martin Schongauer, Albrecht Dürer's master. (Schongauer also painted the *Virgin in the Rosebush*, now located at the Dominican church.) Throughout the museum you'll see small photos of engravings illustrating how painters were influenced by other artists' engravings. Most German painters of the time were also engravers (that's how they made money—making lots of copies for sale). The following rooms are filled with paintings that are wonderfully described by the audioguide. As you enjoy the art, remember that Alsace was historically German and part of the upper Rhine River Valley. (This museum boasts France's only painting by Lucas Cranach.) Remember those Three Kings (of Bethlehem fame) from St. Martin Cathedral? They're prominently featured throughout this region, because their heads ended up as relics in Köln's cathedral (on the Rhine). You'll pass several more works by Martin Schongauer before reaching the...

Isenheim Altarpiece: The highlight of the museum (and, for me, the city) is Matthias Grünewald's gripping *Isenheim Altarpiece* (c. 1515), actually a series of three different paintings on hinges that pivot like shutters (study the little models on the wall, with English explanations nearby). Designed to help people in a medieval hospital endure horrible skin diseases (such as St. Anthony's Fire, later called rye ergotism)—long before the age of painkillers—it's one of the most powerful paintings ever produced. Germans know this painting like Americans know the *Mona Lisa.*

Stand in front of the centerpiece as if you were a medieval peasant, and let the agony and suffering of the Crucifixion drag its fingers down your face. It's an intimate drama. The point—Jesus' suffering—is drilled home: the weight of his body bends the crossbar (unrealistically, creating to some eyes an almost crossbow effect). His elbows are pulled from their sockets by the weight of his dead body. People who are crucified die of asphyxiation, as Jesus' chest implies. His mangled feet are swollen with blood. The

grief on Mary's face is agonizing. In hopes that the intended viewers (the hospital's patients) would know that Jesus understood their suffering, Jesus himself was even painted to appear as if he had a skin disease. Study the faces and the Christian symbolism. Mary is wrapped in the shroud that will cover Jesus. The sorrowful composition on the left is powerful. On the far left stands St. Sebastian (called upon by those with the plague) and on the right is St. Anthony (called upon by those with ergot poisoning from rotten rye).

Walk to the back of this panel. The Resurrection scene is

unique in art history (Grünewald had no master and no students). Jesus rockets out of the tomb as man is transformed into God. As if proclaiming once again, "I am the Light," he is radiant. His shroud is the color of light: Roy G. Biv. Around the rainbow is the "resurrection of the flesh." Jesus' perfect pink flesh would appeal to the patients who meditated on the scene. The right half of this panel depicts the Annunciation, with the normally sanguine Mary looking unsettled, as if she's been hit by some unexpected news. You wouldn't think she'd be shocked to learn of her pregnancy—she's shown reading the Bible passage that tells of this event. Find the translucent dove near Mary.

In the nativity scene on the next panel—set in the Rhineland—the much-adored Mary is tender and loving, true to the Dominican belief that she was the intercessor for all in heaven. The three scenes of the painting changed with the church calendar. The happy ending—a psychedelic explosion of Resurrection joy—is the spiritual equivalent of jumping from the dentist's chair directly into a whirlpool tub. The scene on the left is the Concert of Angels.

Look at the last panel—zoom in on the agonizing Temptation of St. Anthony. Patients who meditated on this painting were reminded that they didn't have it so bad. They were also reminded to stay the course (religiously) and to not stray from the path of salvation. The other panel shows Anthony's visit to St. Paul the hermit. The final scene (behind you), carved in wood by Nikolaus Hagenauer, is St. Anthony on his throne.

The Rest of the Museum: The upstairs rooms, displaying local and folk history, are worth a look. You'll see everything from iron store signs, massive church bells, and chests with intricate locking systems, to ornate armoires, medieval armor, muskets, old-time toys, and antique jewelry boxes. Back on the ground floor, near the museum's entrance, you'll find a modern-art section with a small but pleasing permanent collection, including a few works by Monet, Renoir, Picasso, Leger, de Stael, Bonnard, and a wall of Jean Dubuffet. In the basement below are impressively displayed Roman and prehistoric artifacts and temporary exhibits.

▲▲▲Dominican Church (Eglise des Dominicains)

Here's another medieval mindblower. In this church, Martin Schongauer's angelically beautiful *Virgin in the Rosebush* holds court, dating from 1473 but looking as if it were painted yesterday. Here, graceful Mary is shown as a welcoming mother. Jesus clings to her, reminding the viewer of the warmth of his relationship with Mary. The Latin on her halo reads, "Pick me also for your child, O very Holy Virgin." Rather than telling a particular Bible story, this is a general scene, designed to meet the personal devotional needs of any worshipper. Nature is not a backdrop; Mary and Jesus are encircled by it. Schongauer's robins, sparrows, and goldfinches bring extra life to an already impressively natural rosebush (Schongauer was influenced by Roger van der Weyden, who painted the *Last Judgment* in the Hospices de Beaune—described on page 845). The white rose anticipates Jesus' crucifixion. The painting was located in St. Martin Cathedral until 1972, when it was stolen. After being recovered, it was moved to the better-protected Dominican Church (you don't mess with Dominicans). Detailed English explanations are to the left of the painting as you face it. The contrast provided by the simple Dominican setting heightens the flamboyance of this Gothic masterpiece (€1.50, mid-March–Dec daily 10:00–13:00 & 15:00–18:00, last entry 15 minutes before closing, closed Jan–mid-March, no photos).

▲Bartholdi Museum

This little museum recalls the life and work of the local boy who gained fame by sculpting America's much-loved Statue of Liberty. Frédéric-Auguste Bartholdi (1834–1904) was a dynamic painter/ photographer/sculptor with a passion for the defense of liberty and freedom. Although Colmar was his home, he spent most of his career in Paris, unable to move back here without becoming a German (Prussia took control of Alsace in 1871). He devoted years of his life to realizing the vision of a statue of liberty for America that would stand in New York City's harbor. Closer to home, several Bartholdi statues grace Colmar's squares.

Cost and Hours: €5, free on July 4, open March–Dec Wed–Mon 10:00–12:00 & 14:00–18:00, closed Tue and Jan–Feb, in heart of old town at 30 rue des Marchands, tel. 03 89 41 90 60, www .musee-bartholdi.com.

ALSACE

◊ Self-Guided Tour: Curiously, there is no English posted in this museum. The English handouts offer no help navigating the collection, but do give worthwhile background on the Statue of Liberty and *Lion of Belfort* (the document needs an editor). The following commentary helps make sense of the museum, which has three floors.

On the **ground floor,** the room to the right of the ticket desk houses temporary exhibits. To the left are exhibits covering Bartholdi's works commissioned in Alsatian cities, commonly dedicated to military heroes.

Go upstairs to the **first floor,** passing a portrait of the artist at the base of the stairs. Turn left to find the tools of his trade in the glass cases. The rooms beyond re-create Bartholdi's high-society flat in Paris. The dining room is lined with portraits of his aristocratic family. In the next room hangs a beautiful portrait of the sculptor (by Jean Benner), facing his mother (on a red chair). Bartholdi was very close to his mom, writing her daily letters. Many see her features in the Statue of Liberty.

The rest of the first floor shows off Bartholdi's French work. Notice how his patriotic pieces tend to have one arm raised—*Vive la France,* God bless America, *Deutschland über alles...*you can fill in the flag-waving blank.

A room dedicated to Bartholdi's most famous French work, the *Lion of Belfort,* celebrates the Alsatian town that fought so fiercely in 1871 that it was never annexed into Germany. Photos show the red sandstone lion sitting regally below the mighty Vauban fortress of Belfort—a symbol of French spirit standing strong against Germany. Small models give a sense of its gargantuan scale. (If you're linking Burgundy with Alsace by car, you'll pass the city of Belfort and see signs directing you to the *Lion.*)

Next, find Bartholdi's photo (actually a line of six photos) of New York City's harbor in 1876. The first tower of the Brooklyn Bridge is up. Bartholdi added the tiny Statue of Liberty on the far left (along with the boats). This floor ends with the thrilling statue of Gallic leader Vercingétorix victorious over a Roman soldier. In a glass case near this statue, find a lineup of French Who's Who sculpted by Bartholdi, including Claude-Joseph Rouget de Lisle (composer of *La Marseillaise*).

The **second floor** up (top floor) is dedicated to Bartholdi's American works—the paintings, photos, and statues that Bartholdi made during his many travels to the States. You'll see statues of Columbus pointing confidently, and Lafayette (who was only 19 years old when he came to America's aid) with George Washington. One room is dedicated to the evolution and completion of the dream of a Statue of Liberty. Fascinating photos show the Eiffel-designed core, the frame being covered with plaster, and then the hand-hammered copper plating, which was ultimately riveted to the frame. The statue was assembled in Paris, then unriveted and shipped to New York, in 1886...10 years late. The big ear is half-size.

Though the statue was a gift from France, the US had to come up with the cash to build a pedestal. This was a tough sell, but Bartholdi was determined to see his statue erected. On 10 trips to the US, he worked to raise funds and lobbied for construction, bringing with him this painting and a full-size model of the torch—which the statue would ultimately hold. (Lucky for Bartholdi and his cause, his cousin was the French ambassador to the US.) Eventually, the project came together—the pedestal was built, and the Statue of Liberty has welcomed waves of immigrants into New York ever since.

Sleeping in Colmar

Hotels are busy on weekends in May, June, September, and October, and every day in July and August. But there are always rooms—somewhere. Should you have trouble finding a bed, ask the TI for help, or look in a nearby village, where small hotels and bed-and-breakfasts are plentiful (see my recommendations in nearby Eguisheim, later).

In the Center

$$$ Hôtel St. Martin***, ideally situated near the old Customs House, is a family-run place that began as a coaching inn (since 1361). Its 40 traditional yet well-equipped rooms, most with air-conditioning and big beds, are woven into its antique frame. The hotel has three sections (young, middle-aged, and elderly) joined by a peaceful courtyard. All rooms offer good comfort and character, though the better rooms are in the new (young) wing, with traditional furnishings and stone walls. The cheapest rooms are the oldest, with showers instead of tubs, and no elevator (Sb-€82, standard Db-€92-102, bigger Db-€112, still bigger Db-€135, standard Db-€155, Tb/Qb-€135, great breakfast-€12, air-con in all but 3 rooms, free Internet access and Wi-Fi, free public parking nearby at Parking de la Vieille Ville, 38 Grand Rue, tel. 03 89 24 11 51, fax 03 89 23 47 78, www.hotel-saint-martin.com, colmar@hotel-saint-martin.com).

$$$ At Hostellerie le Maréchal****, in the heart of La Petite Venise, Colmar's most famous and characteristic digs are surprisingly affordable. Though the rooms aren't big, the setting is romantic, the decor carefully selected, and the service professional (Sb-€90-100, standard Db-€120-145, Db with whirlpool tub-€165-230, suite Db-€290, breakfast-€15, garage-€15, free Wi-Fi, 4 place des Six Montagnes Noires, tel. 03 89 41 60 32, fax

Sleep Code

(€1 = about $1.25, country code: 33)

S = Single, **D** = Double/Twin, **T** = Triple, **Q** = Quad, **b** = bathroom, **s** = shower only, ***** = French hotel rating system (0–4 stars). Unless otherwise noted, credit cards are accepted and English is spoken.

To help you sort easily through these listings, I've divided the rooms into three categories based on the price for a standard double room with bath:

$$$ **Higher Priced**—Most rooms €90 or more.
$$ **Moderately Priced**—Most rooms between €55–90.
$ **Lower Priced**—Most rooms €55 or less.

Prices can change without notice; verify the hotel's current rates online or by email. For other updates, see www.ricksteves.com/update.

03 89 24 59 40, www.le-marechal.com, info@le-marechal.com). Their well-respected restaurant will melt a romantic's heart, and they'll heartily encourage you to dine here (€38–65 *menus*, reserve ahead).

$$$ Hôtel le Rapp***, well-located off place Rapp and near a big park, holds a variety of rooms for many budgets, a full-service bar, a café, and a nice restaurant. The cheapest rooms are small but comfortable; the bigger rooms are tastefully designed, usually with queen-size beds. There's also a small basement pool, a sauna, and a Turkish bath. It's well-run and family-friendly (Sb–€79, standard Db–€95, bigger Db–€115, junior suite for 2–4 people–€146, good buffet breakfast–€11, air-con, elevator, free Internet access and Wi-Fi, 1 rue Weinemer, tel. 03 89 41 62 10, fax 03 89 24 13 58, www.rapp-hotel.com, rapp-hot@calixo.net).

$$ Hôtel Turenne** is a good, if less central, two-star value (a 10-minute walk from the city center, and a 15-minute walk from the train station). It sits on a busy street with easy, free parking. Rooms vary in size, and many have tight bathrooms, though all are air-conditioned and well-maintained. Rates are hard to pin down (Sb–€52–86, Db–€70–90, Tb–€72–92, family-friendly studios–€105–120, park for free on the street or book ahead to park in their lot–€7, air-con, elevator for most rooms, Internet access, free Wi-Fi, appealing bar and breakfast room, 10 rue de Bâle, tel. 03 89 21 58 58, fax 03 89 41 27 64, www.turenne.com, infos@turenne.com).

$$ Hôtel Ibis Colmar Centre**, on the ring road, rents pleasant rooms with small bathrooms at reasonable rates (Db–€76, bigger Db–€84, breakfast–€8, check for Web deals, air-con, Internet access and Wi-Fi, 10 rue St. Eloi, tel. 03 89 41 30 14, fax 03 89 24 51 49, www.ibishotel.com, h1377@accor.com).

$ Maison Martin Jund holds my favorite budget beds in Colmar. This ramshackle yet historic half-timbered house—the home of likeable winemakers André and Myriam—feels like a medieval tree house soaked in wine and filled with flowers. The rooms are bare-bones simple but comfortable enough, spacious, and equipped with kitchenettes (D–€35, Db/Tb–€45–55; huge family apartment with character and a short, steep staircase–€90 for 2, sleeps up to 6, €5/additional person; breakfast-€6, good organic wine for sale in their tasting room, Internet access, free Wi-Fi, 12 rue de l'Ange, tel. 03 89 41 58 72, fax 03 89 23 15 83, www.martin jund.com, martinjund@hotmail.com). Leave your car at place Scheurer-Kestner. Train travelers can take bus #1, #2, or #3 from the station to the TI, walk from Unterlinden Museum past Monoprix, and veer left on rue des Clefs, left on rue Etroite, and right on rue de l'Ange. This is not a hotel, so there is no real reception—though good-natured Myriam seems to be around, somewhere, most of the time (call if you plan to arrive after 21:00).

$ Hôtel Primo**, near the Unterlinden Museum, is an efficient, nothing-but-the-plastic-and-concrete-basics place to sleep. The easygoing staff will hold a room for you until 18:00 if you call. Rooms facing the big square (*grand place*) are far quieter (S/D/T-€29, Sb-€45, Db-€55, Tb-€65, Qb-€75, small discount for Rick Steves readers in 2011, free Wi-Fi, free parking in big square in front, 5 rue des Ancêtres, tel. 03 89 24 22 24, fax 03 89 24 55 96, www.hotel-primo.fr, reservation@hotel-primo.fr). Half the beds have footboards—a problem if you're more than six feet tall.

Near the Train Station

$$$ Grand Hôtel Bristol*** has little personality but works if you need three-star comfort at the train station (standard Db-€100–130, big Db-€170, overpriced breakfast-€15, some rooms with air-con, free Wi-Fi, 7 place de la Gare, tel. 03 89 23 59 59, fax 03 89 23 92 26, www.grand-hotel-bristol.com, reservation@grand-hotel-bristol.com).

$$ At Bed-and-Breakfast Chez Leslie, run by engaging Leslie (who is a wealth of information) and her Franco-American family (husband Philippe and daughters Milena and Maya), you'll become a temporary Colmarian. Located in a neighborhood where "real people live," it's a 5-minute walk from the station, a 20-minute walk from the center, and a good place to get a head start on the route du Vin. The rooms are bright, big, and artfully decorated with good beds—and the garden will calm your mind (Sb-€58, Db-€75, family room €85-106, €5 cheaper for stays more than one night, includes breakfast, ask about apartment rental in town, 31 rue de Mulhouse, tel. 03 89 79 98 99, mobile 06 82 58 91 98, www .chezleslie.com, info@chezleslie.com). From the train platform, exit down the stairs into the underground passageway toward rue du Tir (away from station), walk up the stairs at the end, go left down the street, and turn right at the first corner (rue de Soultz). Continue up to the square and turn left on rue de Mulhouse.

Eating in Colmar

Colmar is full of good restaurants offering traditional Alsatian *menus* for €18–30, and expensive places with lighter fare. (To dine in a smaller town nearby, see "Eating in Eguisheim," later.)

Before Dinner: Slip into **L'un des Sens** wine bar for a glass of wine and an appetizer (long list of wines from many countries) and a short list of foods (meat plates, fancy foie gras, cheese plates). The colorful interior, soothing front terrace, and upbeat waitstaff make this a fun place (Tue–Sat 11:00–21:00, closed Sun–Mon, ask about blind tastings, 18 rue Berthe Molly, tel. 03 89 24 04 37).

After Dinner: Stop by the tiny **Sorbetière d'Isabelle** for Colmar's best sorbet, and ask about her syrup toppings. Get it to go or eat there, inside or out (daily 11:00–22:00, near Maison Pfister at 13 rue des Marchands, tel. 03 89 41 6717). And if you want lively café and bar action, find rue du Conseil Souverain (just below Grand Rue and between rue des Ecoles and rue des Tanneurs).

In Petite Venise

For dining with a canalside view, head into Petite Venise and make your way to the photo-perfect bridge on rue Turenne, where you'll find several picturesque places.

Wistub de la Petite Venise bucks the touristy trend in this area with caring owners Virgine and Julien and a wood-warm, collector's interior (no outside seating). The service is personal, and the menu is limited in selection—heavy on the meats—but generous in quality (daily for dinner, €14–20 *plats*, delicious foie gras, 4 rue de la Poissonnerie, tel. 03 89 41 72 59).

JY's (for chef Jean-Yves) is *the* place to do it up in Petite Venise. It's a trendy spot that draws a young crowd in search of the next Michelin star. The cuisine is a fusion of French and Alsatian classics, tables outside are romantically situated on the canal, and the inside decor is terribly hip (*menus* from €35, closed Sun, 17 rue de la Poissonnerie, tel. 03 89 21 53 60).

La Krutenau's picnic tables sprawl along the canal, offering many desserts and only *tartes flambées*. Come for a light meal with ambience (inside or out, best after dark), a dessert, or a drink on a warm evening (closed Mon, 1 rue de la Poissonnerie, tel. 03 89 41 18 80).

Le Comptoir de Georges, Colmar's unpretentious diner (doing double-duty as a butcher shop), dishes up traditional Alsatian fare alongside French classics. The atmosphere is low-key, with red booths, and your paper placemat doubles as the menu. The best seats are on the tiny terrace that hangs over the canal (€11-16 *plats*, big €10 salads, serves food all day—breakfast, lunch, and dinner, closed Sun-Mon, 1 place des Six Montagnes Noires, tel. 03 89 20 60 72).

La Venezia is a hole-in-the-wall across from the touristy places with a few outdoor tables, serving hot panini sandwiches and other budget snacks (lunch only, daily, rue de Turenne).

In the Old City Center

Winstub Schwendi has the lively feel of a German pub inside (with 10 beers on tap) and a sprawling terrace outside. Choose from a dozen different filling, robust Swiss *rösti* plates or *tarte flambées*; I like the *strasbourgoise* (€10-18 main dishes, good salad options, daily 10:00-24:00, very popular on weekends, facing old Customs House at 3 Grand Rue, tel. 03 89 23 66 26). If the Winstub is full, you'll find a spate of other places with good outdoor seating around place de l'Ancienne Douane.

Chez Hansi, a half-block up from the Customs House, is where Colmarians go for a traditional meal (served by women in Alsatian dresses). This place feels real, even though it's in the thick of the touristic center. Try local specialties like *poulet au Riesling* (chicken in Riesling sauce) or medieval "pub grub" like *choucroute garnie* (€20-44 *menus*, indoor seating only, closed Tue-Wed, 23 rue des Marchands, tel. 03 89 41 37 84).

La Maison Rouge has a folk-museum interior and noisy side-walk seating with good, reasonably priced, traditional Alsatian cuisine. You'll be greeted by the *jambon à l'os*—ham cooking on the bone (€24-40 *menus*), try the veal cordon bleu with Munster or the *tarte flambée au chèvre-basilic,* closed Sun-Mon, 9 rue des Ecoles, tel. 03 89 23 53 22).

Hôtel-Restaurant le Rapp is a traditional place to savor a slow, elegant meal served with grace and fine Alsatian wine. If you want to order high on the menu, this is the perfect place to do it (great *baeckeoffe* for €18 that makes a whole meal, *menus* from €28, good salads, they take their vegetarian options seriously, closed Thu-Fri, air-con, 1 rue Berthe Molly, tel. 03 89 41 62 10).

Le Bartholdi offers Alsatian specialties and French classics (like escargots and foie gras) on a vine-covered and flower-riddled rear terrace (call ahead to hold *un table sur la terrasse*). The service is as formal as the place is local (€22-28 *menus*, good *crudités* and excellent *choucroute,* closed Sun-Mon, 2 rue des Boulangers, tel. 03 89 41 07 74).

Colmar Connections

From Colmar by Train to: Strasbourg (2/hour, 35 minutes), **Reims** (TGV: 10/day, 3 hours, most change in Strasbourg), **Verdun** (8/day, 4–5 hours, possible changes in Metz, Saverne, and Strasbourg), **Beaune** (6/day, 4–5 hours, changes in Besançon, Mulhouse, or Belfort and Dijon), **Paris'** Gare de l'Est (TGV: 12/day, 3 direct, others change in Strasbourg, 3.5 hrs; non-TGV train: 8/day, 5.5 hours, change in Strasbourg, Dijon, or Mulhouse), **Amboise** (TGV: 8/day, 5 hours, most with transfer in Strasbourg and Paris; non-TGV train: 8/day, 9 hours, via Paris), **Basel**, Switzerland (13/day, 1 hour), **Karlsruhe**, Germany (10/day, 2.5 hours, best with change in Strasbourg; from Karlsruhe, it's 1.5 hours to Frankfurt, 3 hours to Munich).

Route du Vin (Wine Road)

Alsace's Route du Vin is an asphalt ribbon that ties 90 miles of vineyards, villages, and feudal fortresses into an understandably popular tourist package. The generally dry climate (with less rain than many parts of southern France) has made for good wine and happy tourists since Roman days. Colmar and Eguisheim are well-located for exploring the 30,000 acres of vineyards blanketing the hills from Marlenheim to Thann. Drivers need a detailed map of the Route du Vin, which they can pick up at any area TI.

As you tour this region, you'll see storks' nests on many church spires and city halls, thanks to a campaign to reintroduce the birds to this area. (Nests can weigh as much as 1,000 pounds.) You'll also see crucifixion monuments scattered about the vineyards. Congregations stopped at these during processions organized to encourage a good harvest. You might want a refresher course on half-timbered architecture, which prevails here (see page 929).

Planning Your Time

If you have only a day, focus on towns within easy striking range of Colmar. World War II left many Route du Vin villages in ruins. These villages have been rebuilt, but offer far less character than those left untouched. Villages that emerged from World

War II unscathed include Eguisheim, Kaysersberg, Hunawihr, Turckheim, Ribeauvillé, and the *très* popular Riquewihr. Be careful not to overdose on all the half-timbered cuteness. Two villages meet the needs of most. For a good sampling of Route du Vin villages and countryside, start in Riquewihr (beat the crowds), then walk, ride, or drive through the vineyards to Kaysersberg. Drivers can tack on Eguisheim, or other villages and sights.

Towns are most alive during their weekly morning (until noon) farmers' markets (Monday-Kaysersberg; Tuesday-Munster; Friday-Turckheim; Saturday-Ribeauvillé and Colmar—behind train station near St. Joseph's Church). Riquewihr and Eguisheim have no market days.

Getting Around the Route du Vin

By Car: A good regional map (1:200,000 scale or better) is helpful. To reach the Route du Vin north of Colmar, leave Colmar following signs to *Ingersheim* and continue to its center, where you can join D-10 north to Sigolsheim, Bennwihr (Kaysersberg is a short detour from here), Riquewihr, Hunawihr, Ribeauvillé, and Château du Haut-Kœnigsbourg. Look for *Route du Vin* signs. For Eguisheim (south of Colmar), leave Colmar on D-83 toward Belfort.

Drivers can use some of the scenic wine service lanes known as *sentiers viticoles*—provided they drive at a snail's pace. I've recommended my favorite segments.

By Bus: Several bus companies connect Colmar with villages along the Route du Vin (except on Sundays, when there are none), but deciphering schedules and locating bus stops in Colmar is a challenge. Before setting out, be clear about bus schedules and stop locations by asking at any TI, or try these bus company websites: www.l-k.fr (French only), www.kunegel.fr/en/ (in English), and www.trace-colmar.fr (French only). When reading schedules, note that *année* means the bus runs all year on days listed, and *scol* (for *solaire*) means buses run only on school days.

All buses to Route du Vin villages stop at Colmar's train station (shelters to the left as you face the station); some also stop in the town center near the TI (verify stops at TI). Some towns (including Eguisheim and Kaysersberg) are served by more than one company, which can use different bus stops.

Kaysersberg has reasonable service (#145 in direction: Le Bonhomme, 7/day, 25 minutes); Riquewihr, Hunawihr, and Ribeauvillé have decent service (#106 in direction: Illhaeusern or #109 in direction: St. Hippolyte; summer 6/day in summer, otherwise 9/day, 30–45 minutes, big midday service gaps in summer). Service to Eguisheim is minimal (look for buses to Guebwiller, 4/day, most in afternoons, 25 minutes). There's also a shuttle bus to

Château du Haut-Kœnigsbourg (explained on page 947). Most schedules are posted where buses stop, though don't count on it. Buy tickets from the driver (€2–4 one-way).

By Train: The only Route du Vin village accessible by train from Colmar is lovely little Turckheim (2/hour, 10 minutes).

By Taxi: Allow €15 from Colmar to Eguisheim and €25 from Colmar or Eguisheim to Kaysersberg or Riquewihr (call friendly William at 06 14 47 21 80, another taxi at 03 89 80 71 71, or ask the TI to call).

By Minivan Tour: Sincere Jean-Claude Werner, who speaks impeccable English with an Alsatian accent, runs **Les Circuits d'Alsace** day trips in a comfortable seven-person minivan (small groups; 2-person minimum, larger groups possible, solo travelers may be able to squeeze in with another group, in English and/or Japanese, great sound system on comfy air-con minibus). His tours include a few enjoyable, very short vineyard walks. Jean-Claude's enthusiasm and personal touches add to the experience. Wine-tastings and gourmet excursions can be arranged on request. Half-day tours visit three towns—generally Kaysersberg, Turckheim, and either Riquewihr or Eguisheim (€53/person). Full-day tours for €99 per person add a couple more towns and Haut-Kœnigsbourg (5 percent discount with this book in 2011, castle admission extra, reserve directly with Jean-Claude, pick-up at your hotel, tel. 03 89 41 90 88, mobile 06 72 37 17 11, www.alsace-travel.com, werner @alsace-travel.com).

Regioscope is another option providing transportation but less commentary (full- and half-day tours in a 15-seat, air-conditioned minivan, departures from Colmar and Strasbourg possible). Morning departures leave Colmar at 9:15; afternoon departures leave at 13:45. Half-day trips return by 12:15 or 18:30. Every morning but Monday, they go to Ribeauvillé and Kaysersberg (€47/person); then, in the afternoon, they head to Haut-Kœnigsbourg and Riquewihr (€55 includes wine-tasting, €98 for both morning and afternoon tours). Excursions from Strasbourg include a morning tour of Mont Sainte-Odile and Obernai (€50), and an afternoon tour of Haut-Kœnigsbourg and Riquewihr (€75; or €120 for both). All prices include entrance fees and guided tours of the castles. In December, ask about Christmas Market excursions (tel. 06 88 21 27 15, www.regioscope.com, info@regioscope.com).

By Bike: With over 2,500 miles of bike-friendly lanes, Alsace is among France's best biking regions. The Route du Vin has an abundance of well-marked trails and *sentier viticole* service roads that run up and down the slopes, offering the best views and the fewest cars but tough pedaling—though more or less level routes exist, too. Start by getting advice and a good map from a TI or from where you're renting your bike.

Bikers can save themselves the ride out of Colmar by renting in Eguisheim, Sigolsheim (near Kaysersberg), or Ribeauvillé (rental options listed for each town). Riding round-trip between Ribeauvillé and Kaysersberg via Hunawihr and Riquewihr along the upper *sentier viticole* yields sensational views but dang hilly terrain (you can reduce some the climbing by following lower wine-service lanes).

Most key roads leaving Colmar have a painted bike lane. One of those lanes leads to Eguisheim and is a level snap, though it's entirely on busy roads.

For a quieter but longer route to Eguisheim, leave Colmar toward Wintzenheim, passing over the train tracks on avenue Général de Gaulle (which becomes route de Wintzenheim; bike lane available). Follow this until you see the *Wettolsheim/Eguisheim* sign (rue du Tiefenbach), take this country road to the signal, and cross D-83. Continue straight into Wettolsheim, turn left at the cemetery, go to the end of the quiet village street, and turn right at the crucifix. Take the first left on rue Marbach, which leads to Eguisheim. The ride from Eguisheim to Turckheim is level, and makes a nice loop ride from Colmar.

On Foot: Hikers can stroll along *sentier viticole* service roads and paths (explained above) into vineyards from each town on short loop trails (each TI has brochures), or connect the villages on longer walks. Consider taking a bus or taxi from Colmar to one village and hiking to another, then taking a bus or taxi back to Colmar (Ribeauvillé and Riquewihr, or Kaysersberg and Riquewihr make good combinations—see details later in this chapter). Hikers can also climb high to the ruined castles of the Vosges Mountains (Eguisheim and Ribeauvillé are good bases).

Route du Vin Wines

Most Route du Vin towns have wineries that give tours (some charge a fee), and scores of small producers open their courtyards with free and fun tastings. The modern cooperatives at Eguisheim, Bennwihr, Hunawihr, and Ribeauvillé, created after the destruction of World War II, provide a good look at modern and efficient methods of production. Before you set off, review "French Wine-Tasting 101" (page 40).

Learn to recognize the basic grapes and wines of this region. The simplest wines are blended from several grapes and usually called **Edelzwicker**. Despite being cheapest, these wines can be delicious and offer very good value.

Here are the key grapes to look for:

Riesling is the king of Alsatian grapes. The name comes from the German word that describes its slightly smoky smell, with a note of petroleum (*goût petrol*).

Alsace's Route du Vin

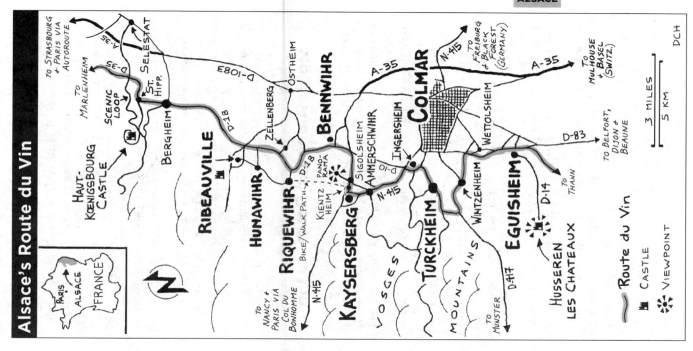

FRANCE

PARIS
ALSACE

N

To STRASBOURG
+ PARIS VIA
AUTOROUTE

A-35

ST. SELESTAT

To
MARLENHEIM

SCENIC
LOOP

ST. HIPP.

D-1B

BERGHEIM

HAUT-
KOENIGSBOURG
CASTLE

ZELLENBERG

OSTHEIM

D-1083

BENNWIHR

COLMAR

A-35

To
FREIBURG
+ BLACK
FOREST
(GERMANY)

N-415

A-35

To
MULHOUSE
+ BASEL
(SWITZ.)

RIBEAUVILLE

HUNAWIHR

RIQUEWIHR

D-1B

PANO-
RAMA

BIKE/WALK PATH

KIENTZ-
HEIM

SIGOLSHEIM

AMMERSCHWIHR

INGERSHEIM

D-10

WETTOLSHEIM

D-83

To BELFORT,
DIJON +
BEAUNE

KAYSERSBERG

N-415

WINTZENHEIM

EGUISHEIM

D-14

To
THANN

N-415

To
NANCY +
PARIS VIA
COL DU
BONHOMME

TURCKHEIM

VOSGES

MOUNTAINS

To
MUNSTER

D-417

HUSSEREN
LES CHATEAUX

3 MILES

5 KM

Route du Vin

CASTLE

VIEWPOINT

DCH

Sylvaner—fresh and light, fruity and cheap—is a good wine for a hot day.

Pinot Gris was called Tokay d'Alsace until recently, when the term was banned to avoid confusion with Tokaji wines in Hungary (where these grapes originated). Still, producers in Alsace call their wines Tokay Pinot Gris. These are more full-bodied, spicier, and distinctly different from other Pinot Gris wines you may have tried.

Muscat is best as a before-dinner wine. Compared with other French muscat wines, the Alsatian version is very dry, usually with a strong floral taste.

Gewürztraminer is "the lady's wine"—its bouquet is like a rosebush, its taste is fruity, and its aftertaste is spicy. In fact, it's named for the German word *gewürtz*, meaning "spicy."

Crémant d'Alsace, the Alsatian sparkling wine, is very good—and much cheaper than Champagne.

If you really get "Alsauced," the French term for headache is *mal à la tête*.

Sights Along the Route du Vin

These sights are listed from south to north, in the order you'll encounter them if you're heading north out of Colmar; except the Viel-Armand WWI Memorial, which is to the south of Colmar.

Eguisheim—This is the most charming village of the region (described on page 948).

Turckheim—With a charming square and a garden-filled moat, this quiet town is refreshingly untouristy, just enough off the beaten path to be overlooked. Bikers appreciate the bike path linking Turckheim with Colmar (see "Getting Around the Route du Vin—By Bike" on page 943). WWII buffs appreciate its "Colmar Pocket" museum, chronicling the American push to take Alsace from the Nazis (minimal English information, but eager-to-help staff, Mon–Sat 14:00–18:00, Sun 10:30–12:00 & 14:00–18:00, tel. 08 89 80 86 66).

Kaysersberg—This town has WWII sights, Dr. Albert Schweitzer's house, and plenty of hiking opportunities (described on page 952).

Bennwihr—After this town was completely destroyed during World War II, the only object left standing was the statue of two girls depicting Alsace and Lorraine (outside the very modern church). The war memorials next to the statue list the names of those who died in both world wars. During World War II, 130,000 Alsatian men aged 17-37 were forced into military service under the German army (after fighting against them); most were sent to the deadly Russian front.

Riquewihr—This adorable town is the most tourristed on the Route du Vin and can feel claustrophobic (described on page 955).

Zellenberg—This place has an impressive setting and is worth a quick stop for the views from either side of its narrow perch.

Hunawihr—This bit of wine-soaked Alsatian cuteness is far less visited than its more famous neighbors, and features a 16th-century fortified church that today is shared by both Catholics and Protestants (the Catholics are buried outside the church; the Protestants are buried next to the church wall). Park at the village washbasin (*lavoir*) and follow the trail up to the church, then loop back through the village. Kids enjoy Hunawihr's small park, Parc des Cigognes, where they'll spot otters, over 150 storks, and more (€8.50, kids–€5.50, April-Sept daily 10:00–12:30 & 14:00–18:00, no midday closing June–Aug, until 17:00 March and Oct–Nov, closed Dec–Feb, other animals take part in the afternoon shows, tel. 03 89 73 72 62, www.cigogne-loutre.com). A nearby butterfly exhibit (Le Jardin des Papillons) houses thousands of the delicate insects from around the world (€3, includes audioguide, daily 10:00–18:00, tel. 03 89 73 33 33, www.jardinsdespapillons.fr).

Ribeauvillé—This pleasant town, less visited by Americans, is well-situated for hiking and biking. It's a linear place with a long pedestrian street (Grande Rue) and feels a tad less tourist-dependent than other towns. A steep but manageable trail leads from the top of the town into the Vosges Mountains, to three castle ruins, and is ideal for hikers wanting a walk the woods to sweeping views. Follow Grand Rue uphill to the Hôtel aux Trois Châteaux and find the cobbled lane leading up from there. St. Ulrich is the most interesting of the three ruins (allow 2 hours round-trip, or 3 hours to see all three castles, or just climb 10 minutes for a view over the town—get info at TI at 1 Grand Rue, tel. 03 89 73 23 23). It's a short, sweet, and hilly bike loop from Ribeauvillé to Hunawihr and Riquewihr (can be extended to Kaysersberg if time and energy permit). You can rent a **bike** at Cycles Binder (82 Grand Rue, tel. 03 89 73 65 87) or Ribo Cycles (17 rue de Landau, tel. 03 89 73 72 94).

▲**Château du Haut-Kœnigsbourg**—This granddaddy of Alsatian castles, strategically situated on a rocky spur 2,500 feet above the flat Rhine plain, protected the passage between Alsace and Lorraine for centuries and provides remarkable insight into the 15th-century mountain fortresses of the Alsace region. The castle's pink stones were quarried from the Vosges Mountains. Rebuilt in the early 20th century, the well-furnished castle highlights Germanic influence in Alsatian history with decorations that illustrate castle life from the 15th through 17th centuries. There's little English, so you'll want the informative one-hour audioguide (€7.80, under 18 free, audioguide–€4, daily June–Aug 9:30–18:00,

April–May and Sept 9:30–17:00, March and Oct 9:30–17:00, Nov–Feb 9:45–12:00 & 13:00–16:30, last entry 30 minutes before closing, about 15 minutes north of Ribeauvillé above St. Hippolyte, tel. 03 88 82 50 60, www.haut-koenigsbourg.fr). A €4 shuttle bus runs here from the Séléstat train station (10/day mid-June to mid-Sept, weekends only rest of year except none Jan–Feb, 30 minutes, timed with trains, call château for schedule or check website). Your shuttle ticket saves you €2 on the château entry fee.

Vieil-Armand WWI Memorial (Hartmannswillerkopf)—This powerful memorial evokes the slaughter of the Western Front in World War I, when Germany and France bashed heads for years in a war of attrition. It's up a windy road above Cernay (20 miles south of Colmar). From the parking lot, walk 10 minutes to the vast cemetery, and walk 30 more minutes through trenches to a hilltop with a grand Alsatian view. Here you'll find a stirring memorial statue of French soldiers storming the trenches in 1915–1916, facing near-certain death.

Eguisheim

Just a few miles south of Colmar's suburbs, this circular, flower-festooned little wine town (pop. 1,600) is overlooked by most tourists. Eguisheim ("aye-gush-Im") is ideal for a relaxing lunch and vineyard walks, and makes a good small-town base for exploring Alsace. It's a cinch by car (easy parking) and manageable by bike (see "Getting Around the Route du Vin—By Bike" on page 943), but barely accessible by bus. Consider taking the bus one way and taxi the other to Colmar or other villages (bus schedules available at TIs and posted at key stops). Eguisheim's stop is at the lower end of the village, near the post office.

Orientation to Eguisheim

The TI has free Wi-Fi and information on accommodations, festivals, vineyard walks, and Vosges mountain hikes (Mon–Fri 9:30–12:00 & 14:00–18:00, Sat 9:30–12:00 & 13:30–17:30, closed Sun, 22 Grand Rue, tel. 03 89 23 40 33, www.ot-eguisheim.fr). They're happy to call a taxi for you.

Winemaker Jean-Luc has **bikes for rent** (4 rue des Trois Châteaux, tel. 03 89 24 53 66).

Self-Guided Walk

Welcome to Eguisheim

Although Eguisheim's wall is gone, the rue des Remparts (Nord and Sud) survives, scenically circling the village. The main drag,

Grand Rue, bisects the circle leading to a town square that's as darling as a Grimm fairy tale.

Start your visit at the bottom of town (near the TI) and circle the ramparts clockwise, walking up rue du Rempart Sud. The most enchanting and higgledy-piggledy view in town is right at the start of the loop (at the tight Y in the road; go left and uphill). Rue du Rempart Sud is more picturesque than rue du Rempart Nord, but I'd walk the entire circle. You'll see that what was once the moat is now lined with 13th- to 17th-century houses—a cancan of half-timbered charm. You're actually walking a lane between the back of fine homes (on the left) and their barns (on the right). Look for emblems of daily life, religious and magical symbols, dates on lintel stones, and so on. (The government pays 15 percent of the cost of any work locals do on their exteriors.) The loop takes a decidedly hip turn along its northern half, as you pass an art gallery, a cool coffee shop, and a trendy bar.

When you've finished the loop, walk up Grand Rue to Eguisheim's main square, **place du Château St. Léon**, and lose all sense of discipline sampling the shops, cafés, and fruits of the local vine. This square, lined with fine Renaissance houses, marks the heart of the old town. The mini-castle is privately owned and closed to the public. Surviving bits of its 13th-century, eight-sided wall circle the chapel, built in Neo-Romanesque style on the site of the castle's keep in 1895. Although it is of little historic importance, it's worth a peek to see how a Romanesque chapel may have been painted (drop any coin into the €0.50 box for light). The 19th-century fountain sports a statue of St. Leo IX (1048–1054), the only Alsatian pope. Eguisheim's most famous son was a saint, to boot.

Exploring the town, you may come upon some of its 20 "tithe courtyards." Farmers who worked on land owned by the church used to come to these courtyards to pay their tithes (10 percent of their production). With so many of these courtyards, it's safe to conclude that the farming around here was excellent.

Sights in Eguisheim

Wine-Tasting—Don't leave without visiting one of Eguisheim's countless cozy wineries. The ambience and quality of wines at **Emile Beyer** is great. Enter through their Old World courtyard on cour Unterlinden (one block from the TI) to find a welcoming counter and ample tables. Ask to visit their aromatic cellar, crammed with old wood vats. They're famous for their Rieslings, but all their wines are worth a taste (free tasting, daily 10:00–19:00, 7 place du Chateau, tel. 03 89 41 40 45). The big, modern **Wine Cooperative Wolfberger** offers tours three times a day and may be able to arrange an English-speaking guide if you call ahead

(Mon–Sat 8:00–12:00 & 14:00–18:00, Sun from 10:00, 6 Grand Rue, tel. 03 89 22 20 20).

Views over Eguisheim—If you have a car, follow signs up to *Husseren Les Cinq Châteaux*, then walk 20 minutes to the ruined castle towers for a good view of the Vosges Mountains above and vineyards below.

By mountain bike or on foot, find any path through the vineyards above Eguisheim for nice views (the TI has a free map). One option is to walk uphill on Grande Rue, cross the ring road leaving Eguisheim's town center, and turn left at the *Camping* arrow. Pass the campground, climb a small hill, and turn right onto the small road leading into the vineyards. From here, climb as high as you like. It's OK to walk on dirt paths between the vines. The five châteaux of Husseren float above. The TI's map shows a longer walk through the vineyards from the same starting point, which should be signposted in English by 2011.

Sleeping in Eguisheim

(€1 = about $1.25, country code: 33)

$$$ Hôtel St. Hubert*** offers 15 rooms with polished, modern, German-hotelesque comfort (and strict management to match), and an indoor pool and sauna (€7). The 10-minute walk from the town center is rewarded with vineyards out your window (Db-€105–125, Tb-€138–168, family suite for four-€185, extra bed-€16, four rooms have patios, free pickup at Colmar's train station if reserved a day in advance, reception open 8:00–12:00 & 15:00–22:00, 6 rue des Trois Pierres, tel. 03 89 41 40 50, fax 03 89 41 46 88, www.hotel-st-hubert.com, contact@hotel-st-hubert.com).

$$$ Hostellerie du Château*** is part art gallery and part hotel, providing contemporary comfort on the pleasant main square (standard Db-€90–110, Db suite with whirlpool tub-€120–175, extra bed-€20, all rooms with tubs, no air-con, Wi-Fi, garage €10/day, 2 place du Château St. Léon IX, tel. 03 89 23 72 00, fax 03 89 41 63 93, www.hostellerieduchateau.com, info@hostellerieduchateau.com, friendly Monsieur Wagner).

$$ Auberge Alsacienne*** is conveniently located near the bus stop, with small, traditionally designed rooms in a picturesque building and rental bikes for guests (Db-€65–75, Tb-€95, 12 Grand Rue, tel. 03 89 41 50 20, fax 03 89 23 89 32, www.auberge-alsacienne.net, auberge-alsacienne@wanadoo.fr).

$$ Auberge du Rempart is a rockin' deal. It's atmospheric, with bright, airy rooms with big beds and surprisingly elaborate decor above a lively café/restaurant deep inside the town (standard Db-€56, grand Db-€72–95; great family suite-€120 for 4 people, €140 for 6; Wi-Fi, 3 rue du Rempart Sud, near TI, tel. 03 89 41 16

87, fax 03 89 41 06 50, www.auberge-du-rempart.com, auberge-du-rempart@wanadoo.fr). The reception desk is in the restaurant and is usually open only during lunch and after 18:00.

Chambres d'Hôtes

Please remember to cancel if you reserve a room and can't use it.

$ Alexandre Freudenreich rents spacious, light, and decent rooms at a good price. He speaks English, and has four rooms in the village center and two more modern rooms in another building up in the vineyards. He can pick you up in Colmar if you book ahead (Db–€42, includes breakfast, cash only, take 2 rights out of the TI to 4 cour Unterlinden, tel. & fax 03 89 23 16 44, maison hote@aol.com).

$ Madame Dirringer rents four traditional, spotless rooms facing an atmospheric courtyard. She speaks no English, but is a creative communicator (Db–€35, good family room, breakfast-€6, cash only, 11 rue du Riesling, tel. 03 89 41 71 87).

$ Madame Bombenger is sweet, speaks some English, and has a modern, graceful home that sits just above Eguisheim with three rooms and nice views into the vineyards and over town (Sb–€35, Db–€45, €2 less for more than one night, includes breakfast, 3 rue des Trois Pierres, tel. & fax 03 89 23 71 19, mobile 06 61 94 31 09, bombenger.marie-therese@wanadoo.fr).

$ Madame Bannwarth has three pleasant, air-conditioned rooms in her modern home a block above the town (Db–€42, includes breakfast, 10 rue de Hautvillers, tel. 03 89 23 74 58, www.bannwarth.eu, ea.bannwarth@wanadoo.fr).

Eating in Eguisheim

Charcuterie-Café A Edel, on place du Château, has killer quiche "to go" and everything you need for a fun picnic, including small tubs of chopped veggies (daily until 19:00, Mon–Fri closes 12:30–14:00). You can picnic by the fountain, or eat at their adjacent restaurant while listening to the trickling of the square's fountain (restaurant closed Tue, €9–12 *tartes flambées* and quiche, 2 place du Château St. Léon, tel. 03 89 41 22 40).

Auberge de Trois Châteaux is very Alsatian, with cozy ambience and traditional cuisine (*menus* from €18 and affordable *plats du jour*, closed Tue–Wed, 26 Grand Rue, tel. 03 89 23 70 61).

Auberge Alsacienne offers regional cuisine in a more refined setting (€23 two-course *menu*, €30 three-course *menu*, closed Sun evening and all day Mon, 12 Grand Rue, tel. 03 89 41 50 20).

Auberge du Rempart is best for outdoor dining in a pleasant courtyard around a big fountain. Come here for less expensive and lighter meals and good *tartes flambées* (€9–17 *plats*, closed Sun–Mon and sometimes Thu evenings Sept–June, 3 rue du Remparts Sud, near TI, tel. 03 89 41 16 87).

Au Vieux Porche is a wood-beamed, white-tablecloth affair, ideal for a leisurely meal or a special occasion (€15–26 *plats*, closed Tue–Wed, upper end of town at 16 rue des Trois Châteaux, tel. 03 89 24 01 90).

Kaysersberg

For much of history, Kaysersberg ("Mountain of the Emperor") was of strategic importance, thanks to its location guarding the important route over the Vosges Mountains that links Colmar with the big city of Nancy. Today, philosopher-physician Albert Schweitzer's hometown offers a cute jumble of 15th-century homes under a romantically ruined castle with easy vineyard trails at its doorstep, and plenty of tourists. Reasonable bus service from Colmar makes Kaysersberg a worthwhile day trip (7–10/day, 30–40 minutes). Catch buses back to Colmar across the road from the bus shelter where riders from Colmar are dropped (a block from post office off the main parking lot, €2 parking).

Orientation to Kaysersberg

The TI is two blocks from the town's main entry, inside the Hôtel de Ville (June–Sept Mon–Sat 9:00–12:30 & 14:00–18:00, Sun 10:00–12:30; Oct–May Mon–Sat 9:30–12:00 & 14:00–17:30, closed Sun; tel. 03 89 78 22 78, www.kaysersberg.com, WCs out the door to left under arch). The TI has free Internet access and rents iPod Nano audioguides for touring Kaysersberg (€5, €150 deposit, allow 1–1.5 hours). Pick up the town map, the free *Sentier Viticole* bike map, detailed descriptions of hiking trails between wine villages (€0.50; see "Walking/Biking Trails from Kaysersberg," later), and bus schedules. You can rent **bikes** nearby in Sigolsheim at La Pommeraie (daily 9:00–19:00, tel. 03 89 78 25 66).

Most buses to Colmar use the Rocade Verte stop, at a parking lot just outside the town walls on the village's south side.

Sights in Kaysersberg

Exploring Kaysersberg—Strolling through Kaysersberg is a treat. The town's main drag is lined with tempting bakeries and colorful shops, and cross-streets merit exploration. There's no

Albert Schweitzer
(1875–1965)

"I don't know what your destiny will be, but one thing I do know: The only ones among you who will be really happy are those who have sought and found how to serve."
—Albert Schweitzer

Albert Schweitzer—theologian, musician, philosopher, and physician—was an unusually gifted individual who never hesitated to question accepted beliefs and practices. He is probably most famous for his work with sufferers of leprosy and tuberculosis in Africa.

Born to German parents in 1875 in Kaysersberg, he studied philosophy and theology at the University of Strasbourg, eventually becoming a pastor at his church. Not satisfied with life as a pastor, Schweitzer studied music and soon gained fame as a musical scholar and organist. After trying his hand at writing with *The Quest of the Historical Jesus*, which challenged contemporary secular views of Jesus, he shifted his attention to medicine. After he married Helene Bresslau, the couple left for Africa and founded a missionary hospital in Gabon (then called Lambaréné). During World War I, Schweitzer and his wife were forced by the French to leave Africa.

After the war, Schweitzer returned to Gabon on his own, where he remained for most of the rest of his life. He received the 1952 Nobel Peace Prize for his service to humanity, particularly for founding the Albert Schweitzer Hospital in Gabon, where he died in 1965. He was 90 years old.

shortage of bakeries selling tasty pretzels and *kugelhopf,* among other tasty treats. Here's a rundown of worthwhile places you'll pass, starting at the TI:

The **Caveau de Kaysersberg** represents all winemakers from around Kaysersberg, including several Grands Crus, and offers free and easy wine-tastings (Wed–Mon 10:00–12:00 & 14:00–18:00 except July–Aug 10:00–19:00, closed Tue year-round, near the TI at 20 rue du Général de Gaulle, tel. 03 89 47 18 43).

Kaysersberg is known for its blown glass, and at **Verrerie d'Art de Kaysersberg** you can see glassblowers at work (nice shop, daily 10:00–18:00, near the church at 30 avenue de Général de Gaulle).

The town's main sight is the medieval **St. Croix Church.** Read the information plaque opposite the entrance, then enter the dark interior. After your eyes adjust, study the unusual crucifix hanging high above (the church is dedicated to the Holy Cross). Next, focus on the sensational 1518 altarpiece—push the button on the right of the altar for light. The 14 brilliantly carved wood panels retrace the Passion of Christ, with Saint Christopher overseeing the event from on top (free, daily 9:00–12:00 & 14:00–17:00, sometimes open later and during lunch).

Vieux Potier is a must for pottery lovers and nostalgic types (steps from the church at 47 place de l'Eglise, tel. 03 89 78 25 15). The courtyard at the **Musée Historique** (#66) has tables with fine ambience and reasonably priced meals.

You'll eventually land on the town's beautiful **16th-century bridge.** As the Nazis were preparing to evacuate, they planned to destroy the bridge. Locals reasoned with the commander, agreeing to dig an anti-tank ditch just beyond the bridge—and the symbol of the town was saved.

At the top end of town, you'll come to **Dr. Albert Schweitzer's house,** a small and disappointing museum. It has two rooms of scattered photos and artifacts from his time in Africa, with some English information (€2, Easter–Oct daily 9:00–12:00 & 14:00–18:00, closed Nov–Easter, 126 rue du Général de Gaulle). The square across the street (place Gouraud) hosts a thriving market each Monday until noon.

Walking/Biking Trails from Kaysersberg—Trails start just outside the TI (get details at the TI). To find the main trail, turn left out of the TI and walk under the arch. A left on the trail leads up to the ruined **castle** (free, always open, fine views and benches, 113 steps up a dark stairway to the tower). Hikers can continue past the castle for more views and trails (TI has detailed map for €0.50, including the long route to **Riquewihr**—2.5 hours). For more great views of Kaysersberg, follow the trail described next (toward Kientzheim) for about 10 minutes.

For an easier 1.5–2-hour hike—or 40-minute bike ride—along a paved lane over vine-covered hills to Riquewihr, turn right on the main trail back down by the TI. You'll start on a bike path (*piste cyclable*) to **Kientzheim** (well-marked with bike icons). In Kientzheim, follow the *sentier viticole* route uphill along service roads past gorgeous views and vineyards to Riquewihr. If you get turned around, stop any biker or vineyard worker and ask, "*à Riquewihr?*" (ah reek-veer?)

Drivers can follow the same signs from Kientzheim to Riquewihr but must be careful of bikers.

World War II Sights—The hill just north of Kaysersberg is soaked in WWII blood. Towns around it have gray rather than red-tiled roofs (indicating that they were entirely destroyed and rebuilt). Kientzheim has an American-made tank parked in its front yard (and a wine museum in its castle grounds). In 2004, the refreshing network of tiny streams trickling down its streets (standard before World War II) was restored. Both Sigolsheim (scene of fierce fighting—note its sterile rebuilt Romanesque church) and Bennwihr are modern, as they were taken and lost a dozen times by the Allies and Nazis, and completely ruined. The hill above is still called "Bloody Hill," as it was nicknamed by German troops. Between its cemeteries, you'll find some of the best vines on the Route du Vin.

A **WWII Monument** stands atop Bloody Hill. The spectacular setting, best at sunset, houses a monument to the American divisions that helped liberate Alsace in World War II (find the American flag). Up the lane, a beautiful cemetery is the final resting place of 1,600 men who fought in the French army (many gravestones are Muslim, for soldiers from France's North African colonies—Morocco, Algeria, and Tunisia). From this brilliant viewpoint you can survey the entire southern section of the Route du Vin and into Germany. The castle hanging high to the north is the Château du Haut-Kœnigsbourg (described on page 947). The road to the memorial leaves from the center of Sigolsheim (follow *Necropole* and *Cimitière* signs turning at Pierre Sparr winery, then keep straight and climb into the vineyards).

Riquewihr

This little village, wrapped in vineyards, is so picturesque today because it was so rich centuries ago. You can recognize its old wealth because it has the most stone houses of any place in Alsace. The circular village is crammed with shops, cafés, galleries, cobblestones, and flowers. Arrive early to experience an almost-peaceful Riquewihr, or sharpen your elbows if you arrive later in the day.

Orientation to Riquewihr

Buses drop you off at the lower end of the village, opposite the post office (drivers can park nearby for €2). Enter the town under the Hôtel de Ville; the main drag runs uphill from here. The **TI** is halfway up at 2 rue de la 1ère Armée (Mon–Sat 9:30–12:00 & 14:00–18:00, Sun 10:00–13:00, tel. 03 89 73 23 23, www.ribeauville-riquewihr.com). A good WC is behind the TI. Quieter lanes lead off the main drag. For a local taxi, call 03 89 73 73 71.

Sights in Riquewihr

Riquewihr Town—Within a few yards of the town entry, you'll see the **tourist train** (€6, next departure time posted, 30 minutes, recorded tour through vineyards). Next up, try the excellent, free wine-tasting at **Caves Dopff et Irion** (€7–10 bottles, just uphill from Hôtel de Ville, daily 10:00–19:00, tel. 03 89 49 08 92). The

Musée de la Communication, a block away (at the town's château), does a good job illustrating the evolution of man's ability to send messages, from mail delivery to mobile phones (€4.50, English brochure, daily 10:00–17:30).

Walking up the main street, you'll pass several **courtyard cafés** with tempting tables. Two levels of nonstop holiday cheer await you at the **Käthe Wohlfahrt** shop, where Christmas comes alive even in July (daily 10:00–12:30 & 13:45–18:00, near the top of town at 1 rue du Cerf). Just beyond, find one of the best **bell towers** in the region (Le Dolder, built in 1291). Look for the engraving of 13th-century Riquewihr by the fountain opposite the tower's entry. The steep-stepped **Dolder Museum,** inside the tower, has small rooms covering its history—but doesn't merit the climb (€3, €5 with Tour des Voleurs, July–Aug daily 10:00–13:00 & 14:00–18:00, Sept–June weekends only). The nearby **Tour des Voleurs** has a small museum of torture (€3, €5 with Dolder Museum, same hours).

Pass under the bell tower, take a left on rue des Remparts, and stroll the picturesque lane. Turn right when you see steps down to the moat (and the big wine press), and double back to the top of the town along the moat. Notice how homes were built right into the defensive walls.

Scenic Walk, Ride, or Drive from Riquewihr—The *sentier viticole* lane to Kientzheim (then Kaysersberg) leads north from the TI out rue de la 1ère Armée, climbs above Riquewihr, then drops into Kientzheim—and delivers beautiful views all the way. Leave town and follow blue signs to *Kientzheim* for a beautiful walk or ride (allow 1.5–2 hours to hike all the way to Kaysersberg). Drivers can follow the same route and get the same great views, but go slow and watch out for bikers.

Strasbourg

Strasbourg is urban Alsace at its best—it feels like a giant Colmar with rivers and streetcars. It's a progressive, livable city, with generous space devoted to pedestrians, scads of bikes, mod trams, meandering waterways, and a young, lively mix of university students, Eurocrats, and street people. This place has an Amsterdam-like feel. Situated just west of the

Rhine River, Strasbourg provides the ultimate blend of Franco-Germanic culture, architecture, and ambience. A living symbol of the perpetual peace between France and Germany, Strasbourg was selected as home to the European Parliament, the European Council (sharing administrative responsibilities for the European Union with Brussels, Belgium), and the European Court of Human Rights.

Planning Your Time

Strasbourg makes a good day trip from Colmar. And, thanks to high-speed TGV-train service, it also makes a handy stop for train travelers en route to or from Paris (baggage storage available). None of its museums is essential (though the Alsatian Museum comes close)—you're here to see the cathedral, wander the waterways, and take a bite out of the big city. Plan on three hours to hit the highlights, starting at Strasbourg's dazzling cathedral (arrive in Strasbourg by 11:30 so you can comfortably make the 12:30 cathedral clock performance) and ending with the district called La Petite France (ideally for lunch).

Orientation to Strasbourg

Tourist Information

Strasbourg's main TI faces the cathedral (daily 9:00–19:00, 17 place de la Cathédrale, tel. 03 88 52 28 28, www.otstrasbourg.fr, info @otstrasbourg.fr). A smaller TI is located in the train station's south hall (across from the station's *Accueil* office, same hours). Buy the €1 city map, which describes a decent walking tour in English, or pay €5.50 to rent an **audioguide** that covers the cathedral and old city in more detail than most need (available only at the main TI, allow 1.5 hours). The TI includes a cute little map of the route, and has bike maps for the city and surrounding areas.

The **Strasbourg Pass** (€12.50, €6.50 for kids), valid three days, is a good value for active travelers. It includes one free museum entry and half-off coupons for others, a discount on the town audioguide, a free half-day bike rental, the boat cruise, and free entry to the cathedral narthex view and the astrological clock tour.

Arrival in Strasbourg

By Train: TGV trains serve Strasbourg's gleaming train station. There is baggage storage at platform 1 (daily 7:45–20:30, airport-type security screening so allow time, WCs nearby—€0.50). A helpful TI is in the station's south hall, opposite the station's *Accueil* office (sells day passes for the tram). Rental bikes are available in the lower level of the glass atrium (see "Helpful Hints," later), and

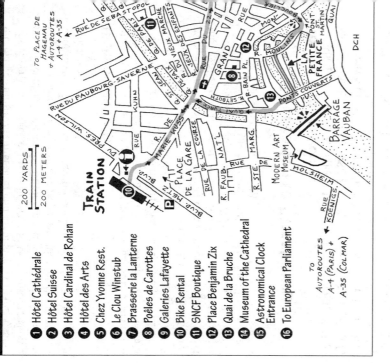

Strasbourg

1. Hôtel Cathédrale
2. Hôtel Suisse
3. Hôtel Cardinal de Rohan
4. Hôtel des Arts
5. Chez Yvonne Rest.
6. Le Clou Winstub
7. Brasserie la Lanterne
8. Poêles de Carottes
9. Galeries Lafayette
10. Bike Rental
11. SNCF Boutique
12. Place Benjamin Zix
13. Quai de la Bruche
14. Museum of the Cathedral
15. Astronomical Clock Entrance
16. To European Parliament

you'll find many budget eating options.

To **walk** to the cathedral in 15 urban minutes, go straight out of the station, cross the big square (place de la Gare), and walk past Hôtel Vendôme and up rue du Maire Kuss. Cross the river, and continue up serpentine, pedestrian-friendly rue du 22 November all the way to place Kléber. Cross bustling place Kléber (whose namesake graces the center of the square), maintaining the same direction, then turn right on the broad pedestrian street (rue des Grandes Arcades). Turn left on rue des Hallebardes (at *Concorde* sign on building), then follow that spire.

To get from the train station to the city center by **public transportation,** catch the caterpillar-like tram that leaves from under the station (buy €1.40 one-way ticket or €3.80 day pass from the station TI, or from machines on platforms—coins only, then validate in skinny machines). Take Tram #A (direction: Illkirch) or Tram #D (direction: Aristide Briand) three stops to Langross-Grande Rue, two blocks from the cathedral. (You can return to

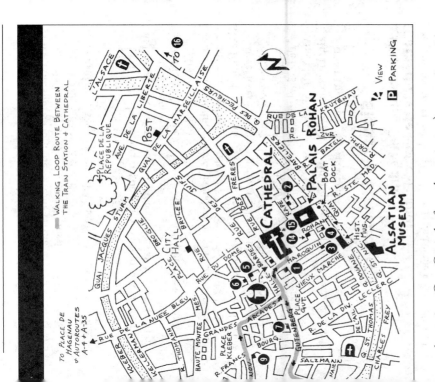

the station, Gare Centrale, from the same stop.)

By Car: You're better off day-tripping in by train. If you drive, you'll see signs on the autoroute for *P+R* (Parking & Relais) lots, which are located at tram stations outside the city center and make for easier driving and cheaper rates (€3/day includes round-trip tram tickets to the center; take tram in direction: Centre-Ville). To park safely in the center, follow *Gare Centrale* signs, then *Parking Aurélie* signs (it's on boulevard de Metz—to the right with your back to the station). To park even closer to the center (and encounter more traffic), follow *Centre-Ville/Cathédrale* signs. In the center, the place Gutenberg has parking near the cathedral, though the larger Austerlitz *parking* works fine. Skip the train station's pricey underground lot (€3/hour).

By Plane: The user-friendly Strasbourg–Entzheim airport (tel. 03 88 64 67 67, www.strasbourg.aeroport.fr), with frequent, often inexpensive flights to Paris, is connected by train to the main rail station (€2.30, 10-minute trip).

Helpful Hints

Quiet Transportation: Beware of virtually silent trams and bicycles—look both ways before crossing streets. Bikes are allowed on pedestrian streets.

US Consulate: It's at 15 avenue d'Alsace (tel. 03 88 35 31 04, fax 03 88 24 06 95).

Internet Access: Several cybercafés lie on the main street into town from the station, rue du Maire Kuss (or ask at the TI).

Car Rental: All major companies have offices at or across from the train station.

Post Office: It's at the cathedral (Mon-Fri 8:00–18:30, Sat 8:00–17:00, closed Sun).

Laundry: You'll find a handy launderette on rue des Veaux, near the recommended hotels.

Bike Rental: You can rent bikes at **Vélocation,** one level below street level at the train station (€5/half-day—either 7:00–13:00 or 13:00–20:00, €8/day; open Mon-Fri 7:00–20:00, Sat-Sun 9:30–12:30 & 13:30–19:30; follow signs for *Parc à Vélo*, Place de la Gare, tel. 03 88 23 56 75, www.velocation.net).

Taxi: Call 03 88 36 13 13 or 03 88 30 13 01.

Train Tickets: The **SNCF Boutique** at 7 quai de Paris sells train tickets and makes reservations.

Sights in Strasbourg

▲▲Strasbourg Cathedral (Cathédrale de Notre-Dame)

Stand in front of Hôtel de la Cathédrale and crane your neck up. If this church, with its cloud-piercing spire and pink sandstone color, wows you today, imagine its impact on medieval tourists. The delicate Gothic style of the cathedral (begun in 1176, not finished until 1429) is another Franco-German mixture that somehow survived the French Revolution, the Franco-Prussian War, World War I, and World War II.

Cost and Hours: Free, daily 7:00–11:40 & 12:45–19:00.

Visiting the Cathedral: Before entering the cathedral, survey the scene. The square in front of the cathedral makes the ideal stage for street performers—it's like a medieval fair. This square was Roman 2,000 years ago. Then, as now, it was the center of activity. The dark half-timbered building to your left, next to the TI, was the home of a wealthy merchant in the 16th century, and symbolizes the virtues of capitalism that Strasbourg has long revered. Goods were sold under the ground-floor arches; owners lived above. Strasbourg made its medieval mark as a trading center, taking advantage of its position at the crossroads of Europe and its access to the important Rhine River to charge tolls for the movement of goods. Its robust economy allowed for the construction of this glorious cathedral. Strasbourg's location also made it susceptible to new ideas. Martin Luther's theses were posted on its main doors, and after the wars of religion, this cathedral was Protestant for more than 100 years. (Louis XIV returned it to Catholicism in 1621.) Strasbourg remains a tolerant city today.

The dark-red stone that differentiates this cathedral from other great Gothic churches in France is quarried from the northern part of the Vosges Mountains (compare it to the yellow stone of St. Martin's in Colmar). You'll see this stone on display in many other buildings as you tour Strasbourg.

As you enter the cathedral, notice the sculpture over the left portal (complacent, spear-toting Virtues getting revenge on those nasty Vices). Enter and walk down the center. English displays at several locations give simple explanations of key aspects of the cathedral. The stained glass on the lower left displays various rulers of Strasbourg; the stained glass on your right depicts Bible stories. An exquisite, gold-leafed organ hangs above the second pillars. Pass the elaborately carved pulpit, then walk to the choir and stare at the stained-glass image of Mary; find the European Union flag at the top.

Inside the right transept is a high-tech, 15th-century **astronomical clock** (restored in 1883, English explanation below) that gives a ho-hum performance every 15 minutes (keep your eye on the little angel about 15 feet up, slightly left of center). The show is better on the half-hour (angel on the right), and best at 12:30 (everybody gets in the act, including a rooster and 12 apostles—for the 12 hours). Arrive by 11:45 outside the right transept, buy your €2 ticket (also available from the souvenir stand inside by the clock), then enter and hear an explanation of the clock's workings while having your pocket picked (be alert).

For €4.80 you can climb 332 steps to the **top of the narthex** for an amazing view (free first Sun of the month, access on right side of cathedral, daily April–Sept 9:00–19:30, June–Aug Fri-Sat nights sometimes until 21:30, Oct–March 10:00–17:15).

Nearby: Before leaving this area, investigate the network of small pedestrian streets that connect the cathedral with the huge place Kléber (home to various outdoor markets, depending on the day of the week). Each street is named for the primary trade that took place there.

Museums near the Cathedral

These museums lie outside the cathedral's right transept and are interesting only for aficionados with particular interests or a full day in Strasbourg. They're all free on the first Sunday of the month (www.musees-strasbourg.org).

Palais Rohan—This stately palace houses three museums: the **Museum of Decorative Arts,** which feels like the Versailles of Strasbourg, with grand reception rooms, a king's bedroom (where Louis XV and Marie-Antoinette both slept), a big library, and rooms displaying ceramic dishes, ancient clocks, and more—borrow the English booklet; the **Museum of Fine Arts,** a small, well-displayed collection of paintings from Middle Ages to Baroque, some by artists you'll recognize; and the **Archaeological Museum,** the best of the three, with a stellar presentation of Alsatian civilization through the millennia (€5 each, includes English audioguide, under 18 free, Wed–Mon 12:00–18:00, closed Tue, 2 place du Château, tel. 03 88 52 50 00).

Museum of the Cathedral (Musée de l'Oeuvre Notre-Dame)—This well-organized museum has plenty of artifacts from the cathedral (€5, includes English audioguide, under 18 free, Tue–Sun 10:00–18:00, Sat from 12:00, closed Mon, 3 place du Château, tel. 03 88 32 88 17).

Alsatian Museum—One of Strasbourg's oldest and most characteristic homes hosts this extensive, well-presented collection of Alsatian folk art. You'll see scenes from daily life, traditional home interiors (including a close-up look at half-timbered construction), lots of tools, and a good overview of the life of a winemaker. The free English audioguide makes this museum a worthwhile detour (€5, Wed–Mon 12:00–18:00, Sun from 10:00, closed Tue, across the river and down a block to the right from the boat dock at 23 quai St. Nicholas, tel. 03 88 52 50 01).

Boat Ride on the Ill River

To see the cityscape from the water, take a loop cruise around Strasbourg. The glass-topped boats are air-conditioned and sufficiently comfortable—both sides have fine views. You'll pass through two locks as you circle the old city clockwise. The highlight for me was cruising by the European Parliament buildings and the European Court of Human Rights (adults–€8.50, under 18-half-price, good English commentary with live guide or audioguide, 2 boats/hour, daily April–Oct 9:30–21:00, May–Sept until 22:00; Nov–March boats depart only at 10:30, 13:00, 14:30, and 16:00; dock is 2 blocks outside cathedral's right transept, where rue Rohan meets the river, tel. 03 88 84 13 13, www.batorama.fr).

▲La Petite France

The historic home to Strasbourg's tanners, millers, and fishermen, this charming area is laced with canals, crowned with magnificent half-timbered homes, carpeted with cobblestones, and filled with tourists.

From the cathedral, walk down rue des Hallebardes to the merry-go-round, then continue straight, following rue Gutenberg. Cross big rue des Francs Bourgeois and keep straight (now on Grande Rue). Turn left on the third little street (rue du Bouclier, street signs are posted behind you), and make your way to the middle of the bridge (pont St. Martin). Gaze at the various locks and the channels that meet here. Find your way down to the river and follow the walkway over the lock deep into La Petite France. Make friends with a leafy café table on **place Benjamin Zix**, or find the siesta-perfect parks between the canals across the bridge at rue des Moulins. Climb the once-fortified grassy wall (Barrage Vauban) for a decent view—the glass structure behind you is the new modern-art museum (interesting more for its architecture than its collection).

La Petite France's coziest cafés line the canal on **quai de la Bruche** near the barrage. From here it's a 10-minute walk back to the station: With the river on your left, walk along quai de Turckheim, cross the third bridge, and find rue du Maire Kuss.

Sleeping in Strasbourg

(€1 = about $1.25, country code: 33)

Strasbourg is quiet in the summer (prices fall) and slammed when the parliament is in session or during major conferences.

$$$ Hôtel Cathédrale** is comfortable and contemporary, with a Jack-and-the-beanstalk spiral stairway (elevator begins one floor up) and a hopelessly confusing floor plan. This modern yet atmospheric place lets you stare at the cathedral point-blank from your room. Skip the cheaper rooms *sans* view (small Db with no view-€93–118, medium Db with no view-€128, larger Db with view-€160, prices sometimes lower on weekends, frequent Web promotions, buffet breakfast-€13, air-con, free Wi-Fi, laundry service, free bicycles can be reserved for up to 2 hours, book ahead for one of 5 parking spaces, 12–13 place de la Cathédrale, tel. 03 88 22 12 12, toll-free in France 08 00 00 00 84, fax 03 88 23 28 00, www .hotel-cathedrale.fr, reserv@hotel-cathedrale.fr).

$$$ Hôtel Suisse*, across from the cathedral's right transept and off place du Château, is a low-profile, dark, central, serious, and solid two-star value (Sb-€67–96, Db-€84–102, Tb-€115, prices €10 less in Jan–Feb and July–Aug—when parliament isn't in session—extra person-€10, elevator, free Wi-Fi, pleasant café, 2 place de la Râpe, tel. 03 88 35 22 11, fax 03 88 25 74 23, www .hotel-suisse.com, info@hotel-suisse.com).

$$$ Hôtel Cardinal de Rohan** has a classy address in the pedestrian zone just steps from the cathedral, with royal public spaces and 36 well-appointed rooms. Eight rooms are small but a good value, and four are good triples (small Db-€78, bigger Db-€160, Tb-€175, buffet breakfast-€13, air-con, free Internet access and Wi-Fi, book ahead for one of 6 parking spaces-€17, rental bikes, 17 rue du Maroquin, tel. 03 88 32 85 11, fax 03 88 75 65 37, www.hotel-rohan.com, info@hotel-rohan.com).

$$ Hôtel des Arts**, located in the thick of things above a busy café, is a young-at-heart, simple place with tight bathrooms. Rooms in front are fun and noisy (Sb/Db-€70–82, Tb-€83–93, cheap breakfast-€6.50, entirely non-smoking, air-con, Wi-Fi, 10 place du Marché aux Cochons de Lait, tel. 03 88 37 98 37, fax 03 88 37 98 97, www.hotel-arts.com, info@hotel-arts.com).

Eating in Strasbourg

Atmospheric *winstubs* (wine bars) serving affordable salads and *tarte flambée* are a snap to find. If the weather is nice, head for **La Petite France** and choose ambience over cuisine—dine outside at any café/*winstub* that appeals to you. Alternatively, stock up on picnic supplies at the terrific grocery store on the main floor of the **Galeries Lafayette** department store (Mon–Sat 9:00–20:00, closed Sun, place Kléber).

For a real meal, skip the touristy restaurants on the cathedral square and along rue de Maroquin. Consider these nearby places instead; both are one block behind the TI (go left out of the TI, then take the first left through the passageway and keep walking): **Chez Yvonne** (marked *S'Burjerstuewel* above windows), right out of a Bruegel painting, has a tradition of good food at fair prices. Try the *coq au Riesling* or *choucroute garnie* (€16 each) or the €11.50 *salade Alsacienne* (reservations smart on weekends and holidays, open late daily, 10 rue du Sanglier, tel. 03 88 32 84 15). Half a block left down rue du Chaudron at #3 lies **Le Clou Winstub,** with €8–11 salads and €13–16 *plats du jour.* This place often looks closed from the outside, but don't be shy (closed Wed lunch and all day Sun, tel. 03 88 32 11 67).

Brasserie La Lanterne, an Alsatian microbrewery and a beloved local hangout for students and locals, is famous for its home brews and convivial ambience (Mon–Sat 12:00–very late, Sun 17:00–late, near place Kléber at 5 rue de la Lanterne, tel. 03 88 32 10 10).

Poêles de Carottes offers vegetarians respite from porky Alsatian cuisine and has a small terrace in front (big €10 salads and stir-fries, closed Sun–Mon, 2 place de Meuniers, tel. 03 88 32 33 23).

Strasbourg Connections

Strasbourg makes a good side-trip from Colmar or a stop on the way to or from Paris.

From Strasbourg by Train to: Colmar (2/hour, 35 minutes), **Reims** (TGV: 10/day, 2 hours, change at Gare Champagne-Ardennes), **Paris'** Gare de l'Est (TGV: hourly, 2.5 hours; non-TGV train: 10/day, 4 hours), **Lyon** (5/day, 5 hours), **Baden-Baden,** Germany (TGV: 3/day, 1.25 hours, change in Karlsruhe; non-TGV train: almost hourly, 70 minutes, change in Appenweier or Offenburg), **Karlsruhe,** Germany (TGV: 4/day, 40 minutes; non-TGV train: 12/day, 1-1.5 hours, most with change in Appenweier or Wissembourg), **Vienna,** Austria (9/day, 9–11 hours, 2–3 changes), **Basel,** Switzerland (TGV: 4/day, 70 minutes; non-TGV train: hourly, 2 hours).

REIMS AND VERDUN

Different as night and day, bubbly Reims and brooding Verdun offer worthwhile stops between Paris and Alsace. The administrative capital of the Champagne region, bustling, modern Reims greets travelers with cellar doors wide open. It features a lively center, a historic cathedral, and, of course, Champagne tasting. Often overlooked, quiet Verdun is famous for the lengthy and brutal World War I battles that surrounded the city and leveled the countryside, and offers an exceptional opportunity to learn about the Great War. High-speed TGV trains make both of these destinations easily accessible to travelers (particularly if coming from Paris).

Planning Your Time

Organized travelers in a hurry can see Reims and Verdun as they travel between Paris and the Alsace, though most will want an overnight (Reims is the better choice) to best appreciate the sights. Plan on most of a day for Reims and a half-day for Verdun. It's about 70 miles between the two towns, making a day trip from Reims to Verdun worth considering if you have a car—but it's too difficult by train. Day-tripping by train from Paris to Reims is a breeze, but day-tripping to Verdun requires careful planning.

Getting Around Reims and Verdun

Driving is a good option, even in the bigger city of Reims, and many find this a good place to pick up a rental car for a longer trip after leaving Paris. Reims offers excellent public transportation, with a new tramway and handy buses linking its major sights. But public transit is nonexistent in Verdun, where it's best to rent a car

Reims & Verdun Area

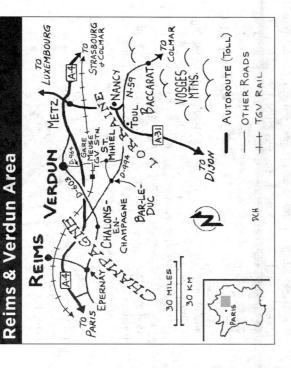

for the day or take a private tour or taxi to visit the battlefields.

Frequent high-speed TGV trains link Paris and Reims in 45 minutes, and rare direct TGV trains link Paris and Verdun in 1.75 hours. Most trains between Reims and Verdun are slow, thanks to required transfers.

Champagne's Cuisine Scene

Because traditional wines are not made here, and the Champagne drink is not often integrated into meals, cuisine in this region suffers from a lack of originality. Much like Paris, Champagne borrows from other regions' recipe books. Still, be on the lookout for anything cooked in Champagne, and try the warm dandelion salad with bacon bits (*salade de pissenlit*). *La potée champenoise* is a blood pudding made from rabbit. Ample rivers make for flavorful trout (*truite*) dishes. Ham wrapped in a pastry shell is popular in Reims, as is *andouillette* (tripe sausage). You may also find rooster cooked in Bouzy wine (*coq au vin de Bouzy*). Brie cheese, made on Champagne's border, is a good choice. Fruit-flavored brandies are a common way to end an evening.

Reims

With its Roman gate, Gothic cathedral, Champagne *caves*, and vibrant pedestrian zone, Reims feels both historic and youthful. And thanks to the TGV bullet train, it's just a 45-minute ride from Paris.

Reims (pronounced "rance," which rhymes with France) has a turbulent history: This is where 26 French kings were crowned, where Champagne first bubbled, where WWI devastation met miraculous reconstruction during the Art Deco age (all but 70 buildings were damaged in 1918), and where the Germans officially surrendered in 1945, bringing World War II to a close in Europe. The town's sights give you an entertaining peek at the entire story.

Planning Your Time

You can see Reims' essential sights in an easy day, either as a day trip from Paris or as a stop en route to or from Paris. Twelve daily TGV trains make the trip from Paris a breeze. Take a morning train from Paris and explore the cathedral and city center before lunch, then spend your afternoon below ground, in a cool, chalky Champagne cellar. You can be back at your Parisian hotel in time for a rest before dinner. Those continuing to destinations farther east find Reims a convenient place to pick up a car.

To best experience contemporary Reims, explore the busy shopping streets between the cathedral and the train station. Rue de Vesle, rue Condorcet, and place Drouet d'Erlon are most interesting.

Orientation to Reims

Reims' hard-to-miss cathedral marks the city center and makes an easy orientation landmark. Most sights of interest are within a 15-minute walk from the Reims-Centre train station. Easy-to-use loop bus routes connect the harder-to-reach Champagne *caves* with the train station and cathedral. The city is ambitiously renovating its downtown, converting large areas into pedestrian-friendly zones. A sleek new tramway line connecting the Reims-Centre train station and the nearby Champagne-Ardenne station should be open when you visit.

Tourist Information

At the TI outside the cathedral's left transept, pick up a free map of the town center and a map of the Champagne *caves* (TI open Easter-mid-Oct Mon-Sat 9:00-19:00, Sun 10:00-18:00; mid-Oct-Easter Mon-Sat 9:00-17:00, Sun 11:00-16:00; public WCs across street, tel. 03 26 77 45 00, www.reims-tourisme.com). The TI can book a visit to any *cave* that accepts visitors, and can call a taxi to get you there. Better yet, go by *cyclopolitain* (tricycle taxi) or bus (for more on both, see "Getting Around Reims," next page). Note that some of the most popular *caves* require advance booking (see "Champagne Tours and Sights" on page 976). The TI also rents pricey audioguides covering the cathedral, city center, and Art Deco architecture (single-€5, each additional set-€4, 1 hour).

Arrival in Reims

By Train: There are three different train routes from Paris' Gare de l'Est station to Reims. The fastest (and most frequent) is the direct TGV to Reims-Centre Station (12/day, 45 minutes, no baggage check at station). Check the schedule before booking to avoid slower trains.

Other TGV trains destined for Germany stop at Reims' Gare de Champagne-Ardenne train station (5 miles away). From there you can take a local TER train to Reims-Centre Station (10-minute ride). Or, if you're here after April 2011, take the new tramway; get off in Reims at the Théâtre stop—one block away from the cathedral and TI (€1, 3–4/hour, buy tickets from machines at stops, tramway ends at Reims-Centre Station).

A few "milk-run" (TER) trains run from Paris through Epernay to Reims (2/day, 2 hours), but these are only convenient if you plan to visit Epernay and Reims.

To get from Reims-Centre Station to the cathedral, it's a 15-minute walk: Head straight out of the station, cross the tree-lined boulevards Joffre and Foch, and stroll up the pedestrian place Drouet d'Erlon. Turn left on rue Condorcet, then right on rue de Talleyrand. To save a little time, you could jump on the tramway for two stops, or take the Citadine bus from the station (see "Getting Around Reims," next page) to the cathedral and to the Taittinger and Martel *caves* (described in "Champagne Tours and Sights" on page 976).

By Car: Day-trippers should take exit #24, follow *Centre-Ville* and *Cathédrale* signs, and park on the street approaching the cathedral (rue Libergier) or in the well-signed Parking Cathédrale structure (€1.50/hour). If you'll be staying the night, take exit #23 (for most of my recommended hotels), follow *Reims-Centre* and *Gare* signs, and park in the Erlon parking garage.

Helpful Hints

Laundry: A launderette is a few blocks south of the cathedral (daily 7:30–21:00, 49 rue Gambetta).

Car Rental: Avis is at the train station (closed Sat afternoon and Sun all day, cours de la Gare, toll tel. 08 20 05 05 05 or 03

26 47 10 08); **Europcar** is at 76 boulevard Lundy (toll tel. 08 25 04 52 82); and **Hertz** is at 26 boulevard Joffre (tel. 03 26 47 98 78). All three are usually open Mon–Sat 8:00–12:00 & 14:00–19:00, closed Sun.

Getting Around Reims

By Citadine Bus: Although many sights are close, most of the Champagne *caves* are a quite a hike from the main train station: Taittinger and Martel are a 30-minute walk; Pommery, Villa Demoiselle, and Veuve Clicquot Ponsardin are a 45-minute walk. Two Citadine bus lines link the historic center with these far-flung cellars in a circular route starting and ending at Reims-Centre Station (every 12 minutes, none on Sun, €1, pay driver). Line #1 does the route clockwise; line #2 does it counterclockwise. To catch the bus, cross the parking lot in front of the train station and look for the yellow Citadine bus stop before crossing the boulevard.

Citadine #1 runs to the cathedral and TI in five minutes (stop: Cathédrale), to Taittinger and Martel in 15 minutes (stop: St. Niçaise), and to Pommery and Villa Demoiselle (stop: St. Niçaise, then a 10-minute walk). To return on line #1, board at the same bus stop where you were dropped off and continue the loop back to the station. To get to Veuve Clicquot Ponsardin, ride bus #F (direction: Farman) from Reims-Centre Station to the Droits de l'Homme stop (4/hour, 20 minutes). Bus line #K also runs from the station (catch it across the street from Hertz car rental, direction: Béthany), getting you close to the Mumm Champagne *cave* (stop: Justice).

By Tramway: Opening in April of 2011, the new tramway connects the two TGV stations, Reims-Centre and TGV Champagne-Ardenne (5 miles apart), and serve a few key stops in town. Trams are expected to run about every seven minutes and cost the same as a bus ticket (€1). To get from Reims-Centre Station to the cathedral, take the tram two stops (direction: Hôpital or Gare Champagne) to Théâtre and walk one block to the cathedral.

By Taxi: A ride from the train station to the farthest Champagne *cave* will cost you about €13. To return, ask the staff at the *caves* to call you a taxi (tel. 03 26 47 05 05). Warning: The meter starts running once they are called, so count on €5 extra for the return trip.

By Cyclopolitain Tricycle: In the summer months, these modern, lightweight, electric tricycles carry one or two passengers and function like taxis, but for shorter trips. The young drivers (called Cyclonautes) speak some English and are happy to take you anywhere within the city limits (€2 per person per trip, €20 for 30-minute tour; flag one down, have the TI call for you, or call

Reims

MUSEUM OF THE SURRENDER

AVE. ROOSEVELT

R. FRANKLIN

R. DE LAON

PORTE DE MARS

BLVD. DU CHAMP DE MARS

MUMM

PLACE DE LA REPUBLIQUE

BLVD. LUNDY

POST CERES

R. ROUSSEAU

R. DE MARS

R. SARR.

R. THIERS

COURS J.B. LANG.

R. TALLEYRAND

PLACE ARISTIDE BRIANDE

BLVD. VOLTAIRE

CATHEDRAL

PALAIS DU TAU & CARNEGIE LIBRARY

RUE CHANZY

PASTEUR

V. HUGO

HENRI

TAITTINGER

CREN.

LUM.

PL. DROITS L'HOMME

70

MARTEL

CERF

SIMON

ST. REMI

ST. REMI BASILICA

BLVD. HENROT

L'UNIVERSITE

R. BARBATRE

R. DE VENISE

GAMBETTA

RUE DU JARD

BLVD. HENRI

CANAL DE L'AISNE A LA MARNE

A-4 E-50

ST. REMI EXIT

REIMS-CENTRE TRAIN STATION

BLVD. JOFFRE

BLVD. FOCH

R. LECLERC

R. ROEDERER

BURELIETTE

R. THILLOIS

R. VESLE

R. LIBERGIER

R. CHATIVESLE

R. NOEL

R. DR.

AV. D'ERLON

BLVD. P. DOUMER

AUTOROUTE

CATHEDRALE EXIT

DCH

400 YARDS
400 METERS

Ⓑ CITADINE BUS STOPS
Ⓟ PARKING
PEDESTRIAN ZONE

1 Grand Hôtel Continental & Micro Brasserie les 3 Brasseurs
2 Grand Hôtel du Nord & L'Apostrophe Rest.
3 Bénédicte et Claude Philippon B&B
4 Claudine Larcher B&B
5 Brasserie du Boulingrin
6 Au Plat du Jour
7 Café du Palais
8 Europcar Car Rental
9 Hertz Car Rental
10 Parking Cathédrale
11 Parking Erlon
12 Laundry
13 Veuve Clicquot Ponsardin
14 To Vranken Pommery & Villa Demoiselle

direct at 06 27 95 54 72). If you take a tour, it'd be nice to tip €2-3; otherwise there's no need to tip for simple transport from point to point.

Sights in Reims

▲▲▲Reims Cathedral

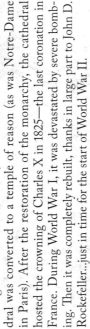

The cathedral of Reims, begun in 1211, is a glorious example of Gothic architecture, and one of Europe's greatest churches. Clovis, the first king of the Franks, was baptized at a church on this site in A.D. 496, establishing France's Christian roots that hold firm today. Since Clovis' baptism, Reims' cathedral has served as *the* place for the coronation of 26 French kings and queens—allowing it to play a more important role in France's political history than Paris' Notre-Dame cathedral. A self-assured Joan of Arc led a less-assured Charles VII to be crowned here in 1429. The French rallied around their new king to push the English out of France and to finally end the Hundred Years' War. During the French Revolution, the cathedral was converted to a temple of reason (as was Notre-Dame in Paris). After the restoration of the monarchy, the cathedral hosted the coronation of Charles X in 1825—the last coronation in France. During World War I, it was devastated by severe bombing. Then it was completely rebuilt, thanks in large part to John D. Rockefeller...just in time for the start of World War II.

Cost and Hours: Free, daily 7:30-19:30.

۞ Self-Guided Tour: Stand on the square in front of the cathedral and admire perhaps the best **west portal** anywhere, with more than 2,000 statues festooning its walls inside and out. (Medieval churches face east, toward the Holy Land, so you almost always enter through a church's west portal.) Like the cathedrals in Paris and in Chartres, this church is dedicated to "Our Lady" (Notre Dame). Statues depicting the crowning of the virgin take center stage on the facade. For eight centuries Catholics have prayed to the "Mother of God," kneeling here to ask her to intervene with God on their behalf. In 1429, Joan of Arc received messages from Mary encouraging her to rally French troops against the English at the Siege of Orléans.

Notice the **flying buttresses** soaring from the sides of the church. These massive "beams" are critical to supporting this structure. The pointed arches inside the church push the weight of the roof outward, rather than downward. The "flying" buttresses support the roof by pushing back inward, creating a delicate balance between the two forces. Gothic architects learned by trial and error—many church roofs caved in as they tested their theories and strove to build ever higher. Work on this cathedral began decades after the Notre-Dame cathedrals in Paris and Chartres, allowing architects to take advantage of what they'd learned from those magnificent earlier structures.

Contemplate the lives of the people who built this huge building, starting in 1211. Construction on a scale like this required a wholesale community effort—all hands on deck. Most townsfolk who participated donated their money or their labor knowing that neither they, nor their children, nor their children's children, would ever see it completed—such was their pride, dedication, and faith. Imagine the effort it took to raise the funds and manage the workforce. Master masons supervised, while the average Jean did much of the sweat work. Labor was something even the poorest medieval peasant could donate generously.

Walk inside. The weight of the roof is supported by a few towering columns that seem to sprout crisscrossing pointed arches. This technique allowed the church to grow higher, and liberated the walls to become window frames. Now, look back at the entry wall, with 120 statues filling the niches. The **rose window** (high above on this wall) contains the best original stained glass in the church (from 1255, removed during World War I to be spared destruction). Most of the windows are clear and newer: 18th- and 19th-century tastes called for more light, and the original, dark stained glass was replaced.

The **south transept windows**, destroyed in World War I, were replaced in 1954 by the local Champagne-makers. The windows show the connection of the Champagne industry to this town and its church with scenes portraying the tending of vines (left), the harvest (center), and the time-honored double-fermentation process (right). Notice, around the edges, the churches representing all the grape-producing villages in the area.

The **apse** (east end, behind the altar) holds a luminous set of Marc Chagall stained-glass windows from 1974. Chagall's inimitable style lent itself to stained glass, and he enjoyed opportunities to adorn great churches with his windows. The left window shows scenes from the Old Testament, and the center features the resurrection of Christ. On the right the tree of Jesse is extended to symbolically include the royalty of France—both affirming the divine power of the monarchs and stressing the responsibility to rule with wisdom and justice. Helpful English explanations offer historical detail.

Palais du Tau—This former Archbishop's Palace, named after the Greek letter T *(tau)* for its shape, houses artifacts from the cathedral (with scant English information). You'll look into the weathered eyes of original statues from the cathedral's facade (taken in from the acidic open air for their own preservation). A set of precious tapestries, telling stories from the life of Mary, are the originals that warmed the walls of the cathedral's choir in the 16th century. Reims hosted the last French coronation—that of Charles X in 1825. Because the coronation jewels, vestments, and other garb were lost a generation earlier in the French Revolution, what you see here was mostly made especially for this event (€7, May–Aug Tue–Sun 9:30–18:30, Sept–April Tue–Sun 9:30–12:30 & 14:00–17:30, closed Mon, tel. 03 26 47 81 79).

More Sights in Reims

▲Museum of the Surrender (Musée de la Reddition)—

World War II buffs enjoy visiting the historic room where the Germans signed the document of surrender of all German forces in the early morning of May 7, 1945. The news was announced the next day, turning May 8 into Victory in Europe (V-E) Day. Anyone interested in World War II will find the extensive collection of artifacts fascinating (particularly the ticker tape with the happy news, old photos, and a worthwhile 10-minute video shown on request). The room of the signing still has the maps with troop positions on the walls and the 13 chairs with name tags, each in its original spot (€3, Wed–Mon 10:00–12:00 & 14:00–18:00, closed Tue, 12 rue Franklin Roosevelt, tel. 03 26 47 84 19).

Porte de Mars—The last vestige of Reims' ancient Roman heritage—an entry gate—is a short walk from the Reims-Centre train station. The Porte de Mars, built in the second century A.D., was one of four principal entrances into the ancient Gallo-Roman town and the only one still standing. Inspired by triumphal arches that Rome built to herald war victories, this one was constructed to celebrate the Pax Romana (a period of peace and stability—after all of Rome's foes were vanquished). Unlike most of the rest of town, the Porte was undamaged in World War I, but it bears the marks of other eras, such as its integration into the medieval ramparts. Find the ruts under the arcade that guided chariots, and look for the depiction of the legend of Romulus and Remus (extremely faint on ceiling under left arch), complete with suckling she-wolf, from which Reims gets its name (free, always open, place du Boulingrin).

▲**Carnegie Library (Bibliothèque Carnegie)**—The legacy of the Carnegie Library network, funded generously by the 19th-century American millionaire Andrew Carnegie and his steel fortune (notice the American flag above the main entrance on the left), extends even to Reims. Built in the flurry of inter-war reconstruction, this beautiful Art Deco building still houses the city's public library. Entrance is free and

it's just behind the cathedral—it's worth a quick look. Visitors are welcome to admire the mosaics, onyx-laden entrance hall, and Jacque Simon chandelier, but are asked not to enter the reading room (some come here to study). Peek through the reading room door to admire the stained-glass windows of this temple of thinking. The gorgeous wood-paneled card-catalogue room takes older visitors back to their childhoods (notice how each card is tediously typed), or even back to 1928, the year the library was inaugurated (free; Tue, Wed, and Fri 10:00–13:00 & 14:00–19:00, Thu 14:00–19:00, Sat 10:00–13:00 & 14:00–18:00, closed Sun–Mon; place Carnegie).

Art Deco on Place Drouet d'Erlon—Place Drouet d'Erlon is a long street-like square marking the commercial center of town. (From the train station, it's directly across the park-like boulevards.) The square's centerpiece, a fountain with a winged figure of victory at the top, celebrates the major rivers of this district. It hasn't worked as a fountain since WWI bombings—a reminder of the devastation brought on this city. All around you'll see the stylized features—geometric reliefs, motifs in iron work, rounded corners, and simple concrete elegance—of Art Deco. The only hints that this was once a Middle Ages town are the narrow lots that struggle to fit today's buildings. Pop into the Waida Pâtisserie (closed Mon, 3 place Drouet d'Erlon) for a pure, typical Art Deco interior. As you stroll about, keep an eye open for "Biscuits Roses"—light, rose-colored egg-and-sugar cookies that date from 1756. They're the locals' favorite munchie to accompany a glass of Champagne—you're supposed to dunk them, but I like them dry (most places that sell the treat offer free samples).

Champagne Tours and Sights

In Reims

▲▲**Champagne Tours**—Reims is the capital of the Champagne region. Although the bubbly stuff's birthplace is closer to Epernay, you can tour several interesting Champagne *caves* right in Reims. All charge for tastings and most are open daily. Most have a few daily English tours, but some require a reservation. Call in advance or email from home before your trip for the schedule and to secure a spot on a tour. Martel offers the most personal and best-value tour. Pommery and Villa Demoiselle have the most impressive cellars. Veuve Clicquot is very popular with Americans and fills up three weeks in advance. Bring a sweater, even in summer, as the *caves* are cool and clammy.

Mumm ("moome"): This *cave* is closest to the train station (15-minute walk) and welcomes the public without reservations. Its "traditional visit" (€10, 1 hour) includes a good 10-minute video, a small museum of old Champagne-making contraptions, and a tour of its industrial-size, modern-feeling chalk cellars where 25 million bottles are stored. The video explains the place's history back to 1827 and the Champagne-making process with the enthusiasm of an advertisement ("Cordon Rouge is dedicated to the audacity and passion of exceptional men and women, with a subtle balance between freshness and intensity"). The tour ends with a glass of bubbly Cordon Rouge. You can pay more for the same tour with extra "guided" tastings—€15 for two tastes, or €20 for three (tours depart March–Oct daily 9:00–11:00 & 14:00–17:00; Nov–Feb weekdays by reservation only, Sat 9:00–11:00 & 14:00–17:00, closed Sun; tel. 03 26 49 59 69, www.mumm.com, guides@mumm.com). Mumm is four blocks left out of the train station, on the other side of place de la République at 34 rue du Champ de Mars (also accessible by bus line #K from the train station). Visits begin in the building on the right, #34, at the end of the courtyard. Follow *Visites des Caves* signs.

Taittinger (tay-tan-zhay): This is one of the biggest and most renowned of Reims' *caves*. They run a few morning and after-noon tours in English through their impressive cellars (show up early or call for times and to reserve a spot, about 20–30 people per tour). After seeing their 10-minute promo-movie (hooray for Taittinger!), follow your guide—mine reminded me of an old-time airline hostess—for 45 chilly minutes and 80 steps down to a chalky underworld of *caves*, the deepest of which were dug by ancient Romans. You'll tour part of the three miles of *caves*, pass some of the three million bottles stored here, and learn all you need to know about the Champagne process from your well-informed guide. Popping corks signal when the tour's done and the tasting's begun (€10, includes tasting, 1 hour, tours daily mid-March–mid-

Nov 9:30–12:00 & 14:00–16:30, closed weekends off-season, 9 place St. Nicaise, tel. 03 26 85 84 33, www.taittinger.com).

Martel: This offers a homey contrast to Taittinger's big-business style. It's a small operation with less extensive *caves* and is *sans* doubt the best deal in town. Call to set up a visit and expect a small group that might be yours alone. Friendly Emmanuel runs the place with a relaxed manner. Only 20 percent of their product is exported (mostly to Europe), so you won't find much of their Champagne in the US. Their €9, 45-minute visit focuses on the basics and includes an informative 10-minute film and a tour of their small cellars peppered with rusted, old wine-making tools. It culminates with a tasting of three different Champagnes in a casual living-room atmosphere (tours depart daily 10:00–18:00, no reservations, open through lunch, 17 rue des Créneaux, tel. 03 26 82 70 67, www.champagnemartel.com, boutique@champagne martel.com).

Getting to Taittinger and Martel: These two places are a few blocks apart, about 30 minutes by foot southeast of the cathedral. It's easiest and cheap by Citadine bus (see "Getting Around Reims" on page 970). A handy Citadine stop is just behind the cathedral (find the yellow stop a block to the left at the rear of the cathedral and take #1). Get off at stop St. Nicaise (stops are digitally displayed on the bus or ask driver) and you'll see the long walls of Taittinger and the green sign to little Martel. If you take a taxi from the train station, figure on €10 one way (cellars will call a cab for you after the tour); the return fare will be a little more. In summer, you can go by *cyclopolitain* tricycle taxi for €2 per person. If you walk, take rue de l'Université (from behind the cathedral's right transept), then rue du Barbâtre.

Vranken Pommery, Villa Demoiselle, and Veuve Clicquot Ponsardin: The next three *caves* are more difficult to reach without a car, require reservations, and are darn pricey (non-drivers should see "Getting Around Reims" on page 970). They are also among the most impressive of Reims' cellars.

Vranken Pommery is a massive domaine. They say reservations are required, but it's easy to get a same-day spot on a tour if you call early. Choose between a one-hour tour of the chalk cellars or a 30-minute Cliffs Notes version (€5 less). All tours finish with a tasting (prices depend on how many glasses you'd like: one glass–€17, two glasses–€21, one glass of the really good stuff–€30). The tour starts with a long, regal staircase down into the cool *caves*. Here, thousands of bottles rest in Gallo-Roman chalk quarries, each 100 feet deep, with glass skylights at ground level. These ancient "underground cathedrals" make it easier to endure the robotic tour guide and spiels lauding Pommery (daily April–mid-mid-Nov 9:30–19:00, mid-Nov–March 10:00–18:00, 5 place du Général

Gouraud, tel. 03 26 61 62 56, www.pommery.com, domaine @vrankenpommery.fr).

Villa Demoiselle, across the street, is also owned by Champagne mogul Vranken, but serves up a different brand. Instead of chalk caves, here you'll tour a beautifully restored Art Nouveau home. Built in the early 1900s, it was bought in 2002 by Vranken, a Belgian who now owns the second-largest Champagne empire in France. It's only been open to the public since 2009. Tours in English are fewer here, but all finish in the tasting room veranda; call or email in advance for the schedule (1-hour tour–€17-25, 30-minute tour–€5 less, prices depend on how many tastings you take, 54 boulevard Henry Vasnier, tel. 03 26 35 80 50, www .champagne-demoiselle.fr, villademoiselle@vrankenpommery.fr).

Veuve Clicquot Ponsardin is widely exported in the US and is popular with American travelers. Reservations are required and fill up three weeks in advance, so book early (easy by email) before you start your trip. They offer a one-hour *cave* visit followed by a one-glass tasting (€16, or €25 for "La Grande Dame" Champagne) or a two-hour tour with a four-glass tasting paired with cheese (€75, April–Oct Tue–Sat 10:30–12:30 & 13:30–18:00, closed Sun–Mon; Nov–March Tue–Fri only, 1 place des Droits de l'Homme, tel. 03 26 89 53 90, www.veuve-clicquot.com, visitscenter@veuve -clicquot.fr).

Near Reims: Route de la Champagne

Drivers can joyride through the pretty Montagne de Reims area just south of Reims and experience the chalky soil and vines that produce Champagne's prestigious wines. At the Reims TI, ask for maps of the Route de la Champagne and *The Discovery Guide* for the Marne region. Roads are clearly marked: Follow signs for *Route Touristique de la Champagne.* The only rail-accessible destination along this route is Epernay.

There are thousands of small-scale producers of Champagne in these villages—unknown outside of France and producing fine-quality Champagne at less cost and without the brand names of the big houses in Reims and Epernay. Visiting these small-time producers (known as *récoltant manipulant* because they harvest the grapes themselves and make wine only from their own grapes) requires a little more planning and perhaps the help of a hotelier or TI, but usually pays off with a more intimate, rewarding cultural experience.

Though most village wineries require a reservation to tour their cellars, a few places are open daily for drop-in tastings. And from April to October, an organization called Les Vignerons Indépendents de Champagne (Independent Winemakers of Champagne) organizes open-house events and tastings (Sat–Sun only, usually 3–4 different wineries a day, tel. 03 26 59 55 22, www .vignerons-independants-champagne.com, contact@vignerons -independants-champagne.com).

Self-Guided Driving Tour: For an afternoon ramble though the vineyards from Reims, try this two- to three-hour loop drive (including stops). Leave Reims on A-4 (direction: Châlons-en-Champagne), then exit south to Cormontreuil on D-9, following signs to *Louvois*, then to the perfectly named village of Bouzy (on D-34, 30-minute drive from Reims).

There are 30 producers of Champagne in little **Bouzy** alone, some of whom are also known for their Bouzy Rouge (a red wine made only from Pinot Noir grapes, and not made every year). To sample the local sauce, try **Champagne Herbert Beaufort**, a rare place that allows tastings without advance reservations (although you do need to reserve to visit the cellar). Check out the list of what's open to taste at the bar, and admire the antique wine press. You'll probably be served by Monsieur Beaufort himself (free tastings, Mon–Fri 9:30–11:30 & 14:00–17:30, Sat 9:30–12:00 & 14:30–17:00, Sun 10:00–12:30 only, first *domaine* on your left coming from Louvois at 28 rue de Tours, tel. 03 26 57 01 34, www .champagnebeaufort.fr).

Before leaving Bouzy, find the **viewpoint** over the vineyards (follow signs uphill for *pointe de vue*; 3 minutes by car). Picnickers will find a bakery in Bouzy and a small grocery in the next village (Ambonnay).

Continue toward Epernay, through Condé-sur-Marne (less interesting), and along the Marne river on D-1, by a chalk quarry, and through the town of Aÿ (pronounced "eye," this larger town boasts 100 percent Grand Cru Champagne from all of its vineyards).

In the next town, **Dizy** (which is what you get after too much Bouzy), follow signs up the hill to Hautvillers, a good second stop.

Hilltop **Hautvillers** ("High Village") is the most attractive hamlet in this area, with strollable lanes, houses adorned with wrought-iron shop signs, and the seventh-century abbey church housing the tombstone of the monk Dom Perignon. According to the story, in about 1700, after much fiddling with double fermentation, it was here that Dom Perignon stumbled onto the bubbly treat. On that happy day, he ran through the abbey, shouting, "Brothers, come quickly...I'm drinking stars!"

To taste your own stars, find **Hautvillers Champagne G. Tribaut**, which offers inexpensive tastes for €1–2. Ask about Ratafia (a local fortified wine served as an apéritif). You can linger over your *coupette* of bubbly in their garden as you survey a sea of vineyards. If you ask nicely, they'll let you picnic there—but you'll have to plan ahead, as there's only a bakery in town (daily 9:00–12:00 & 14:00–18:00; entering from Dizy, turn right at the main junction onto—what else?—rue du Bacchus, and drive 300 yards to 88 rue d'Eguisheim; tel. 03 26 59 40 57, www.champagne.g.tribaut.com, champagne.tribaut@wanadoo.fr).

Exit town following signs to the *Belvedere Dom Perignon* for a good viewpoint over the Marne River and canal. From here it's less than two miles to **Epernay** and the Rodeo Drive of the area, avenue de Champagne. Epernay has restaurants, hotels, and all the expected visitor services. Champagne purists will want to stop in Epernay, where the granddaddy of Champagne companies, **Moët et Chandon**, offers tours with three pricey tasting possibilities (€15 single tasting, €22–27 for 2 tastes, no reservation needed, daily mid-March–mid-Nov 9:30–11:30 & 14:00–16:30, closed weekends off-season, tel. 03 26 51 20 20, www.moet.com, visites@moet.fr). Epernay is the only Champagne town accessible by train: To reach Moët et Chandon from the Epernay train station, walk five minutes straight up rue Gambetta to place de la République, and take a left on avenue de Champagne.

True connoisseurs can continue along the *Route Touristique de Champagne* south of Epernay toward Vertus, along the Chardonnay-grape-filled **Côte des Blancs.**

Sleeping in Reims

The first two of my listings are on place Drouet d'Erlon.

$$$ Grand Hôtel Continental*** is a fine old hotel with well-priced, three-star comfort; stay-awhile public spaces; and helpful Maxeme at the desk. Rooms in the new wing are plush and modern, but smaller. Find the framed print of the original historic building before it became a hotel (classic Db–€85–109, "superior" Db–€130–159, "superior plus" Db–€185, apartments for 3–8 available, 10 percent discount for Rick Steves readers on classic rooms, 20 percent off superior and superior plus rooms, request a non-smoking room, air-con, elevator, laundry service, pricey Wi-Fi, parking–€8, 5-minute walk from train station at 93 place Drouet d'Erlon, tel. 03 26 40 39 35, fax 03 26 47 51 12, www.grandhotel continental.com, reservation@grandhotelcontinental.com).

$$ Grand Hôtel du Nord** delivers two-star comfort in high-ceilinged rooms with wide beds and old-fashioned bathrooms. It's surprisingly quiet despite being right on the square (Db–€71–79 depending on size, Tb–€87, Qb–€98, 75 place Drouet d'Erlon, tel.

Sleep Code

(€1 = about $1.25, country code: 33)

S = Single, **D** = Double/Twin, **T** = Triple, **Q** = Quad, **b** = bathroom, **s** = shower only, ***** = French hotel rating system (0-4 stars). Unless otherwise noted, credit cards are accepted and English is spoken.

To help you sort easily through these listings, I've divided the rooms into three categories based on the price for a standard double room with bath:

$$$ **Higher Priced**—Most rooms €90 or more.
$$ **Moderately Priced**—Most rooms between €60-90.
$ **Lower Priced**—Most rooms less than €60.

Prices can change without notice; verify the hotel's current rates online or by email. For other updates, see www.ricksteves.com/update.

03 26 47 39 03, fax 03 26 40 92 26, www.hotel-nord-reims.com).

$ Bénédicte et Claude Philippon Chambres d'Hôte is a good value. This delightful couple offers two comfortable, homey, and centrally located rooms on place du Chapitre (#21), 100 yards from the cathedral's left transept. Look for the yellow *Chambres d'Hôte* sign (S-€45, D-€55, T-€70, includes French breakfast, cash only, shared bathroom, fourth floor with elevator, parking on square, tel. 03 26 91 06 22, mobile 06 77 76 20 13, claude .philippon@sfr.fr).

$ Claudine Larcher's Chambres d'Hôte is another swinging deal with two traditionally decorated rooms (both with private bathrooms) and helpful, English-speaking Madame Larcher as your host (Db-€55, cash only, includes breakfast, free Wi-Fi, free parking nearby, 11 rue Ponsardin, tel. 03 26 47 32 50, cllarcher @yahoo.fr).

Eating in Reims

Find good people-watching opportunities—if not high cuisine—with the scads of restaurants on place Drouet d'Erlon. All of these recommendations make good lunch or dinner options.

L'Apostrophe, an appealing place with a snazzy-cozy interior, offers a well-presented, creative cuisine that draws a loyal clientele (€15 *plats*, €22 and €30 *menus*, look for specials, daily, 59 place Drouet d'Erlon, tel. 03 26 79 19 89).

Micro Brasserie les 3 Brasseurs is a rollicking, Alsatian-flavored microbrewery with copper vats and a young, inviting feel.

You'll get good brasserie fare and (rare in France) more beer than wine (€9–13 salads, €10–13 *plats*, €16 choucroute, daily, 73 place Drouet d'Erlon, tel. 03 26 47 86 28).

Brasserie du Boulingrin is the oldest brasserie in town, gushing with Art Deco. A Reims institution, it serves traditional French cuisine at blue-collar prices (€15–18 *plats*, €18–25 *menus*, closed Sun; 10-minute walk north of the TI or central train station at 49 rue de Mars, or take the Citadine bus #2, stop Boulingrin; tel. 03 26 40 96 22).

Au Plat du Jour, near the Martel and Taittinger *caves*, makes a useful pre- or post-Champagne-tasting option. Casually elegant, with old posters and Champagne labels adorning the walls, this is a good spot to enjoy hearty, classic French cuisine (€14–19 *plats*, €16–21 *menus*, daily but closed for lunch Sat–Sun, 219 rue Barbâtre, tel. 03 26 85 27 60).

Café du Palais is appreciated by older locals who don't mind paying a premium to eat a meal or sip coffee wrapped in 1930s ambience. Reims' most venerable café-bistro stands across from the Grand Theater (€32 *menus*, €20–30 *plats*, daily but closed for dinner Sun–Mon, 14 place Myron Herrick, tel. 03 26 47 52 54).

Reims Connections

There are two train stations in Reims (Reims-Centre and Gare Champagne-Ardennes). Most trains to/from Paris use the Reims-Centre Station, while TGV trains to/from points east (i.e., Strasbourg or Colmar) use Gare Champagne-Ardennes (5 miles from the center of Reims; frequent connection by shuttle train or—after April of 2011—tramway to Reims-Centre Station). Trains that stop at Reims-Centre don't stop at Champagne-Ardennes. For more on Reims' train stations, see "Arrival in Reims" on page 969.

From Reims-Centre Station by Train to: Paris' Gare de l'Est (via TGV: 12/day, 45 minutes; by slow, local train: 2/day, 2 hours), **Epernay** (12/day, 30 minutes), **Verdun** (8/day, 2–5 hours, most with change in Châlons or Metz).

From Reims' Gare Champagne-Ardennes by Train to: Paris' Gare de l'Est (via TGV: 3/day, 45 minutes), **Strasbourg** (via TGV: 10/day, 2 hours), **Colmar** (via TGV: 10/day, 3 hours, most change in Strasbourg).

Verdun

Few traces of World War I remain in Europe today, but the battlefields of Verdun provide an appropriately hard-hitting tribute to the 800,000 lives lost here in the horrific war of 1914–1918. The lunar landscape left by World War I battles is buried under thick forests. Millions of live bombs are scattered in vast cordoned-off areas—it's not unusual for French farmers or hikers to be injured by until-now-unexploded mines. Drive or ride through the eerie moguls surrounding Verdun, stopping at melted-sugar-cube forts and plaques marking spots where towns once existed. With three hours and a car, a tour (operated by the TI), or easy taxi rides, you can see the most important sights and appreciate the horrific scale of the battles. The town of Verdun is not your destination, but a starting point for your visit into the nearby battlefields.

Tourist Information

The TI is just across the river (cross pont Chausée), east of Verdun's city center on place de la Nation (April Mon–Sat 9:00–12:00 & 13:30–18:00, Sun 9:00–16:00; May–Sept Mon–Sat 8:30–12:30 & 13:30–18:30, Sun 9:00–16:00; Oct–March Mon–Sat 9:00–12:00 & 14:00–17:00, closed Sun; tel. 03 29 86 14 18, excellent website—www.tourisme-verdun.fr). The TI has a good selection of books in English, maps of the city center with English descriptions of key monuments, and maps of the battlefields. Most importantly for non-drivers, this is where tours to the battlefields depart (see page 984; drivers don't need to stop here). The TI can arrange for private guides, but you'll need your own car and must book in advance (€150/2 hours). The pleasant park across the street provides a good picnic setting and a more cheerful break from the heavy sights.

Arrival in Verdun

By Train: Scarce TGV trains serve the **Gare Meuse TGV station**, where a 30-minute shuttle bus ride (€4, leaves 5–10 minutes after train arrives) takes you to Verdun's central station (described below). This high-speed service puts the city of Verdun within 1.75 hours of Paris, but with only two direct trips a day, it's critical to confirm the schedule in advance. Less convenient trains are also available (see "Verdun Connections" at the end of this chapter) that route you through Metz or Chalóns-sur-Champagne.

Verdun's **central station,** called Verdun SNCF, is 15 minutes by foot from the TI. To reach the town center, walk straight out of the station (no baggage check), cross the parking lot and the roundabout, and keep straight down avenue Garibaldi, then follow *Centre-Ville* signs on rue St. Paul. (You'll pass a grocery store and a recommended car-rental agency soon after leaving the station.) Turn left on the first traffic-free street in the old center (rue Chausée, good lunch options) and walk past the towers and across the river to the TI.

By Car: Drivers can bypass the town center and TI and head straight for the battlefields. Follow signs reading *Verdun Centre-Ville*, then signs toward *Longwy*, then find signs to *Douaumont* and *Champs de Bataille* (battlefields) on D-112, then D-913. By following signs for *Fort de Douaumont* and *Ossuaire*, you'll pass Memorial–Musée de Fleury, your first stop. To reach the TI, follow signs to *Centre-Ville*, then *Office du Tourisme* (you'll pass the TI just before crossing the river).

Getting Around the Verdun Battlefields

The battlefield remains are situated on both sides of the Meuse River; the *rive droite* (right bank)—where we'll go—has more sights.

Verdun has sparse train service—plan your arrival and departure carefully. Once here, you have three choices for touring the battlefields:

By Car: Dirt-cheap car rental is available a block from the train station at **AS Location** (about €44/day with 100 km/60 miles included—easily enough to do the battlefields, Mon-Fri 8:30–12:00 & 14:00–18:00, no office hours Sat-Sun but pre-booked rentals possible, 22 rue Louis Maury, tel. 03 29 86 58 58 or 06 08 91 81 71, fax 03 29 86 26 55). Book ahead if possible, though they usually have cars available.

By Tour: Verdun's TI offers four-hour group tours of the battle sites described in this section. Though the tour is in French, the guides usually speak a little English (€29, includes entry fees and transportation, reserve ahead and save €2, May–mid-Sept departures Mon–Sat at 14:00, none on Sun; see "Tourist Information," earlier).

By Taxi: For about €40 round-trip, taxis can drop a carload at one sight and pick up at another (walk between sights). Ask to be dropped off at the Mémorial–Musée de Fleury and picked up at the Fort de Douaumont four hours later (visiting l'Ossuaire in between); it's about two miles from one sight to the other, so expect to walk a minimum of four miles for this plan. For less walking, ask to be dropped off at l'Ossuaire and picked up at either Fort de Douaumont or Mémorial–Musée de Fleury. Taxis normally meet trains at the station; otherwise they park at the TI (taxi tel. 06 07 02 24 16). It's easiest to arrange a taxi with the help of the TI.

Self-Guided Tour

▲▲The Battlefields of Verdun

Verdun's battlefields are littered with monuments and ruined forts. For most travelers, a half-day is enough, though historians could spend days here. We'll concentrate on the three most important sights: Mémorial–Musée de Fleury, l'Ossuaire de Douaumont, and Fort de Douaumont. Each offers a different perspective on the war.

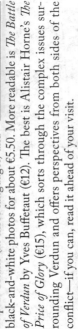

Information: Sights are adequately described in English. If you want more, the TI and all sights sell helpful books in English describing the Battle of Verdun. The simple but adequate booklet *Verdun: Images of War* provides helpful details (in three languages) and black-and-white photos for about €5.50. More readable is *The Battle of Verdun* by Yves Buffetaut (€12). The best is Alistair Horne's *The Price of Glory* (€15), which sorts through the complex issues surrounding Verdun and offers perspectives from both sides of the conflict—if you can, read it ahead of your visit.

Background: After the annexation of Alsace and Lorraine following the German victory in the Franco-Prussian War in 1871, Verdun found itself just 25 miles from the German border. This was too close for comfort for the French, who invested mightily in the fortification of Verdun, hoping to discourage German thoughts of invasion. The plan failed. World War I erupted in August of 1914, and after a lengthy stalemate, the Germans elected to strike a powerful knockout punch at the heart of the French defense, to demoralize them and force a quick surrender. They chose Verdun as their target. By defeating the best of the French defenses, the Germans would cripple the French military and morale. The French chose to fight to the bitter end. Three hundred days of nonstop trench warfare ensued. France eventually prevailed, but at a terrible cost.

Soft, forested lands hide the memories of World War I's longest battles, which raged here for over 300 days in 1916. Only small monuments remind us that they ever existed. It's difficult to imagine today's lush terrain as it was just a few generations ago...a gray, treeless, crater-filled landscape, smothered in mud and littered with shattered stone.

⊙ Self-Guided Tour: Drivers (and cabbies) leave Verdun on D-603 (direction: Logwy), then take a left on D-112 (direction: Douaumont). Take the first turnoff possible (see map, next page)

Verdun

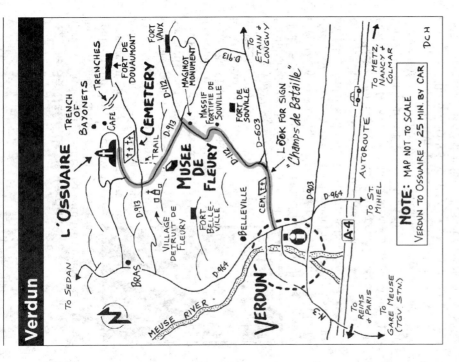

into the...

Massif Fortifié de Souville: At this parking and picnic area, find a curving trench and craters, similar to those that mark so much of the land here. A few communication trenches like this remain, though all fortified trenches were destroyed during the battles or have since been filled in. After leaving the parking area, you'll soon pass a monument to André Maginot, creator of the Maginot Line of forts erected following World War I to defend France against all future attacks from the east. Maginot was wounded during the battle of Verdun.

• Continue following signs to Ossuaire and Douaumont, turning left on D-913.

Mémorial–Musée de Fleury (Verdun Memorial): This museum makes a good first visit. It's built near the site of a village (Fleury) destroyed during the fighting. The museum provides a helpful visual presentation of this war that would see the potential of mankind's destructive creativity—machine guns, flamethrowers, poisonous gas, airplanes, and observation balloons were all first used in World War I. The museum houses a manageable number of displays of weapons, uniforms (note the French colonies' contributions), models, and photos. Its centerpiece is the re-creation of a battlefield (built by veterans of the battle), and a faded-but-worthwhile 15-minute movie (request English version or read English subtitles; less important if you see the better film at l'Ossuaire de Douaumont—described below). Look for the model of the unblemished Fort de Douaumont, and remember this when you visit the fort. Basic information is posted in English throughout the museum (€7, daily April–mid-Nov 9:00–18:00, mid-Nov–mid-Dec and Feb–March 9:00–12:00 & 14:00–18:00, closed mid-Dec–Jan).

• *From the museum, look for signs leading to the* Village Détruit de Fleury.

Village Détruit (Destroyed Village) de Fleury: Detour in and find the church, then locate the public fountain plaque (the heart of the village) and the plaques with names of original residents and their occupations. Thirteen area villages like this one were caught in the battles and obliterated, never to be resurrected (signposted as *Villages Détruits*). Though gone, these villages have not been forgotten: Nine still have mayors and city councils.

• *Next, follow signs to the tall, missile-like building....*

L'Ossuaire de Douaumont: This is the tomb of 130,000 French and Germans whose last homes were the muddy trenches of Verdun. (Drivers can park at the rear.) The artillery shell-shaped tower and cross design of this building symbolizes war and peace. Look through the low windows for a bony memorial to those whose political and military leaders asked them to make the "ultimate sacrifice" for their countries. The building has 22 sections with 46 granite graves, each holding remains from a different sector of the battlefield. Enter down the steps and start with the thought-provoking 20-minute film that remains relevant today (€4, ask for English headphones—you can adjust volume). The little picture boxes in the gift shop are worth a look if you don't visit Mémorial–Musée de Fleury. Climb upstairs and experience a humbling and moving tribute to the soldiers who were convinced that this war would end all wars and that their children would grow up in a world at peace. The red lettering on the walls lists a soldier's name, rank ("Lt" is lieutenant, "Cal" is corporal, "St" is sergeant), regiment, and dates of birth and death. Skip the 204 steps up the tower (daily April–June 9:00–18:00, July–Aug 9:00–18:30, March and Sept–Nov 9:00–12:00 & 14:00–17:00 or 17:30, Dec and Feb 14:00–17:00, closed Jan, tel. 03 29 84 54 81).

Walk out to the **cemetery** and listen for the eerie buzz of silence and peace. Reflect on a war that ruined an entire generation, leaving half of all Frenchmen aged 15 to 30 dead or wounded. Rows of 15,000 Christian crosses and Muslim headstones (oriented toward Mecca), all with roses, decorate the cemetery. Moroccan soldiers were instrumental in France's ultimate victory at Verdun, a fact often overlooked by anti-immigration, right-wing politicians in France today.

Looking over the cemetery from above, the road on the lower left leads 1.5 miles to Fort de Douaumont (described next). Also to the left, but behind you, a road leads to a good little café, **Abri des Pèlerins** (salads, omelets, €14 *menu*, March–Nov daily until 18:00, tel. 03 29 85 50 58). Although it's too far for walkers and there's not much to see there now, those interested can continue down the road to **Tranchée des Baïonnettes** (Trench of Bayonets). Here, an entire company of soldiers was buried alive in their trench (the soldiers' bayonets remained aboveground for decades). The bulky concrete monument to this tragic event was donated by the US. *"Leurs frères d'Amérique"* translates as "Brothers from America."
• *Now head for…*

Fort de Douaumont: This was the most important stronghold in the network of forts built to protect Verdun after the annexation of Alsace and Lorraine to Germany in 1871. First constructed in 1882, it was built into the hillside and ultimately served as a strategic command center for both sides at various times. Soldiers were protected by a thick layer of sand (to muffle explosions) and a wall of concrete five to seven feet thick. In spite of this, German shelling in 1916 rocked the structure, leaving it useless. Inside, there's little to see except two miles of cold, damp hallways. Experiencing these corridors will add to your sympathy for the soldiers who were forced to live here like moles (€3, ask for English descriptions, daily May–Aug 10:00–18:30, April and Sept until 18:00, Oct until 17:30, Nov–Dec and Feb–March until 17:00, closed Jan). Climb to the bombed-out top of the fort and check out the round, iron-gun emplacements that could rise and revolve.

Between l'Ossuaire and Fort de Douaumont, on either side of the road, you'll pass what remains of the London Communication Trench. This served as a means of communication and resupply for the Fort de Douaumont. Notice the concrete-reinforced sides. You'll see the ruins of several *abri* (shelters) on the hillside above the trench—these provided safe haven for the trench's soldiers.

Sights in Verdun

Unless you're arriving by train and have some time to spare, there's no reason to visit central Verdun's sights. The severe **Victory Monument** (Monument à la Victoire) is a block from the river, overlooking the pedestrian zone. Seventy-three steps follow a watery path to a crypt storing records of the soldiers who fought here (both French and German). The **Citadelle Souterraine** offers a disappointing walk through the tunnels of the French Command. And though it tries to re-create the Battle of Verdun scene, it's not worth your time or money (€6, daily April-Sept 9:00–18:00—except July-Aug until 19:00, March and Oct-Nov 9:30–17:00, Feb and Dec 10:00–12:00 & 14:00–17:00, closed Jan, last entry 45 minutes before closing).

Near Verdun

St-Mihiel—To better understand the American role in the battles, drive 17 miles south of Verdun to the town of St-Mihiel. Here, American and French forces joined in 1918 under the command of General John Pershing, in hopes of breaking the Germans' will by gaining the important city of Metz. The joint attack on the St-Mihiel salient (a salient is territory surrounded on three sides by the enemy) caught the Germans by surprise and was initially successful, but later became bogged down by poor roads and related supply problems. The Americans didn't make it to Metz, and the Germans were able to regroup and hunker down.

Today at St-Mihiel, you can see the best examples of WWI trenches in the Verdun region (some are reconstructions) and appreciate how close the opposing trenches were to one another. You can also visit the St-Mihiel American Cemetery and Memorial at Thiaucourt (with 4,153 graves), appreciate views over the battlefields from the Montsec Monument (marks the conquest of St-Mihiel by the First US Army), and see the ruins of several forts. There is no TI in St-Mihiel, so get informed at Verdun's TI before you head out.

Eating in Verdun

You'll find several inexpensive restaurants in the pedestrian zone and along the river. There's also a good café near l'Ossuaire in the battlefields, **Abri des Pelerins.**

Verdun Connections

Remember, a few high-speed TGV trains serve the Verdun area from the Gare Meuse TGV station, 30 minutes south of Verdun, whereas non-TGV trains run to Verdun's central station. For TGV connections listed below, allow an additional 30 minutes to reach Verdun's central station by shuttle bus (€4).

From Verdun by Train to: Strasbourg (9/day, 3–4 hours, most change in Metz), **Colmar** (8/day, 4–5 hours, possible changes

FRANCE:
PAST AND PRESENT

"La Marseillaise"

There's a movement in France to soften the lyrics of their national anthem. Sing it now...before it's too late.

Allons enfants de la Patrie, (Let's go, children of the motherland,)
Le jour de gloire est arrivé. (The day of glory has arrived.)
Contre nous de la tyrannie (The blood-covered flag of tyranny)
L'étendard sanglant est levé. (Is raised against us.)
L'étendard sanglant est levé. (Is raised against us.)
Entendez-vous dans les campagnes (Do you hear these ferocious soldiers)

Mugir ces féroces soldats? (Howling in the countryside?)
Qui viennent jusque dans nos bras (They're nearly in our grasp)
Egorger vos fils et vos compagnes. (To slit the throats of your sons and your women.)

Aux armes citoyens, (Grab your weapons, citizens,)
Formez vos bataillons, (Form your battalions,)
Marchons, marchons, (March on, march on,)
Qu'un sang impur (So that their impure blood)
Abreuve nos sillons. (Will fill our trenches.)

French History in an Escargot Shell

About the time of Christ, Romans "Latinized" the land of the Gauls. With the fifth-century fall of Rome, the barbarian Franks and Burgundians invaded. Today's France evolved from this unique mix of Latin and Celtic cultures.

While France wallowed with the rest of Europe in medieval darkness, it got a head start in its development as a nation-state. In 507, Clovis established Paris as the capital of his Christian

Typical Church Architecture

History comes to life when you visit a centuries-old church. Even if you wouldn't know your apse from a hole in the ground, learning a few simple terms will enrich your experience. Note that not every church has every feature, and a "cathedral" isn't a type of church architecture, but rather a designation for a church that's a governing center for a local bishop.

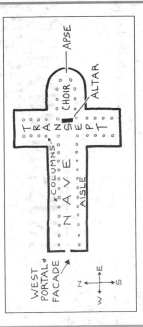

Aisles: The long, generally low-ceilinged arcades that flank the nave.

Altar: The raised area with a ceremonial table (often adorned with candles or a crucifix), where the priest prepares and serves the bread and wine for Communion.

Apse: The space beyond the altar, often bordered with small chapels.

Choir: A cozy area, often screened off, located within the church nave and near the high altar where services are sung in a more intimate setting.

Cloister: A square-shaped series of hallways surrounding an open-air courtyard, traditionally where monks and nuns got fresh air.

Facade: The outer wall of the church's main (west) entrance, viewable from outside and usually highly decorated.

Groin Vault: An arched ceiling formed where two equal barrel vaults meet at right angles. Less common usage: term for a medieval jock strap.

Narthex: The area (portico or foyer) between the main entry and the nave.

Nave: The long, central section of the church (running west to east, from the entrance to the altar) where the congregation stood through the service.

Transept: The north-south part of the church, which crosses (perpendicularly) the east-west nave. In a traditional Latin cross-shaped floor plan, the transept forms the "arms" of the cross.

West Portal: The main entry to the church (on the west end, opposite the main altar).

Merovingian dynasty. Clovis and the Franks would eventually become Louis and the French. Charles Martel stopped the spread of Islam by beating the Spanish Moors at the Battle of Poitiers. And Charlemagne ("Charles the Great"), the most important of the "Dark Age" Frankish kings, was crowned Holy Roman Emperor by the pope in 800. Charlemagne presided over the "Carolingian Renaissance" and effectively ruled a vast-for-the-time empire.

The Treaty of Verdun (843), which divided Charlemagne's empire among his grandsons, marks what could be considered the birth of Europe. For the first time, a treaty was signed in vernacular languages (French and German), rather than in Latin. This split established a Franco-Germanic divide, and heralded an age of fragmentation. While petty princes took the reigns, the Frankish king ruled only Ile de France, a small region around Paris.

Vikings, or Norsemen, settled in what became Normandy. Later, in 1066, these "Normans" invaded England. The Norman king, William the Conqueror, consolidated his English domain, accelerating the formation of modern England. But his rule also muddied the political waters between England and France, kicking off a centuries-long struggle between the two nations.

In the 12th century, Eleanor of Aquitaine (a separate country in southwest France) married Louis VII, king of France, bringing Aquitaine under French rule. They divorced, and she married Henry of Normandy, soon-to-be Henry II of England. This marital union gave England control of a huge swath of land from the English Channel to the Pyrenees. For 300 years, France and England would struggle over control of Aquitaine. Any enemy of the French king would find a natural ally in the English king.

In 1328, a French king (Charles IV) died without a son. The English king (Edward III) was his nephew and interested in the throne, but the French resisted. This quandary pitted France, the biggest and richest country in Europe, against England, which had the biggest army. They fought from 1337 to 1453 in what was modestly called the Hundred Years' War.

Regional powers from within France actually sided with England. Burgundy took Paris, captured the royal family, and recognized the English king as heir to the French throne. England controlled France from the Loire north, and things looked bleak for the French king.

Enter Joan of Arc, a 16-year-old peasant girl driven by religious voices. France's national heroine left home to support Charles VII, the dauphin (boy prince, heir to the throne but too young to rule). Joan rallied the French, ultimately inspiring them to throw out the English. In 1430 Joan was captured by the Burgundians, who sold her to the English, who convicted her of heresy and burned her at the stake in Rouen. But the inspiration of Joan of Arc lived on, and

Typical Castle Architecture

Castles were fortified residences for medieval nobles. Castles come in all shapes and sizes, but knowing a few general terms will help you understand them.

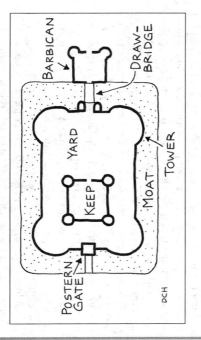

Barbican: A fortified gatehouse, sometimes a stand-alone building located outside the main walls.

Crenellation: A gap-toothed pattern of stones atop the parapet.

Drawbridge: A bridge that could be raised or lowered, using counterweights or a chain-and-winch.

Great Hall: The largest room in the castle, serving as throne room, conference center, and dining hall.

Hoardings (or Gallery or Brattice): Wooden huts built onto the

by 1453 English holdings on the Continent had dwindled to the port of Calais.

By 1500, a strong, centralized France had emerged, with borders similar to today's. Its kings (from the Renaissance François I through the Henrys and all those Louises) were model divine monarchs, setting the standards for absolute rule in Europe.

Outrage over the power plays and spending sprees of the kings, coupled with the modern thinking of the Enlightenment—whose leaders were the French *philosophes*—led to the French Revolution (1789). In France, it was the end of the *ancien régime*, as well as its notion that some are born to rule, while others are born to be ruled.

The excesses of the Revolution in turn led to the rise of Napoleon, who ruled the French empire as a dictator. Eventually, *his* excesses ushered him into a South Atlantic exile, and the French settled on a compromise role for their leader. The modern French king was himself ruled by a constitution. Rather than dress upper parts of the stone walls. They served as watch towers, living quarters, and fighting platforms.

The Keep (or Donjon): A high, strong stone tower in the center of the castle complex that was the lord's home and refuge of last resort.

Loopholes: Narrow slits in the walls (also called embrasures, arrow slits, or arrow loops) through which soldiers could shoot arrows at the enemy.

Machicolation: A stone ledge jutting out from the wall, fitted with holes in the bottom. If the enemy was scaling the walls, soldiers could drop rocks or boiling oil down through the holes and onto the enemy below.

Moat: A ditch encircling the wall, often filled with water.

Parapet: Outer railing of the wall walk.

Portcullis: A heavy iron grille that could be lowered across the entrance.

Postern Gate: A small, unfortified side or rear entrance used during peacetime. In wartime, it could become a "sally-port" used to launch surprise attacks, or as an escape route.

Towers: Tall structures serving as lookouts, chapels, living quarters, or the dungeon. Towers could be square or round, with either crenellated tops or conical roofs.

Turret: A small lookout tower projecting up from the top of the wall.

Wall Walk (or Allure): A pathway atop the wall where guards could patrol and where soldiers stood to fire at the enemy.

The Yard (or Bailey or Ward): An open courtyard inside the castle walls.

in leotards and powdered wigs, he went to work in a suit with a briefcase.

The 20th century spelled the end of France's reign as a military and political superpower. Devastating wars with Germany in 1870, 1914, and 1940—and the loss of her colonial holdings—left France with not quite enough land, people, or production to be a top player on a global scale. But the 21st century may see France rise again: Paris is once again the cultural capital of Europe, and France—under the EU banner—is a key player in integrating Europe as one unified economic power. And when Europe is a superpower, Paris may yet be its capital.

Contemporary Politics in France

Today, the key political issues in France (like everywhere) are mainly about the economy. And though the French have suffered less than the US (they didn't get involved in risky home loans and are less invested in the stock market), unemployment is high

Top French Notables in History

Madame and Monsieur Cro-Magnon: Prehistoric hunter-gatherers who moved to France (c. 30,000 B.C.), painted cave walls at Lascaux and Font-de-Gaume, and eventually settled down as farmers (c. 10,000 B.C.).

Vercingétorix (72 B.C.–46 B.C.): This long-haired warrior rallied the Gauls against Julius Caesar's invading Roman legions (52 B.C.). Defeated by Caesar, France fell under Roman domination, resulting in 500 years of peace and prosperity. During that time, the Romans established cities, built roads, taught in Latin, and converted people to Christianity.

Charlemagne (A.D. 742–814): For Christmas in A.D. 800, the pope gave King Charlemagne the title of Emperor, thus uniting much of Europe under the leadership of the Franks ("France"). Charlemagne stabilized France amid centuries of barbarian invasions. After his death, the empire was split, carving the outlines of modern France and Germany.

Eleanor of Aquitaine (c. 1122–1204): The beautiful, sophisticated ex-wife of the King of France married the King of England, creating an uneasy union between the two countries. During her lifetime, French culture was spread across Europe by roving troubadours, theological scholars, and skilled architects pioneering "the French style"—Gothic.

Joan of Arc (1412–1431): When France and England fought the Hundred Years' War to settle who would rule (1337–1453), teenager Joan of Arc—guided by voices in her head—rallied the French troops. Though Joan was captured and burned as a heretic, the French eventually drove England out of their country for good, establishing the current borders. Over the centuries, the church upgraded Joan's status from heretic to saint (canonized in 1920).

François I (1494–1547): This Renaissance king ruled a united, modern nation, making it a cultural center that hosted the Italian Leonardo da Vinci. François set the tone for future absolute monarchs, punctuating his commands with the phrase "For such is our pleasure."

Louis XIV (1638–1715): Charismatic and cunning, the "Sun King" ruled Europe's richest, most populous, most powerful nation-state. Every educated European spoke French, dressed in Louis-style leotards and powdered wigs, and built Versailles-like palaces. Though Louis ruled as an absolute monarch (distracting the nobility with courtly games), his reign also fostered the arts and philosophy, sowing the seeds of democracy and revolution.

Marie-Antoinette (1755–1793): As the wife of Louis XVI, she came to symbolize (probably unfairly) the decadence of France's ruling class. When Revolution broke out (1789), she was arrested, imprisoned, and executed—one of thousands who were guillotined on Paris' place de la Concorde as an enemy of the people.

Napoleon Bonaparte (1769–1821): This daring young military man became a hero during the Revolution, fighting Europe's royalty. He went on to conquer much of the Continent, become leader of France, and eventually rule as a dictator with the title of Emperor. In 1815, an allied Europe defeated and exiled Napoleon, reinstating the French monarchy—though future kings (including Napoleon's nephew, who ruled as Napoleon III) were subject to democratic constraints.

Claude Monet (1840–1926): Monet's Impressionist paintings captured the soft-focus beauty of the belle époque—middle-class men and women enjoying drinks in cafés, walks in gardens, and picnics along the Seine. At the turn of the 20th century, French culture reigned supreme while its economic and political clout was fading, soon to be shattered by the violence of World War I.

Charles de Gaulle (1890–1970): A career military man, de Gaulle helped France survive occupation by Nazi Germany during World War II with his rousing radio broadcasts and unbending faith in France. As president he led the country through its postwar rebuilding, divisive wars in Vietnam and Algeria (trying to preserve France's colonial empire), and turbulent student riots in the 1960s.

Contemporary French: Which recent French people will history remember? President François Mitterrand (1916–1996), the driving force behind La Grande Arche and Opéra Bastille? Marcel Marceau (1923–2007), white-faced mime? Chef Paul Bocuse (b. 1926), inventor of *nouvelle cuisine*? Brigitte Bardot (b. 1934), film actress, crusader for animal rights, and popularizer of the bikini? Yves Saint Laurent (1936–2008), one of the world's greatest fashion designers? Jean-Marie Le Pen (b. 1928), founder of the far-right Front National party, with staunch anti-immigration policies? Bernard Kouchner (b. 1939), co-founder of Doctors without Borders and minister of foreign affairs under President Sarkozy? Or Zinédine Zidane (b. 1972), France's greatest soccer player ever, whose Algerian roots helped raise the status of Arabs in France?

(about 10 percent) and taxes are higher (about 44 percent of the gross domestic product). Other French concerns are the cultural strains caused by a steadily increasing percentage of ethnic minorities (10 percent of France's population is of North African descent), the extent of the European Union's power, and balancing cushy workers' benefits against the need to compete in a global marketplace. The challenge for the French leadership is to address these issues while maintaining the level of social services that the French expect from their government.

France is part of the 27-member European Union (a kind of "United States of Europe") that has successfully dissolved borders and implemented a single currency, the euro. France's governments have been decidedly pro-EU; however, its people are more skeptical. In 2005 the French voted against ratifying an EU constitution that would have increased the EU's political powers. Many French fear that a more powerful EU would ultimately result in lost job security and social benefits (a huge issue in France).

Another controversy involves the increased presence of Muslim immigrants. The French have debated whether it makes sense to ban women from wearing head scarves and veils. Does banning the veil enforce democracy...or squelch diversity?

French national politics are complex but fascinating. The two biggest parties are President Nicolas Sarkozy's center-right Popular Movement Union (UMP) and the center-left Socialists (PS).

But unlike America's two-party system, France has many small parties, and any major player must form coalitions in order to rule. There's the MoDem (Democratic Movement) party, fighting for the center of the political landscape. To the left lie the once-powerful, now-marginal Communists (PCF); the "Green" environmental party (Les Verts); and—on the extreme left—the New Anti-Capitalists (NPA). These leftists have to work with the more centrist Socialist party to have a national voice. The French left tends to see its popularity rise when the economy is strong and fall when it's weak.

To the right of Sarkozy lies the National Front party (FN), led by 82-year-old Jean-Marie Le Pen. He campaigns on a "France for the French" platform, calling for expulsion of ethnic minorities, restoration of the French franc, and broader police powers. The situation in the country became especially tense in the fall of 2005, when disadvantaged youths (primarily of North African descent) rioted in Parisian suburbs, protesting discrimination. Although the Front Nationalists have a staunch voter base of only about 13 percent, rising unemployment and globalization worries have increased its following, allowing Le Pen to nudge the political agenda to the right. In the 2010 regional elections, Le Pen won 20 percent of the vote in his home province, and his daughter won

18 percent in hers.

The French president is elected by popular vote every five years. The prime minister is chosen by the president, then confirmed by the parliament (Assemblée Nationale), and is a very powerful position when the president's party loses its majority in parliament. With seven major parties, a single majority is rare, so it takes a coalition to confirm a prime minister. Over the past 13 years, the right has been more successful than the left in marshaling supporters. Previous President Jacques Chirac (who served two terms) and current President Sarkozy (elected in 2007) are both conservatives.

Sarkozy is pro-American (though he doesn't speak English) and pro-EU. He is tough on crime and on unchecked immigration. To address a sluggish economy, he proposes a tough-love, carrot-and-stick approach—limiting the power of unions and cutting workers' benefits, while offering tax incentives to workers who work overtime (above the current 35–39-hour workweek). His policies generate predictable resistance from unions: Expect at least one major strike somewhere in France during your trip.

More French eyebrows have been raised by Sarkozy's personal life. Within a year of becoming president, he divorced his wife of 11 years and married sexy Italian model-turned-singer Carla Bruni (who has been linked romantically with Mick Jagger and Eric Clapton). Google "Sarkozy," and you'll turn up almost as many hits for Carla. Their bedroom life is a constant topic of paparazzi gossip, as are their eccentricities. Sarkozy likes to jog, and even wears sweats when relaxing (*quelle horreur!*). The press has nicknamed Sarkozy "President Bling Bling" for his love of shiny things (Ray-Ban sunglasses, expensive watches, yachts, Italian supermodels), his jet-set lifestyle, and consorting with celebrities.

APPENDIX

Contents

Tourist Information

The French national tourist office **in the US** is a wealth of information. Before your trip, scan their website, www.franceguide.com. You can ask questions and request information (such as city maps and schedules of upcoming festivals) by emailing info.us@franceguide.com or calling 514/288-1904. Expect a small shipping fee if anything is mailed to you; note that their website offers many brochures downloadable free of charge.

In France, your best first stop in a new city is generally the tourist information office—abbreviated **TI** in this book—except in Paris, where they aren't very necessary. Throughout France you'll find TIs are well organized, with English-speaking staff. A TI is a great place to get a city map, advice on public transportation (including bus and train schedules), information on special events, and recommendations for nightlife. Most TIs will help you find a room by calling hotels (for free or for a small fee) or by giving you a complete listing of available bed-and-breakfasts. Towns with a lot of tourism generally have English-speaking guides available for private hire (about $140 for a 2-hour guided town walk). Many TIs have information on nearby regions and cities, so try to pick up maps for towns you'll be visiting later in your trip. If you're arriving in town after the TI closes, call ahead or pick up a map in a neighboring town.

The French call TIs by different names. *Office de Tourisme* and *Bureau de Tourisme* are used in cities; *Syndicat d'Initiative* or *Information Touristique* are used in small towns. Also look for *Accueil* signs in airports and at popular sights. These are information booths staffed with seasonal helpers who provide tourists with limited, though generally sufficient, information. Smaller TIs often close from 12:00 to 14:00.

Communicating

The Language Barrier and That French Attitude

You've probably heard that the French are "mean and cold and refuse to speak English." This is an out-of-date preconception left over from the days of Charles de Gaulle. Be reasonable in your expectations: French waiters are paid to be efficient, not chatty. And postal clerks are every bit as speedy, cheery, and multilingual as ours are back home.

The biggest mistake most Americans make when traveling to France is trying to do too much with limited time. This approach is a mistake in the bustling north, and a virtual sin in the laid-back south. Hurried, impatient travelers who miss the subtle pleasures of people-watching from a sun-dappled café often misinterpret French attitudes. By slowing your pace and making an effort to understand French culture by living it, you're far more likely to have a richer experience. With the five weeks of paid vacation and 35-hour work week that many French workers consider as non-negotiable rights, your hosts can't fathom why anyone would rush through their vacation.

The French take great pride in their customs, clinging to their belief in cultural superiority despite the fact that they're no longer a world superpower. Let's face it: It's tough to keep on smiling when you've been crushed by a Big Mac, Mickey Moused by Disney, and drowned in instant coffee. Your hosts are cold only if you decide to see them that way. Polite and formal, the French respect the fine points of culture and tradition. Here, strolling down the street with a big grin on your face and saying hello to strangers is a sign of senility (seriously). They think that Americans, though friendly, are hesitant to pursue more serious friendships. Recognize sincerity and look for kindness. Give them the benefit of the doubt.

French communication difficulties are exaggerated. To hurdle the language barrier, bring a small English/French dictionary, a phrase book (look for mine, which contains a dictionary and menu decoder), a menu reader (if you're a gourmet eater), and a good supply of patience (for a list of survival phrases, see page 1047). In transactions, a small notepad and pen minimize misunderstandings about prices; have vendors write the price down.

If you learn only five phrases, learn and use these: *bonjour* (good day), *pardon* (pardon me), *s'il vous plaît* (please), *merci* (thank you), and *au revoir* (goodbye). The French value politeness. Begin every encounter with: *Bonjour* (or *S'il vous plaît*), *madame* or *monsieur*. End every encounter with: *Au revoir, madame* or *monsieur*. Though many French people—especially those in the tourist trade, and in big cities—speak English, you'll get better treatment if you learn and use these French pleasantries.

When you do make an effort to speak French, expect to be politely corrected—*c'est normal*. The French are language perfectionists—they take their language (and other languages) seriously. Often they speak more English than they let on. This isn't a tourist-baiting tactic, but timidity on their part about speaking another language less than fluently. Start any conversation with: *Bonjour, madame* or *monsieur. Parlez-vous anglais?* And hope they speak more English than you speak French.

Telephones

Smart travelers use the telephone to reserve or reconfirm rooms, get tourist information, reserve restaurants, confirm tour times, or phone home. When spelling out your name on the phone, you'll find that most letters are pronounced very differently in French: *a* is pronounced "ah," *e* is pronounced "eh," and *i* is pronounced "ee." To avoid confusion, say *a*, Anne," *e*, euro," and "*i*," Isabelle."

Generally the easiest, cheapest way to call home is to use an international phone card purchased in France. This section covers dialing instructions, phone cards, and types of phones (for more in-depth information, see www.ricksteves.com/phoning).

How to Dial

Calling from the US to France, or vice versa, is simple—once you break the code. The European calling chart in this chapter will walk you through it.

Dialing Domestically Within France

France has a direct-dial 10-digit phone system (no area codes).

European Calling Chart

Just smile and dial, using this key:
AC = Area Code, LN = Local Number.

European Country	Calling long distance within …	Calling from the US or Canada to …	Calling from a European country to …
Austria	AC + LN	011 + 43 + AC (without the initial zero) + LN	00 + 43 + AC (without the initial zero) + LN
Belgium	LN	011 + 32 + LN (without initial zero)	00 + 32 + LN (without initial zero)
Bosnia-Herzegovina	AC + LN	011 + 387 + AC (without initial zero) + LN	00 + 387 + AC (without initial zero) + LN
Britain	AC + LN	011 + 44 + AC (without initial zero) + LN	00 + 44 + AC (without initial zero) + LN
Croatia	AC + LN	011 + 385 + AC (without initial zero) + LN	00 + 385 + AC (without initial zero) + LN
Czech Republic	LN	011 + 420 + LN	00 + 420 + LN
Denmark	LN	011 + 45 + LN	00 + 45 + LN
Estonia	LN	011 + 372 + LN	00 + 372 + LN
Finland	AC + LN	011 + 358 + AC (without initial zero) + LN	999 (or other 900 number) + 358 + AC (without initial zero) + LN
France	LN	011 + 33 + LN (without initial zero)	00 + 33 + LN (without initial zero)
Germany	AC + LN	011 + 49 + AC (without initial zero) + LN	00 + 49 + AC (without initial zero) + LN
Gibraltar	LN	011 + 350 + LN	00 + 350 + LN
Greece	LN	011 + 30 + LN	00 + 30 + LN
Hungary	06 + AC + LN	011 + 36 + AC + LN	00 + 36 + AC + LN
Ireland	AC + LN	011 + 353 + AC (without initial zero) + LN	00 + 353 + AC (without initial zero) + LN

European Country	Calling long distance within...	Calling from the US or Canada to...	Calling from a European country to...
Italy	LN	011 + 39 + LN	00 + 39 + LN
Montenegro	AC + LN	011 + 382 + AC (without initial zero) + LN	00 + 382 + AC (without initial zero) + LN
Morocco	LN	011 + 212 + LN	00 + 212 + LN
Netherlands	AC + LN	011 + 31 + AC (without initial zero) + LN	00 + 31 + AC (without initial zero) + LN
Norway	LN	011 + 47 + LN	00 + 47 + LN
Poland	LN	011 + 48 + LN	00 + 48 + LN
Portugal	LN	011 + 351 + LN	00 + 351 + LN
Slovakia	AC + LN	011 + 421 + AC (without initial zero) + LN	00 + 421 + AC (without initial zero) + LN
Slovenia	AC + LN	011 + 386 + AC (without initial zero) + LN	00 + 386 + AC (without initial zero) + LN
Spain	LN	011 + 34 + LN	00 + 34 + LN
Sweden	AC + LN	011 + 46 + AC (without initial zero) + LN	00 + 46 + AC (without initial zero) + LN
Switzerland	LN	011 + 41 + LN	00 + 41 + LN
Turkey	AC (if there's no initial zero, add one) + LN	011 + 90 + AC (without initial zero) + LN	00 + 90 + AC (without initial zero) + LN

- The instructions above apply whether you're calling a land line or mobile phone.
- The international access codes (the first numbers you dial when making an international call) are 011 if you're calling from the US or Canada, or 00 if you're calling from virtually anywhere in Europe (except Finland, where it's 999 or another 900 number, depending on the phone service you're using).
- To call the US or Canada from Europe, dial 00, then 1 (the country code for the US and Canada), then the area code and number. In short, 00 + 1 + AC + LN = Hi, Mom!

To make domestic calls anywhere within France, just dial the number.

For example, the number of one of my recommended hotels in Nice is 04 97 03 10 70. That's the number you dial whether you're calling it from across the street or across the country.

Dialing Internationally to or from France

If you want to make an international call, follow these steps:

1. Dial the international access code (00 if you're calling from Europe, 011 from the US or Canada).

2. Dial the country code of the country you're calling (33 for France, or 1 for the US or Canada).

3. Dial the local number. If you're calling France, drop the initial zero of the phone number (the European calling chart lists specifics per country).

Calling from the US to France: To call the Nice hotel from the US, dial 011 (the US international access code), 33 (France's country code), then 4 97 03 10 70 (the hotel's number without its initial zero).

Calling from any European Country to the US: To call my office in Edmonds, Washington, from anywhere in Europe, I dial 00 (Europe's international access code), 1 (the US country code), 425 (Edmonds' area code), and 771-8303.

Note: You might see a + in front of a European number. When dialing the number, replace the + with the international access code of the country you're calling from (00 from Europe, 011 from the US or Canada).

Public Phones and Hotel-Room Phones

To make calls from public phones, you'll need a prepaid phone card. There are two kinds of phone cards: insertable and international. Both types work only in France. If you have a live card at the end of your trip, give it to another traveler to use up. (Coin-op phones are virtually extinct.)

Insertable Phone Cards: Called a *télécarte* (tay-lay-kart), this type of card can be used only at pay phones. These cards are handy and affordable for local and domestic calls, but more expensive than international phone cards for international calls. To use the card, insert it into a slot in the pay phone. They're sold in two denominations—*une petite* costs about €7.50; *une grande* about €15—at *tabacs*, newsstands, post offices, and train stations. Though you can use a *télécarte* to call anywhere in the world, it's only a good deal for making quick local calls from a phone booth.

International Phone Cards: Called "code cards" (*cartes à code*, cart ah code), these are the cheapest way to make international calls from Europe—with the best cards, it costs literally pennies a minute. They also can be used to make local calls, and work from any type of phone, including your hotel-room phone (but ask at the front desk if you'll be charged for making toll-free calls).

The cards are sold at newsstand kiosks and tobacco shops (*tabacs*). Ask the clerk which of the various brands has the best rates for calls to America. Because cards are occasionally duds, avoid the more expensive denominations. Some shops also sell cardless codes, printed right on the receipt.

To use the card, scratch to reveal your code, then dial the free (usually 4-digit) access number. If the access code on the card doesn't work from your hotel-room phone, try the card's 10-digit, toll-free code that starts with 08. A voice in French (followed by English) tells you to enter your code. Before or after entering your code, you may need to press (or "*touche*," pronounced toosh) the pound key (#, *dièse*, dee-ehz) or the star key (*, *étoile*, eh-twahl). At the next message, dial the number you're calling (possibly followed by pound or star key; you don't have to listen through the entire sales pitch).

Remember that you don't need the actual card to use a card account, so it's shareable. You can write down the access number and code in your notebook and share it with friends.

Hotel-Room Phones: Calling from your room can be cheap for local calls (ask for the rates at the front desk first), but is often a rip-off for long-distance calls (unless you use an international phone card, explained above). Incoming calls are free, making this a cheap way for friends and family to stay in touch (provided they have a good long-distance plan for calls to Europe—and a list of your hotels' phone numbers).

US Calling Cards: These cards, such as the ones offered by AT&T, Verizon, or Sprint, are the worst option. You'll nearly always save a lot of money by using a locally purchased phone card instead.

Mobile Phones

Many travelers enjoy the convenience of traveling with a mobile phone.

Using Your Mobile Phone: Your US mobile phone works in Europe if it's GSM-enabled, tri-band or quad-band, and on a calling plan that includes international calls. Phones from T-Mobile and AT&T, which use the same GSM technology that Europe does, are more likely to work overseas than Verizon or Sprint phones (if you're not sure, ask your service provider). Most US providers charge $1.29 per minute while roaming internationally to make or receive calls, and 20–50 cents to send or receive text messages.

You'll pay cheaper rates if your phone is electronically

"unlocked" (ask your provider about this); then in Europe, you can simply buy a tiny **SIM card,** which gives you a European phone number. SIM cards are sold at mobile-phone stores and some newsstand kiosks for about $5–10, and generally include several minutes' worth of prepaid domestic calling time. When you buy a SIM card, you may need to show ID, such as your passport. Insert the SIM card in your phone (usually in a slot behind the battery), and it'll work like a European mobile phone. When buying a SIM card, always ask about fees for domestic and international calls, roaming charges, and how to check your credit balance and buy more time.

Many **smartphones,** such as the iPhone or BlackBerry, work in Europe—but beware of sky-high fees, especially for data downloading (checking email, browsing the Internet, watching videos, and so on). Ask your provider in advance how to avoid unwittingly roaming your way to a huge bill. Some applications allow for cheap or free smartphone calls over a Wi-Fi connection (see "Calling over the Internet," below).

Using a European Mobile Phone: Mobile-phone shops all over Europe sell basic phones. Phones that are "locked" to work with a single provider start at around $30; "unlocked" phones (which allow you to switch out SIM cards to use your choice of provider) start at around $60. You'll also need to buy a SIM card and prepaid credit (called à la carte in France) for making calls. When you're in the phone's home country, domestic calls are reasonable, and incoming calls are free, even if you've run out of credit. Adding credit is easy and cheap at any store selling your service plan. (My French friends tell me that SFR is a reliable French mobile-phone company.) You'll pay more if you're roaming in another country.

Calling over the Internet

Some things that seem too good to be true...actually are true. If you're traveling with a laptop, you can make calls using VoIP (Voice over Internet Protocol). With VoIP, two computers act as the phones, and the Internet-based calls are free (or you can pay a few cents to call from your computer to a telephone). If both computers have webcams, you can even see each other while you chat. The major providers are Skype (www.skype.com) and Google Talk (www.google.com/talk).

Useful Phone Numbers

Understand the various prefixes. France's toll-free numbers start with 0800 (like US 800 numbers, though in France you dial a 0 first rather than a 1). In France, these 0800 numbers—called *numéro vert* (green number)—can be dialed free from any phone without using a phone card. But you can't call France's toll-free numbers from America, nor can you count on reaching US toll-free numbers from France.

Any 08 number that does not have a 00 directly following is a toll call, generally costing €0.10–0.50 per minute.

Emergency Needs

Police: tel. 17

Emergency Medical Assistance: tel. 15

Ambulance in Paris: tel. 01 45 67 50 50 (message asks for your address and name)

Embassies and Consulates

US Consulate and Embassy in Paris: tel. 01 43 12 22 22, emergency walk-in passport services available Mon–Fri 9:00–11:00, nonemergency online appointments possible, closed Sat–Sun (4 avenue Gabriel, to the left as you face Hôtel Crillon, Mo: Concorde, http://france.usembassy.gov)

Canadian Consulate and Embassy in Paris: tel. 01 44 43 29 00, reception open daily 9:00–12:00, 14:00–17:00 (35 avenue Montaigne, Mo: Franklin D. Roosevelt, www.amb-canada.fr)

Australian Consulate in Paris: tel. 01 40 59 33 00, Mon–Fri 9:00–12:00 & 14:00–16:00, closed Sat–Sun (4 rue Jean Rey, Mo: Bir-Hakeim, www.france.embassy.gov.au)

US Consulate in Lyon: tel. 04 78 38 33 03 (1 quai Jules Courmant)

Canadian Consulate in Lyon: tel. 04 72 77 64 07 (17 rue Bourgelat)

US Consulate in Marseille: tel. 04 91 54 92 00, fax 04 91 55 09 47 (place Varian Fry, http://france.usembassy.gov/marseille.html)

US Consulate in Nice: tel. 04 93 88 89 55, fax 04 93 87 07 38 (7 avenue Gustave V, http://france.usembassy.gov/nice.html; does *not* provide visa services—Paris is the nearest office for these services)

Canadian Consulate in Nice: tel. 04 93 92 93 22, fax 04 93 92 55 51 (2 place Franklin)

US Consulate in Strasbourg: tel. 03 88 35 31 04, fax 03 88 24 06 95 (15 avenue d'Alsace)

Travel Advisories

US Department of State: tel. 202/647-5225, www.travel.state.gov

Canadian Department of Foreign Affairs: Canadian tel. 800-267-6788, www.dfait-maeci.gc.ca

US Centers for Disease Control and Prevention: tel. 800-CDC-INFO (800-232-4636), www.cdc.gov/travel

Directory Assistance

Directory Assistance for France (some English spoken): tel. 12

Collect Calls to the US: tel. 00 00 11

Trip-Planning Assistance

Detours in France: tel. 03 80 22 06 03, planning and rooms anywhere in France (www.detours-in-france.com)

Paris Webservices: tel. 01 53 62 02 29, booking service for hotels, transportation, restaurants, and other tourist activities (111 avenue Victor Hugo, www.pariswebservices.com, contactpws@parisweb services.com, helpful Gérard)

Paris Information

Tourist Information: toll tel. 08 92 68 30 00 (recorded info with long menu, €0.34/minute, www.parisinfo.com)

American Church: tel. 01 40 62 05 00 (65 quai d'Orsay, Mo: Invalides, www.acparis.org)

American Hospital: tel. 01 46 41 25 25 (63 boulevard Victor Hugo, in Neuilly suburb, Mo: Porte Maillot, then bus #82, www .american-hospital.org)

Trains

Train (SNCF) Reservations and Information: tel. 3635 (in French only)

Airports

Paris: Charles de Gaulle and Orly Airports share the same phone number (toll tel. 3950; €0.34/minute) and website (www.adp.fr).

Beauvais Airport: toll tel. 08 92 68 20 66, www.aeroportbeauvais .com

Lyon: Saint-Exupéry Airport—toll tel. 08 26 80 08 26 (€0.15/minute), www.lyon.aeroport.fr

Marseille: Aéroport Marseille–Provence—tel. 04 42 14 14 14, www.marseille.aeroport.fr

Nice: Aéroport de Nice—toll tel. 08 20 42 33 33 (€0.12/minute), www.nice.aeroport.fr

Airlines

The following 08 numbers are toll calls; the per-minute fee generally ranges from €0.10 to €0.50.

Aer Lingus: tel. 08 21 23 02 67

Air Canada: tel. 08 25 88 08 81

Air France: tel. 3654 or 08 20 82 36 54

Alitalia: tel. 08 20 31 53 15

American Airlines: tel. 01 55 17 43 41

Austrian Airlines: tel. 08 02 81 68 16

British Airways: tel. 08 25 82 54 00
Continental: tel. 01 71 23 03 35
Delta: tel. 08 11 64 00 05
easyJet: tel. 08 26 10 33 20
Iberia: tel. 08 25 80 09 65
Icelandair: tel. 01 44 51 60 51
KLM: tel. 08 92 70 26 08
Lufthansa: tel. 08 92 23 16 90
Olympic: tel. 01 44 94 58 58
Royal Air Maroc: tel. 08 20 82 18 21
SAS: tel. 08 25 32 53 35
Swiss International: tel. 08 92 23 25 01
United: tel. 08 10 72 72 72
US Airways: tel. 08 10 63 22 22

Car Leasing in France

Europe by Car: US tel. 800-223-1516, US fax 212/246-1458, www.ebctravel.com
Auto France: US tel. 800-572-9655, US fax 201/393-7800, www.autofrance.net
Kemwel: US tel. 877-820-0668, www.kemwel.com

RV Rental

French RVs are much smaller than those you see at home.
Van It: mobile 06 70 43 11 86, www.van-it.com
Idea Merge: US tel. 888-297-0001, US fax 503/296-2625, www.ideamerge.com

Hotel Chains

Accor Hotels (huge chain, including Ibis, Mercure, and Novotel): US tel. 800-221-4542, www.accorhotels.com
Ibis Hotels: toll tel. 08 92 68 66 86, US tel. 800-221-4542, www.ibishotel.com
Formule 1 Hotels: toll tel. 08 92 68 56 85 (€0.34/minute), www.hotelformule1.com,
Mercure Hotels: toll tel. 08 25 88 33 33, US tel. 800-221-4542, www.mercure.com
Kyriad Hotels: toll tel. 08 25 02 80 38, from US dial 011 33 1 64 62 59 70, www.kyriad.com,
Best Western Hotels: tel. 08 00 90 44 90, US tel. 800-780-7324, www.bestwestern.com
Château Hotels: www.chateaucountry.com
Country Home Rental: www.gites-de-france.com or www.gite.com; France Homestyle, US tel. 206/325-0132, www.francehomestyle.com, info@francehomestyle.com; Ville et Village, US tel. 510/559-8080, www.villeetvillage.com, rentals@villeetvillage.com

Youth Hostels

Hostelling International, US Office: www.hiusa.org

Hostelling International, Canada Office: www.hihostels.ca

Hotel Barges

Papillon Barge: www.hotelbarge.com, US tel. 781/631-5414, mobile 06 86 28 11 55

Barge Nilaya: www.bargenilaya.com, mobile 06 70 82 47 60

Internet Access

It's useful to get online periodically while you travel—to confirm trip plans, check train or bus schedules, get weather forecasts, catch up on email, blog or post photos from your trip, or call folks back home (explained earlier, under "Calling over the Internet").

Many hotels offer a computer in the lobby with Internet access for guests. Smaller places may sometimes let you sit at their desk for a few minutes just to check your email, if you ask politely. If your hotel doesn't have access, ask your hotelier to direct you to the nearest place to get online. Little hole-in-the-wall Internet-access shops, while common in the rest of Europe, are not prevalent in France. If you can't find an Internet café, look for a post office that offers Internet access (*cyberposte*); buy a chip-card (about same prices as phone cards, rechargeable for €4 per hour) and you're in business.

Traveling with a Laptop: With a laptop or netbook, it's easy to get online if your hotel has Wi-Fi (wireless Internet access, pronounced "wee-fee" by the French) or a port in your room for plugging in a cable. Some hotels offer Wi-Fi for free; others charge by the minute or hour. In France's key cities—Paris, Nice, Lyon, and Avignon—you'll find plenty of coffee shops that offer Wi-Fi to travelers with laptop computers. Every McDonald's in France offers free Wi-Fi (handy for drivers as McD's are omnipresent on town outskirts). A cellular modem—which lets your laptop access the Internet over a mobile phone network—provides more extensive coverage, but is much more expensive than Wi-Fi.

Mail

French post offices are sometimes called PTT, for "Post, Telegraph, and Telephone"—look for signs for *La Poste.* Hours vary, though most are open weekdays 8:00–19:00 and Saturday morning 8:00–12:00. Stamps are also sold at *tabacs.* It costs about €1 to mail a postcard to the US. Federal Express makes pricey two-day deliveries. One convenient, if pricey, way to send packages home is to use the PTT's Colissimo International XL postage-paid mailing box (allow 6 days to reach the US). It costs €36–41 to ship boxes weighing 5–7 kilos (about 11–15 pounds).

You can arrange for mail delivery to your hotel (allow 10 days for a letter to arrive), but phoning and emailing are so easy that I've dispensed with mail stops altogether.

Transportation

By Car or Public Transportation?

Cars are best for three or more traveling together (especially families with small kids), those packing heavy, and those scouring the countryside. Trains and buses are best for solo travelers, blitz tourists, and city-to-city travelers.

Train stations are usually centrally located in cities, which makes hotel-hunting and sightseeing easy. But in France, many of your destinations are likely to be small, remote places, such as Honfleur, Mont St. Michel, D-Day beaches, Loire châteaux, Dordogne caves, and villages in Provence and Burgundy. In such places, taking trains and buses can require great patience, planning, and time. If relying on public transportation, focus on fewer destinations, or hire one of the excellent minivan tour guides I recommend.

I've included two sample itineraries—by car and by public transportation—to help you explore France smoothly; you'll find these in the Introduction.

Trains

France's rail system (SNCF) sets the pace in Europe. Its super TGV (tay zhay vay; *train à grande vitesse*) system has inspired bullet trains throughout the world. The TGV runs at 170–220 mph. Its rails are fused into one long, continuous track for a faster and smoother ride. The TGV has changed commuting patterns in much of France by putting most of the country within day-trip distance of Paris.

At any train station, you can get schedule information, make reservations, and buy tickets for any destination.

Schedules

Schedules change by season, weekday, and weekend. Verify train times shown in this book—on the Web, visit http://bahn.hafas.de /bin/query.exe/en (Germany's excellent all-Europe schedule site), or check at local train stations.

Bigger stations have helpful information agents (wearing red or blue vests) roaming the station and at *Accueil* offices or booths. They can answer rail questions more quickly than the clerks at the information or ticket windows. Make use of their help; don't stand in a ticket line if all you need is a train schedule.

French Train Terms and Abbreviations

SNCF (*Société Nationale Chemins de Fer*): This is the Amtrak of France, operating all national train lines that link cities and towns.

TGV (*Train à Grande Vitesse*): SNCF's network of high-speed trains (twice as fast as regular trains) that connect major cities in France. These trains always require a reservation.

CORAIL: These trains are next best compared to the TGV in terms of speed and comfort.

TER (*Trains Express Régionale*): These trains serve smaller stops within a region. For example, you'll find trains called TER de Bourgogne (trains operating only in Burgundy) and TER Provence (Provence-only trains).

Rapide and *Express:* Trains designated as *Rapide* stop only at major cities; *Express* trains serve long-distance destinations and stop at both large and middle-sized cities.

Paris Region Only

For more on Paris transit, see "Getting Around Paris" on page 58.

RATP (*Réseau Autonome de Transport Parisienne*): This organization operates subways and buses within Paris.

Le Métro: This network of subway lines serves central Paris.

RER (*Réseau Express Régional*): This commuter rail and subway system links central Paris with suburban destinations.

Transilien: It's similar to the RER system, but travels farther afield, serving the Île de France region around Paris. Railpasses cover these lines.

Railpasses

Long-distance travelers can save money with a France Railpass, sold only outside Europe (through travel agents or Europe Through the Back Door). For roughly the cost of a full-fare Paris–Avignon–Paris ticket, the France Railpass offers three days of travel (within a month) anywhere in France. You can add up to six more days for the cost of a two-hour ride. You can save money by getting the second-class instead of the first-class version, but first class gives you more options when reserving popular TGV routes (seats are very limited for passholders, so reserving these fast trains at least several weeks in advance is recommended). The Saverpass version gives two or more people traveling together a 15 percent discount. Each day of use allows you to take as many trips as you want on one calendar day (you could go from Paris to Beaune in Burgundy, enjoy wine-tasting, then continue to Avignon, stay a few hours, and end in Nice—though I wouldn't recommend it). Buy second-

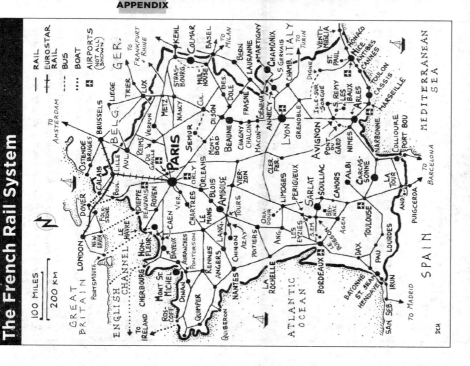

The French Rail System

RAIL
EUROSTAR RAIL
BUS
BOAT
AIRPORTS (NOT ALL SHOWN)

100 MILES
200 KM

class tickets in France for shorter trips, and save your valuable pass days for longer trips. Note that if you're connecting the French Alps with Alsace, you might travel through Switzerland, a route that requires France railpass holders to buy a ticket for that segment (about €50).

For a free summary of railpass deals and the latest prices, check my Guide to Eurail Passes at www.ricksteves.com/rail. If you decide to get a railpass, this guide will help you know you're getting the right one for your trip.

Buying Tickets

If traveling *sans* railpass, and buying tickets as you go, remember that second-class tickets provide the same transportation for up to 33 percent less than first class (and many regional trains to

Cost of Railpasses

Prices listed are for 2010 and are subject to change. For the latest prices, details, and train schedules (and easy online ordering), see my comprehensive Guide to Eurail Passes at www.ricksteves.com/rail.

"Saver" prices are per person for two or more people traveling together. "Youth" means under age 26. The fare for children 4–11 is half the adult individual fare or Saver fare. Kids under age 4 travel free.

FRANCE PASS

	Adult 1st Class	Adult 2nd Class	Senior 1st Class	Youth 1st Class	Youth 2nd Class
3 days in 1 month	$291	$248	$266	$215	$182
Extra rail days (max 6)	40–44	32–38	37–41	30–33	26–29

Senior = 60 and up.

FRANCE SAVERPASS

	1st Class	2nd Class
3 days in 1 month	$249	$214
Extra rail days (max 6)	36–38	30–31

FRANCE RAIL & DRIVE PASS

Any 2 rail days and 2 car days in 1 month.

Car Category	1st Class	Extra Car Day
Economy	$289	$47
Compact	297	55
Intermediate	309	67
Full Size	340	98
Premium Automatic	357	115
Minivan	336	94

Prices are per person, two traveling together. Solo travelers pay about $100 extra; third and fourth adults pay $207 per person. Extra rail days (3 max) cost $39 per day. To order a Rail & Drive pass, call your travel agent or Rail Europe at 800-438-7245. *This pass is not sold by Europe Through the Back Door.*

Map key:

Approximate point-to-point one-way second-class rail fares in US dollars. First class costs 50 percent more. Add up fares for your itinerary to see if a railpass will save you money.

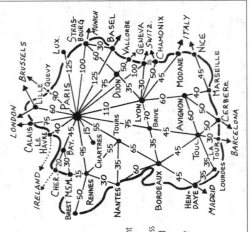

SELECTPASS

This pass covers travel in three adjacent countries. For four- and five-country options, please visit www.ricksteves.com/rail.

	Individual 1st Class	Saver 1st Class	Youth 2nd Class
5 days in 2 months	$408	$346	$266
6 days in 2 months	450	384	295
8 days in 2 months	534	456	346
10 days in 2 months	619	524	400

FRANCE–SWITZERLAND PASS

	Individual 1st Class	Saver 1st Class	Youth 2nd Class
4 days in 2 months	$360	$306	$253
Extra rail days (max 6)	42	36	28-30

FRANCE–ITALY PASS

	Individual 1st Class	Individual 2nd Class	Saver 1st Class	Saver 2nd Class	Youth 2nd Class
4 days in 2 months	$335	$286	$286	$243	$218
Extra rail days (max 6)	39-41	33-35	33-35	28-30	25-27

Be aware of your route. Many daytime connections from Paris to Italy pass through Switzerland (e.g., connecting in Basel, Geneve, or Lausanne) which costs an additional $60 or more in second class if Switzerland is not covered by your pass. Direct Paris-Italy day or night trains are covered by the pass, regardless of their route. Routes via Nice, Torino, or Modane will bypass Switzerland (consult a good timetable for details).

FRANCE–SPAIN PASS

	Individual 1st Class	Individual 2nd Class	Saver 1st Class	Saver 2nd Class	Youth 2nd Class
4 days in 2 months	$366	$328	$331	$299	$256
Extra rail days (max 6)	39-41	33-35	33-35	28-30	25-27

If you're only dipping into a bit of Spain, you may not need the France-Spain pass. For instance, a ticket from the French border at Cerbere to Barcelona costs only $30. From the border at Hendaye to Madrid costs $75, but if you cover this ground via the fancy Paris–Madrid "Elipsos" night train, the same passholder fares ($70 and up) apply whether your pass covers one or both countries.

FRANCE–GERMANY PASS

	Individual 1st Class	Individual 2nd Class	Saver 1st Class	Saver 2nd Class	Youth 2nd Class
4 days in 2 months	$366	$281	$286	$239	$210
5 days in 2 months	405	364	328	283	
6 days in 2 months	443	400	356	310	
8 days in 2 months	521	468	408	366	
10 days in 2 months	598	538	468	423	

FRANCE–BENELUX PASS

	Individual 1st Class	Individual 2nd Class	Saver 1st Class	Saver 2nd Class	Youth 2nd Class
4 days in 2 months	$335	$281	$286	$239	$210
5 days in 2 months	366	312	312	265	236
6 days in 2 months	401	343	341	291	262
8 days in 2 months	467	408	397	347	313
10 days in 2 months	531	474	452	404	364

Coping with Strikes

Going on strike (en grève) is a popular pastime in this revolution-happy country. President Sarkozy is pushing unions to their limits, and because bargaining between management and employees is not standard procedure, workers strike to get attention. Truckers and tractors block main roads and autoroutes (they call it Opération Escargot: "Operation Snail's Pace"), baggage handlers bring airports to their knees, and museum workers make Mona Lisa off-limits to tourists. Métro and train personnel seem to strike every year—probably during your trip. What does the traveler do? You could jetter l'éponge (literally, throw in the sponge) and go somewhere less strike-prone (Switzerland's nice), or learn to accept certain events as out of your control. Strikes in France generally last no longer than a day or two, and if you're aware of them, you can usually plan around them. Your hotelier will know the latest (or can find out). Make a habit of asking your hotel receptionist about strikes, or check www.americansinfrance .net (look under "Daily Life").

less-trafficked places often have only second-class cars).

You can buy tickets online at www.raileurope.com (a US company that delivers tickets to your home but doesn't always have the lowest rates). It's usually cheaper to use www.tgv-europe.com /en/home; if you choose a country other than the US and outside of western Europe, you'll be able to print tickets at home or pick them up in any French train station (if you choose, say, France, the site will be in French, and if you choose the US, you'll be redirected to www.raileurope.com).

On the Train: You can buy tickets on the train for a small surcharge, but you must find the conductor immediately upon boarding; otherwise it's a €35 minimum charge.

Automatic Train-Ticket Machines

The ticket machines available at most stations are great time-savers for short trips when ticket window lines are long (but your American credit card won't work, so you'll need euro coins). Some have English instructions, but for those that don't, here is what you are prompted to do. (The default is usually what you want; turn the dial or move the cursor to your choice, and press "Validez" to agree to each step.)

1. Quelle est votre destination? (What's your destination?)
2. Billet Plein Tarif (Full-fare ticket—yes for most.)
3. 1ère ou 2ème (First or second class; normally second is fine.)
4. Aller simple ou aller-retour? (One-way or round-trip?)
5. Prix en Euro (The price should be shown if you get this far.)

Reservations

Reservations are required for any TGV train, *couchettes* (sleeping berths) on night trains, and some other trains when indicated in timetables. You can reserve any train at any station or through SNCF Boutiques (small offices in city centers).

Fast and popular TGV trains usually fill up quickly, making reservations a challenge (particularly for railpass-holders, who are allocated a limited number of seats). It's wise to book ahead for any TGV, especially on the busy Paris–Avignon–Nice line. Reservations cost €3 (more during peak periods) and are possible up to 90 days in advance.

Reservations are generally unnecessary for non-TGV trains (verify ahead), but they are advisable during busy times (e.g., Fri and Sun afternoons, Sat mornings, weekday rush hours, and holiday weekends; see "Major Holidays and Weekends" on page 14). International trains (such as Eurostar, Thalys, Artesia, and international TGV) have different reservation price ranges.

Validating Tickets, Reservations, and Railpasses

You are required to validate (*composter*, kohm-poh-stay) all train tickets and reservations before boarding any SNCF train. Look for a yellow machine nearby to stamp your ticket or reservation. If you have a railpass, validate it at a ticket window before the first time you use it; don't stamp it in the yellow machine.

Baggage Storage

Baggage storage (*consigne* or *Espaces Bagages*) is available only at the biggest train stations (about €4–10 per bag depending on size), and is noted where available in this book (depends on security concerns, so be prepared to keep your bag). For security reasons, all luggage must carry a tag with the traveler's first and last name and current address. This applies to hand luggage as well as bigger bags that are stowed. Free tags are available at train stations in France.

Other baggage-check options in cities are also listed in this book (where available). Here's a tip: Major museums and monuments usually have free baggage check for visitors. Even if the sight is not particularly interesting to you, the entry fee may be worth it if you need to stow your bags for a few hours.

Train Tips

• Arrive at the station with plenty of time before your departure to find the right platform, confirm connections, and so on.

• Small stations are minimally staffed; if there is no agent at the station, go directly to the tracks and look for the overhead sign that confirms your train stops at that track.

• Larger stations have platforms with monitors showing each

Key Travel Phrases

Bonjour, monsieur or ***madame, parlez-vous anglais?***
Pron: bohn-zhoor, muhs-yur/mah-dahm, par-lay-voo ahn-glay?
Meaning: Hello, sir or madam, do you speak English?

Je voudrais un départ pour _____ (destination), ***pour le***
_____ (date), ***vers*** _____ (general time of day). ***la plus
direct possible.***
Pron: zhuh voo-dray uhn day-par poor _____ (destination),
poor luh _____ (date), vehr _____ (time), lah ploo dee-rehk
poh-see-bluh.
Meaning/Example: I would like a departure for Avignon, on
23 May, about 9:00, the most direct way possible.

car's layout (numbered forward or backward) so you can figure out where your *voiture* will stop on the long platform and where to board each car.

• Check schedules and reservation requirements in advance. Upon arrival at a station, learn your departure possibilities. Large stations have an information window or office; at small stations, the ticket office gives information.

• If you have a rail flexipass, write the date on your pass each day you travel (before or immediately after boarding you board your first train).

• Validate tickets (not passes) and reservations in yellow machines before boarding. If you're traveling with a pass and have a reservation for a certain trip, you must validate the reservation.

• Before getting on a train, confirm that it's going where you think it is. For example, if you want to go to Bayeux, ask the conductor or any local passenger, *"A Bayeux?"* (ah bah-yuh; meaning, "To Bayeux?").

• Some trains split cars en route. Make sure your train car is continuing to your destination by asking, for example, *"Cette voiture va à Bayeux?"* (set vwah-toor vah ah bah-yuh; meaning, "This car goes to Bayeux?"). On my last trip, the train from Marseilles to Arles split off some cars along the way—which wasn't mentioned when I asked the conductor if this train went to Arles.

• If you don't understand an announcement, ask your neighbor to explain, "Pardon madame/monsieur, qu'est-ce qui se passe?" (kess key suh pahs; meaning, "Excuse me, what's going on?").

• Verify with the conductor all of the transfers you must make: *"Correspondance à?"*; meaning, "Transfer to where?"

• The early boarder gets the best storage space. To guard against theft, it's best to keep your bags directly overhead. If you want to store them in the lower racks (available in most cars), make sure you can see them from your seat. Your bags are most vulnerable to theft before the train takes off and whenever it stops.

- Note your arrival time, so you'll be ready to get off.
- Use the trains' free WCs before you get off (but not while the train is stopped).

Buses

You can get nearly anywhere in France by rail and bus...if you're well-organized, patient, and not in a hurry. Review my bus schedule information in advance and verify times at the local TI or bus station. Regional buses work well for many destinations not served by trains. Buses are almost always comfortable and air-conditioned.

A few bus lines are run by SNCF (France's rail system) and are included with your railpass (show railpass at station to get free bus ticket), but most bus lines are independent of the rail system and are not covered by railpasses. Bus stations (*gare routière*) are usually located next to train stations. Train stations usually have bus information where train-to-bus connections are important—and vice versa for bus companies. On Sunday, regional bus service virtually disappears.

Bus Tips

- Read the train tips described earlier, and use those that apply (check schedules in advance, arrive at the station early, confirm the destination before you board, find out if you need to transfer, etc.).
- Use TIs often to help plan your trip; they have regional bus schedules and are happy to assist you.
- Remember that service is sparse or even nonexistent on Sunday. Wednesday bus schedules often are different during the school year, because school is out this day (and regional buses generally operate school service).
- Be at bus stops at least five minutes early.
- On schedules, *en semaine* means Monday through Saturday, *dimanche* is Sunday, and *jours fériés* are holidays.

Regional Minivan Excursions

Worthwhile day tours generally are available in regions where bus and train service is sparse. For the D-Day beaches, châteaux of the Loire Valley, Dordogne Valley villages and caves, Provence's villages and vineyards, the Route du Vin (Wine Road) in Alsace, Brittany sights (including Mont St. Michel), and wine-tasting in Burgundy, I list reliable companies that provide this helpful service at fair rates. Some of these minivan excursions simply offer transportation between the sights; others add a running commentary and information on regional history.

Renting a Car

To rent a car in France, you must be at least 18 years old and have held your license for one year. An International Driving Permit—a translation of your driver's license—is recommended, but not required, if your driver's license has been renewed within the last year ($15 through your local AAA, plus two passport photos, www.aaa.com). However, I've frequently rented cars in France and traveled problem-free with just my US license.

Drivers under the age of 25 may incur a young-driver surcharge, and some rental companies do not rent to anyone 75 and over. If you're considered too young or old, look into leasing, described later, which has less-stringent age restrictions.

Research car rentals before you go. It's cheaper to arrange most car rentals from the US. Call several companies and look online to compare rates, or arrange a rental through your hometown travel agent.

Most of the major US rental agencies (such as Alamo/National, Avis, Budget, Dollar, Hertz, and Thrifty) have offices in France. It can be cheaper to use a consolidator, such as Auto Europe (www.autoeurope.com) or Europe by Car (www.ebctravel.com), but by using a middleman, you risk trading customer service for lower prices; if you have a problem with the rental company, you can't count on the consolidator to intervene on your behalf.

For the best rental deal, rent by the week with unlimited mileage. I normally rent the least expensive model with a stick-shift. Almost all rentals are manual by default, so if you need an automatic, you must request one in advance; beware that these cars usually are larger models and more expensive. Roads and parking spaces are narrow in France, so you'll do yourself a favor by renting the smallest car that meets your needs. If you want to save money on gas, ask for a diesel car.

For a three-week rental, allow $900 per person (based on two people sharing a car), including insurance, tolls, gas, and parking. For longer trips, consider leasing (explained later); you'll save money on insurance and taxes. Compare pick-up costs (downtown can be cheaper than the airport) and explore drop-off options. Returning a car at a big-city train station can be tricky; get precise details on the car drop-off location and hours. Except in major cities, rental offices are usually closed during lunch and on Sundays.

If you want a car for only a day or two (e.g., for the D-Day beaches or Loire châteaux), you'll likely find it cheaper to rent it in France—most US-arranged rentals make financial sense only for three days or more. You can rent a car on the spot just about anywhere in France. In many cases, this is a worthwhile splurge. All you need is your American driver's license and a major credit card (figure €65–80/day, including at least 100 kilometers, or 60 miles, per day).

When you pick up the car, check it thoroughly and make sure any damage is noted on your rental agreement. Find out how your car's lights, turn signals, wipers, and gas cap function. Be sure you know what type of fuel your car takes before you fill up. When you return the car, make sure the agent verifies its condition with you.

A **rail-and-drive pass** (such as a EurailDrive, Selectpass Drive, or France Rail and Drive) allows you to mix car and train travel economically (sold only outside France, from your travel agent). Generally big-city connections are best done by train, and rural regions are best done by car. With a rail-and-drive pass, you can take advantage of the speed and comfort of the TGV trains for longer trips, and rent a car for as little as one day at a time for day trips that can't be done without one (such as the Loire, the Dordogne, and Provence).

The basic France Rail and Drive Pass comes with two days of car rental and two days of rail in one month. You can pick up a car in one city and drop it off in another. Though you're only required to reserve the first car day, it's safer to reserve all days, as cars are not always available on short notice.

Car Insurance Options

Accidents can happen anywhere, but when you're on vacation, the last thing you need is stress over car insurance. When you rent a car, you are liable for a very high deductible, sometimes equal to the entire value of the car. Limit your financial risk by choosing one of these three options: buy Collision Damage Waiver (CDW) coverage from the car-rental company, get coverage through your credit card (free, but more complicated), or buy coverage through Travel Guard.

CDW includes a very high deductible (typically $1,000–1,500). Though each rental company has its own variation, the basic CDW costs $15–25 a day (figure roughly 25 percent extra) and reduces your liability, but does not eliminate it. When you pick up the car, you'll be offered the chance to "buy down" the deductible to zero (for an additional $15–30/day; this is sometimes called "super CDW").

If you opt for **credit-card coverage,** there's a catch: You'll technically have to decline all coverage offered by the car-rental company, which means they can place a hold on your card (up to the full value of the car). In case of damage, it can be time-consuming to resolve the charges with your credit-card company. Before you decide on this option, quiz your credit-card company about how it works.

Finally, you can buy car-rental insurance from **Travel Guard** ($9/day plus a one-time $3 service fee covers you for up to $35,000,

$250 deductible, tel. 800-826-4919, www.travelguard.com). It's valid everywhere in Europe except the Republic of Ireland, and some Italian car-rental companies refuse to honor it. Residents of Texas and Washington state aren't eligible for this coverage.

For more on car-rental insurance, see www.ricksteves.com /cdw.

Leasing

For trips of three weeks or more, consider a tax-free lease (no VAT to pay), which also includes zero-deductible collision and theft insurance. By technically buying and then selling back the car, you save lots of money on tax and insurance. Leasing provides you a brand-new car with unlimited mileage and a 24-hour emergency assistance program. You can lease for as little as 17 days to as long as 6 months (possibly longer if you're a teacher or student on sabbatical). Car leases must be arranged in the US at least 30–45 days prior to departing for Europe.

Three reliable companies offering 17-day lease packages from about $1,000 for a small car ($1,400 for a midsize) are Auto France (Peugeot cars only, US tel. 800-572-9655, fax 201/393-7800, www .autofrance.net), Europe by Car (Peugeot, Citroën, and Renault cars, US tel. 800-223-1516, www.ebctravel.com), and Kemwel (Peugeot cars only, US tel. 877-820-0668, www.kemwel.com). Anyone age 18 or over with a driver's license is eligible. You can pick up or return cars in major cities outside of France, but you'll have to pay an additional fee.

Driving in France

Remember to bring your driver's license. Seat belts are mandatory for all, and children under age 10 must be in the back seat.

Your US credit and debit cards are unlikely to work at self-service gas pumps, automated tollbooths, and automated parking garages. Alternative options are mentioned below. The easiest thing to do is carry sufficient cash in euros.

Fuel: Gas (essence) is expensive, costing about $7 per gallon. Diesel (gazole) is less (about $6 per gallon), and

AND LEARN THESE ROAD SIGNS

STOP · Speed Limit (km/hr) · Speed Limit No Longer Applies · No Passing · End of No Passing Zone · SENS UNIQUE One Way · Danger · Intersection · Main Road · Freeway · No Entry · No Entry for Cars · All Vehicles Prohibited · Parking · No Parking · Customs · Yield diesel cars get better mileage. Fuel is most expensive on autoroutes and cheapest at big supermarkets (closed at night and on Sun). Many gas stations close on Sunday. Avoid self-service gas pumps and automated stations; instead find a station with attendants (you'll normally pump first, then pay with cash or plastic inside).

Autoroute: Four hours on the autoroute costs about €26 in tolls (for which you'll need to pay cash, since US credit and debit cards won't work), but the alternative to these super "feeways" usually means being marooned behind sluggish tractors in countryside traffic. Autoroutes save enough time, gas, and nausea to justify the splurge. Mix high-speed "autorouting" with scenic country-road rambling. You'll usually take a ticket when entering an autoroute and pay when you leave. Avoid the *Télépéage* tollbooths and those with a credit-card icon, and look instead for tollbooths sporting green arrows, indicating they accept cash. Some exits are entirely automated, with machines that take any denomination of euro bills. Shorter autoroute sections have periodic tollbooths, where you can pay by dropping coins into a basket (change given, but keep a good supply of coins handy to avoid waiting for an attendant). Autoroute gas stations usually come with well-stocked mini-marts, clean restrooms, sandwiches, maps, local products, and cheap vending-machine coffee (€1.20—I dig the sweet *cappuccino sucré*). Many have small cafés or more elaborate cafeterias with reasonable prices.

Road Designations: Roads are classified into departmental (D), national (N), and autoroutes (A). D routes (usually yellow lines on maps) can be slower, but often are the most scenic. N routes and important D routes (usually red lines) are the fastest after autoroutes (orange lines). Green road signs are for national routes; blue are for autoroutes. Note that some key roads in France are undergoing letter designation and number changes (mostly N roads converting to D roads). If you are using an older map, the actual route number may differ from what's on your map. Navigate by destination rather than by road number, or buy a new map. There are plenty of good facilities, gas stations (most closed Sun), and rest stops.

Speed Limits: Because speed limits are by road type, they typically aren't posted, so it's best to memorize them:

- Two-lane D and N routes outside cities and towns: 90 km/hour
- Divided highways outside cities and towns: 110 km/hour
- Autoroutes: 130 km/hour

If it's raining, subtract 10 km/hour on D and N routes and 20 km/hour on divided highways and autoroutes. Speed limit signs are a red circle around a number; when you see that same number

Road Signs and Driving Tips

Instructional Signs That You Must Obey

Cédez le Passage	Yield
Priorité à Droite	Right-of-way is for cars coming from the right
Vous n'avez pas la priorité	You don't have the right of way (when merging)
Rappel	Remember to obey the sign
Déviation	Detour
Allumez vos feux	Turn on your lights
Doublage Interdit	No passing
Parking Interdit/ Stationnement Interdit	No parking

Signs for Your Information

Route Barrée	Road blocked
Sortie des Camions	Work truck exit
Centre Commercial	Grouping of large, suburban stores (not city center)
Centre-Ville	City center
Feux	Traffic signal
Horadateur	Remote parking meter, usually at the end of the block
Parc de Stationnement	Parking lot
Rue Piétonne	Pedestrian-only street
Sauf Riverains	Local access only

Signs Unique to Autoroutes

Aire	Rest stop with WCs, telephones, and sometimes gas stations
Bouchon	Traffic jam ahead
Fluide	No slowing ahead (fluid conditions)
Péage	Toll
Télépéage	Toll booths—automatic toll payment only
Toutes Directions	All directions (passing through a city)
Autres Directions	Other directions (passing through a city)
Par temps de Pluie	When raining (modifies speed limit signs)

Driving in France: Distance & Time

Note: Your times may vary based on traffic, construction, and road conditions.

m = miles   h = hours

again in gray with a broken line diagonally across it, this means that limit no longer applies. Speed limits drop to 30–50 km/hour in villages (always posted) and must be respected.

Beware of traffic cameras. These portable cameras are sometimes positioned to trap unsuspecting drivers, particularly in 30–50 km/hour zones. You can get busted for going even a few kilometers over the limit (believe me).

Parking: Parking is a headache in larger cities, and theft is a problem. Ask your hotelier for ideas, and pay to park at well-patrolled lots (blue P signs direct you to parking lots in French cities). Parking garages usually require that you take a ticket with you and pay at a machine (called a *caisse*) on your way back to the car. Be aware that US credit cards probably won't work in these automated machines, but euro bills will. Overnight parking (usually 19:00–8:00) in lots and garages is generally reasonable, except in Paris and Nice. Curbside metered parking also works (usually free 12:00–14:00 & 19:00–9:00, and all day and night in Aug). Look for a small machine selling time (called *horadateur*, usually one per block), plug in a few coins (€1.50 buys about an hour, varies by city), push the button, get a receipt showing the amount of time you have, and display it inside your windshield.

Driving Tips

• Be aware that in city and town centers, traffic merging from the right (even from tiny side streets) normally has the right-of-way (*priorité à droite*). So, even when merging on to a major road, pay attention to cars merging from the right. In contrast, cars entering the many suburban roundabouts must yield (*cédez le passage*).

• Be ready for many roundabouts—navigating them is an art. The key is to know your direction and be ready for your turnoff. If you miss it, take another lap.

• When navigating into cities, approach intersections cautiously, stow the map, and follow the signs to *Centre-Ville* (city center). From there, head to the TI (*Office de Tourisme*) or your hotel.

• When leaving or just passing through cities, follow the signs for *Toutes Directions* or *Autres Directions* (meaning "anywhere else") until you see a sign for your specific destination.

• Driving on any roads but autoroutes will take longer than you anticipated, so allow yourself plenty of time for slower traffic (tractors, trucks, traffic, and hard-to-decipher signs all deserve blame). First-timers should estimate how long they think a drive will take...then double it. I pretend that kilometers are miles (for distances) and base my time estimates accordingly.

• While locals are eating lunch (12:00–14:00), many sights (and gas stations) are closed, so you can make great time driving— but keep it slow when passing through villages.

• U-turns are illegal throughout France, and you cannot turn right on red lights.

• Be very careful when driving on smaller roads—many are narrow, flanked by little ditches that lure inattentive drivers. I've met several readers who "ditched" their cars (which were later successfully pulled out by local farmers).

• On autoroutes, keep to the right lanes to let fast drivers by, and be careful when merging into a left lane, as cars can be coming at very high speeds. Cars and trucks commonly keep their left blinker on while in a passing lane, indicating that they plan to get back over to the right.

• Motorcycles will scream between cars in traffic. Be ready— they expect you to make space so that they can pass.

• Gas is tricky to find in rural areas on Sunday, so fill up on Saturday. Autoroute filling stations are always open and always staffed.

• Keep a stash of coins in your ashtray for parking and small autoroute tolls.

Biking

Throughout France you'll find areas where public transportation is limited and bicycle touring might be a good idea. For many, biking is a romantic notion whose novelty wears off after the first hill or headwind—realistically evaluate your physical condition and be clear on the limitations bikes present. Start with an easy pedal to a nearby village or through the vineyards, then decide how ambitious you feel. Most find that two hours on a narrow, hard seat is enough. I've listed bike-rental shops where appropriate and suggested a few of my favorite rides. TIs always have addresses for bike-rental places. For a good touring bike, figure about €10 for a half-day and €16 for a full day. You'll pay more for better equipment; generally the best is available through bike shops, not at train stations or other outlets. French cyclists often do not wear helmets, though most rental outfits have them (for a small fee). Some shops even rent electric bikes.

Cheap Flights

If you're visiting other countries in Europe, consider intra-European airlines. Though trains are still the best way to connect most cities in France, a flight can save both time and money on international journeys. When comparing a flight to a train trip, factor in the time it takes to get to and through the airport—and how early you'll need to arrive to check in before the flight. Most flights make sense only as an alternate to a train ride five or more hours in length.

One of the best websites for comparing inexpensive flights is www.skyscanner.net. Other comparison search engines include www.wegolo.com and www.whichbudget.com. Airlines offering inexpensive flights include easyJet (www.easyjet.com) and Ryanair (www.ryanair.com). Airport websites may list smaller airlines that serve your destination.

Be aware of the potential drawbacks of flying on the cheap: nonrefundable and nonchangeable tickets, minimal or nonexistent customer service, treks to airports far outside town, and pricey baggage fees. If you're traveling with lots of luggage, a cheap flight can quickly become a bad deal. To avoid unpleasant surprises, read the small print—especially baggage policies—before you book.

Resources

Resources from Rick Steves

Books: *Rick Steves' France 2011* is one of many books in my series on European travel, which includes country guidebooks, city guidebooks (Paris, Rome, Florence, London, etc.), Snapshot guides (excerpted chapters from my country guides), Pocket guides (full-color little books on big cities), and my budget-travel skills handbook, *Rick Steves' Europe Through the Back Door*. My phrase books—for French, Italian, German, Spanish, and Portuguese—are practical and budget-oriented. My other books include *Europe 101* (a crash course on art and history) and *Travel as a Political Act* (a travelogue sprinkled with tips for bringing home a global perspective). For a list of my books, see the inside of the last page of this book.

Video: My public television series, *Rick Steves' Europe*, covers European destinations in 100 shows, with nine episodes on France. To watch episodes, visit www.hulu.com/rick-steves-europe; for scripts and other details, see www.ricksteves.com/tv.

Audio: My weekly public radio show, *Travel with Rick Steves*, features interviews with travel experts from around the world. I've also produced free self-guided audio tours of the top sights and neighborhoods in Paris, London, Florence, Venice, and Rome. All of this audio content is available for free at Rick Steves Audio Europe, an extensive online library organized by destination. Choose whatever interests you, and download it for free to your iPod, smartphone, or computer at www.ricksteves.com or iTunes.

Maps

The black-and-white maps in this book, drawn by Dave Hoerlein, are concise and simple. The maps are intended to help you locate recommended places and reach TIs, where you'll find more in-depth maps of cities or regions (usually free). Better maps are sold at newsstands and bookstores. Before you buy a map, look at it to be sure it has the level of detail you want.

Michelin maps are available throughout France at bookstores, newsstands, and gas stations (about €5 each, cheaper than in the

Begin Your Trip at www.ricksteves.com

At our travel website, you'll find a wealth of free information on European destinations, including fresh monthly news and helpful tips from thousands of fellow travelers. You'll also find my latest guidebook updates (www.ricksteves.com/update) and my travel blog.

Our **online Travel Store** offers travel bags and accessories specially designed by me and my staff to help you travel smarter and lighter. These include my popular carry-on bags (roll-aboard and rucksack versions), money belts, totes, toiletries kits, adapters, other accessories, and a wide selection of guidebooks, planning maps, and DVDs.

Choosing the right **railpass** for your trip—amid hundreds of options—can drive you nutty. We'll help you choose the best pass for your needs, plus give you a bunch of free extras.

Rick Steves' Europe Through the Back Door travel company offers **tours** with more than three dozen itineraries and about 400 departures reaching the best destinations in this book...and beyond. Our France tours include Paris and the South of France in 15 days (focusing on Paris, the Loire, the Dordogne, Provence, and the Riviera); Paris and the Heart of France in 11 days (focusing on Paris, the Loire, and Normandy); Villages and Vineyards of Eastern France in 14 days (visiting Champagne, Alsace, Burgundy, the Alps, Provence, and the Riviera); and a one-week Paris city tour. You'll enjoy great guides, a fun bunch of travel partners (with small groups of generally around 28), and plenty of room to spread out in a big, comfy bus. You'll find European adventures to fit every vacation length. For all the details, and to get our Tour Catalog and a free Rick Steves Tour Experience DVD (filmed on location during an actual tour), visit www.ricksteves.com or call us at 425/608-4217.

US). The Michelin #721 France map (1:1,000,000 scale) covers this book's destinations with generally enough detail for drivers (those delving deeper into a region will want to pick up that region's detailed map). Drivers should consider the soft-cover Michelin France atlas (the entire country at 1:200,000, well-organized in a €16 book with an index and maps of major cities). Spend a few minutes learning the Michelin key to get the most sightseeing value out of these maps.

Train travelers do fine with a simple rail map (such as the one that comes with a railpass) and city maps from the TI offices.

Other Guidebooks

If you're like most travelers, this book is all you need. But if you're heading beyond my recommended destinations, $40 for extra maps and books can be money well spent. Note that none of the following guidebooks are updated annually; check the publication date before you buy.

I like Cadogan guides for their well-presented background information and coverage of cultural issues. Their recommendations suit upscale travelers. Lonely Planet's *France* is well-researched, with good maps and hotel recommendations for low- to moderate-budget travelers. But because it tries to cover every city in France, you'll likely find too little information on the most important places and too much information on the minor places you don't care about. The highly opinionated *Let's Go: France* is ideal for students and vagabonds traveling by train and staying in hostels. The popular, skinny, green Michelin guides are dry but informative, especially for drivers. They're known for their city and sightseeing maps, and for their succinct, helpful information on all major sights. English editions, covering most of the regions you'll want to visit, are sold in France for about €14 (or $20 in the US).

Recommended Books and Movies

To learn more about France past and present, check out a few of these books or films.

Nonfiction

For a good introduction to the French culture and people, read *Sixty Million Frenchmen Can't Be Wrong* (Jean-Benoit Nadeau and Julie Barlow), *Culture Shock: France* (Sally Adamson Taylor), and/ or *French or Foe* (Polly Platt).

For a readable history of the country, try *The Course of French History* (Pierre Goubert). *Portraits of France* (Robert Daley) is an interesting travelogue that roams from Paris to the Pyrenees. A mix of writers explore French culture in *Travelers Tales: France*

The Rules of *Boules*

Throughout France you'll see people playing *boules* (also known as *pétanque*). Each player starts with three iron balls, with the object of getting them close to the target, a small wooden ball called a *cochonnet*. The first player tosses the *cochonnet* about 30 feet, then throws the first of his iron balls near the target. The next player takes a turn. As soon as a player's ball is closest, it's the other guy's turn. Once all balls have been thrown, the score is tallied—the player with the closest ball gets one point for each ball closer to the target than his opponent's. The loser gets zero. Games are generally to 15 points.

A regulation *boules* field is 10 feet by 43 feet, but the game is played everywhere—just scratch a throwing circle in the sand, toss the *cochonnet*, and you're off. Strategists can try to knock the opponent's balls out of position, knock the *cochonnet* itself out of position, or guard their best ball with the other two.

(edited by James O'Reilly, Larry Habegger, and Sean O'Reilly).

Many great memoirs take place in Paris. Consider reading Ernest Hemingway's *A Moveable Feast*, Art Buchwald's *I'll Always Have Paris*, and/or *Paris to the Moon* by *New Yorker* writer Adam Gopnik, who takes his young son for a carousel ride in the Luxembourg Garden.

If you'll be visiting Provence, pick up Peter Mayle's memoirs, *A Year in Provence* and *Toujours Provence*. Ina Caro's *The Road from the Past* is filled with enjoyable essays on her travels through France, with an accent on history. *The Da Vinci Code* fans will enjoy reading the book that inspired that book—*Holy Blood, Holy Grail* (Michael Baigent, Richard Leigh, and Henry Lincoln)—which takes place mostly in southern France. *Labyrinth* (Kate Mosse) is an intriguing tale, much of which takes place in medieval southern France during the Cathar crusade.

War buffs may want to read these classics before visiting the D-Day Beaches: *The Longest Day* (Cornelius Ryan) and *Wine & War: The French, the Nazis, and the Battle for France's Greatest Treasure* (Donald and Petie Kladstrup). *Is Paris Burning?*, set in the last days of the Nazi occupation, tells the story of the French resistance and how a German general disobeyed Hitler's order to destroy Paris (Larry Collins and Dominique Lapierre).

If you'll be enjoying an extended stay in France, consider *Living Abroad in France* (Terry Link) or *Almost French* (Sarah Turnbull), a funny take on living as a Parisian native. Gourmands appreciate the *Marling Menu-Master for France* (William E.

Marling). Travelers seeking green and vegetarian options in France could consider *Traveling Naturally in France* (Dorian Yates).

Fiction

"It was the best of times, it was the worst of times," begins Charles Dickens' gripping tale of the French Revolution, *A Tale of Two Cities*. In *Les Misérables* (Victor Hugo), a Frenchman tries to escape his criminal past, fleeing from a determined police captain and becoming wrapped up in the Revolutionary battles between the rich and the starving. Another recommended book set during this time is *City of Darkness, City of Light*, by Marge Piercy.

Ernest Hemingway was a fan of Georges Simenon, a Belgian who wrote mysteries based in Paris, including *The Hotel Majestic*. Other mysteries using Paris as the backdrop are *Murder in Montparnasse* (Howard Engel), *Murder in the Marais* (Cara Black), and *Sandman* (J. Robert Janes).

A Very Long Engagement (Sebastien Japrisot) is a love story set during the bleak years when World War I raged. Using a similar timeframe, *Birdsong* (Sebastian Faulks) follows a 20-year-old Englishman into France, and into the romance that follows.

Chocolat (Joanne Harris)—a book and a 2000 movie with Johnny Depp and Juliette Binoche—charms readers with its story of magic and romance.

Suite Française (Irène Némirovsky) plunges readers into the chaos of the evacuation of Paris during World War II, as well as daily life in a small rural town during the ensuing German occupation. The author, a Russian Jew living in France, wrote her account within weeks of the actual events, and died at Auschwitz in 1942.

Films

In *The Grand Illusion* (1937, directed by Jean Renoir), WWI prisoners of war hatch an escape plan. Considered a masterpiece of French film, the movie was later banned by the Nazis for its anti-fascism message.

Stanley Kubrick's *Paths of Glory* (1957) is a WWI story about the futility and irony of war. François Truffaut, a filmmaker of the French New Wave school, shows the Parisian streets in *Jules and Jim* (1962). Wander the streets of Paris with a small boy as he chases *The Red Balloon* (1956).

Jean de Florette (1986), a marvelous tale of greed and intolerance, follows a hunchback as he fights for the property he inherited. Its sequel, *Manon of the Spring* (1986), continues with his daughter's story. *Blue/White/Red* (1990s) is a stylish trilogy of films by Krzystof Kieslowski, based on France's national motto—"Liberty, Equality, and Fraternity."

Cyrano de Bergerac (1990) is about a homely, romantic poet who woos his love with the help of another, better-looking man. Fans of crime films—and Robert De Niro—will like *Ronin* (1998), with multiple scenes shot in France. *Saving Private Ryan* (1998) is Steven Spielberg's intense and brilliant story of the D-Day landings.

The Gleaners & I (2000), a quiet, meditative film by Agnès Varda, follows a few working-class men and women as they gather sustenance from what's been thrown away. In *Amélie* (2001), a charming young waitress in Paris searches for love. If you'll be heading to Versailles, consider seeing *Marie Antoinette* (2006), which stars Kirsten Dunst as the infamous French queen (with a California accent).

Holidays and Festivals

This list includes many—but not all—major festivals, plus national holidays observed throughout France. Many sights close down on national holidays, and weekends around those holidays often are wildly crowded with vacationers (book your hotel room for the entire holiday weekend well in advance). Before planning a trip around a festival, make sure that you verify the festival dates on the website for the festival or the France TI (listed at the beginning of the appendix).

Here is a sampling of events and holidays in 2011:

Jan 1	New Year's Day
Jan 6	Epiphany
Late Feb	Carnival (Mardi Gras) parades and fireworks, Nice (www.nicecarnaval.com)
March	Grenoble Jazz Festival, near Lyon (www.jazzgrenoble.com)
April 24	Easter Sunday
April 25	Easter Monday
May–Mid-Oct	Festival of Gardens, Chaumont-sur-Loire (www.domaine-chaumont.fr)
May	Versailles Festival (arts), Versailles; Festival Jeanne d'Arc (pageants), Rouen
May 1	Labor Day
May 8	VE Day
May 11–22	Cannes Film Festival, Cannes (www.festival-cannes.fr)
May 26–29	Monaco Grand Prix, auto race, Monaco (www.yourmonaco.com/grand_prix)
June 2	Ascension
June 6	67th Anniversary of the D-Day Landing, Normandy

2011

JANUARY
S	M	T	W	T	F	S
						1
2	3	4	5	6	7	8
9	10	11	12	13	14	15
16	17	18	19	20	21	22
23/30	24/31	25	26	27	28	29

FEBRUARY
S	M	T	W	T	F	S
		1	2	3	4	5
6	7	8	9	10	11	12
13	14	15	16	17	18	19
20	21	22	23	24	25	26
27	28					

MARCH
S	M	T	W	T	F	S
		1	2	3	4	5
6	7	8	9	10	11	12
13	14	15	16	17	18	19
20	21	22	23	24	25	26
27	28	29	30	31		

APRIL
S	M	T	W	T	F	S
					1	2
3	4	5	6	7	8	9
10	11	12	13	14	15	16
17	18	19	20	21	22	23
24	25	26	27	28	29	30

MAY
S	M	T	W	T	F	S
1	2	3	4	5	6	7
8	9	10	11	12	13	14
15	16	17	18	19	20	21
22	23	24	25	26	27	28
29	30	31				

JUNE
S	M	T	W	T	F	S
			1	2	3	4
5	6	7	8	9	10	11
12	13	14	15	16	17	18
19	20	21	22	23	24	25
26	27	28	29	30		

JULY
S	M	T	W	T	F	S
					1	2
3	4	5	6	7	8	9
10	11	12	13	14	15	16
17	18	19	20	21	22	23
24/31	25	26	27	28	29	30

AUGUST
S	M	T	W	T	F	S
	1	2	3	4	5	6
7	8	9	10	11	12	13
14	15	16	17	18	19	20
21	22	23	24	25	26	27
28	29	30	31			

SEPTEMBER
S	M	T	W	T	F	S
				1	2	3
4	5	6	7	8	9	10
11	12	13	14	15	16	17
18	19	20	21	22	23	24
25	26	27	28	29	30	

OCTOBER
S	M	T	W	T	F	S
						1
2	3	4	5	6	7	8
9	10	11	12	13	14	15
16	17	18	19	20	21	22
23/30	24/31	25	26	27	28	29

NOVEMBER
S	M	T	W	T	F	S
		1	2	3	4	5
6	7	8	9	10	11	12
13	14	15	16	17	18	19
20	21	22	23	24	25	26
27	28	29	30			

DECEMBER
S	M	T	W	T	F	S
				1	2	3
4	5	6	7	8	9	10
11	12	13	14	15	16	17
18	19	20	21	22	23	24
25	26	27	28	29	30	31

June 12 Pentecost
June Marais Festival (arts), Paris
Mid-June Le Mans Auto Race, Le Mans—near Loire Valley (www.lemans.org)
June 21 Fête de la Musique, concerts and dancing in the streets throughout France
July Nice Jazz Festival (www.nicejazzfestival .fr); Avignon Festival, theater, dance, music (www.festival-avignon.com); Beaune International Music Festival; Chorégies d'Orange, Orange (performed in Roman theater, www .choregies.asso.fr); "Jazz à Juan" International Jazz Festival, Antibes/ Juan-les-Pins (www.jazzajuan .fr); Jousting matches and medieval festivities, Carcassonne; Nights of

	Fourvière, Lyon (theater and music in a Roman theater, www.nuits-de-fourviere.org); Colmar International Music Festival, www.festival-colmar.com); International Music and Opera Festival, Aix-en-Provence (www.festival-aix.com)
July	Tour de France, national bicycle race culminating on the Champs-Élysées in Paris (www.letour.fr)
July 14	Bastille Day (fireworks, dancing, and revelry all over France)
July–Aug	International Fireworks Festival, Cannes (www.festival-pyrotechnique-cannes.com)
Aug 15	Assumption of Mary
Late Aug	Jazz at La Villette Festival, Paris (www.villette.com)
Sept	Fall Arts Festival (Fête d'Automne), Paris; Wine harvest festivals in many towns
Early Oct	Grape Harvest Festival in Montmartre, Paris (www.commanderie-montmartre.com)
Nov 1	All Saints' Day
Early Nov	Dijon International and Gastronomic Fair, Dijon, Burgundy
Nov 11	Armistice Day
Late Nov	Wine Auction and Festival (Les Trois Glorieuses), Beaune
Late Nov–Dec 24	Christmas Markets, Strasbourg and Colmar
Dec 8	Festival of Lights (celebration of Virgin Mary, candlelit windows), Lyon
Dec 25	Christmas Day
Dec 31	New Year's Eve

Conversions and Climate

Numbers and Stumblers

- Europeans write a few of their numbers differently than we do: 1 = 1, 4 = 4, 7 = 7.
- In Europe, dates appear as day/month/year, so Christmas is 25/12/11.
- Commas are decimal points and decimals commas. A dollar and a half is 1,50, and there are 5.280 feet in a mile.
- When pointing, use your whole hand, palm down.
- When counting with fingers, start with your thumb. If you hold up your first finger to request one item, you'll probably get two.
- What Americans call the second floor of a building is the first floor in Europe.
- On escalators and moving sidewalks, Europeans keep the left "lane" open for passing. Keep to the right.

Metric Conversions (approximate)

A kilogram is 2.2 pounds, and 1 liter is about a quart, or almost four to a gallon. A kilometer is six-tenths of a mile. I figure kilometers to miles by cutting them in half and adding back 10 percent of the original (120 km: 60 + 12 = 72 miles, 300 km: 150 + 30 = 180 miles).

1 foot = 0.3 meter	1 square yard = 0.8 square meter
1 yard = 0.9 meter	1 square mile = 2.6 square kilometers
1 mile = 1.6 kilometers	1 ounce = 28 grams
1 centimeter = 0.4 inch	1 quart = 0.95 liter
1 meter = 39.4 inches	1 kilogram = 2.2 pounds
1 kilometer = 0.62 mile	32°F = 0°C

Clothing Sizes

When shopping for clothing, use these US-to-France comparisons as general guidelines (but note that no conversion is perfect).

- Women's dresses and blouses: Add 30
  (US women's size 10 = French size 40)
- Men's suits and jackets: Add 10
  (US size 40 regular = French size 50)
- Men's shirts: Multiply by 2 and add about 8
  (US men's size 15 collar = French size 38)
- Women's shoes: Add about 31
  (US size 8 = French size 38–39)
- Men's shoes: Add 32–34
  (US size 9 US = French size 43; US size 11 = French size 45)

Climate

First line, average daily high; second line, average daily low; third line, average days without rain. For more-detailed weather statistics for destinations in this book (as well as the rest of the world), check www.worldclimate.com.

Paris

	J	F	M	A	M	J	J	A	S	O	N	D
	43°	45°	54°	60°	68°	73°	76°	75°	70°	60°	50°	44°
	34°	34°	39°	43°	49°	55°	58°	58°	53°	46°	40°	36°
	14	14	19	17	19	18	18	19	17	18	15	15

Nice

	J	F	M	A	M	J	J	A	S	O	N	D
	50°	53°	59°	64°	71°	79°	84°	83°	77°	68°	58°	52°
	35°	36°	41°	46°	52°	58°	63°	63°	58°	51°	43°	37°
	23	22	24	23	23	26	29	26	24	23	21	21

Temperature Conversion: Fahrenheit and Celsius

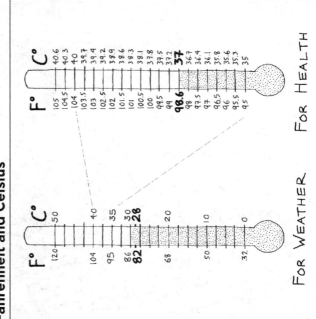

FOR WEATHER   FOR HEALTH

Europe takes its temperature using the Celsius scale, whereas we opt for Fahrenheit. For a rough conversion from Celsius to Fahrenheit, double the number and add 30. For weather, remember that 28°C is 82°F—perfect. For health, 37°C is just right.

Essential Packing Checklist

Whether you're traveling for five days or five weeks, here's what you'll need to bring. Remember to pack light to enjoy the sweet freedom of true mobility. Happy travels!

- [ ] 5 shirts
- [ ] 1 sweater or lightweight fleece jacket
- [ ] 2 pairs pants
- [ ] 1 pair shorts
- [ ] 1 swimsuit (women only—men can use shorts)
- [ ] 5 pairs underwear and socks
- [ ] 1 pair shoes
- [ ] 1 rain-proof jacket
- [ ] Tie or scarf
- [ ] Money belt
- [ ] Money—your mix of:
  - [ ] Debit card for ATM withdrawals
  - [ ] Credit card
  - [ ] Hard cash in dollars or euros (in \$20s or €20s)
- [ ] Documents (and back-up photocopies):
  - [ ] Passport
  - [ ] Printout of airline e-ticket
  - [ ] Driver's license
  - [ ] Student ID and hostel card
  - [ ] Railpass/car rental voucher
  - [ ] Insurance details

- [ ] Daypack
- [ ] Sealable plastic baggies
- [ ] Camera and related gear
- [ ] Empty water bottle
- [ ] Wristwatch and alarm clock
- [ ] Earplugs
- [ ] First-aid kit
- [ ] Medicine (labeled)
- [ ] Extra glasses/contacts and prescriptions
- [ ] Sunscreen and sunglasses
- [ ] Toiletries kit
- [ ] Soap
- [ ] Laundry soap
- [ ] Clothesline
- [ ] Small towel
- [ ] Sewing kit
- [ ] Travel information
- [ ] Necessary map(s)
- [ ] Address list (email and mailing addresses)
- [ ] Postcards and photos from home
- [ ] Notepad and pen
- [ ] Journal

If you plan to carry on your luggage, note that all liquids must be in three-ounce or smaller containers and fit within a single quart-size baggie. For details, see www.tsa.gov/travelers.

Hotel Reservation

To: _____
_____hotel_____ / _____email or fax_____

From: _____
_____name_____ / _____email or fax_____

Today's date: _____ / _____ / _____
                day   month   year

Dear Hotel _____,

Please make this reservation for me:

Name: _____

Total # of people: _____ # of rooms: _____ # of nights: _____

Arriving: _____ / _____ / _____   My time of arrival (24-hr clock): _____
           day   month   year   (I will telephone if I will be late)

Departing: _____ / _____ / _____
            day   month   year

Room(s): Single _____ Double _____ Twin _____ Triple _____ Quad _____

With: Toilet _____ Shower _____ Bath _____ Sink only _____

Special needs: View _____ Quiet _____ Cheapest _____ Ground Floor _____

Please email or fax confirmation of my reservation, along with the type of room reserved and the price. Please also inform me of your cancellation policy. After I hear from you, I will quickly send my credit-card information as a deposit to hold the room. Thank you.

Name _____

Address _____

City _____ **State** _____ **Zip Code** _____ **Country** _____

Before hoteliers can make your reservation, they want to know the information listed above. You can use this form as the basis for your email, or you can photocopy this page, fill in the information, and send it as a fax (also available online at www.ricksteves.com/reservation).

Pronunciation Guide for Place Names

When using the phonetics: Try to nasalize the n sound (let the sound come through your nose). Note that the "ahn" combination uses the "ah" sound in "father," but the "an" combination uses the "a" sound in "sack." Pronounce the "i" as the long "i" in "light." If your best attempt at pronunciation meets with a puzzled look, just point to the place name on the list.

In Paris

Arc de Triomphe ark duh tree-ohnf
arrondissement ah-rohn-dees-mohn
Bateaux-Mouches bah-toh moosh
Bon Marché bohn mar-shay
Carnavalet kar-nah-vah-lay
Champ de Mars shahn duh mar
Champs-Elysées shahn-zay-lee-zay
Conciergerie kon-see-ehr-zhuh-ree
Ecole Militaire eh-kohl mee-lee-tehr
Egouts ay-goo
Fauchon foh-shohn
Galeries Lafayette gah-luh-ree lah-fay-yet
gare gar
Gare d'Austerlitz gar doh-stehr-leets
Gare de l'Est gar duh less
Gare de Lyon gar duh lee-ohn
Gare du Nord gar dew nor
Gare St. Lazare gar san lah-zar
Garnier gar-nee-ay
Grand Palais grahn pah-lay
Grande Arche de la Défense grahnd arsh duh lah day-fahns
Ile de la Cité eel duh lah see-tay
Ile St. Louis eel san loo-ee
Jacquemart-André zhahk-mar-ahn-dray
Jardin des Plantes zhar-dan day plahnt
Jeu de Paume juh duh pohm
La Madeleine lah mah-duh-lehn
Le Hameau luh ah-moh
Les Halles lay ahl

Les Invalides lay-zan-vah-leed
Orangerie oh-rahn-zhuh-ree
Louvre loov-ruh
Marais mah-ray
marché aux puces mar-shay oh poos
Marmottan mar-moh-tahn
Métro may-troh
Monge mohnzh
Montmartre mohn-mart
Montparnasse mohn-par-nahs
Moulin Rouge moo-lan roozh
Musée d'Orsay mew-zay dor-say
Musée de l'Armée mew-zay duh lar-may
Notre-Dame noh-truh-dahm
Opéra Garnier oh-pay-rah gar-nee-ay
Orsay or-say
palais pah-lay
Palais de Justice pah-lay duh zhew-stees
Palais Royal pah-lay roh-yahl
Parc de la Villette park duh la vee-leht
Parc Monceau park mohn-soh
Père Lachaise pehr lah-shehz
Petit Palais puh-tee pah-lay
Pigalle pee-gahl
place Dauphine plahs doh-feen
place de la Bastille plahs duh lah bah-steel
place de la Concorde plahs duh lah kohn-kord
place de la République plahs duh lah ray-poo-bleek
place des Vosges plahs day vohzh
place du Tertre plahs dew tehr-truh
place St. André-des-Arts plahs san tahn-dray day-zart

place **Vendôme** plahs vahn-dohm
Pompidou pohn-pee-doo
pont pohn
pont Alexandre III pohn ah-leks-ahn-druh twah
pont Neuf pohn nuhf
Promenade Plantée proh-mehn-ahd plahn-tay
quai kay
Rive Droite reeve dwaht
Rive Gauche reeve gohsh
Rodin roh-dan
rue rew
rue Cler rew klehr
rue Daguerre rew dah-gehr
rue de Rivoli rew duh ree-voh-lee
rue des Rosiers rew day roz-ee-ay
rue Montorgueil rew mohn-tor-goy
rue Mouffetard rew moof-tar
Sacré-Cœur sah-kray-koor
Sainte-Chapelle sant-shah-pehl
Seine sehn
Sèvres-Babylone seh-vruh-bah-bee-lohn
Sorbonne sor-buhn
St. Germain-des-Prés san zhehr-man-day-pray
St. Julien-le-Pauvre san zhew-lee-ehn-luh-poh-vruh
St. Séverin sahn say-vuh-ran
St. Sulpice sahn sool-pees
Tour Eiffel toor ee-fehl
Trianon tree-ahn-ohn
Trocadéro troh-kah-day-roh
Tuileries twee-lay-ree
Venus de Milo vuh-news duh mee-loh

Outside of Paris

Abri du Cap Blanc ah-bree dew cah blahn
Aiguille du Midi ah-gwee dew mee-dee
Ainhoa an-oh-ah
Albi ahl-bee
Alet ah-lay
Alise Ste. Reine ah-leez sant rehn
Aloxe-Corton ah-lohx kor-tohn
Alsace ahl-sahs

Amboise ahm-bwahz
Annecy ahn-see
Antibes ahn-teeb
Aosta (Italy) ay-oh-stah
Apt ahp
Aquitaine ah-kee-tehn
Arles arl
Arromanches ah-roh-mahnsh
Autoire oh-twahr
Auvergne oh-vehrn
Avignon ah-veen-yohn
Azay-le-Rideau ah-zay luh ree-doh
Balazuc bah-lah-zook
Bayeux bi-yuh
Bayonne bi-yuhn
Beaucaire boh-kehr
Beaujolais boh-zhoh-lay
Beaune bohn
Bedoin buh-dwan
Bennwihr behn-veer
Beynac bay-nak
Biarritz bee-ah-reetz
Blois blah
Bonnieux bohn-yuh
Bordeaux bor-doh
Brancion brahn-see-ohn
Brittany bree-tah-nee
Bruniquel brew-nee-kehl
Caen kahn
Cahors kah-or
Cajarc kah-zhark
Calais kah-lay
Camargue kah-marg
Cambord kahn-bor
Cancale kahn-kahl
Carcassonne kar-kah-suhn
Carennac kah-rehn-ahk
Carsac kar-sahk
Castelnaud kah-stehl-noh
Castelnau-de-Montmiral kah-stehl-noh-duh-mohn-mee-rahl
Caussade koh-sahd
Cavaillon kah-vi-ohn
Cénac say-nahk
Céret say-ray
Chambord shahn-bor
Chamonix shah-moh-nee
Champagne shahn-pahn-yuh
Chapaize shah-pehz
Chartres shart
Château de Chatonnière shah-toh duh shah-tuhn-yehr
Château de Rivau shah-toh duh ree-voh

Château du Haut-Kœnigsbourg shah-toh dew oh-koh-neegs-boorg
Châteauneuf-du-Pape shah-toh-nuhf-dew-pahp
Châteauneuf-en-Auxois shah-toh-nuhf-eh<u>n</u>-ohx-wah
Chaumont-sur-Loire shoh-moh<u>n</u>-sewr-lwahr
Chenonceau shuh-noh<u>n</u>-soh
Chenonceaux shuh-noh<u>n</u>-soh
Cherbourg shehr-boor
Cheverny shuh-vehr-nee
Chinon shee-noh<u>n</u>
Cluny klew-nee
Colleville kohl-veel
Collioure kohl-yoor
Collonges-la-Rouge koh-lohnzh-lah-roozh
Colmar kohl-mar
Cordes-sur-Ciel kord-sewr-see-yehl
Côte d'Azur koht dah-zewr
Cougnac koon-yahk
Courseulles-sur-Mer koor-suhl-sewr-mehr
Coustellet koo-stuh-lay
Digne deen-yuh
Dijon dee-zhoh<u>n</u>
Dinan dee-nah<u>n</u>
Dinard dee-nar
Domme dohm
Dordogne dor-dohn-yuh
Eguisheim eh-geh-shim
Entrevaux ah<u>n</u>-truh-voh
Epernay ay-pehr-nay
Espelette eh-speh-leht
Eze-Bord-de-Mer ehz-bor-duh-mehr
Eze-le-Village ehz-luh-vee-lahzh
Faucon foh-koh<u>n</u>
Flavigny-sur-Ozerain flah-veen-yee-sewr-oh-zuh-ra<u>n</u>
Font-de-Gaume foh<u>n</u>-duh-gohm
Fontenay foh<u>n</u>-tuh-nay
Fontevraud fohn-tuh-vroh
Fontvieille foh<u>n</u>-vee-yeh-ee
Fougères foo-zher
Fougères-sur-Bièvre foo-zher-sewr-bee-ehv
Gaillac gï-yahk
Gigondas zhee-goh<u>n</u>-dahs
Giverny zhee-vehr-nee
Gordes gord

Gorges de l'Ardèche gorzh duh lar-dehsh
Grenoble gruh-noh-bluh
Grouin groo-a<u>n</u>
Guédelon gway-duh-loh<u>n</u>
Hautes Corbières oht kor-bee-yehr
Hendaye eh<u>n</u>-dï
Honfleur oh<u>n</u>-flur
Huisnes-sur-Mer ween-sewr-mehr
Hunawihr uhn-ah-veer
Ile Besnard eel bay-nar
Isle-sur-la-Sorgue eel-sewr-lah-sorg
Juan-les-Pins zhwa<u>n</u>-lay-pa<u>n</u>
Kaysersberg kï-zehrs-behrg
Kientzheim keentz-īm
La Charente lah shah-rah<u>n</u>t
La Rhune lah rewn
La Rochepot lah rohsh-poh
La Roque St. Christophe lah rohk sa<u>n</u> kree-stohf
La Roque-Gageac lah rohk-gah-zhahk
La Trophée des Alpes lah troh-fay dayz ahlp
La Turbie lah tewr-bee
Lacoste lah-kohst
Langeais lah<u>n</u>-zhay
Languedoc long-dohk
Lascaux lah-skoh
Lastours lahs-toor
Le Bugue luh bewg
Le Crestet luh kruh-stay
Le Havre luh hah-vruh
Le Ruquet luh rew-kay
Lémeré lay-muh-ray
Les Baux lay boh
Les Eyzies-de-Tayac lay zay-zee-duh-tï-yahk
Les Praz lay prah
Les Vosges lay vohzh
Limoges lee-mohzh
Loches lohsh
Loire lwahr
Longues-sur-Mer long-sewr-mehr
Loubressac loo-bruh-sahk
Lourmarin loo-mah-ra<u>n</u>
Luberon lew-beh-roh<u>n</u>
Lyon lee-oh<u>n</u>
Malaucène mah-loh-sehn
Marne-la-Vallée-Chessy marn-lah-vah-lay-shuh-see
Marseille mar-say

Martel mar-tehl
Mausanne moh-sahn
Ménerbes may-nehrb
Millau mee-yoh
Minerve mee-nerv
Mirabel mee-rah-behl
Modreuc mohd-rewk
Mont Blanc mohn blahn
Mont St. Michel mohn san mee-shehl
Mont Ventoux mohn vehn-too
Montenvers mohn-tuh-vehr
Montfort mohn-for
Montignac mohn-teen-yahk
Mortemart mort-mar
Munster mewn-stehr
Nantes nahnt
Nice nees
Normandy nor-mahn-dee
Nyons nee-yohns
Oradour-sur-Glane oh-rah-door-sewr-glahn
Orange oh-rahnzh
Padirac pah-dee-rahk
Paris pah-ree
Pech Merle pehsh mehrl
Peyrepertuse pay-ruh-per-tewz
Pointe du Hoc pwant dew ohk
Pont du Gard pohn dew gahr
Pontorson pohn-tor-sohn
Provence proh-vahns
Puycelci pew-suhl-cee
Puyméras pwee-may-rahs
Queribus kehr-ee-bews
Reims rans (rhymes with France)
Remoulins ruh-moo-lan
Rennes rehn
Ribeauvillé ree-boh-vee-yay
Riquewihr reek-veer
Rocamadour roh-kah-mah-door
Rouen roo-ahn
Rouffignac roo-feen-yahk
Roussillon roo-see-yohn
Route du Vin root dew van
Sablet sah-blay
Sare sahr
Sarlat sar-lah
Savigny-lès-Beaune sah-veen-yee-lay-bohn
Savoie sah-vwah
Séguret say-goo-ray
Semur-en-Auxois suh-moor-ehn-ohx-wah

Sigolsheim see-gohl-shīm
Souillac soo-ee-yahk
St. Cirq Lapopie san seerk lah-poh-pee
St. Cyprien san seep-ree-ehn
St. Emilion san tay-meel-yohn
St. Geniès san zhuh-nyehs
St. Jean-de-Luz san zhahn-duh-looz
St. Jean-Pied-de-Port san zhahn-pee-yay-duh-por
St. Malo san mah-loh
St. Marcellin-lès-Vaison san mar-suh-lan-lay-vay-zohn
St. Rémy san ray-mee
St. Romain-en-Viennois san roh-man-ehn-vee-ehn-nwah
St. Suliac san soo-lee-ahk
St-Paul-de-Vence san-pohl-duh-vahns
Ste. Mère Eglise sant mehr ay-gleez
Stes-Maries-de-la-Mer sant-mah-ree-duh-lah-mehr
Strasbourg strahs-boorg
Suzette soo-zeht
Taizé teh-zay
Tarascon tah-rah-skohn
Tours toor
Turckheim tewrk-hīm
Ussé oo-say
Uzès oo-zehs
Vacqueyras vah-kee-rahs
Vaison la Romaine vay-zohn lah roh-mehn
Valançay vah-lahn-say
Valréas vahl-ray-ahs
Vence vahns
Verdun vehr-duhn
Versailles vehr-sī
Veynes vay-nuh
Vézelay vay-zuh-lay
Vierville-sur-Mer vee-yehr-veel-sewr-mehr
Villandry vee-lahn-dry
Villefranche-de-Rouergue veel-frahnsh-duh-roo-ehrg
Villefranche-sur-Mer veel-frahnsh-sewr-mehr
Villeneuve-lès-Avignon veel-nuhv-lay-zah-veeh-yohn
Vitrac vee-trahk
Vouvray voo-vray
Villedieu vee-luh-dyuh

French Survival Phrases

When using the phonetics, try to nasalize the n̲ sound.

English	French	Phonetics
Good day.	Bonjour.	bohn̲-zhoor
Mrs. / Mr.	Madame / Monsieur	mah-dahm / muhs-yur
Do you speak English?	Parlez-vous anglais?	par-lay-voo ahn̲-glay
Yes. / No.	Oui. / Non.	wee / nohn̲
I understand.	Je comprends.	zhuh kohn̲-prahn̲
I don't understand.	Je ne comprends pas.	zhuh nuh kohn̲-prahn̲ pah
Please.	S'il vous plaît.	see voo play
Thank you.	Merci.	mehr-see
I'm sorry.	Désolé.	day-zoh-lay
Excuse me.	Pardon.	par-dohn̲
(No) problem.	(Pas de) problème.	(pah duh) proh-blehm
It's good.	C'est bon.	say bohn̲
Goodbye.	Au revoir.	oh vwahr
one / two	un / deux	uhn̲ / duh
three / four	trois / quatre	twah / kah-truh
five / six	cinq / six	san̲k / sees
seven / eight	sept / huit	seht / weet
nine / ten	neuf / dix	nuhf / dees
How much is it?	Combien?	kohn̲-bee-an̲
Write it?	Ecrivez?	ay-kree-vay
Is it free?	C'est gratuit?	say grah-twee
Included?	Inclus?	an̲-klew
Where can I buy / find...?	Où puis-je acheter / trouver...?	oo pwee-zhuh ah-shuh-tay / troo-vay
I'd like / We'd like...	Je voudrais / Nous voudrions...	zhuh voo-dray / noo voo-dree-ohn̲
...a room.	...une chambre.	ewn shahn̲-bruh
...a ticket to ___.	...un billet pour ___.	uhn̲ bee-yay poor
Is it possible?	C'est possible?	say poh-see-bluh
Where is...?	Où est...?	oo ay
...the train station	...la gare	lah gar
...the bus station	...la gare routière	lah gar root-yehr
...tourist information	...l'office du tourisme	loh-fees dew too-reez-muh
Where are the toilets?	Où sont les toilettes?	oo sohn̲ lay twah-leht
men	hommes	ohm
women	dames	dahm
left / right	à gauche / à droite	ah gohsh / ah dwaht
straight	tout droit	too dwah
When does this open / close?	Ça ouvre / ferme à quelle heure?	sah oo-vruh / fehrm ah kehl ur
At what time?	À quelle heure?	ah kehl ur
Just a moment.	Un moment.	uhn̲ moh-mahn̲
now / soon / later	maintenant / bientôt / plus tard	man̲-tuh-nahn̲ / bee-an̲-toh / plew tar
today / tomorrow	aujourd'hui / demain	oh-zhoor-dwee / duh-man̲

APPENDIX

In the Restaurant

English	French	Pronunciation
I'd like / We'd like...	Je voudrais / Nous voudrions...	zhuh voo-dray / noo voo-dree-ohn
...to reserve...	...réserver...	ray-zehr-vay
...a table for one / two.	...une table pour un / deux.	ewn tah-bluh poor uhn / duh
Non-smoking.	Non fumeur.	nohn few-mur
Is this seat free?	C'est libre?	say lee-bruh
The menu (in English), please.	La carte (en anglais), s'il vous plaît.	lah kart (ahn ahn-glay) see voo play
service (not) included	service (non) compris	sehr-vees (nohn) kohn-pree
to go	à emporter	ah ahn-por-tay
with / without	avec / sans	ah-vehk / sahn
and / or	et / ou	ay / oo
special of the day	plat du jour	plah dew zhoor
specialty of the house	spécialité de la maison	spay-see-ah-lee-tay duh lah may-zohn
appetizers	hors-d'oeuvre	or-duh-vruh
first course (soup, salad)	entrée	ahn-tray
main course (meat, fish)	plat principal	plah pran-see-pahl
bread	pain	pan
cheese	fromage	froh-mahzh
sandwich	sandwich	sahnd-weech
soup	soupe	soop
salad	salade	sah-lahd
meat	viande	vee-ahnd
chicken	poulet	poo-lay
fish	poisson	pwah-sohn
seafood	fruits de mer	frwee duh mehr
fruit	fruit	frwee
vegetables	légumes	lay-gewm
dessert	dessert	duh-sehr
mineral water	eau minérale	oh mee-nay-rahl
tap water	l'eau du robinet	loh dew roh-bee-nay
milk	lait	lay
(orange) juice	jus (d'orange)	zhew (doh-rahnzh)
coffee	café	kah-fay
tea	thé	tay
wine	vin	van
red / white	rouge / blanc	roozh / blahn
glass / bottle	verre / bouteille	vehr / boo-teh-ee
beer	bière	bee-ehr
Cheers!	Santé!	sahn-tay
More. / Another.	Plus. / Un autre.	plew / uhn oh-truh
The same.	La même chose.	lah mehm shohz
The bill, please.	L'addition, s'il vous plaît.	lah-dee-see-ohn see voo play
tip	pourboire	poor-bwar
Delicious!	Délicieux!	day-lee-see-uh

For more user-friendly French phrases, check out *Rick Steves' French Phrase Book and Dictionary* or *Rick Steves' French, Italian & German Phrase Book*.

INDEX

MAP INDEX

Audio Europe

Free mobile app (and podcast)

With the **Rick Steves Audio Europe** app, your iPhone or smartphone becomes a powerful travel tool.

This exciting app organizes Rick's entire audio library by country—giving you a playlist of all his audio walking tours, radio interviews, and travel tips for wherever you're going in Europe.

Let the experts Rick interviews enrich your understanding. Let Rick's self-guided tours amplify your guidebook. With Rick in your ear, Europe gets even better.

Thanks Facebook fans for submitting photos while on location! From top: John Kuijper in Florence, Brenda Mamer with her mother in Rome, Angel Capobianco in London, and Alyssa Passey with her friend in Paris.

Find out more at ricksteves.com/audioeurope

Free information and great gear to

▶ Plan Your Trip

Browse thousands of articles and a wealth of money-saving tips for planning your dream trip. You'll find up-to-date information on Europe's best destinations, packing smart, getting around, finding rooms, staying healthy, avoiding scams and more.

▶ Eurail Passes

Find out, step-by-step, if a railpass makes sense for your trip—and how to avoid buying more than you need. Get a bunch of free extras!

▶ Graffiti Wall & Travelers' Helpline

Learn, ask, share—our online community of savvy travelers is a great resource for first-time travelers to Europe, as well as seasoned pros.

Rick Steves' Europe Through the Back Door, Inc.

turn your travel dreams into affordable reality

▶ Free Audio Tours & Travel Newsletter

Get your nose out of this guide book and focus on what you'll be seeing with Rick's free audio tours of the greatest sights in Paris, London, Rome, Florence and Venice.

Subscribe to our free Travel News e-newsletter, and get monthly articles from Rick on what's happening in Europe.

▶ Great Gear from Rick's Travel Store

Pack light and right—on a budget—with Rick's custom-designed carry-on bags, roll-aboards, day packs, travel accessories, guidebooks, journals, maps and DVDs of his TV shows.

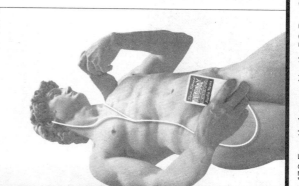

130 Fourth Avenue North, PO Box 2009 • Edmonds, WA 98020 USA
Phone: (425) 771-8303 • Fax: (425) 771-0833 • www.ricksteves.com

www.ricksteves.com

Rick Steves guidebooks are published by Avalon Travel,
a member of the Perseus Books Group.

NOW AVAILABLE: eBOOKS, APPS, DVDS, & BLU-RAY

eBOOKS

Most guides available as eBooks from Amazon, Barnes & Noble, Borders, Apple iBook and Sony eReader, beginning January 2011

RICK STEVES' EUROPE DVDs

Austria & the Alps
Eastern Europe, Israel & Egypt
England & Wales
European Travel Skills & Specials
France
Germany, Benelux & More
Greece & Turkey
Iran
Ireland & Scotland
Italy's Cities
Italy's Countryside
Rick Steves' European Christmas
Scandinavia
Spain & Portugal

BLU-RAY

Celtic Charms
Eastern Europe Favorites
European Christmas
Italy Through the Back Door
Surprising Cities of Europe

PHRASE BOOKS & DICTIONARIES

French
French, Italian & German
German
Italian
Portuguese
Spanish

JOURNALS

Rick Steves' Pocket Travel Journal
Rick Steves' Travel Journal

APPS

Rick Steves' Ancient Rome Tour
Rick Steves' Historic Paris Walk
Rick Steves' Louvre Tour
Rick Steves' Orsay Museum Tour
Rick Steves' St. Peter's Basilica Tour
Rick Steves' Versailles

PLANNING MAPS

Britain, Ireland & London
Europe
France & Paris
Germany, Austria & Switzerland
Ireland
Italy
Spain & Portugal

Rick Steves books and DVDs are available at bookstores and through online booksellers.

Credits

Researchers

In addition to Rick Steves and Steve Smith, the following researchers helped update this book:

Kristen Kusnic Michel

Kristen, a native of Seattle, first came to Europe as an exchange student, studying theater. Years later, she is fluent in French, German, red wine, and dark chocolate. For the last decade she's been leading tours and researching guidebooks for Rick Steves. She lives in Paris with her husband, Sylvain.

Caitlin Woodbury

Caitlin splits time each year between Santa Rosa, California, and an old stone house in southwest France, where she runs a B&B with her husband, Albert. She has worked in wineries and as an editorial assistant at a newspaper. She loves good food, good wines, and lively conversation—and is an excellent speller.

Jennifer Gouge

Jennifer, a one-time tax accountant, abandoned her adding machine to move to France. She has skied the Alps' highest peaks, explored Angkor Wat in Cambodia, and bargained in Moroccan bazaars. Now a tour guide and guidebook researcher for Rick Steves, Jennifer lives in Seattle, where she enjoys hosting dinner parties.

Contributor
Gene Openshaw

Gene is the co-author of seven Rick Steves books. For this book he wrote material on Europe's art, history, and contemporary culture. When not traveling, Gene enjoys composing music, recovering from his 1973 trip to Europe with Rick, and living everyday life with his daughter.

Images

Location	Photographer
Title Page: Villefranche-sur-Mer	Steve Smith
Full-Page Color: Collioure	Dominic Bonuccelli
Paris: Louvre	Rick Steves
Near Paris: Versailles	Rick Steves
Normandy: Mont St. Michel	Rick Steves
Brittany: Dinan	Steve Smith
The Loire: Château d'Amboise	Steve Smith
Dordogne: Dordogne River Valley	David C. Hoerlein
Basque Country: St. Jean-de-Luz	Cameron Hewitt
Languedoc: Carcassonne	Dominic Bonuccelli
Provence: Pont du Gard Aqueduct	Rick Steves
The French Riviera: Cannes	Steve Smith
The French Alps: Chamonix Valley	David C. Hoerlein
Burgundy: Château de la Rochepot	Steve Smith
Lyon: Saône River and Bonaparte Bridge	Steve Smith
Alsace and Northern France: Kaysersberg	Steve Smith
Reims and Verdun:	
The Five Defenders of Verdun	Abe Bringolf

Acknowledgments

Thanks to Steve's wife, Karen Lewis Smith, for her assistance covering French cuisine; and to Steve's children, Travis and Maria, for help with children's activities.

Thanks to Aaron Harting for his help with the "Winter Sports in Chamonix" section. Aaron is a travel advisor and assistant video editor in our Edmonds office, assists on a multitude of tours, and has skied his way through much of the Alps.

Rick Steves' Guidebook Series

Country Guides

Rick Steves' Best of Europe
Rick Steves' Croatia &
  Slovenia
Rick Steves' Eastern Europe
Rick Steves' England
Rick Steves' France
Rick Steves' Germany
Rick Steves' Great Britain
Rick Steves' Ireland
Rick Steves' Italy
Rick Steves' Portugal
Rick Steves' Scandinavia
Rick Steves' Spain
Rick Steves' Switzerland

City and Regional Guides

Rick Steves' Amsterdam,
  Bruges & Brussels
Rick Steves' Athens &
  the Peloponnese
Rick Steves' Budapest
Rick Steves' Florence &
  Tuscany
Rick Steves' Istanbul
Rick Steves' London
Rick Steves' Paris
Rick Steves' Prague &
  the Czech Republic
Rick Steves' Provence &
  the French Riviera
Rick Steves' Rome
Rick Steves' Venice
Rick Steves' Vienna,
  Salzburg & Tirol

Rick Steves' Phrase Books

French
French/Italian/German
German
Italian
Portuguese
Spanish

Snapshot Guides

Excerpted chapters from country guides, such as Rick Steves'
Snapshot Barcelona, Rick Steves' Snapshot Scotland, and
Rick Steves' Snapshot Hill Towns of Central Italy.

Pocket Guides (new in 2011)

Condensed, pocket-size, full-color guides to Europe's top
cities: Paris, London, and Rome.

Other Books

Rick Steves' Europe 101: History and Art for the Traveler
Rick Steves' Europe Through the Back Door
Rick Steves' European Christmas
Rick Steves' Postcards from Europe
Rick Steves' Travel as a Political Act

Avalon Travel
a member of the Perseus Books Group
1700 Fourth Street
Berkeley, California 94710

Printed in the USA by Worzalla. First printing November 2010.

For the latest on Rick's lectures, guidebooks, tours, public radio show, and public television series, contact Europe Through the Back Door, Box 2009, Edmonds, WA 98020, 425/771-8303, fax 425/771-0833, rick@ricksteves.com, www.ricksteves.com.

ISBN 978-1-59880-663-2
ISSN 1084-4406

Europe Through the Back Door Reviewing Editors: Cameron Hewitt, Jennifer Madison Davis
ETBD Editors: Cathy McDonald, Tom Griffin, Sarah McCormic, Gretchen Strauch, Cathy Lu
ETBD Managing Editor: Risa Laib
Research Assistance: Kristin Kusnic Michel, Caitlin Woodbury, Jennifer Gouge
Avalon Travel Senior Editor and Series Manager: Madhu Prasher
Avalon Travel Project Editor: Kelly Lydick
Copy Editor: Jennifer Malnick
Proofreader: Ellie Winters
Indexer: Claire Splan
Production & Typesetting: McGuire Barber Design
Cover Design: Kimberly Glyder Design
Graphic Content Director: Laura VanDeventer
Maps & Graphics: David C. Hoerlein, Laura VanDeventer, Lauren Mills, Barb Geisler, Mike Morgenfeld, Brice Ticen
Photography: Rick Steves, Steve Smith, David C. Hoerlein, Cameron Hewitt, Dominic Bonuccelli, Laura VanDeventer, Lauren Mills, Julie Coen, Barb Geisler, Robyn Cronin, Abe Bringolf, Paul Orcutt, Mike Potter, Carol Ries, Dorian Yates, Rob Unck
Front Cover Photo: Castelnaud © Steve Smith

Foldout Color Map ▶

The foldout map on the opposite page includes:
- A map of France on one side
- City map of Paris, an inset of Montmarte, and a Paris Métro map on the other side

MOTHER'S DAY

"It is the character's business as an organizer that makes her successful as an amateur sleuth. . . . The story flows well."—*RT Book Reviews*

MILKSHAKES, MERMAIDS, AND MURDER

"Rosett's latest Ellie Avery mystery is less about solving a mystery and more about finding out the truth. The story becomes more about a woman trying to protect her family, and that's a message most of us can relate to."
—*RT Book Reviews*, 4.5 Stars

MISTLETOE, MERRIMENT, AND MURDER

"Sara Rosett's Ellie Avery series is a winner. Rosett always delivers a terrific mystery with believable characters and lots of heart. The insider look at the life of a military spouse makes this series a fascinating read. I look forward to each new book."
—*Denise Swanson*, *New York Times* bestselling author of the Scumble River and Devereaux's Dime mystery series

"Intriguing characters, a strong setting, more than a dash of humor and a suspenseful plot that ably keeps us guessing until the end. . . . Yet, what places Air Force wife Ellie Avery at the top of my list are the poignant descriptions of what military families face each and every day."
—*Katherine Hall Page*, Agatha Award-winning author of *The Body in the Boudoir*

MIMOSAS, MISCHIEF, AND MURDER

"What fun is a funeral without a corpse? Ellie Avery steps into snooping mode, and not a moment too soon. . . . Rosett's grasp of the minutiae of mommyhood is excellent."—*Kirkus Reviews*

"A winning mystery . . . A rumor of hidden money, secret letters from a famous recluse, a fire, a threatening message, and a crazed gunman add to the cozy mischief."
—*Publishers Weekly*

"Charm, Southern sass, and suspense abound in the sixth delightful cozy mystery in Sara Rosett's series featuring Ellie Avery—mom, military wife, part-time professional organizer, and amateur sleuth."
—*Fresh Fiction*

MINT JULEPS, MAYHEM, AND MURDER

"A nifty mystery . . . Fans of TV's *Air Force Wives* will especially appreciate Ellie, a smart crime solver who successfully navigates the challenges of military life."
—*Publishers Weekly*

"Some cozies just hit on all cylinders, and Rosett's Ellie Avery titles are among the best. Her books recall the early Carolyn Hart."—*Library Journal*

"Tightly constructed with many well-fitted, suspenseful turns, and flows like a country creek after an all-day rain."
—*Shine*

MAGNOLIAS, MOONLIGHT, AND MURDER

"Rosett's engaging fourth Mom Zone mystery finds super efficient crime-solver Ellie Avery living in a new subdivision in North Dawkins, GA . . . Some nifty party tips help keep the sleuthing on the cozy side."
—*Publishers Weekly*

GETTING AWAY IS DEADLY

"No mystery is a match for the likeable, efficient Ellie, who unravels this multilayered plot with skill and class."
—*Romantic Times Book Reviews* (four stars)

"*Getting Away Is Deadly* keeps readers moving down some surprising paths—and on the edge of their chairs—until the very end."—*Cozy Library*

"Sparkling . . . Rosett skillfully interweaves a subplot and provides practical travel tips."—*Publishers Weekly*

"Hyperorganized Ellie is an engaging heroine, always ready with tips for ordering your life."—*Kirkus Reviews*

STAYING HOME IS A KILLER

"A satisfying, well-executed cozy . . . The author includes practical tips for organizing closets, but the novel's most valuable insight is its window into women's lives on a military base."—*Publishers Weekly*

"If you like cozy mysteries that have plenty of action and lots of suspects and clues, *Staying Home Is a Killer* will be a fun romp through murder and mayhem. This is a mystery with a 'mommy lit' flavor. . . . A fun read."
—*Armchair Interviews*

"Thoroughly entertaining. The author's smooth, succinct writing style enables the plot to flow effortlessly until its captivating conclusion."
—*Romantic Times Book Reviews* (four stars)

MOVING IS MURDER

"A fun debut for an appealing young heroine."
—*Carolyn Hart,* author of the Death on Demand mystery series

"A squadron of suspects, a unique setting, and a twisted plot will keep you turning pages!"
—*Nancy J. Cohen,* author of the Bad Hair Day mystery series

"Everyone should snap to attention and salute this fresh new voice."
—**Denise Swanson,** nationally bestselling author of the Scumble River mystery series

"An absorbing read that combines sharp writing and tight plotting with a fascinating peek into the world of military wives. Jump in!"
—**Cynthia Baxter,** author of the Reigning Cats & Dogs mystery series

"Reading Sara Rosett's *Moving Is Murder* is like making a new friend—I can't wait to brew a pot of tea and read all about sleuth Ellie Avery's next adventure!"
—**Leslie Meier,** author of the Lucy Stone mystery series

"Mayhem, murder, and the military! Rosett is an author to watch."
—**Alesia Holliday,** author of the December Vaughn mystery series

"A cozy debut that'll help you get organized and provide entertainment in your newfound spare time."
—**Kirkus Reviews**

"Packed with helpful moving tips, Rosett's cute cozy debut introduces Ellie Avery . . . an appealing heroine, an intriguing insider peek into air force life."
—**Publishers Weekly**

"Ellie's intelligent investigation highlights this mystery. There are plenty of red herrings along her path to solving the murderous puzzle—along with expert tips on organizing a move. The stunning conclusion should delight readers."—**Romantic Times Book Reviews**

Mother's Day,
Muffins,
and Murder

Mother's Day, Muffins, and Murder

Sara Rosett

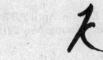

KENSINGTON BOOKS
http://www.kensingtonbooks.com

KENSINGTON BOOKS are published by

Kensington Publishing Corp.
119 West 40th Street
New York, NY 10018

All Kensington titles, imprints, and distributed lines are available at special quantity discounts for bulk purchases for sales promotion, premiums, fund-raising, educational, or institutional use. Special book excerpts or customized printings can also be created to fit specific needs. For details, write or phone the office of the Kensington Special Sales Manager: Attn. Special Sales Department. Kensington Publishing Corp., 119 West 40th Street, New York, NY 10018. Phone: 1-800-221-2647.

Kensington and the K logo Reg. U.S. Pat. & TM Off.

ISBN-13: 978-1-61773-151-8
ISBN-10: 1-61773-151-X
First Kensington Hardcover Edition: April 2017
First Kensington Mass Market Printing: May 2018

eISBN-13: 978-1-61773-152-5
eISBN-10: 1-61773-152-8

10 9 8 7 6 5 4 3 2 1

Printed in the United States of America

To
Mom

Chapter One

"How many more days of school are left?" Livvy asked.

"I'm not sure." I waited until Nathan climbed out of the minivan after Livvy, then picked up the plastic container of blueberry muffins, as well as paper plates and napkins, and clicked the button on the key fob to lock the minivan. "Let's see—it's the second week of May, so you probably have around fifteen days or so left."

We turned toward the low, flat-roofed brick elementary school building. Despite it being thirty minutes before the first bell of the day, the school parking lot was packed, and I'd had to park at the farthest point away from the school, on the grass near the fence that enclosed the school grounds. The sun was barely over the tops of the tall pines that ringed the outer edge of the back of the school's property, but the air was already dense and muggy. Spring was a fleeting season in middle Georgia. Ninety-degree days had been our norm for several weeks, and today would be just the same, sunny and humid.

I'd parked beside an old Subaru. The hatchback was open and a small, gray-headed woman was pulling something out of the back of the car. "Twelve," she said as we came even with her. "Twelve days left in the school year, not counting today—for students, that is. Teachers have seventeen."

"Mrs. Harris," Livvy said with delight as she moved to give the woman a hug. I smiled, glad to see that despite the grown-up veneer Livvy had acquired over the last year or so—she was a big fifth-grader now—she was still happy to see her former first-grade teaching assistant.

Mrs. Harris pulled Livvy in for a tight hug against her flat chest. I wasn't sure how old Mrs. Harris was. Wrinkles scored her face, and she'd tamed her iron-colored hair, which was wiry with white strands, into a flat bowl cut that just brushed her eyebrows, earlobes, and the back of her neck, a few inches above her collar. With her inquisitive dark eyes and delicate frame, she reminded me of a sparrow. She had a way of nudging the students toward the right answer with her encouraging smile and expressive face, something I'd seen firsthand when I'd volunteered in the classroom, first with Livvy and then with Nathan.

The first-grade teachers might rotate in and out, but Mrs. Harris was a steady, unchanging presence in the first-grade hallway. She worked with Mrs. Dunst, who had been Nathan's first-grade teacher last year.

Nathan played it a bit cooler, but he gave her his full attention when Mrs. Harris looked toward him and asked, "So how is your year going, Nathan? Isn't that nice Mr. Spagnatilli your teacher this year for second grade?"

Nathan nodded. "Yes, Mr. S. That's what we call him. He's great."

I exchanged a glance with Mrs. Harris. "High praise, indeed," she said, and I agreed.

"He likes science, and he has a snake," Nathan said. "In the classroom."

Livvy rolled her eyes. "It's in a tank."

"So I've heard," Mrs. Harris said. "And fish, too."

Nathan's head bobbed again. "Yep. And a full-size skeleton, so we can learn about bones and everything. He's cool. He let us decorate Mr. Metacarpal—that's the skeleton—for Halloween."

"Excellent," Mrs. Harris said. "Now, I wonder if you could help me?" she asked, and I recognized the inquisitive tone she used in the classroom. She managed to convey that Livvy and Nathan helping her would be both a privilege and an honor. I'd seen her in action when the kids had been in first grade, and she always had kids straining, their arms raised high in the air, in hopes that they would be the lucky one she singled out to help her.

Both kids instantly said yes, and she turned to the open hatchback. "I have quite a load of muffins in here, and I have to get them to the first-grade classrooms."

Livvy had already shifted a plastic tub into her arms. Nathan said, "I can take two. No, three."

Mrs. Harris removed the top tub, which was teetering dangerously, from Nathan's arms. "Two is more than enough, Nathan. Thank you. Just drop them in the classroom, and go to the cafeteria."

The classrooms didn't open until eight o'clock, and students who arrived between seven-fifty and eight o'clock went directly to the cafeteria to wait for the bell that signaled they could go to their classrooms. The kids hurried away at their quick pace, while I waited for Mrs. Harris. She picked up the last tub of muffins, closed the hatchback, then fell into step with me.

"So you're the designated muffin person today?" I asked.

"Oh, yes. I always think it's a bit sad to ask the mothers to bake and bring muffins for their own celebration," she said with a birdlike tilt of her head toward the plastic container I carried. Today, as the sign in front of the school proclaimed, was WEDNESDAY—5/10—MUFFINS WITH MOM DAY, the school's nod to Mother's Day. The sign also listed the next end-of-year activity, Field Day, which was scheduled for Thursday and Friday. I had pretty much cleared my calendar for the rest of this week because I knew I would be at the school for Field Day, and next week was Teacher Appreciation Week, which I had agreed to coordinate.

"After all," Mrs. Harris continued, "we don't ask the fathers to bring donuts for Donuts with Dad Day."

"Funny how it always works out that way, isn't it?" I missed the days of having my kids in Mrs. Harris's classroom. She was as much about looking after the parents as she was about caring for the kids. I was now a seasoned "room mom," and looking back, I could see that Mrs. Harris had done a lot, and she didn't focus only on the kids. She'd also helped ease the parents through the transition to sending their kids to class each day.

A car pulled into the lot, and we both shifted to the left, as far as we could get from the blue Ford Fiesta. It whipped through the parking lot, bumped off the edge of the asphalt, and surged onto the grass between the two wavy rows of cars that had parked rather haphazardly in an open area, the elementary school's makeshift overflow lot. A tight turn slewed the car into a slot barely wide enough for it, between two hulking SUVs. The door opened a crack, and a blond head popped out. The woman worked her way out of the car, contorting herself in the narrow space, reminding me of those nature shows where you see a butterfly fighting its way out of a chrysalis.

She wrestled a huge tote bag out of the car behind her, then emerged from between the two cars and smoothed her Peter Pan shirt collar. "Hello, Mrs. Harris," she said as she caught sight of us.

"Ms. McCormick," Mrs. Harris said with a nod. I slid my gaze toward Mrs. Harris. There was something in her tone, a reservation, that hadn't been there moments before.

Ms. McCormick was all breathless smiles. "Gorgeous day, isn't it?" Her eyes were startling blue, so much so that I wondered if they were those fake contact lenses that you can get to change your eye color. Dark lashes fringed her vibrant eyes, and a bright shade of red lipstick highlighted her full lips. "Hectic morning. I'm running late." She slung a tote bag over her shoulder. "Have to dash." She motored away, her heels sinking into the grass, making her work even harder to cover the ground to the parking lot.

"She's the new teacher?" I asked. I knew one of the fifth-grade math teachers had moved in January, and Ms. McCormick was the new math teacher. Mid-year moves weren't that unusual in North Dawkins since it was a community that surrounded an Air Force base, which was where my husband, Mitch, worked.

Livvy had Ms. McCormick for one class period each day and had mentioned her. I now understood why she said Ms. McCormick was like a Disney princess. My part-time organizing business had taken up a lot of my time lately, and I hadn't been at the school volunteering as much during the last few months, so I hadn't met Ms. McCormick yet. I had asked my friend Abby, who was a teacher at the school and a fellow military spouse, if she'd met Ms. McCormick, and Abby had described her as a big-eyed beauty with a perky disposition. The profusion of happy faces and exclamation notes on home-work pages suddenly made more sense, as did all the smiley-face emoticons in my email updates from Livvy's math teacher.

"Yes. She's been with us since Christmas break." Mrs. Harris's head was tilted back, her eyes narrowed thoughtfully as she watched the progress of Ms. McCormick across the asphalt to the school. "It's just not natural, you know," she muttered under her breath.

"What?" I asked.

"That buoyant disposition, not when you're in the public education system, anyway. I'm waiting for her to crack. It worries me." She raised her eyebrows and glanced over at me, seeming to realize that she'd spoken her thoughts aloud. "Of course, she seems to be an excellent teacher, and I shouldn't have—"

"Don't worry, Mrs. Harris," I said. "I won't say anything. But I know what you mean." I realized that Mrs. Harris had touched on the exact thing that had struck me. "I get her biweekly class update emails." The frequency of the emails surprised me. Most teachers only sent out the required quarterly grade report. "Her emails are very upbeat, rah-rah-type updates." I'd assumed that she was layering on the encouragement to motivate her students, but it did seem a little over the top.

"Yes," Mrs. Harris said. "Well, she is young. First teaching assignment, I believe."

We walked by the bus circle, then followed the sidewalk around the main parking area until we came to the school's wide, covered porch-like entry. I tugged open the heavy door for Mrs. Harris, then stepped inside behind her.

"Ellie," a voice thick with a Southern accent called, and I turned to see the woman who had been my arch-nemesis in the organizing world, Gabrielle Matheson, emerging from the school office into the lobby. I'd been the sole professional organizer in the small town of North Dawkins, Georgia, until newly divorced Gabrielle moved here and set up shop. After a rather rocky start, we'd become . . . well, not exactly friends. More like business associates with very different temperaments who managed to get along . . . most of the time. "I didn't know you'd be here today, honey."

To Gabrielle, everyone was "honey" or "sweetie."

The men in her orbit ate it up. The women were less enthusiastic—at least that had been my observation. I would be the first person to admit that statement sounded catty, but it was true. Gabrielle was a gorgeous woman in her early forties—long black hair, beautiful green eyes, and high cheekbones coupled with a figure that curved in all the right places—it was easy to see why she was such a hit with the male portion of the population. She normally wore power suits with nipped-in waists and filmy shells with deep necklines, but today she was dressed down in a sleeveless green cotton tank and black skinny jeans.

I held up the plastic tub. "Muffins with Mom."

She looked toward the painted banner hanging across the wall that welcomed the moms to the school. "Oh, yes. That is so sweet, that you have time to come here and relax with your children."

So it was going to be one of those days. I fixed a smile on my face. "Yes, that is my favorite way to relax, supervising twenty-two eight-year-olds hyped up on sugar at eight in the morning."

She put her hand on my arm. "Oh, Ellie, you are so funny. I'd love to stay and chat, but I have to get these forms copied and distributed. It's the final stage of my de-cluttering plan for the classrooms. I'm implementing it personally in each school." She shrugged her shoulder slightly. "It's just so exciting and rewarding to see it all come together."

I wrinkled my nose at her. "I bet it is." The fact that Gabrielle had snagged the contract to help the school district reduce their paper consumption and increase efficiency was still a sore spot with me. She'd parlayed the initial job into several additional contracts that kept her very busy. I knew about the new contracts because she was always sure to give me an update whenever our paths crossed.

Take the high road, I mentally recited. It was a mantra that I tended to repeat when I was around Gabrielle. "I'll let you get to it," I said, and moved to the school's office to sign in and get my volunteer sticker. Student safety was always a concern, and anyone entering the school had to check in at the office, no matter how brief the visit.

Several moms were on their way out of the office, rectangular labels with their names and student associations stuck to their shirts. I put the muffins down on the tall counter that ran across the office, dividing it from the desks and the principal's enclosed office area in the back. As I typed my name into the search bar on the computer, I said hello to one of the "office ladies," as the kids called them. In the course of the last few years, I'd volunteered so much that I knew most of the women. "Is Marie out?" I asked, looking toward the first desk on the left, which didn't have Marie's usual pink cardigan draped over the rolling desk chair. There were also no papers or file folders stacked on the desk, only a couple of gnome figurines, a name plate that read MARIE ORMSBY, and one of those calendars made of two block letters that have different digits cut on each side and can be rotated to display the correct date. I'd seen them everywhere around the school. All the teachers and staff had one because Mrs. Kirk had given them out at the beginning of the year at the first staff meeting.

"No." Peg Watson shook her head, but didn't turn from stuffing pale blue envelopes into the wall of cubbyholes, the teachers' mailboxes. "She's on vacation this week. Jekyll Island."

"Oh, we went to one of the barrier islands last year," I said. "For a wedding. It was . . . well, it turned out to be quite an event."

"Hmm . . ." murmured Peg, but she didn't turn or look my way, so I didn't say anything else. I'd never heard Peg say more than five words anytime I'd been in. The most I saw of her was the top of her dark brown hair because she usually had her head bent over some task at her desk and let the other ladies in the office do all the chatting with the moms who came to check in for volunteer work. I thought she was in her thirties, but I wasn't sure because I'd never really gotten a good look at her.

"So Marie was able to work in one last vacation before her retirement? That's nice," I said.

"Yes." Peg picked up a stack of orange interoffice envelopes and moved back to the first cubbyhole.

The computer designated for volunteer check-in was an old model, and I had to wait while it processed my entry. Without Marie there to chat with, the office seemed very quiet except for the snick of paper going into the cubbies and the distant hum of the air conditioner unit outside the window. The small printer beside the computer finally spit out my name tag, sounding extremely loud in the small room. At the back of the room, the office for the principal, Mrs. Kirk, was empty. I knew she was outside, keeping an eye on the arrival of students, as she did every morning.

I'd once asked Marie if I'd done something to offend Peg—you never want to tick off the office ladies—but Marie had waved her hand and said, "Oh, she's just shy. Don't give it a second thought."

Marie was Peg's opposite, a sweet, cheerful, and chatty motherly woman with determinedly blond hair fluffing out around her face. She had been at the school since it opened its doors in 1985, and she was retiring at the end of this school year. I'd gotten to know her quite well this year because I had helped coordinate the gift wrap fundraising sale before Christmas.

A couple of moms on the PTA had argued that we needed to do another fundraiser before the school year ended, but that idea had gone down in flames at the last PTA meeting. Marie had been very interested in whether or not the idea of another fundraiser would go forward. She was the person who handled all the details for the PTA, placing orders, making deposits, following up on deliveries. A second round of fundraising would mean a lot of work for her.

I should let her know she was off the hook. "I need to leave a message for Marie," I said as another mom entered the office and headed for the check-in computer.

Peg tilted her head toward the end of the counter. "There's a sticky note and pen."

I jotted a quick note to Marie with the news that the idea for another fundraiser was a no-go, then pushed through the swinging half door at the end of the counter. "I'll leave it on her desk," I said as I stuck it on the one and zero of her block calendar. She'd be sure to see it there. I wasn't too confident that, if I left it with Peg, it would actually reach Marie.

Kids and moms were flowing into the lobby as I left the office to hurry down the hallway to Nathan's room. His teacher, Mr. Spagnatilli, and I quickly set up the muffins, paper plates, and napkins as well as the cartons of juice that he'd brought before the first bell rang, signaling that kids could go to their classrooms. The Muffins with Mom event took place during the twenty-minute window when the kids could arrive and go directly to their classrooms. Nathan arrived, and he and I ate muffins, with me squeezed into a little chair beside his desk. "We're making something for our moms this week," Nathan informed me as we munched on our blueberry muffins.

"Interesting. Should I ask what it is?"

"No." He shook his head, his expression somber. "Don't ask, because I can't tell."

"Okay. I won't, but I'm looking forward to seeing it . . . whatever it is." I brushed the crumbs from my lap. "All right, buddy, I have to scoot over to Livvy's room and have a muffin with her before the last bell. I'll see you in the pickup line this afternoon."

The school was set up with several hallways branching off the central area of the school, which contained the school office, cafeteria, library, and nurse's office. As I moved through the central lobby area, I passed several moms who, like me, were packing in multiple stops during the short morning so that they could have muffins with all of their kids. Considering the muffins that the kids and I had eaten at home to "test" the recipe, plus the ones I would have this morning, I was glad they were mini-muffins; otherwise, I would have needed to go to the gym next instead of to the organizing appointment that was on my schedule.

I dropped into Livvy's classroom, which had a completely different atmosphere from Nathan's room. The bulletin boards were still covered with decorations and informative charts about reading tips and common spelling mistakes, and the desks were only slightly bigger, but there was a more grown-up ambiance. There were less crafts and more paper-work in these classrooms. The oh-so-sophisticated fifth-graders changed classes for every subject, so their backpacks hung on the back of their chairs. A few students were trying to send texts discreetly, their phones hidden in their laps under their desks. The cell phone thing was a sore spot with Livvy. She wanted one, and we'd decided that there was no need for her to have one until middle school, which was only next year, a fact that amazed me. Where had the grade-school years gone? I pushed that thought away and focused on chatting with Livvy while eating my cranberry muffin. I asked Livvy what book she'd picked up at the library.

"*The Mysterious Benedict Society.* I've only read the first few pages, and I think it's going to be good."

"Wonderful." Livvy was happiest when she had a good book. The trouble was keeping her in books. I recently introduced her to Nancy Drew and Trixie Belden. She'd run through all those books in a few weeks. "Oh, there's the eight-twenty warning bell," I said. I had five minutes to help clean up in Nathan's classroom and get off campus before the school day officially began with announcements immediately after the eight-twenty-five bell. I gave Livvy a quick one-armed hug. She glanced around, obviously hoping not too many of her friends had seen the display of affection, but I'd been fast.

I hurried back through the hallways, threading through moms and kids doing a good imitation of race-walking as they scurried to their classrooms and tried to beat the last bell. In Nathan's classroom, I brushed the crumbs into the empty plastic tub, swept up the extra plates and cups, and dumped the empty juice boxes in the trash before waving to Nathan and hurrying down the hallway to the lobby. I didn't want to get stuck listening to the morning announcements and the pledge of allegiance. It wasn't that I wasn't patriotic—Mitch was in the military, after all. Couldn't get much more patriotic than that. But the timing to get to my organizing appointment was tight, and the announcements often ran long, especially on a day like today when parents were in the building.

I was scooting along, making great time, when Gabrielle backed out of a doorway and collided with me, sending the plastic container spinning off across the white tile floor.

"Gabrielle, what on earth—" I broke off as I looked up from retrieving the plastic tub. Her face was a washed-out, pale color, the same tone as the shiny industrial tiles that lined the floor. "What's wrong?"

"There's somebody in there. A body." She pointed at the storage closet door.

"What? No, you must be mistaken." It was such a bizarre thing to say that I would have thought she was joking, but her color wasn't good and, except for the quick glance she'd sent me when we banged into each other, her eyes were wide and fixed on the door.

I reached for the handle, thinking that it must be a bundle of clothes leftover from some event, but the door wouldn't budge. The slim bar handle twisted down, but when I pulled, the door didn't open. "It's locked." I looked back at Gabrielle. "Do you have a key?" With all the organizing she'd been doing, it wouldn't be impossible that she'd have a key to one of the storage closets around the school.

"No." She shook her head, her ponytail slapping her shoulders. "It wasn't completely closed before. There was about an inch gap when I went in. The lights were off, and when I flicked them on . . . I saw her."

"Her?" That was pretty specific. "You're sure it was a woman?"

Gabrielle's head bobbed. "Yes. It was a woman." Gabrielle swallowed. "I could tell from the hand—long, narrow fingers and a ring with a big oval stone. It's definitely a woman."

"That's all you saw? A hand?" I asked.

"Yes, sticking up out of a trash can." She shifted her gaze from the door to my face. "I know what I saw."

I looked up and down the hallway, but it was the final moments before the tardy bell, and the hall was deserted.

"Come on, let's go to the office." Gabrielle didn't move. I wrapped an arm around her shoulders and propelled her in the direction of the lobby. "They'll have a key. I bet it was something else. . . ."

She stopped walking. "No. Ellie, it was a body. There is a woman in there, and she's dead; I know it. The skin was so white, it has to be . . ." She shivered and looked like she might be sick.

Before I could say anything, the tardy bell rang, and then the public address system crackled. Gabrielle started as if someone had given her an electric shock. Mrs. Kirk's voice came through the speakers, which were positioned in each of the classrooms as well as the hallways.

"Welcome, mothers, to Muffins with Mom Day. We're so happy you could join us this morning. We know you do so much to help your kids succeed, and we wanted to take a little time today to honor you. Students, let's give a round of applause for your fantastic moms."

Mrs. Kirk paused, and little bursts of clapping sounded from the classrooms on either side of the hallway as Gabrielle and I walked on toward the lobby.

Mrs. Kirk continued, "Moms, thank you for coming today. We're glad you could start your day with us, but after announcements, students must get to work, so all parents must leave campus after announcements. Today's lunch menu is a crispy taco, salad, milk, and a pudding cup. Teachers, don't forget—"

A high-pitched buzzing sound that hurt my ears cut through Mrs. Kirk's words. Gabrielle and I paused and looked at each other.

"That's not the fire alarm, is it?" I asked.

Gabrielle nodded. "No. They had a drill when I was here last week. Surely, they wouldn't have another drill so soon."

"And not in the middle of announcements," I said.

Mrs. Kirk's voice resumed, carrying on through the continued siren-like blasts. "Students, teachers, and parents, please exit the building in an orderly fashion."

Up and down the hall, teachers emerged from their classrooms, the students following in undulating lines as they marched down the hallway. Gabrielle and I started moving again. When we got to the lobby, I glanced in the office, but it was empty. Mrs. Kirk stood at the doors, watching the children file by and shushing any talking students into silence. Peg stood at Mrs. Kirk's side, a clipboard and bullhorn tucked into the crook of her elbow.

I looked toward Gabrielle, but she was still pale and shaken, her gaze darting around the entrance. Where was the take-charge dynamo who was always stampeding forward, snapping up organizing clients and jobs? I steered Gabrielle toward Peg and the principal.

I had expected Gabrielle to tell Mrs. Kirk what she'd seen, but Gabrielle looked at me with her wide eyes, so I said, "Mrs. Kirk, Gabrielle—"

Mrs. Kirk held up a hand, palm out. "Ladies, this is not the time. We must make sure all students and staff are out of the building. Please take your place in line over there." Mrs. Kirk was a sturdy woman in her fifties who liked to joke that she was tougher than Captain Kirk, a comment that went right over the heads of most of her students, but today she was all business.

I exchanged a look with Gabrielle, then glanced at the lines of kids still filing out of the school. Mrs. Kirk was right. The first priority had to be making sure the kids were safely out of the school, in case there was a fire. And any mention of . . . something . . . possibly a body, might be picked up on by the kids, who somehow always seemed to hear the very things we didn't want them to hear.

Mrs. Kirk raised her eyebrows at Gabrielle and me. At her elbow, Peg sent us a disapproving look.

"Of course, we'll wait," I said. "But it is very urgent that we speak to you as soon as possible. Very urgent," I repeated.

Mrs. Kirk's eyebrows came down in a frown as her gaze went from me to Gabrielle. She lingered, looking over Gabrielle for a moment. "Mrs. Matheson, do you need anything? To sit down?"

Gabrielle blinked, then seemed to pull herself together. "No. No, I'm . . . okay, I guess."

Mrs. Kirk gave a slow nod. "All right. I'll find you as soon as I can. Wait for me there, by the line of kindergartners."

"Right." We moved off through the line of benches that edged the circular car pickup lanes to wait with the smallest kids.

I turned to Gabrielle and said in a low voice, "Are you sure what you saw was a hand? Could it have been . . . I don't know . . . maybe a glove—a plastic glove—or something like that?"

My doubting tone shook Gabrielle out of her daze. "No," she said in a loud, adamant whisper. "It was a hand. I'm positive."

One of the kindergarten teachers frowned at us and made a zipping-her-lips motion. I mouthed, *Sorry,* and didn't say anything else.

We waited there, Gabrielle and I, until the last student had filed out. Occasional whispers, which were quickly silenced, floated on the morning air between pulses of the fire alarm. The wail of a fire engine joined the sound of the alarm, and less than a minute later, a fire truck lumbered up into the car circle pickup lane and came to a halt at the front doors of the school.

The kids went quiet for a moment—obviously this wasn't normal fire drill procedure—then there was a fresh burst of talking, which the teachers quickly squashed. The firefighters swung down from their truck, conferred with Mrs. Kirk, then entered the building.

We waited in the growing warmth of the sun. Eventually, the pulsing fire alarm stopped, and the firefighters emerged from the building and spoke to Mrs. Kirk again. She took the bullhorn from Peg and announced, "Thank you, students and parents, for following directions so well this morning. You may return to your classrooms." The teachers led their charges back into the school. Now, the kids were chattering and pointing as the fire truck pulled away.

Mrs. Kirk watched the first classes return to the building, then came over to us. "Now, what can I help you with?"

Gabrielle shot a look at me out of the corner of her eye, then licked her lips. "There's a body in the storage closet in the blue hallway." The hallways were color-coded to help the kids navigate them, which came in handy, especially during the first weeks of the school year. The first- and second-grade class-rooms were in the blue hallway.

Mrs. Kirk's gaze had been divided between us and the children filing back into the school, but at Gabrielle's words, her attention snapped to her. "A body?"

"Yes," Gabrielle said firmly. "I know it sounds crazy, but I know what I saw."

"You saw this . . . when?"

"Right before the fire alarm went off. The door wasn't closed. I went in, turned on the light, and saw . . . her."

Mrs. Kirk looked to me. "You saw it, too?"

"No, the door closed and locked when Gabrielle came out."

Mrs. Kirk's gaze shifted from Gabrielle to me for a moment. Then she said, "Very well, come into the office while we check it out."

We followed her into the office, where she motioned for us to have a seat on the bench that ran along the wall opposite the tall counter, saying she would check the storage closet herself. "Best if you wait here. I don't want to draw too much attention to . . . this situation until we know what is going on, and having several parents in the hallway will do that."

I knew it was silly, but as I sat down on the smooth wood, I couldn't help but feel that I was back in grade school and had been called to the principal's office for some infraction.

Peg went behind the counter, stowed the bull-horn in a cabinet at the back of the room in the little nook that contained a bar sink and a coffee machine, then sat down at her desk without a look in our direction.

It was probably less than a minute before Mrs. Kirk returned, a concerned look on her face. She sat down beside Gabrielle on the bench. "Mrs. Matheson, there is nothing in the storage closet except cleaning supplies and extra paper."

Chapter Two

Gabrielle's spine straightened. "What are you talking about? Of course, there's a body there. I saw it." She surged up from the bench and strode out the door.

Mrs. Kirk shot an exasperated look at me, then hurried after her. After a beat, I hopped up and strode down the hallway, too, stepping through the last group of the moms who had walked their kids back to class and were now leaving the campus.

Gabrielle was tugging at the storage-room door as Mrs. Kirk arrived with me on her heels. Mrs. Kirk had a set of keys in her hand. "Here, let me show you."

Gabrielle stepped back, her arms crossed and a determined look on her face. "I don't know how you could have overlooked it."

The shell-shocked look had worn off, and in a strange way, I was glad to see the old assertive—or perhaps aggressive was a better word—Gabrielle that I knew.

With a jangle of the keys, Mrs. Kirk unlocked the door and pulled it open.

"It's right there—"

Gabrielle stared inside the storage room for a second, then marched into the tiny room, flicking on the lights. "It's impossible. It's got to be here." She turned in a circle, her gaze raking every inch of the small closet, but there was nowhere for a body to be hidden.

The small square of space contained two sets of metal shelves, which were filled with cleaning supplies and paper products. Two tables with the legs folded leaned against the far wall and kid-sized chairs were stacked next to them.

Mrs. Kirk gazed at Gabrielle, a concerned look on her face. "It must have been a shadow or a trick of the light . . . or something." She half stepped into the closet and put a hand on Gabrielle's shoulder. "Let me make you a cup of coffee," Mrs. Kirk said as she drew Gabrielle out of the closet.

"I know what I saw." Gabrielle allowed herself to be maneuvered out of the closet, but shrugged her shoulder so that Mrs. Kirk's hand dropped away.

"Was the light on when you looked inside the closet?" I asked. If Gabrielle had only opened the door an inch and it had been dark in the room . . .

A boy I recognized from Nathan's class came down the hallway, carrying a piece of paper. His steps slowed as he reached us.

"No," Gabrielle snapped. "The light was off, but I could see the arm sticking up out of the trash can just fine. It *had* to be a body. It couldn't be anything else."

Mrs. Kirk smiled at the boy. "Hurry along, Ned. No dawdling." He picked up his pace, but snuck several glances at us over his shoulder.

Mrs. Kirk turned off the light. I'd been holding the closet door open, looking at every inch of the room, hoping to see something odd—a dropped rubber glove or piece of cloth that might have resembled a hand in a poorly lit space, but that didn't seem to be a possibility. Not even a bit of dust or scrap of paper marred the spick-and-span floor. I released the door and it sighed on its pneumatic hinge as it closed slowly.

"Wait." Gabrielle stuck out a hand, halting the door. "Where is the trash can?"

"I'm not following," Mrs. Kirk said.

"The trash can," Gabrielle said, her voice triumphant. "It was one of those big ones—you know, the thirty-gallon ones on wheels, like the kind in the cafeteria. It was right here by the door. Where is the trash can now?"

Mrs. Kirk blinked a few times. "Klea probably moved it to the cafeteria," she said gently, referring to the one of the school's janitors. With her cap of curly dark hair and a quick smile, Klea was a familiar sight around the school. I'd met her a few years ago when I'd helped with the annual book sale, which had been held in the library. Setup had involved rearranging furniture to make room for the book displays. Klea had helped me pack away the unneeded tables and chairs from the library and found space to store them at the back of the stage, which filled one side of the cafeteria. (For plays and events, the cafeteria could be turned into a makeshift auditorium.) Klea and I, along with a few other moms, had lugged tables and chairs up the stairs to the stage for a couple of hours. She could have left the moving of everything to us, but she'd pitched in and helped. I'd also met with Klea two weeks ago for an organizing consultation. I made a mental note to check in with her today and see if she'd made a decision about whether or not to hire me.

Gabrielle looked mulish. "I know what I saw. It was here."

"I'm sure you *thought* you saw something," Mrs. Kirk said in a soothing tone, one that I'd heard her use with especially upset kindergarteners during the first week of a new school year. "But whatever you saw, it's not there now. Let's go back to the office. We can talk there." Mrs. Kirk motioned for Gabrielle to release the door.

Gabrielle didn't look happy, but she let the door close and followed Mrs. Kirk back to the office. I fell into step beside Gabrielle, consulting my phone as I walked. I still had time to get to my appointment if I left now. Gabrielle *must* have been imagining things. I'd learned that she was a bit prone to exaggeration. She must have seen a shadow . . . or something . . . and jumped to the conclusion that it was a body.

Mrs. Kirk went into the main office, and Gabrielle was about to follow Mrs. Kirk into her separate office at the back of the room when she noticed that I'd peeled off from their little group. I swiveled the mouse and waited for the screen to come up so I could check out, another requirement for all visitors to the school campus.

"Ellie, what are you doing?" Gabrielle saw the checkout screen load, and she widened her eyes. "You can't leave now. We have to figure out what happened."

"Gabrielle, I have an appointment with a client in twenty minutes." Gabrielle was a businesswoman and I figured she—of all people—would understand that I needed to leave. She shot a quick glance over her shoulder to make sure Mrs. Kirk was inside her separate office, then turned back to me and whispered, "You heard Mrs. Kirk. She doesn't believe me. She spoke to me like I was a pre-K kid who'd had a bad dream during naptime. I can't have her thinking I'm . . . losing it. I need to stay in good standing with the school district. You know how much bad word of mouth can hurt an organizer."

I sighed. She was worried. I could see it in her strained expression. And I'd learned a while back that even though Gabrielle presented a tough and confident exterior to the world, she had issues—and some of them had been financial issues. As much as I would have liked to have landed the organizing contract with the school, I knew she needed it and I wouldn't want to see her in a precarious financial position.

"And there's your kids," Gabrielle continued. "They go to school here. Don't you want to make sure everything is really okay?" she asked, sensing that I was wavering.

"Of course I want to make sure they're safe, but like Mrs. Kirk said, there's nothing in the storage closet."

"You saw me seconds after I looked in there. Did I look like someone who'd imagined . . . a body?" She lowered her voice as she said the last two words and looked out of the corner of her eye at Peg. She had been sitting motionless at her desk on the other side of the counter, but suddenly became very busy, quickly unwinding the string that held an interoffice envelope closed.

"No, you didn't." Gabrielle had looked truly shaken to the core.

I picked up my phone and called my client, asking if I could reschedule. I could tell from her voice that she wasn't thrilled with the idea, but she did agree that we could reschedule for next week.

I ended the call and followed Gabrielle into Mrs. Kirk's office. She had an insulated carafe on a credenza and handed us each a cup of coffee, then waved us into chairs across from her desk before closing the door on Peg's curious gaze.

"We should call the police," Gabrielle said.

Mrs. Kirk sat down behind her desk and sipped her own coffee before saying, "I know you've been putting in quite a few hours on the organizing project, Mrs. Matheson. You could probably use a break. I think you should take the rest of the day off."

Gabrielle shook her head and looked briefly at me in amazement before turning back to Mrs. Kirk. "I don't need time off. We need—"

"To find that body," Mrs. Kirk said. "Yes, I understand that's your concern. But what would you suggest we tell the police? You saw for yourself that there is nothing for them to investigate in the storage closet."

"Well, then it must have been moved."

"Where?" Mrs. Kirk set her coffee down. "Where could it have been moved that it wouldn't have been noticed? I did think there might be some sort of prank going on when I went to look in the storage room after you told me what you thought you saw. When it was empty, I checked the bathrooms on this hallway as well as the other storage closet in the next hallway. As you know, that is the only other storage closet we have. There was nothing out of place. Every classroom we have is in use, and the cafeteria as well as the library and the gym are open and staffed at this time of day. There are very few quiet, disused places here. If there were a body on this campus, I assure you, Mrs. Matheson, we would have heard about it by now."

I took a small sip of my coffee. It wasn't my favorite drink, but I didn't want to be impolite. I thought that while Mrs. Kirk was mostly right, there were a few places that weren't always bustling, like the gloomy backstage area. And each classroom had storage closets, but I didn't suppose we could go from room to room and search without alarming the students. Mrs. Kirk didn't look like she'd allow it.

Gabrielle seemed to be winding up to continue arguing her point, but Mrs. Kirk looked immovable. I put my coffee cup down on the edge of the desk and said, "Perhaps we could check and make sure all the teachers and staff are accounted for?" I looked at Gabrielle. "You thought it—the body— was an adult, right? You said it was a woman, didn't you?"

Gabrielle nodded, her gaze fixed absently on the desk. "Yes. It was definitely a woman. I just—knew." She suddenly looked up. "There was a ring on one of the fingers. Not a wedding band. It was silver with a large dark stone. Maybe it was green. I'm not sure. But it was feminine. The stone was a big oval, maybe half an inch long. A man wouldn't wear something like that. And the arm was thin and didn't have any hair on it."

"You couldn't see a sleeve?"

"No."

"So." I looked toward Mrs. Kirk. "Would it be possible for you to check and make sure everyone is accounted for—all the teachers and staff? That would make Gabrielle feel better, right?"

Gabrielle looked as if she was about to argue, but I kicked her foot, and she nodded after a second.

Mrs. Kirk seemed to be suppressing a sigh, but then she said, "Yes. We can do that." She stood and walked around her desk. As she opened the door and spoke to Peg, Gabrielle leaned toward me and said in a whisper, "That's a start, but you know as well as I do that there are places in this building where someone could stash a body."

"Let's make sure everyone is accounted for first," I said in an undertone.

Mrs. Kirk returned to the office. "Peg says that we have only one substitute today. Mrs. Patel is out." Mrs. Kirk sat down and brought up a file on her computer, then dialed a phone number. After a few seconds, she said, "Mrs. Patel, this is Mrs. Kirk. Sorry to bother you today. We've had a bit of a mix-up here in the office and I just needed to speak with you to confirm that you're out today. . . . Yes, the substitute is here and everything is fine. . . . Okay. We will see you tomorrow."

Mrs. Kirk hung up the phone. "She's traveling to her son's graduation ceremony in Florida."

"What about the staff?" Gabrielle said quickly, as she glanced over her shoulder to the empty desk in the office. "What about . . . Mary, isn't it? Where is she?"

"It's Marie," Mrs. Kirk said. "She's on vacation." She didn't bother to disguise her sigh this time. "I'd rather not bother her, but I can see that you're quite determined to track down everyone." She consulted her computer again and dialed another number.

"Marie. It's Mrs. Kirk," she said, shooting a rather disapproving glance at Gabrielle. "Sorry to bother you, but I needed to check on when you'll be back in the office. . . . Monday? Excellent. That's what I thought, but I didn't have a note of it here. How is your vacation? Oh, that's a pity. I hope it clears up for you soon. . . . All right. See you next week."

Mrs. Kirk replaced the phone. "She's on Jekyll Island, waiting out a thunderstorm."

Peg appeared in the doorway. "If you're checking on the staff as well as the teachers, everyone is here, except for Klea. I just got a text from her saying she didn't feel well and was going home. Vaughn said he can cover for her for the rest of the day."

Mrs. Kirk shook her head impatiently. "Put it in the system, then. Klea never has liked using the computerized personnel system."

As Peg stepped away from the door, Gabrielle said, "And what about the moms who were here today? How can you be sure that they're all . . . okay?"

Mrs. Kirk tapped a few keys and studied her monitor. "The only people who signed in this morning before the first bell who haven't signed out are you and Mrs. Avery. And before you say someone could have signed out another person . . ." She swiveled her chair and looked out the windows behind her desk, which overlooked the front of the school. "The overflow lot is almost empty. I see only two extra cars, which I suspect are yours and Mrs. Avery's. So I do believe we can rest assured that all visitors to the campus have left . . . except you and Mrs. Avery."

Mrs. Kirk linked her fingers together and placed them on her desk. "As you can see, everyone is accounted for. No need to worry. Now, Mrs. Matheson, I do think you should take a break."

Gabrielle stood up. "Oh, no. I couldn't possibly do that. I have too much to do. I know you think I'm imagining things, but I assure you I did see a body. I can't explain what happened to it, but I know what I saw." She gave a sharp nod of her head and left the office.

Mrs. Kirk leaned over her desk and said in a low voice, "She told me yesterday that she would finish today by noon. Can you keep an eye on her for a bit this morning?"

"As it works out, my schedule is clear, so yes."

I caught up with Gabrielle in the lobby. "What are you going to do?" I asked.

She crossed to the little nook where the janitors had their office. "Look around."

"What about implementing your de-cluttering plan?"

"That will have to wait." She tapped on the door, then opened it. The little office was empty. A messy desk filled one side of the room and a short section of lockers covered the wall opposite the desk. A few scruffy plastic chairs and a small, round table with some books and papers filled the remaining space in the center of the room. "Nothing here. Let's check the workroom next."

I didn't argue with her or try to talk her out of her search. I knew her well enough to know that nothing short of an act of God—something like a hurricane or tornado—would slow her down. And I did want to be completely confident that everything was okay at the school.

The workroom contained two copy machines, a set of cubbyholes stocked with papers in a rainbow of shades, and a long table with staplers, pens, and sticky notepads ranging over it. I had spent many hours in this room copying and collating for various teachers. It didn't take long to confirm the room was empty. Next door, the teachers' lounge with its scattering of tables and chairs was also deserted.

We entered the cafeteria, which was already filled with the smell of ground beef and spices. The long rows of tables were empty and no one popped out of the kitchen to ask us what we were doing as we made our way up the stairs at the side of the stage. The red curtains were open, but the main lights weren't on. "There's a switch over here," I said, and found the panel on the wall. I flicked on a few. Gabrielle took stage right, and I took stage left. There was nothing but stacks of extra chairs on my side. We met in the middle of the area behind the back curtain and poked around, checking behind the scenery leftover from the first-grade play, a couple of trees painted on plywood, and a five-foot-high house that looked like so many of Livvy and Nathan's simple line drawings that they'd made when they were in pre-school.

"Nothing here," I said.

"I know." Gabrielle's hands were on her hips. She surveyed the area once more. "On to the gym."

"Mrs. Morrison isn't going to let us look in the storage room in the gym," I said.

"She will if I tell her I need to see them for my organizing project," Gabrielle said.

And Mrs. Morrison did. In fact, she handed over her keys and said, "I have to get out on the field. It's a tee ball day," before disappearing out the open double doors.

As Gabrielle took the keys, she must have caught the disapproving expression on my face.

"It's not a total lie," Gabrielle said as she unlocked the door. "I am working on another proposal for the school district and need to do a survey of a typical school. This is a typical school. I hadn't planned to do the survey today, but I can do it now instead of next week."

Gabrielle threw open the doors to the gym's storage room. A quick circuit of the room revealed nothing more than rolling racks of basketballs, portable netted goals for soccer, miniature orange cones, Hula-Hoops, and vests for playing capture the flag. It was the same situation in the library, except the librarian, Mrs. Roberts, unlocked the door to the storage room herself and watched us as we surveyed boxes, rolled-up posters, and a few dusty stacks of books with damaged spines or wavy, water-damaged pages. "Perhaps you'd like a notepad?" she asked, a thread of suspicion in her voice.

Gabrielle smiled brightly at her as she said, "I use my phone," and proceeded to take pictures of the room.

As we left the library, Gabrielle caught sight of the school's other janitor in the hallway. "Vaughn, could you unlock the records room for us? I just need to take a quick peek. It's for more organizing stuff."

Vaughn didn't seem to think the request was odd. In his fifties, he was a big, broad-shouldered man, pudgy around the middle, with thinning gray hair. We followed his lumbering stride down the hall to the main lobby, where the door to the records room was located, adjacent to the door to the main office. His hefty key ring tinkled like jingle bells as he spun it in the lock. He opened the door and stepped back, then waited for us to have a look around.

The fluorescent lights flickered on, illuminating four rows of filing cabinets. Gabrielle snapped a few photos. We both walked the aisles, then exited the room.

"Thank you, Vaughn. That was very helpful," Gabrielle said. Vaughn shrugged a shoulder as he relocked the door, then clipped the key ring to a belt loop and ambled away. He wasn't nearly as personable as Klea, I thought, glad that she had been the one to help with the book sale setup.

Gabrielle eyed a classroom door. "If only we could get into the classrooms . . ."

"No, Gabrielle," I said, using the firm tone that I took with the kids when I absolutely wouldn't let them do something. "That is where I draw the line. We've looked everywhere we can. There is no way Mrs. Kirk would approve of you going from classroom to classroom."

Gabrielle scowled at me.

"You do want to keep your organizing contact with the school, right?" I asked. "Disturbing every classroom would really tick off Mrs. Kirk, I can promise you that."

She sighed. "I know. You're right. But what if some poor teacher opens her storage closet door and a body tumbles out? Think of the trauma to the kids. It would be awful."

"It would be terrible, but I think you've got to let it go. Since nothing has happened so far, I think we can probably assume . . . it . . . the body . . . whatever it was . . . wasn't moved to a classroom." I tried to keep the doubt out of my voice, but she zeroed in on it.

"I know you're thinking that I hallucinated or something, and you've been humoring me, but I didn't imagine it."

"Okay, let's say it was a body, and it was moved," I said. "Why would someone move it to a classroom? It would probably be discovered very quickly, if that were the case. I think the areas we've just searched, the out-of-the-way places, would be a much more likely place to leave a body, and we didn't find anything."

"I know." She closed her eyes for a second, then snapped them open. "Okay. Have it your way. We'll stop. But if some poor kid is scarred for life, it's your fault. I guess I better try and do some actual work, although I have no idea how I'll be able to concentrate. You're so lucky that you're just a part-time organizer. At least all you've got to worry about is end-of-year parties and Teacher Appreciation Week."

I gritted my teeth and went to the office to sign out.

* * *

I negotiated through the car circle's double one-
way pickup lines at the school that afternoon, stopping even with the front doors of the school when it
was finally my turn. As Mrs. Kirk slid open the van's
door, the walkie-talkie she held in her hand crackled with static, then a voice stated that bus number
twelve was departing.

Afternoon pickup at the elementary school was
as practiced and as tightly timed as a symphony performance. Parents swooped in through the parking
lot, bypassing the turn for the rows of parked cars
that filled the back half of the lot. Instead, they followed carefully marked-out yellow lines, which separated us into two lanes that curved up to the front
of the school and then continued on to the exit on
the other side of the lot.

The car circle was a loop that, in theory, should
move smoothly and let cars flow through with a
brief pause to pick up their students. In reality, the
double lines moved in fits and starts. Drop-off or
pickup time meant gridlock for the streets surrounding the school as the car circle line backed up
and clogged the roads. Kids waited on benches in
areas designated according to their grade, and the
teachers and staff sorted the kids into appropriate
cars, relaying names of students along the walkie-
talkie network as their turn arrived. Like a conductor,
Mrs. Kirk supervised it all, directing all the various
players so that the line moved fairly smoothly—most
of the time.

To Livvy and Nathan's great disappointment, we
lived too close to the school to be included on the
bus route. I'd told them they would have to wait

until they were in middle school to enjoy riding the bus. I wasn't looking forward to Livvy riding the bus to school next year—as a friend said to me once, all the bad stuff seemed to happen on the bus—but I thought it would probably be one of those things that appeared to be great at a distance, when they were impossible, but quickly lost their luster with day-to-day familiarity. But that was still several months away, and although I was really good at worrying about things in the future, I put those worries away and concentrated on the here and now.

Gabrielle's worry about the body turning up in a classroom must not have been realized because all was normal. Otherwise, I doubted the car line would move smoothly and that the kids would be as relaxed as they were. Shrieks and laughter and chatter flowed in through the open door as Livvy and Nathan climbed in.

As Nathan settled into his booster seat, he asked, "Mom, is it true that there was a zombie in the storage closet?"

Okay, so not everything was completely normal . . .

"And so now a kid in Nathan's class told everyone that he saw a zombie in the closet," I said into the phone later that night.

"So I bet that made bedtime fun." Mitch's voice came over the line faintly. Usually the connection was good no matter where he was in the world, but this time he really did sound like he was on the other side of the ocean, which he was. His job as an Air Force pilot had taken him to Europe, where he was participating in exercises that would last for the next two weeks. It was the middle of the night where he was, but he'd just finished a night sortie and had called after he landed. We worked in our phone calls whenever we could because the time zone difference made it a challenge to connect.

I had been walking around the living room, picking up action figures and books with one hand while we talked. "Yes. Livvy said the zombie thing was 'moronic.'" Livvy had taken to dropping words she'd learned while reading into conversation, which I thought was great. I was glad her vocabulary was growing, but Nathan had thought she'd accused him of being a moron, which had resulted in an argument.

"That's my little word geek," Mitch said after I related the story. Then his voice turned serious. "But do you think Gabrielle really saw a body?"

I put the books and action figures on the coffee table and curled up on the couch, tucking my feet under me. "I don't know. She was certainly frightened when she backed out of the closet, but there was nothing there when we checked later. And I mean literally nothing. Not even a scrap of paper or a bit of dust. And Mrs. Kirk checked on all the teachers and staff. Everyone was accounted for."

"But the school was full of parents—moms—right?"

"Yes, but Mrs. Kirk checked the sign-in system and everyone had signed out again, and there weren't any stray cars left in the parking lot." I picked up one of the action figures and propped it up on the arm of the couch. "And Gabrielle and I looked everywhere we could think of around the school, except in every classroom. Gabrielle wanted to check the storage closets in each room, but I knew

Mrs. Kirk wouldn't stand for that." I sighed. "I don't know what Gabrielle saw."

"Probably nothing," Mitch said. "She probably imagined the whole thing."

I didn't really agree with him. Gabrielle was about the least imaginative person I knew, but I knew Mitch was trying to help me not worry. And with him thousands of miles away, I didn't want him to be anxious about us, so I said, "Maybe." I knew being stranded in a foreign country was no fun for him when things went wrong. Of course, we were usually talking about fairly minor things, like leaky pipes or the washing machine suddenly not working.

But he must have had reservations as well because he said, "Ellie, be careful, okay?"

I heard a noise from down the hall and uncurled my legs. "I will. Zombies or no zombies, I'll watch out. I think Nathan's up. I've got to go."

"Okay, put the little man on," Mitch said.

Nathan's head appeared around the corner.

"Oh good, you're up," I said, and Nathan looked surprised. "Dad wants to talk to you."

I held out the phone and listened to Nathan say, "Okay" about seven times. He hung up and said, "Dad says not to worry, that zombies don't really exist. They're just made up."

"Good. That's good," I said, and didn't add that I'd told him the same thing at least twenty times tonight. "Let's go back to bed." I escorted him back to his room, tucked him into bed, read him a *Nate the Great* book, and didn't hear a peep out of him the rest of the night.

Organizing Tips for PTA Moms

<u>Routines to keep school year running smoothly</u>

Use a wall calendar to keep track of doctor and dentist appointments, music lessons, sports practices, and school events.

Try to schedule activities into blocks to save time. Can you coordinate music lessons for one child with the orthodontist appointment for another child? Try and plan evening activities so that they fall on a few nights of the week, giving you some "at home" nights each week.

Do as much the night before as possible. Pack lunches, lay out clothes, and prep backpacks with homework.

Chapter Three

"Sunscreen, bug spray, water, snack bars, camera, and water bottle," I said as I checked my tote bag. I removed my folding chair from the back of the van and closed the hatch. "I think I'm ready for Field Day."

Abby, standing next to me by her car, said, "You forgot a hat," and handed me a baseball cap, then squinted up at the clear blue sky. "I think we'll need it." Field Day was scheduled for the coolest time of the day, first thing in the morning, but the air already had a steamy quality, and I knew that by the time we left in a few hours, we'd both be drenched in sweat.

"At least you get to wear blue tomorrow." Abby repositioned her orange cap, which matched the orange T-shirt she wore. Abby taught third grade at the school, but she'd taken today off so she could spend all of Field Day cheering on her son, Charlie. Otherwise she'd have had to spend the whole time on another part of the field with her class and missed seeing Charlie participate in any of the events. There were a couple of other teachers who were also moms, and they were covering for each other during Field Day.

Each grade wore a different color for Field Day. Nathan and Charlie were the orange group. Tomorrow, the older grades would have their Field Day, and Livvy was in the blue group. To encourage school spirit—and raise funds for the school—the parents also ordered matching shirts, which meant that I had an orange, as well as a baby-blue, Field Day T-shirt.

We joined the throng of parents making their way into the school. We stopped off at the office and signed in; then, with our name-tag stickers on our T-shirts, we headed through to the back of the lobby and out the doors that led outside. We crossed the blacktop marked out with lines for a basketball court and joined the mass of kids and parents on the wide open stretch of grass directly behind the school that was known as the back field. A thick belt of tall pines lined the right-hand side of the back field, extending from the school to the far end of the property. The open, grassy area beside the wooded area wrapped around to the front of the school, and that area was called the side field, even though there was no clear separation between the fields. A chain-link fence enclosed the side and back fields, but not the woods.

Unlike so many of the newer neighborhoods that had popped up around North Dawkins before the housing bubble popped, the school was located in an older neighborhood. Small Craftsman-style homes from the twenties, thirties, and forties ringed the school, and I could see some parents departing from them and making their way along the chain-link fence to the school's main doors.

A few parents slipped in through the woods, which were strictly off-limits to the kids during recess, but I didn't blame the parents for taking the shortcut. Mrs. Harris was there in her yellow first-grade shirt and wide-brimmed straw hat, fluttering around the parents who emerged from the trail that cut through the woods, welcoming them to Field Day, and then shifting them toward the school building, reminding them to check in at the office before staking out a spot on the sidelines. The shade under the tall pines looked cool and inviting, and I thought longingly of the little trail that ran in a rough diagonal line through the trees and came out on the far side of them, at the street that ran along that side of the school. I knew many kids who lived on that side of the school took the tree-lined path home, a route that cut their walk in half. I'd taken a turn on it myself a few times.

I wasn't big on running or aerobics, so I tried to walk as much as I could. That usually meant walking in our neighborhood after dinner, when the sun had dropped below the treetops and the air was a bit cooler, but I also tried to add walks in during the day when I could. Sometimes I finished up my volunteer work at the school and had a little time to burn before dismissal. If the weather wasn't too sweltering, I'd check out at the office, go through the woods, and then walk through the surrounding neighborhood streets, working my way around to the parking lot, making a loop, and getting in some steps before waiting in the car line.

"Here's second grade," Abby said, staking out a spot beside a fresh chalk line. I turned my back on the woods and unfolded my chair, got my camera ready, and settled in to wait for the first event. It was a carnival-like atmosphere, with the kids and parents in their brightly colored shirts and the happy chatter of several hundred kids.

Abby and I were scheduled to man the refreshment booth, a table under a blue shade canopy stocked with bottled water and juice bags, during the second hour, so we were free to be spectators during the first round of events.

The classes in each grade competed against each other, and I spotted Nathan in line behind Mr. Spagnatilli. Nathan was talking to Charlie, who was in line beside him in another line for another classroom. The word "upset" didn't begin to describe how he and Charlie had felt when they had been assigned to different teachers this year, but although the beginning of the year had been rough, it had worked out to be a good thing. Nathan now had a few more friends, and I thought Charlie did as well.

The bullhorn screeched, and we all cringed. Then Mrs. Kirk's magnified, yet hollow, voice said, "Welcome to Field Day, students and parents." She usually wore suits, but today she had on a T-shirt, jeans, and tennis shoes.

A high-pitched shout of excitement went up from the student sections, which were spaced around the schoolyard. The parents clapped, and a few of them, including Abby, whooped. Mrs. Kirk gave detailed instructions that I'm sure most of the kids totally missed, but the teachers knew what to do and got their classes lined up for the first event, the three-legged relay race.

Nathan and his partner, a girl with her blond hair in dog ears, both looked embarrassed—until Mrs. Morrison, the P.E. teacher, took over the bullhorn and raised a starting pistol high over her head as she announced the first event.

Silence fell over the field like a blanket, muffling all sounds except for the distant bark of a dog. Mrs. Morrison's voice came through the bullhorn. "Three—two—one." When the report of the blank echoed over the field, the students and parents came to life, shouting and cheering. I managed to get some photos of Nathan and his partner, who both suddenly became so focused on making it from one end of their narrow lane to the other and back to the starting point that they forgot to be embarrassed. They loped back and touched the next group of kids, then collapsed, giggling, on the grass.

Nathan's class came in second, and the results were reported to a group of teachers stationed near the blacktop, who kept track of the outcome of each event. At the end of the day, each kid would go home with a collection of different-colored ribbons for the place their class had finished in the different events.

The next event was the egg race, and instead of focusing on speed, the kids were now carefully treading with a heel-to-toe stride as they balanced an egg on a spoon. Next up was the bottle-fill race, which took forever as the kids carried a single cup of water to a huge bottle at the far end of the their

lane. Charlie's class won that event, and he grinned
happily at Abby as the kids high-fived each other.
The second-graders went off for a break and ate
Popsicles under several shade canopies while Abby
and I went to man the refreshment booth, where we
handed out water bottles dripping with condensation to students and parents; then we went back for
the second half of Field Day, which included sack
races, the fifty-yard-dash relay, and the Frisbee toss.

By the time we got to the last event, the Frisbee
toss, the sun was high in the sky and the back of my
shirt was plastered to my shoulder blades. The kids'
faces shone with sweat, but most of them were grinning and looking forward to the promised treat of
ice cream bars for dessert after lunch in the cafeteria. I knew that the rest of the day would pretty
much be a write-off in the classroom, with lots of educational videos being shown. Nathan had already
had his turn at the Frisbee throw, and I was lounging back in the chair, fanning myself with the brim
of my hat, when one of the boys in Mrs. Dunst's line
put all he had into throwing the Frisbee, but his aim
was way off. The Frisbee went sailing over the line of
spectators and into the woods.

Under her sun visor, Mrs. Dunst, who was seven
months pregnant, looked exhausted. "I'll get it," I
said, and hopped up.

I walked along the hard-packed dirt path that ran
along the edge of the woods, then followed it as it
turned into the shadow of the trees. The red Frisbee rested a few feet away on a layer of dead leaves
and pine needles that lined the path. A woman
holding a large ice chest was farther along the trail,

deeper in the woods, and stood with her back to me, looking into the trees.

I tossed the Frisbee back toward Mrs. Dunst. My aim was terrible, too, and it went wide, but Mr. Spagnatilli caught it and handed it off.

I started back toward the schoolyard, but glanced back at the woman. She hadn't moved and still stood motionless, her gaze fixed on something off the path. It looked like Karen Hopkins, one of the other moms from Charlie's class. Her white-blond hair, cut in an inverted bob, was easy to recognize. "Hey, Karen, are you okay?" I called.

She turned slowly toward me and blinked. She didn't seem to recognize me.

"It's Ellie. Nathan's mom," I said, but there was something in her face that made me hurry down the path to her. "What's wrong?"

She carefully set down the ice chest as if it were made of delicate crystal. "Get Mrs. Kirk," she said in an unsteady voice. "There's a body over there."

She pointed through the trees, and I saw it immediately, a trash can turned on its side, half hidden by several pine branches. At the same time, I noticed a low hum as flies buzzed around the trash can. An unmistakably human form, a woman's head and shoulders, had tumbled partially out of the can. She was turned away from us, but her short dark hair was visible through the screen of pine branches and needles that covered her. I felt sick as my gaze traveled over what I could see of the figure. One arm extended out from the body, and rested in a pile of fallen leaves. I saw a silver ring with a large oval stone on one of the slender fingers.

Chapter Four

Karen spoke and I jumped as she said, "You can see the trail it left." She motioned at the ground near our feet, tracing the four lines of compressed dirt, leaves, and pine needles that branched off from the main path.

"I was going to run the ice chest home," Karen said in her shaky voice. "I didn't want to lug it all the way through the school and around the fence. It's so much faster this way. I live on Chestnut, right over there. This way is faster, but then I saw the gray color—the trash can. The light hit it just right, and it caught my eye." She swallowed and looked away from the trash can and the figure in the woods. "I wonder how long . . . it . . . has been there? Do you think it was there this morning when I walked over?" she asked, her voice cracking.

"I don't know," I said, but the low drone of the flies made me think it probably had been. "You're right. We do need to get Mrs. Kirk." I glanced over my shoulder. The kids must have finished the last event. Through the trees, I could see the kids returning to the school in orderly lines with parents and teachers streaming along beside them. A few teachers remained on the rapidly clearing field, picking up equipment.

"You go," Karen said. "I'll wait here." She glanced at the trash can, then quickly looked away again. "I'll sit down here and wait." She plopped onto the ice chest.

"Are you okay?"

"Yes." She ran a hand over her forehead. "I don't think I could walk if I wanted to. One of us has to stay here to make sure none of the kids come by. . . . Some of the early release students go home this way."

"Of course." I'd forgotten about the half-day kindergarten students. They would be dismissed now that Field Day was over. I shivered, thinking that at least it had been an adult, not a student, who had discovered the body. "I'll be as quick as I can."

Karen nodded, and I trotted away. It didn't take long to cover the short distance under the trees. I emerged from the woods and surveyed the almost empty field. Abby waved to me. She'd collapsed both our chairs and had packed up all our extraneous stuff. "What happened to you?"

"I'll tell you in a minute," I called as I spotted Mrs. Kirk at the refreshment station. She and Ms. McCormick were stacking unused water bottles on a cart. I hurried in their direction, and reached the table just as Ms. McCormick left, pushing the full cart over the bumpy grass.

"There's been a death, in the woods," I said.

Mrs. Kirk had gripped the edge of the table to tilt

it on its side and fold in the legs, but she stopped, arms braced on the tabletop. "What?"

Ms. McCormick stopped wheeling the cart away and turned back to us.

I motioned toward the school building. "You've got to stop the parents who are leaving," I said to Mrs. Kirk. "The police will want to talk to them."

"So it's an accident?" Her face was concerned and a little frightened.

"No. It's . . . well . . . you better see for yourself."

She nodded and walked swiftly across the grass with me. "It's along the trail." We turned into the shadow of the tall pines, and I shuddered. The buzzing of the flies seemed louder, but maybe I was just aware of it now.

Mrs. Kirk hurried along the trail and stopped beside Karen, who was still sitting on the ice chest, her face pale and scared. "Mrs. Hopkins—" Mrs. Kirk began, her voice concerned, but then her gaze was drawn to the trash can a few feet away as Karen pointed at it.

Mrs. Kirk darted through the trees, circling around so that she could see the face. She stopped abruptly, sucked in a breath, and put her hand to her mouth. "That's Klea," she said in a high-pitched, breathless tone that I'd never heard her use. Her voice was tinged with surprise and disbelief.

"Not Klea," I said, thinking of the way she always smiled at me in the hall. And when I'd entered her jumbled house for a consultation, she'd shrugged and laughingly said, "It's a mess, I know, but I have the excuse that I just moved." Of course, anyone dying out here alone in the woods was awful, but to think it was someone I knew and had chatted with at the school and even met in their home . . .

"I'm surprised it's not Peg," muttered a voice behind me. Startled, I jerked around. I hadn't realized anyone else had followed us into the woods, but Ms. McCormick stood beside me, her face almost perplexed, and behind her, Abby was just making her way up the path.

Ms. McCormick saw my sharp look and waved a hand. "Sorry. I didn't mean to scare you. It's the hair. . . . They both have short brown hair." I heard the wail of a siren in the distance.

Abby reached Ms. McCormick's side and halted as she took in the scene. "Oh, no," she whispered. "How awful. Is it . . . anyone we know?"

"Klea," I said, and because she looked puzzled, I added, "One of the school's janitors."

"Oh, Klea," Abby said as realization dawned. "I thought it might be a parent . . . you know, with so many visitors on campus." She looked toward the trash can and the crumpled body. "How terrible. But how did she get out here? What happened? I mean, it can't have been an accident or something like that. . . . Someone put her there. So that means . . . but why would someone kill a janitor?"

Abby had a tendency to chatter when she was upset or nervous. I sent her a warning glance. "We don't know anything yet."

"Mrs. Avery is correct," Mrs. Kirk said. She seemed to have braced herself and spoke in her normal tones as she walked back through the trees to the trail. "I suggest everyone return to the school. I will stay here until the police arrive." She removed a cell phone from her pocket, but Karen held up her phone.

"I already called," she said to Mrs. Kirk, then looked at me. "When you left to get Mrs. Kirk . . . I realized we should do that first. I'm a little muddled"—she gave a brief smile—"but I did think of that."

"Good. Then they are on the way—"

A siren had grown louder and seemed to be coming from the front of the school. "I wish we could have caught them and told them to come here instead of the main entrance to the school. It will upset the students." Mrs. Kirk unclipped a walkie-talkie from the waistband of her jeans. "Peg, send the police to the back field as discreetly as possible." Mrs. Kirk nodded at Ms. McCormick. "Go meet them at the back door and bring them here."

Ms. McCormick licked her lips and tucked a strand of blond hair behind her ear. "Couldn't someone else do that? I have to get those water bottles. . . ." She quailed under Mrs. Kirk's disapproving gaze. "Yes. All right," she said, and hurried down the trail.

"At this point, I think we should all wait here," Mrs. Kirk said. "Since the police are on the scene now, I'm sure they will want to speak to each of us."

The investigators did want to speak to us, but it took a long time to get around to it. It was actually the sheriff's office that responded to Karen's 911 call because the school was in an unincorporated area of Dawkins County. The uniformed deputy who arrived first took one look at the scene in the woods and called for a detective and the forensic team.

After the first deputy took our names and the bare facts about the discovery of the body, we were told to wait on the field. More police arrived and moved in and out of the woods; then plainclothes officers began to arrive. We were moved to the school office when a deputy began to unroll the crime scene tape to cordon off the woods. As we walked to the building, I saw Detective Dave Waraday striding across the field from the school to the woods. He didn't see me, and I was relieved.

There had been a little misunderstanding between Detective Waraday and me in the past. He'd thought I was an excellent suspect in a murder investigation. If he was assigned to this case, then I knew I would have to talk to him, but later was certainly fine with me.

Unfortunately, it was sooner rather than later. I sat on the hard wooden bench in the school office for only a few minutes before a deputy entered and asked me to come with him. He escorted me to one of the pre-K classrooms. The classroom must only be used in the morning, because there were no backpacks hanging on the hooks and the cubbyholes for lunch boxes and take-home folders were empty.

Detective Waraday sat at the teacher's desk, looking a little out of place surrounded by kids' artwork and posters illustrating the letters of the alphabet. He wore a black polo shirt embroidered with the words DAWKINS COUNTY SHERIFF'S DEPARTMENT. He stood when I entered, and his badge, which was clipped to the waistband of his khaki pants, caught the light as he moved.

He gestured for me to have a seat in a chair that had been pulled up across from the desk. Detective Waraday had one of those baby faces that made him look far younger than his actual years. As I sat down across from him in the folding chair, I noticed a couple of fine lines radiating out from the corners of his eyes, but that was the only thing that made him look slightly older. His short hair was still brown and thick and he was as trim as ever. I'd known him for several years, so I supposed he must be in his thirties by now, but he looked younger than that.

"So, Mrs. Avery," he said as he sat down. "Why don't you tell me why your phone number is in the victim's incoming call log?"

"Oh." I blinked. It wasn't the question I expected. I'd thought he'd want to know about this morning on the field, but I switched gears mentally. "I'd forgotten about that. I called her yesterday. I had an organizing consultation with her two weeks ago. I was following up to see if she wanted to hire me."

"So you called and left her a message?" Detective Waraday asked.

I relaxed my shoulders a bit. His tone wasn't accusing, and he wasn't nearly as hostile as the last time we'd interacted.

"Yes. I didn't hear back."

"Because she was already dead by then," Detective Waraday muttered more to himself than to me as he made a note. "The organizing consultation," he said, giving the words a special emphasis. "What does that involve?"

"It depends on what the client is interested in. That's what the appointment is for, actually. Some people just want help with one specific thing, and other people wave a hand at their garage or a bedroom or a closet, and say, 'Take care of this.'"

"And what did Mrs. Burris want?"

"Mrs. Burris—? Oh, Klea, you mean. I think of her as Klea," I said, realizing that it was sort of odd that all the other adults at the school, the teachers and the parents, were addressed by their surnames, but not the janitors or the office staff. Now that I thought about it, it made me slightly uncomfortable. It was a bit patronizing. I gave myself a mental shake and focused on answering Detective Waraday's question. "She had moved to a smaller house—on Maple—right across from the school," I said. "She wanted some help downsizing. She had too much stuff."

"So it would have been a big job?"

"Yes, if she decided to hire me, but I hadn't heard back from her. That's why I called."

"And is that normal?" Detective Waraday looked up from his notepad. "For potential clients to not make a decision?"

"Oh, yes. All the time. I'd love it if all my consultations turned into actual jobs, but that doesn't happen. People decide they can do it themselves, or they don't want to pay my fee, or they put it off until later. Some people, I just never hear from again," I said with a shrug of one shoulder. "That's why I like to follow up at least once. If I haven't heard from someone after a week or two, I contact them once to see if they're interested. If they're not, I leave it at that."

"And how did Mrs. Burris seem when you met with her for the appointment?"

"Um . . . fine. She wasn't self-conscious about the state of her house. Some people are embarrassed about their clutter, but she wasn't."

"Did she seem worried or nervous?" Detective Waraday asked as he wrote.

"No."

"She didn't say anything to indicate she was frightened?"

I shook my head, then stopped. "There was one thing, but . . ." I shrugged. "It was probably nothing."

Detective Waraday looked up. "What is it, Mrs. Avery? Everything is important at this point."

"Okay. Right. Well, I asked her if the traffic bothered her—you know, from the school. It can get pretty hectic during drop-off and pickup times. Klea laughed and said train tracks could run right through her backyard, and she wouldn't care. Then she said, 'Anywhere away from Ace is peaceful, no matter how much traffic there is.' She didn't say anything else, and I didn't ask, but I assumed Ace was a relative."

I expected him to wave off the comment as unimportant, but he only nodded and made a note. Then he said, "Now tell me about today, finding the body."

"I think I better tell you about yesterday first." No one else from the little group who had found the body had been called for an interview, so I didn't think he would have heard the story from anyone else.

He raised his eyebrows. "Why?"

"Because Gabrielle Matheson—you remember her from . . . that other case a while back?"

"Yes, ma'am. I don't think anyone forgets Gabrielle Matheson after they meet her," he said with a hint of a smile.

"That's probably true. She's working here at the school as a consultant. Yesterday, she thought she saw a body in a storage closet."

Organizing Tips for PTA Moms

Room Mom Tips

Send a welcome message to the parents in the classroom, introducing yourself and highlighting the upcoming volunteer opportunities.

Contact parents early in the school year and set up a tentative event calendar for the whole year so that the events at the end of the year are covered.

Be specific when asking for volunteers. Outline the time commitment (a volunteer for carnival night will have a "one-hour shift manning the ring-toss booth") and clarify any additional requirements. A field trip chaperone may need to complete additional forms for background checks before being cleared to participate.

Ask about food allergies and plan accordingly.

Coordinate with the teacher for party planning, asking what has worked well in the past and what hasn't.

For Teacher Appreciation Week, make a list of the teacher's favorite foods and activities, which you can either share with other parents or use to coordinate for a classroom gift.

Give parents a variety of ways to help. Some parents can donate their time while others can provide a monetary donation for campaigns and events, while still other parents may be able to prep crafts or send snacks or supplies.

Chapter Five

Detective Waraday raised his eyebrows. "A body? As in a dead body?"

I nodded and described what had happened from the moment Gabrielle backed out of the closet to the informal search of the school that Gabrielle and I had conducted.

Detective Waraday put his pen down and rubbed his forehead for a moment, muttering something that I couldn't hear. He looked up. "You know, I promised myself I wouldn't make any comments about you being in the thick of another murder investigation, but I'm very tempted to break that promise. The law of averages . . ." He shrugged and seemed to be speechless for a moment, then finally said, "Statistically, you're a menace to the community. Wherever you go, dead bodies pop up."

"That's not true." I shifted in my seat. Well, it was sort of true. I had gotten involved in quite a few investigations, but it's not like I went looking for trouble. But trouble did seem to cross my path frequently. "I didn't find the body this time," I said a bit defensively.

"No, but you managed to be on hand at the scene of the crime—both times, in fact. You were there at the initial discovery and also later when the body was found in the woods." Detective Waraday again massaged his forehead, then dropped his hand and refocused on me. "And no one thought to call the police or the sheriff's office yesterday?"

"Gabrielle wanted to, but Mrs. Kirk talked her out of it. There wasn't a body in the storage closet or anywhere on campus after the fire drill, and no one was missing. All the teachers and staff were accounted for." I sat up straighter. "Oh, I just remembered, Peg said she got a text from Klea that morning that said Klea wasn't feeling well and had gone home. Gabrielle insisted Mrs. Kirk check on all the adults."

Detective Waraday nodded. "Yes, that text is in Mrs. Burris's phone."

"But then—that means Klea was fine after the fire drill?" I asked, perplexed. "Gabrielle saw the body *before* the fire drill. It was after the drill when Peg said she'd received a text from Klea that she was going home." I got that same sick feeling that I'd had earlier. "You don't think . . . there couldn't be two dead bodies, could there?"

"No," Detective Waraday said decisively. "I think that, after Mrs. Burris was killed, the murderer used Mrs. Burris's phone to send the text so no one would realize she was missing. Apparently, the victim kept the phone in her pocket, not in her locker with her other belongings, so it would have been on her body."

"Oh." I fell back against the chair, not liking the word "victim" and its ramifications. I didn't like how it depersonalized Klea. She had become a tag, a descriptor, but it also meant something else, something that scared me. "Then it *was* murder?"

Detective Waraday pressed his lips together and sighed. "I'm afraid so. She was strangled."

"Poor Klea. That's . . . awful," I said. "I keep saying that—that it's awful and terrible—but it doesn't do the situation justice." I noticed Detective Waraday looking at me very closely, and I had the feeling that he had told me how she died to watch my reaction to his words.

"There never are words for something like this," he said quietly. After a few seconds of silence, he picked up his pen and beat out a quick tap on the paper. "Getting back to yesterday, what did you do after you and Mrs. Matheson looked around the school?"

"I went to the Comm," I said. "That's the grocery store on base," I added, not sure how familiar Detective Waraday was with military jargon. The full name of the store was actually the Commissary, but Mitch and I always used the shorthand name of "the Comm" when we talked about it. "I was supposed to have an appointment with a client, but when I had to reschedule the appointment, I went to the store instead. I went directly there from the school." I reached for my phone. "I remember the checkout line I went through. It was Janelle. She's there all the time and it seems like I always get her line for some reason. She might remember I was in—the computers had a glitch and she couldn't get my paper towels to ring up and she had to call for a price check. Do you want her information?"

"No, that won't be necessary."

I put my phone away, realizing that if Detective Waraday wasn't concerned with my movements during the late morning, he—or the medical examiner or whoever had examined Klea's body this morning—must be pretty sure Klea had died before early afternoon. And Gabrielle was sure she had seen a dead body, and that had happened in the morning, before the announcements, which had occurred right after the eight-twenty-five bell.

Detective Waraday opened his mouth to ask another question, but stopped and said, "You're frowning, Mrs. Avery. Is something wrong?"

My thoughts coalesced, and I said slowly, "If Klea was killed Wednesday morning before the eight-twenty-five bell—which is when Gabrielle thought she saw something in the storage closet—why did no one notice Klea was missing during the fire drill? Don't they have procedures for that? It can't just be the kids that they keep track of. They have to account for the adults in the building too."

"There are procedures in place, but the procedures only work when people follow them. The janitors are supposed to exit the building and line up on the field with the cafeteria workers. Vaughn Lang, the other janitor on duty that morning, didn't see Klea, but he assumed she'd been caught on the other side of the school when the alarm sounded. He thought she had exited through the other doors and was in the group that lines up near the bus circle. He says that he was about to speak up, but then the firefighters came out of the building with the news that it was a false alarm. If the fire had been a real one, he says he would have said something, but he didn't want to get Mrs. Burris in trouble."

"Did anyone see her at all yesterday morning—alive, I mean? Maybe she didn't even come to the school. Maybe Gabrielle *didn't* see her body in the closet, after all. Maybe she just imagined it," I said, thinking that Gabrielle would be so upset if she could hear me. As terrible as it was that Klea was dead, the thought that it might not have happened on school grounds made me feel a little better. I didn't want to think that someone had committed a murder in the school where my kids spent so much of their days. "Klea lived right across the street, and I know she walked to work. I usually see—I mean, I usually saw her walking along the chain-link fence when I dropped the kids off in the morning."

"Mr. Lang had a short conversation with her yesterday morning at seven-thirty in the janitor's office."

"Well, if he's the only one who saw her . . ."

"He's not," Detective Waraday said quickly. "And her belongings—a purse and a sweater—were retrieved from her locker. I doubt she left them there overnight."

"No," I said with a sigh. Which meant the death *had* probably occurred on school property. I shivered. "No woman would go off and leave her purse."

Detective Waraday said, "Glad we agree about something. Now then, tell me about today. I understand you went into the woods during the Field Day event?"

"Yes, to get a Frisbee. I saw Karen standing beside the path. She was very still. I called out and asked if she was okay, and when she turned to look at me, I could tell from her expression that something was wrong."

He asked me questions, taking me through the morning, and jotted down my answers. Finally, he put his pen down. "Okay, Mrs. Avery. I think that's all we need for now, unless there is something else that you think is relevant?" he asked.

I searched his face for a trace of condescension, but he seemed to be completely serious. "Um, no, I can't think of anything else."

He nodded and stood, then walked with me through the miniature tables and chairs, which, while they were the perfect size for five-year-olds, made me feel like a giant.

Before we reached the classroom door, I stopped. "Detective Waraday, do you think the students here are in any . . . well, I don't want to be alarmist, but do you think there's any danger? If Klea was killed in the school . . ." I paused, trying to think how to put things, but gave up trying to think of a diplomatic way to phrase my question. "I have two kids in school here. If there's any chance that they might be in danger, you would let Mrs. Kirk know, wouldn't you?" After the discovery of Klea's body, Mrs. Kirk had decided not to dismiss school. Aside from the chaos an unexpected early dismissal would cause, Mrs. Kirk had said she wanted to keep everything as normal as possible for the students.

I expected Detective Waraday to brush off my concern, but he looked at me with sympathy. "We don't know all the details yet, so I can't say anything

with one hundred percent certainty, but I assure
you that if I thought there was a threat to the students here, I would make sure they were all escorted home, if need be. No, early indications point
to . . ." He pursed his lips and tilted his head. "Let's
say off-campus issues in Klea's life will be our primary line of pursuit at this time. I had to ask you all
the questions about yesterday and this morning to
make sure I had the full picture."

"Right. Thank you for the information. That
makes me feel a little better."

"I'd appreciate it if you kept the information
about what Mrs. Matheson saw—or thinks she
saw—in that storage closet quiet."

"I won't say anything else, but Mrs. Kirk knows
about it as well as Peg. She works in the office, so if
either of them mentioned it to someone, the story
is already out."

He nodded, then said, "I understand that, but if
you'd not talk about it with anyone else, that would
be best."

"Of course."

He opened the door of the classroom, and his
sheriff's deputy badge and shirt were quite a contrast to the brightly colored spring flowers that were
taped to the door. He lifted his chin at a waiting
deputy and said, "Escort Mrs. Avery back to the office. She's cleared to leave. I need to speak to Karen
Hopkins."

The deputy and I walked side by side through the
quiet hallways, his equipment belt jangling with
each step. Voices of teachers and students floated
out of classrooms as we walked by, which was a little
jarring. It was odd to think that school was still

going on a short distance from where Klea's body had been found, but as I'd found out a few years ago, Detective Waraday was a very thorough investigator, and if he felt that Klea's death wasn't related to the school, then there was no need to panic and pull the kids out before the school year ended.

I sincerely hoped Detective Waraday was right, but I knew that sometimes the initial line of inquiry didn't always pan out, and I resolved to be a little more active in my volunteering. I was already scheduled to be at the school quite a bit over the next few weeks for all the end-of-the-school-year activities. I might just have to expand those volunteer hours even more until Klea's murderer was caught.

Organizing Tips for PTA Moms

When to say no to volunteering:

- If a volunteer job makes you anxious.
- If you don't have the skills to accomplish what is asked of you.
- If your schedule is already full and you don't have the time.
- If you are in a season of life like new motherhood or caring for elderly relatives that consumes your time.
- Remember, you don't have to give a reason or excuse. Say that you can't take on the job and then don't let anyone guilt-trip you into changing your mind.

Chapter Six

I was worried about how the kids would react to the news about Klea's death, which I broke to them after school on the way to the special parent-teacher meeting that Mrs. Kirk had announced would take place immediately after dismissal. But while Livvy and Nathan seemed surprised by the news, they both displayed the typical resiliency of kids. When we got home after the meeting, Livvy said it was sad and sat still without saying anything else while she ate a clementine. Then she asked, "Will school be cancelled tomorrow?"

"No. Mrs. Kirk says everything will go on as scheduled."

Livvy nodded, slid off her chair, and reached down to pet Rex, our overly friendly Rottweiler. "I want to get the computer game Ms. McCormick has," she said.

I was used to abrupt topic shifts from the kids, so I said, "What's it about?" Livvy didn't spend a lot of time on the computer and I liked that she usually picked books over games, so I wasn't sure I wanted to encourage her to shift her priorities.

"It's called *Adventure-matics*. You know, like part adventure, part math. It's really cool. The first levels are easy, but then it gets harder and harder. Ms. McCormick lets us play it if we finish our classroom work early."

"I see." The school classrooms had all been outfitted with computers during the summer. Not every desk had a computer, but all the rooms now had a computer section.

"I finished the treasure hunt level today," she said.

The way she said it, I could tell it was an achievement.

"Good job. What was it about?"

"Well, it's kind of sneaky, actually. You land on this island, and you have to do all sorts of fractions to figure out the map and get across the island. The lagoon with the piranha was really tough. If you get it wrong, you fall into the lagoon and get eaten, but if you get it right you get more of the map. Then, when you get all the way across the island and work that last problem, it unlocks the treasure chest and then you can go on to the Jungle Trek. That's where I am."

"Sounds like something worth looking into. I'll check for it online."

"Oh, Ms. McCormick says it's not available yet, that she's got a special test version but she'll tell us when it's out."

Livvy went off to find her book. After a few seconds, Nathan, who was still sitting at the table twisting the rind of the clementine into different shapes, said, "So it really wasn't a zombie." He looked relieved, and I realized he was still thinking about the news about Klea. I guess a death was better than a zombie in his way of thinking.

Later that night, over a plate of cookies, Abby asked, "So what are you going to do?" She touched a white piece of paper on the counter beside a plate. "Do you believe this? That everything is okay?"

The note had gone home with all the kids and explained that Klea's body had been discovered and that the sheriff's department was investigating. Detective Waraday, along with the school superintendent and counselors, had been there after dismissal to answer questions at the special Parent-Teacher Association meeting. Abby picked up a cookie. "They really didn't tell us anything at that meeting today."

"I know. It was vague," I said. Detective Waraday hadn't mentioned anything about primary lines of inquiry being off campus, so I kept that bit of news to myself, but I did wonder why he'd told me that earlier today. Had he again been watching for my reaction? Had he been trying to catch me out, or scare me? He had tried to use those tactics in the past, but I didn't think that was what was going on this time. The meeting at the school had been full of generalizations and reassurances: *working around the clock to find the culprit, stepped-up law enforcement presence at the school, no specific or credible links from the murder to the school—at this time.* "I'm sure they're doing everything they can, and if they do have any leads, they can't really announce them to the whole school."

Abby frowned. "Wow, you're cutting Detective Waraday a lot of slack—much more than you did before."

"I'm not a suspect—thank goodness—this time . . . just a concerned parent. At least that's how it felt today when he talked to me. A lot less threats and more sympathy. It was a nice change," I said.

"So I guess the question is—are you sending the kids to school tomorrow?" Abby glanced into the living room, where Livvy was sprawled in a chair with a book in her lap while Nathan and Charlie had practically every action figure they owned strewn around every flat surface in the room. Rex had uncurled himself from his cushion by the window and trotted through the room, knocking down the action figures and poking his nose over Nathan's and Charlie's shoulders to breathe heavily in their faces for a while before loping off to patrol the backyard for squirrels.

"I think so," I said slowly. "Mitch and I talked about it on the phone a little while this afternoon. The kids don't seem frightened or traumatized. And I'm sure there will be lots of law enforcement types on campus at least for a few days."

Abby dusted the cookie crumbs from her fingers and said, "It's not like we have a rigorous academic schedule for the next few weeks. I could keep Charlie home, and he wouldn't fall behind."

"But you have to be there," I said. "Or are you thinking of staying home as well?" Mrs. Kirk had made it clear that attendance for both students and staff, at least for the rest of the week, was optional.

Abby sighed. "I'd like to, but then I think of all my kids. I know at least some of them will be there tomorrow, and I hate to think of them having a substitute in case they're worried or scared." She sighed and pushed away from the counter. "No, I don't think we'll stay home. I'd feel better being there on campus."

I was glad Abby would be there tomorrow. I knew I couldn't actually spend every minute of the day in the school, so having her there sort of as my backup for Livvy and Nathan made me feel better. "I'll be there, too," I said, "for Field Day again."

"Right, the upper grades. I'd forgotten about that."

"And if I wasn't scheduled to be there tomorrow, I think I'd drop in and volunteer anyway."

I'd never seen so many volunteers the next morning. Apparently, I wasn't the only parent who liked the idea of being on campus. I think it must have been the best attended Field Day in the school's history. The back field was packed with parents. Apparently, the investigators had finished examining the school building, and were now concentrating only on the woods, which had been completely blocked off. Even the hard-packed dirt path that ran from the corner of the blacktop to the woods had been cordoned off with barricades.

It wasn't as hot today, and a thin screen of clouds coupled with a light breeze made the day feel pleasant. Even at the mid-point of the event, when I went to take my turn at the refreshment station, the weather was still nice. Since the day wasn't sweltering, I wasn't as busy handing out water bottles, and I watched the investigators moving around the trees beyond the crime scene tape. It looked as if they were methodically searching the whole wooded area.

Mrs. Kirk had opened Field Day that morning with a moment of silence for Klea, and except for the flutter of crime scene tape along the perimeter of the woods, once the event began, I thought that anyone strolling into the event would never know that a body had been discovered in the woods yesterday. Well, unless they listened to the conversations among the parents.

As I returned to the section of the field where Livvy's class was stationed, I dropped into my chair beside two moms who were deep in conversation.

". . . can't believe they're going on with Field Day as if nothing has happened. I mean, it's upsetting enough for the kids as it is, but to have to be out here—within sight of where it happened—it's just . . . I don't know . . . *not right.* And I told Mrs. Kirk exactly that, but she said she didn't agree—that the kids need the normalcy of routine and to cancel the second day of Field Day would only emphasize the tragedy in their minds. Can you believe that?"

The second mom rolled her eyes. "And if Field Day is going on, the kids are going to insist on going to school. Any other day and they'd gladly stay home, but not today."

The announcement of the next event drew my attention back to the field, and I spent the rest of the time snapping more pictures and cheering for Livvy and her class. They came in first in two events, one of them the fifty-yard relay, which the whole class was happy about since that event was the finale of Field Day for the upper grades. She was in a little huddle with two other friends as they walked back to the school for lunch, so instead of breaking up the group, I waved and shouted that she'd done a good job.

She smiled and waved back, then moved away with her friends as I packed up my chair. While I loved that she was a reader, it was good to see her interacting with her friends, too. I was in the lobby, making my way toward the office to sign out, when a hand gripped my elbow and a voice heavy with a Southern accent said, "Ellie, I can't believe you didn't call me yesterday. I *told* you there was a body in that closet."

A couple of parents moving around us shot disapproving glances our way. It seemed the parents were fine discussing Klea's death among themselves, but they didn't want it mentioned in front of the kids. "Hi, Gabrielle," I said, stepping out of the flow of parents and students streaming in the doors. "I did think about calling you, but it was too late by the time I was able to do it. I was kind of busy earlier in the day—being interviewed by the sheriff's department and then dealing with the kids."

She immediately looked contrite. "Oh, that's right. I wasn't thinking about your kids. How are they taking it? Are they scared?"

"No. They think it's very sad, but they're doing okay. Mostly, I think because they didn't really know Klea. Did you know her at all?"

"Not really. Only to say hello to in the hall, that sort of thing. That detective—you know, the one who looks like he graduated from high school about two minutes ago? He came by my house yesterday afternoon. It was shocking to hear that they'd found Klea . . . like that, but at the same time

I was half expecting it—not that it would be Klea, of course." She shook her head as she added, "Just someone." She gave a little shiver that made the silky material of her camp shirt shimmer. Her gaze traveled over the parents, students, and teachers coming inside the building through the double doors from the field; then she lowered her voice. "It's scary to think the murderer had to be someone here at the school."

"Why do you say that?" I wasn't surprised that she'd called it a murder, but that she was sure the murderer had come from the school. I'd watched last night's news, which had reported the discovery of the body in the field adjacent to the school. The news anchor had said the death was being treated as a homicide, so that was common knowledge. "I got the impression that the investigation wouldn't focus on the school."

Gabrielle's smooth forehead wrinkled into a frown as she scowled at me. "Not have something to do with the school? Of course it has something to do with the school. The body was discovered here."

"No, it wasn't. It was discovered in the woods."

"Well, I saw it here. So that means it was here, at least for a while. Then it was moved. And it was in a trash can from the school."

"How do you know that . . . for sure, I mean?" I'd thought the trash can in the woods had probably come from the school, but I hadn't looked closely at it. "Someone could have just taken a trash can off the grounds. There are usually two big trash cans on wheels by the back door on the blacktop. I know there were some on the field yesterday for the first day of Field Day."

"I asked—that's how I know." Gabrielle folded her arms. "Detective Waraday told me the trash can had the school's name on the side, and he had someone do an inventory. One trash can was missing. It *must* be someone associated with the school." She chewed on a corner of her lip for a moment. "It's a shame, really, that it happened on the morning of the muffins and mommy thing. It makes it so much more complicated . . . so many more people were here on campus. I printed off a list of everyone who checked in that morning from the sign-in system." As she spoke, she reached into a legal-size leather portfolio and removed several pages of paper.

"How did you do that?" I asked.

"I can run reports. It's all part of my organizing projects. I needed to know when the high-traffic times are for the office so I could help them streamline their routines. Of course, they can't afford to upgrade that check-in computer," she said in an aside. "If they could speed that up, it would help to reduce the line and get everyone out of there so much faster. But back to the point—I figured we could split the list. You check half, and I'll check half." She held out several printed pages.

"For what?"

"Alibis, of course. What else would we check?"

I blinked. There were so many objections . . . I didn't quite know where to start. "Gabrielle . . ." I said warningly.

"Oh, don't go all huffy on me. I remember how that detective treated you . . . last time," she said. She looked away and focused her gaze on the field outside the doors for a moment, and I realized she was regaining her composure.

The last time, when Detective Waraday and I had had that misunderstanding—when he'd suspected me of being a murderer—Gabrielle had been related to the victim. It was something she didn't like to talk about. She usually avoided the subject, and that was what she did now. She shifted her shoulders and looked back to me, then plowed on again, speaking quickly—well, as quickly as she could with her languid Southern accent. "That Detective Waraday made your life he—" She smiled at an inquisitive stare from one of the kindergarteners walking by on his way to the library, then cleared her throat. "He made your life very uncomfortable, all because you were the first person on the scene. That's *me* this time. Even though I didn't see her face, I *know* that was Klea's body in the storage closet. I can't risk a smidgen of rumor being associated with me. You know people won't call me if they think I had anything to do with Klea's death. No one is going to invite a suspected murderer into their home or business for an organizing consultation. My business would dry up faster than a puddle after a July rain shower."

"You do have a point," I said slowly. I knew she needed to keep the clients she had, but I wasn't about to start sleuthing. My conscience immediately prickled. I'd already promised myself I'd spend as much time at the school as I could, possibly poking around—to make sure everything was safe for my kids, of course—but that was totally different from teaming up with Gabrielle to look for a murderer. I'd been on a team with her before, and I wasn't looking to repeat that wild ride. "I don't think—"

"Oh, look, here's Vaughn." She nodded at the doors that opened onto the back field, where the janitor was carrying a table with the legs flattened against the tabletop. He paused to let a group of students go first, then maneuvered through the door. I switched my lawn chair to my other hand and caught one door to hold it open for him as Gabrielle tucked her portfolio under an arm and gripped one end of the table. "Vaughn, you are just the person I wanted to talk to," she said. As she helped him carry the table inside, she looked back at me and gave a jerk of her head.

I hitched my tote bag higher on my shoulder and walked behind them into the cafeteria, which today smelled like chicken nuggets. I didn't like following Gabrielle's directions, and I certainly wasn't signing on to be her sleuthing buddy, but I had wondered what Vaughn had to say about Klea's death. After all, he was her closest work associate.

Gabrielle and Vaughn placed the table against the wall, and she brushed her hands on her skinny jeans. Again, today, she was dressed down—at least for her. The lemon-colored camp shirt with rolled sleeves, jeans, and leopard-print heels that were only two inches instead of her usual three-inch stilettos must mean it was another hands-on workday for her. Just looking at her shoes made my feet hurt, but she always wore heels. I had a feeling she could run a marathon in them without blinking an eye. She placed a hand on his arm. "Vaughn, honey, how are you doing? We're so sorry about Klea. Were you close?"

Vaughn had been at the school as long as I could remember. With his thin silver hair, bushy gray eyebrows, and wrinkled face, he certainly had to be near retirement age, and was probably at least fifteen years older than Gabrielle, but he responded as I'd seen almost every other male respond to her. Like a bee attracted to a bright flower, he focused on her, giving her all his attention. "It's very sad," he said with a shake of his head. He gave the table a shove with his foot to make sure it was secure against the wall. "But I didn't really know her. She kept to herself," Vaughn said, and moved to leave the cafeteria.

"Did she?" Gabrielle asked as we walked with him through the lobby. "In what way?"

He shrugged one of his broad shoulders as he came even with the door to the janitor's office. "She didn't talk about . . . anything personal . . . nothing about kids, husband, family, that sort of thing. Not at all like that Rosa, who worked here before her. She talked so much, she couldn't get her work done. It was a relief to have Klea. I don't think she had many friends, actually," he said. "She never talked about meeting anyone for drinks after work or traveling to meet family. She didn't jabber all day. Just came in and put her purse away, then went straight to work."

"Did you see her put her purse away Wednesday morning? You know, before the fire drill?" I asked, glancing inside the little room at the row of lockers, curious to see if he'd tell us what he'd told Detective Waraday.

"Yeah. She was here when I got here at seven-thirty-five. She'd already unlocked the doors. That's the advantage of living across the street—no traffic, she used to say. She'd kid me about being late sometimes. I live on the other side of North Dawkins," he said with a grin. Then the smile dropped off his face. "That was one of the few things we talked about, traffic. It's a shame what happened to her—ignoble, you know."

The word choice of *ignoble* surprised me a bit. It wasn't a word that usually came up in conversation, but when I glanced in the room, I saw a crossword puzzle book, folded back to a partially completed puzzle, on the round table. A hardback dictionary was propped up on the windowsill behind the table. He caught my glance and said, "I like crosswords. I had Klea hooked on them, too. Maybe that's why she didn't talk much. If we both happened to be in here on a break, we worked puzzles."

"Did she say anything that morning?" I asked.

"No, Mrs. Kirk came in with a list of things to do to prep for Field Day, so Klea and I didn't talk."

"I see." So it had been Mrs. Kirk who backed up Vaughn's statement about seeing Klea that morning. No wonder Detective Waraday hadn't seemed to think there was any issue to investigate further. You couldn't get much better than the principal of the school seconding your statements.

"Did you see her again that morning?" Gabrielle asked.

"No," Vaughn said, and I thought, with a cold feeling creeping over me, that he hadn't seen her because she had been in the storage closet. Sometime between seven-thirty and eight-twenty-five, when the announcements started, Klea had been killed. "Mrs. Kirk had a list of things she needed moved to prep for Field Day, so I went with her to the cafeteria to figure out if we had any extra tables we could move that day or if we'd have to wait until the next morning."

"But the fire drill . . ." Gabrielle said. I sent Gabrielle a warning glance, and she must have received the same warning from Detective Waraday about talking about what she'd seen in the closet as I had, because she stopped. After a second's pause, she ended with, "I mean, she wasn't there, was she?"

Vaughn shook his head. "No, and I wish I had spoken up, but I didn't want to make trouble for her. I figured she was at the other end of the school. Most of the school goes out these central doors," he said as he tilted his head toward the main doors that opened onto the covered porch, where the car circle pickup line curved in front of the school. "But there are several classes that go out the south doors," he said, referring to a set of doors at the end of one hallway that opened to the area near the bus circle.

Vaughn lifted his powerful shoulder again. "I thought she was over there. And then it was a false alarm. . . ."

"Yes, it was," I said, and realized Gabrielle was sending me a significant look. When I didn't respond—because I had no idea what she was trying to convey—she rolled her eyes.

"Who set off the alarm? That's the question, isn't it?" Gabrielle said.

Even though the question wasn't addressed to Vaughn, he answered. "One of the fifth-graders, most likely. We have that problem during the last weeks of school. High spirits, you know." He rubbed his hand across the back of his neck, then said, "A false alarm is nothing unusual this time of year. No, what bothered me was the trash can. I sure didn't like that, when I heard about it."

"What do you mean?" I asked.

"Well, she was a janitor. Was it some sort of statement? You know, was someone insinuating that she was trash, or does someone have it in for janitors?"

"Like it was some sort of . . . serial killer?" Gabrielle asked, her expression incredulous.

Vaughn immediately looked like he wished he could take the words back. "I'm not saying that's what happened, but you got to wonder. At least, I do. A janitor is killed, and her body is found in a trash can. You got to wonder." He shifted around us. "Excuse me, I've got to get back to work."

"Wait, Vaughn," I said before he got too far away. "Do you know where the trash can went missing from?"

"Oh sure, it was from the main office. The detective showed me a picture of it, and I recognized it right away. It had a streak of yellow paint on the handle from when the office was painted last summer. It usually sits in the corner by the cubbyholes in the main office." He caught sight of Mrs. Kirk coming out of the office and moved away quickly.

Gabrielle and I did the same. I headed for the checkout computer in the main office, noticing that a new, smaller trash can stood by the row of teacher cubbyholes. Gabrielle followed me, signing out after I did.

As I headed out the main doors to the overflow parking lot, I heard Gabrielle calling me. "Ellie, wait."

I'd arrived early this morning, so my van was

fairly close, and I was opening the back of the van so I could stow the chair and my tote bag by the time she caught up with me. As Gabrielle hurried over, she waved the sheets of paper at me. "You forgot your portion of the list."

"Gabrielle," I sighed, not sure where to start. "I know you want to get this thing cleared up, and I understand that you're worried about your clients, but I don't think you need to worry about being a suspect."

"No? Are you sure? Did you think you'd be a suspect last time? I bet you didn't. I don't want to be blindsided."

She flapped the papers at me. "Come on, Ellie. At least take a look."

"And," I continued as if she hadn't spoken, "I know Detective Waraday would not be happy for you to be poking around in his investigation."

"But we'd be helping him," she said, her eyes wide.

"Trust me, he doesn't want our help."

"Well, whether or not you help me, I'm doing it. You don't even have to talk to anyone. Just *look* at the list. Please," she said, drawing out the word like Livvy did when she asked if a friend could stay for a sleepover, but my impassive face must have gotten across the message that pleading wouldn't work with me. I had years of practicing that *it's not going to happen* expression with the kids.

Gabrielle glanced around the empty parking lot and her voice went completely serious as she took a step closer. "I'm not going to stand around and wait to show up on the evening news. And I promise you that if I show up on the news, you'll be next, because who was with me when I saw the body?"

"I wasn't with you."

"You were there on the scene."

On the scene. Detective Waraday had used those same words, and they echoed in my head.

"I'll make that very clear to anyone who asks. You were there."

"That's blackmail," I said.

She grinned. "No, don't think of it that way. It's just a little motivator."

I blew out a breath. I couldn't tell her what Detective Waraday had said about the investigation focusing on Klea's personal life—he'd asked me not to talk about that—so I couldn't use that as an argument to convince Gabrielle to back off.

Gabrielle waved the papers again, her expression expectant and hopeful. The phrase *a dog with a bone* came to mind. She was as persistent as Rex when he wanted a treat. Gabrielle wasn't going to give up. I sighed again and took the papers. "I will look through them, but I am *not* chasing down half the parents from Muffins with Mom Day and asking them for an alibi."

She must have sensed that she wouldn't get any more out of me today because she said quickly, "That's okay. I'll do all the asking. I just want you to read over them, see if anything pops out. You know more of the parents than I do." She gave my upper arm a quick squeeze. "Thanks, Ellie. I knew I could count on you. I'll call you later so we can compare notes." She marched off, her heels clicking across the asphalt of the parking lot.

I stood there for a second, scanning the list in my hand, then let out a snort. She hadn't given me half of the list. Of course not. Once I'd agreed to look it over, she'd given me the *whole* list, a complete print-out of every parent or volunteer who had signed in from when the doors opened at seven-thirty until the eight-twenty-five bell rang on Wednesday. Hundreds of names. I stuffed the list in my tote bag, then put it in the back of the van, along with my lawn chair and closed the hatchback door.

"Excuse me, Mrs. Avery," said a voice behind me, and I turned to see Detective Waraday.

Chapter Seven

"Oh, hello," I said. "I didn't see you there." I glanced around, looking to see if Gabrielle was still in the vicinity, but she was already motoring out of the parking lot in her compact SUV.

"Do you have a moment?" Detective Waraday asked.

I checked my watch. It was only a little after noon. "Yes. I have some time." It was noon, but I didn't have any other plans, except to go home and work on an ad for Everything In Its Place, my organizing business, and to clean house. Everything seemed fine at the school, and although part of me wanted to camp out in the workroom all day, I knew that realistically I couldn't do that.

"Good. I have a request." Detective Waraday looked away, squinting as he gazed across the tops of the cars. "I'd like for you to look at Mrs. Burris's house."

"Um—why?" I'd been braced for questions that

would rehash everything that Detective Waraday had asked me yesterday.

"Mrs. Burris lived alone. You saw her house a few weeks ago. I'd like to know if it is in the same state it was when you saw it."

"Oh. Sure." I paused uncertainly. "Um, should we walk?"

"If you don't mind."

"No. It's not far." Leaving my stuff inside the van, I clicked the button on the key fob to lock it, then pocketed the keys and fell into step beside Detective Waraday. We crossed the parking lot and walked on the grassy verge outside of the chain-link fence that ran along the side field, stepping over a few rutted tracks where the tires of a car had dug into the soft turf. This morning, when Field Day began, each side of the street had been lined with cars parked parallel, bumper to bumper. Parents who had arrived to find the overflow lot full had wedged their cars in somewhere on the surrounding residential streets. The extra cars were gone, and only one class was having recess as students ran back and forth across the field.

Klea's house was about halfway up the block, and we glanced up and down the now-quiet street before crossing to the other side. Klea's Craftsman bungalow looked a little rough around the edges. The white trim on the porch pillars was peeling, and the grass in the small yard was ankle high. A paved driveway ran down the right side of the property to a carport that listed to the side, following the sloping line of the ground, which plunged from Klea's property to a rainwater drain set into the grass on her neighbor's property a few feet below. A huge oak tree, with a trunk so thick that my fingers wouldn't touch if I tried to put both arms around it, threw a blanket of shade over the entire front yard.

"You said she lived alone. Was she a widow?" I asked, thinking of what Vaughn had said about how Klea never mentioned family. "I knew her from school, but not that well," I explained.

"She was getting a divorce." Detective Waraday looked at me sharply as he stopped so that I would walk in front of him along the little strip of concrete to the wide set of steps at the foot of the porch. "I'm surprised you didn't know that."

"I'd only talked to her a few times, really. I saw her around the school a lot, but we were acquaintances, not close friends. We didn't know each other well. When I came for the consultation, we talked about organizing her things and that was all."

Now that I thought about it, that was rather strange. There is something about looking through a person's possessions that is very intimate. By the end of most organizing consultations, I usually knew quite a bit about the person. Analyzing clutter typically led to at least brief mentions of family members and situations. I often knew a potential client's background and life situation—kid going off to college, or death of a relative who had left them furniture or boxes to shift through, or even mundane things like the hobbies and interests—because it was often stuff related to those very things that the client wanted help with.

One husband had called me hoping I could settle a dispute between him and his wife about how they should use an extra bedroom. He wanted to

store his vintage record collection there. She
wanted to turn it into a darkroom for her hobby of
taking pictures with vintage cameras and develop-
ing the film herself. Those were details that I normally wouldn't have known about near strangers.
But Klea hadn't been chatty or forthcoming, I realized, now that I thought about it.

"And that seems odd to you?" Detective Waraday
said as he took out a key ring and unlocked a dead
bolt on the front door.

"At the time, I didn't notice it, but it does now,
since I've thought about it. Most people chat and
tell me about their life. And seeing their belongings, well, you always learn things about people
from their stuff."

"And what did you learn about Mrs. Burris from
your appointment?" Detective Waraday switched to
another key and unlocked a second dead bolt.

"Hardly anything," I said slowly. "She said she'd
bought the house about a month ago and had too
much stuff. She was downsizing." I thought back
over the meeting, then shook my head. "No, I think
that was it. That was all she said about herself."

He nodded. "From what I've found out about
her, that was typical. She was a loner. Didn't have
any kids. Her parents were both dead. A relative—a
sister—lives in Missouri, but she didn't keep in
close touch with her."

"What about friends?" I asked, thinking of Vaughn
saying that Klea kept to herself.

"I can't find anyone she kept in touch with regularly. Except for her work, she didn't have contact
with many people."

"That's so sad," I said, wishing that I had taken

the time to talk to her and gotten to know her a little bit.

"Some people don't want lots of social interaction." Detective Waraday pushed the door open and stepped inside. I followed him in, and he closed the door behind me, but didn't flip the dead bolts. The air was stale and muggy in the little house. The blinds were drawn, and with the heavy shade from the tree outside, it was so dark inside the house that it almost felt like night.

Waraday opened the curtains in the front room and crossed to a floor lamp, which he switched on. The front door opened directly into a living area, which was so filled with boxes that I could only see a couple of inches of the golden oak floorboards. A bit of breathing room had been carved out for a couch, a coffee table, and an older television at one end of the room.

"Look around," Waraday said as he moved into the dining room directly behind the living area and turned on more lights. As he went into the kitchen at the back of the house, he called out, "Tell me what's changed."

I felt a bit like I was looking at one of those Find the Hidden Item books that the kids liked so much as I scanned the room. "Not much in here . . . I think," I said. I remembered the room being filled with boxes. I reached for my phone. It had been a while since I'd been there and I couldn't remember exactly what was in each room, but—like Gabrielle—I often took pictures of rooms to help me jog my memory.

I found the pictures I'd taken of Klea's front room and compared them to the room as it was now. "She opened some boxes that were stacked here by the wall," I said to Waraday as he came back into the room. I showed him my phone. "Look, you can see the fireplace now, and it was totally blocked by boxes when I was here."

Detective Waraday nodded. "I'd like a copy of those." He handed me a business card. "You can text them to this number."

"Okay," I said. "I would have mentioned them yesterday, but I didn't think about them—that you might be interested in them." I tapped on my phone as I spoke, sending the images. "I only have this room and a few pictures of the spare bedroom."

"Anything will be helpful." Detective Waraday's phone dinged, and as he checked it, he pulled at the collar of his polo shirt. "Got them. Thanks. It's stuffy in here. Let me see if there's central air." He walked off down the hall. A low rumble sounded, and he came back with a shake of the head. "Just window coolers. I turned one on, but I doubt it will do much good out here."

"Yeah, I love the architecture of these homes—they have plenty of charm—but I don't think I could get by without air-conditioning here in Georgia."

Mitch and I had lived in what we'd come to think of as our antique starter home during his last assignment in Washington state. We hadn't had air-conditioning there. It had been bearable, but only because the summers were so short. I looked toward the window at the front of the house, thinking of all the times I'd opened windows in Washington and set up fans in an effort to get a cross breeze. Except for the windows with the AC units, Klea's windows were painted shut, and in addition to the old sash locks that had been painted over, all the windows had an extra set of what looked to be brand-new bolt locks. Not a speck of paint marred their shiny silver surface, unlike the rest of the windowsills, which had thick coats of paint on them.

I moved into the dining room. A large cabinet stocked with antique china and a dining room table with eight chairs filled the small space. "She did a lot of work in here. There were boxes stacked all along that wall, but they're gone now. The table looks . . . about the same," I said.

Klea had been using the dining room table, a huge rectangle of dark wood that was too big for the room, as a desk when I'd come through for the appointment. I remembered that her laptop had been at the head of the table, with piles of papers, folders, notepads, and bank boxes arranged around it. The paper stacks and the boxes remained, but the laptop was gone now. The police had probably taken it to examine it.

"Can I look in the boxes?" I asked.

Detective Waraday waved his hand. "Go ahead. We've already fingerprinted everything and removed what looked significant."

I peered in a few of the bank boxes, which had their lids off. They contained old bills and file folders of tax returns from prior years. "There were boxes on the table that day I was here. Klea and I talked about going through them, throwing away old paperwork, and setting up a filing cabinet to store the records she needed to keep. I recommended using the extra bedroom as an office."

I picked up a lid from the seat of a nearby dining

room chair and replaced it. I could only suppress my instincts to tidy things for so long. Klea must have used the box lid as a notepad because it had scribbles all over it. The word "dentist," along with a time and next Tuesday's date, filled one corner.

I ran my finger over the indentations the pen had made in the cardboard, thinking how sad it was that her life had been cut off so abruptly and how fragile all our connections were. Klea had been moving through her days, planning for next week and next month with no idea that everything would end so abruptly. I let my finger trail over another jotted note for her to buy a shredder, which had been checked off; then I paused at a list of names.

"What is it?" Detective Waraday asked.

"This list of names. I know the first person, Mrs. Harris, and the last four, Ms. McCormick, Mrs. Kirk, Peg, and Marie—they all work at the school—but I don't know who Alexa Wells is." Her name was second on the list and bracketed in parentheses. A question mark was written to the side of the names. Did Klea have some question about the whole list or one person in particular? Or was it only a doodle, something she had randomly written while waiting on hold when she was on the phone? "I wonder why one name is set off from the others in parentheses? Maybe she's a new teacher, and I just don't know her."

"Or maybe a parent," Waraday said, looking over my shoulder. "It's probably nothing." He seemed more interested in a phone number jotted down across one corner and made a note of it.

After checking some of the papers on the table and the contents of some of the boxes, I said, "It looks like she was working her way through the boxes, sorting which things to keep and which to get rid of." I pointed to the different stacks on the table. A paper shredder sat by the table, its bin full of confetti.

I stepped away from the table, and Detective Waraday gestured for me to go ahead of him through the kitchen door. "Klea said she didn't like to cook and didn't need any help with organizing or de-cluttering the kitchen so I didn't even go in here—"

I glanced into the tiny galley kitchen, which was old-fashioned and decorated in lime green, but what caught my attention was a piece of wood in the window over the sink, where a pane of glass should have been. "But I would have noticed if that window was broken. It wasn't like that."

A faint smile crossed Detective Waraday's face. "That's another reason I asked you to look around. We found the window broken when we checked the house yesterday. It must have happened Thursday, after she was killed. I doubt she would have gone off to work without putting something in the window or making a call on her cell phone or a search on her computer for glass repair. Someone's been in here. It looks as if they tried the back door, but couldn't get in that way—there are scrapes and scratches around the frame—but these old houses are pretty solid."

I studied the back door, which opened onto the carport and driveway, for a second. It looked as if it was more than the craftsmanship of the home that had kept the intruder out. Like the front door, the back door also had two thick dead bolts.

Someone had swept up the big pieces of the glass

from the counter and sink, but tiny shards speckled the Formica. Two partial prints from the sole of a shoe marred the clean surface of the white sink. The treads were bumpy and patterned like the sole of a tennis shoe.

"They only came in for a look around, it seems," Detective Waraday said. "No fingerprints, nothing identifiable, except those shoe prints. The only thing I can figure is that someone wanted something from this house." Waraday put his hands on his hips and looked back toward the living room. "The question is, what? Nothing obvious is missing—no jewelry, no valuable electronics—the laptop was still here—and the neighbors didn't notice anyone coming or going. I thought you might be able to tell us more about Mrs. Burris's possessions. Did she mention any sort of collection or anything valuable at all?"

"No. Nothing like that came up." I heard a faint ringing, and recognized the school bell. I checked the time, but saw it wasn't the last bell of the day. I still had some time before I had to get back to pick up the kids. I wasn't surprised that you could hear the school bells from inside Klea's house. Since she was right across the street, she probably got so used to them that she just tuned them out.

Detective Waraday didn't seem to notice the school bell and went on. "It was a long shot. She didn't seem the type of woman to own jewelry or valuable decorative things. Why don't you take a look in the bedrooms?"

"Okay," I said, doubtfully. "But I was only in those rooms for a few minutes." Now that I knew why I was here, I felt overwhelmed. It had been weeks since I was in this house, and I hadn't been looking at and memorizing each individual thing. I'd focused on the big picture, the clutter, and tried to figure out how to help Klea get it under control. I retraced my steps through the dining room and the living room, and down the short hallway that branched off the living room to the two bedrooms.

The first bedroom was Klea's. The window unit was pumping out cool air. I shivered as I walked into the room, but it wasn't because of the temperature. A pair of flats was discarded in front of the closet, and a jumble of earrings, lipstick, and a phone-charging cord covered the dresser. It looked as if Klea had stepped out and would be back at any moment.

I swallowed and moved to the closet. "Nothing's changed in here that I can see. Klea showed it to me so I could see how much storage she had in this room and the other room, but I told her she was better off using this for clothes and converting the extra bedroom to an office with storage in there." As I glanced around the room a final time, I noticed that in addition to the regular sash locks, each window had shiny new metal locks.

Detective Waraday nodded and stepped back from the doorway, where he was waiting. I moved by him to the last room. It was still a mishmash of extraneous stuff that Klea hadn't known where to put: packing boxes, unhung pictures, a coat rack, folded lawn chairs, and a treadmill filled the room. I looked from the pictures on my phone to the room and sighed. "I don't think anything's changed in here, but I'm not sure at all. I measured the room and tried to help Klea imagine what it would look like without all the clutter." After a quick survey of the room, my gaze stopped at the window. It, too, had the new, extra locks installed.

Detective Waraday noticed what I was looking at. "Security seemed to be a high priority for her," he said.

"Yes. Now that I think about it, I do remember that it was a nice day—unusually cool—when I was here, and I said something about how it was pleasant enough that I'd opened some windows at my house to enjoy the cool air. She said she never did that, and when I came inside, she locked both dead bolts on the front door. At the time, I thought it was a bit strange. The multiple locks seemed like something out of a television show—you know, something you'd see on a show set in a rough, downtown area, but I didn't think about it again until now," I said as I followed Detective Waraday back down the hall to the living room.

"Did she have a security system, too?" I asked.

"No." His gaze went from lock to lock on the windows in the front room. "It looks as if she wanted one—there was a search on her computer for home security companies—but I think she probably couldn't afford to have one installed. Her finances were . . . um, tight after purchasing the house."

"I know that feeling," I said, thinking of all the unexpected expenses that pop up after buying a house.

"It looks like the locks were her cost-effective alternative to installing a whole house-monitoring system," Detective Waraday said. "So nothing stands out to you?"

"Except for the locks?" I frowned and looked

around the small rooms with their thick trim, coved ceilings, and freshly painted white walls. "No. The only thing I'm sure of is that some boxes in here and in the dining room are gone."

Detective Waraday said, "I doubt the person who broke in here did it to steal cardboard boxes, but I'll check. There is a stack of flattened cardboard boxes in the carport—probably boxes that Mrs. Burris had gone through, as you indicated. I'll have my team compare your pictures to the boxes out there. I have a feeling that they'll be a match. Well, thank you for taking a look, Mrs. Avery," he said as he walked me to the door. "I won't keep you any longer. I have to turn everything off and lock up, but you don't need to stay."

He thanked me again for my help, which was a rather odd thing for me—I was used to Detective Waraday warning me off or even accusing me, not thanking me. I walked down the street and back to the school parking lot, wondering why Klea had needed so many locks.

Despite being packed with activities, the weekend was uneventful. Soccer games for Livvy on Saturday took up most of the day, and Sunday, after church, we had a birthday party for one of Nathan's friends, which left enough time to run home and prep lunches, wash clothes, do the bath and bedtime routine. Then I called the parents who had signed up to bring food on Monday for Teacher Appreciation Week and remind them of their commitment to bring a breakfast-type food. The rest of the week was planned, and each day had a menu. Tuesday was snacks and desserts, Wednesday was catered sub rolls for lunch, Thursday was breakfast again, and then on Friday we had a catered barbecue buffet scheduled for lunch.

Another mom, Mia, and I had coordinated the whole thing, but her twins had gotten into poison ivy. She'd said, "My life is all about calamine lotion and oatmeal baths. Can you handle this week on your own? They're both very sensitive to it and taking prescriptions to help, but the doctor says it could be a week before we're back to normal."

I told her not to worry, that the hard part—getting parents to sign up to bring food or donate money—was done. All I had to do was make reminder calls and make sure the food was put out and later cleared away each day. It would actually be a great way to unobtrusively check in at the school every day.

With the kids in bed, I settled into my favorite overstuffed chair for some downtime. Rex was sprawled on the floor, snoring so loudly that I wondered if he'd keep the kids awake. I had the television on more for company than because I was interested in the sitcom rerun. Without Mitch around, the house always seemed a little empty, so I liked the low murmur of the television show in the background.

I read the first chapter of the novel for the book club, which the back cover described as "hauntingly evocative and moving," but I couldn't get into it, so I put it aside. I'd try it again later when I wasn't so . . . what? Edgy. Despite being tired from doing the parenting thing solo for several days, I felt twitchy and unsettled. I knew it was Klea's death and the questions around it that had me feeling off. This was the first time I'd slowed down all weekend, and of course my mind went directly to Klea.

I thought of her stuffy, deserted house and its abandoned air. I shifted in the chair, reaching for the list of parents who had signed up to bring food this week for Teacher Appreciation. I scanned down the list of names. The unfamiliar name of Alexa Wells tugged at me. I didn't remember seeing that name on the list, but I had been more focused on getting the calls made than concentrating on names. I ran my finger down the lists for each day of the week, but there was no Alexa Wells.

I uncurled my legs and went to find the list that Gabrielle had pressed on me. I hadn't had time to look at that list either and studied it as I walked back to the chair. It was much longer—several pages—but I reached the end of it without seeing the name Alexa Wells there either. I frowned over the list for a while because I knew that Gabrielle would ask me about it the next time I saw her, but I couldn't for the life of me see how we could use this list of names to figure out who had killed Klea.

Yes, all the people had been at the school that morning, but unless we planned to interview each person and trace their movements around the school—and I knew Gabrielle and I couldn't do that—it wouldn't do us much good. No, those were tasks more suited to someone like Detective Waraday. He could interview everyone and plot movements, and I was sure he already had a copy of the list. I turned off the television and gave Rex a rub on his belly before I went to switch off lights around the house. Somehow I doubted Gabrielle would see it the same way.

Organizing Tips for PTA Moms

To keep from getting roped into doing more than you're able, choose the type of volunteer activities that work best with your schedule. If you are juggling a job outside the home as well as volunteering at school, pick one-time events like a field trip or yearly events like Field Day or holiday parties. If you have the ability to be at the school more often, you could volunteer to help in a certain area on a recurring basis, like in your child's classroom or in the library.

Chapter Eight

"**W**hat are you talking about?" Gabrielle asked the next morning, her eyes wide. "That list is *the* key."

A group of second-grade boys walked through the school lobby, their gazes fastened on Gabrielle and me. She rotated her shoulders and lowered her voice. "We have to use it."

"How?" I asked.

I'd arrived at the school early to help set up food for Teacher Appreciation and had run into Gabrielle on my way into the office to sign in. She was on her way out the door, a stack of papers tucked into her elbow, and had nearly collided with me. I'd side-stepped and managed not to drop the bag of paper cups, the gallon of orange juice, and the platter of breakfast biscuits I'd picked up on the way to school.

"What do you mean, how?" Gabrielle said. "I told you. We ask everyone where they were that morning. If they were in any other hallway besides the blue hallway, then we mark them off the list."

"And what if they were in several hallways, like me?" I shifted my grip on the cold orange juice container, which was already beaded with condensation. "I visited Nathan and Livvy's classrooms."

"Then we'll put them down for both. We'll need a spreadsheet. You can take care of that, right? I have a meeting today with the school board to update them on the progress of the implementation." She smoothed a hand over the lapel of her black suit jacket. With her black skirt and heels, she looked much dressier than most of the teachers and parents at the school.

"And what if they lie?" I asked.

"Lie? Why would they lie?" she asked, her tone indicating I'd suggested something as impossible as snow in Georgia, a very rare occurrence.

"Lots of reasons . . . maybe just to be difficult. But it will only confuse the issue, if we try and do it. It's something Detective Waraday should do, and I bet he already is. People don't have to talk to us, but they do have to answer to the police."

She frowned at me a moment, then said, "Ellie, you are as obstinate as a mule, do you know that? You could argue with a wall and win. Just because this was my idea . . ."

"No, that's not it, Gabrielle," I said quickly. "I think we can use our time in a better way."

She narrowed her eyes. "How?"

"By focusing on the things that Detective Waraday won't see or overhear. He'll get the official story, but we're in the school with the parents and teachers in a way that Detective Waraday can't be. We're here every day—or it seems like I'm here every day right now. We listen and pay attention. That's all we can do."

"Listen and pay attention," she said slowly as if those were foreign concepts. "I don't know. It seems kind of . . . vague." She pursed her lips to one side, then said, "Okay, I don't like it, but we can try it—for a bit. If it doesn't work . . ." She looked at her watch and gave a little shriek. "Oh, I have to get on the road to be at the district office on time."

She swept off, her heels clacking over the tile floor. As I walked inside the office and set the food and drink down on the counter to sign in, Marie followed me in, looking a little breathless. "Hi, Ellie," she said as she hurried around the end of the counter to her desk. She patted her fluffy blond hair into place. "I know better than to wait until after seven-thirty to leave. I just could not get out the door this morning."

"Hi, Marie," I said over the clatter of the little printer as it spit out my volunteer sticker, glad to see Marie's friendly face, which was such a contrast to Peg's usually sour looks. Abby had told me that Marie's husband had worked for an accounting firm that went under because of a financial scandal several years ago. He'd had a heart attack shortly after he lost his job, and Marie had found herself on her own without a retirement plan or investments because they'd lost everything when his company shut down, and up to that point she'd been a part-time employee. Abby said Marie had switched to a full-time position the next year, and I admired

Marie for always being upbeat, despite having had a rather rough time, and wondered if any of her sunny disposition would ever rub off on Peg.

I peeled the sticker off the paper and attached it to my shirt. "How was your vacation? Did you go to the beach with some friends?"

"No, just me."

"Oh," I said, surprised and a little saddened for her.

"Don't feel sorry for me. I shopped a lot and read two novels, and started knitting a new sweater," she said as she plucked a sticky note off her wooden cube calendar. Still standing, she read the note and looked up at me. "So, no second round of fundraising?"

I paused, the platter of food balanced in one hand and the juice dangling from my other hand. "Oh, right. I'd completely forgotten about that note. I left it for you last week when I found out the second fundraiser was off the table."

Marie nodded and tossed the note in the trash. "Glad to hear it. There's enough going on during the final weeks of school. The last thing we need is another fundraiser." She flipped the wooden blocks around so that the combination of numbers reflected the correct date, then took off her pink cardigan and draped it over her chair. She gave a quick glance around the office, then lowered her voice as she sat down in her rolling chair. "Of course, you didn't hear that from me."

I smiled conspiratorially at her. "Hear what?"

Marie shifted her chair closer to the desk and punched her computer to turn it on. "Where's Peg? I want all the details about what happened to Klea."

We both looked at Peg's desk, which was cluttered with papers, interoffice envelopes, and a folder. A mug of coffee steamed to one side. "She must be around," Marie said. "Probably in the workroom, running copies. I swear she spends half her day in the workroom."

"Really? I never see her in there, and I'm in there a lot."

Marie raised one eyebrow. "Well, that's where she tells Mrs. Kirk she is." Mrs. Kirk's office light was on, but the room itself was empty. I'd seen Mrs. Kirk a few minutes ago when I dropped the kids off, so I knew she wouldn't be back until after the tardy bell rang.

Marie waved a plump hand with pink nails. "You'll have to tell me." She came around the counter and picked up the juice. "Let me help you with this, and you can fill me in on the way. Teachers' lounge?"

I nodded, and we headed out of the office, Marie's pale pink skirt swishing as she walked beside me, her pumps tapping out a sturdy beat as we crossed the lobby, dodging kids streaming in from the drop-off as they hurried to class, their backpacks thumping against their backs. I was in my usual mom uniform of jeans, a casual T-shirt, and boat shoes. I didn't make a sound as we walked along.

Once we'd cleared the lobby and the door to the teachers' lounge swung shut behind us, Marie said, "I heard the news about Klea as soon as I got back in town last night. I couldn't believe it. Poor Klea. What happened?"

I shrugged. "No one knows. The sheriff's department is investigating."

"And she was found during Field Day?"

I nodded as I arranged the paper cups. I summa-
rized what had happened, skipping over Gabrielle's
sighting of the body in the closet, as Marie found
paper napkins and set them on the table. I removed
the cover from the food, and she shook her head as
she picked up one of the biscuits and put it on a
napkin. "It's shocking, that something like that could
happen here at the school." She shook her head again
and muttered, "Just shocking," again before taking a
bite. I agreed and wadded up the plastic wrap and
dusted a few crumbs from the table.

"I bet it was her ex." Marie pointed the half-eaten
biscuit at me to emphasize her point.

"Her ex?" I asked. "Why do you say that? I thought
she was in the process of getting a divorce."

Marie waved floury fingertips. "All but done.
Only a few more days and the papers would have
been filed. I heard her telling Mrs. Kirk in the office
the other day. Klea was already calling him her ex
even though it wasn't official yet. He is apparently
quite a character. In fact, you probably know him—
or would recognize him. You've heard of Ace Burris
Auto Sales?"

"You mean Screaming Ace? That guy that runs
commercials on the local channels?"

Marie nodded as she polished off the last bite,
then mimicked the announcer's voice, but in a quieter
tone than the one I'd heard on the commercials, "Get
a screaming good deal from Burris Auto!" Marie's
voice returned to normal. "Yep, that's Klea's ex. Or was
her soon-to-be ex."

"Really?" I asked, amazed. "I never would have
pictured them together. Klea was so quiet and reserved." At the end of every commercial, "Scream-

ing Ace" gave a loud "yee-haw" before his signature pitch line.

"It just goes to show, doesn't it? I don't know the whole story—Klea was a very private person—but I do know that she had a restraining order on him. He wasn't allowed on school property at all."

"Wow. That's kind of scary. I wonder what he'd done."

Marie glanced quickly at the door. "I think—I don't know this for sure—but I think he beat her up."

"Oh, that's terrible."

Marie nodded as she wiped her fingers on the napkin. "It was. Klea came in to work one day, and she was moving stiffly. Mrs. Kirk noticed. You know what Mrs. Kirk is like when she focuses on something. Mrs. Kirk must have suspected something because she had Klea in her office with the door closed as soon as the announcements were over. Klea came out, her eyes all red, and Mrs. Kirk said she'd be out of the office for a few hours. She bundled Klea into her car. Klea took some vacation days, and I didn't think anything else about it until a parent, Mrs. Hudson—she had a daughter in fourth grade at that time, I think—she came in a couple of days later for something at the office, and she asked how Klea's ribs were doing. She's a nurse at the urgent-care walk-in clinic over on Tyler Avenue. Mrs. Kirk came flying out of her office and got Mrs. Hudson out of the office quick as a duck on a June bug. Nothing else was said, but about a week later, I heard that Klea had moved into an apartment. It was right after that happened that Mrs. Kirk told me and Peg that Mr. Burris was not allowed on school grounds, and if we saw him we should call the school district's resource officer."

"When was this?" I asked. No wonder Klea had sturdy locks all over her house and Detective Waraday said the investigation would focus on off-campus issues.

"Let's see, she put that offer in on that cute little house across the street a few months ago, so I think this was about six months before that. Last fall sometime, anyway. There's the second bell. I have to get back. Let me know if you hear anything else, will you?"

Peg opened the door and held it so another mom could walk in with a plastic container of fruit salad. Another mom followed her in with a breakfast casserole. Marie and I moved to the door as I said in a quiet voice, "I'm sure the sheriff's office will keep Mrs. Kirk updated. You'll probably hear any news before me."

She patted my arm. "But you somehow always manage to find things out. It must be your knack for organizing that lets you put it all together. Keep me in the loop."

Abby came through the door, spotted the food, and said, "Oh, isn't this sweet? I love Teacher Appreciation Week. So thoughtful of everyone." Her smile included me and the other moms who had put out food. A group of teachers arrived and picked up paper plates, commenting on how good everything looked. The word was out that the food was here, and I knew the room would be busy until the eight-twenty-five bell, with teachers slipping down for a quick bite to eat.

Abby filled her plate and came back to stand by me on the side of the room. "So how are things in the classroom? Are the kids worried or scared?" I asked.

"They are doing okay for the most part. I've had a few kids who have been more clingy than usual, but that's all I've noticed."

"What about the teachers?"

Abby sipped some juice, her face thoughtful. "Well, it's certainly a topic of conversation, but no one seems to know anything specific about what happened. I have heard a few . . . I don't know what you'd call them . . . insinuations, I guess, that Klea was probably poking her nose in where she shouldn't have."

"Really? I hadn't heard that. Only that she was very private."

Abby popped a grape in her mouth and chewed while a group of teachers passed us. When they were clear, she said, "Klea did keep to herself, but there was once that I came back to the school for something I'd left here—a jacket or something like that—and when I walked into my classroom she was at my desk and jumped. She said I'd startled her, and I apologized. We had a laugh, but"—Abby paused, her forehead crinkling into a frown—"I had the impression that she was closing one of my desk drawers when I came through the door."

She took a bite of a biscuit and shook her head as she chewed. "I could be totally wrong. That's why I didn't say anything, but I made sure I didn't leave anything on my desk—or in it—that I didn't mind anyone seeing. I've gotten the impression from a few other teachers that they were . . . let's say, a little wary of her." Abby frowned again. "Or someone. There's a definite atmosphere lately of tension."

"That's understandable with the circumstances."

Abby tossed her empty plate in a trash can as she said, "No, it's more than just generally being worried. Something is up—and it has been for a while. Klea's death has magnified it—or perhaps given it a focus, would be a better way to say it. I can't put my finger on exactly what it is, but there's definitely an uneasy atmosphere around here." Abby glanced at the clock on the wall. "I have to get back. Thanks for breakfast," she said, and turned to leave.

"Oh, Abby, wait. Do you know Alexa Wells?"

I probably wouldn't have noticed Mrs. Harris, except she was standing directly behind Abby in my line of sight. When I said the name Alexa Wells, Mrs. Harris's whole body went completely still. She had been leaning over the table, scooping a spoonful of the fruit salad onto her plate. But at my words, she froze, the spoon suspended in the air.

Abby's face split into a grin. "I don't know her, but I know *of* her."

Her words broke the spell around Mrs. Harris, and she glanced around with the same expression I'd seen on Nathan's face when I mentioned Rex had suddenly taken to digging holes in the backyard. I hadn't thought the divots in the grass were Rex's doing, but Nathan had confessed that he and Charlie had been pretending they were pirates. Mrs. Harris's face had that same guilty cast to it for a few seconds; then she dumped the fruit on her plate and moved to stand close to us. She kept her gaze focused on the windows, but I had the feeling she was listening intently to every word we said.

"So Alexa Wells doesn't work at the school?" I asked. "Her name sounded familiar, but I couldn't place it."

"Because we talked about reading her book for the book club," Abby said.

"Oh, right," I said as the light bulb went on. "Alexa Wells, the author. Super steamy."

Abby cocked an eyebrow. "More than that. Erotica, actually."

"Oh, is that what she writes? I got a phone call when we were discussing which book to read next at the book club and missed the discussion." I'd returned from my phone call to find that the Alexa Wells title was off the table and the group had agreed on the evocative and haunting women's fiction book that I'd tried to read last night.

"Are you thinking about picking up a copy?" Abby asked. "If you do, I'd keep it out of Livvy's sight. I know what a voracious reader she is. You might not want to have to explain some of the things in there to Livvy."

"No, it's not that. I saw the name on a list that Klea had written." I didn't mention where I'd seen it. I thought it would be better to keep my visit to Klea's house quiet. "The weird thing is that the rest of the list was names of teachers and staff from the school."

Mrs. Harris was standing just behind Abby's shoulder, facing slightly away from me. She had been eating chopped fruit with mechanical movements, but she suddenly sprang to life, tossing her plate that was still half-filled with food into the trash can and striding out of the room. Another teacher was on the way inside and backed out of the doorway as Mrs. Harris motored through.

Abby hadn't noticed Mrs. Harris's abrupt exit.

"Well, maybe Klea wanted to read one of her books and jotted the name down," Abby said.

"But it was in the middle of a list of names, not just scribbled randomly on the page." Right under Mrs. Harris's name, I thought to myself, but didn't say aloud.

"Weird," Abby said in a tone of voice that indicated that it was nothing significant. "Got to run," she said. "Will you be around today?"

"Yes, I think so," I said, already trying to think of when the best time would be to get a minute alone with Mrs. Harris.

Chapter Nine

It was lunchtime before I saw Mrs. Harris again. I'd hung around in the workroom for about an hour, intermittently cruising up and down the first-grade hallway a few times, but Mrs. Harris was always busy moving from student to student, along with the teacher, so I went back to the teachers' lounge and cleaned up the breakfast spread, left the campus and ran a few errands, then returned to the school with two Subway sandwiches and surprised Nathan when I joined him for lunch. He was still cool with his mom sitting beside him in the cafeteria. I wasn't sure Livvy would be too excited about me eating lunch with her, but I'd offer to bring her lunch later in the week and see how she reacted.

As I said good-bye to Nathan when his class left for their after-lunch recess, I spotted Mrs. Harris moving down the hallway toward the workroom. I scooted along and followed her into the empty room. She stood at the copier, one veined hand holding down the lid, while pages whirred out into the bin. She saw me as I walked into the room and she froze again like she had in the teachers' lounge for a second. The copier ejected the last page with a click, then went silent.

I couldn't transfer the questions that had been bumping around in my mind into words. Standing there in her plain white cotton top, sensible dark knit pants, and flat-soled loafers, she looked like the last person in the world who would know anything about Alexa Wells.

She cleared her throat and nodded at me as she opened the copier lid and picked up a book. "Mrs. Avery." The ends of her gray bowl haircut brushed at her cheekbones as she reached down to retrieve the copies from the bin.

"Mrs. Harris, there's something—"

"Let's go outside for a moment," she said, clasping the papers and the book to her flat chest and marching by me.

I turned and followed her through the lobby and out the heavy doors. She glanced around the school's empty porch, then moved to benches that lined the covered area, taking a seat on the one farthest from the school building.

She sat down and balanced the papers and books carefully on her knees. I'd barely had time to sit down beside her on the metal bench before she said, "You want to know why I reacted so oddly in the teachers' lounge this morning when you mentioned Alexa Wells."

I shifted a bit uncomfortably on the bench. "Yes.

You seemed to be shocked or startled to hear the name."

She looked at me for a moment, her dark eyes studying me, reminding me of the sparrow that was hopping around the patch of grass behind her. Finally, she said, "And I assume this list that you saw my name on was at Klea's house?"

"How did you know about that?" I asked.

She shifted her dark gaze to the side field and pointed. "Klea's house is just over there. I was on the side field last Friday during recess when I saw Detective Waraday speak to you in the parking lot. Then you walked with him to Klea's house and were in there for quite a while."

"He asked me to look around her house because I'd been inside a few weeks ago for an organizing consultation," I said, figuring that if I shared some information she might return the favor.

"Ah, I see." She squinted across the parking lot, then nodded her head decisively. She turned to me and tilted her head to one side. "I am Alexa Wells."

I blinked. "Oh."

"You half suspected it, didn't you? From my reaction when you mentioned the name."

"The thought crossed my mind—fleetingly. You looked so . . . well, guilty, is the word that comes to mind. But then I thought I must be mistaken."

"Because an old woman like me could never write"—she leaned forward, her eyes twinkling—"erotica?"

I opened my mouth, but she leaned back, a smile on her face, and waved away my response.

"Perfectly logical explanation. Nice old ladies

don't write erotica," she said in her normal tone of voice. "Usually. Except in my case. You see, years ago, my husband was diagnosed with a degenerative disease. Eventually, he couldn't work." She gazed at the field surrounding the school, but I could tell her thoughts were turned inward. After a second, she breathed out a little sigh and said, "We'd been fine with both our incomes, but even with insurance, it was difficult to make ends meet on my salary alone. After he passed away, there was a bit of a pension, but it didn't amount to much. Being a teacher's aide doesn't pay well, so I had to either find a way to supplement my income or find a new job. But I do love working with the children here so much that I hated to leave. And everything else I looked into paid a pittance as well. If I was going to be on my feet all day, I'd rather be here at the school with the children than in a department store or something like that."

She straightened the edges of the papers stacked in her lap. "So I decided to try my hand at one thing I've always loved—books. I wrote a historical novel first. It was one of those sweeping family sagas, an epic that covered three—no, four—generations. I sent it to a few agents and the verdict was that it was well written, but nobody wanted epic family sagas. Too dated."

Her laugh lines creased the skin around her eyes. "I put it on the top shelf of my closet. I thought that was that. I should move on to something more practical, but then I heard about erotica and how well some authors were doing. I thought, why not? I'd give it a try. I could write under a pen name and no one would know it was me. That's how things are now. You can be a totally different person on the Internet, and no one has a clue. Well, unless you slip up."

My mind was reeling. I pushed down the many questions that were crowding to the front of my thoughts and focused instead on her last words. I didn't think she was talking about me. "So Klea found out?" I asked.

Mrs. Harris nodded, her face clouding over. "I was foolish. I'm so careful. I never bring anything to school with that name on it—no manuscripts to proofread or anything like that. I never open any of my accounts with that name on any of the school's computers. I always tried to keep Alexa separate from my life here, but I do have a Facebook account in my pen name. I forgot my phone in the workroom one day—set it down while I was making copies and walked off and left it."

Mrs. Harris smoothed back a strand of hair that the breeze had teased across her face. "Klea found it. I'd remembered I'd left the phone and went rushing back to get it, but she'd picked it up and opened the Facebook app, thinking that was the fastest way to see who the phone belonged to." Mrs. Harris's voice became practical. "Very smart of her. Our phones have so much information on them, but sometimes the hardest thing to find is the owner's name."

She lifted a shoulder. "So Klea knew my secret. She'd heard of the books. I could see it in her face when she looked from the phone to me, but she was kind about it. She handed back my phone and said, 'Is this yours? I wasn't sure who it belonged to.' But of course she knew. My picture was right there at the top where you can choose which profile you want to use to post. Next to my public profile about me as everyone knew me, Mrs. Harris, was the profile . . . with a much racier picture for Alexa Wells."

My thoughts skipped ahead. I knew that Mrs. Harris wouldn't want the school to know about her side job. No matter how sweet Mrs. Harris was, there would be some parents who wouldn't want her working with their children. So Klea had to be a threat to Mrs. Harris—whether or not Klea seemed inclined to keep Mrs. Harris's secret. But Mrs. Harris, a murderer . . . ? No, I just couldn't see it.

"Now, I know you're smart and can put two and two together," Mrs. Harris said. "I did, without a doubt, have a reason to silence Klea if I was afraid she'd tell my secret, but I didn't do that. I didn't like that she knew, but I wasn't worried that she'd talk about it. She never mentioned it again, and she wasn't a gossip, so I felt I had nothing to worry about."

"When did this happen? Do you remember?"

"I believe it was right after spring break last year. April or May. I have no idea of the exact date." She waved a hand, brushing away that detail, but I thought it was important.

If Mrs. Harris were worried about keeping Klea quiet, why would she wait nearly a year to kill her? That didn't make sense at all. I breathed a little easier at the thought.

"I have let you in on my little secret for a reason," Mrs. Harris said, her voice brisk. "I know you have an aptitude for finding out interesting things. I could tell from your face this morning that I'd given myself away. And I know you, Mrs. Avery. You're not one to let questions go unanswered, so I decided to take you into my confidence in the hope that you will keep my identity as Alexa hidden."

She held up a finger as I was about to break into her speech. "I know what you're going to say—that this is something that can't be kept from the people investigating Klea's death, and you're absolutely right. I will contact the sheriff's department today and tell the detective in charge the whole story."

One corner of her mouth quirked down. "I had hoped it wouldn't have to come out, but I will certainly explain everything and ask for the investigator's discretion. The detective in charge seemed like a nice young man. I understand that he is interested in the time from seven to nine on Wednesday morning. Fortunately, I have you, Mrs. Dunst, and a whole classroom of six-year-olds who can vouch for me during that time."

"How do you know the times?" I asked, surprised at her exact knowledge.

"Oh, that tidbit was one of the first details to circulate through the school's grapevine after the police began interviewing us. The detective talked to all of us, every teacher, asking each of us about our movements during that time. It wasn't that difficult to deduce when they think Klea was killed."

I nodded, but didn't say anything, thinking that Detective Waraday must have widened the window he was asking about so he wouldn't give away the exact time of death. I knew from talking to Vaughn and being with Gabrielle when she saw the body that it was the time before school started that mattered the most, seven-thirty to eight-thirty. Mrs. Harris had arrived at school Wednesday morning the same time I had. We'd walked into the school together. She didn't realize it, but I was her most critical alibi.

She picked up the papers and pressed them to her chest. "Mrs. Dunst is probably wondering what happened to me. I have to get back. Can I count on you?"

"As long as you tell Detective Waraday, I won't say a word."

"Thank you, Mrs. Avery." She tensed to stand, then stopped and swiveled toward me on the bench. "I have begun to think about retiring. My knees are not what they used to be. All the time sitting criss-cross applesauce with the children is taking its toll, but I would like to be the one to make that decision and not have it made for me."

"I can understand that," I said. I hesitated for a second, then said, "Mrs. Harris, can I ask you a question?" She nodded. "Are you doing all right with your writing? No financial worries?" I asked because I'd discovered that some people were really good at hiding their problems. If she needed help, I wanted her to know that she had plenty of friends who would be happy to step in, as well as several resources in the community, like the local food bank, where I sometimes volunteered.

For the first time since we'd begun talking, her shoulders relaxed completely. "I said I was thinking of retiring, didn't I? I wouldn't—or couldn't—do that without my little side business." She winked as she stood to go back into the school.

After she'd left, I sat on the bench for a few more minutes, my thoughts whirling. I wasn't sure what was going on at the school, but one thing I knew for sure was that Klea's list of names *did* mean something.

Organizing Tips for PTA Moms

<u>Timeline for Planning an Event</u>

- Get permission from school/principal
- Decide on date
- Coordinate with room moms to recruit volunteers
- Announce event:
  —PA announcements
  —Flyers posted around school
  —Banner for hallways/drop-off area
  —Social media
- Send reminders to volunteers one week before
- Send reminders to volunteers one day before
- Thank volunteers after the event

Chapter Ten

The next morning, Tuesday, I drove up to the school drop-off line, and Mrs. Kirk slid the van door back. "Bye, kids," I called as they scrambled out.

Mrs. Harris was on car line duty today, standing between the two lanes of one-way traffic, waving cars through or motioning for them to stop to let kids walk through the crosswalk to the building. I waved to her as I went by, and she sent me a cheery smile. Mrs. Harris was Alexa Wells. I still had trouble taking that news in.

I spun the steering wheel and accelerated slowly, mentally shifting my thoughts to the rest of my day. I had an appointment with Margo Wilkins, a mom I knew through the school. She was remodeling her kitchen and wanted me to help her plan the cabinet and pantry layout of her new kitchen so she'd get the most storage out of the space, but before I went to her house, I exited the car circle, then parked on the grassy verge by the side field and walked back into the school.

I stopped by the office to sign in and said hello to Marie and Peg. Marie had walked into the office a few steps ahead of me, and as she stowed her purse beneath her desk and reached over to flip the calendar blocks to the new date, she raised her eyebrows and asked, "So . . . any news? Heard anything?"

"Nope," I said, mentally adding, *not that I can talk about.*

She sat down and tilted her head, looking at me out of the corner of her eye. "You're not holding out on us, are you?"

"Of course not," I said quickly.

She turned on her computer, then flicked open a file on her desk. "I only ask because you always seem to find out things," she said with a smile. "You're always in the know."

"Not really. I usually feel like I'm in the dark," I said lightly. "Sometimes people just tell me things," I added, thinking of Mrs. Harris and how she'd spilled the whole story of her secret pen name without me hardly having to ask her anything. She must have been longing to talk about it with someone. It would be hard to have a whole separate life and not be able to share it with anyone. It was only because I'd seen her face at a critical moment when she'd given herself away that I had discovered her secret . . . well, that and the fact that she'd wanted to head me off at the pass, so to speak. She'd taken the direct approach and volunteered her secret in the hopes that I would keep quiet. If she'd kept up her end of the bargain with Detective Waraday, then I certainly wasn't going to say anything to Marie about it.

"People trust you," Marie said with a nod. "And I bet you're a good listener." She dropped the file into a metal bin and looked up at me, her face serious. "Don't keep everything to yourself. That could be dangerous."

Peg, who hadn't said a word, let out a snort, and both Marie and I looked toward her. She turned from the cubbyholes, where she had been depositing papers. "Like a mom is going to uncover some deep, dark secret in the school that could endanger her life."

It was the first time Peg had said anything to me that wasn't directly related to school business.

"Peg!" Marie said, her tone scandalized. She shot a quick glance at the door that opened into the lobby, but none of the students were near the door at the moment. "A staff member has been killed," she said in a whisper. "*Someone* did it."

"I thought you were sure it was her husband," Peg said as she banged a stack of papers on the counter to align the edges.

Gabrielle, attired in casual work clothes, an oxford shirt, and khaki pants, came through the door from the lobby as Peg finished her sentence. Gabrielle sang out, "Morning, ladies."

Peg and Marie ignored Gabrielle.

"How did you—?" Marie shifted her glance toward me. I gave a tiny shake of my head to indicate that I hadn't said anything to Peg about what Marie had told me about Klea's husband. Marie spun her chair so that she faced Peg directly. "You were listening at the door to the teachers' lounge." Her voice was accusatory. "I can't believe you would do something so low as eavesdrop."

"I did not eavesdrop." Peg said. "If you don't want people to hear what you have to say, you shouldn't talk about it in a public place where people come and go constantly." She tucked the papers into the crook of her arm and strode out the door of the office, causing Gabrielle to have to sidestep around her.

"Well, I never," Marie said.

Gabrielle watched Peg walk out the door, then swiveled back to face Marie and me. "What's going on?"

Marie waved a hand dismissively at Peg's desk. "Just ignore her. She's having one of her snits. She does that. No big deal."

"What's this about a husband?" Gabrielle asked, her face eager as she looked from Marie to me. "You're not talking about Klea's husband, are you?"

"Why would we be talking about Klea's husband?" Marie said quickly.

Gabrielle dropped her expensive leather purse with heavy gold embellishments onto the tall counter with a *thunk*. "Because Klea is all anyone is talking about." She looked over her shoulder and amended, "Well, when the kids aren't around. But it is the main topic of conversation." She stepped closer and hunched her shoulders over the counter. "Come on, give. What do you know?"

Marie said, reluctantly, "I don't know anything for sure, except that Klea's soon-to-be-ex-husband, Ace Burris, was a first-class louse. He's *got* to be the prime suspect. It's always the spouse, right?"

Gabrielle reared back from the counter. "Ace Burris? But he can't be the prime suspect."

"Why not?" Marie asked in a challenging tone.

"He was at a chamber of commerce breakfast meeting on Wednesday."

"How do you know this?" I asked, thinking that the whole school system and everyone associated with it must have figured out that the time of Klea's death was Wednesday morning.

"Because I'm a member—you really should get involved, Ellie. It will do wonders for your networking," Gabrielle said in an aside. "Anyway, Ace was on the agenda to speak, but I absolutely had to be *here* to do my organizing work, you know, so I had to miss it. But one of my other clients, Crissy Monroe— she's in the chamber, and she went. I talked to her yesterday about the meeting. She said Ace was there. As I said, he was the speaker."

"How long do these meetings go?"

"Let's see, the breakfast meeting starts at seven-thirty and ends about nine or nine-thirty. Since he was speaking, he'd need to be there early. Crissy said he had a PowerPoint and everything. He would have had to get there early to set it up. There's no way he could have . . ."

A student walked into the office with a slip of paper. Marie hopped up and took the paper. "Thank you, Holly," she said, and the girl left.

Gabrielle waited until the girl was in the lobby, then said, "There's no way Ace murdered Klea. He couldn't have."

The three of us looked from one to the other. "That's not good news," Marie said.

I agreed. I wanted Klea's murderer caught, and I wanted it to be someone not associated with the school. All through yesterday afternoon and last night, what Mrs. Harris had told me had been on my mind. I'd managed to convince myself that it didn't really matter that Klea knew a secret about Mrs. Harris that the teacher's aide wanted kept quiet.

I'd turned on the news this morning, hoping—half expecting—to hear that an arrest had been made. Not that I expected Mrs. Harris to be arrested, but I'd hoped that Detective Waraday might have turned up a suspect in his original line of investigation that he'd hinted involved someone off campus.

After learning about Klea's soon-to-be ex and the restraining order, and seeing firsthand Klea's DIY security measures at her house, the logical conclusion would seem to be that the murderer was Ace Burris. But if Gabrielle was right and he did have an alibi—and it sounded like an airtight alibi, at that—then it was looking more and more likely that the murderer was associated with the school. Vaughn and Detective Waraday had said Klea kept to herself. Without any close family or friends, where else could the murderer have come from but the school? Everything seemed so normal this morning at the school—kids crisscrossing the lobby, their high-pitched voices filling the halls, the aroma of Tater Tots wafting out from the cafeteria, and the faint sound of basketballs smacking against the blacktop as the first P.E. class of the day began. A cold feeling of dread washed over me at the thought that someone here at the school was a murderer.

Gabrielle leveled her gaze at me. "This listening and waiting isn't working," she said in a low voice. "We need to get serious and find out who killed Klea. The police don't seem to be doing anything."

"You know that's not true," I said to Gabrielle.

"They're working on it. They're just not keeping us updated on their progress."

Gabrielle gave an impatient toss of her head and returned to her normal tones. "But it amounts to nothing. Have they arrested anyone? No. What are they doing? Who are their suspects?"

"If Ace is out of the running, I don't know who else could have done it. It's not like Klea had . . . enemies," Marie said.

Mrs. Kirk entered the office and our group immediately broke up, Marie moving to her desk, and Gabrielle going to sign in. I went to the teachers' lounge to check on the food for the day, and was happy to see that the parents on the Tuesday Teacher Appreciation crew had come through. Snacks and drinks were spread across the table. A tray of homemade brownies tempted me, but I resisted, promising I'd treat myself to a Hershey's Kiss. They were my Achilles' heel when it came to chocolate, but at least they were small doses of chocolate.

Ms. McCormick was helping herself to one of the delicious brownies, and I thought of the list of names Klea had written down. Mrs. Harris's name had been on it, along with her pen name, something she wanted to hide.

Ms. McCormick's name had been on that, too. Maybe Ms. McCormick was hiding something as well? Her blue dress looked nothing like a ball gown, but with her blond hair up and the color of her dress making her eyes look even more intently blue, she reminded me more than ever of an illustration of a fairy tale princess.

She caught sight of me as she took a bite of the

brownie. She put a hand over her pink lips and looked a little embarrassed. Swallowing quickly, she said, "I know it's early, but I just couldn't wait. They looked so good."

"I'm not throwing stones," I said, picking up some napkins that had fallen on the floor and throwing them in the trash. "I love chocolate. And the food is here for you—you're supposed to enjoy it."

"Thanks. I can't believe that the parents bring in food all week. This really is the nicest school. The one I was at before didn't do anything for Teacher Appreciation. Not even a card."

"Really? I thought this was your first teaching assignment."

For a second, a stricken look crossed her face and I had the funniest feeling that internally she was muttering a curse word. Moments later, her face transformed as she smiled brightly at me. "Oh, it is." She picked up a few almonds and added them to her plate. "I mean, it is my first teaching *job*. I was a substitute before."

I took more napkins out of a cabinet and placed them on the table. "Where was that?"

"Oh, it was in another state. Look, someone made a fruit tart—I just adore those." She moved a wedge of the tart onto her plate. "So you're"—she checked my name tag—"Livvy's mom. She's great."

"Thanks," I said, noticing how fast she'd changed the subject. She really didn't want to talk about her other job.

"I enjoy having her in my math class."

"How is everything going . . . after Klea, I mean? Do you think the kids are okay?"

"Oh, yes. Now that we're back in a routine, the

kids are fine. Well, you know what I mean. It's hard to have a routine the last weeks of school, but I think they feel safe and that's the important thing."

"Yes, it is. That's what we all want, to feel safe, but I can't help worrying. Did you know Klea?"

"No." She shook her head and leaned back against the counter as she cut a bite of the tart. I could have sworn she looked completely at ease. She didn't mind discussing Klea at all. "So horrible what happened to her. I mean, I never even talked to her, but to think about that happening . . ." She shivered.

Gabrielle poked her head in the door. "Ellie, there you are," she said in an accusatory tone, as if I'd been hiding from her. Peg followed her into the room and picked up a plate.

Ms. McCormick stiffened, and her face changed back to a guarded look. She gave me a quick nod. "Nice chatting with you," she said, and left the room. I glanced between Gabrielle and Peg. It seemed that just the arrival of one of the women had caused Ms. McCormick to leave the room immediately. Which one was it?

"I had to check and make sure everything was set up here," I said to Gabrielle. Peg didn't say anything, just filled her plate and left the room without looking at either one of us.

Gabrielle watched her go. "Well, she must have gotten up on the wrong side of the bed."

"I'm glad I don't work in the office." I glanced at the clock on the wall. "Speaking of work, I have to go."

Gabrielle held up a hand. "Oh, no. You can't just run out of here. We need to talk. What have you found out? I'll walk with you."

"Gabrielle—" I sighed. "I don't have anything to tell. It seemed like Klea's husband might be . . . involved, but apparently not. That's all I know." I wasn't about to tell her about Mrs. Harris's pen name, and the only other bit of information that I'd picked up—the list of names—was so vague that I didn't want to mention it. Gabrielle was the sort to charge ahead without thinking, and I didn't want her to do anything that would endanger herself—or make Detective Waraday angry with me. "All we can do is try and find someone with a connection to Klea— someone who was either angry enough or scared enough of her to want her dead."

Gabrielle had been walking with me as we spoke in low voices. We paused in the lobby, and she sent me a frustrated look. "There's got to be more we can do."

I decided the only way to deal with Gabrielle was to handle her the same way I did when the kids were determined to help me do something—usually with something that I didn't want their assistance with, like painting a room. "Okay, here's something. See if you can find out if anyone at the school was close to Klea. As far as I can tell, she didn't have any friends."

"Not have any friends? How could that be?"

"She kept her distance."

"That's . . . weird," Gabrielle said. Clearly keeping people at a distance was a foreign concept for her. "Okay, I'll ask around."

The faint sound of a horn honking repeatedly filtered through the closed doors at the front of the school as someone's car alarm went off.

"Well, weird or not, that's how she was," I said.

"See if you can find anyone she talked to or confided in."

Gabrielle nodded. "I can do that."

"Subtly," I said.

"Pshaw," Gabrielle said with a wave of her hand, and moved down the hall.

I'd never actually heard anyone use the southern expression *pshaw*, except in old movies, and I wasn't exactly sure what it meant, but I had a feeling from Gabrielle's attitude that it translated loosely to something along the lines of *don't be an idiot*.

I shook my head and went into the office to sign out. Peg was there, her plate of food on her desk. She didn't look up from her monitor. Marie, on the other hand, smiled at me as I signed out. I motioned to her with a tilt of my head, and she hopped up from her chair and walked with me across the lobby. "Do you know anything about Ms. McCormick?" I asked as I pushed open the heavy door. Humid air swept inside and the volume of the car alarm, which was still going on, increased.

"No, just that she's from somewhere out of state."

"Is this her first teaching job?" I asked, to see what Marie would say.

"Yes, I think so. I can do a . . . little digging, see what her application says. Discreetly, of course."

I smiled at her, knowing that she would keep anything she found to herself. "That would be great. I don't know anything, but I have a feeling it might be important."

"Gotcha. Check in with me tomorrow."

"Okay. Thanks."

Marie tilted her head and looked over my shoulder out the door I held half open. "Isn't that your minivan?"

I turned. The taillights of the van were flickering on and off in time with the honking horn. "Yes. How embarrassing." I felt my pockets for the key. "I probably pressed the panic button on the key fob somehow."

I found my keys, clicked the button, and silence fell for a moment until the school bell rang. I waved to Marie and headed across the school property to walk along the chain-link fence by the side yard, but when I rounded the side of the van, I stopped in my tracks. A spider web of cracks covered the driver's-side window around a gaping, concave hole.

Chapter Eleven

I don't know how long I stood there, stunned by the vandalism. This was a nice, safe neighborhood. Things like windows getting broken—especially in the middle of the day—didn't happen. I shook myself out of my frozen state and took a few steps closer to the door. I peered inside the van though the hole radiating out from the hole.

I didn't touch anything because a network of jagged cracks radiated out from the hole, but I saw that a brick rested on the driver's seat. Tiny chunks of glass pooled around it, glittering in the sunlight like diamonds. I twisted around and scanned the street and surrounding houses, but the front yards were empty of neighbors—not a single person moving a sprinkler or weeding a flowerbed. Faint shouts from the kids at recess were the only sounds.

With a sigh, I took out my phone. I'd already rescheduled once with Margo when Gabrielle convinced me to search the school with her on the morning of Muffins with Mom. Now I called Margo to tell her I needed to postpone our appointment again.

"Random vandalism?" Mitch asked later that night, disbelief heavy in his voice.

"I know," I said. "I don't really believe it either." I sat down on the bed and held the phone in place with my shoulder while I tied the laces of my tennis shoes. Dinner was over, the dishes were washed, and the kids were in their rooms doing the last bits of homework. There wasn't much homework at this time of year, but the teachers were still sending a few assignments home for the kids to do in the evening.

Rex was prancing back and forth letting out low-level whines, sensing that a walk around the neighborhood was imminent. In Rex's mind, footwear signaled a trip around the block, which was what I had planned, but the walk could wait while I talked to Mitch. I had no idea when he'd be able to call again.

"Ellie," Mitch said with a sigh in his voice, "what *have* you been doing?"

I flopped back on the bed and stared at the ceiling fan. "Just all the usual stuff—running the household, taking care of the kids, *trying* to meet with clients."

"All the usual stuff," Mitch repeated, "which, I know, means that you're also keeping your eyes and ears open for anything that might be a tad off or strange. And possibly dropping a few questions here and there. Am I right?"

"Since we're not on a video call, I should tell you that I'm rolling my eyes."

"I know you are." Mitch's chuckle came over the phone. "Do I know you or what?"

"Yes, and that is both a blessing and a curse," I said.

"I wish I was there with you," Mitch said, his tone becoming more serious.

"I know. That would be really nice. How many more days?" Mitch was much better at keeping track of how many days he had left on his trips than I was. His constantly changing schedule was hard to keep up with, to begin with, and if he was gone on a long deployment, it was easier for me if I didn't focus on the exact number of days until he came home. Anything over a week was a little depressing to contemplate. It was usually easier to roll with the punches until the trip was over.

"Ten days until I'm back, and we can have your delayed Mother's Day celebration." Mother's Day had actually been last Sunday, but because of Mitch's rather unpredictable schedule, we celebrated events and special days when we were together and that wasn't always when those days showed up on the calendar. Since Mitch's training exercise happened to fall over Mother's Day, we postponed celebrating that day until he got back. We did the same with birthdays and holidays.

"I'm looking forward to it," I said.

Letting out another round of low whimpers, Rex pressed against my leg. I rubbed his side with my foot.

"So back to the car," Mitch said. "Did you call the police?"

"Yes, and the insurance. It's all covered. I have a copy of the police report, but the officer spent about as long on it as Livvy did on the first draft of her science report."

"So about ten minutes."

"Yep. Even after I told him about Klea's death. He said he'd mention it to Detective Waraday, but I could tell the officer didn't think it was related. Like I said, random vandalism was his assessment."

"I don't agree. Have you heard or seen anything that could make someone nervous?"

"Possibly," I said, thinking of Mrs. Harris. But she'd told Detective Waraday her secret—hadn't she?

I should ask Detective Waraday and make sure she had followed through with him. But even if she hadn't talked to Detective Waraday, I couldn't see her throwing a brick through the van window any more than I could see her strangling Klea. Without giving away her secret or mentioning her pen name, I gave Mitch an outline of what Mrs. Harris had told me.

"And you don't want to share names or specifics?" Mitch asked.

"No, I can't. I promised, but I will check with Detective Waraday and make sure he knows. If he does know about the situation, what would be the good of tossing a brick at my car? The secret is already out—to a limited audience, granted—but it's not totally hidden anymore."

"Maybe this person changed their mind and regretted telling you the secret. Maybe it was a warning to continue to keep quiet. You know, no talking to the other teachers."

"Kind of an unspecific way to do it." Rex walked around to the foot of the bed and poked his nose over the edge, fixing me with the saddest brown-eyed expression that I'd seen since yesterday at this time.

"Oh, I think they got their message across." Mitch paused a moment, then said, "Or maybe it was a completely different person. Any other tidbits you've heard or prodding questions you've asked?"

"Ms. McCormick is hiding something, I'm sure of it. But I don't know specifically what it is." I recounted my conversation with her as Rex kept his gaze fastened on me and whined a few times just to make sure I didn't forget about him.

"Breaking car windows after a conversation like that would be going to quite an extreme," Mitch said, "but it looks as if you've made someone nervous."

"Or I've been the random victim of senseless vandalism."

"Odd that I actually like the sound of that better. Look, there's a chance this exercise may get cut short. Weather issues. I could be home in a day or two."

"That would be great," I said. "And you don't have to say it. I'll be careful."

We said good-bye, and I hung up. "Come on, Rex, let's go."

With a joyful spasm that shook his whole body, he pranced to the back door.

When we returned a few minutes later, I punched in the code to open the garage and then walked by the van. The new window had been ordered and should arrive tomorrow. But, for now, a clear piece of plastic covered the window, a temporary fix that the repair shop had put in place in case it rained, which was always a possibility in Georgia. After the police had finished, I'd gone back to the school and found Vaughn, who'd brought a cardboard box for me, along with a dustpan. We'd cleaned up the glass from inside the van, then scoured the grass, looking for any tiny pieces that we might have missed, but it seemed all the glass was inside the van, not outside it.

I went inside the house, hung up Rex's leash, and then quizzed Livvy on the words for her last spelling test of the school year. An hour later, the kids were tucked in bed and I had an old movie playing on television, the barely audible dialogue filling the quiet house. I was seated at the dining room table going over my "homework" with Rex curled up under the table at my feet. I rubbed my foot along his back as I flipped from one page to the next in Nathan's homework folder, dutifully scribbling my initials on each page near the letter or number grade.

Tuesdays were homework folder days, which meant the kids brought home their work for the week, and I went over it. I thought it was absurd that the teachers required that the parents initial each paper. I didn't need a threat to keep up with my kids' homework, but it seemed that some parents did because some teachers dropped students' grades if they didn't return the homework papers with their parents' initials.

I had already gone through both Livvy's and Nathan's folders earlier in the evening while they were with me, going over the questions that they'd missed and praising them for their good grades. I signed Nathan's last homework paper, slid them all back into the pocket, and flipped to the front of the folder, where I recorded the date and signed my John Hancock on one of the last lines of the form. I was glad it was the end of the year and the avalanche of paperwork was tapering off.

I slapped the folder closed, then pulled Livvy's folder to me and worked my way through this week's stack, signing off on all papers. Finished, I stacked the papers and slid them back into the pocket, but something blocked them. The sheaf of papers wouldn't go in all the way. I removed them and pulled out a folded note that I must have missed earlier.

It was a piece of white copy paper, folded in thirds and held together with a piece of tape. Folded and taped notes placed in take-home folders were not a good thing. Usually, they were a message from the office about some sort of problem. Livvy and Nathan were both good students. They kept up with their work, mostly, and behaved in class, so we didn't usually receive notes from the office.

I smoothed the wrinkles out, worked the tape free, and unfolded the note, expecting it to contain a list of Livvy's overdue library books or something along those lines, but it was only a few lines of text, carefully hand printed. It read, *Back off. Klea was nosy and look what happened to her.*

Organizing Tips for PTA Moms

Staying in touch with other parents is critical and it's easier than ever with digital tools. Yahoo Groups allows you to create a group and invite members, then share information through emails and a group calendar. Companies like SignUpGenius and Volunteer Spot provide free online volunteer sign-up forms and reminders, which are sent through emails and texts. The advantage to this type of system is that the contact list is maintained for you through the site. You can easily send an invite to members of the list and not have to weed through long "reply all" emails.

Chapter Twelve

D etective Waraday placed the note inside a plastic sleeve. "How much did you handle it?"

"Quite a bit, I'm afraid. It got pushed to the bottom of the folder, and I ran my hand across it to flatten out the wrinkles."

Detective Waraday made a "hmm" sound and read over the note again.

Rex, now fully awake, was sitting by my knee at the table, keeping a sharp eye on Detective Waraday.

"And you found it when?" Detective Waraday asked.

"Just now. I dropped it and called you."

Well, I'd actually dropped it on the table and contemplated doing several things, from ignoring it to burning it, but in the end, I'd known I had to call Detective Waraday. I was glad the kids were asleep— and they had to be or they would have popped into the living room at the sound of a deep male voice, expecting to see Mitch, whose job had him arriving and departing at all hours. I was relieved I didn't have to explain why a detective was at our house.

Detective Waraday pointed to the folders with their lines of signatures on the outside. "Tell me about these homework folders. Who has access to them?"

"Livvy is in fifth grade and those students change classes for different subjects, but they have a home-room classroom. That's where each teacher sends all the papers for the week. Either the teacher, the teacher's aide, or a parent volunteer sorts the papers into the files for each student. Once a week, the papers are transferred from the files to a folder and the kids bring them home. I sign off on everything, and it all goes back the next day. I did it last year for Nathan's class." It was a fairly mindless volunteer job, but I actually preferred other ways of helping out, like helping with the book fair or Field Day, which were more active and not so monotonous.

Detective Waraday tapped the plastic sleeve with the note on the table. Rex's ears pricked at the sound. "And the classrooms aren't locked during the day when students are out of them for recess or lunch." He looked up from the paper. "I found that out last week when I was at the school."

"No, they're not."

"So anyone—teacher, staff, or student—could have written this note and slipped it in your daughter's folder, knowing that it would go home to you today. I'll send it to the techs, but there probably won't be any distinguishable prints on it since it has been handled so much. But we'll check." He rubbed his hand across his forehead as he said, "Someone is not happy with you, Mrs. Avery."

A statement like that would have normally "gotten my back up," a description I'd heard members of Mitch's very Southern family use, but Detective Waraday said it in a flat tone, not as if he was laying blame. The bags under his eyes made him look almost mature, and the way he'd wearily dropped into the chair at the table indicated that he was tired. I wondered how many hours he'd worked today.

"I really don't know who it could be," I said. "Ms. McCormick did act kind of strange today when I asked her where she taught before she came to North Dawkins. But other than Ms. McCormick and one other person . . . I'm not sure . . . were you contacted . . . ?"

"A certain person from the school got in touch with me and told me about her . . . um"—a smile flickered at the corners of his mouth—"literary activities, let's call them. I don't think this note has anything to do with that."

"That's good. I was wondering because, if she had changed her mind and hadn't talked to you, then this could have been from her, but since you know about the situation . . ."

"Yes, the cat is out of the bag, at least where the investigation is concerned. She came forward voluntarily, so I doubt she'd double back and attack you. She doesn't seem the sort to regret her actions."

"No, I agree."

"This Ms. McCormick you mentioned who acted odd—what happened?"

I told him how she'd hadn't wanted to talk about her other job and how the general impression at the school was that this was her first job. "But when I asked her about it today, she said it *was* her first teaching job—that she'd only been a substitute before. I got the impression that she wasn't telling the truth . . . or not the whole truth."

Detective Waraday raised his eyebrows, looking energized for the first time that night. "A possible lie, then. Lies are always interesting. And her name was on that list you spotted in Mrs. Burris's house." He didn't say anything else, but he wrote something in the notebook that he removed from his pocket. "Anyone else upset with you?"

Noting that he seemed to have changed his opinion about the list from Klea's house, I said, "No, not unless you count my client I keep canceling on or Peg in the school office, but she seems to be upset with everyone all the time."

"An Eeyore," he said with a nod.

"I'm sorry?"

"I met her the other day when I interviewed all the teachers and staff. She's an Eeyore. We have had one at our office. Generally gloomy disposition and always looking on the dark side."

"Yes, I think that's a good description of her."

"Melancholy," Detective Waraday said. "So I don't know that we should mark her down as an enemy of yours just yet."

"She was on Klea's list."

"As was Marie Ormsby."

"That's true," I said, "But I don't think Marie is upset with me."

Detective Waraday didn't reply, just made another note, and I had a feeling that he would be chatting with both Peg and Marie tomorrow.

"I did ask Marie what she knew about Ms. McCormick," I said, hoping that getting that fact out there now might preempt any recriminations from Detective Waraday later. "Marie said that Ms. McCormick was from out of state."

Detective Waraday nodded as he studied the note in the plastic sleeve. He tilted it toward me. "Do you recognize the handwriting?"

I'd had plenty of time after I made the call and waited for him to arrive to study the note. "No. It's so perfect, it's almost like it was printed on a computer." Each stroke of every letter in the hand-printed note was made with precision. None of the letters were higher, lower, wider, or fatter than the others. None of the letters had a stroke that trailed off below or soared above the others. "It does remind me a little of the printing I've seen on architects' drawings, but those have some style . . . or flare to them with some of the strokes extended or angled. This writing is even more precise than that."

"Presumably done to disguise the handwriting."

"Why wouldn't someone just have used a computer? Why go to the trouble of handwriting it?" I asked. It was one of the many questions that had been going through my mind while I waited for Detective Waraday.

"Maybe they didn't have time. If someone wanted to get a note into the folders, they'd have to slip in the classroom when it was empty. Maybe the person saw their opportunity and took it—a spur-of-the-moment kind of thing. And then there is also the fact that most documents created on a computer are traceable even if they are deleted. Perhaps the person knew that and didn't want any record of these words on their computer, which would be pretty far thinking. But it would also be very wise. With all the school computers linked to the school district's database, it would probably be more difficult to make sure no record of the words existed."

He inched his chair back from the table. "After we check for prints, I'll send it off to the state crime lab, see what they can come up with related to the handwriting. And then there is your car. I got the message about it this evening. Mind if I have a look?"

"No, not at all." I stood, and he followed me to the garage. I flicked on the light, and he moved around to the driver's side, where he examined the doorframe. I waited in the doorway. Rex positioned himself by my leg.

"It was a brick, you said?"

"Yes. It was inside the car."

"Where is it now?"

"Probably in a Dumpster at the school." I told him how Vaughn had helped me clean up.

Detective Waraday nodded. "Perfectly reasonable for the officer who arrived in response to your call to assume it was random, but in light of this"—he held up the note—"well, maybe not so random. The brick probably wouldn't hold fingerprints very well, but I'll send someone out to look for it tomorrow and canvass the street to see if anyone saw anything."

"Thank you. That would make me feel a little better."

He came inside and headed for the front door. I

locked the door to the garage, then followed him to the front door, Rex at my heels. "The brick through your car window could have been random, but this"— he raised the paper and the plastic sleeve caught the reflection of the porch light—"is a threat, directed specifically at you. I suggest you lock up and keep your head down. The farther you stay away from the investigation, the better off you'll be."

"I know. Don't worry. I'm not asking any more questions. It's too dangerous."

And that was my intention. I'd had plenty of time to think things over while I stared at the note, jumping at each little creak the house made. It was just too dangerous to keep asking questions. I had two kids to think of. For their sake, I had to back off. I knew Gabrielle wouldn't agree, but she'd have to deal with it.

Despite knowing that Detective Waraday had the note and that the brick-throwing incident was being investigated more thoroughly, I didn't sleep too well. The next morning, I was afraid that the bags under my eyes rivaled Detective Waraday's.

With the temporary plastic covering on the driver's window pulsating as I drove, I dropped the kids at school, then went to the glass repair shop. It was next door to a shopping center, which contained a gym and a newly opened boutique that sold decorative knickknacks and personal items. While my window was being fixed, I walked over to the boutique to look for Teacher Appreciation gifts for the kids to give to their teachers. I'd been so busy with everything going on at the school that buying gifts for the teachers had fallen completely off my to-do list. I found several cute notebooks embellished with different school themes—math and science problems and the titles of classic children's stories—and purchased one for each of the teachers, along with some cool pens.

As I walked back to the window repair shop, the repairman, a guy in his mid-twenties, stepped into the parking lot. He waved and crossed the lot to me. "All fixed. We're running it through the car wash and will have it out here in a minute. You can pay at the desk inside," he said, handing me an invoice.

"So have you had a lot of these types of repairs lately?" I asked as we walked to the office portion of the shop.

"Vandalism, you mean? Nah, you're the first we've had in, oh, probably two or three months. We see mostly chips and cracks from rocks hitting cars while they are on the road." He opened the door for me.

"Thanks," I said, and went in to pay my bill. Since this was the only repair shop in this area, they'd know if there had been an uptick in vandalism of car windows. It looked more and more likely that the brick through the window had been a random incident.

I powered the new window up and down a few times to make sure it worked, then set out to mark off the rest of the items on my to-do list, putting thoughts of Klea, bricks through windows, and threatening notes out of my mind. I ran by an ice cream shop, bought some gift cards, and tucked them into each notebook. I'd have the kids wrap them tonight—well, gift-bag them—and we'd be set.

Then I ran home, switched the load of laundry that I'd started that morning to the dryer, and tossed in a new load to wash. I hit the road again to pick up today's food for Teacher Appreciation. It was Wednesday, so that meant sub sandwiches were on the menu.

I swung by the sub shop to pick up a platter of sandwiches, glad that Mia had coordinated all the details, even the payment, beforehand. All I had to do was take the sandwiches and chips to the school.

A few minutes later, I parked in the school parking lot, as close to the main doors as I could get. I wouldn't be parking along the chain-link fence anymore. My phone rang. I saw it was Gabrielle and braced myself. "Gabrielle, I'm so glad you called," I said. "Quite a bit has happened—"

"For me, too, honey. That's why I called. You won't believe what I found out. Talk about juicy gossip—"

"I'm not really interested in gossip," I said quickly.

"But it's not any old gossip. This has to do with the school. There are some mighty shady things going on at that school."

"Gabrielle, before you say anything else, you should know that I'm done with poking around, trying to find out what happened to Klea."

Gabrielle's rich chuckle sounded through the line. "I don't believe that for a minute."

"Well, it's true. A brick was thrown through my van window, and I got a threatening note. I can't continue to ask questions and snoop around. It's too dangerous."

"What did the note say? Did it demand money?"

I'd gotten out of the van, slid the side door open, and reached to pick up the sandwiches, but I paused. "Money? No, of course not. The note said I should back off and that Klea was nosy and 'look what happened to her,' to be exact. It was a threat."

The line was silent a few beats. "Oh. Well. That is a bit disconcerting," Gabrielle said quietly. Then her voice changed to a more upbeat tone. "But I know you. You won't let that sidetrack you."

"No, I'm afraid it has. I'm done."

"Of course you're not. You only think you are. Now, I have a meeting starting in two minutes, so I can't talk any longer, but I want to get together with you and discuss this info I have."

"Gabrielle—" I sighed as the buzz of the disconnected line sounded in my ear. I picked up the sandwiches, dropped my phone into the van's console, and locked the van. I'd only be in the school for a few minutes and didn't need to bring in my purse and phone.

I was backing though the main door, using my shoulder to open it as I balanced the tray of sandwiches, when a voice near my ear said, "There you are." I nearly dropped the tray.

Marie, today in a pink shirt and white short-sleeved sweater, reached out to steady the tray of sandwiches. "I've been watching for you all morning. You said you'd check with me first thing this morning about . . ." She stopped speaking abruptly as a line of students walked through the lobby. Ms. McCormick, the skirt of her blue shirtwaist dress swishing, was in the lead. As she passed us, she glared at me, and instinctively I fell back a step. She looked nothing like Livvy's description of a fairy tale princess. Instead, with her angry face, she looked more like an evil villainess.

As Ms. McCormick disappeared into the cafeteria,

Marie let out a whoosh of breath. "I'm glad I wasn't standing any closer to you. We'd both be in cinders if looks could kill."

"Why is she mad at me? What's happened?" I asked.

"Detective Waraday was in first thing this morning, asking all sorts of questions about Klea," Marie said. "He started with me and Peg in the office. Why didn't you tell me about the note you received?"

"Detective Waraday told you about the note?"

"Showed us a copy, even."

"Oh." I hadn't expected Detective Waraday to show the note to anyone at school, but of course that was silly. How could he question people unless he mentioned the note? And if he showed them a copy he could watch their reactions.

"Of course we were floored," Marie continued. "But then he wanted to speak to Ms. McCormick, which I thought was odd. Why her, of all the teachers? But now that I've done that little bit of research for you, I think I understand."

It didn't seem odd to me. Mrs. Kirk, Marie, Peg, and Ms. McCormick were the four people left on Klea's list, but of course Marie didn't know about the list. Although why Detective Waraday would include Marie in his questioning, I didn't understand. Marie had been out of town the morning Klea died, but I guessed he was just being thorough.

"Oh, it's sub sandwiches today," exclaimed a teacher coming out of the cafeteria, and I said to Marie, "I'd better get this set up."

She nodded. "Meet you back here in a jiffy."

I put the tray in the teachers' lounge and set up

bags of chips alongside it, with napkins and paper plates, then headed back to the lobby. Marie emerged from the office with some papers, which she handed to me. "Look at this."

The page on top was a job application form.

"Ms. McCormick's job application? How did you get this?" I asked.

Marie smiled. "I have my ways."

She was the longest employed person at the school. She'd been here even longer than Mrs. Kirk, so I supposed she knew how to get a hold of files. "Remind me never to cross you," I said with a grin.

"Wouldn't be wise. Now, look at that." She pointed to the job history.

"It's blank . . . but she said she worked before. Even if it was only substitute teaching, shouldn't she have put it down as prior experience?"

"Yes, she should have," Marie said as I quickly scanned the rest of the form. Ms. McCormick had a degree in elementary education from a university in North Carolina and had listed her address as an apartment in Charlotte.

I thought of Detective Waraday's comment about Ms. McCormick and a potential lie.

"There's more," Marie said.

I flipped to the next page and realized it was a wage and earnings statement. I pushed the papers back into Marie's hands. "No. That's too personal."

Marie frowned at me. "This has nothing to do with the amount of money she makes. Look here, at her name. See how it's spelled?" Marie pointed to the wage form.

"Jill McCormick," I said, not seeing her point.

Marie flipped back to the other page. "And here, on the job application? I don't think you looked at it very carefully."

She pushed both papers back at me, pointing to the names. I *had* read them too quickly. The name on the job application had an extra letter. She'd listed her name as "Jill MacCormick."

"So the job application has MacCormick, but her wage and earning statement has McCormick? Which one is right?"

"Her name is Jill McCormick. I checked the database. We have to verify everyone's name with a government-issued ID, so I'm pretty sure that's her real name," Marie said.

"So the name on the application must be a typo," I said. "It looked like it was filled in on one of those online application systems. It would be easy to make a mistake. She probably caught it when she was hired."

"I don't think so. I know the process. The job application is the basis for the background check. Jill *Mac*Cormick would have been the name that was checked, not her real name. Once an individual clears the district's background check, and they're hired, then they fill out all the tax paperwork. I was curious what a background check on the name 'Jill McCormick' would bring up in North Carolina, so I did a little searching online on my own this morning."

She handed me the last sheet of paper. It was a printout of a newspaper article. I recognized Ms. McCormick's face under the headline, which I whispered, "'Teacher arrested in drug bust'? *Ms. McCormick* was involved in a drug arrest?"

Marie nodded, her lips pressed together.

"Oh, this is not good," I said, looking at the ceiling. While parents might not like a teacher writing erotica, a teacher with a drug arrest in her past was a completely different level of complication. Just for starters, the school district held Red Ribbon Week, which taught students the dangers of drugs and warned them away from them, every year. Everyone—the parents, Mrs. Kirk, the other teachers— would be upset at the news about Ms. McCormick.

Marie said, "You can see why she changed her name. Just one little letter, and she becomes a whole new person. The background check doesn't show anything—no drug bust—nothing." Marie pointed to the name of the newspaper. "That's actually in South Carolina, so I assume she put North Carolina as her permanent address, hoping to confuse the issue even more. I found a record of a Jill McCormick employed at an elementary school in Lexington, South Carolina."

"Which didn't show up on the background search because the name that was checked was spelled with an extra 'a.' "

"Right. And then once she had the job here, she gave us the correct name and Social Security number, probably hoping that the district wouldn't check into it again. And, of course, they didn't. We can't afford to do yearly background checks." Marie fiddled with a rubber band that was around her wrist. "Do you think Ms. McCormick had anything to do with Klea?"

"I honestly don't know, but this is quite a secret."

Marie nodded. "Something worth killing for." She lowered her voice. "She'll lose her job, for sure, once this comes out. And then what will she do? She won't be able to find work again."

"Well, she found this job, didn't she?" I said grimly.

Marie's forehead wrinkled. "Do you think she could do it again? I don't know. I think she was lucky. Someone should have cross-checked her ID with the name on the background check and her application. If Klea found out somehow . . ."

"How could she have known?" I asked.

Marie shrugged. "I don't know. Klea was always going through the trash. She was supposed to just dump it, but I saw her, digging around in the papers. She liked to know things. If she *did* find out about Ms. McCormick . . ."

"Have you shown this to Detective Waraday?" I asked.

"No, I didn't dig into it until after he asked to see Ms. McCormick this morning when he finished talking to Peg and me."

"So did he talk to Ms. McCormick?"

"No, she was in the office and told him that she had classes to teach, but she could talk to him during lunch. We're shorthanded today. Mrs. Kirk has already had to call for another substitute for a second-grade teacher who got sick. Mrs. Kirk is actually covering the class until the sub arrives."

"But this must be Ms. McCormick's lunch," I said. "Remember, she just went into the cafeteria."

"That's her students' lunch. She stays with them until they go out to recess, then she gets a thirty-minute lunch while they are outside." Marie glanced at the hall clock. "I'm sure she'll be along shortly."

A sheriff's car pulled up into the drop-off circle

and parked in front of the main doors. "There's Detective Waraday," I said. "You better make sure he sees those papers before he talks to her."

"Me? But you asked me for it. Remember, you wanted me to do a little digging?" She pushed the papers toward me.

"No." I held up a hand. "I can't. You heard about the note. I'm out. No more questions. It's too dangerous. I told Detective Waraday last night that I'm done. I can't go running up to him with all this now. You found it. You should be the one to tell him about it."

A car door slammed, and Marie went a shade paler. "I'm not supposed to be in these files. I could lose my job."

I looked at her, trying to imitate Rex's pleading look. "You're retiring in—what?—two weeks. What can they do to you?"

"My pension may be tiny, but I want it." She flapped the papers. "Say you found them on the counter with your name on them. A little bird left them for you. Please, Ellie." She looked at me beseechingly. "I need that pension."

"Oh, all right."

She pressed the papers into my hands and twirled away, her pink skirt flaring out as she skittered back to the office.

I turned toward Detective Waraday. As he came in the doors, I held out the papers. "You know what I said about not being involved anymore? Well, turns out it's not so easy to bow out. People know I'm involved. I was given this today."

Detective Waraday frowned as he took it. "Did this person have a name?"

"Yes, but they would prefer you didn't know it came from them."

Detective Waraday scanned the documents. "Well, we'll see if that is possible. Depends on what . . ."

He must have picked up on the discrepancy in the last names because he looked back and forth from the first two pages for a few moments, then went on to the last page, the newspaper article. He looked up at me. "What did I tell you? Lies are always interesting." He went into the office, and a short time later, Peg came out of the office and went into the cafeteria. I went into the teachers' lounge, checked the sub platter, put out more napkins, and cleaned up a plate with crumbs someone had forgotten. When I left, I automatically headed for the office, but realized I'd forgotten to sign in in the first place.

I'd barely cleared the threshold of the office when Peg burst in, bumping into my shoulder and causing me to stumble. "Ms. McCormick is gone."

Chapter Thirteen

I caught the counter and steadied myself.

"What do you mean, she's gone?" Detective Waraday asked.

Peg drew in a breath. She'd obviously been hurrying through the hallways. "She's not in the cafeteria or the teachers' lounge or her classroom."

Mrs. Kirk came out of her office. "What is the problem?"

"It's Ms. McCormick," Peg said. "She's gone."

"Gone?" Mrs. Kirk said. "She didn't schedule the afternoon off." She scowled. "And I just got a substitute in for second grade."

"She's probably in the restroom," Marie said.

"No. I think she left the campus," Peg said. "Her purse is gone. I checked when I was in her room."

"Why did you do that?" Detective Waraday asked.

Peg, whose face had been bright with excitement, suddenly looked uncomfortable. "I'm not sure . . . except when I walked in there . . . it felt like she was gone. The lights were off in her room. No one turns their lights off except when they leave for the day. I know she keeps her purse in her desk—most of the teachers do, and I've seen her put hers away. So I checked. Bottom left drawer. It's gone."

Marie turned toward the windows. "Her car is a little blue one."

We all moved to the windows and spotted a blue Ford Fiesta as it careened along the aisle, then turned at the exit. Its brake lights flared for an instant, contrasting with the royal-blue bumper sticker that read, KEEP CALM AND MATH ON; then the car surged out of the parking lot and went down the residential street, breaking all the school-zone speed limits.

Detective Waraday ran out of the office, and in a few seconds, we heard the wail of his siren as he pulled away from the front doors of the school. His car disappeared down the street. With the sound of the siren fading, we all looked at each other for a few seconds. Then Mrs. Kirk said, "What could have happened?"

I caught Marie's eye, then let my gaze fall on the papers that I had given to Detective Waraday. He must have set them down on the counter while he was waiting for Ms. McCormick and forgotten them when he left to pursue her out of the parking lot.

"I think it had something to do with these papers." I pushed them across the counter to Mrs. Kirk. She marched across the room and swiped them off the counter so quickly that the papers snapped. Mrs. Kirk read over the pages, her frown of irritation transforming into an expression of alarm. Marie hovered behind her shoulder, her hands linked together at her waist in such a tight grip that her knuckles showed white. Peg moved back around the counter to her desk, but her pace slowed to almost non-movement as she strained to get a glimpse of the papers.

Mrs. Kirk reached the last page, scanned it quickly, then briefly closed her eyes. She opened her eyes, noticed Peg and Marie hovering, and folded the papers in half. Peg and Marie retreated to their desks as Mrs. Kirk said, "Let me know the moment Detective Waraday returns."

"Do you think he'll be back?" Peg asked.

"I'm sure of it," Mrs. Kirk said, and braced her shoulders. She turned back toward her office. "For now, we must do something about Ms. McCormick's classroom." She looked at the clock. "Recess will be over in five minutes. I believe she has her planning period after this period. I can ask Mrs. Cross to cover for her after that, but we are already stretched quite thin today." She sighed and then a speculative look came into her eye as she turned her attention to me. "Mrs. Avery. May I impose on you for an hour of your time?"

"What?"

"I believe your daughter, Livvy, is in Ms. McCormick's class, correct?"

"Yes."

"And you've volunteered in that classroom before, haven't you?" Mrs. Kirk's voice was becoming more upbeat as she spoke.

I had a feeling I knew what was coming. "A little, yes. But it was before Christmas break—"

"Excellent. You have already done so much for the school that I hate to ask for anything else, but we're in a sort of emergency situation right now.

Could you monitor Ms. McCormick's classroom for the next hour until Mrs. Cross can take over? I'd do it myself, but"—she glanced at the papers—"I have some calls that absolutely must be made, and then I'm sure Detective Waraday will return and need to speak to me as well."

"Mrs. Kirk," Peg said, pointing out the windows, where the sheriff's car was pulling slowly to the curb. "There he is now."

"I can give you an hour," I said, partially because I wanted to see what happened, but also because Mrs. Kirk looked more frazzled than I'd ever seen her. She was always upbeat and encouraging, and exuded an air of calm competence. Seeing that the school had hired someone with a drug arrest in her past, Mrs. Kirk had been shaken. I was sure she was wondering what the fallout would be.

Detective Waraday came into the office. "She had too much of a head start for me to catch her, but the county and the city police will be on the lookout for her." He spotted the papers in Mrs. Kirk's hands. "I'll need to take those with me."

"Yes, I assumed so," Mrs. Kirk said, her shoulders braced again. "And I believe you have a few questions for me as well?"

"Yes."

Mrs. Kirk nodded and handed off the papers. "Fine. If you'll wait in my office, I'll be right with you. I must get Ms. McCormick's class settled."

The bell rang, indicating the end of the period, and I knew the fifth-grade students would be trudging in from recess.

Detective Waraday frowned and looked as if he was about to protest, but Mrs. Kirk said, "I assure you, Detective, I will not go AWOL. It is important that I speak with Ms. McCormick's class. I don't want to have any rumors circulating. Well, any more than are already going around."

She motioned for me to come with her, and I followed her across the lobby to the fifth-grade hallway. I let her enter Ms. McCormick's room first. Students were milling around and talking. The volume level dropped immediately when they caught sight of Mrs. Kirk. Students quickly slid into their seats.

"Something unexpected came up, and Ms. Mc-Cormick is not here this period. Mrs. Avery has kindly agreed to fill in for her and monitor your class today." She looked toward the board. "I see your assignment for the day is listed. I suggest you get to work. Mrs. Avery, if you'll see me at the end of the hour?" She looked toward me, and I nodded. Then she ran her gaze over the class. "I'm sure you won't have any problems because fifth-grade students are really so grown up and responsible." She nodded her head and exited the room.

Every head in the class swiveled to look at me, except for Livvy, who had her attention focused on her stack of textbooks. She looked like she wanted the floor to open up and swallow her.

I glanced at the board. "Well, let's get on with this. Chapter ten, lesson seven," I said, reading the board while mentally estimating how far away Abby's classroom was in case a question came up that I couldn't answer or a riot broke out. Moving so slowly that they reminded me of the sloths we'd seen on a recent visit to the zoo, the students took out textbooks and flipped pages.

Remembering Livvy's mention of the computer game in Ms. McCormick's classroom, I said, "And if you get your lesson done and there is still time left, you can take turns playing the game on the computers." Monitors lined the back wall of the classroom, their screens dark. A murmur of what sounded like halfhearted approval ran through the room and several students, including Livvy, bent over their desks.

Ms. McCormick's desk was at the back of the room. I went and perched on her chair. I checked the clock. Only forty-seven minutes to go.

I swiveled in the chair and studied the desk, which was covered with papers, sticky notes, pens, and books. An aloe vera plant in a clay pot perched on one corner beside the computer. A couple of framed pictures were also propped up on the desk, including one of an older couple on a golf course, whom I supposed were Ms. McCormick's parents. Another showed Ms. McCormick with a man with longish brown hair who looked to be about her age. They stood on a beach, smiling happily and holding up sand dollars. Several sheets of stickers were scattered around the desk. Lots of them were happy faces of many varieties, along with stars, rainbows, and several sheets that proclaimed, *You're a Star!* and *Good Job!* The graded papers were liberally spotted with the stickers and plenty of hand-drawn happy faces and exclamation points.

I debated for a moment, knowing that poking around in the desk drawers was snooping, but then I thought of Klea's body in the woods. I inched open each drawer and found nothing more exciting than extra office supplies and a stash of gummy bears at the back of a lower drawer.

I closed the last drawer and sat back in the seat, wishing I'd brought my phone with me, but it was locked inside the van in the parking lot. I watched the kids for a bit. Most of them had settled down to their task and were working through the problems.

Livvy looked back over her shoulder at me. I smiled at her, then crossed my eyes. She grinned before she could help it and quickly turned back to her paper.

More out of habit than anything else, I tidied the desk, sorting papers into stacks and dropping paper clips and rubber bands into the pencil tray. Most of the papers were easy to sort—obvious homework papers or memos from the office, but there were a couple that I frowned over.

One was a schematic of some sort. A hand-drawn sketch, it was filled with lines that traveled from one geometric shape to another. *It must be some sort of flowchart,* I decided as I tried to make out the notes inside the shapes, but the words—whatever they were—were abbreviated and I couldn't decipher them. There were four similar sheets and the only words I could actually read were across the top of the pages: *Undersea Exploration, Mayan Temple, Egyptian Pyramid,* and *Jungle Trek.*

I fingered the sheets, paging back and forth. They all began with the same set of shapes running in a smooth line down the left-hand side of the page, but after a few shapes, the lines branched off in different directions without a pattern that I could see repeated anywhere among the four sheets of paper. Perhaps it was some sort of quiz or puzzle for her class?

A whisper of conversation floated my way. I got up and paced up and down the rows of desks, and the room fell silent again. Most of the students had made at least some progress on the problems and several were near the end. The minutes were ticking down in the class. I wandered around the classroom and even helped a few students get unstuck on their problems.

One student finished his last problem and hopped up. He dropped the paper into a basket on a table at the front of the room, then looked at me questioningly as he pointed to the computers.

I nodded, and he headed to the back of the room, where he logged in and was soon playing a game. Livvy was the third student to finish and headed for the back of the room. Soon, all the chairs around the computers were full, and I had instituted a ten-minute limit so that everyone could have a turn. Low groans and cheers sounded from around the computers as the kids moved through the bright images on the screen, cartoony versions of a deserted island or the jungle.

The bell rang and there was a scramble for backpacks and a surge for the door. Livvy gave me a little raised-eyebrow look with a lift of her head, which I took to mean *Bye, Mom*, and then the room was quiet.

Ms. McCormick had a schedule taped to her desktop and it showed that the next hour was her planning period, so there wasn't a flow of kids coming in for the next class. I walked around the room, picking up a stray pencil and a page of homework that hadn't been deposited in the basket. I shut down the computers, then walked back to Ms. McCormick's desk and paused, looking over it, taking in the framed photos and the plant and the super-cheerful stickers and notes. Could this really be the desk of a killer?

I shook my head and was about to leave the room when the flowchart pages caught my eye again. It must have been because I was standing a little distance away and looking at them upside down that I noticed it. I wasn't trying to read them individually, but looking at the page as a whole, I could see what I hadn't noticed before—that the printed abbreviations on the flowchart page were made with precise, even strokes. The perfectly spaced letters looked exactly like the printing on the threatening note I'd received.

Organizing Tips for PTA Moms

<u>End-of-Year Tips</u>

- Write a thank-you note to your children's teachers.
- Get contact information for your child's friends so you can stay in touch over the summer.
- Have a plan for sorting the reams of paper that will come home as the school year ends, deciding which papers or artwork to keep.
- Have an end-of-school ritual like a trip to get ice cream or a visit to a pool to mark the last day of school and celebrate the beginning of summer.

Chapter Fourteen

I hurried over to the desk, and compared the writing on the flowcharts, which was careful and exact, to the flowing writing on the graded papers. They weren't exactly the same, but they were similar enough that it looked as if the same person had written both things. When Ms. McCormick wrote on the graded papers, her letters were printed and small, but not nearly as perfectly formed. Those notes looked as if she'd been in a hurry, jotting down short notes to the students and scribbling the grades quickly across the top of the papers. The painfully exact lettering on the flowchart looked like the printing on the note I'd received in Livvy's take-home folder.

I snatched up one of the flowchart papers and dashed out the door. Once I entered the hallway, which was a mass of kids and bumping backpacks, I had to slow down. I spotted Livvy at the other end of the hallway. She stood outside the door to her science classroom, talking to another girl. I waved, catching her eye.

Her easy stance shifted so that she looked as stiff as one of Nathan's action figures. I waved for her to come to me, figuring that would be slightly less embarrassing for her than me going into her classroom. After a second of hesitation, she motored down the hall to me.

"*Mom*," she said, drawing out the syllable and infusing it with as much chagrin as any tween can. "What is it?"

"Did you ever see Ms. McCormick working on papers like this?"

"Sure," Livvy said without a moment's hesitation. "It's for the game," she said easily, and then her eyes widened. "I wasn't supposed to tell."

"Tell what?"

Livvy clamped her lips together and sent me a mulish look.

"This is not the time for secrets, Livvy." I said it so sharply that, after a sigh, Livvy nodded, then looked up and down the hall. "It's Ms. McCormick's secret project, her game," she said in a voice that made me lean close to her to hear. "She was letting us test it, but didn't want us to tell anyone." Livvy pointed to the words at the top. "See, this one is for the Egyptian Pyramid." Livvy's finger traced along the line of shapes. "They all start out this way, with a really easy problem." She paused over the first geometric shape, then traced the line on down the page. "But they get harder."

"Did you ever see her actually writing on these flowcharts? Is this her writing?"

"Sure," Livvy said, back in her normal voice.

"It's very different from the way she writes on your homework papers."

Livvy shrugged. "She says math is exact and you have to be neat when you're working problems. Ms. McCormick said that writing stuff for the game is the same way. You should see her when she works problems on the whiteboard, it looks like something from a computer."

"You said it was her game. Did Ms. McCormick have early access to the game, or was it actually her game?"

"It was her game. She was making it up as she went along. That's why she wanted us to play it, so that she could make it better before she told everyone about it." Livvy looked around the almost empty hall. "Mom, I've got to go."

"Of course. I'll see you after school."

Livvy scooted down the hall and into her classroom. She made it before the bell rang. I went slowly back into Ms. McCormick's room. I stopped inside the doorway and looked at the lesson that was printed on the side of the whiteboard. The letters were exact. They did look like a computer printout . . . just like the flowchart and the printing on the threatening note.

"I don't know why I didn't see it right away," I said to Detective Waraday.

After Peg fled, he must have gotten a search warrant because when I stepped out into the hall to track him down and share the news about the handwriting, he was already in the hallway, leading a group of crime scene technicians to Ms. McCormick's room. As the technicians worked around us, Detective Waraday and I stood at the whiteboard where Ms. McCormick had written the day's lesson.

Detective Waraday slipped the papers with the flowcharts into plastic sleeves. "It's not surprising. You weren't looking for it. I'm sure you were only thinking about keeping the kids in line for fifty minutes, which is enough to occupy anyone's mind."

One of the crime scene techs was going through Ms. McCormick's desk while another had opened the storage closet and was removing items one at a time and examining them. Detective Waraday had looked disgruntled when he arrived with the crime scene technicians. If Ms. McCormick was the murderer, then she'd had plenty of time to get rid of any evidence that might have been left behind, but it looked as if they were going to go over the room inch by inch.

Detective Waraday pointed to the flowchart. "You say this had something to do with a game?"

"Yes. My daughter—she's in Ms. McCormick's class—I asked her about the paper, and she told me just now that it was a secret. Apparently, Ms. McCormick was designing a game about math and was letting the kids play it on the computers. Livvy had mentioned the game before, but not that Ms. McCormick had created it."

"And that was the word your daughter used, 'secret'?" Detective Waraday asked thoughtfully. "Something like that wouldn't be allowed on school time?"

"I don't know. You'd have to ask Mrs. Kirk, but Livvy said they only were allowed to play it if they finished their schoolwork, so it wasn't like Ms. McCormick was ignoring the kids or their studies."

Detective Waraday said, "Perhaps there would be some sort of conflict of interest with the school district or her contract or something."

"I suppose that could be a possibility," I said. "If Ms. McCormick left those papers out on her desk—and they were out today—and Klea saw them and realized what they were . . ."

Detective Waraday frowned. "Did you know what these were?"

"No."

"And you'd actually heard of the game. I'm not sure someone not associated with the class would make that assumption. In fact, I think most people wouldn't know what these were."

The sound of a voice came from the doorway. "Oh, sorry, I didn't realize . . ."

Abby stood uncertainly. "Sorry," she said again. "I heard that you had to wrangle Ms. McCormick's class, and I popped down to make sure you were okay." Her gaze traveled from Detective Waraday to the crime scene techs going through drawers and closets.

"No, that was last period. It went fine," I said. I turned to Detective Waraday. "Do you need anything else from me?"

"Not at this time," he said. He closed the door behind me as I left.

"What is going on in there?" Abby asked in a whisper as I fell into step with her in the quiet hall, which was as still as a library on Friday night.

"Detective Waraday wanted to talk to Ms. McCormick, but she bolted. Left her class and drove off campus right after lunch. I think she wrote the note."

"What note?" Abby asked.

"That's right—I haven't had a chance to tell you."
I quickly caught Abby up on what had happened,
describing the smashed window, the threatening
note, and the scandal in Ms. McCormick's past, figuring that if Marie and Peg knew about it, it would
only be a short time before the word spread through
the school, at least to the teachers. "That should
probably be confidential, but I don't think there's
any way that the news won't get out."

"I won't tell anyone," Abby said, then shook her
head. "A drug bust?" She mouthed the words, not
even wanting to speak them aloud. "How did she
ever get hired?"

"It's a long, complicated story that I don't think I
should go into," I said as we arrived at the door to
Abby's classroom. A low murmur of conversation
broke off when she peered inside, called a few
names, and pointed out that they still had one more
quiz left to take this week.

She turned back to me. "Call me if anything else
happens, okay? I can't believe you're dealing with
vandalism and threats and you didn't call."

"It was late when it happened, and you're busy," I
said.

"Not that busy," she said firmly. "I'm calling you
tonight to check on you."

"Okay," I said with a grin. "Hey, before I go, did
you ever hear Ms. McCormick talk about a game?"

"No . . . what kind of game? Playground game or
board game or what?"

"A computer game. It looks like Ms. McCormick
was working on one and letting the kids test it for

her. I saw her notes for it, and the handwriting looked exactly like the writing on the note."

Abby frowned at the tile floor for a second. "No, she never mentioned it, but we aren't on the same team—not even the same grade. I've only spoken to her a few times, in fact. But it sounds like you should steer clear of her."

I sighed. "I vowed I was going to stay out of all this, but that's not going so well."

"Hmm. Well, you do have a way of getting at the truth, so perhaps it's not all bad, especially if it was Ms. McCormick." She shivered. "I hate to think that she . . . hurt Klea. I mean, that's what the detective must think since they're going through her classroom."

"Well, I think they have to check into it since she ran off campus instead of talking to Detective Waraday. Just doing that by itself looks suspicious. It is possible that Klea found out what Ms. McCormick was doing with the game or maybe Klea found out about that thing from Ms. McCormick's past," I said, being intentionally vague since we were standing at the door of Abby's classroom, even though I was speaking softly. "You aren't the only person I've heard say that Klea was nosy. Maybe Klea figured out Ms. McCormick's secret—at least one of them."

"And Klea threatened to expose Ms. McCormick, so Ms. McCormick killed Klea?" Abby whispered. "Ugh. I don't even like to think about it." She glanced at her watch. "It can't already be one-thirty," she said. "And we haven't even started going over homework. I've got to go. I'll call you tonight."

I waved at her, distractedly. One-thirty. I had a bad feeling that I had something on my calendar today at one-thirty. "Oh, great," I muttered as I remembered my schedule for the day. I half walked, half ran down the hallway. I could not postpone my organizing appointment with Margo *again*.

Fortunately, Margo lived in the neighborhood that surrounded the school. I was only a few minutes late when I rang the doorbell of her brick rancher. I'd met Margo once last year when her youngest was still at school with my kids, but he was now at the middle school, so I hadn't seen as much of Margo as I used to. I'd been surprised to hear from her a few weeks ago when she filled out the online contact form on my website. She wanted to use one of my *à la carte* services, a one-time consultation to help work out the cabinet design of her kitchen remodel.

When she opened the door, she looked just the same, slender with a sprinkling of freckles across her cheeks. She taught yoga at the local gym, and I'd always seen her in workout clothes, which was how she was dressed today. She had a phone tucked between her ear and her shoulder, and mouthed *hello*, and then raised a finger. *One minute.*

I nodded, and she waved me inside, motioning for me to go down the hallway to the kitchen. She followed me into the small square of space that was walled off from the living room as she wrapped up her conversation.

She ended the call and ran her hand through her short red curls. "Well, here it is. It will be completely gutted, and we'll start from scratch." She waved her hand around the kitchen. Formica countertops, faded linoleum, and a dropped ceiling with fluorescent lights showed the house had been built in another era. She motioned to the wall that separated the kitchen from the living room. "That wall will come down to open up the room. And in here—" She took a few steps into the breakfast nook next to the kitchen and moved to the wall of windows that overlooked the backyard. "We're blowing out this wall to give us more space. This whole area"—she circled her hand around the breakfast nook—"will actually be where the sandbox is now."

"Wow. That's a big job," I said.

She ran her hands through her curls again. "Don't I know it. I'm lying awake at night, trying to figure out whether to put in a lazy Susan or those rollout shelf things. That's when I decided to call you. If you can help me configure the cabinet design, then I'll only have to worry about the tile, counters, fixtures, hardware, and lights," she said with a grimace.

"What are your thoughts right now?"

Margo pointed to the round table in the breakfast nook. It was covered with sketches on grid paper, as well as glossy brochures featuring gorgeous kitchen cabinets and paint chips. We settled into the chairs, and it was a relief to focus on organizing and debate the pros and cons of drawer depths and dividers. After about thirty minutes, we had roughed out a way to maximize as much storage space in the new kitchen as possible. I was usually limited by what the client had in place. It wasn't often that I had a blank slate to work with, so to speak, and I had a great time exploring possibilities.

It was also nice to leave all the questions and

problems surrounding Klea's death behind, and I wasn't even thinking about any of those things when Margo said, "I can't believe everything that's going on at the elementary school. So scary. I never thought I'd say this, but I'm glad my kids are at the middle school." She refolded brochures and shuffled them into a stack. "Of course, there's always been rumors about sketchy stuff going on at the elementary school, so I shouldn't be so surprised, I guess."

I handed her the list of cabinetry and organizing items I'd made while we were talking so she could order them. "Sketchy stuff? Like what?"

Margo waved a hand. "I shouldn't have said anything. I don't know anything for sure. Just rumors."

"Margo, my kids are there every day. I'm in and out of the school all the time, and I've never heard anything."

"Well, you wouldn't. You're not the type to have any problems."

"What do you mean?"

Margo wrinkled her nose. "You know . . . you're happily married—at least you seem to be. You're not the type to get yourself into a sticky situation and be . . . vulnerable."

I stared at her a moment. "I'm not sure I'm following you," I said, but I was afraid I did know what she was hinting at.

Margo sighed. "I've really put my foot in it now. Oh, well. It's all rumors, anyway." She scrubbed her hand through her curls. "It's probably totally wrong, but I heard that one of the moms who had been fooling around got a note from the office in their kid's take-home folder, demanding she pay a certain amount of money or her husband would be contacted."

I fell back against the chair. "A blackmail note?"

"Yes, but, as I said, it's all rumor."

"What did she do?"

"Paid it, I guess." Margo shrugged. "Since she didn't end up getting a divorce."

"So you know who it was?"

"No, not really. I mean, not one hundred percent. I *think* I know, but I'm not sure. It was one of those things that you hear third-or-fourth person, so I have no idea if there's even a bit of truth in it."

"Wow." I blinked, stunned that something like that was going on in the school—if it was true. But then I thought of Gabrielle's call this morning and her juicy gossip about something shady going on at the school. And Gabrielle had asked if the note I received demanded money. . . . Maybe there *was* some truth to what Margo had overheard.

"Wait," I said as I sat forward. "You said it came from the office."

"Did I?" Margo looked flustered. "I hadn't realized . . ." She gazed off into space, then said, "But I think that's right."

"How would someone know it came from the office?" As Detective Waraday and I had worked out, almost anyone could slip a note into the papers that went into the take-home folders.

"I don't know." Margo shrugged and looked like she wished she'd never brought up the subject. "I suppose someone said it was one of those folded and taped notes. Isn't that how all the notes from the office look? I know whenever I got one of those, it was from the main office."

"That's true, but it could be someone imitating that. It's not hard to fold a piece of copy paper in thirds and put tape on it. It could have been from anyone in the school—a teacher, the staff, or even another parent."

She closed a folder with a thump. "I probably shouldn't have said anything at all."

"No, it could be very important. Will you tell the sheriff's department about it? I can give you the name of the detective—"

"Oh, no. I could never do that." She looked like I'd asked her to rob a bank. "In the first place, Dave would not like it," she said, referring to her husband. "And, in the second, it's just a rumor. I'm not even sure who mentioned it. It came up after a yoga class. I overheard a couple of the moms talking as I was cleaning up the room. It was a tight little group, and I don't even remember all the names of the people who were there. It was last year, too, so it's probably nothing to do with anything this year." She pushed her chair back. "Would you like a cup of coffee?"

The subject was closed, and I could tell she wasn't going to give an inch, so I declined the coffee and gathered up my organizing materials. I gave her an invoice and left, wishing that we hadn't ended on such a strained note.

Chapter Fifteen

The next morning, I was the first person to pull into the school parking lot, and my conversation with Margo was still on my mind. I'd debated calling Detective Waraday yesterday, but in the end, I just couldn't see telling him about the rumors and then expecting him to take them seriously when I couldn't give him a single name or solid fact, especially since Margo refused to talk to him.

I was still second-guessing my decision as I parked near the main doors to the school. I must have arrived even before Vaughn, who was supposed to be here a few minutes early to open the doors for me. I was here to meet Joy Peel, the owner of the catering company providing the breakfast buffet for today's Teacher Appreciation.

While we had some parents who wanted to bring homemade food, there was another set of parents who were just as happy to write a check and let someone else bring the food. We'd sent home a letter with the students a month ago and asked for either sign-ups to bring food or a donation to purchase catering. The donations had provided enough money to cover Thursday's breakfast and Friday's barbecue lunch. The only glitch was that the catering company had two events this morning. If we wanted our food, someone had to be at the school at seven to make sure Joy was able to get inside and set up. Abby had offered to help me by bringing the kids with her at eight, and I'd taken her up on the offer, figuring it would be easier to coordinate the food if both kids weren't underfoot.

The catering van lumbered into the parking lot, followed by Vaughn, who pulled into the drop-off line and unlocked the main doors for us before he went to park his car. I grabbed my phone, hopped out of the van, and went to prop open the school's door. Then I flipped on the lights in the lobby and the teachers' lounge. Joy was a military spouse who I knew through the squadron's spouse club. She came through the doors, carrying a container of muffins. "I figured I better get right to it, since I've got to run."

"That's fine. Through here," I said, directing her to the teachers' lounge. We ferried the rest of the food inside, arranged it, and then set out coffee and juice. I could hear Vaughn's keys jangling as he moved through the school, unlocking doors.

Joy put the last tray in place and removed the cover.

"Looks great," I said.

"Excellent. Thanks for the business," Joy said before departing. "I'll close that main door on my way out. Anything else?"

"Nope."

I tweaked the card with Joy's company name so that it was more visible, then noticed a book with a flowery cover on one of the tables. It was a date-book. When I flicked the cover open, I saw the name Hillary Cross, one of the fifth-grade teachers, on the first page. She must have forgotten it here yesterday, I thought. I had some time. I'd run it down to her room and drop it off.

As I paced through the empty halls, I could hear Vaughn bumping around in the janitor's office, but other than that, it was quiet. The calm before the storm, I thought. In about twenty minutes, the halls would be flooded with scurrying kids and teachers.

Mrs. Cross's room was one room beyond Ms. Mc-Cormick's, and I couldn't help but glance in as I approached the door. I'd almost expected to see crime scene tape sealing off the room, but the door was open and the swath of room that I could see as I passed looked completely normal. Detective Wara-day must not have found anything significant enough to warrant sealing the room. I dropped the datebook on Mrs. Cross's desk, then returned to the hallway, again looking into Ms. McCormick's room as I approached.

A flicker of movement within the room caught my eye, and I veered toward the door. I had thought for a second I'd seen Ms. McCormick, but that couldn't be right. It was probably just another teacher with a slender figure and blond hair—the substitute teacher for the day, most likely.

But as I paused by the door, I saw it wasn't some-one else. It *was* Ms. McCormick. She was bent over the desk at the back of the room. She glanced up and saw me an instant after I spotted her. I suppose if I had been smart I would have ducked out of the door as quickly as I could, but I was so shocked to see her that my feet stayed planted to the floor. For a second, I wondered if everything had been cleared up. Perhaps the newspaper article and the two different names were some sort of mix-up that had been explained, and she was back at work today.

But after one look at her haggard face, I dismissed that thought. She looked like one of the kids when they come home from a slumber party where they didn't sleep at all. Ms. McCormick's makeup looked like she had stayed up all night, with her eyeliner smudged and her mascara flaking off, making the dark circles under her eyes look even worse. Her dress was wrinkled and creased, and I realized it was the same dress she had been wearing yesterday. Her golden hair was in a lopsided ponytail, and her lipstick had been chewed off. She looked like a weird, distorted modern-art version of a cartoon princess.

She stood there a moment, her eyes wide. "What are you doing to do? Call the police on me again?"

"I had nothing to do with that. I didn't call the police," I said.

"But it's your fault. You wanted to know about my other job. No one else *ever* asked about that. You set everything in motion. You and your questions." She slammed a drawer closed, rifled through the papers on the top of the desk, then stood back and scanned the rest of the room.

"Where are they?" she demanded.

"What?"

"My notes for the game." She came around the

desk, fingering the zipper on the cross-body bag that was slung over her shoulder. "I *know* you were in here yesterday. If you want to know anything that's going on in a school, just follow some of the kids on social media. They have no filters and post about absolutely everything."

I did not have a good feeling about her hostile tone. Was anyone else in the school besides Vaughn? And where was Vaughn? I listened, but didn't hear the jingle of his key ring. "But if you knew that the kids were so unguarded, I'm surprised that you would let them play the computer game. It was supposed to be a secret, right?" I asked.

She gave a sharp nod. "You're right. I shouldn't have let them see the game, but I was stupid. I needed their help to get through beta. I figured the risk was worth it. I *need* those notes. That game is all I have."

I was about to make some excuse and slip out of the room, but her words surprised me. "What do you mean, it's all you have?"

"You're kidding, right? Even I understand that I'll never get another job at a school again after all this comes out. My teaching career is over, but the game—the kids like it. It has potential. I can upload it and sell it myself. No one will care that I happened to be too stupid to realize a friend had put *her* drugs in *my* car. One mistake. I made *one* mistake."

She rotated her shoulders, relaxing them slightly. "But that's over. No more trying to hide my past. I'm a game designer now, and I need those notes. They're critical for the app version."

"I'm sorry, but I don't know where they are. They're not on your desk?"

"No, they're not on my desk," she said, raising her voice. "They're not *anywhere* in this room." She pulled a gun from her bag. "Now, what did you do with them?"

I put my hands up, palms facing her, and backed away. "Ms. McCormick—"

She laughed, but it wasn't a normal laugh. The sound had a slightly hysterical edge to it. "You don't have to look so terrified. It's not a gun. Not a real one, anyway." She twisted her hand for a second so that I could see the gun from the side. "It's a Taser," she said.

It was boxier than a real gun and seemed to be made of plastic, I realized and calmed down a bit.

She shifted it back so that it was aimed it at me. "Handy to have. I got it when I was in college for those long walks across the campus after my night class. Who would have thought that the first time I would use it would be in my classroom?"

I was pretty sure that even mace violated the school's no-weapons policy, so a Taser would definitely be against the rules, but I wasn't about to mention that at this moment. Instead, I moved an inch toward the door.

"It won't do you any good to run. The range on these things is quite impressive," she said. "Now come inside the room. Yes, that's good," she said, indicating that I should stop between two of the rows of desks.

I kept my eyes on her face, which was now a bit flushed, as I listened for the sound of the first teachers arriving. Surely it wouldn't be long before there would be several teachers in the hallway and surrounding classrooms.

I swallowed, going back to the issue that seemed to have set her off. "If your papers aren't here, then Detective Waraday probably took them."

She lowered the Taser an inch. "Why would he do that? Why would he even care? He's investigating Klea's death. My game has nothing to do with Klea."

"Well, then you'll get the papers back, no problem. You're sure Klea didn't know about the game? Or . . . anything else?" Were those footsteps echoing down the hall?

"My past, you mean," Ms. McCormick said. "Oh, no, it wasn't Klea who knew."

She put a slight emphasis on the name Klea. "But someone else knew," I said slowly, working it out as I remembered Ms. McCormick's comment when Klea was discovered in the woods and the way Ms. McCormick had stiffened when Peg and Gabrielle came into the teachers' lounge and then departed as quickly as she could. "Peg. Peg knows?" I asked, dropping my hands to my side at the thought. The footsteps faded, probably a teacher going into another room closer to the main hall, but I only half noticed.

Ms. McCormick's shoulders sagged. "I think so. It's someone in the office, that's all I know for sure. Peg always has a sort of superior smirk on her face when she sees me, so I think it's her. But that's hardly evidence."

My thoughts were churning. If Peg knew about Ms. McCormick's past, why hadn't she said anything? But then I thought of the rumors Margo had mentioned—the rumors that focused on someone in the office. "You were being blackmailed," I guessed.

Ms. McCormick closed her eyes for a second, then snapped them open and tossed her head. "I suppose since it's all out now, it doesn't matter anyway. I might as well take her down with me. Yes, I was being blackmailed, and I do think it was Peg."

"Not Klea?" I asked just to be sure.

"No, of course it wasn't Klea. It couldn't have been her."

"Why?"

"Because the note that said I had to pay up came from the office. It thoughtfully included an envelope that I was to fill with my cash and then return to the office in one of those inter-office envelopes—you know, the kind with the lines on the side and the string tie to hold down the flap. Who sorts the inter-office mail? Peg. It *has* to be her."

It did sound logical. Peg handled the paper that came into the office, as well as distributing the papers that went out. She was always over at the pigeonholes, shifting paper into the slots for teachers to pick up.

"I knew I shouldn't pay, but what else could I do? The envelopes came like clockwork every other Monday," she said with a bitter laugh. "And I filled them with cash and returned them."

"How long has this been going on?"

"Since the week after I arrived." Her arms were now sagging, and she shifted over so that she could prop one hip on a student desk, suddenly looking drained.

Some of the tension had eased out of me when

Ms. McCormick lowered the Taser, but she still held it in her hand, even if it wasn't aimed at me right now. I decided that I wouldn't make any sudden moves. I didn't want to startle her now that she seemed to be calming down.

"You thought I hurt Klea?" She dropped the Taser to her lap. "I would never do that. Besides, when would I have had time? I was with my class all that morning."

It was a good point, except that the critical time wasn't during the Muffins with Mom; it was earlier, when teachers were moving around the hallways before the students and parents arrived in the classrooms. It wouldn't be hard for a teacher to slip out and strangle someone unnoticed at that time of the morning, especially if the murderer caught Klea going either into or out of the closet and attacked her there, then left her body in the closet until it could be moved. With a jolt, I realized that that line of reasoning meant that Mrs. Harris could still be a suspect, too. She could have arrived earlier, then returned to the parking lot to remove the food from her car. I hadn't seen her arrive at the school, only met her standing in the parking lot.

"It had to have been Peg who did it," Ms. McCormick said, interrupting my thoughts. "I mean, everyone knew Klea liked to snoop in drawers and files and stuff. She must have found out what Peg was doing, and Peg killed her."

"Why didn't you tell Detective Waraday that instead of running away yesterday?"

"Because how could I tell him what was going on without telling him about the blackmail? And I have no proof, only my suspicions."

"You don't have any of the envelopes or the original note? Did you get a note every time?" I asked, my thoughts swerving all over the place.

"No, only that first time. Believe me, the envelope was sufficient for me to know what was being demanded."

"And that first note?"

"I burned it on the barbecue grill at my apartment complex. So, no evidence, just Peg's smug looks."

"Still, you should tell Detective Waraday. You can talk to him about your notes for the computer game at the same time. I'm sure that you can get them back, at least a copy, especially since they don't seem to have any relation to Klea's death."

She jumped up from the desk where she'd been perched. "No. I'm not talking to him. I have a criminal record. He's not going to believe anything I say, especially after—" She stopped speaking and looked down at the Taser, fidgeting with one of the little flap-type things that covered the end of the barrel.

Watching her pick at the flap of the Taser made me nervous—it was still pointed loosely in my direction—but the guilty cast of her face looked just like Nathan's when I pointed out to him that I knew from the crumbs all over the counter that he'd had a snack when I told him not to.

"That wasn't the only note," I said. "There was also the note you wrote to me."

Her head popped up. "You can't prove that."

"Oh, I'm afraid I can. Or, at least, Detective Waraday can." I glanced at the handwritten lesson that was still on the whiteboard. "You left a sample of your handwriting here on the board as well as in the game notes. Why did you write that note to me, if you didn't kill Klea?" I asked, realizing that despite all her lies and misdirection, I really did believe her when she said she hadn't killed Klea.

Ms. McCormick swiped at a strand of hair that had fallen over her forehead. She pushed it back. "It was stupid. I see that now, but I thought if I could just get you to keep quiet and not ask any more questions . . . then it would all be okay. No one had been interested in my previous job—or whether or not I'd even *had* a previous job. If I could get you to leave it alone, it would all be fine."

I'd been so focused on what Ms. McCormick was saying that I hadn't been paying attention to what was going on in the hallway outside the door, but we both realized that there were several sets of footsteps ringing out on the tile.

"I have to go," Ms. McCormick said quickly. "Tell that Detective Waraday everything I told you, okay?" Ms. McCormick moved across the room. As she flitted by me, she stuffed the Taser back in her purse, but kept her hand around the handle, inside the bag. She reached the door at the same time that Mrs. Kirk appeared. They almost ran into each other, but Mrs. Kirk stepped back, her face shocked. "Ms. McCormick! What are you doing . . . ?" She trailed off as she took in Ms. McCormick's rough appearance.

Ms. McCormick pushed by Mrs. Kirk and hurried down the hall. I rushed into the hallway and grabbed Mrs. Kirk's arm to help steady her. Ms. McCormick had pushed her off balance, and Mrs. Kirk had half-fallen against the wall.

She righted herself and we both started after Ms. McCormick, but she was too fast for us. By the time we got to the end of the hallway where it met the lobby, all we could see of Ms. McCormick was a glimpse of her blue dress as she disappeared out the front doors of the school. We hurried to the doors and saw Ms. McCormick's little blue car already bumping over the dip at the exit of the parking lot and accelerating into the street.

Organizing Tips for PTA Moms

Social Media and Schools

If your school doesn't have social media accounts and you enjoy social media, volunteer to create and maintain a profile for your school on one of the social media websites. Facebook probably has the widest reach so it would be a good starting point.

Use the account to post information and reminders about upcoming events, link to volunteer signup opportunities, and promote school spirit with images and reports about events, but check with your school district about their policy on photography releases before posting any images of students.

Chapter Sixteen

Mrs. Kirk shook her head. "I can't believe it . . . that she showed up here." She turned and went into the main office. I followed her more slowly, my thoughts spinning. Should I tell Mrs. Kirk what Ms. McCormick had told me—her suspicions about Peg? Ms. McCormick was sure it was Peg who was blackmailing her, and it seemed like that was the logical conclusion, but what if Ms. McCormick was wrong? What if it was someone else who worked in the office . . . ? Marie and Mrs. Kirk worked in the office, too.

I didn't want to go there—not even in my thoughts, but all three women worked in the office . . . and then there was Klea's list as well. After discovering that Mrs. Harris was writing under the name Alexa Wells, I couldn't help but wonder why the other names were on the list with those two. Could it be that everyone on the list had something to hide? Ms. McCormick certainly did. And now it appeared Peg did as well. Marie and Mrs. Kirk's names were on that list, too . . . so perhaps keeping the news to myself until I could tell Detective Waraday about it was the better call.

I went to the main office and headed for the computer, intending to sign out before I left the campus, but I realized I hadn't signed in at all, which was getting to be a bad habit. It was the second time I'd forgotten to sign in, but the shock of spotting Ms. McCormick had pushed everything out of my mind.

Mrs. Kirk was in her office, on the telephone with the door closed, but she saw me through the glass panel that ran along the side of her door. She stood and walked to the door, but kept the phone pressed to her ear. She tilted the lower portion of it away from her mouth as she said, "Ellie, you're not leaving, are you? I'm on the line with the sheriff's department. I'm sure they'll want to speak to you."

"Yes, of course," I said. Of course Mrs. Kirk would call Detective Waraday. He needed to be informed that Ms. McCormick had shown up at the school. I sat down on the long wooden bench, mentally kicking myself for not immediately telling Detective Waraday about the rumors Margo had mentioned. There was definitely something shady going on in the school.

Peg's desk was off to the side and, despite the tall counter that blocked Mrs. Kirk and Marie from my view, I could see Peg. She sat at her desk, tapping away on her computer, looking completely calm, occasionally taking a sip from her coffee mug. Could she be a blackmailer? A stack of orange inter-office folders sat in a basket on the corner of her desk. I wished I

could get a peek at them, but that was crazy. I
shifted on the bench, recrossing my legs in the
other direction. I was too nosy. Maybe Gabrielle was
right that even if I wanted to leave the questions
around Klea's death alone, I just couldn't do it.

I glanced back at Peg. When I'd first met her, I'd
wondered if she was shy because she hardly ever
spoke to anyone and only answered if she was asked
a direct question, but as time went by, I'd decided
she wasn't reticent because she was nervous or embarrassed. I'd realized that there was a sullenness to
her personality that came through in every interaction we'd had.

She must have felt my gaze on her because she
looked over at me and raised her eyebrows. "Did
you need something?" she said, her tone sharp.

"No, nothing. Sorry."

I took out my phone and checked my calls, then
noticed a message had come in a few minutes ago
through my website, a request for an organizing
consultation. The person, Marguerite, had left the
section for the last name blank. She wanted to meet
this afternoon and had checked off kitchen and
closets as the areas she wanted help with. I ran over
my schedule in my mind. I'd planned on stopping
at the office supply store, but I could put that off. It
would be best to get in as many appointments as I
could before summer hit and the kids were home
all the time.

A strange sound—a half gulp, half gasp—made
me look up, my mom senses on full alert. I knew
that sound. It was the prelude to someone throwing
up. Peg, one hand clasped over her mouth and the
other over her stomach, lurched to the door and

disappeared into the restroom across the hall.

I stood up and looked at Marie. "Do you think she's okay?"

"I better go see." Marie bustled around the tall counter, her sky-blue shirt swishing with every step.

I waited a moment, then decided that Peg didn't need a second person hovering over her in the bathroom and sat back down. My phone buzzed with a new text. It was from Abby, letting me know that she and the kids had arrived at school.

I went into the lobby in time to catch the kids and say hello to them. They answered distractedly and hurried on to the cafeteria, where they could talk quietly with their friends until the bell to go to class sounded. I turned to Abby. "Everything go okay?"

"Oh, sure. We had a short panic when Charlie couldn't find his math homework." She rolled her eyes. "I really should get you to organize his room. It's a disaster."

"I could do that. This summer?"

"Yes, please." She shifted her feet, and I knew she wanted to get to class, so I said quickly, "Have you ever heard any rumors about . . . well, shady things going on here at the school?"

She went still and tilted her head. "What do you mean, shady?"

Two teachers passed us, and I waited until they were in the teachers' lounge before I said, "There's really no way to phrase it subtly. Have you heard anything about people being blackmailed?"

I'd expected Abby to look shocked and immediately say how crazy that thought was, but she didn't. She shifted her gaze around the lobby, where more teachers were entering the building. She grabbed my arm and pulled me down to the turn where the second-grade hallway branched off the lobby. "What have you heard?"

"You mean it's true?" I asked.

"I don't know, but I have heard . . . rumblings . . . nothing concrete—that's why I didn't say anything to you. I figured it was just some moms exaggerating."

"It was moms—parents—you heard talking about it?"

"Two moms. I walked into the workroom one day and heard what I thought was the word 'blackmail.' The two women shifted their conversation to something else right away, and I decided it was just too absurd. I must have misheard them."

"Who were they?"

"I don't know. Not any parents I've come in contact with before, but the school is pretty big. There are lots of parents that I don't know. And people are always moving in and out, coming and going. I don't know everyone. But you've obviously heard something, too—something more than the word blackmail."

"I've heard a couple of things—"

The bell rang, and Abby sighed. "I'm late. I have car circle duty today. I have to go, but we have to talk later."

I nodded and went back to the office, passing Mrs. Kirk. "Detective Waraday is on his way," she said. "He does want to speak to you." She moved to the main doors, her walkie-talkie in hand.

A runaway teacher might have returned unexpectedly, but the routines of the school day, like monitoring morning drop-off, continued.

"I'll wait in the office," I said, and returned there to find Marie making a *tsking* sound as she picked up the stack of papers Peg had been working on. Marie dropped them in the basket on top of the inter-office envelopes, and carried the whole thing over to her desk. She went back to Peg's desk and switched off the computer, then picked up her coffee mug. Marie took it to the back of the room, where there was a little bar-type sink in the counter next to a coffeepot. She dumped the coffee, rinsed out the mug, and returned it to Peg's desk. "I just hope none of the rest of us come down with it."

"Oh, no. What does Peg have?" I asked.

"I hope it's food poisoning. She said she had a fast-food breakfast roll on the way to work today. Otherwise, we're all in for it."

"I hate to wish food poisoning on anyone, but I hope that's it and not something else contagious," I said, thinking of how quickly viruses and flu bugs spread through the school.

Marie moved back to her desk. "I told Peg to go on home. She didn't want to, but she looked as green as the grass out that window. No use her sitting around, spreading germs, if she is contagious."

"And she seemed fine a few minutes ago."

"You know how those things are," Marie said. "They come on sudden."

Marie attacked the pile of papers she'd transferred to her desk, and I went back to my phone, automatically tapping out a reply that I could meet my new client at two o'clock, wondering if it was too much of a coincidence that Peg had become ill and had to leave the school shortly after Ms. McCormick returned. Had Peg somehow overheard what she'd said? I bit my lip, trying to remember how busy the hallway had been. A few people had been moving around—teachers, I'd assumed, going to their classrooms. But from the point when Ms. McCormick mentioned blackmail, I had been so focused on her that I hadn't noticed anyone in the hall.

I supposed Peg could have been hovering outside the room listening to part of the conversation. I couldn't be sure, so I sent a long text to Detective Waraday, summarizing what Ms. McCormick had told me, and sat back to wait, hoping that Marie might get called away, and I could sneak a look at the basket of inter-office envelopes.

Chapter Seventeen

"**I** was caught completely off guard," Mrs. Kirk said.

Mrs. Kirk, Detective Waraday, and I were in Mrs. Kirk's office with the door closed. It was close to noon. I had spent the morning hanging about the school, waiting for Detective Waraday. I had lingered for a good hour in the office, but Marie hadn't left her desk once.

After retrieving my laptop—which I'd gotten into the habit of bringing with me because I could get a lot of work done while waiting in the car circle line at the end of the school day—from the van, I'd finally moved down to the workroom and cleared my email inbox, then created a checklist for a client who was moving soon.

Detective Waraday had arrived, and I'd been called to the office shortly before noon. I'd thought it might have taken him so long to arrive because he had gone to Peg's house to speak to her, but he'd explained that he'd been delayed because a report had come in that he had to investigate. Ms. McCormick's car had been spotted at a park on the other side of North Dawkins. It had been abandoned, and there'd been no sign of her, but a search of the surrounding area had to be made.

Mrs. Kirk tapped a pencil on her desktop. "I find it very disturbing, Detective, that Ms. McCormick returned to the school this morning and slipped in before the students arrived."

"I can understand your worries," Detective Waraday said. "I've instructed an officer to be here from the time the doors open until the school is locked at night. He should arrive soon. I've told him to check in with you, but I doubt Ms. McCormick will return to the school. I understand that what she was looking for wasn't here," he said, glancing at me.

Mrs. Kirk sat forward, her surprised gaze fixed on me. "She spoke to you? Why didn't you say anything?"

"You had drop-off, and with Peg getting sick . . . there was so much going on, I thought I'd tell you both, at once."

Mrs. Kirk frowned. "Well, what did she want?"

I looked at Detective Waraday, and he gave a nod of his head, indicating I should tell her. "The notes for her game."

Mrs. Kirk's chin came down, and she looked at me with raised eyebrows. "She came back to the school for a *game*?"

I was surprised that Detective Waraday hadn't told Mrs. Kirk about the game. He'd definitely known about it yesterday and could have informed Mrs. Kirk about it then.

Detective Waraday said, "Yes. It appears Ms. Mc-Cormick was creating a computer game. I think Mrs. Avery can explain it better than I can." He motioned that I had the floor.

I gave Mrs. Kirk a quick summary of the game, noticing that while Mrs. Kirk's attention was focused on me, Detective Waraday was watching her intently. I said, "So Ms. McCormick wanted those notes, the flowchart schematic thing. That's what she was looking for today."

Mrs. Kirk shook her head. "Of all the things . . ." She picked up a pencil and tapped the pencil's eraser on the desktop rapidly. "And they weren't there? She didn't find them?" Mrs. Kirk's voice had an edge to it. She wasn't happy that I hadn't informed her of all this before Detective Waraday arrived.

"No," Detective Waraday said, "I have them."

"I see," Mrs. Kirk said, and gave him a long look that I was sure made the kids squirm in their chairs, but it didn't seem to bother Detective Waraday. After a second, Mrs. Kirk went on. "Well, creating a game on the school's computer system and using students to beta test it, as you called it, is certainly something she should have run by me."

The beat of the eraser increased, then stopped abruptly as Mrs. Kirk replaced it in a pencil cup. "But, as we all now know, Ms. McCormick had quite a few things that she preferred to keep to herself, things that she should have informed me of." She inched her chair back. "If that's all you need from us, Detective . . . ?"

He said, "That's not quite all. Do you have an extra classroom where I can speak with Mrs. Avery?"

I had been wondering if I should launch into the whole blackmail story of Ms. McCormick's in front of Mrs. Kirk. It seemed that Detective Waraday wasn't sharing all the details of the investigation with her, and I didn't want to give anything away.

Mrs. Kirk stared at him a moment, a frown on her face. "At the moment, no, there is not a free classroom, as we have a substitute in Ms. McCormick's classroom today, but you may use my office."

She stood and left, closing the door behind her.

Detective Waraday looked at the door for a moment, then turned back to me. His expression seemed to say, *I'm not getting any bonus points here, thanks to you.* He cleared his throat and adjusted his sport coat as he shifted in his chair so that he was fully facing me. Today he wore a dress shirt, tie, and jacket with his khakis. I wondered if he'd had to testify in court or attend some other important meeting. "So, blackmail?" he asked.

"I know it sounds crazy, but that is what Ms. McCormick said."

He took me through Ms. McCormick's story, then circled back and asked me about certain points again. Finally, he put his notebook and pen away. "It would make this whole situation much easier if she'd kept the note demanding money from her," he said.

"Do you think it could be true?" I asked. "I've heard some other . . . rumors. Nothing substantial, but . . ."

He took out his notebook again, and I recounted what Margo had told me without mentioning her name. "And then Gabrielle Matheson called me and told me she had some juicy gossip about something shady going on in the office, but I haven't heard back from her, so I don't know exactly what she was talking about." I frowned. "In fact, it's odd that she hasn't called me back. That's not like her."

Detective Waraday's chest heaved with a silent sigh as he added Gabrielle's name to his notebook. "I wouldn't worry about it. If there is one person who knows how to look out for herself, it's Mrs. Matheson."

I raised my eyebrows. "That's true."

He rubbed his hand down over his face, muffling his next words. "That was an inappropriate comment. I'm putting in too many hours, if I'm not censoring myself."

"I suppose something can be inappropriate but still true," I said with a grin.

"If that means I can count on you not to pass that comment on to Mrs. Matheson, then thank you." He stood and moved to open the door for me, but paused with his hand on the doorknob. "I thought you were giving up sleuthing," he said.

I threw up a hand. "I'm trying. It's not like I was camped out, waiting for Ms. McCormick to come back to the school. And about the blackmail, what M—" I cleared my throat, realizing I'd almost given away Margo's name. ". . . my friend told me about the rumors . . . well, I'm sure you can imagine what the number-one topic of conversation is among people connected to the school—Klea's death—so it's not like I'm seeking this out."

Detective Waraday nodded. "Right. Just be careful. The possibilities are narrowing. That's got to make the murderer nervous."

"Are you narrowing things down?"

"Oh, yes. We may have this resolved shortly.

About the note and the handwriting samples . . . I have a local consultant—a person I've used a few times. I called her in, and she took a look at the two samples before I sent everything off to the state crime lab. She's confident the same person wrote both the note you received and the gaming flow-chart."

"So Ms. McCormick did write the note that was in Livvy's take-home folder."

Detective Waraday nodded. "And probably threw the brick through the window of your van. I checked with the teachers in the rooms on either side of Ms. McCormick's room, asking them about the time period after you spoke to Ms. McCormick in the teachers' lounge. Ms. McCormick wasn't in her classroom when the bell rang for that next period. One of the teachers in the room next door to her classroom said she had to go over and tell Ms. McCormick's class to be quiet. Ms. McCormick arrived a minute or so later, slightly out of breath and with her hair windblown. Would she have known which car was yours?"

"Yes. All the teachers take turns monitoring drop-off and pickup. I'm sure she'd remember that I had a minivan. If she didn't remember exactly which one, she'd just have to look for the one with my kids' name tags hanging from the rearview mirror." The school required parents to hang laminated tags from their rearview mirror with the names of their students on it, to help keep the drop-off and pickup lines moving. "She didn't actually admit to throwing a brick at my van, but she told me she wanted me to back off."

"So now it's just a question of running down this

blackmail thing, seeing if there is any truth in that," Detective Waraday said.

"But Ms. McCormick didn't think it was Klea who was blackmailing her."

"Right. But she's lied before," Detective Waraday said simply.

He opened the door, and let me precede him out of the office. Mrs. Kirk was at the counter, speaking to a teacher. Marie's desk was finally empty and the basket of inter-office envelopes sat invitingly unattended, but I thought that Detective Waraday would definitely see it as stepping on his toes if I tried to get a look at them. I settled for pointing out the envelopes quietly to Detective Waraday while Mrs. Kirk finished up at the counter. When she turned around, Detective Waraday thanked her for the use of her office, then said, "I'd like to make sure that Ms. McCormick didn't put any of her other papers in your inter-office mail. It would be helpful if I could check that. I can have the search warrant extended to include the office. . . ."

Mrs. Kirk said, "No need," and gestured to Marie's desk and the stack of envelopes. "There they are. Help yourself. You can even use Marie's desk. She's at lunch."

Detective Waraday sat down and began to unwind the string on the top envelope. I left the office and spotted Livvy's class going into the lunchroom. She had late lunch today. She waved and slowed down. "Are you here to have lunch with me?"

I checked my watch and saw that I had some time. "If you'd like that," I said, and she nodded.

I wasn't sure what had brought on the sudden change of her being okay being seen with me, but I figured I'd enjoy it while I could. I ate a lunch of watery spaghetti and heard all about Livvy's science class and their last experiment of the year, building a suspension bridge for toy cars using clothespins, paper, and yarn. Her team had built the only bridge that hadn't collapsed. Watching her animated face and listening to her and her friends describe their design, often speaking over each other in their excitement, I wished the rest of the school year could be more like the end of the year.

The end of the year—when the standardized tests were over—was when the kids got to do all the fun stuff. Instead of studying for the standardized tests, why couldn't the kids do more hands-on activities like this throughout the year? Abby and I discussed this topic often—in fact, I knew not to get her started on it unless I had plenty of time to listen.

We turned in our trays, and I said good-bye to Livvy and her friends. "See you at the end-of-school party, Mrs. Avery," one of Livvy's friends called as I left. The parties were still a week away, but the kids were already looking forward to them.

I gathered up my laptop and left the school for the organizing appointment with my new client. I wished Marguerite-with-the-last-name-left-blank had given me more details. It would have been nice to have a better idea of what she was hoping for, but she hadn't filled in any of the additional fields except the one for how she heard about me. She'd marked *From a Friend*, but that was it, except for the address.

North Dawkins was an interesting mix of densely packed stands of pines, sprawling rural areas with small ranch homes on large lots, and pockets of suburbia with street grids and modern homes. Marguerite lived in one of the more rural areas, and I was glad I had used my GPS as I turned onto the unmarked and slightly rutted lane that ran through a thick copse of pines.

The trees fell away, and I drove into a small clearing with a pale yellow frame house with a connected carport, which was obviously a more modern addition, tacked on to the side. A little flowerbed of orange and yellow flowers ringed the foundation of the house and a pair of white iron chairs were positioned at the side of the clearing in the shade of the pines.

I followed the rutted tracks to the carport and parked behind a silver two-door sedan. It was another muggy day, and the air felt heavy and stagnant as I walked around to the back of the van to gather my tote bag with all my organizing paraphernalia. Except for the faint call of a bird, the clearing was absolutely quiet and still. Not even a gust of wind ruffled the tops of the pines.

I climbed the steps to the wooden porch and rang the bell next to the door, which had a metal screen door mounted in front of it. I waited, surveying the porch swing with its flowered cushion and the hanging pots of petunias. A bee buzzed lazily from one bright pink flower to another. After a few minutes, I rang the bell again, leaning a bit longer on the button, but I didn't hear any sounds from inside to indicate someone was on his or her way to the door. Despite the car parked to the side of the house, it felt like no one was home. I knocked on the frame of the metal screen door. It clattered, sounding extra loud in the stillness, and the bee bobbed off around the side of the house.

It certainly wasn't the first time someone had forgotten an appointment with me, but it *was* unusual that someone would not show up for an appointment they'd made only a few hours earlier. With sweat already beading along my hairline, I shifted over a few steps, taking a peek in the windows on either side of the front door. Through the window on the left, I could see a dining room table and a corner cabinet with antique plates displayed. Clearly, Marguerite didn't need my help organizing that spotless room. I moved to the other window and caught my breath.

A woman lay sprawled on a couch. My hands began to shake as I reached for my phone to call 911 even though I knew it was too late to help her. There could be no mistake—with her white skin and jaw hanging open, she was dead. But what was worse was that it wasn't some stranger named Marguerite. It was Peg.

Chapter Eighteen

I don't know how long it was until I heard the low rev of an engine. I looked up and saw a sheriff's car bump down the rutted road toward me. I'd dialed 911 and then called Detective Waraday and left him a message when he didn't answer.

My legs had felt unsteady, and I'd moved over to the porch steps. I had dropped down onto the lowest step and put my elbows on my knees and my head in my hands, fighting off the surge of nausea that hit me as I thought about Peg's slack and lifeless face.

The deputy parked the car near the steps. He came out of his vehicle slowly. He was a young man in his twenties with dark hair and eyes. RAMIREZ was printed on his name tag. "You made the emergency call?"

I nodded, grabbed the step's handrail, and levered myself up. "Yes. I had an appointment here at two—I'm a professional organizer—but no one answered the door, so I looked in the window and saw her. She's on the couch," I said, looking over my shoulder to the house.

"Name?"

"She's Peg Watson. She worked at the elementary school."

"No, your name."

"Oh. Ellie Avery."

He methodically took down my name and contact information, then told me to stay where I was and climbed the steps to the porch. He peered in both windows for a moment, then went to the front door. He tugged on the screen door's handle, and it opened with a screech. He raised his hand and knocked on the wooden front door, but it swung open at the first touch of his knuckles.

He turned back to me. "Did you go inside?"

"No. I just rang the bell and knocked on the screen."

"You didn't notice that the door wasn't closed?"

"No."

He was about to enter the house when the sound of another car engine filled the air. It was Detective Waraday. He parked beside the sheriff's car and crossed quickly to the steps. He must have received my message because he said, "It's Peg Watson? You're sure?"

I nodded. "I could see her through the window." He went up the steps, paused to glance in the front window, then moved to the front door. "William," Detective Waraday said in greeting.

The deputy nodded. "Detective. I haven't been in yet." He glanced over Detective Waraday's shoulder to me. "Witness states that she didn't enter the house." He waved at the door. "It opened when I knocked."

Detective Waraday removed some plastic gloves from his pocket and handed a pair to Deputy Ramirez. "I have a feeling we'll need these." He lifted his chin toward the open door as he worked his fingers into the gloves, indicating that the deputy should move into the house.

They were in the house for about five minutes before Detective Waraday came back outside and moved slowly down the steps, his face grim.

"You didn't enter the house?"

"No. I rang the bell and knocked. I didn't even know Peg lived here. I mean, she does live here, right?"

"Yes. This is her residence. Let's move over to those chairs in the shade." Detective Waraday pulled off the plastic gloves and stuffed them in his pocket, then wiped his forehead with the back of his hand. I realized that I was sweaty, too. Normally, I spent as little time as possible outdoors when it was hot and muggy, but the heat hadn't even registered. My shirt pressed damply against the skin between my shoulder blades, but I felt cold. The warm metal of the chair against the back of my legs actually felt soothing.

Detective Waraday sat down across from me and said, "Why are you here?"

I explained about the online appointment system and even showed him the message on my phone. "See, it says the client is Marguerite. Why would someone put in a fake name and then give this address?" I asked. I'd been pondering that question while I waited for the officers to come back out of the house.

"It wasn't a fake name," Detective Waraday said. "Not technically. Ms. Watson's full name is Marguerite Erica Watson. Peg is a nickname. When did you get that message?" Detective Waraday asked.

"This morning."

"Had Ms. Watson ever mentioned setting up an appointment with you?"

"No, never." I shook my head. "In fact, she hardly ever spoke to me . . . or anyone, really, that I saw. She was very, um, antisocial. Kept to herself."

He handed my phone back. "I'd like to have my tech people take a look at that message."

"Of course." I put my phone back in my pocket. "What happened?"

"Overdose," Detective Waraday said. "Prescription painkillers."

"That's—that's terrible."

"Unfortunately, we're seeing it more and more—accidental overdose, I mean," he said, his face bleak.

"I had no idea that she had any sort of . . . problem like that."

"Oh, not her. I meant in general we're seeing more and more deaths related to painkillers. No, I didn't see any evidence that she was an addict. It appears that she used painkillers that were prescribed to her several months ago by a reputable local dentist, probably after a dental surgery."

I frowned. "I do remember back around January, right after Christmas break, that Peg was extra . . . um, grumpy." I cleared my throat, feeling guilty about talking about Peg this way, but it was true and if it could help Detective Waraday narrow down the possibilities, then I should tell him.

He nodded, and I went on, "Anyway, it was during that time—right after school started in January—that Marie told me that Peg had her wisdom teeth removed."

"That makes sense," he said. "In cases with addicts, it is common to find meds from these fake 'pain centers' that have popped up. We're cracking down on them, and we've made a lot of progress, but there are still some out there. It doesn't seem that was what was going on here."

"Peg was sick earlier today," I said, "but I can't imagine she would have taken a prescription painkiller for a virus or flu or whatever it was that she had. At least, not intentionally. Is there a chance that she got—I don't know—mixed up or something and took the wrong medicine?"

"I'm afraid not." He reached inside his jacket and removed a white sheet of paper that was already encased in plastic. "Suicide," he said as he handed it to me.

I blinked and scanned the typed page with Peg's signature at the bottom. I read a few lines, then looked up at him. It wasn't long and began without a salutation: *I can't stand it anymore. It's too difficult. Now that everyone will know, I don't want to go on. It's true that I took money from people, but they were so dumb that they deserved it. If they hadn't been doing things they shouldn't, they wouldn't have had anything to worry about. Same thing with Klea. If she had minded her own business, I wouldn't have had to kill her.*

The typed signature was Peg's full name, Marguerite Erica Watson, and under her name was a date, today's date. I looked up at Detective Waraday. "She says she did it—that she killed Klea," I said, amazed.

He nodded. "And admits to the blackmail, too."

"How terrible," I said again, and handed the paper back to him. I felt even colder than I had before and wrapped my arms across my waist.

Detective Waraday's phone rang, and he took the call, saying only a few words and listening for long moments. I stared at the tall pines behind Detective Waraday, my thoughts swirling—Peg, dead. It was so shocking. And the things that were coming out— blackmail at the school, not to mention murder. I thought back to the morning that Klea had gone missing. While moms were squeezing into tiny chairs and nibbling muffins with their kids, Peg had killed Klea. Something—some stray thought—flitted in and out of my mind, but before I could grasp it, it disappeared. It had been there, something that seemed important, too. But now it was gone like a wisp of ground fog that appeared in the morning, then vanished as soon as the sun hit it.

Detective Waraday hung up and shifted back to me. "Would you say Ms. Watson had been depressed or frightened lately?"

"I suppose I should say that I didn't know her well enough to answer that question, but as little as I knew her, I would say no. She didn't seem at all like someone who would commit suicide." I paused, thinking over my interactions, then said, "But Marie is who you should talk to about that." I sat forward suddenly. "Why would someone make an appointment to organize their closets, then kill themselves later that day? That just seems odd."

"I agree, but if she made the appointment, then later realized the net was closing around her . . . perhaps she decided she'd rather die than face the consequences of her actions. Could she have overheard Ms. McCormick's accusations?"

"It's possible she could have," I said. "Anyone could have been in the hallway and heard us, but I didn't see Peg. But then Peg got sick and left the school. Could it be . . . ? You're sure her death *was* an overdose, not something else? I wonder if she had some sort of medical condition. . . ."

"I'm not the medical examiner, but that will all be sorted out. There will be an autopsy. But you're forgetting about the suicide note."

"Yes. Right," I said, rubbing my forehead. "So many notes lately—Klea's note, blackmail notes to teachers and parents, and now a suicide note."

"I'm glad that's resolved," Mitch said later that night when I told him what happened with Peg. I could hear the relief in his tone. "I mean, it's a horrible situation for everyone involved, but selfishly I'm glad it's over. Especially since there's no chance of this exercise ending early. The weather's cleared and everything is back on schedule."

"Oh, that's too bad." I curled my legs under me and settled against the headboard. The kids were tucked in bed, and I was in our bedroom with the door closed. I hadn't mentioned what had happened with Peg to the kids. I'd been able to make it back to the school in time to pick them up. Then I'd been happy to throw myself into the normal afterschool routine of snacks, homework, and cooking dinner. I'd debated talking to the kids about Peg later that night, but in the end, I'd decided that I would wait. The kids hadn't had any interactions with Peg, and if they knew her at all, it would only be as one of the "office ladies." I would see how the school handled it and go from there.

I adjusted one of the pillows behind my neck and settled down to catch up with Mitch. He had a gap in his schedule, and we hadn't been able to have an uninterrupted call for a few days. "I was hoping you'd be home early."

"Me too, but it doesn't look like it's going to happen. At least now I don't have to worry about you."

"You never worry," I said. "That's my department."

"I agree, you are the chief worrier in our family, but I have my moments, too. You're not one to let things go, and I know that this thing with Klea was weighing on you."

"Yeah, about that . . ." I cleared my throat.

"Ellie," Mitch said warningly.

"What?"

His sigh came through the phone line loud and clear. "I know that tone. You think something about Peg's death is off—that's it, isn't it?"

"Well, yes. I do. Several things, actually."

"I suppose you've made a list," Mitch said.

"I have." I reached for the notepad on the nightstand.

"I knew it," Mitch said, half exasperated, half joking.

"It's everything that is weird or doesn't fit."

"I don't know if you can make suicide 'fit,'" Mitch said, his tone serious again.

"I know, but these things . . . they're just strange. I mean, who makes an appointment with an organizer, then kills herself?"

"Okay, I wouldn't think someone would do that either, but you can't know what's going on in someone's head. Or maybe she made the appointment, then realized she was about to be found out. Once she knew that, nothing else mattered."

"That's what Detective Waraday said," I admitted. "But I still think it doesn't fit. And then there was her note. It was typed, which seems a little . . . formal . . . to me."

"Maybe she did most things on the computer. People don't write longhand anymore, not really."

"I know, but if that's the case, why wouldn't she just . . . I don't know . . . send a text? That's more in keeping with how we communicate with each other now. It seems odd that she'd type up a suicide note and print it out, then sign it. And the tone—I can't remember it word for word, but it wasn't sad or morose. It was almost . . . defiant," I said, finally hitting on the word I was searching for.

"So she saw her suicide as a final in-your-face gesture. There's no rule that suicidal people must be depressed," Mitch said. I could tell from his thoughtful tone of voice that he was arguing the other side of my points, but was giving serious consideration to what I was saying. "Although, taken all together, I can see what you're saying. I hope you're wrong about all this. I mean, I hope that Peg's death is exactly what it seems. You haven't talked to anyone else about this?" he asked sharply.

"Only Detective Waraday."

"And what did he say?"

"Not much. He raised some of the points that you did."

"Keep all this to yourself, okay? If you're right . . ."

I felt my insides twist. "Then the murderer is still out there."

Organizing Tips for PTA Moms

<u>How to find your volunteering sweet spot</u>

Here are some questions to consider and some volunteer ideas:

Do I like this type of activity?

If you don't enjoy being outdoors, then Field Day is probably not the best place to volunteer. If you love to read, the library is an obvious starting place. If you're crafty, then planning holiday party crafts or volunteering on art days could be just the thing for you.

Do I like to be front and center or behind the scenes?

A fundraising coordinator needs a specific set of skills (comfort with public speaking, to parents and students; vision casting; and the ability to get everyone excited about the campaign), while volunteers who set up or tear down for plays or events like the book fair enjoy working behind the scenes.

Do I like to work in a group or alone?

Managing the phone or text chain requires someone who likes detailed work, is methodical, and likes to work alone. Someone who loves working cooperatively would be great at planning parties, dances, or teacher appreciation events, which require the input and coordination of many people.

Do I like to have a fixed schedule or play it by ear?

If you like to know ahead of time what your schedule is, then you'll probably enjoy volunteering in your child's classroom on a fixed day of the week. If you hate feeling pinned down by a schedule, volunteer to help when your school is shorthanded or when someone gets sick.

Chapter Nineteen

When I walked into the school on Friday before lunch, I sensed a change in the atmosphere. The first person I saw was Vaughn, striding across the lobby, whistling as he pushed a rolling trash can. He nodded to me. Two teachers had paused on the side of the lobby to chat for a moment. As I passed them, I caught a few words.

". . . so horrible to know it was Peg, but I'm so glad. That's terrible to say, but it means it's over."

The other teacher nodded. "I know exactly what you mean. We can put it all behind us now. No more looking at everyone and wondering, *Was it you?*"

I went in the office and saw that Detective Waraday was at Peg's desk. He nodded and said, "Mrs. Avery," in greeting, and I said hello. Two of Peg's desk drawers hung open as he methodically picked up sheets of paper and examined them. The computer was missing, and I assumed it had been taken so that the tech-savvy investigators could search the files.

Mrs. Kirk was walking briskly toward the door, but she paused by the sign-in computer as I waited for my name tag to print. "Good afternoon, Mrs. Avery. Such a shame about Peg, and I'm terribly sorry that you were the one to find her."

"It was distressing," I said, feeling that the word was inadequate, but Mrs. Kirk just nodded.

"Of course it would be." She frowned. "The end of the year has been quite difficult, but at least we can start over with a fresh slate next fall." She glanced at Detective Waraday, who had moved on to another drawer at Peg's desk. "Thank goodness it wasn't during the middle of the school year. By the time August rolls around, most people will have forgotten what happened." She patted my arm. "Again, I'm sorry you were involved, but we can all rest easy now."

She left, and I glanced at Marie as I stuck the name tag to my shirt. She picked up a stack of papers and came around the counter. "How are you holding up?"

"Okay, I guess. I didn't really know Peg."

"Apparently none of us did." She looked through the door into the lobby and lowered her voice. "Can you believe it? Peg!"

"No," I said quite truthfully. I felt Detective Waraday look at me sharply so I didn't say anything else.

"It's made a complete difference in the atmosphere here at the school," Marie said. "Can you feel it?"

I nodded, and she added, "I didn't realize how on edge we all were, but now that we know . . . who . . . er, I mean, what happened . . . it's like everyone has relaxed."

Through the office's windows I saw a van with the words SOUTHERN BARBECUE on it arrive. It lumbered around the drop-off line circle and came to a stop at the school's front doors. "There's lunch. I have to go."

Today was the last day of Teacher Appreciation Week, and for a finale, we had a catered barbecue buffet scheduled. I met the two restaurant employees, a young man and a young woman who looked to be about college age, at the door and guided them through the sign-in process and then showed them the teachers' lounge. I had them set up the food on the counter that ran across the back of the room. They'd barely finished putting the last pan of coleslaw out when a couple of teachers poked their heads in the room. "Is it ready? It smells delicious." I waved them in, told them to help themselves, then walked the restaurant employees back to the office so they could check out.

"Will you return this afternoon for the containers?" I asked.

"No. It's all disposable," the young woman said as I walked them out the main doors. "Hopefully, there will be some leftovers for you to take home."

"I doubt that." When we had come out of the main office, the line of teachers waiting to dip a plate of food and return to either the cafeteria or their classrooms had already been out the door of the teachers' lounge.

I was on my way back inside when a car horn tooted. Gabrielle waved from the driver's seat of a compact SUV. I saw that she had upgraded her advertising. She used to have metallic signs attached to each side that read GET ORGANIZED WITH GABRIELLE, but those were gone. Now the whole car had been encased—wrapped, I think it's called—so that the same slogan marched from the front to the rear bumper in giant font. Her website and phone number were also listed. Near the back of the car, a four-foot image of Gabrielle's face smiled out at me.

The catering van pulled away, and Gabrielle punched the gas. Her car surged forward and stopped by the main door; then she hit the brakes and hopped out.

"Wow." I pointed to the side of her car. "Nice advertising. How's that working out?"

Her long hair bouncing against her shoulders, she came around to the passenger side of the car and studied the ad on her car. She was again in a nice tailored suit and heels. Today's combination was a purple jacket with a black skirt. "Great! I've only had it for a couple of days and already gotten three calls because of it."

"Good for you," I said, as I contemplated doing something similar. I was always looking for ways to grow my business, but after thinking about it for a second, I decided that the approach wasn't quite me. So far, my best advertising had been satisfied clients who told their friends. A discount coupon for people to give their friends seemed like a better idea for my business.

"I wanted to catch you before you went inside." Gabrielle took a few steps in her high heels, but only moved to the edge of the sidewalk and stopped. "You heard about Peg?" she asked.

"Yes," I said, leaving out the fact that I'd been the person to find her. I was sure Gabrielle would be upset she hadn't been my first phone call.

"Can you believe it? I always thought she was a

sneaky one, but my, I never expected that. When I heard the rumors about what was going on here at the school, I never would have put it together with her."

"We didn't get to talk about that message you left for me," I said.

"I know. I've been so busy. Fitzgerald called me."

"Oh," I said, recognizing that she wasn't talking about a person, but a company. Fitzgerald was one of the big paper companies in the area. They had a paper-manufacturing plant in North Dawkins, and their name came up frequently as a sponsor of various local events like the North Dawkins Fourth of July fireworks display.

"They want my input on a couple of changes they are considering." Gabrielle looked pleased. "I've just come from their main offices, in fact."

"That's quite a coup," I said, and for once, I didn't envy her. I didn't have a great desire to do freelance corporate work, especially if I had to dress in hose and heels on the job.

"I'm enjoying it," she said, then lowered her voice. "Anyway, I know you're up on all the news. Detective Waraday called me the other day and had all sorts of questions about the rumor I'd heard. I wasn't able to tell him much, but I did pass along what I knew—that someone was making money off people who had been naughty. But when I asked him what was going on, he wouldn't tell me anything."

"Well, he was probably still investigating," I said, not quite believing that I was defending Detective Waraday.

She made an impatient movement with her hand. "Still. He could have given me a *hint*."

"I think that might be frowned on in the sheriff's office." She looked like she was about to protest again, so I hurried on and said, "Anyway, it appears to be all sorted out now." I didn't wholeheartedly agree with that statement, but I didn't want Gabrielle insisting that we had more to investigate.

"Yes, it is good that it's all straightened out. I doubt that the executives at Fitzgerald would have called me in if they knew I was involved in what happened here." She tilted her head toward the school building. "No matter how remotely I was involved, it would be a black mark. They're such nervous nellies, these corporate bigwigs."

Her phone buzzed with a text and she checked the display. "Oh, this is Fitzgerald." She read the message and quickly sent one back. "They want me to drop by the office to clarify a few points, which is a good sign. I better get out there right away." She held the folder in her hand out toward me. "Ellie, will you be a dear and drop this with Mrs. Kirk? Tell her I'll be by tomorrow to explain everything."

"Um, sure." I took the folder. Her SUV with the ad on the side was out of the parking lot before I made it to the school doors. I dropped off the folder with Mrs. Kirk, who opened it, read the title, then looked from it to me.

"Mrs. Matheson's recommendation for the digital organization class for the teachers, I assume?" Mrs. Kirk said, eyebrows raised.

"I'm not sure."

A shade of disapproval came into Mrs. Kirk's

voice. "I thought she wanted to go over this with me. She was very insistent."

"She had to leave unexpectedly. I'm sure she'll contact you."

Mrs. Kirk made a harrumphing sound as I left her office. I went back to the teachers' lounge and found that about half of the food was gone, and the teachers for late lunch were lining up, their plates ready. I was glad they were enjoying the food, and I was also happy it was the last day I'd have to monitor the food. Now, all I had to get through were the end-of-school parties next week and another school year would be over. Mrs. Harris, plate in hand, came over to me. "This has been wonderful, Ellie. Thanks for coordinating the food."

"You're welcome. We do appreciate everything you all do for the students."

"Well, this is an excellent way to show it," Mrs. Harris said, pointing at her plate with her fork. "I'm glad I caught you," she said. "I thought you'd be interested to know that this will be my last year here at the school."

"Really? Oh, I'm . . . happy for you . . . ?" I asked with an uncertain grin.

She laughed. "Thank you. Yes, I am looking forward to it. I can still volunteer at the school. They always need help—volunteers don't have to be parents—but I can dedicate more time to . . . other things. I'm considering trying something new . . . more mainstream, you might say."

I fell into step beside her as we left the teachers' lounge. "Well, good luck with it," I said, glancing at her out of the corner of my eye, my thoughts about

Klea's list coming back to me, as well as my realization that Mrs. Harris's alibi wasn't as solid as I'd first
thought. But she looked so frail and had such a kind
disposition. Could she really be a murderer? Everyone seemed to think that Peg's death had wrapped
up the investigation, but there were too many questions around Peg's suicide and that had me second-
guessing everything. At first glance, Mrs. Harris didn't
look like a murderer, but she was also very good at
hiding a part of her life from nearly everyone at
school. Could she be hiding something else?

As we crossed the lobby, a strange swishing sound
interrupted my thoughts, but before I could look
for the source, Vaughn hurried by, his heavy tread
thudding loudly. With a mop and bucket in hand,
he nearly ran me over. "Sorry," he called over his
shoulder.

I'd never seen him move that fast. He slowed
down as he approached the records room next to
the main office and stepped more carefully as he
paused to prop the mop and bucket against the
wall. That was when I saw water rushing out from
the gap under the door to the records room. As he
flicked through his key ring, the water coursed over
his shoes and splashed at the ankles of his pants. He
inserted the key and opened the door. A flood of
water rushed out, soaking him to the knees, and
spread out across the lobby floor like an incoming
tide.

Organizing Tips for PTA Moms

<u>Social Media Ideas for Schools</u>

Facebook
Facebook is a great platform for posting announcements and reminders, and for providing a platform for parents to connect.

Twitter
The short format of Twitter works great for announcements and reminders for events, as well as for notifications of school closures or changes in schedules.

Pinterest
Room moms can create a pinboard for party planning and invite other moms to participate in pinning ideas for food, decorations, and games.

School clubs can create pinboards for upcoming activities to gather ideas and inspiration.

A general pinboard for the school could feature events and activities, but check with the school district for their photography policy before posting images of students.

Chapter Twenty

The water slid across the floor toward me. I automatically stepped back, but it reached me and sloshed over the tops of my boat shoes. Mrs. Harris said, "Oh my," as the water soaked into her sensible rubber-soled flats. A few teachers came out of the teachers' lounge, saw the flood of water, and screeched as the water pushed toward them.

Now that Vaughn had opened the door and released the water that had been pent up in the records room, the water flowing out of the door was lower. He stepped into the room, and the water came up to his shins. It coursed down the hallway, reaching some of the classrooms. Exclamations and the scrapes of chairs sounded from the nearby classrooms.

Marie and Mrs. Kirk emerged from the main office. Mrs. Kirk took one look around and said, "I'll call maintenance. Thank goodness we have tile floors and not carpet."

Vaughn came splashing out of the records room. "It's a broken pipe in the ceiling. The sprinkler system. I'll turn off the main." He strode quickly away, water splashing with each step as he hurried across the lobby to the doors that opened to the back field. Water continued to flow out the door of the records room, but as it spread through the hallways, the level of it went down.

Marie still stood in the door of the office, an appalled look on her face. "This is awful. We should get some towels . . . or something," she said.

Mrs. Kirk reappeared. "No, that won't do us any good. There's too much water already. Marie, help me open the main doors. Let's get as much of this water outside as possible." Mrs. Kirk sloshed through the water to the main doors. Marie followed her, and they opened the row of doors.

Mrs. Harris and I moved to the doors at the other side of the lobby, the ones that opened to the back field, and propped them open as well. Vaughn, holding a wrench, was on his way back. The water was streaming out the doors and rushing across the blacktop, soaking the grass. Vaughn shook his head as he hurried by. "This is going to be a mess."

He was right. Vaughn was able to get the water turned off, but it took an hour to clear the standing water out of the school. I pitched in and helped, along with several other teachers who were on their planning period and some parent volunteers who happened to be in the building at that time. We used mops and brooms to shift the standing water out the doors, and we were all soaked to the knees by the time the worst of it was cleared out. The school district's maintenance people arrived in a van and went to work repairing the pipe in the records room.

I gave the still damp floor in the hallway a final swipe with a push broom and returned to the lobby. I paused beside Marie, who stood in the doorway of the records room. "Such a shame," she said. "All that paper, ruined."

Two maintenance men were on ladders, working on the pipes overhead. The ceiling tiles had been soaked. Some had fallen to the floor, and others hung limply in their metal grids, looking more like soaked towels than acoustical tiles. The leak had been at the back of the room, but because the door had been closed and trapped most of the water, it had backed up and soaked into the lower drawers of the filing cabinets.

"I opened a couple of the files to see how bad it is," Marie said, nodding toward several of the lowest file drawers, which had been pulled out. The file folders and papers were waterlogged, the pages wavy and the ink smeared. "They'll have to be destroyed . . . somehow," Marie said. "These are confidential files. We can't just throw them away. They have Social Security numbers and test scores on them."

"That will be difficult," I said. "But I'm sure there are companies that handle that sort of thing. Maybe the people who repair the water damage will have some suggestions, or I can ask around."

Before Marie could answer, Mrs. Kirk appeared behind our shoulders. "A team is on the way. We should have fans set up, and the tile floors dry before the end of the day." Mrs. Kirk had made an announcement that the teachers should keep the students in their current classrooms until the water was cleaned up.

One of the repairmen clattered down the ladder. "That should do it," he said. "We'll turn on the water and test it, make sure everything is okay."

"Excellent. Thank you for arriving so quickly." Mrs. Kirk looked around and spotted Vaughn, who was collecting mops and brooms from the volunteers. She motioned him over. "Vaughn will show you the water main."

The other repairman stayed on the ladder, to monitor for leaks when the water was turned back on, I imagined.

"Could you tell us what happened?" Mrs. Kirk asked. "What caused the leak?"

The repairman had been about to follow Vaughn, but he stopped and pulled a short section of pipe from the pocket of the cargo pants he wore. He pointed at the pipe with a grimy finger. "See that? That's a pinhole leak. It happens with these copper pipes sometimes. Corrosion," he said with a shrug. "These older buildings all have it. I wouldn't be surprised to see more instances of this. The district really should look into replacing it all, but—you know—the cost." He pointed to the area where they had been working. "We replaced the whole section in the ceiling to be on the safe side. You shouldn't have any more problems—well, at least not from that pipe," he said, and left to go with Vaughn.

Mrs. Kirk put her hands on her hips and surveyed the damage. "And this was all to be digitized this summer," she said. "I suppose the only good thing about this situation is that they are old files."

"Oh, they weren't current information?" I asked,

thinking that was one bit of positive news in the midst of the mess.

"No," Mrs. Kirk said. "We've used digital records for years now." She tapped the card label on one of the filing cabinet drawers near her. The writing on the label was runny, but I could still read it. *A-H, 1989.* "These files were from years ago when we used a paper system—seems like ancient times, doesn't it? Well, all except for yours, Marie," Mrs. Kirk said as she gestured at a stack of banker boxes along the floor. "They'll have to be disposed of now."

"I'll make some calls and see that it's done," Marie said.

Vaughn, his head poking in the open doorway at the back of the lobby, called for Mrs. Kirk, and she strode away.

Marie reached down and picked up some sodden papers that were plastered to the floor. "If only I hadn't moved these boxes in here yesterday." She held the dripping sheet of paper away from her body. "All that work . . . just gone." She smiled bleakly. "If I'd known all my files were going to be destroyed, I wouldn't have worked so hard to get everything organized before I retired."

"That's right. I forgot, you only have a few days left."

Marie tossed the limp paper into a trash can. "All that work, for nothing." She wiped her damp fingers on her skirt. "I don't know why I'm so upset. I mean, files of fundraising activities really are trivial when you compare it to student grades."

"Yes, but it was your work. No one likes to see something they've put time into damaged." She murmured an agreement, but was moving from box to box, lifting lids and shaking her head. "No, they're all a complete loss."

"Have you had anything to eat? No? Then come have a plate of food from the teachers' lounge," I said, thinking that getting her out of the records room would do more than anything else to cheer her up. She nodded and headed in that direction. I followed her, and was relieved to see that there was still some food. I left her microwaving a plate and went back to the lobby.

I intended to go home and change out of my wet shoes, but as my shoes squished across the lobby, I saw a petite woman hesitating in the open doors as she brushed her bangs from her eyes while she scanned the damp floor and the disarray of mops and brooms propped around the walls. I studied her oval face with its upturned nose and blue eyes, trying to place her. Was she a parent? A substitute teacher?

Since she looked like she wasn't sure where to go, I said, "Can I help you?"

"Ah—yes. I'm Jane Guthrie, Klea Burris's sister."

"Oh," I said, and immediately realized she looked slightly familiar because her build was similar to Klea's—she was slender and small, and she had the same upturned nose that Klea had had. "I'm so sorry about Klea," I said. "We all are."

"Thank you. It's still—I can't quite take it in. But at least now we know who did it and can move on." She blinked and swallowed. "I stopped by because the principal—Mrs. Kirk, I think it was—contacted me and said she had some of Klea's belongings, but"—her gaze ranged around the chaotic scene of the lobby—"this doesn't look like a good time."

"There was a water leak," I said. "It's a little crazy right now."

"No problem," Jane said. "I'm here for a few days, sorting through Klea's belongings and getting her house in order so it can go on the market. I can come back next week."

"That would probably be best. I'm Ellie Avery, by the way."

"Nice to meet you," she said, then paused. "That name—you're the organizer, aren't you?"

"Yes," I said.

"Klea mentioned you. She said that you came to her house and gave her some suggestions. I think she wanted to hire you, but money was tight and then—" She cleared her throat and hurried on. "Anyway, she said you were very helpful."

"I'm glad."

"In fact, I intended to get your phone number from the school, if they would give it to me," she said with a small smile. "Or look for you online. I have a few things I need help with and thought you might be just the person I need."

Jane brushed her bangs off her forehead again. It was a gesture that I remembered Klea making, too. On that day Klea and I had hauled the tables up to the stage when we'd finished, she'd swept her hair off her forehead and said, "Well, that was my workout for the day." We'd laughed together, and I'd said, "Who would have thought that volunteering at the school was as good as going to the gym?"

A wave of sadness swept over me. It was still hard to believe that Klea was gone. "What kind of help are you looking for?" I asked, refocusing on Jane.

"I've been sorting through her belongings, deciding what to keep and what to give away. I should be done with that soon, but next week I have to go back to Missouri—that's where I live—so I can't be here on Friday, when I have several pickups scheduled. That was the first day I could get on their schedules. A charity is coming to pick up the boxes of belongings I'm giving away, and I have a consignment shop scheduled to pick up the furniture. Could you be there to let them in and make sure they only take what I have marked for them?"

"Yes, of course. I can do that," I said, relieved that it was a simple job. If she wanted help cleaning out every room in Klea's house, there was no way I could get it done before school was out, and my time was limited in the summer.

"I'll pay your usual rate," she said.

"There's no need for that. I'd be happy to do it, no charge."

"Oh, it's not a problem—"

"No, please let me do this. I'd like to," I said.

After a moment, she nodded. "Thank you."

She suggested we meet during the weekend so she could show me which items should be picked up, and then we exchanged phone numbers. She was about to leave when I said, "There's something I was wondering about. . . . I may not have heard because I'm in and out of the school," I said, mentally amending that phrase in my mind—*except for this week*—because I'd been at the school more than I'd been home, it seemed. "But I didn't hear about a memorial service or funeral for Klea. Will it be in Missouri? I know the teachers and staff here will want to know what is planned."

Jane looked away for a second, gazing across the busy lobby. "There will be a small memorial service in Missouri. Klea wanted to be cremated. That's already been taken care of. I'm taking her ashes home next week."

"Oh, I see," I said quickly.

Jane sighed. "It seemed better this way. I know it's selfish of me, but if we planned something here, then Ace would show up, and I absolutely will not have him contaminating anything to do with Klea's memory. It's so unfair," she said, her tone becoming heated, "that she finally got away from him, and then she was killed. I'd wanted her to leave him for years, even offered to help her move back to Missouri. She could have lived with us until she got on her feet, but . . ." Her voice changed, and the vigor and passion she spoke with drained out of her as she said, "She wouldn't do it."

Jane shook her head. "She had to do it in her own way. I never could talk her into anything, not even when it was good for her," she said with a weak smile. "Excuse me, I should go." She hurried away, and I knew she was leaving before she cried. I could see the tears glistening in her eyes before she turned away.

I watched her walk along the school's car circle lane. Then she turned and walked beside the chain-link fence. About halfway down the block, she crossed the street to Klea's Craftsman, climbed the steps, and went in the front door.

The weekend was actually fairly quiet, except for a soccer game and a trip to the North Dawkins library for Livvy to pick up new books. The school library had closed. All books had to be returned, so she was in book-withdrawal. We returned from the library with a tower of books for each of the kids, which at first glance would seem to keep them in books all summer, but I knew it would only be a week or two before Livvy would want to make another trip because she had "read all the good ones."

It was late Sunday evening when I met Jane at Klea's house. Jane walked me through the rooms, which looked so different with all their contents stowed in boxes. She had marked everything clearly, and I didn't have any questions. Jane gave me the keys to the front door dead bolts, then said, "If you could do me one more favor, I'd appreciate it." I could tell she'd been working hard for several days, packing and cleaning. She looked exhausted and leaned against the doorframe.

I paused on the top porch step. "Sure. What do you need?"

"Well, I thought I could stay here until Tuesday, but I have to leave tomorrow. I intended to go over to the school on Monday to pick up Klea's things, but I have to be at the airport in Atlanta at eight tomorrow morning, so there's no way . . ."

"I can pick them up from Mrs. Kirk. I'll bring them back here."

"Oh, that would be a relief. Mrs. Kirk said it's nothing really significant—just some odds and ends—but they were Klea's, and I'm afraid that if something comes up at home, I may not get back here before the school closes for the summer."

"No worries. I'll take care of it." I said good-bye

to her, then got in the van to get back to the kids, who were at home.

I'd called in their favorite babysitter, but I knew it wouldn't be long before I wouldn't need her services. Livvy would soon be a teenager—teenager!—and I knew that soon she would be perfectly capable of holding down the fort while I was gone. I'd even had a few moms, who were looking for sitters, ask me if she was available. I had said we weren't quite ready for that, and Livvy had countered that *she* was ready. "You may be ready for it, but I don't think I am," I'd said with a laugh, and since Livvy was more interested in playing soccer, reading, and spending time with her friends than watching other people's kids, that had been the end of the that conversation.

I glanced at the school as I crept by with my foot on the brake. Even though school wasn't in session, the school speed zone was still in effect. The school had a forlorn, deserted air with the empty parking lot and all the windows dark.

Abby had told me that Mrs. Kirk had sent the teachers an alert, letting them know that a water remediation crew would work all day Saturday at the school to repair the worst of the water damage so that school could continue until the end of the year. Then, in the summer, any large-scale repairs that needed to be done would be undertaken. Fortunately, there wasn't a lot they had to do.

"That's the beauty of tile floors and cinderblock walls," Abby had quipped. "No wood or drywall to replace."

They must have finished the temporary repairs

because the school was quiet. The sun was already low in the sky, casting long shadows from the tall pines that filled the front lawns of the houses across from the school. The patches of shade stretched all the way across the parking lot and engulfed the school, the surrounding fields, and the belt of trees behind the school. I shivered, thinking of Klea's body in the wooded area. I didn't think I'd ever want to walk through that shortcut again.

As I came even with the front of the school, I thought I saw a flash of light in one of the office windows, but it must have been a reflection of another car's headlights because when I looked again, all the windows were black squares.

The next morning, the atmosphere of the school was completely different as I pulled into the drop-off line on Monday at fifteen minutes after eight. Kids, some with parent escorts, others on their own, walked toward the school. Buses inched through the traffic, then lumbered into the bus circle and disgorged kids. Cars circulated through the drop-off circle like parts on a conveyer belt that moved in fits and starts.

The kids and I were cutting it close on time today—it had been one of the those mornings when nothing goes right—so I completed the circuit, dropping the kids at the main doors so they could make it to class before the bell. Then, knowing that if I deviated from the pattern I would gum up the works of the car circle, to say nothing of making parents, teachers, and staff angry with me, I exited the parking lot. Then I returned, but this time, instead of going to the car circle drop-off line, I turned into a parking slot and went into the school, after giving Mrs. Kirk a wave on the way in. She barely acknowledged my greeting, and looked rather harried, but I didn't feel snubbed. I was sure her mind was on making sure that drop-off ran smoothly.

Since I'd promised Jane that I would pick up Klea's belongings, I wanted to do it first thing so that I didn't forget it. I hurried in the main doors along with the last of the late-arriving kids, surprised to see a square of plywood covering a section of one of the main doors.

I crossed the lobby and walked to the office. Even though Mrs. Kirk was busy outside, I was sure that Marie would know where to find Klea's things. I was surprised to see that the door to the office was closed. It was never closed.

I turned the handle and stepped inside, then stopped dead in my tracks. The office looked like a tornado had hit it.

Chapter Twenty-one

"**A**nd I thought my day had started badly," I said, shaking my head over the destruction.

Shattered glass, bits of plastic, and paper covered the floor of the office. The desks had been flipped on their sides and chairs upended. The wooden bench was overturned, and a spray-paint scrawl of curses covered the rich dark wood. In the middle of it all stood Marie, her hands limp by her sides, and expression of disbelief on her face. She saw me and started. "Did I not lock that door?" She crunched toward me and pushed the door closed. "I thought I'd locked it," she said distractedly. She flipped the lock into place. "We can't have the students in here— all this glass and . . . and mess." She picked up an inbox tray from the floor and set it on the counter. It clattered against fragments of plastic and metal scattered over the counter.

"This is awful," I said as the full amount of destruction sank in. The glass window in the wall next to Mrs. Kirk's office had been shattered. The computer monitors were gaping holes and a couple of computer towers looked as if someone had taken a mallet to them.

"Yes. Shocking, isn't it?" Marie said. "I feel like I'm in a daze." She reached down and picked up something else, one of the wooden cubes with numbers carved into the sides that was part of her desk calendar. "I'll probably never find the other one," she said. "If it wasn't against school policy, I think I might bring my pistol to school," she said.

I must have looked surprised because she said, "It's been one thing on top of the other, you know? Klea and Peg, and now this. I'm beginning to wonder if it will stop."

"I can understand that," I said. "I was just surprised that you own a gun. You don't seem to be the type, you know."

"I bought it after Heath died. I didn't like being alone in the house at night. It was silly, I know. I mean, I live in a great neighborhood, just a few blocks from here, in fact. But it was difficult after Heath passed away, especially at night, so I got a gun and went to classes to learn how to use it and everything." She looked less skittish and more like her normal, cheerful self, but then the door handle rattled, and she jumped as a knock sounded.

Marie unlocked the door, opened it a crack, then stepped back so that Vaughn could maneuver through the door with a broom and a rolling trash can. He wore a pair of thick work gloves and also carried a dustpan. It was going to take more than a trash can to clear up this mess, but they had to start somewhere, I supposed.

Marie locked the door behind him, and Vaughn set to work as he cleared a trail from the door to the counter.

"Marie," I said. "I hate to be a bother right now, but I only ran in to pick up Klea's things. Her sister was going to come in and get them today, but she had to leave town early and asked me to do it. Do you know if they were in here?" I asked, scanning the scattered pieces of office equipment and reams of paper that covered the floor. I was already dreading calling Jane and telling her that it might be a while—maybe never—before Klea's things were found.

My question seemed to give Marie a purpose and help her focus. She put a finger to her lips and turned in a circle. "Yes, Mrs. Kirk mentioned that the sister would be coming by to pick up Klea's things. Now, where were they? Mrs. Kirk had them in her office for a few days, but—ah!—you're in luck, or I guess her sister is in luck." Marie focused on a cardboard box on the back counter near the coffeepot. "Mrs. Kirk moved it out here yesterday." Marie crunched across the floor and retrieved a cardboard box. "Somehow this escaped the destruction," she said. The flaps of the box were open, and as she handed it to me I could see it only held a few items—two coffee mugs, some paperback books, a calendar made of wooden cubes, and a sweater. That weird half-formed thought . . . or perhaps impression was a better word . . . threaded through my mind, but I couldn't quite grasp it.

I realized Marie was speaking, and I blinked, refocusing on her. "I'm sorry. What did you say?"

Marie waved her hand around the room. "Whoever did this probably didn't think this"—she tapped the box—"was worth destroying . . . unlike the computers."

"It's so sad that someone would do this," I said, looking around the office. "It happened during the weekend?"

"It must have been either late Saturday night or sometime during Sunday. The crew cleaning up the water damage was here all day Saturday."

Vaughn dumped a pile of debris into the trash can. "Everything was fine when they left. I made sure before I locked up."

"And they got in the main doors?" I asked, thinking of the square of plywood that I'd noticed on my way in. Had it been broken on Sunday night when I'd driven by the school? I didn't remember it, but would I have noticed it with all the lights off inside the school and the windows dark?

Vaughn nodded. "Yep. I got that cleaned up. First thing I did today. Couldn't have the kids walking through broken glass this morning."

"And it didn't set off an alarm, or anything?"

Vaughn snorted. "No alarms in a building this old. Only the district's newer buildings have alarms." He leaned on his broom. "But with all this computer equipment, they should have alarms in all the buildings. All the schools have computers now." He straightened and poked at the remains of a shattered computer monitor with the bristles of the broom. "Someone could have had a nice haul of computers—if they'd wanted to steal things instead of destroying them."

"And nothing else was vandalized?" I asked.

"No," Marie said. "Only the office." She ran her hand over her upper arms as if she were cold. "It seems whoever did this hates the school . . . or someone who works here."

I set the box by the door and picked up one of the gnome figurines that usually decorated Marie's desk. The tip of the figurine's red hat had broken off. "I can help you for a bit," I said as I put the gnome on the counter.

"You don't have to do that," Marie said, and there was something guarded in her tone. It appeared the wariness and distrust that had been almost palpable before Peg's death was back.

Vaughn waved me off, too. "No, you don't have any gloves or the right kind of shoes," he said, pointing at my ballet flats. Marie unlocked the door for me, and I picked up the box, but before I could step out the door, Mrs. Kirk appeared and pushed inside. She looked surprised to see me in the office, but her gaze rested on me for only a second, then swept around the room.

She put a hand to her temple and rubbed. "It's utter destruction," she said in a frazzled tone of voice. "What else can go wrong? This is absolutely the worst end of a school year we've ever had."

I had never seen her look so upset. Every time I saw her, she was calm and in control. She was a steadying influence on the students. Her high expectations made the unruliest kids curb their behavior while her firm belief that her students were bright and smart and could do anything inspired and encouraged them.

The tardy bell rang, and it seemed to snap Mrs. Kirk out of her gloomy state. She drew in a deep breath and made her way carefully through the wreckage to her office. "At least the PA system wasn't destroyed. I'll make the usual morning announcements. Perhaps we can be back to normal—or some sort of version of it—by lunch."

Mrs. Kirk's voice came through the speakers. I detected a slight quaver in her first words, but after a few sentences, she was soon back to her normal tone. I paused by the door, reciting the pledge along with Marie and Vaughn; then, as Mrs. Kirk announced that the office would be closed until further notice, I picked up the box and slipped out. Marie clicked the lock into place as soon as I was in the lobby.

I hefted the box in my arms and headed for the doors, my attention drawn to the square of plywood over one of the panes. Detective Waraday stood outside the door, examining it. I picked another one of the doors farther down from him and used my shoulder to push it open; then I angled the box through. Detective Waraday came over and held the door open for me.

"Are you here about the office?" I asked, wondering why Vaughn was cleaning up if the police had been called.

"Anything that happens here, dispatch figures I'll want to know about it," he said with a faint smile.

"Then you don't think it's related to the other things that have happened?"

"Mrs. Burris and Ms. Watson's deaths? No. This is probably end-of-year hijinks."

"Hmm," I said, thinking that he might change his mind when he saw the viciousness of the destruction. "Well, I should tell you that I drove by here on Sunday night, and I thought I saw a light in one of the window."

"The light was on in the office?"

"No, I don't think so. I'm not even sure it was inside the school. It was just a flash of light. At the time, I thought it was the reflection from another car's headlights, but I suppose it could have been a flashlight."

"Did you notice the broken pane in the door?" he asked.

"No. I wasn't looking closely. I saw the flash of light as I drove by and then went on. I only mentioned it because of what happened. That's quite a mess in there."

Detective Waraday nodded, but he looked distracted, as if his thoughts were elsewhere. He put his hands in the pockets of his khakis and surveyed the parking lot. No one else was in sight. "I want you to know the autopsy of Ms. Watson is in."

"You have the results already? That was fast," I said, surprised.

"I called in a favor," he said. "The autopsy showed Ms. Watson ingested a lethal amount of painkillers. There was no sign of any medical complication either."

"Oh," I said. "I'd thought that the results might be different. There were so many little details that seemed a bit . . . off." It wasn't that I was hoping she hadn't killed herself—if that was the case, it would only make things much more complicated and also mean that the killer was still out there—but I didn't like the rather strange details surrounding her death, like the almost hostile typed note and, in particular, the fact that she'd scheduled an organizing appointment shortly before her death.

Detective Waraday nodded. "I know the appointment she made with you troubled you. That's why I wanted a quick word with you. Our computer forensics team tracked the IP address of the computer that was used to fill out your online appointment form. It was Ms. Watson's computer, here at the school."

"Really?" I said. I hadn't expected that. I shifted the box from one arm to another because one of the flaps kept popping up and cutting into my arm.

Detective Waraday continued, "And as far as we can tell, she had no other long-term issues with prescription painkiller addiction. The amount of medicine missing from the prescription bottle correlates with what was prescribed for her after her dental surgery. It looks as if she took two pain pills shortly after her surgery, which would be completely normal, then put the pill bottle away and didn't take any more until Thursday. And her bank account also shows multiple cash deposits at regular intervals, indicating that Ms. McCormick didn't lie about the blackmail. She was right about that. Ms. Watson had a nice little side income from her activities." He reached for the door handle. "Sometimes things don't fit together in a neat pattern. I know you're all about making things neat and tidy, but people don't behave like you expect them to, especially when someone is suicidal."

"So the investigations into Peg's death and Klea's murder are closed?" The flap released again and dug into my arm.

"Yes, they are officially closed."

I forgot about the pressure of the box flap. There

was something, some slight reservation in his tone, that made me frown at him. "Are you satisfied? Personally, I mean?"

He pulled open the door. "I don't think I'm ever one hundred percent satisfied that I have all the answers, no matter what the case, Mrs. Avery." He went inside, and I stood there a moment, thinking about what he'd said. Then I set the box down on the ground and tucked the flaps under each other.

A mom approached at a quick pace. A little girl, a toddler with her fine blond hair in dog ears, ambled along behind her mom. The mom wrenched open the door with the plywood panel and held it for her daughter, but she didn't follow her mom inside. The toddler, squatting with perfect form, was trying to pick up something shiny from behind the metal doorstop that was set in the concrete.

"No! Dirty!" the mom said, and backtracked. As she took the toddler's hand and moved her toward the door, the mom used her foot to sweep away the thing that had fascinated the little girl. The mom and I exchanged a look. "Why is it that whatever is on the ground is always irresistible?" she asked.

I picked up the box. "Yep, I remember those days," I said as the mom went into the door, coaxing the toddler along with her.

I transferred the box onto my hip and went over to the bed of shrubs next to the main doors. A thin shard of glass glittered in the dirt.

An uneasy atmosphere settled over the school. I wasn't in the building as often as I had been during the previous week, but the few trips I had made inside, I noticed the tension among the staff. The teachers snapped, and even Vaughn, who had always seemed easygoing, was jumpy. I ran by the school to drop off Nathan's forgotten lunch box one afternoon and turned the corner into a hallway and bumped into Vaughn, who was moving backward as he mopped the floor. "Watch where you're going," he said sharply, then immediately apologized.

Despite the uneasiness that the adults clearly felt, within a day, the office had been returned to a semblance of order. Computers and phones had been transferred from other parts of the school. The wooden bench was now upright, the graffiti on the back turned to the wall. Mrs. Kirk had said that she had a furniture restorer scheduled to pick up the piece as soon as the school year was over. They would strip it and re-stain it. The glass panel beside Mrs. Kirk's door was back in place, and Marie had even been able to find both wooden blocks from her calendar. I'd seen a large truck with the company name SECURE DOCUMENT DISPOSAL on it parked at the school during the week, and supposed that they had been hired to remove and destroy the sodden files from the records room.

Abby, who was usually so buoyant and positive, noticed it as well. She called me on Tuesday night to see if I could give Charlie a ride to school on Wednesday morning, as she had drop-off duty. I said of course, and then she said, "It's so weird at the school right now. I'm always glad when the school year is over, but this is so different. Everyone is tense and suspicious. I don't like it."

I didn't like it either, but there were only a few days left in the school year. I'd again considered keeping the kids home during the remainder of the week, but when I floated the idea, they'd both been adamant. They wanted to go. There was no way they were missing their year-end activities, which were mostly the fun things that they didn't get to do all year, including picking up their memory books and participating in the end-of-year assembly, when awards were handed out.

Friday, the last day of the school year, the kids literally bounced out of the van when I dropped them off. I negotiated the congestion around the school and had to park on the grassy overflow area. I would be bouncing between Klea's house and the school today. I had two charity donation pickups to supervise at Klea's house, one at nine-thirty and another at two. In between those two appointments, I had two end-of-year parties to attend.

Instead of driving the short distance back and forth between Klea's house and the school, I'd decided it would be smarter to park in the school lot and walk the short distance. With all that had been going on lately, my walks with the Stroller Brigade, my neighborhood walking group, had been sadly ignored. Getting in some extra footsteps during my day was exactly what I needed.

I left the school parking lot and walked down the grassy verge next to the chain-link fence, then crossed the street and unlocked the front door to Klea's house with the keys Jane had given me. The house was again stuffy and dark with all the blinds drawn. I snapped on lights as I made a rapid survey of the house, making sure that everything was ready for the charity pickups. Once I was sure everything was fine, I went to the porch to wait. I didn't turn on the air conditioner, figuring it wasn't worth it for the short time I would be at the house. And the people loading boxes and furniture would probably prop the doors open anyway.

But I wished I had turned it on because the charity picking up the boxes arrived forty-five minutes late. The two men used dollies to ferry stacks of boxes from the house to the truck. It took them about twenty minutes to clear all the boxes, and when they left, the house seemed much emptier. One of the guys had attempted to take the box of personal items from the school, but I'd rescued it before it disappeared onto the truck. While there wasn't anything inherently valuable in the box, Jane wanted to go through it. After I'd picked up the box of Klea's belongings from the school, I'd brought it to Klea's house and left it on the kitchen counter with a note that it wasn't part of the charity donation, but the guy must not have seen the note.

Most of the furniture was going next. Jane said she couldn't afford to move all the furniture halfway across the country. The only things that were staying were a rocking chair and a small end table that Jane said had belonged to their mother. Jane would take them back with her to Missouri after her next trip back here.

I transferred the box of belongings to the seat of the rocking chair in the living room, where I could keep an eye on it while they loaded the rest of the boxes. After they finished, I had enough time to hike down to the van, go to the nearby sub shop, and have a turkey sandwich before I returned to the school to help with the parties.

Nathan's party in Mr. Spagnatilli's room involved

lots of frosted cupcakes and the traditional decorating of Mr. Metacarpal, the skeleton, for summer. "It gives the kids something to do—besides run around the room and scream," Mr. Spagnatilli said.

I thought it was a very clever idea. Each of the kids had brought some contribution. Nathan's was a beat-up straw hat. By the end of the party, in addition to the hat, the skeleton was decked out in swim shorts, sunglasses, swim flippers, and sunglasses.

A more grown-up atmosphere permeated Livvy's classroom. There were still cupcakes, but no special activities or games—those were for babies, I was informed—but the kids were allowed to talk among themselves and most of the time was spent signing memory books.

As I left both parties, I promised each of the kids that I would be back as soon as the furniture pickup was over, to sign them out early. I offered to take them with me then—there was no need for the kids to stay for the full day—but they both wanted to spend the last hour with their friends so I went back to the office to sign out.

Since the sign-in computer was in smithereens, a paper on a clipboard had replaced it. *Last time I'll sign out this year*, I thought as I wrote the time I was leaving on the line next to my name. I had that funny half-sad feeling that a phase of my life was coming to a close. This was the last year Livvy would be in elementary school. We rush through our days so quickly and have so many little rituals that we do, day in and day out, but then a moment like the last day of school comes along. It's a milestone that makes a definite break in the continuum and emphasizes that one phase is ending and another beginning.

I waved to get Mrs. Kirk's attention. She was in her office, but her door was open. "Where's Marie?" I asked.

"She left early. Before lunch, actually."

"She left?" I repeated, surprised that she wouldn't stay for the whole day. "But perfect attendance has always been so important to her." I saw that the individual touches, like her block calendar, the gnome figurines, and the sweater that was usually draped over the back of her chair, were gone.

Mrs. Kirk smiled. "I guess she figured she could slack off on her last day. She's retired now." Mrs. Kirk lowered her voice. "And after these last few weeks, I don't blame her for wanting to leave early. I would if I could," she said with a mock grimace. "Anyway, Marie said something about going out of town on a short vacation to celebrate."

"How nice for her," I said, then glanced at the clock. "Oh, I've got to go."

I hoofed it back to Klea's house and turned on one of the window coolers, in case the next pickup was delayed. But the consignment shop people were right on time and began wheeling out furniture as soon as I let them in. It didn't take long to clear the living room. The dining room was more of a challenge with the large table in such a small area. They took out the table first, then the heavy china cabinet. They removed the top of the china cabinet with the glass doors and carried it out, then returned for the base. As they tilted it on the dolly and moved it carefully out the front door, one of the men said, "Hey, look at this. Hold up." The other man paused with the dolly balanced at the top of the metal ramp they'd positioned over the porch steps.

"Did you know that was down there?" the first guy asked, pointing to something flat taped to the bottom of the cabinet.

"No," I said.

He reached down, brushed away some dust, and pried the thing off, then handed it to me. It was an inter-office envelope.

Chapter Twenty-two

The envelope was thick and filled with what felt like paper. It flexed slightly as I handled it. The envelope was so full that the flap barely covered the opening of the envelope, but the red string was tightly wound around the little bracket and held it closed.

"Might be the Declaration of Independence," the man said with a laugh, putting out his hand to steady the base of the cabinet as the other man backed slowly down the metal ramp.

"I doubt it," I said. As they loaded the china cabinet in the truck, I unwound the string and peered inside. It contained a thick stack of paper and a leather notebook. I was about to close the flap and tuck the envelope away in the box with Klea's belongings when a design on the top paper caught my eye. It was the logo for the Hoops for Healthy Hearts event, which was a fundraiser that the students participated in each year. The school had held the event

last month, and Livvy and Nathan had both collected pledges for the number of basketball goals
they could shoot during the event.

Still standing on the porch, I slid out the paper
and scanned it. It was the final accounting form with
the figures for the money the school had raised.
Marie's flowing signature was across the bottom of
the page, next to the total amount of money raised.
My eyebrows shot up as I took in the number with
several zeros. I had no idea that the kids had raised
that much money. I remembered Mrs. Kirk had
praised the kids for doing a good job, but she'd
never mentioned a specific amount of money.

These were obviously school records and should be
at the school, not Klea's house. I tipped the leather
journal out of the envelope and glanced through it as
the men continued to remove the rest of the furniture from the house, wondering if the journal belonged to Klea or if it belonged to the school and
should go back with all the papers.

But as I flipped through the book, I saw that the
handwriting looked like Marie's smooth cursive. I'd
seen her handwriting so many times in the school
office when she signed off on hall passes after I
brought the kids back to school after a dentist or
doctor appointment.

I fanned the pages of the journal. It contained a
long, ledger-like list with dates, a brief description,
and then amounts entered in neat, handwritten
columns. I skimmed down a random page and recognized most of the descriptions as fundraisers the
school had conducted. Besides Hoops for Healthy
Hearts, there were entries for the school's booster
club activities, like the Friday Store, where kids

could purchase pencils or candy and the profits went toward purchasing more books for the library and upgrades for computers. But there were some entries that I didn't understand at all, just a row of random numbers and letters.

I reached the end of the pages with handwriting. The last entry caught my eye. It was for Hoops for a Healthy Heart and the date was last month. Like all the other entries, it had two numbers following the description. The first column was more than the second column. It was five hundred dollars higher, in fact.

I looked at the sheet of paper that I'd first taken out of the envelope and checked it again, comparing it to the final fundraising total in the ledger, thinking that I must have misread the numbers. But I hadn't. The amount reported to Hoops for a Healthy Heart was definitely the lower amount.

"We're done, ma'am."

I looked up to find one of the men holding out a paper, the receipt for the items they'd picked up. The other man was in the truck with the engine running, ready to leave.

"Oh. Great. Before you leave, let me check inside the house, okay?" I asked, belatedly remembering I was supposed to be monitoring what the men had taken. I left him holding the receipt and quickly moved through the rooms. Everything looked as it should. The rocking chair, the box of Klea's belongings, and the side table were still there, but all the other furniture was loaded. I returned to the porch, thanked him for waiting, and took the receipt.

He climbed in the truck, and it trundled away. I glanced at the school. Parents were already arriving, lining up for the car circle line, but I had some time before the school was out. If what I suspected was true . . . well, I wanted to make sure I was right before I showed any of this to Mrs. Kirk.

I went back in Klea's house and locked both dead bolts on the front door. I needed somewhere quiet and private to check the ledger and the papers. With the blinds drawn and all the bolts on the doors locked, I felt safe.

I moved the cardboard box out of the rocking chair to the floor and sat down in the rocker. I pulled the entire stack of papers out of the folder and looked through them, comparing the dates on the papers with the dates in the ledger. Many of the pages were like the Hoops for a Healthy Heart form, summary sheets of fundraising totals, and my heart sank as I looked up each one and found a discrepancy between the total on the sheets and the total in the ledger. The total in the first column in the ledger was always higher, sometimes by a couple of hundred dollars, but other times by several thousand, and it was always the smaller amount that was listed on the reporting forms.

Then there were some forms that had the school district name printed at the top, contract work requests and purchase requests. Each request had a number associated with it on the form, and that number was also recorded in the ledger—the seemingly random strings of letters and numbers. When I went through the purchase requests, I found the amounts on the forms requesting money from the district were higher than the amounts in the ledger.

I finally sat back with a thud that set the rocking chair moving. I shook my head while I surveyed the stacks of paper I'd set on the floor as I progressed through the forms. I didn't want to believe it, but Marie had been skimming money from the school, and not just ten or twenty dollars here or there. She had taken thousands of dollars. Maybe hundreds of thousands. The ledger didn't have a running total, but the amounts were significant.

I rubbed my hand over my eyes, thinking that it was awful. She had been at the school so long. Everyone trusted her implicitly—even Mrs. Kirk, who must never have suspected anything because she'd let Marie handle the money. And Marie had handled *all* the money. She collected the cash for the fundraisers and counted it. Obviously, no one else had checked her totals. As the ledger showed, she just kept some of the money and turned in the lower numbers.

I wasn't completely sure about the requests to the district, but it looked like she'd done the opposite thing there, turning in a higher amount to the district and then paying out a lower amount to the company or contractor and keeping the difference for herself. She must have been doctoring the files as well as the receipts. I suddenly thought of the water damage to the records room and the vandalism. . . . Could Marie be behind those things as well? Was it an effort to cover her tracks completely before she retired?

I closed the ledger, feeling incredibly sad and somewhat betrayed. Someone I thought I knew had been siphoning money from the school. Stealing from kids . . . that was low.

And somehow Klea had figured it out. She must have. She had all the evidence here, even Marie's ledger. How had she gotten these papers, the fundraising forms and the district purchase requests? Had she found them while she was snooping and gradually built up a stack of evidence that Marie couldn't deny? And the ledger, how had she gotten that?

I pulled my phone out of my pocket, suddenly nervous. I wasn't sure how it all fit together, but my gut feeling was that this was why Klea had been killed. Perhaps Peg had committed suicide, but this paper trail went back years and years, and I could imagine Marie killing to keep it a secret.

I was about to dial, but stopped as a thought hit me. Marie couldn't have killed Klea. Marie had been out of town Wednesday morning, the morning of the fire drill, the morning Klea was killed. Marie had been miles away on Jekyll Island.

Had she really been on Jekyll Island? I pushed my foot against the floor and set the rocking chair in motion as I considered everything. We had only Marie's word that she had been out of town. Mrs. Kirk had called her cell phone and talked to her that morning. Marie had said she was on the coast of Georgia, but she could have been blocks away or even inside the school.

What if Marie had arrived at the school Wednesday morning and either she'd caught Klea in the act of collecting incriminating papers, or maybe Klea had confronted her? I let the scenario play out in my mind. Vaughn and Mrs. Kirk had seen Klea that morning around seven-thirty. Students would have begun arriving at seven-fifty. If Marie killed Klea, she'd need someplace to stash Klea's body until she could get it out of the school. What better place than a rarely used storage closet?

And maybe it wasn't some student prankster who'd set off the fire drill, but Marie. It would be one way to clear the school. While everyone was out front on the grass waiting for the firefighters to arrive, Marie would have had a few minutes to move Klea's body out of the school. If Klea's body had been in the rolling trash can, Marie could have easily pushed it through the school and out the back doors of the lobby, then across the blacktop to the woods. It would have been harder to move the trash can over the dirt path, but it was hard-packed earth. It would have taken some effort to move it along the path, but it could have been done. With all the students, teachers, and staff in the front of the school, the building would have shielded her from their view as she moved from the school building to the woods.

Once Marie was in the woods, she could have dumped the trash can, then continued on to the other side of the woods and come out at the street on the far side of the school. The neighborhood was full of walkers and joggers. No one would give her a second glance. Then all she would have had to do would be walk back around to the school and get her car and leave. If she'd even had her car at the school. She lived close by. She'd mentioned that the other day. She could walk the few blocks back to her house and be in her car on the way to the coast to establish her alibi.

I stopped rocking. I had to get these papers to Detective Waraday. I checked my watch, automatically calculating whether I had enough time to drop everything off at the sheriff's office, but it was too close to dismissal. I certainly didn't want to be driving around with this stuff in the van when I had the kids with me, and I wasn't going to take the chance of leaving the papers and the ledger at the school with Mrs. Kirk. I didn't think she was involved, but . . . well, Marie had worked for her. Mrs. Kirk should have looked over the school's finances. I suddenly wondered where Marie was right that moment.

With shaking fingers, I sent a text to Abby. **Emergency. Can you get the kids for me? I promised I'd get them out of school early, but can't. I'm still at Klea's house.**

Her text was a quick affirmative reply. I spread some of the pages out and photographed them, then took pictures of the matching pages in the ledger. I attached the images and tapped out a short message to Detective Waraday, saying that I'd found what looked to be some important files at Klea's house.

After a few minutes, he replied. **In your area. I'll come pick them up.**

I texted back that I would wait there. I quickly stacked the pages and the ledger, then returned everything to the envelope. I wound the string around the brad to keep the flap closed and stood up. I hurried across the living room, intending to peek out the blinds so that I could watch for Detective Waraday, but my foot connected with the cardboard box and sent items flying across the room. I'd forgotten that I'd set the box on the floor.

Hand to my heart, I quickly collected the sweater, books, and coffee mugs, tossing them back in the box. I spotted one of the little wooden cubes from the calendar under the rocking chair. I retrieved it and tossed it back in the box, then stopped as a thought struck me.

Slowly, I picked up the second cube of wood with the numbers on each side and looked at it. That elusive fragment of thought that had been teasing at my mind suddenly came to me, blooming into completeness like those time-lapse pictures of flowers that transition from bud to blowsy fullness in seconds. *Marie was at the school the Wednesday morning that Klea died.*

I traced the number cut into the wooden cube with my finger. On the morning of the Muffins with Mom event, I had left Marie a note, saying that idea of a final fundraiser for the school had been shot down at the PTA meeting. I'd put the sticky note with the news on the two wooden cubes that made up her calendar. They had been positioned so that the numbers one and zero formed the date, the tenth of May.

My mind scrolled back through the many times I had arrived at the office at the same time as Marie. The first thing she did was lean over her desk and arrange the numbers on the wooden cubes so that they reflected the correct date. She did it even before putting her purse away, taking off her jacket, or sitting down at her desk. In fact, she'd arrived late that next Monday after Klea's body had found. I'd been in the office signing in at the check-in computer when she'd arrived. She'd hurried over to her desk and plucked the sticky note I'd left her from the calendar, then changed the blocks to reflect the new date, her purse still in her hand.

Marie must have arrived at the school Wednesday morning for some reason and then done what she always did first thing, change the date on her calendar. It was a habit—an unconscious rote behavior.

She probably didn't even think about it when she did it.

Marie had been there Wednesday morning, not in Jekyll Island. It wasn't evidence that Detective Waraday could use. He would say anyone could have changed the date on the calendar, but combined with the evidence in the envelope—

At a whisper of sound, I jerked around. Marie stood in the doorway of the dining room.

Chapter Twenty-three

"Hello, Ellie," Marie said. "I let myself in." She jingled a pair of keys, the clatter of metal sounding loud, even against the constant hum of the window cooler. But it wasn't the keys that caught my attention—it was the gun she held loosely in her other hand. "It was so thoughtful of Klea to leave a second set of keys for me so that I didn't have to climb in that window over the sink again."

Her fluffy blond hair haloed her face as it always did, but she wasn't wearing one of her pastel shirts and matching skirt. She had on a loose, flowing black top and pants with a bright, primary-colored pattern. A choker necklace with small rocks spaced along stiff wires encircled her throat, and huge hoop earrings of the same design dangled from her ears.

She waved the barrel of the gun up and down her figure. "I can see you're surprised by my new look. What do you think? This is the real me." She widened her eyes. "You have no idea how sick I am of baby blue, pale pink, and yellow. And twin sets and those bell skirts and sensible pumps. Ugh. I wanted to burn them all—it would have been such fun—but I simply don't have time. Of course, the clothes served their purpose. Stereotypes are so useful, you know? Harmless, middle-aged woman . . . who would ever think that I would do that?" She jabbed the gun at the envelope on the floor by my knee. I'd put it down when I picked up the items I'd kicked out of the box.

"Marie, I'm not sure what is wrong," I said. "Why don't you put the gun down, and we'll sort this out?" I said, wondering how far away "in the area" was for Detective Waraday. Did that mean he was close, like a few miles, or merely on this side of North Dawkins? If it was the latter, then it could be ten or fifteen minutes before he arrived. I licked my lips and took a steadying breath. A lot could happen in ten minutes, I thought, glancing at the gun, but at least Detective Waraday was on his way. If I could just keep her here, once Detective Waraday was on the scene . . . well, it would probably be chaos, but at least he'd have a gun, too, which would go a long way to even the odds.

"Really, Ellie. I expected more of you," Marie said, her tone heavy with disappointment. "I know you're aware of what's going on."

"I'm not sure what you mean," I hedged, listening for the sound of a car pulling up outside, mentally running through what would happen when Detective Waraday arrived. He would come to the front door, but what would he do when I didn't open it? I knew he had a set of keys because he'd opened the door with them that first time he asked me to look around. How long would he wait before he decided to use the keys? Would he even have the keys with him? I could shout at him that Marie was inside and had a gun, but he might not be able to understand me through the closed door, and I couldn't imagine Marie not firing at the door if she thought a sheriff's detective was on the other side.

My stomach plunged at the thought of Marie firing the gun. School would be out soon . . . all those kids and parents swarming around the school. No, I had to keep her in the house and somehow keep her from firing the gun. Maybe I could distract her somehow or trip her or . . . something. My insides twisted again at the thought of getting any closer to her when she had a gun in her hand.

Marie sighed, then said rapidly, "Don't pretend, Ellie. You know Klea was a snoop. She found those papers and my ledger. She was going to expose me, so I killed her. There. Now you don't have to pretend you don't know." She made two little movements with the gun barrel and my heartbeat kicked. "Move away from that box, please," she said.

I was still kneeling on the floor and made a move to stand up, but she said, "No. Stay there. Just scoot backward." I moved back a few inches. I still held one of the wooden cubes from the calendar in my hand. I curled my fingers around it and held it behind my leg.

"That's right," Marie said. "Sit crisscross applesauce, like a good girl."

While I was so scared I was jittery and my palms were sweaty, her stance was relaxed and her grip on the gun was casual and familiar. I heard a car engine and tensed, but it didn't slow down. "Okay," I said, "if we aren't pretending any more, what about Peg?"

"Did I kill her?" Marie asked. "Yes, of course," she said matter-of-factly. "She was the perfect opportunity to distract everyone. I couldn't pass it up. I knew all about her little blackmail thing," she said, her tone dismissive. "Nothing like what I had going, of course, but she was trying, I give her that. I knew that if Peg appeared to commit suicide, it would wrap everything up so neatly. Because Peg was blackmailing people, the police would assume Klea had discovered her secret. They would think Peg had killed Klea to keep her blackmail quiet. You know how the rest of it played out. With the police closing in, Peg killed herself. Did you like the suicide note?"

"Marie—"

"I went to her house on my lunch hour," Marie said, speaking over me. "It is a relief to talk about this," she said in an aside. "You see, it's rather ingenious, and it's a shame that no one knows. I took a bowl of chicken soup—doctored with the pain pills from my medicine cabinet, you understand—and told Peg we needed her signature for a file at work. Poor dear, she was still feeling awful from that ipecac—from the nurse's office, you know. I put it in her coffee that morning, and she signed the paper without looking at it closely. I had another sheet of paper over the top so she wouldn't see, but she didn't even give it a second glance. Then she tried the soup and"—Marie lifted both shoulders in a shrug and smiled—"that was that. So easy. All I had to do after that was remove a few pills from Peg's medicine cabinet and leave the prescription bottle beside the note, and it was done." Marie gave me a disappointed look. "And you didn't even appreciate the setup I gave you. I made that appointment on Peg's computer so that you'd be the first one on the scene. I know how you fancy yourself a sort of sleuth, but you didn't seem to enjoy it at all."

Marie looked rational, and her tone of voice was completely normal, but the words coming out of her mouth . . . I was stunned. I had been totally fooled. She wasn't who I'd thought she was at all. She was talking about killing a woman—no, two women— without a trace of remorse. "I don't know what to say," I finally said. "You sound as if you think I should say how clever you are."

"I *am* clever," she snapped. "Clever enough to put my life back together after Heath's company went belly-up. Years and years, Heath invested in that company, trusting them when they said their pension plan was terrific, and then suddenly—the money is gone because of some financial accounting scandal? He couldn't take it. I don't care what the doctors said about his heart. He couldn't handle the pressure of the job hunt. He should have been looking forward to his retirement, not filling out job applications. And once he was gone, I should have had the spouse pension, but no, I had to rely on the little job at the school that we'd been using as side income. Instead of a little bonus, suddenly my check had to provide for *everything*."

She pressed her lips together for a second, then said, "Do you know what a level-one admin makes in this school district? Of course you don't. You're just like all the other stay-at-home moms with their comfy income from their husbands. The money rolls in, and you spend it."

As she spoke, her easy stance disappeared, and her face contorted. I'd always thought that Marie was pretty in a faded sort of way, but now she looked ugly.

"You don't have to work for anything in your cushy world," she said. "It only took me a couple of years to realize I didn't have to work quite so hard to get what I deserved." She gave a sharp nod. "I was cheated out of what was rightfully mine, so got it back."

She was quite worked up, speaking more passionately than I had ever seen her. She shifted her shoulders and took a deep breath, then seemed to calm down a bit. She pointed the gun at the envelope. "Where was it?"

"Taped to the bottom of the china cabinet."

She snorted. "And to think I spent hours in this house, night after night, looking for my ledger. I knew Klea had found it."

Faintly, I heard the school bell ring. It was the last bell of the day, the final bell of the school year, in fact. Outside, the street and the school parking lot, only half a block away, would be flooded with parents, which was hard to believe in the dim cocoon of the living room with its closed blinds and the hum of the window unit.

"Did Klea tell you?" I asked, straining to listen for any movement outside, but I only heard more cars drive by and then the louder rev of a bus engine as it cruised by.

"No. I discovered what the little sneak was doing," Marie said. "She thought I was on vacation, so I'm sure she thought she was in the clear. But I'd forgotten my sunglasses at the school. It's a long drive to Jekyll Island. Directly into the sun. Good thing, too, that I had to go back, or she would have told Mrs. Kirk and ruined everything. Odd, when you think about it, that a pair of sunglasses did her in. I left them on my desk, so I walked over to the school that morning. It's so much easier to walk over during morning drop-off, isn't it? You know how congested the street and parking lot get. Anyway, they were right where I'd left them, but one of my desk drawers was open."

Her eyes narrowed. "I *knew* it was Klea. I'd caught her snooping around the desks in the office before. So I waited in Mrs. Kirk's office, behind the door, watching out the crack between the hinges. It was Klea all right. She came in, bold as you please. She must have been making copies of my files because she returned some papers to my drawer, but kept some others. Then she came in Mrs. Kirk's office, and left the pages she'd copied on Mrs. Kirk's desk with a note."

Marie was getting agitated again, her face flushing pink as she said, "Klea left Mrs. Kirk's office—walked right by me without knowing I was on the other side of the door. As soon as she left the main office, I slipped over to Mrs. Kirk's desk to read her note. Klea wanted to meet with Mrs. Kirk later that day. She said she had more papers like the ones she'd left, and she had my ledger in a safe place, that she could bring it later."

The flush deepened on Marie's face, and I could see the muscles in her hand flex as she squeezed the handle of the gun. "Klea must have slipped the ledger out of my purse a day or two before. I'd looked for it earlier in the week, but it wasn't there. I'd assumed I'd left it at home, but as soon as I saw her note, I knew what had happened. She'd stolen it," she said, her tone incensed.

The irony of Marie being angry over something being stolen from her was lost on her, and I wasn't about to point it out to her. She was worked up enough.

Marie raised her eyebrows and said emphatically, "There was only one thing to do. It was so simple, really. Klea came back in the office, and was so surprised to see me that she stood stock-still for a moment. That was all I needed. The phone cord was right there. It only took a second to get it around her neck." She rotated her shoulders again as if she were working a kink out of her neck. "And the rest was incredibly simple. I suppose you've worked it out?"

"I think so. You hid her in the storage closet, then moved her after you set off the fire alarm."

"Very good. The only bad bit was when I had to wait in the janitor's office until the last bell of the morning. I knew if I pulled the fire alarm during drop-off, it would be a madhouse. I needed the school to be cleared in an orderly fashion so that I could get out of there without being seen." She eyed me, considering. "Of course, you will be more of a challenge. It's too bad I can't leave you here, but my car is parked out front. With the craziness of the last day of school, no one will probably remember seeing it, but I can't take that chance, if I leave your body here. No, I suppose you'll have to come with me and have a little accident. Nearby, of course—" She cocked her head. "What was that?"

Chapter Twenty-four

I had heard it, too. The sound of a car engine idling close by, then the engine shutting off.

"Probably just someone picking up their kids from school," I said quickly, but Marie was already moving across the room to the window, her gun still trained on me.

Before she could twitch the curtain back, I flung the block at her and dived for the dining room. The block must have connected with at least some part of her because I heard a gasp as I sprinted through the dining room to the kitchen. I fumbled with the levers on the dead bolts, my fingers slipping. The floor in the dining room creaked as she came after me. I was glad she'd come after me, away from the window and the kids and the school—but glad in a terrified way.

The locks unfastened. I yanked the door open and sprinted down the two steps to the carport. Klea's street didn't have an alley, so I couldn't leave the back way. I ran past Klea's hatchback in the carport. Parked behind the hatchback in the single drive was a gray four-door sedan, Marie's car, I assumed.

I slowed my pace as I came to the front yard, expecting to see Detective Waraday's unmarked sedan parked on the street and him on the porch, but he wasn't anywhere in sight. A large SUV was in front of the house, and the person who I assumed was the driver, a woman dressed in shorts, a tank top, and flip-flops, was several paces away, moving rapidly toward the school.

I spun back around. Marie was already down the steps and coming out of the shade of the carport. She walked with the gun angled slightly up, the barrel pointed at the limbs of the tree overhead, but as soon as she came out of the carport, she leveled the gun at me, her arm straight and steady. "Ellie, stop," she called, but her words about needing only a few seconds to kill Klea popped into my head, and I kept moving.

I skittered backward around her car, moving away from the school and putting the trunk of the sedan between us. She made an impatient exclamation, and my hyper-aware senses picked up the sound of her sandals slapping on the driveway as she hurried toward the back of her car.

With the car shielding me, I crouched and ran down the side yard that sloped away from Klea's property to a rainwater drainage grid set in a square of concrete. The grass was wet and my ballet slippers had zero traction. I slid down the little slope, but I got my balance back as I hit the concrete surrounding the drain. Marie was right behind me.

Her sandals must have had as little traction as my shoes because she slid down and bumped into me before I could even take a step.

She had the gun in her right hand, and I lunged for that arm, grabbing her wrist and twisting it away from me. She grunted and jerked backward, but the gun fell from her hand, clattering onto the metal drainage grid. I cringed, thinking it might go off. But like a coin pushed into a slot, it fell through the space between the metal squares and landed with a faint, watery *plink*.

For half a second, we both stared down the drain, our arms interlinked, then I jerked away and scrambled up the little hill toward the school. Marie wasn't quite so scary without the gun, but I still didn't want to be too close to her. She had strangled a woman, after all.

I heard her coming up the slope behind me, but I didn't stop to look back. I managed a quick glance both ways before I sprinted across the street to the grassy verge that ran along the edge of the chain-link fence. I wanted to get to the school, which was still a mass of cars, parents, and kids. Traffic was always bad at the open and close of the school day, but the first and last days of the year were the worst. Parents who usually had their kids ride the bus picked them up instead as a special treat for the last day, and as a result, the car circle pickup line was always extra long.

I ran down the street, feeling every pebble and uneven clump of grass through the thin soles of my flats. I heard the screech of tires and glanced quickly over my shoulder. Marie, in the gray sedan, had backed out of the driveway, into the street. I slowed my pace, expecting her to turn in the opposite direction from the school and accelerate away, but she spun the wheel and turned the car toward me. Her gaze locked with mine, and she gunned the engine, aiming straight for me.

Great, no gun, but she still had a car. The thought flicked through my mind even as I twisted around and made for the school. The long line of the fence hemmed me in on one side, and the row of stationary cars, waiting for their turn to inch into the car circle line, filled one lane of the street.

I came even with the tail end of the car circle line and felt relieved. I was inside the labyrinth of the pickup zone and would be okay. But then I heard the growl of the engine and looked back. With a shock, I realized Marie was driving on the wrong side of the road, in the lane that was open, the one that cars flowing out of the car circle would take.

The engine roared and the car closed in on me. Mitch was the runner in our family, but I put on a burst of speed that would have made him proud. I sprinted, legs pumping, for the end of the fence. I rounded the metal pole that marked the end of the chain-link and raced into the double car circle lane, palms out, arms waving a warning for the two cars that were waiting while kids climbed into them.

The screech of metal on metal filled the air as Marie careened around the fence post and barreled toward the two minivans that were about to pull away from the school. I darted to the side to the parking area, getting out of the path of the car circle and all the vehicles.

With a squeal of brakes, Marie stopped inches before her bumper made contact with one of the vans.

A cacophony of horns sounded from farther

back in the car circle, and both moms in the mini-vans at the front of the line gestured impatiently at Marie to back up out of their way. I raced over to Mrs. Kirk, who had whirled around, a look of severe displeasure on her face.

"It's Marie," I panted as I wove between the cars toward Mrs. Kirk. "She did it. . . . She killed Klea. And Peg, too," I added.

Mrs. Kirk stared at me for a second, but the sound of an engine growling snapped all our attention back to Marie's car. Marie reversed away from the double minivans that barred her way, backed into a parked car with a crunch, then put her car in drive.

Mrs. Kirk unclipped the walkie-talkie from her waist as she scanned the parking lot. Her gaze fixed on a yellow school bus that had turned into the street at the far end. Normally, the bus would wait on the street behind the cars as they filtered through the car circle pickup line, then continue on to the bus circle, which was positioned past the car circle. "Bus six, do you have any students on board?" Mrs. Kirk asked.

Static cracked; then a faraway-sounding voice said, "No."

"I need you to turn into the exit lane of the car circle and park there."

"Did you say the exit of the car circle?"

The space where Marie was trying to turn was narrow and she had to inch forward, then put the car in reverse again and move back a few more inches before she could make the turn.

Mrs. Kirk put the walkie-talkie to her mouth. "Yes. I did. Come in the car circle exit and park."

The faint voice came out of the speaker again as the bus lumbered closer to the school. "I can't do that. Mrs. Kirk would kill me."

Marie had finally gotten the car turned around. The horns and shouting continued. Some of the parents had half emerged from their cars to yell, adding to the confusion. "This *is* Mrs. Kirk," she said into the walkie-talkie above the din. "Now go around that line of cars that are stopped and come in the exit. Do it quickly."

"Yes, ma'am."

The bus swung around the cars, taking the lane the wrong way as Marie had. The bus turned its nose into the exit just as Marie accelerated. The front of her car crashed into the front bumper of the bus. Her hood crumbled and the air bags deployed just as Detective Waraday appeared on foot, running along the chain-link fence, his gun drawn but held pointed toward the sky.

He dodged around the bus and, as he circled the car to the driver's side, lowered the gun so that it was aimed at Marie. He reached out and cautiously opened the door, peered inside, then holstered his gun. Marie's body sagged forward over the air bag. I moved quickly around the two minivans that were still trapped in the double lanes. "Is she . . . ?" I called as I neared him.

Over the melee of angry shouts, car horns, and the kids' excited chatter, he said, "No, but she is out cold. I'll call for an ambulance. . . . I don't know how it will get here, but I'll call for one."

* * * *

It took over an hour to sort out the mess that was the car circle. Eventually, the students and parents were matched up and the car circle line cleared. The bus driver was unharmed, and the bus itself only had one long scratch on its bumper. Marie came around in the ambulance, and Detective Waraday questioned her there, but she refused to say anything. He called for a deputy, who accompanied Marie to the hospital. She wasn't severely injured. Detective Waraday said she would probably be treated and released from the hospital, and then the deputy would take her into custody.

Detective Waraday tapped the ledger and papers that now sat on Mrs. Kirk's desk. "This will be all we need to hold her until we can charge her with the murders of Mrs. Burris and Ms. Watson." As soon as things had settled down in the parking lot, and a search of Marie's car hadn't turned up the envelope with all the evidence that Klea gathered, I'd told Detective Waraday that it must still be in Klea's house. Detective Waraday dispatched a deputy, who returned with the envelope, saying that it had been on the floor of the living room. In her pursuit of me, Marie had run out without it.

Detective Waraday, Mrs. Kirk, and I were all in Mrs. Kirk's office with the door closed. Abby had taken the kids home with her and told me she wanted a full rundown later. Detective Waraday had asked me to go through what had happened this afternoon. I was glad Mrs. Kirk was sitting down as I recounted what Marie had said.

Mrs. Kirk shook her head. "Marie? I'm so— stunned. I don't even know what to say. I would never have thought she would do anything like steal money from the school. And the thought of what she did to Klea and Peg . . ." Mrs. Kirk's voice faded as she gazed at the papers spread across her desk. "I trusted her. She'd been here longer than me. I never once thought she was anything but honest."

"That's what she counted on," Detective Waraday said. "These all-cash fundraising things are the easiest way to skim money."

"Well, we're going to have some very strict rules around her from now on . . . if I get to keep my job, that is."

"In most cases of this sort," Detective Waraday said, motioning to the ledger, "the organization doesn't press charges. I know the DA will be much more concerned with the murder cases."

Mrs. Kirk nodded, but didn't seem to be too reassured. She looked like she was still stunned at the news, and I felt a little guilty that the thought she could be involved in the murder had even crossed my mind. Since Mrs. Kirk was still processing the details of what had happened, I turned toward Detective Waraday. "Klea's list . . . she must have suspected . . ."

"That either the blackmailer or the person skimming money worked in the office," Detective Waraday said, finishing my sentence. "She seemed to be a collector of secrets."

I agreed, knowing he was referring to Mrs. Harris's pen name.

"Do you think she knew about Ms. McCormick's past?" I asked, avoiding mentioning Mrs. Harris.

"I haven't seen anything that proves she did. We do know that she liked to know things so it's possible she found out."

"But her list," I said. "Those names, every one of those people had a secret, except Mrs. Kirk."

Startled, Mrs. Kirk rejoined the conversation. "Sorry, I was a bit distracted. Did you say Klea had my name on a list?"

Detective Waraday said in a soothing tone, "No need to get upset. Whether or not Mrs. Burris knew about the other . . . illegal things going on in the school, we know she was aware of the skimming." He tapped the envelope. "These pages prove that she was collecting evidence. She probably made that list when she first discovered the skimming and listed the people she thought could be involved . . . for one reason or another."

He didn't say it, but I thought that Mrs. Harris had probably been at the top of the list because Klea had known she'd hidden her pen name. Klea had probably wondered if Mrs. Harris was hiding other activities as well.

"She must have narrowed it down to the office staff as the most likely culprits," Detective Waraday continued. "That's why the list included people who worked here, like you, Mrs. Kirk."

"I promise you, I had no knowledge of what she was doing," Mrs. Kirk said.

"I understand that, and a preliminary look through Marie Ormsby's check register—she was old school and still wrote down everything in her checkbook—matches up with amounts in the ledger. She was an excellent record keeper, I'll give her that. No, she kept everything for herself. I don't see any indication that she gave anyone else a cut."

"Well, thank goodness for that," Mrs. Kirk said faintly.

"Speaking of Ms. McCormick," Detective Waraday said, "you'll be happy to know she came into the sheriff's office of her own accord this morning. Apparently, her boyfriend convinced her to come in, with a lawyer, of course."

"What will happen to her?" I asked.

"That's another matter for the school board. If she had bribed someone to falsify records, it could be a criminal matter, but there's no evidence of that. She's claiming the misspelling of her name on the original application was a mistake and that she never noticed it. She thought that somehow her record hadn't come up in the background search. She decided to keep her head down, do her job well, and hope it never came up again. I'm afraid this will be another of those cases where the district would rather the whole mess go away and it will fade away," he said, his tone regretful.

"Well, I know one thing—she will not teach again after this. I've already had several calls from the media, asking for a comment. The story is out and has been reported. Someone must have spoken to the media about it. She won't be able to pull the same trick again in another state."

"I don't think she has any interest in that," Detective Waraday said.

"She's going to release the computer game?" I asked.

"I believe so. Her lawyer was insistent that they get the flowchart schematics back or, at the very least, copies of them, because they had no direct bearing on the case. I expect to see *Adventure-matics* for sale in a few months."

"It's a shame because she was a good teacher. Livvy did really well with her in math," I said.

"I think she's much more suited to working outside the classroom," Mrs. Kirk said with finality.

Detective Waraday said to Mrs. Kirk, "Moving back to the other incidents here at the school over the last few weeks, the broken pipe and vandalism. It appears they were related."

Mrs. Kirk closed her eyes briefly. "You're saying that Marie was responsible for those things, too? I see what you're thinking, that Marie did those things to make sure no one could discover what she did after she retired. It does explain why we've had such a run . . . of . . . bad luck. Marie moved all her old files into the records room right before the leak, and she handled the destruction of the damaged files," Mrs. Kirk said, her voice getting tighter and tighter. "And I didn't have a second thought about it when she said she would take care of the removal of the damaged files—that gave her a free hand to destroy whatever she wanted."

Detective Waraday said, "And the damage to the office could have been to cover the real reason for the attack, the destruction of her hard drive. I had my suspicions that something was off with the vandalism once I saw the destruction."

Mrs. Kirk said, "What do you mean?"

"Well, in the first place, your janitor described cleaning up some glass from the concrete porch. It could have been tracked there if someone walked through the glass, but it did make me wonder if someone had entered the school with a key, then broken the glass out from the inside to make it appear as if there had been a break-in. She must not have realized that breaking the glass from the inside would give away that it was an inside job."

Mrs. Kirk sighed. "Marie occasionally had access to my keys to the main doors. I keep them with me, but there have been times when I was out of town on vacation when I gave them to her as my backup."

"And then the damage inside the office was uneven. . . . Special attention had been given to the computers. They were pulverized, in particular the hard drives," Detective Waraday added.

"But you didn't say anything at all," Mrs. Kirk said.

"I couldn't," Detective Waraday said, then looked at me. "Just like I couldn't say anything to you to confirm your suspicion that Ms. Watson's death wasn't a suicide."

"So you didn't think she'd killed herself?"

Detective Waraday said, "No, but I couldn't reveal that to you. The less you knew, the better. Several things brought up questions, including the ones you mentioned, the typed suicide note, and the appointment. But there were also other strange things. The autopsy showed Ms. Watson had ingested chicken soup, but we couldn't find a trace of any can or container of chicken soup. If she was as sick as everyone reported her to have been, I couldn't picture her going home and making chicken soup from scratch. If she'd picked up some at a store or restaurant, there should have been something in the trash, but there was nothing."

"Marie must have taken the container away in case it had residue of the drugs in it," I said.

"I was interviewing the employees at the sub shop a few blocks over when I got your initial text,

Mrs. Avery," Detective Waraday said. "They serve soup there and the owner recognized a photo of Marie as a customer who came in and purchased a bowl of soup to go on Thursday afternoon."

"If you were so close, why did it take you so long to get here?" I asked, thinking of the long minutes inside Klea's house.

Detective Waraday shook his head. "I came in from the south. I wasn't thinking about the time of day and got caught in the traffic around the school."

"Oh, I see," I said. "No wonder." The traffic, especially the road that Detective Waraday had arrived on, was awful in the afternoon. Parents began lining up in the car circle line twenty to thirty minutes before school let out, causing terrible gridlock.

"It took me fifteen minutes just to get to a place were I could park and come in on foot. I had no idea that Marie was there, or I would have sent a deputy."

A tap sounded on the door, and we all looked up to see Gabrielle poking her head through a crack in the door. "Oh, am I interrupting?"

Detective Waraday gathered the papers from Mrs. Kirk's desk. "No, I think we're done for now. I'll contact you both for formal statements later."

He shook hands with Mrs. Kirk, then turned to me. "Stay safe, Mrs. Avery," he said. I looked at him closely to see if it was a dig, but he seemed to be completely sincere.

He left, and Gabrielle came in the office, then dropped into the chair he'd been in. "Such excitement. I heard all about it. Sweet little Marie! Hard to believe," she said as she put a folder on the desk.

"So glad that's all cleared up, and so glad I caught you both. I have a proposal."

I blinked, marveling that this was the woman who had been so freaked out about being associated with a possible murder that she'd dragged me into investigating Klea's death. Her ability to switch tacks was truly amazing. I wasn't in the mood to hear any proposal. I just wanted to get home, hug my kids, and see Mitch. He was due to arrive back from his trip later tonight.

Mrs. Kirk said, "I don't think this is the time—"

"But it is," Gabrielle said. "It's perfect, really. You know I've finished the last of my organizing projects, except for the digital organization class for the teachers proposed for next year." She tapped the folder. "But an opportunity has come up that I just can't say no to. Fitzgerald has asked me to take on a complete overhaul of their systems." She grinned as she looked from me to Mrs. Kirk. Clearly, she expected congratulations.

"That's great," I said.

"Thanks." She wrinkled her nose. "I'm so excited, but the downside is that I can't do any more work for the district. I simply won't have the time. But Ellie will. She can take over the digital organization class. Mrs. Kirk, I'm sure if you recommend her, the district will approve. And, Ellie, you're here at the school all the time anyway. You might as well get paid for it."

"I'm not sure I'll have any pull left at the district after today," Mrs. Kirk said, dampeningly.

Gabrielle flapped her hand at her. "Don't be so pessimistic," she said, then leaned forward and whispered, "Just between you and me, out of all the schools I've worked in here in the district, you are the best principal, hands down. I'll be happy to put in a good word for you, and I'm sure your students and teachers will as well."

"It's true," I said, for once agreeing wholeheartedly with Gabrielle. "I'd be happy to let the district know that I wouldn't want anyone else as principal, and I'm sure the teachers and parents feel the same."

"That is very nice of you both," Mrs. Kirk said. "I'm touched. It makes this day not quite so bad."

"Bad?" Gabrielle said, rearing back in her chair. "What are you talking about? Ellie rooted out a murderer from the school and you," she said, speaking to Mrs. Kirk, "were instrumental in capturing her. I heard about your quick thinking, having the bus block Marie in the parking lot. You've got to frame these things the right way. You're a hero, not a victim."

"You know, I think you're wasted in organizing," I said to Gabrielle. "I think you should be in public relations."

"Oh, no. I have plenty to do with Fitzgerald, which brings us back to the district's contract with me," she said, eyeing first Mrs. Kirk and then me.

Mrs. Kirk said, "If the district is interested in my opinion, I'd certainly be in favor of working with you, Ellie."

"You're giving me the contract you have with the school district?" I asked Gabrielle in what I was sure was an unbelieving tone.

"Yes. Don't you think it's a perfect solution?"

* * *

"And you think she won't demand you give it back to her later?" Mitch asked the next morning as we stood in the hallway, waiting for Nathan to find his shoes so we could go to lunch for my delayed Mother's Day celebration. Mitch had arrived last night after the kids were asleep. I'd been glad about his late arrival because it had given us time alone, and I'd been able to tell him everything that had happened. Once we'd rehashed everything, he'd said, "So, next year, private school?"

Livvy appeared in the hallway. "Where are we going to lunch?"

Mitch looked at me with eyebrows raised. "It's your day."

"Portofino's," I said, naming North Dawkins's fanciest Italian restaurant.

"I better get another book," Livvy said and turned away. Portofino's had more leisurely service than the restaurants that we usually frequented. As she went to her room, I said, "Getting back to Gabrielle, I wouldn't put anything past her, but I have a feeling Fitzgerald will keep her too busy to worry about one contract with the North Dawkins School District. Imagine the contacts she'll make! I bet her business will be one hundred percent corporate by this time next year."

"So you don't mind that?"

"Are you kidding? I don't like the corporate stuff. I'll stick with the school and helping individuals. That's my line."

Nathan came around the corner holding a rather crushed gift bag with a picture of Spider-Man on the outside. I recognized it as one of the extra bags I'd saved after his last birthday celebration. He held out the bag. "Happy Mother's Day."

Livvy, who had just returned with books, said, "Oh, I have something for you, too," and darted away.

Mitch sighed. "Glad we don't have reservations."

I shushed him, and Livvy was back in seconds with another package wrapped in newspaper and decorated with hand-drawn flowers.

"This is so nice," I said, reaching for the single sheet of tissue paper stuffed in the gift bag that Nathan had handed to me.

"Hadn't you better wait and open them at the restaurant? You know, during the official Mother's Day lunch celebration," Mitch said with a twinkle in his eye.

"No way. I've waited long enough. Mother's Day celebration starts now." I took out the tissue and removed two potholders. Each one had an imprint of Nathan's hands and the words *Mother's Helper* across the top.

"Oh, I love them," I said, squeezing him close. He wiggled away quickly, but I could tell he was pleased.

I took the paper off the box Livvy gave me. It contained a pair of leather flip-flops decorated with a flower motif. "I need flip-flops," I said, hugging Livvy. "These will be perfect for summer."

She grinned and hugged me back. "Dad and I went shopping before he left on his trip."

"There's a little something else in there, too," Mitch said.

I checked the tissue under the shoes and found a pair of silver earrings. "I love them, too," I said, and gave Mitch a kiss. "What a perfect Mother's Day."

"So you're good?" Mitch asked. "Because there's a game on I'd like to catch. Want to eat here? You could use your new potholders."

"Funny. To the car, everyone."

Livvy and Nathan both charged for the door and bumped shoulders.

"Ouch."

"Hey!"

Arguing about who truly was at fault, they made their way to the van.

Mitch grabbed my hand. "Ah, the return to normalcy. Glad to see nothing has changed."

"It's a pretty good normal. Overall, I mean." I squeezed his hand.

He returned the pressure. "I agree."

Acknowledgments

Ten Ellie books! I am amazed and very happy to get to this point. I would never have reached this milestone without Faith, who enabled me to start this wonderful writing journey. To Michaela, thanks for choosing Ellie and company, and thanks for shepherding me through the publishing process for ten books. To the crew at Kensington, thanks for all your hard work that makes the Ellie books look wonderful. To the Ellie readers, I appreciate so much the kind words you send my way. Thank you for reading and reviewing the books and for spreading the word about the series. You are the best! And, of course, to my family, thanks for your encouragement, your support, and your endless patience while I finish one more sentence.

In case you missed the first delightful Ellie Avery
mystery

MOVING IS MURDER

Here is an excerpt for your reading pleasure . . .

Chapter One

Light bled across the horizon, but it was still night below the towering pines where the figure in black slipped up the driveway toward the slumbering house and slithered under the parked minivan. A small flashlight beam illuminated the engine and its hoses. The beam found the right hose and followed it until it was within reach. Metal glinted in the light. A small prick, not a slash, produced a drop of brake fluid that bubbled out and dripped to the ground. The figure twisted around and repeated the procedure on the other hoses. The person allowed a small smile as tiny puddles formed.

With a backward push, the dark form emerged from under the van, grabbed the knife, and shoved it into a deep pocket before joining the early morning joggers trotting through the still neighborhood.

Nothing had gone wrong—yet. It made me nervous. Something always went wrong when we moved. There was the time our mattress became a sponge in the mover's leaky storage unit and another time our hand-made silk rug vanished from our shipment but, so far, our move to Vernon in Eastern Washington State had been uneventful.

I set down a box brimming with crumpled packing paper that threatened to spill over its edge like froth on a cappuccino and watched the moving van lumber away. Its top grazed the leaves of the maple trees that arched over Nineteenth Street, making the street into a leafy tunnel. Sweat trickled down between my shoulder blades.

My fingers itched to get back inside our new house, rip open the butterscotch-colored tape on the boxes, and bring order out of chaos, but inside the heat magnified the smells of fresh paint, floor wax, and dusty cardboard from the boxes that were stacked almost to the coved ceiling.

The heat wasn't as bad outside because there was a breeze, but it was still ninety-nine degrees. Since we didn't have air-conditioning, stepping outside was like moving from inside a heated oven to the fringe of a campfire.

I pushed my damp bangs off my face as a black pickup slowed in front of our house. The driver draped his arm over the open window and called to my husband, "Mitch Avery, is that you?" A bright shoulder patch contrasted with the olive drab of the driver's flight suit. "I didn't know you were moving into Base Housing–East," he continued.

"Steven?" Mitch trotted down the sidewalk. I followed slowly. I'd probably heard him wrong. We were miles from base housing.

Mitch's friend parked his truck on the curb beside a pile of wardrobe boxes that needed to go to the shed since our bedroom closet was roughly the size of a matchbox. Patches on our visitor's chest and upper arms identified him as Captain Steven Givens, a member of the 52nd ARS, or in real language without the acronyms, the 52nd Air Refueling Squadron, Mitch's new squadron. They did the guy equivalent of air kisses: a handshake and a half-hug with slaps on the back.

Mitch introduced Steven.

"This is my wife, Ellie," he said. "And this is my daughter, Olivia." He patted Livvy's head, barely visible in the BabyBjörn carrier I had strapped on my chest.

Steven smiled and shook my hand in a firm, eager grip. "This is great that you're moving in. We live on Twentieth." He had thick burnt almond–colored hair cut neatly to regulation above sincere hazel eyes. His smooth complexion made him look young, even though I knew he had to be older than Mitch.

I glanced at Mitch. His smile was relaxed, so apparently he didn't mind that Steven lived one block away.

"So what do you think of Base Housing–East?" Steven asked, gesturing to the empty street.

Mitch and I looked at each other blankly.

"You didn't know half the squadron lives up here?" Steven asked.

"Here? In Vernon?" I asked.

"Right here, on Black Rock Hill. Most everyone lives within a few blocks," Steven said.

So much for our flawless moving day. Mitch and I exchanged glances. This was much worse than damage to our household goods.

"Well, it won't be like living on-base. We're not next door to each other, right?" Mitch asked.

"No, but Joe, our 'C' Flight Commander, and his wife live across the street from you. The McCarters are on Twentieth with us. There're too many to count, probably ten or fifteen couples, now that you're moving in." Steven beamed like this was the best news he could give us. Why hadn't my friend Abby, who had also just moved here, mentioned this?

"At least the squadron commander is still on-base," Mitch joked.

"No, with the remodeling going on in base housing they don't have many houses open. Colonel Briman lives down your street." Mitch looked like he'd been punched in the stomach.

Steven thumped him on the shoulder. "Welcome to the neighborhood." Steven hoisted up a box, spoke around it. "Where do you want this? I can help you out for a few hours. I was coming home to meet Gwen," he glanced at me and explained, "that's my wife, for lunch. But she's tied up at work. She's the manager at Tate's and has a heck of a time getting away from there."

"So the old bachelor finally got hitched?" Mitch seemed to have recovered from Steven's bombshell. A smile tilted up the corners of his mouth as he kidded with Steven.

"Yeah. I gave in." Steven shrugged.

Mitch's smile widened as he transferred his gaze to me, but spoke to Steven. "It's great, isn't it?"

"Sure is. Now, where do you want this box?"

Mitch pointed to the shed. "Over there. Anywhere inside."

I touched Mitch's shoulder to hold him back from following Steven. I kept my voice low. "I can't believe we bought a house in the wrong neighborhood," I said. "I mean, we've moved how many times? Four?"

"In five years," Mitch confirmed. I felt a sigh bubble up inside me. I squashed it. When I married Mitch I knew we'd have to move. After all, he was a pilot in the Air Force. Moves came with the job. We'd talked about our next assignment and I'd pictured somewhere exotic and foreign, Europe or Asia, Germany or Japan. Not Washington State. And certainly not Vernon, Washington, during a heat wave. And my vision of our next assignment *definitely* hadn't included living next door to everyone else in the squad.

I needed chocolate. I dug into my shorts pocket and pulled out a Hershey Kiss. Chocolate makes even the worst situation look better. It was mushy from the heat, but I managed to peel the foil away and pop it in my mouth. I felt as weak as a wet paper towel.

I lifted Livvy out of the BabyBjörn and transferred her to the bouncy chair in the shade of the pines beside Mitch's makeshift table, a wardrobe box, where he'd checked off each box or piece of furniture on our inventory as the movers unloaded it.

I surveyed the quiet street and came back to what was really bothering me. "Four moves and we make a mistake like this."

We'd researched everything. At least, we thought we had. To avoid living with Mitch's coworkers twenty-four hours a day, we'd decided to live off-base. We wanted privacy and Vernon, Washington, the major city thirty miles from Mitch's new assignment, Greenly Air Force Base, seemed like the perfect place to buy our first home.

We picked an arts-and-crafts-style bungalow on Black Rock Hill, a "regeneration area," our realtor, Elsa, had called it. As the original owners retired and moved to sunnier climates, young professionals moved in and updated. Apparently, everyone else from Greenly AFB had picked Black Rock Hill, too.

"This is one of the best neighborhoods in town." Mitch wiped the sweat off his forehead with the back of his arm. "Great schools, there's a park one block down the road, and it's only thirty minutes from the base."

"I know. I know. You're right," I said. "But it's not our property values I'm worried about. Well," I amended, "I certainly don't want them to go down." My stomach flip-flopped every time I thought of the money we'd plunked down on the house. Buying a house was kind of risky for us. Unlike corporate America, there weren't any moving packages for military folks. Either we sold our house when our three years at Greenly were up or we took the financial hit.

"Buyer's remorse?" Mitch asked. "You look a little sick."

"No. It's the thought of people from the squadron dropping in at any moment or watching us."

Mitch stepped on the paper in a box to flatten it. "At least they can't make us shovel our sidewalk or mow the lawn."

"You're right." I removed the Björn carrier and pulled my sweaty T-shirt away from my back.

"Come on," Mitch said. "It won't be so bad. Everybody's so busy that most people won't even notice us."

"I don't know. Ten or fifteen couples. And the squadron commander," I said, thinking of nosy neighbors checking our driveway for Mitch's car to see if he knocked off work early. "You can park in the empty side of the garage," I offered. "But only until it starts to snow. Then I get it."

"Deal," Mitch said. "You'll have the boxes on the other side of the garage sorted out in a few weeks. How's it going inside?"

"Great, if I want to do some baking. So far I've found the placemats, cake pans, and measuring spoons and cups, but no plates or silverware. Or glasses."

I'd made sure the boxes we needed with our essential things were the last items loaded on the truck, so they'd be the first off. I hadn't counted on the movers unloading our stuff, storing it for two weeks, and then reloading it on another truck in random order.

Mitch considered the seven empty boxes stacked by the curb. "You know, it's not too late to move again. Almost everything is still in boxes."

I was tempted for a moment, but then I looked at the neighborhood and our house. Bungalows with broad porches and sturdy pillars rested in the shade of towering maple and pine trees. A few houses, like ours, had an English influence. Its steep A-line roof sloped down to honey-colored bricks, leaded-glass windows, and an arched front door. It was a gingerbread cottage out of a fairy tale and I loved it. A warm breeze stirred the trees and lifted the strands of hair off my sweaty neck. "No way. We'll just have to be mildly friendly and keep our distance."

Three hours later, I plodded along, gritty with dried sweat, mentally running down my Day One Moving Checklist while I pushed Livvy's stroller. We'd found sheets, but towels were still a no-show. No sign of plates, silverware, and glasses either.

Livvy let out a half-cry, more a squawk, then fell silent to study the dappled sunlight and shade as it flicked over her stroller canopy. She'd been content most of the day to watch the parade of movers, but half an hour ago her patience ran out. I'd fed, burped, and changed her, but she still squeezed her eyes shut and shrieked. She didn't like walking, humming, or singing either. I used to rely on a quick car ride to soothe her, but her enchantment with the car seat evaporated during our road trip from Southern California to Washington State. That meant I had to resort to the big guns, a walk.

Where else could the towels be? We definitely needed showers tonight. We'd unpacked all the boxes labeled BATHROOM. Maybe LINEN CLOSET?

"Ellie, did you hear me?"

"Sorry. I was wondering where the towels might be packed," I said to my friend Abby, the one person I didn't mind dropping in on me. She was such a good friend I put her to work as soon as she had showed up this afternoon even though her style was a shotgun approach compared with my more methodical way. She tore open the boxes and pulled everything out.

Her curly black hair, pulled back in a ponytail,

bounced in time with her steady stride as she motored down the sidewalk. "I'll bring over some of our towels for you. I'm so glad you're finally moving in," she said. "You can run with me. I go every morning." Her white sleeveless shirt and jean cut-offs showed off her tanned, toned arms and legs. She claimed her figure tended toward stockiness, but with her energy and huge smile she looked great to me. I couldn't get into last summer's shorts because of pregnancy weight still hanging around, especially on my tummy and thighs.

"Yeah, right. I can't stand running, remember?" Before my pregnancy I ran a few times with Abby, but it reminded me of how much I hated it. Abby and I met two years ago in one of those prefabricated friendship opportunities that arise in military life. Mitch and Abby's husband, Jeff, were friends at the Air Force Academy. More than once, I had found myself straining to carry on a conversation with another wife over dinner while Mitch and his friend caught up. But Abby and I hit it off right away, except for her love of jogging.

"Why didn't you tell me there were so many people from the squadron in this neighborhood?" I asked.

"I didn't realize until we moved in and started unpacking." Abby bounced along beside me. "It'll be great—just like base housing, only better because these houses are newer."

Before I could argue with this overly optimistic view she pointed to a gray stucco house with black shutters. Blooms of roses, hollyhocks, and mums layered color and texture around the base of the trees and house. "That's Cass and Joe Vincent's house," Abby said. A spade and pruning shears had been tossed on the ground beside a bucket sprouting uprooted weeds and grass. "He's Jeff's flight commander, 'C' Flight. She's into gardening and ecology—the environment and all that. She writes about it." Abby's voice had an edge to it.

"You don't like her?" Abby's bubbly personality blended with most people's.

"She's all right," Abby said.

"Cass, from that gardening column in the newspaper, 'Clippings with Cass'?"

"Yes. And she writes articles for environmental Web sites and magazines. A few months ago she headed up a crusade to keep Wal-Mart from building a supercenter on Black Rock Hill. You know, the usual—local neighborhood versus big retailer. But she found some restriction and she was on that news show, *24/7*, as the local environmental expert. I think it went to her head." Abby waved her hand, shuffling the subject away. "Enough about that. How about going to the spouse coffee with me tomorrow night?"

I felt Abby look at me out of the corner of her eye to gauge my reaction before she said, "I know you just got here, but please go with me tomorrow night."

"Abby." My voice had a warning tone.

"I know you don't like the coffees, but I need you to go with me. The times I've gotten together with the spouses here it's been strained, or, I don't know, tense."

"Sounds normal."

Abby sighed as I maneuvered the stroller onto the bumpy walking path of the park down the block from our house. "I know you don't want to go, but I really want to make a good impression. And I want to get involved, too," she added, almost defiantly. "When I finally got to Hunter, they announced the base closing and the coffees just sort of fizzled out."

"Thank God," I muttered.

"You can sneer all you want. You've done it, but I want to give it a shot."

"Abby, they're boring. No fun." This was the most convincing argument I could think of to persuade Abby not to go. She always wanted to experience new things, but she wanted them to be fun and exciting. "It's just the wives of the higher-ranking officers and enlisted trying to outdo each other."

"Well, I don't care if it is boring. We'll make it fun. I want to support Jeff and if it can help him, I'm doing it."

"Slow down," I pleaded. She'd picked up the pace and we were nearly running around the rolling path that circled the playground and duck pond of Windemere Park. "Mitch says if his career depends on how many cookies I bake, then he doesn't want an Air Force career."

"Jeff supports me in my teaching," Abby countered. "He doesn't say a word about the extra time I put in getting ready for school. And last year I bought so many school supplies I thought I should just stay in line at Wal-Mart, but he didn't mind. I want to support him, too."

We left the park and crossed Birch Street to head back down Nineteenth Street. "How much is the Vernon Public School District going to ask of Jeff? Monthly meetings? Two dozen cookies?"

I knew that set look on Abby's face, so I gave up

trying to argue with her and looked down the street to our new house. Even from this end of the block I could see it. Warm yellow light shone from every window. Why hadn't Mitch closed the curtains in the growing dusk?

I did a quick mental tour of the house, then groaned. "Look. The sellers took every curtain and we didn't even notice during the walk-through before we signed the closing paperwork." Yep, we were first-time home buyers, all right. No wonder our house glowed like a birthday cake for a retiree.

"I guess we'll have to do some shopping," Abby said. I nodded, wondering if our budget could stretch to include curtains.

As we paced along the twilight sounds were loud in the silence between us: the racket of the crickets, the swish of sprinklers, the yells of the kids on their bikes as they took one last ride down the sidewalk.

A burgundy minivan backed out of the Vincents' driveway. "That's Cass," Abby said. Cass slammed on the brakes to let a kid swoop across the street on his bike, then she zipped down the street toward us.

Instead of making the slight adjustment to follow the gentle curve of the street, the van stayed on its current track with its nose pointed straight at us. "What's she doing?" I quickened my steps and steered the stroller away from the street.

"I don't know—" The blare of the horn cut into Abby's words. The stroller wheels caught on the uneven sidewalk and the handle slammed into my stomach. "The yard," Abby said. We wrenched the stroller back, shoved it across a driveway. I stumbled. The cement bit into my knee.

Abby steadied the stroller. "Are you all right?" The headlights closed on us.

"Yeah—" We rushed into the grass.

My vision turned to glaring white. I blinked in the black that descended, but I was aware of the solid mass of metal and glass as the van swept past us. I turned and my eyes adjusted. The van's front wheel bounced onto the curb of the driveway we'd just ran across. It bumped along the sidewalk a few feet, then dropped back onto the street before barreling into the intersection next to the park. My shoulders tensed.

Brakes screeched and a crunch of metal sounded as the front of a car grazed the back bumper of the van. The car stopped beside the park. Cass's minivan jumped the curb and sped across Windemere Park, its tires kicking up little branches and pinecones. The van jolted along the walking path, headed up a slight rise near the playground, and took out a wide section of low bushes, which slowed it down. It rolled to a stop on the next rise of ground, then settled back into the little gully.

My fingers trembled as I pushed back the stroller awning to check on Livvy. Her eyes were closed and she had her thumb tucked in her mouth. I guess she'd liked the bumpy dash across the neighborhood.

The driver of the car beat us to the van. My knee stung with each step. A woman in a turquoise tank top and brightly flowered capri pants sat on the grass. She ignored the driver of the car, who muttered about reckless drivers and the crushed headlight of his Volvo.

"Cass, are you all right? What happened?" Abby bent over her, touched her freckled shoulder.

Cass's voice trembled. "No brakes."

An Everything in Its Place Tip for an Organized Move

Create and label an "Open First" box with:
- Sheets
- Pillows
- Towels
- Shower curtain
- Paper plates, cups, utensils
- Alarm clock
- Phone
- Answering machine